REEDS

Boat Owner
BRITAIN'S BIGGEST SELLING YACHTING MAGAZINE | SAIL AND

C000157596

SMALL CRAFT
ALMANAC
2009

EDITORS

Neville Featherstone & Andy Du Port

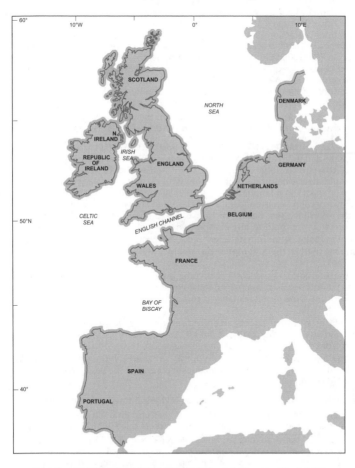

THE UNITED KINGDOM AND IRELAND
AND DENMARK TO GIBRALTAR

REEDS
SMALL CRAFT ALMANAC
2009

Editors: Neville Featherstone & Andy Du Port

The Editors would like to thank the many official bodies who have kindly provided essential information in the preparation of this Almanac. They include the UK Hydrographic Office, Trinity House, Northern Lighthouse Board, Irish Lights, HM Nautical Almanac Office, HM Stationery Office, HM Customs, Meteorological Office and the Maritime and Coastguard Agency.

Information from the Admiralty List of Lights, Admiralty Tide Tables and the Admiralty List of Radio Signals is reproduced with the permission of the UK Hydrographic Office and the Controller of HMSO. Extracts from the following are published by permission of the Controller of HM Stationery Office: International Code of Signals, 1969; Meteorological Office Weather Services for Shipping. Phases of the Moon and Sun/Moon rising and setting times are derived from the current editions of the Channel and Eastern Almanacs, and are included by permission of HM Nautical Almanac Office. UK and Foreign tidal predictions are supplied by the UK Hydrographic Office, Taunton TA1 2DN. Acknowledgment is also made to the following authorities for permission to use tidal predictions stated: Royal Danish Administration of Navigation and Hydrography, Farvandsvæsnet: Esbjerg. SHOM, France: Dunkerque, Dieppe, Le Havre, Cherbourg, St Malo, Brest, Pointe de Grave, Authorisation (No 160/2008). Rijkswaterstaat, The Netherlands: Vlissingen, and Hoek van Holland. BSH, Hamburg and Rostock: Helgoland, Wilhelmshaven and Cuxhaven (BSH 11123/2005-09). Marina Institute Hidrográfico, Portugal: Lisboa, Authorisation (No 24/2008). **Warning:** The UK Hydrographic Office has not verified the reproduced data and does not accept any liability for the accuracy of reproduction or any modifications made thereafter.

Corrections Any necessary corrections will be published on the website www.reedsalmanac.co.uk. Data in this almanac is corrected up to Edition 25/2008 of the *Admiralty Notices to Mariners*.

IMPORTANT SAFETY NOTE AND LEGAL DISCLAIMER

This Almanac is intended as an aid to navigation only and to assist with basic planning for your passage. The information, charts, maps and diagrams in this Almanac should not be relied on for navigational purposes and should always be used in conjunction with current official hydrographic data. Whilst every care has been taken in its compilation, this Almanac may contain inaccuracies and is no substitute for the relevant official hydrographic charts and data, which should always be consulted in advance of, and whilst, navigating in the relevant area. Before setting out you should also check local conditions with the harbourmaster or other appropriate office responsible for your intended area of navigation.

Before using any waypoint or coordinate listed in this Almanac it must first be plotted on an appropriate official hydrographic chart to check its usefulness, accuracy and appropriateness for the prevailing weather and tidal conditions.

To the extent that the editors or publishers become aware that corrections are required, these will be published on the website www.reedsalmanac.co.uk. Readers should therefore regularly check the website for any such corrections. Data in this Almanac is corrected up to Edition 25/2008 of the Admiralty Notices to Mariners.

The publishers, editors and their agents accept no responsibility for any errors or omissions, or for any accident, loss or damage (including without limitation any indirect, consequential, special or exemplary damages) arising from the use or misuse of, or reliance upon, the information contained in this Almanac.

The decision to use and rely on any of the data in this Almanac is entirely at the discretion of, and is the sole responsibility of, the Skipper or other individual in control of the vessel in connection with which it is being used or relied upon.

Correspondence Letters on nautical matters should be addressed to editors@reedsalmanacs.co.uk

Practical Boat Owner is published monthly by IPC Magazines Ltd, Blue Fin Building, 110 Southwark Street, London SE1 0SU. For subscription enquiries and overseas orders call 0845 676 7778 (fax: 01444 445599).

Almanac manager: Chris Stevens
Cartography & production: Chris Stevens

Adlard Coles Nautical
38 Soho Square, London W1D 3HB
Tel: +44 (0)207 758 0200 Fax: +44 (0)207 758 0222
www.reedsalmanac.co.uk

Foreword

This book is the skipper's essential companion, both at home and onboard your boat. It contains all the information you need to plan a day sail or long-distance cruise, plus handy reference guides to help you deal with situations on the way.

Work out your route and tidal timings with the distance tables and tide charts – there are even suggested waypoints to get you started. Then, with the latest marine forecast, sourced with the help of this book's weather section, you're set to go.

We hope the only checking you need to do en route is tidal streams, the odd forgotten ship lights, and the VHF channel or phone number of that marina you decide to pop in to. But this book covers emergency situations too, including first aid and how to send a distress call.

It's amazing how much information the Almanac's expert editors have crammed in to this handy-size book. Whether you're cruising all the way from Denmark to Gibraltar, or just pottering around your local bay, don't be without your 2009 Small Craft Almanac!

Sarah Norbury
Editor
Practical Boat Owner
Britain's biggest-selling yachting magazine

Contents

ABBREVIATIONS

AC, ACA	Admiralty chart, chart agent
AC	Shore power (electrical)
ACN	Adlard Coles Nautical
Al	Alternating lt
ALL	Admiralty list of lights
ALRS	Admiralty list of radio signals
ASD	Admiralty sailing directions (Pilot)
ATT	Admiralty tide tables
ATT	Atterisage (landfall/SWM) buoy
Bcn, Bn	Beacon
Bkwtr	Breakwater
BST	British summer time (DST)
CD	Chart datum
Cf	Compare, cross-refer to
CG	Coastguard
Ch	Channel (VHF)
chan.	Channel (navigational)
CROSS	Centre régional opérationnel de surveillance et sauvetage (MRCC)
CRS	Coast radio station(s)
DF	Direction finding
Dia	Diaphone (fog signal)
Dir Lt	Directional light
DSC	Digital selective calling
DST	Daylight saving time
DZ	Danger zone (buoy)
E	East
ECM	East cardinal mark (buoy/beacon)
ED	Existence doubtful, European datum
EPIRB	Emergency position indicating radio bn
F	Fixed light. Beaufort wind force
FFL	Fixed and flashing lt
Fl	Flashing light
FM	Frequency modulation
FV	Fishing vessel
G	Green. Gravel
GMDSS	Global maritime distress & safety system
H, Hrs, h	Hour(s)
H24	Continuous
HAT	Highest astronomical tide
Hbr	Harbour
Hd	Head, headland
HF	High frequency
HJ	Day service, sunrise to sunset
HO	Office hours, Hydrographic office
ht	Height
HW	High water
HX	No fixed hours
Hz	Hertz
IALA	Int'l association of lt ho authorities
IDM	Isolated danger mark (buoy/bcn)
IMO	Int'l maritime organisation
Inmarsat	Int'l maritime satellite system
IPTS	Int'l port traffic signals
Is, I	Island, Islet
Iso	Isophase light
ITZ	Inshore traffic zone
Kn	Knot(s)
Lanby	Large automatic navigational buoy
Lat	Latitude
LB	Lifeboat
Ldg	Leading (lt)
LF	Low frequency
Long	Longitude
LT	Local time
Lt(s)	Light(s)
Lt F	Light float
Lt Ho	Lighthouse
Lt V	Light vessel
LW	Low water
M	Nautical mile(s)
m	Metre(s)
MCA	Maritime & Coastguard Agency
Météo	Météorologie/weather
MF	Medium frequency
MHWN	Mean HW neaps
MHWS	Mean HW springs
MHz	Megahertz
MLWN	Mean LW neaps
MLWS	Mean LW springs
MMSI	Maritime mobile service identity
Mo	Morse
MRCC	Maritime rescue co-ordination centre
MRSC	Maritime rescue sub-centre (not in UK)
MSI	Maritime safety information
N	North
NCM	North cardinal mark (buoy/bcn)
Oc	Occulting light
PHM	Port-hand mark (buoy/bcn)
Pt(e), (a)	Point(e), Punta
Q	Quick flashing
R	Red. River
Ra	Coast radar station
Racon	Radar transponder beacon
RG	Emergency RDF station
R/T	Radiotelephony
S	South
s	second(s) of time
SAR	Search and rescue
SCM	South cardinal mark (buoy/bcn)
SHM	Starboard-hand mark (buoy/bcn)
Sig Stn	Signal station
SMS	Short message service (texting)
SNSM	Société nationale de sauvetage en mer (French LB service)
SOG	Speed over the ground
SOLAS	Safety of life at sea (Convention)
SPM	Special mark (buoy/bcn)
SRR	SAR Region
SSB	Single sideband (radio)
Stn	Station
SWM	Safe water mark, landfall buoy
Tfc	Traffic
TSS	Traffic separation scheme
UQ	Ultra quick flashing lt
UT	Universal time
VHF	Very high frequency
VNF	Voie navigable de France (canals)
VQ	Very quick flashing lt
VTS	Vessel traffic service
W	West, White
WCM	West cardinal mark (buoy/bcn)
WGS	World geodetic system (datum)
WIP	Work in progress
WPT	Waypoint
Y	Yellow, orange, amber

GENERAL VOCABULARY. See also weather vocabulary on page 94

ENGLISH	GERMAN	FRENCH	SPANISH	DUTCH
ASHORE				
Ashore	An Land	A terre	A tierra	Aan land
Airport	Flughafen	Aéroport	Aeropuerto	Vliegveld
Bank	Bank	Banque	Banco	Bank
Boathoist	Bootskran	Travelift	Travelift	Botenlift
Boatyard	Bootswerft	Chantier naval	Astilleros	Jachtwerf
Bureau de change	Wechselstelle	Bureau de change	Cambio	Geldwisselkantoor
Bus	Bus	Autobus	Autobús	Bus
Chandlery	Yachtausrüster	Shipchandler	Efectos navales	Scheepswinkel
Chemist	Apotheke	Pharmacie	Farmacia	Apotheek
Dentist	Zahnarzt	Dentiste	Dentista	Tandarts
Doctor	Arzt	Médecin	Médico	Dokter
Engineer	Motorenservice	Ingénieur/mécanique	Mecánico	Ingenieur
Ferry	Fähre	Ferry/transbordeur	Ferry	Veer/Pont
Garage	Autowerkstatt	Station service	Garage	Garage
Harbour	Hafen	Port	Puerto	Haven
Hospital	Krankenhaus	Hôpital	Hospital	Ziekenhuis
Mast crane	Mastenkran	Grue	Grúa	Masten kraan
Post office	Postamt	Bureau de poste/PTT	Correos	Postkantoor
Railway station	Bahnhof	Gare de chemin de fer	Estación de ferrocanil	Station
Sailmaker	Segelmacher	Voilier	Velero	Zeilmaker
Shops	Geschäfte	Boutiques	Tiendas	Winkels
Slip	Slip	Cale	Varadero	Helling
Supermarket	Supermarkt	Supermarché	Supermercado	Supermarkt
Taxi	Taxi	Taxi	Taxis	Taxi
Village	Ort	Village	Pueblo	Dorp
Yacht club	Yachtclub	Club nautique	Club náutico	Jacht club
NAVIGATION				
Abeam	Querab	A côté	Por el través	Naast
Ahead	Voraus	Avant	Avante	Voor
Astern	Achteraus	Arrière	Atrás	Achter
Bearing	Peilung	Cap	Maración	Peiling
Buoy	Tonne	Bouée	Boya	Boei
Binoculars	Fernglas	Jumelles	Prismáticos	Verrekijker
Channel	Kanal	Chenal	Canal	Kanaal
Chart	Seekarte	Carte	Carta náutica	Zeekaart
Compass	Kompass	Compas	Compás	Kompas
Compass course	Kompass Kurs	Cap du compas	Rumbo de aguja	Kompas koers
Current	Strömung	Courant	Coriente	Stroom
Dead reckoning	Koppelnavigation	Estime	Estimación	Gegist bestek
Degree	Grad	Degré	Grado	Graden
Deviation	Deviation	Déviation	Desvio	Deviatie
Distance	Entfernung	Distance	Distancia	Afstand
Downstream	Flußabwärts	En aval	Río abajo	Stroom afwaards
East	Ost	Est	Este	Oost
Ebb	Ebbe	Jusant	Marea menguante	Eb
Echosounder	Echolot	Sondeur	Sonda	Dieptemeter
Estimated position	Gegißte Position	Point estimé	Posición estimado	Gegiste positie
Fathom	Faden	Une brasse	Braza	Vadem
Feet	Fuß	Pieds	Pie	Voet
Flood	Flut	Flot	Flujo de marea	Vloed
Handbearing compass	Handpeilkompass	Compas de relèvement	Compás de marcaciones	Handpeil kompas

ENGLISH	GERMAN	FRENCH	SPANISH	DUTCH
Harbour guide	Hafenhandbuch	Guide du port	Guia del Puerto	Havengids
High water	Hochwasser	Peine mer	Altamer	Hoog water
Latitude	Geographische Breite	Latitude	Latitud	Breedte
Leading lights	Feuer in Linie	Alignement	Luz de enfilación	Geleide lichten
Leeway	Abdrift	Dérive	Hacia sotavento	Drift
Lighthouse	Leuchtturm	Phare	Faro	Vuurtoren
List of lights	Leuchtfeuer Verzeichnis	Liste des feux	Listude de Luces	Lichtenlijst
Log	Logge	Loch	Corredera	Log
Longitude	Geographische Länge	Longitude	Longitud	Lengte
Low water	Niedrigwasser	Basse mer	Bajamar	Laag water
Metre	Meter	Mètre	Metro	Meter
Minute	Minute	Minute	Minuto	Minuut
Nautical almanac	Nautischer Almanach	Almanach nautique	Almanaque náutico	Almanak
Nautical mile	Seemeile	Mille nautique	Milla marina	Zeemijl
Neap tide	Nipptide	Morte-eau	Marea muerta	Dood tij
North	Nord	Nord	Norte	Noord
Pilot	Lotse	Pilote	Práctico	Loods/Gids
Pilotage book	Handbuch	Instructions nautiques	Derrotero	Vaarwijzer
RDF	Funkpeiler	Radio gonio	Radio-gonió	Radio richtingzoeker
Radar	Radar	Radar	Radar	Radar
Radio receiver	Radio, Empfänger	Récepteur radio	Receptor de radio	Radio ontvanger
Radio transmitter	Sender	Emetteur radio	Radio-transmisor	Radio zender
River outlet	Flußmündung	Embouchure	Embocadura	Riviermond
South	Süd	Sud	Sud, Sur	Zuid
Spring tide	Springtide	Vive-eau	Marea viva	Springtij/ springvloed
Tide	Tide, Gezeit	Marée	Marea	Getijde
Tide tables	Tidenkalender	Annuaire des marées	Anuario de mareas	Getijdetafel
True course	Wahrer Kurs	Vrai cap	Rumbo	Ware Koers
Upstream	Flußaufwärts	En amont	Río arriba	Stroom opwaards
VHF	UKW	VHF	VHF	Marifoon
Variation	Mißweisung	Variation	Variación	Variatie
Waypoint	Wegpunkt	Point de rapport	Waypoint	Waypoint/Route punt
West	West	Ouest	Oeste	West

OFFICIALDOM

ENGLISH	GERMAN	FRENCH	SPANISH	DUTCH
Certificate of registry	Schiffszertifikat	Acte de franchisation	Doc de matrícuia	Zeebrief
Check in	Einklarieren	Enregistrement	Registrar	Check-in
Customs	Zoll	Douanes	Aduana	Douane
Declare	Verzollen	Déclarer	Declarar	Aangeven
Harbour master	Hafenmeister	Capitaine du port	Capitán del puerto	Havenmeester
Insurance	Versicherung	Assurance	Seguro	Verzekering
Insurance certificate	Versicherungspolice	Certificat d'assurance	Certificado deseguro	Verzekeringsbewijs
Passport	Paß	Passeport	Pasaporte	Paspoort
Police	Polizei	Police	Policía	Politie
Pratique	Verkehrserlaubnis	Pratique	Prático	Verlof tot ontscheping
Prohibited area	Sperrgebiet	Zone interdite	Zona de prohibida	Verboden gebied
Register	Register	Liste de passagers	Lista de tripulantes/rol	Register
Ship's log	Logbuch	Livre de bord	Cuaderno de bitácora	Logboek
Ship's papers	Schiffspapiere	Papiers de bateau	Documentos del barco	Scheepspapieren
Surveyor	Gutachter	Expert maritime	Inspector	Opzichter

Chapter 1 - Navigation

PASSAGE PLANNING CHECKLIST

DATE .... FROM ....ETD .... VIA .... TO .... ETA ....

TIMES OF SUNRISE .... SUNSET .... MOON RISE .... MOONSET .... WATCH SYSTEM ☐

CHARTS ☐   DOCUMENTS ☐   CUSTOMS ☐   PAY DUES ☐   CG (T/R) ☐   FUEL ☐   WATER ☐   FOOD ☐

WEATHER FORECAST ....

DEPARTURE PORT VHF .... HM ☎ ....

BRIDGE TIMES ....

LOCK/GATE TIMES ....

BAR CROSSING TIMES ....

DEPARTURE WINDOW ....

DEPARTURE PROCEDURE ....

....

....

VTS DETAILS ....

....

....

STANDARD PORT, TIDES (SP/NP, HW/LW TIMES & HEIGHTS)

....

....

....

DEPARTURE PORT TIDES (HW/LW TIMES & HEIGHTS) ....

....

TIDAL STREAMS ON DEPARTURE ....

....

....

EN ROUTE

TIDAL STREAM ANALYSIS ....

....

....

....

....

TIDAL GATES (TIMES) ....

....

TIDE RACES ....

TRAFFIC SEPARATION SCHEMES ....

PROHIBITED AREAS/DANGERS ....

PRINCIPAL LIGHTS/MARKS

....

....

LEG DETAILS

FROM	TO	WPT	TRK°M	DIST	TIME	REMARKS

DESTINATION PORT VHF .... HM ☎ ....

ARRIVAL PROCEDURE ....

....

BAR CROSSING TIMES ....

LOCK/GATE/SILL TIMES ....

BRIDGE TIMES ....

ACCESS WINDOW ....

ALTERNATE PORT VHF .... HM ☎ ....

ARRIVAL PROCEDURE ....

....

BAR CROSSING TIMES ....

LOCK/GATE/SILL TIMES ....

BRIDGE TIMES ....

ACCESS WINDOW ....

PASSAGE PLANNING AND SOLAS V

Before you start to navigate you need to plan: where you are going, how to get there and what factors may influence the plan. To most people this is commonsense, but now it is also the law; see Regulation 34 in chapter V of the International Convention for Safety of Life at Sea (SOLAS).

Regulation 34 **Safe Navigation and avoidance of dangerous situations** is actually quite short and bland. The MCA have provided extra guidance for small craft skippers at www.mcga.gov.uk.

Legally all voyages/passages by any vessel that goes to sea must be pre-planned. 'Going to sea' is defined as proceeding beyond sheltered waters. Even in very familiar waters every passage, however short, must be pre-planned, but for small craft the degree of planning may be less than for big ships.

The passage plan need not be in writing – which makes it hard to consult. However a written plan, in the event of legal action, is clear proof that planning has been done. A checklist, which when completed forms the passage plan, is therefore included on the previous page; it may be photocopied and enlarged to suit individual needs.

The MCA states that Regulation 34 does not herald a regime of pre-departure or spot checks on small craft. But obviously it might apply to an incident or accident involving a pleasure craft where it can be proved that the skipper did not carry out any form of passage planning; in which case the MCA would have clear authority to take action under the Merchant Shipping Act. For small craft skippers the emphasis on passage planning has shifted from good practice to a legal requirement.

SOLAS V, Regulation 34 (as paraphrased)

All passage plans, however short, should consider or better still answer the following questions:

- **Limitations of the vessel:** Is your craft suitable for the intended passage? Is proper safety equipment and enough fuel, water and stores onboard?
- **Crew:** Is the crew sufficiently experienced and physically capable? Cold, tiredness and seasickness can soon render crew incapable of performing their tasks properly, thus overburdening the skipper both physically and mentally.
- **Navigational dangers:** Are you aware of navigational dangers which may affect the passage? If not, check up-to-date charts, pilot books and the current PBO Almanac.
- **Tides:** Do you know times/heights of HW & LW at departure, destination and alternate ports? Are you aware of tidal streams and races expected on passage? Does your passage plan make best use of all tidal data?
- **Weather:** Before leaving, is the forecast suitable for the likely duration of the passage? Whilst at sea what updates can be obtained for destination and alternate?
- **Contingency plan:** Have you an alternative plan to cope with weather deterioration, gear failure, accident or injury? Which ports of refuge or bolt-holes are available?
- **GPS**: Do not become over-reliant on it. It *can* fail, usually at the most awkward moment. Can you navigate safely without it? Do you have a back-up set?
- **Information ashore:** Does someone ashore know your plans and what to do should he/she become concerned? If you get into difficulties the CG Voluntary Identification Scheme (CG66) helps the Coastguard to help you more quickly. It is easy to join – and free.

Passage planning checklist

Before reaching the checklist stage, much thought and study must go into drafting the plan. Any plan for any project goes through some or all of the following phases:

- Deciding the aim – not always obvious.
- Gathering the facts – time consuming but essential.
- Assessing the information now available.
- Formulating the plan. Think laterally.

A checklist ensures that the plan has been methodically prepared and minimises the risk of errors or omissions. Use a checklist in which the user must actively tick off items and/or insert data into boxes – rather than passively glancing at a screed and saying 'Yes, done all that'. That may well not be the case.

The following notes amplify some of the checklist items:

- Tidal streams around headlands tend to form gates, especially on a coastal passage. Note when the tides are fair or foul and the times of slack water.
- Times of entry/exit at a harbour may be affected by bars, sills and locks.
- A detailed pilotage plan/sketch for any unfamiliar harbour always helps.
- Involve your crew with passage plans.

DISTANCES (M) ACROSS THE ENGLISH CHANNEL

FRANCE/CI \ ENGLAND	Longships	Falmouth	Fowey	Plymouth bkwtr	Salcombe	Dartmouth	Torbay	Weymouth	Poole Hbr Ent	Needles Lt Ho	Nab Tower	Littlehampton	Shoreham	Brighton	Newhaven	Eastbourne	Folkestone	Dover
Le Conquet	112	112	123	125	125	137	144	172	188	194	212	230	240	245	249	261	295	301
L'Aberwrac'h	102	97	106	107	105	117	124	153	168	174	192	211	219	224	228	239	275	280
Roscoff	110	97	101	97	91	100	107	130	144	149	165	184	193	197	200	211	246	252
Trébeurden	120	105	106	102	94	102	109	129	142	147	164	181	190	194	197	208	244	249
Tréguier	132	112	110	101	94	98	102	116	128	132	147	162	170	174	177	188	224	229
Lézardrieux	142	121	118	107	94	100	105	115	126	130	140	157	165	169	172	184	219	224
St Q.-Portrieux	159	137	135	124	111	115	121	127	135	135	146	162	171	174	178	189	225	230
St Malo	172	149	146	133	118	120	124	125	130	130	143	157	166	170	173	184	220	225
St Helier	155	130	123	108	93	95	100	99	104	104	115	132	140	144	147	158	194	199
St Peter Port	139	113	104	89	73	70	75	71	79	83	97	112	120	124	127	135	174	179
Braye (Alderney)	146	116	106	89	72	69	71	54	60	62	73	91	100	103	106	114	153	159
Cherbourg	168	138	125	107	92	87	88	66	64	63	68	81	90	92	96	102	140	145
St Vaast	194	164	150	132	116	111	112	83	76	72	71	80	87	88	90	96	132	138
Ouistreham	229	198	185	167	151	146	147	117	107	100	86	91	92	91	90	92	125	130
Deauville	236	205	192	174	158	153	154	122	111	104	88	89	88	87	85	87	120	125
Le Havre	231	200	187	169	153	148	148	118	105	97	82	82	83	82	79	80	115	120
Fécamp	242	212	197	179	163	157	157	120	105	96	75	71	68	65	62	62	90	95
Dieppe	268	237	222	204	188	180	180	142	125	117	91	80	75	70	64	63	70	75
Boulogne	290	258	242	224	208	198	195	153	135	127	97	81	71	66	59	47	28	25
Calais	305	272	257	239	223	213	210	168	150	141	111	96	86	81	74	62	26	22

NOTES

1. This Table applies to Areas 1–3, and 14–16, each of which also contains its own internal Distance Table. Approximate distances in nautical miles are by the most direct route, while avoiding dangers and allowing for Traffic Separation Schemes.

2. For ports within the Solent, add the appropriate distances given in Area 2 to those shown above under either Needles Lighthouse or Nab Tower.

AREA 1 South West England - *Isles of Scilly to Anvil Point*

SELECTED LIGHTS, BUOYS & WAYPOINTS

Positions are referenced to WGS84

ISLES OF SCILLY TO THE LIZARD

ISLES OF SCILLY

Bishop Rock ☆ Fl (2) 15s 44m **24M**; part obsc 204°-211°, obsc 211°-233° and 236°-259°; Gy ○ twr with helo platform; *Racon T, 18M, 254°-215°*; 49°52'·37N 06°26'·74W.

Round Rock ⌿ 49°53'·10N 06°25'·19W.

Gunner ⌿ 49°53'·64N 06°25'·08W.

Old Wreck ⌀ VQ; 49°54'·26N 06°22'·81W.

Peninnis Hd ☆ Fl 20s 36m **17M**; 231°-117° but partially obsc 048°-083° within 5M; W ○ twr on B frame, B cupola; 49°54'·28N 06°18'·22W.

Spanish Ledge ⌀ Q (3) 10s; *Bell;* 49°53'·94N 06°18'·86W.

N Bartholomew ⌀ Fl R 5s; 49°54'·49N 06°19'·99W.

Bacon Ledge ⌀ Fl (4) R 5s; 49°55'·22N 06°19'·27W.

Tresco Flats, Hulman ⌀ Fl G 4s, 49°56'·29N 06°20'·31W.

Little Rag Ledge ⌀ Fl (2) R 5s; 49°56'·43N 06°20'·43W.

Bryher, Bar Quay ⌀ Q (3) 10s, 49°57'·35N 06°20'·85W.

Crow Rock ⌀ Fl (2) 10s; 49°56'·26N 06°18'·49W.

Hats ⌀ VQ (6) + L Fl 10s; 49°56'·21N 06°17'·14W.

Spencers Ledge ⌀ Q (6) + L Fl 15s; 49°54'·78N 06°22'·06W.

St Agnes, Porth Conger ⌀ QG, 49°53'·76N 06°20'·40W.

Steeple Rock ⌀ Q (9) 15s; 49°55'·46N 06°24'·24W.

Round Island ☆ Fl 10s 55m **18M**; 021°-288°; *Horn (4) 60s; Racon M, 10M;* 49°58'·74N 06°19'·40W.

St Martin's, Higher Town quay ⌀ Fl R 5s, 49°57'·45N 06°16'·84W.

SCILLY TO LAND'S END

Seven Stones ⌀ Fl (3) 30s 12m **25M**; H24; *Horn (3) 60s; Racon O, 15M;* 50°03'·62N 06°04'·34W.

Wolf Rock ☆ Fl 15s 34m **16M**; H24; *Horn 30s; Racon T, 10M;* 49°56'·72N 05°48'·57W.

Longships ☆ Fl (2) WR 10s 35m **W16M**, R11M; 189°-R-327°-W-189°; Gy ○ twr with helicopter platform; *Horn 10s;* 50°04'·01N 05°44'·81W.

Runnel Stone ⌀ Q (6) + L Fl 15s; *Bell;* 50°01'·19N 05°40'·36W.

Tater-du ☆ Fl (3) 15s 34m **20M**; 241°-074°; W ○ twr 50°03'·14N 05°34'·68W. Same twr FR 31m 13M, 060°-074° over Runnel Stone and in places 074°-077° (3°) within 4M; *Horn (2) 30s.*

NEWLYN and PENZANCE

S Pier ⌀ Fl 5s 10m 9M; W ○ twr; 253°-336°; 50°06'·19N 05°32'·57W.

N Pier ⌀ F WG 4m 2M; 238°-G-248°, W over hbr; 50°06'·19N 05°32'·62W.

Penzance S Pier ⌀ Fl WR 5s 11m **W17M**, R12M; 159°-R-268°-W-344·5°-R-shore; 50°07'·07N 05°31'·68W.

Lizard ☆ Fl 3s 70m **26M**; H24; 250°-120°, partly visible 235°-250°; W 8-sided twr; *Horn 30s;* 49°57'·61N 05°12'·13W.

FALMOUTH TO START POINT

FALMOUTH

St Anthony Head ☆ Iso WR 15s 22m, **W16M**, R14M, H24; 295°-W-004°-R-022°-W-172°; W 8-sided twr; *Horn 30s;* 50°08'·47N 05°00'·96W.

Black Rock ⌀ Fl (2) 10s 3M; 50°08'·72N 05°02'·00W.

St Mawes ⌀ Q (6) + L Fl 15s; 50°09'·10N 05°01'·42W.

Mylor chan ⌀ Fl G 6s; 50°10'·79N 05°02'·70W.

MEVAGISSEY

Victoria Pier ⌀ Fl (2) 10s 9m 12M; *Dia 30s;* 50°16'·15N 04°46'·93W.

FOWEY

Cannis Rock ⌀ Q (6) + L Fl 15s; *Bell;* 50°18'·38N 04°39'·95W.

Fowey ⌀ L Fl WR 5s 28m W11M, R9M; 284°-R-295°-W-028°-R-054°; 50°19'·62N 04°38'·84W.

Whitehouse Pt ⌀ Iso WRG 3s 11m W11M, R/G8M; 017°-G-022°- W-032°-R-037°; R col; 50°19'·98N 04°38'·24W.

POLPERRO

Spy House Pt ⌀ Iso WR 6s 30m 7M; W288°-060°, R060°-288°; 50°19'·81N 04°30'·70W.

LOOE and EDDYSTONE

Banjo Pier ☆ Oc WR 3s 8m **W15M**, R12M; 207°-R267°- W-313°-R-332°; 50°21'·05N 04°27'·06W.

Eddystone ☆ Fl (2) 10s 41m **17M**; Gy twr, helicopter platform; *Horn 30s; Racon T, 10M,* 50°10'·85N 04°15'·94W. Same twr, Iso R 10s 28m 8M; 110·5°-130·5° over Hand Deeps.

PLYMOUTH

Draystone ⌀ Fl (2) R 5s; 50°18'·85N 04°11'·07W.

Plymouth W bkwtr ⌀ Fl WR 10s 19m W12M, R9M; 262°-W-208°-R-262°; W ○ twr. Same twr, Iso 4s 12m 10M; vis 033°-037°; *Horn 15s;* 50°20'·07N 04°09'·53W.

The Bridge Channel. No 1, ⌀ QG 4m; 50°21'·03N 04°09'·53W. No 2, ⌀ QR 4m.

E Bkwtr ⌀ L Fl WR 10s 9m W8M, R6M; 190°-R-353°-W-001°-R-018°-W-190°; 50°20'·01N 04°08'·25W.

Ldg lts 349°. Front, Mallard Shoal ⌀ Q WRG 5m W10M, R/G3M; 233°-G-043°- R-067°-G-087°-W-099°-R-108°; 50°21'·60N 04°08'·33W. Rear, Hoe ⌀ Oc G 1·3s 11m 3M, 310°-040°; W ▽, Or bands.

Queen Anne's Battery (QAB) ldg lts ⌀ 048·5°. Front, Oc R 8s; R/W bcn; 50°21'·84N 04°07'·84W. Rear, Oc R 8s 14m 3M; 50°21'·89N 04°07'·75W.

Fisher's Nose, Fl (3) R 10s 4M; 50°21'·80N 04°08'·01W.

Sutton Hbr lock; IPTS; 50°21'·98N 04°07'·96W.

Plymouth Yacht Haven (PYH), outer bkwtr, E end, 2 FG (vert); 50°21'·59N 04°07'·15W.

Mayflower marina, outer bkwtr, E end, 2 FR (vert).

RIVER YEALM
The Sand Bar ⌇ Fl R 5s; 50°18'·59N 04°04'·12W.

SALCOMBE
Sandhill Pt Dir ⚡ 000°: Fl WRG 2s 27m W10M, R/G7M; 182·5°-G-357·5°-W-002·5°-R-182·5°; R/W ◇ on W mast; 50°13'·77N 03°46'·67W. 000° on with Pound Stone R/W ⚓, 230m S.

Start Pt ☆ Fl (3) 10s 62m **25M**; 184°-068°. Same twr: FR 55m 12M; 210°-255° over Skerries Bank; *Horn 60s;* 50°13'·33N 03°38'·54W.

START POINT TO ANVIL POINT

DARTMOUTH
Kingswear Dir ⚡ 328°: Iso WRG 3s 9m 8M; 318°-G-325°-W-331°-R-340°; W ○ twr; 50°20'·81N 03°34'·10W.
Mewstone ⚓ VQ (6) + L Fl 10s; 50°19'·92N 03°31'·89W.
West Rock ⚓ Q (6) + L Fl 15s; 50°19'·86N 03°32'·47W.
Homestone ⌇ QR; 50°19'·61N 03°33'·55W.
Castle Ledge ▲ Fl G 5s; 50°19'·99N 03°33'·12W.

BRIXHAM
Berry Head ☆ Fl (2) 15s 58m 14M; vis 100°-023°; W twr; 50°23'·97N 03°29'·01W. R lts on radio mast 5·7M NW, inland of Paignton.
Victoria bkwtr ⚡ Oc R 15s 9m 6M; W twr; 50°24'·33N 03°30'·78W.
Fairway Dir ⚡ 159°: Iso WRG 5s 4m 6M; 145°-G-157°-W-161°-R-173°; 50°23'·83N 03°30'·57W.

TORQUAY
▲ QG (May-Sep); 50°27'·42N 03°31'·80W.

TEIGNMOUTH
Outfall ⌇ Fl Y 5, 288°/1·3M to hbr ent.
Spratt Sand ▲ Fl G 2s; 50°32'·39N 03°29'·77W.
The Point ⚓ Oc G 6s 3M & FG (vert); 50°32'·42N 03°30'·05W.

RIVER EXE
Exe ⌇ Mo (A) 10s; 50°35'·90N 03°23'·70W.
No. 1 ▲ 50°36'·03N 03°23'·88W.

No. 7 ⚓ QG; 50°36'·43N 03°24'·09W.
Ldg lts 305°. Front, Iso 2s 6m 7M, 50°36'·99N 03°25'·34W. Rear, Q 12m 7M, 57m from front.
No. 10 ⌇ Fl R 3s; 50°36'·73N 03°24'·77W.
No. 12 Warren Pt ⌇ 50°36'·91N 03°25'·40W.

LYME REGIS
Outfall ⚓ Q (6) + L Fl 15s; 50°43'·17N 02°55'·66W.
Ldg lts 284°: Front, Victoria Pier ⚡ Oc WR 8s 6m, W9M, R7M; 296°-R-116°-W-296°; 50°43'·19N 02°56'·17W. Rear, FG 8m 9M, 240m from front.

WEST BAY (BRIDPORT)
W pier root, Dir ⚡ F WRG 5m 4M; 165°-G-331°-W-341°-R-165°; 50°42'·62N 02°45'·89W.
W pier ⚡ Iso R 2s 5m 4M; 50°42'·51N 02°45'·83W.
E pier ⚡ Iso G 2s 5m 4M; 50°42'·53N 02°45'·80W.

PORTLAND
Portland Bill lt ho ⚡ Fl (4) 20s 43m **25M**. vis 221°-244° (gradual change from 1 Fl to 4 Fl); 244°-117° (shows 4 Fl); 117°-141° (gradual change from 4 Fl to 1 Fl). W ○ twr; *Dia 30s;* 50°30'·85N 02°27'·38W. Same twr, FR 19m 13M; 271°-291° over Shambles.
W Shambles ⚓ Q (9) 15s; *Bell;* 50°29'·78N 02°24'·40W.
E Shambles ⚓ Q (3) 10s; *Bell;* 50°30'·78N 02°20'·08W.
Portland hbr, outer bkwtr (N end) ⚡ QR 14m 5M; 013°-268°; 50°35'·11N 02°24'·87W.
NE Bkwtr (A Hd) ⚡ Fl 2·5s 22m **20M**; 50°35'·16N 02°25'·07W.
NE Bkwtr (B Hd) ⚡ Oc R 15s 11m 5M; 50°35'·65N 02°25'·88W.

WEYMOUTH TO ANVIL POINT
Weymouth ldg lts 239·6°: both FR 5/7m 7M; Front 50°36'·46N 02°26'·87W, R ♦ on W post; rear 17m from front, R ♦ on W mast.
N Pier hd ⚡ 2 FG (vert) 9m 6M; 50°36'·59N 02°26'·63W.
S Pier hd ⚡ Q 10m 9M; 50°36'·57N 02°26'·49W.
IPTS 190m SW.

Lulworth Cove, E point 50°37'·00N 02°14'·78W.

Anvil Pt ☆ Fl 10s 45m **19M**; vis 237°-076° (H24); W ○ twr and dwelling; 50°35'·51N 01°57'·60W.

		1	2	3	4	5	6	7	8	9	10	11	12	13	14	15	16	17
1	Longships	1																
2	Scilly (Crow Rock)	22	2															
3	Penzance	15	35	3														
4	Lizard Point	23	42	16	4													
5	Falmouth	39	60	32	16	5												
6	Mevagissey	52	69	46	28	17	6											
7	Fowey	57	76	49	34	22	7	7										
8	Looe	63	80	57	39	29	16	11	8									
9	Plymouth (bkwtr)	70	92	64	49	39	25	22	11	9								
10	River Yealm (ent)	72	89	66	49	39	28	23	16	4	10							
11	Salcombe	81	102	74	59	50	40	36	29	22	17	11						
12	Start Point	86	103	80	63	55	45	40	33	24	22	7	12					
13	Dartmouth	95	116	88	72	63	54	48	42	35	31	14	9	13				
14	Torbay	101	118	96	78	70	62	55	50	39	38	24	15	11	14			
15	Exmouth	113	131	107	90	82	73	67	61	51	49	33	27	24	12	15		
16	Lyme Regis	126	144	120	104	96	86	81	74	63	62	48	41	35	30	21	16	
17	Portland Bill	135	151	128	112	104	93	89	81	73	70	55	49	45	42	36	22	17

DISTANCE TABLES
Approx distances in nautical miles are by the most direct route allowing for dangers and TSS.

NAVAL EXERCISE AREAS: Isles of Scilly to Start Point

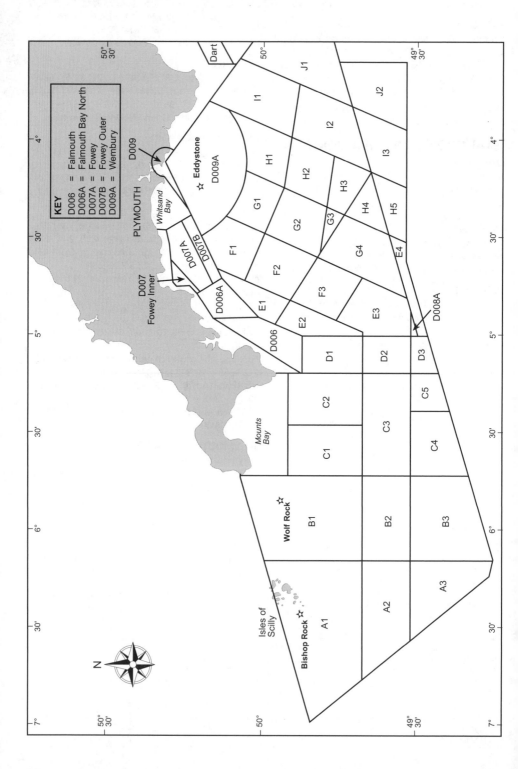

KEY

D006 = Falmouth
D006A = Falmouth Bay North
D007A = Fowey
D007B = Fowey Outer
D009A = Wembury

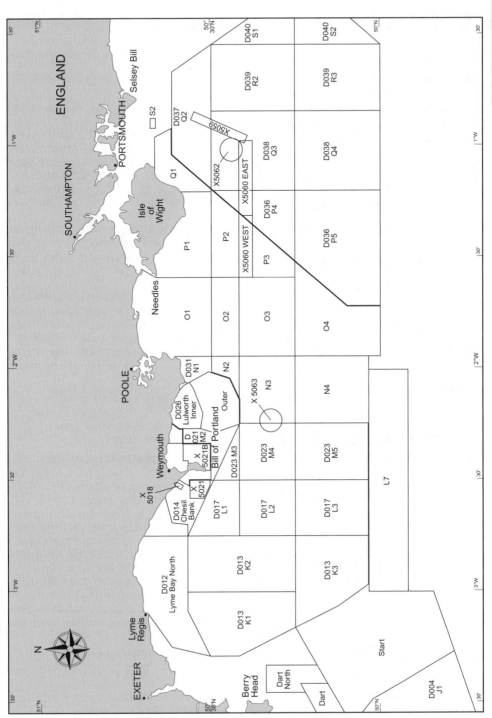

AREA 2 South Central England – *Anvil Point to Selsey Bill*

SELECTED LIGHTS, BUOYS & WAYPOINTS | Positions are referenced to WGS84

SWANAGE TO ISLE OF WIGHT

SWANAGE
Pier Hd ⌁ 2 FR (vert) 6m 3M; 50°36'·56N 01°56'·95W.
Peveril Ledge ⌁ QR; 50°36'·41N 01°56'·10W.

POOLE HARBOUR and APPROACHES
Poole Bar (No.1) ▲ QG; *Bell.*; 50°39·32N 01°55'·16W.

SWASH CHANNEL/EAST LOOE CHANNEL
South Hook *ℓ*; 50°39'·70N 01°55'·20W.
No. 3 ▲ Fl G 3s; 50°39'·76N 01°55'·49W.
Training Bank ⌁ 2 FR (vert); 50°39'·84N 01°55'·92W.
Channel (No. 8) ⌁ Fl R 2s; 50°40'·45N 01°56'·26W.
Swash (No.9) *ℓ* Q (9) 15s; 50°40'·88N 01°56'·70W.
East Looe 1 ▲ Fl G 5s; 50°41'·09N 01°55'·82W.
East Looe 4 (Limit 10 knots) ⌁ Fl R 2s; 50°41'·09N 01°56'·17W.
South Deep. Marked by lit and unlit Bns from ent South of Brownsea Castle to Furzey Is.

MIDDLE SHIP and NORTH CHANNELS
Bell (No. 15) *ℓ* Q (6) + L Fl 15s; *Bell;* 50°41'·36N 01°57'·12W.
Marked by PHM and SHM Lt buoys.
Aunt Betty (No.22) *ℓ* Q (3)10s; 50°41'·96N 01°57'·39W.
Diver (No. 25) *ℓ* Q (9) 15s; 50°42'·28N 01°58'·34W.
Stakes (No. 29) *ℓ* Q (6) + L Fl 15s; 50°42'·43N 01°59'·01W.

WAREHAM CHANNEL
Wareham Chan initially m'kd by ▲'s and ⌁'s and then by stakes.

WESTERN APPROACHES TO SOLENT

NEEDLES and NORTH CHANNELS
Needles Fairway *ℓ* L Fl 10s; *Bell;* 50°38'·24N 01°38'·98W.
SW Shingles *ℓ*Fl R 2·5s;50°38'·24N 01°38'·98W.
Bridge *ℓ* VQ (9) 10s; *Racon (T) 10M;* 50°39'·63N 01°36'·88W.
Needles 50°39'·73N 01°35'·50W; Oc (2) WRG 20s 24m **W17M**, R14M, R13M G14M; ○ Twr, R band and lantern; vis: shore-R-300°-W-083°-R (unintens)-212°-W-217°-G-224°. *Horn (2) 30s* H24. 01°33'·55W.
NE Shingles *ℓ* Q (3) 10s; 50°41'·96N 01°33'·41W.
Hurst Point ☆ 50°42'·48N 01°33'·03W; FL (4) WR 15s 23m W13M, R11M; W ○ Twr; vis:080°-W(unintens)-104°, 234°-W-244°-R-250°-W-053°. Same structure, Iso WRG 4s 19m **W21M, R18M, G17M**; vis: 038·8°-G-040·8°-W-041·8°-R- 043·8°; By day W7M, R5M, G5M.
N Head ▲ Fl (3) G 10s; 50°42'·69N 01°35'·52W.

YARMOUTH/LYMINGTON
Sconce *ℓ* Q; *Bell;* 50°42'·53N 01°31'·43W.
Black Rock ▲ Fl G 5s; 50°42'·58N 01°30'·64W.

Y'mouth E F'wy ⌁ Fl R 2s. 50°42'·64N 01°29'·88W.
Pier Head, centre, ⌁ 2 FR (vert) 2M; G col. High intensity FW (occas); 50°42'·51N 01°29'·97W.
Jack in the Basket *ℓ* Fl R 2s 9m; 50°44'·27N 01°30'·57W.
No. 1 *ℓ* Fl G 2s 2m 3M; G △ on pile; 50°44'·41N 01°30'·48W.
Lymington Bank ⌁ Fl (2) R 5s. *Bell;* 50°43'·10N 01°30'·85W.
Solent Bank ⌁ Fl (3) R 10s; 50°44'·23N 01°27'·37W.
Hamstead Ledge ▲ Fl (2) G 5s; 50°43'·87N 01°26'18W.
Newtown River ⌁ Fl R 4s; 50°43'·75N 01°24'·91W.
W Lepe ⌁ Fl R 5s; 50°45'·24N 01°24'·09W.
Salt Mead ▲ Fl (3) G 10s; 50°44'·51N 01°23'·04W.
Gurnard Ledge ▲ Fl (4) G 15s; 50°45'·51N 01°20'·59W.
E Lepe ⌁ Fl (2) R 5s; *Bell;* 50°45'·93N 01°21'·07W.
Lepe Spit *ℓ* Q (6) + L Fl 15s; 50°46'·78N 01°20'·64W.
Beaulieu Millenium Dir lt 334°. ⌁ Oc Q WRG 4s 13m W4M, R3M, G3M; vis: 321°-G-331°-W-337°-R-347°; 50°47'·12N 01°21'·90W.
NE Gurnard ▲ Fl (3) R 10s; 50°47'·06N 01°19'·42W.
W Bramble *ℓ* VQ (9) 10s; *Bell;* **Racon (T) 3M.;** 50°47'·20N 01°18'·65W.
W Knoll ⌁ Fl Y 2·5s; 50°47'·43N 01°17'·84W.
Williams Ship'g ⌁ (or) Fl Y 4s; 50°47'·11N01°18'·08W.
S Bramble ▲ Fl G 2·5s; 50°46'·98N 01°17'·72W.

COWES
Gurnard *ℓ* Q; 50°46'·22N 01°18'·84W.
Prince Consort *ℓ* VQ; 50°46'·42N 01°17'·55W.
No. 1 ▲ Fl G 3s; 50°46'·07N 01°18'·03W.
No. 2 ⌁ QR; 50°46'·07N 01°17'·87W.

SOUTHAMPTON WATER/RIVER HAMBLE
CALSHOT SPIT ⌁ Fl 5s 12m 11M; R hull, Lt Twr amidships; *Horn (2) 60s;* 50°48'·35N 01°17'·64W.
Calshot *ℓ* VQ; *Bell* ; 50°48'·44N 01°17'·03W.
Black Jack ⌁ Fl (2) R 4s; 50°49'·13N 01°18'·09W.
Hook ▲ QG; *Horn (1) 15s;* 50°49'·52N 01°18'·30W.
Bald Head ▲ Fl G 2·5s; 50°49'·80N 01°18'·06W.
Hamble Pt *ℓ* Q (6) + L Fl 15s; 50°50'·15N 01°18'·66W.
No. 1 *ℓ* QG 2m 2M; 50°50'·34N 01°18'·65W.
No. 2 *ℓ* Q (3) 10s 2m 2M; 50°50'·39N 01°18'·77W.
Greenland ▲ IQ G 10s; 50°51'·11N 01°20'·38W.
Weston Shelf ▲ Fl (3) G 15s; 50°52'·71N 01°23'·26W.
Hythe Pier Hd ⌁ 2 FR (vert) 12m 5M; 50°52'·49N 01°23'·61W.

SOUTHAMPTON/ITCHEN/TEST
Swinging Ground No. 1 ▲ Oc G 4s; 50°53'·00N 01°23'·44W.
Queen Elizabeth II Terminal, S end ⌁ 4 FG (vert) 16m 3M; 50°53'·00N 01°23'·71W.
Gymp ⌁ QR; 50°53'·17N 01°24'·30W.

THE EAST SOLENT

NORTH CHANNEL/HILLHEAD
Hillhead ₄Fl R 2·5s; 50°48'·07N 01°16'·00W.
Hillhead ⅃ Or Bn; 50°49'·06N 01°14'·78W.
E Bramble ⅃ VQ (3) 5s; 50°47'·23N 01°13'·64W.

EASTERN SOLENT MARKS/WOOTTON
W Ryde Middle ⅃ Q (9) 15s; 50°46'·48N 01°15'·79W.
Norris ₄ Fl (3) R 10s; 50°45'·97N 01°15'·51W.
N Ryde Middle ₄ Fl (4) R 20s; 50°46'·61N 01°14'·31W.
S Ryde Middle ▲ Fl G 5s; 50°46'·13N 01°14'·16W.
Peel Bank ₄ Fl (2) R 5s; 50°45'·49N 01°13'·35W.
SE Ryde Middle ⅃ VQ (6)+L Fl 10s; 50°45'·93N 01°12'·10W.
NE Ryde Middle ₄ Fl (2) R 10s; 50°46'·21N 01°11'·88W.
Wootton Bn ⅃ Q 1M; (NB); 50°44'·53N 01°12'·13W.
Mother Bank ₄ Fl R 3s; 50°45'·49N 01°11'·21W.
Browndown ▲ Fl G 15s; 50°46'·57N 01°10'·95W.

PORTSMOUTH and APPROACHES
Horse Sand Ft ⅃ Iso G 2s 21m 8M; 50°45'·01N 01°04'·34W.
Horse Sand ▲ Fl G 2·5s; 50°45'·53N 01°05'·27W.
Outer Spit ⅃ Q (6) + L Fl 15s; 50°45'·58N 01°05'·50W.
Mary Rose ₄ Fl Y 5s; 50°45'·80N 01°06'·20W.
No. 1 Bar (NB) ▲ Fl (3) G 10s; 50°46'·77N 01°05'·81W.
No. 2 ₄ Fl (3) R 10s; 50°46'·69N 01°05'·97W.
No. 4 (NB) ₄ QR; 50°47'·01N 01°06'·36W.
BC Outer ⅃ Oc R 15s; 50°47'·32N 01°06'·68W.
Fort Blockhouse ⅃ Dir lt 320°; WRG 6m W13M, R5M, G5M; vis: 310°- Oc G-316°-Al WG(W phase incr with brg), 318·5°-Oc-321·5°-Al WR (R phase incr with brg), 324°-Oc R-330°. 2 FR (vert) 20m E; 50°47'·37N 01°06'·74W.
Ballast ⅃ Fl R 2·5s; 50°47'·62N 01°06'·83W.

EASTERN APPROACHES TO THE SOLENT
Outer Nab 1 ⅃ VQ (9) 10s; 50°38'·18N 00°56'·88W.
Outer Nab 2 ⅃ VQ (3) 5s; 50°38'·43N 00°57'·70W.

Nab Tower ☆ 50°40'·08N 00°57'·15W; Fl 10s 27m 16M, *Horn (2) 30s; Racon (T) 10M.*
N 2 ⅃ Fl Y 2·5s. 6M; 50°41'·03N 00°56'·74W.
N 1 ⅃ Fl Y (4)10s; 50°41'·26N 00°56'·52W.
N 7 ⅃ Fl Y 2·5s; 50°42'·35N 00°57'·20W.
New Grounds ⅃ VQ (3) 5s; 50°41'·84N 00°58'·49W.
Nab End ₄ Fl R 5s; *Whis*; 50°42'·63N 00°59'·49W.
Dean Tail ▲ Fl G 5s; 50°42'·99N 00°59'·17W.
Dean Tail S ⅃ Q (6) + L Fl 10s; 50°43'·04N 00°59'·57W.
Dean Tail N ⅃ Q; 50°43'·13N 00°59'·57W.
St Helens ₄ Fl (3) R 15s; 50°43'·36N 01°02'·41W.
Horse Elbow ▲QG; 50°44'·26N 01°03'·88W.
Cambrian Wreck ⅃ 50°44'·43N 01°03'·43W.
Warner ₄ QR; *Whis*; 50°43'·87N 01°03'·99W.
W Princessa ⅃ Q (9) 15s; 50°40'·16N 01°03'·65W.
Bembridge Ledge ⅃ Q (3) 10s; 50°41'·15N 01°02'·81W
St Helen's Fort ☆ (IOW) Fl (3) 10s 16m 8M; large ○ stone structure; 50°42'·30N 01°05'·05W.

SE COAST OF THE ISLE OF WIGHT
St Catherine's Point ☆ 50°34'·54N 01°17'·87W; Fl 5s 41m **27M**; vis: 257°-117°; FR 35m **17M** (same Twr) vis: 099°-116°.
Ventnor Haven W Bwtr ⅃ 2 FR (vert) 3M; 50°35'·50N 01°12'·30W.

LANGSTONE and APPROACHES
Winner ⅃; 50°45'·10N 01°00'·10W.
Langstone F'wy ⅃ L Fl 10s; 50°46'·32N 01°01'·36W.

CHICHESTER ENTRANCE
West Pole (tripod) ⅃ Fl R 5s 14m 7M; 50°45'·45N 00°56'·59W.
Bar ⅃ Fl(2) R 10s 10m 4M; 50°46'·02N 00°56'·38W.
Eastoke ⅃ QR 2m 3M; 50°46'·66N 00°56'·16W.
West Winner ⅃ QG; Tide gauge. 50°46'·88N 00°55'·98W.

		1	2	3	4	5	6	7	8	9	10	11	12	13	14	15	16	17	18
1	Portland Bill	1																	
2	Weymouth	8	2																
3	Swanage	22	22	3															
4	Poole Hbr ent	28	26	6	4														
5	Needles Lt Ho	35	34	14	14	5													
6	Lymington	42	40	20	24	6	6												
7	Yarmouth (IOW)	40	39	18	22	4	2	7											
8	Beaulieu River ent	46	45	25	29	11	7	7	8										
9	Cowes	49	46	28	27	14	10	9	2	9									
10	Southampton	55	54	34	34	20	16	16	9	9	10								
11	R. Hamble (ent)	53	51	32	34	18	12	13	6	6	5	11							
12	Portsmouth	58	57	37	35	23	19	19	12	10	18	13	12						
13	Langstone Hbr	61	59	39	39	25	21	21	14	12	21	18	5	13					
14	Chichester Bar	63	62	42	42	28	23	24	17	15	23	18	8	5	14				
15	Bembridge	59	58	38	39	24	18	19	13	10	18	15	5	6	8	15			
16	Nab Tower	64	63	43	44	29	23	24	18	15	24	19	10	7	6	6	16		
17	St Catherine's Pt	45	44	25	25	12	19	21	27	15	36	29	20	20	19	17	15	17	
18	Littlehampton	79	79	60	61	46	44	45	38	36	45	42	31	28	25	28	22	35	18

DISTANCE TABLES
Approx distances in nautical miles are by the most direct route allowing for dangers and TSS.

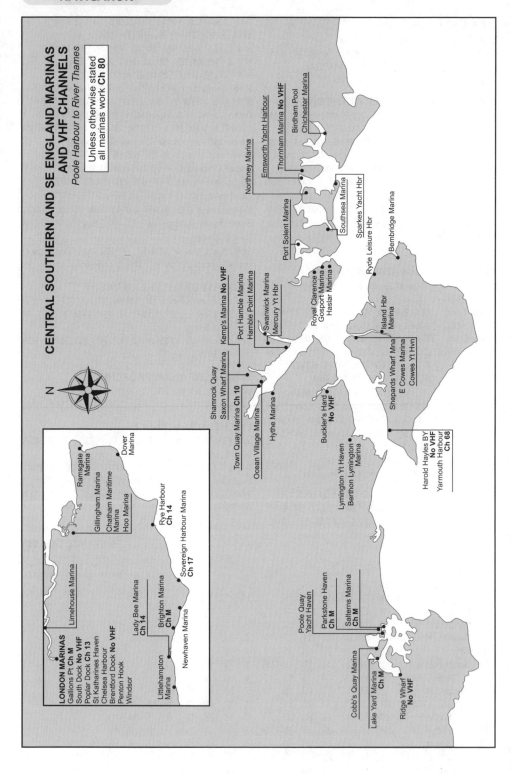

CENTRAL SOUTHERN AND SE ENGLAND MARINAS AND VHF CHANNELS

Poole Harbour to River Thames

Unless otherwise stated all marinas work **Ch 80**

N

LONDON MARINAS
Gallions Pt **Ch M**
South Dock **No VHF**
Poplar Dock **Ch 13**
St Katharines Haven
Chelsea Harbour
Brentford Dock **No VHF**
Penton Hook
Windsor

Limehouse Marina

Ramsgate Marina
Gillingham Marina
Chatham Maritime Marina
Hoo Marina
Dover Marina

Rye Harbour **Ch 14**

Lady Bee Marina **Ch 14**
Brighton Marina **Ch M**

Sovereign Harbour Marina **Ch 17**

Littlehampton Marina

Newhaven Marina

Northney Marina
Emsworth Yacht Harbour
Thornham Marina **No VHF**
Birdham Pool
Chichester Marina

Port Solent Marina
Southsea Marina
Sparkes Yacht Hbr
Bembridge Marina
Ryde Leisure Hbr

Kemp's Marina **No VHF**
Port Hamble Marina
Hamble Point Marina
Swanwick Marina
Mercury Yt Hbr

Royal Clarence
Gosport Marina
Haslar Marina

Island Hbr Marina

Shamrock Quay
Saxon Wharf Marina

Town Quay Marina **Ch 10**
Ocean Village Marina

Hythe Marina

Shepards Wharf Mna
E Cowes Marina
Cowes Yt Hvn

Buckler's Hard **No VHF**

Harold Hayles BY **No VHF**
Yarmouth Harbour **Ch 68**

Lymington Yt Haven
Berthon Lymington Marina

Poole Quay Yacht Haven
Parkstone Haven **Ch M**
Salterns Marina **Ch M**

Cobb's Quay Marina **Ch M**

Lake Yard Marina
Ridge Wharf **No VHF**

AREA 3 South East England – *Selsey Bill to North Foreland*

SELECTED LIGHTS, BUOYS & WAYPOINTS

Positions are referenced to WGS84

SELSEY BILL TO NORTH FORELAND

SELSEY BILL AND THE OWERS
S Pullar ⚓ VQ (6) + L Fl 10s; 50°38'·84N 00°49'·29W.
Boulder ⚓ Fl G 2·5s; 50°41'·56N 00°49'·09W.
Street ⚓ QR; 50°41'·69N 00°48'·89W.
Mixon ⚓ Fl R 5s; 50°42'·35N 00°46'·21W.
Owers ⚓ Q (6) + L Fl 15s; *Whis*; *Racon (O) 10M.*;
50°38'·63N 00°41'·19W.
E'Boro Hd ⚓ Q (3) 10s *Bell*; 50°41'·54N 00°39'·09W

LITTLEHAMPTON/SHOREHAM
Littlehampton W Pier Hd ⚓ QR 7m 6M; 50°47'·88N
00°32'·46W.
Shoreham E Bkwtr Hd ⚓ Fl G 5s 8M; *Siren 120s*;
50°49'·54N 00°14'·80W.

BRIGHTON MARINA
W Bkwtr Hd ⚓ QR 10m 7M; W○ structure, R bands;
Horn (2) 30s; 50°48'·50N 00°06'·38W.
E Bkwtr Hd ⚓ QG 8m 7M and Fl (4) WR 20s 16m
W10M, R8M; W pillar, G bands; vis: 260°-R- 295°-W-
100°; 50°48'·47N 00°06'·37W.

NEWHAVEN TO DUNGENESS
Newhaven Bkwtr Hd ⚓ Oc (2) 10s 17m 12M;
50°46'·56N 00°03'·50E.
GREENWICH ⚓ 50°24'·54N 00°00'·10E; Fl 5s 12m
15M; Riding lt FW; R hull; *Racon (M) 10M; Horn 30s*.
Beachy Head ☆ 50°44'·03N 00°14'·49E; Fl (2) 20s
31m **20M**; W round twr, R band and lantern; vis:
248°-101°; (H24); *Horn 30s.*
Royal Sovereign ☆ Fl 20s 28m 12M; W ○ twr, R band
on W cabin on col; *Horn (2) 30s*; 50°43'·45N
00°26'·09E.

SOVEREIGN HBR/RYE
Sovereign Hr Marina ⚓ Fl (3) 15s 12m 7M.;
50°47'·24N 00°19'·83E.
Rye Fairway , L Fl 10s; 50°54'·04N 00°48'·04E.

DUNGENESS - DOVER STRAIT
Dungeness ☆ 50°54'·81N 00°58'·56E; Fl 10s 40m
21M; B ○ twr, W bands and lantern, floodlit; Part
obsc 078°-shore; (H24). F RG 37m 10M (same twr);
vis: 057°-R-073°-G-078°-196°-R-216°; *Horn (3) 60s;*FR
Lts shown between 2·4M and 5·2M WNW when
firing taking place. QR on radio mast 1·2M NW.
Folkestone Bkwtr Hd ⚓ 51°04'·56N 01°11'·69E; Fl
(2) 10s 14m **22M**; *Dia (4) 60s*. In fog Fl 2s; vis: 246°-
306°, intens 271·5°-280·5°.

VARNE ⚓ 51°01'·29N 01°23'·90E; Fl R 20s12m
19M; *Racon (T)10M*; *Horn 30s*.

DOVER TO NORTH FORELAND
Dover Admiralty Pier Extension Hd ⚓ 51°06'·69N
01°19'·66E; Fl 7·5s 21m **20M**; W twr; vis: 096°-090°,
obsc in The Downs by S Foreland inshore of 226°;
Horn 10s; Int Port Tfc sigs.
Knuckle ☆ 51°07'·04N 01°20'·49E; Fl (4) WR 10s
15m **W15M**, R13M; W twr; vis: 059°-R-239°-W-059°.
SW Goodwin ⚓ Q (6) + L Fl 15s;51°08'·50N
01°28'·88E.

E GOODWIN ⚓ 51°13'·26N 01°36'·37E; Fl 15s 12m
23M; R hull with lt twr amidships; *Racon (T) 10M*;
Horn 30s.
NE Goodwin ⚓ Q (3) 10s; *Racon (M) 10M*. 51°20'·31N
01°34'·16E.
Goodwin Fork ⚓ Q (6) + L Fl 15s; *Bell*; 51°14'·33N
01°26'·86E.
NW Goodwin ⚓ Q (9) 15s; *Bell*; 51°16'·65N
01°28'·50E.
Gull Stream ⚓ QR; 51°18'·26N 01°29'·69E.

RAMSGATE/BROADSTAIRS
RA ⚓ Q(6) + L Fl 15s; 51°19'·60N 01°30'·13E.
E Brake ⚓ Fl R 5s; 51°19'·47N 01°29'·20E.
Broadstairs Knoll ⚓ Fl R 2·5s; 51°20'·88N 01°29'·48E.

North Foreland ☆ 51°22'·49N 01°26'·70E; Fl (5) WR
20s 57m **W19M, R16M, R15M**; W 8-sided twr; vis:
shore-W-150°-R(**16M**)-181°-R(**15M**)-200°-W-011°;
H24.

DISTANCE TABLES
Approx distances in nautical
miles are by the most direct
route allowing for dangers
and TSS.

		1															
1	Nab Tower	1															
2	Boulder Lt Buoy	5	2														
3	Owers Lt Buoy	11	8	3													
4	Littlehampton	19	13	12	4												
5	Shoreham	32	24	21	13	5											
6	Brighton	35	28	24	17	5	6										
7	Newhaven	40	34	29	24	12	7	7									
8	Beachy Head Lt	46	41	36	30	20	14	8	8								
9	Eastbourne	51	45	40	34	24	19	12	7	9							
10	Rye	72	67	62	56	46	41	34	25	23	10						
11	Dungeness Lt	76	71	66	60	50	44	38	30	26	9	11					
12	Folkestone	92	84	81	76	65	60	53	43	40	23	13	12				
13	Dover	97	89	86	81	70	65	58	48	45	28	18	5	13			
14	Ramsgate	112	104	101	96	85	80	73	63	60	43	33	20	15	14		
15	N Foreland Lt	115	107	104	99	88	83	76	66	63	46	36	23	18	3	15	
16	Sheerness	146	139	135	132	119	114	107	97	96	79	67	54	49	34	31	16
17	London Bridge	188	184	177	177	161	156	149	139	141	124	109	96	91	76	73	45	17

AREA 4 East England – *North Foreland to Berwick-upon-Tweed*

SELECTED LIGHTS, BUOYS & WAYPOINTS | Positions are referenced to WGS84

THAMES ESTUARY – SOUTHERN

(Direction of buoyage generally East to West)

IMPORTANT NOTE. Regular changes are made to Thames Estuary buoyage. Check Notices to Mariners for the latest information.

OUTER APPROACHES

Foxtrot 3 ⌐ 51°24'·2N 02°00'·4E; Fl 10s 12m **15M**; *Racon (T) 10M*; *Horn 10s*.
Drill Stone ⌠ Q (3) 10s ; 51°25'·88N 01°42'·89E.
NE Spit ⌠ VQ (3) 5s; 51°27'·93N 01°29'·89E.

N KENT COAST/THE SWALE

East Margate ⌐ Fl R 2·5s; 51°27'·03N 01°26'·40E.
Foreness Pt O'fall ⌐ Fl R 5s; 51°24'·61N 01°26'·02E.
SE Margate ⌠ Q (3) 10s; 51°24'·05N 01°20'·40E.
Hook Spit ▲ QG; 51°24'·08N 01°12'·26E.
Spaniard ⌠ Q (3) 10s; 51°26'·23N 01°04'·00E.
Spile ▲ Fl G 2·5s; 51°26'·43N 00°55'·70E.
Whitstable Street ⌐ ; 51°24'·00N 01°01'·54E.
Pollard Spit ⌐ Fl R 2s; 51°22'·98N 00° 58'·57E.
Queenboro Spit ⌠ Q (3) 10s; 51°25'·81N 00°43'·93E.

PRINCES CHANNEL /MEDWAY/SEA REACH

Outer Tongue ⌠ L Fl 10s; *Racon (T) 10M*; 51°30'·73N 01°26'·40E.
Princes Appr ⌠ Mo (A) 10s; 51°28'·32N 01°23'·75E.
E Redsand ⌐ Fl (2) R 5s; 51°29'·41N 01°04'·05E.
Sea Reach 1 ⌠ Fl Y 2·5s; *Racon (T) 10M*; 51°29'·45N 00°52'·57E.
Medway ⌠ Mo (A) 6s; 51°28'·83N 00°52'·81E.

FOULGER'S - FISHERMAN'S GATS

Long Sand Inner ⌐ Mo 'A' 15s; 51°38'·80N 01°25'·60E.
Long Sand Outer ⌐ L Fl 10s; 51°35'·90N 01°26'·00E.
Outer Fisherman ⌠Q (3) 10s; 51°33'·89N 01°25'·01E.
Inner Fisherman ⌐ Q R; 51°36'·07N 01°19'·87E.

THAMES ESTUARY – NORTHERN

KENTISH KNOCK

Kentish Knock ⌠ Q (3) 10s; *Whis*; 51°38'·08N 01°40·43E.
S Knock ⌠ Q (6) + L Fl 15s; *Bell*; 51°34'·13N 01°34'·29E.

BLACK DEEP

No. 9 ⌠ Q (6) + L Fl 15s; 51°35'·13N 01°15'·09E.
No. 2 ⌐ Fl (4) R 15s; 51°45'·63N 01°32'·20E.
Sunk Hd Tr ⌠ Q; *Whis*; 51°46'·63N 01°30'·51E.
Black Deep ⌐ QR. 51°47'·50N 01°35'·64E.
Long Sand Hd ⌠ VQ; *Bell*; 51°47'·90N 01°39'·42E.

BARROW DEEP

SW Barrow ⌠ Q(6) + L Fl 15s; *Bell*; 51°32'·29N 01°00'·31E.
Barrow No. 9 ⌠ VQ 5s; 51°35'·34N 01°10'·30E.

Barrow No. 5 ▲ Fl G 10s; 51°40'·03N 01°16'·20E.
Barrow No. 3 ⌠ Q (3) 10s; *Racon (M)10M*; 51°42'·02N 01°20'·24E.

WEST SWIN AND MIDDLE DEEP

Blacktail Spit ▲ Fl (3) G 10s; 51°31'·47N 00°56'·74E.
Maplin ▲ Q G; *Bell*; 51°33'·66N 01°01'·59E.
W Swin ⌐ QR; 51°33'·40N 01°01'·97E.
Maplin Edge ▲ 51°35'·33N 01°03'·64E.
Maplin Bank ⌐ Fl (3) R 10s; 51°35'·50N 01°04'·70E.

EAST SWIN (KING'S) CHANNEL

NE Maplin ▲ Fl G 5s; *Bell*; 51°37'·43N 01°04'·90E.
S Whitaker ▲ Fl (2) G 10s; 51°40'·23N 01°09'·05E.
W Sunk ⌠ Q (9) 15s; 51°44'·33N 01°25'·80E.
Gunfleet Spit ⌠ Q (6) + L Fl 15s; *Bell*; 51°45'·33N 01°21'·70E.
Gunfleet Old Lt Ho 51°46'·09N 01°20'·39E.

WHITAKER CHANNEL AND RIVER CROUCH

Whitaker ⌠ Q (3) 10s; *Bell*; 51°41'·43N 01°10'·51E.
Swin Spitway ⌠ Iso 10s; *Bell*; 51°41'·95N 01°08'·35E.
Whitaker ⌐ 51°39'·64N 01°06'·16E.
Ridge ⌐ Fl R 10s; 51°40'·13N 01°04'·87E.
Sunken Buxey ⌠ Q; 51°39'·54N 01°00'·59E.
Outer Crouch ⌠Q(6)+LFl 15s; 51°38'·38N 00°58'·48E.

GOLDMER GAT/WALLET/COLNE BAR

NE Gunfleet ⌠ Q (3) 10s; 51°49'·93N 01°27'·79E.
Wallet No. 2 ⌐ Fl R 5s; 51°48'·88N 01°22'·99E.
Wallet No. 4 ⌐ Fl (4) R 10s; 51°46'·53N 01°17'·23E.
Wallet Spitway ⌐ L Fl 10s; *Bell*; 51°42'·86N 01°07'·30E.
Knoll ⌠ Q; 51°43'·88N 01°05'·07E.
N Eagle ⌠ Q; 51°44'·71N 01°04'·32E.
NW Knoll ⌐ Fl (2) R 5s; 51°44'·35N 01°02'·17E.
Colne Bar ▲ Fl (2) G 5s; 51°44'·61N 01°02'·57E.
Bench Head ▲ Fl (3) G 10s; 51°44'·69N 01°01'·10E.
Inner Bench Hd ⌐ Fl (2) R 5s; 51°45'·96N 01°01'·74E.
Brightlingsea Spit ⌠ Q (6) + L Fl 15s; 51°48'·08N 01°00'·70E.

RIVER BLACKWATER/WALTON BACKWATERS

The Nass ⌠ VQ (3) 5s 6m 2M; 51°45'·83N 00°54'·83E.
Thirslet ▲ Fl (3) G 10s; 51°43'·73N 00°50'·39E. 00°57'·10E.
Naze Tower; 51°51'·87N 01°17'·29E.
Pye End ⌐ L Fl 10s; 51°55'·03N 01°17'·90E.
Crab Knoll No. 3 ▲ Fl G 5s; 51°54'·41N 01°16'·41E.
Island Point ⌠ Q; 51°53'·36N 01°15'·36E.

HARWICH APPROACHES

(Direction of buoyage North to South)

MEDUSA CHAN/CORK SAND/ROUGHS

Medusa ▲ Fl G 5s; 51°51'·23N 01°20'·35E.
Stone Banks ⌐ FlR 5s; 51°53'·19N 01°19'·23E.
S Cork ⌠ Q (6) + L Fl 15s; 51°51'·33N 01°24'·09E.

Roughs Tr SE ⚓ Q (3) 10s; 51°53'·64N 01°28'·94E.
Cork Sand Yacht Bn ⚓ VQ ; 51°55'·21N 01°25'·20E.

HARWICH CHANNEL
Sunk Inner ⚓ Mo(A), *Racon (T)*; 51°51'·03N 01°34'·89E.
S Shipwash ⚓⚓ 2 By(s) Q (6) + L Fl 15s; 51°52'·71N 01°33'·97E.
Outer Tidal Bn ⚓ Mo (U) 15s 2m 3M; 51°52'·85N 01°32'·34E.
SW Shipwash ⚓ Q (9)15s; 51°54'·75N 01°34'·21E.
Haven ⚓ Mo (A) 5s; 51°55'·76N 01°35'·56E.
HA ⚓ Iso 5s; 51°56'·75N 01°30'·66E.
Harwich Chan No. 1 ⚓ Fl Y 2·5s; *Racon (T)10M*; 51°56'·13N 01°27'·06E.
S Bawdsey ⚓ Q (6) + L Fl 15s; *Whis*; 51°57'·23N 01°30'·19E.
Platters ⚓ Q (6) + L Fl 15s; 51°55'·64N 01°20'·97E.
Rolling Ground ⚓ QG; 51°55'·55N 01°19'·75E.
Inner Ridge ⚓ QR; 51°55'·38N 01°20'·20E.
Landguard ⚓ Q; 51°55'·45N 01°18'·84E.

HARWICH TO ORFORDNESS
OFFSHORE MARKS
E Shipwash ⚓ VQ (3) 5s; 51°57'·08N 01°37'·89E.
N Shipwash ⚓ Q 7M; *Racon (M) 10M*; *Bell*; 52°01'·73N 01°38'·27E.
S Galloper ⚓ Q (6) L Fl 15s; *Racon (T)10M*; 51°43'·98N 01°56'·43E.
Outer Gabbard ⚓ Q (3) 10s; *Racon (O)10M*; 51°57'·83N 02°04'·19E.

DEBEN/ORE/SUFFOLK COAST
Woodbridge Haven ⚓ Mo(A)15s; 51°58'·20N 01°23'·85E.
Cutler ⚓ QG; 51°58'·51N 01°27'·48E.
SW Whiting ⚓ Q (6) + L Fl 10s; 52°00'·96N 01°30'·69E.
Orford Haven ⚓ L Fl 10s; *Bell*. 52°01'·62N 01°28'·00E.
NE Whiting ⚓ Q (3) 10s; 52°03'·61N 01°33'·32E.
NE Bawdsey ⚓ Fl G 10s; 52°01'·73N 01°36'·09E.

ORFORDNESS TO GT YARMOUTH
(Direction of buoyage is South to North)
Orford Ness ☆ 52°05'·03N 01°34'·46E; Fl 5s 28m **20M**; W ○ twr, R bands. F WRG 14m **W17M**, R13M, **G15M** (same twr). vis: R shore-210°, 038°-R-047°-G-shore; *Racon (T) 18M*. FR 13m 12M vis: 026°- 038° over Whiting Bank.
Aldeburgh Ridge ⚓ QR; 52°06'·72N 01°36'·95E.
Southwold ☆ 52°19'·63N 01°40'·89E; Fl (4) WR 20s 37m **W16M**, **R12M**, R14M; vis 204°-R (intens)- 215°-W-001°.

LOWESTOFT/GT YARMOUTH APPROACHES
E Barnard ⚓ Q (3) 10s; 52°25'·14N 01°46'·38E .
Newcome Sand ⚓ QR; 52°26'·28N 01°46'·97E.
S Holm ⚓ VQ (6) + L Fl 10s; 52°27'·05N 01°47'·15E.
N Newcome ⚓ Fl (4) R 15s; 52°28'·39N 01°46'·37E.

Lowestoft ☆ 52°29'·22N 01°45'·35; Fl 15s 37m **23M**; W twr; part obscd 347°- shore;
E Newcome ⚓ Fl (2) R 5s; 52°28'·51N 01°49'·21E.
Corton ⚓ Q (3) 10s; *Whis*; 52°31'·13N 01°51'·39E.
E. Holm ⚓ Fl (3) R 10s; 52°30'·64N 01°49'·72E.
S Corton ⚓ Q (6) + L Fl 15s; *Bell*; 52°32'·70N 01°49'·50E.
Holm Sand ⚓ Q. 52°33'·36N 01°46'·85E.
W Corton ⚓ Q (9) 15s; 52°34'·59N 01°46'·62E.
Gorleston South Pier Hd ⚓ Fl R 3s 11m 11M; vis: 235°-340°; *Horn (3) 60s*; 52°34'·33N 01°44'·28E.

GREAT YARMOUTH TO THE WASH
(Direction of buoyage ⇧ South to North)

GT YARMOUTH/COCKLE GATWAY/OFFSHORE
SW Scroby ⚓ Fl G 2·5s; 52°35'·82N 01°46'·26E.
Scroby Sands Wind Farm, 30 turbines centred on 52°39'·00N 01°47'·00E. NW, NE, SW, SE extremities (F.R Lts) Fl Y 5s 5M Horn Mo (U) 30s.
N Scroby ⚓ VQ; 52°41'·39N 01°46'·47E.
Cockle ⚓ VQ (3) 5s; *Bell*; 52°44'·03N 01°43'·59E.
Winterton Church *Racon (T) 10M*; 52°42'·92N 01°41'·21E.
Cross Sand ⚓ L Fl 10s 6m 5M; *Racon (T)10M*; 52°37'·03N 01°59'·14E.
NE Cross Sand ⚓ VQ (3) 5s; 52°44'·22N 01° 58'·80E.
Smith's Knoll ⚓ Q (6) + L Fl 15s 7M; *Racon (T) 10M*; 52°43'·52N 02°17'·89E.
S Winterton Ridge ⚓ Q (6) + L Fl 15s; 52°47'·21N 02°03'·44E.
Newarp ⚓ L Fl 10s 7M; *Racon (O) 10M*; 52°48'·37N 01°55'·69E.
S Haisbro ⚓ Q (6) + L Fl 15s; *Bell*; 52°50'·82N 01°48'·29E.
N Haisbro ⚓ Q; *Racon (T) 10M*; *Bell*; 53°00'·22N 01°32'·29E.
Happisburgh ☆ Fl (3) 30s 41m 14M; 52°49'·21N 01°32'·18E.

N NORFOLK COAST/THE WASH
Cromer ☆ 52°55'·45N 01°19'·01E; Fl 5s 84m **21M**; W 8-sided twr; vis: 102°-307° H24; *Racon (O) 25M*.
E Sheringham ⚓ Q (3) 10s; 53°02'·21N 01°14'·84E.
Blakeney O'falls ⚓ Fl (2) R 5s; *Bell*; 53°03'·01N 01°01'·37E.
Wells Leading Buoy ⚓ Fl (2) R 5s; 52°59'·80N 00°50'·49E.
S Race ⚓ Q (6) + L Fl 15s; *Bell*; 53°07'·81N 00°57'·34E.
S Inner Dowsing ⚓ Q (6) + L Fl 15s; *Bell*; 53°12'·12N 00°33'·69E.
Burnham Flats ⚓ Q (9) 15s; *Bell*; 53°07'·53N 00°34'·89E.
N Well ⚓ L Fl 10s; *Whis*; *Racon (T) 10M*; 53°03'·02N 00°27'·90E.
Roaring Middle ⚓ L Fl 10s 7m 8M; 52°58'·64N 00°21'·08E.

Sunk ↙ Q (9) 15s; 52°56'·29N 00°23'·40E.
Boston Roads ◔ L Fl 10s; 52°57'·66N 00°16'·04E.

THE WASH TO THE RIVER HUMBER

Dudgeon↙Q (9) 15s 7M; *Racon (O) 10M*; 53°16'·62N 01°16'·90E.
E Dudgeon ↙ Q (3) 10s; 53°19'·72N 00°58'·69E.
N Outer Dowsing ↙ Q; 53°33'·52N 00°59'·59E.

B.1D Platform Dowsing ◌ 53°33'·68N 00°52'·63E; Fl (2) 10s 28m **22M**; Morse (U) R 15s 28m 3M; *Horn (2) 60s*; *Racon (T) 10M*.
Inner Dowsing ↙ Q (3) 10s 7M, *Racon (T) 10M*; *Horn 60s*; 53°19'·10N 00°34'·80E.
Protector ◔ Fl R 2·5s; 53°24'·84N 00°25'·12E.
Humber ⚓ L Fl 10s 7M; *Horn (2) 30s*; *Racon (T) 7M*; 53°38'·83N 00°20'·17E.

SPURN ⚓ Q (3) 10s 10m 8M; *Horn 20s*; *Racon (M) 5M*; 53°33'·56N 00°14'·20E.

RIVER HUMBER TO RIVER TYNE
BRIDLINGTON/FILEY

SW Smithic ↙ Q (9) 15s; 54°02'·41N 00°09'·21W.
Flamborough Hd ☆ 54°06'·98N 00°04'·96W; Fl (4) 15s 65m **24M**; W ◯ twr; *Horn (2) 90s*.
Filey Brigg ↙ Q (3) 10s; *Bell*; 54°12'·74N 00°14'·60W.

SCARBOROUGH/WHITBY

Scarborough Pier ⚡ Iso 5s 17m 9M; W ◯ twr; vis: 219°-039° (tide sigs); *Dia 60s*; 54°16'·91N 00°23'·40W.
Whitby ↙ Q; *Bell*; 54°30'·33N 00°36'·58W.
Whitby High ☆ 54°28'·67N 00°34'·10W; Ling Hill Fl WR 5s 73m **18M**, R16M; W 8-sided twr and dwellings; vis: 128°-R-143°-W- 319°.
Salt Scar ↙ 54°38'·12N 01°00'·12W VQ; *Bell*.

TEES BAY/HARTLEPOOL/SUNDERLAND

Tees Fairway ↙Iso 4s 8m 8M; *Racon (B) unknown range*; *Horn (1) 5s*; 54°40'·94N 01°06'·48W.
Bkwtr Hd S Gare ☆ 54°38'·85N 01°08'·27W; Fl WR 12s 16m **W20M, R17M**; W ◯ twr; vis: 020°-W-274°-R-357°; Sig Stn; *Horn 30s*.
Longscar ↙ Q (3) 10s; *Bell*; 54°40'·86N 01°09'·89W.
The Heugh ☆ 54°41'·79N 01°10'·56W; Fl (2) 10s 19m**19M** ; W twr.
Hartlepool Old Pier Hd ⚡ Fl WG 3s 13m 7M; vis: 317°-

W-325°-G- 317°; 54°41'·60N 01°11'·09W.

Sunderland Roker Pier Hd ☆ 54°55'·28N 01°21'·15W; Fl 5s 25m **23M**; W ☐ twr, 3 R bands and cupola: vis: 211°- 357°; *Siren 20s*.

TYNE ENTRANCE/NORTH SHIELDS
Ent North Pier Hd ☆ 55°00'·88N 01°24'·18W; Fl (3) 10s 26m **26M**; Gy ☐ twr, W lantern; *Horn 10s*.

RIVER TYNE TO BERWICK-ON-TWEED
BLYTH/COQUET ISLAND/ AMBLE

Blyth F'w'y ◣ Fl G 3s; *Bell*;55°06'·59N 01°28'·60W.
Blyth E Pier Hd ☆ 55°06'·98N 01°29'·37W; Fl (4) 10s 19m **21M**, W twr; same structure FR 13m 13M, vis:152°-249°; *Horn (3) 30s*.
Coquet ☆ 55°20'·03N 01°32'·39W; Fl (3) WR 20s 25m **W19M, R15M**; W ☐ twr, turreted parapet, lower half Gy; vis: 330°-R-140°-W-163°-R-180°-W-330°; sector boundaries are indeterminate and may appear as Alt WR; *Horn 30s*.
Amble N Pier Hd ⚡ Fl G 6s 12m 6M; 55°20'·39N 01°34'·25W.

BAMBURGH/FARNE ISLANDS

The Falls ◔ Fl R 2·5s; 55°34'·61N 01°37'·12W.
Shoreston Outcars ◔ QR; 55°35'·88N 01°39'·34W.
Bamburgh Black Rocks Point ☆ 55°36'·99N 01°43'·45W; Oc(2) WRG 8s 12m **W14M**, R11M, G11M; W bldg; vis: 122°-G-165°-W-175°-R-191°-W-238°-R- 275°-W- 289°-G-300°.
Inner Farne ⚡ Fl (2) WR 15s 27m W10M, R7M; W ◯ twr; vis: 119°-R-280°-W-119°; 55°36'·92N 01°39'·35W.
Longstone ☆ **W side** 55°38'·62N 01°36'·65W; Fl 20s 23m **24M**; R twr, W band; *Horn (2) 60s*.
Swedman ◣ Fl G 2·5s; 55°37'·65N 01°41'·63W.

HOLY ISLAND

Ridge ↙ Q (3) 10s; 55°39'·70N 01°45'·97W.
Triton ↙ QG; 55°39'·59N 01°46'·82W.
Plough Seat ◔ QR; 55°40'·37N 01°44'·97W.
Goldstone ↙ QG; 55°40'·25N 01°43'·64W.

BERWICK-ON-TWEED

Bkwtr Hd ⚡ Fl 5s 15m 6M; vis: 201°-009°, (obscured 155°-201°); W ◯ twr, R cupola and base; FG (same twr) 8m 1M; vis 009°-G-155°; 55°45'·88N 01°59'·06W.

		1	2	3	4	5	6	7	8	9	10	11			
1	Ramsgate	1				11	31	61	78	91	107	126	189	205	205	232	Berwick-upon-Tweed	11
2	Sheerness	34	2				10	27	42	65	81	102	157	176	185	203	Amble	10
3	Gravesend	56	22	3				9	16	36	51	70	138	149	156	180	Sunderland	9
4	London Bridge	76	45	23	4				8	24	39	58	122	137	140	169	Hartlepool	8
5	Burnham-on-Crouch	44	34	53	76	5				7	16	35	88	114	121	143	Whitby	7
6	Brightlingsea	41	28	47	71	22	6				6	20	81	98	105	130	Scarborough	6
7	Harwich	40	50	65	83	31	20	7				5	58	83	87	114	Bridlington	5
8	River Deben (ent)	45	55	71	89	35	23	6	8				4	72	75	113	Hull	4
9	Southwold	62	80	95	113	58	46	30	23	9				3	34	83	Boston	3
10	Lowestoft	72	90	105	123	68	56	40	33	10	10				2	85	King's Lynn	2
11	Great Yarmouth	79	97	112	130	76	63	52	41	18	7	11				1	Great Yarmouth	1

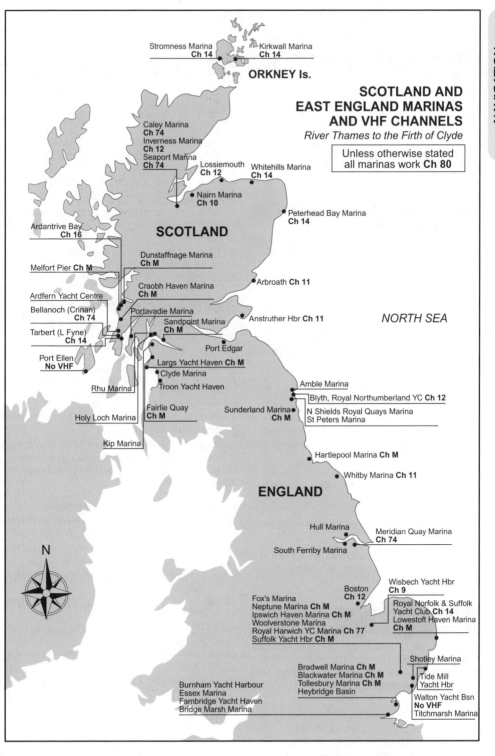

Stromness Marina
Ch 14

Kirkwall Marina
Ch 14

ORKNEY Is.

**SCOTLAND AND
EAST ENGLAND MARINAS
AND VHF CHANNELS**
River Thames to the Firth of Clyde

Unless otherwise stated
all marinas work **Ch 80**

Caley Marina
Ch 74
Inverness Marina
Ch 12
Seaport Marina
Ch 74

Lossiemouth
Ch 12

Whitehills Marina
Ch 14

Nairn Marina
Ch 10

Peterhead Bay Marina
Ch 14

Ardantrive Bay
Ch 16

SCOTLAND

Dunstaffnage Marina
Ch M

Melfort Pier **Ch M**

Craobh Haven Marina
Ch M

Arbroath **Ch 11**

Ardfern Yacht Centre

Bellanoch (Crinan)
Ch 74

Portavadie Marina

Sandpoint Marina
Ch M

Anstruther Hbr **Ch 11**

NORTH SEA

Tarbert (L Fyne)
Ch 14

Port Edgar

Port Ellen
No VHF

Largs Yacht Haven **Ch M**

Clyde Marina

Rhu Marina

Troon Yacht Haven

Amble Marina

Blyth, Royal Northumberland YC **Ch 12**

Fairlie Quay
Ch M

Sunderland Marina
Ch M

N Shields Royal Quays Marina
St Peters Marina

Holy Loch Marina

Kip Marina

Hartlepool Marina **Ch M**

Whitby Marina **Ch 11**

ENGLAND

Hull Marina

Meridian Quay Marina
Ch 74

South Ferriby Marina

N

Wisbech Yacht Hbr
Ch 9

Boston
Ch 12

Fox's Marina
Neptune Marina **Ch M**
Ipswich Haven Marina **Ch M**
Woolverstone Marina
Royal Harwich YC Marina **Ch 77**
Suffolk Yacht Hbr **Ch M**

Royal Norfolk & Suffolk
Yacht Club **Ch 14**
Lowestoft Haven Marina
Ch M

Shotley Marina

Bradwell Marina **Ch M**
Blackwater Marina **Ch M**
Tollesbury Marina **Ch M**
Heybridge Basin

Tide Mill
Yacht Hbr

Walton Yacht Bsn
No VHF
Titchmarsh Marina

Burnham Yacht Harbour
Essex Marina
Fambridge Yacht Haven
Bridge Marsh Marina

AREA 5 E Scotland – *Berwick-upon-Tweed to C Wrath & N Isles*

SELECTED LIGHTS, BUOYS & WAYPOINTS

Positions are referenced to WGS84

BERWICK-UPON-TWEED TO BASS ROCK

EYEMOUTH/ST ABB'S/DUNBAR

Blind Buss ↓ Q; 55°52'·80N 02°05'·25E.

Eyemouth E Bkwtr Hd ⊀ Iso R 2s 8m 8M; 55°52'·50N 02°05'·29W.

St Abb's Hd ☆ 55°54'·96N 02°08'·29W; Fl 10s 68m **26M**; W twr; *Racon (T) 18M*.

Bass Rock, S side, ☆ Fl (3) 20s 46m 10M; W twr; vis: 241°-107°; 56°04'·61N 02°38'·48W.

FIRTH OF FORTH - SOUTH SHORE

SOUTH SIDE TO LEITH/PORT EDGAR

Fidra ☆ 56°04'·39N 02°47'·13W; Fl (4) 30s 34m **24M**; W twr; obsc by Bass Rk, Craig Leith & Lamb Is.

Wreck ↺ Fl (2) R 10s; 56°04'·39N 02°52'·39W.

Inchkeith F'wy ↺ Iso 2s; *Racon (T) 5M*; 56°03'·49N 03°00'·10W.

Narrow Deep ↺ Fl (2) R 10s; 56°01'·46N 03°04'·59W.

Craigh Waugh ↓ Q;56°00'·26N 03°04'·47W.

Leith Approach ↺ Fl R 3s; 55°59'·95N 03°11'·51W.

Inch Garvie, NW ⊀ L Fl 5s 9m 11M; 56°00'·10N 03°23'·37W.

Forth Rail Br. Centres of spans have W Lts and ends of cantilevers R Lts, defining N and S chans. Centre Piers; 2 Aero FR 47m 5M; 56°00'·33N 03°21'·79W.

Forth Road Br. N susp twr Iso G 4s 7m 6M on E and W sides. S susp twr Iso R 4s 7m 6M on E and W sides.

Port Edgar W Bkwtr Hd ⊀ Fl R 4s 4m 8M; 55°59'·86N 03°24'·78W. W blockhouse

NORTH CHANNEL/MIDDLE BANK

Inchkeith ☆ 56°02'·01N 03°08'·17W; Fl 15s 67m **22M**; stone twr.

No. 7 ↘ QG; *Bell; Racon (T) 5M*; 56°02'·80N 03°10'·97W.

Oxcars ☆ Fl (2) WR 7s 16m W13M, R12M; W twr, R band; vis: 072°-W-087°-R-196°-W-313°-R-072°; 56°01'·36N 03°16'·84W.

FIRTH OF FORTH - N SHORE; ELIE TO FIFE NESS/RIVER TAY/ARBROATH

Elie Ness ☆ 56°11'·04N 02°48'·77W; Fl 6s 15m **18M**; W twr.

St Monans Bkwtr Hd ⊀ Oc WRG 6s 5m W7M, R4M, G4M; vis: 282°-G-355°-W-026°-R-038°; 56°12'·20N 02°45'·94W.

Anstruther, W Pier Hd ⊀ 2 FR (vert) 5m 4M; Gy mast; *Horn (3) 60s (occas)*; 56°13'·18N 02°41'·84W.

Isle of May ☆ 56°11'·12N 02°33'·46W(Summit); Fl (2) 15s 73m **22M**; ☐ twr on stone dwelling.

Fife Ness ☆ 56°16'·74N 02°35'·19W; Iso WR 10s 12m **W21M, R20M**; W bldg; vis: 143°-W-197°-R-217°-W-023°.

N Carr ↓ Q (3) 10s 3m 5M; 56°18'·05N 02°32'·94W.

Bell Rk ☆ 56°26'·08N 02°23'·21W; Fl 5s 28m **18M**; *Racon (M) 18M*.

Tay F'wy ↺ L Fl 10s; 56°28'·30N 02°36'·60W.

Abertay N ↓ Q (3) 10s; *Racon (T) 8M*; 56°27'·39N 02°40'·36W.

Horse Shoe ↓ Q (6) + L Fl 15s; 56°27'·28N 02°50'·20W.

Tayport High Lt Ho ☆ 56°27'·17N 02°53'·96W; Dir lt 269°; Iso WRG3s 24m **W22M, R17M, G16M**; W twr; vis:267°-G-268°-W-270°-R-271°;56°27'·04N 02°56'·55W.

Arbroath E Pier S Elbow ⊀ Fl G 3s 8m 5M; W twr; shows FR when hbr closed; *Siren (3) 60s* (occas); 56°33'·25N 02°34'·97W.

MONTROSE TO RATTRAY HEAD

MONTROSE/JOHNSHAVEN/GOURDON

Scurdie Ness ☆ 56°42'·10N 02°26'·24W; Fl (3) 20s 38m **23M**; W twr; *Racon (T) 14-16M*.

Montrose Ldg Lts 271·5°. Front, FR 11m 5M; W twin pillars, R bands; 56°42'·21N 02°27'·41W. Rear, 272m from front, FR 18m 5M; W twr, R cupola.

Johnshaven, Ldg Lts 316°. Front, FR 5m; 56°47'·62N 02°20'·26W . Rear, 85m from front, FG 20m; shows R when unsafe to enter hbr.

Gourdon Hbr, Ldg Lts 358°. Front, FR 5m 5M; W twr; shows G when unsafe to enter; *Siren (2) 60s* (occas); 56°49'·69N 02°17'·24W. Rear, 120m from front, FR 30m 5M; W twr.

STONEHAVEN/ABERDEEN/PETERHEAD

Stonehaven Outer Pier Hd ⊀ Iso WRG 4s 7m W11M, R7M, G8M; vis: 214°-G-246°-W-268°-R-280°; 56°57'·59N 02°12'·00W.

Girdle Ness ☆ Fl (2) 20s 56m **22M**; obsc by Greg Ness when brg more than about 020°; *Racon (G) 25M*; 57°08'·34N 02°02'·91W.

Aberdeen F'wy ↺ Mo (A) 5s; *Racon (T) 7M*; 57°09'·31N 02°01'·95W.

Torry Ldg lts 235·7°. Front, FR or FG 14m 5M; FR entry safe, FG when entry dangerous; vis: 195°-279°; 57°08'·37N 02°04'·51W. Rear, FR 19m 5M.

Buchan Ness ☆ Fl 5s 40m **28M**; W twr, R bands; *Racon (O) 14-16M*; 57°28'·23N 01°46'·51W.

Cruden Skares ↺ Fl R 10s; 57°23'·17N 01°50'·36W.

Peterhead Marina N Bkwtr Hd ⊀ QG 5m 2M; vis: 185°-300°; 57°29'·81N 01°47'·49W.

Rattray Hd ☆ 57°36'·61N 01°49'·03W; Fl (3) 30s 28m **24M**; W twr; *Racon (M) 15M*.

RATTRAY HEAD TO INVERNESS

Rattray Hd ☆ 57°36'·61N 01°49'·03W Fl (3) 30s 28m **24M**; W twr; **Racon (M) 15M**; *Horn (2) 45s.*

FRASERBURGH/MACDUFF/BANFF

Fraserburgh, Balaclava Bkwtr Head ⚓ Fl (2) G 8s 26m 6M; dome on W twr; vis: 178°-326°; 57°41'·51N 01°59'·70W.

Kinnaird Hd ☆ 57°41'·87N 02°00'·26W Fl 5s 25m **22M**; vis: 092°-297°.

Macduff Pier Hd ⚓ Fl (2) WRG 6s 12m W9M, R7M; W twr; vis: shore-G-115°-W-174°-R-210°; 57°40'·25N 02°30'·02W.

Banff N Pier Hd ⚓ Fl 4s; 57°40'·22N 02°31'·27W.

WHITEHILLS/PORTSOY/FINDOCHTY

Whitehills Pier Hd ⚓ 57°40'·80N 02°34'·88W Fl WR 3s 7m W9M, R6M; W twr; vis: 132°-R-212°-W-245°.

Portsoy Pier Ldg Lts 160°, Front F 12m 5M; twr; 57°41'·17N 02°41'·49W. Rear FR 17m 5M; mast.

Findochty Middle Pier Ldg Lts 166°, Front FR 6m 3M; 57°41'·90N 02°54'·20W. Rear FR 10m 3M.

BUCKIE/LOSSIEMOUTH/HOPEMAN

West Muck ⚓ QR 5m 7M; tripod; 57°41'·06N 02°58'·01W.

N Pier 60m from Hd ☆ 57°40'·9N 02°57'·5W Oc R 10s 15m **15M** W twr.

BURGHEAD/FINDHORN/NAIRN

Lossiemouth S Pier Hd ⚓ Fl R 6s 11m 5M; *Siren 60s;* 57°43'·42N 03°16'·69W.

Covesea Skerries ☆ 57°43'·47N 03°20'·45W Fl WR 20s 49m **W24M, R20M**; W twr; vis: 076°-W-267°-R-282°.

Hopeman W Pier Hd ⚓ Oc G 4s 8m 4M; 57°42'·69N 03°26'·29W.

Burghead N Bkwtr Hd ⚓ Oc 8s 7m 5M; 57°42'·09N 03°30'·03W.

Findhorn Landfall ⚓ LF 10s; 57°40'·33N 03°38'·94W.

Nairn W Pier Hd ⚓ QG 5m 1M; Gy post; 57°35'·60N 03°51'·63W.

INVERNESS FIRTH/CALEDONIAN CANAL

Navity Bk ⚓ Fl (3) G 15s; 57°38'·16N 04°01'·18W.

Riff Bank S ⚓ Q (6) + L Fl 15s; 57°36'·73N 04°00'·97W.

Craigmee ⚓ Fl R 6s 3m 4M; 57°35'·30N 04°05'·04W.

Chanonry ☆ 57°34'·44N 04°05'·57W Oc 6s 12m **15M**; W twr; vis: 148°-073°.

Kessock Bridge Centre , Or △; **Racon (K) 6M**; 57°29'·97N 04°13'·79W.

Clachnaharry, S Tr'ng Wall Hd ⚓ Iso G 4s 5m 2M; tfc sigs; 57°29'·43N 04°15'·86W.

INVERNESS TO DUNCANSBY HEAD

CROMARTY FIRTH

Fairway ⚓ L Fl 10s; **Racon (M) 5M**; 57°39'·96N 03°54'·19W.

Cromarty Bank ⚓ Fl (2) G 10s; 57°40'·66N 03°56'·78W.

Buss Bank ⚓ Fl R 3s 57°40'·97N 03°59'·54W.

The Ness ☆ 57°40'·98N 04°02'·20W Oc WR 10s 18m **W15M**, R11M; W twr; vis: 079°-R-088°-W-275°, obsc by N Sutor when brg less than 253°.

Three Kings ⚓ Q (3) 10s; 57°43'·73N 03°54'·25W.

DORNOCH FIRTH/LYBSTER/WICK

Tarbat Ness ☆ 57°51'·88N 03°46'·76W Fl (4) 30s 53m **24M**; W twr, R bands; *Racon (T) 14-16M*.

Lybster, S Pier Hd ⚓ Oc R 6s 10m 3M; 58°17'·79N 03°17'·41W.

Clyth Ness ☆ Fl (2) 30s 45m 14M; 58°18'·64N 03°12'·74W.

Wick S Pier Hd ⚓ Fl WRG 3s 12m W12M, R9M, G9M; W 8-sided twr; vis: 253°-G-270°-W-286°-R-329°; Bell (2) 10s (occas); 58°26'·34N 03°04'·73W.

Noss Hd ☆ 58°28'·71N 03°03'·09W Fl WR 20s 53m **W25M, R21M**; W twr; vis: shore-R-191°-W-shore.

DUNCANSBY HEAD TO CAPE WRATH

Duncansby Hd ☆ 58°38'·65N 03°01'·58W Fl 12s 67m **22M**; W twr; **Racon (T)**.

Pentland Skerries ☆ 58°41'·41N 02°55'·49W Fl (3) 30s 52m **23M**; W twr.

Lother Rock ⚓ Fl 2s 13m 6M; *Racon (M)10M*; 58°43'·79N 02°58'·69W.

Swona N Hd ⚓ Fl (3) 10s 16m 10M; 58°45'·11N 03°03'·10W.

Stroma ☆, Swilkie Point 58°41'·75N 03°07'·01W Fl (2) 20s 32m **26M**; W twr.

Dunnet Hd ☆ 58°40'·28N 03°22'·60W Fl (4) 30s 105m **23M**.

Scrabster Q. E. Pier Hd ⚓ Fl (2) 4s 8m 8M 58°36'·66N 03°32'·31W.

Strathy Pt ☆ 58°36'·04N 04°01'·12W Fl 20s 45m **26M**; W twr on W dwelling. F.R. on chy 100° 8·5M.

Sule Skerry ☆ 59°05'·09N 04°24'·38W Fl (2) 15s 34m **21M**; W twr; *Racon (T)*.

North Rona ☆ 59°07'·27N 05°48'·91W Fl (3) 20s 114m **24M**.

Sula Sgeir ⚓ Fl 15s 74m 11M; □ structure; 59°05'·61N 06°09'·57W.

Loch Eriboll, White Hd ⚓ Fl WR10s 18m W13M, R12M; W twr and bldg; vis: 030°-W-172°-R-191°-W-212°; 58°31'·01N 04°38'·90W.

Cape Wrath ☆ 58°37'·54N 04°59'·94W Fl (4) 30s 122m **22M**; W twr.

ORKNEY ISLANDS

Tor Ness ☆ 58°46'·78N 03°17'·86W Fl 5s 21m **17M**; W twr.

Cantick Hd (S Walls, SE end) ☆ 58°47'·23N 03°07'·88W Fl 20s 35m **18M**; W twr.

SCAPA FLOW AND APPROACHES

Ruff Reef, off Cantick Hd ⚡Fl 10s 10m 6M; 58°47'·43N 03°07'·80W.

Hoxa Hd ⚡ Fl WR 3s 15m W9M, R6M; W twr; vis: 026°-W-163°-R-201°-W-215°; 58°49'·31N 03°02'·09W.

Stanger Hd ⚡ Fl R 5s 25m 8M 58°48'·96N 03°04'·74W.

CLESTRAN SOUND/HOY SOUND

Peter Skerry ▲ Fl G 6s; 58°55'·25N 03°13'·51W.

Riddock Shoal ⚲ Fl (2) R 12s; 58°55'·89N 03°15'·00W.

Graemsay Is Hoy Sound Low ☆ Ldg Lts 104°. **Front,** 58°56'·42N 03°18'·60W Iso 3s 17m **15M**; W twr; vis: 070°-255°. **High Rear**, 1·2M from front, Oc WR 8s 35m **W20M, R16M**; W twr; vis: 097°-R-112°-W-163°-R-178°-W-332°; obsc on Ldg line within 0·5M.

STROMNESS

Stromness ⚲ QR; 58°57'·25N 03°17'·61W.

N Pier Hd ⚡ Fl R 3s 8m 5M; 58°57'·75N 03°17'·71W.

AUSKERRY/KIRKWALL

Copinsay ☆ 58°53'·77N 02°40'·35W Fl (5) 30s 79m **21M**; W twr.

Auskerry ☆ 59°01'·51N 02°34'·34W Fl 20s 34m **20M**; W twr.

Scargun Shoal v Q (3) 10s; 59°00'·69N 02°58'·58W.

Kirkwall Pier N end ☆ 58°59'·29N 02°57'·72W Iso WRG 5s 8m **W15M**, R13M, G13M; W twr; vis: 153°-G-183°-W-192°-R-210°.

WIDE FIRTH

Linga Skerry ⚑ Q (3) 10s; 59°02'·39N 02°57'·56W.

Boray Skerries ⚑ Q (6) + L Fl 15s; 59°03'·65N 02°57'·66W.

Skertours ⚑ Q; 59°04'·11N 02°56'·72W.

Galt Skerry ⚑ Q; 59°05'·21N 02°54'·20W.

Brough of Birsay ☆ 59°08'·19N 03°20'·41W Fl (3) 25s 52m **18M**.

Papa Stronsay NE end, The Ness Fl(4)20s 8m 9M; W twr; 59°09'·34N 02°34'·93W

STRONSAY, PAPA SOUND

Quiabow ▲ Fl (2) G 12s; 59°09'·82N 02°36'·30W.

No. 1 ▲ Fl G 5s; (off Jacks Reef) 59°09'·16N 02°36'·51W.

Whitehall Pier Hd ⚡ 2 FG (vert) 8m 4M; 50°08'·61N 02°35'·96W.

SANDAY ISLAND/NORTH RONALDSAY

Start Pt ☆ 59°16'·69N 02°22'·71W Fl (2) 20s 24m **18M**.

N Ronaldsay ☆ NE end, 59°23'·37N 02°23'·03W Fl 10s 43m **24M**; R twr, W bands; **Racon (T) 14-17M**.

WESTRAY/PIEROWALL

Noup Head ☆ 59°19'·86N 03°04'·23W Fl 30s 79m **20M**; W twr; vis: about 335°-282° but partially obsc 240°-275°.

Pierowall E Pier Head ⚡ Fl WRG 3s 7m W11M, R7M, G7M; vis: 254°-G-276°-W-291°-R-308°-G-215°; 59°19'·35N 02°58'·53W.

Papa Westray, Moclett Bay Pier Head ⚡ Fl WRG 5s 7m W5M, R3M, G3M; vis: 306°-G-341°-W-040°-R-074°; 59°19'·60N 02°53'·52W.

SHETLAND ISLES

FAIR ISLE

Skadan South ☆, 59°30'·84N 01°39'·16W Fl (4) 30s 32m **22M**; W twr; vis: 260°-146°, obsc inshore 260°-282°; *Horn (2) 60s.*

Skroo ☆ N end 59°33'·13N 01°36'·58W Fl (2) 30s 80m **22M**; W twr; vis: 086·7°-358°.

MAINLAND, SOUTH

Sumburgh Head ☆ 59°51'·21N 01°16'·58W Fl (3) 30s 91m **23M**.

Pool of Virkie, Marina E Bkwtr Head ⚡ 2 FG (vert) 6m 5M; 59°53'·01N 01°17'·16W.

BRESSAY/LERWICK

Bressay, Kirkabister Ness ☆ 60°07'·20N 01°07'·29W; Fl (2) 20s 32m **23M**.

Soldian Rock ⚑ Q (6) + L Fl 15s; 60°12'·51N 01°04'·73W.

Gremista Marina S Hd ⚡ Iso R 4s 3m 2M; 60°10'·20N 01°09'·61W.

Rova Hd ⚡ 60°11'·46N 01°08'·60W Fl (3) WRG 18s 12m W12M, R9M, G9M; W twr; vis: 090°-R-182°-W-191°-G-213°-R-241°-W-261·5°-G-009°-R-040°. Same structure and synhcronised: Fl (3) WRG 18s 14m **W16M**, R13M, G13M; vis: 176·5°-R-182°-W-191°-G-196·5°.

The Brethren Rock ⚑ Q (9) 15s; 60°12'·35N 01°08'·24W.

The Unicorn Rock ⚑ VQ (3) 5s; 60°13'·51N 01°08'·48W.

Dales Voe ⚡ Fl (2) WRG 8s 5m W4M, R3M, G3M; vis: 220°-G-227°-W-233°-R-240°; 60°11'·79N 01°11'·23W.

Dales Voe Quay ⚡ 2 FR (vert) 9m 3M; 60°11'·60N 01°10'·48W.

1	Berwick-upon-Tweed	1			11	155	79	47	76	104	144	126	120	125	145	Cape Wrath	11
2	Eyemouth	10	2			10	95	124	120	148	190	170	162	156	160	Lerwick	10
3	Dunbar	26	17	3			9	50	46	74	114	104	90	95	115	Kirkwall	9
4	Port Edgar	58	50	34	4			8	31	59	99	89	75	80	100	Scrabster	8
5	Methil	45	36	20	20	5			7	29	69	58	44	50	72	Wick	7
6	Fife Ness	38	29	17	34	16	6			6	43	32	26	44	74	Helmsdale	6
7	Dundee	58	49	37	54	36	20	7			5	13	34	59	90	Inverness	5
8	Montrose	59	51	43	61	43	27	27	8			4	23	48	79	Nairn	4
9	Stonehaven	72	66	60	78	60	44	45	20	9			3	25	56	Lossiemouth	3
10	Aberdeen	82	78	73	90	72	56	57	32	13	10			2	33	Banff/Macduff	2
11	Peterhead	105	98	93	108	94	78	80	54	35	25	11			1	Peterhead	1

AREA 6 NW Scotland – C *Wrath to Oban including The Western Isles*
SELECTED LIGHTS, BUOYS & WAYPOINTS

Positions are referenced to WGS84

CAPE WRATH TO LOCH TORRIDON

Cape Wrath ☆ 58°37'·54N 04°59'·99W Fl (4) 30s 122m **22M**; W twr.

LOCH INCHARD/LOCH LAXFORD
Bodha Ceann na Saile ⚓ Q; 58°27'·24N 05°04'·01W.
Kinlochbervie Dir lt 327° ☆. 58°27'·49N 05°03'·08W WRG 15m **16M**; vis: 326°-FG-326·5°-Al GW-326·75°-FW-327·25°-Al RW-327·5°-FR-328°.
Stoer Head ☆ 58°14'·43N 05°24'·07W Fl 15s 59m **24M**; W twr.

LOCH INVER/SUMMER ISLES/ULLAPOOL
Soyea I ⚓ Fl (2) 10s 34m 6M; 58°08'·56N 05°19'·67W.
Glas Leac ⚓ Fl WRG 3s 7m 5M; 58°08'·68N 05°16'·36W.
Rubha Cadail ⚓ Fl WRG 6s 11m W9M, R6M, G6M; W twr; vis: 311°-G-320°-W-325°-R-103°-W-111°-G-118°-W-127°-R-157°-W-199°; 57°55'·51N 05°13'·40W.
Ullapool Pt ⚓ QR; 57°53'·70N 05°10'·68W.
Cailleach Head ⚓ Fl (2) 12s 60m 9M; W twr; vis: 015°-236°; 57°55'·81N 05°24'·23W.

LOCH EWE/LOCH GAIRLOCH
Fairway ⚓ L Fl 10s; 57°51'·98N 05°40'·09W.
Rubha Reidh ☆ 57°51'·52N 05°48'·72W Fl (4) 15s 37m **24M**.
Glas Eilean ⚓ Fl WRG 6s 9m W6M, R4M; vis: 080°-W-102°-R-296°-W-333°-G-080°; 57°42'·79N 05°42'·42W.
Gairloch Pier ⚓ 57°42'·59N 05°41'·03W QR 6m 2M.

OUTER HEBRIDES – EAST SIDE
LEWIS
Butt of Lewis ☆ 58°30'·89N 06°15'·84W Fl 5s 52m **25M**; R twr; vis: 056°-320°.
Tiumpan Head ☆ 58°15'·66N 06°08'·29W Fl (2) 15s 55m **25M**; W twr.
Reef Rock ⚓ QR; 58°11'·58N 06°21'·97W.
Arnish Point ☆ Fl WR 10s 17m W9M, R7M; W ○ twr; vis: 088°-W-198°-R-302°-W-013°; 58°11'·50N 06°22'·16W.
Rubh' Uisenis ⚓ Fl 5s 24m 11M; W twr; 57°56'·25N 06°28'·36W.
Shiants ⚓ QG; 57°54'·57N 06°25'·70W.
Sgeir Inoe ⚓ Fl G 6s; *Racon (M) 5M*; 57°50'·93N 06°33'·93W.
Scalpay, **Eilean Glas** ☆ 57°51'·41N 06°38'·55W Fl (3) 20s 43m **23M**; W twr, R bands; *Racon (T) 16-18M*.
Sgeir Bràigh Mor ⚓ Fl G 6s; 57°51'·51N 06°43'·84W.
Sgeir Graidach ⚓ Q (6) + L Fl 15s; 57°50'·36N 06°41'·37W.
Tarbert ⚓ Oc WRG 6s 10m 5M; 57°53'·82N 06°47'·93W

SOUND OF HARRIS/BERNERAY
Fairway ⚓ L Fl 10s; 57°40'·35N 07°02'·15W.

Cabbage ⚓ Fl (2) R 6s; *Racon (T) 5M (3cm)*; 57°42'·13N 07°03'·96W.
Bo Stainan ⚓ 57°45'·76N 07°02'·40W VQ(6) + LF 10s.
Trench ⚓ Q (3) G 10s; 57°41'·89N 07°09'·00W.

LOCH MADDY
Weaver's Pt ⚓ 57°36'·49N 07°06'·00W Fl 3s 24m 7M; W hut.
Glas Eilean Mòr ⚓ 57°35'·95N 07°06'·70W Fl (2) G 4s 8m 5M.

SOUTH UIST, LOCH CARNAN
Landfall ⚓ L Fl 10s; 57°22'·27N 07°11'·52W.
Ushenish ☆ (S Uist) 57°17'·89N 07°11'·58W Fl WR 20s 54m **W19M, R15M**; W twr; vis: 193°-W-356°-R-018°.

LOCH BOISDALE/BARRA/CASTLEBAY
MacKenzie Rk ⚓ Fl (3) R 15s 3m 4M; 57°08'·24N 07°13'·71W.
Calvay E End ⚓ Fl (2) WRG 10s 16m W7M, R4M, G4M; W twr; vis: 111°-W-190°-G-202°-W-286°-R-111°; 57°08'·53N 07°15'·38W.
Binch Rock ⚓ Q (6) + L Fl 15s; 57°01'·60N 07°17'·12W.
Bo Vich Chuan ⚓ Q (6) + L Fl 15s; *Racon (M) 5M*; 56°56'·15N 07°23'·31W.
Castle Bay S ⚓ Fl (2) R 8s; *Racon (T) 7M*; 56°56'·09N 07°27'·21W.
Barra Hd ☆ 56°47'·11N 07°39'·26W Fl 15s 208m **18M**; W twr; obsc by islands to NE.

OUTER HEBRIDES – WEST SIDE
Flannan I ☆, Eilean Mór 58°17'·32N 07°35'·23W Fl (2) 30s 101m **20M**; W twr; obsc in places by ls to W of Eilean Mór.
Haskeir I ☆ 57°41'·98N 07°41·36W Fl 20s 44m **23M**; W twr.

LOCH TORRIDON TO MULL
LITTLE MINCH/NORTH SKYE/RONA
Eugenie Rk ⚓ Q 6 + LF 15s; 57°46'·47N 06°27'·28W.
Eilean Trodday ⚓ Fl (2) WRG 10s 52m W12M, R9M, G9M; W Bn; vis: W062°-R088°-130°-W-322°-G-062°; 57°43'·64N 06°17'·89W.
Comet Rock ⚓ Fl R 6s; 57°44'·60N 06°20'·50W.
Rona NE Point £ 57°34'·68N 05°57'·56W Fl 12s 69m 19M; W twr; vis: 050°-358°.

CROWLIN ISLANDS/RAASAY
Sgeir Mhór ⚓ Fl G 5s; 57°24'·57N 06°10'·53W.
Eilean Beag ⚓ Fl 6s 32m 6M; W Bn; 57°21'·21N 05°51'·42W.
Eyre Pt ⚓ Fl WR 3s 6m W9M, R6M; W twr; vis: 215°-W-266°-R- 288°-W-063°; 57°20'·01N 06°01'·29W.

KYLE AKIN AND KYLE OF LOCH ALSH
Carragh Rk ⚓ Fl (2) G 12s; *Racon (T) 5M*; 57°17'·18N 05°45'·36W.
Skye Br Centre ⚹ Oc 6s; 57°16'·57N 05°44'·58W.
String Rock ⚓ Fl R 6s; 57°16'·50N 05°42'·89W.
Sgeir-na-Caillich ⚹ Fl (2) R 6s 3m 4M; 57°15'·59N 05°38'·90W.

SOUND OF SLEAT
Kyle Rhea ⚹ Fl WRG 3s 7m W8M, R5M, G5M; W Bn; vis: shore-R-219°-W-228°-G-338°-W-346°-R-shore.

Ornsay, SE end ☆ 57°08'·59N 05°46'·88W Oc 8s 18m **15M**; W twr; vis: 157°-030°.
Pt. of Sleat ⚹ Fl 3s 20m 9M; W twr; 57°01'·08N 06°01'·08W.

MALLAIG
Sgeir Dhearg ⚓ QG; 57°00'·74N 05°49'·50W.
N Pier, E end ⚹ Iso WRG 4s 6m W9M, R6M, G6M; Gy twr; vis: 181°-G-185°-W-197°-R-201°. Fl G 3s 14m 6M; same structure; 57°00'·47N 05°49'·50W.

NW SKYE
Neist Point ☆ 57°25'·41N 06°47'·30W Fl 5s 43m **16M**; W twr.

WEST OF MULL AND SMALL ISLES
Hyskeir ☆ 56°58'·14N 06°40'·87W Fl (3) 30s 41m **24M**; W twr. *Racon (T) 14-17M.*
Bogha Ruadh ⚹ Fl G 5s 4m 3M; 56°49'·56N 06°13'·05W.
Bo Faskadale ⚓ Fl (3) G 18s; 56°48'·18N 06°06'·37W.
Ardnamurchan ☆ 56°43'·63N 06°13'·58W Fl (2) 20s 55m **24M**; Gy twr; vis: 002°-217°.

TIREE
Roan Bogha ⚐ Q (6) + L Fl 15s 3m 5M; 56°32'·23N 06°40'·18W.
Placaid Bogha ⚓ Fl G 4s; 56°33'·22N 06°44'·06W.
Scarinish ☆, S side of ent 56°30'·01N 06°48'·27W Fl 3s 11m **16M**; W □ twr; vis: 210°-030°.
Skerryvore ☆ 56°19'·36N 07°06'·88W Fl 10s 46m **23M**; Gy twr; *Racon (M) 18M; Horn 60s.*

Cairn na Burgh More (Treshnish Is), Fl (3) 15s 36m 8M; solar panels on framework tr; 56°31'·05N 06°22'·95W.

LOCH NA LÀTHAICH (LOCH LATHAICH)
Dubh Artach ☆ 56°07'·94N 06°38'·08W; Fl (2)30s 44m **20M**; Gy twr, R band.

SOUND OF MULL
LOCH SUNART/TOBERMORY/LOCH ALINE
Ardmore Pt ⚹ Fl (2) 10s 18m 13M; 56°39'·37N 06°07'·70W.
New Rks ⚓ Fl G 6s 56°39'·05N 06°03'·30W.
Rubha nan Gall ☆ 56°38'·33N 06°04'·00W Fl 3s 17m **15M**; W twr.
Avon Rock ⚓ Fl (4) R 12s; 56°30'·78N 05°46'·80W.
Yule Rocks ⚓ Fl R 15s; 56°30'·01N 05°43'·96W.
Glas Eileanan Gy Rks ⚹ Fl 3s 11m 6M; W ○ twr on W base; 56°29'·77N 05°42'·83W.
Craignure Ldg Lts 240·9°. Front, FR 10m; 56°28'·26N 05°42'·28W. Rear, 150m from front, FR 12m; vis: 225·8°-255·8°.

MULL TO OBAN
Lismore ☆, SW end 56°27'·34N 05°36'·45W Fl 10s 31m **17M**; W twr; vis: 237°-208°.
Lady's Rk ⚐ Fl 6s 12m 5M; 56°26'·92N 05°37'·05W.
Duart Pt ⚹ Fl (3) WR 18s 14m W5M, R3M; vis: 162°-W-261°-R-275°-W-353°-R-shore; 56°26'·84N 05°38'·77W.

DUNSTAFFNAGE BAY
Pier Hd ⚹ NE end, 2 FG (vert) 4m 2M; 56°27'·21N 05°26'·18W.

OBAN
N spit of Kerrera ⚹ Fl R 3s 9m 5M; W col, R bands; 56°25'·49N 05°29'·56W.
Dunollie ⚹ Fl (2) WRG 6s 7m W8M, G6M, R6M; vis: 351°-G- 020°- W-047°-R-120°-W-138°-G-143°; 56°25'·37N 05°29'·05W.
Corran Ledge ⚐ VQ (9) 10s; 56°25'·19N 05°29'·11W.
Oban N Pier Mid ⚹ 2 FG (vert) 8m 5M; 56°24'·87N 05°28'·49W.

		1															
1	Cape Wrath	**1**															
2	Ullapool	54	**2**														
3	Stornoway	53	45	**3**													
4	East Loch Tarbert	75	56	33	**4**												
5	Portree	83	57	53	42	**5**											
6	Kyle of Lochalsh	91	63	62	63	21	**6**										
7	Mallaig	112	82	83	84	42	21	**7**									
8	Eigg	123	98	97	75	54	35	14	**8**								
9	Castlebay (Barra)	133	105	92	69	97	76	59	46	**9**							
10	Tobermory	144	114	115	87	74	53	32	20	53	**10**						
11	Loch Aline	157	127	128	100	87	66	45	33	66	13	**11**					
12	Fort William	198	161	162	134	121	98	75	63	96	43	34	**12**				
13	Oban	169	138	139	111	100	77	56	44	77	24	13	29	**13**			
14	Loch Melfort	184	154	155	117	114	93	69	61	92	40	27	45	18	**14**		
15	Craobh Haven	184	155	155	117	114	92	70	60	93	40	27	50	21	5	**15**	
16	Crinan	187	157	158	129	112	95	74	63	97	42	30	54	25	14	9	**16**
17	Mull of Kintyre	232	203	189	175	159	143	121	105	120	89	87	98	72	62	57	51	**17**

DISTANCE TABLES
Approx distances in nautical miles are by the most direct route allowing for dangers and TSS.

NAVAL EXERCISE AREAS

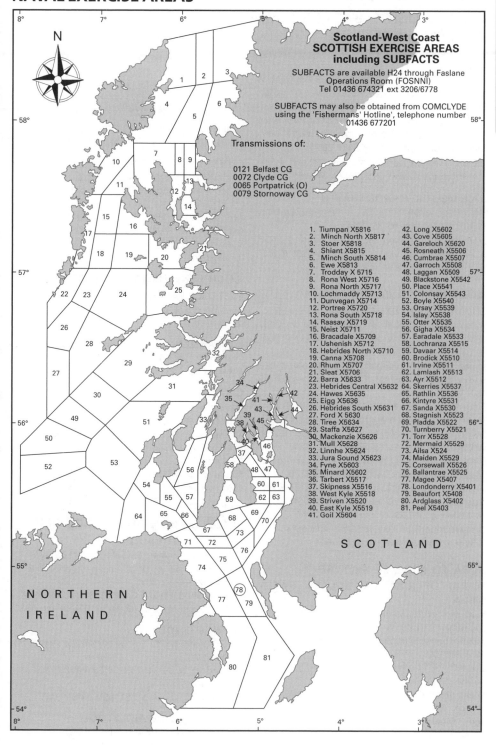

Scotland-West Coast
SCOTTISH EXERCISE AREAS
including SUBFACTS

SUBFACTS are available H24 through Faslane
Operations Room (FOSNNI)
Tel 01436 674321 ext 3206/6778

SUBFACTS may also be obtained from COMCLYDE
using the 'Fishermans' Hotline', telephone number
01436 677201

Transmissions of:

0121 Belfast CG
0072 Clyde CG
0065 Portpatrick (O)
0079 Stornoway CG

1. Tiumpan X5816
2. Minch North X5817
3. Stoer X5818
4. Shiant X5815
5. Minch South X5814
6. Ewe X5813
7. Trodday X 5715
8. Rona West X5716
9. Rona North X5717
10. Lochmaddy X5713
11. Dunvegan X5714
12. Portree X5720
13. Rona South X5718
14. Raasay X5719
15. Neist X5711
16. Bracadale X5709
17. Ushenish X5712
18. Hebrides North X5710
19. Canna X5708
20. Rhum X5707
21. Sleat X5706
22. Barra X5633
23. Hebrides Central X5632
24. Hawes X5635
25. Eigg X5636
26. Hebrides South X5631
27. Ford X 5630
28. Tiree X5634
29. Staffa X5627
30. Mackenzie X5626
31. Mull X5628
32. Linnhe X5624
33. Jura Sound X5623
34. Fyne X5603
35. Minard X5602
36. Tarbert X5517
37. Skipness X5516
38. West Kyle X5518
39. Striven X5520
40. East Kyle X5519
41. Goil X5604

42. Long X5602
43. Cove X5605
44. Gareloch X5620
45. Rosneath X5506
46. Cumbrae X5507
47. Garroch X5508
48. Laggan X5509
49. Blackstone X5542
50. Place X5541
51. Colonsay X5543
52. Boyle X5540
53. Orsay X5539
54. Islay X5538
55. Otter X5535
56. Gigha X5534
57. Earadale X5533
58. Lochranza X5515
59. Davaar X5514
60. Brodick X5510
61. Irvine X5511
62. Lamlash X5513
63. Ayr X5512
64. Skerries X5537
65. Rathlin X5536
66. Kintyre X5531
67. Sanda X5530
68. Stagnish X5523
69. Pladda X5522
70. Turnberry X5521
71. Torr X5528
72. Mermaid X5529
73. Ailsa X524
74. Maiden X5529
75. Corsewall X5526
76. Ballantrae X5525
77. Magee X5407
78. Londonderry X5401
79. Beaufort X5408
80. Ardglass X5402
81. Peel X5403

SCOTLAND

NORTHERN IRELAND

AREA 7 SW Scotland – *Oban to Kirkcudbright*

SELECTED LIGHTS, BUOYS & WAYPOINTS | Positions are referenced to WGS84

OBAN TO LOCH CRAIGNISH

Bogha Nuadh ⚓ Q (6) + LFl 15s; 56°21'·69N 05°37'·88W.

Fladda ⚡ Fl (2) WRG 9s 13m W11M, R9M, G9M; W twr; vis: 169°-R-186°-W-337°-G-344°-W-356°-R-026°; 56°14'·89N 05°40'·83W.

Dubh Sgeir (Luing) ⚡ Fl WRG 6s 9m W6M, R4M. G4M; W twr; vis: W000°- R010°- W025°- G199°-000°; *Racon (M) 5M*; 56°14'·76N 05°40'·20W.

The Garvellachs, Eileach an Naoimh, SW end ⚡ Fl 6s 21m 9M; W Bn; vis: 240°-215°; 56°13'·04N 05°49'·06W.

LOCH MELFORT/CRAOBH HAVEN

Melfort Pier ⚡ Dir FR 6m 3M; (Private shown 1/4 to 31/10); 56°16'·14N 05°30'·19W.

Craobh Marina Bkwtr Hd ⚡ Iso WRG 5s 10m, W5M, R3M, G3M; vis:114°-G-162°-W-183°-R-200°; 56°12'·78N 05°33'·52W.

COLONSAY TO ISLAY

COLONSAY/SOUND OF ISLAY/PORT ELLEN

Scalasaig, Rubha Dubh ⚡ Fl (2) WR 10s 8m W8M, R6M; W bldg; vis: shore-R- 230°-W-337°-R-354°; 56°04'·01N 06°10'·90W.

Rhubh' a Mháil (Ruvaal) ☆ 55°56'·18N 06°07'·46W Fl (3) WR 15s 45m **W24M, R21M**; W twr; vis: 075°-R-180°-W-075°.

Black Rocks ▲ Fl G 6s; 55°47'·50N 06°04'·09W.

McArthur's Hd ⚡ Fl (2) WR 10s 39m W14M, R11M; W twr; W in Sound of Islay from NE coast,159°-R-244°-W-E coast of Islay; 55°45'·84N 06°02'·90W.

Eilean a Chùirn ⚡ Fl (3) 18s 26m 8M;   W Bn; obsc when brg more than 040°; 55°40'·12N 06°01'·22W.

Gigha Rocks ⚓ Q (9) 15s; 55°39'·20N 05°43'·65W.

Otter Rk ⚓ Q (6) + L Fl 15s; 55°33'·86N 06°07'·92W.

Port Ellen ▲ QG; 55°37'·00N 06°12'·27W.

Orsay Is, **Rhinns of Islay** ☆ 55°40'·40N 06°30'·84W Fl 5s 46m **24M**; W twr; vis: 256°-184°.

JURA TO MULL OF KINTYRE

SOUND OF JURA/CRAIGHOUSE/L SWEEN/GIGHA

Reisa an t-Struith, S end of Is ⚡ Fl (2) 12s 12m 7M; W col; 56°07'·77N 05°38'·91W.

Ruadh Sgeir ⚡ Fl 6s 15m 9M; W ○ twr; 56°04'·32N 05°39'·77W.

Skervuile ⚡ Fl 15s 22m 9M; W twr; 55°52'·46N 05°49'·85W.

Eilean nan Gabhar ⚡ Fl 5s 7m 8M; framework twr; vis: 225°-010°; 55°50'·04N 05°56'·25W.

Sgeir Gigalum ▲ Fl G 6s 3m 4M; 55°39'·96N 05°42'·67W.

Cath Sgeir ⚓ Q (9) 15s; 55°39'·66N 05°47'·50W.

Gigalum Rks ⚓ Q (9) 15s; 55°39'·20N 05°43'·70W.

WEST LOCH TARBERT

Dunskeig Bay ⚡ Q (2) 10s 11m 8M; 55°45'·22N 05°35'·00W.

Eileen Tráighe (off S side) ⏚ Fl (2) R 5s 5m 3M; R post; 55°45'·37N 05°35'·75W.

Mull of Kintyre ☆ 55°18'·64N 05°48'·25W Fl (2) 20s 91m **24M**; W twr on W bldg; vis: 347°-178°.

CRINAN CANAL/ARDRISHAIG

Crinan, E of lock ent ⚡ Fl WG 3s 8m 4M; W twr, R band; vis: shore-W-146°-G-shore; 56°05'·48N 05°33'·37W.

Ardrishaig Bkwtr Hd ⚡ L Fl WRG 6s 9m 4M; vis: 287°-G-339°-W-350°-R-035°; 56°00'·76N 05°26'·59W.

Sgeir Sgalag No. 49 ▲ Fl G 5s; 56°00'·36N 05°26'·30W.

LOCH FYNE TO SANDA ISLAND

EAST LOCH TARBERT

Madadh Maol ⚡ Fl R 2·5s 4m 3M; 55°52'·02N 05°24'·25W.

KILBRANNAN SOUND/CARRADALE BAY

Crubon Rk ⌇ Fl (2) R 12s; 55°34'·48N 05°27'·07W.

Otterard Rk ⚓ Q (3) 10s; 55°27'·07N 05°31'·11W.

CAMPBELTOWN LOCH

Davaar N Pt ☆ 55°25'·69N 05°32'·42W Fl (2) 10s 37m **23M**; W twr; vis: 073°-330°.

Methe Bk 'C' ⚓ Fl (2) 6s; 55°25'·30N 05°34'·42W.

Arranman's Barrels ⌇ Fl (2) R 12s; 55°19'·40N 05°32'·87W.

Sanda Island ☆ 55°16'·50N 05°35'·01W Fl 10s 50m **15M**; W twr.

Patersons Rk ⌇ Fl (3) R 18s; 55°16'·90N 05°32'·48W.

KYLES OF BUTE TO RIVER CLYDE

KYLES OF BUTE/CALADH

Rubha Ban ⌇ Fl R 4s; 55°54'·95N 05°12'·40W.

Burnt I No. 42 ⌇ (S of Eilean Buidhe) Fl R 2s; 55°55'·76N 05°10'·39W.

Rubha á Bhodaich ▲ Fl G; 55°55'·38N 05°09'·59W.

Ardmaleish Pt No. 41 ⚓ Q; 55°53'·02N 05°04'·70W.

FIRTH OF CLYDE

Ascog Patches No. 13 ⚓ Fl (2) 10s 5m 5M; 55°49'·71N 05°00'·25W.

Toward Pt ☆ 55°51'·73N 04°58'·79W Fl 10s 21m **22M**; W twr.

Skelmorlie ⚓ Iso 5s; 55°51'·65N 04°56'·34W.

WEMYSS/INVERKIP/HOLY LOCH

Kip ▲ Fl G 5s; 55°54'·49N 04°52'·98W.

Warden Bank ▲ Fl G 2s; 55°54'·77N 04°54'·54W.

Cowal ⚓ L Fl 10s; 55°56'·00N 04°54'·83W.
The Gantocks ⚓ Fl R 6s 12m 6M; ○ twr; 55°56'·45N 04°55'·08W.
Cloch Point ⚡ Fl 3s 24m 8M; W ○ twr, B band, W dwellings; 55°56'·55N 04°52'·74W.
Holy Loch Marina 2 FR (vert) 4m 1M; 55°59'·00N 04°56'·80W.

LOCH LONG/LOCH GOIL/GOUROCK
Loch Long ⚓ Oc 6s; 55°59'·15N 04°52'·42W.
Ashton ⚓ Iso 5s; 55°58'·10N 04°50'·65W.
Whiteforeland ⚓ L Fl 10s; 55°58'·11N 04°47'·28W.
Rosneath Patch ⚓ Fl (2) 10s 5m 10M; 55°58'·52N 04°47'·45W.

ROSNEATH/RHU NARROWS/GARELOCH
Ldg Lts 356°. **Front, No. 7N** ⚓ 56°00'·05N 04°45'·36W Dir lt 356°. WRG 5m **W16M**, R13M, G13M; vis: 353°-Al WG- 355°- FW-357°-Al WR-000°-FR-002°.
Dir lt 115° WRG 5m **W16M**, R13M, G13M; vis: 111°-Al WG-114°-FW- 116°-Al WR-119°-FR-121°.
Row ▲ Fl G 5s; 55°59'·84N 04°45'·13W.
Cairndhu ▲ Fl G 2·5s; 56°00'·35N 04°46'·00W.
Rhu SE ▲ Fl G 3s; 56°00'·64N 04°47'·17W.
Rhu NE ▲ QG; 56°01'·02N 04°47'·58W.
Rhu Spit ⚓ Fl 3s 6m 6M; 56°00'·84N 04°47'·34W. 8m 8M. are Fl G and Lts on N bank are Fl R.

CLYDE TO LOCH RYAN
LARGS/FAIRLIE
Approach ⚓ L Fl 10s; 55°46'·40N 04°51'·85W.
Largs Marina S Bkwtr Hd ⚡ Oc G 10s 4m 4M; 55°46'·36N 04°51'·73W.
Fairlie Patch ▲ Fl G 1·5s; 55°45'·38N 04°52'·34W.

MILLPORT, GREAT CUMBRAE
The Eileans, W end ⚡ QG 5m 2M; 55°44'·89N 04°55'·59W.
Mountstuart ⚓ L Fl 10s; 55°48'·00N 04°57'·57W.
Portachur ▲ Fl G 3s; 55°44'·35N 04°58'·52W.
Little Cumbrae Is, Cumbrae Elbow ⚡ Fl 6s 28m 14M; W twr; vis: 334°-193°; 55°43'·22N 04°58'·06W.

ARDROSSAN/TROON
Ardrossan N Bkwtr Hd ⚡ Fl R 5s 7m 5M; R gantry; 55°38'·53N 04°49'·64W.
W Crinan Rk ⚓ Fl R 4s; 55°38'·47N 04°49'·89W.
Eagle Rock ▲ 55°38'·21N 04°49'·69W Fl G 5s.
Troon ▲ Fl G 4s; 55°33'·06N 04°41'·35W.
Lady I ⚓ Fl 2s 19m 8M; W Bn; 55°31'·63N 04°44'·04W.

ARRAN/RANZA/LAMLASH
Hamilton Rk ⚓ Fl R 6s; 55°32'·63N 05°04'·90W.
Pillar Rk Pt ☆ (Holy Island), 55°31'·04N 05°03'·67W Fl (2) 20s 38m **25M**; W □ twr.
Pladda ☆ 55°25'·50N 05°07'·12W Fl (3) 30s 40m **17M**; W twr.

AYR/GIRVAN/LOCH RYAN
S. Nicholas ▲ 55°28'·12N 04°39'·44W Fl G 2s.
Turnberry Point ☆, near castle ruins 55°19'·56N 04°50'·71W Fl 15s 29m **24M**; W twr.
Ailsa Craig ☆ 55°15'·12N 05°06'·52W Fl 4s 18m **17M**; W twr; vis: 145°-028°.
Girvan S Pier Hd 2 FG (vert) 8m 4M; W twr; 55°14'·72N 04°51'·90W.
Milleur Point ⚓ Q; 55°01'·28N 05°05'·66W.
Cairn Pt ⚡ Fl (2) R 10s 14m 12M; W twr; 54°58'·46N 05°01'·85W.

LOCH RYAN TO KIRKUDBRIGHT
Corsewall Point ☆ 55°00'·41N 05°09'·58W Fl (5) 30s 34m **22M**; W twr; vis: 027°-257°.
Crammag Hd ☆ 54°39'·90N 04°57'·92W Fl 10s 35m **18M**; W twr.
Mull of Galloway ☆, SE end 54°38'·08N 04°51'·45W Fl 20s 99m **28M**; W twr; vis: 182°-105°.

KIRKUDBRIGHT BAY
Hestan I, E end ⚡ Fl (2) 10s 42m 9M; 54°49'·95N 03°48'·53W.

1	Loch Craignish	1												
2	Crinan	5	2											
3	Ardrishaig	14	9	3										
6	East Loch Tarbert	24	19	10	4									
5	Campbeltown	55	50	39	31	5								
6	Lamlash	48	43	34	25	24	6							
7	Largs	48	43	34	24	39	17	7						
8	Kip Marina	53	48	39	28	50	25	10	8					
9	Greenock	59	54	45	36	53	31	16	6	9				
10	Rhu (Helensburgh)	62	57	48	37	59	33	19	9	4	10			
11	Troon	54	49	40	33	33	16	20	29	34	38	11		
12	Girvan	67	62	53	43	29	20	33	46	49	51	21	12	
13	Stranraer	89	84	75	65	34	39	56	69	65	74	44	23	13
14	Kirkcudbright	136	131	122	114	88	92	110	116	124	125	97	94	71	14

DISTANCE TABLES
Approx distances in nautical miles are by the most direct route allowing for dangers and TSS.

AREA 8 NW England & Wales – *Kirkcudbright & Isle of Man to Swansea*

SELECTED LIGHTS, BUOYS & WAYPOINTS

Positions are referenced to WGS84

SOLWAY FIRTH TO BARROW-IN-FURNESS

SILLOTH/MARYPORT
Two Feet Bk ⚓ Q (9) 15s; 54°42'·90N 03°47'·10W.
Solway ⚓ Fl G 4s; 54°46'·80N 03°30'·14W.
Maryport S Pier Hd ⚲.Fl 1·5s 10m 6M;54°43'·07N 03°30'·64W.
S Workington ⚓ VQ (6) + L Fl 10s; 54°37'·01N 03°38'·58W.
Whitehaven W Pier Hd ⚲ Fl G 5s 16m 13M; W○ twr; 54°33'·17N 03°35'·92W.

Saint Bees Hd ☆ 54°30'·81N 03°38'·23W Fl (2) 20s 102m **18M**; W○ twr; obsc shore-340°.
Selker ⚓ Fl (3) G 10s; *Bell;* 54°16'·14N 03°29'·58W.
Lightning Knoll ⚓ L Fl 10s; *Bell;* 53°59'·83N 03°14'·28W.
Isle of Walney ☆ 54°02'·92N 03°10'·64W Fl 15s 21m **23M**; stone twr; obsc 122°-127° within 3M of shore.

ISLE OF MAN

Whitestone Bk ⚓ Q (9) 15s; 54°24'·58N 04°20'·41W.
Point of Ayre ☆ 54°24'·94N 04°22'·13W Fl (4) 20s 32m **19M**; W twr, two R bands; *Racon (M) 13-15M*.
Low Lt ⚲ 54°25'·03N 04°21'·86W Fl 3s 10m 8M; R twr, lower part W, on B Base; part obsc 335°-341°.
Thousla Rk ⚲ Fl R 3s 9m 4M; 54°03'·73N 04°48'·05W.
Calf of Man Lighthouse (disused), white 8-sided tower.
Chicken Rk ⚲ Fl 5s 38m 21M; twr; 54°02'·26N 04°50'·32W.
Douglas Head ☆ 54°08'·60N 04°27'·95W Fl 10s 32m **24M**; W twr; obsc brg more than 037°. FR Lts on radio masts 1 and 3M West.
Maughold Head ☆ 54°17'·72N 04°18'·58W Fl (3) 30s 65m **21M**.
Bahama ⚓ VQ (6) + L Fl 10s; 54°20'·01N 04°08'·57W.
King William Bank ⚓ Q (3) 10s; 54°26'·01N 04°00'·08W.

BARROW TO RIVERS MERSEY AND DEE

MORECAMBE/FLEETWOOD/RIVER RIBBLE
Morecambe ⚓ Q (9) 15s; 53°52'·01N 03°24'·10W.
Lune Deep ⚓ Q (6) + L Fl 15s; *Racon (T);* 53°56'·07N 03°12'·9W.
R Lune ⚓ Q (9) 15s; 53°58'·63N 03°00'·03W. 53°58'·89N 02°52'·96W.
Gut ⚓ L Fl 10s; 53°41'·74N 03°08'·98W.
Jordan's Spit ⚓ Q (9) 15s; 53°35'·76N 03°19'·28W.

RIVER MERSEY APPROACHES

Bar ⚓ L Fl 10s; *Racon (T) 10M;* 53°32'·01N 03°20'·98W.
Q1 ⚓ VQ; 53°31'·00N 03°16'·72W.

Formby ⚓ Iso 4s 11m 6M; R hull, W stripes; 53°31'·13N 03°13'·50W.
Crosby ⚓ Oc 5s 11m 8M; R hull, W stripes; 53°30'·72N 03°06'·29W.
Brazil ⚓ QG; G hull; 53°26'·84N 03°02'·24W.

RIVER DEE

HE1 ⚓ Q (9) 15s; 53°26'·33N 03°18'·08W.
Hilbre I ⚲ Fl R 3s 14m 5M; W twr; 53°22'·99N 03°13'·72W.
Salisbury Mid ⚓ Fl (3) R 10s; 53°21'·30N 03°16'·39W.
Dee ⚓ Q (6) + L Fl 15s; 53°21'·99N 03°18'·68W.

N AND NW WALES COAST

RIVER DEE TO CONWY
N Hoyle ⚓ VQ; 53°26'·68N 03°30'·58W.
S Hoyle Outer ⚓ Fl R 2·5s; 53°21'·47N 03°24'·70W.
Prestatyn ⚓ QG; 53°21'·51N 03°28'·51W.
N Hoyle Wind Farm (30 turbines) centred on 53°25'·00N 03°27'·00W. NW, NE, SW, SE extremities (F.R Lts) Fl Y 2.5s 5M Horn Mo (U) 30s.
W Constable ⚓ Q (9) 15s; *Racon (M) 10M;* 53°23'·14N 03°49'·26W.
N Constable ⚓ VQ; 53°23'·76N 03°41'·42W.
Conwy F'wy ⚓ L Fl 10s; 53°17'·95N 03°55'·58W.
C2 ⚓ Fl (2) R 10s; 53°17'·64N 03°54'·71W.

MENAI STRIAT - N APPROACHES
Trwyn-Du ⚲ Fl 5s 19m 12M; W○ castellated twr, B bands; vis: 101°-023°; *Bell (1) 30s,* sounded continuously; 53°18'·77N 04°02'·44W.
Ten Feet Bank ⚓ QR; 53°19'·47N 04°02'·82W.

ANGLESEY
Point Lynas ☆ 53°24'·98N 04°17'·35W Oc 10s 39m **18M**; W castellated twr; vis: 109°-315°; *Horn 45s;* H24 in periods of reduced visibility.
Archdeacon Rock ⚓ Q; 53°26'·71N 04°30'·87W.
The Skerries ☆ 53°25'·27N 04°36'·55W Fl (2) 15s 36m **20M**; W○ twr, R band; *Racon (T) 25M*. Iso R 4s 26m 10M; same twr; vis: 233°-253°; *Horn (2) 60s.* H24 in periods of reduced visibility.
Langdon ⚓ Q (9) 15s; 53°22'·74N 04°38'·74W.
Holyhead Bkwtr Hd ⚲ Fl (3) G 10s 21m 14M; W☐ twr, B band; Fl Y vis: 174°-226°; *Siren 20s;* 53°19'·86N 04°37'·16W.
Marina Bkwtr Hd ⚲ 2 FR (vert); 53°19'·31N 04°38'·63W.
South Stack ☆ 53°19'·31N 04°41'·98W Fl 10s 60m **24M**; (H24); W○ twr; obsc to N by N Stack and part obsc in Penrhos bay; *Horn 30s.* Fog Det lt vis: 145°-325°.

MENAI STRAIT TO BARDSEY ISLAND

CAERNARFON APPROACHES
(Direction of buoyage ⚓ SW to NE)
C2 ⚓ Fl R 10s; 53°07'·07N 04°24'·52W.

Llanddwyn I ⚡Fl WR 2·5s 12m W7M, R4M; W twr; vis: 280°-R- 015°-W-120°; 53°08'·05N 04°24'·79W.
Mussel Bank ⚓ Fl (2) R 5s; 53°07'·27N 04°20'·81W.

LLEYN PENINSULA/BARDSEY ISLAND

Porth Dinllaen, Careg y Chwislen ↓ 52°56'·99N 04°33'·51W.

Bardsey I ☆ 52°44'·97N 04°48'·02W Fl (5) 15s 39m **26M**; W ☐ twr, R bands; obsc by Bardsey Is 198°-250° and in Tremadoc B when brg less than 260°; *Horn Mo (N) 45s*; H24.

CARDIGAN BAY

St Tudwal's ⚡ Fl WR 15s 46m W14, R10M; vis: 349°-W-169°-R- 221°-W-243°-R-259°-W-293°-R-349°; obsc by East I 211°-231°; 52°47'·92N 04°28'·30W.

PWLLHELI/PORTHMADOG/BARMOUTH/ ABERDOVEY

Pwllheli App ↓ Iso 2s; 52°53'·02N 04°23'·07W.
Porthmadog Fairway ⚓ L Fl 10s; 52°52'·97N 04°11'·18W.
Barmouth Outer ↓ L Fl 10s; 52°42'·62N 04°04'·83W.
Sarn Badrig Causeway ↓Q (9) 15s; *Bell*; 52°41'·19N 04°25'·36W .
Sarn-y-Bwch ↓ VQ (9) 10s; 52°34'·81N 04°13'·58W.
Aberdovey Outer ⚓ Iso 4s; 52°32'·00N 04°05'·56W.
Patches ↓ Q (9) 15s; 52°25'·83N 04°16'·41W.

ABERYSTWYTH/FISHGUARD

Aberystwyth S Bkwtr Hd ⚡ Fl (2) WG 10s 12m 10M; vis: 030°-G- 053°-W-210°; 52°24'·40N 04°05'·52W.
Fishguard N Bkwtr Hd ⚡ Fl G 4·5s 18m 13M; *Bell (1) 8s*; 52°00'·76N 04°58'·23W. 89m 5M.

Strumble Head ☆ 52°01'·79N 05°04'·43W Fl (4) 15s 45m **26M**; vis: 038°-257°; (H24).

BISHOPS AND SMALLS

South Bishop ☆ 51°51'·14N 05°24'·74W Fl 5s 44m **16M**; W ○ twr; *Horn (3) 45s; Racon (O)10M*; (H24).
The Smalls ☆ 51°43'·27N 05°40'·19W Fl (3) 15s 36m **18M**; *Racon (T)* ; *Horn (2) 60s*. Same twr, Iso R 4s 33m 13M; vis: 253°-285° over Hats & Barrels Rk;

both Lts shown H24 in periods of reduced visibility.
Skokholm I ☆, 51°41'·64N 05°17'·22W Fl WR 10s 54m **W18M, R15M**; vis: 301°-W-154°-R-301°; partially obsc 226°-258°.

W & S WALES - BRISTOL CHANNEL
MILFORD HAVEN

St Ann's Head ☆ 51°40'·87N 05°10'·42W Fl WR 5s 48m **W18M, R17M**, R14M; W 8-sided twr; vis: 233°-W-247°-R-285°-R(intens)-314°-R-332°-W131°, partially obscured between 124°-129°; *Horn (2) 60s*.
W Blockhouse Pt ↓ Ldg Lts 022·5°. Front, F 54m 13M; B stripe on W twr; vis: 004·5°-040·5°; intens on lead. By day 10M; vis: 004·5°-040·5°; *Racon (Q) range unknown*; 51°41'·31N 05°09'·56W.
Watwick Point Common Rear ☆, 0·5M from front, F 80m **15M**; vis: 013·5°-031·5°. By day 10M; vis: 013·5°-031·5°; *Racon (Y)*.
St Ann's ⚓ Fl R 2·5s; 51°40'·25N 05°10'·51W.
Sheep ▲ QG; 51°40'·06N 05°08'·31W.
Dakotian ↓ Q (3) 10s; 51°42'·15N 05°08'·29W.
Turbot Bk ↓ VQ (9) 10s; 51°37'·41N 05°10'·08W.
St Gowan ↓Q (6) + L Fl 15s, *Whis, Racon (T) 10M*; 51°31'·93N 04°59'·77W.

TENBY/CARMARTHEN BAY/BURRY INLET

Caldey I ⚡ Fl (3) WR 20s 65m W13M, R9M; vis: R173°- W212°- R088°-102°; 51°37'·90N 04°41'·08W.
Spaniel ↓ Q (3) 10s; 51°38'·06N 04°39'·74W.
Tenby Pier Hd ⚡ FR 7m 7M; 51°40'·40N 04°41'·89W.
DZ7 ⚓ Fl Y 10s; 51°38'·09N 04°30'·12W.
DZ5 ⚓ Fl Y 2·5s; 51°36'·37N 04°24'·39W.
Burry Port ⚡ 51°40'·62N 04°15'·06W Fl 5s 7m **15M**.
W. Helwick (W HWK) ↓ (9) 15s; *Racon (T) 10M*; *Whis*; 51°31'·40N 04°23'·65W Q.
E. Helwick ↓ VQ (3) 5s; *Bell*; 51°31'·80N 04°12'·68W.

SWANSEA BAY

Ledge ↓ VQ (6) + L Fl 5s; 51°29'·93N 03°58'·77W.
Mixon ⚓ Fl (2) R 5s; *Bell*; 51°33'·12N 03°58'·78W.

		1	2	3	4	5	6	7	8	9	10	11	12	13	14	15	16	17
1	Portpatrick	1																
2	Mull of Galloway	16	2															
3	Kirkcudbright	48	32	3														
4	Maryport	65	49	26	4													
5	Workington	63	47	25	6	5												
6	Ravenglass	70	54	40	30	23	6											
7	Point of Ayre	38	22	46	37	31	34	7										
8	Peel	41	26	46	55	49	52	18	8									
9	Douglas	60	42	46	50	44	39	19	30	9								
10	Glasson Dock	101	85	74	66	60	37	64	85	63	10							
11	Fleetwood	95	79	68	59	53	30	58	80	57	10	11						
12	Liverpool	118	102	97	89	83	60	80	86	70	52	46	12					
13	Conwy	111	95	95	92	86	58	72	72	59	62	56	46	13				
14	Beaumaris	109	93	94	95	89	72	71	73	58	66	60	49	12	14			
15	Caernarfon	117	103	104	105	99	82	81	73	68	76	70	59	22	10	15		
16	Holyhead	93	81	94	96	90	69	68	62	50	79	73	68	36	32	26	16	
17	Fishguard	171	158	175	175	169	160	153	140	134	153	147	136	100	88	78	89	17

DISTANCE TABLES

Approx distances in nautical miles are by the most direct route allowing for dangers and TSS.

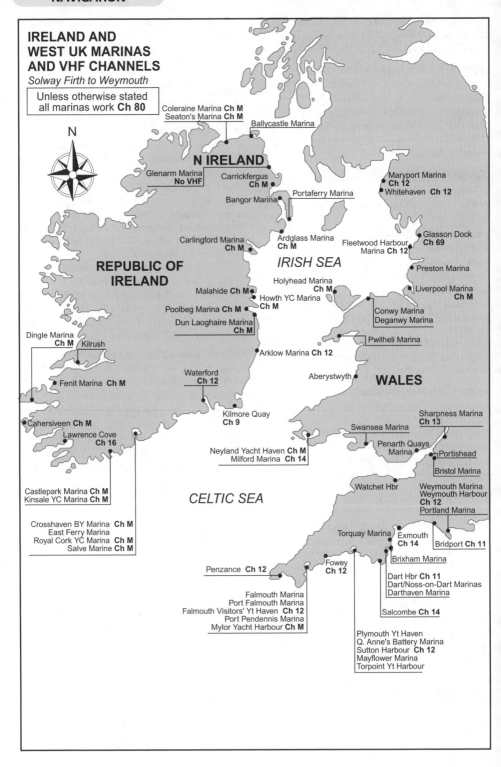

IRELAND AND WEST UK MARINAS AND VHF CHANNELS

Solway Firth to Weymouth

Unless otherwise stated all marinas work **Ch 80**

N

Coleraine Marina **Ch M**
Seaton's Marina **Ch M**
Ballycastle Marina

N IRELAND

Glenarm Marina **No VHF**
Carrickfergus **Ch M**
Maryport Marina **Ch 12**
Whitehaven **Ch 12**
Portaferry Marina
Bangor Marina

REPUBLIC OF IRELAND

Carlingford Marina **Ch M**
Ardglass Marina **Ch M**
Fleetwood Harbour Marina **Ch 12**
Glasson Dock **Ch 69**

IRISH SEA

Preston Marina

Malahide **Ch M**
Holyhead Marina **Ch M**
Howth YC Marina **Ch M**
Liverpool Marina **Ch M**

Poolbeg Marina **Ch M**
Dun Laoghaire Marina **Ch M**
Conwy Marina
Deganwy Marina

Dingle Marina **Ch M**
Kilrush
Pwllheli Marina

Arklow Marina **Ch 12**

Fenit Marina **Ch M**
Waterford **Ch 12**
Aberystwyth
WALES

Cahersiveen **Ch M**
Kilmore Quay **Ch 9**
Sharpness Marina **Ch 13**

Lawrence Cove **Ch 16**
Swansea Marina
Penarth Quays Marina
Portishead

Neyland Yacht Haven **Ch M**
Milford Marina **Ch 14**
Bristol Marina

Castlepark Marina **Ch M**
Kinsale YC Marina **Ch M**
Watchet Hbr
Weymouth Marina
Weymouth Harbour **Ch 12**
Portland Marina

CELTIC SEA

Crosshaven BY Marina **Ch M**
East Ferry Marina
Royal Cork YC Marina **Ch M**
Salve Marine **Ch M**

Torquay Marina
Exmouth **Ch 14**
Bridport **Ch 11**

Brixham Marina

Penzance **Ch 12**
Fowey **Ch 12**
Dart Hbr **Ch 11**
Dart/Noss-on-Dart Marinas
Darthaven Marina

Falmouth Marina
Port Falmouth Marina
Falmouth Visitors' Yt Haven **Ch 12**
Port Pendennis Marina
Mylor Yacht Harbour **Ch M**
Salcombe **Ch 14**

Plymouth Yt Haven
Q. Anne's Battery Marina
Sutton Harbour **Ch 12**
Mayflower Marina
Torpoint Yt Harbour

SELECTED LIGHTS, BUOYS & WAYPOINTS

Positions are referenced to WGS84

NAVIGATION

BRISTOL CHANNEL (NORTH SHORE)

SWANSEA BAY/PORT TALBOT/PORTHCAWL

Mixon ⌐ Fl (2) R 5s; *Bell;* 51°33'·12N 03°58'·78W.

Grounds ⌐ VQ (3) 5s; 51°32'·81N 03°53'·47W.

Mumbles ☆ 51°34'·01N 03°58'·27W Fl (4) 20s 35m **15M**; W twr; *Horn (3) 60s.*

SW Inner Green Grounds ⌐ Q (6) + L Fl 15s; *Bell;* 51°34'·06N 03°57'·03W.

Cabenda ⌐ VQ (6) + L Fl 10s; *Racon (Q);* 51°33'·36N 03°52'·23W.

P Talbot N Outer ⌐ Fl R 5s; 51°33'·78N 03°51'·38W.

Kenfig ⌐ VQ (3) 5s; 51°29'·44N 03°46'·06W.

W Scar ⌐ Q (9) 15s, *Bell,* **Racon (T) 10M;** 51°28'·31N 03°55'·57W.

S Scar ⌐ Q (6) + L Fl 15s; 51°27'·61N 03°51'·58W.

E Scar ⌐ Q (3) 10s; *Bell;* 51°27'·98N 03°46'·76W.

Fairy ⌐ Q (9) 15s; *Bell;* 51°27'·86N 03°42'·07W.

Tusker ⌐ Fl (2) R 5s *Bell;* 51°26'·85N 03°40'·74W.

W Nash ⌐ VQ (9) 10s ; *Bell;* 51°25'·99N 03°45'·95W.

East Nash ⌐ Q (3) 10s; 51°24'·06N 03°34'·10W.

Nash ☆ 51°24'·03N 03°33'·06W Fl (2) WR 15s 56m **W21M, R16M**; vis: 280°-R-290°-W-100°-R-120°-W-128°.

BARRY/CARDIFF/PENARTH/NEWPORT

Breaksea ⌐ L Fl 10s; *Racon (T) 10M;* 51°19'·88N 03°19'·08W.

Merkur ⌐ QR; 51°21'·88N 03°15'·95W.

Barry W Bkwtr Hd ⌁ Fl 2·5s 12m 10M; 51°23'·46N 03°15'·52W.

Lavernock Spit ⌐ VQ (6) + L Fl 10s; 51°23'·02N 03°10'·82W.

Mackenzie ⌐ QR; 51°21'·75N 03°08'·24W.

Wolves ⌐ VQ; 51°23'·13N 03°08'·88W.

Flat Holm ☆, SE Pt 51°22'·54N 03°07'·14W Fl (3) WR 10s 50m **W15M**, R12M; W ○ twr; vis: 106°-R-140°-W-151°-R-203°-W-106°; (H24).

Weston ⌐ Fl (2) R 5s; 51°22'·60N 03°05'·75W.

Monkstone Rk ⌁ Fl 5s 13m 12M; 51°24'·89N 03°06'·02W.

Ranie ⌐ Fl (2) R 5s; 51°24'·23N 03°09'·39W.

S Cardiff ⌐ Q (6) + L Fl 15s; *Bell;* 51°24'·18N 03°08'·57W.

Outer Wrach ⌐ Q (9) 15s; 51°26'·20N 03°09'·46W.

N Cardiff ⌐ QG; 51°26'·52N 03°07'·19W.

EW Grounds ⌐ L Fl 10s 7M; *Bell;* **Racon (T) 7M;** 51°27'·12N 02°59'·95W.

Newport Deep ⌐ Fl (3) G 10s; *Bell;*51°29'·36N 02°59'·12W.

East Usk ☆ 51°32'·40N 02°58'·01W Fl (2) WRG 10s 11m W11M,R10M, G10M; vis: 284°-W-290° -obscd shore-324°-R-017°-W-037°-G-115°-W-120°.

Also Oc WRG 10s 10m W11M, R9M, G9M; vis: 018°-G-022°-W- 024°-R-028°.

SEVERN ESTUARY

THE SHOOTS

Lower Shoots ⌐ Q (9) 15s 6m 7M; 51°33'·85N 02°42'·05W.

2nd Severn Crossing, Centre span ⌁ Q Bu 5M; *Racon (O) (3cm) range unknown*; 51°34'·45N 02°42'·03W.

Old Man's Hd ⌐ VQ (9) W 10s 6m 7M; 51°34'·74N 02°41'·69W.

Lady Bench (Lts in line 234°) ⌐ QR 6m 6M; 51°34'·85N 02°42'·20W. Rear, Oc R 5s 38m 3M.

Charston Rk ⌁ Fl 3s 5m 8M; 51°35'·35N 02°41'·68W.

Chapel Rk ⌁ Fl WRG 2·6s 6m 8M, vis: W213°- G284°-W049°-R051·5°-160°; 51°36'·44N 02°39'·21W.

SEVERN BRIDGE TO SHARPNESS

Aust ⌁ 2 QG (vert) 11m 6M; 51°36'·16N 02°38'·00W.

West Tower ⌁ 3 QR (hor) on upstream/downstream sides; *Siren (3) 30s*; obscured 040°-065°; 51°36'·73N 02°38'·80W.

Centre of span ⌁ Q Bu, each side; 51°36'·59N 02°38'·43W.

Lyde Rock ⌁ Q WR 5m 5M; vis: 148°-R-237°-W-336°-R-067°; 51°36'·89N 02°38'·67W.

COUNTS ⚓ Q; 51°39'·48N 02°35'·84W .

LEDGES ⚓ 51°39'·77N 02°34'·15W Fl (3) G 10s.

Bull Rock ⌁ Fl 3s 6m 8M; 51°41'·80N 02°29'·89W.

Sharpness S Pier Hd ⌁ 2 FG (vert) 6m 3M; *Siren 20s*; 51°42'·97N 02°29'·12W.

BRISTOL CHANNEL (SOUTH SHORE)

BRISTOL DEEP

N Elbow ⌐ QG; *Bell;* 51°26'·97N 02°58'·65W.

S Mid Grounds ⌐ VQ (6) + L Fl 10s; 51°27'·62N 02°58'·68W.

E Mid Grounds ⌐ Fl R 5s; 51°27'·75N 02°54'·98W.

Clevedon ⌐ VQ; 51°27'·39N 02°54'·93W.

Welsh Hook ⌐ Q (6) + L Fl 15s; *Bell;* 51°28'·53N 02°51'·86W.

Avon ⌐ Fl G 2·5s; 51°27'·92N 02°51'·73W.

Black Nore Pt ☆ 51°29'·09N 02°48'·05W Fl (2) 10s 11m **17M**; obsc by Sand Pt when brg less than 049°; vis: 044°-243°.

Firefly ⌐ Fl (2) G 5s; 51°29'·96N 02°45'·35W.

Portishead Pt ☆ 51°29'·68N 02°46'·42W Q (3) 10s 9m **16M**; B twr, W base; vis: 060°-262°; *Horn 20s.*

AVONMOUTH/RIVER AVON

Royal Edward Dock N Pier Hd ⌁ Fl 4s 15m 10M; vis: 060°-228·5°; 51°30'·49N 02°43'·09W.

Avonmouth S Pier Hd ⌁ Oc RG 30s 9m 10M; vis: 294°-R-036°-G-194°; 51°30'·37N 02°43'·10W.

BRISTOL CHANNEL (SOUTH SHORE)

E Culver ⚓ Q (3) 10s; 51°18'·00N 03°15'·44W.
W Culver ⚓ VQ (9) 10s; 51°17'·37N 03°18'·68W.
Gore ⚓ Iso 5s; *Bell;* 51°13'·94N 03°09'·79W.

BURNHAM-ON-SEA/RIVER PARRETT

Lower Lt Ent ⚓ Fl 7·5s 7m 12M; vis: 074°-164°; 51°14'·89N 03°00'·36W.Dir lt 076°. F WRG 4m W12M, R10M, G10M; vis: 071°-G- 075°-W-077°- R-081°.
Bridgewater Bar No. 1 ⚓ QR; 51°14'·53N 03°03'·75W.

WATCHET/MINEHEAD

Watchet W Bkwtr Hd ⚓ Oc G 3s 9m 9M; 51°11'·03N 03°19'·74W.
Minehead Bkwtr Hd ⚓ Fl (2) G 5s 4M; vis: 127°-262°; 51°12'·81N 03°28'·36W.
Lynmouth Foreland ☆ 51°14'·73N 03°47'·21W Fl (4) 15s 67m **18M**; W ○ twr; vis: 083°-275°; (H24).

LYNMOUTH/WATERMOUTH/ILFRACOMBE

Lynmouth Harbour Arm ⚓ 2 FG (vert) 6m 5M; 51°13'·92N 03°49'·84W.
Sand Ridge ⚓ Q G; 51°15'·01N 03°49'·77W.
Copperas Rock ⚓ 51°13'·78N 04°00'·60W.
Watermouth ⚓ Oc WRG 5s 1m 3M; W △; vis: 149·5°-G-151·5°-W- 154·5°-R-156·5°; 51°12'·93N 04°04'·60W.
Lantern Hill ⚓ Fl G 2·5s 39m 6M; 51°12'·66N 04°06'·78W.
Horseshoe ⚓ Q; 51°15'·02N 04°12'·96W.
Bull Point ☆ 51°11'·94N 04°12'·09W Fl (3) 10s 54m **20M**; W ○ twr, obscd shore-056°. Same twr; FR 48m 12M; vis: 058°-096°.
Morte Stone ⚓ 51°11'·30N 04°14'·95W.
Baggy Leap ⚓ 51°08'·92N 04°16'·97W.

BIDEFORD, RIVERS TAW AND TORRIDGE

Bideford F'wy ⚓ L Fl 10s; *Bell;* 51°05'·25N 04°16'·25W.
Bideford Bar ⚓ Q G; 51°04'·89N 04°14'·62W.
Pulley ⚓ Fl G 10s; 51°04'·08N 04°12'·70W.
Instow ☆ Ldg Lts 118°. **Front,** 51°03'·62N 04°10'·67W Oc 6s 22m **15M**; vis: 104·5°-131·5°.
Rear, 427m from front, Oc 10s 38m **15M**; vis: 104°-132°; (H24).

Crow Pt ⚓ Fl WR 2. 5s 8m W6M R5M; vis: 225°-R-232°-W-237°-R-358°-W-015°-R-045°; 51°03'·96N 04°11'·39W.

CLOVELLY/HARTLAND/LUNDY

Clovelly Hbr Quay Hd ⚓ 50°59'·92N 04°23'·83W Fl G 5s 5m 5M.
Lundy Near North Pt ☆ 51°12'·10N 04°40'·65W Fl 15s 48m **17M**; vis: 009°-285°.
Lundy South East Pt ☆ 51°09'·72N 04°39'·37W Fl 5s 53m **15M**; vis: 170°-073°; *Horn 25s.*
Jetty Head ⚓ Fl R 3s 8m 3M; 51°09'·80N 04°39'·20W.
Hartland Point ☆ 51°01'·29N 04°31'·59W Fl (6) 15s 37m **25M**; (H24); *Horn 60s.*

NORTH CORNWALL

PADSTOW/NEWQUAY

Stepper Point ⚓ L Fl 10s 12m 4M; 50°34'·12N 04°56'·72W.
Greenaway ⚓ Fl (2) R 10s; 50°33'·78N 04°56'·06W.
Bar ⚓ Fl G 5s; 50°33'·46N 04°56'·12W.
Padstow N Quay Hd ⚓ 2 FG (vert) 6m 2M; 50°32'·50N 04°56'·16W.
Trevose Head ☆ 50°32'·94N 05°02'·13W Fl 7·5s 62m **21M**; *Horn (2) 30s.*
Newquay N Pier Hd ⚓ 2 FG (vert) 5m 2M; 50°25'·07N 05°05'·19W..

HAYLE/ST IVES

The Stones ⚓ Q; 50°15'·64N 05°25'·51W.
Godrevy I ⚓ Fl WR 10s 37m W12M, R9M; vis: 022°-W-101°-R-145°-W-272°; 50°14'·54N 05°24'·04W.
Hayle App ⚓ QR; 50°12'·26N 05°26'·30W.
St Ives App ⚓ 50°12'·85N 05°28'·42W
East Pier Hd ⚓ 2 FG (vert) 8m 5M; 50°12'·80N 05°28'·61W.
West Pier Hd ⚓ 2 FR (vert) 5m 3M; 50°12'·77N 05°28'·73W.
Pendeen ☆ 50°09'·90N 05°40'·32W Fl (4) 15s 59m **16M**; vis: 042°-240°; in bay between Gurnard Hd and Pendeen it shows to coast; *Horn 20s.*

For Lts further W see Area 1 SW England - *Isles of Scilly to Anvil Point.*

#	Port														Port	#
1	Aberystwyth	1	12	64	66	122	164	192	224	254	286	299	318	361	Kilrush	12
2	Fishguard	40	2	11	13	69	111	139	171	201	233	246	265	308	Dingle	11
3	Milford Haven	84	48	3	10	56	102	131	165	188	227	242	252	295	Valentia	10
4	Tenby	107	71	28	4	9	42	70	102	132	164	177	196	239	Baltimore	9
5	Swansea	130	94	55	36	5	8	35	69	95	135	150	168	202	Kinsale	8
6	Cardiff	161	125	86	66	46	6	7	34	65	100	115	133	172	Youghal	7
7	Sharpness	192	156	117	106	75	33	7	6	32	69	84	102	139	Dunmore East	6
8	Avonmouth	175	139	100	89	58	20	18	8	5	34	47	66	108	Rosslare	5
9	Burnham-on-Sea	169	133	94	70	48	53	50	33	9	4	15	36	75	Arklow	4
10	Ilfracombe	128	92	53	35	25	44	74	57	45	10	3	21	63	Wicklow	3
11	Padstow	142	106	70	70	76	97	127	110	98	55	11	2	48	Dun Laoghaire	2
12	Longships	169	133	105	110	120	139	169	152	140	95	50	12	1	Carlingford Lough	1

AREA 10 Ireland – *South and Westwards from Rockabill to Inisheer*

SELECTED LIGHTS, BUOYS & WAYPOINTS | Positions are referenced to WGS84

NAVIGATION

LAMBAY ISLAND TO TUSKAR ROCK
MALAHIDE/LAMBAY ISLAND/HOWTH
Taylor Rks ⟨ Q; 53°30'·21N 06°01'·87W.

Rowan Rocks ⟨ Q (3) 10s; 53°23'·88N 06°03'·27W.

Howth E Pier Hd ⚡ Fl (2) WR 7·5s 13m W12M, R9M; W twr; vis: W256°-R295°-256°; 53°23'·66N 06°04'·03W.

Baily ☆ 53°21'·70N 06°03'·14W Fl 15s 41m **26M**; twr.

Rosbeg E ⟨ Q (3) 10s; 53°21'·02N 06°03'·45W.

Rosbeg S ⟨ Q (6) + L Fl 15s; 53°20'·22N 06°04'·17W.

S Burford ⟨ VQ (6) + L Fl 10s; *Whis;* 53°18'·07N 06°01'·27W.

PORT OF DUBLIN/DUN LAOGHAIRE
Dublin Bay ⟨ Mo (A) 10s; *Racon (M);* 53°19'·92N 06°04'·64W.

Great S Wall Hd Poolbeg ☆ Fl R 4s 20m 10M*(synchro with N.Bull)*; R ◯ twr; *Horn (2) 60s;* 53°20'·53N 06°09'·08W

Dublin N Bank ☆ 53°20'·69N 06°10'·59W Oc G 8s 10m **16M**; G ☐ twr.

Dun Laoghaire E Bkwtr Hd ⚡ 53°18'·15N 06°07'·62W Fl (2) R 10s 16m **17M**; twr, R lantern; *Horn 30s (or Bell (1) 6s).*

Muglins ⚡Fl R 5s 14m 11M; 53°16'·55N 06°04'·58W.

Bennett Bk ⟨ Q (6) + L Fl 15s; 53°20'·17N 05°55'·11W.

Kish Bank ☆ 53°18'·64N 05°55'·48W Fl (2) 20s 29m **22M**; W twr, R band; *Racon (T) 15M; Horn (2) 30s.*

S Codling ⟨ VQ (6) + L Fl 10s; 53°04'·74N 05°49'·76W.

S India ⟨ Q (6) + L Fl 15s; 53°00'·36N 05°53'·31W.

CODLING LANBY ⌐ 53°03'·02N 05°40'·76W Fl 4s 12m **15M**; tubular structure on By; *Racon (G)10M; Horn 20s.*

WICKLOW/ARKLOW
Wicklow E Pier Hd ⚡ Fl WR 5s 11m 6M; W twr, R base and cupola; vis: 136°-R-293°-W-136°; 52°58'·99N 06°02'·07W.

Wicklow Head ☆ 52°57'·95N 05°59'·89W; Fl (3) 15s 37m **23M**; W twr.

N Arklow ⟨ Q; 52°53'·86N 05°55'·21W.

Arklow Bank Wind Farm from 52°48'·47N 05°56'·57W to 52°46'·47N 05°57'·11W, N and S Turbines Fl Y 5s14m 10M + Fl W Aero lts. AIS transmitters. Other turbines Fl Y 5s.

S Arklow ⟨ VQ (6) + L Fl 10s; 52°40'·82N 05°59'·21W.

ARKLOW LANBY ⌐ 52°39'·52N 05°58'·16W Fl (2) 12s 12m **15M**; *Racon (O)10M; Horn Mo (A) 30s.*

No. 2 Glassgorman ⟨ Fl (4) R 10s; 52°44'·52N 06°05'·36W.

S Blackwater ⟨ Q (6) + L Fl 15s; 52°22'·76N 06°12'·86W.

WEXFORD/ROSSLARE
S Long ⟨ VQ (6) + L Fl 10s; 52°14'·84N 06°15'·64W.

Splaugh ⟨ Fl (2) R 6s; 52°14'·37N 06°16'·76W.

Tuskar ☆ 52°12'·17N 06°12'·42W Q (2) 7·5s 33m **24M**; W twr; *Horn (4) 45s, Racon (T) 18M.*

TUSKAR ROCK TO OLD HD OF KINSALE
S Rock ⟨ Q (6) + L Fl 15s; 52°10'·80N 06°12'·84W.

Barrels ⟨ Q (3) 10s; 52°08'·32N 06°22'·05W.

KILMORE/WATERFORD
St Patrick's Bridge ⟨ Fl R 6s; (Apr-Sep); 52°09'·30N 06°34'·71W.

Kilmore Quay SWM ⟨ Iso 10s; (Apr-Sep); 52°09'·20N 06°35'·30W.

Coningbeg ⟨ Q(6)+LFl 15s, Racon, AIS; 52°03'·20N 06°38'·57W.

Hook Hd ☆ 52°07'·32N 06°55'·85W Fl 3s 46m **23M**; W twr, two B bands; *Racon (K) 10M vis 237°-177°; Horn (2) 45s.*

Waterford ⟨ Fl R 3s. Fl (3) R 10s; 52°08'·95N 06°57'·00W.

Dunmore East Pier Head ☆ 52°08'·93N 06°59'·37W Fl WR 8s 13m **W17M**, R13M; Gy twr, vis: W225°-R310°-004°.

DUNGARVAN
Helvick ⟨ Q (3) 10s; 52°03'·61N 07°32'·25W.

Mine Head ☆ 51°59'·52N 07°35'·25W Fl (4) 20s 87m **20M**; W twr, B band; vis: 228°-052°.

YOUGHAL/BALLYCOTTON
Youghal W side of ent ☆ 51°56'·57N 07°50'·53W Fl WR 2·5s 24m **W17M**, R13M; W twr; vis: W183°-R273°- W295°- R307°- W351°-003°.

Ballycotton ☆ 51°49'·52N 07° 59'·09W Fl WR 10s 59m **W21M, R17M**; B twr, within W walls, B lantern; vis: W238°- R048°-238°; *Horn (4) 90s.*

CORK
Cork ⟨ L Fl 10s; *Racon (T) 7M*; 51°42'·92N 08°15'·60W.

Fort Davis Ldg lts 354·1°. Front, 51°48'·82N 08°15'·80W Dir WRG 29m **17M**; vis: FG351·5°-AlWG352·25°-FW353°-AlWR355°-FR355·75°-356·5°. Rear, Dognose Quay, 203m from front, Oc 5s 37m 10M; Or 3, synch with front.

Roche's Point ☆ 51°47'·59N 08°15'·29W Fl WR 3s 30m **W20M, R16M**; vis: Rshore- W292°- R016°- 033°, W(unintens) 033°- R159°- shore.

KINSALE/OYSTER HAVEN
Bulman ⟨ Q (6) + L Fl 15s; 51°40'·14N 08°29'·74W.

Charle's Fort ⚡ Fl WRG 5s 18m W9M, R6M, G7M; vis: G348°- W358°- R004°-168°; H24; 51°41'·74N 08°29'·97W.

OLD HEAD OF KINSALE TO MIZEN HEAD

Old Head of Kinsale ☆, S point 51°36'·28N 08°32'·03W Fl (2) 10s 72m **20M**; B twr, two W bands; *Horn (3) 45s.*

Galley Head ☆ summit 51°31'·80N 08°57'·19W Fl (5) 20s 53m **23M**; W twr; vis: 256°-065°.

Kowloon Br ⟨ Q (6) + L Fl 15s; 51°27'·58N 09°13'·75W.

BALTIMORE/SCHULL/CROOKHAVEN

Barrack Pt ⚡ Fl (2) WR 6s 40m W6M, R3M; vis: R168°-W294°-038°; 51°28'·33N 09°23'·65W.

Fastnet ☆, W end 51°23'·35N 09°36'·19W Fl 5s 49m **27M**; Gy twr, *Horn (4) 60s, Racon (G) 18M.*

Mizen Head ☆ 51°27'·00N 09°49'·24W Iso 4s 55m **15M**; vis: 313°-133°.

MIZEN HEAD TO DINGLE BAY

Sheep's Hd ☆ 51°32'·60N 09°50'·95W Fl (3) WR 15s 83m **W18M, R15M**; W bldg; vis: 007°-R-017°-W-212°.

BANTRY BAY/KENMARE RIVER

Roancarrigmore ☆ 51°39'·19N 09°44'·83W Fl WR 3s 18m **W18M**, R14M; W □ twr, B band; vis: 312°-W-050°-R-122°-R(unintens)-242°-R-312°. Reserve lt W8M, R6M obsc 140°-220°.

Ardnakinna Pt ☆ 51°37'·11N 09°55'·08W Fl (2) WR 10s 62m **W17M**, R14M; W ○ twr; vis: 319°-R- 348°-W- 066°-R-shore.

Bull Rock ☆ 51°35'·51N 10°18'·08W Fl 15s 83m **21M**; W twr; vis: 220°-186°.

Skelligs Rock ☆ 51°46'·12N 10°32'·51W Fl (3) 15s 53m **19M**; W twr; vis: 262°-115°; part obsc within 6M 110°-115°.

VALENTIA/PORTMAGEE

Fort (Cromwell) Point ☆ 51°56'·02N 10°19'·27W Fl WR 2s 16m **W17M, R15M**; W twr; vis: 304°-R-351°,102°-W-304°; obsc from seaward by Doulus Head when brg more than 180°.

DINGLE BAY TO LOOP HEAD

DINGLE BAY/VENTRY/DINGLE/FENIT

Inishtearaght ☆, W end Blasket Islands 52°04'·55N 10°39'·68W Fl (2) 20s 84m **19M**; W twr; vis: 318°-221°; *Racon (O).*

Little Samphire Is ☆ 52°16'·26N 09°52'·91W Fl WRG 5s 17m **W16M**, R13M; G13M; Bu ○ twr; vis: 262°-R-275°, 280-R-090°-G-140°-W- 152°-R-172°.

SHANNON ESTUARY

Ballybunnion ⟨ VQ; *Racon (M) 6M*; 52°32'·52N 09°46'·93W.

Kilcredaune Hd ☆ Fl 6s 41m **15M**; W twr; 52°34'·79N 09°42'·58W; obsc 224°-247° by hill within 1M. twr; vis: 208°-092°; 52°36'·32N 09°31'·03W.

Loop Head ☆ 52°33'·68N 09°55'·96W Fl (4) 20s 84m **23M**.

Positions are referenced to WGS84

North and Westwards from Rockabill to Inisheer

LAMBAY ISLAND TO DONAGHADEE

Rockabill ☆ 53°35'·82N 06°00'·25W Fl WR 12s 45m **W22M, R18M**; W twr, B band; vis: 178°-W-329°-R-178°; H24.

DROGHEDA/DUNDALK

Drogheda Port Appr Dir lt 53°43'·30N 06°14'·73W WRG 10m **W19M, R15M**, G15M; vis: 268°-FG- 269°-Al WG-269·5°-FW-270·5°-Al WR-271°-FR-272°; H24.

Dundalk Pile Light ☆ 53°58'·56N 06°17'·70W Fl 15s 10m **21M**; W Ho; vis: 124°-W-151°-R-284°-W-313°-R-124°. Fog Det lt VQ 7m, vis: when brg 358°; *Horn (3) 60s.*

CARLINGFORD LOUGH

Carlingford ⚲ L Fl 10s; 53°58'·76N 06°01'·06W.

Hellyhunter ⟨ Q (6) + L Fl 15s; *Racon;* 54°00'·35N 06°02'·10W.

Haulbowline ☆ 54°01'·19N 06°04'·74W Fl (3) 10s 32m **17M**; Gy twr; reserve lt 15M; Fog Det lt VQ 26m; vis: 330°. Turning lt ⚡ FR 21m 9M; same twr; vis: 196°-208°; *Horn 30s.*

DUNDRUM BAY

St John's Point ☆ 54°13'·61N 05°39'·30W Q (2) 7·5s 37m **25M**; B twr, Y bands; H24 when horn is operating. **Auxiliary Light** ☆ Fl WR 3s 14m **W15M**, R11M; same twr, vis: 064°-W-078°-R-shore; Fog Det lt VQ 14m vis: 270°; *Horn (2) 60s.*

STRANGFORD LOUGH/ARDS PENINSULA

Strangford ⚲ L Fl 10s; 54°18'·61N 05°28'·67W.

Bar Pladdy ⟨ Q (6) + L Fl 15s; 54°19'·34N 05°30'·51W.

Butter Pladdy ⟨ Q (3) 10s; 54°22'·45N 05°25'·74W.

SOUTH ROCK ⛴ 54°24'·49N 05°22'·02W Fl (3) R 30s 12m **20M**; R hull and lt twr, W Mast, *Horn (3) 45s, Racon (T) 13M.*

BALLYWATER/DONAGHADEE

Skulmartin ⚲ L Fl 10s; *Whis;* 54°31'·82N 05°24'·80W.

Donaghadee ☆, S Pier Hd 54°38'·70N 05°31'·86W Iso WR 4s 17m **W18M**, R14M; W twr; vis: shore-W-326°-R-shore; *Siren 12s.*

DONAGHADEE TO RATHLIN ISLAND

BELFAST LOUGH/BANGOR

Mew I ☆ NE end 54°41'·91N 05°30'·79W Fl (4) 30s 37m; B twr, W band; *Racon (O) 14M.*

S Briggs ⚲ 54°41'·19N 05°35'·72W Fl (2) R 10s.

BangorN Pier Hd ⚡ Iso R 12s 9m14M; 54°40'·03N 05°40'·34W.

Belfast Fairway ⟨ LFl10s; *Horn (1) 16s; Racon(G);* 54°41'·71N 05°46'·24W

CARRICKFERGUS/LARNE
Carrickfergus Marina E Bkwtr Hd ⚡ QG 8m 3M; 54°42'·58N 05°48'·69W.

Black Hd ☆ 54°45'·99N 05°41'·33W Fl 3s 45m **27M**; W 8-sided twr.

N Hunter Rock ⚓ Q; 54°53'·04N 05°45'·13W.

Larne Chaine Twr ☆ Iso WR 5s 23m **16M**; Gy twr; vis: 230°-W-240°-240°-R-shore; 54°51'·27N 05°47'·90W.

East Maiden ⚡ Fl (3) 20s 29m 24M; W twr, B band; *Racon (M) 11-21M.* Auxiliary lt Fl R 5s 15m 8M; 54°55'·74N 05°43'·65W; same twr; vis:142°-182° over Russel and Highland Rks.

RATHLIN ISLAND TO INISHTRAHULL
RATHLIN ISLAND
Altacarry Head Rathlin East ☆ 55°18'·06N 06°10'·30W Fl (4) 20s 74m **26M**; W twr, B band; vis: 110°-006° and 036°-058°; *Racon (G) 15-27M.*

Rathlin W 0·5M NE of Bull Pt ⚡ 55°18'·05N 06°16'·82W Fl R 5s 62m **22M**; W twr, lantern at base; vis: 015°-225°; H24.

LOUGH FOYLE
Foyle ⚓ L Fl 10s; 55°15'·32N 06°52'·60W.

Inishowen ☆ 55°13'·56N 06°55'·75W Fl (2) WRG 10s 28m **W18M**, R14M, G14M; W twr, 2 B bands; vis: 197°-G-211°-W-249°-R-000°; *Horn (2) 30s.* Fog Det lt VQ 16m vis: 270°.

Inishtrahull ☆ 55°25'·86N 07°14'·62W Fl (3) 15s 59m **19M**; W twr; obscd 256°-261° within 3M; *Racon (T) 24M 060°-310°.*

INISHTRAHULL TO BLOODY FORELAND
L SWILLY/MULROY BAY/SHEEPHAVEN
Fanad Head ☆ 55°16'·57N 07°37'·91W Fl (5) WR 20s 39m **W18M**, R14M; W twr; vis 100°-R-110°-W-313°-R-345°-W-100°.

Limeburner ⚓ Q Fl; 55°18'·54N 07°48'·40W.

Tory Island ☆ 55°16'·36N 08°14'·97W Fl (4) 30s 40m **27M**; B twr, W band; vis: 302°-277°; *Racon (M) 12-23M*; H24.

Bloody Foreland ⚡ Fl WG 7·5s 14m W6M, G4M; vis: 062°-W-232°-G-062°; 55°09'·51N 08°17'·03W.

BLOODY F'LD TO RATHLIN O'BIRNE
Aranmore, Rinrawros Pt ☆ 55°00'·90N 08°33'·66W Fl (2) 20s 71m **27M**; W twr; obsc by land about 234°-007° and about 013°. Auxiliary lt Fl R 3s 61m 13M, same twr; vis: 203°-234°.

Rathlin O'Birne, W side ☆ 54°39'·80N 08°49'·94W Fl WR 15s 35m **W18M**, R14M; W twr; vis: 195°-R-307°-W-195°; *Racon (O) 13M, vis 284°-203°.*

RATHLIN O'BIRNE TO EAGLE ISLAND
St John's Pt ⚡ Fl 6s 30m 14M; W twr; 54°34'·16N 08°27'·64W.

Rotten I ⚡ 54°36'·97N 08°26'·41W; Fl WR 4s 20m **W15M**, R11M; W twr; vis: W255°-R008°- W039°-208°.

SLIGO
Wheat Rk ⚓ Q (6) + LFl 15s; 54°18'·84N 08°39'·10W.

EAGLE ISLAND TO SLYNE HEAD
Eagle Is, W end ☆ 54°17'·02N 10°05'·56W Fl (3) 15s 67m **19M**; W twr.

Black Rk ☆ 54°04'·03N 10°19'·25W Fl WR 12s 86m **W20M, R16M**; W twr; vis: 276°-W-212°-R-276°.

BROAD HAVEN/BLACKSOD/CLEW BAYS
Gubacashel Pt ⚡ Iso WR 4s 27m W17M, R12M; 110°-R-133°-W-355°-R-021° W twr; 54°16'·06N 09°53'·33W.

Blacksod ⚓ Q (3) 10s; 54°05'·89N 10°03'·01W.

Achillbeg I S Point ☆ 53°51'·51N 09°56'·85W Fl WR 5s 56m **W18M, R18M, R15M**; W □ twr on □ building; vis: 262°-R-281°-W-342°-R- 060°-W- 092°-R(intens)-099°-W-118°.

Inishgort S Point ⚡ L Fl 10s 11m 10M; W twr. Shown H24; 53°49'·61N 09°40'·25W.

Slyne Hd, North twr, Illaunamid ☆ 53°23'·99N 10°14'·06W; Fl (2) 15s 35m **19M**; B twr.

SLYNE HEAD TO BLACK HEAD
GALWAY BAY/INISHMORE
Eeragh, Rock Is ☆ 53°08'·10N 09°51'·39W Fl 15s 35m **23M**; W twr, two B bands; vis: 297°-262°.

Straw Is ☆ 53°07'·06N 09°37'·85W Fl (2) 5s 11m **15M**; W twr.

Black Hd ⚡ Fl WR 5s 20m W11M, R8M, W □ twr; vis: 045°- R268°-276°; 53°09'·26N 09°15'·83W.

Inisheer ☆ 53°02'·78N 09°31'·58W Iso WR 12s 34m **W20M, R16M**; vis: 225°-W(partially vis >7M)-231°, 231°-W-245°-R-269°-W-115°; *Racon (K) 13M.*

See table on page 36 for distances anticlockwise between Kilrush and Carlingford Lough

DISTANCE TABLES
Approx distances in nautical miles are by the most direct route allowing for dangers and TSS.

		1	2	3	4	5	6	7	8	9	10	11	12	13	14	15
1	Strangford Lough	1														
2	Bangor	34	2													
3	Carrickfergus	39	6	3												
4	Larne	45	16	16	4											
5	Carnlough	50	25	26	11	5										
6	Portrush	87	58	60	48	35	6									
7	Lough Foyle	92	72	73	55	47	11	7								
8	L Swilly (Fahan)	138	109	104	96	81	48	42	8							
9	Burtonport	153	130	130	116	108	74	68	49	9						
10	Killybegs	204	175	171	163	148	115	109	93	43	10					
11	Sligo	218	189	179	177	156	123	117	107	51	30	11				
12	Eagle Island	234	205	198	193	175	147	136	123	72	62	59	12			
13	Westport	295	266	249	240	226	193	187	168	120	108	100	57	13		
14	Galway	338	309	307	297	284	253	245	227	178	166	163	104	94	14	
15	Kilrush	364	335	332	323	309	276	270	251	203	191	183	142	119	76	15

AREA 11 West Denmark – *Skagen to Rømø*
SELECTED LIGHTS, BUOYS & WAYPOINTS

Positions are referenced to WGS84

SKAGEN
Skagen W ☆ Fl (3) WR 10s 31m **W17M**/R12M; 053°-W-248°-R-323°; W ○ twr; 57°44'·92N 10°35·66E.
Skagen ☆ Fl 4s 44m **23M**; Gy ○ twr; *Racon G, 20M*; 57°44'·11N 10°37'·76E.
Skagen No 1A ⸬ L Fl 10s; *Racon N*; 57°43'·42N 10°53'·51E.

HIRTSHALS
Hirtshals ☆ F Fl 30s 57m **F 18M**; **Fl 25M**; W ○ twr, approx 1M SSW of hbr ent; 57°35'·07N 09°56'·45E.
Outer W mole ⸍ Fl G 3s 14m 6M; G mast; *Horn 15s*; 57°35'·97N 09°57'·36E.

HANSTHOLM
Hanstholm ☆ Fl (3) 20s 65m **26M**; shown by day in poor vis; W 8-sided twr; 57°06'·65N 08°35'·74E, approx 1M S of the hbr ent.
Hanstholm ⸬ LFl 10s; 57°08'·10N 08°34'·94E.

THYBORØN
Landfall ⸬ L Fl 10s; *Racon T, 10m*; 56°42'·55N 08°08'·70E.
Approach ☆ Fl (3) 10s 24m 12M; 56°42'·49N 08°12'·90E.
Bovbjerg ☆ L Fl (2) 15s 62m **16M**; 56°30'·74N 08°07'·13E.

THORSMINDE HAVN (Positions approx)
Lt ho ⸍ F 30m 13M; 56°22'·34N 08°06'·99E.
S mole ⸍ Iso G 2s 9m 4M; 56°22'·26N 08°06'·92E.

HVIDE SANDE
Lyngvig ☆ Fl 5s 53m **22M**; 56°02'·95N 08°06'·17E.
N outer bkwtr ⸍ Fl R 3s 7m 8M; 55°59'·94N 08°06'·55E.
Lt ho ⸍ F 27m 14M; 56°00'·00N 08°07'·35E.

HORNS REV
Blåvands Huk ☆ Fl (3) 20s 55m **23M**; W □ twr; 55°33'·46N 08°04'·95E.

Horns Rev is encircled clockwise by:
Tuxen ⸬ Q; 55°34'·22N 07°41'·92E on the N side.
Vyl ⸬ Q (6) + L Fl 15s; 55°26'·22N 07°49'·99E.
No. 2 ⸬ L Fl 10s; 55°28'·74N 07°36'·49E, SW side.
Horns Rev W ⸬ Q (9) 15s; 55°34'·47N 07°26'·05E.
Slugen Channel (crosses Horns Rev ESE/WNW)
▲ L Fl G 10s; 55°33'·99N 07°49'·38E.
⸺ Fl (3) R 10s; 55°29'·42N 08°02'·56E.
Wind farm in □ 2·7M x 2·5M, centred on 55°29'·22N 07°50'·21E: 80 turbines all R lts, the 12 perimeter turbines are lit Fl (3) Y 10s. NE and SW turbines, *Racon (U)*.

APPROACHES TO ESBJERG
Grådyb ⸬ L Fl 10s; *Racon G, 10M*; 55°24'·63N 08°11'·59E.
Sædding Strand 053·8° triple ldg lts: to Nos 7/8 buoys; H24: **Front** Iso 2s 13m **21M**; 052°-056°; R bldg; 55°29'·74N 08°23'·87E.
Middle Iso 4s 26m **21M**; 051°-057°; R twr, W bands; 55°29'·94N 08°24'·33E, 630m from front.
Rear F 37m **18M**; 052°-056°; R twr; 55°30'·18N 08°24'·92E, 0·75M from front.
Ldg lts 067°, to Nos 9/10 buoys. Both FG 10/25m **16M**, H24. Front, Gy tripod; rear, Gy twr, 55°28'·76N 08°24'·70E.
Ldg lts 049°, to No 16 buoy/Jerg. Both FR 16/27m **16M**, H24. Front, W twr; rear, Gy twr, 55°29'·92N 08°23'·75E.

FANØ
Slunden outer ldg lts 242°, both Iso 2s 5/8m 3M; 227°-257°. Front, twr; 55°27'·20N 08°24'·53E. Rear, twr, 106m from front.
Nordby marina 55°26'·65N 08°24'·53E.

APPROACHES (Lister Tief) TO RØMØ
Rode Klit Sand ⸬ Q (9) 15s, 55°11'·11N 08°04'·88E, (130°/9M to Lister Tief ⸬).
Lister Tief ⸬ Iso 8s; *Whis*; 55°05'·32N 08°16'·80E.
Lister Landtief No 5 ▲ 55°03'·68N 08°24'·73E.
Rømø S mole ⸍ Fl R 3s 7m 2M; Gy twr; 55°05'·19N 08°34'·31E.

		1	2	3	4	5	6	7	8	9	10	11	12	13	14	15	16	17	18
1	Skagen	1																	
2	Hirtshals	33	2																
3	Hanstholm	85	52	3															
4	Thyborøn	114	84	32	4														
5	Torsminde	141	108	56	24	5													
6	Hvide Sande	162	179	77	45	24	6												
7	Esbjerg	200	174	122	90	76	54	7											
8	Fanø	210	177	125	93	79	57	3	8										
9	Rømø	233	200	148	116	94	73	30	33	9									
10	Hörnum	248	215	163	131	108	86	70	73	29	10								
11	Husum	275	247	195	163	152	131	95	98	68	45	11							
12	Kiel/Holtenau	261	233	281	249	232	208	180	183	189	126	129	12						
13	Bremerhaven	306	285	233	201	185	163	127	129	107	83	82	123	13					
14	Wilhelmshaven	414	296	242	310	184	162	125	128	106	82	82	123	45	14				
15	Helgoland	259	238	186	154	141	119	83	85	63	39	47	104	44	43	15			
16	Cuxhaven	304	284	232	200	162	138	110	113	85	56	66	70	58	56	38	16		
17	Wangerooge	283	262	210	178	168	147	109	112	94	68	52	108	38	27	24	42	17	
18	Hamburg	338	317	265	233	216	192	163	167	139	99	113	90	81	110	88	54	61	18

DISTANCE TABLES
Approx distances in nautical miles are by the most direct route allowing for dangers and TSS.

SELECTED LIGHTS, BUOYS & WAYPOINTS | Positions are referenced to WGS84

SYLT

Lister Tief ⚓ Iso 8s; *Whis;* 55°05'·33N 08°16'·79E.

List West ⚡ Oc WRG 6s 19m W14M, R11M, G10M; 040°-R-133°-W-227°-R-266·4°-W-268°-G-285°-W-310°-W(unintens)-040°; W twr, R lantern; 55°03'·15N 08°24'·00E.

List Ost ⚡ Iso WRG 6s 22m W14M, R11M, G10M; 010·5°-W(unintens)-098°-W-262°-R-278°-W-296°-R-323·3°-W-324·5°-G-350°-W-010·5°; W twr, R band; 55°02'·93N 08°26'·58E.

List Hafen, N mole ⚡ FG 8m 4M; 218°-038°; G mast; 55°01'·03N 08°26'·52E.

Kampen, Rote Kliff ☆ L Fl WR 10s 62m **W20M, R16M**; 193°-W-260°- W (unintens)-339°-W-165°-R-193°; W twr, B band; 54°56'·76N 08°20'·38E.

Hörnum ☆ Fl (2) 9s 48m **20M**; 54°45'·23N 08°17'·47E. Hbr, N pier ⚡ FG 6m 4M, 024°-260°.

Vortrapptief ⚓ Iso 4s; 54°34'·88N 08°13'·06E.

AMRUM ISLAND

Norddorf ☆ Oc WRG 6s 22m **W15M**, R12M, G11M; 031-W-097°-R-176·5°-W-178·5°-G-188°; W ○ twr, R lantern; 54°40'·13N 08°18'·46E.

Amrum ☆ Fl 7·5s 63m **23M**; R twr, W bands; 54°37'·84N 08°21'·23E.

FÖHR ISLAND

Nieblum Dir lt ☆ Oc (2) WRG 10s 11m **W19M, R/G15M**; 028°-G-031°-W-032·5°-R-035·5°; R twr, W band; 54°41'·10N 08°29'·20E.

DAGEBÜLL

Dagebüll Iso WRG 8s 23m **W18M, R/G15M**; 042°-G-043°-W-044·5°- R-047°; G mast; 54°43'·82N 08°41'·43E. FW lts on N and S moles.

RIVER HEVER

Hever ⚓ Iso 4s; *Whis;* 54°20'·41N 08°18'·82E.

Westerheversand ☆ Oc (3) WRG 15s 41m **W21M, R17M, G16M**; 012·2°-W-069°-G-079·5°-W-080·5°-R-107°-W-233°-R-248°; 54°22'·37N 08°38'·36E.

RIVER EIDER

Eider ⚓ Iso 4s; 54°14'·54N 08°27'·61E.

St Peter ☆ L Fl (2) WR 15s 23m **W15M**, R12M; 271°-R-280·5°-W-035°-R-055°-W-068°-R-091°-W-120°; R twr, B lantern; 54°17'·24N 08°39'·10E.

BÜSUM

Süderpiep ⚓ Iso 8s; *Whis;* 54°05'·82N 08°25'·70E.

Büsum ☆ Iso WR 6s 22m **W19M**, R12M; 248°-W-317°-R-024°-W-148°; 54°07'·60N 08°51'·48E.

GB Light V 🛟 Iso 8s 12m **17M**; *Horn Mo (R) 30s; Racon, T, 8M;* 54°10'·80N 07°27'·60E.

HELGOLAND

Helgoland ☆ Fl 5s 82m **28M**; brown ☐ twr, B lantern, W balcony; 54°10'·91N 07°52'·93E.

Vorhafen. Ostmole, S elbow ⚡ Oc WG 6s 5m W6M, G3M; 203°-W-250°-G-109°; G post; fog det lt; 54°10'·31N 07°53'·94E.

Düne. Ldg lts 020°. Front ⚡ Iso 4s 11m 8M; 54°10'·87N 07°54'·80E. Rear, Iso WRG 4s 17m W11M, R/ G10M; synch; 010°-G-018·5°-W-021°-R-030; 106°-G-125°-W-130°-R-144°.

RIVER ELBE APPROACHES

Elbe ⚓ Iso 10s; *Racon T, 8M;* 53°59'·95N 08°06'·49E. No.1 ⚓ QG; 53°59'·21N 08°13'·20E.

Neuwerk ☆, S side, L Fl (3) WRG 20s 38m **W16M**, R12M, G11M; 165·3°-G-215·3°-W-238·8°-R-321°; 343°-R-100°; 53°54'·92N 08°29'·73E.

CUXHAVEN/OTTERNDORF

Marina, F WR & F WG ⚡; 53°52'·43N 08°42'·49E. Medem ⚡ Fl (3) 12s 6m 5M; B △, on B col; 53°50'·15N 08°53'·85E.

BRUNSBÜTTEL

Ldg lts 065·5°: both Iso 3s 24/46m **16/21M**; synch; R twrs, W bands. Front ☆ 53°53'·32N 09°08'·47E. Alter Vorhafen ⚡ F WG 14m W10M, G6M; 266·3°-W-273·9°-G-088·8°; 53°53'·27N 09°08'·59E.

HAMBURG, WEDEL YACHT HAFEN

E ent ⚡ FG 5m 3M; 53°34'·25N 09°40'·79E. City Sport Hafen ⚡ Iso Or 2s; 53°32'·52N 09°58'·81E.

RIVER WESER APPROACH CHANNELS

ALTE WESER

Schlüsseltonne ⚓ Iso 8s; 53°56'·25N 07°54'·76E.

Alte Weser ☆ F WRG 33m **W23M, R19M, G18M**; 288°-W-352°-R-003°-W-017°- G-045°-W-074°-G-118°- W-123°- R-140°-G-175°-W-183°-R-196°-W-238°; *Horn Mo (AL) 60s;* 53°51'·79N 08°07'·65E.

NEUE WESER

3/Jade 2 ⚓ Fl (2+1) G 15s; *Racon T, 8M;* 53°52'·40N 07°44'·00E.

Tegeler Plate ☆ Oc (3) WRG 12s 21m **W21M, R17M, G16M**; 329°-W-340°-R-014°-W-100°-G-116°-W-119°-R-123°-G-144°-W-147°-R-264°; 53°47'·87N 08°11'·45E.

BREMERHAVEN

No. 61 ⚓ QG; 53°32'·26N 08°33'·93E (Km 66·0). Vorhafen S pier hd ⚡ FG 15m 5M; 355°-265°; 53°32'·09N 08°34'·50E.

BREMEN
Hasenbüren Sporthafen ⚓ 2 FY (vert); 53°07'·51N 08°40'·03E.

RIVER JADE APPROACHES

Jade-Weser ⚓ Oc 4s; *Racon T, 8M;* 53°58'·33N 07°38'·83E.
Mellumplate ☆ FW 28m **24M**; 116·1°-116·4°; R ☐ twr, W band; 53°46'·28N 08°05'·51E.

HOOKSIEL
No. 37/Hooksiel 1 ⚓ IQ G 13s; 53°39'·37N 08°06'·58E.
Vorhafen ent ⚓ L Fl R 6s 9m 3M; 53°38'·63N 08°05'·25E.

WILHELMSHAVEN
Fluthafen N mole ⚓ F WG 9m,W6M, G3M; 216°-W-280°-G-010°-W-020°-G-130°; 53°30'·86N 08°09'·32E.

WANGEROOGE
Harle ⚓ Iso 8s; 53°49'·24N 07°48'·92E.
Buhne W bkwtr ⚓ FR 3m 4M; 53°46'·33N 07°51'·93E.

SPIEKEROOG
Otzumer Balje ⚓ Iso 4s; 53°48'·11N 07°37'·12E.
Spiekeroog ⚓ FR 6m 4M; 53°45'·0N 07°37'·7E.

LANGEOOG
Accumer Ee ⚓ Iso 8s; 53°46·93N 07°25·73E.
W mole ⚓ Oc WRG 6s 8m W7M, R5M, G4M; 064°-G-070°-W-074°-R-326°-W-330°-G-335°-R-064°; *Horn Mo (L) 30s*; 53°43'·42N 07°30'·13E .

NORDERNEY
Norderney N ⚓ Q; 53°46'·06N 07°17'·12E.
Dovetief ⚓ Iso 4s; 53°45'·48N 07°12'·70E.
Schluchter ⚓Iso 8s; 53°44'·48N 07°02'·27E.
W mole ⚓ Oc (2) R 9s 13m 4M; 53°41'·9N 07°09'·9E.
Norderney ☆ Fl (3) 12s 59m **23M**; unintens 067°-077° and 270°-280°; R 8-sided twr; 53°42'·58N 07°13'·83E.

BENSERSIEL
E training wall head ⚓ Oc WRG 6s 6m W5M, R3M, G2M; 110°-G-119°-W-121°-R-110°; R post & platform; 53° 41'·80N 07°32'·84E.
Ldg lts 138°, both Iso 6s 12/18m 9M.
Inner hbr, W mole hd FG; E mole hd FR.

DORNUMER-ACCUMERSIEL
AB3 ⚓ IQ G 13s; 53°41'·50N 07°29'·34E.
W bkwtr head, approx 53°41'·04N 07°29'·30E.

NESSMERSIEL
N mole ⚓ Oc 4s 6m 5M; G mast; 53°41'·9N 07°21'·7E.

NORDDEICH
W trng wall head ⚓ FG 8m 4M, 021°-327°; G framework twr; 53°38'·7N 07°09'·0E.
Outer ldg lts 144°, both B masts. Front, Iso WR 6s 6m W6M, R5M; 078°-R-122°-W-150°. Rear, Iso 6s 9m 6M; synch, 140m from front.

RIVER EMS APPROACHES

GW/EMS 🛟 Iso 8s 12m **17M**; *Horn Mo (R) 30s (H24)*; *Racon T, 8M;* 54°09'·96N 06°20'·72E.
Borkumriff ⚓ Oc 4s; *Racon T, 8M;* 53°47'·44N 06°22'·05E.
Osterems ⚓ Iso 4s; 53°41'·91N 06°36'·17E.
Riffgat ⚓ Iso 8s; 53°38'·96N 06°27'·10E.
Westerems ⚓ Iso 4s; *Racon T, 8M;* 53°36'·93N 06°19'·39E.
H1⚓ 53°34'·91N 06°17'·97E.

BORKUM
Borkum Grosser ☆ Fl (2) 12s 63m **24M**; 53°35'·32N 06°39'·64E. Same twr, ⚓ F WRG 46m **W19M, R/G15M**; 107·4°-G-109°-W-111·2°- R-112·6°.
Fischerbalje ☆ Oc (2) 16s 15m **3M**; 260°-W-123°; Fog det lt; R/W twr on tripod; 53°33'·18N 06°42'·90E.

EMDEN
Outer hbr, W pier ⚓ FR 10m 4M; R 8-sided twr; *Horn Mo (ED) 30s*; 53°20'·06N 07°10'·49E.
E pier ⚓ FG 7m 5M; 53°20'·05N 07°10'·84E.

		1																
1	Esbjerg	**1**																
2	Hörnum Lt (Sylt)	47	**2**															
3	Husum	95	48	**3**														
4	Hamburg	163	112	113	**4**													
5	Kiel/Holtenau	179	128	129	90	**5**												
6	Brunsbüttel	126	75	76	37	53	**6**											
7	Cuxhaven	110	63	66	54	70	17	**7**										
8	Bremerhaven	127	80	82	81	131	78	58	**8**									
9	Wilhelmshaven	125	78	82	110	123	70	56	45	**9**								
10	Hooksiel	116	69	73	101	117	64	47	36	9	**10**							
11	Helgoland	83	38	47	88	104	51	38	44	43	35	**11**						
12	Wangerooge	109	60	52	61	108	55	42	38	27	19	24	**12**					
13	Langeoog	119	72	77	114	130	77	60	47	43	34	35	21	**13**				
14	Norderney	123	77	85	81	137	84	69	62	53	44	44	29	18	**14**			
15	Emden	165	129	137	174	190	137	120	115	106	97	85	80	63	47	**15**		
16	Borkum	133	97	105	104	163	110	95	88	80	71	67	55	46	31	32	**16**	
17	Delfzijl	155	119	127	159	173	120	105	100	89	83	81	65	56	41	10	22	**17**
18	Den Helder	187	192	198	229	245	192	175	180	159	150	153	148	130	115	125	95	115	**18**

DISTANCE TABLES
Approx distances in nautical miles are by the most direct route allowing for dangers and TSS.

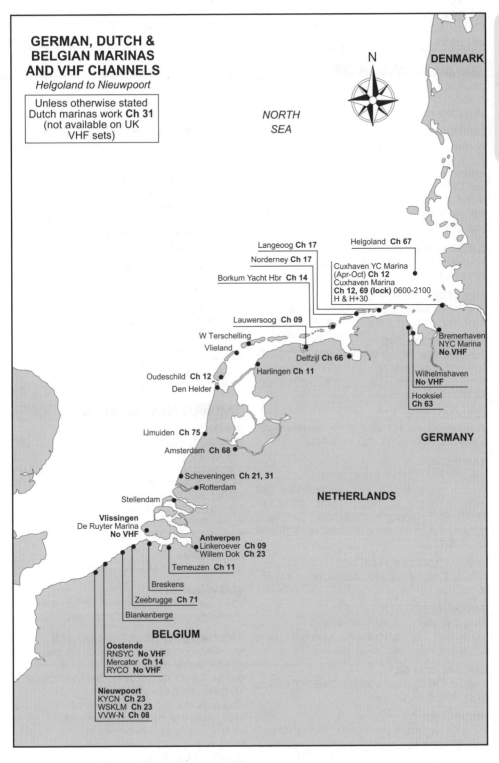

GERMAN, DUTCH &
BELGIAN MARINAS
AND VHF CHANNELS
Helgoland to Nieuwpoort

Unless otherwise stated
Dutch marinas work **Ch 31**
(not available on UK
VHF sets)

N

DENMARK

NORTH
SEA

Langeoog **Ch 17**
Norderney **Ch 17**
Borkum Yacht Hbr **Ch 14**

Helgoland **Ch 67**

Cuxhaven YC Marina
(Apr-Oct) **Ch 12**
Cuxhaven Marina
Ch 12, 69 (lock) 0600-2100
H & H+30

Lauwersoog **Ch 09**

W Terschelling
Vlieland

Bremerhaven
NYC Marina
No VHF

Delfzijl **Ch 66**
Harlingen **Ch 11**

Oudeschild **Ch 12**
Den Helder

Wilhelmshaven
No VHF

Hooksiel
Ch 63

IJmuiden **Ch 75**

GERMANY

Amsterdam **Ch 68**

Scheveningen **Ch 21, 31**
Rotterdam

NETHERLANDS

Stellendam

Vlissingen
De Ruyter Marina
No VHF

Antwerpen
Linkeroever **Ch 09**
Willem Dok **Ch 23**

Terneuzen **Ch 11**

Breskens

Zeebrugge **Ch 71**

Blankenberge

BELGIUM

Oostende
RNSYC **No VHF**
Mercator **Ch 14**
RYCO **No VHF**

Nieuwpoort
KYCN **Ch 23**
WSKLM **Ch 23**
VVW-N **Ch 08**

43

AREA 13 Netherlands & Belgium – *Delfzijl to Nieuwpoort*

SELECTED LIGHTS, BUOYS & WAYPOINTS

Positions are referenced to WGS84

DELFZIJL TO DEN HELDER

DELFZIJL
W mole ⚓ FG; 53°19'·01N 07°00'·26E.
Ldg lts 203° both Iso 4s. Front, 53°18'·62N 07°00'·16E.

LAUWERSOOG
W mole head ⚓ FG 3M; *Horn (2) 30s;* 53°24'·68N 06°12'·00E.
Schiermonnikoog ☆ Fl (4) 20s 43m **28M**; dark R ○ twr; 53°29'·19N 06°08'·76E. Same twr: FWR 29m **W15M**, R12M; W210°-221°, R221°-230°.
WG (Westgat) ℚ Iso 8s; *Racon Z;* 53°32'·00N 05°58'·54E.

ZEEGAT VAN AMELAND
Ameland, W end ☆ Fl (3) 15s 57m **30M**; 53°26'·92N 05°37'·52E.

ZEEGAT VAN TERSCHELLING
ZS ℚ Iso 4s; *Racon T;* 53°19'·71N 04°55'·86E.
SM1-ZS10 ⚓ Fl(2+1) G 10s; 53°18'·99N 05°03'·60E.

WEST TERSCHELLING
Brandaris Twr ☆ Fl 5s 54m **29M**, Y ☐ twr; 53°21'·61N 05°12'·85E.
W hbr mole ⚓ FR 5m 5M; R post, W bands; *Horn 15s;* 53°21'·25N 05°13'·09E.

VLIELAND
Vuurduin ☆ Iso 4s 54m **20M**; 53°17'·69N 05°03'·46E.
E mole hd ⚓ FG; 53°17'·68N 05°05'·51E.

HARLINGEN
P9/BO44 ⚓ VQ; 53°10'·59N 05°23'·88E.
Pollendam ldg lts 112°, both Iso 6s 8/19m 13M (H24); B masts, W bands. Front, 53°10'·51N 05°24'·18E. Rear, vis 104·5°-119·5°.
N mole hd ⚓ FR 9m 4M; R/W pedestal; 53°10'·59N 05°24'·32E.

KORNWERDERZAND SEALOCK
W mole ⚓ FG 9m 7M; *Horn Mo(N) 30s;* 53°04'·77N 05°20'·03E.

DEN OEVER SEALOCK
LW ℚ L Fl 10s; 52°59'·51N 04°55'·90E,.
Ldg lts 131°, both Oc 10s 6m 7M; 127°-137°. Front, 52°56'·32N 05°02'·98E. Rear, 280m SE.

EIERLANDSCHE GAT
Eierland ☆ Fl (2) 10s 52m **29M**; R ○ twr; 53°10'·93N 04°51'·30E, N tip of Texel.

OUDESCHILD
Dir ⚓ Oc 6s; intens 291°; 53°02'·40N 04°50'·94E; leads 291° into hbr. N mole hd FG 6m. S mole hd ⚓ FR 6m; *Horn (2) 30s;* 53°02'·33N 04°51'·17E.
ZH ⚓ VQ (6) + L Fl 10s; 52°54'·65N 04°34'·71E.

TX1 ⚓ Fl G 5s; 52°48'·01N 04°15'·50E.
Vinca G ⚓ Q (9) 15s; *Racon D*; 52°45'·93N 04°12'·35E.

MOLENGAT (from the N)
MG ⚓ Mo (A) 8s; 53°03'·91N 04°39'·36E.
MG1 ⚓ Iso G 4s; 53°02'·89N 04°40'·84E.
S14-MG17 ⚓ VQ (6) + L Fl 10s; 52°58'·50N 04°43'·60E.

DEN HELDER
Ldg lts 191°, both Oc G 5s 15/24m 14M, synch. Front, vis 161°-221°; 52°57'·37N 04°47'·08E.
Marinehaven, W bkwtr head ⚓ QG 11m 8M; *Horn 20s;* 52°57'·95N 04°47'·07E (Harssens Is).
Ent W side, ⚓ Fl G 5s 9m 4M (H24); 180°-067°; 52°57'·78N 04°47'·08E. Marina ent FG and FR.

SCHULPENGAT (from the SSW)
Ldg lts 026·5°, both Oc 8s **18M** (by day 9M); vis 024·5°-028·5°. **Front** ☆, 53°00'·85N 04°44'·42E (on Texel). Rear, **Den Hoorn** ☆.
SG ⚓ Mo (A) 8s; *Racon Z*; 52°52'·90N 04°37'·90E.
Schilbolsnol ☆ F WRG 27m **W15M**, R12M, G11M; 338°-W-002°-G-035°-W(ldg sector)-038°-R-051°-W-068°; post; 53°00'·50N 04°45'·68E (on Texel).
Kijkduin ☆ Fl (4) 20s 56m **30M**; vis 360°; brown twr; 52°57'·33N 04°43'·58E.

IJMUIDEN TO STELLENDAM

IJMUIDEN
ℚ Mo (A) 8s; *Racon Y, 10M*; 52°28'·44N 04°23'·78E.
Ldg lts 100·5°. **Front** ☆ F WR 30m **W16M**, R13M; 050°-W-122°-R-145°-W-160°; dark R ○ twrs; 52°27'·70N 04°34'·47E. **Rear** ☆ Fl 5s 52m **29M**; 019°-199°. FW 4M by day; 090·5°-110·5°.
S bkwtr hd ⚓ FG 14m 10M (in fog Fl 3s); *Horn (2) 30s;* W twr, G bands; 52°27'·82N 04°31'·94E.
N bkwtr hd ⚓ FR 15m 10M; 52°28'·05N 04°32'·55E.

AMSTERDAM
IJ8 ℚ Iso R 8s (for Sixhaven); 52°22'·84N 04°54'·29E.

SCHEVENINGEN
SCH ℚ Iso 4s; 52°07'·75N 04°14'·14E. W mole ⚓ FG 12m 9M; G twr, W bands; 52°06'·22N 04°15'·16E.

APPROACHES to HOEK VAN HOLLAND
Noord Hinder ℚ Fl (2) 10s; *Horn (2) 30s; Racon T, 12-15M;* 52°00'·04N 02° 51'·03E.
Goeree ☆ Fl (4) 20s 32m **28M**; *Horn (4) 30s; Racon T, 12-15M;* 51°55'·42N 03°40'·03E.
Indusbank N ⚓ VQ; 52°02'·88N 04°03'·55E.
MO ℚ Mo (A) 8s; 52°00'97N 03°58'·06E.
MVN ⚓ VQ; 51°59'·59N 04°00'·19E.
MV ⚓ Q (9) 15s; 51°57'·44N 03°58'·40E.
Westhoofd, Fl (3) 15s 55m **30M**; R ☐ tr. 51°48'·78N 03°51'·82E.

HOEK VAN HOLLAND
Nieuwe Waterweg ldg lts 107°: both Iso R 6s 29/43m **18M**; 099.5°-114.5°; Front, 51°58'·55N 04°07'·53E.
Maasvlakte ☆ Fl (5) 20s 67m **28M**, H24; 340°-267°; 51°58'·20N 04°00'·85E.
Nieuwe Zuiderdam ⚟ FG 25m 10M; *Horn 10s*; G twr, W bands; 51°59'·13N 04°02'·47E.

SLIJKGAT and STELLENDAM
SG ℺ Iso 4s; 51°51'·93N 03°51'·40E.
N mole ⚟ FG; *Horn (2) 15s;* 51°49'·87N 04°02'·01E.

ROOMPOTSLUIS TO TERNEUZEN
Schouwenbank ℺ Mo (A) 8s; *Racon O, 10M;* 51°44'·94N 03°14'·32E.
West Schouwen ☆ Fl (2+1)15s 57m **30M**; Gy twr, R diagonals; 51°42'·53N 03°41'·48E
Westpit ℺ Iso 8s; 51°33'·65N 03°09'·92E.

ROOMPOTSLUIS
N bkwtr ⚟ FR 7m; 51°37'·30N 03°40'·09E.
Kaloo ℺ Iso 8s; 51°35'·56N 03°23'·23E.
Westkapelle ☆, Common rear, Fl 3s 49m **28M**; partially obsc'd; ☐ twr; 51°31'·75N 03°26'·80E.

OOSTGAT
Ldg lts 149·5°: Front, Noorderhoofd Oc WRG 10s 20m; W13M, R/G10M; 353°-R-008°-G-029°-W-169°; R ○ twr, W band; 51°32'·40N 03°26'·21E.
OG5 ⚟ Iso G 8s; 51°33'·95N 03°25'·92E.

VLISSINGEN
Songa ⚟ QG; 51°25'·16N 03°33'·66E.
Koopmanshaven, W mole root, ⚟ Iso WRG 3s 15m W12M, R10M, G9M; 253°-R-277°-W-284°-R-297°-W-306·5°-G-013°-W-024°-G-033°-W-035°-G-039°-W-055°-G-084·5°-R-092°-G-111°-W-114°; R pylon; 51°26'·37N 03°34'·52E.
E mole ⚟ FG 7m; W mast; 51°26'·32N 03°34'·66E.

BRESKENS
ARV-VH ⚟ Q; 51°24'·71N 03°33'·89E.
Yacht hbr, W mole ⚟ FG 7m; 51°24'·04N 03°34'·06E.

TERNEUZEN
W mole ⚟ Oc WRG 5s 15m W9M, R7M, G6M; 090°-R-115°-W-120°-G-130°-W-245°-G-249°-W-279°-R-004°; B & W post; 51°20'·54N 03°49'·58E.

BELGIUM
ANTWERPEN
Royerssluis, ldg lts 091°, both FR. FR/FG,ent to Willemdok ④. Linkeroever marina ent, FR/FG.

ZEEBRUGGE
A2 ⚟ Iso 8s; 51°22'·42N 03°07'·05E.
Ldg lts 136°, both Oc 5s 22/45m 8M; 131°-141°; H24, synch; W cols, R bands. Front, 51°20'·71N 03°13'·11E.
W outer mole ⚟ Oc G 7s 31m 7M; *Horn (3) 30s;* IPTS; 51°21'·73N 03°11'·17E.
Leopold II mole ☆ Oc WR 15s 22m, **W20M, R18M**; 068°-W-145°-R-212°-W-296°; IPTS; *Horn (3+1) 90s;* 51°20'·85N 03°12'·17E.

BLANKENBERGE
Lt ho ☆ Fl (2) 8s 30m **20M**; 065°-245°; W twr, B top; 51°18'·76N 03°06'·87E.
E pier ⚟ FR 12m 11M; 290°-245°; W ○ twr; *Bell (2) 15s;* 51°18'·91N 03°06'·56E.
W pier ⚟ FG 14m 11M; intens 065°-290°, unintens 290°-335°; W ○ twr; 51°18'·89N 03°06'·43E.

OOSTENDE
A1 ⚟ Iso 8s; 51°22'·37N 02°53'·34E.
Ldg lts 128°: both Iso 4s (triple vert) 22/32m 4M; 051°-201°. Front, 51°14'·13N 02°55'·55E.
Oostende lt ho ☆ Fl (3) 10s 65m **27M**; obsc 069·5°-071°; 51°14'·18N 02°55'·83E.
E pier ⚟ and *Horn* have been withdrawn. The E pier has been demolished (2008) and a new pier is being built further east; WIP until 2012 is marked by 1 NCM buoy Q; 2 SPM buoys QY; and 3 PHM buoys QR.

NIEUWPOORT
Lt ho ☆ Fl (2) R 14s 28m **16M**; R ○ twr, W bands; 51°09'·28N 02°43'·80E, 2 ca E of E pier root.
E pier ⚟ FR 11m 10M; vis 025°-250° & 307°-347°; 51°09'·42N 02°43'·08E.
W pier ⚟ FG 11m 9M; vis 025°-250° & 284°-324°; IPTS; *Bell (2) 10s;* 51°09'·35N 02°43'·00E.

1	Delfzijl	**1**															
2	Terschelling	85	**2**														
3	Harlingen	102	19	**3**													
4	Den Oever	110	34	21	**4**												
5	Den Helder	115	39	30	11	**5**											
6	Amsterdam	159	83	81	62	51	**6**										
7	IJmuiden	146	70	68	49	38	13	**7**									
8	Scheveningen	171	95	93	74	63	38	25	**8**								
9	Rotterdam	205	129	127	108	97	72	59	34	**9**							
10	Hook of Holland	185	109	107	88	77	52	39	14	20	**10**						
11	Stellendam	201	125	123	104	93	68	55	30	36	16	**11**					
12	Roompotsluis	233	157	155	136	125	100	87	50	68	48	32	**12**				
13	Vlissingen	228	152	150	131	120	99	86	61	67	47	45	24	**13**			
14	Zeebrugge	239	163	161	142	131	106	93	68	74	54	50	28	16	**14**		
15	Blankenberge	244	168	166	147	136	111	98	73	79	59	55	33	21	5	**15**	
16	Oostende	239	163	161	142	131	110	106	81	87	67	72	40	29	13	9	**16**
17	Nieuwpoort	262	186	184	165	154	129	116	91	97	77	83	51	39	23	18	9	**17**

DISTANCE TABLES
Approx distances in nautical miles are by the most direct route allowing for dangers and TSS.

AREA 14 North France – *Dunkerque to Cap de la Hague*
SELECTED LIGHTS, BUOYS & WAYPOINTS | Positions are referenced to WGS84

BELGIAN BORDER TO CAP GRIS-NEZ
OFFSHORE MARKS
WH Zuid ⚓ Q (6) + L Fl 15s; 51°22'·78N 02°26'·25E.
Bergues N ⚓ Q; 51°19'·92N 02°24'·50E.
Oostdyck radar twr; ☆ Mo (U) 15s 15m 12M; *Horn Mo (U) 30s; Racon O*; 51°16'·49N 02°26'·83E.
Bergues ⚓ Fl G 4s; 51°17'·15N 02°18'·62E.
Ruytingen N ⚓ 51°13'·10N 02°10'·28E, VQ.
Ruytingen SE ⚓ VQ (3) 15s; 51°09'·20N 02°08'·92E.
Sandettié SW ⚓ Q (9) 15s 5M; 51°09'·72N 01°45'·60E.
Sandettié 🛳 Fl 5s 12m **12M**; R hull; *Horn 30s; Racon T, 10M*; 51°09'·34N 01°47'·10E.

PASSE DE ZUYDCOOTE
E12 ⚓ VQ (6) + L Fl 10s; 51°07'·90N 02°30'·80E.
E11 ⚓ Fl G 4s; 51°06'·90N 02°30'·91E.
E9 ⚓ Fl (2) G 6s; 51°05'·66N 02°29'·68E.

PASSE DE L'EST
E6 ⚓ QR; 51°04'·86N 02°27'·08E.
E2 ⚓ Fl (2) R 6s; 51°04'·32N 02°22'·31E.
⚓ Q (6) + L Fl 15s; 51°04'·29N 02°21'·72E.

DUNKERQUE PORT EST
Jetée Est ☆ Fl (2) R 6s 12m **10M**; 51°03'·59N 02°21'·20E. **Jetée Ouest** ☆ Fl (2) G 6s 35m **10M**.
Dunkerque lt ho ☆ Fl (2) 10s 59m **26M**; 51°02'·93N 02°21'·86E. 137·5° ldg lts, both Oc (2) 6s 7/10m 12M.

GRAVELINES
W jetty ≤ Fl (2) WG 6s 9m W8M, G6M; 317°-W-327°-G-085°-W-244°; 51°00'·94N 02°05'·48E.

DUNKERQUE, WEST APPROACH
DW29 ⚓ Fl (3) G 12s; 51°03'·85N 02°20'·21E.
DW18 ⚓ Fl (3) R 12s; 51°03'·47N 02°10'·37E.
RCE ⚓ Iso G 4s; 51°02'·43N 01°53'·21E.
Dyck ⚓ Fl 3s; *Racon B*; 51°02'·99N 01°51'·78E.

CALAIS
Jetée Est ☆ Fl (2) R 6s 12m **17M**; Gy twr, R top; *Horn (2) 40s*; 50°58'·40N 01°50'·46E.
Jetée Ouest ≤ Iso G 3s 12m 9M; W twr, G top; *Bell 5s*; 50°58'·24N 01°50'·40E.
Calais ☆ Fl (4) 15s 59m **22M**; vis 073°-260°; W 8-sided twr, B top; 50°57'·68N 01°51'·21E.

CALAIS, WESTERN APPROACH
Calais Approche ⚓ VQ (9) 10s; 50°58'·89N 01°45'·10E.
CA2 ⚓ Fl R 4s; 50°58'·15N 01°45'·68E.
CA1 ⚓ Fl G 4s; 50°57'·64N 01°46'·14E.
Sangatte ≤ Oc WG 4s 13m W8M, G5M; 065°-G-089°-W-152°-G-245°; 50°57'·19N 01°46'·47E.
CA4 ⚓ Fl (2) R 6s; 50°58'·38N 01°48'·65E.
Cap Gris-Nez ☆ Fl 5s 72m **29M**; 005°-232°; W twr, B top; *Horn 60s*; 50°52'·09N 01°34'·94E.

CAP GRIS-NEZ TO LE HAVRE
DOVER STRAIT TSS, French side
Ruytingen SW ⚓ Fl (3) G 12s; 51°04'·98N 01°46'·83E.
ZC2 ⚓ Fl (2+1) Y 15s; 50°53'·53N 01°30'·88E.
ZC1 ⚓ Fl (4) Y 15s; 50°44'·99N 01°27'·21E.
Vergoyer N ⚓ VQ; *Racon C, 5-8M*; 50°39'·64N 01°22'·18E.
Vergoyer E ⚓ VQ (3) 5s; 50°35'·74N 01°19'·65E.
Bassurelle ⚓ Fl (4) R 15s 6M; *Racon B, 5-8m*; 50°32'·74N 00°57'·69E.
Vergoyer SW ⚓ VQ (9) 10s; 50°26'·98N 01°00'·00E.

BOULOGNE
Approche Boulogne ⚓ VQ (6) + L Fl 10s 8m 6M; 50°45'·31N 01°31'·07E.
Digue Carnot (S) ☆ Fl (2+1) 15s 25m **19M**; W twr, G top; *Horn (2+1) 60s*; 50°44'·44N 01°34'·05E.
Cap d'Alprech ☆ Fl (3) 15s 62m **23M**; W twr, B top; 50°41'·90N 01°33'·75E, 2·5M S of hbr ent.

LE TOUQUET and ÉTAPLES
Le Touquet ☆ Fl (2) 10s 54m **25M**; Or twr, brown band, W&G top; 50°31'·43N 01°35'·49E.
Pointe du Haut-Blanc ☆ Fl 5s 44m **23M**; W twr, R bands, G top; 50°23'·89N 01°33'·62E.

ST VALÉRY-SUR-SOMME
ATSO ⚓ Mo (A) 12s; 50°14'·00N 01°28'·08E.
Trng wall hd, ⚓ Fl G 2.5s 2m 1M; 50°12'·25N 01°35'·85E.
Cayeux-sur-Mer ☆ Fl R 5s 32m **22M**; W twr, R top; 50°11'·65N 01°30'·67E.

LE TRÉPORT
Ault ☆ Oc (3) WR 12s 95m **W15M**, R11M; 040°-W-175°-R-220°; W twr, R top; 50°06'·28N 01°27'·23E.
Jetée Ouest ☆ Fl (2) G 10s 15m **20M**; W twr, G top; *Horn (2) 30s*; 50°03'·87N 01°22'·13E.

DIEPPE
DI ⚓ VQ (3) 5s; 49°57'·05N 01°01'·25E.
Jetée Ouest ≤ Iso G 4s 11m 8M; W twr, G top; *Horn 30s*; 49°56'·27N 01°04'·95E.
Pte d'Ailly ☆ Fl (3) 20s 95m **31M**; W ☐ twr, G top; *Horn (3) 60s*; 49°54'·96N 00°57'·49E.

SAINT VALÉRY-EN-CAUX
Jetée Est ≤ Fl (2) R 6s 8m 4M; 49°52'·40N 00°42'·70E.

FÉCAMP
Jetée Nord ☆ Fl (2) 10s 15m **16M**; Gy twr, R top; *Horn (2) 30s*; 49°45'·93N 00°21'·78E.
Jetée Sud ≤ QG 14m 9M; Gy twr, G top; 49°45'·88N 00°21'·80E.
Cap d'Antifer ☆ Fl 20s 128m **29M**; 021°-222°; Gy 8-sided twr, G top; 49°41'·01N 00°09'·90E.

LE HAVRE

Cap de la Hève ☆ Fl 5s 123m **24M**; 225°-196°; W 8-sided twr, R top; 49°30'·74N 00°04'·15E.

LHA ⌐ Mo (A) 12s 10m 9M; R&W; *Racon, 8-10M*; 49°31'·38N 00°09'·88W.

Digue Nord ☆ Fl R 5s 15m **21M**; IPTS; W ○ twr, R top; *Horn 15s;* 49°29'·19N 00°05'·44E.

LE HAVRE TO CAP DE LA HAGUE

CHENAL DE ROUEN/HONFLEUR

No. 2 ☖ QR; *Racon T*; 49°27'·40N 00°01'·35E.

Ratier NW ☖ Fl G 2·5s; 49°26'·85N 00°02'·50E.

No. 20 ☖ QR; 49°25'·85N 00°13'·51E. Honfleur Digue Ouest ⚓ QG 10m 6M; 49°25'·68N 00°13'·81E.

DEAUVILLE/TROUVILLE

Ratelets ☖ Q (9) 15s; 49°25'·29N 00°01'·71E.

E jetty ⚓ Fl (4) WR 12s 8m W7M, R4M; 131°-W-175°-R-131°; 49°22'·22N 00°04'·33E.

DIVES-SUR-MER

DI ☖ L Fl 10s; 49°19'·18N 00°05'·84W.

No. 1 ☖ 49°18'·50N 00°05'·67W.

Dir lt 159·5°, Oc (2+1) WRG 12s 6m, W12M, R/G9M; 125°-G-157°-W-162°-R-194°;49°17'·80N 00°05'·24W.

OUISTREHAM

Ldg lts 185°, both Dir Oc (3+1) R 12s 10/30m **17M**.

Front, 49°17'·09N 00°14'·80W.

Lt ho ☆ Oc WR 4s 37m **W17M**, R13M; 115°-R-151°-W-115°; 49°16'·85N 00°14'·80W.

COURSEULLES-SUR-MER

Courseulles ☖ Iso 4s; 49°21'·28N 00°27'·69W.

W jetty ⚓ Iso WG 4s 7m; W9M, G6M; 135°-W-235°-G-135°; 49°20'·41N 00°27'·37W.

Ver ☆ Fl (3)15s 42m **26M**; 49°20'·39N 00°31'·15W.

Arromanches Ent buoys: ☖ 49°21'·35N 00°37'·26W; ☖ 49°21'·25N 00°37'·30W.

PORT-EN-BESSIN

W mole ⚓ Fl WG 4s 14m, W10M, G7M; G065°-114·5°, W114·5°-065°; 49°21'·17N 00°45'·39W.

GRANDCAMP

Ldg lts 146°, both Dir Q 9/12m **15M**, 144·5°-147·5°.

Front ☆, 49°23'·42N 01°02'·92W.

Jetée Est ⚓ Oc (2) R 6s 9m 9M; 49°23'·52N 01°02'·98W.

CARENTAN

C-I ☖ Iso 4s; 49°25'·44N 01°07'·08W.

Trng wall ☖ Fl (4) G 15s; 49°21'·94N 01°09'·96W.

Iles St-Marcouf ⚓ VQ (3) 5s 18m 8M; □ Gy twr, G top; 49°29'·86N 01°08'·82W.

ST VAAST-LA-HOUGUE

Le Gavendest ☖ Q (6) + L Fl 15s; *Whis;* 49°34'·36N 01°13'·89W.

Jetty ⚓ Dir Oc (2) WRG 6s 12m W10M, R/G7M; 219°-R-237°-G-310°-W-350°-R-040°; *Siren Mo (N) 30s;* 49°35'·17N 01°15'·41W.

BARFLEUR

Ldg lts 219·5°, both Oc (3) 12s 7/13m 10M; synch. Front, W □ twr;49°40'·18N 01°15'·61W.

W jetty ⚓ Fl G 4s 8m 6M; 49°40'·32N 01°15'·57W.

Pte de Barfleur ☆ Fl (2) 10s 72m **29M**; Gy twr, B top; *Horn (2) 60s;* 49°41'·78N 01°15'·96W.

Les Équets ☖ Q 8m 3M; 49°43'·62N 01°18'·36W.

La Pierre Noire ☖ Q (9) 15s 8m 4M;49°43'·53N 01°29'·09W.

CHERBOURG

La Truite ☖ Fl (4) R 15s; 49°40'·33N 01°35'·50W.

Fort de l'Est ⚓ Iso G 4s 19m 9M; 49°40'·28N 01°35'·93W.

CH1 ☖ L Fl 10s 8m 4M; *Whis;* 49°43'·24N 01°42'·09W.

Fort de l'Ouest ☆ Fl (3) WR 15s 19m **W24M, R20M**; 122°-W-355°-R-122°; Gy twr, R top; *Horn (3) 60s;* 49°40'·45N 01°38'·87W.

Digue de Querqueville ⚓ Fl (4) G 15s 8m 4M; W col, G top; 49°40'·30N 01°39'·80W.

Marina W mole ⚓ Fl (3) G 12s 7m 6M; G pylon; 49°38'·87N 01°37'·15W. E side, ⚓ Fl (3) R 12s 6m 6M; W col, R lantern; 49°38'·91N 01°37'·08W.

OMONVILLE-LA-ROGUE

L'Étonnard ☖ 49°42'·32N 01°49'·85W.

Cap de la Hague ☆ Fl 5s 48m **23M**; Gy twr, W top; *Horn 30s;* 49°43'·31N 01° 57'·28W.

	1. Dunkerque-Est	1																	
	2. **Calais**	28	**2**																
	3. **Boulogne**	49	21	**3**															
	4. St Valéry-sur-Somme	86	58	37	**4**														
	5. **Le Tréport**	90	62	41	16	**6**													
	6. **Dieppe**	100	74	53	30	15	**5**												
	7. St Valéry-en-Caux	109	81	62	42	28	16	**6**											
	8. **Fécamp**	121	93	76	57	44	32	17	**7**										
	9. **Le Havre**	148	121	103	84	71	61	47	27	**8**									
	10. **Honfleur**	157	129	108	92	80	67	51	35	13	**10**								
	11. **Deauville/Trouville**	152	125	108	91	79	61	53	34	9	13	**11**							
	12. Dives-sur-Mer	155	129	110	94	83	66	55	38	16	19	9	**12**						
	13. **Ouistreham**	160	138	115	97	85	73	59	41	20	24	15	9	**13**					
	14. **Courseulles**	162	136	115	100	87	75	60	44	24	30	23	18	14	**14**				
	15. Grandcamp	177	150	130	118	104	94	80	62	47	52	45	41	37	27	**15**			
	16. Carentan	187	159	139	126	112	100	85	69	56	61	55	50	45	36	13	**16**		
	17. **St Vaast**	179	151	131	120	107	96	80	65	54	61	54	50	46	35	16	20	**17**	
	18. Barfleur	175	147	128	118	105	94	78	64	56	62	57	53	48	39	21	26	10	**18**
	19. **Cherbourg**	188	160	142	131	120	108	94	80	71	77	73	69	66	57	40	44	28	21	**19**

DISTANCE TABLES

Approx distances in nautical miles are by the most direct route allowing for dangers and TSS.

AREA 15 N Central France (*Cap de la Hague to St Quay*) & Channel Is

SELECTED LIGHTS, BUOYS & WAYPOINTS | Positions are referenced to WGS84

DIELETTE TO ST MALO

DIELETTE
W bkwtr Dir lt 140°, Iso WRG 4s 12m W10M, R/G7M; 070°-G-135°-W-145°-R-180°; 49°33'·18N 01°51'·81W.
E bkwtr ⚓ Fl R 4s 6m 2M; 49°33'·21N 01°51'·78W.

CARTERET
Cap de Carteret ☆ Fl (2+1) 15s 81m **26M**; Gy twr, G top; 49°22'·40N 01°48'·41W.
W bkwtr ⚓ Oc R 4s 7m 7M; W post, R top; 49°22'·17N 01°47'·30W.

PORTBAIL
PB ⓘ 49°18'·37N 01°44'·75W.
Ldg lts 042°: Front, Q 14m 10M, 49°19'·75N 01°42'·50W. Rear, Oc 4s 20m 10M; stubby ch spire.

PASSAGE DE LA DÉROUTE
Les Trois-Grunes ⓘ Q (9) 15s, 49°21'·84N 01°55'·21W.
Le Sénéquet ⚓ Fl (3) WR 12s 18m W13M, R10M; 083·5°-R-116·5°-W-083·5°; 49°05'·48N 01°39'·73W.
NE Minquiers ⓘ VQ (3) 5s; *Bell;* 49°00'·85N 01°55'·30W.
S Minquiers ⓘ Q (6) + L Fl 15s; 48°53'·09N 02°10'·10W.

ÎLES CHAUSEY
L'Enseigne, W twr, B top; 48°53'·67N 01°50'·37W.
Grande Île ☆ Fl 5s 39m **23M**; Gy ☐ twr, G top; *Horn 30s;* 48°52'·17N 01°49'·34W.
La Crabière Est ⓘ Oc WRG 4s 5m, W9M, R/G 6M; 079°-W-291°-G-329°-W-335°-R-079°; 48°52'·46N 01°49'·39W.
Le Pignon ⚓ Fl (2) WR 6s 10m, W9M, R6M; 005°-150°-W-005°; B twr, W band; 48°53'·49N 01°43'·36W.

GRANVILLE
Pte du Roc ☆ Fl (4) 15s 49m **23M**; 48°50'·06N 01°36'·78W.
Le Loup ⓘ Fl (2) 6s 8m 11M; 48°49'·57N 01°36'·24W.
Marina S bkwtr ⚓ Fl (2) R 6s 12m 5M; W post, R top; *Horn (2) 40s;* 48°49'·89N 01°35'·90W. Marina sill, E & W sides: Oc (2) G 6s & Oc (2) R 6s.

CANCALE
Pierre-de-Herpin ☆ Oc (2) 6s 20m **17M**; 48°43'·77N 01°48'·92W.
Jetty ⚓ Oc (3) G 12s 12m 7M; 48°40'·10N 01°51'·11W.

ST MALO TO ST QUAY-PORTRIEUX

ST MALO, CHENAL DE LA PETITE PORTE
Outer ldg lts 129·7°: **Front, Le Grand Jardin** ☆ Fl (2) R 10s 24m **15M**, 48°40'·20N 02°04'·97W. Rear, **La Balue** ☆ FG 20m 22M; 48°37'·60N 02°00'·24W.
St Malo Fairway ⓘ Iso 4s; 48°41'·39N 02°07'·28W.
Inner ldg lts 128·6°, both Dir FG 20/69m **22/25M**; H24. Front, **Les Bas Sablons** ☆; W ☐ twr, B top; 48°38'·16N 02°01'·30W. Rear, **La Balue** ☆, above.

CHENAL DE LA GRANDE PORTE
Outer ldg lts 089·1°: **Front, Le Grand Jardin** ☆ (as above). Rear, **Rochebonne** ☆ Dir FR 40m **24M**; 48°40'·26N 01°58'·71W.
Môle des Noires hd ⚓ Fl R 5s 11m 13M; W twr, R top; *Horn (2) 20s;* 48°38'·52N 02°01'·91W.
Bas-Sablons marina ⚓ Fl G 4s 7m 5M; 48°38'·42N 02°01'·70W.

LA RANCE BARRAGE
La Jument ⚓ Fl G 4s 6m 4M; G twr, 48°37'·44N 02°01'·76W. Barrage lock, NW wall ⚓ Fl (2) G 6s 6m 5M,191°-291°; 48°37'·06N 02°01'·73W.

ST CAST
Môle ⚓ Iso WG 4s 11m, W11M, G8M; 204°-W-217°-G-233°-W-245°-G-204°; 48°38'·41N 02°14'·61W.
Cap Fréhel ☆ Fl (2) 10s 85m **29M**; Gy ☐ twr, G lantern; *Horn (2) 60s;* 48°41'·05N 02°19'·13W.

ERQUY
S môle ⚓ Fl (2) WRG 6s 11m W7M, R/G5M; 055°-R-081°-W-094°-G-111°-W-120°-R-134°; W twr; 48°38'·07N 02°28'·66W.

DAHOUET
La Petite Muette ⓘ Fl WRG 4s 10m W9M, R/G6M; 055°-G-114°-W-146°-R-196°; 48°34'·82N 02°34'·19W.

BAIE DE SAINT BRIEUC and LE LÉGUÉ
Grand Léjon ☆ Fl (5) WR 20s 17m **W18M**, R14M; 015°-R-058°-W-283°-R-350°-W-015°; R twr, W bands; 48°44'·91N 02°39'·87W.
Le Rohein ⓘ VQ (9) WRG 10s 13m, W10M, R/G7M; 072°-R-105°-W-180°-G-193°-W-237°-G-282°-W-301°-G-330°-W-072°; Y twr, B band; 48°38'·80N 02°37'·77W.
Le Légué ⓘ Mo (A) 10s; 48°34'·32N 02°41'·15W.
Pte à l'Aigle ⚓ VQ G 13m 8M; 48°32'·12N 02°43'·11W.

BINIC
N môle ⚓ Oc (3) 12s 12m 11M; unintens 020°-110°; W twr, G lantern; 48°36'·07N 02°48'·92W.

SAINT QUAY-PORTRIEUX
La Roselière ⓘ VQ (6) + L Fl 10s; 48°37'·29N 02°46'·18W.
Herflux ⓘ Dir ⚓ 130°, Fl (2) WRG 6s 10m, W 8M, R/G 6M; 115°-G-125°-W-135°-R-145°; 48°39'·07N 02°47'·95W.
Île Harbour ⚓ Fl WRG 4s 16m, W10M, R/G 8M; 011°-R-133°-G-270°-R-306°-G-358°-W-011°; 48°39'·99N 02°48'·49W.
Marina, **NE mole elbow,** Dir lt 318·2°: Iso WRG 4s 16m **W15M**, R/G11M; 159°-W-179°-G-316°- W-320·5°-R-159°; 48°38'·99N 02°49'·09W.
NE môle hd ⚓ Fl (3) G 12s 10m 2M; 48°38'·84N 02°48'·91W.

CHANNEL ISLANDS

THE CASQUETS AND ALDERNEY

Casquets ☆ Fl (5) 30s 37m **24M**, H24; *Horn (2) 60s*; *Racon T, 25M*; 49°43'·32N 02°22'·63W.

Quenard Pt ☆ Fl (4) 15s 37m **23M**, H24; 085°-027°; *Horn 30s*; 49°43'·75N 02°09'·86W.

Braye, ldg lts 215°: both Q 8/17m 9/12M, synch; 210°-220°. Front, old pier, 49°43'·40N 02°11'·91W.

Admiralty bkwtr ⚓ L Fl 10s; 49°43'·82N 02°11'·67W.

GUERNSEY, LITTLE RUSSEL CHANNEL

Platte Fougère ☆ Fl WR 10s 15m **16M**; 155°-W-085°-R-155°; W 8-sided twr, B band; *Horn 45s*; *Racon P*; 49°30'·83N 02°29'·14W.

Petite Canupe ⚓ Q (6) + L Fl 15s; 49°30'·20N 02°29'·14W. ⚓ L Fl 10s 49°30'·15N 02°29'·66W.

Beaucette marina Ldg lts 276°, both FR. Front, 49°30'·19N 02°30'·23W.

Roustel ⚓ Q 8m 7M; 49°29'·23N 02°28'·79W.

Platte ⚓, Fl WR 3s 6m, W7M, R5M; 024°-R-219°-W-024°; G conical twr; 49°29'·08N 02°29'·57W.

Brehon ⚓ Iso 4s 19m 9M, 49°28'·28N 02°29'·28W.

BIG RUSSEL

Noire Pute ⚓ Fl (2) WR 15s 8m 6M; 220°-W-040°-R-220°; on 2m high rock; 49°28'·21N 02°25'·02W.

Lower Heads ⚓ Q (6) + L Fl 15s; *Bell;* 49°25'·85N 02°28'·55W.

ST PETER PORT

Outer ldg lts 220°: **Front**, Castle bkwtr, Al WR 10s 14m **16M**; 187°-007°; *Horn 15s;* 49°27'·31N 02°30'·45W. Rear, Oc 10s 61m 14M; 179°-269°.

White Rock pier ⚓ Oc G 5s 11m 14M; tfc sigs; 49°27'·38N 02°31'·59W.

S Fairway ⚓ QG; 49°27'·30N 02°31'·76W.

HAVELET BAY

Oyster Rock ⚓ QG; 49°27'·04N 02°31'·47W.

Moulinet ⚓ QR; 49°26'·97N 02°31'·54W. Two inner buoys are also ⚓ QG and ⚓ QR.

HERM Hbr ldg lts 078° ⚓ 2F occas; W drums; 49°28'·25N 02°27'·11W.

SARK

Corbée du Nez ⚓ Fl (4) WR 15s 14m 8M; 057°-W-230°-R-057°; W structure; 49°27'·09N 02°22'·17W.

Point Robert ☆ Fl 15s 65m **20M**; W 8-sided twr; *Horn (2) 30s;* 49°26'·19N 02°20'·75W.

LES ÉCREHOU

Écrevière ⚓ Q (6) + L Fl 15s; 49°15'·26N 01°52'·15W.

JERSEY (North coast)

Sorel Point ☆ L Fl WR 7·5s 50m **15M**; 095°-W-112°-R-173°-W-230°-R-269°-W-273°; 49°15'·60N 02°09'·54W.

JERSEY (West and South coasts)

Grosnez Point ☆ Fl (2) WR 15s 50m **W19M, R17M**; 081°-W-188°-R-241°; 49°15'·50N 02°14'·80W.

La Corbière ☆ Iso WR 10s 36m **W18M, R16M**; shore-W-294°-R-328°-W-148°-R-shore; W ○ twr; *Horn Mo (C) 60s;* 49°10'·79N 02°15'·01W.

WESTERN PASSAGE

Ldg lts 082°. Front Oc 5s 23m 14M; 034°-129°; 49°10'·16N 02°05'·09W. Rear, Oc R 5s 46m 12M.

Noirmont Pt ⚓ Fl (4) 12s 18m 10M; B twr, W band; 49°09'·91N 02°10'·08W.

ST HELIER

Elizabeth marina: Dir ⚓ 106°: F WRG 4m 1M; 096°-G-104°-W-108°-R-119°; 49°10'·76N 02°07'·12W.

Marina ent ⚓ Oc G 4s 2M; 49°10'·83N 02°07'·13W.

Red & Green Passage, ldg lts 022·7° on dayglo R dolphins: Front, ⚓ Oc G 5s 10m 11M; 49°10'·63N 02°06'·94W. Rear, ⚓ Oc R 5s 18m 12M.

East Rock ⚓ QG; 49°09'·95N 02°07'·29W.

Victoria pier hd, Port control twr; IPTS; 49°10'·57N 02°06'·88W.

JERSEY (South-East coast)

Demie de Pas ⚓ Mo (D) WR 12s 11m, W14M, R10M; 130°-R-303°-W-130°; *Horn (3) 60s; Racon T, 10M*; B bn twr, Y top; 49°09'·01N 02°06'·15W.

Violet ⚓ L Fl 10s; 49°07'·81N 01°57'·14W.

GOREY

Ldg lts 298°: Front, ⚓ Oc RG 5s; 304°-R-353°-G-304°; 49°11'·80N 02°01'·34W. Rear, ⚓ Oc R 5s 24m 8M.

ST CATHERINE BAY

Verclut bkwtr ⚓ Fl 1·5s 18m 13M; 49°13'·34N 02°00'·64W.

1	Cherbourg	**1**																
2	Omonville	10	**2**															
3	Braye (Alderney)	25	15	**3**														
4	St Peter Port	44	34	23	**4**													
5	Creux (Sark)	37	29	22	10	**5**												
6	St Helier	64	51	46	29	24	**6**											
7	Carteret	41	29	28	31	23	26	**7**										
8	Portbail	49	33	32	35	27	25	5	**8**									
9	Iles Chausey	69	61	58	48	43	25	33	30	**9**								
10	Granville	75	67	66	55	50	30	38	35	9	**10**							
11	Dinan	102	91	85	66	64	50	62	59	29	35	**11**						
12	St Malo	90	79	73	54	52	38	50	47	17	23	12	**12**					
13	Dahouet	88	80	72	54	52	41	60	59	37	45	41	29	**13**				
14	Le Légué/St Brieuc	96	86	76	57	56	46	69	69	41	49	45	33	8	**14**			
15	Binic	95	84	75	56	55	46	70	70	43	51	45	33	10	8	**15**		
16	St Quay-Portrieux	88	80	73	56	51	46	64	64	47	54	47	35	11	7	4	**16**	
17	Lézardrieux	88	80	68	48	38	47	68	71	53	54	61	49	33	32	30	21	**17**

DISTANCE TABLES

Approx distances in nautical miles are by the most direct route allowing for dangers and TSS.

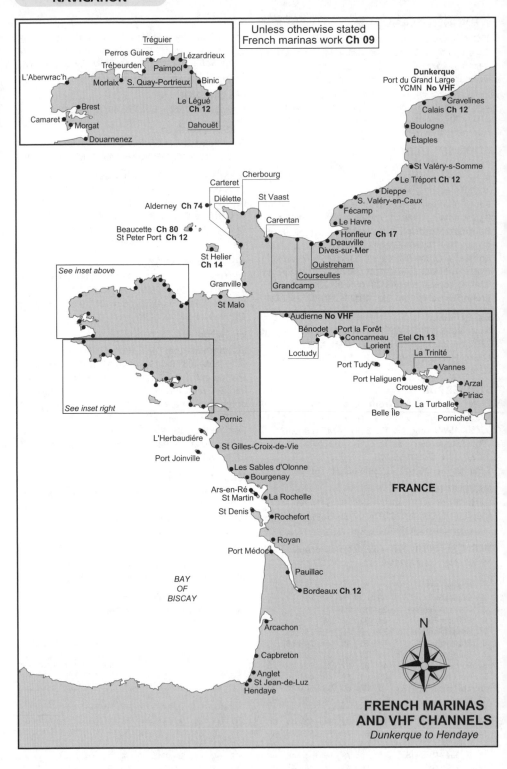

Unless otherwise stated
French marinas work **Ch 09**

Tréguier
Perros Guirec
Lézardrieux
Trébeurden
Paimpol
L'Aberwrac'h
Morlaix
S. Quay-Portrieux
Binic
Brest
Le Légué
Ch 12
Camaret
Dahouët
Morgat
Douarnenez

Dunkerque
Port du Grand Large
YCMN **No VHF**
Gravelines
Calais **Ch 12**
Boulogne
Étaples
St Valéry-s-Somme
Le Tréport **Ch 12**
Dieppe
S. Valéry-en-Caux
Fécamp
Le Havre
Honfleur **Ch 17**
Deauville
Dives-sur-Mer
Ouistreham
Courseulles
Grandcamp

Cherbourg
Carteret
Diélette
St Vaast
Carentan
Alderney **Ch 74**
Beaucette **Ch 80**
St Peter Port **Ch 12**
St Helier
Ch 14
Granville
St Malo

See inset above

Audierne **No VHF**
Bénodet
Port la Forêt
Concarneau
Lorient
Etel **Ch 13**
Loctudy
La Trinité
Port Tudy
Vannes
Port Haliguen
Crouesty
Arzal
Piriac
La Turballe
Belle Île
Pornichet

See inset right

Pornic
L'Herbaudiére
St Gilles-Croix-de-Vie
Port Joinville
Les Sables d'Olonne
Bourgenay
Ars-en-Ré
St Martin
La Rochelle
St Denis
Rochefort
Royan
Port Médoc
FRANCE
Pauillac
Bordeaux **Ch 12**

*BAY
OF
BISCAY*

Arcachon

Capbreton
Anglet
St Jean-de-Luz
Hendaye

N

**FRENCH MARINAS
AND VHF CHANNELS**
Dunkerque to Hendaye

SELECTED LIGHTS, BUOYS & WAYPOINTS | Positions are referenced to WGS84

PAIMPOL TO L'ABERWRAC'H

OFFSHORE MARKS

Roches Douvres ☆ Fl 5s 60m **28M**; 49°06'·28N 02°48'·89W.

PAIMPOL

L'Ost Pic ⚡ Oc WR 4s 20m, W11M, R8M; 105°-W-116°-R-221°-W-253°-R-291°-W-329°; 48°46'·76N 02°56'·44W. La Jument ⌁ 48°47'·34N 02°57'·97W. Ldg lts 262·2°, both QR 5/12m 7/14M. Front, Kernoa jetty; W & R hut; 48°47'·09N 03°02'·44W.

ÎLE DE BRÉHAT

Rosédo ☆ Fl 5s 29m **20M**; 48°51'·45N 03°00'·30W. Le Paon ⚡ Oc WRG 4s 22m W11M, R/G8M; 033°-W-078°-G-181°-W-196°-R-307°-W-316°-R-348°; Y twr; 48°51'·93N 02°59'·17W.

LÉZARDRIEUX

Ldg lts 224·7°: Front, **La Croix** ☆ Q 15m **18M**; 48°50'·22N 03°03'·24W. Rear **Bodic** ☆ Dir Q 55m **22M**. Coatmer ldg lts 218·7°: Front, Q RG 16m R/G7M; 200°-R-250°-G-053°; 48°48'·26N 03°05'·75W. Rear, QR 50m 7M; vis 197°-242°.

JAUDY (TRÉGUIER) RIVER

Les Héaux de Bréhat ☆ Oc (3) WRG 12s 48m, **W15M**, R/G11M; 227°-R-247°-W-270°-G-302°-W-227°; Gy ○ twr; 48°54'·50N 03°05'·18W. Ldg lts 137°: Front, Oc 4s 12m 11M; 042°-232°; 48°51'·55N 03°07'·90W. Rear, Dir Oc R 4s 34m **15M**. La Corne ⚡ Fl (3) WRG 12s 14m W8M, R/G6M; 052°-W-059°-R-173°-G-213°-W-220°-R-052°; W twr, R base; 48°51'·34N 03°10'·63W.

PERROS-GUIREC

Passe de l'Est, ldg lts 224·5°. Front ☆ Dir Oc (4) 12s 28m **15M**; 48°47'·87N 03°26'·66W. Rear ☆, Dir Q 79m **21M**; intens 221°-228°.

PLOUMANAC'H

Men-Ruz ⚡ Oc WR 4s 26m W12M, R9M; 226°-W-242°-R-226°; pink ☐ twr; 48°50'·26N 03°29'·03W.

TRÉBEURDEN

Ar Gouredec ⚡ VQ (6) + L Fl 10s; 48°46'·41N 03°36'·60W. NW bkwtr ⚡ Fl G 2·5s 8m 2M; IPTS; 48°46'·34N 03°35'·20W.

PRIMEL-TRÉGASTEL

Ldg lts 152°, both ⚡ QR 35/56m 7M, R vert stripe on W ☐. Front, 48°42'·45N 03°49'·20W.

BAIE DE MORLAIX

Chenal du Tréguier ldg lts 190·5°: Front, ⚡ Île Noire Oc (2) WRG 6s 15m, W11M, R/G8M; 051°-G-135°-R-211°-W-051°; 48°40'·34N 03°52'·56W. **La Lande** ☆

Fl 5s 85m **23M**; 48°38'·19N 03°53'·16W. Common rear for both channels.

Grande Chenal ldg lts 176·4°: Front, **Île Louet** ☆ Oc (3) WG 12s 17m **W15M**,G10M; 305°-W-244°-G-305°; W ☐ twr, B top; 48°40'·40N 03°53'·34W.

CANAL DE L'ÎLE DE BATZ

Ar-Chaden ⚓ Q (6) + L Fl WR 15s 14m, W8M, R6M; 262°-R-289·5°-W-293°-R-326°- W-110°; YB twr; 48°43'·93N 03°58'·26W.
Men-Guen-Bras ⚓ Q WRG 14m, W9M, R/ G6M; 068°-W-073°-R-197°-W-257°-G-068°; BY twr; 48°43'·76N 03°58'·07W.
Lt ho ☆ Fl (4) 25s 69m **23M**; 48°44'·71N 04°01'·63W.

L'ABER WRAC'H

Île-Vierge ☆ Fl 5s 77m **27M**; 337°-325°; Gy twr; 48°38'·33N 04°34'·06W.
Libenter ⚡ Q (9) 15s 6M; 48°37'·50N 04°38'·37W.
Outer ldg lts 100·1°: Front ⚡ QR 20m 7M; 48°36'·88N 04°34'·56W. Rear ⚡ Dir Q 55m 12M.

CHENAL DU FOUR TO RAZ DE SEIN

Le Four ☆ Fl (5) 15s 28m **18M**; Gy ○ twr; *Horn (3+2) 60s*; 48°31'·38N 04°48'·32W.
Ldg lts 158·5°. Front, **Kermorvan** ☆ Fl 5s 20m **22M**; W ☐ twr; *Horn 60s*; 48°21'·72N 04°47'·42W.
Rear, **Pte de St Mathieu** ☆ Fl 15s 56m **29M**; W twr, R top; 48°19'·79N 04°46'·27W.
Grande Vinotière ⚓ L Fl R 10s; 48°21'·93N 04°48'·43W.
Les Vieux-Moines ⚓ Fl R 4s 16m 5M; 280°-133°; R 8-sided twr; 48°19'·33N 04°46'·63W.
Pte du Toulinguet ☆ Oc (3) WR 12s **W15M**, R11M; shore-W-028°-R-090°-W-shore; 48°16'·82N 04°37'·73W.

BREST

Moulin Blanc ⚡ Fl (3) R 12s; 48°22'·79N 04°25'·99W.

CAMARET

N môle ⚡ Iso WG 4s 7m W12M, G9M; 135°-W-182°-G-027°; 48°16'·85N 04°35'·32W.

MORGAT

Pte de Morgat ☆ Oc (4) WRG 12s 77m **W15M**, R11M, G10M; Shore-W-281°-G-301°-W-021°-R-043°; 48°13'·17N 04°29'·81W.

DOUARNENEZ

Île Tristan ⚡ Oc (3) WR 12s 35m, W13M, R10M; shore-W-138°-R-153°-W-shore; 48°06'·14N 04°20'·25W.

RAZ DE SEIN

Tévennec ⚡ Q WR 28m W9M R6M; 090°-W-345°-R-090°; 48°04'·28N 04°47'·73W. Same twr, Dir ⚡ Fl 4s 24m 12M; intens 324°-332°.

La Vieille ☆ Oc (2+1) WRG 12s 33m **W18M**, R13M, G14M; 290°-W-298°-R-325°-W-355°-G-017°- W-035°-G-105°-W-123°-R-158°-W-205°; Gy □ twr; *Horn (2+1) 60s;* 48°02'·43N 04°45'·43W.

La Plate ⛯ VQ (9) 10s 8M; 48°02'·35N 04°45'·61W.

RAZ DE SEIN TO PORNICHET

AUDIERNE

Kergadec Dir ✧ 006°: Q WRG 43m 12/9M; 000°-G-005·3°-W-006·7°-R-017°; 48°00'·95N 04°32'·78W.

LOCTUDY

Pte de Langoz ☆ Fl (4) WRG 12s 12m, **W15M**, R/G11M; 115°-W-257°-G-284°-W-295°-R-318°-W-328°-R-025°; 47°49'·87N 04°09'·59W.

BENODET

Ldg lts 345·5°: Front Dir Oc (2+1) G 12s 11m **17M**; W ○ twr, G stripe; 47°52'·31N 04°06'·70W. Rear ✧ Oc (2+1) 12s 48m 11M; 338°-016°, synch.

PORT-LA-FORÊT

Cap Coz ✧ Fl (2) WRG 6s 5m, 7/5M; shore-R-335°-G-340°-W-346°-R-shore; 47°53'·48N 03°58'·28W.

ÎLES DE GLÉNAN

Penfret ☆ Fl R 5s 36m **21M**; W □ twr, R top; 47°43'·26N 03°57'·17W.

CONCARNEAU

Ldg lts 028·5°: Front, ✧ Q 14m 13M; 006·5°-093°; 47°52'·15N 03°55'·08W. **Rear** ☆ Dir Q 87m **23M**; intens 026·5°-030·5°; spire, 1·34M from front.

Marina ✧ Fl (4) R 15s 3m 1M; 47°52'·20N 03°54'·72W.

ÎLE DE GROIX

Pen Men ☆ Fl (4) 25s 60m **29M**; 309°-275°; W □ twr, B top; 47°38'·86N 03°30'·54W.

Port Tudy, ✧ Iso G 4s 12m 6M; 47°38'·70N 03°26'·74W.

LORIENT

Passe de l'Ouest ldg lts 057°: both Dir Q 11/22m 13/**18M**. Front, 47°42'·13N 03°21'·83W

BELLE ÎLE

Pte des Poulains ☆ Fl 5s 34m **23M**; 023°-291°; W □ twr and dwelling; 47°23'·28N 03°15'·17W.

Sauzon, ✧ Fl G 4s 8m 8M; 47°22'·51N 03°13'·10W.

Le Palais, N jetty ✧ QG 11m 7M, obsc 298°-170°; W twr, G top; 47°20'·84N 03°09'·04W. S jetty QR.

La Teignouse ☆ Fl WR 4s 20m **W15M**, R11M; 033°-W-039°-R-033°; 47°27'·45N 03°02'·79W.

ÎLE DE HOUAT

Port St-Gildas N môle ✧ Fl (2) WG 6s 8m W9M, G6M; 168°-W-198°-G-210°-W-240°-G-168°; W twr, G top; 47°23'·57N 02°57'·34W.

ÎLE DE HOËDIC

Port de l'Argol bkwtr ✧ Fl WG 4s 10m W9M, G6M; 143°-W-163°-G-183°-W-194°-G-143°; W twr, G top; 47°20'·69N 02°52'·56W.

PORT HALIGUEN

E bkwtr hd ✧ Oc (2) WR 6s 10m, W11M, R8M; 233°-W-240·5°-R-299°-W-306°-R-233°; W twr, R top; 47°29'·30N 03°05'·99W.

LA TRINITÉ-SUR-MER

Ldg lts 347°: Front, ✧ Q WRG 11m W10M, R/G7M; 321°-G-345°-W-013·5°-R-080°; 47°34'·08N 03°00'·37W. **Rear,** Dir Q 21m **15M**; synch.

Marina ✧ Iso R 4s 8m 5M; 47°35'·27N 03°01'·47W.

CROUESTY

Ldg lts 058°, Dir Q 10/27m **19M**: **Front**; 47°32'·54N 02°53'·94W. **Rear** ☆, grey lt ho.

VILAINE RIVER

Pte de Penlan ☆ Oc (2) WRG 6s 26m, **W15M**, R/G11M; 292·5°-R-025°-G-052°-W-060°-R-138°-G-180°; W twr, R bands; 47°30'·98N 02°30'·13W.

PIRIAC-SUR-MER

Inner mole ✧ Oc (2) WRG 6s 8m, W10M, R/G7M; 066°-R-148°-G-194°-W-201°-R-221°; *Siren 120s (occas);* 47°22'·93N 02°32'·72W.

LA TURBALLE

Ldg lts 006·5°, both Dir Iso R 4s 11/19m 3M; intens 004°-009°; Front, 47°20'·80N 02°30'·87W.

Jetée de Garlahy ✧ Fl (4) WR 12s 13m, W10M, R7M; 060°-R-315°-W-060°; W pylon, R top; 47°20'·70N 02°30'·93W.

PORNICHET (La Baule)

S bkwtr ✧ Iso WRG 4s 11m, W10M, R/G7M; 303°-G-081°-W-084°-R-180°; 47°15'·49N 02°21'·15W.

1	Lézardrieux	**1**		**12**	16	18	24	42	43	45	72	97	100	105	124	Pornic	**12**
2	Tréguier	22	**2**		**11**	12	24	39	40	41	66	87	90	95	113	St Nazaire	**11**
3	Perros-Guirec	28	21	**3**		**10**	13	30	30	34	55	78	80	85	106	La Baule/Pornichet	**10**
4	Trébeurden	40	32	17	**4**		**9**	18	22	27	48	73	75	79	100	Le Croisic	**9**
5	Morlaix	60	46	36	23	**5**		**8**	28	36	57	78	80	84	105	Arzal/Camöel	**8**
6	Roscoff	54	41	28	17	12	**6**		**7**	16	37	58	60	64	85	Crouesty	**7**
7	L'Aberwrac'h	84	72	60	49	48	32	**7**		**6**	26	47	48	54	74	Le Palais (Belle Ile)	**6**
8	Le Conquet	106	98	83	72	68	55	29	**8**		**5**	32	33	38	61	Lorient	**5**
9	Brest (marina)	114	107	92	83	79	67	42	18	**9**		**4**	4	12	37	Concarneau	**4**
10	Morgat	126	118	103	92	88	75	49	20	24	**10**		**3**	12	36	Port-la-Forêt	**3**
11	Douarnenez	131	123	108	97	93	80	54	25	29	11	**11**		**2**	30	Loctudy	**2**
12	Audierne	135	128	113	102	98	86	55	30	34	27	30	**12**		**1**	Audierne	**1**

SELECTED LIGHTS, BUOYS & WAYPOINTS | Positions are referenced to WGS84

RIVER LOIRE TO ÎLE D'OLÉRON

Pte de Saint-Gildas ☆ Q WRG 20m, W14M, R/G10M; 264°-R-308°-G-078°-W-088°-R-174°-W-180°-G-264°; col on W house; 47°08'·02N 02°14'·76W.

PORNIC

Appr buoy ↺ L Fl 10s; 47°06'·45N 02°06'·64W.

Pte de Noëveillard ☆ Oc (4) WRG 12s 22m W13M, R/G9M; Shore-G-051°-W-079°-R-shore; W☐twr, G top, W dwelling; 47°06'·62N 02°06'·92W.

ÎLE DE NOIRMOUTIER

Île du Pilier ☆ Fl (3) 20s 33m **29M**; Gy twr; 47°02'·55N 02°21'·61W. Same twr, ☆ QR 10m 11M, 321°-034°.

Les Boeufs ↺ VQ (9) 10s; 46°55'·04N 02°28'·02W.

L'Herbaudière, ldg lts 187·5°, both Q 5/21m 7M, Gy masts. Front, 47°01'·59N 02°17'·85W. Martroger ↺, Q WRG 11m W9M, R/G6M; 033°-G-055°-W-060°-R-095°-G-124°-W-153°-R-201°-W-240°-R-033°; 47°02'·60N 02°17'·12W. W jetty ☆ Oc (2+1) WG 12s 9m W10M, G7M; 187·5°-W-190°-G-187·5°; 47°01'·63N 02°17'·86W.

Noirmoutier-en-L'Île jetty ☆ Oc (2) R 6s 6m 6M; W col, R top; 46°59'·27N 02°13'·14W.

ÎLE D'YEU

Petite Foule (main lt) ☆ Fl 5s 56m **24M**; W☐twr, G lantern; 46°43'·05N 02°22'·96W.

Port Joinville ldg lts 219°, both QR 11/16m 6M, 169°-269°: Front 46°43'·61N 02°20'·95W. NW jetty ☆ Oc (3) WG 12s 7m, W11M, G8M; Shore-G-150°-W-232°-G-279°-W-285°-G-shore; W 8-sided twr, G top; 46°43'·77N 02°20'·82W.

Pte des Corbeaux ☆ Fl (2+1) R 15s 25m **20M**; 083°-143° obsc by Île d'Yeu; 46°41'·42N 02°17'·11W. Port de la Meule ☆ Oc WRG 4s 9m, W9M, R/G6M; 007·5°-G-018°-W-027·5°-R-041·5°; Gy twr, R top; 46°41'·66N 02°20'·75W.

SAINT GILLES-CROIX-DE-VIE

Pte de Grosse Terre ☆ Fl (4) WR 12s 25m, **W18M, R15M**; 290°- R-339°-W-125°-R-145°; W truncated twr; 46°41'·54N 01°57'·92W.

Ldg lts 043·7°,Q 7/28m **15M**; 033·5°-053·5°: Front, 46°41'·85N 01°56'·67W

Pilours ↺ Q (6) + L Fl 15s; *Bell*; 46°40'·98N 01°58'·10W. Jetée de la Garenne ☆ Fl G 4s 8m 6M; 46°41'·45N 01°57'·26W.

LES SABLES D'OLONNE

Les Barges ☆ Fl (2) R 10s 25m 13M; Gy twr; 46°29'·70N 01°50'·50W.

L'Armandèche ☆ Fl (2+1) 15s 42m **24M**; 295°-130°; W 6-sided twr, R top; 46°29'·40N 01°48'·29W.

Nouch Sud ↺ Q (6) + L Fl 15s; 46°28'·55N 01°47'·42W. SW Pass, ldg lts 032·5°, Iso 4s 12/33m **16M**, H24: **Front** ☆, 46°29'·42N 01°46'·37W. SE Pass, ldg lts 320°:   Front ☆ QG 11m 8M; 46°29'·44N 01°47'·51W. Rear ☆ Q 33m 13M. Jetée St Nicolas (W jetty) ☆ QR 16m 8M; 143°-094°; W twr, R top; 46°29'·23N 01°47'·52W.

BOURGENAY

Ldg lts 040°, QG 9/19m 7M. Front; 46°26'·37N 01°40'·61W. Rear, 010°-070°; 162m from front. Landfall ↺ L Fl 10s; 46°25'·28N 01°41'·91W. Ent ☆ Fl R 4s & ☆ Iso G 4s; 46°26'·29N 01°40'·75W.

ÎLE-DE-RÉ

Les Baleineaux ☆ VQ 23m 7M; pink twr, R top; 46°15'·81N 01°35'·22W.

Les Baleines ☆ Fl (4) 15s 53m **27M**; conspic Gy 8-sided twr, R lantern; 46°14'·64N 01°33'·69W. Chanchardon ☆ Fl WR 4s 15m W11M, R8M; 118°-R-290°-W-118°; 46°09'·73N 01°28'·44W. **Chauveau** ☆ Oc (3) WR 12s 27m **W15M**, R11M; 057°-W-094°-R-104°-W-342°-R-057°; W○ twr, R top; 46°08'·03N 01°16'·42W.

ARS-EN-RÉ

Les Islattes ↺ Q 13m 3M; BY bcn twr; 46°14'·03N 01°23'·33W. Dir ☆ 268° Oc WRG 4s, W10M, R/G 7M; 275·5°-G-267·5°-W-268·5°-R-274·5°; 46°14'·05N 01°28'·60W. Le Fier d'Ars, inner ldg lts 232·5°: ☆ Q 5/13m 9/11M; 46°12'·76N 01°30'·60W. Rear ☆ Q 11M.

ST MARTIN DE RÉ

Rocha ↺ Q; 46°14'·74N 01°20'·64W. Lt ho, E of ent ☆ Oc (2) WR 6s 18m W10M, R7M; Shore-W-245°-R-281°-W-shore; W twr, R top; 46°12'·44N 01°21'·89W. W mole   ☆ Fl G 2·5s 10m 6M; 46°12'·49N 01°21'·89W.

LA ROCHELLE

Ldg lts 059°, both Dir Q 15/25m 13/14M; synch; by day Fl 4s. Front; 46°09'·35N 01°09'·16W. Pte des Minimes ☆ Fl (3) WG 12s 8m; W8M, G5M; 059°-W-213°; 313°-G-059°; 46°08'·33N 01°10'·68W. Tour Richelieu ↺ Fl R 4s 10m 9M; 46°08'·90N 01°10'·34W. Marina ☆ Fl (2)G 6s 9m 7M; 46°08'·82N 01°10'·15W.

LA CHARENTE

Ldg lts 115°, Dir QR 8/21m **19/20M**: Front ☆, 45°57'·96N 01°04'·38W. Fort Boyard ☆ Q (9) 15s; 45°59'·96N 01°12'·87W. **Île d'Aix** ☆ Fl WR 5s 24m **W24M, R20M**; 103°-R-118°-W-103°; 46°00'·60N 01°10'·67W.

ÎLE D'OLÉRON

Chassiron ☆ Fl 10s **28M**; 46°02'·80N 01°24'·61W.
Antioche ₤ Q 20m 11M; 46°03'·94N 01°23'·71W.

ST DENIS

Dir ⚡ 205°, Iso WRG 4s 14m, W11M, R/G8M; 190°-G-204°-W-206°-R-220°;46°01'·61N 01°21'·91W.
E jetty ⚡ Fl (2) WG 6s 6m, W9M, G6M; 205°-G-277°-W-292°-G-165°; 46°02'·10N 01°22'·06W.

R GIRONDE TO THE SPANISH BORDER

GIRONDE, PASSE DE L'OUEST

Pte de la Coubre ☆ Fl (2) 10s 64m **28M**; 45°41'·78N 01°13'·99W. Also, F RG 42m, R12M, G10M; 030°-R-043°-G-060°-R-110°.
BXA ₤ Iso 4s 8m 7M; *Whis*; **Racon** ; 45°37'·53N 01°28'·69W.
Ldg lts 081·5° (not valid E of Nos 4 & 5 buoys). **Front** ☆, Dir Iso 4s 21m **20M**; 45°39'·56N 01°08'·76W. Same structure, Q (2) 5s 10m 3M.
La Palmyre, common rear ☆ Dir Q 57m **27M**; 45°39'·71N 01°07'·24W. Same twr, Dir FR **17M**.
Cordouan ☆ Oc (2+1) WRG 12s 60m, **W22M, R/G18M**; 014°-W-126°-G-178·5°-W-267°-R -294·5°-R-014°; 45°35'·16N 01°10'·39W.

PASSE SUD (or DE GRAVE)

Ldg lts 063°: **Front**, Dir QG 22m **16M**; 45°33'·72N 01°05'·03W. **Rear**, Oc WRG 4s 26m, **W19M, R/G15M**; 033°-W-233·5°-R-303°-W-312°-G-330°-W-341°-025°.
G ₤ 45°30'·32N 01°15'·56W.
G3 ₤ 45°32'·78N 01°07'·72W.
Ldg lts 041°, both Dir QR 33/61m **18M. Front, Le Chay** ☆ intens 039·5°-042·5°; W twr, R top; 45°37'·30N 01°02'·40W. **Rear, St Pierre** ☆, intens 039°-043°; R water twr, 0·97M from front.
G5 ₤ 45°33'·97N 01°06'·39W.
G4 ₤ 45°34'·70N 01°05'·79W.
G6 ₤ 45°34'·88N 01°04'·81W.

ROYAN

R1 ₤ Iso G 4s; 45°36'·56N 01°01'·96W.
NE jetty ⚡ Fl (3) G 12s 2m 5M; 45°37'·23N 01°01'·49W.

PORT-MÉDOC

N bkwtr ⚡ QG 4M; 45°33'·42N 01°03'·48W.
S bkwtr ⚡ QR 4M; 45°33'·37N 01°03'·44W.

PAUILLAC

Pauillac, NE elbow ⚡ Fl G 4s 7m 5M; 45°11'·96N 00°44'·61W.
Ent E side ⚡ QG 7m 4M; 45°11'·86N 00°44'·60W.

BORDEAUX

Lock into Bassins Nos 1 & 2, 44°51'·74N 00°32'·94W.

ARCACHON, PASSE NORD

Cap Ferret ☆ Fl R 5s 53m **27M**; W ○ twr, R top; 44°34'·05N 01°18'·71W. Same twr, ⚡ Oc (3) 12s.
ATT-ARC ₤ L Fl 10s 8m 5M; 44°33'·80N 01°18'·69W.
Note: Buoys are moved as the channel shifts.

1N	₤	44°33'·74N 01°17'·78W.
3N	₤	44°34'·49N 01°16'·43W.
5N	₤	44°34'·78N 01°15'·92W.
7N	₤	44°35'·44N 01°14'·76W.
9N	₤	44°36'·96N 01°14'·34W.
11	₤	44°37'·35N 01°14'·10W.
15	▲	44°39'·85N 01°12'·04W.

Marina ⚡ QG 6m 6M; 44°39'·77N 01°09'·15W.

CAPBRETON

Digue Nord ⚡ Fl (2) R 6s 13m 12M; W ○ twr, R top; *Horn 30s*; 43°39'·38N 01°27'·01W.
Estacade Sud ⚡ Fl (2) G 6s 9m 8M; 43°39'·25N 01°26'·89W. Marina ent, Fl G 4s and Fl R 4s.

ANGLET/BAYONNE

BA ₤ L Fl 10s; 43°32'·59N 01°32'·76W.
Outer ldg lts 090°, both Q 9/15m 19M.
Outer S bkwtr ₤ Q (9) 15s 15m 6M; 43°31'·60N 01°31'·68W. Anglet marina ent ⚡ Fl G 2s 5m 2M; 43°31'·57N 01°30'·51W.

ST JEAN DE LUZ

Inner ldg lts 150·7°, both Dir QG 18/27m **16M**; intens 149·5°-152·2°. **Front, E jetty** ☆ W □ twr, R stripe; 43°23'·25N 01°40'·15W. **Rear** ☆, W □ twr, G stripe; at S corner of marina.

HENDAYE

Cabo Higuer ☆ Fl (2) 10s 63m **23M**; 43°23'·51N 01°47'·53W (in Spain).
W trng wall ⚡ Fl (3) G 9s 9m 5M; 43°22'·82N 01°47'·36W. E trng wall ₤ L Fl R 10s 7m 5M.
Marina ent, E side ⚡ Fl Y 4s 5m 3M.

1	Port Joinville	**1**														
2	St Gilles-C-de-Vie	18	**2**													
3	Sables d'Olonne	31	16	**3**												
4	Bourgenay	40	25	9	**4**											
5	St Martin (I de Ré)	55	44	27	20	**5**										
6	La Rochelle	66	51	36	29	12	**6**									
7	Rochefort	84	75	61	54	36	26	**7**								
8	R La Seudre	89	71	58	52	33	24	30	**8**							
9	Port St Denis	59	48	33	30	21	13	26	22	**9**						
10	Port Bloc/Royan	97	85	71	60	56	52	68	27	42	**10**					
11	Bordeaux	152	140	126	115	111	107	123	82	97	55	**11**				
12	Cap Ferret	138	130	113	110	102	98	114	75	88	68	123	**12**			
13	Capbreton	192	186	169	166	165	156	172	131	145	124	179	58	**13**		
14	Anglet/Bayonne	200	195	181	178	177	168	184	143	157	132	187	70	12	**14**	
15	Santander	212	210	204	204	206	202	218	184	192	180	235	133	106	103	**15**
16	Cabo Finisterre	377	395	393	394	406	407	423	399	397	401	456	376	370	373	274	**16**

DISTANCE TABLES
Approx distances in nautical miles are by the most direct route allowing for dangers and TSS.

LANDES FIRING RANGE: Pointe de la Négade to Capbreton

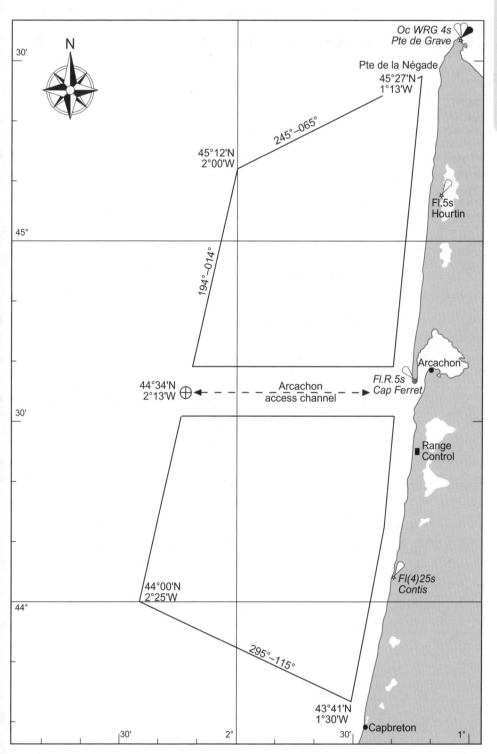

AREA 18 N & NW Spain – *French border to Portuguese border*

SELECTED LIGHTS, BUOYS & WAYPOINTS

Positions are referenced to WGS84

FRENCH BORDER TO GIJON

FUENTERRABIA (See Hendaye, previous page)
Marina ent, ⚓ Fl (4) G 11s 9m 3m; 43°22'·59N 01°47'·51W. ⚓ Fl (4) R 11s 9m 1M, close SW.

PASAJES
⚓ Mo (A) 6s 11M; 43°21'·19N 01°56'·12W.
Senocozulúa Dir ⚓ 155·75°: Oc (2) WRG 12s 50m W6M, R/G3M; 129·5°-G-154·5°-W-157°-R-190°; W twr; *Racon M*; 43°19'·90N 01°55'·61W.

SAN SEBASTIÁN
Ldg lts 158°: Front ⚓ QR 10m 7M; 143°-173°; 43°18'·89N 01°59'·47W. Rear ⚓ Oc R 4s 16m 7M.
Igueldo ☆ Fl (2+1) 15s 132m **26M**; 43°19'·35N 02°00'·64W.

GUETARIA

I. de San Antón ☆ Fl (4) 15s 91m **21M**; 43°18'·62N 02°12'·09W.
N mole ⚓ Fl (3) G 9s 11m 5M; 43°18'·26N 02°11'·91W.

ZUMAYA

Lt ho ⚓ Oc (1+3) 12s 39m 12M; Port sigs; 43°18'·14N 02°15'·07W. Marina ent, ⚓ Fl (3) R 9s 6m 1M and ⚓ Fl (2+1) G 10s 6m 1M.

LEQUEITIO

Pta Amandarri ⚓ Fl G 4s 8m 5M; 43°21'·99N 02°29'·94W.
Cabo de Santa Catalina ☆ Fl (1+3) 20s 44m **17M**; *Horn Mo (L) 20s;* 43°22'·67N 02°30'·69W.

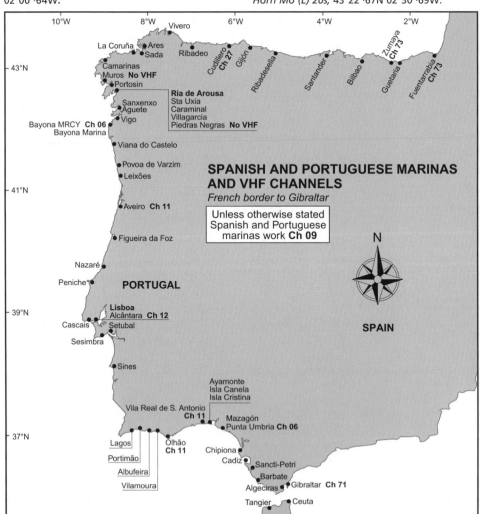

ELANCHOVE

Digue N ⚓ Fl G 3s 8m 4M. **Cabo Machichaco** ☆ Fl 7s 120m **24M**; *Siren Mo (M) 60s;* 43°27'·30N 02°45'·19W.

BILBAO

Punta Galea ☆ Fl (3) 8s 82m **19M**; 011°-227°; *Siren Mo (G) 30s;* 43°22'·30N 03°02'·14W.

Pta Lucero bkwtr head ⚓ Fl G 5s 21m 10M; *Racon X, 20M;* 43°22'·67N 03°05'·04W.

Getxo marina bkwtr ⚓QR 3m 2M, R col; 43°20'·23N 03°01'·02W.

Las Arenas marina (RCMA) ⚓ Oc G 4s 1m 1M; 43°19'·83N 03°00'·98W; and Oc R 4s 2m 1M.

CASTRO URDIALES

Castillo de Santa Ana ☆ Fl (4) 24s 47m **20M**; W twr; *Siren Mo (C) 60s;* 43°23'·06N 03°12'·89W.

N bkwtr ⚓ Fl G 3s 12m 6M; 43°22'·86N 03°12'·54W.

LAREDO and RIA DE SANTOÑA

Laredo N bkwtr ⚓ Fl (4) R 11s 9m 5M; 43°24'·89'N 03°25'·20W.

Santoña ldg lts 283·5°: Front, ⚓ Fl 2s 5m 8M; 43°26'·33N 03°27'·62W. Rear, ⚓ Oc (2) 5s 12m 11M.

C. Ajo ☆ Oc (3) 16s 69m **17M**; 43°30'·70N 03°35'·72W.

SANTANDER

Cabo Mayor ☆ Fl (2) 10s 89m **21M**; *Horn Mo (M) 40s;* 43°29'·37N 03°47'·51W.

Marina de Santander, ldg lts 235·6°: Front ⚓ Iso 2s 9m 2M; 43°25'·75N 03°48'·83W. Rear ⚓ Oc 5s.

Marina ent QR and QG.

Pta del Torco de Afuera ☆ Fl (1+2) 24s 33m **22M**; W twr; 43°26'·51N 04°02'·61W.

RIBADESELLA

Pta del Caballo ⚓ Fl (4) R 11s 10m 5M; 278·4°-212·9°; ○ twr; 43°28'·08N 05°03'·98W.

Marina trng wall ⚓ Q; approx 43°27'·83N 05°03'·70W.

Somos ☆ Fl (2+1) 12s 113m **25M**; twr; 43°28'·08N 05°03'·98W.

C. Lastres ☆ Fl (5) 25s 116m **23M**. W ○ twr; 43°32'·03N 05°18'·07W.

GIJÓN

Piedra Sacramento ⚓ Fl (2) G 6s 9m 5M; 8-sided twr; 43°32'·90N 05°40'·21W.

Marina, N bkwtr ⚓ Fl (2) R 6s 7m 3M; 05°40'·08W.

Cabo de Torres ☆ Fl (2) 10s 80m **18M**; 43°34'·29N 05°41'·97W.

Cabo Peñas ☆ Fl (3) 15s 115m **35M**; Gy 8-sided twr; *Siren Mo (P) 60s;* 43°39'·31N 05°50'·90W.

GIJON TO LA CORUÑA

CUDILLERO

Pta Rebollera ☆ Oc (4) 16s 42m **16M**; W 8-sided twr;

Siren Mo (D) 30s; 43°33'·96N 06°08'·68W.
Ent, N bkwtr ⚓ Fl (3) G 9s 3m 2M.

Cabo Vidio ☆ Fl 5s 99m **25M**; *Siren Mo (V) 60s;* 43°35'·60N 06°14'·79W.

Cabo Busto ☆ Fl (4) 20s 84m **25M**; 43°34'·13N 06°28'·23W.

LUARCA

Punta Altaya ⚓ Oc (3) 15s 63m 14M; W □ twr; *Siren Mo (L) 30s;* 43°33'·03N 06°31'·85W.

Ldg lts 170°, W cols, R bands: Front ⚓ Fl 5s 18m 2M; 43°32'·78N 06°32'·11W. Rear ⚓ Oc 4s 25m 2M.

RÍA DE RIBADEO

Pta de la Cruz ⚓ Fl (4) R 11s 16m 7M; 43°33'·40N 07°01'·75W.

Isla Pancha ☆ Fl (3+1) 20s 26m **21M**; *Siren Mo (R) 30s;* 43°33'·39N 07°02'·53W, W side of entrance.

1st ldg lts 140°, both R ◊s, W twrs. Front ⚓ Iso R 18m 5M; 43°32'·83N 07°01'·53W. Rear ⚓ Oc R 4s.

2nd ldg lts 205°. Front, ⚓ VQ R 8m 3M; R ◊, W twr; 43°32'·49N 07°02'·24W. Rear ⚓ Oc R 2s 18m 3M.

Yacht hbr, ⚓ Fl G 5s 9m 3M; 43°32'·45N 07°02'·16W.

RÍA DE VIVERO

Pta de Faro ⚓ Fl R 5s 18m 7M; 43°42'·74N 07°35'·03W.

Pta Socastro ⚓ Fl G 5s 18m 7M; 43°43'·08N 07°36'·42W.

Cillero, outer bkwtr ⚓ Fl (2) R 7s 8m 5M; 43°40'·93N 07°36'·16W.

Marina ent ⚓ Fl (3) G 9s 7m 1M; 43°40'·22N 07°35'·62W.

Pta de la Estaca de Bares ☆ Fl (2) 7·5s 99m **25M**; *Siren Mo (B) 60s;* 43°47'·21N 07°41'·14W.

Cabo Ortegal ☆ Oc 8s 122m **18M**; W ○ twr, R band; 43°46'·22N 07°52'·30W,.

RÍA DE CEDEIRA

Piedras de Media Mar ⚓ Fl (2) 5s 12m 4M; BRB twr; 43°39'·37N 08°04'·79W.

Bkwtr ⚓ Fl (2) R 7s 10m 4M; 43°39'·30N 08°04'·20W.

Cabo Prior ☆ Fl (1+2) 15s 105m **22M**; 055·5°-310°; 6-sided twr; 43°34'·05N 08°18'·87W.

Punta del Castro ⚓ Fl (2) 7s 42m 8M; W 6-sided twr; 43°30'·47N 08°19'·73W.

RÍA DE FERROL

Cabo Prioriño Chico ☆ Fl 5s 34m **23M**; 225°-129·5°; W 8-sided twr; 43°27'·52N 08°20'·40W.

RÍAs DE ARES & DE BETANZOS

Ares bkwtr ⚓ Fl (3) R 9s; 43°25'·35N 08°14'·27W.
Sada marina ⚓ Fl (4) G 11s; 43°21'·76N 08°14'·54W.

LA CORUÑA

Torre de Hércules ☆ Fl (4) 20s 104m **23M**; *Siren Mo (L) 30s;* 43°23'·15N 08°24'·39W.

Ldg lts 108·5°: Front ⚓ Oc WR 4s 54m, W8M R3M; 000°-R-023°; 100·5°-R-105·5°-W-114·5°-R-153°; *Racon M, 18M; 020°-196°;* 43°23'·00N 08°21'·28W.

Rear ⚡ Fl 4s 79m 8M; 357·5°-177·5°.
Ldg lts 182°: Front, ⚡ Iso WRG 2s 27m, W10M, R/G7M; 146·4°-G-180°-W-184°-R-217·6°; *Racon X, 11-21M;* 43°20'·59N 08°22'·25W. Rear ⚡ Oc R 4s.
Darsena de la Marina ⚡ Fl (3) G 9s 8m 3M; 43°21'·01N 08°23'·66W.

LA CORUÑA TO BAYONA

RÍA DE CORME Y LAGE
Pta Lage ☆ Fl (5) 20s 64m **20M**; 43°13'·84N 09°00'·65W.
Lage, N mole ⚡ Fl G 3s 15m 4M; 43°13'·34N 08°59'·96W.
Corme, mole ⚡ Fl (2) R 5s 12m 3M; 43°15'·64N 08°57'·83W.
C. Villano ☆ Fl (2) 15s 102m **28M**; *Siren Mo (V) 60s; Racon M, 35M;* 43°09'·60N 09°12'·70W

RÍA DE CAMARIÑAS
Ldg lts 081°: Front ⚡ Fl 5s 13m 9M; 43°07'·37N 09°11'·56W. Rear ⚡ Iso 4s 25m 11M.
Outer bkwtr ⚡ Fl R 5s 7m 3M; 43°07'·45N 09°10'·70W.
Cabo Toriñana ☆ Fl (2+1) 15s 63m **24M**; *Racon T, 35M (1.7M SE of ☆);* 43°03'·17N 09°18'·01W.
Cabo Finisterre ☆ Fl 5s 141m **23M**; *Racon O, 35M;* 42°52'·93N 09°16'·29W.

RÍA DE MUROS
Pta Queixal ⚡ Fl (2+1) 12s; 42°44'·36N 09°04'·75W.
Muros ⚡ Fl (4) R 11s 4m 5M; 42°46'·54N 09°03'·14W.
Portosin ⚡ Fl (3) G 9s 8m 5M; 42°45'·94N 08°56'·93W.
Pta Cabeiro ⚡ Oc WR 3s 35m 9/6M; 050°-R-054·5°-W-058·5°-R-099·5°-W-189·5°;42°44'·37N 08°59'·44W.

RÍA DE AROUSA (Selected lights only)
Isla Sálvora ☆ Fl (3+1) 20s 38m **21M**; 42°27'·82N 09°00'·80W. Same twr, ⚡ Fl (3) 20s; 126°-160°.
Santa Uxia ⚡ Fl (2) R 7s 7m 4M; 42°33'·58N 08°59'·24W. 50m SE, ⚡ Fl R 5s 8m 5M.

Isla Rúa ⚡ Fl (2) WR 7s 25m 12M; 121·5°-R-211·5°-W-121·5°; *Racon K, 211°-121°, 10-20M;* 42°32'·95N 08°56'·38W.
Pobra do Caramiñal E bkwtr ⚡ Fl (3) G 9s 9m 5M; W ○ twr, G band; 42°36'·28N 08°55'·87W.
Villagarcia, N mole ⚡ Iso 2s 2m 10M; 42°36'·11N 08°46'·33W. Marina ent, QG & QR, both 6m 3M.
Piedras Negras marina ⚡ Fl (4) WR 11s 5m, W4M R3M; 305°-W-315°-R-305; 42°27'·49N 08°55'·11W.

RÍA DE PONTEVEDRA
Isla Ons ☆ Fl (4) 24s 125m **25M**; 8-sided twr; 42°22'·94N 08°56'·17W.
Sangenjo ⚡ QR 5m 4M; 42°23'·81N 08°48'·06W.
Combarro ⚡ Fl (2) R 8s 7m 3M; 42°25'·78N 08°42'·23W.
Aguete ≀ Fl (4) G 11s 3M, 42°22'·66N 08°44'·21W.

RÍA DE VIGO
Ldg lts 129°: Front, ⚡ Fl 3s 36m 9M; 42°15'·15N 08°52'·37W. Rear ⚡ Oc 6s 53m 11M.
S Chan ldg lts 069·3°: **Front** ☆ Iso 2s 16m **18M**; *Horn Mo (V) 60s; Racon B, 22M;* 42°11'·12N 08°48'·89W. **Rear** Oc 4s 48m **18M**.
Marina, QG/ QR, 10m 5M, 42°14'·56N 08°43'·41W.

BAYONA
Las Serralleiras ≀ Q (9) 15s 4M; 42°09'·23N 08°53'·35W.
Ldg lts 084°: Front ⚡ Fl 6s 8m 10M; 42°08'·24N 08°50'·09W.
Rear, **Panjón Dir** ⚡ 084°, Oc WRG 4s **W18M, R15M,** G14M; 079°-G-083°-W-085°-R-088°; 42°08'·34N 08°48'·84W.
C. Silleiro ☆ Fl (2+1) 15s 84m **24M**; W 8-sided twr, R bands; 42°06'·27N 08°53'·80W.
≀ Q; 42°07'·29N 08°54'·73W, 9ca NW of C. Silleiro.

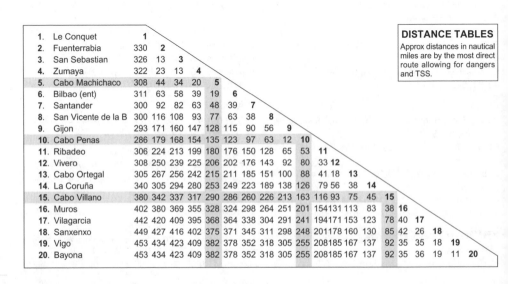

		1	2	3	4	5	6	7	8	9	10	11	12	13	14	15	16	17	18	19	20
1.	Le Conquet	**1**																			
2.	Fuenterrabia	330	**2**																		
3.	San Sebastian	326	13	**3**																	
4.	Zumaya	322	23	13	**4**																
5.	Cabo Machichaco	308	44	34	20	**5**															
6.	Bilbao (ent)	311	63	58	39	19	**6**														
7.	Santander	300	92	82	63	48	39	**7**													
8.	San Vicente de la B	300	116	108	93	77	63	38	**8**												
9.	Gijon	293	171	160	147	128	115	90	56	**9**											
10.	Cabo Penas	286	179	168	154	135	123	97	63	12	**10**										
11.	Ribadeo	306	224	213	199	180	176	150	128	65	53	**11**									
12.	Vivero	308	250	239	225	206	202	176	143	92	80	33	**12**								
13.	Cabo Ortegal	305	267	256	242	215	211	185	151	100	88	41	18	**13**							
14.	La Coruña	340	305	294	280	253	249	223	189	138	126	79	56	38	**14**						
15.	Cabo Villano	380	342	337	317	290	286	260	226	213	163	116	93	75	45	**15**					
16.	Muros	402	380	369	355	328	324	298	264	251	201	154	131	113	83	38	**16**				
17.	Vilagarcia	442	420	409	395	368	364	338	304	291	241	194	171	153	123	78	40	**17**			
18.	Sanxenxo	449	427	416	402	375	371	345	311	298	248	201	178	160	130	85	42	26	**18**		
19.	Vigo	453	434	423	409	382	378	352	318	305	255	208	185	167	137	92	35	35	18	**19**	
20.	Bayona	453	434	423	409	382	378	352	318	305	255	208	185	167	137	92	35	36	19	11	**20**

DISTANCE TABLES
Approx distances in nautical miles are by the most direct route allowing for dangers and TSS.

AREA 19 Portugal – *Viana do Castelo to Vila Real de Santo Antonio*
SELECTED LIGHTS, BUOYS & WAYPOINTS | Positions are referenced to WGS84

SPANISH BORDER TO CASCAIS
Montedor ☆ Fl (2) 9·5s 102m 22M; R twr; *Horn Mo (S) 25s;* 41°45'·09N 08°52'·49W.

VIANA DO CASTELO
Dir lt Oc WRG 4s 15m 8/6M; 350°-G-005°-W-010°-R-025°; 41°41'·12N 08°50'·21W.
Outer mole ✟ Fl R 3s 9M; *Horn 30s;* 41°40'·46N 08°50'·66W.
No. 2 ⌐ Fl R 3s; 41°40'·53N 08°50'·48W.
E mole ✟ Fl G 3s 9M; 41°40'·67N 08°50'·25W.
No. 1 ▲ Fl G 3s; 41°40'·68N 08°50'·29W.
No. 3 ▲ Fl (2) G 3s; 41°40'·86N 08°50'·24W.
No. 4 ⌐ Fl (2+1) R 5s; 41°40'·89N 08°50'·36W.
Nos. 5-13 ▲s are Fl G 3s. Nos. 6-14 ⌐s are Fl R 3s.
No. 13 ▲ Fl G 3s; 41°41'·49N 08°49'·27W, SSE of marina ent at 41°41'·59N 08°49'·33W.

PÓVOA DE VARZIM
Molhe N ✟ Fl R 3s 14m 12M; *Siren 40s;* 41°22'·29N 08°46'·23W. Molhe S ✟ L Fl G 6s 4M.

LEIXÕES
Tanker mooring ⌀ Fl (3) 15s 6M; *Horn (U) 30s;* 41°12'·10N 08°45'·07W.
Leça ☆ Fl (3) 14s 56m 28M; W twr, B bands; 41°12'·08N 08°42'·73W.
Outer N mole ✟ Fl WR 5s 23m W12M, R9M; 001°-R-180°-W-001°; *Horn 20s;* 41°10'·37N 08°42'·49W.
S mole ✟ Fl G 4s 16m 7M; 328°-285°; *Horn 30s;* 41°10'·68N 08°42'·35W.
Marina ✟ L Fl (2) R 12s 4m 2M; 41°11'·08N 08°42'·27W.

AVEIRO
Lt ho Aero ☆ Fl (4) 13s 65m 23M; R/W twr; 40°38'·57N 08°44'·88W. Same twr ✟ Fl G 4s 53m 9M, rear 085·4° ldg lt. Front 085·4° ldg lt Fl G 3s 16m 9M; 40°38'·54N 08°45'·48W.
Ldg lts 065·6°: Front ✟ Oc R 3s 7m 9M; 40°38'·82N 08°44'·99W. Rear ✟ Oc R 6s 8M, 440m from front.
Molhe N ✟ Fl R 3s 11m 8M; W col, R bands; *Horn 15s;* 40°38'·61N 08°45'·81W.
Molhe S ✟ Fl G 3s 16m 9M; front 085·4° ldg lt. Molhe Central ✟ L Fl G 5s; 40°38'·64N 08°44'·95W.
Baia de São Jacinto, S bkwtr Fl R 3s; 40°39'·21N 08°43'·96W. N bkwtr Fl G 4s, 40°38'·39N 08°43'·77W.

FIGUEIRA DA FOZ
Cabo Mondego ☆ Fl 5s 96m 28M; W twr and house; *Horn 30s;* 40°11'·43N 08°54'·32W.
Ldg lts 081·5°, W cols, R bands: Front ✟ Iso R 5s 6m 8M; 40°08'·83N 08°51'·23W. Rear, ✟ Oc R 6s.
Molhe N ✟ Fl R 6s 14m 9M; *Horn 35s;* 40°08'·74N 08°52'·50W. Marina ent Fl (2) R 8s and Fl (2) G 8s.
Molhe S ✟ Fl G 6s 13m 7M; 40°08'·59N 08°52'·41W.

Penedo da Saudade ☆ Fl (2) 15s 54m 30M; ☐ twr, and house; 39°45'·84N 09°01'·89W.

NAZARÉ
Pontal da Nazaré ✟ Oc 3s 49m 14M; twr & bldg; *Siren 35s;* 39°36'·25N 09°05'·18W.
Molhe S ✟ L Fl G 5s 14m 8M; 39°35'·34N 09°04'·76W. Molhe N ✟ L Fl R 5s 14m 9M.

FARILHÃO and ILHA DA BERLENGA
Farilhão Grande ✟ Fl (2) 5s 99m 13M; 39°28'·73N 09°32'·72W.
Ilha da Berlenga ☆ Fl 10s 120m 27M; W ☐ twr and houses; *Horn 28s;* 39°24'·90N 09°30'·63W.
Cabo Carvoeiro ☆ Fl (3) R 15s 56m 15M; W ☐ twr; *Horn 35s;* 39°21'·61N 09°24'·51W.

PENICHE
Molhe W ✟ Fl R 3s 13m 9M; W twr, R bands; *Siren 120s;* 39°20'·85N 09°22'·56W.
C. da Roca ☆ Fl (4) 18s 164m 26M; W twr and bldgs; 38°46'·88N 09°29'·90W.
Cabo Raso ☆ Fl (3) 9s 22m 15M; 324°-189°; R twr; *Horn Mo (I) 60s;* 38°42'·56N 09°29'·15W.

CASCAIS TO CAPE ST VINCENT
CASCAIS
Ldg lts 284·7°: Front, ☆ Oc WR 6s 24m W18M, R14M; 233°-R-334°-W-098°; *Horn 10s;* 38°41'·42N 09°25'·27W. Rear, ☆ Iso WR 2s W19M, R16M; 326°-W-092°; 278°-R-292°; W twr. Marina S mole ✟ Fl (3) R 4s 8m 6M; 38°41'·58N 09°24'·84W.

LISBOA
Triple ldg lts 047·1°: Front, ☆ Oc R 3s 30m 21M; 38°41'·94N 09°15'·97W. Middle, ☆ Oc R 6s 81m 21M; *Racon Q, 15M.* Rear, ☆ Iso 6s 153m 21M; 38°43'·65N 09°13'·63W.
No. 1 ᶘ Fl G 2s; 38°39'·55N 09°18'·79W.
Forte Bugio ✟ Fl G 5s 27m 9M; ○ twr on fortress; *Horn Mo (B) 30s;* 38°39'·62N 09°17'·93W.
No. 5 ᶘ Fl G 4s; 38°40'·43N 09°17'·66W.
No. 7 ᶘ Fl G 5s; 38°40'·64N 09°16'·90W.
No. 9 ᶘ Fl G 6s; 38°40'·63N 09°14'·49W.
Ponte 25 de Abril: Fl (3) G 9s and Fl (3) R 9s on the N (38°41'·64N 09°10'·69W) and S pillars.
Cabo Espichel ☆ Fl 4s 167m 26M; W 6-sided twr; *Horn 31s;* 38°24'·94N 09°13'·05W.

SESIMBRA
Ldg lts 003·5°, L Fl R 5s 9/21m 7/6M: Front, 38°26'·56N 09°06'·16W. Rear 34m from front.

SETÚBAL
Ldg lts 039·7°, both Iso Y 6s 12/60m 22M. Front, R structure, W stripes; 38°31'·08N 08°54'·01W.

No. 1 ⚓ Fl G 3s 5M; 38°26'·98N 08°58'·18W.
No. 2 ⚓ Fl (2) R 10s 13m 9M; *Racon B, 15M*;
38°27'·21N 08°58'·45W.
Forte de Outão ⚡ Oc R 6s 33m 12M; 38°29'·31N
08°56'·06W.
Pinheiro da Cruz ⚡ Fl 3s; 38°15'·46N 08°46'·34W.

SINES
Cabo de Sines ☆ Fl (2) 15s 55m **26M**; 37°57'·56N
08°52'·83W.
W mole ⚡ Fl 3s 20m 12M; 37°56'·48N 08°53'·33W.
Sines W ⚓ Fl R 3s 6M; 37°56'·12N 08°53'·25W.
Marina mole ⚡ Fl G 4s 4M; W twr, G bands;
37°57'·03N 08°52'·03W.

C. Sardão ☆ Fl (3) 15s 67m **23M**; 37°35'·94N
08°49'·02W.

CAPE ST VINCENT/SAGRES
Cabo de São Vicente ☆ Fl 5s 84m **32M**; *Horn Mo (I)
30s;* 37°01'·36N 08°59'·78W.
Ponta de Sagres ⚡ Iso R 2s 52m 11M; 36°59'·66N
08°56'·94W.
Baleeira mole ⚡ Fl WR 4s 12m, W14M, R11M; 254°-
W-355°-R-254°; 37°00'·67N 08°55'·46W.

CAPE ST VINCENT TO SPANISH BORDER
LAGOS
Pta da Piedade ☆ Fl 7s 50m **20M**; 37°04'·81N
08°40'·20W.
W mole ⚡ Fl (2) R 6s 5M; W col, R bands; 37°05'·85N
08°40'·02W.
E mole ⚡ Fl (2) G 6s 5M; W col, G bands; 37°05'·96N
08°39'·96W.
Alvor ent, ⚡ Fl R/G 4s; W twrs, R/G bands; 37°07'·13N
08°37'·14W.

PORTIMÃO
Ponta do Altar ☆ L Fl 5s 31m **16M**; 290°-170°;
W twr and bldg; 37°06'·34N 08°31'·17W.
Ldg lts 019·1°: Both ⚡ Iso R 6s 18/30m 6M; W cols, R
bands. Front 37°07'·35N 08°31'·31W. Rear 54m
from front.
E mole ⚡ Fl G 5s 9m 7M; 37°06'·50N 08°31'·59W.
W mole ⚡ Fl R 5s 9m 7M; 37°06'·52N 08°31'·77W.
No. 2 ⚓ Fl R 4s; 37°06'·96N 08°31'·53W.
Marina ent, S side ⚡ Fl R 6s 3M; 37°07'·10N
08°31'·58W.
N side ⚡ Fl G 6s 3M; 37°07'·14N 08°31'·58W.

N Mole ⚡ Iso R 4s 8m 3M; 37°07'·33N 08°31'·59W.
Pta de Alfanzina ☆ Fl (2) 15s 62m **29M**; 37°05'·22N
08°26'·59W.

ALBUFEIRA
Ponta da Baleeira ⚡ Oc 6s 30m 11M; 37°04'·84N
08°15'·85W.
N bkwtr ⚡, Fl (2) G 5s 9m 4M, approx 37°04'·90N
08°15'·52W.
S bkwtr ⚡, Fl (2) R 5s 9m 4M.
Praia da Albufeira, E end of bay, Olhos de Água ⚡
L Fl 5s 29m 7M; 37°05'·47N 08°11'·40W.

VILAMOURA
Vilamoura ☆, Fl 5s 17m **19M**; 37°04'·50N
08°07'·42W.
Marina, W mole ⚡ Fl R 4s 13m 5M; 37°04'·19N
08°07'·49W.
E mole ⚡ Fl G 4s 13m 5M; 37°04'·22N 08°07'·42W.

FARO, OLHÃO and TAVIRA
Ent from sea: E mole ⚡ Fl G 4s 9m 6M; 36°57'·79N
07°52'·14W.
W mole ⚡ Fl R 4s 9m 6M; 37°57'·84N 08°52'·26W,
appr on 352°.
Access ldg lts 020·9°: Front, Barra Nova ⚡ Oc 4s 8m
6M; 37°58'·22N 07°52'·00W. Rear, **Cabo de Santa
Maria** ☆ Fl (4) 17s 49m **25M**; W ○ twr; 36°58'·48N
07°51'·88W.
No. 6 ⚓ Fl R 6s; 36°58'·49N 07°52'·12W (NW to Faro;
NE to Olhão).
No. 20 ⚓ Fl R 6s, 37°00'·13N 07°55'·11W (edge of AC
83 approx 2M before **Faro** proper).
No. 8 ⚓ Fl R 3s; 36°59'·90N 07°51'·07W, thence N &
E to **Olhão**.

Tavira ldg lts 325·9°: Front, ⚡ Fl R 3s 6m 4M. Rear,
Iso ⚡ R 6s 9m 5M. W mole ⚡ Fl R 2·5s 7m 7M;
37°06'·79N 07°37'·10W.

VILA REAL DE SANTO ANTONIO
Lt ho ☆ Fl 6·5s 51m **26M**; W twr, B bands;
37°11'·23N 07°25'·00W.
R. Guadiano, Bar buoys ⚓ Q (3) G 6s; 37°08'·90N
07°23'·44W.
No. 2 ⚓ Fl R 4s; 37°08'·83N 07°23'·74W.
W bkwtr ⚡ Fl R 5s 4M; 37°09'·75N 07°24'·03W.
Marina, Fl R 3s at S corner; Fl R 3s/Fl G 3s at ent; Fl
R 3s at N corner.

See also Area 20 Distance Table

		1	2	3	4	5	6	7	8	9	10	11	12
1	Longships	1											
2	Ushant (Créac'h)	100	2										
3	La Coruña	418	338	3									
4	Cabo Villano	439	365	43	4								
5	Bayona	510	436	114	71	5							
6	Viana do Castelo	537	468	141	98	32	6						
7	Leixões (Pôrto)	565	491	169	126	63	33	7					
8	Nazaré	659	585	263	220	156	127	97	8				
9	Cabo Carvoeiro	670	596	274	231	171	143	114	22	9			
10	Cabo Raso	710	636	314	271	211	183	154	62	40	10		
11	Lisboa (bridge)	686	652	330	287	227	199	170	78	56	16	11	
12	Cabo Espichel	692	658	336	293	233	205	176	84	62	22	23	12

DISTANCE TABLES
Approx distances in nautical
miles are by the most direct
route allowing for dangers
and TSS.

AZORES – SELECTED LIGHTS

Positions are referenced to WGS 84

ILHA DAS FLORES

Ponta do Albarnaz ∡, Fl 5s 103m 22M, 035°-258°; W twr, R cupola. 39°31'·20N 31°14'·12W.
Ponta das Lajes ☆, Fl (3) 28s 98m **26M**, 263°-054°; W twr, R cupola. 39°22'·56N 31°10'·59W.
PORTO DAS LAJES, ldg lts 250·8°: Front, L Fl G 7s 17m 2M, 39°22'·74N 31°10'·24W; rear Oc G 4s.
Bkwtr hd ∡ Fl (2) R 10s 2M; 39°22'·75N 31°09'·94W.

ILHA DO FAIAL

Ponta dos Cedros ∡, Fl 7s 144m 12M; 38°38'·29N 28°43'·36W.
Ponta da Ribeirinha ∡, Fl (3) 20s 131m 12M; post; 38°35'·73N 28°36'·15W, E end of island.

HORTA

Boa Viagem ∡ Iso G 1·5s 12m 9M; appr brg 285°; B column on R cupola; 38°32'·28N 28°37'·49W.
Bkwtr hd ∡ Fl R 3s 20m 11M; W structure. 38°32'·03N 28°37'·27W.

Ldg lts 194·9°: both Iso G 2s 13/15m 2M; Red X on W posts, R bands. Front 38°31'·67N 28°37'·51W.

ILHA DO PICO (Pico mountain 38°28'·11N 28°23'·92W) Ponta de São Mateus ∡ Fl 5s 33m 13M, 284°-118°; W twr, R cupola. 38°25'·35N 28°26'·93W, SW side of island. **Ponta da Ilha** ☆ Fl (3) 15s 28m **24M**, 166°-070°; W twr, R cupola and bldg; 38°24'·84N 28°01'·83W, E tip of island.

ILHA DE SÃO JORGE

Ponta dos Rosais ∡ Fl (2) 10s 259m 8M. 38°45'·24N 28°18'·71W, WNW tip of island.
Ponta da Topo ☆ Fl (3) 20s 57m **20M**, 133°-033°; W twr, R bldg. 38°32'·92N 27°45'·24W, E tip of island.

ILHA TERCEIRA

Ponta da Sereta ☆ Fl (3) 15s 95m **21M**; W col, R top; 38°45'·97N 27°22'·45W, NW end of island.
Lajes ☆ Aero Al Fl WG 10s 132m **W28M, G23M**.

Praia da Vitoria, N mole Fl G 5s 11m 6M; G lantern, Gy post; 38°43'·56N 27°03'·04W. S mole Fl R 3s 8M; W twr, R bands; 38°43'·24N 27°02'·92W.
Ponta das Contendas ☆ Fl (4) WR 15s 190m **W23M, R20M**; 220°-W-020°-R-044°-W-072°-R-093°; W twr, R top; 38°38'·62N 27°05'·07W.
Monte Brasil, Oc WR 10s 21m 12M; 191°-R-295°-W-057°; W col, R bands; 38°38'·60N 27°13'·04W.

ANGRA DO HEROISMO

Ldg lts 340·9°: front, Fl R 4s 29m 7M, R mast; 38°39'·25N 27°13'·09W. Rear, Oc R 6s 54m 7M.
Marina ent, S side (Porto Pipas) ∡ Fl G 3s 14m 6M.
N mole, ∡ Fl (2) R 6s 8m 3M; 38°39'·12N 27°12'·95W.

ILHA DE SAO MIGUEL

Ponta da Ferraria ☆ Fl (3) 20s 106m **27M**; 339°-174°; W twr, R cupola. 37°51'·21N 25°51'·02W.
Airport ☆ Aero Al Fl WG 10s 83m **W28M, G23M**; 282°-124°; control twr; 37°44'·64N 25°42'·46W.
Santa Clara ☆ L Fl 5s 26m **15M**; 282°-102°; R lantern; 37°43'·99N 25°41'·15W.
Ponta Garça ☆ L Fl WR 5s 100m **W16M**, R13M; 240°-W-080-R-100°; 37°42'·85N 25°22'·18W.
Ponta do Arnel ☆ Aeromarine Fl 5s 65m **25M**; 157°-355°; W twr on ho; 37°49'·43N 25°08'·12W.

PONTA DELGADA

Bkwtr head ∡ L Fl R 6s 16m 10M; W twr, R bands; 37°44'·18N 25°39'·40W.
Naval Club Dir lt 309°: Fl (2) WRG 5s 24m 10M H24; 306°-G-308°-W-310°-R-312°; 37°44'·39N 25°39'·42W.
Marina mole hd ∡ Fl G 3s 12m 10M; W twr, G bands; 37°44'·32N 25°39'·57W.
Forte S. Bras Dir lt 262°: Fl (4) WRG 8s 13m 10M H24; 259°-G-261°-W-263°-R-265°; 37°44'·08N 25°40'·39W.

Ilhéus das Formigas ∡ Fl (2) 12s 21m 9M; W twr. 37°16'·29N 24°46'·87W (20M NE of Santa Maria).

ILHA DE SANTA MARIA

Ponta do Castelo ☆ Aeromarine Fl (3) 13·5s 113m **25M**; 181°-089°; W ☐ twr and bldg. 36°55'·75N 25°00'·97W, SE corner of island.

1	Falmouth	**1**										
2	Brest	136	**2**									
3	La Coruña	440	350	**3**								
4	Bayona	554	456	114	**4**							
5	Leixões (Pôrto)	617	526	176	63	**5**						
6	HORTA	1235	1202	966	927	937	**6**					
7	PONTA DELGADA	1183	1145	862	813	815	151	**7**				
8	Lisboa	780	658	327	227	163	904	771	**8**			
9	Cabo São Vicente	888	757	426	318	263	934	794	102	**9**		
10	Cádiz	1022	901	560	452	397	1068	928	236	134	**10**	
11	Europa Point	1087	960	618	506	455	1125	984	294	192	72	**11**
12	Casablanca	1114	978	637	525	474	1065	918	313	211	187	188	**12**

1	131	152	190	282	320	Flores	1
2	48	69	152	191		Horta	2
3		44	138	185		Graciosa	3
4			94	143		Terceira	4
5				54		Ponta Delgada	5
6						Sta Maria	6

DISTANCE TABLES
Approx distances in nautical miles are by the most direct route allowing for dangers and TSS.

AREA 20 SW Spain & Gibraltar – *Ayamonte to Gibraltar and Ceuta*

SELECTED LIGHTS, BUOYS & WAYPOINTS

Positions are referenced to WGS84

PORTUGUESE BORDER TO CADIZ

AYAMONTE (E side of Rio Guadiana)
Bar buoys ⚓ Q (3) G 6s; 37°08'·90N 07°23'·44W.
⚓ Fl R 4s; 37°09'·14N 07°23'·82W.
W trng wall ⚓ Fl R 5s 4M; 37°09'·75N 07°24'·03W.
E trng wall ⚓ Fl G 3s 4M; 37°09'·93N 07°23'·63W.
Vila Real de Santo Antònio ☆ Fl 6·5s 51m **26M**; W twr, B bands; 37°11'·23N 07°25'·00W (Portugal).
Marina ent, ⚓ QR & ⚓ QG; 37°12'·61N 07°24'·43W.

ISLA CANELA and ISLA CRISTINA
Appr ⚓ Fl 10s; 37°10'·51N 07°19'·49W.
W mole ⚓ VQ (2) R 5s 9m 4M; 37°10'·83N 07°19'·58W.
Ldg lts 313°: Front ⚓ Q 8m 5M; 37°11'·50N 07°20'·40W approx. Rear ⚓ Fl 4s 13m 5M.
Both marina entrances are QR and QG.

RIO DE LAS PIEDRAS
No 1 Bar ⚓ L Fl 10s; 37°11'·64N 07°03'·00W. The shifting chan is marked by lateral lt buoys.
El Rompido ☆ Fl (2) 10s 41m **24M**; W twr, B bands; 37°13'·12N 07°07'·69W.

RIA DE HUELVA
Punta Umbria, ⚓ L Fl 10s; 37°08'·78N 06°56'·74W.
No. 1 ⚓ Fl (2) G 10s; No. 2 ⚓ Fl (2) R 10s; 37°09'·14N 06°56'·60W.
Bkwtr hd ⚓ VQ (6) + L Fl 10s 8m 5M; 37°09'·85N 06°56'·93W.
Marina wavebreak, S hd, Fl (2) R 10s 1M; 37°10'·40N 06°56'·38W.
N head, Fl (3) R 15s 1M; 37°10'·40N 06°56'·48W.
Dir ⚓ 339·2°, WRG 59m 8M; 337·5°- Fl G-338°-FG-338·6°-OcG-339·1°-FW-339·3°-OcR-339·8°-FR-340·4°-Fl R-340·9°; W twr; 37°08'·57N 06°50'·66W.
No. 1 ⚓ Fl G 5s; 37°06'·26N 06°49'·46W.
No. 2 ⚓ Fl R 5s; 37°06'·33N 06°49'·72W.
Bkwtr hd ⚓ Fl (3+1) WR 20s 29m, W12M, R9M; 165°-W-100°-R-125°; *Racon K, 12M;* 37°06'·47N 06°49'·93W.
No. 3 ⚓ Fl (2) G 10s; 37°06'·87N 06°49'·77W.
No. 5 ⚓ Fl (3) G 15s; 37°07'·38N 06°50'·03W.
No. 7 ⚓ Fl (4) G 20s; 37°07'·77N 06°50'·29W.

MAZAGÓN
Picacho lt ho ☆ Fl (2+4) 30s 52m **25M**; 37°08'·10N 06°49'·56W.
Marina, S pier ⚓ QG 7m 2M; 37°07'·91N 06°50'·03W.
⚓ Fl (2) 10s; 37°04'·22N 06°43'·67W.
La Higuera ☆ Fl (3) 20s 45m **20M**; 37°00'·47N 06°34'·16W.

CHIPIONA
Bajo Salmedina ⚓ Q (9) 15s 9m 5M; 36°44'·27N 06°28'·64W.

Pta de Chipiona ☆ Fl 10s 67m **25M**; 36°44'·26N 06°26'·53W.
Marina, No. 2 ⚓ Fl (2) R 7s; 36°45'·14N 06°25'·59W.
N bkwtr ⚓ Fl (2) G 10s 6m 5M; 36°44'·96N 06°25'·70W.

RÍO GUADALQUIVIR
No. 1 ⚓ L Fl 10s; *Racon M, 10M;* 36°45'·74N 06°27'·03W.
Ldg lts 068·9°: Front ⚓ Q 28m 10M; 36°47'·84N 06°20'·24W. Rear, ⚓ Iso 4s 60m 10M.
No. 3 ⚓ Fl G 5s; 36°46'·16N 06°25'·36W.
Selected buoys in sequence as far as Bonanza:
No. 7 ⚓ Fl (3) G 10s; 36°46'·61N 06°24'·02W.
No. 8 ⚓ Fl (3) R 10s; 36°46'·67N 06°24'·12W.
No. 11 ⚓ Fl G 5s; 36°46'·96N 06°22'·90W.
No. 12 ⚓ Fl R 5s; 36°47'·05N 06°22'·94W.
No. 14 ⚓ Fl (2) R 6s; 36°47'·21N 06°22'·39W.
No.13 ⚓ Fl (2) G 6s; 36°47'·12N 06°22'·36W.
No.17 ⚓ Fl (4) G 12s; 36°47'·46N 06°21'·23W.
No. 20 ⚓ Fl R 5s; 36°47'·81N 06°20'·70W.
Bonanza lt ho Fl 5s 22m 6M; 36°48'·17N 06°20'·15W.

SEVILLA
No. 52 bcn ⚓ Fl (2+1) R 21s 9m 5M; 37°18'·97N 06°00'·83W. Gelves marina Fl R 5s; 37°20'·42N 06°01'·39W; and Fl G 3s.
Lock, 37°19'·86N 05°59'·74W, for city centre.
CN Sevilla pontoons, 37°22'·20N 05°59'·59W.

BAY OF CADIZ
Rota Aero ☆ Alt Fl WG 9s 79m **17M**; R/W chequered water twr, conspic; 36°38'·13N 06°20'·84W.
Rota ⚓ Oc 4s 33m 13M; W lt ho, R band; 36°36'·96N 06°21'·44W.
Marina, S pier ⚓ Fl (3) R 10s 8m 9M; 36°36'·96N 06°21'·44W.

P'TO SHERRY/P'TO DE SANTA MARIA
Puerto Sherry marina, S bkwtr ⚓ Oc R 4s 4M; 36°34'·64N 06°15'·25W. N bkwtr ⚓ Oc G 5s 3M.
Santa María ldg lts 040°: Front ⚓ QG 16m 4M; 36°35'·77N 06°13'·36W. Rear ⚓ Iso G 4s 20m 4M.
W trng wall ⚓ Fl R 5s 10m 3M; 36°34'·34N 06°14'·96W.

CÁDIZ CITY and PUERTO AMERICA
⚓ L Fl 10s; 36°33'·99N 06°19'·80W.
No. 1 ⚓ Fl G 3s; 36°33'·12N 06°19'·07W.
No. 3 ⚓ Fl (2) G 4s; 36°33'·17N 06°18'·14W.
No. 5 ⚓ Fl (3) G 13s; 36°33'·03N 06°17'·38W.
San Felipe mole ⚓ Fl G 3s 10m 5M; G twr; 36°32'·56N 06°16'·77W.
P'to America marina, NE bkwtr, ⚓ Fl (4) G 16s 1M. RCN pier ⚓ FG; 36°32'·34N 06°17'·13W.

International Free Zone hbr: No. 1 ↙ Fl (3) G 9s; 36°30'·66N 06°15'·45W.

Puerto Elcano marina 36°30'·08N 06°15'·45W.

Castillo de San Sebastián ☆ Fl (2) 10s 38m **25M**; *Horn Mo (N) 20s;* 36°31'·70N 06°18'·97W.

CADIZ TO GIBRALTAR

SANCTI PETRI

Punta del Arrecife ↙ Q (9) 15s 7m 3M; 36°23'·71N 06°13'·58W.

Castle ↙ Fl 3s 18m 9M; 36°22'·75N 06°13'·33W.

Outer ldg lts 050°: Front ↙ Fl 5s 12m 6M. Rear ↙ Oc (2) 6s 16m 6M.

No. 1 ↙ Fl (3) G 9s; 36°22'·50N 06°12'·93W.

No. 2 ↙ Fl (3) R 9s; 36°22'·46N 06°12'·81W.

No. 3 ↙ Fl (4) G 11s; 36°22'·64N 06°12'·65W.

No. 4 ↙ Fl (4) R 11s; 36°22'·66N 06°12'·71W.

Inner ldg lts 346·5°: Front ↙ Fl 5s 11m 6M. Rear ↙ Oc (2) 6s 21m.

↙ Fl G 5s 8m 2M & ↙ Fl R 5s; 36°23'·10N 06°12'·65W.

Cabo Roche ☆ Fl (4) 24s 44m **20M**; 36°17'·75N 06°08'·59W.

Cabo Trafalgar ☆ Fl (2+1) 15s 50m **22M**; 36°10'·95N 06°02'·12W.

BARBATE

Lt ho ↙ Fl (2) WR 7s 22m, W10M, R7M; 281°-W-015°-R-095°; W twr, R bands; 36°11'·21N 05°55'·43W.

SW mole ↙ Fl R 4s 11m 5M; 36°10'·78N 05°55'·56W.

Marina ent, Fl (4) Y 20s 1M (anti-oil boom) and Fl R 4s 2M.

↙ Q; 36°10'·75N 05°55'·40W (1ca E of hbr ent) marks N end of a roughly △-shaped tunny net.

Torre de Gracia ↙ Oc (2) 5s 74m 13M; 36°05'·38N 05°48'·69W.

TARIFA

Tarifa ☆ Fl (3) WR 10s 40m **W26M, R18M**; 113°-W-089°-R-113°; W twr; *Siren Mo (O) 60s; Racon C, 20M;* 36°00'·06N 05°36'·60W.

Outer SE mole ↙ Fl G 5s 11m 5M; vis 249°-045°; G twr with statue; 36°00'·38N 05°36'·24W.

ALGECIRAS

Pta Carnero ☆ Fl (4) WR 20s 42m, **W16M**, R13M; 018°-W-325°-R-018°; *Siren Mo (K) 30s;* 36°04'·61N 05°25'·57W.

↙ Q (3) 10s; 36°06'·73N 05°24'·76W.

Marina, outer S jetty ↙ Q (3) R 9s 7m 3M; 36°07'·10N 05°26'·13W.

LA LÍNEA

↙ Fl (3) G 6s; 36°09'·53N 05°22'·03W.

Dique de Abrigo ↙ Fl (2) G 7s 8m 4M; 36°09'·51N 05°22'·05W.

GIBRALTAR

Aero ↙ Mo (GB) R 10s 405m **30M**; 36°08'·57N 05°20'·60W.

Europa Pt ☆ Iso 10s 49m **19/15M**; vis 197°-042° & 067°-125°; W twr, R band; 36°06'·58N 05°20'·69W.
Also ↙ FR 44m **15M**; 042°-067°; *Horn 20s.*
Same twr ↙ Oc R 10s 49m **15M**; 042°-067°.

'A' Head ☆ Fl 2s 18m **15M**; *Horn 10s;* 36°08'·03N 05°21'·85W.

'B' head ↙ QR 9m 5M; 36°08'·14N 05°21'·84W.

Queensway Quay marina, N ent ↙ FR/FG, 36°08'·16N 05°21'·39W.

Yacht fuelling station; 36°08'·90N 05°21'·37W.

MOROCCO (WEST TO EAST)

Cap Spartel ☆ Fl (4) 20s 95m **30M**; Y ☐ twr; *Dia (4) 90s;* 35°47'·47N 05°55'·43W.

TANGIER

Navaids are reported unreliable. They may be missing, unlit, off station or not as charted.

Monte Dirección (Le Charf) ☆ Oc (3) WRG 12s 88m **W16M**, R12M, G11M; 140°-G-174·5°-W-200°-R-225°; 35°45'·98N 05°47'·35W.

↙ L Fl 10s; 35°47'·66N 05°47'·03W.

N pier ↙ Fl (3) 12s 20m 14M; 35°47'·47N 05°47'·60W.

Jetée des Yachts ↙ Iso G 4s 6m 6M; 35°47'·23N 05°48'·14W.

Pta Malabata ☆ Fl 5s 77m **22M**. W ☐ twr; 35°48'·99N 05°44'·92W.

Pte Cires ↙ Fl (3) 12s 44m **18M**; 060°-330°; 35°54'·51N 05°28'·92W.

CEUTA (Spanish enclave)

Punta Almina ↙ Fl (2) 10s 148m 22M; 35°53'·90N 05°16'·85W.

W pier ↙ Fl G 5s 13m 15M; *Siren 15s; Racon O, 12M;* 35°53'·75N 05°18'·68W.

E pier ↙ Fl R 5s 13m 5M; vis 245°-210°; 35°53'·73N 05°18'·47W.

Marina ent, N bkwtr ↙ Fl (4) R 11s 8m 1M; 35°53'·45N 05°18'·90W.

1	Nazaré	1											
2	Cabo Carvoeiro	22	2										
3	Cabo Raso	62	40	3									
4	Lisboa (bridge)	78	56	16	4								
5	Cabo Espichel	84	62	22	23	5							
6	Sines	118	96	54	57	34	6						
7	Cabo São Vicente	169	147	104	108	85	57	7					
8	Lagos	189	167	124	128	105	77	20	8				
9	Vilamoura	212	190	147	151	128	100	43	27	9			
10	Cádiz	303	281	238	242	219	191	134	120	95	10		
11	Cabo Trafalgar	320	298	255	259	236	208	151	139	115	28	11	
12	Tarifa	344	322	279	283	260	232	175	163	139	52	24	12
13	Gibraltar	360	338	295	299	276	248	191	179	155	68	40	16	13

DISTANCE TABLES

Approx distances in nautical miles are by the most direct route allowing for dangers and TSS.

Times are UT - add 1 hour in non-shaded months to convert to Summer Time

SUN RISE/SET LATITUDE 56°N – 2009

	Rise JAN	Set JAN	Rise FEB	Set FEB	Rise MAR	Set MAR	Rise APR	Set APR	Rise MAY	Set MAY	Rise JUN	Set JUN
1	0831	1536	0755	1633	0651	1734	0530	1838	0416	1940	0322	2035
4	0830	1540	0749	1640	0644	1741	0523	1845	0409	1946	0319	2038
7	0828	1545	0743	1646	0636	1747	0515	1851	0403	1952	0317	2042
10	0826	1550	0736	1653	0628	1753	0507	1857	0357	1957	0315	2045
13	0823	1555	0730	1700	0620	1800	0459	1903	0351	2003	0314	2047
16	0820	1600	0723	1706	0613	1806	0452	1909	0345	2009	0313	2049
19	0816	1606	0716	1713	0605	1812	0444	1915	0340	2014	0313	2050
22	0812	1612	0709	1719	0557	1818	0437	1921	0335	2019	0313	2051
25	0807	1618	0701	1726	0549	1824	0430	1927	0331	2024	0315	2051
28	0802	1625	0654	1732	0541	1830	0423	1934	0327	2029	0316	2050
31	0757	1631			0533	1836			0323	2033		

	Rise JUL	Set JUL	Rise AUG	Set AUG	Rise SEP	Set SEP	Rise OCT	Set OCT	Rise NOV	Set NOV	Rise DEC	Set DEC
1	0318	2049	0404	2007	0504	1854	0603	1735	0707	1619	0807	1531
4	0321	2047	0410	2001	0510	1846	0609	1727	0714	1613	0812	1528
7	0324	2045	0415	1955	0516	1839	0615	1719	0720	1607	0816	1527
10	0328	2042	0421	1948	0522	1831	0621	1712	0726	1601	0820	1526
13	0332	2039	0427	1941	0528	1823	0627	1704	0733	1555	0823	1525
16	0336	2035	0433	1934	0534	1815	0633	1657	0739	1550	0826	1525
19	0341	2030	0439	1927	0539	1807	0640	1649	0745	1545	0829	1526
22	0346	2026	0445	1920	0545	1759	0646	1642	0751	1541	0830	1527
25	0351	2021	0451	1912	0551	1751	0652	1635	0756	1537	0831	1529
28	0357	2015	0457	1905	0557	1743	0659	1628	0802	1534	0832	1532
31	0402	2009	0502	1857			0705	1621			0831	1535

SUN RISE/SET LATITUDE 48°N – 2009

	Rise JAN	Set JAN	Rise FEB	Set FEB	Rise MAR	Set MAR	Rise APR	Set APR	Rise MAY	Set MAY	Rise JUN	Set JUN
1	0750	1618	0728	1700	0641	1744	0538	1830	0442	1913	0405	1952
4	0750	1621	0724	1705	0635	1749	0532	1835	0437	1917	0403	1954
7	0749	1624	0719	1710	0629	1754	0526	1839	0432	1922	0402	1957
10	0748	1628	0715	1715	0623	1758	0520	1843	0428	1926	0401	1959
13	0746	1632	0710	1719	0617	1803	0514	1847	0424	1930	0400	2000
16	0744	1636	0705	1724	0611	1807	0509	1852	0420	1934	0400	2002
19	0742	1640	0659	1729	0605	1811	0503	1856	0416	1937	0400	2003
22	0739	1645	0654	1734	0559	1816	0458	1900	0413	1941	0401	2003
25	0736	1649	0649	1738	0553	1820	0452	1905	0410	1944	0402	2004
28	0733	1654	0643	1743	0547	1824	0447	1909	0408	1948	0403	2004
31	0729	1659			0540	1829			0405	1951		

	Rise JUL	Set JUL	Rise AUG	Set AUG	Rise SEP	Set SEP	Rise OCT	Set OCT	Rise NOV	Set NOV	Rise DEC	Set DEC
1	0405	2003	0436	1936	0518	1841	0559	1739	0645	1642	0729	1609
4	0407	2002	0440	1931	0522	1835	0603	1733	0650	1637	0732	1608
7	0409	2001	0444	1927	0526	1829	0608	1727	0654	1633	0736	1607
10	0411	1959	0448	1922	0530	1823	0612	1721	0659	1629	0739	1607
13	0414	1957	0452	1917	0534	1817	0616	1715	0703	1625	0742	1607
16	0417	1954	0456	1911	0538	1810	0621	1710	0708	1621	0744	1607
19	0420	1952	0500	1906	0543	1804	0625	1704	0712	1618	0746	1608
22	0424	1948	0504	1900	0547	1758	0630	1658	0717	1615	0748	1610
25	0427	1945	0508	1855	0551	1752	0634	1653	0721	1613	0749	1612
28	0431	1941	0513	1849	0555	1745	0639	1648	0725	1611	0750	1614
31	0435	1937	0517	1843			0643	1643			0750	1616

Times are UT - add 1 hour in non-shaded months to convert to Summer Time

SUN RISE/SET LATITUDE 40°N – 2009

	Rise	Set	Rise	Set	Rise	Set	Rise	Set	Rise	Set	Rise	Set
	JANUARY		FEBRUARY		MARCH		APRIL		MAY		JUNE	
1	07 22	16 46	07 09	17 19	06 33	17 52	05 44	18 24	05 00	18 55	04 33	19 23
4	07 22	16 48	07 06	17 23	06 29	17 55	05 39	18 27	04 56	18 58	04 32	19 25
7	07 22	16 51	07 02	17 26	06 24	17 58	05 35	18 30	04 53	19 01	04 31	19 27
10	07 22	16 54	06 59	17 30	06 20	18 02	05 30	18 33	04 50	19 04	04 31	19 28
13	07 21	16 57	06 55	17 34	06 15	18 05	05 25	18 36	04 47	19 07	04 31	19 30
16	07 20	17 00	06 52	17 37	06 10	18 08	05 21	18 40	04 44	19 09	04 31	19 31
19	07 18	17 04	06 48	17 41	06 05	18 11	05 16	18 43	04 41	19 12	04 31	19 32
22	07 16	17 07	06 44	17 44	06 00	18 14	05 12	18 46	04 39	19 15	04 32	19 33
25	07 14	17 11	06 39	17 47	05 55	18 17	05 08	18 49	04 37	19 17	04 32	19 33
28	07 12	17 14	06 35	17 51	05 51	18 20	05 04	18 52	04 35	19 20	04 34	19 33
31	07 09	17 18			05 46	18 23			04 34	19 22		

	Rise	Set	Rise	Set	Rise	Set	Rise	Set	Rise	Set	Rise	Set
	JULY		AUGUST		SEPTEMBER		OCTOBER		NOVEMBER		DECEMBER	
1	04 35	19 33	04 58	19 14	05 28	18 31	05 56	17 42	06 29	16 58	07 03	16 35
4	04 36	19 32	05 01	19 10	05 31	18 27	05 59	17 38	06 33	16 54	07 06	16 35
7	04 38	19 31	05 04	19 07	05 33	18 22	06 02	17 33	06 36	16 51	07 08	16 35
10	04 40	19 30	05 07	19 03	05 36	18 17	06 05	17 28	06 39	16 48	07 11	16 35
13	04 42	19 29	05 10	18 59	05 39	18 12	06 08	17 23	06 43	16 45	07 13	16 35
16	04 45	19 27	05 13	18 55	05 42	18 07	06 12	17 19	06 46	16 43	07 15	16 36
19	04 47	19 25	05 15	18 51	05 45	18 02	06 15	17 15	06 50	16 41	07 17	16 37
22	04 49	19 23	05 18	18 47	05 48	17 57	06 18	17 10	06 53	16 39	07 19	16 39
25	04 52	19 21	05 21	18 42	05 50	17 52	06 21	17 06	06 56	16 37	07 20	16 40
28	04 55	19 18	05 24	18 38	05 53	17 47	06 25	17 02	07 00	16 36	07 21	16 42
31	04 57	19 15	05 27	18 33			06 28	16 59			07 22	16 45

MOON RISE/SET LATITUDE 56°N – 2009

	Rise	Set	Rise	Set	Rise	Set	Rise	Set	Rise	Set	Rise	Set
	JANUARY		FEBRUARY		MARCH		APRIL		MAY		JUNE	
1	10 26	21 28	09 07	** **	07 28	** **	07 46	01 55	09 52	01 47	13 31	00 42
4	10 48	00 09	10 07	03 48	08 50	02 56	12 06	03 42	14 19	02 25	17 39	01 12
7	11 36	04 40	13 40	06 50	12 49	05 17	16 34	04 16	18 30	02 52	21 14	02 20
10	14 42	08 21	18 34	07 42	17 31	05 59	20 50	04 44	22 24	03 46	22 56	05 14
13	19 39	09 26	22 56	08 08	21 52	06 26	** **	05 45	00 03	06 15	23 32	09 02
16	23 59	09 52	01 42	08 47	00 38	07 14	02 06	08 28	01 05	10 00	23 56	12 53
19	02 42	10 24	05 02	10 40	03 37	09 32	02 59	12 19	01 32	13 54	00 21	17 15
22	06 18	11 53	06 23	14 20	04 42	13 20	03 25	16 19	02 02	18 15	02 08	21 08
25	08 01	15 18	06 53	18 21	05 10	17 21	03 58	20 48	03 27	22 30	06 40	22 28
28	08 35	19 16	07 17	22 32	05 37	21 43	05 40	** **	07 33	** **	11 16	22 59
31	08 58	23 19			06 51	00 42			12 07	00 33		

	Rise	Set	Rise	Set	Rise	Set	Rise	Set	Rise	Set	Rise	Set
	JULY		AUGUST		SEPTEMBER		OCTOBER		NOVEMBER		DECEMBER	
1	15 27	23 34	17 58	23 49	17 48	01 07	16 26	02 40	15 12	05 35	14 20	07 27
4	19 09	00 21	19 26	02 04	18 17	04 57	16 53	06 35	16 27	09 54	17 39	10 39
7	21 01	03 02	19 59	05 54	18 44	08 52	17 49	10 51	20 00	12 41	22 19	11 43
10	21 41	06 50	20 23	09 44	19 45	13 06	20 43	14 07	** **	13 36	01 13	12 16
13	22 05	10 38	21 10	13 56	22 56	16 08	** **	15 16	03 25	14 08	05 26	13 01
16	22 42	14 47	23 50	17 32	02 06	17 10	04 17	15 49	07 42	14 58	08 52	14 59
19	** **	18 52	03 01	18 52	06 45	17 42	08 41	16 32	10 58	17 10	10 21	18 33
22	04 00	20 32	07 48	19 24	11 10	18 29	12 20	18 22	12 16	20 49	10 56	22 16
25	08 51	21 07	12 13	20 03	14 32	20 32	13 57	21 50	12 49	** **	11 23	00 45
28	13 11	21 41	15 52	21 43	15 53	** **	14 33	00 22	13 17	03 08	12 14	04 54
31	17 02	22 59	17 32	** **			15 00	04 12			15 05	08 29

Times are UT - add 1 hour in non-shaded months to convert to Summer Time

MOON RISE/SET LATITUDE 48°N – 2009

	Rise Set JANUARY	Rise Set FEBRUARY	Rise Set MARCH	Rise Set APRIL	Rise Set MAY	Rise Set JUNE
1	10 14 21 36	09 29 ****	07 57 23 24	08 45 00 56	10 26 01 10	13 25 00 43
4	11 03 ****	11 01 02 55	09 49 01 57	12 37 03 08	14 20 02 19	17 03 01 40
7	12 24 03 54	14 28 06 01	13 29 04 35	16 32 04 13	18 01 03 14	20 16 03 15
10	15 35 07 26	18 43 07 28	17 35 05 50	20 17 05 10	21 27 04 37	22 15 06 02
13	19 54 09 07	22 34 08 24	21 25 06 46	23 39 06 39	23 45 07 08	23 18 09 22
16	23 42 10 02	00 59 09 33	**** 08 04	01 13 09 19	00 37 10 26	**** 12 45
19	02 05 11 03	04 01 11 41	02 39 10 29	02 34 12 41	01 30 13 52	00 52 16 34
22	05 17 12 54	05 46 14 55	04 11 13 48	03 27 16 12	02 28 17 40	03 06 20 13
25	07 18 15 59	06 44 18 25	05 06 17 20	04 29 20 08	04 24 21 32	07 11 22 06
28	08 21 19 27	07 36 22 06	06 02 21 09	06 38 23 46	08 11 23 40	11 13 23 06
31	09 10 23 01		07 47 ****		12 11 00 25	

	JULY	AUGUST	SEPTEMBER	OCTOBER	NOVEMBER	DECEMBER
1	14 54 ****	17 00 ****	17 17 01 45	16 18 02 54	15 35 05 15	15 09 06 40
4	18 11 01 14	18 49 02 49	18 12 05 07	17 11 06 21	17 19 09 04	18 25 09 51
7	20 18 03 53	19 49 06 10	19 05 08 34	18 36 10 05	20 42 11 57	22 31 11 27
10	21 25 07 12	20 38 09 33	20 35 12 17	21 33 13 16	**** 13 23	01 05 12 27
13	22 13 10 33	21 54 13 13	23 44 15 19	00 13 14 56	03 14 14 22	04 47 13 41
16	23 20 14 12	**** 16 38	02 30 16 53	04 12 15 58	07 00 15 41	07 57 15 54
19	00 46 17 55	03 32 18 29	06 36 17 55	08 05 17 10	10 04 18 04	09 47 19 09
22	04 38 20 05	07 44 19 33	10 28 19 12	11 24 19 18	11 45 21 18	10 47 22 21
25	08 52 21 11	11 37 20 42	13 35 21 28	13 19 22 25	12 42 ****	11 38 00 34
28	12 41 22 13	14 54 22 41	15 19 ****	14 22 00 38	13 36 02 52	12 58 04 12
31	16 05 23 56	16 52 00 39		15 14 04 02		15 56 07 38

MOON RISE/SET LATITUDE 40°N – 2009

	Rise Set JANUARY	Rise Set FEBRUARY	Rise Set MARCH	Rise Set APRIL	Rise Set MAY	Rise Set JUNE
1	10 05 21 42	09 44 23 56	08 18 22 59	09 23 00 18	10 50 00 45	13 21 00 43
4	11 14 ****	11 37 02 21	10 26 01 21	12 58 02 44	14 21 02 14	16 38 02 01
7	12 56 03 23	14 59 05 28	13 56 04 07	16 31 04 11	17 41 03 30	19 39 03 51
10	16 09 06 51	18 50 07 18	17 38 05 44	19 54 05 28	20 51 05 10	21 48 06 33
13	20 04 08 53	22 19 08 35	21 06 07 00	23 02 07 14	23 14 07 43	23 08 09 35
16	23 31 10 10	00 30 10 18	**** 08 37	00 39 09 52	00 17 10 44	**** 12 39
19	01 40 11 30	03 23 12 18	02 03 11 05	02 16 12 56	01 28 13 50	01 15 16 07
22	04 38 13 33	05 21 15 19	03 50 14 08	03 28 16 08	02 46 17 17	03 43 19 38
25	06 48 16 27	06 38 18 29	05 04 17 19	04 51 19 41	05 00 20 55	07 32 21 50
28	08 11 19 35	07 49 21 48	06 20 20 46	07 15 23 10	08 36 23 19	11 11 23 11
31	09 19 22 48		08 23 ****		12 14 00 18	

	JULY	AUGUST	SEPTEMBER	OCTOBER	NOVEMBER	DECEMBER
1	14 31 00 04	16 23 00 32	16 55 02 11	16 12 03 03	15 52 05 01	15 40 06 09
4	17 35 01 49	18 23 03 19	18 09 05 14	17 24 06 11	17 52 08 31	18 55 09 20
7	19 49 04 26	19 41 06 22	19 20 08 21	19 08 09 35	21 10 11 27	22 39 11 16
10	21 13 07 28	20 49 09 25	21 08 11 44	22 06 12 42	**** 13 13	00 59 12 36
13	22 20 10 30	22 24 12 45	**** 14 46	00 32 14 41	03 06 14 33	04 21 14 09
16	23 47 13 47	00 09 16 02	02 47 16 41	04 09 16 04	06 32 16 11	07 22 16 29
19	01 22 17 18	03 53 18 13	06 30 18 05	07 40 17 36	09 29 18 39	09 23 19 28
22	05 03 19 45	07 42 19 39	10 01 19 41	10 48 19 54	11 23 21 38	10 40 22 26
25	08 54 21 13	11 12 21 08	12 59 22 04	12 54 22 50	12 37 ****	11 49 00 25
28	12 21 22 35	14 17 23 18	14 55 00 01	14 13 00 50	13 50 02 41	13 27 03 44
31	15 29 ****	16 24 01 11		15 24 03 55		16 29 07 04

SPEED, TIME AND DISTANCE (NAUTICAL MILES)

Time in minutes \ Speed in knots	1	2	3	4	5	6	7	8	9	10	15	20
1	0·0	0·0	0·1	0·1	0·1	0·1	0·1	0·1	0·2	0·2	0·3	0·3
2	0·0	0·1	0·1	0·1	0·2	0·2	0·2	0·3	0·3	0·3	0·5	0·7
3	0·1	0·1	0·2	0·2	0·3	0·3	0·4	0·4	0·5	0·5	0·8	1·0
4	0·1	0·1	0·2	0·3	0·3	0·4	0·5	0·5	0·6	0·7	1·0	1·3
5	0·1	0·2	0·3	0·3	0·4	0·5	0·6	0·7	0·8	0·8	1·3	1·7
6	0·1	0·2	0·3	0·4	0·5	0·6	0·7	0·8	0·9	1·0	1·5	2·0
7	0·1	0·2	0·4	0·5	0·6	0·7	0·8	0·9	1·1	1·2	1·8	2·3
8	0·1	0·3	0·4	0·5	0·7	0·8	0·9	1·1	1·2	1·3	2·0	2·7
9	0·2	0·3	0·5	0·6	0·8	0·9	1·1	1·2	1·4	1·5	2·3	3·0
10	0·2	0·3	0·5	0·7	0·8	1·0	1·2	1·3	1·5	1·7	2·5	3·3
11	0·2	0·4	0·6	0·7	0·9	1·1	1·3	1·5	1·7	1·8	2·8	3·7
12	0·2	0·4	0·6	0·8	1·0	1·2	1·4	1·6	1·8	2·0	3·0	4·0
13	0·2	0·4	0·7	0·9	1·1	1·3	1·5	1·7	2·0	2·2	3·3	4·3
14	0·2	0·5	0·7	0·9	1·2	1·4	1·6	1·9	2·1	2·3	3·5	4·7
15	0·3	0·5	0·8	1·0	1·3	1·5	1·8	2·0	2·3	2·5	3·8	5·0
16	0·3	0·5	0·8	1·1	1·3	1·6	1·9	2·1	2·4	2·7	4·0	5·3
17	0·3	0·6	0·9	1·1	1·4	1·7	2·0	2·3	2·6	2·8	4·3	5·7
18	0·3	0·6	0·9	1·2	1·5	1·8	2·1	2·4	2·7	3·0	4·5	6·0
19	0·3	0·6	1·0	1·3	1·6	1·9	2·2	2·5	2·9	3·2	4·8	6·3
20	0·3	0·7	1·0	1·3	1·7	2·0	2·3	2·7	3·0	3·3	5·0	6·7
21	0·4	0·7	1·1	1·4	1·8	2·1	2·5	2·8	3·2	3·5	5·3	7·0
22	0·4	0·7	1·1	1·5	1·8	2·2	2·6	2·9	3·3	3·7	5·5	7·3
23	0·4	0·8	1·2	1·5	1·9	2·3	2·7	3·1	3·5	3·8	5·8	7·7
24	0·4	0·8	1·2	1·6	2·0	2·4	2·8	3·2	3·6	4·0	6·0	8·0
25	0·4	0·8	1·3	1·7	2·1	2·5	2·9	3·3	3·8	4·2	6·3	8·3
30	0·5	1·0	1·5	2·0	2·5	3·0	3·5	4·0	4·5	5·0	7·5	10·0
35	0·6	1·2	1·8	2·3	2·9	3·5	4·1	4·7	5·3	5·8	8·8	11·7
40	0·7	1·3	2·0	2·7	3·3	4·0	4·7	5·3	6·0	6·7	10·0	13·3
45	0·8	1·5	2·3	3·0	3·8	4·5	5·3	6·0	6·8	7·5	11·3	15·0
50	0·8	1·7	2·5	3·3	4·2	5·0	5·8	6·7	7·5	8·3	12·5	16·7

DISTANCE (NAUTICAL MILES) OFF RISING/DIPPING LIGHTS

Height of light in metres \ Height of eye in feet	2	3	4	5	6	7	8	9	10	20	30	40	50
2	4·6	4·9	5·2	5·5	5·7	6·0	6·2	6·4	6·6	8·1	9·2	10·2	11·0
3	5·2	5·6	5·9	6·2	6·4	6·6	6·8	7·0	7·2	8·7	9·9	10·8	11·7
4	5·8	6·1	6·4	6·7	6·9	7·2	7·4	7·6	7·8	9·3	10·4	11·4	12·2
5	6·3	6·6	6·9	7·2	7·4	7·7	7·9	8·1	8·3	9·8	10·9	11·9	12·7
6	6·7	7·1	7·4	7·6	7·9	8·1	8·3	8·5	8·7	10·2	11·3	12·3	13·2
7	7·1	7·5	7·8	8·0	8·3	8·5	8·7	8·9	9·1	10·6	11·8	12·7	13·6
8	7·5	7·8	8·2	8·4	8·7	8·9	9·1	9·3	9·5	11·0	12·1	13·1	14·0
9	7·8	8·2	8·5	8·8	9·0	9·2	9·5	9·7	9·8	11·3	12·5	13·5	14·3
10	8·2	8·5	8·8	9·1	9·4	9·6	9·8	10·0	10·2	11·7	12·8	13·8	14·6
11	8·5	8·9	9·2	9·4	9·7	9·9	10·1	10·3	10·5	12·0	13·1	14·1	15·0
12	8·8	9·2	9·5	9·7	10·0	10·2	10·4	10·6	10·8	12·3	13·4	14·4	15·3
13	9·1	9·5	9·8	10·0	10·3	10·5	10·7	10·9	11·1	12·6	13·7	14·7	15·6
14	9·4	9·7	10·0	10·3	10·6	10·8	11·0	11·2	11·4	12·9	14·0	15·0	15·8
15	9·6	10·0	10·3	10·6	10·8	11·1	11·3	11·5	11·6	13·1	14·3	15·3	16·1
16	9·9	10·3	10·6	10·8	11·1	11·3	11·5	11·7	11·9	13·4	14·6	15·5	16·4
17	10·2	10·5	10·8	11·1	11·3	11·6	11·8	12·0	12·2	13·7	14·8	15·8	16·6
18	10·4	10·8	11·1	11·4	11·6	11·8	12·0	12·2	12·4	13·9	15·1	16·0	16·9
19	10·7	11·0	11·3	11·6	11·8	12·1	12·3	12·5	12·7	14·2	15·3	16·3	17·1
20	10·9	11·3	11·6	11·8	12·1	12·3	12·5	12·7	12·9	14·4	15·5	16·5	17·3
25	12·0	12·3	12·6	12·9	13·2	13·4	13·6	13·8	14·0	15·5	16·6	17·6	18·4
30	13·0	13·3	13·6	13·9	14·1	14·4	14·6	14·8	15·0	16·5	17·6	18·6	19·4
40	14·7	15·1	15·4	15·7	15·9	16·1	16·3	16·5	16·7	18·2	19·4	20·3	21·2
50	16·3	16·6	16·9	17·2	17·4	17·7	17·9	18·1	18·3	19·8	20·9	21·9	22·7
60	17·7	18·0	18·3	18·6	18·8	19·1	19·3	19·5	19·7	21·2	22·3	23·3	24·1

CONVERSION TABLE

Sq inches to sq millimetres *multiply by* **645.20**	**Sq millimetres to sq inches** *multiply by* **0.0016**
Inches to millimetres *multiply by* **25.40**	**Millimetres to inches** *multiply by* **0.0394**
Sq feet to square metres *multiply by* **0.093**	**Sq metres to sq feet** *multiply by* **10.7640**
Inches to centimetres *multiply by* **2.54**	**Centimetres to inches** *multiply by* **0.3937**
Feet to metres *multiply by* **0.305**	**Metres to feet** *multiply by* **3.2810**
Nautical miles to kilometres *multiply by* **1.852**	**Kilometres to nautical miles** *multiply by* **0.5400**
Statute miles to kilometres *multiply by* **1.609**	**Kilometres to statute miles** *multiply by* **0.6214**
Statute miles to nautical miles *multiply by* **0.8684**	**Nautical miles to statute miles** *multiply by* **1.1515**
HP to metric HP *multiply by* **1.014**	**Metric HP to HP** *multiply by* **0.9862**
Pounds per sq inch to kg per sq centimetre *multiply by* **0.0703**	**Kg per sq centimetre to pounds per sq inch** *multiply by* **14.2200**
HP to kilowatts *multiply by* **0.746**	**Kilowatts to HP** *multiply by* **1.341**
Cu inches to cu centimetres *multiply by* **16.39**	**Cu centimetres to cu inches** *multiply by* **0.0610**
Imperial gallons to litres *multiply by* **4.540**	**Litres to imperial gallons** *multiply by* **0.2200**
Pints to litres *multiply by* **0.5680**	**Litres to pints** *multiply by* **1.7600**
Pounds to kilogrammes *multiply by* **0.4536**	**Kilogrammes to pounds** *multiply by* **2.2050**

LIGHT CHARACTERISTICS

CLASS OF LIGHT	International abbreviations	National abbreviations	Illustration Period shown ⊢——————⊣
FIXED	F		
OCCULTING *(total duration of light longer than dark)*			
Single-occulting	Oc	Occ	
Group-occulting	eg Oc(2)	Gp Occ(2)	
Composite group-occulting	eg Oc(2+3)	Gp Occ(2+3)	
ISOPHASE *(light and dark equal)*	Iso		
FLASHING *(total duration of light shorter than dark)*			
Single-flashing	Fl		
Long-flashing *(flash 2s or longer)*		L Fl	
Group-flashing	eg Fl(3)	Gp Fl(3)	
Composite group-flashing	eg Fl(2+1)	Gp Fl(2+1)	
QUICK *(50 to 79, usually either 50 or 60, flashes per min.)*			
Continuous quick	Q	Qk Fl	
Group quick	eg Q(3)	Qk Fl(3)	
Interrupted quick	IQ	Int Qk Fl	
VERY QUICK *(80 to 159, usually either 100 or 120, flashes per min.)*			
Continuous very quick	VQ	V Qk Fl	
Group very quick	eg VQ(3)	V Qk Fl(3)	
Interrupted very quick	IVQ	Int V Qk Fl	
ULTRA QUICK *(160 or more, usually 240 to 300, flashes per min.)*			
Continuous ultra quick	UQ		
Interrupted ultra quick	IUQ		
MORSE CODE	eg Mo(K)		
FIXED AND FLASHING	F Fl		
ALTERNATING	eg Al. WR	Alt. WR	

COLOUR	International abbreviations	NOMINAL RANGE in miles	International abbreviations
White	W *(may be omitted)*	Light with single range	eg 15M
Red	R	Light with two different ranges	eg 15/10M
Green	G	Light with three or more ranges	eg 15-7M
Blue	Bu		
Violet	Vi	**PERIOD** is given in seconds	eg 90s
Yellow	Y	**DISPOSITION** horizontally disposed	(hor)
Orange	Y		
Amber	Y	**ELEVATION** is given in metres (m) or feet (ft) above MHWS	

Chapter 2 - Weather

Beaufort scale

Force	Wind speed (knots)	(km/h)	(m/sec)	Description	State of sea	Probable wave ht(m)
0	0–1	0–2	0–0·5	Calm	Like a mirror	0
1	1–3	2–6	0·5–1·5	Light airs	Ripples like scales are formed	0
2	4–6	7–11	2–3	Light breeze	Small wavelets, still short but more pronounced, not breaking	0·1
3	7–10	13–19	4–5	Gentle breeze	Large wavelets, crests begin to break; a few white horses	0·4
4	11–16	20–30	6–8	Moderate breeze	Small waves growing longer; fairly frequent white horses	1
5	17–21	31–39	8–11	Fresh breeze	Moderate waves, taking more pronounced form; many white horses, perhaps some spray	2
6	22–27	41–50	11–14	Strong breeze	Large waves forming; white foam crests more extensive; probably some spray	3
7	28–33	52–61	14–17	Near gale	Sea heaps up; white foam from breaking waves begins to blow in streaks	4
8	34–40	63–74	17–21	Gale	Moderately high waves of greater length; edge of crests break into spindrift; foam blown in well-marked streaks	5·5

WEATHER

Terminology used in forecasts
Pressure systems' speed of movement

Slowly	< 15 knots
Steadily	15–25 knots
Rather quickly	25–35 knots
Rapidly	35–45 knots
Very rapidly	> 45 knots

Visibility

Good	> 5 miles
Moderate	2–5 miles
Poor	1000 metres–2 miles
Fog	< 1000 metres

Barometric pressure tendency

Rising/falling slowly: Change of 0·1 to 1·5 hPa/mb in the preceding 3 hours.

Rising/falling: Change of 1·6 to 3·5 hPa/mb in the preceding 3 hours.

Rising/falling quickly: Change of 3·6 to 6 hPa/mb in the preceding 3 hours.

Rising/falling very rapidly: Change of > 6 hPa/mb in the preceding 3 hours.

Now rising/falling: Pressure has been falling (rising) or steady in the preceding 3 hours, but was definitely rising (falling) at the time of observation.

Gale warnings

A *Gale* warning means that winds of at least F8 (34-40kn) or gusts up to 43-51kn are expected somewhere within the area, but not necessarily over the whole area

Severe Gale means winds of at least F9 (41-47kn) or gusts reaching 52-60kn

Storm means winds of F10 (48-55kn) or gusts of 61-68kn

Violent Storm means winds of F11 (56-63kn) or gusts of 69+ kn

Hurricane Force means winds of F12 (64+ kn)

Gale warnings remain in force until amended or cancelled. If a gale persists for >24 hours the warning is re-issued.

Timing of gale warnings from time of issue

Imminent	<6 hrs
Soon	6–12 hrs
Later	>12 hrs

Strong wind warnings

Issued, if possible 6 hrs in advance, when winds F6 or more are expected up to 5M offshore; valid for 12 hrs.

MAP OF UK SHIPPING FORECAST AREAS

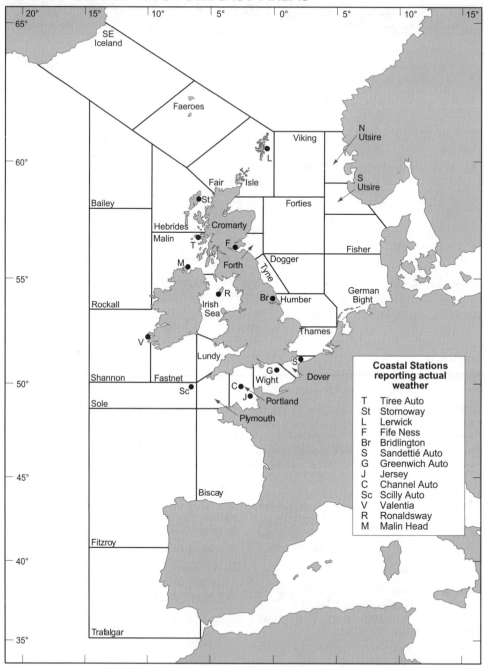

Coastal Stations reporting actual weather

T	Tiree Auto
St	Stornoway
L	Lerwick
F	Fife Ness
Br	Bridlington
S	Sandettié Auto
G	Greenwich Auto
J	Jersey
C	Channel Auto
Sc	Scilly Auto
V	Valentia
R	Ronaldsway
M	Malin Head

SHIPPING FORECAST RECORD Time/Day/Date ....

GENERAL SYNOPSIS

at .... UT/BST

System position	Present position at	Movement	Forecast	

Gales	SEA AREA FORECAST	Wind		Weather	Visibility
		(At first)	(Later)		
	VIKING				
	NORTH UTSIRE				
	SOUTH UTSIRE				
	FORTIES				
	CROMARTY				
	FORTH				
	TYNE				
	DOGGER				
	FISHER				
	GERMAN BIGHT				
	HUMBER				
	THAMES				
	DOVER				
	WIGHT				
	PORTLAND				
	PLYMOUTH				
	BISCAY				
	FITZROY				
	TRAFALGAR				
	SOLE				
	LUNDY				
	FASTNET				
	IRISH SEA				
	SHANNON				
	ROCKALL				
	MALIN				
	HEBRIDES				
	BAILEY				
	FAIR ISLE				
	FAEROES				
	S E ICELAND				

COASTAL REPORTS BST at .... UTC	Wind Direction	Force	Weather	Visibility	Pressure	Change	COASTAL REPORTS	Wind Direction	Force	Weather	Visibility	Pressure	Change
Tiree Auto (T)							Greenwich Lt V (G)						
Stornoway (St)							Jersey (J)						
Lerwick (L)							Channel Auto (C)						
Fife Ness (F)							Scilly Auto (Sc)						
Bridlington (Br)							Valentia (V)						
Sandettie Auto (S)							Ronaldsway (R)						
							Malin Head (M)						

WEATHER

SOURCES OF WEATHER INFORMATION IN THE UK

BBC Radio 4 Shipping forecasts
are broadcast at:

0048 LT[1]	LW, MW, FM
0520 LT[1]	LW, MW, FM
1201 LT	LW only
1754 LT	LW, FM (Sat/Sun)

[1] Includes weather reports from coastal stations

Frequencies

LW		198 kHz
MW	Tyneside	603 kHz
	London & N Ireland	720 kHz
	Redruth	756 kHz
	Plymouth & Enniskillen	774 kHz
	Aberdeen	1449 kHz
	Carlisle	1485 kHz
FM	England	92·4–94·6 MHz
	Scotland	91·3–96·1 MHz
		103·5–104·9 MHz
	Wales	92·8–96·1 MHz
		103·5–104·9 MHz
	N Ireland	93·2–96·0 MHz
		103·5–104·6 MHz
	Channel Islands	94·8 MHz

The Shipping forecast contains:

A summary of gale warnings in force at time of issue; a general synopsis of weather systems and their expected development over the next 24 hours; and a forecast of wind direction/force, weather and visibility in each sea area for the next 24 hours.

Gale warnings are also broadcast at the earliest juncture in Radio 4 programmes after receipt, as well as after the next news bulletin. Sea area **Trafalgar** is only included in the 0048 forecast.

Shipping forecasts cover large sea areas, and rarely include the detailed variations that may occur near land. The Inshore waters forecast can be more helpful to mariners on coastal passages.

Weather reports from coastal stations follow the 0048 and 0520 forecasts. They include wind direction and force, present weather, visibility, and sea-level pressure and tendency, if available. The stations are shown overleaf on the previous page.

BBC Radio 4 Inshore waters forecast
A forecast for inshore waters (up to 12M offshore) around the UK and N Ireland, valid until 1800, is broadcast after the 0048 and 0520 coastal station reports. It includes a general synopsis, forecasts of wind direction and force, visibility and weather for stretches of inshore waters. These are defined by well-known places and headlands from C. Wrath clockwise via Orkney, Rattray Hd, Berwick-upon-Tweed, Whitby, Gibraltar Pt, N Foreland, Selsey Bill, Lyme Regis, Land's End, St David's Hd, Great Ormes Hd, Isle of Man, Mull of Galloway, Carlingford Lough, Lough Foyle, Mull of Kintyre, Ardnamurchan Pt and Shetland.

Strong wind warnings are issued by the Met Office whenever winds of Force 6 or more are expected over coastal waters up to 5M offshore.

Reports of actual weather at the stations below are broadcast only after the 0048 Inshore waters forecast: Boulmer, *Bridlington*, Sheerness, St Catherine's Pt*, *Scilly**, Milford Haven, Aberporth, Valley, Liverpool/Crosby, *Ronaldsway*, Larne, Machrihanish*, Greenock, *Stornoway*, *Lerwick*, Wick*, Aberdeen and Leuchars. Asterisk* denotes an automatic station. Stations in italics also feature in the 0048 and 0520 shipping forecasts.

BBC general (land) forecasts
Land area forecasts may include an outlook period up to 48 hours beyond the shipping forecast, plus more details of frontal systems and weather along the coasts. The most comprehensive land area forecasts are broadcast by BBC Radio 4 on the frequencies above.

Land area forecasts – Wind strength
Wind descriptions used in land forecasts, with their Beaufort scale equivalents, are:

Calm	0	Fresh	5
Light	1–3	Strong	6–7
Moderate	4	Gale	8

Land area forecasts – Visibility
The following visibility definitions are used in land forecasts:

Mist	2000m–1000m
Fog	<1000m
Dense fog	< 50m

NAVTEX

Navtex uses a dedicated aerial, receiver and integral printer or LCD screen. The user programmes the receiver for the required station(s) and message categories. It automatically prints or displays MSI, ie weather, navigational and safety data.

Two frequencies are used: 518 kHz and *490 kHz*. 518 kHz messages are in English (occasionally in the national language as well), with excellent coverage of Europe. Interference between stations is avoided by time sharing and by limiting the range of transmitters to about 300M; see Fig. 5(4). Navtex information applies only to the geographic area for which each station is responsible.

490 kHz (for clarity shown in italics throughout this chapter) is used abroad for transmissions in the national language. In the UK it is used for inshore waters forecasts in English. Identification letters for 490 kHz stations differ from 518 kHz stations.

Weather information accounts for about 75% of all messages and Navtex is particularly valuable when out of range of other sources, otherwise occupied or if there is a language problem.

Messages

Each message is prefixed by a four-character group:

The first character is the code letter of the transmitting station (eg **E** for Niton).

The second character is the message category, see below.

The third and fourth are message serial numbers, running from 01 to 99 and then re-starting at 01.

The serial number 00 denotes urgent messages which are always printed.

Messages which are corrupt or have already been printed are rejected.

Weather messages, and certain other message types, are dated and timed.

Message categories

A*	Navigational warnings
B*	Meteorological warnings
C	Ice reports
D*	SAR info and piracy warnings
E	Weather forecasts
F	Pilot service
H	Loran-C
J	Satellite navigation
K	Other electronic navaids
L	Subfacts and Gunfacts (UK)
V	Amplifies Navwarnings initially sent under A; plus weekly oil/gas rig moves.
W-Y	Special service, trials
Z	No messages on hand at scheduled time

Missing category letters are unallocated.

*The receiver cannot reject these categories.

Navtex stations/areas – UK & W Europe

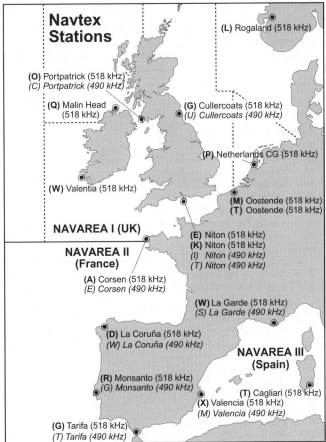

Navtex Stations

(L) Rogaland (518 kHz)

(O) Portpatrick (518 kHz)
(C) Portpatrick (490 kHz)

(Q) Malin Head (518 kHz)

(G) Cullercoats (518 kHz)
(U) Cullercoats (490 kHz)

(P) Netherlands CG (518 kHz)

(W) Valentia (518 kHz)

NAVAREA I (UK)

(M) Oostende (518 kHz)
(T) Oostende (518 kHz)

NAVAREA II (France)

(E) Niton (518 kHz)
(K) Niton (518 kHz)
(I) Niton (490 kHz)
(T) Niton (490 kHz)

(A) Corsen (518 kHz)
(E) Corsen (490 kHz)

(W) La Garde (518 kHz)
(S) La Garde (490 kHz)

(D) La Coruña (518 kHz)
(W) La Coruña (490 kHz)

NAVAREA III (Spain)

(R) Monsanto (518 kHz)
(G) Monsanto (490 kHz)

(T) Cagliari (518 kHz)
(X) Valencia (518 kHz)
(M) Valencia (490 kHz)

(G) Tarifa (518 kHz)
(T) Tarifa (490 kHz)

WEATHER

UK 518 kHz stations

The times (UT) of weather messages are in bold; the times of an extended outlook (a further 2 or 3 days beyond the shipping forecast period) are in italics.

G –	**Cullercoats**	*0100*	0500	**0900**	1300	1700	**2100**
	Fair Isle clockwise to Thames, excluding N & S Utsire, Fisher and German Bight.							
O –	**Portpatrick**	*0220*	**0620**	1020	1420	**1820**	2220
	Lundy clockwise to SE Iceland.							
E –	**Niton**	*0040*	0440	**0840**	1240	1640	**2040**
	Thames clockwise to Fastnet, excluding Trafalgar.							

UK 490 kHz stations (in yellow) provide forecasts for UK inshore waters, a national 3 day outlook for inshore waters and, at times in bold, reports of actual weather at some or all of the places listed below. To receive these reports select message category 'V' on the receiver. Times (UT) are listed in chronological order. Reports include some or all of: Sea level pressure (hPa/mb), wind direction and speed (kn), weather, visibility (M), air and sea temperatures (°C), dewpoint temperature (°C) and mean wave height (m).

C – Portpatrick Land's End to Shetland   **0020 0420** 0820 **1220 1620** 2020
N Rona, Stornoway, S Uist, Lusa (Skye), Tiree, Macrihanish, Belfast, Malin Hd, Belmullet, St Bees Hd, Ronaldsway, Crosby, Valley, Aberporth, Roches Pt, Valentia, St Mawgan.

I – Niton The Wash to St David's Head   **0120** 0520 **0920 1320** 1720 **2120**
Sandettie Lt V, Greenwich Lt V, Solent, Hurn airport, Guernsey airport, Jersey airport, Portland, Channel Lt V, Plymouth, Culdrose, Seven Stones Lt V, St Mawgan & Roches Pt.

U – Cullercoats Cape Wrath to N Foreland **0320** 0720 **1120 1520** 1920 **2320**
Sandettie Lt V, Manston, Shoeburyness, Weybourne, Donna Nook, Boulmer, Leuchars, Aberdeen, Lossiemouth, Wick, Kirkwall, Lerwick, Foula, K7 Met buoy, Sule Skerry.

Navtex coverage abroad

Selected Navtex stations in Metareas I and II, with identity codes and transmission times, are listed below. Times of weather messages are shown in **bold**. Gale warnings are usually transmitted 4 hourly.

METAREA I (Co-ordinator – UK)	Transmission times (UT)					
K – **Niton** (Note 1)	0140	0540	0940	1340	1740	2140
L – Pinneberg, Hamburg	*0150*	*0550*	*0950*	*1350*	*1750*	*2150*
M – **Oostende**, Belgium (Note 2)	0200	0600	1000	1400	1800	2200
P – **Netherlands CG**, Den Helder	**0230**	0630	1030	**1430**	1830	2230
Q – **Malin Head**, Eire	0240	**0640**	**1040**	1440	**1840**	2240
S – **Pinneberg**, Hamburg	**0300**	**0700**	**1100**	**1500**	**1900**	**2300**
T – **Oostende**, Belgium (Note 3)	0310	**0710**	1110	1510	**1910**	2310
W – **Valentia**, Eire	0340	**0740**	**1140**	1540	**1940**	2340

Notes:
1 In English, no weather; only Nav warnings for waters from Cap Gris Nez to Île de Bréhat.
2 No weather information, only Nav warnings for NavArea Juliett.
3 Forecasts and strong wind warnings for Thames and Dover, plus Nav info for Belgium.

METAREA II (Co-ordinator – France)						
A – **Corsen**, Le Stiff, France	0000	0400	0800	**1200**	1600	2000
E – Corsen, Le Stiff, France (In French)	*0040*	*0440*	*0840*	*1240*	*1640*	*2040*
D – **Coruña**, Spain	0030	0430	**0830**	1230	1630	**2030**
W – Coruña, Spain (in Spanish)	*0340*	*0740*	*1140*	*1540*	*1940*	*2340*
F – **Horta**, Açores, Portugal	**0050**	0450	**0850**	**1250**	1650	**2050**
J – Horta, Açores, (In Portuguese)	*0130*	*0530*	*0930*	*1330*	*1730*	*2130*
G – **Tarifa**, Spain (English & Spanish)	0100	0500	0900	1300	1700	2100
T – Tarifa, Spain (in Spanish)	*0310*	*0710*	*1110*	*1510*	*1910*	*2310*
R – **Monsanto**, Portugal	**0250**	**0650**	**1050**	**1450**	**1850**	**2250**
G – Monsanto, Portugal (In Portuguese)	*0100*	*0500*	*0900*	*1300*	*1700*	*2100*

WEATHER BY TELEPHONE

Marinecall offers 3 types of recorded forecasts as shown below. You can use Marinecall from any landline or mobile network within the UK (inc Channel Islands).

Actual weather

Current weather, updated hourly, gives hourly summaries for next 6 hours at over 160 locations around the UK. Dial **09068 969** + the required area number below.

5-day forecasts for Inshore waters

For UK inshore areas, call **09068 969** + the **Area number** shown below. For an inshore waters forecast covering the whole UK for 3 to 5 days ahead, dial **09068 969** 640.

Forecasts cover the waters out to 12M offshore for up to 5 days and include: General situation, strong wind or gale warnings in force, wind, weather, visibility, sea state, max air temp and mean sea temp.

The local inshore forecast for Shetland is only available from Shetland CG ☎ 01595 692976. 09068 calls cost 60p/min from a landline.

Offshore planning forecasts

For 2 to 5-day planning forecasts for offshore areas, updated by 0700, call **09068 969** + the number for the offshore area:

657 English Channel. **658** S North Sea. **659** Irish Sea. **660** Biscay. **661** NW Scotland **662** Northern North Sea

For further information contact:

Marinecall Customer Services, Avalon House, 57-63 Scrutton St, London EC2A 4PF. ☎ 0871 200 3985; ✉ 0870 600 4229. www.marinecall.co.uk   marinecall@itouch.co.uk

European weather by phone & Fax

Marinecall offers forecasts, updated 2x daily, of wind, cloud, temperature, visibility and general conditions for the European areas below.

For recorded bulletins call 09064 700 plus the 3 digit suffix below. Calls cost 60p/min.

For fax call 09065 501 and the 3 digit suffix. Calls cost £1.00/min.

NE France
☎ 421, ✉ 611

N France
☎ 422, ✉ 612

N Brittany
☎ 423, ✉ 613

S Brittany
☎ 424, ✉ 614

S Biscay
☎ 425, ✉ 615

N & W Spain
☎ 426, ✉ 616

SW Spain
☎ 427, ✉ 617

Portugal
☎ 428, ✉ 618

Inshore & offshore forecast areas by telephone

WEATHER

Telephone recordings
☎ 09068 9696 + Area No

Weather by Fax
✉ 09065 2223 + Area No

61

54 Ardnamurchan Point to Cape Wrath

41 Cape Wrath to Rattray Head

62

42 Rattray Head to Berwick-upon-Tweed

53 Mull of Kintyre to Ardnamurchan Point

58

52 Mull of Galloway to the Mull of Kintyre

43 Berwick-upon-Tweed to Whitby

55 Loch Foyle to Carlingford Lough

59   51 Great Ormes Head to Mull of Galloway

44 Whitby to Gibraltar Point

45 Gibraltar Point to North Foreland

50 St Davids Head to Great Ormes Head

49 Hartland Point St Davids Head

46 North Foreland to Selsey Bill

47 Selsey Bill to Lyme Regis

60   48 Lyme Regis to Hartland Point

57

WEATHER BY FAX

Inshore and offshore forecasts by fax are available at Standard (£1/min) and Advance levels of service (£1.50/min). The Fax numbers given are for the Advance service.

Inshore waters forecasts

• The 2 page Standard inshore forecast is for up to 48 hrs and includes synoptic charts for today and tomorrow.

The forecast includes any gale and strong wind warnings, the general situation, wind speed/direction, strength of gusts, weather, visibility and sea state.

• The 3 page Advance inshore forecast includes the above, plus a tabulated hourly forecast over the next 6 hrs for 4 key places in the Area.

• To obtain the Advance inshore forecast dial 🖥 **09065 222** + the Area No above. For a National inshore 3–5 day forecast dial 🖥 **09065 222 340**.

Offshore planning forecasts

• The 2 page Standard offshore forecast includes 2–5 day planning forecasts and 2–5 day synoptic charts for the offshore Areas. The forecast includes wind, weather, visibility and sea states.

• The 3 page Advance offshore forecast includes the above, plus four diagrams showing contours of significant wave heights in the forecast area. It takes about 6 mins to receive/print.

• To obtain the Advance offshore forecast dial 🖥 **09065 222** + Area Number required.

WEATHER BY MOBILE PHONE

Use your mobile to obtain forecasts by:

• **SMS** (Short Message Service, or texting). A message includes: current weather and a forecast for 6 hrs later, at one of 161 coastal locations (below); updated hrly. Format: Location, date, time; max temp °C; mean wind direction/speed; visibility; % risk of precipitation. For example:

> Exmouth: 1/4/09
>
> 10am: 11c, WD 250d, WS 12kt, VIS 17.59km, RAIN 10%.
>
> 4pm: 12c, WD 290d, WS 14kt, VIS 13.50km, RAIN 12%.

To obtain this message, by return @ 25p per message, type **AC** and the location's name; then send it to 83141.

Or, for data received by 0900 daily @ £1.50 for 6 messages, type **AC Sub** and location's name; send it to 83141.

The message also contains an embedded Marinecall Tel No; press 'Dial' for a 2–5 day recorded forecast as in 5.8.2.

Coastal locations in Areas 1–11 and 15 are listed alphabetically below.

Area 1, SW England

Anvil Point	Newton Ferrers
Brixham	Penzance
Dart marina	Plymouth
Exmouth	Portland Bill
Falmouth	Salcombe
Fowey	St Mary's (Scilly)
Helford River	Start Point
Lizard Point	Torquay
Longships	Weymouth
Lyme Regis	

Area 2, S England

Bembridge	Poole
Buckler's Hard	Portsmouth
Chichester	St Catherine's Point
Christchurch	Solent
Cowes	Southampton
Hamble Point	Southsea
Lymington	Wootton Creek
Needles Fairway	Yarmouth (IoW)

Area 3, SE England

Brighton	Newhaven
Dover	Ramsgate
Dungeness	Rye
Eastbourne	Selsey Bill
Littlehampton	Shoreham

Area 4, E England

Bradwell marina	Lowestoft
Brightlingsea	North Foreland
Burnham-on-Crouch	Orford Ness
Chatham	Sheerness
Great Yarmouth	Southend-on-sea
Ipswich	Southwold
Landguard Point	Tidemill
London	Walton-on-the-Naze

Area 5, NE England

Amble	Holy Island
Berwick-upon-Tweed	Hull
Blyth	Kings Lynn
Boston	Royal Quays marina
Cromer	Spurn Head
Flamborough Head	Sunderland
Grimsby	Wells-next-the-Sea
Hartlepool	Whitby

Area 6, SE Scotland

Aberdeen	Peterhead
Dundee	Port Edgar
Eyemouth	Stonehaven
Montrose	

Area 7, NE Scotland

Caledonian Canal	Lossiemouth
Cape Wrath	Whitehills
Duncansby Head	Wick

Area 8, NW Scotland

Craobh marina	Oban
Iona	Tobermory

Area 9, SW Scotland

Ardrossan	Lamlash
Burrow Head	Largs
Campbeltown	Mull of Kintyre
East Loch Tarbert	Portpatrick
Kip marina	Rhu marina
Kirkcudbright	Troon

Area 10, NW England

Beaumaris	Liverpool
Caernarfon	Maryport
Conwy	Preston
Glasson Dock	Whitehaven
Holyhead	Wyre Dock (Fleetwood)

Area 11, Wales – Land's End

Aberystwyth	Padstow
Bardsey Island	Penarth (Cardiff)
Bristol	Portishead
Milford Dock	Pwllheli
Newquay (Cornwall)	Swansea

Area 15, Channel Islands

Channel Isles	Jersey
Guernsey	

METMARINE, a wholly separate company from Marinecall, sends Area forecasts to your mobile by texting. Metmarine contact details are:

☎ +44 (0)207 6177817;
info@metmarine.com:
www.metmarine.com

• Current coverage is the UK S coast, French N and W coasts and the Mediterranean coasts of Spain and France, Greece and Turkey). Messages are in English and require a UK-registered mobile (foreign mobile networks are planned); no prior registration is needed.

• To request a forecast, text MET followed by a space before the code for the required area; then send it to 80818, whether you are in the UK or abroad.

For example, to obtain Area 'Brest to Ploumanac'h', text MET FR13 and send to 80818. The forecasts will appear on your mobile without delay.

• An area forecast contains up to 3 text messages each costing £1: the first message covers Today (12 hr period), the second Tonight (12 hrs) and the third Tomorrow (12 hrs). Costs are billed direct to the mobile account.

• Forecasts for coastal waters out to 20M offshore are valid for 36 hrs and updated every 6 hours. Contents include: Time/date; pressure and trend; wind direction/strength and tendency; visibility and weather; air and sea temperatures.

For example:

Message 1
Today from 0700 BST 10/9/08. 1008mb rising slowly to 1009mb. Wind NE2, backing NNE2. Visibility good, drizzle.
Max temp 23°C. Sea temp 17°C.

Message 2
Tonight from 1900 BST 10/9/08. 1011mb rising slowly to 1012mb. Wind E1, backing NNE2. Visibility good, drizzle. Min temp 16°C. Sea temp 17°C.

Message 3
Tomorrow from 0700 BST 11/9/08. 1014mb rising slowly to 1016mb. Wind NNE2, backing N2. Visibility good, over-cast. Min temp 20°C. Sea temp 17°C.

The N and W coasts of France are divided into 14 Areas as listed below:

Code	Boundaries
FR13	Brest to Ploumanac'h
FR14	Ploumanac'h to Cap Fréhel
FR15	Cap Fréhel to Granville
FR16	Channel Islands to Cherbourg
FR17	Cherbourg to Courseulles
FR18	Courseulles to St Valéry-en-Caux
FR19	St Valéry-en-Caux to Étaples
UK1	Étaples to Calais
FR6	Spanish border to Arcachon
FR7	Arcachon to Pointe de Grave
FR8	Pte de Grave to Sables d'Olonne
FR9	Sables d'Olonne to Pte de Croisic
FR10	Pointe de Croisic to Lorient
FR11	Lorient to Pointe de Penmarc'h
FR12	Pointe de Penmarc'h to Brest

OTHER WEATHER SOURCES

Internet www.metoffice.com (UK Met Office site) has 2 day and 3–5 day inshore forecasts, 2–5 day planning data, shipping forecasts, gale warnings, coastal reports, surface pressure charts and satellite images. Other UK weather sites and foreign Met Offices provide further data.

Press Some national and regional papers include a synoptic chart which can help to interpret the shipping forecast.

Television Most TV forecasts show a synoptic chart and satellite pictures – a useful guide to the weather situation. In remote areas abroad a TV forecast in a bar, café or even shop window may be the best or only source of weather data.

In the UK Ceefax (BBC) gives the weather index on Ceefax page 400, weather warnings on page 405 and inshore waters forecasts on page 409.

Teletext (ITN) has general forecasts on page 151, shipping forecasts on page 157 and inshore waters forecasts on page 158.

Broadcasts of shipping and inshore waters forecasts by HM Coastguard

HM CG Centres routinely broadcast MSI every 3 hours at the local times below.

Each broadcast contains one of 3 different Groups of MSI:

Group A, the full broadcast, contains the Shipping forecast, a new Inshore waters forecast and 24 hrs outlook, Gale warnings, a 3 day forecast for Fishermen in the winter months*, Navigational (WZ) warnings and Subfacts & Gunfacts where relevant ‡. 'A' broadcast times are in bold type.

Group B contains a new Inshore waters forecast, plus the previous outlook, and Gale warnings. 'B' broadcast times are in plain type.

Group C is a repeat of the Inshore forecast and Gale warnings (as per the previous Group A or B) plus new Strong wind warnings. 'C' broadcast times are italicised.

Notes
*Fisherman's 3 day forecast (1 Oct–31 Mar).
‡ Subfacts & Gunfacts.

Coastguard	Shipping forecast areas	Inshore areas	B	C	A	C	B	C	A	C
South Coast			B	C	A	C	B	C	A	C
Falmouth‡	Portland, Plymouth, Sole, Shannon, Fastnet	8, 9	0110	*0410*	**0710**	*1010*	1310	*1610*	**1910**	*2210*
Brixham‡	Same as Falmouth CG	8, 9	0110	*0410*	**0710**	*1010*	1310	*1610*	**1910**	*2210*
Portland	Plymouth, Portland, Wight	6–8	0130	*0430*	**0730**	*1030*	1330	*1630*	**1930**	*2230*
Solent	Plymouth, Portland, Wight	6–8	0130	*0430*	**0730**	*1030*	1330	*1630*	**1930**	*2230*
Dover	Dover, Wight, Thames, Humber	5, 6	0110	*0410*	**0710**	*1010*	1310	*1610*	**1910**	*2210*
East Coast			B	C	A	C	B	C	A	C
Thames	Dover, Wight, Thames, Humber	5, 6	0110	*0410*	**0710**	*1010*	1310	*1610*	**1910**	*2210*
Yarmouth	Humber, German Bight, Dogger, Tyne	3–5	0150	*0450*	**0750**	*1050*	1350	*1650*	**1950**	*2250*
Humber	Same as Yarmouth CG	3–5	0150	*0450*	**0750**	*1050*	1350	*1650*	**1950**	*2250*
Forth	Tyne, Forth, Cromarty, Forties, Fair Isle	1, 2	0130	*0430*	**0730**	*1030*	1330	*1630*	**1930**	*2230*
Aberdeen‡	Same as Forth CG	1, 2	0130	*0430*	**0730**	*1030*	1330	*1630*	**1930**	*2230*
Shetland	Cromarty, Viking, Fair Isle, Faeroes	1, 16	0110	*0410*	**0710**	*1010*	1310	*1610*	**1910**	*2210*
West Coast			B	C	A	C	B	C	A	C
Stornoway‡	Rockall, Malin, Hebrides, Bailey, Fair Is, Faeroes, SE Iceland	16	0110	*0410*	**0710**	*1010*	1310	*1610*	**1910**	*2210*
Clyde‡	Rockall, Malin, Hebrides, Bailey	14, 15	0210	*0510*	**0810**	*1110*	1410	*1710*	**2010**	*2310*
Belfast‡	Irish Sea, Malin	12–14	0110	*0410*	**0710**	*1010*	1310	*1610*	**1910**	*2210*
Liverpool	Irish Sea	11, 12	0130	*0430*	**0730**	*1030*	1330	*1630*	**1930**	*2230*
Holyhead	Irish Sea	10, 11	0150	*0450*	**0750**	*1050*	1350	*1650*	**1950**	*2250*
Milford Hvn	Lundy, Fastnet, Irish Sea	9, 10	0150	*0450*	**0750**	*1050*	1350	*1650*	**1950**	*2250*
Swansea	Lundy, Fastnet, Irish Sea	9, 10	0150	*0450*	**0750**	*1050*	1350	*1650*	**1950**	*2250*

MSI broadcasts are transmitted via remote aerial sites geographically selected to give optimum coverage. The table below lists their positions and the VHF broadcast channel to be used. It will be one of channels 10, 23, 84 or 86 and is also specified in a prior announcement on Ch 16.

To minimise the risk of missing a broadcast, pre-select Ch 16 on Dual watch with the relevant (clearest) channel; and/or monitor the prior announcement to verify the working channel. **MF frequencies** (kHz), as quoted below, are also used for the broadcasts, primarily for fishermen.

Falmouth CG

Trevose Head	84	50°33′N 05°02′W
St Mary's (Scilly)	86	49°56′N 06°18′W
Lizard*	2226kHz, 23	49°58′N 05°12′W
Falmouth	84	50°09′N 05°03′W

Brixham CG

Fowey	10	50°20′N 04°38′W
Rame Head	86	50°19′N 04°13′W
East Prawle	84	50°13′N 03°42′W
Dartmouth	10	50°21′N 03°35′W
Berry Head	23	50°24′N 03°29′W

Portland CG

Beer Head	86	50°41′N 03°05′W
Grove Pt (Portland Bill)	84	50°33′N 02°25′W

Solent CG

Needles	86	50°39′N 01°35′W
Boniface (Ventnor, IoW)	23	50°36′N 01°12′W
Newhaven	86	50°47′N 00°03′E

Dover CG

Fairlight (Hastings)	84	50°52′N 00°39′E
Langdon (Dover)	86	51°08′N 01°21′E

Thames CG

Shoeburyness	23	51°31′N 00°47′E
Bradwell (R Blackwater)	86	51°44′N 00°53′E
Walton-on-the-Naze	23	51°51′N 01°17′E
Bawdsey (R Deben)	84	52°00′N 01°25′E

Yarmouth CG

Lowestoft	23	52°29′N 01°46′E
Great Yarmouth	86	52°36′N 01°43′E
Trimingham (Cromer)	23	52°54′N 01°21′E
Langham (Blakeney)	86	52°57′N 00°58′E
Guy's Head (Wisbech)	23	52°48′N 00°13′E

Humber CG

Easington (Spurn Hd)	86	53°39′N 00°06′E
Flamborough*	2226kHz, 23	54°07′N 00°05′W
Ravenscar	86	54°24′N 00°30′W
Hartlepool	23	54°42′N 01°10′W
Cullercoats (Blyth)	86	55°04′N 01°28′W
Newton	23	55°31′N 01°37′W

Forth CG

St Abbs/Cross Law	86	55°54′N 02°12′W
Craigkelly (Burntisland)	23	56°04′N 03°14′W
Fife Ness	84	56°17′N 02°35′W
Inverbervie	23	56°51′N 02°16′W

Aberdeen CG

Greg Ness*	2226kHz, 86	57°08′N 02°03′W

Windyheads Hill	23	57°39′N 02°14′W
Rosemarkie (Cromarty)	86	57°38′N 04°05′W
Noss Head (Wick)	84	58°29′N 03°03′W
Durness (Loch Eriboll)	23	58°34′N 04°44′W

Shetland CG

Wideford Hill (Kirkwall)	86	58°59′N 03°01′W
Fitful Head (Sumburgh)	23	59°54′N 01°23′W
Lerwick (Shetland)	84	60°10′N 01°08′W
Collafirth*	2226kHz, 86	60°32′N 01°23′W
Saxa Vord (Unst)	23	60°42′N 00°51′W

Stornoway CG

Butt of Lewis	1743kHz, 86	58°28′N 06°14′W
Portnaguran (Stornoway)	84	58°15′N 06°10′W
Forsnaval (W Lewis)	23	58°13′N 07°00′W
Melvaig (Loch Ewe)	23	57°50′N 05°47′W
Rodel (S Harris)	86	57°45′N 06°57′W
Clettreval (N Uist)	84	57°37′N 07°26′W
Skriag (Portree, Skye)	84	57°23′N 06°15′W
Drumfearn (SE Skye)	86	57°12′N 05°48′W
Barra	10	57°01′N 07°30′W
Arisaig (S of Mallaig)	23	56°55′N 06°50′W

Clyde CG

Glengorm (N Mull)	23	56°38′N 06°08′W
Tiree	1883kHz, 86	56°31′N 06°57′W
Torosay (E Mull)	10	56°27′N 05°43′W
Clyde CG (Greenock)	84	55°58′N 04°48′W
South Knapdale (Loch Fyne)	23	55°55′N 05°28′W
Kilchiaran (W Islay)	84	55°46′N 06°27′W
Lawhill (Ardrossan)	86	55°42′N 04°50′W
Rhu Staffnish (Kintyre)	10	55°22′N 05°32′W

Belfast CG

Navar (Lower L Erne)	86	54°28′N 07°54′W
Limvady (Lough Foyle)	84	55°06′N 06°53′W
West Torr (Fair Head)	86	55°12′N 06°06′W
Black Mountain (Belfast)	23	54°35′N 06°01′W
Orlock Point (Bangor)	84	54°40′N 05°35′W
Slievemartin (Rostrevor)	86	54°06′N 06°10′W

Liverpool CG

Caldbeck (Carlisle)	23	54°46′N 03°07′W
Snaefell (Isle of Man)	86	54°16′N 04°28′W
Langthwaite (Lancaster)	84	54°02′N 02°46′W
Moel-y-Parc (Anglesey)	23	53°13′N 04°28′W

Holyhead CG

Great Ormes Head	86	53°20′N 03°51′W
South Stack (Holyhead)	23	53°19′N 04°41′W

Continued overleaf

WEATHER

WEATHER

Milford Haven CG			Swansea CG		
Blaenplwyf			Mumbles	86	51°34'N 03°59'W
(Aberystwyth)	84	52°22'N 04°06'W	St Hilary (Barry)	23	51°27'N 03°25'W
Dinas Hd (Fishguard)	86	52°00'N 04°54'W	Severn Bridges	86	51°36'N 02°38'W
St Ann's Head	84	51°40'N 05°11'W	Combe Martin	23	51°12'N 04°03'W
Monkstone (Tenby)	84	51°42'N 04°41'W	Hartland Point	86	51°01'N 04°31'W

Inshore waters forecasts: Area boundaries used by the Coastguard

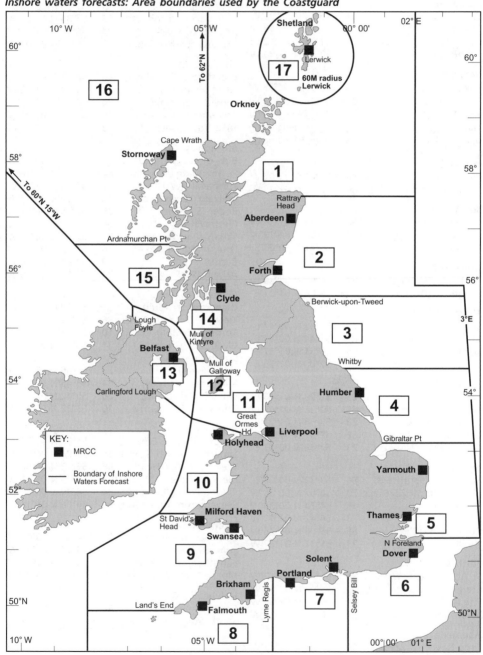

CHANNEL ISLANDS
Jersey Meteorological department
From the CI and UK call ☎ 0900 665 0022 for the Channel Islands recorded shipping forecast. From France call ☎ +44 1534 448787. For Guernsey only, call ☎ 06969 8800; it is chargeable. For more detailed info call ☎ +44 1534 745550, 📠 746351.

Forecasts include: general situation, 24hr forecast for wind, weather, vis, sea state, swell, sea temperature, plus 2 & 4 day outlooks and St Helier tide times/heights. The area is bounded by 50°N, 03°W and the mainland from Cap de la Hague to Ile de Bréhat.

Weather broadcasts and bulletins
BBC Radio Guernsey 93·2 MHz, 1116 kHz
Bulletins for the waters around Guernsey, Herm and Sark are broadcast Mon-Fri at 0630, 0730 and 0830 LT; Sat/Sun at 0730 and 0830 LT. They contain forecast, synopsis, coastal forecast, storm warnings and wind strength.
In the summer coastal reports are included from: Portland, Chan lt V, Alderney, Guernsey, Jersey, Cherbourg, Cap de la Hague and Dinard.

BBC Radio Jersey 1026 kHz, 88·8 MHz.
Storm warnings on receipt. Wind info for Jersey waters: Mon-Fri 0725, 0825, 1325, 1725 LT; Sat/Sun 0825.
Shipping forecast for local waters: Mon-Fri @ H+00 (0600-1900, after the news) and 0625 & 1825 LT; Sat/Sun @ H+00 (0700-1300, after the news) and 0725 LT.

Jersey Coastguard Ch 25, 82. Gale warnings at 0307, 0907, 1507, 2107UT. Gale warnings, synopsis, 24h forecast, outlook for next 24 hrs, plus reports from observation stations, are broadcast on request and at 0645*, 0745*, 0845*, 1245, 1845, 2245 UT; *broadcast 1 hr earlier when DST in force

IRELAND
Met Éireann (Irish Met Office) is at Glasnevin Hill, Dublin 9, Ireland. ☎ 1 806 4250, 📠 1 806 4250, www.met.ie. General forecasting division: ☎ 1 806 4255, 📠 1 806 4275 (H24, charges may apply).

Coast radio stations
CRS and their VHF channels are listed below (anti-clockwise from Malin Head) and shown overleaf. Weather bulletins for 30M offshore and the Irish Sea are broadcast on VHF at 0103, 0403, 0703, 1003, 1303, 1603, 1903 and 2203UT after an announcement on Ch 16. Broadcasts are made 1 hour earlier when DST is in force. Bulletins include gale warnings, synopsis and a 24-hour forecast.

Malin Head	23	Bantry	23
Glen Head	24	Mizen Head	04
Donegal Bay	02	Cork	26
Belmullet	83	Mine Head	83
Clifden	26	Rosslare	23
Galway	04	Wicklow Head	02
Shannon	28	Dublin	83
Valentia	24	Carlingford	04

Gale warnings are broadcast on these VHF channels on receipt and at 0033, 0633, 1233 and 1833 UT, after an announcement Ch 16.

MF Valentia Radio broadcasts forecasts for sea areas Shannon and Fastnet on 1752 kHz at 0833 & 2033 UT, and on request.

Gale warnings are broadcast on 1752 kHz on receipt and at 0303, 0903, 1503 and 2103 (UT) after an announcement on 2182 kHz.

Malin Head does not broadcast weather information on 1677 kHz. At Dublin there is no MF transmitter.

Radio Telefís Éireann (RTE) Radio 1
RTE Radio 1 broadcasts weather bulletins daily at 0602, 1253, 1650 & 2355LT on 252kHz (LW) Summerhill (15M W ofDublin airport) and FM (88·2-95·2MHz).

Bulletins contain a situation, forecast and coastal reports. Forecasts include: wind, weather, vis, swell (if higher than 4m) and a 24 hrs outlook.

Gale warnings are included in hourly news bulletins on FM & MF.

Coastal reports include wind, weather, visibility, pressure and pressure tendency. The change over the last 3 hrs is described as:

Steady	= 0–0·4hPa
Rising/falling slowly	= 0·5–1·9
Rising/falling	= 2·0–3·4
Rising/falling rapidly	= 3·5–5·9
Rising/falling very rapidly	= > 6·0

Weather by telephone
The latest sea area forecast and gale warnings are available as recorded messages H24 from Weatherdial. Dial ☎

1550 123 plus the suffixes below:

850	Munster
851	Leinster
852	Connaught
853	Ulster
854	Dublin (plus winds in Dublin Bay and HW times)
855	Coastal waters and Irish Sea.

Weather by fax

Similar information, plus isobaric, swell and wave charts and any small craft warnings (>F6 up to 10M offshore; Apr-Sep inc) is available H24 by Weatherdial Fax.

Dial 📠 1550 131 838 (from within ROI only). From the menu below select the required 4-digit product code (see 0400 for full listing):

0015: Latest analysis chart
0016: Forecast valid for next 24 hrs

0017: Forecast valid for next 36 hrs
0018: Forecast valid for next 48 hrs
0021: Forecasts for coastal waters and Irish Sea
0031, 0032, 0033, 0034: Forecast (days 1-4) for sea/swell wave hts/periods

5-day forecasts (plain language, farming/national) 0001: Munster. 0002: Leinster. 0003: Connaught. 0004: Ulster. 0005: Dublin.

Sea Planners provide graphic forecasts for up to 5 days (updated at 0430 daily) of expected winds and waves at the following seven offshore positions:

0041:	53°N	05°30'W
0042:	51°N	06°W
0043:	51°N	10°30'W
0044:	53°N	11°W
0045:	54°N	11°W
0046:	55°N	10°W
0047:	56°N	08°W

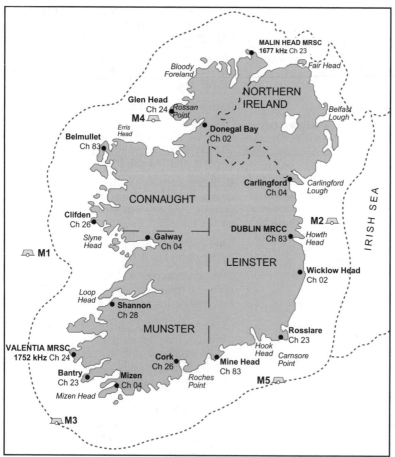

Provinces, headlands, sea areas and coastal stations referred to in weather broadcasts are shown here. Forecasts for coastal waters cover areas within 30M of the shore.

DENMARK

Gale warnings and forecasts are broadcast on receipt, on request and at 0133, 0533, 0933, 1333, 1733, 2133 UT in Danish/English by remote CRS, callsign *Lyngby Radio:*

Areas	VHF Channels
2 South Baltic	02, 04,
3 West Baltic	01, 02, 03, 04, 07, 28
4 The Belts & Sound	01, 02, 03, 04, 05, 07, 28, 65, 83
5 Kattegat	03, 04, 05, 07, 64, 65, 66, 83
6 Skagerrack	01, 02, 04, 64, 66
8 Fisher	01, 02, 23, 26
9 German Bight	02, 23

Forecast areas: see above. Skagen and Blåvand CRS broadcast on MF gale warnings for all areas on receipt.

Areas 2–5 are north of the Kiel Canal and east of 10°E.
MF: Blåvand 1734 kHz, Skagen 1758 kHz, Skamlebæk 1704 kHz and Rønne 2586 kHz broadcast gale warnings for all areas in Danish/**English** on receipt.

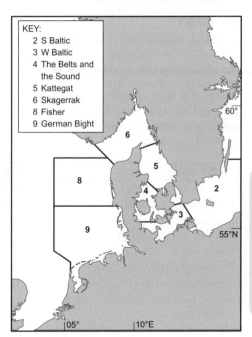

KEY:
2 S Baltic
3 W Baltic
4 The Belts and the Sound
5 Kattegat
6 Skagerrak
8 Fisher
9 German Bight

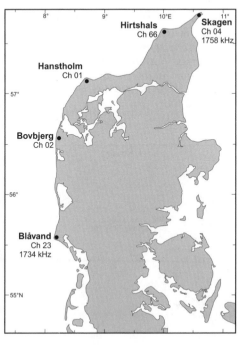

Hirtshals Ch 66
Skagen Ch 04 1758 kHz
Hanstholm Ch 01
Bovbjerg Ch 02
Blåvand Ch 23 1734 kHz

Danmarks Radio, Programme 1

Kalundborg (55°44'N 11°E) broadcasts on MW 1062 kHz:

• Gale warnings, weather reports and forecast for areas 2-6, 8, 9 at 0545, 0845, 1145, 1745LT.

• A 5 day forecast for areas 2-6, 8 and 9 at 1145 & 1745LT.

6.16.3 Danmarks Meteorologiske Institut (DM)

provides marine forecasts in Danish, **English** and German on www.dmi.dk/dmi/index/

GERMANY

Deutsche Wetterdienst (DWD)

DWD (German weather service) provides Met info through a databank which is updated twice daily; more often for weather reports and text forecasts.

DWD ☎ + 49 (0) 40 6690 1851. 🖷 + 49 (0) 40 6690 1946. www.dwd.de seeschifffahrt@dwd.de.

Traffic Centres

Traffic Centres, below, broadcast local storm warnings, weather bulletins, visibility (and when appropriate ice reports) in German or **English** on request.

Traffic Centre	VHF Ch	Every
German Bight Traffic	80	H+00
Cuxhaven-Elbe Traffic	71 (outer Elbe)	H+35
Brunsbüttel-Elbe Traffic	68 (lower Elbe)	H+05
Kiel Kanal II (E-bound)	02	H+15 & H+45
Kiel Kanal III (W-bound)	03	H+20 & H+50
Bremerhaven-Weser Traffic	02, 04, 05, 07, 21, 22, 82	H+20
Bremen-Weser Traffic	19, 78, 81	H+30
Hunte Traffic	63	H+30
Jade Traffic	20, 63	H+10
Ems Traffic	15, 18, 20, 21	H+50

Coast Radio Stations

DP07 (Seefunk) has commercial CRS, below, at:

Nordfriesland (Sylt) Ch 26. **Elbe-Weser** Ch 01, 24. **Hamburg** (Control centre) Ch 83. **Bremen** Ch 25. **Borkum** Ch 28.

DP07 broadcasts (only in German): gale and strong wind warnings on receipt. At 0745Ⓐ, 0945, 1245, 1645 and 1945Ⓐ UT for Fisher, German Bight and Humber, DP07 broadcasts: a synopsis, 12hr forecast, 24hrs outlook and coastal station reports. Ⓐsummer only. Also a 4–5 day outlook for the North Sea (and Baltic) at 0945 and 1645.

Radio broadcasting: Nord Deutscher Rundfunk (NDR)

NDR 1 Welle Nord (FM)

A summary, outlook and wind forecast for the German Bight are broadcast after the news at H (0600-2200LT) and at H +30 (0530-17300LT) by:

Sylt 90·9 MHz; **Helgoland** 88·9 MHz;

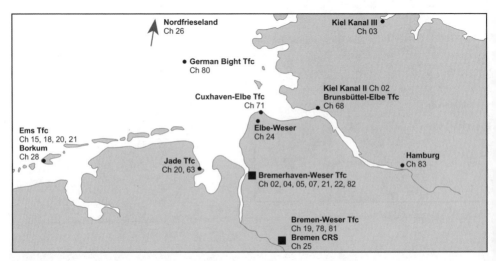

Hamburg 89·5 MHz; **Flensburg** 89·6 MHz; **Heide** 90·5 MHz; **Kiel** 91·3 MHz.

NDR Info (AM)
Synopsis, forecast and coastal station reports for the North Sea (and Baltic) are broadcast at 0005, 0830 and 2205 UT on 972 (Hamburg) & 702 (Flensburg) kHz.

Radio Bremen (MW and FM)
Warnings of extreme weather conditions in German Bight, with associated hazards, are broadcast after the news by: **Bremerhaven** 936 kHz; 89·3, 92·1, 95·4 & 100·8 MHz; and by **Bremen** 88·3, 93·8, 96·7 & 101·2 MHz.

Telephone forecasts (Marineweather)
For wind forecast and outlook (1 April – 30 Sept) call 0190 1160 (only within Germany) plus two digits for the following areas:

45	North Frisian Islands and Helgoland
46	R Elbe, Cuxhaven to Hamburg
47	Weser , Jade Bay and Helgoland
48	East Frisians and Ems Estuary
53	For pleasure craft

For year-round weather synopsis, forecast and outlook, call 0190 1169 plus two digits:

20	General information
21	North Sea and Baltic
22	German Bight, Fisher and SW North Sea
31	Reports for North Sea and Baltic

For the latest wind warnings (greater than F6) and storm warnings for individual areas of the North Sea coasts, call +49 40 66901209 (H24). If no warning is in force, a wind forecast for the German Bight, west and southern Baltic is given.

NETHERLANDS
VHF MSI broadcasts
Forecasts for 7 areas to 30M offshore and 3 inland waterways (IJsselmeer, Marken and Zierikzee) are broadcast in **English** and Dutch at 0805, 1305, 1905, 2305 LT on VHF as shown below, **without** prior announcement on Ch 16 or 70.

VHF Ch 23: Schiermonnikoog, Kornwerderzand, Wezep, Huisduinen (Den Helder), IJmuiden, Renesse, Woensdrecht.

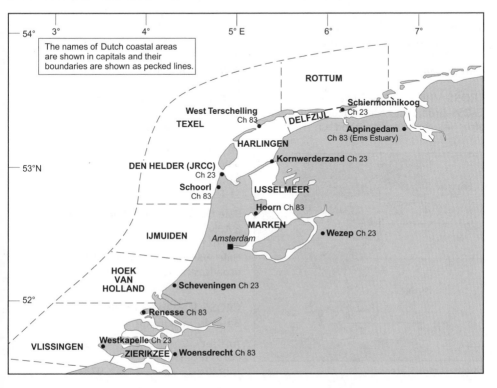

VHF Ch 83: Appingedam, West Terschelling, Hoorn, Schoorl, Scheveningen, Westkapelle. All stations monitor Ch 16.

MF weather broadcasts

Forecasts for areas Dover, Thames, Humber, German Bight, Dogger, Fisher, Forties and Viking are broadcast by Scheveningen in **English** at 0940 & 2140 UT on 3673 kHz. Gale warnings for these areas are broadcast in **English** on receipt and at 0333, 0733, 1133, 1533, 1933 and 2333 UT.

Radio Noord-Holland (FM)

Coastal forecasts for northern areas, gale warnings and wind strength are broadcast in Dutch, Mon-Fri at 0730, 0838, 1005, 1230 and 1705LT; Sat/Sun 1005, by: **Haarlem** 97.6 MHz and **Wieringermeer** 93.9 MHz.

Omroep Zeeland (FM)

Coastal forecasts for southern areas, synopsis, gale warnings and wind strength are broadcast in Dutch, Mon-Fri at 0715, 0915, 1215 and 1715LT; Sat/Sun 1015, by:

Philippine 97.8 MHz and **Goes** 101.9 MHz.

BELGIUM, Coast radio stations

Oostende Radio, after prior notice on VHF 16, DSC 70 and 2182kHz, broadcasts in **English** and Dutch on VHF 27, MF 2256, 2376 and 2761 kHz: Strong wind warnings on receipt and after the next 2 silent periods. Forecasts for Thames, Dover and the Belgian coast at 0720 LT and 0820, 1720 UT.

Antwerpen Radio broadcasts in **English** and Dutch on VHF Ch 24 for the Schelde estuary: Gale warnings on receipt and at every H+55. Also strong wind warnings (F6+) on receipt and at every H+55.

FRANCE

Le Guide Marine is a useful, free annual booklet which summarises the various means by which weather forecasts and warnings are broadcast or otherwise disseminated. It is available from marinas or Météo-France, 1 quai Branly, 75340 Paris. ☎ 01.45.56.74.36; 📠 01.45.56.71.70. marine@meteo.fr   www.meteo.fr

CROSS VHF and MF broadcasts

CROSS broadcasts Met bulletins in French, after an announcement on Ch 16. In the English Channel broadcasts can be given in English, on request Ch 16. Broadcasts include: Any gale warnings, general situation, 24 hrs forecast (actual weather, wind, sea state and vis) and further trends for coastal waters, which extend 20M offshore. VHF channels, remote stations and local times are shown below.

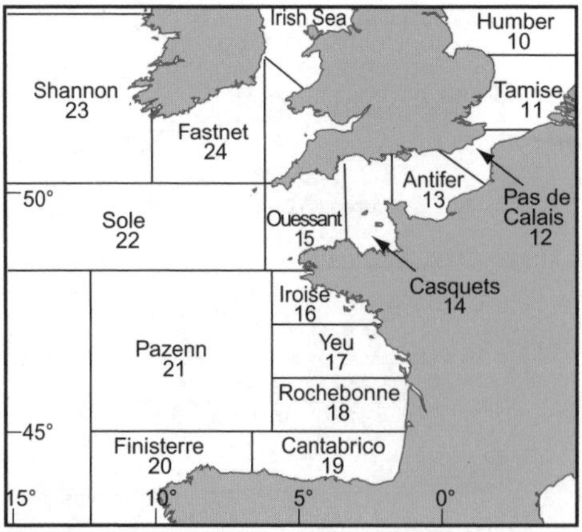

Gale warnings feature in Special Met Bulletins (*Bulletins Météorologiques Spéciaux* or BMS). They are broadcast in French by all CROSS on VHF at H+03 and at other times on MF frequencies as shown below.

CROSS GRIS-NEZ Ch 79
Belgian border to Baie de la Somme

Dunkerque	0720,	1603,	1920
St Frieux	0710,	1545,	1910

Baie de la Somme to Cap de la Hague
L'Ailly
0703, 1533, 1903
Gale warnings for areas 12-13 are broadcast in French on MF 1650 & 2677 kHz at 0833 & 2033LT

CROSS JOBOURG Ch 80
Baie de la Somme to Cap de la Hague

Antifer	0803,	1633,	2003
Port-en-Bessin	0745,	1615,	1945
Jobourg	0733,	1603,	1933

French forecast areas

CROSS JOBOURG *continued*

Cap de la Hague to Pointe de Penmarc'h

Jobourg	0715, 1545, 1915
Granville	0703, 1533, 1903

Gale warnings for areas 13-14 in **English** on receipt and at H+20 and H+50. No gale warnings on MF.

CROSS CORSEN Ch 79

Cap de la Hague to Pte de Penmarc'h
(Times in bold = 1 May to 30 Sep only).

Cap Fréhel	0545, 0803, **1203**, 1633, 2003
Bodic	0533, 0745, **1145**, 1615, 1945
Ile de Batz	0515, 0733, **1133**, 1603, 1933
Le Stiff	0503, 0715, **1115**, 1545, 1915

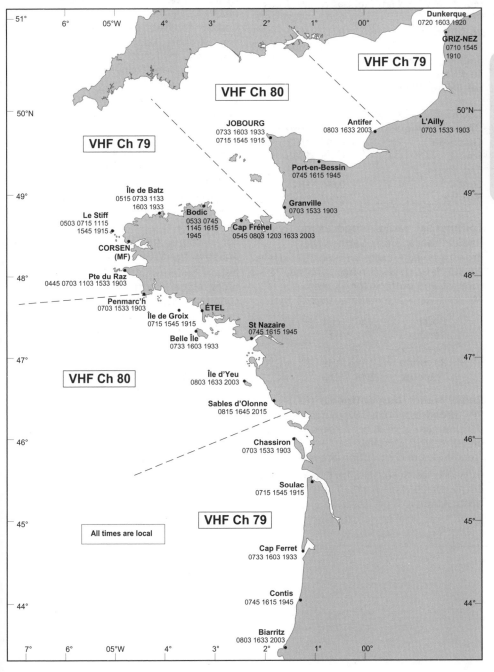

WEATHER

Pte du Raz   0445, 0703, **1103**, 1533, 1903 Corsen broadcasts gale warnings for areas 13-22 in French at 0815 and 2015LT on MF 1650 & 2677 khz.

CROSS ÉTEL Ch 80
Pte de Penmarc'h to l'Anse de l'Aiguillon
(46° 15'N 01°10'W). Étel has no MF freqs

Penmarc'h	0703, 1533, 1903
Ile de Groix	0715, 1545, 1915
Belle Ile	0733, 1603, 1933
Saint-Nazaire	0745, 1615, 1945
Ile d'Yeu	0803, 1633, 2003
Les Sables d'Olonne	0815, 1645, 2015

CROSS ÉTEL Ch 79
L'Anse de l'Aiguillon to Spanish border

Chassiron	0703, 1533, 1903
Soulac	0715, 1545, 1915
Cap Ferret	0733, 1603, 1933
Contis	0745, 1615, 1945
Biarritz	0803, 1633, 2003

Commercial radio broadcasting
Radio France (Inter-Service-Mer)
Broadcasts in French on LW 162 kHz at 2003LT daily: gale warnings, synopsis, 24 hrs forecast and outlook for all areas.
MF broadcasts are made at 0640LT by:

Brest	1404 kHz
Rennes	711 kHz
Bordeaux	1206 kHz
Bayonne	1494 kHz
Toulouse	945 kHz

Radio France Internationale (RFI)
RFI broadcasts gale warnings, synopsis, development and 24 hrs forecasts in French on HF at 1130 UT daily.
Frequencies and reception areas are:

6175 kHz: North Sea, English Channel, Bay of Biscay. 15300, 15515, 17570 and 21645 kHz: North Atlantic, E of 50°W.

See opposite for the High Seas forecast areas in the Eastern Atlantic.
Engineering bulletins giving any changes in frequency are transmitted between H+53 and H+00.

Local radio (FM)
Radio France Cherbourg broadcasts daily at 0829 LT:
Coastal forecast, gale warnings, visibility, wind strength, tidal information, small craft warnings, in French, for the Cherbourg peninsula on the following frequencies:

St Vaast-la-Hougue	85·0 MHz
Cherbourg	100·7 MHz
Cap de la Hague	99·8 MHz
Carteret	99·9 MHz

Forecasts by telephone
For recorded Inshore and Coastal forecasts. Dial 08·92·68·02·dd (dd is the number, as given, for the *département*); press the * key then 1 to access the main menu. Follow instructions:

For Inshore (*rivage*) or Coastal (*côte*) bulletins, say 'STOP' as your choice is spoken. Inshore bulletins contain 7 day forecasts, tide times, actual reports, sea temperature, surf conditions, etc.

Coastal bulletins contain strong wind/gale warnings, general synopsis, 24 hrs forecast and outlook. Five bulletins cover the N & W coasts, out to 20M offshore.

For Offshore bulletins (*large*), out to 200M offshore, dial ☎ 08·92·68·08·77. Select one of three offshore areas (English Channel & southern North Sea, Bay of Biscay or the N part of the western Mediterranean) by saying 'STOP' as it is named. Offshore bulletins contain strong wind/gale warnings, the general synopsis and forecast, and the outlook for up to 7 days.

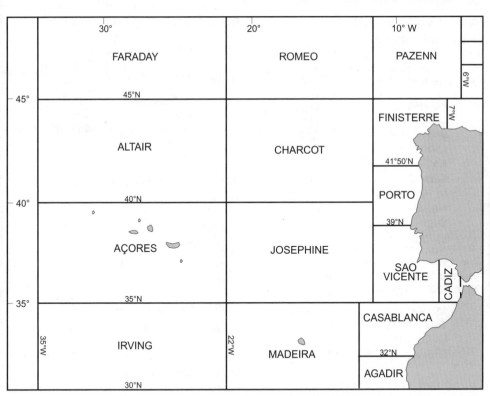

Forecast areas for the Eastern Atlantic and Coastal/Offshore Areas off France, Spain, Portugal and North West Africa

NOTES

NORTH WEST SPAIN

Coast radio stations
VHF weather warnings and 48h coastal forecasts are broadcast in Spanish at 0840, 1240 and 2010 UT by:

Pasajes	Ch 27
Bilbao	Ch 26
Santander	Ch 24
Cabo Peñas	Ch 26
Navia	Ch 60
Cabo Ortegal	Ch 02
La Coruña	Ch 26
Finisterre	Ch 22
Vigo	Ch 65
La Guardia	Ch 21

Gale warnings, synopsis and 24h/48h forecasts for Atlantic areas are broadcast on MF at 0703, 1303 and 1903 UT by:

Machichaco	1707 kHz
Cabo Peñas	1677 kHz
La Coruña	1698 kHz
Finisterre	1764 kHz

Coastguard weather broadcasts
Gale warnings and coastal forecasts are broadcast in Spanish and English on receipt and as listed below:

Bilbao*	Ch 10	4 hrly from 0033, except 0633
Santander	Ch 74	0245, 0445, 0645, 0845, 1045, 1445, 1845, 2245
Gijón	Ch 10	2 hrly (0215-2215)
Coruña	Ch 10	4 hrly from 0005
Finisterre	Ch 11	4 hrly from 0233
Vigo	Ch 10	4 hrly from 0015

*Bilbao also broadcasts High Seas gale warnings and forecasts 4 hourly from 0233.

Navtex
Coruna Navtex (D) transmits on 518 kHz at 0830 and 2030 UT: gale warnings, synopsis and the forecast for the following 24 hrs, valid out to 450M offshore.
Coruna Navtex (W) transmits in Spanish on 490 kHz at 1140 & 1940 UT: the same weather information as above.

Radio Nacional de España (MW)
Broadcasts storm warnings, synopsis and 12h or 18h forecasts for Cantábrico and Galicia at 1100, 1400, 1800 & 2200 LT in Spanish. Stations/frequencies are:

San Sebastián	774 kHz
Bilbao	639 kHz
Santander	855 kHz
Oviedo	729 kHz
La Coruña	639 kHz

Recorded telephone forecasts
This service is only available within Spain and for vessels equipped with Autolink. For a recorded weather bulletin in Spanish, call:

☎ 906 365 372 for the coasts of Cantábrico and Galicia.

☎ 906 365 374 for High Seas bulletins.

PORTUGAL AND THE AZORES

Broadcasts by Radionaval Portugal
Broadcasts in Portuguese and **English** are on Ch 11 at the times (UT) below. They contain:

Storm, gale and poor visibility warnings; synopsis and 24 hrs forecasts for three coastal zones out to 20M offshore; see opposite:

Leixões 0705, 1905
Coastal waters of N and Central zones.

Alges (also on MF 2657 kHz) 0905, 2105
Coastal waters of all 3 zones.

Faro 0805, 2005
Coastal waters of Central and S Zones.

Horta (Azores, LT) 0900, 2100
Waters off Faial, Pico, Graciosa, São Jorge and Terceira

Waters off Corvo and Flores 1000, 1900

Radiofusão Portuguesa
Broadcasts weather bulletins for coastal waters in Portuguese at 1100 UT. Stations (N-S) and frequencies are:

Porto	720 kHz
Viseu	666 kHz
Montemer (Coimbra)	630 kHz
Lisboa 1	666 kHz
Miranda do Douro	630 kHz
Elvas	720 kHz
Faro	97·6 MHz, 720 kHz

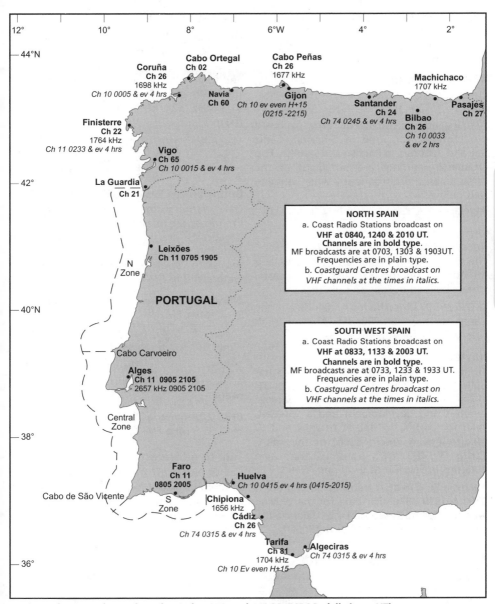

Spain and Portugal: MSI broadcasts by CRS and MRCCs/MRSCs (all times UT)

SOUTH WEST SPAIN

Coast radio stations

CRS broadcast gale warnings, synopsis, 24h and 48h forecasts for Atlantic and Mediterranean areas, in Spanish, at the times (UT) and on the VHF and MF frequencies shown below:

Chipiona	1656 kHz	0733	1233	1933
Cadiz	Ch 26	0833	1133	2003
Tarifa	Ch 81	0833	1133	2003
	1704 kHz	0733	1233	1933
Malaga	Ch 26	0833	1133	2003
Cabo Gata	Ch 27	0833	1133	2003

Continued overleaf

Coastguard broadcasts

Weather bulletins are broadcast in Spanish and **English** on the VHF channels and times (UT) below:

Huelva	Ch 10	4 hrly (0415-2015)
Cadiz	Ch 74	4 hrly from 0315
Tarifa	Ch 10, 67	Every even H+15.

Actual wind and visibility at Tarifa, followed by a forecast for Strait of Gibraltar, Cádiz Bay and Alborán, in **English** and Spanish. Fog (visibility) warnings are broadcast at the same times, more frequently when visibility falls below 2M.

Algeciras	Ch 74	4 hrly from 0315 and at 0515.

Recorded telephone forecasts

The service is only available within Spain and for Autolink-equipped vessels. For a coastal waters bulletin in Spanish call:

☎ 906 365 373 for Atlantic Andalucia and the Canaries.   ☎ 906 365 374 for High Seas bulletin for Atlantic areas.

Navtex

Tarifa (G, 518 kHz) transmits weather bulletins in English at 0900 and 2100 UT. These include: Gale warnings, general synopsis and development and a forecast, valid for 24 hrs, for the N Atlantic and W Mediterranean within 450M of the coast. Tarifa (T, 490 kHz) transmits the same bulletins in Spanish at 0710 and 1910 UT.

Valencia (X, 518 kHz) transmits in English at 0750 & 1950 UT similar data for the W Med within 450M of the coast. Ditto Valencia (M, 490 kHz) in Spanish at 1000 & 1800UT.

GIBRALTAR

Gibraltar Broadcasting Corporation (GBC) Gibraltar Radio broadcasts in English: General synopsis, situation, wind direction and force, visibility and sea state, radius 5M from Gibraltar. Frequencies are 1458 kHz, 91·3 MHz, 92·6 MHz and 100·5 MHz. Times (UT):

Mon-Fri:	0530, 0630, 0730, 1030, 1230
Sat:	0530, 0630, 0730, 1030
Sun:	0630, 0730, 1030

British Forces Broadcasting Service (BFBS)
Gale warnings for the Gibraltar area are broadcast on receipt by BFBS 1 and 2. All broadcasts are in English and comprise: Shipping forecast, wind, weather, visibility, sea state, swell, HW and LW times for waters within 5M of Gibraltar.

BFBS 1 frequencies and times (Local): 93·5, 97·8* MHz FM.

Mon-Fri:	0745, 0845, 1005, 1605
Sat:	0845, 0945, 1202
Sun:	0845, 0945, 1202, 1602

* This frequency is reported to have greater range.

BFBS 2 frequencies and time:
89·4, 99·5 MHz FM. Mon-Fri: 1200 Local time

Talk to a forecaster

Call ☎ 08700 767 818 to talk to a forecaster in Gibraltar about local weather in the Med or Canaries. Pay a flat rate of £17·00 by credit card, for a typical 5–10 mins briefing.

WEATHER VOCABULARY

English	German	French	Spanish	Dutch
Air mass	Luftmasse	Masse d'air	Massa de aire	Luchtmassa
Anticyclone	Antizyklonisch	Anticyclone	Anticiclón	Hogedrukgebied
Area	Gebiet	Zone	Zona	Gebied
Backing wind	Rückdrehender Wind	Vent reculant	Rolar el viento	Krimpende wind
Barometer	Barometer	Baromètre	Barómetro	Barometer
Breeze	Brise	Brise	Brisa	Bries
Calm	Flaute	Calme	Calma	Kalmte
Centre	Zentrum	Centre	Centro	Centum
Clouds	Wolken	Nuages	Nube	Wolken
Cold	Kalt	Froid	Frio	Koud
Cold front	Kaltfront	Front froid	Frente frio	Kou front
Cyclonic	Zyklonisch	Cyclonique	Ciclonica	Cycloonachtig
Decrease	Abnahme	Affaiblissement	Disminución	Afnemen
Deep	Tief	Profond	Profundo	Diep
Deepening	Vertiefend	Approfondissant	Ahondamiento	Verdiepend
Depression	Sturmtief	Dépression	Depresión	Depressie

English	German	French	Spanish	Dutch
Direction	Richtung	Direction	Dirección	Richting
Dispersing	Auflösend	Se dispersant	Disipación	Oplossend
Disturbance	Störung	Perturbation	Perturbación	Verstoving
Drizzle	Niesel	Bruine	Lioviena	Motregen
East	Ost	Est	Este	Oosten
Extending	Ausdehnung	S'étendant	Extension	Uitstrekkend
Extensive	Ausgedehnt	Etendu	General	Uitgebreid
Falling	Fallend	Descendant	Bajando	Dalen
Filling	Auffüllend	Secomblant	Relleno	Vullend
Fog	Nebel	Brouillard	Niebla	Nevel
Fog bank	Nebelbank	Ligne de brouillard	Banco de niebla	Mist bank
Forecast	Vorhersage	Prévision	Previsión	Vooruitzicht
Frequent	Häufig	Fréquent	Frecuenta	Veelvuldig
Fresh	Frisch	Frais	Fresco	Fris
Front	Front	Front	Frente	Front
Gale	Sturm	Coup de vent	Temporal	Storm
Gale warning	Sturmwarnung	Avis de coup de vent	Aviso de temporal	Stormwaarschuwing
Good	Gut	Bon	Bueno	Goed
Gradient	Druckunterschied	Gradient	Gradiente	Gradiatie
Gust, squall	Bö	Rafalle	Ráfaga	Windvlaag
Hail	Hagel	Grêle	Granizo	Hagel
Haze	Diesig	Brume	Calina	Nevel
Heavy	Schwer	Abondant	Abunante	Zwaar
High	Hoch	Anticyclone	Alta presión	Hoog
Increasing	Zunehmend	Augmentant	Aumentar	Toenemend
Isobar	Isobar	Isobare	Isobara	Isobar
Isolated	Vereinzelt	Isolé	Aislado	Verspreid
Lightning	Blitze	Eclair de foudre	Relampago	Bliksem
Local	Örtlich	Locale	Local	Plaatselijk
Low	Tief	Dépression	Baja presión	Laag
Mist	Dunst	Brume légere	Nablina	Mist
Moderate	Mäßig	Modéré	Moderado	Matig
Moderating	Abnehmend	Se modérant	Medianente	Matigend
Moving	Bewegend	Se déplacant	Movimiento	Bewegend
North	Nord	Nord	Septentrional	Noorden
Occluded	Okklusion	Couvert	Okklusie	Bewolkt
Poor	Schlecht	Mauvais	Mal	Slecht
Precipitation	Niederschlag	Précipitation	Precipitación	Neerslag
Pressure	Druck	Pression	Presión	Druk
Rain	Regen	Pluie	lluvia	Regen
Ridge	Hochdruckbrücke	Crête	Cresta	Rug
Rising	Ansteigend	Montant	Subiendo	Stijgen
Rough	Rauh	Agitée	Bravo o alborotado	Ruw
Sea	See	Mer	Mar	Zee
Seaway	Seegang	Haute mer	Alta mar	Zee
Scattered	Vereinzelt	Sporadiques	Difuso	Verspreid
Shower	Schauer	Averse	Aguacero	Bui
Slight	Leicht	Un peu	Leicht	Licht
Slow	Langsam	Lent	Lent	Langzaam
Snow	Schnee	Neige	Nieve	Sneeuw
South	Süd	Sud	Sur	Zuiden
Storm	Sturm	Tempête	Temporal	Storm
Sun	Sonne	Soleil	Sol	Zon
Swell	Schwell	Houle	Mar de fondo	Deining
Thunder	Donner	Tonnerre	Tormenta	Donder
Thunderstorm	Gewitter	Orage	Tronada	Onweer
Trough	Trog, Tiefausläufer	Creux	Seno	Trog
Variable	Umlaufend	Variable	Variable	Veranderlijk
Veering	Rechtdrehend	Virement de vent	Dextrogiro	Ruimende wind
Warm front	Warmfront	Front chaud	Frente calido	Warm front
Weather	Wetter	Temps	Tiempo	Weer
Wind	Wind	Vent	Viento	Wind
Weather report	Wetterbericht	Météo	Previsión	Weer bericht meteorologica

Chapter 3 - Communications

RADIO OPERATION

Avoiding interference
Before transmitting, first listen on the VHF channel. If occupied, wait for a break before transmitting, or choose another channel. If you cause interference you must comply immediately with any request from a Coastguard or Coast radio station to stop transmitting.

Control of communications
Ship-to-Shore: Communications between ship and shore stations are controlled by the latter, except in distress, urgency or safety cases.

Intership: The ship *called* controls communication. If you call another ship, then it has control. If you are called by a ship, you assume control. If a shore-based station breaks in, both ships must comply with instructions given.

Radio confidentiality
Private conversations heard on the radio must not be reproduced, passed on or otherwise used.

Making yourself understood
Clear R/T speech is vital. If a message cannot be understood by the receiver it is useless. Messages which have to be written down at the receiving station should be spoken slowly. This gives time for it to be written down by the receiving operator. If the transmitting operator himself writes it down all should be well. The average reading speed is 250 words a minute, whilst average writing speed is only 20.

When speaking, consider the following:

- **What** to say, ie *voice Procedure*
- **How** to say it, ie *voice Technique*

Voice Procedure is discussed below and overleaf. It includes procedural words, callsigns, making contact etc.

Voice Technique depends on a few simple rules:

Hold the microphone a few inches in front of the mouth and speak directly into it at a normal level. Speak clearly so that there can be no confusion. The voice should be pitched up at a higher level than normal. Do not drop the voice pitch at the end of a phrase or sentence. Emphasise words with weak syllables; 'Tower', if badly pronounced, could sound like 'tar'. People with strong regional or foreign accents must try to pronounce words as clearly as possible.

Difficult words may be spelled phonetically, preceded with 'I spell'. If the word can be pronounced, include it before and after it has been spelt. For example, the message 'I will berth on the yacht *Coila*' would be sent as: 'I will berth on the yacht *Coila* – I spell – Charlie Oscar India Lima Alfa – *Coila*'.

The phonetic alphabet
The syllables to emphasise are underlined

Letter	Morse	Phonetic	Spoken as
A	• –	Alfa	AL-fah
B	– • • •	Bravo	BRAH-voh
C	– • – •	Charlie	CHAR-lee
D	– • •	Delta	DELL-tah
E	•	Echo	ECK-oh
F	• • – •	Foxtrot	FOKS-trot
G	– – •	Golf	GOLF
H	• • • •	Hotel	hoh-TELL
I	• •	India	IN-dee-ah
J	• – – –	Juliett	JEW-lee-ett
K	– • –	Kilo	KEY-loh
L	• – • •	Lima	LEE-mah
M	– –	Mike	MIKE
N	– •	November	no-VEM-ber
O	– – –	Oscar	OSS-car
P	• – – •	Papa	pa-PAH
Q	– – • –	Quebec	keh-BECK
R	• – •	Romeo	ROW-me-oh
S	• • •	Sierra	see-AIR-rah
T	–	Tango	TANG-go
U	• • –	Uniform	OO-nee-form
V	• • • –	Victor	VIK-tah
W	• – –	Whiskey	WISS-key
X	– • • –	X-Ray	ECKS-ray
Y	– • – –	Yankee	YANG-key
Z	– – • •	Zulu	ZOO-loo

Phonetic numerals
When numerals are transmitted, the following pronunciations make them easier to understand.

No	Morse	Spoken	No	Morse	Spoken
1	• – – – –	WUN	6	– • • • •	SIX
2	• • – – –	TOO	7	– – • • •	SEV-EN
3	• • • – –	TREE	8	– – – • •	AIT
4	• • • • –	FOW-ER	9	– – – – •	NIN-ER
5	• • • • •	FIFE	0	– – – – –	ZERO

Numerals are transmitted digit by digit except that multiples of thousands may be spoken as follows:

Numeral	Spoken as
44	FOW-ER FOW-ER
90	NIN-ER ZERO
136	WUN TREE SIX
500	FIFE ZERO ZERO
1478	WUN FOW-ER SEV-EN AIT
7000	SEV-EN THOU-SAND

COMMUNICATIONS

Punctuation

Punctuation marks should be used only where their omission would cause confusion.

Mark	Word	Spoken as
.	Decimal	DAY-SEE-MAL
,	Comma	COMMA
.	Stop	STOP

Procedural words or 'prowords'

These are used to shorten transmissions

All after and **All before.** Used after proword *'say again'* to request repetition of a part of a message

Correct Reply to repeat of message that was preceded by prowords *'read back for check'* when it has been correctly repeated. Often said twice

Correction Cancel the last word or group of words. The correct word or group follows. Spoken when an error has been made in a transmission.

I say again I repeat the transmission or the part indicated (see 'All after' and 'All before').

I spell I shall spell the next word or group of letters phonetically

Out This is the end of working to you

Over Invitation to reply

Read back If the receiver is doubtful about accuracy of all or part of message he may repeat it back to the sending station, preceding the repetition with prowords *'I read back'*

Station calling Used when a station is uncertain of the calling station's identification/callsign

This is This transmission is from the station whose callsign or name immediately follows

Wait If a called station cannot accept traffic immediately, it will reply **'WAIT.......MINUTES'**, with reason if delay may exceed 10 minutes

Word after or Word before Used after the proword *'say again'* to request repetition

Wrong Reply to repetition of message preceded by prowords *'read back'* when it has been incorrectly repeated

Calls, calling and callsigns

Shore stations normally use a callsign of their geographic name followed by Coastguard or Radio, eg Solent Coastguard, Dublin Radio etc. Vessels usually identify themselves by the ship's name but the International callsign may be used in certain cases. If two yachts have the same or confusingly similar names, give your International callsign when starting communications, and thereafter use your ship's name as callsign.

'All ships' broadcast

Address used by Coastguard Radio where broadcast information is to be received or used by all who intercept it, eg gale warnings etc. No reply is needed.

Communicating with a coast radio station

Call initially on a working channel or very briefly on channel 16 to establish a working channel.

- Pause to check the working channel is clear before transmitting
- Use low power *(1 watt)* if close enough , ie up to 10 miles away. High power *(25 watts)* drains more from the battery
- The callsign of calling station up to three times only, and prowords 'This is'
- Say how many R/T calls you have to make
- Proword 'Over'

Using high power decreases battery state and the range your VHF will achieve. Continued calling also clutters up the channel and denies access to other users.

Aerial faults commonly reduce your transmitting range. Possibly the station aerial for the channel chosen is directionally orientated and you are on the wrong side. Try another channel or station. Call again when closer.

RADIO DATA

SHORT, MEDIUM and LONG RANGE RADIO COMMUNICATIONS

A suitable radio receiver on board will provide weather forecasts and time signals at scheduled times on a number of frequencies in various wavebands. With a maritime receiver you are not limited to the familiar BBC and commercial broadcasts. HM Coastguard transmit navigation warnings, storm warnings and weather messages for shipping in their respective sea areas.

Short range radiotelephony (RT) transmits and receives on VHF channels in the marine VHF (Very High Frequency) band. The equipment and procedures are simple, but range is normally limited to about 20 miles from ship to shore, rather less from ship to ship. Interconnection with national telephone systems is possible on certain VHF/RT channels when a yacht is within range of a Coast Radio Station, although there are now no such stations on the mainland of the UK, France or the Netherlands. Mobile telephones are now by far the most common form of ship to shore communication.

Medium range two-way communication operate in the marine MF (medium frequency) RT band, the 2MHz 'trawler band'. Single sideband techniques are employed on these medium frequencies and SSB equipment is essential. The effective range depends on the power of the transmitter and the sensitivity of the associated receiver; in general this might be up to 200 miles from certain (but not all) Coast Radio Stations.

THE MARINE VHF BAND

VHF is used by most vessels, Coast Radio Stations, CG centres and other rescue services. Its range is slightly better than the line of sight between the transmitting and receiving aerials. A good aerial, as high as possible, is most important.

In the Marine VHF band (156·00–174·00 MHz) the individual frequencies are separated from their neighbours by exactly 25kHz 'elbow-room' to eliminate mutual interference. Each frequency is given a channel number, not necessarily consecutive. Thus 55 channels are available, plus some with special purposes (see below).

VHF Channel Grouping

Channels are grouped for three main purposes, but some can be used for more than one purpose. They are listed below in their preferred order of usage:

• *Public correspondence* (ie link calls via CRS into the shore telephone system): Ch 26, 27, 25, 24, 23, 28, 04, 01, 03, 02, 07, 05, 84, 87, 86, 83, 85, 88, 61, 64, 65, 62, 66, 63, 60, 82, 78, 81.

• *Inter-ship:* Ch 06, 08, 10, 13, 09, 72, 73, 67, 69, 77, 15, 17. Remember these, so that if another vessel calls you, you can swiftly nominate a working channel from within this group.

• *Port Operations:*
Ch 12, 14, 11, 13, 09, 68, 71, 74, 69, 73, 17, 15, 20, 22, 18, 19, 21, 05, 07, 02, 03, 01, 04, 78, 82, 79, 81, 80, 60, 63, 66, 62, 65, 64, 61, 84.

Special purposes. The following channels have one specific purpose only:

Ch 0 (156·00 MHz): SAR ops, not available to yachts.

Ch's 10 (156·500 MHz), 23 (161·750 MHz) 84 (161·825 MHz) and 86 (161·925 MHz): for MSI broadcasts by HMCG.

Ch 13 (156·650 MHz): Intership safety of navigation (sometimes referred to as bridge-to-bridge); a possible channel for calling a merchant ship if no contact on Ch 16.

Ch 16 (156·80 MHz): Distress, Safety and calling. *See Chapter 4 for Distress and Safety.* Ch 16 will be monitored by ships, CG centres (and, in some areas, any remaining Coast Radio Stations) for Distress and Safety until at least 2005, in parallel with DSC Ch 70. Yachts should monitor Ch 16. After an initial call, the stations concerned **must** switch to a working channel, except for Safety matters.

Ch 67 (156·375 MHz): the Small Craft Safety channel in the UK, accessed via Ch 16.

Ch 70 (156·525 MHz): exclusively for digital selective calling for Distress and Safety purposes.

Ch 80 (157·025 MHz): the primary working channel between yachts and UK marinas.

Ch M (157·85 MHz): the secondary working channel between yachts and UK marinas; previously known as Ch 37.

Ch M2 (161·425 MHz): for race control, with Ch M as stand-by. YCs may apply to use Ch M2.

SILENCE PERIODS

The periods are the 3 minutes immediately after the whole and half hours, ie H to H+03 and H+30 to H+33, when no transmissions should be made.

MEDIUM RANGE MF RADIO

Single sideband MF/RT provides communications in the offshore waters of the UK and Western Europe where small craft may be out of VHF contact. A receiver alone gives the ability to hear weather bulletins, storm and navigation warnings for local sea areas broadcast from CRS in the 1.6 to 4.0MHz maritime band, ie on frequencies from 1605 to 4200 kHz.

MF transmissions tend to follow the curvature of the earth, which makes them suitable for direction-finding. For this reason, and because of their good range, the marine Distress R/T frequency (2182 kHz) is in the MF band.

TRAFFIC LISTS

If a Coast Radio station has messages for a vessel, but is unable to contact her, that vessel's name will be added to the Traffic List broadcast at (usually) two hour intervals. This is not a system much used by yachts and small craft.

LONG RANGE HF RADIO

HF radios use short wave frequencies in the 4, 8, 12, 16 and 22 MHz bands, as chosen to suit propagation conditions. HF is more expensive than MF and requires more power, but can provide worldwide coverage. A good installation and skilled operating techniques are essential for satisfactory results.

COMMUNICATIONS

GLOBAL COMMUNICATIONS

Wireless Telephony (Mobile Phone)

Mobile phones are not suitable for emergency situations, except in extremis, but are often carried, in addition to VHF radio, for communicating with marinas. The digital GSM system also permits SMS text messaging as well as roaming between different countries.

Wireless telephony also has a definite role to play in data communication, allowing a PC to connect wirelessly to the Internet at a speed of 9.6kbps (thousand bits per second) in most areas when close to the shore; this is quite slow, but nevertheless sufficient for sending and receiving basic emails and browsing text-only websites.

Enhancements: GPRS (Global Packet Radio Service) works on mobile phone networks and boosts download rates to around 36kbps within about 5M of most NW European coasts. 3G (3rd Generation mobiles) data services provide data rates between 384kbps and 1,800kbps, though currently only in urban and more populated areas. Emerging UMTS/EDGE (Universal Mobile Telecommunications System/Enhanced Data Rates for GSM Evolution) standards promise even greater speeds, up to 14,000kbps.

These services are charged by the amount of data transmitted, not the duration of the call and therefore an 'always on' connection can be used. GPRS/G3/UMTS and EDGE all require compatible handsets and for the service to be activated on your account with the phone company.

Availability of each service from base stations varies and range offshore cannot be relied upon, especially off sparsely populated coasts where only a limited service is provided.

Wired Internet (VOIP and Data)

Internet Protocol, or IP, is the 'language' that drives the Internet, and VOIP (Voice over IP) is a system where voice communication is encoded and transmitted very efficiently as computer data. This provides free voice communication between two (or more) VOIP equipped yachts; and also (usually for a small charge) with normal land-line telephones. A broadband Internet connection is required, often available on the marina pontoons.

In addition to VOIP, a plug-in broadband Internet connection may be used by an onboard PC (or Macintosh) to send and receive email, to access weather websites and download updates and chart corrections, in exactly the same way as from a home PC.

Wireless Internet (Wi-Fi/Wi-MAX)

Wireless telephony services are primarily geared-up for voice but also have some data capability. Wireless Internet systems on the other hand mainly provide fast broadband Internet access (although with VOIP, they can happily be used for voice communication).

Wi-Fi is an increasingly common wireless system that provides broadband Internet access via 'hotspots', or 'wireless access points'. Increasingly marinas include Wi-Fi Internet access as part of their berthing fees, though paid-for access is also provided by specialist companies.

Even with special antennae, range is limited and this prevents Wi-Fi being useful to yachts while at sea, but speeds of up to 10,000kbps in the marina are typical and are perfectly suited to normal Internet use like web browsing and downloading Notices to Mariners or Almanac updates.

Wi-Max is an emerging, ie within 2 years, technology that promises to deliver marine users Internet access at much higher speeds with ranges exceeding 10 miles offshore.

Satellite Radio

Satellite radio is a receive-only digital radio broadcast signal transmitted via satellites. Services are subscription based, main providers being WorldSpace, XM Radio and Sirius. A digital decoding receiver is required (usually included with the subscription). Programming includes news, sport and music and some providers offer weather synopsis and forecast imagery, transmitted as a digital signal that is decoded using on board software.

Satellite Communications (Satcoms)

Satcoms offer simpler-to-operate and more reliable voice (and data) communications than HF SSB radio; they operate with either a dedicated ship installation or a standalone handheld terminal. Apart from the equipment purchase (and installation if necessary), ongoing costs usually include a monthly service fee and usage charges that will be related to either the amount of time used, or the volume of data transmitted and received.

For two-way voice communications, the 'Ship Station' (aka 'Mobile Earth Station') transmits to a visible satellite that is simultaneously in sight of a 'Land Earth Station', eg Goonhilly, Cornwall. From there, the call is routed to its destination through the normal terrestrial telephone network.

The satellite 'constellations' have different architectures. Inmarsat for example has four geostationary (GEO) satellites, one each positioned over the Pacific and Indian oceans and two over the Atlantic. Because they are comparatively high up (19,400M/36,000km), each satellite has a large signal 'footprint', overlapping the next one and thus world-wide coverage is provided (although not in the polar regions above about 70°N and 70°S). Other systems employ many more Low Earth Orbit (LEO) satellites orbiting the Earth about (540M/1,000km) above the surface.

The smaller, low-data rate, handheld voice terminals incorporate an omni-directional antenna that works best with an unobstructed view of the satellite. Fixed installations use an external gyro-stabilised antenna (to keep it pointing at the satellite as the boat moves); more powerful systems that support higher data rates employ antenna radomes that are really too large for installation aboard a 10–15m yacht.

The GMDSS provides automatic distress, urgency and safety communications, with some systems (eg Inmarsat C) providing a red button that alerts a Maritime Rescue Coordination Centre (MRCC) when pressed.

There are several providers of satellite communications services (see table below), each offering an array of capabilities and services. But note that this is a fast moving market place and you should check with manufacturers/retailers for up-to-date specifications and prices.

SATELLITE COMMUNICATION SERVICES

System	Antenna	Satellites	Coverage	GMDSS	Phone (voice)	Fax	SMS text	Position tracking	Data rate
INMARSAT C	Omni-directional	4 GEO	Global excepting polar regions	Yes	No	Yes	Yes	Yes (GPS)	Very low, uneconomic for email
INMARSAT Mini-M	Gyro-stabilised 40cms diameter	4 GEO	Global excepting polar regions	No	Yes	Yes	No	No	2.4kbps
INMARSAT D+	Omni-directional	4 GEO	Global excepting polar regions	No	No	No	No	Yes (GPS)	Very low, uneconomic for email
Fleet 33	Gyro-stabilised 40cms diameter	4 GEO	Global excepting polar regions	No	Yes	Yes	Yes	No	9.6kbps uncom-pressed
Iridium	Omni-directional	66 LEO	Global	No	Yes	Out only	Yes	No	Data kit required 2.4kbps, higher with compression
Globalstar	Omni-directional	40 LEO	Global excepting polar regions	No	Yes	Yes	Yes	To 10km	9.6kbps uncom-pressed, 38.6kbps compressed, 56k with data kit
Thuraya	Omni-directional	1 GEO	Europe, N Africa & Middle East, India	No	Yes	Yes	Yes	Yes (GPS)	9.6kbps (144kbps possible with land *DSL receiver)

*DSL (Digital Subscriber Line) allows broadband Internet access via normal copper telephone lines. It is used in the wireless/Satcoms arena to denote broadband-like speeds over the wireless link. This usually means data transfer speeds of 5 to 24mbps which is fast for Satcoms.

COMMUNICATIONS

101

PORT and/or MARINA VHF channels & telephone numbers

NOTES. Ch 16 is almost universally guarded, so is omitted. *In larger ports it is sensible to monitor the VTS channel (if any) or the primary port channel (in bold) before changing to a marina channel.* Times are local, unless marked UT. Abbreviations are at the front of the book. Telephone codes are shown only once unless more than one applies.

ENGLAND – SOUTH COAST

ISLES OF SCILLY, St Mary's HM Ch 14 (0800-1700); ☎ 01720 422768. *Falmouth CG* covers Scilly and the TSS off Land's End on Ch 23. **Tresco** HM ☎ 422849, mob 07778 601237.

NEWLYN HM Ch 09, **12** (M-F: 0800-1700, Sat: 0800-1200). ☎ 01736 362523.

PENZANCE HM Ch 09, **12** (M-F: 0830-1730 and HW −2 to +1). ☎ 01736 366113.

FALMOUTH *Falmouth Hbr Radio* Ch 11, **12**, 14 (M-F 0800-1700). ☎ 01326 312285.
Ch 80: Falmouth ☎ 316620 and Port Pendennis marinas ☎ 311113. **Ch 12**: Visitors Yacht Haven ☎ 310991; St Mawes HM ☎ 270553. **Ch M** (HO): Mylor Yacht Hbr ☎ 372121.

TRURO HM *Carrick One* Ch 12. ☎ 01872 272130. **Ch M** (HO): Malpas Marine ☎ 271260.

MEVAGISSEY HM Ch 14 (Summer: 0900-2100, Winter: 0900-1700). ☎ 01726 843305.

CHARLESTOWN HM Ch 14, HW −2 to +1, only when a vessel is expected. ☎ 01726 70241.

PAR HM Ch 12 (HO). ☎ 01726 817337.

FOWEY HM Ch 12 (0900-1700); also Hbr Patrol (0900-2000). ☎ 01726 832471. Water taxi: Ch 06.

LOOE. HM Ch 16, occas. ☎ 01503 262839.

PLYMOUTH *Long Room Port Control* Ch 14 H24, ☎ 01752 836528. **QAB** Ch 80, ☎ 671142. **Sutton Hbr lock**: Ch 12 H24, ☎ 204737. **Cattewater HM** Ch 14 (M-F 0900-1700), ☎ 836528. **Plymouth Yacht Haven**, Ch 80, M; ☎ 404231. **Mayflower marina**, Ch 80; ☎ 556633.

SALCOMBE HM & launch: Ch 14, May to mid-Sep: 7/7, 0600-2100; otherwise: M-F 0900-1600; ☎ 01548 843791. *Hbr Taxi* Ch 12. Fuel barge Ch 06, ☎ 07801 798862. *Egremont* (ICC) Ch M.

DARTMOUTH HM *Dartnav* Ch 11, 7/7 0730-dusk; ☎ 01803 832337. Darthaven marina Ch 80, ☎ 752545. Dart & Noss-on-Dart marinas Ch 80, ☎ 833351. Fuel barge Ch 06. Water taxi Ch 08.

TORBAY HBRS Brixham Marina Ch 80, ☎ 01803 882929; YC, ☎ 853332, & Water taxi *Shuttle* Ch M. Torquay Marina Ch 80, ☎ 200210. Fuel Ch M.

EXETER Exmouth Marina Ch 14, ☎ 01395 269314. **Retreat BY**: Ch M, ☎ 01392 874720. **Port of Exeter** HM Ch 12, M-F: 0730-1730 and when vessel due; ☎ 274306.

LYME REGIS HM Ch 14. Summer 0800-2000, winter 1000-1500. ☎ 01297 442137.

BRIDPORT HM Ch 11. ☎ 01308 423222.

PORTLAND PORT Port Control Ch 74 (H24). ☎ 01305 824044. **Sailing Academy** ☎ 866000.

WEYMOUTH HM & Town Bridge: Ch 12, M-F 0800-2000 summer & when vessel due; ☎ 01305 838423. **Marina** Ch 80, ☎ 767576. **Fuel** Ch 60.

POOLE
HM/bridge Ch 14 (H24); Code 01202 ☎ 440233. **Marinas Ch 80 M**: Salterns ☎ 709971. Parkstone YC ☎ 743610. Poole Quay ☎ 649488. Cobbs Quay ☎ 674299. **Poole Bay Fuels**: **Ch M** M-F: 0900-1730; Sat/Sun 0800-1800. ☎ 07768 71511.

YARMOUTH (IoW)
HM & Yar bridge **Ch 68** H24. ☎ 01983 760321. Water taxi **Ch 15**.

LYMINGTON
Marinas **Ch 80, M**: Yacht Haven ☎ 01590 677071. Berthon Marina ☎ 01590 673312.

COWES
Harbour Radio, Chain Ferry & Folly Inn Ch 69 Mon-Fri: 0800-1700. Marinas **Ch 80, M**. Tel code 01983: Yacht Haven ☎ 299975. Shepards ☎ 297821. East Cowes ☎ 293983. Island Hbr **Ch 80**, ☎ 822999. Water Taxi **Ch 06**.

NEWPORT HM & Yacht Hbr Ch 69 0800-1600. ☎ 01983 525994.

RYDE HM Ch 80. Summer 0900-2000, Winter HX. ☎ 01983 613879. Access HW±2.

BEMBRIDGE Marina **Ch 80**, ☎ 01983 872828. Hbr launch **Ch M**.

SOUTHAMPTON
Port Ops and VTS Ch 12 14. Marinas **Ch 80, M**. Tel code 02380: Hythe ☎ 207073. Ocean Village ☎ 229385. Shamrock Quay ☎ 229461. Kemp's ☎ 632323.

HAMBLE
Hbr Radio Ch 68 Apr-Sep daily 0600-2200; Oct-Mar 0700-1830. Marinas **Ch 80, M**. Tel code 02380: Hamble Pt ☎ 452464. Port Hamble ☎ 452741. Mercury ☎ 455994. Water Taxi **Ch 77**, ☎ 454512. Tel code 01489: Universal ☎ 574272. Swanwick ☎ 885000.

PORTSMOUTH
VTS **Ch 11** (& *QHM* if essential). Marinas **80**. Tel code 02392: Haslar ☎ 601201. Gosport ☎ 524811. Royal Clarence ☎ 523810. Port Solent ☎ 210765. THE CAMBER (Commercial Hbr): *Portsmouth Hbr Radio* **Ch 11** 14 (H24).

LANGSTONE HBR
HM **Ch 12**. Summer, daily 0830-1700; Winter, M-F 0830-1700; Sat/Sun 0830-1300. Southsea Marina **Ch 80, M,** ☎ 02392 822719.

CHICHESTER
HM *Chichester Hbr Radio* **Ch 14**. 1 Apr-Sep: M-Fri: 0830-1700. Sat: 0900-1300. 1 Oct - 31 Mar: 0900-1300, 1400-1700. Marinas **Ch 80, M.** Sparkes ☎ 02392 463572. Tel code 01243: Northney ☎ 466321. Emsworth Yacht Hbr ☎ 377727. Thornham ☎ 375335. Birdham Pool ☎ 512310. Chichester ☎ 512731. Water taxi **Ch 08** 0900-1800, mobile 07970 378350

LITTLEHAMPTON HM/Bridge **Ch 71** 0900-1700. Marina **Ch 80, M;** ☎ 01903 241663.

SHOREHAM HM & lock *Shoreham Hbr Radio* **Ch 14** (H24). Marina ☎ 01273 593801.

BRIGHTON
Marina *Brighton Control* **Ch M 80;** ☎ 01273 819919.

NEWHAVEN HM & Bridge *Newhaven Radio* **Ch 12**. Marina **Ch 80, M;** ☎ 01273 513881.

EASTBOURNE
Sovereign Hbr, inc lock/berthing: **Ch 17**. ☎ 01323 470099.

RYE *Hbr Radio,* **Ch 14** 0900-1700 or when ship due. ☎ 01797 225225.

FOLKESTONE
Port Control **Ch 15** for entry; ☎ 01303 254597.

DOVER
Port Control **Ch 74** for entry. Marina **Ch 80;** ☎ 01304 241663.

RAMSGATE
Port Control **Ch 14**. Marina **Ch 80;** ☎ 01843 572110.

ENGLAND – EAST COAST

WHITSTABLE
Hbr Radio Ch 09 12, Mon-Fri: 0830-1700 and –3HW+1. ☎ 01227 274086.

MEDWAY
Medway VTS **Ch 74.** Kingsferry Bridge (W Swale) **Ch 10** H24. Marinas **Ch 80, M.** Tel code 01634: Gillingham ☎ 280022. Hoo ☎ 250311. Chatham ☎ 899200.

PORT OF LONDON
LONDON VTS: Ch 69 from sea to Sea Reach No 4 buoy. **Ch 68** Sea Reach No 4 to Crayford Ness. **Ch 14, 22,** W of Crayford Ness.
Thames Barrier Ch 14. ☎ 020 8855 0315.

RIVER THAMES
Patrol Launches *Thames Patrol* **Ch 06, 13, 14, 68**
King George V Dock lock *KG Control* **Ch 13.**
West India Dock lock **Ch 13**
Greenwich Yacht Club **Ch M**

Thames lock (Brentford) **Ch 74** Summer 0800-1800; Winter 0800-1630.
Cadogan Pier **Ch 14** 0900-1700.
Marinas Ch 80, M; Tel code 0207: Gallions Point ☎ 4767054. Poplar Dock ☎ 5151046. South Dock ☎ 2522244. Limehouse Basin ☎ 3089930. St Katherine Haven ☎ 2645312. Chelsea Hbr ☎ 2259100. Brentford Dock ☎ 0208 2328941.

RIVER ROACH Havengore Bridge **Ch 72** *Shoe Bridge* HW±2. ☎ 01702 383436.

BURNHAM-ON-CROUCH
Ch 80: HM Launch 0900-1700. Yacht Hbr ☎ 01621 782150. Essex Marina ☎ 01702 258531.

RIVER BLACKWATER
Marinas **Ch 80, M;** Tel code 01621: Tollesbury ☎ 869202. Bradwell ☎ 776235. **Ch M:** Blackwater ☎ 740264. Heybridge Lock, **Ch 80** ☎ 853506.

RIVER COLNE
Brightlingsea Hbr Radio **Ch 68** 0800-2000. ☎ 01206 302200, mob 07952 734814.

WALTON BACKWATERS
Titchmarsh Marina **Ch 80,** ☎ 01255 672185.

RIVERS STOUR AND ORWELL
HARWICH VTS **Ch 71,** 11, 20, H24
SUNK VTS **Ch 14,** H24
Ipswich Port Radio (for R Orwell) **Ch 68,** H24
Marinas **Ch 80, M.** Tel code 01473: Shotley ☎ 788982. Suffolk Hbr ☎ 659240. Woolverstone ☎ 780206. Fox's ☎ 689111. Neptune ☎ 215204. Ipswich Haven ☎ 236644.

RIVER DEBEN HM *Odd Times* **Ch 08.** Tidemill Yacht Hbr ☎ 01394 385745.

SOUTHWOLD *Port Radio* **Ch 09** **12.** HM ☎ 01502 724712.

LOWESTOFT
Hbr Control **Ch 11, 14.** HM ☎ 01502 572286.
Royal Norfolk & Suffolk YC **Ch 80.** ☎ 566726.
Haven Marina **Ch 80** ☎ 580300. **Mutford Bridge & Lock Ch 09, 14** ☎ 531778.

GREAT YARMOUTH
Yarmouth Radio **Ch 12.** HM ☎ 01493 335511.
Haven & Breydon bridges **Ch 12.**

WELLS-NEXT-THE-SEA
Wells Hbr **Ch 12,** HJ, HW±2 and when vessel expected. HM ☎ 01328 711646.

WISBECH Ch 09 HW–3 when vessel expected. HM 01945 588059. Sutton Bridge **Ch 09**

KING'S LYNN
Harbour Radio **Ch 14** 11 Mon-Fri: 0800-1700 and –3HW+1. HM ☎ 01553 773411.

BOSTON
Port Control **Ch 12** Mon-Fri 0800-1700 and HW HW -2½ to HW + 1½. HM ☎ 01205 362328.
Grand Sluice **Ch 74** only when lock operates. Marina ☎ 364420.

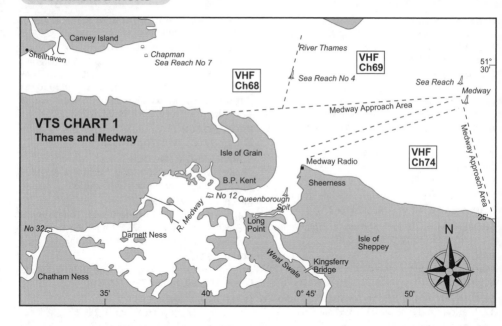

VTS CHART 1
Thames and Medway

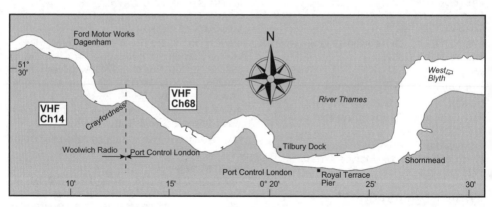

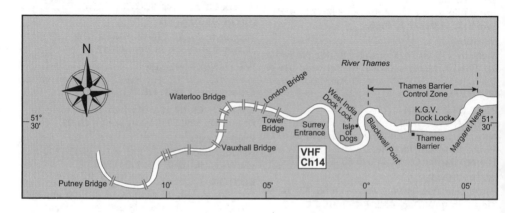

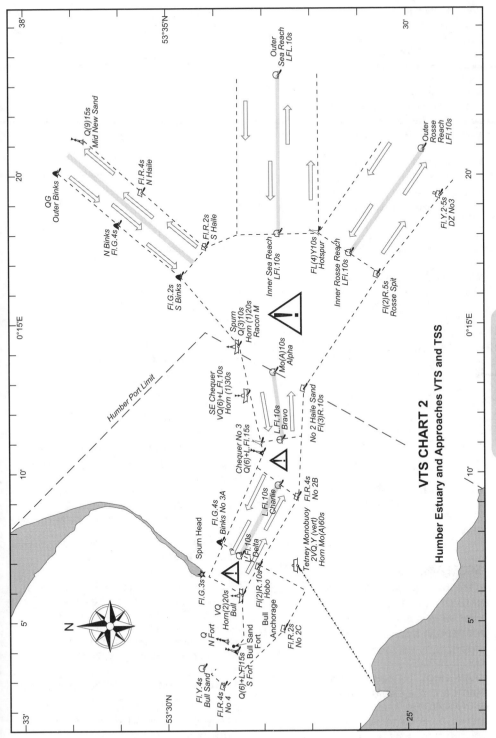

VTS CHART 2
Humber Estuary and Approaches VTS and TSS

RIVER HUMBER
VTS 1, Ch 14 to seaward of Clee Ness Lt F
VTS 2, Ch 12 Clee Ness–Gainsborough (R Trent) & Goole (R Ouse). MSI broadcasts Ch 12 & 14 every 2 hrs from 0103LT.
Grimsby Docks Radio **Ch 74**; 18 79 H24
Marinas: Grimsby, Meridian Quay **Ch 74,** ☎ 01472 268424. **Hull, Ch 80,** ☎ 01482 330508.
South Ferriby, Sluice **Ch 74. Brough,** Humber Yawl club ☎ 01482 667224. **Goole** Boathouse ☎ 01405 763985.

BRIDLINGTON
HM, call Ch 16; work **Ch 12.** ☎ 01262 670148.

SCARBOROUGH
HM *Scarborough Port Control* **Ch 12** H24. ☎01723 373530.

WHITBY
HM, Bridge & Marina **Ch 11,** 12 H24. ☎ 01947 602354.

RIVER TEES and HARTLEPOOL
Monitor *Tees Port control* **Ch 14,** 08, 11, 12, 22. Hartlepool Marina **Ch 80, M** H24. ☎01429 865744.

SEAHAM
HM **Ch 12,** M-F 0800-1800. ☎ 0191 5161700.

SUNDERLAND
Hbr Radio **Ch 14** (H24). Marina **Ch 80, M.** ☎ 0191 5144721.

RIVER TYNE
Tyne VTS **Ch 12,** 08, 11, inc Info service.
Royal Quays Marina **Ch 80.** ☎ 0191 2728282.
St Peter's Marina **Ch 80.** ☎ 0191 2654472.

BLYTH
Port control **Ch 12,** 11. ☎ 01670 352066. Marina ☎ 01670 353636 (R Northumberland YC).

WARKWORTH HARBOUR (Amble)
HM Ch 16, work **Ch 14.** ☎ 01665 710306. Marina **Ch 80,** ☎ 01665 712168.

BERWICK-UPON-TWEED
HM **Ch 12,** M-F 0800-1700. ☎ 01289 307404.

SCOTLAND

EYEMOUTH HM **Ch 12,** 06 HO. ☎ 01890 750223.
FIRTH OF FORTH
Forth Navigation **Ch 71;** may work 12, 20.
PORT EDGAR Marina **Ch 80, M.** ☎ 0131 3313330.
GRANTON, Royal Forth YC, Call *Boswell* **Ch M.** ☎ 0131 5523006.
GRANGEMOUTH Docks **Ch 14.** ☎ 01324 498566.
FORTH & CLYDE CANAL *Carron Sea Lock* **Ch 74.** ☎ 01324 483034.
METHIL Docks **Ch 14.** ☎ 01324 498585.
ANSTRUTHER Ch 11. ☎ 01333 310836.
DUNDEE *Harbour Radio* **Ch 12.** ☎ 01382 224121. Royal Tay YC **Ch M.** ☎ 01382 477516.

PERTH *Perth Harbour* **Ch 09.** ☎ 01738 624056.
ARBROATH *Port Control* **Ch 11.** ☎ 01241 872166.
MONTROSE *Port Control* **Ch 12.** ☎ 01674 672302.
STONEHAVEN HM **Ch 11.** ☎ 01569 762741.
ABERDEEN VTS **Ch 12,** ☎ 01224 597000.
PETERHEAD *Peterhead Hbrs* **Ch 14** for cl'nce to enter/exit. Marina ☎ 01779 477868.
FRASERBURGH Ch 12 H24, ☎ 01346 515858.
MACDUFF Ch 12 H24, ☎ 01261 832336.
BANFF Ch 12, ☎ 01261 815544.
WHITEHILLS *Whitehills Hbr Radio* **Ch 14,** ☎01261 861291.
BUCKIE Ch 12, 16 (H24), ☎ 01542 831700.
LOSSIEMOUTH
HM **Ch 12** 0700-1700. Marina, ☎ 01343 813066.
HOPEMAN and BURGHEAD
Same HM: *Burghead Radio* **Ch 14** HX, ☎ 01343 835337.
NAIRN HM/Marina ☎ 01667 454330. No VHF.
INVERNESS
HM **Ch 12,** M-Fri 0900-1700; Tel code 01463: ☎ 715715.
Clachnaharry Sealock **Ch 74,** ☎ 713896. HW ±4.
Inverness Marina ☎ 07526 446348.
Seaport Marina ☎ 239745.
Caley Marina ☎ 236539.
HELMSDALE Ch 13, ☎ 01431 821692.
WICK Ch 14 HX, ☎ 01955 602030.
SCRABSTER
HM **Ch 12** H24. Call on arr/dep, ☎ 01847 892779.
ORKNEY HARBOURS NAVIGATION SERVICE
Orkney Harbour Radio **Ch 09 11** 12
Stromness HM **Ch 14** M-Fri 0900-1700; Tel code 01856: ☎ 850744. Marina, ☎ 465825.
Kirkwall *Hbr Radio* **Ch 14,** ☎ 872292. M-Fri, 0800-1700.
Westray Pier, *Pierowall Hbr* **Ch 14** when vessel expected. ☎ 01857 677216.
SHETLAND
Lerwick Hbr Radio **Ch 11,** 12 ☎ 01595 692991.
Scalloway Hbr Radio **Ch 09, 12,** M-F 0700-1800, Sat 0900-1230. Piermaster ☎ 01595 880574.
Sullom Voe VTS **Ch 14** for tfc info, weather & radar assistance on request. ☎ 01806 242551.
Balta Sound Harbour **Ch 16, 20** HO
OUTER HEBRIDES
STORNOWAY HM **Ch 12** H24, ☎ 01851 702688.
Loch Maddy, N Uist Ch 12, ☎ 01876 500337.
St Kilda, *Kilda Radio* **Ch 16,** ☎ 01870 604406.
MAINLAND
Kinlochbervie Ch 14 HX, ☎ 01971 521235.
Loch Inver Ch 09 HX, ☎ 01571 844265.

ULLAPOOL Ch 14, ☎ 01854 612091.

Loch Gairloch Hbr Ch 16, ☎ 01445 712140.

ISLE OF SKYE
Portree Ch 12 (occas), ☎ 01478 612926.

Kyle Akin Ch 11, ☎ 01599 534167.

KYLE OF LOCH ALSH Ch 11, ☎ 01599 534589.

Mallaig Ch 09 HO, ☎ 01687 462154.

Tiree, Gott Bay Pier, Ch 31, ☎ 01879 230337.

Coll, Arinagour Pier, Ch 31, ☎ 01879 230347.

L Sunart, Salen Bay, Ch 16, ☎ 01967 431333.

ISLAND OF MULL
Tobermory, Ch 12, M HJ, ☎ 01688 302017.

Loch Lathaich; Sound of Iona; Craignure Pier.

Corpach basin & lock/Caledonian Canal Ch 74, ☎ 01397 772249.

DUNSTAFFNAGE Marina, Ch M, ☎ 01631 566555.

Oban North Bay Ch 12. Marina, ☎ 01631 565333.

L Melfort, Kilmelford Haven, Ch M, ☎ 01852 200248.

L Shuna, Craobh Marina, Ch M, ☎ 01852 500222.

L Craignish, Ardfern Ch 80, M, ☎ 01852 500247.

CRINAN CANAL, Ch 74. BWB, ☎ 01546 603210.

Islay, Port Ellen, ☎ 01496 300301; no VHF.

Tarbert, Loch Fyne Ch 14, ☎ 01880 820344.

Portavadie Marina Ch 80, ☎ 01700 811075.

CAMPBELTOWN Ch 12, 13, ☎ 01586 552552.

ROTHESAY, Bute Ch 12, ☎ 01700 500630.

LARGS Yacht Haven Ch 80, M, ☎ 01475 675333.

KIP Marina Ch 80, M, ☎ 01475 521485.

HOLY LOCH Marina Ch 80, M, ☎ 01369 701800.

RHU Marina Ch 80, M, ☎ 01436 820238.

ARDROSSAN Marina Ch 80, M, ☎ 01294 607077.

IRVINE HM/Bridge Ch 12, ☎ 01292 487286.

TROON Ch 14. Marina Ch 80, M, ☎ 01294 315553.

GIRVAN HM Ch 12, ☎ 01465 713648.

KIRKCUDBRIGHT HM Ch 12, ☎ 01557 331135.

ENGLAND W COAST AND WALES

MARYPORT Marina Ch 80, ☎ 01900 814431.

WORKINGTON HM Ch 14, ☎ 01900 602301.

WHITEHAVEN Marina Ch 12, ☎ 01946 692435.

ISLE OF MAN (Tel code 01624) If unable to contact IoM hbrs below, call Douglas.

Douglas Hbr Control Ch 12 H24.

Port St Mary HM Ch 12 HJ, ☎ 833205.

Peel HM Ch 12 HJ, ☎ 842338.

Ramsey HM Ch 12 0800-1600. HO, ☎ 812245.

MAINLAND
GLASSON DOCK Marina Ch 69, ☎ 01524 751491.

FLEETWOOD Dock Radio Ch 12 for Marina, ☎ 01253 879062.

PRESTON Lock Riversway Ch 14. Marina Ch 80, ☎ 01772 733595.

LIVERPOOL Mersey Radio Ch 12. Info Ch 09. Radar Ch 18. Liverpool Marina (Brunswick Dock) Ch M, ☎ 0151 7076777. Albert Dock Ch M, ☎ 0151 7096558; access via Canning Dock lock.

CONWY HM Ch 14. Marinas, both Ch 80: Conwy, ☎ 01492 593000. Deganwy 576888.

MENAI STRAIT and ANGLESEY
Beaumaris/Menai HM Ch 69, ☎ 01248 712312.

Caernarfon, HM & Victoria Dock Ch 80, ☎ 01286 672118. Mon-Fri: 0900-1700 Sat: 0900-1200

HOLYHEAD Port Control Ch 14, ☎ 01407 606700. Marina 764242.

MAINLAND
PWLLHELI, HM Ch 12. Marina Ch 80, M, ☎ 01758 704081.

PORTHMADOG Hbr Ch 12, ☎ 01766 512927.

BARMOUTH HM Barmouth Hbr Ch 12, ☎ 01341 280671.

ABERDOVEY Aberdovey Hbr Ch 12, ☎ 01654 767626.

ABERYSTWYTH HM Ch 14. Marina Ch 80, ☎ 01970 611422.

FISHGUARD HM Ch 14, ☎ 01348 873369.

MILFORD HAVEN Monitor Port Control (and Patrol launch) Ch 12, whilst under way. Milford Docks Pierhead Ch 18. Milford Dock Marina Ch 14, ☎ 01646 696312. Neyland Yacht Haven Ch 80, M, ☎ 01646 601601.

Tenby Ch 80, ☎ 01834 842717.

Saundersfoot Ch 11

SWANSEA
Tawe Lock Ch 18. Marina Ch 80, ☎ 01792 470310.

BARRY Barry Radio Ch 11. HM ☎ 01446 732665.

CARDIFF Cardiff Radio Ch 14. Barrage control Ch 18. Penarth Marina Ch 80, ☎ 02920 705021.

NEWPORT HM Ch 71, ☎ 0870 6096699.

SHARPNESS Sharpness Radio Ch 13 for lock. Marina, ☎ 01453 811476. Canal Ch 74

BRISTOL Bristol VTS Ch 12 with intentions. City Docks Radio Ch 14 (low power) to confirm. Bristol Floating Hbr Ch 73. Bristol Marina Ch 80, ☎ 0117 9213198.

PORTISHEAD Marina Ch 80, ☎ 0198 4631264.

BURNHAM-ON-SEA HM Ch 08, ☎ 01278 782180.

WATCHET Marina Ch 80, ☎ 01255 841941.

ILFRACOMBE HM Ch 80, ☎ 01271 862108.

COMMUNICATIONS

APPLEDORE-BIDEFORD HM *Two Rivers* **Ch 12,** Appledore ☎ 01237 474569.

BUDE HM **Ch 12,** ☎ 01288 353111.

PADSTOW HM **Ch 12,** ☎ 01841 532239.

ST IVES HM **Ch 12,** ☎ 01736 795018.

IRELAND

ROSSAVEEL Ch 12, ☎ 091 572108.

GALWAY, HM Ch 12, ☎ 091 561874.

SHANNON ESTUARY *Shannon Ports Radio* **Ch 11** (HO), ☎ 087 2560427.

KILRUSH Marina Ch 80, ☎ 06590 52072.

LIMERICK HBR Ch 12 13, ☎ 061 315377.

MFENIT HM **Ch 14, M,** ☎ 066 7136231.

DINGLE HM **Ch 14** (no calls req'd), ☎ 066 9151629.

CAHERSIVEEN (Valentia) Marina Ch 80, ☎ 066 9472777.

BANTRY BAY, Lawrence Cove Marina **Ch M,** ☎ 027 75044.

CASTLETOWN BEARHAVEN ⚓, ☎ 027 70220.

CROOKHAVEN ⚓, ☎ 028 35319.

SCHULL ⚓, mobile ☎ 086 1039105.

BALTIMORE Ch 09, mobile 087 2351485.

GLANDORE HM **Ch 06,** ☎ 028 34737.

COURTMACSHERRY HM/RNLI ☎ 023 46170.

KINSALE HM **Ch 14** ☎ 021 4772503. Marinas **Ch M:** KYC ☎ 4772196. Castlepark ☎ 4774959.

CORK *Cork Hbr Radio* **Ch 12,** 14 H24. HM ☎ 021 4273125. Marinas **Ch M:** Crosshaven ☎ 4831161. Salve ☎ 4831145. Royal Cork YC ☎ 4831023. East Ferry ☎ 4813390.

YOUGHAL HM/Pilots **Ch 14** Mon-Fri 0900-1700 and when ships expected. ☎ 024 92577.

DUNMORE EAST HM/Pilots **Ch 14** ☎ 051 383166.

WATERFORD & **NEW ROSS Ch 12, 14.** ☎ 051 873501.

KILMORE QUAY Ch 09. Marina, ☎ 053 29955.

ROSSLARE HM **Ch 12** H24, ☎ 053 33114.

WEXFORD Hbr Boat club. **Ch 16,** ☎ 053 22039.

ARKLOW HM **Ch 12,** ☎ 0402 32466. Marina 39901.

WICKLOW HM **Ch 14** 12, ☎ 0404 67455.

DUN LAOGHAIRE HM **Ch 14,** ☎ 01 2801130. YCs & Marina **Ch M:** Marina 2020040. National 2805725. R. St George 2801811. R. Irish 2809452. DL Motor YC 2801371.

DUBLIN HM and VTS *Port Radio* **Ch 12,** 13. Poolbeg Marina **Ch M,** ☎ 01 6689983. Lifting bridge *Eastlink* **Ch 12, 13.** City moorings, ☎ 01 8183300.

HOWTH HM **Ch 11.** Marina Ch M, 80, ☎ 01 8392777.

MALAHIDE Marina **Ch 80, M,** ☎ 01 8454129.

CARLINGFORDFORD LOUGH
Carlingford Marina **Ch M,** ☎ 042 93730739.

Warrenpoint Ch 12, ☎ 028 41752878.

Kilkeel Ch 12, ☎ 028 41762287.

ARDGLASS (Phennick Cove) Marina **Ch M, 80,** ☎ 028 44842332.

STRANGFORD LOUGH
HM **Ch 12 14,** ☎ 028 44881637.

Portaferry Marina Ch 80, M, ☎ 07703 209780.

Donaghadee Copelands Marina, ☎ 028 91882184.

BELFAST VTS *Belfast Hbr Radio* **Ch 12.** **Marinas Ch 80, M:** Carrickfergus, ☎ 028 93366666. Bangor, ☎ 028 91453217.

LARNE *Port Control* **Ch 14,** 11.

Glenarm HM/Marina, mobile ☎ 07703 606763.

Ballycastle HM/Marina, mob ☎ 07803 505084.

PORTRUSH HM **Ch 12,** ☎ 028 70822307.

COLERAINE HM **Ch 12.** Marina, ☎ 028 70832086.

LONDONDERRY *Hbr radio* **Ch 14,** ☎ 028 71860555.

L SWILLY Fahan Marina, ☎ 074 9360008.

KILLYBEGS HM **Ch 14,** ☎ 07497 31032.

Burton Port HM **Ch 06, 12, 14,** ☎ 075 42155.

SLIGO HM **Ch 12,** 14, ☎ 071 9161197.

DENMARK

Skagen HM **Ch 12** 13 HX, ☎ 98 941346.

Hirtshals HM **Ch 12** 13 HX, ☎ 98 941422.

Torup Strand HM **Ch 12** 13 HX.

Hanstholm HM **Ch 12** 13 HX, ☎ 97 961833.

THYBORØN HM **Ch 12** 13 H24, ☎ 97 831188.

Thisted (Limfjord) Ch 12 13 HX, ☎ 97 911400.

Torsminde HM **Ch 12** 13, ☎ 24 233345.

Hvide Sande HM **Ch 12** HX, ☎ 97 311633.

ESBJERG *Hbr Control* **Ch 12** 13 14 H24, ☎ 75 124000. **Fanø** HM, ☎ 75 163100.

Rømø HM **Ch 10, 12, 13** HX, ☎ 74 755245.

GERMANY

HELGOLAND HM **Ch 67,** ☎ 04725 81593583. **May-Aug** Mon-Thu 0700-1200, 1300-2000. Fri-Sun 0700-1200.
Sep-Apr Mon-Thu 0700-1200, 1300-1600. Fri 0700-1200.

List HM **Ch 11**, ☎ 046 51870374.
Hörnum HM **67**, ☎ 046 51881027.
Wyk HM **Ch 11**, ☎ 046 81500430.
Pellworm HM **Ch 11**, ☎ 048 44726.
Husum HM **Ch 11**, ☎ 048 16670.
R. **Eider** sealock **Ch 14**, ☎ 04833 4535211.
Büsum HM **Ch 11**, ☎ 048 413607.

INNER DEUTSCHE BUCHT (GERMAN BIGHT)
VTS, Eastern part **Ch 80**, ☎ 04421 489282.
VTS, Western part **Ch 79**

BRUNSBÜTTEL HM **Ch 06**, ☎ 04852 88418.

NORD-OSTSEE KANAL (KIEL CANAL)
VTS Canal I   **Ch 13**, ☎ 04852 885371.
VTS Canal II   **Ch 02**, ☎ 04852 885369.
VTS Canal III **Ch 03**, ☎ 0431 3603456.
VTS Canal IV   **Ch 12**, ☎ 0431 3603465.
Brieholz, Ch 73
Ostermoor, **Ch 73**

RIVER ELBE
CUXHAVEN HM **Ch 69** HX, ☎ 04721 500150.
Cuxhaven Marina, ☎ 37363. YC Marina, ☎ 34111.
R. **Stör Lock Ch 09** Bridge opens on request.
Glückstadt HM **Ch 08**, ☎ 04124 913200.

HAMBURG Port HM **Ch 12**, ☎ 040 7411540.

VTS *Hamburg Port Traffic* **Ch 13**, **14**, **74**. Wedel
Yacht Hbr, ☎ 040 1034438. City Sporthafen, ☎ 040
364297.

BREMERHAVEN *Weser VTS* **Ch 22**. Port **Ch 12**, ☎
0471 59613401. **Locks Ch 69**, **70**. **Marinas** Weser
YC, ☎ 23531. NYC, ☎ 77555. WVW, ☎ 73268.

BREMEN *Port Radio* **Ch 03**, ☎ 0421 3618504.

JADE VTS *Jade Traffic* **Ch 63**, **20**.

WILHEMSHAVEN
Port **Ch 11**, ☎ 04421 154580. **Sealock Ch 13**.
Bridges Ch 11. **Marinas** Nassauhafen, ☎ 41439.
Wiking Sportsboothafen, ☎ 41301.

HOOKSIEL Ch 63. Alterhafen Marina.

WANGEROOGE HM **Ch 17**, ☎ 04469 630. Marina,
☎ 942126.

SPIEKEROOG HM No VHF, ☎ 04976 9193133.

DORNUMER-ACCUMERSIEL HM No VHF, ☎
04933 2510. YC ☎ 2240.

LANGEOOG HM **Ch 17**, ☎ 04972 301.

NORDERNEY HM **Ch 17**, ☎ 04932 82826.

NORDDEICH HM **Ch 17**, ☎ 04931 81317.

BORKUM HM **Ch 14**, ☎ 04922 81317.

EMS VTS *Ems Traffic* **Ch 15**, **18**, **20**, **21**

EMDEN HM & locks **Ch 13**, ☎ 04921 897260.
YC Marina, ☎ 997147. Mariners' Club, ☎ 953795.
City Marina, ☎ 8907211.

NETHERLANDS

DELFZIJL/EEMSHAVEN VTS is not compulsory for
leisure craft. **Delfzijl Radar Ch 03** gives radar assistance when visibility falls below 2000m.
Eemshaven Radar Ch 01. **Port Control Ch 66**
broadcasts info every even H+10.

DELFZIJL HBR. HM **Ch 14**; ☎ 0596 640400. **Locks
Ch 26**, M-Sat H24, Sun & hols on request; ☎
693293. **Bridges:** Weiwerder **Ch 11**. Heemskes &
Handelshaven **Ch 14**. **Farmsumerhaven**, **Ch 66**,
☎ 640494.

EEMSHAVEN HM **Ch 14**; ☎ 516142. Radar **Ch 19**.

LAUWERSOOG. HM, *Havendienst*, **Ch 09**; ☎ 0519
39023. Mon 0000-1700; Tu-Wed 0800-1700; Th-Sat
0700-1500.

TERSCHELLING VTS Call/monitor *Brandaris* **Ch
02**; ☎ 0562 443100. **Marina, Ch 31**; ☎ 443337.

VLIELAND. HM **Ch 12**. **Marina, Ch 31**; ☎ 0562
451729.

HARLINGEN HM **Ch 11** (not on Sun); ☎ 0517
413423. **Locks Ch 22**.

OUDESCHILD HM **Ch 12**; ☎ 0222 312710. **Marina,
Ch 31**; ☎ 0222 321227. See Den Helder VTS.

DEN HELDER VTS. Monitor *Tfc Centre* **Ch 62**, H24;
broadcasts info and gives radar surveillance.
PORT CONTROL Ch 14; ☎ 0223 62770. **Marina** ☎
652645. **Bridge:** Moormanbrug **Ch 18**. **Lock:**
Koopvaarders **Ch 22**.

IJSSELMEER Den Oever lock Ch 20, ☎ 0227
511383. **Port Ch 11**, ☎ 511303. Marina ☎ 511789.
Kornwerderzand lock Ch 18, ☎ 0517 57441.

ENKHUIZEN Naviduct (also Krabbersgat) **Ch 22**.

IJMUIDEN VTS. Traffic Centre **Ch 07**, Roads (W
of IJmuiden buoy). Thence **Port Control Ch 61**
to Noordzeesluizen (locks).
Seaport Marina **Ch 75**, ☎ 0255 560300.

NORDZEEKANAAL VTS
Noordzeesluizen. *Sluis IJmuiden* **Ch 22**.
Noordzeekanaal. **Ch 03**, from locks to km 11·2.

AMSTERDAM
Port Control Ch 68 (Km 11·2 to Oranjesluisen).
Port Info Ch 14. Access to Standing Mast route:
Westerkeersluis Ch 22. **Haarlem hbr Ch 18**.
Marinas: Sixhaven, ☎ 020 6329429. **WV Aeolus**,
☎ 6360791. **Aquadam**, ☎ 6320616.
Access to Markermeer: **Oranjesluisen Ch 18**.

SCHEVENINGEN. Traffic Centre & Port **Ch 21**; ☎
070 3527711. **Marina Ch 31**; ☎ 070 3520017.

HOEK VAN HOLLAND ROADSTEAD
To cross the mouth of the Maas, call *Maas
Entrance* **Ch 03**, with vessel's name, position and
course. Follow a track close W of a line joining
buoys MV, MVN and Indusbank N. See VTS Chart
No 4. Whilst crossing, maintain continuous
listening watch and keep a very sharp lookout.

COMMUNICATIONS

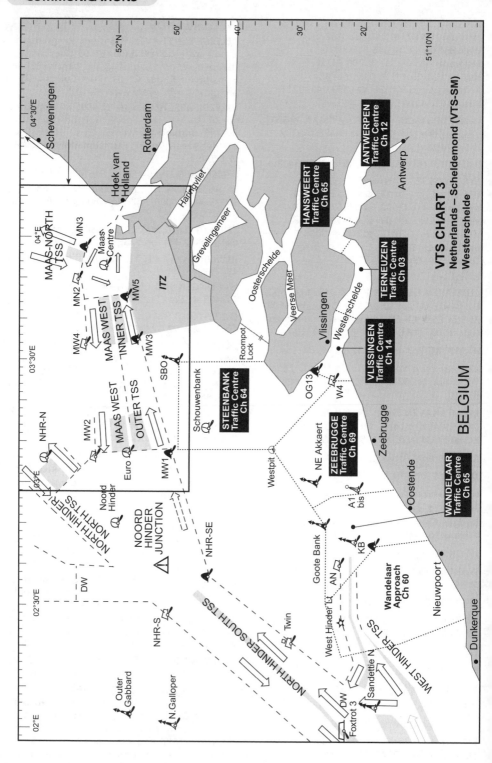

VTS CHART 3
Netherlands – Scheldemond (VTS-SM)
Westerschelde

ANTWERPEN Traffic Centre Ch 12

HANSWEERT Traffic Centre Ch 65

TERNEUZEN Traffic Centre Ch 03

VLISSINGEN Traffic Centre Ch 14

STEENBANK Traffic Centre Ch 64

ZEEBRUGGE Traffic Centre Ch 69

WANDELAAR Traffic Centre Ch 65

Wandelaar Approach Ch 60

BELGIUM

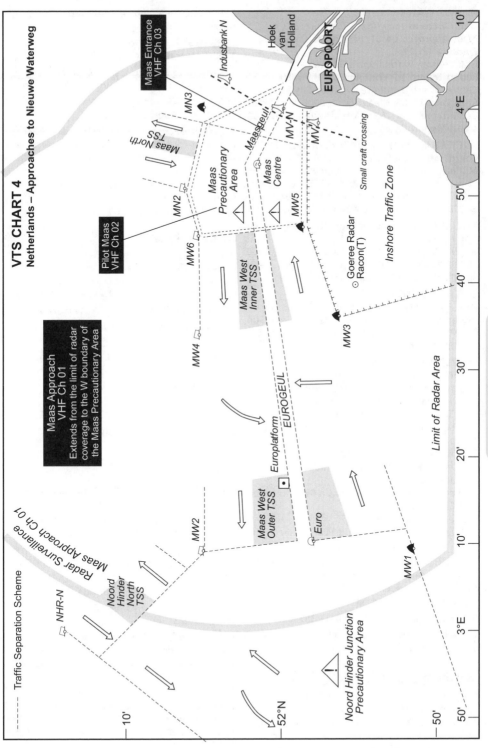

VTS CHART 4
Netherlands – Approaches to Nieuwe Waterweg

Maas Entrance
VHF Ch 03

Indusbank N

Hoek van Holland

EUROPOORT

MN3

Maas North TSS

Maasgeul

MV-N

MV-C

MV-S

Small craft crossing

Maas Precautionary Area

Maas Centre

MW5

Inshore Traffic Zone

Pilot Maas
VHF Ch 02

MN2

MW6

Maas West Inner TSS

Goeree Radar
Racon(T)

MW3

Maas Approach
VHF Ch 01
Extends from the limit of radar coverage to the W boundary of the Maas Precautionary Area

MW4

EUROGEUL

Limit of Radar Area

Europlatform

Maas West Outer TSS

Euro

MW2

Radar Surveillance
Maas Approach Ch 01

Noord Hinder North TSS

NHR-N

MW1

Traffic Separation Scheme

Noord Hinder Junction Precautionary Area

10'

52°N

3°E

50'

10'

4°E

50'

40'

30'

20'

10'

COMMUNICATIONS

111

COMMUNICATIONS

NIEUWE WATERWEG VTS.

Outer areas as shown on VTS Charts 3 & 4: *Maas Approach* Ch 01. *Pilot Maas* Ch 02. *Maas Entrance* Ch 03.

HCC *Central Traffic Control* Ch 14 19.

Report to/monitor continuously the relevant Tfc Centre, as listed from seaward to City Marina: Rozenburg Ch 65; Maassluis Ch 80; Botlek Ch 61; Eemhaven Ch 63; Waalhaven Ch 60; Maasbruggen Ch 81.

ROTTERDAM Rotterdam Tfc Centre Ch 11. Hbr Coordination Centre (HCC) Ch 19. Marinas/Yacht hbrs: Vlaardingen ☎ 010 4346786; Lock Ch 20. Spuihaven ☎ 4667765. Coolhaven ☎ 4738614. Veerhaven ☎ 4365446. City Marina ☎ 0187 48540986, via Erasmus bridge Ch 18.

STELLENDAM Haringvliet lock & lifting bridge: *Goereese Sluis* Ch 20, ☎ 0187 497350. Opening hrs: M-F 0000-2200. 1 Nov - 1 Apr: Sat 0800-2200; Sun 0800-1000, 1600-1800. 1 Apr - 1 Nov: Sat & Sun 0800-2000. Marina Ch 31, ☎ 493769.

OOSTERSCHELDE

Lock *Roompotsluis* Ch 18, ☎ 0111 659265. Opening hours: Mon & Thu, 0000-2200; Tue & Sun, 0600-0000; Wed H24; Fri & Sat: 0600-2200. Roompot Marina Ch 31.

WESTERSCHELDE VTS

See VTS Chart No 3. Reporting is not compulsory for leisure craft, but they should monitor the VHF channel for the appropriate Traffic Area. Each Traffic Area is controlled by a Traffic Centre and bounded by buoys. *In emergency call the relevant Traffic Centre: Ch 67.*

Tfc Centre Steenbank & Radar Ch 64.
Tfc Centre Vlissingen Ch 14. Radar Ch 21. Info broadcast Ch 14 H+55.
Tfc Centre Terneuzen & Radar Ch 03. Info broadcast Ch 11 H+00.
Tfc Centre Hansweert Ch 65.

Antwerpen, Zeebrugge and Wandelaar Traffic Areas are listed under Belgium.

VLISSINGEN De Ruyter Marina no VHF, ☎ 0118 414498, mobile 06 5353 7181. *Flushing Port Control* Ch 09. Sealocks & canal bridge Ch 22. VVW Schelde Marina Ch 14, ☎ 465912.

BRESKENS Marina, Ch 31, ☎ 0117 381902.

TERNEUZEN Port control Ch 11. Marina, ☎ 0115 697089. Oostsluis (E lock, small craft) Ch 18.

BELGIUM

ANTWERPEN, *Tfc Centre Zandvliet* Ch 12. Info broadcast Ch 12 H+35.

ANTWERPEN PORT Calling and safety Ch 74. Royerssluis Ch 22. Siberia & Londen bridges Ch 62. Willemdok Marina Ch 23, ☎ 03 2315066. Linkeroever Marina Ch 09, ☎ 03 2190895.

ZEEBRUGGE *Tfc Centre Zeebrugge* Ch 69. Info broadcasts Ch 69 H+15.

ZEEBRUGGE Port Control Ch 71 H24, ☎ 050 546867. Marina ☎ 544903. E lock Ch 68.

BLANKENBERGE Marinas: VNZ, ☎ 050 429150, & SYCB, ☎ 411420, Ch 31. VVW ☎ 417536, Ch 23.

WANDELAAR Tfc Centre Wandelaar Ch 65. Wandelaar Approach Ch 60.

OOSTENDE Port Control Ch 09 H24, ☎ 059 566313. Mercator lock, ☎ 321669, & marina, ☎ 705762: Ch 14 H24. Marinas: RNSYC, ☎ 505912. RYCO, ☎ 321452.

NIEUWPOORT Port HM Ch 09 H24, ☎ 058 233000. Marinas: KYCN, Ch 23, ☎ 234413. WSKLM, Ch 23, ☎ 5233641. VVW-N, Ch 08, ☎ 235232.

NORTH FRANCE

DUNKERQUE Port & VTS Ch 73, H24. The VTS does not affect leisure craft, but monitor Ch 73. Marinas Ch 09: Grande Large ☎ 03.28.63.23.00. YCMN ☎ 03.28.66.79.90. Trystram lock Ch 73.

GRAVELINES HM/Marina, Ch 09, ☎ 03.28.23.19.45.

CALAIS VTS, Port Control & Marina Ch 17 H24, ☎ 03.21.34.55.23.

BOULOGNE *Boulogne Port*, ☎ 03.21.31.52.43, Ch 12, H24. Marina Ch 09, ☎ 03.21.31.70.01.

LE TOUQUET/ÉTAPLES-SUR-MER Ch 09, 77. Étaples Marina, ☎ 03.21.84.54.03.

LE TRÉPORT Marina/lock Ch 12, 72, ☎ 02.35.50.63.06

DIEPPE Port HM Ch 12, HO. Marina Ch 09, ☎ 02.35.40.19.79.

ST VALÉRY-EN-CAUX Entry gate & marina Ch 09, ☎ 02.35.97.01.30.

FÉCAMP Port HM, Ch 10, 12, ☎ 02.35.28.25.53. Marina & Bérigny lock, Ch 09, ☎ 02.35.28.13.58.

LE HAVRE *Control Tower* Ch 12, 20. Port Ops Ch 67, 69. Marina, Ch 09, ☎ 02.35.21.23.95.

LA SEINE VTS Rouen Port Control Ch 73 (Estuary), 68 (River). Honfleur radar Ch 15, 19, 73.

HONFLEUR HM Ch 17, 73 HX, ☎ 02.31.14.61.09. Lock, ☎ 02.31.98.72.82, & Bridge Ch 17 H24.

ROUEN Port HM Ch 73, 68 H24. Halte Nautique, ☎ 02.32.08.31.40.

ROUEN – PARIS, LOCKS Amfreville Ch 18. Notre-Dame-de-la-Garenne Ch 22. Mericourt Ch 18. Andrésy Ch 22. Bougival Ch 22. Chatou Ch 18. Suresnes Ch 22.

PARIS-ARSENAL Marina Ch 09, ☎ 01.43.41.39.32.

DEAUVILLE Port Deauville lock, ☎ 02.31.88.95.66; Marina ☎ 02.31.98.30.01, Ch 09 0800-1730. Port Morny gate ☎ 02.31.88.57.89; Marina, Ch 09, ☎ 02.31.98.50.40.

DIVES-SUR-MER. Marina Ch 09, ☎ 02.31.24.48.00.

OUISTREHAM Port 74; lock Ch 12, ☎ 02.31.36.22.00. Marina Ch 09, ☎ 02.31.96.91.37. Canal Ch 68.

CAEN HM/Marina Ch 74, ☎ 02.31.95.24.47.

COURSEULLES-SUR-MER Marina Ch 09, ☎ 02.31.37.51.69.

PORT-EN-BESSIN HM, ☎ 02.31.21.70.49. Gate/bridge Ch 18, ☎ 02.31.21.71.77.

GRANDCAMP Marina Ch 09, ☎ 02.31.22.63.16.

CARENTAN Lock Ch 09, ☎ 02.33.71.10.85. Marina Ch 09, ☎ 02.33.42.24.44.

ST VAAST-LA-HOUGUE Marina Ch 09, ☎ 02.33.21.61.00.

BARFLEUR HM, ☎ 02.33.54.08.29. No VHF.

CHERBOURG VTS (yachts to monitor) Vigie du Homet Ch 12 H24. Marina Chantereyne Ch 09, ☎ 02.33.87.65.70. Gate (B du Commerce) Ch 06.

OMONVILLE-LA-ROGUE No VHF/Tel. 6 W ⚓s.

DIÉLETTE Marina Ch 09, ☎ 02.33.53.68.78.

CARTERET Marina Ch 09, ☎ 02.33.04.70.84.

PORTBAIL Yacht hbr Ch 09, ☎ 02.33.04.83.48.

GRANVILLE Port HM Ch 12. Marina Ch 09, ☎ 02.33.50.20.06.

ST MALO Port HM Ch 12 H24. Marinas Ch 09: Bas Sablons, ☎ 02.99.81.71.34. Bassin Vauban, ☎ 02.99.56.51.91. DINARD, ☎ 02.99.46.65.55.

R RANCE barrage lock Ch 13, ☎ 02.99.46.21.87. Chatelier lock Ch 14, ☎ 02.99.39.55.66.

DAHOUËT Marina Ch 09, ☎ 02.96.72.82.85.

LE LÉGUÉ HM/Marina Ch 12, ☎ 02.96.77.49.85.

BINIC Marina Ch 09, ☎ 02.96.73.61.86.

ST QUAY-PORTRIEUX Marina ☎ 02.96.70.81.30. Ch 09.

PAIMPOL Lock/Marina Ch 09, ☎ 02.96.20.47.65.

LÉZARDRIEUX Marina Ch 09, ☎ 02.96.20.14.22.

PONTRIEUX Lock/Marina Ch 12, ☎ 02.96.95.34.87.

TRÉGUIER Marina Ch 09, ☎ 02.96.92.42.37.

PERROS-GUIREC Marina Ch 09, ☎ 02.96.49.80.50.

PLOUMANAC'H Marina Ch 09, ☎ 02.96.91.44.31.

TRÉBEURDEN Marina Ch 09, ☎ 02.96.23.64.00.

MORLAIX Marina Ch 09, ☎ 02.98.62.13.14.

ROSCOFF HM/S Basin Ch 09, ☎ 02.98.69.76.37.

BLOSCON Ferry Port Ch 12, ☎ 02.98.61.27.84.

L'ABERWRACH Marina Ch 09, ☎ 02.98.04.91.62.

CHANNEL ISLANDS

ALDERNEY, Braye Hbr, Alderney Radio Ch 74, ☎ 01481 822620. If no contact, try St Peter Port Radio.

GUERNSEY Beaucette Marina, Ch 80, ☎ 01481 245000. St Sampson Ch 12 H24 via St Peter Port Control Ch 12 H24, ☎ 720229.

Victoria Marina Ch M, 80 HO, ☎ 725987. St Peter Port Radio Ch 20 H24 (only for link calls).

JERSEY St Helier Port Control Ch 14 H24; 8M max range. St Helier Marina, ☎ 01534 885508, has no VHF; call Ch 14 only if essential.

Gorey Ch 74, ☎ 853616.

WEST FRANCE

BREST VTS Brest Port Ch 08 H24. Marina Ch 09, ☎ 02.98.02.20.02.

CAMARET Marina Ch 09, ☎ 02.98.27.95.99.

MORGAT Marina Ch 09, ☎ 02.98.27.01.97.

DOUARNENEZ HM Ch 12. Marinas Ch 09: Tréboul ☎ 02.98.74.02.56; Port Rhu ☎ 02.98.92.00.67.

AUDIERNE No VHF. Marina ☎ 02.98.74.04.93. Ste Evette ☎ 02.98.70.00.28.

LOCTUDY Marina Ch 09, ☎ 02.98.87.51.36.

BENODÉT Marinas Ch 09: Penfoul ☎ 02.98.57.05.78. Ste Marine ☎ 02.98.56.38.72.

PORT-LA-FORÊT Marina Ch 09, ☎ 02.98.56.98.45.

CONCARNEAU Marina Ch 09, ☎ 02.98.97.57.96.

LORIENT Port Ch 12. Marinas Ch 09: Ban-Gâvres ☎ 02.97.65.48.25. Kernével ☎ 02.97.65.48.25. Port Louis ☎ 02.97.83.59.55. Locmiquélic ☎ 02.97.33.59.51. Lorient ☎ 02.97.21.10.14.

PORT TUDY Marina Ch 09, ☎ 02.97.86.54.62.

RIVER ÉTEL Marina Ch 13, ☎ 02.97.55.46.62.

BELLE ILE Sauzon HM Ch 09, ☎ 02.97.31.63.40. Le Palais HM Ch 09, ☎ 02.97.31.42.90.

PORT HALIGUEN Marina Ch 09, ☎ 02.97.50.20.56.

LA TRINITÉ Marina Ch 09, ☎ 02.97.55.71.49.

VANNES Marina Ch 09, ☎ 02.97.54.16.08.

CROUESTY Marina Ch 09, ☎ 02.97.53.73.33.

LA VILAINE Arzal Marina Ch 09, ☎ 02.97.45.02.97.

PIRIAC Marina Ch 09, ☎ 02.40.23.52.32.

LA TURBALLE Marina Ch 09, ☎ 02.40.23.41.65.

LE CROISIC Marina Ch 09, ☎ 02.40.23.10.95.

LE POULIGUEN Marina Ch 09, ☎ 02.40.11.97.97.

PORNICHET Marina Ch 09, ☎ 02.40.61.03.20.

ST-NAZAIRE VTS Loire Ports Control Ch 14. Port HM Ch 14, ☎ 02.40.91.03.17.

PORNIC Marina Ch 09, ☎ 02.40.82.05.40.

L'HERBAUDIÈRE Marina Ch 09, ☎ 02.51.39.05.05.

PORT JOINVILLE Marina Ch 09, ☎ 02.51.58.38.11.

ST GILLES-CROIX-DE-VIE Marina Ch 09, ☎ 02.51.55.30.83.

LES SABLES D'OLONNE Port HM Ch 12, ☎ 02.51.95.11.79. Marina Ch 09, ☎ 02.51.32.51.16.

BOURGENAY Marina Ch 09, ☎ 02.51.22.20.36.

ILE DE RÉ Ars-en-Ré Ch 09, ☎ 05.46.29.08.52. St Martin Ch 09, ☎ 05.46.09.26.69.

COMMUNICATIONS

LA ROCHELLE Marinas Ch 09: Port des Minimes ☎ 05.46.44.41.20. Vieux Port ☎ 05.46.41.32.05.

ROCHEFORT Marina Ch 09, ☎ 05.46.83.99.06.

ILE D'OLÉRON St Denis Ch 09, ☎ 05.46.47.97.97. Boyardville Ch 09, ☎ 05.46.76.48.56.

LA GIRONDE VTS Ch 12 (yachts to monitor). Radar *Bordeaux Port Control* Ch 12 on request. Depths in Gironde broadcast Ch 17 every 5 mins.

ROYAN Marina Ch 09, ☎ 05.46.38.72.22.

PORT-MÉDOC Marina Ch 09, ☎ 05.56.09.69.75.

PAUILLAC Marina Ch 09, ☎ 05.56.59.12.16.

BORDEAUX HM *Bordeaux Traffic* Ch 12, ☎ 05.56.31.58.64. Bassin 2, ☎ 05.56.90.59.57.

ARCACHON Marina Ch 09, ☎ 05.56.22.36.75.

CAPBRETON Marina Ch 09, ☎ 05.58.72.21.23.

ANGLET Marina Ch 09, ☎ 05.59.63.05.45.

ST JEAN-DE-LUZ Marina Ch 09, ☎ 05.59.47.26.81.

HENDAYE Marina Ch 09, ☎ 05.59.48.06.10.

N AND NW SPAIN

FUENTERRABIA Marina Ch 09, ☎ 943 641711.

GUETARIA Marina Ch 09, ☎ 943 580959.

ZUMAYA Marina Ch 73, ☎ 943 860938.

BILBAO *Port Control* Ch 12. Marinas Ch 09: Getxo ☎ 944 912367. Las Arenas ☎ 944 637600.

SANTANDER Marina Ch 09, ☎ 942 369288.

GIJON Marina Ch 09, ☎ 985 344543.

CUDILLERO HM/Yacht hbr Ch 27, ☎ 985 591114.

RIBADEO Marina Ch 09, ☎ 982 131444.

VIVERO Marina Ch 09, ☎ 982 570610.

RÍA DE ARES Marina Ch 09, ☎ 981 468787.

RÍA DE BETANZOS Marina Ch 09, ☎ 981 619015.

LA CORUÑA Marina Ch 09, ☎ 981 914142.

RÍA DE CAMARIÑAS Marina Ch 09, ☎ 981 737130.

RÍA DE MUROS HM Muros, ☎ 981 826005. CN Portosin Marina Ch 09, ☎ 981 766598.

RÍA DE AROUSA Marinas Ch 09: Caraminal, ☎ 981 830970. Sta Uxia, ☎ 981 873801. Vilagarcia, ☎ 986 511175. Piedras Negras, ☎ 986 738430.

RÍA DE PONTEVEDRA Marinas Ch 09: Sangenxo, ☎ 986 720517. Aguete, ☎ 986 702373.

RÍA DE VIGO VTS *Vigo Traffic* Ch 10. Marina Ch 09, ☎ 986 449694.

BAYONA MRCY Ch 06, ☎ 986 385000. Bayona Marina Ch 09, ☎ 986 385107.

PORTUGAL

VIANA DO CASTELO Marina Ch 09, ☎ 258 359546.

PÓVOA DE VARZIM Marina Ch 09, ☎ 252 688121.

LEIXÕES Port Ch 11. Marina Ch 09, ☎ 229 964895.

AVEIRO Port HM Ch 11, 12, 13, ☎ 234 366250.

FIGUEIRA DA FOZ Marina Ch 09, ☎ 233 402910.

NAZARÉ Marina Ch 09, ☎ 262 561401.

PENICHE Marina Ch 09, ☎ 262 783331.

CASCAIS Marina Ch 09, ☎ 214 824800.

LISBOA VTS *Lisboa Port Control* Ch 74. Marina Doca de Alcântara Ch 05, 09, 12, ☎ 213 922048.

SESIMBRA Port Ch 11. Marina Ch 09, ☎ 212 233451.

SETÚBAL VTS (applies to yachts >15m LOA) *Port Control* Ch 73. Marina Ch 09, ☎ 265 452076.

SINES Port Ch 11. Marina Ch 09, ☎ 269 860612.

LAGOS Port Ch 11. Marina Ch 09, ☎ 282 770210.

PORTIMÃO HM Ch 11. Marina Ch 09, ☎ 282 400680.

ALBUFEIRA. Marina Ch 09, ☎ 289 510180.

VILAMOURA. Marina Ch 09, ☎ 289 310560.

FARO ☎ 289 894990; OLHÃO ☎ 703160, Ch 11.

VILA REAL DE SANTO ANTÓNIO Port Ch 11. Marina Ch 09, ☎ 281 541571.

SW SPAIN

AYAMONTE Marina Ch 09, ☎ 959 321294.

IS CANELA, ☎ 959 479000; CRISTINA, ☎ 343501.

MAZAGON Marina Ch 09, ☎ 959 536251.

CHIPIONA Port Ch 12. Marina Ch 09, ☎ 956 373844.

SEVILLA Port Ch 12. Marinas Ch 09: Gelves ☎ 955 761212. Marina Yachting ☎ 954 230326. CN Sevilla ☎ 954 454777.

CÁDIZ Port *Cádiz Trafico* Ch 74. Marinas Ch 09: Rota ☎ 956 454777. Pto Sherry ☎ 870103. Pto de Sta Maria ☎ 852527. Pto America ☎ 223666.

SANCTI PETRI Marina Ch 09, ☎ 956 496169.

BARBATE Marina Ch 09, ☎ 956 431907.

TARIFA VTS *Tarifa Traffic* Ch 10, ☎ 956 684757. Info Ch 67 (on request) inc weather in TSS/ITZ.

ALGECIRAS Marina Ch 09, ☎ 956 572503.

GIBRALTAR AND MOROCCO

GIBRALTAR Port Ch 12, to be monitored whilst under way or at ⚓ in the Bay. Marinas, Ch 71: Queensway Quay, ☎ 350 44700; Marina Bay, ☎ 74322; Sheppards, ☎ 75148. Customs Ch 14. Commercial Port Ch 06.

TANGIER Port Ch 16, ☎ (00 2129) 3993 7495.

CEUTA (Spain) Marina Ch 09, ☎ 956 513753.

COAST RADIO STATIONS

Coast Radio Stations (CRS) deal with public correspondence (and a few other things). They enable a yachtsman to be linked by radio into the public telephone system in order to converse with a subscriber ashore, ie he can make or receive a Link call.

However the mobile 'phone has to a great extent rendered Link calls obsolescent. Thus there are no longer any CRS in the UK, France and Netherlands. In Germany a limited service is provided by a commercial company (see below).

CRS still operate in the Channel Islands, Ireland*, Denmark, Belgium, Spain and Portugal; see below. But they too may gradually be withdrawn. *In Ireland CRS no longer handle commercial link calls, but Medico link calls are still available on both VHF and MF.

The CG does **not** handle Link calls, except in Denmark and Belgium where the functions of CG and CRS have always been co-located.

CHANNEL ISLANDS

ST PETER PORT RADIO 49°27'·00N 02°32'00W
☎ 01481 720672 🖷 01534 714177
Link calls on **Ch 62** only. Ch 20 is used for navigation, pilotage and ships' business

JERSEY RADIO 49°10'·85N 02°14'30W ☎ 01534 885505 🖷 01534 499089
Link calls on **Ch 25** only

REPUBLIC OF IRELAND

A Coast Radio service is provided by the Dept of the Marine, Leeson Lane, Dublin 2, Eire. ☎ +353 (0)1 662 0922; ext 670 for enquiries. Broadcasts are made on a working channel/frequency following a prior announcement on Ch 16 and 2182 kHz. Ch 67 is used for Safety messages only. VHF calls to an Irish Coast Radio Station should be made on a working channel. Only use Ch 16 in case of difficulty or in emergency.

NW and SE Ireland

Weather broadcasts at 0103, 0403, 0703, 1003, 1303, 1603, 1903, 2203 UT and at 0033, 0633, 1233, 1833 UT on the VHF Channels below. Nav warnings are broadcast at 0033, 0433, 0833, 1233, 1633 and 2033 UT.

Clifden Radio	53°30'N 09°56'W	Ch 26
Belmullet Radio	54°16'N 10°03'W	Ch 83
Donegal Bay	54°22'N 08°31'W	Ch 02
Glen Head Radio	54°44'N 08°43'W	Ch 24
MALIN HD RADIO	55°22'N 07°21'W	Ch 23
MF 1677 kHz, ☎ +353 (0) 77 70103		
MMSI 002500100 DSC: 2187·5 kHz		

Carlingford Radio	54°05'N 06°19'W	Ch 04
DUBLIN RADIO	53°23'N 06°04'W	Ch 83
Wicklow Hd Radio	52°58'N 06°00'W	Ch 02
Rosslare Radio	52°15'N 06°20'W	Ch 23
Mine Hd Radio	52°00'N 07°35'W	Ch 83

SW Ireland

Weather is broadcast at 0103, 0403, 0703, 1003, 1303, 1603, 1903, 2203 and at 0033, 0633, 1233, 1833 UT on the VHF Channels listed.
Navwarnings are broadcast every 4 hrs from 0233.

Cork Radio	51°51'N 08°29'W	Ch 26
Mizen Radio	51°34'N 09°33'W	Ch 04
Bantry Radio	51°38'N 10°00'W	Ch 23
VALENTIA RADIO	51°56'N 10°21'W	Ch 24
MF 1752 kHz, ☎ + 353 (0) 66947 6109		
MMSI 002500200, DSC: 2187·5 kHz		
Shannon Radio	52°31'N 09°36'W	Ch 28
Galway Bay Radio	53°18'N 09°07'W	Ch 04

DENMARK

All VHF/MF CRS are remotely controlled from Lyngby Radio (55°50N 11°25'E) (MMSI 002191000). The callsign for all stations is Lyngby Radio. Call on working frequencies to help keep Ch 16 clear. The stations listed below monitor Ch 16 H24 and Ch 70 DSC. Traffic lists are broadcast on all VHF channels every odd H+05. All MF stations, except Skagen, keep watch H24 on 2182 kHz. Blåvand, Skagen and Lyngby also monitor MF 2187·5 kHz DSC. MF DSC Public correspondence facilities are available from Blåvand and Skagen on 1624·5 and 2177 kHz.

VHF & MF CRS

Skagen	57°44'N 10°35'E	Ch 04
	MF: Tx 1758, Rx 2045, 2102	
Hirtshals	57°31'N 09°57'E	Ch 66
Hanstholm	57°07'N 08°39'E	Ch 01
Bovbjerg	56°32'N 08°10'E	Ch 02
	MF: Tx 1767, Rx 2045, 2111	
Blåvand	55°33'N 08°07'E	Ch 23
	MF: Tx 1734, Rx 2045, 2078	

GERMANY

CRS: DPO7 – Seefunk (Hamburg) *(MMSI 002113100).* All stns monitor DSC Ch 70 and 16. Traffic lists are broadcast: 0745, 0945, 1245, 1645, 1945 and H & H+30 on request Ch 16.

Nordfriesland	54°31'N 08°41'E	Ch 26
Elbe-Weser	53°50'N 08°39'E	Ch 24
Hamburg	53°33'N 09°58'E	Ch 83
Bremen	53°05'N 08°48'E	Ch 25
Accumersiel	53°40'N 07°29'E	Ch 28
Borkum	53°35'N 06°40'E	Ch 61

COMMUNICATIONS

NORTH SPAIN

All stns guard DSC Ch 70 H24. Ch 16 is not continuously guarded. Call on working channel below; the callsign is the name of the station followed by Radio; all are remotely controlled by Bilbao Comms Centre. Navigation warnings on VHF at 0840 & 2010 after weather broadcast.

Pasajes	43°17'N 01°55'W	Ch 27
Machichaco	43°27'N 02°45'W MF 1707 kHz	No VHF
BILBAO	43°22'N 03°02'W	Ch 26
Santander	43°25'N 03°36'W	Ch 24
Cabo Peñas	43°26'N 05°35'W MF 1677 kHz	Ch 26
Navia	43°25'N 06°50'W	Ch 60

NORTH WEST SPAIN

Details as for N Spain. All stations are remotely controlled by Coruña Comms Centre.

Cabo Ortegal	43°35'N 07°47'W	Ch 02
CORUÑA	43°22'N 08°27'W MF 1698 kHz	Ch 26
Finisterre	42°54'N 09°16'W	Ch 22
Vigo	42°10'N 08°41'W	Ch 65
La Guardia	41°53'N 08°52'W	Ch 21

PORTUGAL

Stations are remotely controlled by Lisboa. All monitor Ch 16 H24. The callsign is the name of the station followed by Radio.

Arga	41°48'N 08°41'W	24, 25, 28, 83
Arestal	40°46'N 08°21'W	12, 24-26, 85
Montejunto	39°10'N 09°03'W	24, 25, 27, 86
LISBOA	38°33'N 09°11'W	12, 23, 25, 26, 83
		MF 2182 kHz
Atalaia	38°10'N 08°38'W	12, 23-25, 85
Foia	37°50'N 08°35'W	23, 24, 27, 28
Estoi	37°10'N 07°50'W	24, 27, 28, 86

AZORES

Stations are remotely controlled by Lisboa. All monitor Ch 16 H24. The callsign is the name of the station followed by Radio.

Flores	39°27'N 31°32'W	Ch 23-26
Faial	38°35'N 28°43'W	Ch 24-26, 28
Pico	38°24'N 28°44'W	Ch 23, 24, 26
Sao Miguel	37°45'N 25°40'W	Ch 23-27

SOUTH WEST SPAIN

Stations are remotely controlled from Malaga. Initially call Ch 16 H24 using station callsign, ie name + Radio. Navwarnings 0833 & 2033 after the weather.

Chipiona	36°42'N 06°25'W MF 1656kHz	No VHF
Cádiz	36°22'N 06°17'W	Ch 26
Tarifa	36°03'N 05°33'W MF 1704 kHz	Ch 81

SHAPES

◆	Towing vessel - length of tow > 200m	Rule 24
▼	Yacht under sail *and* power	Rule 25
✕	Vessel fishing or trawling	Rule 26
✕ + ▲	Vessel fishing with outlying gear >150mlong	Rule 26
● ◆ ●	Vessel restricted in her ability to manoeuvre	Rule 27
● ●	Vessel not under command	Rule 27
▮	Vessel constrained by her draught	Rule 28
●	Vessel at anchor	Rule 30

SOUND SIGNALS

MANOEUVRING AND WARNING Rule 34

•	A short blast = about 1 second.
—	A prolonged blast = 4 – 6 seconds.
•	I am altering course to **Starboard**
••	I am altering course to **Port**
•••	My engines are going **Astern**
•••••	I do not understand your intentions/ actions

Note: The above sound signals may be supplemented by light signals flashed on an all-round white light with least range of 5 miles.

In a narrow channel

— — •	I intend to overtake on your starboard side.
— — ••	I intend to overtake on your port side.
— • — •	I agree with your overtaking signal
—	Warning by vessel nearing a bend where other vessels may not be seen
—	Approaching vessel acknowledges.

VESSELS IN RESTRICTED VISIBILITY Rule 35

–	Power-driven vessel making way.
– –	Power-driven vessel underway, but stopped and not making way.
– ••	**A sailing vessel**; vessels not under command; restricted in ability to manoeuvre; constrained by draught; engaged in fishing, towing or pushing.
– •••	Vessel being towed or, if more than one vessel is towed, the last vessel in the tow.

Vessels at anchor

⌓	Bell, ring for 5 seconds every minute
⌓⟍	Vessel >100m: Bell forward, ring for 5 seconds every minute; plus
⊙	Gong aft, for 5 seconds every minute.
– • –	Optional extra to warn any approaching vessel

Sailing vessels < 12m at ⚓ do not have to sound the above fog signals. But if they do not, they *must* make an efficient noise every 2 minutes.

INTERNATIONAL PORT TRAFFIC SIGNALS (IPTS)

IPTS are widely used on the Continent, but less so around the UK. They may also be used to control traffic at locks and bridges.

- The main movement signal is always 3 lights in a vertical column, to which no extra light shall be added. Thus it is always recognisable as IPTS, as distinct from some kind of navigational lights.

- Red lights ® indicate *Do not proceed*.

- Green lights Ⓖ indicate *Proceed, subject to the conditions stipulated*. To avoid confusion ® and Ⓖ lights are never displayed together.

- Signals may be omni-directional ie seen by all vessels simultaneously; or directional, ie seen only from outside or from inside the harbour.

- Some ports may only use signals 2 and 4, or only Signal 1 when necessary

- Signal 1 *Serious Emergency* must show at least 60 flashes/minute.

- All other signals may be fixed or slow occulting, eg every 10s (helpful when background glare poses a problem), but never a mixture of both.

- Signal 5 assumes that VHF, signal lamp, loud-hailer, auxiliary signal or other means of communication will specifically inform a vessel that she may proceed.

- Exemption signals. A single Ⓨ light, shown to the left of signals 2 or 5 and level with the upper light, means *Vessels which can safely navigate outside the main channel need not comply with the main message*. This signal is obviously important to small craft, which nevertheless have a

No	Lights		Main message
1	☀®☀ ☀®☀ ☀®☀	Flashing	Serious emergency – all vessels to stop or divert according to instructions
2	® ® ®		Vessels shall not proceed (*Note:* Some ports may use an exemption signal, as in 2a below)
3	Ⓖ Ⓖ Ⓖ		Vessels may proceed. One-way traffic
4	Ⓖ Ⓖ Ⓦ	Fixed or Slow Occulting	Vessels may proceed. Two-way traffic
5	Ⓖ Ⓦ Ⓖ		A vessel may proceed only when she has received specific orders to do so. (*Note:* Some ports may use an exemption signal, as in 5a below)
	Exemption signals and messages		
2a	Ⓨ ® ® ®	Fixed or Slow Occulting	Vessels shall not proceed, except that vessels which navigate outside the main channel need not comply with the main message
5a	Ⓨ Ⓖ Ⓦ Ⓖ		A vessel may proceed when she has received specific orders to do so, except that vessels which navigate outside the main channel need not comply with the main message
	Auxiliary signals and messages		
	White and/or yellow lights, displayed with the main lights		

clear duty to keep clear of manoeuvring vessels.

- Auxiliary signals (only Ⓦ and/or Ⓨ lights) may be locally authorised and displayed to the right of the main signal. Their meanings must be promulgated.

COMMUNICATIONS

117

Chapter 4 - Safety

THINK SAFETY - BE PREPARED

Many 'incidents' at sea are preventable by the sensible application of knowledge and experience. Experience can only be gained by going to sea and building up a mental 'database' from which to draw when we are faced with a problem which demands quick, decisive actions to bring the situation under control. There are no short cuts, and no qualifications or classroom work that can substitute for time spent underway.

Knowledge, on the other hand, can be acquired ashore and there is no lack of courses and facilities available where one can learn or brush up on the theory. For example, before venturing afloat we should all acquire an instinctive working knowledge of the Collision Regulations. A dark, wet and windy night is no time to start looking in books to find out what lights a fishing vessel displays when trawling, what red-white-red shown vertically might signify, or what action to take to avoid a collision in fog.

Occasionally, genuine accidents do happen. Despite the most rigorous checks, rigging and engines can fail unexpectedly, the weather does sometimes defy the forecasters, and semi-submerged containers do get in the way. In these circumstances we can only do our best to mitigate the damage and, if necessary, call for help. In this chapter you will find definitions of Distress, Urgency and Safety; how to make a MAYDAY call; a brief description of GMDSS; an outline of services provided by the Coastguard, Coast Radio Stations, the RNLI and the National Coastwatch Institution; and advice on how to cope with medical emergencies. A few minutes spent reading now could pay off if you are ever unfortunate enough to find yourself in difficulties.

Most 'accidents', though, can be averted by thorough maintenance, careful preparation and a continuously critical eye on the boat, the weather, the crew – and yourself. A tired skipper is unlikely to be an effective skipper, especially when he or she needs to take charge of an anxious crew facing a difficult situation. A good skipper will continuously be asking 'What if ...?' for all conceivable eventualities: What if the engine dies? What if someone falls overboard? What if the visibility reduces? The list is endless. Most of us have never experienced a fire at sea; even a small one can be extremely dangerous, very frightening, and often produces lots of smoke. Are all your extinguishers in date? Does everyone know where they are? Do they all know how to operate them? And if it all goes wrong, are your flares in date and do you know how to use them - in the dark?

The Marine Accident Investigation Branch (MAIB) recently reported a tragic case of a life lost when a man went over the side following an uncontrolled gybe in a Force 5-6 and rough seas. In those conditions all the crew should have been wearing properly fitted lifejackets. If they had been, it is possible that the man could have been saved. However, he wasn't even brought back on board, so the case also illustrated just how difficult it is to recover someone from the water - even in a fully crewed yacht. No amount of MOB drills with a fender can prepare you for the real thing. Unless you are extremely lucky and the weather is benign, the chances of recovering a cold, semi-conscious or heavy person are very slight indeed.

The Fastnet Race of 1979 showed that it is much safer to remain with the yacht (if she is not actually sinking under you) rather than take to a liferaft. The same applies to involuntarily falling over the side. In many circumstances, wearing a lifejacket is a wise precaution - at night, in fog, in the dinghy - but it only comes into its own when you are in the water! Far, far better to stay onboard by using a well adjusted harness securely clipped on to the boat.

So far, yachting is relatively free of burdensome regulations. The safer we keep ourselves while afloat, the less excuse there is for introducing more rules and restrictions. Let's keep it that way.

DEFINITIONS OF DISTRESS, URGENCY AND SAFETY

Distress (MAYDAY): *A ship or person is in grave and imminent danger and requires immediate assistance.* Appropriate for a man overboard if not quickly recovered.

Urgency (PAN-PAN): *A very urgent message concerning the safety of a vessel or person.* May be used for urgent medical advice.

Safety (SÉCURITÉ): Used typically by coast stations to announce navigational or weather warnings. May be used to report a hazard, eg a buoy adrift.

HOW TO MAKE A DISTRESS CALL

- Switch on the VHF Radio
- Select **Channel 16**
- Make sure Dual Watch is disabled
- Select **HIGH POWER (25W)**
- Hold down the transmit button on the microphone; say slowly and clearly:
- **MAYDAY, MAYDAY, MAYDAY**
- This is.....................................(Say your boat's name 3 times)
- **MAYDAY**...........(Repeat your boat's name once)
- My position is................... (See below)
- *Tell them what is wrong:* For example, the boat is sinking; how many people (including you) on board; if you have fired flares; if you are abandoning ship etc. If there is time, repeat your position
- **I require immediate assistance. Over** - This means: please reply
- Release the microphone button and listen for an acknowledgement
- If you can't hear clearly, adjust the volume and/or squelch controls

If there is no reply, check the radio switches and repeat the message

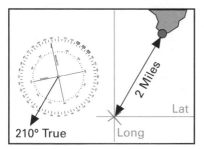

210° True   Long   Lat

Give your position as either:

Lat and Long (from the GPS); or

Bearing and distance from a known landmark or feature (see left for eg: 'My position is 210° True, 2 miles from Portland Bill'); or

General location if appropriate (eg: 'Aground on the Bramble Bank')

Say if you are not sure – do not guess!

MAYDAY RELAY

- **If you hear a MAYDAY call, write it down**
- If practicable to give assistance, acknowledge the call

- If you can't offer assistance and no acknowledgement is heard:
- Select VHF **Channel 16**
- Select **HIGH POWER (25W)**
- Make sure Dual Watch is disabled
- Hold down the transmit button on the microphone; say slowly and clearly:
- **MAYDAY RELAY, MAYDAY RELAY, MAYDAY RELAY**
- **This is**......................(say your boat's name 3 times)
- **State the MAYDAY message, exactly as you wrote it down**
- **Over** - This means: please reply
- Release the button and listen

HELICOPTER RESCUE

- **COMMUNICATE ON CHANNEL 16**
- Use flares or smoke when helicopter is seen or heard
- Helicopter may ask you to drop sails and motor on a specific course
- You may be asked to stream the casualty astern in the dinghy
- Brief yourcrew early (too noisy when helicopter is close)
- **HELM MUST KEEP ON COURSE** and not be distracted
- Weighted line lowered
- Let it touch boat or water first (to earth any static charge)
- Take in slack line only
- **PULL IN AS DIRECTED**
- **DO NOT SECURE IT TO THE BOAT**
- **DO AS YOU ARE TOLD**
  Note: The text and sketch relate to a Hi-line transfer, one of several techniques which may be used

MEDICAL HELP

- **CH 16, High power, Dual watch off**
- **PAN PAN** .... (repeat 3 times)
- **ALL STATIONS** .... (repeat 3 times)
- **This is** .... (repeat 3 times)
- Over
  Next message should contain:
  Yacht's name, callsign, nationality
  Yacht's position and nearest harbour
  Patient's details, symptoms and advice wanted
  The medication you have on board

FIRST AID

The objectives of First Aid at sea are to:

• **Preserve life** • **Prevent further damage**
• **Relieve pain and distress** • **Deliver a live casualty ashore**

With any casualty be calm, reassuring and methodical. But first ensure your own safety and that of the vessel. If in doubt call for advice and assistance.

MEDICAL ADVICE can be obtained almost anywhere in European waters by making an All-Stations 'PAN PAN' call or a DSC Urgency Alert to the Coastguard or to a Coast Radio Station. They will connect you to a doctor or to the nearest hospital.

The Urgency signal 'PAN PAN' is always advised, especially abroad, because it is internationally understood and eliminates most language problems; it is also free.

As a layman you are not qualified to judge how serious the casualty's condition is – so get the best possible advice and/or help as quickly as possible. *Urgent help needed* is shown below against the more serious medical problems.

Be ready to describe the patient's symptoms, eg consciousness, pulse rate, breathing rate, temperature, skin colour, site and type of injury, any pain, amount of blood lost etc. If a doctor needs to come aboard, or a casualty has to be landed, the Coastguard will arrange.

If non-urgent, wait until in harbour. Consider calling the port authority before arrival so that a doctor or paramedic can meet you on arrival.

MEDICAL CARE ABROAD It is sensible to carry the European Health Insurance Card (EHIC) which entitles you to medical treatment on a reciprocal basis, although it may not cover the full charge. See *www.dh.gov.uk* for full details.

EMERGENCY RESUSCITATION (ABC)

The immediate procedure for any collapsed or apparently unconscious person is: Assess whether or not the casualty is conscious. Carefully shake his/her shoulders and ask loudly 'What's happened?' or 'Are you all right?' or give a command such as 'Open your eyes'. An unconscious casualty will not respond.

A = Airway

Remove any visible obstruction from the casualty's mouth (leave well-fitting dentures in place). Listen at the mouth for breathing. Tilt the head backwards, using head tilt and chin lift to maintain a clear airway.

Check the area is clear of danger. Place casualty in recovery position if breathing.

B = Breathing

Keeping the airway open, check whether the casualty is breathing normally by **looking** for chest movement, **listening** at the mouth for breathing sounds and **feeling** for breath on your cheek. Look, listen and feel for 10 seconds before deciding that breathing is absent.

If the casualty is not breathing and the airway is clear, mouth to mouth ventilation can be started, in conjunction with 'External chest compression' below: kneel beside the casualty, maintain head tilt and chin lift, and pinch the nostrils. Take a deep breath and blow two full breaths into patient's mouth. Watch for rise and fall of chest.

C = Circulation

Assess the casualty for signs of circulation by looking, listening and feeling for normal breathing, coughing, any movement or improvement in colour. Check for signs of circulation for no more than 10 seconds. If the circulation stops, the breathing will also stop.

If there are no signs of a circulation or you are at all unsure, assume that the heart has stopped. This is called **cardiac arrest**. The casualty will be unconscious and may appear very pale, grey or bluish in colour.

An artificial circulation will have to be provided by chest compression. Casualties with cardiac arrest will need both rescue breathing and chest compression, a combination known as Cardio Pulmonary Resuscitation (**CPR**).

External chest compression

To start external chest compression, lay the casualty face up on a hard, flat surface. Kneel beside casualty. The point at which pressure will be applied is the centre of the chest.

Place the heel of your hand on top of the other hand and interlock your fingers.

Depress breastbone 4–5cm (1½–2in) then release.

With either one or two operators give 30 chest compressions and continue cycles of 2 breaths to 30 compressions. Use a compression rate of 100 per minute. Chest compression must always be combined with rescue breathing so after every 30 compressions, give 2 effective rescue breaths. *Do not stop.*

Action plan for the resuscitation of adults
Casualty unconscious but is breathing normally:

• *Urgent help needed*
• Turn casualty into the recovery position
• Check for continued breathing

Casualty is unconscious and not breathing:
- **Urgent help needed**
- Give 2 effective rescue breaths
- Check for signs of circulation

If no sign of a circulation, give 30 chest compressions and continue cycles of 2 breaths to 30 compressions.

If breathing restarts, place casualty in the recovery position.

BITES AND STINGS Injected poison from bites and stings usually only causes local swelling and discomfort, but some people may react severely. For insect stings, resuscitate if collapse occurs; otherwise give rest, painkillers, antihistamines (eg chlorpheniramine).

BLEEDING – OPEN WOUND Bleeding is often very dramatic, but is virtually always controllable.
- Apply firm continuous direct pressure; bandage on a large pad. If bleeding continues, bandage more pads on top of initial pads; then press directly over wound for at least 10 minutes (blood takes this long to clot).
- Elevate if wound is on a limb.
- Do *not* apply a tourniquet. This practice is out of date due to the danger of losing a limb.

BLEEDING – INTERNAL (CLOSED INJURY)
Follows fractured bones, crush injuries, or rupture of organs such as the liver or spleen. Treat for shock which may appear rapidly. *Urgent help needed*.

BURNS AND SCALDS Move the victim into fresh air to avoid inhaling smoke.

ABC – Airway, Breathing, Circulation
Stop further injury: dip the whole of the burnt part into cold water for 10–15 minutes. Seawater is excellent but may be very painful.

Remove only loose clothing. Do not pull off clothing stuck to the skin.

Cover with sterile dressing. If skin is broken or blistered, use sterile paraffin gauze beneath the dressing. Separate burnt fingers with paraffin gauze. Never use adhesive dressings.

Do not prick blisters or apply ointments.

Elevate burnt limb and immobilise.

Give strong painkillers.

Treat for shock: give frequent and copious drinks of water.

Start giving antibiotics for major burns. If burns extensive or deep, *urgent help needed*.

CHOKING If blockage by some object (eg a peanut) is suspected, turn the casualty on his side and give up to 5 sharp back slaps with the flat of the hand between the shoulder blades. Check mouth and remove any obstruction.

If unsuccessful, wrap both arms around the victim's waist from behind, and give 5 sharp upward thrusts with both fists into the abdomen above the navel but below the ribs so as to cause coughing. Clear object from mouth.

CUTS AND WOUNDS Often dramatic but only potentially serious if nerves, tendons or blood vessels are severed.

Clean thoroughly with antiseptic. Remove dirt or other foreign bodies. Small clean cuts can be closed using as many Steristrips as necessary to keep the skin edges together. Skin must be dry. Leave for 5 days at least. Larger deep cuts may require stitches; apply a dressing and seek help. Do not try amateur surgery at sea.

Ragged lacerations or very dirty wounds – do not attempt to close these. Clean as well as possible, sprinkle antibiotic powder in wound and apply a dressing. Seek help. If in doubt a wound is best left open and lightly covered to keep it clean and dry.

Fingers and toes Blood may collect under the nail following an injury. Release the blood by piercing the nail with a red hot needle or paper clip. It will not hurt!

DENTAL PAIN seems worse at sea; prevention is better than cure. Dentanurse is an emergency treatment pack which enables an amateur to make temporary repairs, eg replacing crowns, lost fillings. It contains zinc oxide and Eugenol.

Throbbing toothache made worse by hot or cold or when bitten on. Clean out any cavity and apply temporary filling. Take painkiller.

Dull toothache tender to bite on; gum swollen or red with possible discharge. Treat as above but also take an antibiotic.

Broken tooth or filling Cover exposed surfaces with zinc oxide paste. Teeth knocked out should be put in a clean container with milk or moist gauze for a dentist to re-implant asap. This can be attempted onboard - ideally within 1 hour

Bleeding gums Clean teeth more thoroughly. Use regular hot salt water rinses and antibiotics.

Pain round wisdom tooth Clean area with toothbrush; use hot salt water rinses; take antibiotics and painkillers.

Mouth ulcers Hot salt water rinses.

DIARRHOEA Can become serious, especially in young children if much fluid is lost. Stop food, give plenty of fluid. Plain water is usually sufficient, or add salt (1 teaspoonful/litre) and sugar (4–5 teaspoons/litre). Lomotil or Imodium tablets are very effective in adults.

DROWNING ABC Clear seaweed, dentures. If not breathing start mouth to mouth ventilation

SAFETY

123

as soon as possible and in the water if practicable. If no pulse, start chest compression as soon as on board. Keep the head low so that vomit is not inhaled and water can drain.

If stomach is bulging, turn casualty on to side to empty water and avoid inhaling it. Prevent cooling. Remove wet clothes; wrap casualty in blankets to warm him/her.

Continue resuscitation until the casualty revives or death is certain. Hypothermia may mimic death. Do not abandon resuscitation until the casualty has been warmed or signs of death persist despite attempts at warming.

Once revived, put in the recovery position.

Any person rescued from drowning may collapse in the next 24 hours as the lungs react to inhaled water. *Urgent help needed*.

EYE INJURIES are potentially serious. Never put old or previously opened ointment or drops into an eye; serious infection could result.

Foreign object Flush with clean water, pull the lower lid out to inspect, remove object with a clean tissue. For objects under upper eyelid, ask casualty to grasp lashes and pull the upper lid over the lower lid. An eye-bath is very effective. Blinking under water may help. After removal of object, insert sterile antibiotic ointment inside pulled out lower lid. Cover with pad.

Corrosive fluid Flush continuously with water for 15 minutes. Give painkillers and chloramphenicol ointment; cover with pad. *Seek help asap*.

Conjunctivitis Sticky, weeping eye with yellow discharge. Chloramphenicol 4 times a day.

FISH HOOKS Push the hook round until the point and barb can be cut off; withdraw the hook. Dress the holes and give an antibiotic.

FRACTURES AND DISLOCATIONS Fracture is a broken bone. Dislocation is a displaced joint. Both produce pain (aggravated by attempted movement), localised swelling, abnormal shape, and a grating feeling on movement (if it is a fracture). Blood vessels or nerves around the fracture or dislocation may also be damaged causing a cold, pale, or numb limb below the site of the injury.

Fractures of large bones such as the femur (upper leg) will result in major internal bleeding and may cause shock. When complications occur *urgent help is needed*.

Early application of a splint and raising the injured limb where possible will reduce pain and complications. Treat for shock and pain.

Specific fractures and dislocations
Cheek Caused by a direct blow. Rarely serious but requires specialist care.

Jaw Beware of associated brain or spinal injury. Remove blood and teeth fragments; leave loose teeth in place; protect broken teeth. Ensure airway is clear. Start regular antiseptic mouth washes and antibiotics. Support jaw with bandage over top of the head. Give only fluids by mouth.

Neck May result from a direct blow, a fall or a whiplash type injury. If conscious, casualty may complain of pain, tingling, numbness or weakness in limbs below the injury. *Mishandling may damage the spinal cord, causing paralysis or death*. Avoid movement and support the head. Immobilise by wrapping a folded towel around the neck. If movement is necessary then lift the victim as one rigid piece, never allowing the neck to bend. *Urgent help needed*.

Nose Control bleeding by pinching.

Ribs Very painful. Strapping is not advised.

Spine Fracture of the spine below the neck, may cause *paralysis or death*. Mishandling of the victim may greatly worsen the damage. Avoid movement if possible. Lift the casualty without allowing the spine to sag. *Urgent help needed*.

Collar bone Support arm in sling.

Dislocated shoulder If this has happened before, the casualty may remedy the dislocation himself; otherwise do not attempt to remedy it in case a fracture exists.

Upper arm Support the arm with a collar and cuff inside the shirt, ie tie a clove hitch around the wrist and loop the ends behind the neck.

Forearm and wrist Splint (eg with battens or wood). Do not bandage tightly. Elevate or support in a sling.

Fingers Elevate hand and, unless badly crushed, leave unbandaged; keep moving. If very wobbly, bandage to adjacent finger.

Lower limb
Thigh Shock may be considerable. Strap to other leg with padding between. Gently straighten the lower leg. If necessary apply traction at the ankle to help straighten the leg. Do not bandage too tightly.

Knee Twisting injuries or falls damage the ligaments and cartilages of the knee. Very painful and swollen. Treat as for fracture.

Lower leg Pad very well. Splint using oar, broom handle or similar pieces of wood.

Ankle Fracture or severe sprain may be indistinguishable. Immobilise in neutral position with foot at right angles. Raise the limb.

HEART ATTACK Severe 'crushing' chest pain; may spread to shoulders, neck or arms. Sweating, then bluish lips, then collapse.

Breathing and heart may stop. Give one 300mg aspirin tablet (to chew) **Urgent help needed.**

Rest, reassure. If unconscious: recovery position; observe breathing and pulse. If breathing stops or no pulse, start mouth to mouth ventilation and chest compression immediately; do not stop.

HEAT STROKE Cool casualty by spraying with cold water or wrap the casualty in a cold wet sheet until their temperature under the tongue falls to 38°C. Encourage drinking (1 teaspoon of salt/half litre of water). If casualty stops sweating, has a rapid pounding pulse and is becoming unconscious: **Urgent help needed.**

HYPOTHERMIA will follow immersion in the sea or prolonged exposure on deck. Symptoms include: unreasonable behaviour, apathy and confusion; unsteady gait, stumbling; slurring of speech; pale, cold skin; slow, weak pulse; slow breathing; shivering. It leads to collapse, unconsciousness and ultimately death.

ABC Put in recovery position. If not breathing, start mouth to mouth ventilation. Be prepared to use chest compressions.

Remove wet clothing. Avoid wind chill. Dry and wrap in blankets or sleeping bag plus warm hat and cover, if available, in foil survival bag. **Urgent help needed.**

Give hot sweet drinks if conscious. Do not give alcohol, or rub the skin, or place very hot objects against skin.

SEASICKNESS is a motion-induced inner ear disturbance, aggravated by fear, anxiety, fatigue and boredom. Symptoms: lethargy, dizziness, headache, nausea and vomiting. Take preventative drugs.

Avoid strong food tastes and too much alcohol. Take small amounts of fluid and food (eg biscuits) frequently if you feel ill. Avoid fatigue; adequate sleep will often give relief. Keep warm. Stay on deck, and concentrate on some task if possible. Sick crew on deck must be secured by lifeline. Turn in if all else fails. Prolonged seasickness may cause serious loss of fluid – seek advice. See First Aid kit for drugs.

SHOCK can result from almost any accident or medical emergency; it can lead to collapse.

Signs and symptoms Thirst, apathy, nausea, restlessness. Pale, cold, clammy skin, sweating. Rapid, weak pulse. Rapid, shallow breathing. Dull, sunken eyes, bluish lips.

ABC Control any bleeding. Lay the casualty flat or in recovery position; raise legs 20°. Splint any fractures; avoid movement. Avoid chilling, keep warm. Give pain killers. Reassure the casualty. Do not let the casualty eat, drink, smoke or move unnecessarily. If complaining of thirst, moisten the lips with a little water. Note: Fluids may be life saving in cases of dehydration (eg diarrhoea, vomiting, severe burns).

FIRST AID KIT

Stow the following items in a waterproof container, readily accessible and clearly marked:

Triangular bandage x 2 (doubles as a sling)
Crepe bandage 75mm x 2
Gauze bandage 50mm x 2
Elastoplast 75mm x 1
Band Aids (or similar) various shapes and sizes
Wound dressings, 1 large, 1 medium
Sterile non-adhesive dressing (Melolin) x 5
Steristrips x 5 packs
Cotton wool. Safety pins. Thermometer.
Scissors and forceps, good quality stainless steel
Disposable gloves
Antiseptic solution (eg Savlon)
Sunscreen with high protection factor
Antifungal powder or cream (athlete's foot)
Insect repellent (DEET, diethyltoluamide)
Individual choice of anti-seasick tablets
Antibiotic eye ointment (prescription only)

Additional items for extended cruising

Vaccinations – a course may need to start as much as 6 months before departure.
Syringes 2ml x 2 (if carrying injections)
Dental kit – see Dental pain.
Moisture cream (for cracked hands and lips)

DRUGS

*Prescriptions are needed for asterisked drugs. Out of date drugs are potentially dangerous – destroy them.

Drug, purpose and dose

Paracetamol, painkiller. 1-2 500mg tablets 4 hrly.

*Dihydrocodeine, strong painkiller. 1-2 30mg tablets 4 hrly.

Chlorpheniramine, antihistamine. 1 x 4mg tablet 8 hrly.

Aludrox, indigestion. 1-2 before meals.

Loperamide, diarrhoea. 2 x 2mg capsules initially, then 1 after each loose stool; max 8 day.

Senokot, constipation. 2-4 tablets per day.

Tetracycline, antibiotic. 1 x 250mg capsule, 4 times per day.

*Amoxycillin, antibiotic. 2 x 250 mg capsules 8 hrly. (Beware penicillin allergy)

*Erythromycin, antibiotic for penicillin-allergic adults. 4 x 250mg tablets daily.

Cinnarizine, seasickness. 2 x 15mg tablets before sailing, then 1 every 8 hrs.

OBSERVATION FORM

The information recorded by you on this form will be invaluable in helping doctors and/or paramedics ashore to diagnose the problem and arrange the best possible treatment for your casualty.

This is particularly important if there may be a considerable time lapse between requesting medical help and the casualty reaching hospital.

- Keep photocopies of this form in your First Aid kit so as to preserve the original.
- Whilst awaiting help, record your careful observations by ticking or annotating the various boxes at 10 minute intervals. This will help doctors detect any improvement or deterioration in the casualty's condition.

- If within radio range of shore attempt to pass the observations via the Coastguard to a medical authority; or ask a ship to relay.

- Before the casualty is taken off the yacht ensure that this form and personal documents (money, passport, EHIC and mobile 'phone) are securely tied to him/her.

DATE .... CASUALTY'S NAME .... AGE .... M/F ....

Times of observations @ 10 minute intervals:		10	20	30	40	50	60
EYES Observe for reactions whilst testing other responses	Open spontaneously						
	Open when spoken to						
	Open to painful stimulus						
	Nil response						
MOVEMENT Apply painful stimulus: Pinch ear lobe or skin on back of hand	Obeys commands						
	Responds						
	Nil response						
SPEECH Speak clearly and directly, close to the casualty's ear	Responds sensibly to queries						
	Seems confused						
	Uses inappropriate words						
	Incomprehensible sounds						
	Nil response						
PULSE (Beats per minute) Take adult' pulse at wrist or neck. Note rate and whether beats are: weak (w); strong (s); regular (reg) or irregular (irreg)	Over 110						
	101-110						
	91-100						
	81-90						
	71-80						
	61-70						
	Below 61						
BREATHING (Breaths per minute) Note rate and whether breathing is: quiet (q); noisy (n); easy (e); or difficult (d)	Over 40						
	31-40						
	21-30						
	11-20						
	Below 11						

GMDSS

The Global Maritime Distress and Safety System (GMDSS) is a sophisticated, but complex, semi-automatic, third-generation communications system. Although not compulsory for yachts, its potential for saving life, particularly when far offshore and out of VHF range, is so great that every yachtsman should seriously consider it. Equipment costs continue to fall. Training courses, leading to the award of the Short Range Certificate (SRC) of Competence, are widely available. The Long Range Certificate covers MF, HF, SatCom, EPIRBs and SART.

Recommended reading:

- *ALRS, Vol 5* (UK Hydrographic Office)
- *GMDSS: a User's Handbook* (Bréhaut/ACN)
- *GMDSS for small craft* (Clemmetsen/Fernhurst)
- *Reeds VHF/DSC Handbook* (Fletcher/ACN)

Purpose

GMDSS enables a coordinated SAR operation to be mounted rapidly and reliably anywhere at sea. To this end, terrestrial and satellite communications and navigation equipment is used to alert SAR authorities ashore and ships in the vicinity to a Distress incident or Urgency situation. GMDSS also promulgates Maritime Safety Information.

Sea areas

For the purposes of GMDSS, the world's sea areas are divided into 4 categories (A1-4), defined mainly by the range of radio communications. These are:

A1 An area within R/T coverage of at least one VHF Coastguard or Coast radio station in which continuous VHF alerting is available via DSC. Range: 20–50M from the CG/CRS.

A2 An area, excluding sea area A1, within R/T coverage of at least one MF CG/CRS in which continuous DSC alerting is available. Range: approx 50–250M from the CG/CRS.

A3 An area between 70°N and 70°S, excluding sea areas A1 and A2, within coverage of HF or an Inmarsat satellite in which continuous alerting is available.

A4 An area outside sea areas A1, A2 and A3, ie the polar regions, within coverage of HF.

In each category of sea area certain types of radio equipment must be carried. In A1 areas VHF DSC; A2 areas MF or HF DSC; A3 areas SatCom; A4 MF/HF.

Most UK yachtsmen will operate in A1 areas (the English Channel, for example, is an A1 area) where a simple VHF radio and a Navtex receiver will initially meet GMDSS requirements. As equipment becomes more affordable, yachtsmen may decide to fit GMDSS. This will become increasingly necessary as the present system for sending and receiving Distress calls is run down. The CG will continue a loudspeaker watch on VHF Ch 16 until further notice.

Functions

Regardless of the sea areas in which they operate, vessels complying with GMDSS must be able to perform certain functions:

- transmit ship-to-shore Distress alerts by two independent means
- receive shore-to-ship Distress alerts
- transmit & receive ship-to-ship Distress alerts
- transmit signals for locating incidents
- transmit and receive communications for SAR co-ordination
- transmit/receive maritime safety info, eg navigation and weather warnings

Distress alerts

A Distress alert is simply a Distress call using DSC. It is transmitted on Ch 70 and is automatically repeated five times. Whenever possible, a Distress alert should always include the last known position and time in UT. The position is normally entered automatically from an interfaced GPS, but can be entered manually if required. The nature of the distress can also be selected from the receiver's menu. The vessel's identity (MMSI number) is automatically included.

GMDSS requires participating ships to be able to send Distress alerts by two out of three independent means. These are:

- Digital Selective Calling (DSC) using terrestrial communications, ie VHF Ch 70,

SAFETY

127

MF 2187·5 kHz, or HF distress and alerting frequencies in the 4, 6, 8,12 and 16 MHz bands.

- Emergency Position Indicating Radio Beacons (EPIRBs), either float-free or manually released, using the Cospas/Sarsat satellites on 406 MHz with homing on 121·5 MHz; or those using Inmarsat satellites in the 1·6 GHz band. Both types transmit Distress messages which include the position and identification of the vessel in distress. See below for further details of EPIRBs.
- Inmarsat, via ship terminals.

Digital Selective Calling

DSC is an essential component of GMDSS. It is so called because information is sent by a burst of digital code; selective because it can be addressed to a specific DSC-equipped vessel or to a selected group of vessels.

In all DSC messages every vessel and relevant shore station has a 9-digit identification number, or MMSI (Maritime Mobile Service Identity), which is in effect an automatic, electronic callsign.

DSC is used to transmit Distress alerts from ships, to receive Distress acknowledgements from ships or shore stations; to send Urgency and Safety alerts; to relay Distress alerts; and for routine calling & answering. A thorough working knowledge is needed.

Using the procedures and switches applicable to your particular VHF/DSC radio, a VHF/DSC Distress alert might be sent as follows:

- Briefly press the (red, guarded) Distress button. The set automatically switches to Ch 70 (DSC Distress chan). Press again for 5 seconds to transmit a basic Distress alert with position & time. It then reverts to Ch l6.
- If time permits, select the nature of distress from the menu, eg Collision, then press the Distress button for 5 seconds to send a full Distress alert.

A CG/CRS automatically sends a Distress acknowledgement on Ch 70, before replying on Ch 16. Ships in range should reply directly on Ch 16.

If a Distress acknowledgement is not received from a CG/CRS, the Distress alert will automatically be repeated every four minutes.

- When a DSC Distress acknowledgement has been received, or after about 15 seconds, the vessel in distress should transmit a MAYDAY message by voice on Ch 16, adding its MMSI.

NB: If a Distress alert is inadvertently transmitted, an All stations DSC message cancelling the false alert (by date and time) must be sent at once.

Maritime Safety Information (MSI)

MSI consists of the vital navigational, weather and safety messages which traditionally were sent to vessels at sea by CRS in Morse, but by R/T on VHF and MF in more recent years – and now by GMDSS. For navigation and weather warnings see this and chapter 2 respectively.

GMDSS transmits MSI in English by two independent but complementary means, Navtex and SafetyNet.

- Navtex on MF (518 kHz and 490 kHz) which can be received out to about 300 miles offshore, see Chapter 2.
- SafetyNet uses Inmarsat-C satellites to cover beyond MF range. Enhanced Group Calling (EGC) is a part of SafetyNet which enables MSI to be sent to selected groups of users in any of the four oceans.

SATELLITES FOR SAR

Inmarsat (International Maritime Satellite system) and COSPAS/SARSAT (joint Russian-American system) provide satellite alerts and communications for SAR.

Inmarsat

Near-global communications are provided by four Inmarsat geostationary satellites, each positioned 19,300M above the four oceans (Pacific, Indian, East Atlantic & West Atlantic). The polar regions, ie N of about 70°N and S of 70°S, are not covered. Inmarsat-E enables distress alerting in the L-band 1.6 GHz frequency. From pressing the red button in a yacht to reception at an MRCC usually takes less than 2 minutes. From 1 Feb 2009 the 121·5 MHz service will be discontinued.

COSPAS/SARSAT (C/S)

These Russian/US C/S satellites were specifically designed for SAR operations. They not only detect a 406 MHz Distress alert transmitted by an EPIRB, but also locate it with a high degree of accuracy. There are 10 ground receiving stations in 9 countries worldwide.

There are four geostationary satellites (GEOSAR) in a 24 hr orbit at 19,400M above the equator, ie apparently fixed in relation to the earth. Four more low earth orbit (LEOSAR) satellites, about 450M high, pass over both poles every 100 minutes.

These 8 satellites give global coverage and receive both 406 and 121.5 MHz signals. But coverage is not quite continuous due to possible delays in detection by the LEOSAR system; waiting time is greater in equatorial regions.

LEOSAR satellites calculate an EPIRB's position by Doppler effect. GEOSAR satellites cannot do this since there is no Doppler shift between beacon and satellite. However this problem is solved by newer (and dearer) EPIRBs which have a built-in GPS receiver to provide location directly and with continuous updating.

EPIRBs

These are best categorised by their frequencies, ie:

- 406 MHz, as specifically designed to be processed by C/S. They emit a powerful and frequency-stable signal which ensures proven success in detection and location. C/S has established its own beacon specification and issues type approvals.

- 1·6 GHz, as used exclusively with Inmarsat satellites. L-band EPIRBs, known as Inmarsat-E, provide global distress alerting (as an alternative to 406 MHz EPIRBs in the C/S system). Inmarsat-E EPIRBs can also be equipped with an optional 121·5 MHz locator beacon for homing purposes and/or a Search and Rescue Radar Transponder (SART).

- 121·5 MHz (civilian aeronautical distress). These simple, inexpensive beacons are mainly used in conjunction with 406 MHz beacons for homing purposes. However their outdated technology was never designed to be detected by satellites. As a result from 1 Feb 2009 they will no longer be used at sea for satellite alerting.

If you own a basic 121·5 MHz beacon, do not throw it away; it can still be detected at long range by overflying airliners/Nimrods and at short range by homing lifeboats and helicopters.

- 243·0 MHz (military aeronautical distress). These too will be phased out from 1 Feb 2009 since their limitations are similar to 121·5 MHz beacons.

EPIRBs can be hand-held or float-free. Hand-held are popular in small craft because of their smaller size and portability. Many have lanyards for securing them to a liferaft or person in the water; these must not be secured to the yacht.

Float-free must be correctly installed so that they can indeed float free without snagging on a sinking vessel.

Most modern EPIRBs have a built-in GPS and a 48 hrs battery life. Costs range from £500 to £1200 for float-free, built-in GPS models. Inmarsat-E beacons cost about £1500.

Accuracy

All frequencies can be detected by C/S satellites. The processed positions are automatically passed to a Mission Control Centre (MCC) for assessment of any SAR action required; the UK MCC is co-located with the ARCC at Kinloss, NE Scotland.

C/S location accuracy is normally better than 5 km on 406 MHz, but no better than 20 km on 121·5 and 243·0 MHz. Dedicated SAR aircraft can home on 121·5 MHz and 243·0 MHz, but not on 406 MHz. Typically a helicopter at 1000 feet can receive homing signals from about 30M range whilst fixed-wing aircraft at higher altitudes can home from about 60M.

Best results will invariably be obtained from those 406 MHz EPIRBs with a built-in GPS receiver which transmits continuously updated positions.

SAFETY

UK EMERGENCY VHF DIRECTION FINDING SERVICE

VHF DF is for emergency use only, ie 'one stage down' from real distress. It is remotely controlled H24 by a CG Centre (MRCC) and is not a free navigational service. After contact on Ch 16, invariably Ch 67 is used for the DF procedure; this may be a count from 1-10. Note that the bearing obtained is in °True *from the station to the vessel*. VHF-DF stations are marked on charts by a dot and magenta circle, suffixed 'RG'.

STATION	CONTROLLED BY MRCC	POSITION	
St Mary's, Isles of Scilly	Falmouth	49°55'·73N	06°18'·25W
Lands End	Falmouth	50°08'·13N	05°38'·19W
Lizard	Falmouth	49°57'·60N	05°12'·06W
Rame Head	Brixham	50°19'·03N	04°13'·20W
East Prawle	Brixham	50°13'·10N	03°42'·50W
Berry Head	Brixham	50°23'·97N	03°29'·05W
Grove Point	Portland	50°32'·93N	02°25'·20W
Hengistbury Head	Portland	50°42'·95N	01°45'·64W
Boniface	Solent	50°36'·21N	01°12'·03W
Selsey	Solent	50°43'·80N	00°48'·22W
Newhaven	Solent	50°46'·93N	00°03'·01E
Fairlight	Dover	50°52'·19N	00°38'·74E
Langdon Battery	Dover	51°07'·97N	01°20'·59E
North Foreland	Dover	51°22'·53N	01°26'·72E
Shoeburyness	Thames	51°31'·38N	00°46'·50E
Bawdsey	Thames	51°59'·60N	01°25'·00E
Lowestoft	Yarmouth	52°28'·60N	01°42'·20E
Trimingham	Yarmouth	52°54'·57N	01°20'·60E
Skegness	Yarmouth	53°09'·00N	00°21'·00E
Easington	Humber	53°39'·13N	00°05'·90E
Flamborough	Humber	54°07'·06N	00°05'·07W
Ravenscar	Humber	54°23'·83N	00°30'·68W
Hartlepool	Humber	54°41'·79N	01°10'·57W
Tynemouth	Humber	55°01'·07N	01°24'·99W
Cullercoats	Humber	55°04'·00N	01°28'·00W
Newton	Humber	55°31'·01N	01°37'·10W
Crosslaw	Forth	55°54'·48N	02°12'·31W
Fife Ness	Forth	56°16'·70N	02°35'·30W
Inverbervie	Forth	56°51'·10N	02°15'·65W
Windyhead	Aberdeen	57°38'·90N	02°14'·50W
Noss Head	Aberdeen	58°28'·80N	03°03'·00W
Wideford Hill	Shetland	58°59'·29N	03°01'·40W
Compass Head	Shetland	59°52'·05N	01°16'·30W
Dunnet Head	Aberdeen	58°40'·31N	03°22'·52W
Sandwick	Stornoway	58°12'·65N	06°21'·27W
Rodel	Stornoway	57°44'·90N	06°57'·41W
Barra	Stornoway	57°00'·81N	07°30'·42W
Tiree	Clyde	56°30'·62N	06°57'·68W
Kilchiaran	Clyde	55°45'·90N	06°27'·19W
Law Hill	Clyde	55°41'·76N	04°50'·46W
Snaefell	Liverpool	54°15'·84N	04°27'·66W
Walney Island	Liverpool	54°06'·61N	03°16'·00W
Great Ormes Head	Holyhead	53°19'·96N	03°51'·25W
Rhiw	Holyhead	52°50'·00N	04°37'·82W
St Ann's Head	Milford Haven	51°40'·97N	05°10'·52W
Hartland Pt	Swansea	51°01'·22N	04°31'·40W
Trevose Head	Falmouth	50°32'·91N	05°01'·99W
NORTHERN IRELAND			
Orlock Head	Belfast	54°40'·41N	05°34'·97W
West Torr	Belfast	55°11'·70N	06°05'·20W
CHANNEL ISLANDS			
Guernsey	Ship transmits on Ch 16 (Distress only)	49°26'·27N	02°35'·77W
Jersey	or Ch 67 (Guernsey) or Ch 82 (Jersey)	49°10'·85N	02°14'·30W

VHF EMERGENCY DIRECTION FINDING SERVICES

N

Compass Head
Wideford Hill
Dunnett Head
Sandwick
Noss Head
Rodel
Windyhead
Barra
Inverbervie
Tiree
Fife Ness
Kilchiaran
Crosslaw
Law Hill
Newton
Cullercoats
Tynemouth
West Torr
Hartlepool
Orlock Head
Ravenscar
Snaefell
Flamborough
Walney Island
Easington
Great Ormes Head
Skegness
Rhiw
Trimingham
Lowestoft
Bawdsey
St Ann's Head
Shoeburyness
North Foreland
Langdon Battery
Dunkerque
Hartland
Fairlight
Hengistbury Head
Selsey Bill
Gris-Nez
Trevose Head
Boniface
Newhaven
Boulogne
Grove Point
Rame Head
Land's End
Berry Head
Levy
Ault
E Prawle
Homet
Barfleur
Dieppe
St Mary's
Lizard
Jobourg
Saint-Vaast
Fécamp
La Hague
La Hève
Guernsey
Carteret
Roches-Douvres
Villerville
Ploumanach
Jersey
Port-en-Bessin
Batz
Bréhat
Le Roc
Brignogan
Grouin
Créach
Saint-Cast
Saint-Mathieu
Toulinguet
Cap de la Chèvre
S-Quay-Portrieux
Pointe du Raz
Beg-Meil
Penmarc'h
Étel
Beg Melen
Saint-Julien
Port Louis
Piriac
Le Talut
Chemoulin
Taillefer
Saint-Sauveur
Les Baleines
Chassiron
La Coubre
Pointe de Grave
Cap Ferret
Messanges
Socoa

United Kingdom	Ch 16 (Distress only) Ch 67
Guernsey	Ch 16 (Distress) Ch 67
Jersey	Ch 16 (Distress) Ch 82
France	Ch 16 11 67

HM COASTGUARD - MRCC CONTACT DETAILS

EASTERN REGION

PORTLAND COASTGUARD
50°36'N 02°27'W. DSC MMSI 002320012
Custom House Quay, Weymouth DT4 8BE.
☎ 01305 760439. ᴁ 01305 760451.
Area: Topsham to Chewton Bunney
(50°44'N 01°42'W).

SOLENT COASTGUARD
50°48'N 01°12'W. DSC MMSI 002320011
44A Marine Parade West, Lee-on-Solent,
PO13 9NR. ☎ 02392 552100. ᴁ 02392
554131. Area: Chewton Bunney to Beachy
Hd. Call on Ch 67 to keep Ch 16 clear.

DOVER COASTGUARD
50°08'N 01°20'E. DSC MMSI 002320010
Langdon Battery, Dover CT15 5NA.
☎ 01304 210008. ᴁ 01304 225762.
Area: Beachy Head to Reculver Towers
(51°23'N 01°12'E). Operates Channel
Navigation Information Service.

THAMES COASTGUARD
51°51'N 01°17'E. MMSI 002320009
East Terrace, Walton-on-the-Naze CO14
8PY. ☎ 01255 675518. ᴁ 01255 679415.
Area: Reculver Towers to Southwold.

LONDON COASTGUARD
51°30'N 00°03'E. MMSI 002320063
Thames Barrier Navigation Centre, Unit 28,
34 Bowater Rd, Woolwich, London SE18 5TF.
☎ 0208 312 7380. ᴁ 0208 309 8196.
Area: River Thames from Shell Haven Pt (N
bank) & Egypt Bay (S bank) up-river to
Teddington Lock.

YARMOUTH COASTGUARD
52°37'N 01°43'E. MMSI 002320008
Haven Bridge House, North Quay, Great
Yarmouth NR30 1HZ.
☎ 01493 851338. ᴁ 01493 331975.
Area: Southwold to Haile Sand Fort.

†HUMBER COASTGUARD
54°06'N 00°11'W. MMSI 002320007
Lime Kiln Lane, Bridlington, N Humberside
YO15 2LX.
☎ 01262 672317. ᴁ 01262 400779.
Area: Haile Sand Fort to Scottish border.

SCOTLAND & NORTHERN IRELAND

FORTH COASTGUARD
56°17'N 02°35'W. MMSI 002320005
Fifeness, Crail, Fife KY10 3XN.
☎ 01333 450666. ᴁ 01333 450703.
Area: English border to Doonies Pt
(57°01'N 02°10'W).

†ABERDEEN COASTGUARD
57°08'N 02°05'W. MMSI 002320004
Marine House, Blaikies Quay, Aberdeen
AB11 5PB.
☎ 01224 592334. ᴁ 01224 575920.
Area: Doonies Pt to Cape Wrath, incl
Pentland Firth.

†SHETLAND COASTGUARD
60°09'N 01°08'W. MMSI 002320001
Knab Road, Lerwick ZE1 0AX.
☎ 01595 692976. ᴁ 01595 693634.
Area: Orkney, Fair Isle and Shetland.

†*STORNOWAY COASTGUARD
58°12'N 06°22'W. MMSI 002320024
Battery Pt, Stornoway, Isle of Lewis H51 2RT.
☎ 01851 702013. ᴁ 01851 706796.
Area: Cape Wrath to Ardnamurchan Pt,
Western Isles and St Kilda.

†*CLYDE COASTGUARD
55°58'N 04°48'W. MMSI 002320022
Navy Bldgs, Eldon St, Greenock PA16 7QY.
☎ 01475 729988. ᴁ 01475 888095.
Area: Ardnamurchan Pt to Mull of
Galloway inc islands.

*BELFAST COASTGUARD
54°40'N 05°40'W. MMSI 002320021
Bregenz House, Quay St, Bangor, Co Down
BT20 5ED.
☎ 02891 463933. ᴁ 02891 469854.
Area: Carlingford Lough to Lough Foyle.

WESTERN REGION

LIVERPOOL COASTGUARD
53°30'N 03°03'W. MMSI 002320019
Hall Rd West, Crosby, Liverpool L23 8SY.
☎ 0151 9313341. ᴁ 0151 9320978
Area: Mull of Galloway to Queensferry
(near Chester).

†HOLYHEAD COASTGUARD
53°19'N 04°38'W. MMSI 002320018
Prince of Wales Rd, Holyhead, Anglesey
LL65 1ET.
☎ 01407 762051. ᴁ 01407 761613
Area: Queensferry to Friog (1·6M S of
Barmouth).

†MILFORD HAVEN COASTGUARD
51°42'N 05°03'W. MMSI 002320017
Gorsewood Drive, Hakin, Milford Haven,
SA73 2HD.
☎ 01646 690909. 📠 01646 697287.
Area: Friog to River Towy (11M N of
Worms Head).

SWANSEA COASTGUARD
51°34'N 03°58'W. MMSI 002320016
Tutt Head, Mumbles, Swansea SA3 4EX.
☎ 01792 366534. 📠 01792 368371.
Area: River Towy to Marsland Mouth (near
Bude).

†*FALMOUTH COASTGUARD
50°09'N 05°03'W. MMSI 002320014
Pendennis Point, Castle Drive, Falmouth
TR11 4WZ.
☎ 01326 317575. 📠 01326 315610.
Area: Marsland Mouth (near Bude) to
Dodman Point.

*BRIXHAM COASTGUARD
50°24'N 03°31'W. DSC MMSI 002320013
King's Quay, Brixham TQ5 9TW.
☎ 01803 882704. 📠 01803 859562.
Area: Dodman Point to Topsham (R. Exe).

NOTES: †Monitors DSC MF 2187.5 kHz.
*Broadcasts Gunfacts/Subfacts.

NATIONAL COASTWATCH INSTITUTION
The NCI is a charity dedicated to the safety
of all mariners in UK coastal waters. Since
1994 it has re-introduced visual watch
stations, usually by re-opening abandoned
CG lookouts. Over long stretches of coastline
volunteer NCI watchkeepers alone provide
the vitally important visual watch link with
HM CG, the RNLI and other SAR services.
Many lives have been saved as a direct result
of their actions.

VHF Ch 16 is monitored to detect weak
distress messages. All passing small boats
are logged to assist in the search for missing
craft. By day NCI reports actual weather and
sea states to yachtsmen requesting local
conditions; see ☎ below.

Most NCI stations can warn a yacht of an
apparently dangerous course by light signal,
ie 'U' ••— (You are standing into danger). In
poor visibility some stations keep a radar
watch to 20M offshore. ⑧ = Radar
equipped.

The 35 NCI stations below were/are
operational in 2008/9. They are marked on
the Area maps by ©, for Coastwatch.

Area 1
Gwennap Hd ⑧	01736	871351
Penzance	01736	367063
Lizard ⑧	01326	290212
Helford River	01326	231113
Portscatho (w/ends only)	01872	580180
Charlestown ⑧	01726	817068
Polruan ⑧	01726	870291
Rame Hd ⑧	01752	823706
Prawle Pt ⑧	01548	511259
Froward Pt ⑧	07976	505649
Teignmouth	01626	772377
Exmouth	01395	222492
Portland Bill ⑧	01305	860178
St Alban's Hd ⑧	01929	439220

Area 2
Lee on Solent	02309255	6758
Peveril Pt ⑧	01929	422596

Area 3
Newhaven	01273	516464
Folkestone	01303	227132

Area 4
Herne Bay (w/ends only)	01227	743208
Whitstable (w/ends only)	07932	968707
Holehaven (Canvey Is)	01268	696971
Southend (w/ends only)	07815	945210
Felixstowe	01394	670808
Great Yarmouth ⑧	01493	440384
Mundesley (Norfolk) ⑧	01263	722399
Wells-next-the-sea ⑧	01328	710587
Skegness ⑧	01754	610900
Hartlepool ⑧	01429	274931
Sunderland Life Brigade ⑧	01915	672579
Berwick (w/e; limited hrs)	07950	149865

Area 8
Rossall Pt (Fleetwood)	01253	681378
Worms Hd (Gower)	01792	390167

Area 9
Nells Point (Barry)	01446	420746
Boscastle (N Cornwall) ⑧	01840	250965
Stepper Pt (Padstow) ⑧	07810	898041
St Agnes Hd	01872	552073
St Ives ⑧	01736	799398
Cape Cornwall ⑧	01736	787890

NCI Stations under negotiation: St Mary's
(Scilly), Falmouth, Clacton, Whitby, Walney
Island (Barrow in Furness), Wooltack Point,
Milford Haven. For full details visit:
www.nci.org.uk

SAFETY

Royal National Lifeboat Institution

The RNLI is a registered charity which saves life at sea. It provides, on call H24, a lifeboat service up to 50M off the UK and Irish coasts.

There are 230+ lifeboat stations, 130 all-weather and 191 inshore LBs from 4·9 to 17·0m LOA, plus 3 hovercraft. There are 131 LBs in the reserve fleet. All new LBs are capable of at least 25 knots.

When launched on service, lifeboats >10m keep watch on VHF and MF DSC as well as VHF Ch 16. They can also use alternative frequencies to contact other vessels, SAR aircraft, HM CG, Coast radio stations or other SAR agencies. All lifeboats show a quick-flashing blue light when on operational service.

The RNLI also actively promotes safety at sea by providing a free comprehensive safety service to members and the general public including advice, publications and demonstrations. The RNLI aims to save lives and prevent accidents by helping people be prepared through water safety awareness.

A new and useful A5 size, ring-bound RNLI Handbook covers emergencies, first aid, seamanship, weather, navigation and engines – recommended.

For more details of how the RNLI can help you to be safer at sea, call the RNLI on 0800 328 0600, email seasafety@rnli.org.uk or visit www.rnli.org.uk.

To support the RNLI by becoming a member, contact: RNLI, West Quay Road, Poole, Dorset BH15 1HZ.
☎ 01202 663000. ✉ 01202 663167.

THE CHANNEL ISLANDS

There is no CG as such in the Channel Islands. The HMs at St Peter Port and St Helier direct SAR operations within the Northern and Southern areas respectively.

Communications on VHF, MF and DSC are provided by St Peter Port Radio and Jersey Coastguard (Coast radio stations).

Close liaison is maintained with adjacent French SAR authorities. A distress situation may be controlled by the Channel Islands or France, whichever is more appropriate. For example a British yacht in difficulty in French waters may be handled by St Peter Port or Jersey so as to avoid language problems; and vice versa for a French yacht.

ST PETER PORT RADIO 49°27'·00N 02°32'00W. DSC MMSI 002320064. ☎ 01481 720672. ✉ 714177. Area: Channel Islands North.

JERSEY CG 49°10'·85N 02°14'30W. DSC MMSI 002320060. ☎: 01534 741121. ✉: 499089. Area: Channel Islands South.

SEARCH AND RESCUE ABROAD
THE IRISH REPUBLIC

The Irish CG co-ordinates SAR operations around the coast of Ireland via Dublin MRCC, Malin Head and Valentia MRSCs and remote sites. It may liaise with the UK and France during any rescue operation within 100M of the Irish coast.

It is part of the Dept of Marine, Leeson Lane, Dublin 2. ☎ (01) 6620922; ✉ (01) 6620795. The Irish EPIRB Registry is co-located; ☎ (01) 6199280; ✉ (01) 6621571.

The MRCC/MRSCs are co-located with the Coast radio stations of the same name and manned by the same staff. All stations keep watch H24 on VHF Ch 16 and DSC Ch 70. If ashore dial 999 or 112 in an emergency and ask for Marine Rescue.

Details of the MRCC/MRSCs are as follows:

DUBLIN (MRCC)
53°20'N 06°15W. DSC MMSI 002500300 (+2187·5 kHz).

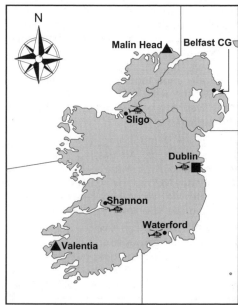

Irish Coastguard centres

☎ +353 1 662 0922/3; 🖷 +353 1 662 0795.
Area: Carlingford Lough to Youghal.

VALENTIA (MRSC)
51°56'N 10°21'W.DSC MMSI 002500200
(+2187·5 kHz).
☎ +353 669 476 109; 🖷 +353 669 476 289.
Area: Youghal to Slyne Head.

MALIN HEAD (MRSC)
55°22'N 07°20W. DSC MMSI 002500100
(+2187·5 kHz).
☎ +353 77 70103; 🖷 +353 77 70221.
Area: Slyne Head to Lough Foyle.

SAR resources
The Irish CG provides some 50 units around the coast and is on call H24. The RNLI maintains 4 stations around the coast and operates 42 lifeboats; six community-run

inshore rescue boats are also available.

Sikorsky S-61 helicopters, based at Dublin, Waterford, Shannon and Sligo, can respond within 15 to 45 minutes and operate to a radius of 200M. They are equipped with infrared search equipment and can uplift 30 survivors.

Military and civilian aircraft and vessels, together with the Garda and lighthouse service, can also be called upon.

Some stations provide specialist cliff climbing services. They are manned by volunteers, who are trained in first aid and equipped with inflatables, breeches buoys, cliff ladders etc. Their ☎ numbers (the Leader's residence) are given, where appropriate, under each port.

DENMARK
The national SAR agency is: Ministry of Defence, 42 Holmens Kanal,DK-1060 København K, Denmark.
☎ +45 339 23320; 🖷 +45 333 20655.

The SAR coordinator for Denmark is MRCC Århus, ☎ +45 894 33099 ext 3203; 🖷 +45 894 33230; mrcc@sok.dk. Århus has no direct communications with vessels in distress, but operates via two MRSCs and several Coast radio stations (CRS). MRSC Kattegat, ☎ +45 992 22255; 🖷 +45 992 22838, deals with the W coast of Denmark.

Lyngby Radio
This is the main Danish CRS and is DSC VHF/ MF/HF equipped (☎ +45 452 89800; 🖷 +45 458 82485, lyngby-radio@tdc.dk MMSI 002191000).

It operates through remote sites at Skagen, Hirtshals, Hantsholm, Bovbjerg and Blavand, all of which guard Ch 16 H24 and use callsign *Lyngby Radio*. Their VHF and MF frequencies are shown in the chartlet opposite.

There are at least 12 lifeboats stationed at the major harbours along the west coast. They are designed to double up as Pilot boats.

Firing practice areas
There are 4 such areas on the W coast as in the chartlet and listed below. Firing times are broadcast daily by Danmarks Radio 1 after the weather at 1645UT. Times can also be obtained from the Range office Ch 16 or ☎.

Ⓐ Tranum & Blokhus ☎ 982 35088 or call *Tranum.*

Ⓑ Nymindegab ☎ 752 89355 or call *Nymindegab.*

Ⓒ Oksbøl ☎ 765 41213 or call *Oksbøl.*

Ⓓ Rømø E ☎ 747 55219; Rømø W ☎ 745 41340 – or call *Fly Rømø.*

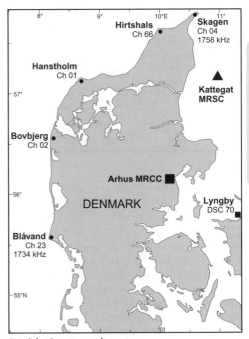

Danish Coastguard centres

GERMANY

The national SAR agency is: *Deutsche Gesellschaft zur Rettung Schiffbrüchiger* (DGzRS), the German Sea Rescue Service. Werderstrasse 2, Hermann-Helms-Haus, D-28199 Bremen. mail@mrcc-bremen.de. ☎ 421 537 070; 🖷 421 537 0714.

DGzRS is responsible for coordinating SAR operations, supported by ships and SAR helicopters of the German Navy.

Bremen MRCC (☎ 421 536870; 🖷 421 5368714; MMSI 002111240), using callsign *Bremen Rescue Radio*, maintains an H24 watch on Ch 16 and DSC Ch 70 via remote Coast radio stations at:

Sylt, Nordfriesland, Eiderstedt, Helgoland, Elbe-Weser, Hamburg and Norddeich.

There are 21 offshore lifeboats, LOA 23–

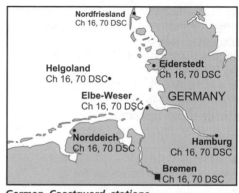

German Coastguard stations

44m, and 21 smaller <10m lifeboats, based at List, Amrum, Helgoland, Cuxhaven, Bremerhaven, Wilhelmshaven, Langeoog, Norderney and Borkum. There are also many inshore lifeboats.

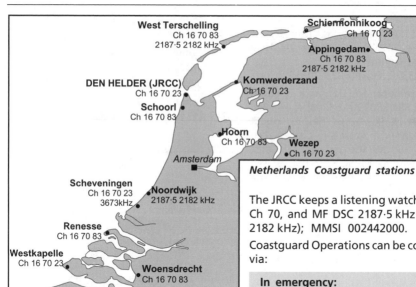

Netherlands Coastguard stations

The JRCC keeps a listening watch H24 on DSC Ch 70, and MF DSC 2187·5 kHz (but not on 2182 kHz); MMSI 002442000.

Coastguard Operations can be contacted H24 via:

In emergency:
☎ + 31 9000 111 or dial 112.

Operational telephone number:
☎ + 31 223 542300. 🖷 + 31 223 658358; ccc@kustwacht.nl If using a mobile phone, call 9000 111, especially if the International emergency number 112 is subject to delays.

Admin/info (HO)
☎+ 31 223 658300. 🖷+31 223 658303. info@kustwacht.nl PO Box 10000, 1780 CA Den Helder.

THE NETHERLANDS

The national SAR agency is: SAR Commission, Directorate Transport Safety (DGG), PO Box 20904, 2500 EX The Hague, Netherlands.

The Netherlands CG at Den Helder, co-located with the Navy HQ, coordinates SAR operations as the Dutch JRCC for A1 and A2 Sea Areas. (JRCC = Joint Rescue Coordination Centre – marine & aeronautical.) Callsign is *Netherlands Coastguard*, but *Den Helder Rescue* during SAR operations.

Remote CG stations are shown above. Working channels are VHF 23 and 83.

BELGIUM

The Belgian CG coordinates SAR operations from Oostende MRCC, callsign *Coastguard Oostende*. The MRCC and *Oostende Radio* (Coast radio rtation) both keep listening watch H24 on Ch 16, 2182 kHz and DSC Ch 70 and 2187·5 kHz.

Coastguard stations

MRCC OOSTENDE
☎ +32 59 701000; 🖷 +32 59 703605.
MMSI 002050480.

MRSC Nieuwpoort
☎ +32 58 230000; 🖷 +32 58 231575.

MRSC Zeebrugge
☎ +32 50 550801; 🖷 +32 50 547400.

RCC Brussels (COSPAS/SARSAT agency)
☎ +32 2 7200338; 🖷 +32 2 7524201.

Coast Radio Stations

OOSTENDE Radio
☎ 59 702438; 🖷 59 701339.
Ch 16, DSC Ch 70 and MF DSC 2187·5 kHz.
MMSI 002050480.

Antwerpen Radio (remotely controlled by Oostende CRS) MMSI 002050485. Ch 16, DSC Ch 70.

Resources

Offshore and inshore lifeboats are based at Nieuwpoort, Oostende and Zeebrugge.

The Belgian Air Force provides helicopters from Koksijde near the French border. The Belgian Navy also participates in SAR operations as required.

FRANCE – CROSS

Four CROSS (Centres Régionaux Opérationnels de Surveillance et de Sauvetage, ie an MRCC) provide a permanent, H24, all weather operational presence along the N and W coasts and liaise with foreign CGs.

CROSS' main functions include:

- Co-ordinating SAR operations.
- Navigational surveillance.
- Broadcasting navigational warnings.
- Broadcasting weather information.
- Anti-pollution control.
- Marine and fishery surveillance.

CROSS locations and areas of responsibility

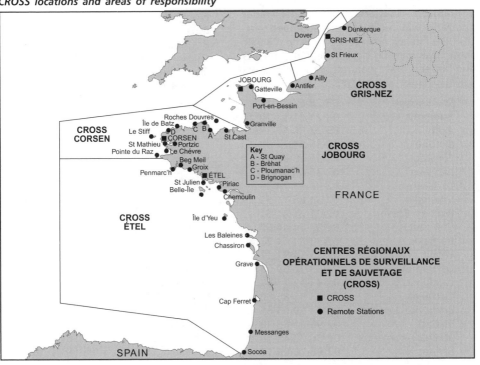

All centres keep watch on VHF Ch 16 as well as Ch 70 (DSC)and co-ordinate SAR on Ch 15, 67, 68, 73. They also broadcast gale warnings, weather forecasts and local navigational warnings.

CROSSA Étel specialises in medical advice and responds to alerts from Cospas/Sarsat satellites.

CROSS can be contacted by R/T, by ☎, through Coast Radio Stations, via the National Gendarmerie or Affaires Maritimes, or via a Semaphore station. Call *Semaphore* stations on Ch 16 (working Ch 10) or by ☎ as listed later in this section.

CROSS also monitor TSS in the Dover Strait, off Casquets and off Ouessant using, for example, the callsign *Corsen Traffic*.

For medical advice call CROSS which will contact a doctor or SAMU (Service d'Aide Médicale Urgente). In harbour/marina SAMU responds faster to a medical emergency than calling a doctor. Simply dial 15.

CROSS stations (Emergency ☎ 1616).

CROSS Gris-Nez
50°52'N 01°35'E   MMSI 002275100
☎ 03 21 87 21 87; ✉ 03 21 87 78 55
Belgian border to Cap d'Antifer.

NavWarnings Ch 79 at every H+10 via Dunkerque, Saint-Frieux and L'Ailly.

CROSS Jobourg
49°41'N 01°54'W   MMSI 002275200
☎ 02 33 52 72 13; ✉ 02 33 52 71 72
Cap de la Hague to Mont St Michel

NavWarnings Ch 80 every H+20 and H+50 via Antifer, Ver-sur-Mer, Gatteville, Jobourg, Granville and Roche Douvres.

CROSS Corsen
48°24'N 04°47'W   MMSI 002275300
☎ 02 98 89 31 31; ✉ 02 98 89 65 75
Mont St Michel to Pointe de Penmarc'h.

NavWarnings Ch 79 every H+10 and H+40 via Cap Fréhel, Bodic, Ile de Batz, Le Stiff and Pte du Raz.

CROSS Étel
47°39'N 03°12'W   MMSI 002275000
☎ 02 97 55 35 35; ✉ 02 97 55 49 34
Pte de Penmarc'h to the Spanish border

NavWarnings Ch 79 for Landes range activity via Chassiron 1903; Soulac 1915; Cap Ferret 1933; Contis 1945; and Biarritz 2003.

Semaphore stations keep visual, radar and radio watch (Ch 16); are equipped with VHF DF; relay emergency calls to CROSS; show gale warning signals, repeat forecasts and offer local weather reports. Hours sunrise-sunset, but * H24.

* Dunkerque	03·28·66·86·18
Boulogne	03·21·31·32·10
Ault	03·22·60·47·33
Dieppe	02·35·84·23·82
* Fécamp	02·35·28·00·91
* La Hève	02·35·46·07·81
* Le Havre	02·35·21·74·39
Villerville	02·31·88·11·13
* Port-en-Bessin	02·31·21·81·51
St-Vaast	02·33·54·44·50
* Barfleur	02·33·54·04·37
Lévy	02·33·54·31·17
* Le Homet	02·33·92·60·08
La Hague	02·33·52·71·07
Carteret	02·33·53·85·08
Barneville Le Roc	02·33·50·05·85
St-Cast	02·96·41·85·30
* St Quay-Portrieux	02.96.70.42.18
Bréhat	02·96·20·00·12
* Ploumanac'h	02·96·91·46·51
Batz	02·98·61·76·06
* Brignogan	02·98·83·50·84
* Ouessant Stiff	02·98·48·81·50
* St-Mathieu	02·98·89·01·59
* Portzic (Ch 08)	02·98·22·21·47
Toulinguet	02·98·27·90·02
Cap-de-la-Chèvre	02·98·27·09·55
* Pointe-du-Raz	02·98·70·66·57
* Penmarc'h	02·98·58·61·00
Beg Meil	02·98·94·98·92
* Port-Louis	02·97·82·52·10
Étel Mât Fenoux	02·97·55·35·35
Beg Melen (Groix)	02·97·86·80·13
Talut (Belle-Île)	02·97·31·85·07
St-Julien	02·97·50·09·35
Piriac-sur-Mer	02·40·23·59·87
* Chemoulin	02·40·91·99·00
St-Sauveur (Yeu)	02·51·58·31·01
Les Baleines (Ré)	05·46·29·42·06
Chassiron (Oléron)	05·46·47·85·43
* Pointe-de-Grave	05·56·09·60·03
Cap Ferret	05·56·60·60·03
Messanges	05·58·48·94·10
* Socoa	05·59·47·18·54

EMERGENCY VHF DF SERVICE

A yacht in emergency can call CROSS on VHF Ch 16, 11 or 67 to obtain a true bearing of the yacht *from* the DF station. These monitor Ch 16 and other continuously scanned frequencies, which include Ch 1-29, 36, 39, 48, 50, 52, 55, 56 and 60-88. The Semaphore stations overleaf are also equipped with VHF DF.

HJ = Day service only.

VHF DF stations, are listed below geographically from NE to W then S:

Station	Lat/Long	Hrs
Dunkerque	51°03'.40N 02°20'.40E	H24
*Gris-Nez	50°52'.20N 01°35'.01E	H24
Boulogne	50°44'.00N 01°36'.00E	HJ
Ault	50°06'.50N 01°27'.50E	HJ
Dieppe	49°56'.00N 01°05'.20E	HJ
Fécamp	49°46'.10N 00°22'.20E	H24
La Hève	49°30'.60N 00°04'.20E	H24
Villerville	49°23'.20N 00°06'.50E	HJ
Port-en-Bessin	49°21'.10N 00°46'.30W	H24
Saint-Vaast	49°34'.50N 01°16'.50W	HJ
Barfleur	49°41'.90N 01°15'.90W	H24
Levy	49°41'.70N 01°28'.20W	HJ
†Homet	49°39'.50N 01°37'.90W	H24
*Jobourg	49°41'.50N 01°54'.50W	H24
La Hague	49°43'.60N 01°56'.30W	HJ
Carteret	49°22'.40N 01°48'.30W	HJ
Le Roc	48°50'.10N 01°36'.90W	HJ
Grouin/Cancale	48°42'.60N 01°50'.60W	HJ
Saint-Cast	48°38'.60N 02°14'.70W	HJ
St-Quay-Port'x	48°39'.30N 02°49'.50W	H24
Bréhat	48°51'.30N 03°00'.10W	HJ
Ploumanac'h	48°49'.50N 03°28'.20W	H24
Batz	48°44'.80N 04°00'.60W	HJ
Brignogan	48°40'.60N 04°19'.70W	H24
Creac'h (Ushant)	48°27'.60N 05°07'.70W	HJ

*Creac'h	48°27'.60N 05°07'.80W	H24
†Saint-Mathieu	48°19'.80N 04°46'.20W	H24
Toulinguet	48°16'.80N 04°37'.50W	HJ
Cap de la Chèvre	48°10'.20N 04°33'.00W	HJ
Pointe du Raz	48°02'.30N 04°43'.80W	H24
Penmarc'h	47°47'.90N 04°22'.40W	H24
Beg-Meil	47°51'.30N 03°58'.40W	HJ
Beg Melen	47°39'.20N 03°30'.10W	HJ
†Port-Louis	47°42'.60N 03°21'.80W	H24
*Etel	47°39'.80N 03°12'.00W	H24
Saint-Julien	47°29'.70N 03°07'.50W	HJ
Taillefer	47°21'.80N 03°09'.00W	HJ
Le Talut	47°17'.70N 03°13'.00W	HJ
Piriac	47°22'.50N 02°33'.40W	HJ
Chemoulin	47°14'.10N 02°17'.80W	H24
Saint-Sauveur	46°41'.70N 02°18'.80W	HJ
Les Baleines	46°14'.60N 01°33'.70W	HJ
Chassiron	46°02'.80N 01°24'.50W	HJ
La Coubre	45°41'.90N 01°13'.40W	H24
Pointe de Grave	45°34'.30N 01°03'.90W	HJ
Cap Ferret	44°37'.50N 01°15'.00W	HJ
Messanges	43°48'.80N 01°23'.90W	HJ
Socoa	43°23'.30N 01°41'.10W	H24

Lifeboats

The lifeboat service Société National de Sauvetage en Mer (SNSM) comes under CROSS, but ashore it is best to contact local lifeboat stations direct. A hefty charge may be levied if a SNSM lifeboat attends a vessel not in distress.

Navigation warnings

Long-range warnings are broadcast by SafetyNet for Navarea II, which includes the W coast of France. The N coast is in Navarea I.

Avurnavs (AVis URgents aux NAVigateurs) are regional, coastal and local warnings issued by Cherbourg and Brest and broadcast by Niton and Brest Navtex and on MF. Warnings are prefixed by 'Sécurité Avurnav'.

SPAIN

The Society for Maritime Rescue and Safety (Sociedad de Salvamento y Seguridad Maritima – SASEMAR) is the national agency for SAR operations (and the prevention of pollution); akin to MCA in the UK.

MRCC Madrid coordinates SAR operations via 3 MRCCs (Bilbao, Gijon and Finisterre) on the N coast and Tarifa MRCC on the SW coast – as listed below.

All Centres monitor (H24) VHF Ch 16, MF 2182 kHz and DSC Ch 70, 2187·5 kHz. They also broadcast weather as shown in Chapter 2 and Nav warnings; but do *not* handle commercial link calls.

North and North West Spain

In N and NW Spain CG Centres do not keep continuous watch on Ch 16, so call on a working channel.

Spanish and Portuguese Coastguard Radio Stations

MADRID MRCC
MMSI 002241008 ☎ 91 7559 132/3; 📠 9I 5261440.

Bilbao MRCC
43°21'N 03°02'W   MMSI 002240996
☎ 944 839411; 📠 944 83 9161.

Santander MRSC
43°28'N 03°43'W   MMSI 002241009
☎ 942 213 030; 📠 942 213 638.

Gijón MRCC
43°34'N 05°42'W   MMSI 002240997
☎ 985 326050; 📠 985 320908.

Finisterre MRCC
42°42'N 08°59'W   MMSI 002240993
☎ 981 767320; 📠 981 767740.

Coruña MRSC
43°22'N 08°23'W   MMSI 002241022
☎ 981 209541; 📠 981 209518.

Vigo MRSC
42°10'N 08°41'W   MMSI 002240998
☎ 986 222230; 📠 986 228957.

PORTUGAL
The Portuguese Navy coordinates SAR in two regions, Lisboa and Santa Maria (Azores) via MRCCs at Lisboa, Ponta Delgada (Azores) and one planned at Horta (Azores). A network of CRS maintains an H24 listening watch on all distress frequencies.
The Naval HQ (Estado Maior da Armada, 3 Divisao) is at: Praca do Comercio, 1188 Lisboa Codex, Portugal.
☎ 21 346 8965. 📠 21 347 9591.

MAINLAND
Lisboa MRCC
38°41'N 09°19'W   MMSI 002630100
☎ 21 4401919; 📠 21 4401954.
mrcclisboa@netc.pt
Planned DSC Ch 70; 2187·5 kHz

Remotely controlled MF DSC stations are planned (2005) at:
Apulia 41°28'N 08°45'W. MMSI 002630200.
Sagres 37°00'N 08°56'W. MMSI 002630400.

AZORES
Ponta Delgada MRCC
37°44'N 25°40'W   MMSI 002040100
☎ 296 281777; 📠 296 281999
mrccdelgada@mail.telepac.pt
Planned DSC Ch 70; 2187·5 kHz.

SOUTH-WEST SPAIN
Tarifa MRCC coordinates SAR in SW Spain and the Gibraltar Strait.

Tarifa MRCC
36°01'N 05°35'W   MMSI 002240994
☎ 956 684740; 📠 956 680 606.

Huelva MRSC
37°13'N 07°07'W   MMSI 002241012
☎ 959 243000; 📠 959 242103.

Cadiz MRSC
36°32'N 06°18'W   MMSI 002241011
☎ 956 214253; 📠 956 226091.

Algeciras MRSC (controlled by Malaga MRCC)
36°08'N 05°26'W   MMSI 002241001
☎ 956 580930; 📠 956 585402.

Chapter 5 – Tides

TIDES

2009 TIMES OF HW DOVER AND MEAN RANGES

JANUARY

Day	HW	Range	HW
1	0122	4.8	1336
2	0155	4.6	1411
3	0234	4.4	1453
4	0320	4.2	1544
5	0416	3.8	1648
6	0526	3.7	1813
7	0646	3.7	1934
8	0759	4.1	2040
9	0904	4.7	2139
10	1003	5.2	2233
11	1058	5.6	2322
12	1147	6.0	—
13	0007	6.1	1234
14	0052	6.1	1318
15	0136	5.9	1402
16	0220	5.4	1447
17	0305	4.9	1533
18	0352	4.2	1625
19	0445	3.5	1725
20	0548	3.2	1835
21	0704	2.9	1950
22	0823	3.2	2057
23	0927	3.7	2148
24	1013	4.2	2229
25	1048	4.6	2303
26	1118	4.9	2334
27	1148	5.1	—
28	0003	5.2	1217
29	0031	5.3	1245
30	0100	5.3	1313
31	0131	5.3	1345

FEBRUARY

Day	HW	Range	HW
1	0207	5.2	1423
2	0248	4.7	1509
3	0338	4.0	1606
4	0442	3.4	1730
5	0621	3.3	1922
6	0757	3.6	2038
7	0909	4.3	2140
8	1009	5.2	2232
9	1059	5.8	2316
10	1143	6.3	2357
11	1222	6.4	—
12	0036	6.4	1300
13	0115	6.2	1336
14	0154	5.8	1414
15	0232	5.1	1454
16	0312	4.3	1538
17	0359	3.5	1635
18	0501	2.8	1747
19	0618	2.5	1908
20	0750	2.6	2029
21	0909	3.3	2126
22	0953	4.1	2205
23	1024	4.7	2236
24	1052	5.0	2306
25	1121	5.3	2335
26	1150	5.5	—
27	0004	5.6	1219
28	0035	5.7	1248

MARCH

Day	HW	Range	HW
1	0106	5.8	1322
2	0142	5.4	1400
3	0223	4.8	1445
4	0312	4.0	1543
5	0421	3.2	1721
6	0624	3.0	1915
7	0758	3.5	2032
8	0908	4.4	2131
9	1003	5.3	2219
10	1048	5.9	2301
11	1126	6.3	2339
12	1201	6.5	—
13	0015	6.3	1235
14	0051	6.1	1309
15	0126	5.7	1344
16	0200	5.1	1419
17	0235	4.3	1458
18	0317	3.5	1551
19	0422	2.7	1705
20	0542	2.3	1825
21	0705	2.5	1944
22	0825	3.2	2045
23	0912	3.9	2126
24	0946	4.6	2159
25	1017	5.1	2231
26	1049	5.4	2303
27	1120	5.7	2335
28	1152	5.8	—
29	0008	5.9	1225
30	0044	5.8	1302
31	0123	5.4	1345

APRIL

Day	HW	Range	HW
1	0207	4.8	1435
2	0303	3.9	1543
3	0429	3.2	1723
4	0622	3.2	1859
5	0748	3.7	2014
6	0854	4.5	2111
7	0945	5.3	2157
8	1026	5.8	2238
9	1102	6.1	2315
10	1136	6.1	2352
11	1209	5.9	—
12	0027	5.7	1244
13	0101	5.4	1318
14	0134	4.9	1352
15	0207	4.3	1428
16	0247	3.6	1516
17	0350	2.9	1625
18	0506	2.5	1739
19	0620	2.6	1849
20	0727	3.1	1949
21	0820	3.8	2036
22	0901	4.5	2115
23	0939	5.0	2152
24	1014	5.4	2229
25	1050	5.8	2307
26	1127	5.9	2345
27	1207	5.9	—
28	0027	5.8	1251
29	0112	5.4	1340
30	0205	4.8	1438

MAY

Day	HW	Range	HW
1	0312	4.2	1547
2	0435	3.7	1705
3	0605	3.7	1828
4	0723	4.0	1942
5	0826	4.5	2040
6	0916	4.9	2128
7	0957	5.3	2211
8	1035	5.5	2251
9	1111	5.5	2329
10	1147	5.3	—
11	0005	5.3	1223
12	0041	5.0	1259
13	0115	4.8	1334
14	0149	4.3	1408
15	0227	3.9	1447
16	0317	3.4	1539
17	0422	3.1	1643
18	0530	3.1	1749
19	0633	3.3	1850
20	0728	3.8	1943
21	0816	4.3	2030
22	0900	4.8	2115
23	0942	5.2	2159
24	1026	5.6	2244
25	1110	5.8	2331
26	1157	5.8	—
27	0019	5.8	1247
28	0111	5.5	1340
29	0209	5.2	1436
30	0312	4.8	1535
31	0419	4.4	1637

JUNE

Day	HW	Range	HW
1	0530	4.3	1744
2	0641	4.1	1856
3	0745	4.2	2001
4	0839	4.4	2057
5	0927	4.6	2146
6	1009	4.8	2230
7	1050	4.9	2311
8	1128	4.9	2349
9	1205	4.8	—
10	0024	4.8	1242
11	0059	4.8	1315
12	0131	4.5	1347
13	0203	4.3	1418
14	0237	4.1	1456
15	0319	3.9	1543
16	0414	3.6	1640
17	0523	3.5	1746
18	0631	3.6	1851
19	0733	4.0	1951
20	0828	4.4	2048
21	0921	4.9	2142
22	1013	5.3	2235
23	1104	5.7	2327
24	1153	5.9	—
25	0018	6.0	1243
26	0110	5.9	1332
27	0202	5.8	1422
28	0255	5.4	1512
29	0348	4.9	1604
30	0444	4.3	1700

JULY

Day	HW	Range	HW
1	0545	4.0	1803
2	0654	3.7	1915
3	0800	3.7	2026
4	0859	3.9	2127
5	0950	4.2	2217
6	1033	4.5	2258
7	1112	4.7	2334
8	1148	4.8	—
9	0007	4.8	1222
10	0038	4.8	1252
11	0107	4.8	1320
12	0133	4.8	1347
13	0201	4.7	1420
14	0235	4.4	1500
15	0319	4.1	1548
16	0414	3.8	1648
17	0528	3.5	1806
18	0700	3.6	1927
19	0813	4.1	2037
20	0915	4.7	2139
21	1010	5.3	2236
22	1100	5.8	2327
23	1147	6.2	—
24	0014	6.3	1232
25	0059	6.3	1316
26	0143	6.2	1400
27	0227	5.8	1445
28	0312	5.1	1531
29	0401	4.3	1621
30	0457	3.5	1719
31	0604	3.2	1831

AUGUST

Day	HW	Range	HW
1	0722	3.0	2000
2	0837	3.3	2117
3	0934	3.8	2207
4	1017	4.4	2244
5	1053	4.8	2314
6	1126	4.9	2342
7	1155	5.1	—
8	0010	5.1	1224
9	0037	5.2	1249
10	0101	5.2	1316
11	0128	5.1	1348
12	0202	4.9	1425
13	0243	4.5	1510
14	0334	3.9	1608
15	0447	3.3	1739
16	0649	3.2	1924
17	0808	3.8	2038
18	0911	4.6	2139
19	1004	5.2	2232
20	1050	6.0	2318
21	1133	6.4	2359
22	1213	6.6	—
23	0037	6.5	1254
24	0116	6.3	1334
25	0155	5.7	1414
26	0236	5.0	1457
27	0323	4.1	1545
28	0418	3.3	1643
29	0525	2.6	1756
30	0645	2.5	1931
31	0811	3.0	2101

SEPTEMBER

Day	HW	Range	HW
1	0911	3.8	2147
2	0953	4.3	2219
3	1026	4.8	2244
4	1055	5.1	2310
5	1123	5.3	2337
6	1150	5.3	—
7	0004	5.3	1218
8	0030	5.4	1246
9	0100	5.3	1319
10	0135	5.0	1356
11	0217	4.4	1442
12	0310	3.7	1544
13	0436	3.0	1747
14	0641	3.1	1921
15	0757	3.8	2033
16	0858	4.7	2130
17	0948	5.5	2218
18	1032	6.1	2259
19	1112	6.4	2336
20	1150	6.4	—
21	0011	6.3	1228
22	0047	6.0	1306
23	0124	5.4	1344
24	0204	4.8	1424
25	0248	4.0	1511
26	0343	3.2	1612
27	0450	2.4	1724
28	0605	2.3	1847
29	0727	2.8	2020
30	0832	3.5	2107

OCTOBER

Day	HW	Range	HW
1	0914	4.3	2137
2	0946	4.8	2204
3	1016	5.2	2233
4	1046	5.3	2302
5	1116	5.5	2332
6	1147	5.7	—
7	0002	5.7	1220
8	0037	5.4	1256
9	0117	5.1	1338
10	0204	4.4	1429
11	0305	3.6	1547
12	0445	3.2	1745
13	0621	3.3	1908
14	0736	4.0	2016
15	0836	4.8	2110
16	0925	5.5	2155
17	1008	5.9	2234
18	1048	6.1	2310
19	1126	6.1	2345
20	1203	5.9	—
21	0022	5.6	1241
22	0059	5.2	1318
23	0138	4.7	1357
24	0219	4.1	1443
25	0309	3.3	1542
26	0411	2.7	1650
27	0520	2.5	1802
28	0630	2.8	1911
29	0733	3.3	2006
30	0821	4.0	2047
31	0859	4.5	2122

NOVEMBER

Day	HW	Range	HW
1	0934	5.0	2156
2	1009	5.4	2230
3	1045	5.5	2305
4	1122	5.7	2342
5	1201	5.7	—
6	0023	5.5	1244
7	0110	5.1	1333
8	0203	4.6	1433
9	0309	4.0	1554
10	0427	3.7	1725
11	0548	3.8	1842
12	0702	4.1	1947
13	0804	4.5	2042
14	0856	5.0	2128
15	0943	5.3	2209
16	1025	5.5	2247
17	1105	5.5	2325
18	1143	5.4	—
19	0002	5.3	1221
20	0041	5.0	1258
21	0118	4.7	1336
22	0155	4.2	1416
23	0235	3.7	1504
24	0322	3.3	1603
25	0421	2.9	1708
26	0526	2.9	1813
27	0629	3.2	1910
28	0724	3.6	1959
29	0812	4.2	2042
30	0856	4.6	2124

DECEMBER

Day	HW	Range	HW
1	0939	5.2	2205
2	1022	5.5	2247
3	1106	5.7	2332
4	1152	5.8	—
5	0018	5.7	1240
6	0108	5.4	1332
7	0201	5.1	1431
8	0258	4.7	1536
9	0400	4.3	1646
10	0505	4.1	1759
11	0616	4.1	1906
12	0725	4.1	2007
13	0827	4.3	2101
14	0921	4.5	2148
15	1009	4.8	2231
16	1051	5.0	2310
17	1130	5.1	2348
18	1207	5.1	—
19	0025	4.9	1243
20	0100	4.8	1316
21	0132	4.6	1348
22	0201	4.3	1419
23	0232	4.0	1453
24	0312	3.7	1539
25	0403	3.4	1642
26	0509	3.2	1803
27	0623	3.3	1911
28	0729	3.7	2009
29	0827	4.3	2102
30	0920	4.9	2152
31	1011	5.4	2240

2009 TIDAL COEFFICIENTS

Date	Jan am	Jan pm	Feb am	Feb pm	Mar am	Mar pm	Apr am	Apr pm	May am	May pm	June am	June pm	July am	July pm	Aug am	Aug pm	Sept am	Sept pm	Oct am	Oct pm	Nov am	Nov pm	Dec am	Dec pm
1	70	68	72	68	88	84	67	60	58	54	57		49		36	39	50	56	60	66	77	81	78	83
2	65	63	63	58	79	74	53	47	51	51	56	57	48	47	43	48	62	67	72	77	85	88	87	90
3	59	57	53	48	67	60	43	43	53		58	59	48	50	52	57	72	77	81	85	91	92	92	93
4	54	51	45	43	53	47	46		56	60	61	64	52	55	62	66	80	84	88	91	93	92	93	92
5	49	48	45		42	40	51	59	64	69	66	68	58	62	70	73	86	88	92	93	91	88	91	88
6	48		49	56	42		66	73	73	77	70	71	64	67	76	79	90	90	93	92	85	81	85	82
7	49	53	63	72	47	55	80	86	80	83	72	73	69	71	81	82	90	89	90	87	76	71	77	73
8	57	63	80	88	64	73	91	95	84	85	74	74	73	74	83	84	87	84	83	78	65	60	69	64
9	69	76	94	100	81	89	97	98	85	85	73	73	75	75	83	82	81	76	73	66	56	53	61	58
10	82	88	104	107	95	100	99	98	84	82	72	70	75	75	80	78	71	65	60	54	52	52	56	
11	93	97	108	108	104	106	96	93	80	77	69	67	74	72	75	71	60	53	48	44	54		55	56
12	100	102	106	102	107	106	89	84	74	70	65	62	71	68	68	63	47	42	43	45	58	62	57	59
13	103	102	98	92	104	101	79	74	66	62	60	57	66	63	58	53	40	40	49		67	71	62	64
14	100	97	85	78	96	90	68	62	58	54	54	52	60	57	49	44	45		56	63	76	79	67	70
15	92	87	70	62	84	77	55	49	50	46	49	47	53	50	42		52	60	71	78	82	85	72	74
16	80	73	54	46	70	62	43	37	42	40	46	45	48	47	42	45	69	78	85	90	86	87	75	76
17	67	59	39	32	55	47	33	30	38	37	46			46	51	58	86	93	94	98	87	86	77	77
18	52	46	27		40	33	29	30	38		47	50	48	51	66	75	100	104	100	100	85	82	77	76
19	41	36	26	27	27	24	34		41	44	54	58	55	61	83	91	107	109	100	98	80	77	75	73
20	34		31	37	24		39	45	49	54	63	68	68	74	98	103	109	107	95	91	73	69	71	69
21	34	36	43	49	28	33	52	58	59	65	74	79	81	88	108	110	104	99	86	81	65	60	66	63
22	39	44	56	62	40	47	65	71	71	76	84	88	94	98	111	110	93	87	75	69	56	52	60	57
23	49	53	68	74	54	61	77	82	81	86	92	95	102	105	107	103	80	72	63	56	47	43	53	50
24	58	63	79	83	68	74	87	92	90	92	97	97	106	105	97	91	64	56	50	44	40	37	47	44
25	67	71	87	90	80	85	95	97	95	95	98	97	103	100	83	75	48	41	38	33	36	36	42	41
26	75	78	93	94	90	93	98	98	95	94	95	92	95	90	67	58	34	29	30	29	37		40	
27	80	83	95	95	96	98	97	95	92	89	88	83	83	76	50	42	26	26	30		39	43	42	44
28	84	85	93	91	99	99	91	87	86	82	78	72	68	61	35	30	30		33	38	47	52	48	53
29	85	85			98	95	81	76	77	73	67	62	53	47	28		35	41	43	49	58	63	59	65
30	83	82			91	87	69	63	68	64	57	53	41	38	29	33	47	54	55	61	68	74	71	77
31	79	76			81	75			61	58			36		38	44			66	72			83	88

Tidal coefficients indicate at a glance the magnitude of the tide on any particular day by assigning a non-dimensional coefficient to the twice-daily range of tide. Coefficients are based on a value of 45 for mean neap (morte eau) and 95 for mean spring (vive eau) ranges. The coefficient is 70 for an average tide. A very small neap tide may have a coefficient of only 20, whilst a very big spring tide might be as high as 120. The ratio of the coefficients of different tides equals the ratio of their ranges; the range, for example, of the largest spring tide (120) is six times that of the smallest neap tide (20). The table above is for Brest, but is valid elsewhere around the coasts of the UK and NW Europe.

French translations of common tidal terms are as follows:

HW	Pleine mer (PM)	LAT	Plus basse mer astronomique (PBMA)
LW	Basse mer (BM)	MHWS	Pleine mer moyenne de VE (PMVE)
Springs	Vive eau (VE)	MHWN	Pleine mer moyenne de ME (PMME)
Neaps	Morte eau (ME)	MLWN	Basse mer moyenne de ME (BMME)
CD	Zero des cartes (Chart Datum)	MLWS	Basse mer moyenne de VE (BMVE)
HAT	Plus haute mer astronomique (PHMA)	ML/MSL	Niveau moyen (NM)

TIDES

TIDAL CALCULATIONS

Find the height at a given time (STANDARD PORT)

1. On Standard Curve diagram, plot heights of HW and LW occuring either side of required time and join by sloping line.
2. Enter HW Time and sufficient others to bracket required time.
3. From required time, proceed vertically to curves, using heights plotted in (1) to help interpolation between Spring and Neaps. Do NOT extrapolate.
4. Proceed horizontally to sloping line, thence vertically to Height scale.
5. Read off height.

EXAMPLE:

Find the height of tide at ULLAPOOL at 1900 on 6th January

From tables	JANUARY	
ULLAPOOL	**6** 0420	4.6
	1033	1.6
	1641	4.6
	F 2308	1.2

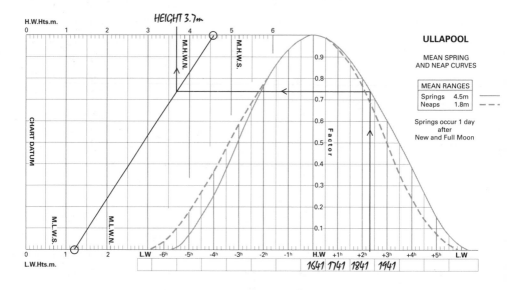

Find the time for a given height (STANDARD PORT)

1. On Standard Curve diagram, plot heights of HW and LW occurring either side of required event and join by sloping line.
2. Enter HW time and those for half-tidal cycle covering required event.
3. From required height, proceed vertically to sloping line, thence horizontally to curves, using heights plotted in (1) to assist interpolation between Spring and Neaps. Do NOT extrapolate.
4. Proceed vertically to Time scale.
5. Read off time.

EXAMPLE:

Find the time at which the afternoon tide at ULLAPOOL falls to 3.7m on 6 January

From tables	JANUARY	
ULLAPOOL	**6** 0420	4.6
	1033	1.6
	1641	4.6
	F 2308	1.2

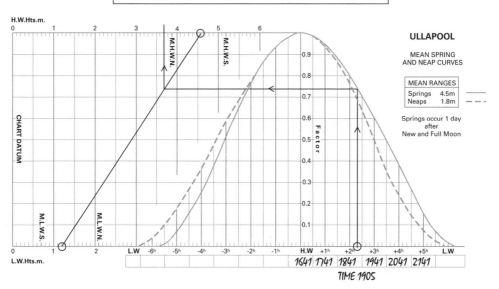

ULLAPOOL

MEAN SPRING
AND NEAP CURVES

MEAN RANGES
Springs 4.5m
Neaps   1.8m

Springs occur 1 day
after
New and Full Moon

TIME 1905

Find the time and height of HW and LW at a Secondary Port

EXAMPLE:

Find the time and height of the afternoon HW and LW at ST MARY's (Isles of Scilly) on 14th July (BST)
Note: *The data used in this example do not refer to the year of these tables.*

From tables	JULY	
PLYMOUTH (DEVONPORT)	**14** 0309	1.0
	0927	5.3
	1532	1.1
	SA 2149	5.0

From tables			High Water		Low Water		MHWS	MHWN	MLWN	MLWS
Location	Lat	Long								
			0000	0600	0000	0600				
DEVONPORT	50°22'N	4°11'W	and	and	and	and	5.5	4.4	2.2	0.8
Standard port			1200	1800	1200	1800				
St Mary's, *Scilly*	49° 55'N	6°19'W	–0035	–0100	–0040	–0025	+0.2	–0.1	–0.2	–0.1

TIDES

TIDAL PREDICTION FORM (NP 204)

STANDARD PORT __Devonport__   TIME/HEIGHT REQUIRED __pm__

SECONDARY PORT __St Mary's__   DATE __14 July__ TIME ZONE __B.S.T__

	TIME		HEIGHT		
STANDARD PORT	HW	LW	HW	LW	RANGE
	1 2149	2 1532	3 5.0	4 1.1	5 3.9
Seasonal change	Standard Ports -		6 0.0	6 0.0	
DIFFERENCES	7* -0044	8 -0032	9 0.1	10 -0.1	
*Seasonal change**	Secondary Ports +		11 0.0	11 0.0	
SECONDARY PORT	12 2105	13 1500	14 5.1	15 1.0	
Duration	16 0605		LW 1500 UT = 1600 BST HW 2105 UT = 2205 BST		

* The seasonal changes are generally less than ± 0.1m and for most purposes can be ignored. See Admiraly Tide Tables Vol 1. for details

CLEARANCE BELOW BRIDGES AND OVERHEAD POWER LINES

Vertical clearance heights are above the level of HAT (Highest Astronomical Tide) instead of MHWS as in the past. HAT is always a higher level than MHWS, as shown in the diagram on the back cover flap. It helps to draw such a diagram and insert the relevant dimensions when calculating overhead clearances. The Height of HAT above Chart Datum is stated at the foot of each page of Standard port tide tables. New editions of Admiralty charts are referenced to HAT; earlier editions to MHWS. Check the title block under **Heights**.

INTERMEDIATE TIMES/HEIGHTS (SECONDARY PORT)

These are the same as the appropriate calculations for a Standard Port except that the Standard Curve diagram for the Standard Port must be entered with HW and LW heights and times for the Secondary Port obtained on Form N.P. 204. When interpolating between the Spring and Neap curves the Range at the Standard Port must be used.

EXAMPLE:

Find the height of the tide at PADSTOW at 1100 on 28th February. Find the time at which the morning tide at PADSTOW falls to 4.9m on 28th February.

Note: The data in these examples do not refer to the year of these tables.

From tables	FEBRUARY	
MILFORD HAVEN	**28** 0315	1.1
	0922	6.6
	1538	1.3
	TU 2145	6.3

From tables Location	Lat	Long	High Water		Low Water		MHWS	MHWN	MLWN	MLWS
MILFORD HAVEN *Standard port*	51°42'N	5°03'W	0100 and 1300	0700 and 1900	0100 and 1300	0700 and 1900	**7.0**	**5.2**	**2.5**	**0.7**
River Camel Padstow	50°33'N	4°56'W	−0055	−0050	−0040	−0050	+0.3	+0.4	+0.1	+0.1
Wadebridge	50°31'N	4°50'W	−0052	−0052	+0235	+0245	−3.8	−3.8	−2.5	−0.4

TIDAL PREDICTION FORM (NP 204)

STANDARD PORT *Milford Haven*   TIME/HEIGHT REQUIRED   *1100 : 4.9*

SECONDARY PORT *Padstow*   DATE *28 Feb*   TIME ZONE   *UT*

	TIME		HEIGHT		
STANDARD PORT	**HW**	**LW**	**HW**	**LW**	**RANGE**
	1 0922	2 1538	3 6.6	4 1.3	5 5.3
Seasonal change	Standard Ports +		6 0.0	6 0.0	
DIFFERENCES	7* −0052	8 −	9 +0.3	10 +0.1	
*Seasonal change *	Secondary Ports -		11 0.0	11 0.0	
SECONDARY PORT	12 0830	13 −	14 6.9	15 1.4	
Duration	16 −				

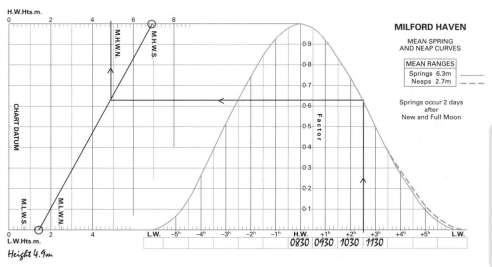

H.W.Hts.m.

CHART DATUM

M.H.W.N. M.H.W.S.

M.L.W.S. M.L.W.N.

L.W.Hts.m.

Height 4.9m

MILFORD HAVEN

MEAN SPRING AND NEAP CURVES

MEAN RANGES
Springs 6.3m
Neaps 2.7m

Springs occur 2 days after New and Full Moon

Factor

L.W. −5ʰ −4ʰ −3ʰ −2ʰ −1ʰ H.W. +1ʰ +2ʰ +3ʰ +4ʰ +5ʰ L.W.

0830 0930 1030 1130

TIDES

SPECIAL INSTRUCTIONS FOR PLACES BETWEEN BOURNEMOUTH AND SELSEY BILL

• Owing to the rapid change of tidal characteristics and distortion of the tidal curve in this area, curves are shown for individual ports. It is a characteristic of the tide here that Low Water is more sharply defined than High Water and these curves have therefore been drawn with their times relative to that of Low Water.

• Apart from differences caused by referring the times to Low Water the procedure for obtaining intermediate heights at places whose curves are shown is identical to that used for normal Secondary Ports.

• The **height** differences for ports between Bournemouth and Yarmouth always refer to the higher High Water, i.e. that which is shown as reaching a factor of 1.0 on the curves. Note that the **time** differences, which are not required for this calculation, also refer to the higher High Water.

• The tide at ports between Bournemouth and Christchurch shows considerable change of shape and duration between Springs and Neaps and it is not practical to define the tide with only two curves. A third curve has therefore been drawn for the range at Portsmouth at which the two High Waters are equal at the port concerned – this range being marked on the body of the graph. Interpolation here should be between this 'critical' curve and either the Spring or Neap curve as appropriate.

Note that while the critical curve extends throughout the tidal cycle the Spring and Neap curves stop at the higher High Water. Thus for a range at Portsmouth of 3.5m the factor for 7 hours after LW at Bournemouth should be referred to the following Low Water, whereas had the range at Portsmouth been 2.5, it should be referred to the preceding Low Water.

NOTES

1. NEWPORT. Owing to the constriction of the River Medina, Newport requires slightly different treatment since the harbour dries out at 1.4m. The calculation should be performed using the Low Water Time and Height Differences for Cowes and the High Water Height Differences for Newport. Any calculated heights which fall below 1.4m should be treated as 1.4m

2. CHRISTCHURCH (Tuckton). Low Waters do not fall below 0.7m except under very low river flow conditions.

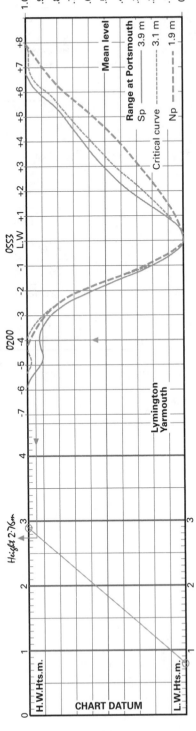

To find the Height of tide at a given time at any Secondary Port between Bournemouth and Selsey Bill

1. Complete top section of N.P. 204 (as below). Omit HW time column (Boxes 1,7,12)
2. On Standard Curve diagram (previous page), plot Secondary Port HW and LW heights and join by sloping line.
3. From the time required, using Secondary Port LW time, proceed vertically to curve, interpolating as necessary using Range at Portsmouth. Do NOT extrapolate.
4. Proceed horizontally to sloping line, thence vertically to Height Scale.
5. Read off height.

EXAMPLE:

Find the height of tide at LYMINGTON at 0200 UT on 18th November

From tables		NOVEMBER	
PORTSMOUTH		**18** 0110	4.6
		0613	1.1
		1318	4.6
		SA 1833	1.0

From tables Location	Lat	Long	High Water		Low Water		MHWS	MHWN	MLWN	MLWS
			0000	0600	0500	1100				
PORTSMOUTH	50°48'N	1°07'W	and	and	and	and	4.7	3.8	1.9	0.8
Standard port			1200	1800	1700	2300				
Lymington	50°46'N	1°32'W	–0110	+0005	–0020	–0020	–1.7	–1.2	–0.5	–0.1

STANDARD PORT ....*Portsmouth*.... TIME/HEIGHT REQUIRED *0200*

SECONDARY PORT *Lymington* .... DATE *18 Nov* .. TIME ZONE .... *UT*

	TIME		HEIGHT		
	HW	LW	HW	LW	RANGE
STANDARD PORT	1 –	2 0613	3 4·6	4 1·1	5 3·5
Seasonal change	Standard Ports –		6 0·0	6 0·0	
DIFFERENCES	7* –	8 –0020	9 –1·7	10 –0·2	
Seasonal change *	Secondary Ports +		11 0·0	11 0·0	
SECONDARY PORT	12 –	13 0553	14 2·9	15 0·9	
Duration	16 –				

* The Seasonal changes are generally less than ± 0.1m and for most purposes can be ignored. See Admiralty Tide Tables Vol 1 for full details.

TIDES

TIDAL CURVES -
BOURNEMOUTH TO FRESHWATER

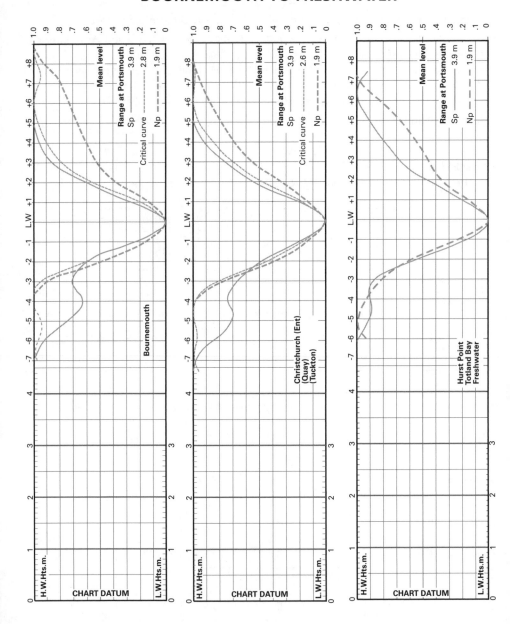

Note: The curves for Lymington and Yarmouth are on page 148, together with a worked example.

TIDAL CURVES -
BUCKLERS HARD TO SELSEY BILL

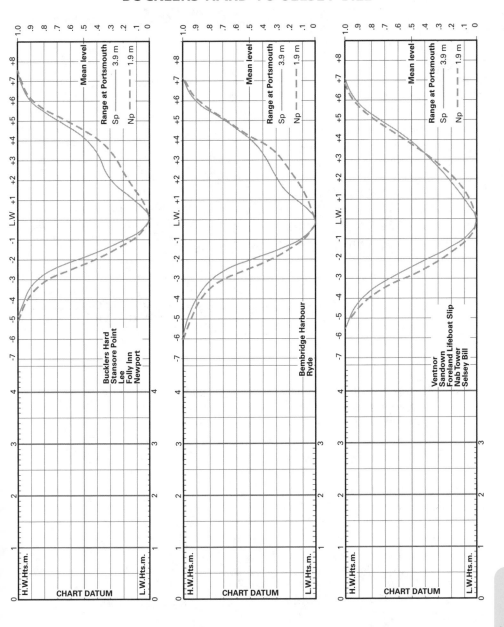

ENGLISH CHANNEL AND SOUTH BRITTANY

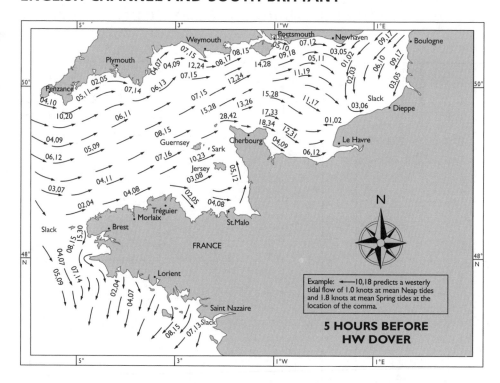

Example: ◄——10,18 predicts a westerly tidal flow of 1.0 knots at mean Neap tides and 1.8 knots at mean Spring tides at the location of the comma.

5 HOURS BEFORE HW DOVER

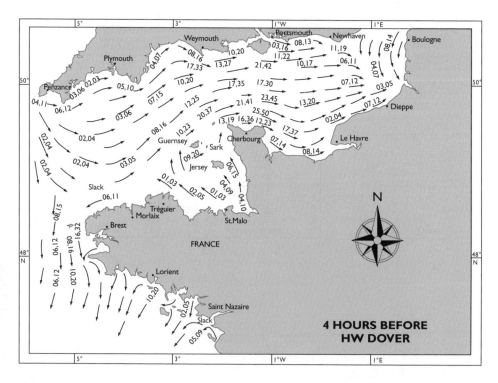

4 HOURS BEFORE HW DOVER

ENGLISH CHANNEL AND SOUTH BRITTANY

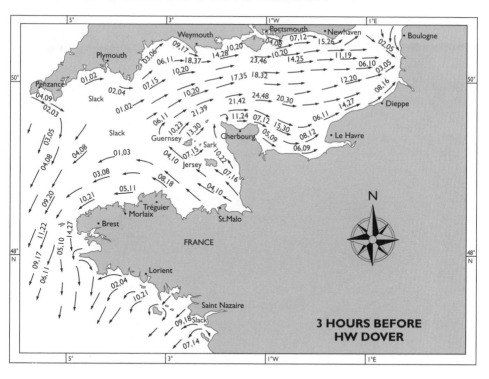

3 HOURS BEFORE HW DOVER

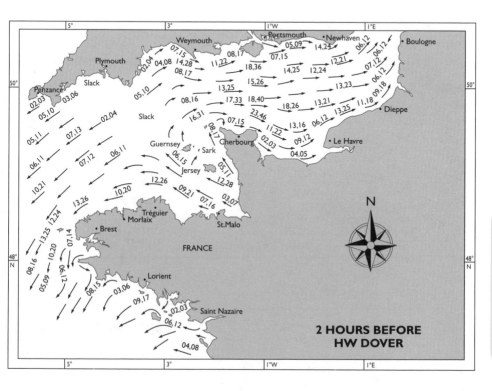

2 HOURS BEFORE HW DOVER

ENGLISH CHANNEL AND SOUTH BRITTANY

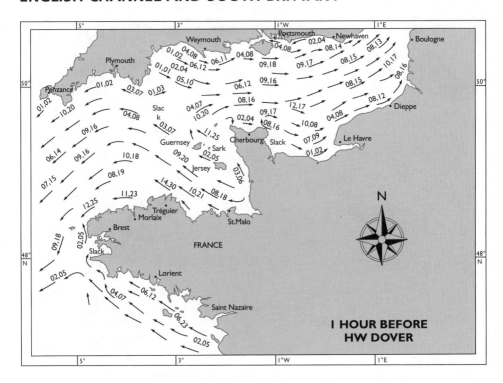

I HOUR BEFORE HW DOVER

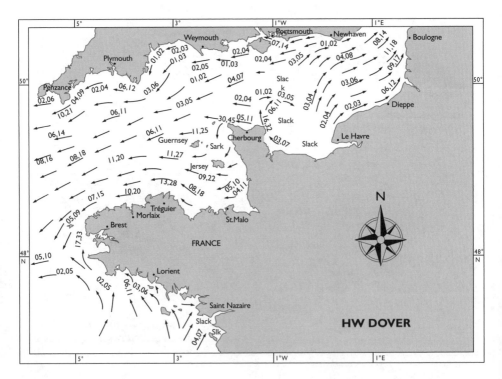

HW DOVER

ENGLISH CHANNEL AND SOUTH BRITTANY

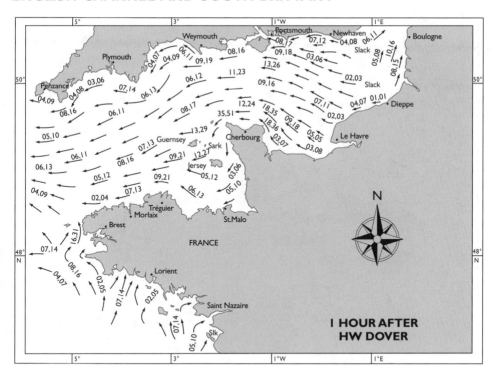

1 HOUR AFTER HW DOVER

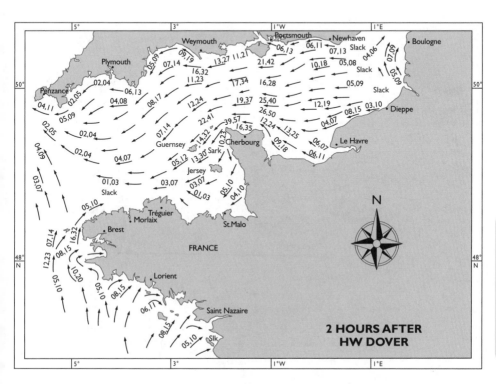

2 HOURS AFTER HW DOVER

ENGLISH CHANNEL AND SOUTH BRITTANY

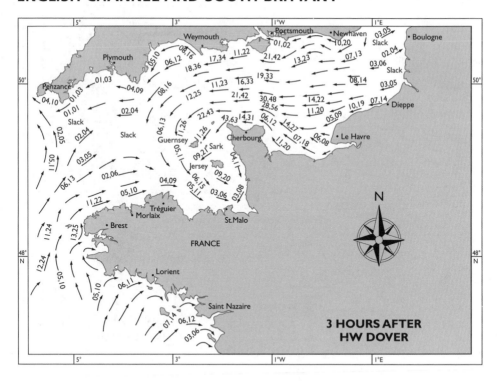

3 HOURS AFTER HW DOVER

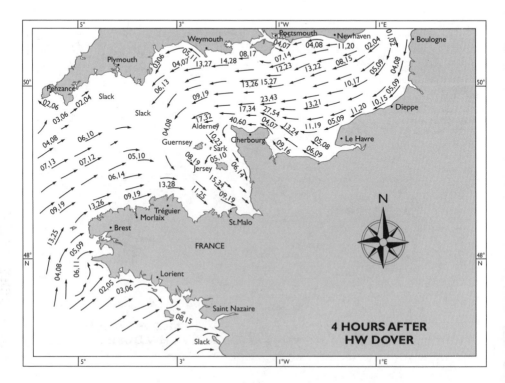

4 HOURS AFTER HW DOVER

ENGLISH CHANNEL AND SOUTH BRITTANY

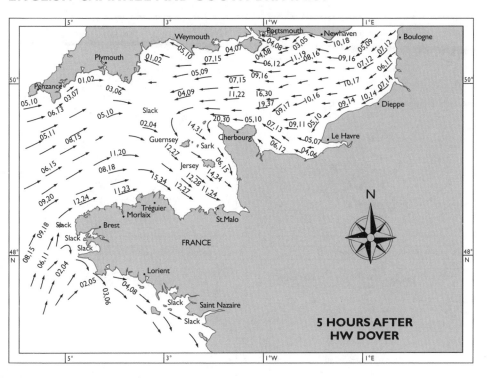

5 HOURS AFTER HW DOVER

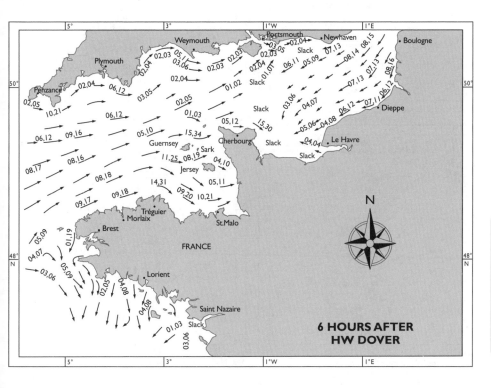

6 HOURS AFTER HW DOVER

PORTLAND

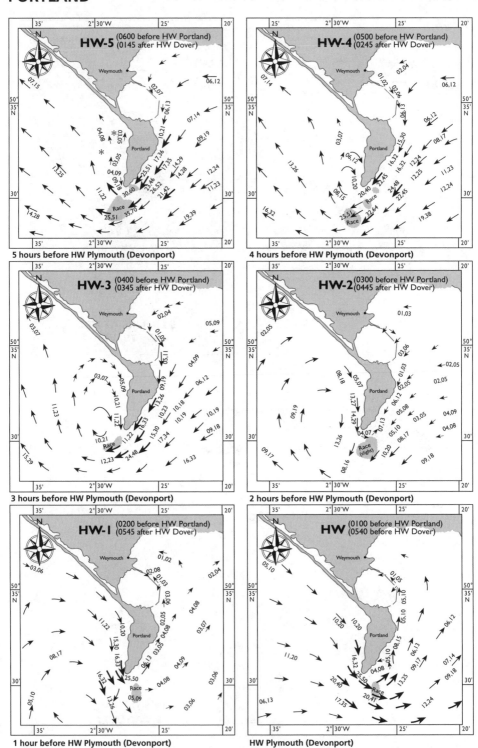

HW-5 (0600 before HW Portland)
(0145 after HW Dover)

5 hours before HW Plymouth (Devonport)

HW-4 (0500 before HW Portland)
(0245 after HW Dover)

4 hours before HW Plymouth (Devonport)

HW-3 (0400 before HW Portland)
(0345 after HW Dover)

3 hours before HW Plymouth (Devonport)

HW-2 (0300 before HW Portland)
(0445 after HW Dover)

2 hours before HW Plymouth (Devonport)

HW-1 (0200 before HW Portland)
(0545 after HW Dover)

1 hour before HW Plymouth (Devonport)

HW (0100 before HW Portland)
(0540 before HW Dover)

HW Plymouth (Devonport)

PORTLAND

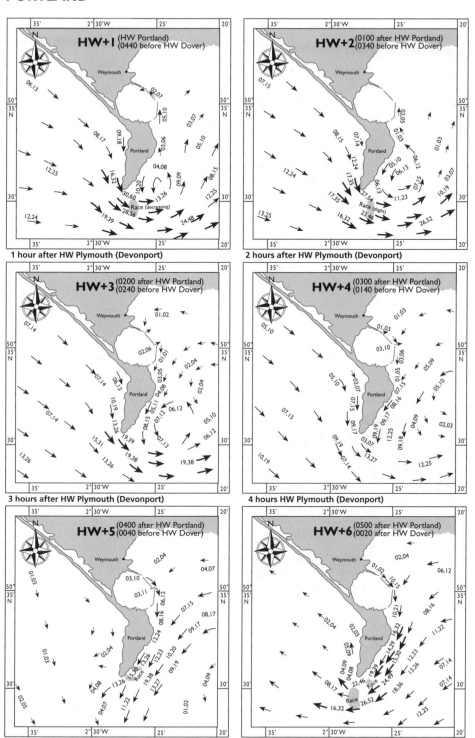

HW+1 (HW Portland)
(0440 before HW Dover)

1 hour after HW Plymouth (Devonport)

HW+2 (0100 after HW Portland)
(0340 before HW Dover)

2 hours after HW Plymouth (Devonport)

HW+3 (0200 after HW Portland)
(0240 before HW Dover)

3 hours after HW Plymouth (Devonport)

HW+4 (0300 after HW Portland)
(0140 before HW Dover)

4 hours HW Plymouth (Devonport)

HW+5 (0400 after HW Portland)
(0040 before HW Dover)

5 hours after HW Plymouth (Devonport)

HW+6 (0500 after HW Portland)
(0020 after HW Dover)

6 hours after HW Plymouth (Devonport)

ISLE OF WIGHT

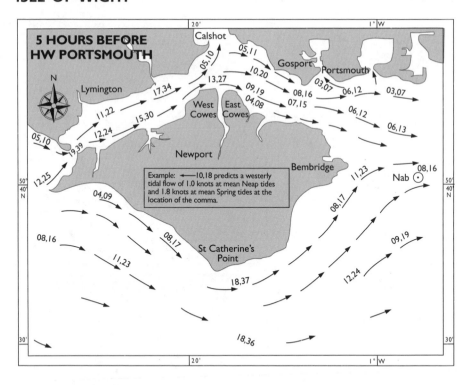

5 HOURS BEFORE HW PORTSMOUTH

Example: ←10,18 predicts a westerly tidal flow of 1.0 knots at mean Neap tides and 1.8 knots at mean Spring tides at the location of the comma.

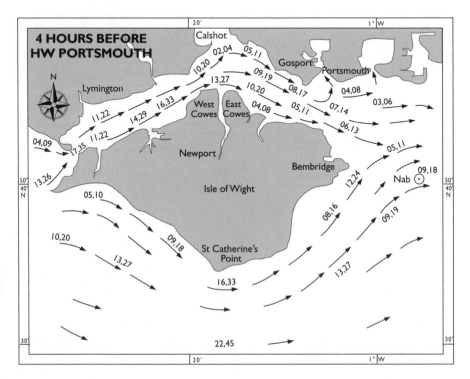

4 HOURS BEFORE HW PORTSMOUTH

ISLE OF WIGHT

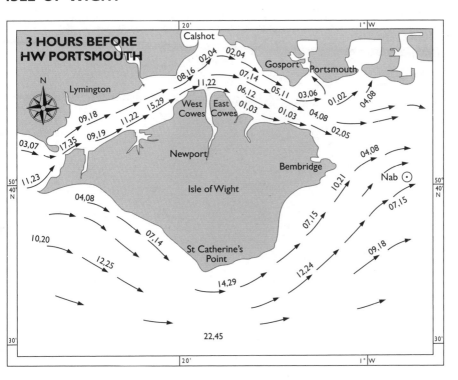

3 HOURS BEFORE HW PORTSMOUTH

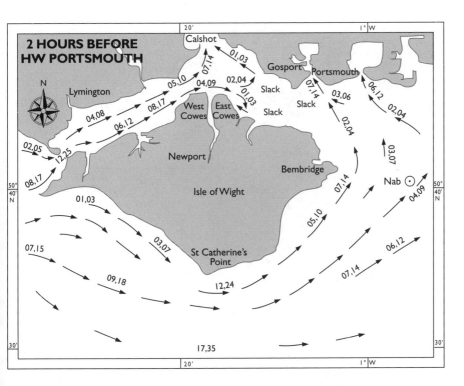

2 HOURS BEFORE HW PORTSMOUTH

ISLE OF WIGHT

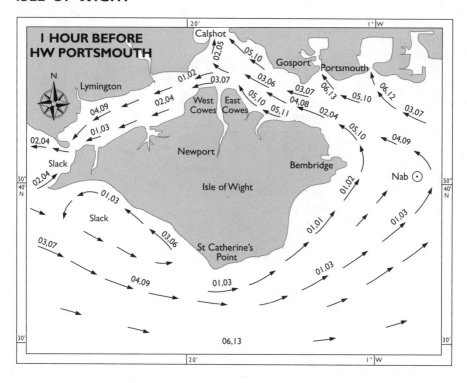

I HOUR BEFORE HW PORTSMOUTH

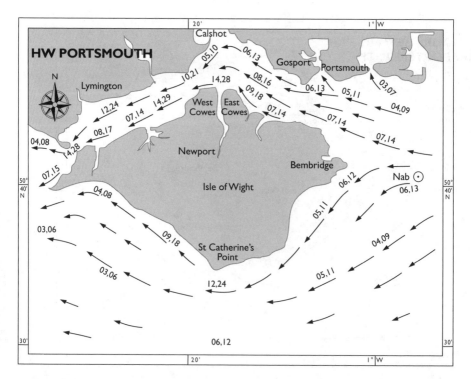

HW PORTSMOUTH

ISLE OF WIGHT

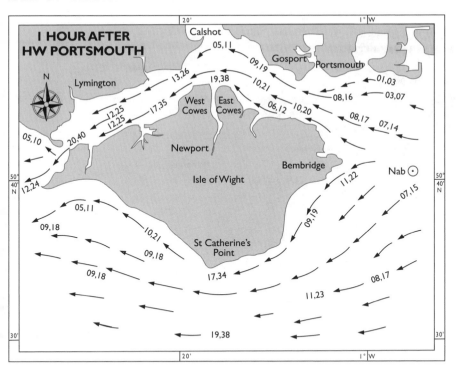

1 HOUR AFTER HW PORTSMOUTH

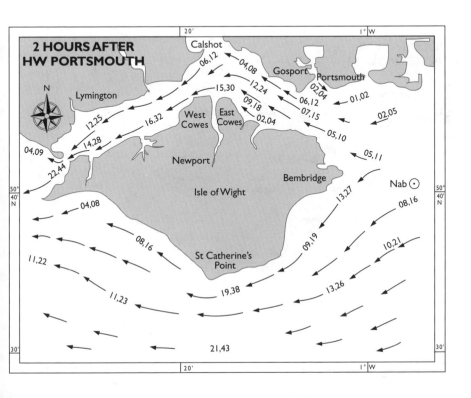

2 HOURS AFTER HW PORTSMOUTH

ISLE OF WIGHT

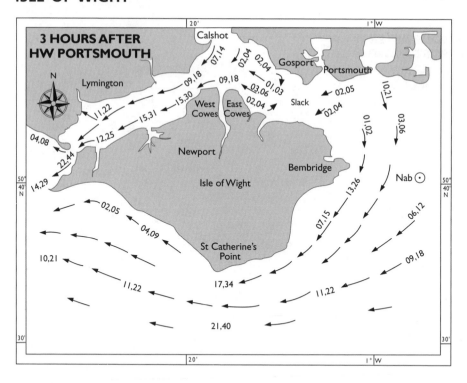

3 HOURS AFTER HW PORTSMOUTH

Calshot
Gosport
Portsmouth
Lymington
West Cowes
East Cowes
Slack
Newport
Bembridge
Isle of Wight
Nab ⊙
St Catherine's Point

07.14 · 02.04 · 02.04 · 01.03 · 02.05 · 10.21
09.18 · 09.18 · 03.06 · 02.04 · 01.02 · 03.06
11.22 · 15.30 · 15.31 · 02.04
04.08 · 12.25 · 22.44
14.29
13.26
07.15 · 06.12
02.05 · 09.18
04.09 · 11.22
10.21
11.22 · 17.34
21.40

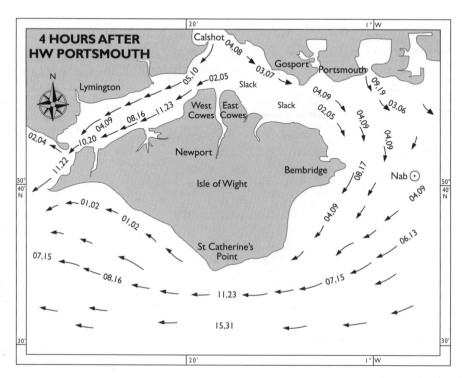

4 HOURS AFTER HW PORTSMOUTH

Calshot
Gosport
Portsmouth
Lymington
West Cowes
East Cowes
Slack
Slack
Newport
Bembridge
Isle of Wight
Nab ⊙
St Catherine's Point

04.08 · 03.07 · 09.19 · 03.06
05.10 · 02.05 · 04.09 · 02.05 · 04.09
04.09 · 08.16 · 11.23 · 04.09
02.04 · 10.20 · 08.17
11.22 · 04.09 · 04.09
01.02 · 06.13
01.02
07.15 · 07.15
08.16
11.23
15.31

ISLE OF WIGHT

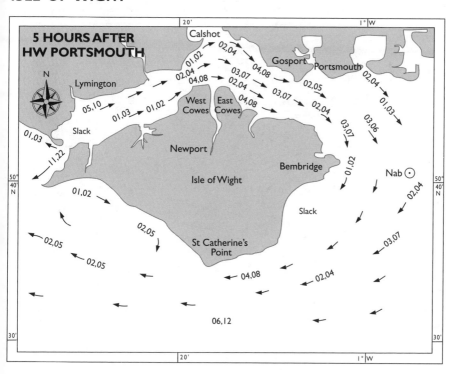

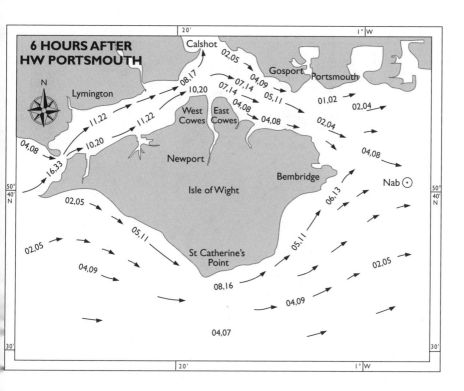

CHANNEL ISLANDS

Example: ◄—10,18 predicts a westerly tidal flow of 1.0 knots at mean Neap tides and 1.8 knots at mean Spring tides at the location of the comma.

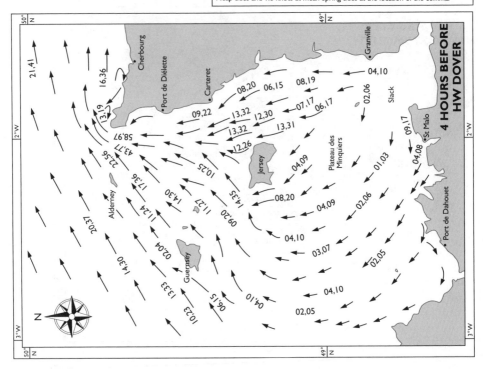

4 HOURS BEFORE HW DOVER

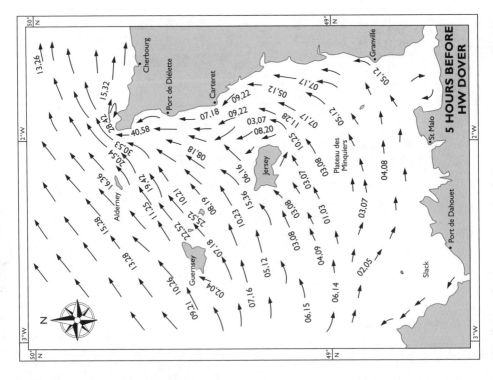

5 HOURS BEFORE HW DOVER

CHANNEL ISLANDS

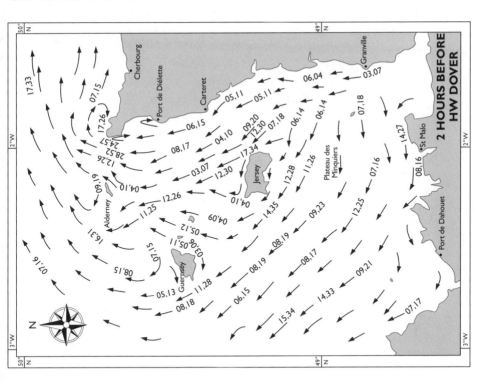

2 HOURS BEFORE HW DOVER

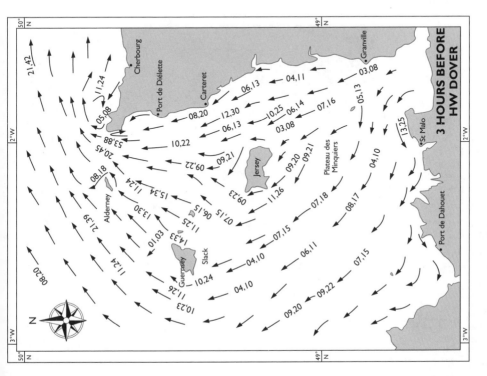

3 HOURS BEFORE HW DOVER

CHANNEL ISLANDS

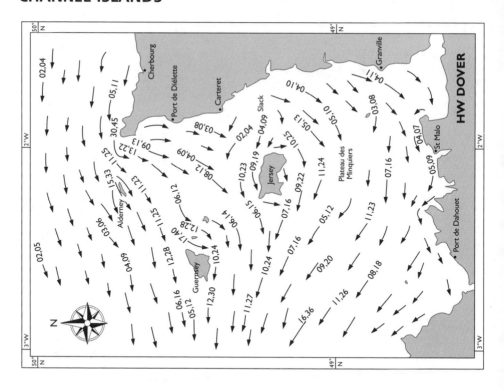

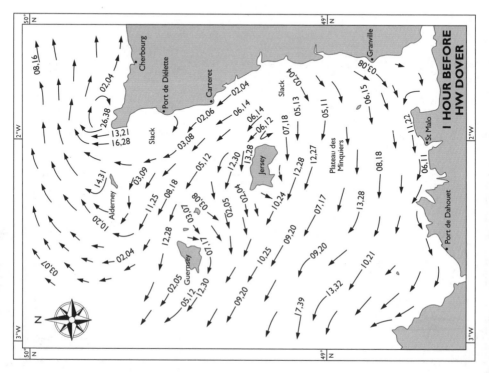

CHANNEL ISLANDS

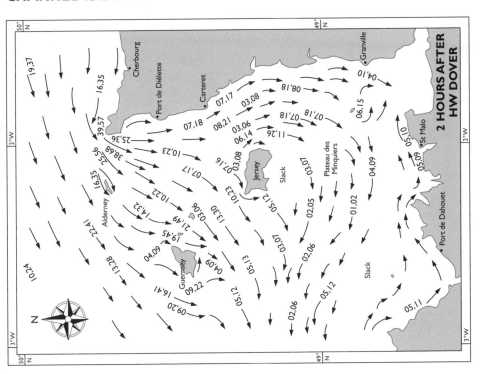

2 HOURS AFTER HW DOVER

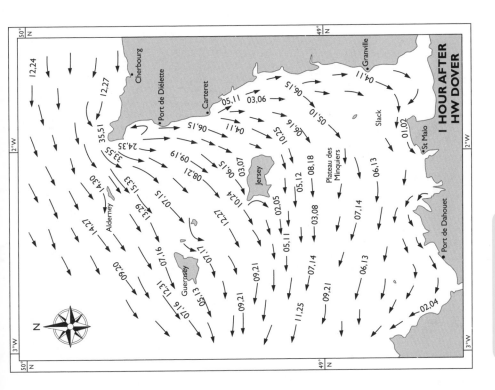

1 HOUR AFTER HW DOVER

TIDES

169

CHANNEL ISLANDS

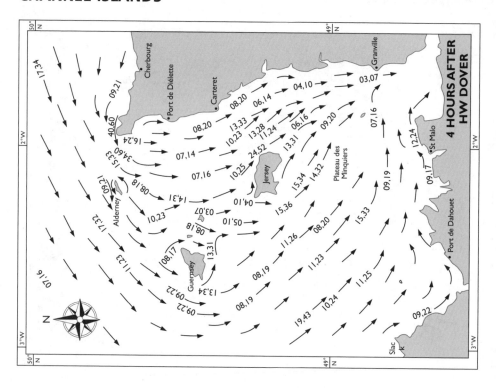

4 HOURS AFTER HW DOVER

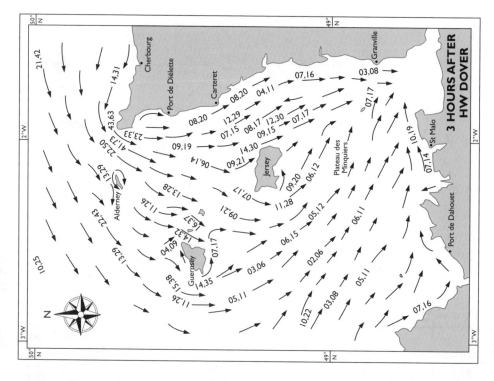

3 HOURS AFTER HW DOVER

CHANNEL ISLANDS

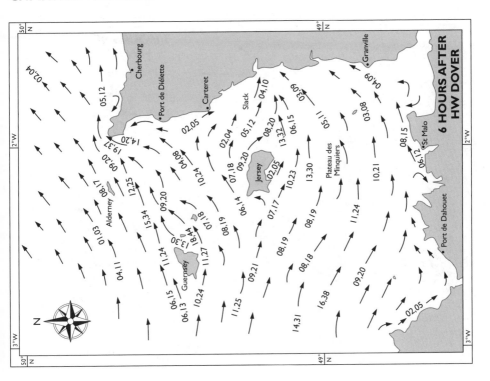

6 HOURS AFTER HW DOVER

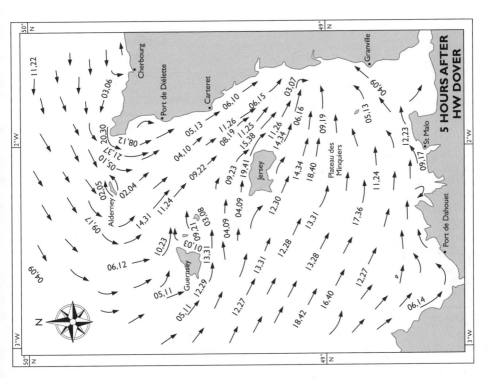

5 HOURS AFTER HW DOVER

NORTH SEA

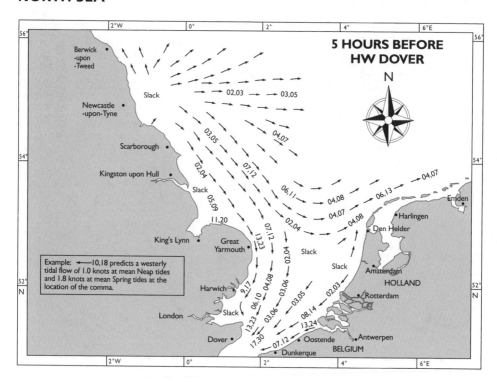

5 HOURS BEFORE HW DOVER

Example: ←10,18 predicts a westerly tidal flow of 1.0 knots at mean Neap tides and 1.8 knots at mean Spring tides at the location of the comma.

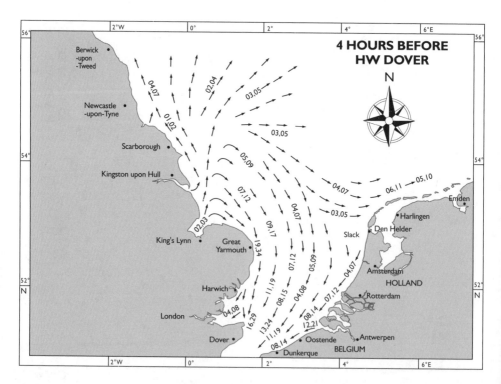

4 HOURS BEFORE HW DOVER

NORTH SEA

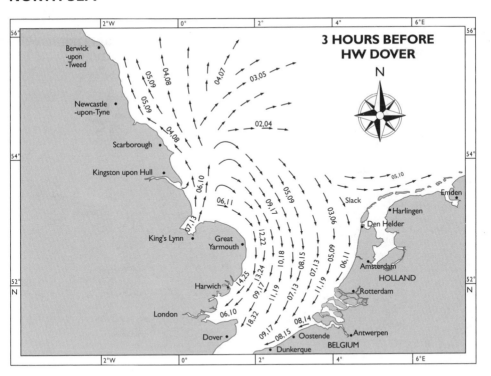

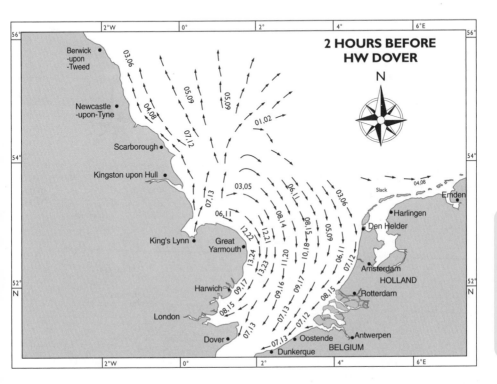

NORTH SEA

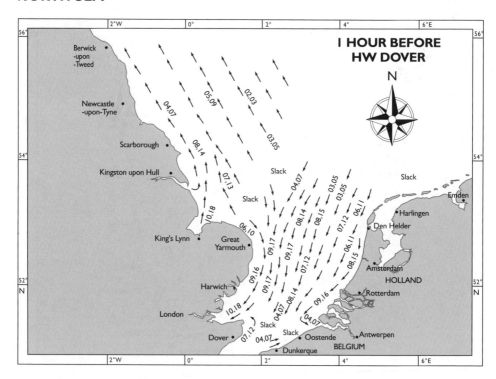

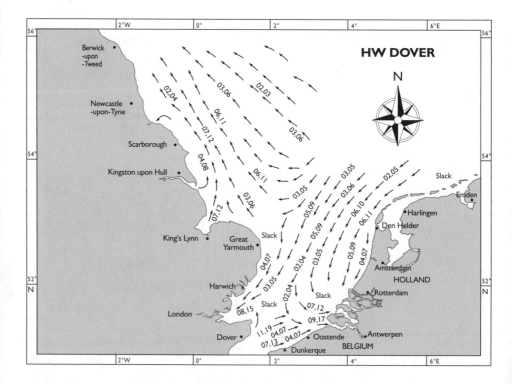

NORTH SEA

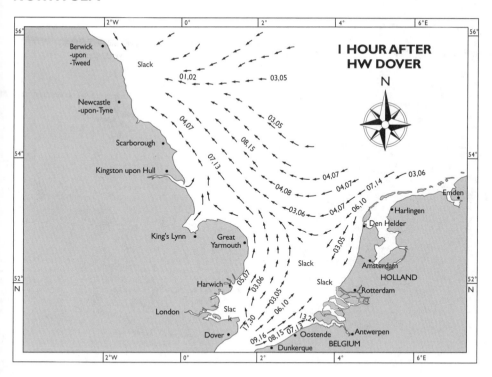

I HOUR AFTER
HW DOVER

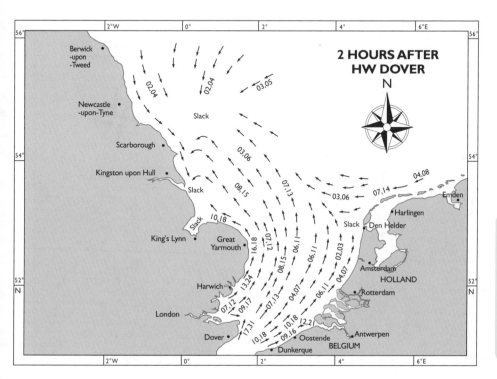

2 HOURS AFTER
HW DOVER

NORTH SEA

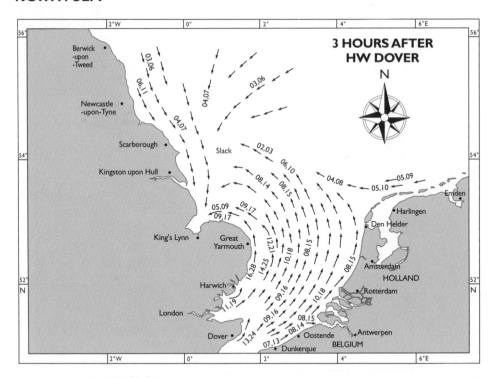

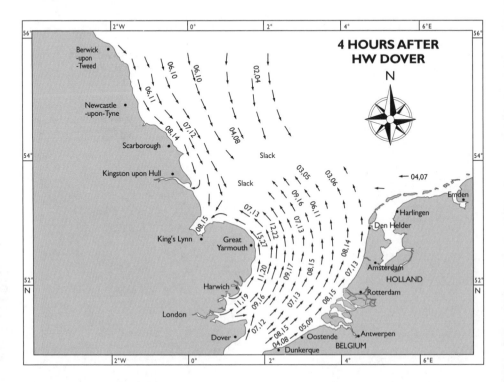

NORTH SEA

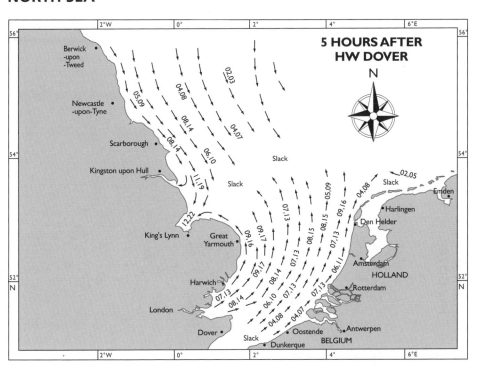

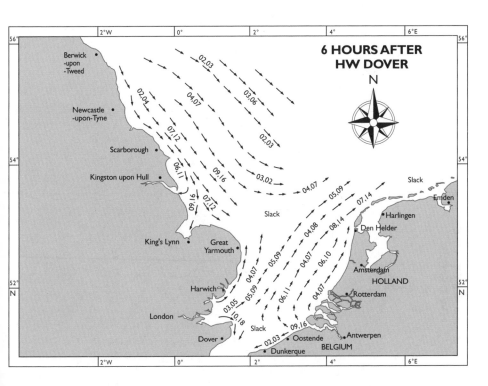

SCOTLAND

Example: ←—10,18 predicts a westerly tidal flow of 1.0 knots at mean Neap tides and 1.8 knots at mean Spring tides at the location of the comma.

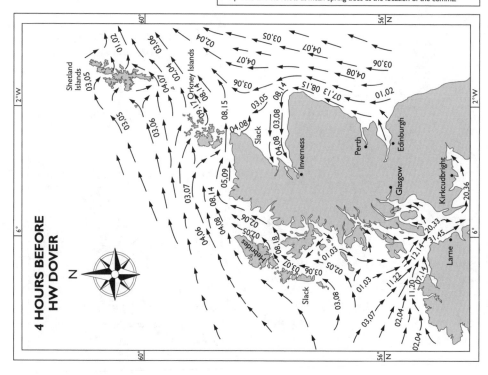

4 HOURS BEFORE HW DOVER

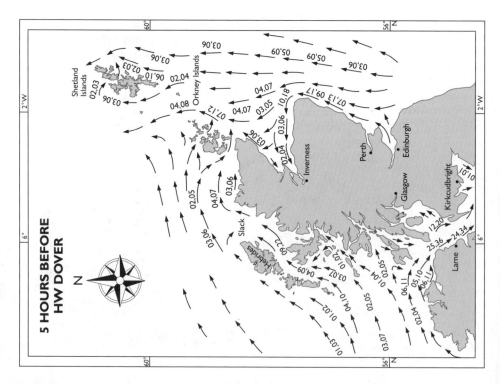

5 HOURS BEFORE HW DOVER

SCOTLAND

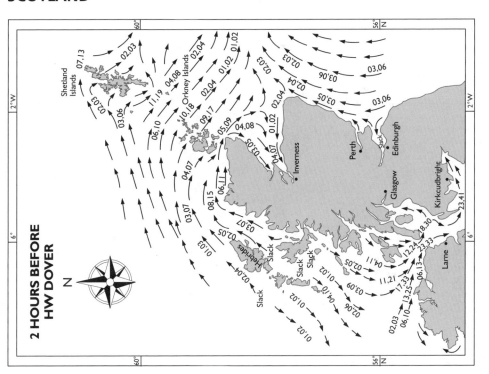

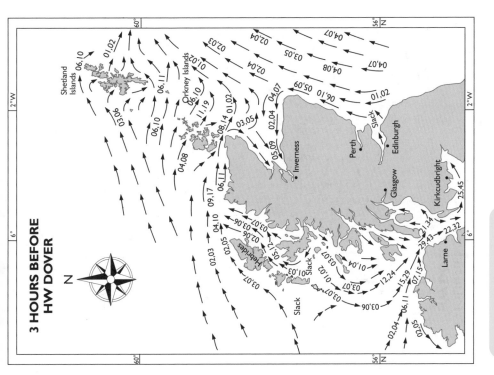

SCOTLAND

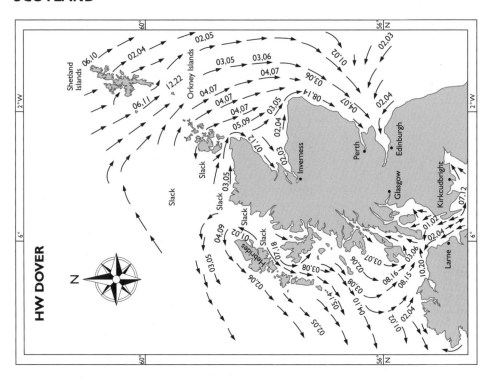

HW DOVER

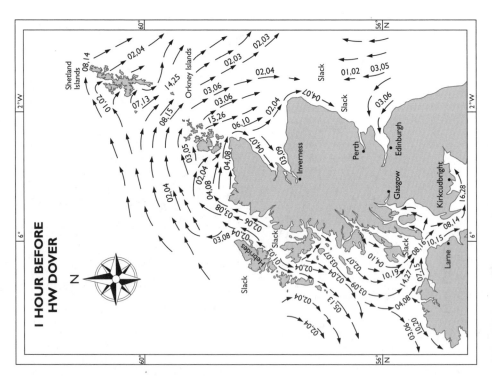

1 HOUR BEFORE HW DOVER

SCOTLAND

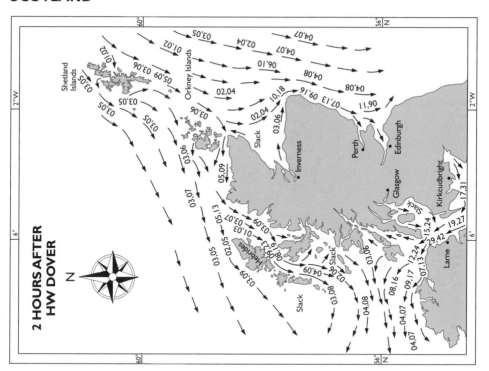

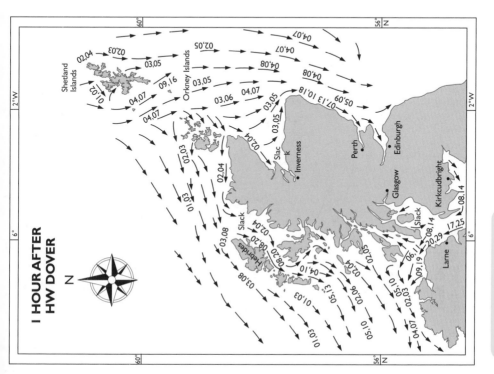

SCOTLAND

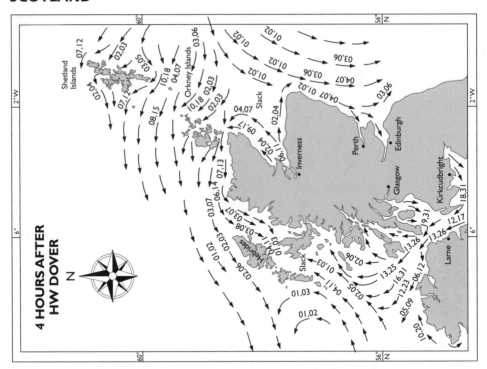

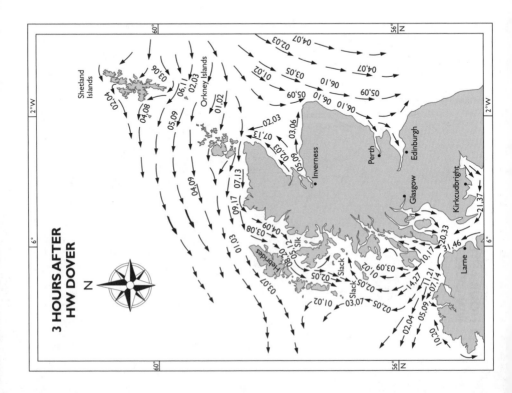

SCOTLAND

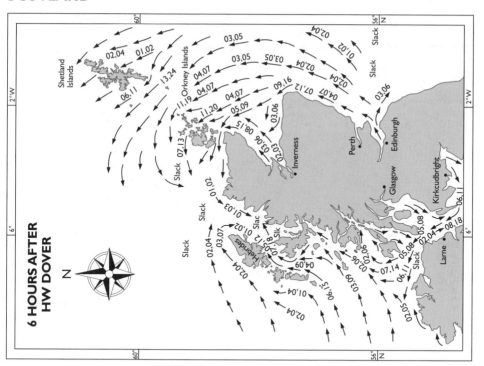

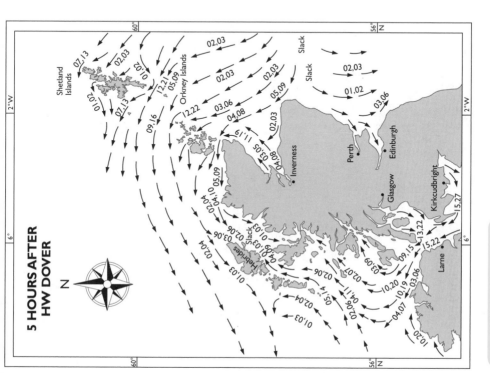

WEST UK AND IRELAND

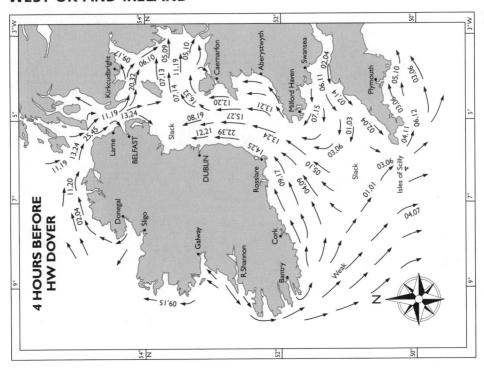

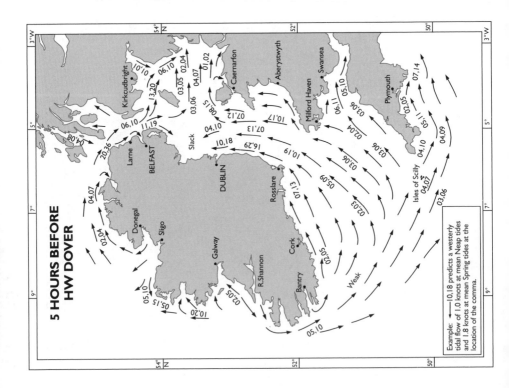

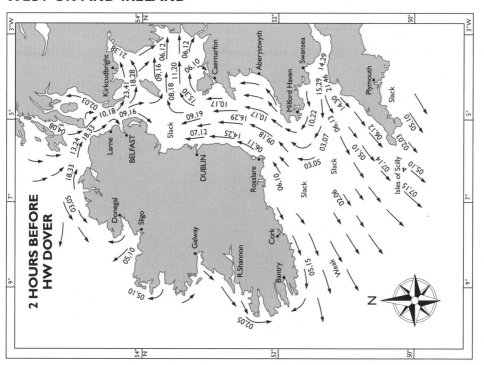

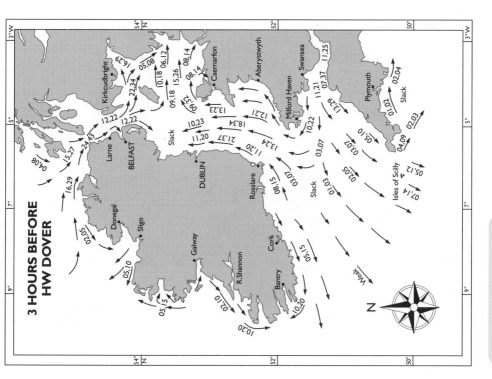

WEST UK AND IRELAND

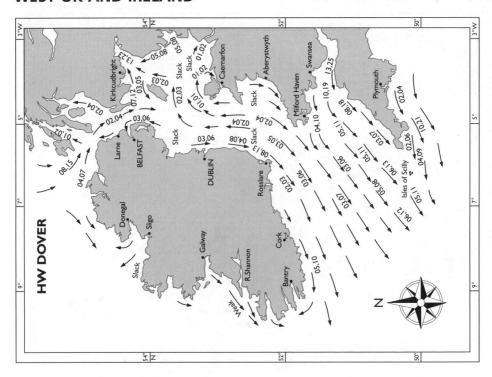

HW DOVER

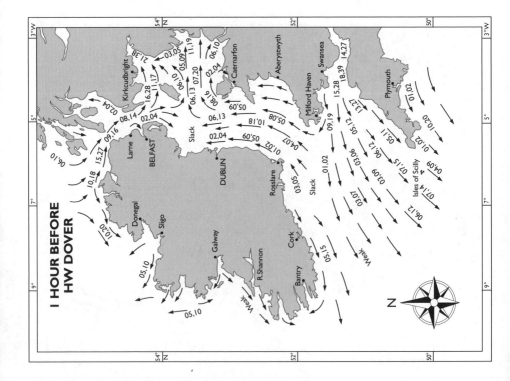

1 HOUR BEFORE HW DOVER

WEST UK AND IRELAND

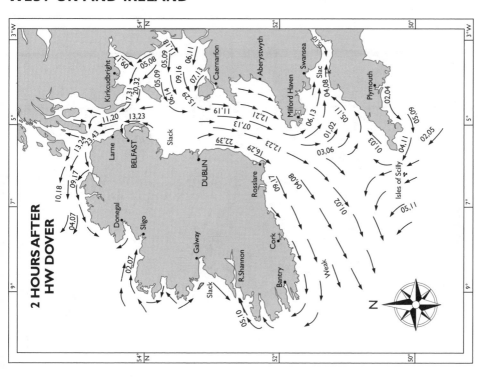

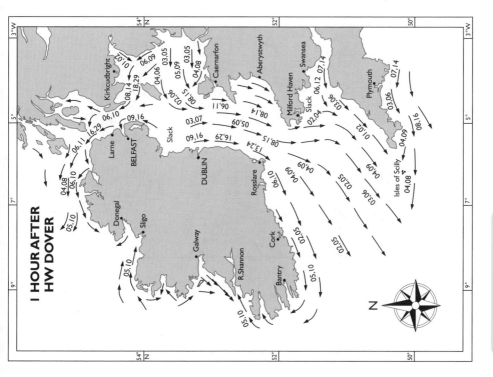

WEST UK AND IRELAND

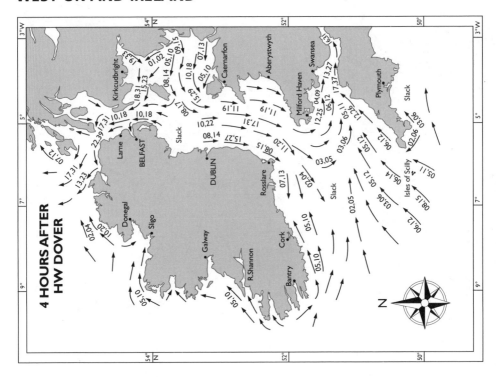

4 HOURS AFTER HW DOVER

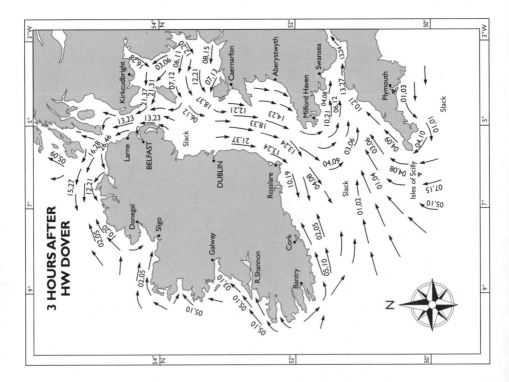

3 HOURS AFTER HW DOVER

WEST UK AND IRELAND

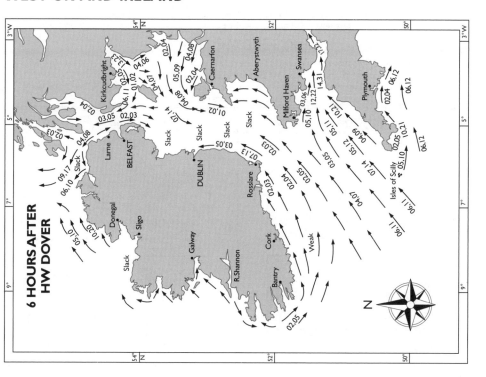

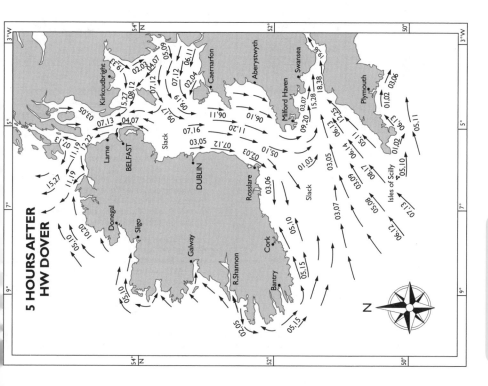

TIDAL GATES - SOUTHERN ENGLAND

A guide to the time of tide turn at tidal gates, the approximate maximum strength of the tidal flow (spring rates shown - neaps are approximately 60% of these), and the position and timing of races, counter tides, etc.

LAND'S END (AC 1148)

Tidal streams set hard north/south round Land's End, and east/west around Gwennap and Pendeen. But the inshore currents run counter to the tidal streams. By staying close inshore, this tidal gate favours a N-bound passage. With careful timing nearly 9½hrs of fair tide can be carried, from HWD–3 to HWD+5. The chartlets, referenced to HW Dover, depict both tidal streams and inshore currents.

FLOOD	EBB

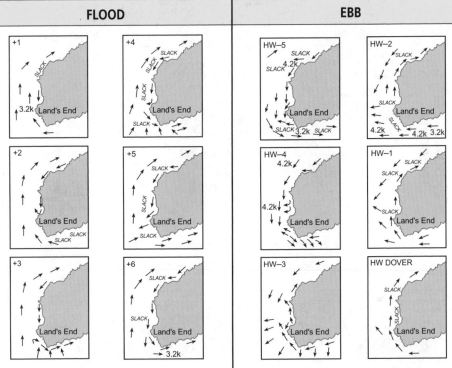

Example N-bound: At HWD+1 the N-going flood starts off Gwennap and does not turn NE along the N Cornish coast until HWD+3. But as early as HWD–3 an inshore current is beginning to set north. Utilise this by arriving off Runnel Stone at HWD–2 and then keeping within ¼M of the shore. If abeam the Brisons at HWD, the tide and current should serve for the next 6 or 7 hours to make good St Ives, or even Newquay and Padstow.

Example S-bound: If S-bound from St Ives to Newlyn, aim to reach the Runnel Stone by HWD+5, ie with 2hrs of E-going tide in hand for the remaining 9M to Newlyn. To achieve this 20M passage, leave St Ives 5 hours earlier, ie at HWD. Buck a foul tide for the first 3 hours, then use the S-going inshore current, keeping as close inshore as is prudent, only moving seaward to clear the Wra and the Brisons. This timing would also suit a passage from S Wales or the Bristol Channel, going inshore of Longships if conditions allow.

From Ireland, ie Cork or further W, the inshore passage would not benefit. But aim to be off the Runnel Stone at HWD+5 if bound for Newlyn; or at HWD+3 if bound for Helford/Falmouth, with the W-going stream slackening and 5hrs of fair tide to cover the remaining 20M past the Lizard.

With acknowledgements to the Royal Cruising Club Pilotage Foundation for their kind permission to use the tidal stream chartlets and text written by Hugh Davies, as first published in Yachting Monthly *magazine.*

TIDAL GATES - SOUTHERN ENGLAND

A guide to the time of tide turn at tidal gates, the approximate maximum strength of the tidal flow (spring rates shown - neaps are approximately 60% of these), and the position and timing of races, counter tides, etc.

FLOOD	EBB

THE LIZARD (AC 777, 2345)

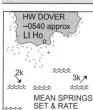

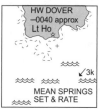

Drying rocks lie approx 5 cables S of the Lizard lt ho and extend westwards. 49°57'N is about as far N as yachts may safely pass inshore of the Race, which extends 2-3M to seaward of these rocks. Race conditions may also exist SE of the Lizard with short, heavy seas in westerlies. If passing S of the Race, route via 49°55'N 05°13'W to clear the worst of the Race.

Inshore the E-going Channel flood, 2kn max @ springs, begins at HW Dover +0145; and outside the Race at approx HWD +0300.	Inshore the W-going Channel ebb, 3kn max @ springs, begins at HW Dover −0345; and outside the Race at HWD −0240.

START POINT (AC 1634)

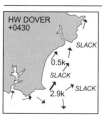

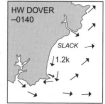

Start Pt, and to a lesser extent Prawle Pt (3.3M WSW), can be slow to round when W-bound with a fair tide against a W'ly wind raising a bad sea. Drying rocks extend 3 cables SSE of the lt ho and a Race may extend up to 1.7M ESE and 1.0M S of the lt ho. It is safe to pass between the Race and the rocks, but in bad weather wiser to go outside the Race. The Skerries Bank (least depth 2.1m) lies 8 cables NE of Start Pt. On both the flood and the ebb back eddies form between Start Pt and Hallsands, 1M NW.

The NE-going Channel flood, 3.1kn max @ springs, begins at HW Dover +0430.	The SW-going Channel ebb, 2.2kn max @ springs, begins at HW Dover −0140, but an hour earlier it is possible to round Start Pt close inshore using the back eddy.

PORTLAND (AC 2255)

A dangerous Race forms between 200 metres and 2 miles south of Portland Bill. The Race shifts westward on the W-going stream and eastward on the E-going stream. In the latter case it is not advisable to pass between the Race and the Shambles Bank. Study carefully the hourly tidal stream chartlets on pp.158-159 or in NP 257. The Race may be avoided either by passing to seaward of it, ie 3-5M south of the Bill and east of the Shambles; or by using the inshore passage – if conditions suit.

Seaward of the Race.

E-bound: The Channel flood sets east from HW Dover +6 to HWD −1.	W-bound: The ebb sets west from HW Dover to HWD +5½.

The inshore passage, (a narrow stretch of relatively smooth water between the Bill and the Race), should be started, in either direction, from a position 2M north of the Bill, keeping close inshore to the Portland peninsula. It should not be used at night (due to pot floats), nor in winds >F4/5, nor at springs especially with wind against tide.

If E-bound via the inshore passage, slackish water or a fair stream occurs around the Bill from HW Portland −3 to +1. The passage across Lyme Bay should be specifically timed to meet this critical window.	W-bound, similar conditions occur from HW Portland +4 to −6. The W-bound timing is easy if you have started from Weymouth, Portland harbour or Lulworth Cove.

ST ALBAN'S HEAD (AC 2610)

A sometimes vicious Race forms over St Alban's Ledge, a rocky dorsal ridge (least depth 8.5m) which extends approx 4M SW from St Alban's Head. Three yellow naval target buoys (DZ A, B and C) straddle the middle and outer sections, but are only occasionally used. In settled weather and at neaps the Race may be barely perceptible in which case it can be crossed with impunity. Avoid it either by keeping to seaward via 50°31'.40N 02°07'.80W; or by using the narrow inshore passage at the foot of St Alban's Head.

Based on a position 1M S of St Alban's Head, the tidal stream windows are:

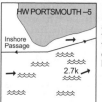

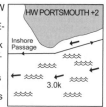

ESE-going stream starts at HW Portsmouth +0530. Spring rates are the same, max 4kn. Along the W side of St Alban's Head the stream runs almost continuously SE due to a back eddy.

WNW-going stream starts at HW Portsmouth. Overfalls extend 2.5M further SW than on the E-going stream and are more dangerous to small craft. Slack water lasts barely half an hour.

The inshore passage lies as close to the foot of St Alban's Head as feels comfortable. It may be hard to see the width of clear water in the inshore passage until committed to it, but except in onshore gales when it is better to stay offshore, the passage will be swiftly made with only a few, if any, overfalls. The NCI station on the Head (☎ 01929 439220) may advise on conditions.

TIDES

TIDAL GATES - SOUTHERN ENGLAND

A guide to the time of tide turn at tidal gates, the approximate maximum strength of the tidal flow (spring rates shown - neaps are approximately 60% of these), and the position and timing of races, counter tides, etc.

FLOOD	EBB

THE NEEDLES CHANNEL (AC 2035)

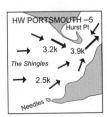

The Needles Channel lies between the SW Shingles PHM buoy and the Bridge WCM buoy. Once through this narrow section the channel widens with the Island shore to starboard and the long, drying 1.2m, Shingles bank to port. Abeam Hurst Castle the channel again narrows (assisted by The Trap, a shoal spit south of Hurst Castle) before opening out into the west Solent.

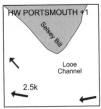

Study carefully the hourly tidal stream chartlets for the Isle of Wight on pp.186-191 and the values shown on AC 2035 at tidal diamonds B, C, D and E.

The ENE-going flood runs from HW Portsmouth +5 until HW P −1½, at springs reaching 3.1kn at The Bridge and 3.9kn at Hurst.	The WSW-going ebb runs from HW P −1 until HW P +4½, reaching 4.4kn at Hurst and 3.4kn at The Bridge, both spring rates. The ebb sets strongly WSW across the Shingles which with adequate rise is routinely crossed by racing yachts; but cruisers should stay clear even in calm conditions when any swell causes the sea to break heavily.

Prevailing W/SW winds, even if only F4, against the ebb raise dangerous breaking seas in the Needles Channel and at The Bridge, a shallow ridge extending 9 cables west from the Needles light. Worst conditions are often found just after LW slack. In such conditions it is safer to go via the North Channel to Hurst. In W/SW gales avoid the Needles altogether by sheltering at Poole or going east-about via Nab Tower.

ON PASSAGE UP CHANNEL

The following 3 tidal gates (Looe Channel, Beachy Head and Dungeness) are components in the tidal conveyor belt which, if stepped onto at the outset, can enable a fastish yacht to carry a fair tide for 88M from Selsey Bill to Dover. Go through the Looe at slackish water, HW Portsmouth +4½ (HW Dover +5). Based on a mean SOG of 7 knots, Beachy Head will be passed at HW D −1, Dungeness at HW D +3 and Dover at HW +5½, only bucking the first of the ebb in the last hour. A faster boat could make Ramsgate. The down-Channel passage is less rewarding and many yachts will pause at Brighton.

LOOE CHANNEL (AC 2045, 1652)

This channel is little shorter than the detour south of the Owers, but is much used by yachts on passage from/to points east of the Solent. Although adequately lit, it is best not attempted at night due to many lobster floats; nor in onshore gales as searoom is limited by extensive shoals on which the sea breaks.

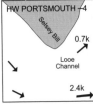

The E-going flood runs from HW Portsmouth +4½ (HW Dover +5) until HW P −1½ (HW D −1), at springs reaching 2.4kn near the Boulder and Street light buoys which mark its narrow western end; they may be hard to see in other than good visibility. Max neap rate is 1.2kn.	The W-going ebb runs from HW P −1½ (HW D −1) until HW P +4½ (HW D +5), at springs reaching 2.6kn near Boulder and Street. Max neap rate is 1.3kn.

At the wider eastern end of the channel (near E Borough Head buoy) rates are greatly reduced.

BEACHY HEAD (AC 1652, 536)

Stay at least 5 cables to seaward of the towering chalk cliffs to avoid isolated boulders and rocky, part-drying ridges such as Head Ledge. The lt ho stands on a drying rock ledge. Close inshore many fishing floats are a trap for the unwary. In bad weather stay 2M offshore to avoid overfalls caused by a ridge of uneven ground which extends 1M SSE from Beachy Head.

2M south of Beachy Head the E-going flood starts at HW Dover +0530, max spring rate 2.6kn.	The W-going ebb starts at HW Dover +0030, max spring rate 2.0kn.

Between 5M and 7M east of Beachy Head avoid breakers and eddies caused by the Horse of Willingdon, Royal Sovereign and other shoals.

DUNGENESS (AC 536, 1892)

Tidal stream atlases: Dungeness is on the east and west edges respectively of NP 250 (English Channel) and NP 233 (Dover Strait). The nearest tidal stream diamond (2.2M SE of Dungeness) is 'H' on AC 536 and 'B' on AC 1892; their positions and values are the same.

The NE-going flood starts at HW Dover −0100, max spring rate 1.9kn.	The SW-going ebb starts at HW Dover +0430, max spring rate 2.1kn.

TIDAL GATES - NORTH EAST SCOTLAND

A guide to the time of tide turn at tidal gates, and in straits and estuaries, showing the approximate strength of the tidal flow (spring rates shown - neaps are approximately 60% of these), and the position and timing of races, counter tides etc.

FLOOD	EBB

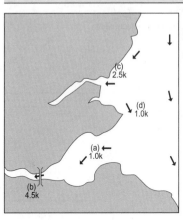

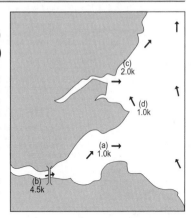

FIRTHS of FORTH (AC 175) & TAY (AC 1481)

Tidal streams are quite weak in the outer part of the Firth, increasing as the narrows at islands and the bridges are approached. Apart from the stream of the Tay, which attains 5 knots in most places, the coastwise tidal streams between Fife Ness and Arbroath are weak.

(a) Dover –0225 to Dover +0330
(b) Dover –0200 to Dover +0400
(c) Dover –0210 to Dover +0420
(d) Dover –0110 to Dover +0520

(a) Dover +0330 to Dover –0225
(b) Dover +0400 to Dover –0200
(c) Dover +0420 to Dover –0210
(d) Dover +0520 to Dover –0110

PASSAGES FROM FORTH & TAY

Northbound. Leave before HW (Dover +0400) to be at N Carr at Dover +0600. Bound from Forth to Tay aim to arrive at Abertay By at LW slack (Dover –0200).
Southbound. Leave before LW (Dover -0200) to be at Bass Rk at HW Dover. Similar timings if bound from Tay to Forth, leave late in ebb to pick up early flood off St Andrews to N Carr and into Forth.

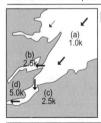

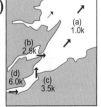

INVERNESS & CROMARTY FIRTHS (AC 1077)

Tidal streams in the Inverness Firth and approaches are not strong, except in the Cromarty Firth Narrows, the Fort George Narrows and the Kessock Road, including off the entrance to the Caledonian Canal.

(a) Dover –0555 to Dover +0030	(a) Dover +0030 to Dover –0555
(b) Dover –0400 to Dover +0115	(b) Dover +0115 to Dover –0400
(c) Dover –0400 to Dover –0220	(c) Dover +0115 to Dover –0440
(d) Dover –0430 to Dover +0100	(d) Dover –0130 to Dover +0545

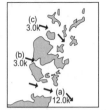

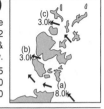

PENTLAND FIRTH & ORKNEYS (AC 1954)

The tide flows strongly around and through the Orkney Islands. The Pentland Firth is a dangerous area for all craft, tidal flows reach 12 knots between Duncansby Head and S Ronaldsay. W of Dunnet Hd & Hoy is less violent. There is little tide within Scapa Flow.

(a) Dover –0500 to Dover +0100	(a) Dover +0115 to Dover –0535
(b) Dover +0500 to Dover –0110	(b) Dover –0110 to Dover +0050
(c) Dover –0530 to Dover +0040	(c) Dover +0040 to Dover –0530

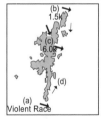

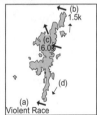

SHETLAND ISLANDS (AC 219)

The tidal flow around the Shetland Islands rotates as the cycle progresses. When the flood begins, at –0400 HW Dover, the tidal flow is to the E, at HW Dover it is S, at Dover +0300 it is W, and at –0600 Dover it is N.

(a) Dover –0410 to Dover +0020	(a) Dover +0050 to Dover –0410
(b) Dover –0400 to Dover +0030	(b) Dover +0130 to Dover –0500
(c) Dover –0530 to Dover +0100	(c) Dover +0100 to Dover –0530
(d) Dover –0400 to Dover –0200	(d) Dover +0200 to Dover +0500

Violent Race

Violent Race

TIDAL GATES - NORTH WEST SCOTLAND

A guide to the time of tide turn at tidal gates, the approximate maximum strength of the tidal flow (spring rates shown - neaps are approximately 60% of these), and the position and timing of races, counter tides, etc.

FLOOD	EBB

SOUND OF HARRIS (AC 2642)

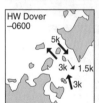

The behaviour of tidal streams in the Sd of Harris varies from day to night, springs to neaps, and winter to summer. The following data applies to daylight, in summer at spring tides in the Cope Channel. Further information can be sought in the Admiralty West of Scotland Pilot.
HW Dover - HW D +0200: SE stream.
HW D +0300 - HW D +0600: Incoming stream from both ends.
HW D −0600 - HW D −0500: NW stream.
HW D −0500 - HW Dover: Outgoing stream from both ends.
At neaps in summer the stream will run SE for most of the day.
Tide rates shown are the maxima likely to be encountered at any time.

THE LITTLE MINCH (AC 1795)

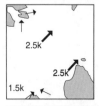

The N going stream on both shores begins at HW Dover +0430 (HW Ullapool -0345), with the strongest flow from mid channel to the Skye coast. There is a W going counter tide E of Vaternish Point.

The S going stream on both shores begins at HW Dover −0130 (HW Ullapool +0240), with the strongest flow from mid channel to the Skye coast. The E going stream in Sound of Scalpay runs at up to 2k.The E going flood and W going ebb in Sound of Scalpay run at up to 2k.

KYLE OF LOCHALSH & KYLERHEA (AC 2540)

NOTE: THESE STREAMS ARE SUBJECT TO VARIATION

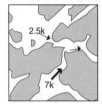

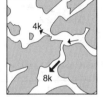

N going stream in Kyle Rhea begins HW Dover +0140 (HW Ullapool +0555) and runs for 6 hours. The E going stream in Kyle Akin begins (Sp) HW Dover +0350 (HW Ullapool −0415). (Nps) HW Dover −0415 (HW Ullapool).

S going stream in Kyle Rhea begins HW Dover -0415 (HW Ullapool) and runs for 6 hours. The W going stream in Kyle Akin begins (Sp) HW Dover −0015 (HW Ullapool +0400). (Nps) HW Dover +0140 (HW Ullapool +0555).

ARDNAMURCHAN POINT (AC 2171)

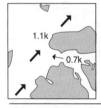

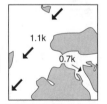

The N going stream off Ardnamurchan begins at HW Dover +0130 (HW Oban −0525). The E going stream in the Sound of Mull begins at HW Dover +0555 (HW Oban −0100).

The S going stream off Ardnamurchan begins at HW Dover −0430 (HW Oban +0100). The W going stream in the Sound of Mull begins at HW Dover −0130 (HW Oban +0400).

SOUND OF MULL - EAST (AC 2171)

The N going stream in the Firth of Lorne begins at HW Dover −0100 (HW Oban +0430). The W going stream in the Sound of Mull begins at HW Dover +0105 (HW Oban −0550). The ingoing tides at Lochs Feochan, Etive and Creran begin at HW Dover +0300, −0100 & +0030.

The S going stream in the Firth of Lorne begins at HW Dover +0500 (HW Oban −0155). The E going stream in the Sound of Mull begins at HW Dover +0555 (HW Oban −0025). The outgoing tides at Lochs Feochan, Etive and Creran begin at HW Dover −0500, −0520 & −0505.

SOUND OF LUING & DORUS MOR (AC 2343)

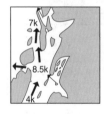

The N or W going stream begins as follows:
Dorus Mor: HW Dover −0200 (HW Oban +0330). Springs: 8 knots.
Corryvreckan: HW D −0120 (HW O +0410). Sp: 8.5 knots.
Cuan Sound: HW D −0110 (HW O +0420). Sp: 6 knots.
Sound of Jura: HW D −0130 (HW O +0400). Sp: 4 knots.
Sound of Luing: HW D −0100 (HW O +0430). Sp: 7 knots.

The S or E going stream begins as follows:
Dorus Mor: HW Dover +0440 (HW Oban −0215). Springs: 8 knots.
Corryvreckan: HW D +0445 (HW O −0210). Sp: 8.5 knots.
Cuan Sound: HW D +0455 (HW O −0200). Sp: 6 knots.
Sound of Jura: HW D +0450 (HW O −0205). Sp: 4 knots.
Sound of Luing: HW D +0500 (HW O −0155). Sp: 7 knots.

TIDAL GATES - SOUTH WEST SCOTLAND

A guide to the time of tide turn at tidal gates, the approximate maximum strength of the tidal flow (spring rates shown - neaps are approximately 60% of these), and the position and timing of races, counter tides, etc.

FLOOD	EBB

SOUNDS OF ISLAY AND GIGHA (AC 2168)

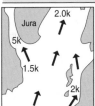

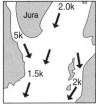

FLOOD	EBB
Main flood begins +0015 HW Dover (HW Oban +0545). Streams turn approx 1 hr earlier in Gigha Sd & at Kintyre & Jura shores. S going stream for 9hrs close inshore between Gigha and Machrihanish starting HW Dover (HW Oban –0530).	Main ebb begins HW Dover –0545 (HW Oban –0015). Streams turn 1 hr earlier in Gigha Sd, Kintyre & Jura shores. Overfalls off McArthur's Hd.

NORTH CHANNEL - NORTH (AC 2798)

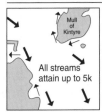

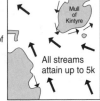

FLOOD	EBB
Main flood begins HW Dover –0600 (HW Greenock +0505). Races off Mull of Kintyre, Altacarry Hd & Fair Hd. Counter tides in bays of Antrim coast. W-going streams in Rathlin Sd, counter tide from Sanda Sd to Machrihanish last 1h30 - 2 hrs.	Main ebb begins HW Dover (HW Greenock –0120). Races off Mull of Kintyre & Altacarry Hd. Counter tides in bays of Antrim coast, counter tide from Macrihanish to Sanda Sd last 1h30 - 2 hrs.

NORTH CHANNEL - SOUTH (AC 2198)

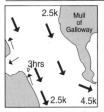

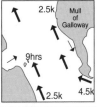

FLOOD	EBB
Irish coast - flood begins HW Dover +0610 (HW Belfast –0600). Scottish coast - HW Dover +0430 (HW Greenock +0310). Races off Copeland Is. & Mull of Galloway. Counter tide off Donaghadee and Island Magee last 3 hrs of flood.	Irish coast - ebb begins HW Dover –0015 (HW Belfast). Scottish coast - HW Dover –0130 (HW Greenock –0250). Races off Copeland Is. & Mull of Galloway. Flood begins 2 hrs early close inshore N of Mull of Galloway.

APPROACHES TO STRANGFORD LOUGH (AC 2156)

The tide cycle is approx 3 hours later than in the N Channel

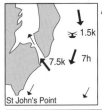

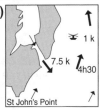

FLOOD	EBB
Flood runs for 6 hours from HW Dover –0345 (HW Belfast –0330), with a maximum rate of 7.5 knots at Rue Point. The strong flow flattens the sea in onshore winds and entrance can be made in strong winds.	Ebb runs for 6 hours from HW Dover +0215 (HW Belfast +0230), max rate 7.5k, E of Angus Rk. If entering against ebb use West Channel with care. Smoothest water near Bar Pladdy Buoy when leaving.

ISLE OF MAN - NORTH (AC 2094)

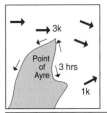

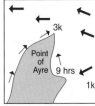

FLOOD	EBB
E going stream at Point of Ayre begins HW Dover –0545 (HW Liverpool –0600). Counter tide inside banks E of Point. In Ramsey Bay the S Going tide runs for 3h from +0530 Dover (+0515 Liverpool).	W going stream at Point of Ayre begins HW Dover +0015 (HW Liverpool). Counter tide inside banks W of Point. In Ramsey Bay the N going tide runs for 9h from –0330 Dover (–0345 Liverpool).

ISLE OF MAN - SOUTH (AC 2094)

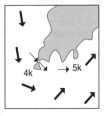

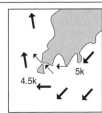

FLOOD	EBB
E going stream begins –0600 Dover (Liverpool +0610). Overfalls and race E of Chicken Rock. Calf Sound: The E going stream begins earlier, at approximately Dover +0400 (Liverpool +0345).	W going stream begins +0015 Dover (HW Liverpool). Overfalls and race N of Chicken Rock. Calf Sound: The W going stream begins earlier, at approximately –0130 Dover (–0145 Liverpool). Note: all times may vary due to weather conditions.

TIDES

MENAI STRAIT (AC 1464) – TIDAL GATES

FLOOD

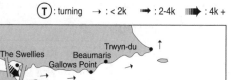
(T): turning   → : < 2k   ⇒ : 2-4k   ⫸ : 4k +

LOCAL LW: Caernarfon: HW Dover –0555. Port Dinorwic: –0620. Menai: –0540. Beaumaris: –0605.

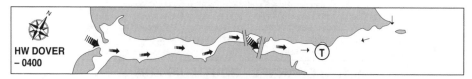

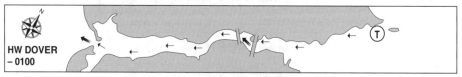

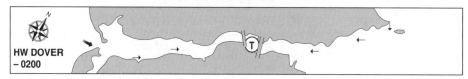

SLACK WATER IN THE SWELLIES: HW Dover –0200 to –0230.

LOCAL HW: Belan: HW Dover –0115. Caernarfon: –0105. Port Dinorwic: –0050.

THE SWELLIES

WESTBOUND: Leave or pass Beaumaris in time to arrive at the Swellies by HW Dover –0230 to –0200. If in doubt about passage speed, leave early; the adverse tide will check your progress. For a first time passage this is useful, as the yacht's speed over the ground is reduced. Late arrival will mean a faster passage, but with perhaps less control.

EASTBOUND: Leave or pass Port Dinorwic in time to arrive at Menai Bridge by HW Dover –0230 to –0200. Progress towards the Swellies should be closely monitored, as you are travelling with the last of the flood. Early arrival will mean a fast, perhaps dangerous passage, being late may make it impossible.

MENAI STRAIT (AC 1464) – TIDAL GATES *contd*

EBB

(T) : turning → : < 2k ⇒ : 2-4k ⟹ : 4k +

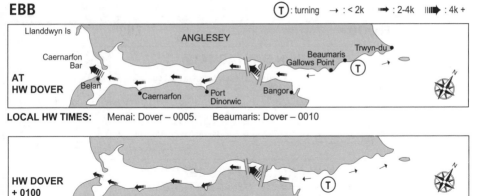

LOCAL HW TIMES: Menai: Dover – 0005. Beaumaris: Dover – 0010

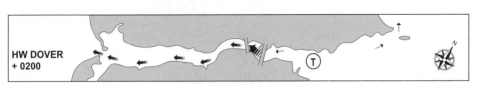

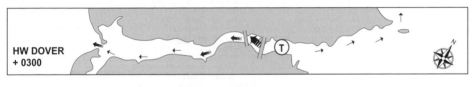

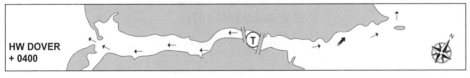

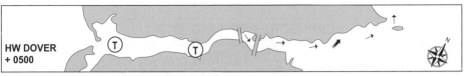

LOCAL LW TIMES: Belan: Dover + 0520.

CAERNARFON BAR

CAERNARFON BAR is without question highly dangerous in certain conditions. Buoys are located to suit changing channel; positions obtainable from Caernarfon Port Radio - VHF Ch 16; 06, 12: 2h–HW, or when vessel expected. Beware cross track tides near high water. Bar impassable during or after fresh or strong onshore weather. Keep strictly in channel.

OUTWARD BOUND: Do not leave Belan Narrows after half tide, better as soon as possible after the ebb commences, which gives maximum depth and duration of fair tide if bound S & W.

INWARD BOUND: Locating the bar buoys may be difficult; head for Llanddwyn I. until they are located. Only cross after half tide (HW Dover –0400), which inevitably limits onward passage to max of 3 hours.

TIDES

TIDAL GATES - IRISH SEA

A guide to the time of tide turn at tidal gates, the approximate strength of the tidal flow (spring rates shown — neaps are approximately 60% of these), and the position and timing of races, counter tides, etc.

FLOOD	EBB

DUBLIN BAY (AC 1415)

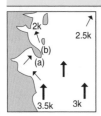
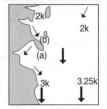

FLOOD: Tide between Rosbeg bank and Howth Hd (a) runs NE from HW Dublin +0300 for 9h30. In Howth Sd (b) the stream is NW going from +0430 to –0130. New flood and ebb tides begin close to the S shore and N of Baily up to 1h before HW Dublin .

EBB: The tide between Rosbeg bank and Howth Hd (a) runs SW from HW Dublin for 3h. In Howth Sd (b) the stream is SE going from –0130 to +0430. Strengths of streams increase S of Dublin Bay, and decrease N of it.

N W ANGLESEY (AC 1977)

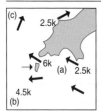
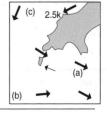

FLOOD: Flood tide close to the coast runs at over 5k springs, and at about 2.5k 7 miles offshore. The brief period of slack water offshore is 1h before HW Dover (1h15 before HW L'pool). Slack water lasts longer in Holyhead Bay.

EBB: Ebb tide close to the coast runs at over 5k springs, and at about 2.5k 7 miles offshore. Slack water is 5h after HW Dover (4h45 after HW L'pool). There is no significant counter tide in Holyhead Bay, but the ebb starts first there, giving about 9h W-going tide N of the harbour (a).

BARDSEY SOUND (AC 1971)

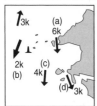
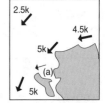

FLOOD: The tide turns to the NW or NE (flood) as follows:
at (a): HW Dover +0300;
at (b): HW D +0500;
at (c): –0545 HW D.
These times are approximate.
There is a strong eddy down tide of Bardsey Island and overfalls throughout the area.

EBB: The tide turns to the SW or SE (ebb) as follows:
at (a): HW Dover –0300;
at (b): HW D –0100 ;
at (c): at HW D –0030.
These times are approximate.
There is a strong eddy down tide of Bardsey Island and overfalls throughout the area.

S W WALES (AC 1478)

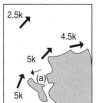
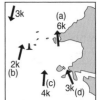

FLOOD: The tide turns to the S or SE (Bristol Channel flood) as follows:
at (a): HW Dover –0200;
at (b) & (c): HW D –0100 ;
at (d): –0300 HW D

EBB: The tide turns to the N or NW (Bristol Channel ebb) as follows:
at (a): HW Dover +0400;
at (b) & (c): HW D +0500 ;
at (d): +0300 HW D

CARNSORE POINT (AC 2049)

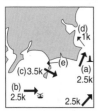
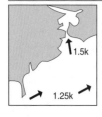

FLOOD: The tide turns to the NE or N (Irish Sea flood) as follows:
at (a): HW Dover +0500; at (b): HW D +0520; at (c): HW D +0600; at (d): –0600 HW D. NE going streams are shorter in duration and weaker than SE going - careful passage planning is essential.

EBB: The tide turns to the SW or S as follows:
at (a): –0200 HW D ; at (b): HW D –0020; at (c): –0015 HW D; at (d): –0300 HW Dover. Leaving Rosslare at –0300 HW D a yacht can carry a fair tide for about 8h until HW D +0515 off Hook Head.

NOTE: The tide turns on St Patrick's Bridge (e) up to 2 hours earlier than in Saltee Sound

CORK COAST (AC 2049)

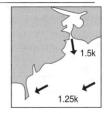

FLOOD: The tide, which flows coastwise, turns to the NE at HW Dover +0045. There is an eddy 5 miles ESE of Old Head of Kinsale at HW Dover +0400. The ingoing Cork Harbour tide begins at HW Dover +0055.

EBB: The tide turns SW at HW Dover +0500. The outgoing Cork Harbour tide begins at HW Dover –0540.

SECONDARY PORTS: TIME & HEIGHT DIFFERENCES
SOUTH COAST OF ENGLAND *Time zone UT*

Location	Lat	Long	High Water		Low Water		MHWS	MHWN	MLWN	MLWS
			0000	0600	0000	0600				
PLYMOUTH (DEVONPORT)	50 22N	4 11W	and	and	and	and	**5.5**	**4.4**	**2.2**	**0.8**
Standard port			1200	1800	1200	1800				
Isles of Scilly, St Mary's	49 55N	6 19W	−0035	−0100	−0040	−0025	+0.2	−0.1	−0.2	−0.1
Penzance & Newlyn	50 06N	5 33W	−0040	−0110	−0035	−0025	+0.1	0.0	−0.2	0.0
Porthleven	50 05N	5 19W	−0045	−0105	−0030	−0025	0.0	−0.1	−0.2	0.0
Lizard Point	49 57N	5 12W	−0045	−0100	−0030	−0030	−0.2	−0.2	−0.3	−0.2
Coverack	50 01N	5 05W	−0030	−0050	−0020	−0015	−0.2	−0.2	−0.3	−0.2
Helford River Entrance	50 05N	5 05W	−0030	−0035	−0015	−0010	−0.2	−0.2	−0.3	−0.2
FALMOUTH	50 09N	5 03W	*Standard port (no Secondaries)*							
River Fal, Truro	50 16N	5 03W	−0020	−0025	*Dries*	*Dries*	−2.0	−2.0	*Dries*	
Mevagissey	50 16N	4 47W	−0015	−0020	−0010	−0005	−0.1	−0.1	−0.2	−0.1
Par	50 21N	4 42W	−0010	−0015	−0010	−0005	−0.4	−0.4	−0.4	−0.2
River Fowey, Fowey	50 20N	4 38W	−0010	−0015	−0010	−0005	−0.1	−0.1	−0.2	−0.2
Lostwithiel	50 24N	4 40W	+0005	−0010	*Dries*	*Dries*	−4.1	−4.1	*Dries*	
Looe	50 21N	4 27W	−0010	−0010	−0005	−0005	−0.1	−0.2	−0.2	−0.2
Whitsand Bay	50 20N	4 15W	0000	0000	0000	0000	0.0	+0.1	−0.1	+0.2
River Tamar										
Saltash	50 24N	4 12W	0000	+0010	0000	−0005	+0.1	+0.1	+0.1	+0.1
Cargreen	50 26N	4 12W	0000	+0010	+0020	+0020	0.0	0.0	−0.1	0.0
Cotehele Quay	50 29N	4 13W	0000	+0020	+0045	+0045	−0.9	−0.9	−0.8	−0.4
River Tavy, Lopwell	50 28N	4 09W	*No data*	*No data*	*Dries*	*Dries*	−2.6	−2.7	*Dries*	
River Lynher, Jupiter Point	50 23N	4 14W	+0010	+0005	0000	−0005	0.0	0.0	+0.1	0.0
St Germans	50 23N	4 18W	0000	0000	+0020	+0020	−0.3	−0.1	0.0	+0.2
Turnchapel	50 22N	4 07W	0000	0000	+0010	−0015	0.0	+0.1	+0.2	+0.1
Bovisand Pier	50 20N	4 08W	0000	−0020	0000	−0010	−0.2	−0.1	0.0	+0.1
River Yealm, Entrance	50 18N	4 04W	+0006	+0006	+0002	+0002	−0.1	−0.1	−0.1	−0.1
			0100	0600	0100	0600				
PLYMOUTH (DEVONPORT)	50 22N	4 11W	and	and	and	and	**5.5**	**4.4**	**2.2**	**0.8**
Standard port			1300	1800	1300	1800				
Salcombe	50 13N	3 47W	0000	+0010	+0005	−0005	−0.2	−0.3	−0.1	−0.1
Start Point	50 13N	3 39W	+0015	+0015	+0005	+0010	−0.1	−0.2	+0.1	+0.2
River Dart										
DARTMOUTH	50 21N	3 34W	*Standard port (no Secondaries)*							
Greenway Quay	50 23N	3 35W	+0030	+0045	+0025	+0005	−0.6	−0.6	−0.2	−0.2
Totnes	50 26N	3 41W	+0030	+0040	+0115	+0030	−2.0	−2.1	*Dries*	
Torquay	50 28N	3 31W	+0025	+0045	+0010	0000	−0.6	−0.7	−0.2	−0.1
Teignmouth, Approaches	50 33N	3 29W	+0020	+0050	+0025	0000	−0.9	−0.8	−0.2	−0.1
Teignmouth, New Quay	50 33N	3 30W	+0025	+0055	+0040	+0005	−0.8	−0.8	−0.2	+0.1
Exmouth Approaches	50 36N	3 23W	+0030	+0050	+0015	+0005	−0.9	−1.0	−0.5	−0.3
River Exe										
Exmouth Dock	50 37N	3 25W	+0035	+0055	+0050	+0020	−1.5	−1.6	−0.9	−0.6
Starcross	50 38N	3 27W	+0040	+0100	+0055	+0025	−1.4	−1.5	−0.8	−0.1
Turf Lock	50 40N	3 28W	+0045	+0100	+0034	*No data*	− 1.6	−1.6	−1.2	*No data*
Topsham	50 41N	3 28W	+0045	+0105	*No data*	*No data*	− 1.5	−1.6	*No data*	
Lyme Regis	50 43N	2 56W	+0040	+0100	+0005	−0005	−1.2	−1.3	−0.5	−0.2
Bridport (West Bay)	50 42N	2 45W	+0025	+0040	0000	0000	−1.4	−1.4	−0.6	−0.2
Chesil Beach	50 37N	2 33W	+0040	+0055	−0005	+0010	−1.6	−1.5	−0.5	0.0
Chesil Cove	50 34N	2 28W	+0035	+0050	−0010	+0005	−1.5	−1.6	−0.5	−0.2
			0100	0700	0100	0700				
PORTLAND	50 34N	2 26W	and	and	and	and	**2.1**	**1.4**	**0.8**	**0.1**
Standard port			1300	1900	1300	1900				
Lulworth Cove, Mupe Bay	50 37N	2 14W	+0005	+0015	−0005	0000	+0.1	+0.1	+0.2	+0.1
			—	—	0500	1100				
POOLE HARBOUR	50 42N	1 59W			and	and	**2.2**	**1.7**	**1.2**	**0.6**
Standard port			—	—	1700	2300				
Swanage	50 37N	1 57W	—	—	−0045	+0055	−0.2	−0.1	0.0	−0.1
Poole Harbour Entrance	50 41N	1 57W	—	—	−0025	−0010	0.0	0.0	0.0	0.0
Ro-Ro terminal	50 42N	1 59W	*Standard port*							
Pottery Pier	50 42N	1 59W	—	—	−0010	0000	−0.2	0.0	+0.1	+0.2
Wareham, River Frome	50 41N	2 06W	—	—	+0130	+0145	0.0	0.0	0.0	+0.3
Cleavel Point	50 40N	2 00W	—	—	−0005	−0005	−0.1	−0.2	0.0	*No data*
			0000	0600	0500	1100				
PORTSMOUTH	50 48N	1 07W	and	and	and	and	**4.7**	**3.8**	**1.9**	**0.8**
Standard port			1200	1800	1700	2300				
Bournemouth	50 43N	1 52W	−0240	+0055	−0050	−0030	−2.7	−2.2	−0.8	−0.3

Location	Lat	Long	High Water		Low Water		MHWS	MHWN	MLWN	MLWS
Christchurch Entrance	50 43N	1 45W	−0230	+0030	−0035	−0035	−2.9	−2.4	−1.2	−0.2
Christchurch Quay	50 44N	1 47W	−0210	+0100	+0105	+0055	−2.9	−2.4	−1.0	0.0
Christchurch, Tuckton	50 44N	1 47W	−0205	+0110	+0110	+0105	−3.0	−2.5	−1.0	+0.1
Hurst Point	50 42N	1 33W	−0115	−0005	−0030	−0025	−2.0	−1.5	−0.5	−0.1
Lymington	50 46N	1 32W	−0110	+0005	−0020	−0020	−1.7	−1.2	−0.5	−0.1
Bucklers Hard	50 48N	1 25W	−0040	−0010	+0010	−0010	−1.0	−0.8	−0.2	−0.3
Stansore Point	50 47N	1 20W	−0050	−0010	−0005	−0010	−0.8	−0.5	−0.3	−0.1
Isle of Wight										
Yarmouth	50 42N	1 30W	−0105	+0005	−0025	−0030	−1.7	−1.2	−0.3	0.0
Totland Bay	50 41N	1 33W	−0130	−0045	−0035	−0045	−2.2	−1.7	−0.4	−0.1
Freshwater	50 40N	1 31W	−0210	+0025	−0040	−0020	−2.1	−1.5	−0.4	0.0
Ventnor	50 36N	1 12W	−0025	−0030	−0025	−0030	−0.8	−0.6	−0.2	+0.2
Sandown	50 39N	1 09W	0000	+0005	+0010	+0025	−0.6	−0.5	−0.2	0.0
Foreland Lifeboat Slip	50 41N	1 04W	−0005	0000	+0005	+0010	+0.1	+0.1	0.0	+0.1
Bembridge Harbour	50 42N	1 07W	+0020	0000	+0100	+0020	−1.5	−1.4	−1.3	−1.0
Ryde	50 44N	1 10W	−0010	+0010	−0005	−0005	−0.1	0.0	0.0	0.0
Medina River										
Cowes	50 46N	1 18W	−0015	+0015	0000	−0020	−0.5	−0.3	−0.1	0.0
Folly Inn	50 44N	1 17W	−0015	+0015	0000	−0020	−0.6	−0.4	−0.1	+0.2
Newport	50 42N	1 17W	No data	No data	No data	No data	−0.6	−0.4	+0.1	+0.8
			0400	**1100**	**0000**	**0600**				
SOUTHAMPTON	50 53N	1 24W	and	and	and	and	4.5	3.7	1.8	0.5
Standard port			**1600**	**2300**	**1200**	**1800**				
Calshot Castle	50 49N	1 18W	0000	+0025	0000	0000	0.0	0.0	+0.2	+0.3
Redbridge	50 55N	1 28W	−0020	+0005	0000	−0005	−0.1	−0.1	−0.1	−0.1
River Hamble										
Warsash	50 51N	1 18W	+0020	+0010	+0010	0000	0.0	+0.1	+0.1	+0.3
Bursledon	50 53N	1 18W	+0020	+0020	+0010	+0010	+0.1	+0.2	+0.2	+0.2
			0500	**1000**	**0000**	**0600**				
PORTSMOUTH	50 48N	1 07W	and	and	and	and	4.7	3.8	1.9	0.8
Standard port			**1700**	**2200**	**1200**	**1800**				
Lee-on-the-Solent	50 48N	1 12W	−0005	+0005	−0015	−0010	−0.2	−0.1	+0.1	+0.2
Chichester Harbour Entrance	50 47N	0 56W	−0010	+0005	+0015	+0020	+0.2	+0.2	0.0	+0.1
Northney	50 50N	0 58W	+0010	+0015	+0015	+0025	+0.2	0.0	−0.2	−0.3
Bosham	50 50N	0 52W	0000	+0010	No data	No data	+0.2	+0.1	No data	
Itchenor	50 48N	0 52W	−0005	+0005	+0005	+0025	+0.1	0.0	−0.2	−0.2
Dell Quay	50 49N	0 49W	+0005	+0015	no data	No data	+0.2	+0.1	No data	
Selsey Bill	50 43N	0 47W	+0010	−0010	+0035	+0020	+0.5	+0.3	−0.1	−0.2
Nab Tower	50 40N	0 57W	+0015	0000	+0015	+0015	−0.2	0.0	+0.2	0.0
			0500	**1000**	**0000**	**0600**				
SHOREHAM	50 50N	0 15W	and	and	and	and	6.3	4.8	1.9	0.6
Standard port			**1700**	**2200**	**1200**	**1800**				
Pagham	50 46N	0 43W	+0015	0000	−0015	−0025	−0.7	−0.5	−0.1	−0.1
Bognor Regis	50 47N	0 40W	+0010	−0005	−0005	−0020	−0.6	−0.5	−0.2	−0.1
River Arun										
Littlehampton Entrance	50 48N	0 33W	+0010	0000	−0005	−0010	−0.4	−0.4	−0.2	−0.2
Littlehampton UMA wharf	50 49N	0 33W	+0015	+0005	0000	+0045	−0.7	−0.7	−0.3	+0.2
Arundel	50 51N	0 33W	No data	+0120	No data	No data	−3.1	−2.8	No data	
Worthing	50 48N	0 22W	+0010	0000	−0005	−0010	−0.1	−0.2	0.0	0.0
Brighton	50 49N	0 08W	0000	−0005	0000	0000	+0.3	+0.2	+0.1	0.0
Newhaven	50 47N	0 04E	−0015	−0010	0000	0000	+0.2	+0.1	−0.1	−0.2
Eastbourne	50 46N	0 17E	−0010	−0005	+0015	+0020	+1.1	+0.6	+0.2	+0.1
			0000	**0600**	**0100**	**0700**				
DOVER	51 07N	1 19E	and	and	and	and	6.8	5.3	2.1	0.8
Standard port			**1200**	**1800**	**1300**	**1900**				
Hastings	50 51N	0 36E	0000	−0010	−0030	−0030	+0.8	+0.5	+0.1	−0.1
Rye Approaches	50 55N	0 47E	+0005	−0010	No data	No data	+1.0	+0.7	No data	
Rye Harbour	50 56N	0 48E	+0005	−0010	Dries	Dries	−1.4	−1.7	Dries	
Dungeness	50 55N	0 58E	−0010	−0015	−0020	−0010	+1.0	+0.6	+0.4	+0.1
Folkestone	51 05N	1 12E	−0020	−0005	−0010	−0010	+0.4	+0.4	0.0	−0.1
Deal	51 13N	1 25E	+0010	+0020	+0010	+0005	−0.6	−0.3	0.0	0.0
Richborough	51 18N	1 21E	+0015	+0015	+0030	+0030	−3.4	−2.6	−1.7	−0.7
Ramsgate	51 20N	1 25E	+0030	+0030	+0017	+0007	−1.6	−1.3	−0.7	−0.2

EAST COAST ENGLAND *Time Zone UT*

			0200	**0800**	**0200**	**0700**				
SHEERNESS	51 27N	0 45E	and	and	and	and	5.8	4.7	1.5	0.6
Standard port			**1400**	**2000**	**1400**	**1900**				
Margate	51 23N	1 23E	−0050	−0040	−0020	−0050	−0.9	−0.9	−0.1	0.0

Location	Lat	Long	High Water		Low Water		MHWS	MHWN	MLWN	MLWS
Herne Bay	51 23N	1 07E	−0025	−0015	0000	−0025	−0.5	−0.5	−0.1	−0.1
Whitstable approaches	51 22N	1 02E	−0008	−0011	+0005	0000	−0.3	−0.3	0.0	−0.1
River Swale										
Grovehurst Jetty	51 22N	0 46E	−0007	0000	0000	+0016	0.0	0.0	0.0	−0.1
Faversham	51 19N	0 54E	*No data*	*No data*	*No data*	*No data*	−0.2	−0.2	*No data*	
River Medway										
Bee Ness	51 25N	0 39E	+0002	+0002	0000	+0005	+0.2	+0.1	0.0	0.0
Bartlett Creek	51 23N	0 38E	+0016	+0008	*No data*	*No data*	+0.1	0.0	*No data*	
Darnett Ness	51 24N	0 36E	+0004	+0004	0000	+0010	+0.2	+0.1	0.0	−0.1
Chatham, Lock approaches	51 24N	0 33E	+0010	+0012	+0012	+0018	+0.3	+0.1	−0.1	−0.2
Upnor	51 25N	0 32E	+0015	+0015	+0015	+0025	+0.2	+0.2	−0.1	−0.1
Rochester, Strood Pier	51 24N	0 30E	+0018	+0018	+0018	+0028	+0.2	+0.2	−0.2	−0.3
Wouldham	51 21N	0 27E	+0030	+0025	+0035	+0120	−0.2	−0.3	−1.0	−0.3
New Hythe	51 19N	0 28E	+0035	+0035	+0220	+0240	−1.6	−1.7	−1.2	−0.3
Allington Lock	51 17N	0 30E	+0050	+0035	*No data*	*No data*	−2.1	−2.2	−1.3	−0.4
River Thames										
Southend–on–Sea	51 31N	0 43E	−0005	−0005	−0005	−0005	0.0	0.0	−0.1	−0.1
Coryton	51 30N	0 31E	+0005	+0010	+0010	+0010	+0.4	+0.3·	0.0	0.0
LONDON BRIDGE	51 30N	0 05W	0300 and 1500	0900 and 2100	0400 and 1600	1100 and 2300	7.1	5.9	1.3	0.5
Standard port										
Tilbury	51 27N	0 22E	−0055	−0040	−0050	−0115	−0.7	−0.5	+0.1	0.0
North Woolwich	51 30N	0 05E	−0020	−0020	−0035	−0045	−0.1	0.0	+0.2	0.0
Albert bridge	51 29N	0 10W	+0025	+0020	+0105	+0110	−0.9	−0.8	−0.7	−0.4
Hammersmith bridge	51 29N	0 14W	+0040	+0035	+0205	+0155	−1.4	−1.3	−1.0	−0.5
Kew bridge	51 29N	0 17W	+0055	+0050	+0255	+0235	−1.8	−1.8	−1.2	−0.5
Richmond lock	51 28N	0 19W	+0105	+0055	+0325	+0305	−2.2	−2.2	−1.3	−0.5
SHEERNESS	51 27N	0 45E	0200 and 1400	0700 and 1900	0100 and 1300	0700 and 1900	5.8	4.7	1.5	0.6
Standard port										
Thames Estuary Shivering Sand	51 30N	1 05E	−0025	−0019	−0008	−0026	−0.6	−0.6	−0.1	−0.1
WALTON-ON-THE-NAZE	51 51N	1 17E	0000 and 1200	0600 and 1800	0500 and 1700	1100 and 2300	4.2	3.4	1.1	0.4
Standard port										
Whitaker Beacon	51 40N	1 06E	+0022	+0024	+0033	+0027	+0.6	+0.5	+0.2	+0.1
Holliwell Point	51 38N	0 56E	+0034	+0037	+0100	+0037	+1.1	+0.9	+0.3	+0.1
River Roach Rochford	51 35N	0 43E	+0050	+0040	*Dries*	*Dries*	−0.8	−1.1	*Dries*	
River Crouch										
North Fambridge	51 38N	0 41E	+0115	+0050	+0130	+0100	+1.1	+0.8	0.0	−0.1
Hullbridge	51 38N	0 38E	+0115	+0050	+0135	+0105	+1.1	+0.8	0.0	−0.1
Battlesbridge	51 37N	0 34E	+0120	+0110	*Dries*	*Dries*	−1.8	−2.0	*Dries*	
River Blackwater										
Bradwell Waterside	51 45N	0 54E	+0035	+0023	+0047	+0004	+1.0	+0.8	+0.2	0.0
Osea Island	51 43N	0 46E	+0057	+0045	+0050	+0007	+1.1	+0.9	+0.1	0.0
Maldon	51 44N	0 42E	+0107	+0055	*No data*	*No data*	−1.3	−1.1	*No data*	
West Mersea	51 47N	0 54E	+0035	+0015	+0055	+0010	+0.9	+0.4	+0.1	+0.1
River Colne										
Brightlingsea	51 48N	1 00E	+0025	+0021	+0046	+0004	+0.8	+0.4	+0.1	0.0
Colchester	51 53N	0 56E	+0035	+0025	*Dries*	*Dries*	0.0	−0.3	*Dries*	
Clacton–on–Sea	51 47N	1 10E	+0012	+0010	+0025	+0008	+0.3	+0.1	+0.1	+0.1
Bramble Creek	51 53N	1 14E	+0010	−0007	−0005	+0010	+0.3	+0.3	+0.3	+0.3
Sunk Head	51 47N	1 30E	0000	+0002	−0002	+0002	−0.3	−0.3	−0.1	−0.1
Harwich	51 57N	1 17E	+0007	+0002	−0010	−0012	−0.2	0.0	0.0	0.0
Mistley	51 57N	1 05E	+0032	+0027	−0010	−0012	0.0	0.0	−0.1	−0.1
Ipswich	52 03N	1 10E	+0022	+0027	0000	−0012	0.0	0.0	−0.1	−0.1
WALTON–ON–THE–NAZE	51 51N	1 17E	0100 and 1300	0700 and 1900	0100 and 1300	0700 and 1900	4.2	3.4	1.1	0.4
Standard port										
Felixstowe Pier	51 57N	1 21E	−0005	−0007	−0018	−0020	−0.5	−0.4	0.0	0.0
River Deben										
Woodbridge Haven	51 59N	1 24E	0000	−0005	−0020	−0025	−0.5	−0.5	−0.1	+0.1
Woodbridge	52 05N	1 19E	+0045	+0025	+0025	−0020	−0.2	−0.3	−0.2	0.0
Bawdsey	52 01N	1 26E	−0016	−0020	−0030	−0032	−0.8	−0.6	−0.1	−0.1
Orford Haven										
Bar	52 02N	1 28E	−0026	−0030	−0036	−0038	−1.0	−0.8	−0.1	0.0
Orford Quay	52 05N	1 32E	+0040	+0040	+0055	+0055	−1.4	−1.1	0.0	+0.2
Slaughden Quay	52 08N	1 36E	+0105	+0105	+0125	+0125	−1.3	−0.8	−0.1	+0.2
Iken Cliffs	52 09N	1 31E	+0130	+0130	+0155	+0155	−1.3	−1.0	0.0	+0.2

TIDES

Location	Lat	Long	High Water		Low Water		MHWS	MHWN	MLWN	MLWS
			0300	0900	0200	0800				
LOWESTOFT	52 28N	1 45E	and	and	and	and	2.4	2.1	1.0	0.5
Standard port			1500	2100	1400	2000				
Orford Ness	52 05N	1 35E	+0135	+0135	+0135	+0125	+0.4	+0.6	−0.1	0.0
Aldeburgh	52 09N	1 36E	+0130	+0130	+0115	+0120	+0.3	+0.2	−0.1	−0.2
Minsmere Sluice	52 14N	1 38E	+0110	+0110	+0110	+0110	0.0	−0.1	−0.2	−0.2
Southwold	52 19N	1 40E	+0105	+0105	+0055	+0055	0.0	0.0	−0.1	0.0
Great Yarmouth										
Gorleston-on-Sea	52 34N	1 44E	−0035	−0035	−0030	−0030	0.0	0.0	0.0	0.0
Britannia Pier	52 36N	1 45E	−0105	−0100	−0040	−0055	+0.1	+0.1	0.0	0.0
Caister-on-Sea	52 39N	1 44E	−0120	−0120	−0100	−0100	0.0	−0.1	0.0	0.0
Winterton-on-Sea	52 43N	1 42E	−0225	−0215	−0135	−0135	+0.8	+0.5	+0.2	+0.1
			0100	0700	0100	0700				
IMMINGHAM	53 38N	0 11W	and	and	and	and	7.3	5.8	2.6	0.9
Standard port			1300	1900	1300	1900				
Cromer	52 56N	1 18E	+0050	+0030	+0050	+0130	−2.1	−1.7	−0.5	−0.1
Blakeney Bar	52 59N	0 59E	+0035	+0025	+0030	+0040	−1.6	−1.3	No data	
Blakeney	52 57N	1 01E	+0115	+0055	No data	No data	−3.9	−3.8	No data	
Wells Bar	52 59N	0 49E	+0020	+0020	+0020	+0020	−1.3	−1.0	No data	
Wells	52 57N	0 51E	+0035	+0045	+0340	+0310	−3.8	−3.8	Not below CD	
Burnham Overy Staithe	52 58N	0 48E	+0045	+0055	No data	No data	−5.0	−4.9	No data	
The Wash										
Hunstanton	52 56N	0 29E	+0010	+0020	+0105	+0025	+0.1	−0.2	−0.1	0.0
West Stones	52 50N	0 21E	+0025	+0025	+0115	+0040	−0.3	−0.4	−0.3	+0.2
King's Lynn	52 45N	0 24E	+0030	+0030	+0305	+0140	−0.5	−0.8	−0.8	+0.1
Outer Westmark Knock	52 53N	0 13E	+0010	+0015	+0040	+0020	−0.2	−0.5	−0.6	−0.4
Wisbech Cut	52 48N	0 13E	+0020	+0010	+0120	+0055	−0.3	−0.7	−0.4 No data	
Port Sutton bridge	52 46N	0 12E	+0030	+0020	+0130	+0105	−0.3	−0.6	−0.6	+0.3
Wisbech	52 40N	0 09E	+0055	+0040	Dries	Dries	−0.2	−0.6	Dries	Dries
Lawyer's Creek	52 53N	0 05E	+0010	+0020	No data	No data	−0.3	−0.6	No data	
Tabs Head	52 56N	0 05E	0000	+0005	+0125	+0020	+0.2	−0.2	−0.2	−0.2
Boston	52 58N	0 01W	0000	+0010	+0140	+0050	−0.5	−1.0	−0.9	−0.5
Skegness	53 09N	0 21E	+0010	+0015	+0030	+0020	−0.4	−0.5	−0.1	0.0
Inner Dowsing Light Tower	53 19N	0 35E	0000	0000	+0010	+0010	−0.9	−0.7	−0.1	+0.3
River Humber										
Bull Sand Fort	53 34N	0 04E	−0020	−0030	−0035	−0015	−0.4	−0.3	+0.1	+0.2
Grimsby	53 35N	0 04W	−0012	−0012	−0015	−0015	−0.2	−0.1	0.0	+0.2
Hull, King George Dock	53 44N	0 16W	+0010	+0010	+0021	+0017	+0.3	+0.2	−0.1	−0.2
Hull, Albert Dock	53 44N	0 21W	+0019	+0019	+0033	+0027	+0.3	+0.1	−0.1	−0.2
Humber Bridge	53 43N	0 27W	+0027	+0022	+0049	+0039	−0.1	−0.4	−0.7	−0.6
River Trent										
Burton Stather	53 39N	0 42W	+0105	+0045	+0335	+0305	−2.1	−2.3	−2.3	Dries
Flixborough Wharf	53 37N	0 42W	+0120	+0100	+0400	+0340	−2.3	−2.6	Dries	
Keadby	53 36N	0 44W	+0135	+0120	+0425	+0410	−2.5	−2.8	Dries	
Owston Ferry	53 29N	0 46W	+0155	+0145	Dries	Dries	−3.5	−3.9	Dries	
River Ouse										
Blacktoft	53 42N	0 43W	+0100	+0055	+0325	+0255	−1.6	−1.8	−2.2	−1.1
Goole	53 42N	0 52W	+0130	+0115	+0355	+0350	−1.6	−2.1	−1.9	−0.6
			0200	0800	0100	0800				
R TYNE, NORTH SHIELDS	55 00N	1 26W	and	and	and	and	5. 0	3.9	1.8	0.7
Standard port			1400	2000	1300	2000				
Bridlington	54 05N	0 11W	+0119	+0109	+0109	+0104	+1.1	+0.8	+0.5	+0.4
Filey Bay	54 13N	0 16W	+0101	+0101	+0101	+0048	+0.8	+1.0	+0.6	+0.3
Scarborough	54 17N	0 23W	+0059	+0059	+0044	+0044	+0.7	+0.7	+0.5	+0.2
Whitby	54 29N	0 37W	+0034	+0049	+0034	+0019	+0.6	+0.4	+0.1	+0.1
Middlesborough Dock ent	54 35N	1 13W	+0019	+0021	+0014	+0011	+0.6	+0.6	+0.3	+0.1
Hartlepool	54 42N	1 12W	+0015	+0015	+0008	+0008	+0.4	+0.3	0.0	+0.1
Seaham	54 50N	1 19W	+0004	+0004	−0001	−0001	+0.2	+0.2	0.0	0.0
Sunderland	54 55N	1 22W	+0002	−0002	−0002	−0002	+0.2	+0.3	+0.2	+0.1
Newcastle-upon-Tyne	54 58N	1 36W	+0003	+0003	+0008	+0008	+0.3	+0.2	+0.1	+0.1
Blyth	55 07N	1 29W	+0005	−0007	−0001	+0009	0.0	0.0	−0.1	+0.1
Coquet Island	55 20N	1 32W	−0010	−0010	−0020	−0020	+0.1	+0.1	0.0	+0.1
Amble	55 20N	1 34W	−0013	−0013	−0016	−0020	0.0	0.0	+0.1	+0.1
North Sunderland	55 35N	1 39W	−0048	−0044	−0058	−0102	−0.2	−0.2	−0.2	0.0
Holy Island	55 40N	1 48W	−0043	−0039	−0105	−0110	−0.2	−0.2	−0.3	−0.1
Berwick	55 46N	1 59W	−0053	−0053	−0109	−0109	−0.3	−0.1	−0.5	−0.1

SCOTLAND *Time Zone UT*

Location	Lat	Long	High Water		Low Water		MHWS	MHWN	MLWN	MLWS
			0300	0900	0300	0900				
LEITH	55 59N	3 11W	and	and	and	and	5.6	4.4	2.0	0.8
Standard port			1500	2100	1500	2100				
Eyemouth	55 52N	2 05W	−0005	+0007	+0012	+0008	−0.4	−0.3	0.0	+0.1
Dunbar	56 00N	2 31W	−0005	+0003	+0003	−0003	−0.3	−0.3	0.0	+0.1
Fidra	56 04N	2 47W	−0001	0000	−0002	+0001	−0.2	−0.2	0.0	0.0
Cockenzie	55 58N	2 57W	−0007	−0015	−0013	−0005	−0.2	0.0	No data	
Granton	55 59N	3 13W	0000	0000	0000	0000	0.0	0.0	0.0	0.0
River Forth Grangemouth	56 02N	3 41W	+0015	+0010	−0050	−0045	0.0	−0.1	−0.2	−0.2
Kincardine	56 04N	3 43W	+0015	+0030	−0030	−0030	0.0	−0.2	−0.5	−0.3
Alloa	56 06N	3 48W	+0040	+0040	+0025	+0025	−0.2	−0.5 No data		−0.7
Stirling	56 07N	3 56W	+0100	+0100	No data		−2.9	−3.1	−2.3	−0.7
Firth of Forth										
Burntisland	56 03N	3 14W	+0013	+0004	−0002	+0007	+0.1	0.0	+0.1	+0.2
Kirkcaldy	56 09N	3 09W	+0005	0000	−0004	−0001	−0.3	−0.3	−0.2	−0.2
Methil	56 11N	3 00W	−0005	−0001	−0001	−0001	−0.1	−0.1	−0.1	−0.1
Anstruther Easter	56 13N	2 42W	−0018	−0012	−0006	−0008	−0.3	−0.2	0.0	0.0
			0000	0600	0100	0700				
ABERDEEN	57 09N	2 04W	and	and	and	and	4.3	3.4	1.6	0.6
Standard port			1200	1800	1300	1900				
River Tay										
Bar	56 28N	2 38W	+0100	+0100	+0050	+0110	+0.9	+0.8	+0.3	+0.1
Dundee	56 27N	2 58W	+0140	+0120	+0055	+0145	+1.3	+0.9	+0.4	+0.2
Newburgh	56 21N	3 14W	+0215	+0200	+0250	+0335	−0.2	−0.4	−1.1	−0.5
Perth	56 24N	3 25W	+0220	+0225	+0510	+0530	−0.9	−1.4	−1.2	−0.3
Arbroath	56 33N	2 35W	+0056	+0037	+0034	+0055	+1.0	+0.8	+0.4	+0.2
Montrose	56 42N	2 28W	+0055	+0055	+0030	+0040	+0.5	+0.4	+0.2	0.0
Stonehaven	56 58N	2 12W	+0013	+0008	+0013	+0009	+0.2	+0.2	+0.1	0.0
Peterhead	57 30N	1 46W	−0035	−0045	−0035	−0040	−0.4	−0.3	+0.1	+0.1
Fraserburgh	57 41N	2 00W	−0105	−0115	−0120	−0110	−0.6	−0.5	−0.2	0.0
			0200	0900	0400	0900				
ABERDEEN	57 09N	2 04W	and	and	and	and	4.3	3.4	1.6	0.6
Standard port			1400	2100	1600	2100				
Banff	57 40N	2 31W	−0100	−0150	−0150	−0050	−0.4	−0.2	−0.1	+0.2
Whitehills	57 41N	2 35W	−0122	−0137	−0117	−0127	−0.4	−0.3	+0.1	+0.1
Buckie	57 41N	2 57W	−0130	−0145	−0125	−0140	−0.2	−0.2	0.0	+0.1
Lossiemouth	57 43N	3 18W	−0125	−0200	−0130	−0130	−0.2	−0.2	0.0	0.0
Burghead	57 42N	3 29W	−0120	−0150	−0135	−0120	−0.2	−0.2	0.0	0.0
Nairn	57 36N	3 52W	−0120	−0150	−0135	−0130	0.0	−0.1	0.0	+0.1
McDermott Base	57 36N	3 59W	−0110	−0140	−0120	−0115	−0.1	−0.1	+0.1	+0.3
			0300	1000	0000	0700				
ABERDEEN	57 09N	2 04W	and	and	and	and	4.3	3.4	1.6	0.6
Standard port			1500	2200	1200	1900				
Inverness Firth										
Fortrose	57 35N	4 08W	−0125	−0125	−0125	−0125	0.0	0.0	No data	
Inverness	57 30N	4 15W	−0050	−0150	−0200	−0150	+0.5	+0.3	+0.2	+0.1
Cromarty Firth										
Cromarty	57 42N	4 03W	−0120	−0155	−0155	−0120	0.0	0.0	+0.1	+0.2
Invergordon	57 41N	4 10W	−0105	−0200	−0200	−0110	+0.1	+0.1	+0.1	+0.1
Dingwall	57 36N	4 25W	−0045	−0145 No data		No data	+0.1	+0.2	No data	
			0300	0800	0200	0800				
ABERDEEN	57 09N	2 04W	and	and	and	and	4.3	3.4	1.6	0.6
Standard port			1500	2000	1400	2000				
Dornoch Firth										
Portmahomack	57 50N	3 50W	−0120	−0210	−0140	−0110	−0.2	−0.1	+0.1	+0.1
Meikle Ferry	57 51N	4 08W	−0100	−0140	−0120	−0055	+0.1	0.0	−0.1	0.0
Golspie	57 58N	3 59W	−0130	−0215	−0155	−0130	−0.3	−0.3	−0.1	0.0
			0000	0700	0200	0700				
WICK	58 26N	3 05W	and	and	and	and	3.5	2.8	1.4	0.7
Standard port			1200	1900	1400	1900				
Helmsdale	58 07N	3 39W	+0025	+0015	+0035	+0030	+0.4	+0.3	+0.1	0.0
Duncansby Head	58 39N	3 02W	−0115	−0115	−0110	−0110	−0.4	−0.4	No data	
Orkney Islands										
Muckle Skerry	58 41N	2 55W	−0025	−0025	−0020	−0020	−0.9	−0.8	−0.4	−0.3
Burray Ness	58 51N	2 52W	+0005	+0005	+0015	+0015	−0.2	−0.3	−0.1	−0.1

TIDES

203

TIDES

Location	Lat	Long	High Water		Low Water		MHWS	MHWN	MLWN	MLWS
Deer Sound	58 58N	2 50W	−0040	−0040	−0035	−0035	−0.3	−0.3	−0.1	−0.1
Kirkwall	58 59N	2 58W	−0042	−0042	−0041	−0041	−0.5	−0.4	−0.1	−0.1
Egilsay	59 09N	2 57W	−0125	−0125	−0125	−0125	−0.1	0.0	+0.2	+0.1
Whitehall	58 09N	2 36W	−0030	−0030	−0025	−0030	−0.1	0.0	+0.2	+0.2
Loth	59 11N	2 42W	−0045	−0045	−00558	−0105	−0.4	−0.3	+0.1	+0.2
Kettletoft Pier	59 14N	2 36W	−0030	−0025	−0025	−0025	0.0	0.0	+0.2	+0.2
Rapness	59 15N	2 52W	−0205	−0205	−0205	−0205	+0.1	0.0	+0.2	0.0
Pierowall	59 19N	2 59W	−0150	−0150	−0145	−0145	+0.2	0.0	0.0	−0.1
Tingwall	59 05N	3 03W	−0200	−0125	−0145	−0125	−0.4	−0.4	−0.1	−0.1
Stromness	58 58N	3 18W	−0225	−0135	−0205	−0205	+0.1	−0.1	0.0	0.0
St Mary's	58 54N	2 55W	−0140	−0140	−0140	−0140	−0.2	−0.2	0.0	−0.1
Widewall Bay	58 49N	3 01W	−0155	−0155	−0150	−0150	+0.1	−0.1	−0.1	−0.3
Bur Wick	58 44N	2 58W	−0100	−0100	−0150	−0150	−0.1	−0.1	+0.2	+0.1
LERWICK *Standard port*	60 09N	1 08W	0000 and 1200	0600 and 1800	0100 and 1300	0800 and 2000	2.1	1.7	0.9	0.5
Fair Isle	59 32N	1 36W	−0006	−0015	−0031	−0037	+0.1	0.0	+0.1	+0.1
Shetland Islands										
Sumburgh (Grutness Voe)	59 53N	1 17W	+0006	+0008	+0004	−0002	−0.3	−0.3	−0.2	−0.1
Dury Voe	60 21N	1 10W	−0015	−0015	−0010	−0010	0.0	−0.1	0.0	−0.2
Out Skerries	60 25N	0 45W	−0025	−0025	−0010	−0010	+0.1	0.0	0.0	−0.1
Toft Pier	60 28N	1 12W	−0105	−0100	−0125	−0115	+0.2	+0.1	−0.1	−0.1
Burra Voe (Yell Sound)	60 30N	1 03W	−0025	−0025	−0025	−0025	+0.2	+0.1	0.0	−0.1
Mid Yell	60 36N	1 03W	−0030	−0020	−0035	−0025	+0.3	+0.2	+0.2	+0.1
Balta Sound	60 46N	0 50W	−0055	−0055	−0045	−0045	+0.2	+0.1	0.0	−0.1
Burra Firth	60 48N	0 52W	−0110	−0110	−0115	−0115	+0.4	+0.2	0.0	0.0
Bluemull Sound	60 42N	1 00W	−0135	−0135	−0155	−0155	+0.5	+0.2	+0.1	0.0
Sullom Voe	60 27N	1 18W	−0135	−0125	−0135	−0120	0.0	0.0	−0.2	−0.2
Hillswick	60 29N	1 29W	−0220	−0220	−0200	−0200	−0.1	−0.1	−0.1	−0.1
Scalloway	60 08N	1 16W	−0150	−0150	−0150	−0150	−0.5	−0.4	−0.3	0.0
Bay of Quendale	59 54N	1 21W	−0025	−0025	−0030	−0030	−0.4	−0.3	0.0	+0.1
Foula	60 07N	2 03W	−0140	−0130	−0140	−0120	−0.1	−0.1	0.0	0.0
WICK *Standard port*	58 26N	3 05W	0200 and 1400	0700 and 1900	0100 and 1300	0700 and 1900	3.5	2.8	1.4	0.7
Stroma	58 40N	3 08W	−0115	−0115	−0110	−0110	−0.4	−0.5	−0.1	−0.2
Gills Bay	58 38N	3 10W	−0150	−0150	−0202	−0202	+0.7	+0.7	+0.6	+0.3
Scrabster	58 37N	3 33W	−0255	−0225	−0240	−0230	+1.5	+1.2	+0.8	+0.3
Sule Skerry	59 05N	4 24W	−0320	−0255	−0315	−0250	+0.4	+0.3	+0.2	+0.1
Loch Eriboll Portnancon	58 30N	4 42W	−0340	−0255	−0315	−0255	+1.6	+1.3	+0.8	+0.4
Kyle of Durness	58 36N	4 47W	−0350	−0350	−0315	−0315	+1.1	+0.7	+0.4	−0.1
Rona	59 08N	5 49W	−0410	−0345	−0330	−0340	−0.1	−0.2	−0.2	−0.1
STORNOWAY *Standard port*	58 12N	6 23W	0100 and 1300	0700 and 1900	0300 and 1500	0900 and 2100	4.8	3.7	2.0	0.7
Outer Hebrides										
Loch Shell	58 00N	6 25W	−0013	0000	0000	−0017	0.0	−0.1	−0.1	0.0
E Loch Tarbert	57 54N	6 48W	−0025	−0010	−0010	−0020	+0.2	0.0	+0.1	+0.1
Leverburgh	57 46N	7 02W	−0041	−0020	−0015	−0025	−0.2	−0.2	−0.2	−0.1
Bays Loch	57 43N	7 10W	−0038	−0013	−0014	−0027	−0.1	−0.2	−0.2	−0.1
Loch Maddy	57 36N	7 09W	−0044	−0014	−0016	−0030	0.0	−0.1	−0.1	0.0
Loch Carnan	57 22N	7 16W	−0050	−0010	−0020	−0040	−0.3	−0.5	−0.1	−0.1
Loch Skiport	57 20N	7 16W	−0100	−0025	−0024	−0024	−0.2	−0.4	−0.3	−0.2
Loch Boisdale	57 09N	7 16W	−0055	−0030	−0020	−0040	−0.7	−0.7	−0.3	−0.2
Barra (North Bay)	57 00N	7 24W	−0103	−0031	−0034	−0048	−0.6	−0.5	−0.2	−0.1
Castle Bay	56 57N	7 29W	−0115	−0040	−0045	−0100	−0.5	−0.6	−0.3	−0.1
Barra Head	56 47N	7 38W	−0115	−0040	−0045	−0055	−0.8	−0.7	−0.2	+0.1
Shillay	57 32N	7 42W	−0103	−0043	−0047	−0107	−0.6	−0.7	−0.7	−0.3
Balivanich	57 29N	7 23W	−0103	−0017	−0031	−0045	−0.7	−0.6	−0.5	−0.2
Scolpaig	57 39N	7 29W	−0033	−0033	−0040	−0040	−1.0	−0.9	−0.5	0.0
W Loch Tarbert	57 55N	6 55W	−0015	−0015	−0046	−0046	−1.1	−0.9	−0.5	0.0
Little Bernera	58 16N	6 52W	−0021	−0011	−0017	−0027	−0.5	−0.6	−0.4	−0.2
Carloway	58 17N	6 47W	−0040	+0020	−0035	−0015	−0.6	−0.5	−0.4	−0.1
St Kilda Village Bay	57 48N	8 34W	−0040	−0040	−0045	−0045	−1.4	−1.2	−0.8	−0.3
Flannan Isles	58 17N	7 35W	−0026	−0016	−0016	−0026	−0.9	−0.7	−0.6	−0.2
Rockall	57 36N	13 41W	−0055	−0055	−0105	−0105	−1.8	−1.5	−0.9	−0.2

Location	Lat	Long	High Water		Low Water		MHWS	MHWN	MLWN	MLWS
			0000	0600	0300	0900				
ULLAPOOL	57 54N	5 09W	and	and	and	and	5.2	3.9	2.1	0.7
Standard port			1200	1800	1500	2100				
Loch Bervie	58 27N	5 03W	+0020	+0010	+0010	+0020	−0.4	−0.3	−0.2	−0.1
Loch Laxford	58 24N	5 05W	+0015	+0015	+0005	+0005	−0.3	−0.4	−0.2	0.0
Eddrachillis Bay										
Badcall Bay	58 19N	5 08W	+0005	+0005	+0005	+0005	−0.7	−0.5	−0.5	+0.2
Loch Nedd	58 14N	5 10W	0000	0000	0000	0000	−0.3	−0.2	−0.2	0.0
Loch Inver	58 09N	5 18W	−0005	−0005	−0005	−0005	−0.2	0.0	0.0	+0.1
Summer Isles Tanera Mor	58 01N	5 24W	−0005	−0005	−0010	−0010	−0.1	+0.1	0.0	+0.1
Loch Ewe Mellon Charles	57 51N	5 38W	−0010	−0010	−0010	−0010	−0.1	−0.1	−0.1	0.0
Loch Gairloch Gairloch	57 43N	5 41W	−0020	−0020	−0010	−0010	0.0	+0.1	−0.3	−0.1
Loch Torridon Shieldaig	57 31N	5 39W	−0020	−0020	−0015	−0015	+0.4	+0.3	+0.1	0.0
Inner Sound Applecross	57 26N	5 49W	−0010	−0015	−0010	−0010	0.0	0.0	0.0	+0.1
Loch Carron Plockton	57 21N	5 39W	+0005	−0025	−0005	−0010	+0.5	+0.5	+0.5	+0.2
Rona Loch a' Bhraige	57 35N	5 58W	−0020	0000	−0010	0000	−0.1	−0.1	−0.1	−0.2
Skye										
Broadford Bay	57 15N	5 54W	−0015	−0015	−0010	−0015	+0.2	+0.1	+0.1	0.0
Portree	57 24N	6 11W	−0025	−0025	−0025	−0025	+0.1	−0.2	−0.2	0.0
Loch Snizort (Uig Bay)	57 35N	6 22W	−0045	−0020	−0005	−0025	+0.1	−0.4	−0.2	0.0
Loch Dunvegan	57 27N	6 38W	−0105	−0030	−0020	−0040	0.0	−0.1	0.0	0.0
Loch Harport	57 20N	6 25W	−0115	−0035	−0020	−0100	−0.1	−0.1	0.0	+0.1
Soay Camus nan Gall	57 09N	6 13W	−0055	−0025	−0025	−0045	−0.4	−0.2	*No data*	
Loch Alsh										
Kyle of Lochalsh	57 17N	5 43W	−0040	−0020	−0005	−0025	+0.1	0.0	0.0	−0.1
Dornie Bridge	57 17N	5 31W	−0040	−0010	−0005	−0020	+0.1	−0.1	0.0	0.0
Kyle Rhea Glenelg Bay	57 13N	5 38W	−0105	−0035	−0035	−0055	−0.4	−0.4	−0.9	−0.1
Loch Hourn	57 06N	5 34W	−0125	−0050	−0040	−0110	−0.2	−0.1	−0.1	+0.1
			0000	0600	0100	0700				
OBAN	56 25N	5 29W	and	and	and	and	4.0	2.9	1.8	0.7
Standard port			1200	1800	1300	1900				
Loch Nevis										
Inverie Bay	57 02N	5 41W	+0030	+0020	+0035	+0020	+1.0	+0.9	+0.2	0.0
Mallaig	57 00N	5 50W	+0017	+0017	+0017	+0017	+1.0	+0.7	+0.3	+0.1
Eigg Bay of Laig	56 55N	6 10W	+0015	+0030	+0040	+0005	+0.7	+0.6	−0.2	− 0.2
Loch Moidart	56 47N	5 53W	+0015	+0015	+0040	+0020	+0.8	+0.6	− 0.2	−0.2
Coll Loch Eatharna	56 37N	6 31W	+0025	+0010	+0015	+0025	+0.4	+0.3	*No data*	
Tiree Gott Bay	56 31N	6 48W	0000	+0010	+0005	+0010	0.0	+0.1	0.0	0.0
			0100	0700	0100	0800				
OBAN	56 25N	5 29W	and	and	and	and	4.0	2.9	1.8	0.7
Standard port			1300	1900	1300	2000				
Mull										
Carsaig Bay	56 19N	5 58W	−0015	−0005	−0030	+0020	+0.1	+0.2	0.0	−0.1
Iona	56 20N	6 23W	−0010	−0005	−0020	+0015	0.0	+0.1	−0.3	−0.2
Bunessan	56 19N	6 14W	−0015	−0015	−0010	−0015	+0.3	+0.1	0.0	−0.1
Ulva Sound	56 29N	6 08W	−0010	−0015	0000	−0005	+0.4	+0.3	0.0	−0.1
Loch Sunart Salen	56 43N	5 47W	−0015	+0015	+0010	+0005	+0.6	+0.5	−0.1	−0.1
Sound of Mull										
Tobermory	56 37N	6 04W	+0025	+0010	+0015	+0025	+0.4	+0.4	0.0	0.0
Salen	56 31N	5 57W	+0045	+0015	+0020	+0030	+0.2	+0.2	−0.1	0.0
Loch Aline	56 32N	5 46W	+0012	+0012	*No data*	*No data*	+0.5	+0.3	*No data*	
Craignure	56 28N	5 42W	+0030	+0005	+0010	+0015	0.0	+0.1	−0.1	−0.1
Loch Linnhe										
Corran	56 43N	5 14W	+0007	+0007	+0004	+0004	+0.4	+0.4	−0.1	0.0
Corpach	56 51N	5 07W	0000	+0020	+0040	0000	0.0	0.0	−0.2	−0.2
Loch Eil Head	56 51N	5 20W	+0025	+0045	+0105	+0025	*No data*		*No data*	
Loch Leven Head	56 43N	5 00W	+0045	+0045	+0045	+0045	*No data*		*No data*	
Loch Linnhe Port Appin	56 33N	5 25W	−0005	−0005	−0030	0000	+0.2	+0.2	+0.1	+0.1
Loch Creran										
Barcaldine Pier	56 32N	5 19W	+0010	+0020	+0040	+0015	+0.1	+0.1	0.0	+0.1
Loch Creran Head	56 33N	5 16W	+0015	+0025	+0120	+0020	−0.3	−0.3	−0.4	−0.3
Loch Etive										
Dunstaffnage Bay	56 27N	5 26W	+0005	0000	0000	+0005	+0.1	+0.1	+0.1	+0.1
Connel	56 27N	5 24W	+0020	+0005	+0010	+0015	−0.3	−0.2	−0.1	+0.1
Bonawe	56 27N	5 13W	+0150	+0205	+0240	+0210	−2.0	−1.7	−1.3	−0.5
Seil Sound	56 18N	5 35W	−0035	−0015	−0040	−0015	−1.3	−0.9	−0.7	−0.3
Colonsay Scalasaig	56 04N	6 11W	−0020	−0005	−0015	+0005	−0.1	−0.2	−0.2	−0.2
Jura Glengarrisdale Bay	56 07N	5 47W	−0020	0000	−0010	0000	−0.4	−0.2	0.0	−0.2

TIDES

Location	Lat	Long	High Water		Low Water		MHWS	MHWN	MLWN	MLWS
Islay										
Rubha A'Mhail	55 56N	6 07W	−0020	0000	+0005	−0015	−0.3	−0.1	−0.3	−0.1
Ardnave Point	55 52N	6 20W	−0035	+0010	0000	−0025	−0.4	−0.2	−0.3	−0.1
Orsay	55 41N	6 31W	−0110	−0110	−0040	−0040	−1.4	−0.6	−0.5	−0.2
Bruichladdich	55 46N	6 22W	−0105	−0035	−0110	−0110	−1.8	−1.3	−0.4	+0.1
Port Ellen	55 38N	6 11W	−0530	−0050	−0045	−0530	−3.1	−2.1	−1.3	−0.4
Port Askaig	55 51N	6 06W	−0110	−0030	−0020	−0020	−1.9	−1.4	−0.8	−0.3
Sound of Jura										
Craighouse	55 50N	5 57W	−0230	−0250	−0150	−0230	−3.0	−2.4	−1.3	−0.6
Loch Melfort	56 15N	5 29W	−0055	−0025	−0040	−0035	−1.2	−0.8	−0.5	−0.1
Loch Beag	56 09N	5 36W	−0110	−0045	−0035	−0045	−1.6	−1.2	−0.8	−0.4
Carsaig Bay	56 02N	5 38W	−0105	−0040	−0050	−0050	−2.1	−1.6	−1.0	−0.4
Sound of Gigha	55 41N	5 44W	−0450	−0210	−0130	−0410	−2.5	−1.6	−1.0	−0.1
Machrihanish	55 25N	5 45W	−0520	−0350	−0340	−0540	*Mean range 0.5 metres*			
			0000	**0600**	**0000**	**0600**				
GREENOCK	55 57N	4 46W	and	and	and	and	**3.4**	**2.8**	**1.0**	**0.3**
Standard port			**1200**	**1800**	**1200**	**1800**				
Firth of Clyde										
Southend, Kintyre	55 19N	5 38W	−0030	−0010	+0005	+0035	−1.3	−1.2	−0.5	−0.2
Campbeltown	55 25N	5 36W	−0025	−0005	−0015	+0005	−0.5	−0.3	+0.1	+0.2
Carradale	55 36N	5 28W	−0015	−0005	−0005	+0005	−0.3	−0.2	+0.1	+0.1
Loch Ranza	55 43N	5 18W	−0015	−0005	−0010	−0005	−0.4	−0.3	−0.1	0.0
Loch Fyne										
East Loch Tarbert	55 52N	5 24W	−0005	−0005	0000	−0005	+0.2	+0.1	0.0	0.0
Inveraray	56 14N	5 04W	+0011	+0011	+0034	+0034	−0.1	+0.1	−0.5	−0.2
Kyles of Bute										
Rubha a'Bhodaich	55 55N	5 09W	−0020	−0010	−0007	−0007	−0.2	−0.1	+0.2	+0.2
Tighnabruich	55 55N	5 13W	+0007	−0010	−0002	−0015	0.0	+0.2	+0.4	+0.5
Firth of Clyde – continued										
Millport	55 45N	4 56W	−0005	−0025	−0025	−0005	0.0	−0.1	0.0	+0.1
Rothesay Bay	55 50N	5 03W	−0020	−0015	−0010	−0002	+0.2	+0.2	+0.2	+0.2
Wemyss Bay	55 53N	4 53W	−0005	−0005	−0005	−0005	0.0	0.0	+0.1	+0.1
Loch Long										
Coulport	56 03N	4 53W	−0011	−0011	−0008	−0008	0.0	0.0	0.0	0.0
Lochgoilhead	56 10N	4 54W	+0015	0000	−0005	−0005	−0.2	−0.3	−0.3	−0.3
Arrochar	56 12N	4 45W	−0005	−0005	−0005	−0005	0.0	0.0	−0.1	−0.1
Gare Loch										
Rhu Marina	56 01N	4 46W	−0007	−0007	−0007	−0007	−0.1	−0.1	−0.1	−0.2
Faslane	56 04N	4 49W	−0010	−0010	−0010	−0010	0.0	0.0	−0.1	−0.2
Garelochhead	56 05N	4 50W	0000	0000	0000	0000	0.0	0.0	0.0	0.0
River Clyde										
Helensburgh	56 00N	4 44W	0000	0000	0000	0000	0.0	0.0	0.0	0.0
Port Glasgow	55 56N	4 41W	+0010	+0005	+0010	+0020	+0.2	+0.1	0.0	0.0
Bowling	55 56N	4 29W	+0020	+0010	+0030	+0055	+0.6	+0.5	+0.3	+0.1
Clydebank (Rothesay Dock)	55 54N	4 24W	+0025	+0015	+0035	+0100	+1.1	+0.9	+0.6	+0.3
Glasgow	55 51N	4 16W	+0025	+0015	+0035	+0105	+1.3	+1.1	+0.7	+0.4
Firth of Clyde – continued										
Brodick Bay	55 35N	5 08W	−0013	−0013	−0008	−0008	−0.2	−0.1	0.0	+0.1
Lamlash	55 32N	5 07W	−0016	−0036	−0024	−0004	−0.2	−0.2	*No data*	
Ardrossan	55 38N	4 49W	−0020	−0010	−0010	−0010	−0.2	−0.2	+0.1	+0.1
Irvine	55 36N	4 42W	−0020	−0020	−0030	−0010	−0.3	−0.3	−0.1	0.0
Troon	55 33N	4 41W	−0025	−0025	−0020	−0020	−0.2	−0.2	0.0	0.0
Ayr	55 28N	4 39W	−0025	−0025	−0030	−0015	−0.4	−0.3	+0.1	+0.1
Girvan	55 15N	4 52W	−0025	−0040	−0035	−0010	−0.3	−0.3	−0.1	0.0
Loch Ryan Stranraer	54 55N	5 02W	−0030	−0025	−0010	−0010	−0.2	−0.1	0.0	+0.1
			0000	**0600**	**0200**	**0800**				
LIVERPOOL	53 24N	3 01W	and	and	and	and	**9.3**	**7.4**	**2.9**	**0.9**
Standard port			**1200**	**1800**	**1400**	**2000**				
Portpatrick	54 51N	5 07W	+0018	+0026	0000	−0035	−5.5	−4.4	−2.0	−0.6
Luce Bay										
Drummore	54 42N	4 53W	+0030	+0040	+0015	+0020	−3.4	−2.5	−0.9	−0.3
Port William	54 46N	4 35W	+0030	+0030	+0025	0000	−2.9	−2.2	−0.8	*No data*
Wigtown Bay										
Isle of Whithorn	54 42N	4 22W	+0020	+0025	+0025	+0005	−2.4	−2.0	−0.8	−0.2
Garlieston	54 47N	4 22W	+0025	+0035	+0030	+0005	−2.3	−1.7	−0.5	*No data*
Solway Firth										
Kirkcudbright Bay	54 48N	4 04W	+0015	+0015	+0010	0000	−1.8	−1.5	−0.5	−0.1
Hestan Islet	54 50N	3 48W	+0025	+0025	+0020	+0025	−1.0	−1.1	−0.5	0.0
Southerness Point	54 52N	3 36W	+0030	+0030	+0030	+0010	−0.7	−0.7	*No data*	

Location	Lat	Long	High Water		Low Water		MHWS	MHWN	MLWN	MLWS
Annan Waterfoot	54 58N	3 16W	+0050	+0105	+0220	+0310	−2.2	−2.6	−2.7	
Torduff Point	54 58N	3 09W	+0105	+0140	+0520	+0410	−4.1	−4.9		
Redkirk	54 59N	3 06W	+0110	+0215	+0715	+0445	−5.5	−6.2		

WEST COAST OF ENGLAND

Location	Lat	Long	High Water		Low Water		MHWS	MHWN	MLWN	MLWS
Silloth	54 52N	3 24W	+0030	+0040	+0045	+0055	−0.1	−0.3	−0.6	−0.1
Maryport	54 43N	3 30W	+0017	+0032	+0020	+0005	−0.7	−0.8	−0.4	0.0
Workington	54 39N	3 34W	+0020	+0020	+0020	+0010	−1.2	−1.1	−0.3	0.0
Whitehaven	54 33N	3 36W	+0005	+0015	+0010	+0005	−1.3	−1.1	−0.5	+0.1
Tarn Point	54 17N	3 25W	+0005	+0005	+0010	0000	−1.0	−1.0	−0.4	0.0
Duddon Bar	54 09N	3 20W	+0003	+0003	+0008	+0002	−0.8	−0.8	−0.3	0.0

Location	Lat	Long	High Water		Low Water		MHWS	MHWN	MLWN	MLWS
			0000	0600	0200	0700				
LIVERPOOL	53 24N	3 01W	and	and	and	and	**9.3**	**7.4**	**2.9**	**0.9**
Standard port			1200	1800	1400	1900				
Barrow-in-Furness	54 06N	3 12W	+0015	+0015	+0015	+0015	0.0	−0.3	+0.1	+0.2
Ulverston	54 11N	3 04W	+0020	+0040	No data	No data	0.0	−0.1		No data
Arnside	54 12N	2 51W	+0100	+0135	No data	No data	+0.5	+0.2		No data
Morecambe	54 04N	2 53W	+0005	+0010	+0030	+0015	+0.2	0.0	0.0	+0.2
Heysham	54 02N	2 55W	+0005	+0005	+0015	0000	+0.1	0.0	0.0	+0.2
River Lune Glasson Dock	54 00N	2 51W	+0020	+0030	+0220	+0240	−2.7	−3.0		No data
Lancaster	54 03N	2 49W	+0110	+0030	*Dries*	*Dries*	−5.0	−4.9		*Dries*
River Wyre										
Wyre Lighthouse	53 57N	3 02W	−0010	−0010	+0005	0000	−0.1	−0.1		No data
Fleetwood	53 56N	3 00W	−0008	−0008	−0003	−0003	−0.1	−0.1	+0.1	+0.3
Blackpool	53 49N	3 04W	−0015	−0005	−0005	−0015	−0.4	−0.4	−0.1	+0.1
River Ribble Preston	53 45N	2 45W	+0010	+0010	+0335	+0310	−4.0	−4.1	−2.8	−0.8
Liverpool Bay										
Southport	53 39N	3 01W	−0020	−0010	No data	No data	−0.3	−0.3		No data
Formby	53 32N	3 07W	−0015	−0010	−0020	−0020	−0.3	−0.1	0.0	+0.1
River Mersey										
Gladstone Dock	53 27N	3 01W	−0003	−0003	−0003	−0003	−0.1	−0.1	0.0	−0.1
Eastham	53 19N	2 57W	+0010	+0010	+0009	+0009	+0.1	+0.1	−0.1	−0.3
Hale Head	53 19N	2 48W	+0030	+0025	No data	No data	−2.4	−2.5		No data
Widnes	53 21N	2 44W	+0040	+0045	+0400	+0345	−4.2	−4.4	−2.5	−0.3
Fiddler's Ferry	53 22N	2 40W	+0100	+0115	+0540	+0450	−5.9	−6.3	−2.4	−0.4
River Dee										
Hilbre Island	53 23N	3 14W	−0015	−0012	−0010	−0015	−0.3	−0.2	+0.2	+0.4
Chester	53 12N	2 54W	+0105	+0105	+0500	+0500	−5.3	−5.4		*Dries*
Connah's Quay (Wales)	53 13N	3 03W	0000	+0015	+0355	+0340	−4.6	−4.4		*Dries*
Mostyn Docks (Wales)	53 19N	3 16W	−0020	−0015	−0020	−0020	−0.8	−0.7		No data
Isle of Man Peel	54 14N	4 42W	+0005	+0005	−0015	−0025	−4.1	−3.1	−1.4	−0.5
Ramsey	54 19N	4 22W	+0005	+0015	−0005	−0015	−1.9	−1.5	−0.6	0.0
Douglas	54 09N	4 28W	+0005	+0015	−0015	−0025	−2.4	−2.0	−0.5	−0.1
Port St Mary	54 04N	4 44W	+0005	+0015	−0010	−0030	−3.4	−2.6	−1.3	−0.4
Calf Sound	54 04N	4 48W	+0005	+0005	−0015	−0025	−3.2	−2.6	−0.9	−0.3
Port Erin	54 05N	4 46W	−0005	+0015	−0010	−0050	−4.1	−3.2	−1.3	−0.5

WALES

Location	Lat	Long	High Water		Low Water		MHWS	MHWN	MLWN	MLWS
Colwyn Bay	53 18N	3 43W	−0020	−0020	No data	No data	−1.5	−1.3		No data
Llandudno	53 20N	3 50W	−0020	−0020	−0035	−0040	−1.7	−1.4	−0.7	−0.3

Location	Lat	Long	High Water		Low Water		MHWS	MHWN	MLWN	MLWS
			0000	0600	0500	1100				
HOLYHEAD	53 19N	4 37W	and	and	and	and	**5.6**	**4.4**	**2.0**	**0.7**
Standard port			1200	1800	1700	2300				
Conwy	53 17N	3 50W	+0025	+0035	+0120	+0105	+2.3	+1.8	+0.6	+0.4
Menai Strait										
Beaumaris	53 16N	4 05W	+0025	+0010	+0055	+0035	+2.0	+1.6	+0.5	+0.1
Menai Bridge	53 13N	4 10W	+0030	+0010	+0100	+0035	+1.7	+1.4	+0.3	0.0
Port Dinorwic	53 11N	4 13W	−0015	−0025	+0030	0000	0.0	0.0	0.0	+0.1
Caernarfon	53 09N	4 16W	−0030	−0030	+0015	−0005	−0.4	−0.4	−0.1	−0.1
Fort Belan	53 07N	4 20W	−0040	−0015	−0025	−0005	−1.0	−0.9	−0.2	−0.1
Trwyn Dinmor	53 19N	4 03W	+0025	+0015	+0050	+0035	+1.9	+1.5	+0.5	+0.2
Moelfre	53 20N	4 14W	+0025	+0020	+0050	+0035	+1.9	+1.4	+0.5	+0.2
Amlwch	53 25N	4 20W	+0020	+0010	+0035	+0025	+1.6	+ 1.3	+0.5	+0.2
Cemaes Bay	53 25N	4 27W	+0020	+0025	+0040	+0035	+1.0	+0.7	+0.3	+0.1
Trearddur Bay	53 16N	4 37W	−0045	−0025	−0015	−0015	−0.4	−0.4	0.0	+0.1
Porth Trecastell	53 12N	4 30W	−0045	−0025	−0005	−0015	−0.6	−0.6	0.0	0.0
Llanddwyn Island	53 08N	4 25W	−0115	−0055	−0030	−0020	−0.7	−0.5	−0.1	0.0
Trefor	53 00N	4 25W	−0115	−0100	−0030	−0020	−0.8	−0.9	−0.2	−0.1
Porth Dinllaen	52 57N	4 34W	−0120	−0105	−0035	−0025	−1.0	−1.0	−0.2	−0.2
Porth Ysgaden	52 54N	4 39W	−0125	−0110	−0040	−0035	−1.1	−1.0	−0.1	−0.1
Bardsey Island	52 46N	4 47W	−0220	−0240	−0145	−0140	−1.2	−1.2	−0.5	−0.1

Location	Lat	Long	High Water		Low Water		MHWS	MHWN	MLWN	MLWS
			0100	0800	0100	0700				
MILFORD HAVEN	51 42N	5 03W	and	and	and	and	7.0	5.2	2.5	0.7
Standard port			1300	2000	1300	1900				
Cardigan Bay										
Aberdaron	52 48N	4 43W	+0210	+0200	+0240	+0310	−2.4	−1.9	−0.6	−0.2
St Tudwal's Roads	52 49N	4 29W	+0155	+0145	+0240	+0310	−2.2	−1.9	−0.7	−0.2
Pwllheli	52 53N	4 24W	+0210	+0150	+0245	+0320	−2.0	− 1.8	−0.6	−0.2
Criccieth	52 55N	4 14W	+0210	+0155	+0255	+0320	−2.0	−1.8	−0.7	−0.3
Porthmadog	52 55N	4 08W	+0235	+0210	*No data*	*No data*	−1.9	−1.8	*No data*	
Barmouth	52 43N	4 03W	+0215	+0205	+0310	+0320	−2.0	−1.7	−0.7	0.0
Aberdovey	52 33N	4 03W	+0215	+0200	+0230	+0305	−2.0	−1.7	−0.5	0.0
Aberystwyth	52 24N	4 05W	+0145	+0130	+0210	+0245	−2.0	−1.7	−0.7	0.0
New Quay	52 13N	4 21W	+0150	+0125	+0155	+0230	−2.1	−1.8	−0.6	−0.1
Aberporth	52 08N	4 33W	+0135	+0120	+0150	+0220	−2.1	−1.8	−0.6	−0.1
Port Cardigan	52 07N	4 41W	+0140	+0120	+0220	+0130	−2.3	−1.8	−0.5	0.0
Cardigan (Town)	52 05N	4 40W	+0220	+0150	*No data*	*No data*	−2.2	−1.6	*No data*	
Fishguard	52 01N	4 59W	+0115	+0100	+0110	+0135	−2.2	−1.8	−0.5	+0.1
Porthgain	51 57N	5 11W	+0055	+0045	+0045	+0100	−2.5	−1.8	−0.6	0.0
Ramsey Sound	51 53N	5 19W	+0030	+0030	+0030	+0030	−1.9	−1.3	−0.3	0.0
Solva	51 52N	5 12W	+0015	+0010	+0035	+0015	−1.5	−1.0	−0.2	0.0
Little Haven	51 46N	5 07W	+0010	+0010	+0025	+0015	−1.1	−0.8	−0.2	0.0
Martin's Haven	51 44N	5 15W	+0010	+0010	+0015	+0015	−0.8	−0.5	+0.1	+0.1
Skomer Island	51 44N	5 17W	−0005	−0005	+0005	+0005	−0.4	−0.1	0.0	0.0
Dale Roads	51 42N	5 09W	−0005	−0005	−0008	−0008	0.0	0.0	0.0	−0.1
Cleddau River										
Neyland	51 42N	4 57W	+0002	+0010	0000	0000	0.0	0.0	0.0	0.0
Black Tar	51 45N	4 54W	+0010	+0020	+0005	0000	+0.1	+0.1	0.0	−0.1
Haverfordwest	51 48N	4 58W	+0010	+0025	*Dries*	*Dries*	−4.8	−4.9	*Dries*	
Stackpole Quay	51 37N	4 54W	−0005	+0025	−0010	−0010	+0.9	+0.7	+0.2	+0.3
Tenby	51 40N	4 42W	−0015	−0010	−0015	−0020	+1.4	+1.1	+0.5	+0.2
Towy River										
Ferryside	51 46N	4 22W	0000	−0010	+0220	0000	−0.3	−0.7	−1.7	−0.6
Carmarthen	51 51N	4 18W	+0010	0000	*Dries*	*Dries*	−4.4	−4.8	*Dries*	
Burry Inlet										
Burry Port	51 41N	4 15W	+0003	+0003	+0007	+0007	+1.6	+1.4	+0.5	+0.4
Llanelli	51 40N	4 10W	−0003	−0003	+0150	+0020	+0.8	+0.6	*No data*	
Mumbles	51 34N	3 58W	+0005	+0010	−0020	−0015	+2.3	+1.7	+0.6	+0.2
River Neath Entrance	51 37N	3 51W	+0002	+0011	*Dries*	*Dries*	+2.7	+2.2	*Dries*	
Port Talbot	51 35N	3 49W	+0003	+0005	−0010	−0005	+2.8	+2.2	+1.0	+0.5
Porthcawl	51 28N	3 42W	+0005	+0010	−0010	−0005	+2.9	+2.3	+0.8	+0.3
			0600	1100	0300	0800				
BRISTOL, AVONMOUTH	51 30N	2 44W	and	and	and	and	13.2	9.8	3.8	1.0
Standard port			1800	2300	1500	2000				
Barry	51 23N	3 16W	−0025	−0025	−0130	−0045	−1.7	−1.0	−0.2	0.0
Flat Holm	51 23N	3 07W	−0015	−0015	−0035	−0035	−1.4	−1.0	−0.5	0.0
Steep Holm	51 20N	3 06W	−0020	−0020	−0040	−0040	−1.7	−1.1	−0.5	−0.4
Cardiff	51 27N	3 10W	−0015	−0015	−0100	−0030	−1.0	−0.5	0.0	0.0
Newport	51 33N	2 59W	−0020	−0010	0000	−0020	−1.1	−0.9	−0.6	−0.6
River Wye Chepstow	51 39N	2 40W	+0020	+0020	*No data*	*No data*	*No data*		*No data*	
			0000	0600	0000	0700				
BRISTOL, AVONMOUTH	51 30N	2 44W	and	and	and	and	13.2	9.8	3.8	1.0
Standard port			1200	1800	1200	1900				

WEST COAST OF ENGLAND

Location	Lat	Long	High Water		Low Water		MHWS	MHWN	MLWN	MLWS
River Severn										
Sudbrook	51 35N	2 43W	+0010	+0010	+0025	+0015	+0.2	+0.1	−0.1	+0.1
Beachley (Aust)	51 36N	2 38W	+0010	+0015	+0040	+0025	−0.2	−0.2	−0.5	−0.3
Inward Rocks	51 39N	2 37W	+0020	+0020	+0105	+0045	−1.0	−1.1	−1.4	−0.6
Narlwood Rocks	51 39N	2 36W	+0025	+0025	+0120	+0100	−1.9	−2.0	−2.3	−0.8
White House	51 40N	2 33W	+0025	+0025	+0145	+0120	−3.0	−3.1	−3.6	−1.0
Berkeley	51 42N	2 30W	+0030	+0045	+0245	+0220	−3.8	−3.9	−3.4	−0.5
Sharpness Dock	51 43N	2 29W	+0035	+0050	+0305	+0245	−3.9	−4.2	−3.3	−0.4
Wellhouse Rock	51 44N	2 29W	+0040	+0055	+0320	+0305	−4.1	−4.4	−3.1	−0.2
Epney	51 42N	2 24W	+0130	*No data*	*No data*	*No data*	−9.4	*No data*	*No data*	
Minsterworth	51 50N	2 23W	+0140	*No data*	*No data*	*No data*	−10.1	*No data*	*No data*	
Llanthony	51 51N	2 21W	+0215	*No data*	*No data*	*No data*	−10.7	*No data*	*No data*	
			0200	0800	0300	0800				
BRISTOL, AVONMOUTH	51 30N	2 44W	and	and	and	and	13.2	9.8	3.8	1.0
Standard port			1400	2000	1500	2000				
River Avon										
Shirehampton	51 29N	2 41W	0000	0000	+0035	+0010	−0.7	−0.7	−0.8	0.0
Sea Mills	51 29N	2 39W	+0005	+0005	+0105	+0030	−1.4	−1.5	−1.7	−0.1
Cumberland Basin Entrance	51 27N	2 37W	+0010	+0010	*Dries*	*Dries*	−2.9	−3.0	*Dries*	

Location	Lat	Long	High Water		Low Water		MHWS	MHWN	MLWN	MLWS
Portishead	51 30N	2 45W	−0002	0000 No data	No data		−0.1	−0.1	No data	
Clevedon	51 27N	2 52W	−0010	−0020	−0025	−0015	−0.4	−0.2	+0.2	0.0
St Thomas Head	51 24N	2 56W	0000	0000	−0030	−0030	−0.4	−0.2	+0.1	+0.1
English & Welsh Grounds	51 28N	2 59W	−0008	−0008	−0030	−0030	−0.5	−0.8	−0.3	0.0
Weston-super-Mare	51 21N	2 59W	−0020	−0030	−0130	−0030	−1.2	−1.0	−0.8	−0.2
River Parrett										
Burnham-on-Sea	51 14N	3 00W	−0020	−0025	−0030	0000	−2.3	−1.9	−1.4	−1.1
Bridgwater	51 08N	3 00W	−0015	−0030	+0305	+0455	−8.6	−8.1	Dries	
Hinkley Point	51 13N	3 08W	−0020	−0025	−0100	−0040	−1.7	−1.4	−0.2	−0.2
Watchet	51 11N	3 20W	−0035	−0050	−0145	−0040	−1.9	−1.5	+0.1	+0.1
Minehead	51 13N	3 28W	−0037	−0052	−0155	−0045	−2.6	−1.9	−0.2	0.0
Porlock Bay	51 13N	3 38W	−0045	−0055	−0205	−0050	−3.0	−2.2	−0.1	−0.1
Lynmouth	51 14N	3 50W	−0055	−0115 No data	No data		−3.6	−2.7	No data	
			0100	**0700**	**0100**	**0700**				
MILFORD HAVEN	51 42N	5 03W	and	and	and	and	7.0	5.2	2.5	0.7
Standard port			1300	1900	1300	1900				
Ilfracombe	51 13N	4 07W	−0016	−0016	−0041	−0031	+2.3	+1.8	+0.6	+0.3
Rivers Taw & Torridge										
Appledore	51 03N	4 12W	−0020	−0025	+0015	−0045	+0.5	0.0	−0.9	−0.5
Yelland Marsh	51 04N	4 10W	−0010	−0015	+0100	−0015	+0.1	−0.4	−1.2	−0.6
Fremington	51 05N	4 07W	−0010	−0015	+0030	−0030	−1.1	−1.8	−2.2	−0.5
Barnstaple	51 05N	4 04W	0000	−0015	−0155	−0245	−2.9	−3.8	−2.2	−0.4
Bideford	51 01N	4 12W	−0020	−0025	0000	0000	−1.1	−1.6	−2.5	−0.7
Clovelly	51 00N	4 24W	−0030	−0030	−0020	−0040	+1.3	+1.1	+0.2	+0.2
Lundy	51 10N	4 39W	−0025	−0025	−0020	−0035	+0.9	+0.7	+0.3	+0.1
Bude	50 50N	4 33W	−0040	−0040	−0035	−0045	+0.7	+0.6	No data	
Boscastle	50 41N	4 42W	−0045	−0010	−0110	−0100	+0.3	+0.4	+0.2	+0.2
Port Isaac	50 35N	4 50W	−0100	−0100	−0100	−0100	+0.5	+0.6	0.0	+0.2
River Camel										
Padstow	50 33N	4 56W	−0055	−0050	−0040	−0050	+0.3	+0.4	+0.1	+0.1
Wadebridge	50 31N	4 50W	−0052	−0052	+0235	+0245	−3.8	−3.8	−2.5	−0.4
Newquay	50 25N	5 05W	−0100	−0110	−0105	−0050	0.0	+0.1	0.0	−0.1
Perranporth	50 21N	5 09W	−0100	−0110	−0110	−0050	−0.1	0.0	0.0	+0.1
St Ives	50 13N	5 29W	−0050	−0115	−0105	−0040	−0.4	−0.3	−0.1	+0.1
Cape Cornwall	50 08N	5 42 W	−0130	−0145	−0120	−0120	−1.0	−0.9	−0.5	−0.1
Sennen Cove	50 05N	5 42W	−0130	−0145	−0125	−0125	−0.9	−0.4	No data	
IRELAND			**0000**	**0700**	**0000**	**0500**				
DUBLIN, NORTH WALL	53 21N	6 13W	and	and	and	and	4.1	3.4	1.5	0.7
Standard port			1200	1900	1200	1700				
Courtown	52 39N	6 13W	−0328	−0242	−0158	−0138	−2.8	−2.4	−0.5	0.0
Arklow	52 48N	6 08W	−0315	−0201	−0140	−0134	−2.7	−2.2	−0.6	−0.1
Wicklow	52 59N	6 02W	−0019	−0019	−0024	−0026	−1.4	−1.1	−0.4	0.0
Greystones	53 09N	6 04W	−0008	−0008	−0008	−0008	−0.5	−0.4	No data	
Dun Laoghaire	53 18N	6 08W	−0006	−0001	−0002	−0003	0.0	0.0	0.0	+0.1
Dublin Bar	53 21N	6 09W	−0006	−0001	−0002	−0003	0.0	0.0	0.0	+0.1
Howth	53 23N	6 04W	−0007	−0005	+0001	+0005	0.0	−0.1	−0.2	−0.2
Malahide	53 27N	6 09W	+0002	+0003	+0009	+0009	+0.1	−0.2	−0.4	−0.2
Balbriggan	53 37N	6 11W	−0021	−0015	+0010	+0002	+0.3	+0.2	No data	
River Boyne Bar	53 43N	6 14W	−0005	0000	+0020	+0030	+0.4	+0.3	−0.1	−0.2
Dunany Point	53 52N	6 14W	−0028	−0018	−0008	−0006	+0.7	+0.9	No data	
Dundalk Soldiers Point	54 00N	6 21W	−0010	−0010	0000	+0045	+1.0	+0.8	+0.1	−0.1

NORTHERN IRELAND

Location	Lat	Long	High Water		Low Water		MHWS	MHWN	MLWN	MLWS
Carlingford Lough										
Cranfield Point	54 01N	6 04W	−0027	−0011	+0005	−0010	+0.7	+0.9	+0.3	+0.2
Warrenpoint	54 06N	6 15W	−0020	−0010	+0025	+0035	+1.0	+0.7	+0.2	+0.0
Newry (Victoria Lock)	54 09N	6 19W	+0005	+0015	+0045	Dries	+1.2	+0.9	+0.1	Dries
			0100	**0700**	**0000**	**0600**				
BELFAST	54 36N	5 55W	and	and	and	and	3.5	3.0	1.1	0.4
Standard port			1300	1900	1200	1800				
Kilkeel	54 03N	5 59W	+0040	+0030	+0010	+0010	+1.2	+1.1	+0.4	+0.4
Newcastle	54 12N	5 53W	+0025	+0035	+0020	+0040	+1.6	+1.1	+0.4	+0.1
Killough Harbour	54 15N	5 38W	0000	+0020 No data	No data		+1.8	+1.6	No data	
Ardglass	54 16N	5 36W	+0010	+0015	+0005	+0010	+1.7	+1.2	+0.6	+0.3
Strangford Lough										
Killard Point	54 19N	5 31W	+0011	+0021	+0005	+0025	+1.0	+0.8	+0.1	+0.1
Strangford	54 22N	5 33W	+0147	+0157	+0148	+0208	+0.1	+0.1	−0.2	0.0
Quoile Barrier	54 22N	5 41W	+0150	+0200	+0150	+0300	+0.2	+0.2	−0.3	−0.1
Killyleagh	54 24N	5 39W	+0157	+0207	+0211	+0231	+0.3	+0.3	No data	
South Rock	54 24N	5 25W	+0023	+0023	+0025	+0025	+1.0	+0.8	+0.1	+0.1
Portavogie	54 27N	5 26W	+0010	+0020	+0010	+0020	+1.2	+0.9	+0.3	+0.2

TIDES

Location	Lat	Long	High Water		Low Water		MHWS	MHWN	MLWN	MLWS
Donaghadee	54 39N	5 32W	+0020	+0020	+0023	+0023	+0.5	+0.4	0.0	+0.1
Carrickfergus	54 43N	5 48W	+0005	+0005	+0005	+0005	−0.3	−0.3	−0.2	−0.1
Larne	54 51N	5 48W	+0005	0000	+0010	−0005	−0.7	−0.5	−0.3	0.0
Red Bay	55 04N	6 03W	+0022	−0010	+0007	−0017	−1.9	−1.5	−0.8	−0.2
Cushendun	55 08N	6 02W	+0010	−0030	0000	−0025	−1.7	−1.5	−0.6	−0.2
Portrush	55 12N	6 40W	−0433	−0433	−0433	−0433	−1.6	−1.6	−0.3	0.0
Coleraine	55 08N	6 40W	−0403	−0403	−0403	−0403	−1.3	−1.2	−0.2	0.0
			0200	**0900**	**0200**	**0800**				
GALWAY	53 16N	9 03W	and	and	and	and	**5.1**	**3.9**	**2.0**	**0.6**
Standard port			**1400**	**2100**	**1400**	**2000**				
Londonderry	55 00N	7 19W	+0254	+0319	+0322	+0321	−2.4	−1.8	−0.8	−0.1

IRELAND

Location	Lat	Long	High Water		Low Water		MHWS	MHWN	MLWN	MLWS
Inishtrahull	55 26N	7 14W	+0100	+0100	+0115	+0200	−1.8	−1.4	−0.4	−0.2
Bulbinbeg	55 22N	7 20W	+0120	+0120	+0135	+0135	−1.3	−1.1	−0.4	−0.1
Trawbreaga Bay	55 19N	7 23W	+0115	+0059	+0109	+0125	−1.1	−0.8	No data	
Lough Swilly										
Rathmullan	55 06N	7 32W	+0125	+0050	+0126	+0118	−0.8	−0.7	−0.1	−0.1
Fanad Head	55 17N	7 38W	+0115	+0040	+0125	+0120	−1.1	−0.9	−0.5	−0.1
Mulroy Bay Bar	55 15N	7 46W	+0108	+0052	+0102	+0118	−1.2	−1.0	No data	
Fanny's Bay	55 12N	7 49W	+0145	+0129	+0151	+0207	−2.2	−1.7	No data	
Seamount Bay	55 11N	7 44W	+0210	+0154	+0226	+0242	−3.1	−2.3	No data	
Cranford Bay	55 09N	7 42W	+0329	+0313	+0351	+0407	−3.7	−2.8	No data	
Sheephaven Downies Bay	55 11N	7 50W	+0057	+0043	+0053	+0107	−1.1	−0.9	No data	
Inishbofin Bay	55 10N	8 10W	+0040	+0026	+0032	+0046	−1.2	−0.9	No data	
			0600	**1100**	**0000**	**0700**				
GALWAY	53 16N	9 03W	and	and	and	and	**5.1**	**3.9**	**2.0**	**0.6**
Standard port			**1800**	**2300**	**1200**	**1900**				
Gweedore Harbour	55 04N	8 19W	+0048	+0100	+0055	+0107	−1.3	−1.0	−0.5	−0.1
Burtonport	54 59N	8 26W	+0042	+0055	+0115	+0055	−1.2	−1.0	−0.6	−0.1
Loughros More Bay	54 47N	8 30W	+0042	+0054	+0046	+0058	−1.1	−0.9	No data	
Donegal Bay										
Killybegs	54 38N	8 26W	+0040	+0050	+0055	+0035	−1.0	−0.9	−0.5	0.0
Donegal Hbr, Salt Hill Quay	54 38N	8 12W	+0038	+0050	+0052	+0104	−1.2	−0.9	No data	
Mullaghmore	54 28N	8 27W	+0036	+0048	+0047	+0059	−1.4	−1.0	−0.4	−0.2
Sligo Hbr (Oyster Island)	54 18N	8 34W	+0043	+0055	+0042	+0054	−1.0	−0.9	−0.5	−0.1
Ballysadare Bay, Culleenamore	54 16N	8 36W	+0059	+0111	+0111	+0123	−1.2	−0.9	No data	
Killala Bay (Inishcrone)	54 13N	9 06W	+0035	+0055	+0030	+0050	−1.3	−1.2	−0.7	−0.2
Broadhaven	54 16N	9 53W	+0040	+0050	+0040	+0050	−1.4	−1.1	−0.4	−0.1
Blacksod Bay										
Blacksod Quay	54 06N	10 04W	+0025	+0035	+0040	+0040	−1.2	−1.0	−0.6	−0.2
Inishbiggle	54 00N	9 53W	+0055	+0100	+0125	+0110	−1.3	− 0.9	−0.5	0.0
Clare Island	53 48N	9 57W	+0015	+0021	+0039	+0027	−0.6	−0.4	−0.1	+0.2
Clew Bay Inishgort	53 50N	9 40W	+0035	+0045	+0115	+0100	−0.7	−0.5	−0.2	+0.2
Killary Harbour	53 38N	9 53W	+0021	+0015	+0035	+0029	−1.0	−0.8	−0.4	−0.1
Inishbofin Bofin Harbour	53 37N	10 12W	+0013	+0009	+0021	+0017	−1.0	−0.8	−0.4	−0.1
Clifden Bay	53 29N	10 04W	+0005	+0005	+0016	+0016	−0.7	−0.5	No data	
Slyne Head	53 24N	10 14W	+0002	+0002	+0010	+0010	−0.7	−0.5	No data	
Roundstone Bay	53 23N	9 55W	+0003	+0003	+0008	+0008	−0.7	−0.5	−0.3	−0.1
Kilkieran Cove	53 19N	9 44W	+0005	+0005	+0016	+0016	−0.3	−0.2	−0.1	0.0
Aran Islands Killeany Bay	53 07N	9 40W	−0008	−0008	+0003	+0003	−0.4	−0.3	−0.2	−0.1
Liscannor	52 56N	9 23W	−0003	−0007	+0006	+0002	−0.4	−0.3	No data	
Seafield Point	52 48N	9 30W	−0006	−0014	+0004	−0004	−0.5	−0.4	No data	
Kilrush	52 38N	9 30W	−0006	+0027	+0057	−0016	−0.1	−0.2	−0.3	−0.1
Limerick Dock	52 40N	8 38W	+0135	+0141	+0141	+0219	+1.0	+0.7	−0.8	−0.2
			0500	**1100**	**0500**	**1100**				
COBH	51 51N	8 18 W	and	and	and	and	**4.1**	**3.2**	**1.3**	**0.4**
Standard port			**1700**	**2300**	**1700**	**2300**				
Tralee Bay Fenit Pier	52 16N	9 52W	−0057	−0017	−0029	−0109	+0.5	+0.2	+0.3	+0.1
Smerwick Harbour	52 12N	10 24W	−0107	−0027	−0041	−0121	−0.3	−0.4	No data	
Dingle Harbour	52 07N	10 15W	−0111	−0041	−0049	−0119	−0.1	0.0	+0.3	+0.4
Castlemaine Hbr Cromane Pt	52 08N	9 54W	−0026	−0006	−0017	−0037	+0.4	+0.2	+0.4	+0.2
Valentia Harbour										
Knights Town	51 56N	10 18W	−0118	−0038	−0056	−0136	−0.6	−0.4	−0.1	0.0
Ballinskelligs Bay Castle	51 49N	10 16W	−0119	−0039	−0054	−0134	−0.5	−0.5	−0.1	0.0
Kenmare River										
West Cove	51 46N	10 03W	−0113	−0033	−0049	−0129	−0.6	−0.5	−0.1	0.0
Dunkerron Harbour	51 52N	9 39W	−0117	−0027	−0050	−0140	−0.2	−0.3	+0.1	0.0

Location	Lat	Long	High Water		Low Water		MHWS	MHWN	MLWN	MLWS
Coulagh Bay										
Ballycrovane Hbr	51 43N	9 57W	−0116	−0036	−0053	−0133	−0.6	−0.5	−0.1	0.0
Black Ball Harbour	51 36N	10 02W	−0115	−0035	−0047	−0127	−0.7	−0.6	−0.1	+0.1
Bantry Bay										
Castletown Bearhaven	51 39N	9 54W	−0048	−0012	−0025	−0101	−0.9	−0.6	−0.1	0.0
Bantry	51 41N	9 28W	−0045	−0025	−0040	−0105	−0.7	−0.6	−0.2	+0.1
Dunmanus Bay										
Dunbeacon Harbour	51 37N	9 33W	−0057	−0025	−0032	−0104	−0.8	−0.7	−0.3	−0.1
Dunmanus Harbour	51 32N	9 40W	−0107	−0031	−0044	−0120	−0.7	−0.6	−0.2	0.0
Crookhaven	51 28N	9 44W	−0057	−0033	−0048	−0112	−0.8	−0.6	−0.4	−0.1
Skull	51 31N	9 32W	−0040	−0015	−0015	−0110	−0.9	−0.6	−0.2	0.0
Baltimore	51 29N	9 23W	−0025	−0005	−0010	−0050	−0.6	−0.3	+0.1	+0.2
Castletownshend	51 32N	9 10W	−0020	−0030	−0020	−0050	−0.4	−0.2	+0.1	+0.3
Clonakilty Bay	51 35N	8 50W	−0033	−0011	−0019	−0041	−0.3	−0.2	No data	
Courtmacsherry	51 38N	8 43W	−0025	−0008	−0008	−0015	−0.1	−0.1	−0.0	+0.1
Kinsale	51 42N	8 31W	−0019	−0005	−0009	−0023	−0.2	0.0	+0.1	+0.2
Roberts Cove	51 45N	8 19W	−0005	−0005	−0005	−0005	−0.1	0.0	0.0	+0.1
Cork Harbour										
Ringaskiddy	51 50N	8 19W	+0005	+0020	+0007	+0013	+0.1	+0.1	+0.1	+0.1
Marino Point	51 53N	8 20W	0000	+0010	0000	+0010	+0.1	+0.1	0.0	0.0
Cork City	51 54N	8 27W	+0005	+0010	+0020	+0010	+0.4	+0.4	+0.3	+0.2
Ballycotton	51 50N	8 01W	−0011	+0001	+0003	−0009	0.0	0.0	−0.1	0.0
Youghal	51 57N	7 51W	0000	+0010	+0010	0000	−0.2	−0.1	−0.1	−0.1
Dungarvan Harbour	52 05N	7 34W	+0004	+0012	+0007	−0001	0.0	+0.1	−0.2	0.0
Waterford Harbour										
Dunmore East	52 09N	6 59W	+0008	+0003	0000	0000	+0.1	0.0	+0.1	+0.2
Cheekpoint	52 16N	7 00W	+0022	+0020	+0020	+0020	+0.3	+0.2	+0.2	+0.1
Kilmokea Point	52 17N	7 00W	+0026	+0022	+0020	+0020	+0.2	+0.1	+0.1	+0.1
Waterford	52 16N	7 07W	+0057	+0057	+0046	+0046	+0.4	+0.3	−0.1	+0.1
New Ross	52 24N	6 57W	+0100	+0030	+0055	+0130	+0.3	+0.4	+0.3	+0.4
Baginbun Head	52 10N	6 50W	+0003	+0003	−0008	−0008	−0.2	−0.1	+0.2	+0.2
Great Saltee	52 07N	6 37W	+0019	+0009	−0004	+0006	−0.3	−0.4	No data	
Carnsore Point	52 10N	6 22W	+0029	+0019	−0002	+0008	−1.1	−1.0	No data	
Rosslare Europort	52 15N	6 21W	+0045	+0035	+0015	−0005	−2.2	−1.8	−0.5	−0.1
Wexford Harbour	52 20N	6 27W	+0126	+0126	+0118	+0108	−2.1	−1.7	−0.3	+0.1

DENMARK *Time zone −0100*

			0300	0700	0100	0800	MHWS	MHWN	MLWN	MLWS
ESBJERG	55 28N	8 27E	and	and	and	and	1.9	1.5	0.5	0.1
Standard port			1500	1900	1300	2000				
Hirtshals	57 36N	9 58E	+0055	+0320	+0340	+0100	−1.6	−1.3	−0.4	−0.1
Hanstholm	57 08N	8 36E	+0100	+0340	+0340	+0130	−1.6	−1.2	−0.4	−0.1
Thyborøn	56 42N	8 14E	+0120	+0230	+0410	+0210	−1.5	−1.2	−0.4	−0.1
Torsminde	56 22N	8 07E	+0045	+0050	+0040	+0010	−1.3	−1.0	−0.4	−0.1
Hvide Sande	56 00N	8 08E	0000	+0010	−0015	−0025	−1.1	−0.8	−0.3	−0.1
Blavands Huk	55 33N	8 05E	−0120	−0110	−0050	−0100	−0.1	−0.1	−0.2	−0.1
Esbjerg, Gradyb Bar	55 26N	8 15E	−0130	−0115	No data	No data	−0.4	−0.3	−0.2	−0.1
Havneby (Rømø)	55 05N	8 34E	−0040	−0005	0000	−0020	0.0	+0.1	−0.2	−0.2
Hojer	54 58N	8 40E	−0020	+0015	No data	No data	+0.5	+0.6	−0.1	−0.1

GERMANY *Time zone −0100*

			0100	0600	0100	0800	MHWS	MHWN	MLWN	MLWS
HELGOLAND	54 11N	7 53E	and	and	and	and	2.7	2.4	0.5	0.0
Standard port			1300	1800	1300	2000				
Lister Tief, List	55 01N	8 26E	+0252	+0240	+0201	+0210	−0.7	−0.6	−0.3	0.0
Hörnum	54 45N	8 18E	+0223	+0218	+0131	+0137	−0.4	−0.3	−0.2	0.0
Amrum - Hafen	54 38N	8 23E	+0138	+0137	+0128	+0134	+0.2	+0.2	−0.1	0.0
Dagebüll	54 44N	8 41E	+0226	+0217	+0211	+0225	+0.5	+0.5	−0.2	0.0
Suderoogsand	54 25N	8 30E	+0116	+0102	+0038	+0122	+0.5	+0.4	0.0	0.0
River Hever, Husum	54 28N	9 01E	+0205	+0152	+0118	+0200	+1.1	+1.0	−0.1	0.0
Suederhoeft	54 16N	8 42E	+0103	+0056	+0051	+0112	+0.7	+0.6	−0.2	0.0
Eidersperrwerk	54 16N	8 51E	+0120	+0115	+0130	+0155	+0.7	+0.6	−0.1	0.0
Linnenplate	54 13N	8 40E	+0047	+0046	+0034	+0046	+0.7	+0.6	−0.1	−0.1
Büsum	54 07N	8 52E	+0054	+0049	−0001	+0027	+0.9	+0.8	−0.1	0.0

			0200	0800	0200	0900	MHWS	MHWN	MLWN	MLWS
CUXHAVEN	53 52N	8 43E	and	and	and	and	3.8	3.4	0.9	0.5
Standard port			1400	2000	1400	2100				
River Elbe Großer Vogelsand	54 00N	8 29E	−0044	−0046	−0101	−0103	0.0	0.0	+0.1	−0.1
Scharhörn	53 58N	8 28E	−0045	−0047	−0101	−0103	0.0	0.0	0.0	−0.1
Otterndorf	53 50N	8 52E	+0029	+0029	+0027	+0027	−0.1	−0.1	−0.1	0.0

TIDES

Location	Lat	Long	High Water		Low Water		MHWS	MHWN	MLWN	MLWS
Brunsbüttel	53 53N	9 08E	+0057	+0105	+0121	+0112	−0.3	−0.2	−0.1	0.0
Glückstadt	53 47N	9 25E	+0205	+0214	+0220	+0213	−0.2	−0.1	−0.1	0.0
Stadersand	53 38N	9 32E	+0241	+0245	+0300	+0254	−0.1	0.0	−0.2	0.0
Schulau	53 34N	9 42E	+0304	+0315	+0337	+0321	+0.1	+0.2	−0.3	−0.1
Seemannshoeft	53 32N	9 53E	+0324	+0332	+0403	+0347	+0.3	+0.3	−0.4	−0.2
Hamburg	53 33N	9 58E	+0338	+0346	+0422	+0406	+0.3	+0.4	−0.4	−0.3
			0200	0800	0200	0900				
WILHELMSHAVEN	53 31N	8 09E	and	and	and	and	**4.3**	**3.8**	**0.6**	**0.0**
Standard port			1400	2000	1400	2100				
River Weser										
Alter Weser lt ho	53 32N	8 08E	−0055	−0048	−0015	−0029	−0.6	−0.5	+0.4	+0.5
Dwarsgat	53 43N	8 18E	−0015	+0002	−0006	−0001	−0.1	0.0	+0.4	+0.5
Bremerhaven	53 33N	8 34E	+0029	+0046	+0033	+0038	−0.2	−0.1	−0.1	−0.1
Nordenham	53 28N	8 29E	+0051	+0109	+0055	+0058	−0.2	−0.1	−0.4	−0.2
Brake	53 19N	8 29E	+0120	+0119	+0143	+0155	−0.3	−0.2	−0.4	−0.2
Elsfleth	53 16N	8 29E	+0137	+0137	+0206	+0216	−0.2	−0.1	−0.3	0.0
Vegesack	53 10N	8 37E	+0208	+0204	+0250	+0254	−0.2	−0.2	−0.5	−0.2
Bremen	53 07N	8 43E	+0216	+0211	+0311	+0314	−0.1	−0.1	−0.6	−0.3
River Jade										
Wangerooge East	53 46N	7 59E	−0058	−0053	−0024	−0034	−0.5	−0.4	+0.5	+0.4
Wangerooge West	53 47N	7 52E	−0101	−0058	−0035	−0045	−0.6	−0.5	+0.4	+0.4
Schillig	53 42N	8 03E	−0031	−0025	−0006	−0014	−0.3	−0.2	+0.4	+0.4
Hooksiel	53 39N	8 05E	−0023	−0022	−0008	−0012	−0.5	−0.4	0.0	0.0
			0200	0700	0200	0800				
HELGOLAND	54 11N	7 53E	and	and	and	and	**2.7**	**2.4**	**0.5**	**0.0**
Standard port			1400	1900	1400	2000				
East Frisian Islands and coast										
Spiekeroog	53 45N	7 41E	+0003	−0003	−0031	−0012	+0.4	+0.3	−0.1	0.0
Neuharlingersiel	53 42N	7 42E	+0014	+0008	−0024	−0013	+0.5	+0.4	−0.1	−0.1
Langeoog	53 43N	7 30E	+0003	−0001	−0034	−0018	+0.3	+0.3	0.0	0.0
Norderney (Riffgat)	53 42N	7 09E	−0024	−0030	−0056	−0045	+0.1	+0.1	0.0	0.0
Norddeich Hafen	53 39N	7 09E	−0018	−0017	−0029	−0012	+0.1	+0.1	−0.1	−0.1
Juist	53 40N	7 00E	−0026	−0032	−0019	−0008	+0.6	+0.5	+0.4	+0.4
River Ems										
Memmert	53 38N	6 54E	−0032	−0038	−0114	−0103	+0.5	+0.5	+0.3	+0.4
Borkum (Fischerbalje)	53 33N	6 45E	−0048	−0052	−0124	−0105	+0.4	+0.4	+0.3	+0.4
Emshorn	53 30N	6 50E	−0037	−0041	−0108	−0047	+0.6	+0.5	+0.3	+0.4
Knock	53 20N	7 02E	+0018	+0005	−0028	+0004	+1.0	+1.0	+0.4	+0.4
Emden	53 20N	7 11E	+0041	+0028	−0011	+0022	+1.3	+1.3	+0.4	+0.4

NETHERLANDS *Time zone −0100*

Location	Lat	Long	High Water		Low Water		MHWS	MHWN	MLWN	MLWS
			0200	0700	0200	0800				
HELGOLAND	54 11N	7 53E	and	and	and	and	**2.7**	**2.4**	**0.5**	**0.0**
Standard port			1400	1900	1400	2000				
Delfzijl	53 20N	6 56E	+0020	−0005	−0040	0000	+1.0	+1.0	+0.3	+0.4
Eemshaven	53 26N	6 52E	−0025	−0045	−0115	−0045	+0.5	+0.5	+0.3	+0.4
Huibergat	53 35N	6 24E	−0150	−0150	−0210	−0210	0.0	0.0	+0.2	+0.3
Schiermonnikoog	53 28N	6 12E	−0120	−0130	−0240	−0220	+0.2	+0.1	+0.2	+0.3
Waddenzee										
Lauwersoog	53 25N	6 12E	−0130	−0145	−0235	−0220	+0.2	+0.2	+0.2	+0.5
Nes	53 26N	5 47E	−0135	−0150	−0245	−0225	+0.2	+0.2	+0.2	+0.5
West Terschelling	53 22N	5 13E	−0220	−0250	−0335	−0310	−0.3	−0.2	+0.1	+0.3
Vlieland-Haven	53 18N	5 06E	−0250	−0320	−0355	−0330	−0.3	−0.2	+0.1	+0.4
Harlingen	53 10N	5 25E	−0155	−0245	−0210	−0130	−0.3	−0.3	0.0	+0.4
Kornwerderzand	53 04N	5 20E	−0210	−0315	−0300	−0215	−0.5	−0.4	0.0	+0.3
Den Oever	52 56N	5 02E	−0245	−0410	−0400	−0305	−0.7	−0.6	−0.1	+0.3
Oudeschild	53 02N	4 51E	−0310	−0420	−0445	−0400	−0.8	−0.7	0.0	+0.3
Den Helder	52 58N	4 45E	−0410	−0520	−0520	−0430	−0.8	−0.7	+0.1	+0.2
Noordwinning (Platform K13–A)	53 13N	3 13E	−0420	−0430	−0520	−0530	−0.9	−0.7	+0.2	+0.3
			0300	0900	0400	1000				
VLISSINGEN	51 27N	3 36E	and	and	and	and	**5.0**	**4.1**	**1.1**	**0.5**
Standard port			1500	2100	1600	2200				
IJmuiden	52 28N	4 35E	+0145	+0140	+0305	+0325	−2.8	−2.3	−0.7	−0.2
Scheveningen	52 06N	4 16E	+0105	+0100	+0220	+0245	−2.7	−2.2	−0.7	−0.2
Europlatform	52 00N	3 17E	+0005	−0005	−0030	−0055	−2.7	−2.2	−0.6	−0.1
Nieuwe Waterweg										
HOEK VAN HOLLAND			*Standard port, no Secondaries*							
Maassluis	51 55N	4 15E	+0155	+0115	+0100	+0310	−2.9	−2.3	−0.8	−0.2
Nieuwe Maas, Vlaardingen	51 54N	4 21E	+0150	+0120	+0130	+0330	−2.9	−2.3	−0.8	−0.2

Location	Lat	Long	High Water		Low Water		MHWS	MHWN	MLWN	MLWS
Haringvlietsluizen	51 50N	4 02E	+0015	+0015	+0015	−0020	−2.0	−1.9	−0.7	−0.2
Ooster Schelde										
Roompot Buiten	51 37N	3 40E	−0015	+0005	+0005	−0020	−1.3	−1.1	−0.4	−0.1
Walcheren, Westkapelle	51 31N	3 27E	−0025	−0015	−0010	−0025	−0.6	−0.6	−0.2	−0.1
Westerschelde										
Terneuzen	51 20N	3 50E	+0020	+0020	+0020	+0030	+0.3	+0.4	0.0	+0.1
Hansweert	51 27N	4 00E	+0100	+0050	+0040	+0100	+0.6	+0.7	0.0	0.0
Bath	51 24N	4 13E	+0125	+0115	+0115	+0140	+1.1	+1.0	+0.1	+0.1

BELGIUM *Time zone −0100*

Location	Lat	Long	High Water		Low Water		MHWS	MHWN	MLWN	MLWS
Antwerpen	51 21N	4 14E	+0128	+0116	+0121	+0144	+1.2	+1.0	+0.1	+0.1
Zeebrugge	51 21N	3 12E	−0035	−0015	−0020	−0035	+0.2	+0.2	+0.4	+0.2
Blankenberge	51 19N	3 07E	−0040	−0040	−0040	−0040	−0.3	0.0	+0.3	+0.2
Oostende	51 14N	2 56E	−0055	−0040	−0030	−0045	+0.5	+0.5	+0.4	+0.2
Nieuwpoort	51 09N	2 43E	−0110	−0050	−0035	−0045	+0.7	+0.6	+0.5	+0.2

FRANCE *Time zone −0100*

Location	Lat	Long	High Water		Low Water		MHWS	MHWN	MLWN	MLWS
DUNKERQUE	51 03N	2 22E	0200 and 1400	0800 and 2000	0200 and 1400	0900 and 2100	6.0	5.0	1.5	0.6
Standard port										
Gravelines	51 01N	2 06E	−0010	−0015	−0010	−0005	+0.4	+0.3	+1.0	0.0
Sandettie Bank	51 09N	1 47E	−0015	−0025	−0020	−0005	+0.1	−0.1	−0.1	−0.1
Calais	51 58N	1 51E	−0020	−0030	−0015	−0005	+1.2	+0.9	+0.6	+0.3
Wissant	50 53N	1 40E	−0035	−0050	−0030	−0010	+1.9	+1.5	+0.8	+0.4
DIEPPE	49 56N	1 05E	0100 and 1300	0600 and 1800	0100 and 1300	0700 and 1900	9.3	7.4	2.5	0.8
Standard port										
Boulogne	50 44N	1 35E	+0014	+0027	+0035	+0033	−0.4	−0.2	+0.1	+0.3
Le Touquet, Étaples	50 31N	1 35E	+0005	+0015	+0030	+0030	+0.2	+0.3	+0.4	+0.4
Berck	50 24N	1 34E	+0005	+0015	+0030	+0030	+0.5	+0.5	+0.4	+0.4
La Somme										
Le Hourdel	50 13N	1 34E	+0020	+0020	*No data*	*No data*	+0.8	+0.6	*No data*	
St Valéry	50 11N	1 37E	+0035	+0035	*No data*	*No data*	+0.9	+0.7	*No data*	
Cayeux	50 11N	1 29E	0000	+0005	+0015	+0010	+0.5	+0.6	+0.4	+0.4
Le Tréport	50 04N	1 22E	+0005	0000	+0007	+0007	+0.1	+0.1	0.0	+0.1
St Valéry–en–Caux	49 52N	0 42E	−0005	−0005	−0015	−0020	−0.5	−0.4	−0.1	−0.1
Fécamp	49 46N	0 22E	−0015	−0010	−0030	−0040	−1.0	−0.6	+0.3	+0.4
Etretat	49 42N	0 12E	−0020	−0020	−0045	−0050	−1.2	−0.8	+0.3	+0.4
LE HAVRE	49 29N	0 07E	0000 and 1200	0500 and 1700	0000 and 1200	0700 and 1900	7.9	6.6	2.8	1.2
Standard port										
Antifer (Le Havre)	49 39N	0 09E	+0025	+0015	+0005	−0005	+0.1	0.0	0.0	0.0
La Seine										
Chenal du Rouen	49 26N	0 07E	0000	0000	−0005	+0015	+0.1	0.0	0.0	−0.1
Honfleur	49 25N	0 14E	−0135	−0135	+0015	+0040	+0.1	+0.1	+0.1	+0.3
Tancarville	49 28N	0 28E	−0105	−0100	+0105	+0140	−0.1	−0.1	0.0	+1.0
Quilleboeuf	49 28N	0 32E	−0045	−0050	+0120	+0200	0.0	−0.1	+0.8	+2.3
Vatteville	49 29N	0 40E	+0005	−0020	+0225	+0250	0.0	−0.1	+0.8	+2.3
Caudebec	49 32N	0 44E	+0020	−0015	+0230	+0300	−0.3	−0.2	+0.9	+2.4
Heurteauville	49 27N	0 49E	+0110	+0025	+0310	+0330	−0.5	−0.2	+1.1	+2.7
Duclair	49 29N	0 53E	+0225	+0150	+0355	+0410	−0.4	−0.3	+1.4	+3.3
Rouen	49 27N	1 06E	+0440	+0415	+0525	+0525	−0.2	−0.1	+1.6	+3.6
Trouville	49 22N	0 05E	−0100	−0010	0000	+0005	+0.4	+0.3	+0.3	+0.1
Dives	49 18N	0 05W	−0100	−0010	0000	0000	+0.3	+0.2	+0.2	+0.1
Ouistreham	49 17N	0 15W	−0045	−0010	−0005	0000	−0.3	−0.3	−0.2	−0.3
Courseulles-sur-Mer	49 20N	0 27W	−0045	−0015	−0020	−0025	−0.5	−0.5	−0.1	−0.1
Arromanches	49 21N	0 37W	−0055	−0025	−0025	−0035	−0.6	−0.6	−0.2	−0.2
Port-en-Bessin	49 21N	0 45W	−0055	−0030	−0030	−0035	−0.7	−0.7	−0.2	−0.1
Alpha-Baie de Seine	49 49N	0 20W	+0030	+0020	−0005	−0020	−1.0	−0.9	−0.4	−0.2
CHERBOURG	49 39N	1 38W	0300 and 1500	1000 and 2200	0400 and 1600	1000 and 2200	6.4	5.0	2.5	1.1
Standard port										
Rade de la Capelle	49 25N	1 05W	+0115	+0050	+0130	+0115	+0.8	+0.9	+0.1	+0.1
Iles Saint Marcouf	49 30N	1 08W	+0115	+0050	+0125	+0110	+0.6	+0.7	+0.1	+0.1
St Vaast-la-Hougue	49 34N	1 16W	+0120	+0050	+0120	+0115	+0.3	+0.5	0.0	−0.1
Barfleur	49 40N	1 15W	+0110	+0055	+0050	+0050	+0.1	+0.3	0.0	0.0
Omonville	49 42N	1 50W	−0010	−0010	−0015	−0015	−0.1	−0.1	0.0	0.0
Goury	49 43N	1 57W	−0100	−0040	−0105	−0120	+1.7	+1.6	+1.0	+0.3

Location	Lat	Long	High Water		Low Water		MHWS	MHWN	MLWN	MLWS

CHANNEL ISLANDS *Time zone UT*

Location	Lat	Long	High Water		Low Water		MHWS	MHWN	MLWN	MLWS
ST HELIER	49 11N	2 07W	0300 and 1500	0900 and 2100	0200 and 1400	0900 and 2100	11.0	8.1	4.0	1.4
Standard port										
Alderney, Braye	49 43N	2 12W	+0050	+0040	+0025	+0105	−4.8	−3.4	−1.5	−0.5
Sark, Maseline Pier	49 26N	2 21W	+0005	+0015	+0005	+0010	−2.1	−1.5	−0.6	−0.3
Guernsey, ST PETER PORT	49 27N	2 31W	*Standard port (no Secondaries)*							
Jersey										
St Catherine Bay	49 13N	2 01W	0000	+0010	+0010	+0010	0.0	−0.1	0.0	+0.1
Bouley Bay	49 14N	2 05W	+0002	+0002	+0004	+0004	−0.3	−0.3	−0.1	−0.1
Les Ecrehou	49 17N	1 56W	+0005	+0009	+0011	+0009	−0.2	+0.1	−0.2	0.0
Les Minquiers	48 57N	2 08W	−0014	−0018	−0001	−0008	+0.5	+0.6	+0.1	+0.1

FRANCE *Time zone −0100*

Location	Lat	Long	High Water		Low Water		MHWS	MHWN	MLWN	MLWS
ST MALO	48 38N	2 02W	0100 and 1300	0800 and 2000	0300 and 1500	0800 and 2000	12.2	9.3	4.2	1.5
Standard port										
Les Ardentes	48 58N	1 52W	+0010	+0010	+0020	+0010	0.0	−0.1	0.0	−0.1
Iles Chausey	48 52N	1 49W	+0005	+0005	+0015	+0015	+0.8	+0.7	+0.6	+0.4
Diélette	49 33N	1 52W	+0045	+0035	+0020	+0035	−2.5	−1.9	−0.7	−0.3
Carteret	49 22N	1 47W	+0030	+0020	+0015	+0030	−1.6	−1.2	−0.5	−0.2
Portbail	49 18N	1 45W	+0030	+0025	+0025	+0030	−0.8	−0.6	−0.2	−0.1
St Germain sur Ay	49 14N	1 36W	+0025	+0025	+0035	+0035	−0.7	−0.5	0.0	+0.1
Le Sénéquet	49 05N	1 40W	+0015	+0015	+0025	+0025	−0.3	−0.3	+0.1	+0.1
Regnéville sur Mer	49 01N	1 33W	+0010	+0010	+0030	+0020	+0.5	+0.4	+0.2	0.0
Granville	48 50N	1 36W	+0005	+0005	+0020	+0010	+0.7	+0.5	+0.3	+0.1
Cancale	48 40N	1 51W	0000	0000	+0010	+0010	+0.8	+0.6	+0.3	+0.1
Ile des Hebihens	48 37N	2 11W	0000	0000	−0005	−0005	−0.2	−0.2	−0.1	−0.1
St Cast	48 38N	2 15W	0000	0000	−0005	−0005	−0.2	−0.2	−0.1	−0.1
Erquy	48 38N	2 28W	−0010	−0005	−0025	−0015	−0.6	−0.5	0.0	0.0
Dahouët	48 35N	2 34W	−0010	−0010	−0025	−0020	−0.9	−0.7	−0.2	−0.2
Le Légué (Buoy)	48 34N	2 41W	−0010	−0005	−0020	−0015	−0.8	−0.5	−0.2	−0.1
Binic	48 36N	2 49W	−0010	−0010	−0030	−0015	−0.8	−0.7	−0.2	−0.2
St Quay-Portrieux	48 38N	2 49W	−0010	−0005	−0025	−0020	−0.9	−0.7	−0.2	−0.1
Paimpol	48 47N	3 02W	−0010	−0005	−0035	−0025	−1.4	−1.0	−0.4	−0.2
Ile de Bréhat	48 51N	3 00W	−0015	−0015	−0045	−0035	−1.9	−1.4	−0.6	−0.3
Les Héaux de Bréhat	48 55N	3 05W	−0020	−0015	−0055	−0045	−2.4	−1.7	−0.7	−0.3
Lézardrieux	48 47N	3 06W	−0020	−0015	−0055	−0045	−1.7	−1.3	−0.5	−0.2
Port-Béni	48 51N	3 10W	−0025	−0025	−0105	−0050	−2.4	−1.7	−0.6	−0.2
Tréguier	48 47N	3 13W	−0020	−0020	−0100	−0045	−2.3	−1.6	−0.6	−0.2
Perros-Guirec	48 49N	3 28W	−0040	−0045	−0120	−0105	−2.9	−2.0	−0.8	−0.3
Ploumanac'h	48 50N	3 29W	−0035	−0040	−0120	−0100	−2.9	−2.0	−0.7	−0.2
BREST	48 23N	4 30W	0000 and 1200	0600 and 1800	0000 and 1200	0600 and 1800	7.0	5.5	2.7	1.1
Standard port										
Trébeurden	48 46N	3 35W	+0100	+0110	+0120	+0100	+2.2	+1.8	+0.8	+0.3
Locquirec	48 42N	3 38W	+0100	+0110	+0120	+0100	+2.1	+1.7	+0.7	+0.2
Anse de Primel	48 43N	3 50W	+0100	+0110	+0120	+0100	+2.0	+1.6	+0.7	+0.2
Chateau du Taureau (Morlaix)	48 41N	3 53W	+0055	+0105	+0115	+0055	+1.9	+1.6	+0.7	+0.2
Roscoff	48 43N	3 58W	+0055	+0105	+0115	+0055	+1.8	+1.5	+0.7	+0.2
Ile de Batz	48 44N	4 00W	+0045	+0100	+0105	+0055	+1.9	+1.5	+0.8	+0.3
Brignogan	48 40N	4 19W	+0040	+0045	+0100	+0040	+1.4	+1.1	+0.5	+0.1
L'Aber Wrac'h	48 36N	4 34W	+0030	+0030	+0040	+0035	+0.7	+0.6	+0.1	−0.1
Aber Benoit	48 35N	4 37W	+0022	+0025	+0035	+0020	+0.9	+0.8	+0.3	+0.1
Portsall	48 34N	4 43W	+0015	+0020	+0025	+0015	+0.5	+0.4	0.0	−0.1
L'Aber Ildut	48 28N	4 45W	+0010	+0010	+0023	+0010	+0.3	+0.2	−0.1	−0.1
Ouessant, Baie de Lampaul	48 27N	5 06W	+0010	+0010	0000	+0005	−0.1	−0.1	−0.1	−0.1
Molene	48 24N	4 58W	+0015	+0010	+0020	+0020	+0.3	+0.3	+0.1	+0.1
Le Conquet	48 22N	4 47W	0000	0000	+0005	+0005	−0.2	−0.2	−0.1	0.0
Le Trez Hir	48 21N	4 42W	−0005	−0005	−0015	−0010	−0.4	−0.4	−0.2	−0.1
Camaret	48 17N	4 35W	−0010	−0010	−0015	−0010	−0.4	−0.4	−0.3	−0.1
Morgat	48 13N	4 30W	−0005	−0010	−0020	−0005	−0.5	−0.4	−0.2	0.0
Douarnenez	48 06N	4 19W	−0010	−0010	−0020	−0010	−0.4	−0.4	−0.2	−0.1

Location	Lat	Long	High Water		Low Water		MHWS	MHWN	MLWN	MLWS
Ile de Sein	48 02N	4 51W	−0005	−0005	−0015	−0010	−0.9	−0.8	−0.4	−0.2
Anse de Feunteun Aod	48 02N	4 42W	−0030	−0040	−0035	−0025	−1.4	−1.2	−0.6	−0.2
Audierne	48 01N	4 33W	−0035	−0030	−0035	−0030	−1.8	−1.4	−0.7	−0.3
Le Guilvinec	47 48N	4 17W	−0010	−0025	−0025	−0015	−1.9	−1.5	−0.7	−0.2
Lesconil	47 48N	4 13W	−0010	−0030	−0030	−0020	−2.0	−1.5	−0.7	−0.2
Pont l'Abbe River, Loctudy	47 50N	4 10W	−0010	−0030	−0030	−0020	−2.1	−1.7	−0.8	−0.4
Odet River										
Bénodet	47 53N	4 07W	0000	−0020	−0025	−0015	−1.8	−1.4	−0.6	−0.2
Corniguel	47 58N	4 06W	+0015	+0010	−0015	−0010	−2.1	−1.7	−1.1	−0.8
Concarneau	47 52N	3 55W	−0010	−0030	−0030	−0020	−2.0	−1.6	−0.8	−0.3
Iles de Glenan, Ile de Penfret	47 44N	3 57W	−0005	−0030	−0030	−0020	−2.0	−1.6	−0.8	−0.3
Port Louis	47 42N	3 21W	+0005	−0020	−0020	−0010	−1.9	−1.5	−0.7	−0.2
Lorient	47 45N	3 21W	+0005	−0020	−0020	−0010	−1.9	−1.5	−0.7	−0.3
Hennebont	47 48N	3 17W	+0015	−0015	+0005	+0003	−2.0	−1.6	−0.9	−0.3
Ile de Groix, Port Tudy	47 39N	3 27W	0000	−0025	−0025	−0015	−1.9	−1.5	−0.7	−0.2
Port d'Etel	47 39N	3 12W	+0020	−0010	+0030	+0010	−2.1	−1.4	−0.5	+0.4
Port Haliguen	47 29N	3 06W	+0010	−0020	−0015	−0010	−1.7	−1.3	−0.7	−0.3
Port Maria	47 29N	3 08W	+0010	−0025	−0025	−0015	−1.7	−1.4	−0.7	−0.2
Belle Ile, Le Palais	47 21N	3 09W	+0005	−0025	−0025	−0010	−1.9	−1.4	−0.8	−0.3
Crac'h River, La Trinité	47 35N	3 01W	+0025	−0020	−0015	−0010	−1.7	−1.2	−0.6	−0.3
Golfe du Morbihan										
Port Navalo	47 33N	2 55W	+0030	−0005	−0010	−0005	−2.1	−1.6	−0.9	−0.4
Auray	47 40N	2 59W	+0035	0000	+0015	−0005	−2.3	−1.9	−1.2	−0.5
Arradon	47 37N	2 50W	+0135	+0145	+0140	+0115	−3.9	−3.1	−1.9	−0.8
Vannes	47 39N	2 46W	+0200	+0150	+0140	+0120	−3.8	−3.0	−2.1	−0.9
St Armel (Le Passage)	47 36N	2 43W	+0200	+0200	+0210	+0135	−3.8	−3.0	−2.0	−0.9
Le Logeo	47 33N	2 51W	+0140	+0140	+0145	+0115	−4.1	−3.2	−2.1	−0.9
Port du Crouesty	47 32N	2 54W	+0010	−0025	−0025	−0030	−2.1	−1.6	−0.9	−0.4
Ile de Houat	47 24N	2 57W	+0005	−0025	−0025	−0010	−1.8	−1.4	−0.7	−0.4
Ile de Hoëdic	47 20N	2 52W	+0010	−0035	−0025	−0020	−1.9	−1.5	−0.8	−0.4
Pénerf	47 31N	2 37W	+0015	−0025	−0015	−0015	−1.6	−1.2	−0.7	−0.4
Tréhiguier	47 30N	2 27W	+0035	−0020	−0005	−0010	−1.5	−1.1	−0.6	−0.4
Le Croisic	47 18N	2 31W	+0015	−0040	−0020	−0015	−1.6	−1.2	−0.7	−0.4
Le Pouliguen	47 17N	2 25W	+0020	−0025	−0020	−0025	−1.6	−1.2	−0.7	−0.4
Le Grand-Charpentier	47 13N	2 19W	+0015	−0045	−0025	−0020	−1.6	−1.2	−0.7	−0.4
Pornichet	47 16N	2 21W	+0020	−0045	−0022	−0022	−1.5	−1.1	−0.6	−0.3
La Loire										
St Nazaire	47 16N	2 12W	+0030	−0040	−0010	−0010	−1.2	−0.9	−0.5	−0.3
Donges	47 18N	2 05W	+0035	−0035	+0005	+0005	−1.1	−0.8	−0.6	−0.5
Cordemais	47 17N	1 54W	+0055	−0005	+0105	+0030	−0.8	−0.6	−0.8	−0.5
Le Pellerin	47 12N	1 46W	+0110	+0010	+0145	+0100	−0.8	−0.6	−1.0	−0.5
Nantes (Chantenay)	47 12N	1 35W	+0135	+0055	+0215	+0125	−0.7	−0.4	−0.9	−0.2
BREST	48 23N	4 30W	0500 and 1700	1100 and 2300	0500 and 1700	1100 and 2300	7.0	5.5	2.7	1.1
Standard port										
Pointe de Saint–Gildas	47 08N	2 15W	−0045	+0025	−0020	−0020	−1.4	−1.1	−0.6	−0.3
Pornic	47 06N	2 07W	−0050	+0030	−0010	−0010	−1.2	−0.9	−0.5	−0.3
Ile de Noirmoutier, L'Herbaudière	47 02N	2 18W	−0045	+0025	−0020	−0020	−1.5	−1.1	−0.6	−0.3
Fromentine	46 54N	2 10W	−0045	+0020	−0015	+0005	−1.8	−1.4	−0.9	−0.2
Ile de Yeu, Port Joinville	46 44N	2 21W	−0040	+0015	−0030	−0035	−2.0	−1.5	−0.8	−0.4
St Gilles-Croix-de-Vie	46 41N	1 56W	−0030	+0015	−0030	−0030	−1.9	−1.4	−0.7	−0.4
Les Sables d'Olonne	46 30N	1 48W	−0030	+0015	−0035	−0035	−1.8	−1.4	−0.7	−0.4
POINTE DE GRAVE	45 34N	1 04W	0000 and 1200	0600 and 1800	0000 and 1200	0500 and 1700	5.4	4.4	2.1	1.0
Standard port										
Ile de Ré, St Martin	46 12N	1 22W	+0005	−0030	−0025	−0030	+0.5	+0.3	+0.2	−0.1
La Pallice	46 10N	1 13W	+0015	−0030	−0020	−0025	+0.6	+0.5	+0.3	−0.1
La Rochelle	46 09N	1 09W	+0015	−0030	−0020	−0025	+0.6	+0.5	+0.3	−0.1
Ile d'Aix	46 01N	1 10W	+0015	−0040	−0025	−0030	+0.7	+0.5	+0.3	−0.1
La Charente, Rochefort	45 57N	0 58W	+0035	−0010	+0125	+0030	+1.1	+0.9	+0.1	−0.2
Le Chapus	45 51N	1 11W	+0015	−0040	−0015	−0025	+0.6	+0.6	+0.4	+0.2
La Cayenne	45 47N	1 08W	+0030	−0015	−0005	−0010	+0.2	+0.2	+0.3	0.0
Pointe de Gatseau	45 48N	1 14W	+0055	0000	−0020	−0015	−0.1	−0.1	+0.2	+0.1
Cordouan	45 35N	1 10W	−0010	−0010	−0025	−0015	−0.5	−0.4	−0.1	−0.2

Location	Lat	Long	High Water		Low Water		MHWS	MHWN	MLWN	MLWS
La Gironde										
Royan	45 37N	1 01W	0000	−0005	0000	0000	−0.2	−0.1	0.0	0.0
Richard	45 27N	0 56W	+0020	+0020	+0035	+0030	−0.1	−0.1	−0.4	−0.5
Lamena	45 20N	0 48W	+0035	+0045	+0125	+0100	+0.2	+0.1	−0.5	−0.3
Pauillac	45 12N	0 45W	+0100	+0100	+0205	+0135	+0.1	0.0	−1.0	−0.5
La Reuille	45 03N	0 36W	+0135	+0145	+0230	+0305	−0.2	−0.3	−1.3	−0.7
La Garonne										
Le Marquis	45 00N	0 33W	+0145	+0150	+0320	+0245	−0.3	−0.4	− 1.5	−0.9
Bordeaux	44 52N	0 33W	+0200	+0225	+0405	+0330	−0.1	−0.2	−1.7	−1.0
La Dordogne										
Libourne	44 55N	0 15W	+0250	+0305	+0540	+0525	−0.7	−0.9	−2.0	−0.4
Bassin d'Arcachon										
Cap Ferret	44 37N	1 15W	−0015	+0005	+0020	−0005	−1.4	−1.2	−0.8	−0.6
Arcachon (Eyrac)	44 40N	1 10W	+0010	+0020	+0030	+0005	−1.1	−1.0	−0.8	−0.6
L'Adour, Boucau	43 31N	1 31W	−0030	−0035	−0040	−0025	−1.2	−1.1	−0.4	−0.3
St Jean de Luz, Socoa	43 23N	1 40W	−0040	−0045	−0045	−0030	−1.1	−1.1	−0.6	−0.4

SPAIN *Time zone −0100*

Location	Lat	Long	High Water		Low Water		MHWS	MHWN	MLWN	MLWS
Pasajes	43 20N	1 56W	−0050	−0030	−0045	−0015	−1.2	−1.3	−0.5	−0.5
San Sebastian	43 19N	1 59W	−0110	−0030	−0040	−0020	−1.2	−1.2	−0.5	−0.4
Guetaria	43 18N	2 12W	−0110	−0030	−0040	−0020	−1.0	−1.0	−0.5	−0.4
Lequeitio	43 22N	2 30W	−0115	−0035	−0045	−0025	−1.2	−1.2	−0.5	−0.4
Bermeo	43 25N	2 43W	−0055	−0015	−0025	−0005	−0.8	−0.7	−0.5	−0.4
Abra de Bilbao	43 21N	3 02W	−0125	−0045	−0055	−0035	−1.2	−1.2	−0.5	−0.4
Portugalete (Bilbao)	43 20N	3 02W	−0100	−0020	−0030	−0010	−0.7	−1.2	−0.2	−0.6
Castro Urdiales	43 23N	3 13W	−0040	−0120	−0110	−0020	−1.4	−1.5	−0.6	−0.6
Ria de Santona	43 26N	3 28W	−0005	−0045	−0035	+0015	−0.7	−1.2	−0.3	−0.7
Santander	43 28N	3 47W	−0020	−0100	−0050	0000	−0.7	−1.2	−0.3	−0.7
Ria de Suances	43 27N	4 03W	0000	−0030	−0020	+0020	−1.5	−1.5	−0.6	−0.6
San Vicente de la Barquera	43 23N	4 24W	−0020	−0100	−0050	0000	−1.5	−1.5	−0.6	−0.6
Ria de Tina Mayor	43 24N	4 31W	−0020	−0100	−0050	0000	−1.4	−1.5	−0.6	−0.6
Ribadesella	43 28N	5 04W	+0005	−0020	−0020	+0020	−1.4	−1.3	−0.6	−0.4
Gijon	43 34N	5 42W	−0005	−0030	−0030	+0010	−1.0	−1.4	−0.4	−0.7
Luanco	43 37N	5 47W	−0010	−0035	−0035	+0005	−1.4	−1.3	−0.6	−0.4
Aviles	43 35N	5 56W	−0100	−0040	−0050	−0015	−1.2	−1.6	−0.5	−0.7
San Esteban de Pravia	43 34N	6 05W	−0005	−0030	−0030	+0010	−1.4	−1.3	−0.6	−0.4
Luarca	43 33N	6 32W	+0010	−0015	−0015	+0025	−1.2	−1.1	−0.5	−0.3
Ribadeo	43 33N	7 02W	+0010	−0015	−0015	+0025	−1.3	−1.5	−0.7	−0.8
Burela	43 39N	7 21W	+0010	−0015	−0015	+0025	−1.5	−1.5	−0.7	−0.6
Ria de Vivero	43 43N	7 36W	+0010	−0015	−0015	+0025	−1.4	−1.3	−0.6	−0.4
Santa Marta de Ortigueira	43 41N	7 51W	−0020	0000	−0020	+0010	−1.3	−1.2	−0.6	−0.4
Ferrol (La Grana)	43 28N	8 16W	−0045	−0100	−0010	−0105	−1.6	−1.4	−0.7	−0.4
La Coruna	43 22N	8 24W	−0110	−0050	−0030	−0100	−1.6	−1.6	−0.6	−0.5
Ria de Corme	43 16N	8 58W	−0025	−0005	+0015	−0015	−1.7	−1.6	−0.6	−0.5
Ria de Camarinas	43 08N	9 11W	−0115	−0055	0000	−0105	−1.6	−1.6	−0.6	−0.5

Location	Lat	Long	High Water		Low Water		MHWS	MHWN	MLWN	MLWS
LISBOA	38 42N	9 07W	0500 and 1700	1000 and 2200	0300 and 1500	0800 and 2000	3.8	2.9	1.5	0.6
Standard port										
Corcubion	42 57N	9 12W	+0055	+0110	+0120	+0135	−0.5	−0.3	−0.3	−0.1
Muros	42 46N	9 03W	+0050	+0105	+0115	+0130	−0.3	−0.2	−0.2	−0.1
Ria de Arosa, Villagarcia	42 37N	8 47W	+0040	+0100	+0110	+0120	−0.3	−0.1	−0.2	−0.1
Ria de Pontevedra, Marin	42 24N	8 42W	+0050	+0110	+0120	+0130	−0.5	−0.3	−0.3	−0.1
Vigo	42 15N	8 43W	+0040	+0100	+0105	+0125	+0.1	−0.3	0.0	−0.3
Bayona	42 07N	8 51W	+0035	+0050	+0100	+0115	−0.3	−0.2	−0.2	−0.1
La Guardia	41 54N	8 53W	+0040	+0055	+0105	+0120	−0.5	−0.3	−0.3	−0.2

PORTUGAL *Time zone UT*

Location	Lat	Long	High Water		Low Water		MHWS	MHWN	MLWN	MLWS
LISBOA	38 42N	9 07W	0400 and 1600	0900 and 2100	0400 and 1600	0900 and 2100	3.8	2.9	1.5	0.6
Standard port										
Viana do Castelo	41 41N	8 50W	−0020	0000	+0010	+0015	−0.4	−0.3	−0.1	−0.1
Esposende	41 32N	8 47W	−0020	0000	+0010	+0015	−0.6	−0.4	−0.2	−0.1

Location	Lat	Long	High Water		Low Water		MHWS	MHWN	MLWN	MLWS
Povoa de Varzim	41 22N	8 46W	−0020	0000	+0010	+0015	−0.3	−0.2	−0.1	−0.1
Porto de Leixoes	41 11N	8 42W	−0025	−0010	0000	+0010	−0.4	−0.3	−0.1	−0.1
Rio Douro										
Entrance	41 09N	8 40W	−0010	+0005	+0015	+0025	−0.6	−0.3	−0.1	+0.1
Oporto (Porto)	41 08N	8 37W	+0002	+0002	+0040	+0040	−0.5	−0.3	−0.2	0.0
Porto de Aveiro	40 39N	8 45W	+0005	+0010	+0010	+0015	−0.5	−0.3	−0.1	0.0
Figueira da Foz	40 09N	8 51W	−0015	0000	+0010	+0020	−0.4	−0.3	−0.1	−0.1
Nazaré (Pederneira)	39 35N	9 04W	−0030	−0015	−0005	+0005	−0.5	−0.3	−0.1	0.0
Peniche	39 21N	9 22W	−0035	−0015	−0005	0000	−0.4	−0.3	−0.1	0.0
Ericeira	38 58N	9 25W	−0040	−0025	−0010	−0010	−0.4	−0.2	−0.1	0.0
River Tagus (Rio Tejo)										
Cascais	38 42N	9 25W	−0040	−0025	−0015	−0010	−0.3	−0.2	0.0	+0.1
Paco de Arcos	38 41N	9 18W	−0020	−0030	−0005	−0005	−0.4	−0.3	−0.2	−0.1
Pedroucos	38 42N	9 13W	−0010	−0015	0000	0000	−0.1	0.0	−0.1	0.0
Sesimbra	38 26N	9 07W	−0045	−0030	−0020	−0010	−0.4	−0.3	−0.1	0.0
Setubal	38 30N	8 54W	−0020	−0015	−0005	+0005	−0.4	−0.3	−0.1	−0.1
Porto de Sines	37 57N	8 53W	−0050	−0030	−0020	−0010	−0.4	−0.3	−0.1	+0.1
Milfontes	37 43N	8 47W	−0040	−0030	*No data*	*No data*	−0.1	0.0	0.0	+0.1
Arrifana	37 17N	8 52W	−0030	−0020	*No data*	*No data*	−0.1	+0.1	−0.1	+0.1
Enseada de Belixe	37 01N	8 58W	−0050	−0030	−0020	−0015	+0.3	+0.3	+0.2	+0.2
Lagos	37 06N	8 40W	−0100	−0040	−0030	−0025	−0.4	−0.3	−0.1	0.0
Portimao	37 07N	8 32W	−0100	−0040	−0030	−0025	−0.5	−0.3	−0.1	+0.1
Ponta do Altar	37 06N	8 31W	−0100	−0040	−0030	−0025	−0.3	−0.2	−0.1	0.0
Enseada de Albufeira	37 05N	8 15W	−0035	+0015	−0005	0000	−0.2	−0.1	0.0	+0.1
Porto de Faro-Olhao	36 59N	7 52W	−0050	−0030	−0015	+0005	−0.5	−0.3	−0.1	0.0
Rio Guadiana										
Vila Real de Santo António	37 12N	7 25W	−0050	−0015	−0010	0000	−0.4	−0.3	−0.1	+0.1
			0500	1000	0500	1100				
LISBOA	38 42N	9 07W	and	and	and	and	3.8	2.9	1.5	0.6
Standard port			1700	2200	1700	2300				

SPAIN *Time zone −0100*

Location	Lat	Long	High Water		Low Water		MHWS	MHWN	MLWN	MLWS
Ayamonte	37 13N	7 25W	+0005	+0015	+0025	+0045	−0.7	−0.5	−0.1	−0.2
Ria de Huelva										
Bar	37 08N	6 52W	0000	+0015	+0035	+0030	−0.1	−0.5	−0.1	−0.4
Rio Guadalquivir										
Bar (Chipiona)	36 45N	6 26W	−0005	+0005	+0020	+0030	−0.6	−0.4	−0.2	−0.2
Bonanza	36 48N	6 20W	+0025	+0040	+0100	+0120	−0.8	−0.5	−0.4	−0.1
Corta de los Jerónimos	37 08N	6 06W	+0210	+0230	+0255	+0345	−1.2	−0.8	−0.5	−0.1
Sevilla	37 23N	6 00W	+0400	+0430	+0510	+0545	−1.7	−1.1	−0.6	−0.1
Bahia de Cadiz										
Rota	36 37N	6 21W	−0010	+0010	+0025	+0015	−0.7	−0.6	−0.3	−0.1
Puerto de Santa Maria	36 36N	6 13W	+0006	+0006	+0027	+0027	−0.6	−0.4	−0.4	−0.1
La Carraca	36 30N	6 11W	+0020	+0050	+0100	+0040	−0.5	−0.4	−0.1	0.0
Cabo Trafalgar	36 11N	6 02W	−0003	−0003	+0026	+0026	−1.4	−1.1	−0.6	−0.1
Barbate	36 11N	5 56W	+0016	+0016	+0045	+0045	−1.9	−1.5	−0.5	+0.1
Punta Camarinal	36 05N	5 48W	−0007	−0007	+0013	+0013	−1.7	−1.4	−0.7	−0.2
			0000	0700	0100	0600				
GIBRALTAR (UK)	36 08N	5 21W	and	and	and	and	1.0	0.7	0.3	0.1
Standard port. Time zone −0100			1200	1900	1300	1800				
Tarifa	36 00N	5 36W	−0038	−0038	−0042	−0042	+0.4	+0.3	+0.3	+0.2
Punta Carnero	36 04N	5 26W	−0010	−0010	0000	0000	0.0	+0.1	+0.1	+0.1
Algeciras	36 07N	5 27W	−0010	−0010	−0010	−0010	+0.1	+0.2	+0.1	+0.1
Ceuta (to Spain)	35 53N	5 16W	−0045	−0045	−0050	−0050	0.0	+0.1	+0.1	+0.1
Morocco, Tangier (*Time UT*)	35 47N	5 48W	−0030	−0030	−0020	−0020	+1.3	+1.0	+0.5	+0.3

TIDES

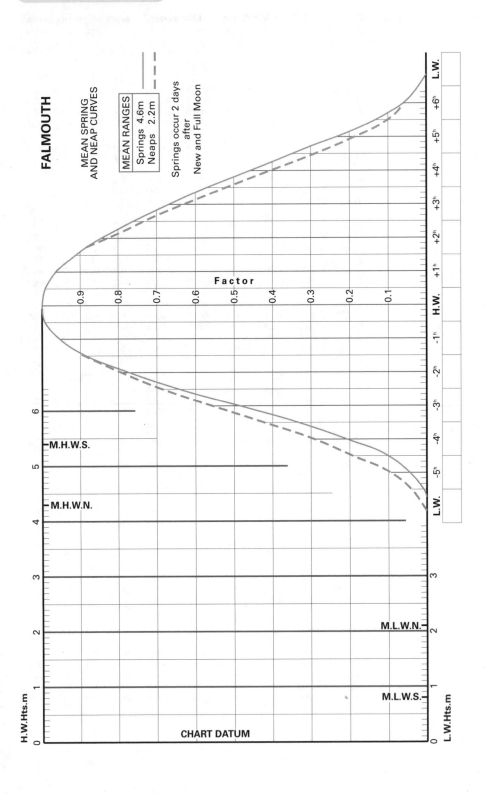

FALMOUTH

MEAN SPRING
AND NEAP CURVES

MEAN RANGES
Springs 4.6m
Neaps 2.2m

Springs occur 2 days
after
New and Full Moon

Factor

0.9 0.8 0.7 0.6 0.5 0.4 0.3 0.2 0.1

L.W. +6ʰ +5ʰ +4ʰ +3ʰ +2ʰ +1ʰ H.W. -1ʰ -2ʰ -3ʰ -4ʰ -5ʰ L.W.

H.W.Hts.m

M.H.W.S.

M.H.W.N.

CHART DATUM

M.L.W.N.

M.L.W.S.

L.W.Hts.m

ENGLAND – FALMOUTH

LAT 50°09′N   LONG 5°03′W

TIMES AND HEIGHTS OF HIGH AND LOW WATERS

2009

JANUARY

Day	Time m	Time m	Time m	Time m
1 TH	0155 1.5	0748 5.0	1420 1.5	2010 4.7
2 F	0227 1.5	0821 4.9	1453 1.5	2044 4.6
3 SA	0302 1.6	0859 4.8	1531 1.5	2126 4.5
4 SU	0344 1.7	0944 4.7	1617 1.8	◐ 2217 4.4
5 M	0438 1.9	1042 4.6	1719 1.8	2322 4.4
6 TU	0550 2.0	1152 4.5	1839 1.9	
7 W	0036 4.4	0721 2.0	1312 4.5	2002 1.8
8 TH	0154 4.6	0842 1.7	1430 4.7	2115 1.5
9 F	0304 4.9	0951 1.5	1537 4.9	2219 1.3
10 SA	0404 5.2	1052 1.1	1637 5.1	2316 1.0
11 SU	0458 5.4	1147 0.8	1730 5.2	○
12 M	0008 0.8	0549 5.6	1238 0.6	1824 5.3
13 TU	0057 0.6	0640 5.7	1325 0.6	1914 5.3
14 W	0142 0.6	0728 5.6	1409 0.5	2000 5.3
15 TH	0223 0.7	0812 5.5	1449 0.7	2041 5.1
16 F	0302 0.9	0854 5.3	1527 1.0	2119 4.9
17 SA	0338 1.3	0930 5.0	1604 1.4	2153 4.7
18 SU	0416 1.5	1006 4.7	1643 1.7	◑ 2231 4.4
19 M	0500 1.9	1047 4.4	1730 2.0	2324 4.3
20 TU	0557 2.2	1151 4.2	1832 2.2	
21 W	0041 4.2	0712 2.3	1320 4.1	1952 2.3
22 TH	0159 4.3	0841 2.2	1432 4.2	2112 2.1
23 F	0300 4.5	0949 1.9	1527 4.4	2210 1.8
24 SA	0349 4.8	1038 1.6	1613 4.6	2255 1.5
25 SU	0431 5.0	1120 1.4	1654 4.8	2334 1.4
26 M	0510 5.1	1158 1.3	1733 4.9	●
27 TU	0010 1.3	0549 5.2	1233 1.1	1812 5.0
28 W	0043 1.2	0626 5.2	1304 1.1	1848 5.0
29 TH	0113 1.1	0702 5.2	1334 1.1	1922 4.9
30 F	0142 1.1	0733 5.1	1403 1.1	1952 4.9
31 SA	0211 1.2	0803 5.1	1433 1.2	2022 4.8

FEBRUARY

Day	Time m	Time m	Time m	Time m
1 SU	0242 1.3	0836 4.9	1505 1.3	2056 4.7
2 M	0318 1.5	0915 4.8	1544 1.5	◑ 2140 4.6
3 TU	0403 1.6	1008 4.6	1636 1.8	2242 4.4
4 W	0507 1.9	1121 4.3	1752 2.0	
5 TH	0004 4.3	0645 2.1	1250 4.3	1936 2.0
6 F	0135 4.4	0828 1.9	1420 4.4	2104 1.7
7 SA	0253 4.7	0945 1.5	1533 4.7	2212 1.4
8 SU	0356 5.1	1046 1.0	1631 5.0	2308 0.9
9 M	0448 5.4	1137 0.6	1721 5.2	○ 2357 0.6
10 TU	0536 5.6	1225 0.3	1809 5.4	
11 W	0042 0.4	0624 5.7	1308 0.2	1853 5.4
12 TH	0123 0.3	0707 5.7	1347 0.2	1932 5.3
13 F	0200 0.5	0745 5.5	1423 0.5	2005 5.2
14 SA	0233 0.7	0818 5.3	1454 0.9	2033 5.0
15 SU	0304 1.1	0844 5.0	1524 1.3	2058 4.8
16 M	0335 1.5	0912 4.7	1554 1.6	2129 4.5
17 TU	0410 1.8	0948 4.4	1632 2.0	2213 4.3
18 W	0501 2.2	1041 4.0	1732 2.3	2323 4.1
19 TH	0617 2.4	1218 3.9	1854 2.5	
20 F	0120 4.1	0751 2.4	1407 4.0	2035 2.3
21 SA	0234 4.3	0927 2.0	1506 4.3	2148 1.9
22 SU	0325 4.6	1018 1.6	1553 4.6	2234 1.5
23 M	0409 4.9	1058 1.3	1634 4.8	2313 1.3
24 TU	0448 5.1	1135 1.1	1711 4.9	2349 1.1
25 W	0526 5.2	1210 0.9	1750 5.0	●
26 TH	0022 0.9	0604 5.3	1243 0.8	1826 5.1
27 F	0054 0.9	0640 5.3	1313 0.8	1859 5.1
28 SA	0123 0.8	0713 5.2	1343 0.8	1929 5.1

MARCH

Day	Time m	Time m	Time m	Time m
1 SU	0152 0.9	0745 5.1	1412 1.0	1959 5.0
2 M	0223 1.0	0818 5.0	1444 1.2	2033 4.9
3 TU	0258 1.3	0857 4.8	1521 1.5	2117 4.7
4 W	0343 1.5	0949 4.5	1611 1.8	◑ 2218 4.4
5 TH	0447 1.9	1105 4.2	1730 2.1	2346 4.2
6 F	0634 2.1	1246 4.1	1927 2.1	
7 SA	0126 4.4	0825 1.8	1420 4.3	2059 1.7
8 SU	0246 4.7	0938 1.4	1528 4.7	2202 1.3
9 M	0345 5.1	1032 0.9	1620 5.0	2253 0.8
10 TU	0434 5.4	1120 0.5	1705 5.2	2338 0.5
11 W	0517 5.6	1203 0.2	1746 5.4	○
12 TH	0020 0.3	0559 5.6	1244 0.2	1825 5.4
13 F	0058 0.3	0638 5.6	1320 0.3	1859 5.3
14 SA	0132 0.4	0712 5.4	1352 0.6	1926 5.2
15 SU	0203 0.7	0739 5.2	1420 0.9	1950 5.1
16 M	0231 1.1	0804 4.9	1446 1.3	2016 4.9
17 TU	0258 1.5	0832 4.6	1511 1.6	2047 4.6
18 W	0328 1.8	0908 4.3	1542 2.0	◑ 2129 4.3
19 TH	0415 2.2	1000 4.0	1642 2.3	2230 4.1
20 F	0537 2.4	1124 3.8	1813 2.5	
21 SA	0021 4.0	0705 2.3	1335 3.9	1943 2.3
22 SU	0200 4.2	0839 2.1	1437 4.2	2105 1.9
23 M	0254 4.5	0938 1.6	1523 4.5	2157 1.5
24 TU	0339 4.8	1022 1.3	1604 4.8	2239 1.3
25 W	0420 5.0	1101 1.0	1643 5.0	2318 1.0
26 TH	0459 5.2	1138 0.8	1720 5.1	● 2354 0.8
27 F	0536 5.3	1215 0.7	1757 5.2	
28 SA	0030 0.7	0615 5.3	1249 0.7	1832 5.2
29 SU	0103 0.7	0651 5.3	1322 0.7	1906 5.2
30 M	0136 0.8	0727 5.2	1354 0.9	1940 5.1
31 TU	0210 1.0	0805 5.0	1429 1.2	2019 5.0

APRIL

Day	Time m	Time m	Time m	Time m
1 W	0248 1.3	0850 4.7	1511 1.5	2105 4.7
2 TH	0338 1.5	0946 4.4	1606 1.8	◑ 2208 4.5
3 F	0449 1.9	1106 4.1	1730 2.1	2339 4.3
4 SA	0635 2.0	1248 4.1	1919 2.0	
5 SU	0116 4.4	0811 1.6	1410 4.4	2041 1.6
6 M	0229 4.7	0917 1.3	1510 4.7	2140 1.3
7 TU	0324 5.1	1009 0.9	1557 5.0	2229 0.9
8 W	0410 5.3	1055 0.6	1639 5.2	2313 0.6
9 TH	0452 5.4	1136 0.5	1716 5.3	2353 0.5
10 F	0530 5.4	1215 0.4	1751 5.3	
11 SA	0031 0.5	0607 5.3	1250 0.6	1823 5.3
12 SU	0104 0.6	0638 5.2	1321 0.8	1849 5.2
13 M	0134 0.9	0706 5.0	1349 1.1	1916 5.1
14 TU	0202 1.2	0733 4.8	1415 1.4	1945 4.9
15 W	0229 1.5	0805 4.6	1440 1.6	2018 4.7
16 TH	0259 1.7	0843 4.3	1509 2.0	2100 4.4
17 F	0344 2.0	0935 4.0	1604 2.2	◑ 2155 4.2
18 SA	0501 2.2	1047 3.9	1734 2.4	2315 4.1
19 SU	0622 2.2	1238 3.9	1855 2.3	
20 M	0102 4.2	0736 2.0	1351 4.2	2006 2.0
21 TU	0210 4.4	0840 1.6	1443 4.4	2106 1.6
22 W	0259 4.7	0933 1.4	1527 4.7	2156 1.4
23 TH	0344 4.9	1020 1.1	1608 4.9	2241 1.1
24 F	0426 5.1	1103 0.9	1648 5.1	2324 0.9
25 SA	0508 5.2	1145 0.7	1727 5.2	
26 SU	0004 0.7	0550 5.3	1225 0.7	1807 5.3
27 M	0044 0.7	0633 5.2	1304 0.8	1847 5.3
28 TU	0124 0.8	0716 5.1	1344 1.0	1928 5.3
29 W	0205 0.9	0801 5.0	1425 1.2	2012 5.1
30 TH	0251 1.2	0852 4.7	1513 1.5	2104 4.9

Chart Datum: 2·91 metres below Ordnance Datum (Newlyn)
HAT is 5·8 metres above Chart Datum

TIDES

ENGLAND – FALMOUTH

TIME ZONE (UT)
For Summer Time add ONE hour in **non-shaded areas**

LAT 50°09′N LONG 5°03′W
TIMES AND HEIGHTS OF HIGH AND LOW WATERS

Dates in amber are **SPRINGS**
Dates in yellow are **NEAPS**

2009

MAY

Day	Time	m	Day	Time	m
1 F	0346 0951 1612 2208	1.5 4.5 1.7 4.6	**16** SA	0325 0918 1541 2129	1.8 4.2 2.0 4.4
2 SA	0455 1109 1728 2331	1.6 4.3 1.9 4.5	**17** SU	0423 1017 1648 2229	2.0 4.1 2.2 4.3
3 SU	0620 1231 1853	1.7 4.3 1.8	**18** M	0534 1129 1802 2344	2.0 4.0 2.1 4.3
4 M	0053 0739 1341 2007	4.6 1.5 4.5 1.6	**19** TU	0642 1243 1911	1.9 4.2 2.0
5 TU	0159 0844 1437 2107	4.7 1.4 4.7 1.4	**20** W	0101 0746 1346 2015	4.4 1.7 4.4 1.7
6 W	0253 0937 1524 2158	4.9 1.1 4.9 1.1	**21** TH	0206 0845 1441 2112	4.6 1.5 4.6 1.5
7 TH	0341 1024 1607 2244	5.0 0.9 5.0 0.9	**22** F	0301 0939 1529 2206	4.8 1.3 4.9 1.2
8 F	0424 1107 1645 2325	5.1 0.8 5.1 0.8	**23** SA	0352 1030 1616 2255	5.0 1.0 5.1 1.0
9 SA	0503 1146 1719	5.1 0.8 5.2	**24** SU	0441 1119 1702 2344	5.1 0.9 5.2 0.8
10 SU	0003 0537 1222 1751	0.9 5.1 0.9 5.2	**25** M	0529 1206 1748	5.2 0.8 5.4
11 M	0038 0612 1254 1822	0.9 5.0 1.1 5.1	**26** TU	0031 0619 1253 1835	0.7 5.2 0.8 5.4
12 TU	0110 0642 1324 1852	1.1 4.9 1.3 5.0	**27** W	0118 0710 1339 1922	0.7 5.1 0.9 5.4
13 W	0140 0715 1352 1925	1.3 4.7 1.5 4.9	**28** TH	0206 0801 1427 2012	0.8 5.0 1.0 5.3
14 TH	0211 0750 1421 2000	1.5 4.5 1.6 4.8	**29** F	0255 0855 1516 2105	1.0 4.9 1.3 5.1
15 F	0244 0830 1455 2040	1.6 4.4 1.8 4.6	**30** SA	0348 0952 1610 2203	1.2 4.7 1.5 4.9
			31 SU	0445 1055 1708 2308	1.4 4.5 1.6 4.7

JUNE

Day	Time	m	Day	Time	m
1 M	0548 1159 1814	1.5 4.5 1.7	**16** TU	0437 1037 1700 2247	1.7 4.2 1.9 4.4
2 TU	0017 0655 1300 1922	4.6 1.5 4.5 1.7	**17** W	0541 1139 1812 2354	1.8 4.3 1.9 4.4
3 W	0120 0801 1356 2027	4.6 1.5 4.6 1.6	**18** TH	0651 1245 1925	1.7 4.4 1.8
4 TH	0216 0900 1447 2124	4.6 1.5 4.7 1.5	**19** F	0107 0800 1352 2033	4.5 1.6 4.5 1.6
5 F	0309 0952 1534 2214	4.7 1.4 4.8 1.4	**20** SA	0219 0903 1453 2135	4.6 1.5 4.8 1.4
6 SA	0355 1038 1616 2300	4.8 1.3 4.9 1.3	**21** SU	0323 1003 1550 2234	4.8 1.2 5.0 1.1
7 SU	0437 1120 1653 2341	4.8 1.2 5.0 1.2	**22** M	0421 1100 1642 2329	5.0 1.0 5.2 0.9
8 M	0515 1158 1728	4.8 1.2 5.1	**23** TU	0514 1153 1733	5.1 0.9 5.4
9 TU	0018 0552 1234 1803	1.2 4.8 1.3 5.1	**24** W	0022 0609 1245 1825	0.7 5.2 0.7 5.5
10 W	0053 0628 1307 1838	1.2 4.8 1.4 5.0	**25** TH	0113 0704 1334 1917	0.6 5.2 0.7 5.5
11 TH	0126 0705 1338 1914	1.3 4.7 1.5 4.9	**26** F	0202 0756 1421 2006	0.5 5.2 0.7 5.4
12 F	0158 0741 1408 1949	1.4 4.6 1.5 4.8	**27** SA	0249 0847 1507 2056	0.6 5.1 0.9 5.3
13 SA	0230 0820 1440 2025	1.5 4.5 1.6 4.7	**28** SU	0334 0935 1551 2143	0.8 4.9 1.1 5.1
14 SU	0305 0900 1516 2104	1.5 4.4 1.7 4.6	**29** M	0420 1024 1637 2233	1.1 4.7 1.4 4.8
15 M	0345 0944 1601 2151	1.6 4.3 1.8 4.5	**30** TU	0508 1116 1729 2330	1.4 4.5 1.6 4.6

JULY

Day	Time	m	Day	Time	m
1 W	0603 1212 1829	1.6 4.4 1.8	**16** TH	0442 1049 1711 2309	1.7 4.3 1.9 4.4
2 TH	0032 0707 1312 1938	4.4 1.8 4.4 1.9	**17** F	0554 1158 1837	1.8 4.3 1.9
3 F	0138 0817 1411 2049	4.3 1.8 4.4 1.8	**18** SA	0026 0720 1316 2003	4.4 1.8 4.4 1.8
4 SA	0238 0921 1504 2149	4.4 1.7 4.6 1.7	**19** SU	0152 0838 1430 2116	4.4 1.6 4.7 1.5
5 SU	0330 1014 1552 2240	4.5 1.6 4.8 1.5	**20** M	0307 0947 1533 2222	4.7 1.4 5.0 1.2
6 M	0416 1101 1633 2325	4.6 1.5 4.9 1.4	**21** TU	0408 1048 1630 2320	4.9 1.1 5.3 0.8
7 TU	0457 1142 1711	4.7 1.4 5.0	**22** W	0505 1144 1721	5.1 0.8 5.5
8 W	0004 0535 1220 1749	1.3 4.8 1.3 5.1	**23** TH	0013 0558 1235 1814	0.5 5.3 0.5 5.6
9 TH	0041 0615 1253 1826	1.2 4.8 1.3 5.1	**24** F	0103 0650 1322 1904	0.3 5.3 0.4 5.7
10 F	0113 0652 1324 1903	1.2 4.8 1.3 5.0	**25** SA	0148 0739 1405 1950	0.3 5.3 0.5 5.6
11 SA	0143 0729 1352 1935	1.2 4.7 1.4 5.0	**26** SU	0230 0824 1446 2032	0.4 5.2 0.6 5.4
12 SU	0211 0803 1420 2007	1.3 4.7 1.4 4.9	**27** M	0309 0904 1524 2111	0.7 5.1 0.9 5.1
13 M	0240 0836 1450 2039	1.4 4.6 1.5 4.8	**28** TU	0347 0941 1601 2146	1.0 4.8 1.3 4.8
14 TU	0312 0910 1525 2117	1.5 4.5 1.5 4.7	**29** W	0425 1019 1643 2224	1.5 4.5 1.6 4.5
15 W	0351 0953 1610 2205	1.5 4.4 1.7 4.5	**30** TH	0509 1108 1735 2322	1.8 4.3 2.0 4.2
			31 F	0607 1221 1845	2.1 4.2 2.2

AUGUST

Day	Time	m	Day	Time	m
1 SA	0058 0726 1339 2016	4.0 2.2 4.2 2.2	**16** SU	0005 0655 1256 1948	4.2 2.0 4.4 1.9
2 SU	0214 0856 1441 2132	4.1 2.1 4.4 1.9	**17** M	0143 0827 1419 2109	4.3 1.8 4.7 1.5
3 M	0312 0957 1531 2225	4.5 1.8 4.7 1.6	**18** TU	0301 0939 1524 2214	4.6 1.4 5.0 1.1
4 TU	0358 1045 1614 2309	4.5 1.5 4.9 1.4	**19** W	0401 1039 1619 2309	4.9 1.0 5.4 0.7
5 W	0440 1126 1653 2348	4.7 1.4 5.0 1.2	**20** TH	0453 1131 1708 2358	5.2 0.6 5.6 0.3
6 TH	0517 1202 1730	4.8 1.2 5.1	**21** F	0542 1218 1755	5.4 0.4 5.7
7 F	0022 0555 1235 1807	1.1 4.9 1.1 5.2	**22** SA	0044 0629 1301 1841	0.2 5.5 0.3 5.7
8 SA	0053 0633 1304 1843	1.0 4.9 1.1 5.1	**23** SU	0125 0712 1341 1923	0.2 5.4 0.3 5.6
9 SU	0121 0708 1331 1916	1.0 4.9 1.1 5.1	**24** M	0203 0750 1417 1959	0.4 5.3 0.6 5.4
10 M	0147 0738 1356 1946	1.1 4.8 1.2 5.0	**25** TU	0238 0823 1451 2030	0.7 5.1 0.9 5.1
11 TU	0213 0808 1424 2015	1.2 4.8 1.3 4.9	**26** W	0309 0851 1524 2056	1.1 4.9 1.4 4.8
12 W	0242 0838 1456 2049	1.3 4.7 1.4 4.8	**27** TH	0341 0919 1600 2128	1.5 4.6 1.7 4.4
13 TH	0317 0918 1536 2134	1.5 4.6 1.6 4.6	**28** F	0419 0958 1649 2215	2.0 4.3 2.2 4.1
14 F	0402 1013 1632 2239	1.7 4.4 1.9 4.3	**29** SA	0515 1105 1801 2354	2.3 4.1 2.3 3.8
15 SA	0510 1128 1804	1.9 4.3 2.1	**30** SU	0638 1308 1943	2.5 4.1 2.4
			31 M	0153 0833 1418 2114	4.0 2.2 4.3 2.0

Chart Datum: 2·91 metres below Ordnance Datum (Newlyn)
HAT is 5·8 metres above Chart Datum

TIME ZONE (UT)
For Summer Time add ONE
hour in **non-shaded areas**

ENGLAND – FALMOUTH
LAT 50°09′N   LONG 5°03′W
TIMES AND HEIGHTS OF HIGH AND LOW WATERS

Dates in amber are **SPRINGS**
Dates in yellow are **NEAPS**

2009

SEPTEMBER
Time	m		Time	m
1 0251	4.3	**16** 0257	4.7	
0936	1.9	0929	1.4	
TU 1509	4.6	W 1513	5.1	
2203	1.6	2200	1.0	
2 0337	4.6	**17** 0351	5.0	
1021	1.5	1023	0.9	
W 1551	4.9	TH 1603	5.4	
2244	1.4	2250	0.6	
3 0416	4.8	**18** 0437	5.3	
1100	1.3	1111	0.6	
TH 1630	5.1	F 1649	5.6	
2320	1.1	● 2336	0.3	
4 0453	5.0	**19** 0518	5.5	
1135	1.1	1155	0.4	
F 1707	5.2	SA 1732	5.7	
○ 2353	1.0			
5 0529	5.0	**20** 0018	0.2	
1208	1.0	0600	5.5	
SA 1743	5.3	SU 1236	0.3	
		1814	5.7	
6 0025	0.9	**21** 0057	0.3	
0606	5.1	0638	5.5	
SU 1237	1.0	M 1313	0.5	
1819	5.2	1851	5.5	
7 0053	0.9	**22** 0132	0.6	
0640	5.1	0712	5.4	
M 1305	1.0	TU 1347	0.7	
1851	5.2	1923	5.3	
8 0121	1.0	**23** 0204	0.9	
0711	5.0	0739	5.2	
TU 1333	1.1	W 1418	1.1	
1922	5.1	1949	5.0	
9 0148	1.1	**24** 0232	1.3	
0740	5.0	0804	4.9	
W 1401	1.2	TH 1449	1.5	
1953	5.0	2016	4.7	
10 0218	1.3	**25** 0300	1.7	
0812	4.9	0834	4.7	
TH 1434	1.4	F 1522	1.9	
2029	4.8	2049	4.4	
11 0252	1.5	**26** 0333	2.1	
0854	4.7	0915	4.4	
F 1514	1.6	SA 1609	2.3	
2118	4.5	◑ 2138	4.1	
12 0338	1.8	**27** 0430	2.4	
0950	4.5	1015	4.1	
SA 1612	1.9	SU 1723	2.5	
◐ 2224	4.3	2255	3.8	
13 0448	2.1	**28** 0558	2.6	
1108	4.3	1218	4.1	
SU 1754	2.2	M 1856	2.5	
2357	4.1			
14 0647	2.2	**29** 0122	3.9	
1246	4.4	0741	2.4	
M 1944	1.9	TU 1346	4.3	
		2033	2.1	
15 0145	4.3	**30** 0222	4.3	
0822	1.8	0858	2.0	
TU 1413	4.7	W 1438	4.6	
2101	1.5	2125	1.7	

OCTOBER
Time	m		Time	m
1 0307	4.6	**16** 0329	5.1	
0944	1.6	1000	1.0	
TH 1521	4.9	F 1543	5.4	
2205	1.4	2226	0.8	
2 0347	4.8	**17** 0413	5.3	
1023	1.4	1046	0.8	
F 1600	5.1	SA 1627	5.5	
2243	1.2	2310	0.6	
3 0425	5.0	**18** 0453	5.4	
1100	1.2	1129	0.6	
SA 1639	5.2	SU 1707	5.6	
2318	1.0	● 2350	0.6	
4 0501	5.2	**19** 0529	5.5	
1135	1.0	1209	0.6	
SU 1715	5.3	M 1745	5.5	
○ 2352	0.9			
5 0536	5.2	**20** 0028	0.7	
1209	0.9	0605	5.4	
M 1752	5.3	TU 1246	0.7	
		1821	5.3	
6 0025	0.9	**21** 0102	0.9	
0612	5.3	0636	5.3	
TU 1241	0.9	W 1319	1.0	
1828	5.3	1850	5.1	
7 0057	1.0	**22** 0133	1.2	
0645	5.2	0704	5.2	
W 1313	1.0	TH 1350	1.3	
1903	5.2	1918	4.9	
8 0128	1.1	**23** 0201	1.5	
0719	5.2	0732	5.0	
TH 1346	1.2	F 1421	1.5	
1938	5.0	1948	4.7	
9 0201	1.3	**24** 0229	1.8	
0756	5.0	0805	4.8	
F 1422	1.4	SA 1454	1.9	
2020	4.8	2026	4.4	
10 0240	1.5	**25** 0301	2.1	
0841	4.8	0848	4.6	
SA 1508	1.6	SU 1538	2.2	
2112	4.5	2114	4.2	
11 0330	1.9	**26** 0351	2.4	
0940	4.6	0943	4.3	
SU 1613	2.0	M 1645	2.4	
◐ 2221	4.3	2222	4.0	
12 0448	2.2	**27** 0513	2.6	
1058	4.4	1102	4.2	
M 1753	2.1	TU 1804	2.4	
2358	4.2			
13 0638	2.2	**28** 0015	4.0	
1236	4.5	0637	2.5	
TU 1931	1.9	W 1247	4.3	
		1921	2.2	
14 0135	4.4	**29** 0134	4.2	
0805	1.8	0753	2.2	
W 1356	4.8	TH 1352	4.5	
2042	1.5	2025	1.9	
15 0240	4.8	**30** 0226	4.5	
0908	1.5	0851	1.8	
TH 1454	5.1	F 1442	4.8	
2137	1.1	2115	1.5	
		31 0310	4.8	
		0939	1.5	
		SA 1525	5.0	
		2159	1.4	

NOVEMBER
Time	m		Time	m
1 0351	5.0	**16** 0426	5.3	
1022	1.3	1104	1.0	
SU 1606	5.1	M 1643	5.3	
2241	1.2	● 2324	1.0	
2 0430	5.2	**17** 0504	5.3	
1102	1.1	1145	1.0	
M 1647	5.2	TU 1721	5.2	
○ 2321	1.0			
3 0508	5.3	**18** 0003	1.0	
1142	1.0	0537	5.3	
TU 1726	5.3	W 1223	1.1	
2359	1.0	1756	5.1	
4 0546	5.4	**19** 0038	1.2	
1221	1.0	0610	5.3	
W 1807	5.3	TH 1258	1.2	
		1829	5.0	
5 0038	1.0	**20** 0110	1.4	
0625	5.4	0642	5.2	
TH 1300	1.0	F 1331	1.4	
1848	5.2	1901	4.9	
6 0116	1.1	**21** 0140	1.5	
0706	5.3	0714	5.1	
F 1340	1.1	SA 1403	1.5	
1932	5.1	1934	4.7	
7 0156	1.3	**22** 0210	1.7	
0749	5.2	0750	4.9	
SA 1424	1.3	SU 1436	1.7	
2020	4.9	2012	4.5	
8 0242	1.5	**23** 0242	1.9	
0838	5.0	0830	4.7	
SU 1515	1.5	M 1514	2.0	
2114	4.7	2058	4.3	
9 0336	1.8	**24** 0322	2.1	
0937	4.8	0918	4.5	
M 1619	1.8	TU 1603	2.1	
2222	4.5	◐ 2152	4.2	
10 0446	2.0	**25** 0418	2.3	
1049	4.7	1015	4.4	
TU 1738	1.9	W 1707	2.2	
2346	4.4	2259	4.1	
11 0611	2.0	**26** 0532	2.4	
1213	4.7	1125	4.4	
W 1900	1.8	TH 1817	2.2	
12 0103	4.5	**27** 0015	4.2	
0732	1.8	0646	2.3	
TU 1325	4.8	F 1239	4.4	
2010	1.5	1922	2.0	
13 0207	4.7	**28** 0124	4.4	
0837	1.5	0753	2.0	
SA 1425	5.0	SA 1346	4.6	
2107	1.4	2022	1.8	
14 0259	5.0	**29** 0221	4.6	
0931	1.4	0851	1.8	
SA 1515	5.1	SU 1442	4.8	
2158	1.1	2117	1.5	
15 0345	5.2	**30** 0312	4.9	
1020	1.1	0944	1.5	
SU 1601	5.2	M 1532	5.0	
2243	1.0	2207	1.4	

DECEMBER
Time	m		Time	m
1 0358	5.1	**16** 0442	5.1	
1033	1.3	1127	1.3	
TU 1620	5.1	W 1703	5.0	
2254	1.2	● 2345	1.3	
2 0442	5.3	**17** 0519	5.2	
1121	1.1	1207	1.3	
W 1707	5.2	TH 1739	5.0	
○ 2340	1.0			
3 0526	5.4	**18** 0022	1.3	
1207	1.0	0554	5.2	
TH 1754	5.3	F 1245	1.3	
		1816	4.9	
4 0026	1.0	**19** 0056	1.4	
0612	5.5	0630	5.2	
F 1254	0.9	SA 1318	1.3	
1841	5.3	1850	4.9	
5 0112	1.0	**20** 0127	1.5	
0659	5.5	0705	5.1	
SA 1341	0.9	SU 1350	1.5	
1930	5.2	1926	4.8	
6 0158	1.1	**21** 0156	1.5	
0747	5.4	0739	5.0	
SU 1428	1.1	M 1420	1.5	
2021	5.1	2002	4.7	
7 0245	1.3	**22** 0225	1.6	
0837	5.3	0816	4.9	
M 1518	1.2	TU 1451	1.6	
2113	4.9	2040	4.6	
8 0335	1.5	**23** 0256	1.7	
0931	5.1	0853	4.7	
TU 1610	1.5	W 1524	1.8	
2211	4.7	2121	4.4	
9 0429	1.6	**24** 0332	1.9	
1030	4.9	0935	4.6	
W 1709	1.6	TH 1605	1.9	
◑ 2314	4.6	◑ 2207	4.3	
10 0532	1.8	**25** 0420	2.1	
1138	4.8	1025	4.5	
TH 1815	1.7	F 1701	2.0	
		2304	4.3	
11 0020	4.5	**26** 0528	2.2	
0644	1.9	1128	4.4	
F 1245	4.7	SA 1815	2.1	
1926	1.7			
12 0125	4.6	**27** 0011	4.3	
0757	1.8	0651	2.1	
SA 1348	4.7	SU 1239	4.4	
2032	1.7	1930	2.0	
13 0223	4.7	**28** 0123	4.4	
0900	1.7	0806	1.9	
SU 1445	4.8	M 1354	4.5	
2129	1.5	2037	1.7	
14 0314	4.9	**29** 0231	4.7	
0955	1.5	0911	1.6	
M 1537	4.9	TU 1501	4.7	
2219	1.5	2138	1.5	
15 0401	5.0	**30** 0330	5.0	
1043	1.4	1011	1.4	
TU 1622	4.9	W 1558	5.0	
2304	1.4	2235	1.3	
		31 0422	5.2	
		1106	1.1	
		TH 1652	5.1	
		○ 2328	1.0	

TIDES

Chart Datum: 2·91 metres below Ordnance Datum (Newlyn)
HAT is 5·8 metres above Chart Datum

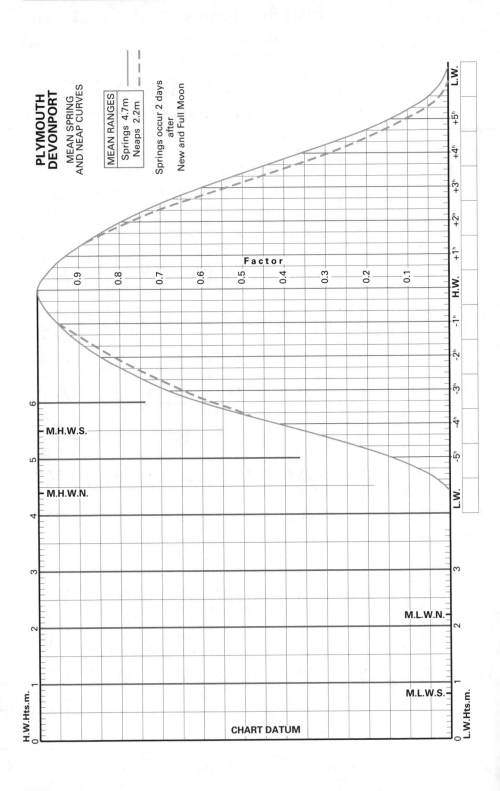

PLYMOUTH
DEVONPORT

MEAN SPRING
AND NEAP CURVES

MEAN RANGES	
Springs 4.7m	
Neaps 2.2m	

Springs occur 2 days
after
New and Full Moon

Factor

0.9 0.8 0.7 0.6 0.5 0.4 0.3 0.2 0.1

H.W.Hts.m.

M.H.W.S.

M.H.W.N.

CHART DATUM

L.W.Hts.m.

M.L.W.N.

M.L.W.S.

L.W.

H.W.

ENGLAND – PLYMOUTH (DEVONPORT)

LAT 50°22'N   LONG 4°11'W

TIMES AND HEIGHTS OF HIGH AND LOW WATERS

Dates in amber are **SPRINGS**
Dates in yellow are **NEAPS**

2009

JANUARY

Time m / Time m

Day	High/Low waters
1 TH	0205 1.5 · 0819 5.1 · 1430 1.5 · 2041 4.8
2 F	0237 1.6 · 0851 5.0 · 1503 1.5 · 2114 4.7
3 SA	0312 1.7 · 0928 4.9 · 1541 1.6 · 2154 4.6
4 SU	0354 1.8 · 1012 4.8 · 1628 1.8 · ◐ 2244 4.5
5 M	0448 2.0 · 1109 4.7 · 1729 1.9 · 2347 4.5
6 TU	0600 2.1 · 1218 4.6 · 1849 2.0
7 W	0103 4.5 · 0731 2.1 · 1340 4.6 · 2012 1.9
8 TH	0223 4.7 · 0852 1.8 · 1500 4.8 · 2125 1.6
9 F	0335 5.0 · 1001 1.5 · 1609 5.0 · 2229 1.3
10 SA	0437 5.3 · 1102 1.1 · 1710 5.2 · 2326 1.0
11 SU	0532 5.5 · 1157 0.8 · 1805 5.3 · ○
12	0018 0.8 · 0623 5.7 · 1248 0.6 · 1857 5.4
13 TU	0107 0.6 · 0713 5.8 · 1335 0.5 · 1946 5.4
14 W	0152 0.6 · 0800 5.8 · 1419 0.5 · 2031 5.4
15 TH	0233 0.7 · 0843 5.6 · 1459 0.7 · 2111 5.2
16 F	0312 0.9 · 0923 5.4 · 1537 1.0 · 2147 5.0
17 SA	0348 1.3 · 0958 5.1 · 1614 1.4 · 2221 4.8
18 SU	0426 1.6 · 1033 4.8 · 1653 1.6 · 2258 4.5
19 M	0510 2.0 · 1114 4.5 · 1740 2.1 · 2349 4.4
20 TU	0607 2.3 · 1217 4.3 · 1842 2.3
21 W	0108 4.3 · 0722 2.4 · 1348 4.2 · 2002 2.4
22 TH	0228 4.4 · 0851 2.3 · 1502 4.3 · 2122 2.2
23 F	0331 4.6 · 0959 2.0 · 1559 4.5 · 2220 1.8
24 SA	0421 4.9 · 1048 1.7 · 1646 4.7 · 2305 1.6
25 SU	0504 5.1 · 1130 1.4 · 1728 4.9 · 2344 1.4
26 M	0545 5.2 · 1208 1.3 · 1808 5.0 · ●
27 TU	0020 1.3 · 0623 5.3 · 1243 1.1 · 1845 5.1
28 W	0053 1.2 · 0659 5.3 · 1314 1.1 · 1921 5.1
29 TH	0123 1.1 · 0734 5.3 · 1344 1.1 · 1954 5.0
30 F	0152 1.1 · 0805 5.2 · 1413 1.1 · 2023 5.0
31 SA	0221 1.2 · 0834 5.2 · 1443 1.2 · 2052 4.9

FEBRUARY

Day	High/Low waters
1 SU	0252 1.3 · 0906 5.0 · 1515 1.3 · 2125 4.8
2 M	0328 1.5 · 0944 4.9 · 1554 1.6 · ◐ 2208 4.7
3 TU	0413 1.7 · 1035 4.7 · 1646 1.9 · 2309 4.5
4 W	0517 2.0 · 1146 4.4 · 1802 2.1
5 TH	0030 4.4 · 0655 2.2 · 1317 4.4 · 1946 2.1
6 F	0203 4.5 · 0838 2.0 · 1450 4.5 · 2114 1.8
7 SA	0324 4.8 · 0955 1.5 · 1605 4.8 · 2222 1.4
8 SU	0428 5.2 · 1056 1.0 · 1704 5.1 · 2318 0.9
9 M	0522 5.5 · 1147 0.6 · 1756 5.3 · ○
10 TU	0007 0.6 · 0611 5.7 · 1235 0.3 · 1843 5.4
11 W	0052 0.4 · 0657 5.8 · 1318 0.2 · 1926 5.5
12 TH	0133 0.3 · 0739 5.8 · 1357 0.3 · 2004 5.4
13 F	0210 0.5 · 0816 5.6 · 1433 0.5 · 2036 5.3
14 SA	0243 0.7 · 0848 5.4 · 1504 0.6 · 2103 5.1
15 SU	0314 1.1 · 0914 5.1 · 1534 1.3 · 2127 4.9
16 M	0345 1.5 · 0941 4.8 · 1604 1.7 · ◑ 2157 4.6
17 TU	0420 1.9 · 1016 4.5 · 1642 2.1 · 2240 4.4
18 W	0511 2.3 · 1108 4.1 · 1742 2.4 · 2348 4.2
19 TH	0627 2.5 · 1244 4.0 · 1904 2.6
20 F	0148 4.2 · 0801 2.5 · 1436 4.1 · 2045 2.4
21 SA	0304 4.4 · 0937 2.1 · 1537 4.4 · 2158 2.0
22 SU	0357 4.7 · 1028 1.7 · 1625 4.7 · 2244 1.6
23 M	0442 5.0 · 1108 1.3 · 1707 4.9 · 2323 1.3
24 TU	0522 5.2 · 1145 1.1 · 1746 5.0 · 2359 1.1
25 W	0601 5.3 · 1220 0.9 · 1824 5.1 · ●
26 TH	0032 0.9 · 0638 5.4 · 1253 0.8 · 1859 5.2
27 F	0104 0.9 · 0713 5.4 · 1323 0.8 · 1931 5.2
28 SA	0133 0.8 · 0745 5.3 · 1353 0.8 · 2001 5.2

MARCH

Day	High/Low waters
1 SU	0202 0.9 · 0816 5.2 · 1422 1.0 · 2030 5.1
2 M	0233 1.0 · 0848 5.1 · 1454 1.2 · 2103 5.0
3 TU	0308 1.3 · 0926 4.9 · 1531 1.5 · 2145 4.8
4 W	0353 1.6 · 1017 4.6 · 1621 1.9 · 2245 4.5
5 TH	0457 2.0 · 1131 4.3 · 1740 2.2
6 F	0011 4.3 · 0644 2.2 · 1313 4.2 · 1937 2.2
7 SA	0154 4.5 · 0835 1.9 · 1450 4.4 · 2109 1.8
8 SU	0317 4.8 · 0948 1.4 · 1600 4.8 · 2212 1.3
9 M	0417 5.2 · 1042 0.9 · 1653 5.1 · 2303 0.9
10 TU	0507 5.5 · 1130 0.5 · 1739 5.3 · 2348 0.6
11 W	0552 5.7 · 1213 0.2 · 1820 5.5 · ○
12 TH	0030 0.3 · 0633 5.7 · 1254 0.2 · 1858 5.4
13 F	0108 0.3 · 0711 5.7 · 1330 0.3 · 1931 5.4
14 SA	0142 0.4 · 0744 5.5 · 1402 0.6 · 1958 5.3
15 SU	0213 0.7 · 0811 5.3 · 1430 0.9 · 2021 5.2
16 M	0241 1.1 · 0835 5.0 · 1456 1.3 · 2046 5.0
17 TU	0308 1.5 · 0902 4.7 · 1521 1.7 · 2116 4.7
18 W	0338 1.9 · 0937 4.4 · 1552 2.1 · ◑ 2157 4.4
19 TH	0425 2.3 · 1028 4.1 · 1652 2.5 · 2257 4.2
20 F	0547 2.5 · 1149 3.9 · 1823 2.6
21 SA	0048 4.1 · 0715 2.4 · 1403 4.0 · 1953 2.4
22 SU	0229 4.3 · 0849 2.1 · 1507 4.3 · 2115 2.0
23 M	0325 4.6 · 0948 1.7 · 1555 4.6 · 2207 1.6
24 TU	0411 4.9 · 1032 1.3 · 1637 4.9 · 2249 1.3
25 W	0453 5.1 · 1111 1.0 · 1717 5.1 · 2328 1.0
26 TH	0533 5.3 · 1148 0.8 · 1755 5.2
27 F	0004 0.7 · 0611 5.4 · 1225 0.7 · 1831 5.3
28 SA	0040 0.7 · 0648 5.4 · 1259 0.7 · 1905 5.3
29 SU	0113 0.7 · 0724 5.4 · 1332 0.7 · 1938 5.3
30 M	0146 0.8 · 0759 5.3 · 1404 0.9 · 2012 5.2
31 TU	0220 1.0 · 0836 5.1 · 1439 1.2 · 2049 5.1

APRIL

Day	High/Low waters
1 W	0258 1.3 · 0919 4.8 · 1521 1.5 · 2134 4.8
2 TH	0348 1.6 · 1014 4.5 · 1616 1.9 · ◐ 2235 4.6
3 F	0459 2.0 · 1132 4.2 · 1740 2.2
4 SA	0004 4.4 · 0645 2.1 · 1315 4.2 · 1929 2.1
5 SU	0144 4.5 · 0821 1.7 · 1439 4.5 · 2051 1.7
6 M	0259 4.8 · 0927 1.3 · 1541 4.8 · 2150 1.3
7 TU	0356 5.2 · 1019 0.9 · 1630 5.1 · 2239 0.9
8 W	0443 5.4 · 1105 0.6 · 1712 5.3 · 2323 0.6
9 TH	0526 5.5 · 1146 0.4 · 1751 5.4 · ○
10 F	0003 0.5 · 0605 5.6 · 1225 0.4 · 1825 5.4
11 SA	0041 0.5 · 0641 5.6 · 1300 0.6 · 1856 5.4
12 SU	0114 0.6 · 0711 5.3 · 1331 0.8 · 1922 5.3
13 M	0144 0.9 · 0738 5.1 · 1359 1.1 · 1948 5.2
14 TU	0212 1.2 · 0805 4.9 · 1425 1.4 · 2016 5.0
15 W	0239 1.5 · 0836 4.7 · 1450 1.7 · 2048 4.8
16 TH	0309 1.8 · 0913 4.4 · 1519 2.1 · 2129 4.5
17 F	0354 2.1 · 1003 4.1 · 1614 2.3 · ◐ 2223 4.3
18 SA	0511 2.3 · 1114 4.0 · 1744 2.5 · 2341 4.2
19 SU	0632 2.3 · 1305 4.0 · 1905 2.4
20 M	0130 4.3 · 0746 2.1 · 1420 4.3 · 2016 2.1
21 TU	0239 4.5 · 0850 1.7 · 1513 4.5 · 2116 1.7
22 W	0330 4.8 · 0943 1.4 · 1559 4.8 · 2206 1.4
23 TH	0416 5.0 · 1030 1.1 · 1641 5.0 · 2251 1.1
24 F	0459 5.2 · 1113 0.9 · 1722 5.2 · 2334 0.9
25 SA	0542 5.3 · 1155 0.7 · 1802 5.3 · ●
26 SU	0014 0.7 · 0624 5.4 · 1235 0.7 · 1841 5.4
27 M	0054 0.7 · 0706 5.3 · 1314 0.8 · 1920 5.4
28 TU	0134 0.8 · 0748 5.3 · 1354 0.9 · 2000 5.4
29 W	0215 0.9 · 0832 5.1 · 1435 1.2 · 2043 5.2
30 TH	0301 1.2 · 0921 4.8 · 1523 1.5 · 2133 5.0

Chart Datum: 3·22 metres below Ordnance Datum (Newlyn)
HAT is 5·9 metres above Chart Datum

TIDES

TIME ZONE (UT)
For Summer Time add ONE hour in **non-shaded areas**

ENGLAND – PLYMOUTH (DEVONPORT)
LAT 50°22'N   LONG 4°11'W
TIMES AND HEIGHTS OF HIGH AND LOW WATERS

Dates in amber are **SPRINGS**
Dates in yellow are **NEAPS**

2009

MAY

Time	m	Time	m	Time	m	Time	m
1 0356	1.5	**16** 0335	1.9	**1** 0558	1.6	**16** 0447	1.8
1019	4.6	0946	4.3	1225	4.6	1104	4.3
F 1622	1.8	SA 1551	2.1	M 1824	1.8	TU 1710	2.0
2235	4.7	2157	4.5			◑ 2314	4.5
2 0505	1.7	**17** 0433	2.1	**2** 0043	4.7	**17** 0551	1.9
1135	4.4	1044	4.2	0705	1.6	1204	4.4
SA 1738	2.0	SU 1658	2.3	TU 1327	4.6	W 1822	2.0
2356	4.6	2256	4.4	◑ 1932	1.8		
3 0630	1.8	**18** 0544	2.1	**3** 0148	4.7	**18** 0020	4.5
1258	4.4	1154	4.1	0811	1.6	0701	1.8
SU 1903	1.9	M 1812	2.2	W 1425	4.7	TH 1312	4.5
		◐		2037	1.7	1935	1.9
4 0120	4.7	**19** 0009	4.4	**4** 0246	4.7	**19** 0135	4.6
0749	1.6	0652	2.0	0910	1.5	0810	1.7
M 1409	4.6	TU 1310	4.3	TH 1518	4.8	F 1421	4.6
◑ 2017	1.7	1921	2.1	2134	1.5	2043	1.7
5 0228	4.8	**20** 0128	4.5	**5** 0340	4.8	**20** 0249	4.7
0854	1.4	0756	1.8	1002	1.4	0913	1.5
TU 1507	4.8	W 1415	4.5	F 1606	4.9	SA 1524	4.9
2117	1.4	2025	1.8	2224	1.4	2145	1.4
6 0324	5.0	**21** 0235	4.7	**6** 0427	4.9	**21** 0355	4.9
0947	1.1	0855	1.5	1048	1.3	1013	1.2
W 1556	5.0	TH 1511	4.7	SA 1649	5.0	SU 1622	5.1
2208	1.1	2122	1.5	2310	1.3	2244	1.1
7 0413	5.1	**22** 0332	4.9	**7** 0510	4.9	**22** 0454	5.1
1034	0.9	0949	1.3	1130	1.2	1110	1.0
TH 1640	5.1	F 1601	5.0	SU 1727	5.1	M 1716	5.3
2254	0.9	2216	1.2	2351	1.2	2339	0.9
8 0457	5.2	**23** 0424	5.1	**8** 0550	4.9	**23** 0549	5.2
1117	0.8	1040	1.0	1208	1.2	1203	0.9
F 1719	5.2	SA 1649	5.2	M 1803	5.2	TU 1808	5.5
2335	0.8	2305	1.0				
9 0537	5.2	**24** 0515	5.2	**9** 0028	1.2	**24** 0032	0.7
1156	0.8	1129	0.9	0626	4.9	0643	5.3
SA 1754	5.3	SU 1736	5.3	TU 1244	1.2	W 1255	0.7
		2354	0.8	○ 1837	5.2	1858	5.6
10 0013	0.9	**25** 0604	5.3	**10** 0103	1.2	**25** 0123	0.6
0612	5.2	1216	0.8	0701	4.9	0736	5.3
SU 1232	0.9	M 1822	5.5	W 1317	1.4	TH 1344	0.7
1825	5.3			1911	5.1	● 1949	5.6
11 0048	0.9	**26** 0041	0.7	**11** 0136	1.3	**26** 0212	0.5
0645	5.1	0652	5.3	0737	4.8	0827	5.3
M 1304	1.1	TU 1303	0.8	TH 1348	1.5	F 1431	0.7
○ 1855	5.2	● 1908	5.5	1946	5.0	2037	5.5
12 0120	1.1	**27** 0128	0.7	**12** 0208	1.4	**27** 0259	0.6
0715	5.0	0742	5.2	0813	4.7	0916	5.2
TU 1334	1.3	W 1349	0.9	F 1418	1.6	SA 1517	0.9
1925	5.1	1954	5.5	2020	4.9	2125	5.4
13 0150	1.3	**28** 0216	0.8	**13** 0240	1.5	**28** 0344	0.8
0747	4.8	0832	5.1	0850	4.6	1003	5.0
W 1402	1.5	TH 1437	1.0	SA 1450	1.7	SU 1601	1.1
1957	5.0	2043	5.4	2055	4.8	2211	5.2
14 0221	1.5	**29** 0305	1.0	**14** 0315	1.6	**29** 0430	1.1
0821	4.6	0924	5.0	0929	4.5	1051	4.8
TH 1431	1.7	F 1526	1.3	SU 1526	1.8	M 1647	1.4
2031	4.9	2134	5.2	2133	4.7	2300	4.9
15 0254	1.7	**30** 0358	1.2	**15** 0355	1.7	**30** 0518	1.4
0900	4.5	1020	4.8	1012	4.4	1142	4.6
F 1505	1.9	SA 1620	1.5	M 1611	1.9	TU 1739	1.7
2110	4.7	2230	5.0	2219	4.6	2355	4.7
		31 0455	1.4				
		1121	4.6				
		SU 1718	1.7				
		2334	4.8				

JUNE

(see columns above under JUNE)

JULY

Time	m	Time	m	Time	m	Time	m
1 0613	1.7	**16** 0452	1.8	**1** 0125	4.1	**16** 0031	4.3
1238	4.5	1115	4.4	0736	2.3	0705	2.1
W 1839	1.9	TH 1721	2.0	SA 1407	4.3	SU 1323	4.5
		2335	4.5	2026	2.3	1958	2.0
2 0059	4.5	**17** 0604	1.9	**2** 0243	4.2	**17** 0211	4.4
0717	1.9	1224	4.4	0906	2.2	0837	1.9
TH 1340	4.5	F 1847	2.0	SU 1511	4.5	M 1449	4.8
1948	2.0			◐ 2142	2.0	◑ 2119	1.6
3 0206	4.4	**18** 0053	4.5	**3** 0343	4.4	**18** 0332	4.7
0827	1.9	0730	1.9	1007	1.9	0949	1.5
F 1440	4.5	SA 1344	4.5	M 1603	4.8	TU 1556	5.1
2059	1.9	◑ 2013	1.9	2235	1.7	2224	1.1
4 0308	4.5	**19** 0221	4.5	**4** 0431	4.6	**19** 0434	5.0
0931	1.8	0848	1.7	1055	1.6	1049	1.0
SA 1535	4.7	SU 1500	4.8	TU 1647	5.0	W 1653	5.5
◑ 2159	1.8	2126	1.6	2319	1.4	2319	0.7
5 0402	4.6	**20** 0338	4.8	**5** 0513	4.8	**20** 0527	5.3
1024	1.7	0957	1.4	1136	1.4	1141	0.6
SU 1624	4.9	M 1605	5.1	W 1727	5.1	TH 1742	5.7
2250	1.6	2232	1.2	2358	1.2		
6 0449	4.7	**21** 0441	5.0	**6** 0552	4.9	**21** 0008	0.3
1111	1.5	1058	1.1	1212	1.2	0616	5.5
M 1706	5.0	TU 1703	5.4	TH 1805	5.2	F 1228	0.4
2335	1.4	2330	0.8			1829	5.8
7 0531	4.8	**22** 0539	5.2	**7** 0032	1.1	**22** 0054	0.2
1152	1.4	1154	0.8	0629	5.0	0702	5.6
TU 1746	5.1	W 1756	5.6	F 1245	1.1	SA 1311	0.3
				1841	5.3	1914	5.8
8 0014	1.3	**23** 0023	0.5	**8** 0103	1.0	**23** 0135	0.2
0610	4.9	0632	5.4	0706	5.0	0744	5.5
W 1230	1.3	TH 1245	0.5	SA 1314	1.1	SU 1351	0.3
1823	5.2	1847	5.7	1916	5.2	1955	5.7
9 0051	1.2	**24** 0113	0.3	**9** 0131	1.0	**24** 0213	0.4
0648	4.9	0723	5.4	0740	5.0	0821	5.3
TH 1303	1.3	F 1332	0.4	SU 1341	1.1	M 1427	0.6
1859	5.2	1936	5.8	○ 1948	5.2	2030	5.5
10 0123	1.2	**25** 0158	0.3	**10** 0157	1.1	**25** 0248	0.7
0725	4.9	0811	5.4	0810	4.9	0853	5.2
F 1334	1.3	SA 1415	0.5	M 1406	1.2	TU 1501	0.9
1935	5.1	2021	5.7	2017	5.1	● 2100	5.2
11 0153	1.2	**26** 0240	0.4	**11** 0223	1.2	**26** 0319	1.1
0801	4.8	0854	5.3	0839	4.9	0920	5.0
SA 1402	1.4	SU 1456	0.6	TU 1434	1.3	W 1534	1.4
○ 2007	5.1	● 2102	5.5	2045	5.0	2125	4.9
12 0221	1.3	**27** 0319	0.7	**12** 0252	1.3	**27** 0351	1.6
0834	4.8	0933	5.2	0908	4.8	0947	4.7
SU 1430	1.4	M 1534	0.9	W 1506	1.4	TH 1610	1.8
2038	5.0	2140	5.2	2118	4.9	2156	4.5
13 0250	1.4	**28** 0357	1.0	**13** 0327	1.5	**28** 0429	2.1
0906	4.7	1009	4.9	0946	4.7	1026	4.4
M 1500	1.5	TU 1611	1.3	TH 1546	1.7	F 1659	2.3
2109	4.9	2214	4.9	2202	4.7	2242	4.2
14 0322	1.5	**29** 0435	1.5	**14** 0412	1.8	**29** 0525	2.4
0939	4.6	1046	4.6	1040	4.5	1131	4.2
TU 1535	1.6	W 1653	1.7	F 1642	2.0	SA 1811	2.5
2145	4.8	2251	4.6	2306	4.4		
15 0401	1.6	**30** 0519	1.9	**15** 0520	2.0	**30** 0020	3.9
1021	4.5	1134	4.4	1153	4.4	0648	2.6
W 1620	1.8	TH 1745	2.1	SA 1814	2.2	SU 1336	4.2
2232	4.6	2347	4.3			1953	2.5
		31 0617	2.2			**31** 0222	4.1
		1248	4.3			0843	2.4
		F 1855	2.3			M 1448	4.4
						2124	2.1

Chart Datum: 3·22 metres below Ordnance Datum (Newlyn)
HAT is 5·9 metres above Chart Datum

TIME ZONE (UT)
For Summer Time add ONE hour in **non-shaded areas**

ENGLAND – PLYMOUTH (DEVONPORT)

LAT 50°22'N   LONG 4°11'W

TIMES AND HEIGHTS OF HIGH AND LOW WATERS

Dates in amber are **SPRINGS**
Dates in yellow are **NEAPS**

2009

SEPTEMBER

Time	m	Time	m
1 0322 4.4		**16** 0328 4.8	
0946 2.0		0939 1.4	
TU 1540 4.7		W 1545 5.2	
2213 1.7		2210 1.0	
2 0409 4.7		**17** 0423 5.1	
1031 1.6		1033 0.9	
W 1623 5.0		TH 1636 5.5	
2254 1.4		2300 0.6	
3 0449 4.9		**18** 0510 5.4	
1110 1.3		1121 0.6	
TH 1703 5.2		F 1723 5.7	
2330 1.1		● 2346 0.3	
4 0527 5.1		**19** 0553 5.6	
1145 1.1		1205 0.4	
F 1741 5.3		SA 1807 5.8	
○			
5 0003 1.0		**20** 0028 0.2	
0604 5.1		0634 5.6	
SA 1218 1.0		SU 1246 0.3	
1817 5.4		1847 5.8	
6 0035 0.9		**21** 0107 0.3	
0640 5.2		0711 5.6	
SU 1247 1.0		M 1323 0.5	
1852 5.3		1924 5.6	
7 0103 0.9		**22** 0142 0.6	
0713 5.2		0744 5.5	
M 1315 1.0		TU 1357 0.7	
1924 5.3		1955 5.4	
8 0131 1.0		**23** 0214 0.9	
0743 5.1		0811 5.3	
TU 1343 1.1		W 1428 1.1	
1954 5.2		2020 5.1	
9 0158 1.1		**24** 0242 1.3	
0812 5.1		0835 5.0	
W 1411 1.2		TH 1459 1.5	
2024 5.1		2046 4.8	
10 0228 1.3		**25** 0310 1.8	
0843 5.0		0904 4.8	
TH 1444 1.4		F 1532 2.0	
2059 4.9		2118 4.5	
11 0302 1.5		**26** 0343 2.2	
0923 4.8		0944 4.5	
F 1524 1.7		SA 1619 2.4	
2146 4.6		◑ 2206 4.2	
12 0348 1.9		**27** 0440 2.5	
1018 4.6		1042 4.2	
SA 1622 2.0		SU 1733 2.6	
◑ 2251 4.4		2321 3.9	
13 0458 2.2		**28** 0608 2.7	
1134 4.4		1245 4.2	
SU 1804 2.3		M 1906 2.6	
14 0023 4.2		**29** 0150 4.0	
0657 2.3		0751 2.5	
M 1313 4.5		TU 1414 4.4	
1954 2.0		2043 2.2	
15 0213 4.4		**30** 0252 4.4	
0832 1.9		0751 2.1	
TU 1442 4.8		W 1508 4.7	
2111 1.5		2135 1.8	

OCTOBER

Time	m	Time	m
1 0338 4.7		**16** 0401 5.2	
0954 1.7		1010 1.0	
TH 1553 5.0		F 1615 5.5	
2215 1.4		2236 0.8	
2 0419 4.9		**17** 0446 5.4	
1033 1.4		1056 0.8	
F 1633 5.2		SA 1700 5.6	
2253 1.2		2320 0.6	
3 0458 5.1		**18** 0527 5.5	
1110 1.2		1139 0.6	
SA 1712 5.3		SU 1741 5.7	
2328 1.0		●	
4 0535 5.3		**19** 0000 0.6	
1145 1.0		0604 5.6	
SU 1750 5.4		M 1219 0.6	
○		1819 5.6	
5 0002 0.9		**20** 0038 0.7	
0611 5.3		0639 5.5	
M 1219 0.9		TU 1256 0.7	
1826 5.4		1854 5.4	
6 0035 0.9		**21** 0112 0.9	
0645 5.4		0709 5.4	
TU 1251 0.9		W 1329 1.0	
1901 5.4		1923 5.2	
7 0107 1.0		**22** 0143 1.2	
0718 5.3		0736 5.3	
W 1323 1.0		TH 1400 1.3	
1935 5.3		1950 5.0	
8 0138 1.1		**23** 0211 1.5	
0751 5.3		0804 5.1	
TH 1356 1.2		F 1431 1.6	
2010 5.1		2019 4.8	
9 0211 1.3		**24** 0239 1.9	
0827 5.1		0836 4.9	
F 1432 1.4		SA 1504 2.0	
2050 4.9		2056 4.5	
10 0250 1.6		**25** 0311 2.2	
0911 4.9		0917 4.7	
SA 1518 1.7		SU 1548 2.3	
2141 4.6		2143 4.3	
11 0340 2.0		**26** 0401 2.5	
1008 4.7		1011 4.4	
SU 1623 2.1		M 1655 2.5	
◑ 2248 4.4		◑ 2249 4.1	
12 0458 2.3		**27** 0523 2.7	
1124 4.5		1128 4.3	
M 1803 2.2		TU 1814 2.5	
13 0024 4.3		**28** 0041 4.1	
0647 2.6		0647 2.6	
TU 1303 4.6		W 1314 4.4	
1941 2.0		1931 2.3	
14 0203 4.5		**29** 0202 4.3	
0815 1.9		0803 2.3	
W 1425 4.9		TH 1421 4.6	
2052 1.5		2035 2.0	
15 0310 4.9		**30** 0256 4.6	
0918 1.5		0901 1.9	
TH 1525 5.2		F 1512 4.9	
2147 1.1		2125 1.6	
		31 0341 4.6	
		0949 1.6	
		SA 1557 5.1	
		2209 1.4	

NOVEMBER

Time	m	Time	m
1 0423 5.1		**16** 0459 5.4	
1032 1.3		1114 1.0	
SU 1639 5.2		M 1717 5.4	
2251 1.2		● 2334 1.0	
2 0503 5.3		**17** 0538 5.4	
1112 1.1		1155 1.0	
M 1721 5.3		TU 1756 5.3	
○ 2331 1.0			
3 0542 5.4		**18** 0013 1.0	
1152 1.0		0612 5.4	
TU 1801 5.4		W 1233 1.1	
		1830 5.2	
4 0009 1.0		**19** 0048 1.2	
0620 5.5		0644 5.4	
W 1231 1.0		TH 1308 1.2	
1841 5.4		1902 5.1	
5 0048 1.0		**20** 0120 1.4	
0658 5.5		0715 5.3	
TH 1310 1.0		F 1341 1.4	
1921 5.3		1933 5.0	
6 0126 1.1		**21** 0150 1.6	
0738 5.4		0746 5.2	
F 1350 1.1		SA 1413 1.6	
2004 5.2		2006 4.8	
7 0206 1.3		**22** 0220 1.8	
0820 5.3		0821 5.0	
SA 1434 1.3		SU 1446 1.8	
2050 5.0		2043 4.6	
8 0252 1.6		**23** 0252 2.0	
0908 5.1		0900 4.8	
SU 1525 1.6		M 1524 2.1	
2143 4.8		2127 4.4	
9 0346 1.9		**24** 0332 2.2	
1005 4.9		0946 4.6	
M 1629 1.9		TU 1613 2.2	
◑ 2249 4.6		◑ 2220 4.3	
10 0456 2.1		**25** 0428 2.4	
1115 4.8		1042 4.5	
TU 1748 2.0		W 1717 2.3	
		2325 4.2	
11 0011 4.5		**26** 0542 2.6	
0621 2.1		1150 4.5	
W 1239 4.8		TH 1827 2.3	
1910 1.9			
12 0131 4.6		**27** 0041 4.3	
0742 1.9		0656 2.4	
TH 1353 4.9		F 1306 4.5	
2020 1.6		1932 2.1	
13 0236 4.8		**28** 0152 4.5	
0847 1.6		0803 2.1	
F 1455 5.1		SA 1414 4.7	
2117 1.4		2032 1.9	
14 0330 5.1		**29** 0251 4.7	
0941 1.4		0901 1.9	
SA 1547 5.2		SU 1512 4.9	
2208 1.1		2127 1.6	
15 0417 5.3		**30** 0343 5.0	
1030 1.1		0954 1.6	
SU 1634 5.3		M 1604 5.1	
2253 1.0		2217 1.4	

DECEMBER

Time	m	Time	m
1 0431 5.2		**16** 0516 5.2	
1043 1.3		1137 1.3	
TU 1653 5.2		W 1737 5.1	
2304 1.2		● 2355 1.3	
2 0516 5.4		**17** 0554 5.3	
1131 1.1		1217 1.3	
W 1741 5.3		TH 1814 5.1	
○ 2350 1.0			
3 0601 5.5		**18** 0032 1.3	
1217 1.0		0628 5.3	
TH 1828 5.4		F 1255 1.3	
		1849 5.0	
4 0036 1.0		**19** 0106 1.4	
0645 5.6		0703 5.3	
F 1304 0.9		SA 1328 1.3	
1914 5.4		1923 5.0	
5 0122 1.0		**20** 0137 1.5	
0731 5.6		0737 5.2	
SA 1351 0.9		SU 1400 1.5	
2002 5.3		1958 4.9	
6 0208 1.1		**21** 0206 1.6	
0818 5.5		0811 5.1	
SU 1438 1.1		M 1430 1.6	
2051 5.2		2033 4.8	
7 0255 1.3		**22** 0235 1.7	
0907 5.4		0846 5.0	
M 1528 1.2		TU 1501 1.7	
2142 5.0		2110 4.7	
8 0345 1.5		**23** 0306 1.8	
0959 5.2		0922 4.8	
TU 1620 1.5		W 1534 1.9	
2238 4.8		2149 4.5	
9 0439 1.7		**24** 0342 2.0	
1057 5.0		1003 4.7	
W 1719 1.7		TH 1615 2.0	
◑ 2340 4.7		◑ 2234 4.4	
10 0542 1.9		**25** 0430 2.2	
1203 4.9		1052 4.6	
TH 1825 1.8		F 1711 2.1	
		2330 4.4	
11 0047 4.6		**26** 0538 2.3	
0654 2.0		1153 4.5	
F 1312 4.8		SA 1825 2.2	
1936 1.8			
12 0153 4.7		**27** 0037 4.4	
0807 1.9		0701 2.2	
SA 1417 4.8		SU 1306 4.5	
2042 1.8		1940 2.1	
13 0253 4.8		**28** 0151 4.5	
0910 1.8		0816 2.0	
SU 1516 4.9		M 1423 4.6	
2139 1.6		2047 1.8	
14 0346 5.0		**29** 0301 4.8	
1005 1.6		0921 1.7	
M 1609 5.0		TU 1532 4.8	
2229 1.5		2148 1.6	
15 0434 5.1		**30** 0402 5.1	
1053 1.4		1021 1.4	
TU 1655 5.0		W 1631 5.1	
2314 1.4		2245 1.3	
		31 0455 5.3	
		1116 1.1	
		TH 1726 5.2	
		○ 2338 1.0	

Chart Datum: 3·22 metres below Ordnance Datum (Newlyn)
HAT is 5·9 metres above Chart Datum

TIDES

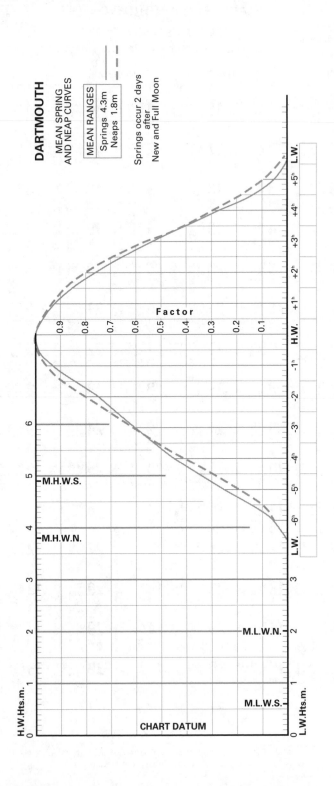

DARTMOUTH

MEAN SPRING
AND NEAP CURVES

MEAN RANGES

Springs 4.3m
Neaps 1.8m

Springs occur 2 days
after
New and Full Moon

Factor

0.9
0.8
0.7
0.6
0.5
0.4
0.3
0.2
0.1

H.W.

L.W.

+1ʰ +2ʰ +3ʰ +4ʰ +5ʰ

-1ʰ -2ʰ -3ʰ -4ʰ -5ʰ -6ʰ

L.W.

M.H.W.S.

M.H.W.N.

M.L.W.N.

M.L.W.S.

H.W.Hts.m.

L.W.Hts.m.

CHART DATUM

JANUARY

Day	Time m	Time m	Day	Time m	Time m
1 TH	0204 1.3	0841 4.5	16 F	0310 0.7	0943 4.8
	1428 1.3	2102 4.2		1534 0.8	2206 4.4
2 F	0235 1.4	0912 4.4	17 SA	0345 1.1	1017 4.5
	1501 1.3	2135 4.1		1641 1.2	2240 4.2
3 SA	0310 1.5	0948 4.3	18 SU	0423 1.4	1051 4.2
	1538 1.4	2213 4.0		1649 1.6	◑ 2316 3.9
4 SU	0351 1.6	1031 4.2	19 M	0506 1.8	1132 3.9
	1625 1.6	◑ 2302 3.9		1735 1.9	
5 M	0444 1.8	1127 4.1	20 TU	0005 3.8	0602 2.1
	1725 1.7			1233 3.7	1838 2.1
6 TU	0003 3.9	0555 1.9	21 W	0123 3.7	0718 2.2
	1234 4.0	1845 1.8		1405 3.6	1958 2.2
7 W	0118 3.9	0727 1.9	22 TH	0246 3.8	0848 2.1
	1356 4.0	2008 1.7		1521 3.7	2119 2.0
8 TH	0241 4.1	0849 1.6	23 F	0351 4.0	0957 1.8
	1519 4.2	2122 1.4		1620 3.9	2218 1.7
9 F	0355 4.4	0959 1.3	24 SA	0443 4.3	1047 1.5
	1630 4.4	2227 1.1		1709 4.1	2304 1.4
10 SA	0459 4.7	1101 0.9	25 SU	0527 4.5	1129 1.2
	1733 4.6	2325 0.8		1752 4.3	2343 1.2
11 SU	0556 4.9	1156 0.6	26 M	0610 4.6	1207 1.1
	1830 4.7 ○			1833 4.4 ●	
12 M	0017 0.6	0648 5.1	27 TU	0019 1.1	0648 4.7
	1248 0.4	1921 4.8		1243 0.9	1909 4.5
13 TU	0107 0.4	0737 5.2	28 W	0053 1.0	0723 4.7
	1334 0.3	2008 4.8		1314 0.9	1944 4.5
14 W	0151 0.4	0822 5.1	29 TH	0123 0.9	0757 4.7
	1418 0.3	2052 4.8		1343 0.9	2016 4.4
15 TH	0231 0.5	0904 5.0	30 F	0151 0.9	0827 4.6
	1457 0.5	2132 4.6		1412 0.9	2045 4.4
			31 SA	0220 1.0	0855 4.6
				1441 1.0	2113 4.3

FEBRUARY

Day	Time m	Time m	Day	Time m	Time m
1 SU	0250 1.1	0927 4.4	16 M	0342 1.3	1001 4.2
	1513 1.1	2145 4.2		1601 1.5	◑ 2216 4.0
2 M	0326 1.3	1004 4.3	17 TU	0417 1.7	1035 3.9
	1551 1.4	◑ 2227 4.1		1638 1.9	2258 3.8
3 TU	0410 1.5	1053 4.1	18 W	0507 2.1	1126 3.5
	1642 1.7	2327 3.9		1737 2.2	
4 W	0513 1.8	1202 3.8	19 TH	0004 3.6	0622 2.3
	1757 1.9			1259 3.4	1900 2.4
5 TH	0045 3.8	0651 2.0	20 F	0205 3.6	0757 2.3
	1333 3.8	1942 1.9		1454 3.5	2042 2.2
6 F	0220 3.9	0835 1.8	21 SA	0323 3.8	0935 1.9
	1509 3.9	2111 1.6		1557 3.8	2156 1.8
7 SA	0344 4.2	0953 1.3	22 SU	0418 4.1	1026 1.5
	1626 4.2	2220 1.2		1647 4.1	2243 1.4
8 SU	0450 4.6	1055 0.8	23 M	0504 4.4	1107 1.1
	1727 4.5	2317 0.7		1730 4.3	2322 1.1
9 M	0546 4.9	1146 0.4	24 TU	0546 4.6	1144 0.9
	1821 4.8			1811 4.4	2358 0.9
10 TU	0006 0.4	0636 5.1	25 W	0626 4.7	1219 0.7
	1235 0.1	1907 4.9		1849 4.5 ●	
11 W	0052 0.2	0721 5.2	26 TH	0032 0.7	0702 4.8
	1318 0.0	1949 4.9		1253 0.6	1923 4.6
12 TH	0132 0.1	0802 5.2	27 F	0104 0.7	0737 4.8
	1356 0.1	2026 4.8		1323 0.6	1954 4.6
13 F	0209 0.3	0838 5.0	28 SA	0132 0.6	0807 4.7
	1431 0.3	2057 4.7		1352 0.6	2023 4.6
14 SA	0241 0.5	0909 4.8			
	1502 0.7	2124 4.5			
15 SU	0312 0.6	0935 4.5			
	1531 1.1	2147 4.3			

MARCH

Day	Time m	Time m	Day	Time m	Time m
1 SU	0201 0.7	0838 4.6	16 M	0239 0.9	0856 4.4
	1421 0.8	2051 4.5		1454 1.1	2107 4.4
2 M	0231 0.8	0909 4.5	17 TU	0306 1.3	0923 4.1
	1452 1.0	2124 4.4		1519 1.5	2136 4.1
3 TU	0306 1.1	0946 4.3	18 W	0335 1.7	0957 3.8
	1528 1.3	2204 4.2		1549 1.9	◑ 2216 3.8
4 W	0350 1.4	1036 4.0	19 TH	0422 2.1	1047 3.5
	1618 1.7	◑ 2303 3.9		1648 2.3	2315 3.6
5 TH	0453 1.8	1148 3.7	20 F	0542 2.3	1205 3.3
	1735 2.0			1818 2.4	
6 F	0027 3.7	0640 2.0	21 SA	0103 3.5	0711 2.2
	1328 3.6	1933 2.0		1420 3.4	1949 2.2
7 SA	0211 3.9	0832 1.7	22 SU	0247 3.7	0846 1.9
	1509 3.8	2106 1.6		1526 3.7	2112 1.8
8 SU	0337 4.2	0946 1.2	23 M	0345 4.0	0946 1.5
	1621 4.2	2210 1.1		1616 4.0	2205 1.4
9 M	0439 4.6	1041 0.7	24 TU	0432 4.3	1031 1.1
	1811 4.5	2302 0.6		1659 4.3	2248 1.1
10 TU	0530 4.9	1129 0.3	25 W	0516 4.5	1110 0.8
	1803 4.7	2347 0.3		1741 4.5	2327 0.8
11 W	0617 5.1	1212 0.0	26 TH	0557 4.7	1147 0.6
	1845 4.9 ○			1820 4.6 ●	
12 TH	0030 0.1	0657 5.1	27 F	0003 0.6	0636 4.8
	1254 0.0	1922 4.9		1224 0.5	1855 4.7
13 F	0108 0.1	0735 5.1	28 SA	0040 0.5	0712 4.8
	1329 0.1	1954 4.8		1259 0.5	1929 4.7
14 SA	0141 0.2	0807 4.9	29 SU	0113 0.5	0747 4.8
	1401 0.4	2020 4.7		1331 0.5	2001 4.7
15 SU	0212 0.5	0833 4.7	30 M	0145 0.6	0821 4.7
	1428 0.7	2043 4.6		1403 0.7	2034 4.6
			31 TU	0219 0.8	0857 4.5
				1437 1.0	2110 4.5

APRIL

Day	Time m	Time m	Day	Time m	Time m
1 W	0256 1.1	0939 4.2	16 TH	0307 1.6	0934 3.8
	1519 1.3	2154 4.2		1517 1.9	2149 3.9
2 TH	0345 1.4	1033 3.9	17 F	0351 1.9	1022 3.5
	1613 1.7	◑ 2253 4.0		1611 2.1	◑ 2242 3.7
3 F	0455 1.8	1149 3.6	18 SA	0507 2.1	1132 3.4
	1735 2.0			1739 2.3	2358 3.6
4 SA	0020 3.8	0641 1.9	19 SU	0628 2.1	1320 3.4
	1331 3.6	1925 1.9		1901 2.2	
5 SU	0200 3.9	0817 1.5	20 M	0146 3.7	0742 1.9
	1457 3.9	2048 1.5		1438 3.7	2012 1.9
6 M	0318 4.2	0924 1.1	21 TU	0257 3.9	0847 1.5
	1601 4.2	2148 1.1		1532 3.9	2113 1.5
7 TU	0417 4.6	1017 0.7	22 W	0350 4.2	0941 1.2
	1652 4.5	2238 0.7		1620 4.2	2204 1.2
8 W	0505 4.8	1104 0.4	23 TH	0438 4.4	1029 0.9
	1735 4.7	2322 0.4		1703 4.4	2250 0.9
9 TH	0550 4.9	1145 0.2	24 F	0522 4.6	1112 0.7
	1816 4.8 ○			1746 4.6	2333 0.7
10 F	0002 0.3	0630 4.9	25 SA	0606 4.7	1154 0.5
	1224 0.2	1850 4.8		1827 4.7 ●	
11 SA	0041 0.3	0705 4.8	26 SU	0013 0.5	0649 4.8
	1300 0.4	1920 4.8		1235 0.5	1905 4.8
12 SU	0114 0.4	0735 4.7	27 M	0054 0.5	0730 4.7
	1330 0.6	1945 4.7		1314 0.6	1943 4.8
13 M	0143 0.7	0801 4.5	28 TU	0133 0.6	0810 4.6
	1358 0.9	2010 4.6		1353 0.7	2022 4.8
14 TU	0211 1.0	0827 4.3	29 W	0214 0.7	0853 4.5
	1424 1.2	2038 4.4		1433 1.0	2104 4.6
15 W	0237 1.3	0857 4.1	30 TH	0259 1.0	0941 4.2
	1448 1.5	2109 4.2		1521 1.3	2153 4.4

Chart Datum: 2·62 metres below Ordnance Datum (Newlyn)
HAT is 5·9 metres above Chart Datum

TIDES

227

TIDES

ENGLAND – DARTMOUTH
LAT 50°21'N   LONG 3°34'W
TIMES AND HEIGHTS OF HIGH AND LOW WATERS

Dates in amber are **SPRINGS**
Dates in yellow are **NEAPS**

2009

MAY

Day	Time	m	Day	Time	m
1 F	0353 / 1038 / 1619 / 2253	1.3 / 4.0 / 1.6 / 4.1	16 SA	0332 / 1005 / 1548 / 2216	1.7 / 3.7 / 1.9 / 3.9
2 SA	0501 / 1152 / 1733	1.5 / 3.8 / 1.8	17 SU	0429 / 1102 / 1654 / 2314	1.9 / 3.6 / 2.1 / 3.8
3 SU	0012 / 0626 / 1313 / 1859	4.0 / 1.6 / 3.8 / 1.7	18 M ◐	0539 / 1210 / 1807	1.9 / 3.5 / 2.0
4 M ◔	0136 / 0745 / 1426 / 2013	4.1 / 1.4 / 4.0 / 1.5	19 TU	0025 / 0648 / 1323 / 1917	3.8 / 1.8 / 3.7 / 1.9
5 TU	0246 / 0851 / 1526 / 2114	4.2 / 1.2 / 4.2 / 1.2	20 W	0144 / 0752 / 1433 / 2021	3.9 / 1.6 / 3.9 / 1.6
6 W	0344 / 0945 / 1617 / 2206	4.4 / 0.9 / 4.4 / 0.9	21 TH	0253 / 0852 / 1530 / 2119	4.1 / 1.3 / 4.1 / 1.3
7 TH	0434 / 1033 / 1702 / 2253	4.5 / 0.7 / 4.5 / 0.7	22 F	0352 / 0947 / 1622 / 2214	4.3 / 1.1 / 4.4 / 1.0
8 F	0520 / 1116 / 1743 / 2334	4.6 / 0.6 / 4.6 / 0.6	23 SA	0446 / 1039 / 1712 / 2304	4.5 / 0.8 / 4.6 / 0.8
9 SA	0601 / 1155 / 1819	4.6 / 0.6 / 4.7	24 SU	0539 / 1128 / 1800 / 2353	4.6 / 0.7 / 4.7 / 0.6
10 SU	0012 / 0637 / 1232 / 1850	0.7 / 4.6 / 0.7 / 4.7	25 M	0629 / 1215 / 1847	4.7 / 0.6 / 4.9
11 M ○	0048 / 0709 / 1304 / 1919	0.7 / 4.5 / 0.9 / 4.6	26 TU ●	0041 / 0716 / 1303 / 1932	0.5 / 4.7 / 0.6 / 4.9
12 TU	0120 / 0738 / 1333 / 1948	0.9 / 4.4 / 1.1 / 4.5	27 W	0128 / 0805 / 1348 / 2016	0.5 / 4.6 / 0.7 / 4.9
13 W	0149 / 0809 / 1401 / 2019	1.1 / 4.2 / 1.3 / 4.4	28 TH	0215 / 0853 / 1435 / 2104	0.6 / 4.5 / 0.8 / 4.8
14 TH	0220 / 0843 / 1429 / 2052	1.3 / 4.0 / 1.5 / 4.3	29 F	0303 / 0944 / 1524 / 2154	0.8 / 4.4 / 1.1 / 4.6
15 F	0252 / 0921 / 1503 / 2131	1.5 / 3.9 / 1.7 / 4.1	30 SA	0355 / 1039 / 1617 / 2248	1.0 / 4.2 / 1.3 / 4.4
			31 SU	0451 / 1138 / 1714 / 2351	1.2 / 4.0 / 1.5 / 4.2

JUNE

Day	Time	m	Day	Time	m
1 M	0553 / 1241 / 1819	1.4 / 4.0 / 1.6	16 TU ◑	0443 / 1122 / 1706 / 2332	1.6 / 3.7 / 1.8 / 3.9
2 TU ◑	0058 / 0701 / 1343 / 1928	4.1 / 1.4 / 4.0 / 1.6	17 W	0546 / 1220 / 1817	1.7 / 3.8 / 1.8
3 W	0205 / 0807 / 1443 / 2034	4.1 / 1.4 / 4.1 / 1.5	18 TH	0036 / 0657 / 1327 / 1931	3.9 / 1.6 / 3.9 / 1.7
4 TH	0305 / 0907 / 1538 / 2132	4.1 / 1.3 / 4.2 / 1.3	19 F	0151 / 0806 / 1439 / 2040	4.0 / 1.5 / 4.0 / 1.5
5 F	0400 / 1000 / 1627 / 2222	4.2 / 1.2 / 4.3 / 1.2	20 SA	0308 / 0910 / 1544 / 2143	4.1 / 1.3 / 4.3 / 1.2
6 SA	0449 / 1047 / 1712 / 2309	4.3 / 1.1 / 4.4 / 1.1	21 SU	0416 / 1011 / 1644 / 2243	4.3 / 1.0 / 4.5 / 0.9
7 SU	0533 / 1129 / 1751 / 2350	4.3 / 1.0 / 4.5 / 1.0	22 M	0517 / 1109 / 1740 / 2338	4.5 / 0.8 / 4.7 / 0.7
8 M	0615 / 1207 / 1828	4.3 / 1.0 / 4.6	23 TU	0614 / 1202 / 1833	4.6 / 0.7 / 4.9
9 TU ○	0027 / 0651 / 1244 / 1901	1.0 / 4.3 / 1.1 / 4.6	24 W	0032 / 0707 / 1255 / 1922	0.5 / 4.7 / 0.5 / 5.0
10 W	0103 / 0725 / 1317 / 1935	1.0 / 4.3 / 1.2 / 4.5	25 TH ●	0123 / 0759 / 1343 / 2011	0.4 / 4.7 / 0.5 / 5.0
11 TH	0135 / 0800 / 1347 / 2008	1.1 / 4.2 / 1.3 / 4.4	26 F	0211 / 0849 / 1429 / 2058	0.3 / 4.7 / 0.5 / 4.9
12 F	0207 / 0835 / 1417 / 2042	1.2 / 4.1 / 1.4 / 4.3	27 SA	0257 / 0936 / 1515 / 2145	0.4 / 4.6 / 0.7 / 4.8
13 SA	0238 / 0911 / 1448 / 2116	1.3 / 4.0 / 1.5 / 4.2	28 SU	0341 / 1022 / 1558 / 2230	0.6 / 4.4 / 0.9 / 4.6
14 SU	0313 / 0949 / 1524 / 2153	1.4 / 3.9 / 1.6 / 4.1	29 M	0426 / 1109 / 1643 / 2318	0.9 / 4.2 / 1.2 / 4.3
15 M	0352 / 1031 / 1608 / 2238	1.5 / 3.8 / 1.7 / 4.0	30 TU	0514 / 1159 / 1734	1.2 / 4.0 / 1.5

JULY

Day	Time	m	Day	Time	m
1 W	0011 / 0608 / 1253 / 1835	4.1 / 1.5 / 3.9 / 1.7	16 TH	0448 / 1132 / 1717 / 2352	1.6 / 3.8 / 1.8 / 3.9
2 TH	0114 / 0713 / 1356 / 1944	3.9 / 1.7 / 3.9 / 1.8	17 F	0559 / 1240 / 1843	1.7 / 3.8 / 1.8
3 F	0223 / 0823 / 1458 / 2056	3.8 / 1.7 / 3.9 / 1.7	18 SA ◑	0108 / 0726 / 1400 / 2009	3.9 / 1.7 / 3.9 / 1.7
4 SA ◑	0327 / 0929 / 1555 / 2157	3.9 / 1.6 / 4.1 / 1.6	19 SU	0239 / 0845 / 1519 / 2123	3.9 / 1.5 / 4.2 / 1.4
5 SU	0423 / 1022 / 1646 / 2249	4.0 / 1.5 / 4.3 / 1.4	20 M	0358 / 0955 / 1626 / 2231	4.2 / 1.2 / 4.5 / 1.0
6 M	0512 / 1110 / 1729 / 2334	4.1 / 1.3 / 4.4 / 1.2	21 TU	0503 / 1057 / 1726 / 2329	4.4 / 0.9 / 4.8 / 0.6
7 TU	0555 / 1151 / 1811	4.2 / 1.2 / 4.5	22 W	0603 / 1153 / 1821	4.6 / 0.6 / 5.0
8 W	0013 / 0635 / 1230 / 1848	1.1 / 4.3 / 1.1 / 4.6	23 TH	0022 / 0656 / 1245 / 1911	0.3 / 4.8 / 0.3 / 5.1
9 TH	0051 / 0712 / 1303 / 1923	1.0 / 4.3 / 1.1 / 4.6	24 F	0113 / 0746 / 1331 / 1959	0.1 / 4.8 / 0.2 / 5.2
10 F	0123 / 0748 / 1333 / 1958	1.0 / 4.3 / 1.1 / 4.5	25 SA	0157 / 0833 / 1414 / 2043	0.1 / 4.8 / 0.3 / 5.1
11 SA ○	0152 / 0823 / 1401 / 2029	1.0 / 4.2 / 1.2 / 4.5	26 SU ●	0238 / 0915 / 1454 / 2123	0.2 / 4.7 / 0.4 / 4.9
12 SU	0220 / 0855 / 1428 / 2059	1.1 / 4.2 / 1.2 / 4.4	27 M	0317 / 0953 / 1531 / 2200	0.5 / 4.6 / 0.7 / 4.6
13 M	0248 / 0927 / 1458 / 2130	1.2 / 4.1 / 1.3 / 4.3	28 TU	0354 / 1028 / 1608 / 2233	0.8 / 4.3 / 1.1 / 4.3
14 TU	0320 / 0959 / 1532 / 2204	1.3 / 4.0 / 1.4 / 4.2	29 W	0431 / 1104 / 1649 / 2309	1.3 / 4.0 / 1.5 / 4.0
15 W	0358 / 1040 / 1617 / 2250	1.4 / 3.9 / 1.6 / 4.0	30 TH	0515 / 1151 / 1740	1.7 / 3.8 / 1.9
			31 F	0003 / 0612 / 1303 / 1851	3.7 / 2.0 / 3.7 / 2.1

AUGUST

Day	Time	m	Day	Time	m
1 SA	0141 / 0732 / 1424 / 2022	3.5 / 2.1 / 3.7 / 2.1	16 SU	0046 / 0701 / 1339 / 1954	3.7 / 1.9 / 3.9 / 1.8
2 SU ◑	0301 / 0903 / 1530 / 2140	3.6 / 2.0 / 3.9 / 1.8	17 M ◑	0228 / 0834 / 1508 / 2116	3.8 / 1.7 / 4.2 / 1.4
3 M	0403 / 1005 / 1624 / 2234	3.8 / 1.7 / 4.2 / 1.5	18 TU	0352 / 0947 / 1617 / 2222	4.1 / 1.2 / 4.5 / 0.9
4 TU	0453 / 1054 / 1710 / 2318	4.0 / 1.4 / 4.4 / 1.2	19 W	0456 / 1048 / 1715 / 2318	4.4 / 0.8 / 4.9 / 0.5
5 W	0536 / 1135 / 1751 / 2357	4.2 / 1.2 / 4.5 / 1.0	20 TH	0551 / 1140 / 1806	4.7 / 0.4 / 5.1
6 TH	0617 / 1211 / 1830	4.3 / 1.0 / 4.6	21 F	0007 / 0641 / 1227 / 1854	0.1 / 4.9 / 0.2 / 5.2
7 F	0032 / 0654 / 1245 / 1905	0.9 / 4.4 / 0.9 / 4.7	22 SA	0054 / 0726 / 1311 / 1938	0.0 / 5.0 / 0.1 / 5.2
8 SA	0103 / 0730 / 1314 / 1939	0.8 / 4.4 / 0.9 / 4.6	23 SU	0134 / 0807 / 1350 / 2017	0.0 / 4.9 / 0.1 / 5.1
9 SU ○	0130 / 0803 / 1340 / 2010	0.8 / 4.4 / 0.9 / 4.6	24 M	0212 / 0843 / 1426 / 2051	0.2 / 4.8 / 0.4 / 4.9
10 M	0156 / 0832 / 1405 / 2039	0.9 / 4.3 / 1.0 / 4.5	25 TU ●	0246 / 0914 / 1459 / 2121	0.5 / 4.6 / 0.7 / 4.6
11 TU	0222 / 0900 / 1432 / 2106	1.0 / 4.3 / 1.1 / 4.4	26 W	0317 / 0940 / 1531 / 2145	0.9 / 4.4 / 1.2 / 4.3
12 W	0250 / 0929 / 1504 / 2138	1.1 / 4.2 / 1.2 / 4.3	27 TH	0348 / 1006 / 1607 / 2215	1.4 / 4.1 / 1.6 / 3.9
13 TH	0325 / 1005 / 1543 / 2221	1.3 / 4.1 / 1.5 / 4.1	28 F	0426 / 1045 / 1655 / 2300	1.9 / 3.8 / 2.1 / 3.6
14 F	0409 / 1058 / 1638 / 2324	1.6 / 3.9 / 1.8 / 3.8	29 SA	0521 / 1148 / 1806	2.2 / 3.6 / 2.3
15 SA	0516 / 1209 / 1809	1.8 / 3.8 / 2.0	30 SU	0036 / 0644 / 1352 / 1949	3.3 / 2.4 / 3.6 / 2.3
			31 M	0240 / 0840 / 1507 / 2121	3.5 / 2.6 / 3.8 / 1.9

Chart Datum: 2·62 metres below Ordnance Datum (Newlyn)
HAT is 5·9 metres above Chart Datum

ENGLAND – DARTMOUTH

LAT 50°21'N   LONG 3°34'W

TIMES AND HEIGHTS OF HIGH AND LOW WATERS

Dates in amber are **SPRINGS**
Dates in yellow are **NEAPS**

2009

SEPTEMBER

Time	m		Time	m
1 TU 0342 0944 1600 2211	3.8 1.8 4.1 1.5		**16** W 0348 0937 1606 2208	4.2 1.2 4.6 0.8
2 W 0430 1030 1645 2253	4.1 1.4 4.4 1.2		**17** TH 0445 1032 1658 2259	4.5 0.7 4.9 0.4
3 TH 0512 1109 1726 2329	4.3 1.1 4.6 0.9		**18** F 0533 1120 1747 ● 2345	4.8 0.4 5.1 0.1
4 F 0551 1144 1805 O	4.5 0.9 4.7		**19** SA 0618 1204 1832	5.0 0.2 5.2
5 SA 0002 0629 1217 1842	0.8 4.5 0.9 4.8		**20** SU 0027 0658 1246 1911	0.0 5.0 0.1 5.2
6 SU 0035 0704 1247 1916	0.7 4.6 0.9 4.7		**21** 0107 0735 1323 1947	0.1 5.0 0.3 5.0
7 M 0103 0737 1315 1947	0.7 4.6 0.8 4.7		**22** TU 0141 0807 1356 2017	0.4 4.9 0.5 4.8
8 TU 0130 0806 1342 2016	0.8 4.5 0.9 4.6		**23** W 0213 0833 1427 2042	0.7 4.7 0.9 4.5
9 W 0157 0834 1410 2046	0.9 4.5 1.0 4.5		**24** TH 0240 0856 1457 2107	1.1 4.4 1.3 4.2
10 TH 0227 0904 1442 2120	1.1 4.4 1.2 4.3		**25** F 0308 0925 1529 2138	1.6 4.2 1.8 3.9
11 F 0300 0943 1522 2205	1.3 4.2 1.5 4.0		**26** SA 0340 1004 1616 ◑ 2225	2.0 3.9 2.2 3.6
12 SA 0345 1037 1619 ◑ 2309	1.7 4.0 1.8 3.8		**27** SU 0436 1100 1728 2338	2.3 3.6 2.4 3.3
13 SU 0454 1151 1759	2.0 3.8 2.1		**28** 0603 1300 1902	2.5 3.6 2.4
14 M 0039 0653 1328 1950	3.6 2.1 3.9 1.8		**29** TU 0207 0747 1431 2040	3.4 2.3 3.8 2.0
15 TU 0230 0829 1500 2108	3.8 1.7 4.2 1.3		**30** W 0311 0905 1527 2133	3.8 1.9 4.1 1.6

OCTOBER

Time	m		Time	m
1 TH 0358 0952 1614 2213	4.1 1.5 4.4 1.2		**16** F 0422 1008 1637 2235	4.6 0.8 4.9 0.6
2 F 0441 1032 1655 2252	4.3 1.2 4.6 1.0		**17** SA 0509 1055 1723 2319	4.8 0.6 5.0 0.4
3 SA 0521 1109 1735 2327	4.5 1.0 4.7 0.8		**18** SU 0551 1138 1805 ● 2359	4.9 0.4 5.1 0.4
4 SU 0559 1144 1815 O	4.7 0.8 4.8		**19** M 0629 1218 1844	5.0 0.4 5.0
5 M 0001 0636 1218 1851	0.7 4.7 0.7 4.8		**20** TU 0038 0703 1256 1918	0.5 4.9 0.5 4.8
6 TU 0035 0709 1251 1925	0.7 4.8 0.7 4.8		**21** W 0112 0733 1329 1946	0.7 4.8 0.8 4.6
7 W 0107 0741 1323 1958	0.8 4.7 0.8 4.7		**22** TH 0142 0759 1359 2012	1.0 4.7 1.1 4.4
8 TH 0137 0813 1355 2032	0.9 4.7 1.0 4.5		**23** F 0210 0826 1429 2041	1.3 4.5 1.4 4.2
9 F 0210 0849 1430 2111	1.1 4.5 1.2 4.3		**24** SA 0237 0857 1502 2117	1.7 4.3 1.8 3.9
10 SA 0248 0932 1516 2201	1.4 4.3 1.5 4.0		**25** SU 0309 0937 1545 2203	2.0 4.1 2.1 3.7
11 SU 0337 1027 1620 ◑ 2306	1.8 4.1 1.9 3.8		**26** M 0358 1030 1651 ◑ 2307	2.3 3.8 2.3 3.5
12 M 0454 1141 1758	2.1 3.9 2.0		**27** TU 0519 1145 1809	2.5 3.7 2.3
13 TU 0040 0644 1318 1937	3.7 2.3 4.0 1.8		**28** W 0056 0643 1329 1927	3.5 2.4 3.8 2.1
14 W 0220 0811 1443 2049	3.9 1.7 4.3 1.3		**29** TH 0219 0759 1439 2032	3.7 2.1 4.0 1.8
15 TH 0329 0915 1545 2145	4.0 1.3 4.6 0.9		**30** F 0315 0858 1531 2122	4.0 1.7 4.3 1.4
			31 SA 0401 0947 1618 2207	4.3 1.4 4.5 1.2

NOVEMBER

Time	m		Time	m
1 SU 0445 1031 1701 2250	4.5 1.1 4.6 1.0		**16** M 0522 1113 1741 ● 2333	4.8 0.8 4.8 0.8
2 M 0526 1111 1745 O 2330	4.7 0.9 4.7 0.8		**17** TU 0602 1154 1821	4.8 0.8 4.7
3 TU 0606 1151 1826	4.8 0.8 4.8		**18** W 0012 0637 1233 1854	0.8 4.8 0.9 4.6
4 W 0008 0645 1231 1905	0.8 4.9 0.8 4.8		**19** TH 0048 0708 1308 1926	1.0 4.8 1.0 4.5
5 TH 0048 0722 1310 1944	0.8 4.9 0.8 4.7		**20** F 0120 0740 1340 1956	1.2 4.7 1.2 4.4
6 F 0126 0801 1349 2026	0.9 4.8 0.9 4.6		**21** SA 0149 0808 1412 2028	1.4 4.6 1.4 4.2
7 SA 0205 0842 1432 2111	1.1 4.7 1.1 4.4		**22** SU 0219 0843 1444 2104	1.6 4.4 1.6 4.0
8 SU 0250 0929 1523 2203	1.4 4.5 1.4 4.2		**23** M 0250 0921 1522 2147	1.8 4.2 1.9 3.8
9 M 0343 1024 1626 ◑ 2307	1.7 4.3 1.7 4.0		**24** TU 0329 1005 1610 ◑ 2239	2.0 4.0 2.0 3.7
10 TU 0452 1132 1743	1.9 4.2 1.8		**25** W 0425 1100 1713 2342	2.2 3.9 2.1 3.6
11 W 0027 0616 1254 1906	3.9 1.9 4.2 1.7		**26** TH 0537 1206 1822	2.3 3.9 2.1
12 TH 0147 0738 1410 2016	4.0 1.7 4.4 1.4		**27** F 0056 0652 1321 1928	3.7 2.2 3.9 1.9
13 F 0254 0844 1514 2114	4.2 1.4 4.5 1.2		**28** SA 0209 0759 1431 2029	3.9 1.9 4.1 1.7
14 SA 0350 0939 1608 2206	4.5 1.2 4.6 0.9		**29** SU 0310 0858 1531 2124	4.1 1.7 4.3 1.4
15 SU 0439 1029 1656 2252	4.7 0.9 4.7 0.8		**30** M 0403 0952 1625 2215	4.4 1.4 4.5 1.2

DECEMBER

Time	m		Time	m
1 TU 0453 1042 1716 2303	4.6 1.1 4.6 1.0		**16** W 0540 1136 1801 ● 2354	4.6 1.1 4.5 1.1
2 W 0540 1130 1805 O 2349	4.8 0.9 4.7 0.8		**17** TH 0619 1216 1839	4.7 1.1 4.5
3 TH 0626 1216 1853	4.9 0.8 4.8		**18** F 0032 0653 1255 1913	1.1 4.7 1.1 4.4
4 F 0036 0709 1304 1938	0.8 5.0 0.7 4.8		**19** SA 0106 0727 1328 1946	1.2 4.7 1.1 4.4
5 SA 0122 0754 1350 2024	0.8 5.0 0.7 4.7		**20** SU 0136 0800 1359 2020	1.3 4.6 1.3 4.3
6 SU 0207 0840 1436 2112	0.9 4.9 0.9 4.6		**21** 0205 0833 1428 2054	1.4 4.5 1.4 4.2
7 M 0253 0928 1526 2202	1.1 4.8 1.0 4.4		**22** TU 0233 0907 1459 2131	1.5 4.4 1.5 4.1
8 TU 0342 1018 1617 2256	1.3 4.6 1.3 4.2		**23** W 0304 0942 1531 2208	1.6 4.2 1.7 3.9
9 W 0435 1115 1715 2357	1.5 4.4 1.5 4.1		**24** TH 0339 1022 1612 ◑ 2252	1.8 4.1 1.8 3.8
10 TH 0537 1219 1820	1.7 4.3 1.6		**25** F 0426 1110 1707 2347	2.0 4.0 1.9 3.8
11 F 0102 0650 1327 1932	4.0 1.8 4.2 1.6		**26** SA 0533 1209 1820	2.1 3.9 2.0
12 SA 0210 0803 1435 2039	4.1 1.7 4.2 1.6		**27** SU 0052 0657 1321 1936	3.8 2.0 3.9 1.9
13 SU 0312 0907 1536 2137	4.2 1.6 4.3 1.4		**28** M 0208 0812 1441 2044	3.9 1.8 4.0 1.6
14 M 0407 1003 1630 2227	4.4 1.4 4.4 1.3		**29** TU 0320 0918 1552 2146	4.2 1.6 4.2 1.4
15 TU 0456 1052 1718 2313	4.5 1.2 4.4 1.2		**30** W 0423 1019 1653 2244	4.5 1.2 4.5 1.1
			31 TH 0518 1115 1750 O 2337	4.7 0.9 4.6 0.8

Chart Datum: 2·62 metres below Ordnance Datum (Newlyn)
HAT is 5·9 metres above Chart Datum

TIDES

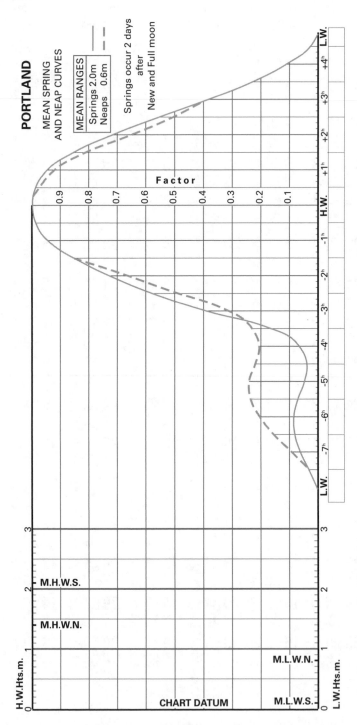

PORTLAND

MEAN SPRING
AND NEAP CURVES

MEAN RANGES	
Springs 2.0m	
Neaps 0.6m	

Springs occur 2 days
after
New and Full moon

Factor

Note - Double LWs occur at Portland. The predictions are for the first LW. The second LW occurs from 3 to 4 Hrs later and may, at Springs, on occasions be lower than the first.

JANUARY

Day	Time m	Time m	Time m	Time m
1 TH	0158 0.4	0908 1.8	1423 0.4	2129 1.6
16 F	0251 0.3	1008 2.0	1523 0.3	2235 1.8
2 F	0227 0.5	0936 1.7	1454 0.4	2200 1.6
17 SA	0329 0.4	1038 1.6	1602 0.4	2306 1.6
3 SA	0258 0.5	1007 1.6	1531 0.4	2236 1.5
18 SU	0409 0.6	1108 1.6	1644 0.5	2341 1.5 ☽
4 SU	0337 0.6	1045 1.6	1620 0.5	2324 1.4 ☽
19 M	0454 0.7	1144 1.4	1732 0.6	
5 M	0430 0.6	1138 1.5	1724 0.5	
20 TU	0027 1.4	0558 0.8	1234 1.3	1834 0.7
6 TU	0028 1.4	0545 0.7	1251 1.5	1840 0.6
21 W	0136 1.4	0726 0.9	1345 1.3	1950 0.8
7 W	0152 1.5	0713 0.7	1426 1.5	1958 0.6
22 TH	0307 1.4	0853 0.8	1521 1.3	2101 0.7
8 TH	0319 1.6	0837 0.7	1556 1.6	2111 0.5
23 F	0415 1.6	0953 0.7	1637 1.4	2157 0.6
9 F	0432 1.8	0950 0.6	1709 1.7	2216 0.4
24 SA	0508 1.7	1038 0.6	1733 1.5	2245 0.5
10 SA	0535 2.0	1050 0.4	1813 1.9	2312 0.3
25 SU	0555 1.8	1120 0.5	1823 1.7	2328 0.4
11 SU	0632 2.2	1143 0.3	1909 2.0 ○	
26 M	0640 2.0	1200 0.3	1907 1.8	
12 M	0002 0.2	0724 2.3	1232 0.2	2000 2.1
27 TU	0009 0.3	0721 2.0	1237 0.3	1947 1.8
13 TU	0049 0.2	0812 2.4	1318 0.1	2045 2.1
28 W	0046 0.2	0759 2.1	1311 0.2	2022 1.9
14 W	0132 0.1	0855 2.3	1401 0.1	2126 2.0
29 TH	0119 0.2	0834 2.0	1341 0.2	2053 1.8
15 TH	0213 0.2	0934 2.2	1443 0.2	2202 1.9
30 F	0149 0.2	0904 1.9	1409 0.2	2119 1.8
31 SA	0217 0.2	0930 1.8	1438 0.2	2143 1.7

FEBRUARY

Day	Time m	Time m	Time m	Time m
1 SU	0245 0.3	0956 1.7	1509 0.3	2212 1.6
16 M	0328 0.4	1027 1.6	1545 0.4	2247 1.5 ☽
2 M	0315 0.4	1027 1.4	1546 0.4	2249 1.5 ☽
17 TU	0356 0.6	1055 1.4	1605 0.6	2323 1.4
3 TU	0355 0.5	1107 1.5	1637 0.5	2341 1.4
18 W	0434 0.7	1136 1.2	1640 0.7	
4 W	0457 0.6	1209 1.4	1757 0.6	
19 TH	0021 1.3	0630 0.8	1249 1.1	1853 0.8
5 TH	0058 1.4	0639 0.7	1345 1.3	1939 0.7
20 F	0155 1.3	0835 0.8	1442 1.2	2035 0.8
6 F	0244 1.5	0833 0.7	1544 1.4	2109 0.6
21 SA	0342 1.4	0937 0.7	1625 1.3	2136 0.6
7 SA	0418 1.7	0953 0.6	1707 1.6	2214 0.4
22 SU	0445 1.6	1019 0.5	1721 1.5	2223 0.5
8 SU	0528 1.9	1049 0.3	1810 1.8	2306 0.3
23 M	0536 1.8	1058 0.4	1809 1.7	2306 0.3
9 M	0625 2.1	1137 0.2	1902 2.0	2352 0.1 ○
24 TU	0622 1.9	1135 0.2	1852 1.8	2345 0.2
10 TU	0715 2.3	1221 0.0	1947 2.1	
25 W	0704 2.1	1211 0.1	1930 1.9 ●	
11 W	0035 0.0	0758 2.4	1303 -0.1	2027 2.2
26 TH	0022 0.1	0743 2.1	1245 0.0	2005 2.0
12 TH	0115 0.0	0837 2.4	1341 -0.1	2102 2.1
27 F	0057 0.0	0818 2.1	1317 0.0	2035 2.0
13 F	0152 0.0	0910 2.2	1418 0.0	2133 2.0
28 SA	0128 0.0	0848 2.0	1348 0.0	2100 1.9
14 SA	0226 0.1	0938 2.0	1451 0.1	2158 1.8
15 SU	0258 0.2	1002 1.8	1521 0.3	2221 1.6

MARCH

Day	Time m	Time m	Time m	Time m
1 SU	0158 0.1	0914 1.9	1418 0.1	2124 1.8
16 M	0229 0.2	0929 1.7	1442 0.3	2143 1.7
2 M	0227 0.2	0941 1.8	1448 0.2	2151 1.7
17 TU	0254 0.4	0952 1.5	1456 0.4	2205 1.5
3 TU	0257 0.3	1011 1.6	1523 0.3	2226 1.6
18 W	0315 0.5	1017 1.3	1511 0.6	2230 1.4 ☽
4 W	0335 0.4	1051 1.5	1609 0.5	2315 1.5 ☽
19 TH	0347 0.7	1053 1.2	1541 0.7	2318 1.3
5 TH	0436 0.6	1154 1.3	1737 0.7	
20 F	0508 0.8	1209 1.1	1659 0.8	
6 F	0032 1.4	0638 0.7	1341 1.3	1938 0.7
21 SA	0056 1.3	0802 0.8	1413 1.1	2002 0.8
7 SA	0229 1.5	0840 0.6	1547 1.4	2105 0.4
22 SU	0253 1.4	0906 0.6	1602 1.3	2106 0.6
8 SU	0408 1.7	0948 0.5	1701 1.6	2203 0.4
23 M	0410 1.6	0948 0.5	1654 1.5	2153 0.5
9 M	0515 1.9	1037 0.2	1755 1.9	2251 0.2
24 TU	0504 1.8	1026 0.3	1740 1.7	2235 0.3
10 TU	0608 2.1	1120 0.1	1842 2.0	2334 0.1
25 W	0552 1.9	1103 0.2	1822 1.9	2315 0.2
11 W	0654 2.3	1201 -0.1	1924 2.2 ○	
26 TH	0636 2.0	1139 0.0	1902 2.0	2352 0.1
12 TH	0014 0.0	0735 2.3	1214 0.0	2001 2.2
27 F	0717 2.1	1214 0.0	1938 2.1	
13 F	0052 -0.1	0811 2.3	1316 -0.1	2034 2.1
28 SA	0028 0.0	0753 2.1	1249 0.0	2010 2.1
14 SA	0127 0.0	0842 2.1	1349 0.0	2101 2.0
29 SU	0102 0.0	0826 2.1	1323 0.0	2038 2.0
15 SU	0200 0.1	0907 2.0	1419 0.1	2123 1.8
30 M	0136 0.1	0857 1.9	1357 0.1	2106 1.9
31 TU	0209 0.2	0927 1.8	1432 0.2	2136 1.8

APRIL

Day	Time m	Time m	Time m	Time m
1 W	0246 0.3	1002 1.6	1511 0.4	2214 1.6
16 TH	0253 0.5	0953 1.3	1443 0.6	2155 1.5
2 TH	0333 0.5	1049 1.5	1607 0.6	2307 1.5 ☽
17 F	0326 0.6	1031 1.2	1515 0.7	2236 1.4 ☽
3 F	0448 0.6	1202 1.3	1741 0.7	
18 SA	0431 0.7	1142 1.1	1628 0.8	
4 SA	0029 1.5	0646 0.7	1359 1.3	1929 0.7
19 SU	0001 1.3	0703 0.7	1333 1.2	1912 0.8
5 SU	0223 1.5	0828 0.6	1534 1.5	2047 0.6
20 M	0155 1.4	0816 0.6	1510 1.3	2025 0.7
6 M	0347 1.7	0927 0.4	1637 1.7	2142 0.5
21 TU	0319 1.5	0904 0.5	1610 1.5	2115 0.5
7 TU	0448 1.9	1013 0.2	1728 1.9	2227 0.3
22 W	0420 1.7	0944 0.3	1659 1.7	2158 0.4
8 W	0540 2.0	1055 0.1	1814 2.0	2309 0.2
23 TH	0513 1.8	1023 0.2	1745 1.9	2239 0.2
9 TH	0627 2.1	1134 0.0	1855 2.1	2348 0.1 ○
24 F	0601 2.0	1102 0.1	1827 2.0	2319 0.1
10 F	0708 2.2	1212 0.0	1932 2.1	
25 SA	0646 2.1	1141 0.0	1907 2.1	2358 0.1 ●
11 SA	0026 0.0	0743 2.1	1248 0.0	2004 2.1
26 SU	0728 2.1	1221 0.0	1945 2.1	
12 SU	0102 0.1	0813 2.0	1321 0.1	2030 2.0
27 M	0037 0.1	0807 2.1	1301 0.1	2020 2.1
13 M	0135 0.1	0838 1.9	1349 0.2	2051 1.9
28 TU	0118 0.0	0844 2.0	1341 0.2	2055 2.0
14 TU	0205 0.3	0901 1.7	1411 0.4	2112 1.7
29 W	0159 0.2	0923 1.8	1424 0.3	2132 1.9
15 W	0230 0.4	0925 1.5	1425 0.5	2133 1.6
30 TH	0245 0.3	1006 1.7	1512 0.5	2216 1.8

TIDES

Chart Datum: 0·93 metres below Ordnance Datum (Newlyn)
HAT is 2·5 metres above Chart Datum

TIME ZONE (UT)	ENGLAND – PORTLAND	Dates in amber are SPRINGS
For Summer Time add ONE hour in **non-shaded areas**	LAT 50°34′N LONG 2°26′W	Dates in yellow are NEAPS
	TIMES AND HEIGHTS OF HIGH AND LOW WATERS	**2009**

MAY

Day	Time m	Time m	Time m	Time m
1 F	0342 0.5	1102 1.5	1613 0.6	2314 1.6
16 SA	0315 0.6	1022 1.3	1511 0.7	2218 1.5
2 SA	0455 0.6	1219 1.5	1732 0.7	
17 SU	0405 0.6	1119 1.2	1611 0.8	2317 1.4
3 SU	0033 1.6	0627 0.6	1348 1.5	1901 0.7
18 M	0523 0.6	1241 1.2	1749 0.8	
4 M	0201 1.6	0753 0.6	1502 1.6	2015 0.7
19 TU	0050 1.4	0656 0.6	1407 1.3	1921 0.7
5 TU	0313 1.7	0853 0.4	1602 1.7	2111 0.5
20 W	0220 1.5	0801 0.5	1516 1.5	2024 0.6
6 W	0414 1.8	0941 0.3	1654 1.8	2158 0.4
21 TH	0331 1.6	0853 0.4	1614 1.7	2115 0.5
7 TH	0507 1.9	1024 0.2	1740 1.9	2241 0.3
22 F	0432 1.7	0940 0.3	1705 1.8	2202 0.4
8 F	0555 1.9	1104 0.2	1823 2.0	2322 0.3
23 SA	0527 1.9	1027 0.2	1754 2.0	2249 0.3
9 SA	0638 2.0	1143 0.2	1901 2.0	
24 SU	0618 2.0	1113 0.2	1841 2.1	2335 0.2
10 SU	0002 0.2	0715 1.9	1221 0.2	1934 2.0
25 M	0708 2.0	1200 0.2	1926 2.2	
11 M	0040 0.2	0746 1.9	1256 0.3	2002 2.0
26 TU	0021 0.2	0754 2.0	1247 0.2	2009 2.2
12 TU	0116 0.3	0814 1.8	1328 0.3	2027 1.9
27 W	0109 0.2	0841 2.0	1334 0.2	2053 2.1
13 W	0149 0.3	0841 1.7	1354 0.4	2052 1.8
28 TH	0157 0.2	0927 1.9	1422 0.3	2138 2.0
14 TH	0218 0.4	0911 1.7	1414 0.5	2116 1.7
29 F	0247 0.3	1016 1.8	1512 0.4	2225 1.9
15 F	0243 0.5	0942 1.4	1436 0.6	2142 1.5
30 SA	0341 0.4	1109 1.7	1606 0.6	2317 1.8
31 SU	0441 0.5	1208 1.6	1707 0.6	

JUNE

Day	Time m	Time m	Time m	Time m
1 M	0016 1.7	0549 0.5	1313 1.6	1816 0.7
16 TU	0429 0.5	1146 1.4	1648 0.7	2347 1.4
2 TU	0122 1.6	0700 0.5	1419 1.6	1927 0.7
17 W	0533 0.5	1255 1.4	1803 0.7	
3 W	0229 1.6	0806 0.5	1521 1.6	2032 0.7
18 TH	0105 1.4	0646 0.5	1413 1.5	1920 0.7
4 TH	0333 1.6	0902 0.5	1617 1.7	2127 0.6
19 F	0233 1.5	0757 0.5	1526 1.6	2030 0.6
5 F	0431 1.6	0951 0.4	1707 1.8	2215 0.5
20 SA	0350 1.6	0902 0.4	1629 1.8	2132 0.5
6 SA	0523 1.7	1036 0.4	1752 1.9	2300 0.5
21 SU	0457 1.7	1002 0.3	1727 1.9	2230 0.4
7 SU	0610 1.7	1118 0.4	1833 1.9	2342 0.4
22 M	0558 1.9	1057 0.3	1822 2.1	2324 0.3
8 M	0651 1.8	1159 0.4	1910 2.0	
23 TU	0656 2.0	1150 0.2	1915 2.2	
9 TU	0023 0.4	0727 1.8	1239 0.4	1942 1.9
24 W	0015 0.2	0749 2.0	1241 0.2	2005 2.3
10 W	0103 0.3	0801 1.9	1315 0.4	2013 1.9
25 TH	0105 0.2	0839 2.1	1329 0.2	2052 2.3
11 TH	0139 0.4	0853 1.7	1347 0.4	2043 1.8
26 F	0153 0.1	0925 2.0	1415 0.2	2136 2.2
12 F	0210 0.4	0905 1.6	1414 0.5	2113 1.7
27 SA	0240 0.2	1009 2.0	1500 0.3	2219 2.1
13 SA	0236 0.4	0938 1.5	1449 0.5	2141 1.6
28 SU	0328 0.2	1053 1.8	1546 0.4	2300 1.9
14 SU	0303 0.4	1012 1.4	1508 0.6	2211 1.5
29 M	0416 0.3	1135 1.7	1634 0.5	2342 1.7
15 M	0340 0.5	1052 1.4	1549 0.6	2250 1.5
30 TU	0507 0.5	1225 1.6	1728 0.6	

JULY

Day	Time m	Time m	Time m	Time m
1 W	0028 1.6	0604 0.6	1323 1.5	1831 0.7
16 TH	0442 0.5	1153 1.4	1706 0.6	
2 TH	0125 1.5	0709 0.6	1432 1.5	1945 0.8
17 F	0004 1.4	0550 0.5	1305 1.4	1827 0.7
3 F	0239 1.4	0818 0.6	1539 1.5	2057 0.7
18 SA	0129 1.4	0715 0.6	1436 1.5	1958 0.7
4 SA	0353 1.4	0921 0.6	1636 1.6	2155 0.7
19 SU	0314 1.5	0841 0.5	1601 1.7	2120 0.6
5 SU	0455 1.5	1013 0.6	1726 1.7	2243 0.6
20 M	0439 1.6	0953 0.4	1710 1.9	2225 0.4
6 M	0548 1.6	1058 0.5	1811 1.8	2326 0.5
21 TU	0549 1.8	1052 0.3	1812 2.1	2320 0.3
7 TU	0634 1.7	1141 0.4	1852 1.9	
22 W	0649 2.0	1144 0.2	1907 2.3	
8 W	0008 0.4	0715 1.7	1223 0.4	1929 2.0
23 TH	0010 0.2	0741 2.1	1232 0.1	1956 2.4
9 TH	0048 0.3	0753 1.8	1301 0.3	2005 2.0
24 F	0057 0.0	0828 2.2	1317 0.0	2041 2.4
10 F	0124 0.3	0826 1.8	1336 0.3	2038 1.9
25 SA	0141 0.0	0910 2.2	1359 0.1	2121 2.3
11 SA	0155 0.3	0858 1.7	1405 0.4	2108 1.8
26 SU	0224 0.0	0948 2.1	1440 0.1	2158 2.2
12 SU	0221 0.3	0927 1.7	1429 0.4	2135 1.7
27 M	0304 0.1	1023 1.9	1519 0.3	2231 1.9
13 M	0246 0.3	0954 1.6	1455 0.4	2201 1.6
28 TU	0344 0.3	1057 1.7	1559 0.4	2302 1.7
14 TU	0315 0.3	1024 1.5	1525 0.5	2229 1.5
29 W	0425 0.4	1132 1.6	1643 0.6	2334 1.5
15 W	0352 0.4	1101 1.5	1606 0.5	2307 1.5
30 TH	0510 0.6	1214 1.4	1740 0.8	
31 F	0017 1.3	0610 0.7	1320 1.4	1901 0.8

AUGUST

Day	Time m	Time m	Time m	Time m
1 SA	0123 1.3	0734 0.8	1500 1.4	2039 0.8
16 SU	0054 1.3	0657 0.7	1401 1.5	1955 0.7
2 SU	0321 1.3	0857 0.7	1612 1.5	2143 0.7
17 M	0301 1.4	0840 0.6	1545 1.6	2122 0.6
3 M	0439 1.4	0953 0.7	1705 1.7	2227 0.6
18 TU	0435 1.6	0949 0.5	1700 1.9	2221 0.4
4 TU	0532 1.5	1038 0.5	1751 1.8	2307 0.5
19 W	0541 1.8	1043 0.3	1800 2.1	2311 0.2
5 W	0619 1.6	1120 0.4	1834 1.9	2346 0.4
20 TH	0636 2.0	1131 0.1	1852 2.3	2356 0.1
6 TH	0700 1.8	1200 0.3	1914 2.0	
21 F	0724 2.2	1215 0.0	1938 2.4	
7 F	0024 0.3	0737 1.9	1239 0.2	1950 2.1
22 SA	0039 -0.1	0806 2.3	1257 0.0	2019 2.4
8 SA	0100 0.2	0811 1.9	1314 0.2	2023 2.0
23 SU	0120 -0.1	0844 2.2	1336 0.0	2056 2.3
9 SU	0132 0.2	0841 1.9	1343 0.2	2054 2.0
24 M	0159 0.0	0918 2.1	1414 0.1	2129 2.2
10 M	0159 0.2	0907 1.8	1409 0.2	2120 1.9
25 TU	0235 0.1	0949 1.9	1449 0.2	2156 1.9
11 TU	0224 0.2	0931 1.7	1433 0.3	2143 1.7
26 W	0308 0.3	1015 1.7	1523 0.4	2220 1.7
12 W	0251 0.3	0956 1.6	1459 0.4	2208 1.6
27 TH	0339 0.5	1040 1.6	1559 0.6	2247 1.4
13 TH	0322 0.4	1028 1.5	1532 0.5	2241 1.5
28 F	0406 0.7	1114 1.4	1649 0.8	2324 1.3
14 F	0403 0.5	1113 1.5	1623 0.6	2330 1.4
29 SA	0443 0.8	1208 1.3	1828 0.9	
15 SA	0510 0.6	1220 1.4	1756 0.7	
30 SU	0029 1.2	0648 0.9	1355 1.3	2028 0.9
31 M	0319 1.2	0831 0.8	1549 1.5	2124 0.7

Chart Datum: 0·93 metres below Ordnance Datum (Newlyn)
HAT is 2·5 metres above Chart Datum

TIME ZONE (UT)		ENGLAND – PORTLAND		Dates in amber are SPRINGS
For Summer Time add ONE hour in **non-shaded areas**		LAT 50°34'N LONG 2°26'W		Dates in yellow are NEAPS
		TIMES AND HEIGHTS OF HIGH AND LOW WATERS		**2009**

SEPTEMBER

Time	m		Time	m
1 0428	1.4	**16**	0429	1.7
0928	0.7		0937	0.5
TU 1640	1.6	W	1644	1.9
2202	0.6		2207	0.4
2 0512	1.5	**17**	0525	1.9
1011	0.5		1026	0.3
W 1724	1.8	TH	1739	2.1
2239	0.4		2251	0.2
3 0554	1.7	**18**	0613	2.1
1052	0.4		1110	0.2
TH 1806	2.0	F	1828	2.3
2317	0.3	●	2334	0.0
4 0633	1.9	**19**	0657	2.2
1131	0.3		1152	0.1
F 1847	2.1	SA	1912	2.4
○ 2353	0.2			
5 0710	2.0	**20**	0014	0.0
1209	0.2		0737	2.3
SA 1925	2.1	SU	1232	0.0
			1951	2.4
6 0028	0.1	**21**	0053	0.0
0747	2.0		0814	2.3
SU 1244	0.1	M	1310	0.1
1959	2.1		2026	2.3
7 0100	0.1	**22**	0129	0.0
0815	2.0		0845	2.1
M 1314	0.1	TU	1345	0.2
2030	2.0		2056	2.1
8 0130	0.1	**23**	0201	0.2
0841	1.9		0911	2.0
TU 1342	0.2	W	1418	0.3
2057	1.9		2119	1.8
9 0158	0.2	**24**	0230	0.4
0904	1.9		0932	1.8
W 1409	0.3	TH	1450	0.5
2121	1.8		2141	1.6
10 0225	0.3	**25**	0250	0.6
0930	1.8		0953	1.6
TH 1436	0.4	F	1520	0.7
2148	1.7		2206	1.4
11 0255	0.4	**26**	0301	0.7
1002	1.6		1019	1.5
F 1509	0.5	SA	1559	0.8
2223	1.5	◐	2240	1.2
12 0334	0.6	**27**	0320	0.9
1047	1.5		1105	1.4
SA 1604	0.7	SU	1757	0.9
◐ 2317	1.4		2349	1.1
13 0449	0.7	**28**	0431	1.0
1156	1.5		1238	1.3
SU 1802	0.8	M	1951	0.9
14 0053	1.3	**29**	0312	1.2
0701	0.8		0753	0.9
M 1348	1.5	TU	1458	1.4
2002	0.7		2048	0.7
15 0311	1.4	**30**	0402	1.4
0836	0.6		0854	0.8
TU 1536	1.7	W	1559	1.6
2115	0.6		2127	0.6

OCTOBER

Time	m		Time	m
1 0440	1.6	**16**	0458	2.0
0938	0.6		1003	0.4
TH 1645	1.8	F	1710	2.1
2204	0.4		2225	0.2
2 0518	1.8	**17**	0544	2.1
1019	0.4		1046	0.3
F 1729	1.9	SA	1758	2.2
2241	0.3		2306	0.1
3 0557	1.9	**18**	0627	2.2
1058	0.3		1127	0.2
SA 1811	2.1	SU	1842	2.2
2317	0.2	●	2346	0.1
4 0636	2.1	**19**	0707	2.3
1134	0.2		1206	0.2
SU 1852	2.1	M	1922	2.2
○ 2351	0.1			
5 0712	2.1	**20**	0023	0.1
1209	0.2		0741	2.2
M 1930	2.1	TU	1244	0.2
			1955	2.1
6 0025	0.1	**21**	0058	0.2
0744	2.1		0811	2.1
TU 1242	0.1	W	1319	0.3
2003	2.1		2023	1.9
7 0058	0.2	**22**	0130	0.3
0814	2.1		0835	2.0
W 1314	0.2	TH	1353	0.4
2033	2.0		2046	1.8
8 0131	0.2	**23**	0156	0.5
0841	2.0		0855	1.9
TH 1346	0.3	F	1425	0.5
2102	1.8		2110	1.6
9 0203	0.4	**24**	0213	0.6
0910	1.9		0916	1.7
F 1421	0.4	SA	1453	0.7
2135	1.7		2137	1.4
10 0238	0.5	**25**	0226	0.7
0945	1.6		0939	1.6
SA 1505	0.6	SU	1528	0.8
2217	1.5		2212	1.3
11 0326	0.7	**26**	0249	0.9
1034	1.6		1014	1.5
SU 1618	0.7	M	1702	0.9
2322	1.4	◐	2318	1.2
12 0457	0.9	**27**	0344	1.0
1148	1.6		1132	1.4
M 1811	0.8	TU	1852	0.8
13 0116	1.4	**28**	0110	1.2
0653	0.9		0657	1.0
TU 1343	1.6	W	1329	1.4
1950	0.7		1957	0.7
14 0303	1.6	**29**	0300	1.4
0818	0.8		0810	0.9
W 1514	1.7	TH	1457	1.6
2053	0.5		2043	0.6
15 0407	1.8	**30**	0352	1.6
0916	0.6		0900	0.7
TH 1617	1.9	F	1556	1.7
2142	0.4		2122	0.4
		31	0436	1.8
			0941	0.6
		SA	1647	1.9
			2200	0.3

NOVEMBER

Time	m		Time	m
1 0518	2.0	**16**	0557	2.1
1020	0.4		1102	0.4
SU 1734	2.0	M	1813	2.0
2237	0.2	●	2317	0.3
2 0600	2.1	**17**	0637	2.1
1058	0.3		1142	0.4
M 1819	2.1	TU	1854	2.0
○ 2314	0.2		2356	0.3
3 0640	2.2	**18**	0713	2.1
1135	0.3		1222	0.4
TU 1901	2.1	W	1929	1.9
2353	0.2			
4 0717	2.2	**19**	0032	0.4
1213	0.3		0743	2.1
W 1940	2.1	TH	1300	0.4
			1958	1.8
5 0031	0.2	**20**	0107	0.4
0752	2.2		0809	2.0
TH 1253	0.3	F	1337	0.5
2017	2.0		2025	1.7
6 0111	0.3	**21**	0137	0.5
0826	2.1		0834	1.9
F 1334	0.4	SA	1411	0.5
2054	1.9		2053	1.6
7 0152	0.4	**22**	0200	0.6
0902	2.0		0859	1.8
SA 1419	0.5	SU	1440	0.6
2135	1.7		2124	1.5
8 0238	0.6	**23**	0219	0.7
0943	1.9		0925	1.7
SU 1513	0.6	M	1509	0.7
2226	1.6		2201	1.4
9 0334	0.7	**24**	0246	0.8
1036	1.9		0956	1.6
M 1625	0.7	TU	1551	0.7
◑ 2335	1.5	◑	2251	1.3
10 0450	0.8	**25**	0331	0.9
1147	1.7		1046	1.5
TU 1751	0.7	W	1709	0.8
11 0107	1.5	**26**	0006	1.3
0620	0.9		0458	0.9
W 1320	1.1	TH	1211	1.4
1913	0.6		1839	0.7
12 0230	1.6	**27**	0136	1.4
0742	0.8		0655	0.9
TH 1440	1.7	F	1348	1.6
2017	0.5		1940	0.6
13 0333	1.8	**28**	0251	1.5
0844	0.7		0804	0.8
F 1543	1.8	SA	1503	1.6
2109	0.5		2028	0.5
14 0425	1.9	**29**	0349	1.7
0935	0.6		0855	0.7
SA 1638	1.9	SU	1605	1.7
2154	0.4		2114	0.4
15 0513	2.0	**30**	0440	1.9
1020	0.5		0940	0.6
SU 1727	2.0	M	1659	1.8
2237	0.4		2159	0.3

DECEMBER

Time	m		Time	m
1 0527	2.0	**16**	0612	2.0
1025	0.5		1126	0.5
TU 1750	1.9	W	1833	1.8
2244	0.3	●	2336	0.4
2 0613	2.1	**17**	0651	2.0
1110	0.4		1207	0.4
W 1839	2.0	TH	1912	1.8
○ 2330	0.3			
3 0657	2.2	**18**	0016	0.4
1156	0.3		0725	2.0
TH 1927	2.0	F	1247	0.4
			1946	1.8
4 0016	0.3	**19**	0054	0.4
0740	2.2		0756	1.9
F 1243	0.3	SA	1325	0.4
2012	2.0		2017	1.7
5 0103	0.3	**20**	0128	0.5
0823	2.2		0826	2.0
SA 1330	0.3	SU	1359	0.4
2058	2.0		2048	1.7
6 0150	0.4	**21**	0157	0.5
0907	2.1		0855	1.9
SU 1420	0.4	M	1428	0.5
2144	1.9		2119	1.6
7 0238	0.5	**22**	0220	0.5
0951	2.0		0924	1.8
M 1512	0.4	TU	1451	0.5
2232	1.8		2151	1.5
8 0329	0.6	**23**	0243	0.6
1040	1.9		0952	1.6
TU 1610	0.5	W	1518	0.5
2326	1.7		2225	1.4
9 0427	0.7	**24**	0315	0.6
1134	1.8		1024	1.5
W 1714	0.6	TH	1557	0.6
◑			◑ 2309	1.4
10 0029	1.6	**25**	0401	0.7
0533	0.8		1111	1.5
TH 1238	1.7	F	1654	0.6
1822	0.6			
11 0139	1.6	**26**	0011	1.4
0647	0.8		0511	0.8
F 1350	1.6	SA	1221	1.4
1928	0.6		1807	0.6
12 0248	1.6	**27**	0133	1.4
0800	0.8		0638	0.8
SA 1500	1.6	SU	1353	1.4
2029	0.6		1922	0.6
13 0349	1.7	**28**	0254	1.5
0904	0.7		0758	0.7
SU 1604	1.7	M	1520	1.5
2122	0.6		2030	0.5
14 0442	1.8	**29**	0401	1.7
0957	0.7		0906	0.6
M 1659	1.7	TU	1629	1.7
2210	0.5		2131	0.4
15 0529	1.9	**30**	0500	1.9
1043	0.6		1004	0.5
TU 1749	1.8	W	1730	1.8
2255	0.5		2227	0.4
		31	0554	2.1
			1058	0.4
		TH	1828	1.9
		○	2320	0.3

Chart Datum: 0·93 metres below Ordnance Datum (Newlyn)
HAT is 2·5 metres above Chart Datum

TIDES

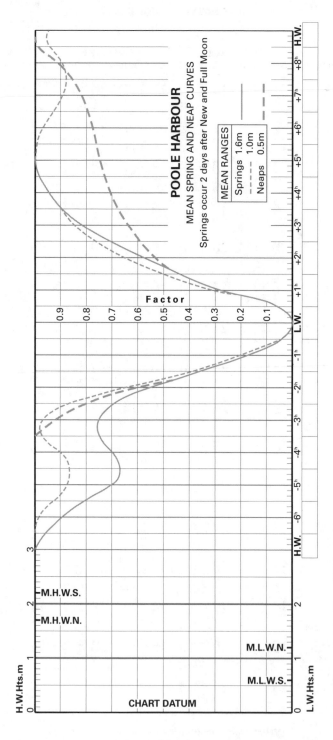

POOLE HARBOUR

MEAN SPRING AND NEAP CURVES

Springs occur 2 days after New and Full Moon

MEAN RANGES
Springs 1.6m
1.0m
Neaps 0.5m

Factor

0.9 0.8 0.7 0.6 0.5 0.4 0.3 0.2 0.1

H.W. +8ʰ +7ʰ +6ʰ +5ʰ +4ʰ +3ʰ +2ʰ +1ʰ L.W. -1ʰ -2ʰ -3ʰ -4ʰ -5ʰ -6ʰ H.W.

H.W.Hts.m

M.H.W.S.
M.H.W.N.

M.L.W.N.
M.L.W.S.

CHART DATUM

L.W.Hts.m

Note - HW times are not shown because they cannot be predicted with reasonable accuracy. Approximate times can be gained using LW times and the Tidal Curves at the start of this section.

TIME ZONE (UT)
For Summer Time add ONE hour in **non-shaded areas**

ENGLAND – POOLE HARBOUR
LAT 50°42'N   LONG 1°59'W
TIMES AND HEIGHTS OF HIGH AND LOW WATERS

Dates in amber are **SPRINGS**
Dates in yellow are **NEAPS**

2009

JANUARY

Time	m	Time	m
1 TH 0654 / 1913	2.0 0.9 / 2.0 0.8	**16** F 0758 / 2019	2.2 0.7 / 2.0 0.7
2 F 0731 / 1950	2.0 1.0 / 1.9 0.9	**17** SA 0842 / 2100	2.1 0.9 / 1.9 0.9
3 SA 0812 / 2033	2.0 1.0 / 1.9 0.9	**18** SU 0929 / 2148	2.0 1.0 / 1.8 1.0
4 SU 0902 / ☽ 2125	1.9 1.9 / 1.9 1.0	**19** M 1026 / 2247	1.9 1.2 / 1.7 1.2
5 M 1002 / 2229	1.9 1.1 / 1.8 1.0	**20** TU 1138	1.8 1.3 / 1.6
6 TU 1114 / 2342	1.9 1.2 / 1.8 1.1	**21** W 1254	0002 1.3 1.7 / 1.3 1.6
7 W 1232	1.9 1.1 / 1.8	**22** TH 1358	0118 1.3 1.8 / 1.2 1.8
8 TH 1345	0059 1.0 2.0 / 1.0 1.9	**23** F 1449	0219 1.2 1.9 / 1.0 1.9
9 F 1448	0209 0.9 2.1 / 0.8 2.1	**24** SA 1531	0307 1.0 1.9 / 0.9 2.0
10 SA 1544	0309 0.8 2.2 / 0.7 2.2	**25** SU 1610	0348 0.9 2.0 / 0.8 2.0
11 SU 1636 / ○	0404 0.7 2.3 / 0.6 2.3	**26** M 1647 / ●	0426 0.9 2.0 / 0.7 2.0
12 M 1725	0455 0.6 2.3 / 0.4	**27** TU 1721	0501 0.8 2.1 / 0.7
13 TU 1811	2.3 0.6 / 2.3 0.4	**28** W 1753	0533 2.1 0.8 / 2.0 0.7
14 W 1855	2.3 0.6 / 2.3 0.5	**29** TH 1822	0604 2.1 0.8 / 2.0 0.7
15 TH 1938	2.3 0.7 / 2.1 0.6	**30** F 1852	0634 2.1 0.7 / 2.0 0.7
		31 SA 1926	0707 2.1 0.8 / 2.0 0.7

FEBRUARY

Time	m	Time	m
1 SU 0745 / 2004	2.0 0.8 / 1.9 0.8	**16** M 0838 / ☽ 2056	2.0 0.9 / 1.8 1.0
2 M 0828 / ☽ 2051	2.0 0.9 / 1.9 0.9	**17** TU 0923 / 2150	1.8 1.1 / 1.7 1.3
3 TU 0923 / 2151	1.9 1.0 / 1.8 1.0	**18** W 1035 / 2318	1.7 1.3 / 1.6 1.4
4 W 1037 / 2314	1.8 1.2 / 1.7 1.2	**19** TH 1214	1.6 1.3 / 1.5
5 TH 1213	1.8 1.2 / 1.8	**20** F 1332	0053 1.4 1.6 / 1.3 1.7
6 F 1340	0049 1.2 1.9 / 1.0 1.9	**21** SA 1426	0202 1.3 1.8 / 1.1 1.8
7 SA 1445	0208 1.0 2.0 / 0.8 1.9	**22** SU 1509	0250 1.1 1.9 / 0.9 1.9
8 SU 1539	0309 0.8 2.0 / 0.6 2.1	**23** M 1547	0329 1.0 1.9 / 0.8 2.0
9 M 1628	0400 0.7 2.1 / 0.5 2.3	**24** TU 1623	0405 0.8 2.0 / 0.7 2.1
10 TU 1712	0447 0.6 2.2 / 0.4	**25** W 1657 / ●	0439 0.7 2.0 / 0.6 2.1
11 W 1754	0530 2.3 0.5 / 2.3 0.4	**26** TH 1729	0511 2.1 0.6 / 2.1 0.6
12 TH 1833	0611 2.3 0.5 / 2.3 0.4	**27** F 1759	0541 2.1 0.6 / 2.1 0.6
13 F 1909	0650 2.3 0.5 / 2.1 0.5	**28** SA 1830	0612 2.1 0.6 / 2.1 0.6
14 SA 1943	0726 2.2 0.6 / 2.1 0.7		
15 SU 2017	0801 2.1 0.6 / 2.0 0.8		

MARCH

Time	m	Time	m
1 SU 0645 / 1903	2.1 0.6 / 2.1 0.7	**16** M 0723 / 1940	2.1 0.7 / 2.0 0.8
2 M 0722 / 1942	2.1 0.7 / 2.0 0.8	**17** TU 0755 / 2016	2.0 0.9 / 1.9 1.0
3 TU 0804 / 2028	2.0 0.8 / 1.9 0.9	**18** W 0834 / ☽ 2104	1.8 1.1 / 1.7 1.3
4 W 0858 / ☽ 2131	1.9 1.0 / 1.8 1.1	**19** TH 0933 / 2235	1.6 1.3 / 1.6 1.4
5 TH 1018 / 2307	1.8 1.2 / 1.7 1.3	**20** F 1127	1.5 1.5 / 1.5
6 F 1207	1.7 1.2 / 1.7	**21** SA 1255	0022 1.4 1.5 / 1.3 1.6
7 SA 1334	0051 1.2 1.8 / 1.0 1.9	**22** SU 1352	0133 1.3 1.6 / 1.1 1.8
8 SU 1436	0206 1.0 1.9 / 0.8 2.0	**23** M 1436	0221 1.1 1.9 / 0.9 1.9
9 M 1526	0302 0.8 2.1 / 0.6 2.2	**24** TU 1515	0300 0.9 2.0 / 0.8 2.0
10 TU 1610	0348 0.6 2.1 / 0.4 2.3	**25** W 1551	0335 0.8 2.1 / 0.7 2.0
11 W 1652 / ○	0431 0.5 2.2 / 0.4 2.3	**26** TH 1626 / ●	0409 0.7 2.0 / 0.6 2.1
12 TH 1730	0511 0.4 2.3 / 0.4	**27** F 1700	0442 0.6 2.2 / 0.6
13 F 1805	0547 2.3 0.4 / 2.2 0.4	**28** SA 1733	0515 2.1 0.5 / 2.1 0.6
14 SA 1838	0622 2.3 0.5 / 2.1 0.6	**29** SU 1808	0549 2.2 0.5 / 2.1 0.6
15 SU 1909	0653 2.2 0.6 / 2.1 0.7	**30** M 1845	0625 2.2 0.5 / 2.1 0.7
		31 TU 1928	0706 2.1 0.6 / 2.1 0.8

APRIL

Time	m	Time	m
1 W 0752 / 2020	2.0 0.8 / 2.0 0.9	**16** TH 0804 / 2035	1.8 1.0 / 1.8 1.3
2 TH 0851 / ☽ 2130	1.9 0.9 / 1.8 1.2	**17** F 0856 / ☽ 2148	1.7 1.2 / 1.6 1.4
3 F 1015 / 2306	1.8 1.1 / 1.8 1.2	**18** SA 1025 / 2330	1.6 1.3 / 1.6 1.4
4 SA 1156	1.7 1.1 / 1.8	**19** SU 1200	1.5 1.3 / 1.7
5 SU 1316	0040 1.2 1.8 / 0.9 1.9	**20** M 1304	0044 1.3 1.6 / 1.1 1.8
6 M 1414	0150 0.9 1.9 / 0.8 2.1	**21** TU 1351	0136 1.1 1.7 / 1.0 1.9
7 TU 1502	0242 0.8 2.0 / 0.6 2.2	**22** W 1433	0218 0.9 1.9 / 0.8 2.0
8 W 1545	0326 0.6 2.1 / 0.6 2.3	**23** TH 1512	0256 0.8 2.0 / 0.7 2.1
9 TH 1625 / ○	0407 0.5 2.2 / 0.5 2.3	**24** F 1550 / ○	0333 0.7 2.0 / 0.6 2.1
10 F 1702	0446 0.5 2.1 / 0.5	**25** SA 1628 / ●	0410 0.6 2.1 / 0.6 2.2
11 SA 1736	0521 2.3 0.5 / 2.1 0.6	**26** SU 1708	0449 2.2 0.5 / 2.2 0.6
12 SU 1808	0553 2.2 0.6 / 2.1 0.6	**27** M 1750	0529 2.2 0.5 / 2.2 0.6
13 M 1840	2.1 0.6 / 2.0 0.8	**28** TU 1834	0612 2.2 0.6 / 2.2 0.7
14 TU 1912	0654 2.0 0.8 / 1.9 0.9	**29** W 1923	0658 2.1 0.6 / 2.1 0.8
15 W 1948	0726 1.9 0.9 / 1.9 1.0	**30** TH 2020	0751 2.0 0.7 / 2.0 0.9

Chart Datum: 1·40 metres below Ordnance Datum (Newlyn)
HAT is 2·6 metres above Chart Datum

TIDES

235

TIDES

TIME ZONE (UT)
For Summer Time add ONE hour in **non-shaded areas**

Dates in amber are **SPRINGS**
Dates in yellow are **NEAPS**
2009

ENGLAND – POOLE HARBOUR
LAT 50°42'N   LONG 1°59'W
TIMES AND HEIGHTS OF HIGH AND LOW WATERS

MAY

Day	Time m	Time m	Day	Time m	Time m
1	0852 1.9 / 0.9	F 2129 1.0	16	0830 1.8 / 1.1	SA 2106 1.3
2	1007 1.8 / 1.0	SA 2250 1.9 / 1.1	17	0929 1.6 / 1.2	SU 2216 1.8 / 1.3
3	1129 1.8	SU 1.9	18	1043 1.6 / 1.2	M 1.8 ☽2331 1.3
4	0011 1.0	M 1242 0.9 / 2.0 ☾	19	1153 1.6 / 1.1	TU 1.8
5	0118 0.9 / 1.9	TU 1341 0.8 / 2.1	20	0033 1.2 / 1.7	W 1252 1.0 / 1.9
6	0212 0.8 / 2.0	W 1431 0.7 / 2.1	21	0125 1.0 / 1.8	TH 1342 0.9 / 2.0
7	0258 0.7 / 2.0	TH 1514 0.7 / 2.1	22	0212 0.9 / 1.9	F 1429 0.8 / 2.1
8	0340 0.7 / 2.1	F 1555 0.7 / 2.1	23	0257 0.7 / 2.0	SA 1516 0.7 / 2.1
9	0419 0.6 / 2.1	SA 1633 0.7 / 2.1	24	0343 0.6 / 2.1	SU 1602 0.7 / 2.2
10	0456 0.7 / 2.1	SU 1710 0.7 / 2.3	25	0429 0.6 / 2.2	M 1650 0.6 / 2.3
11	0529 2.1 / 2.1	M 1744 0.8 ○	26	0517 0.5 / 2.2	TU 1739 0.6 ●
12	0601 0.7 / 2.0	TU 1818 0.8	27	0605 2.3 / 0.6	W 1828 2.2 / 0.7
13	0633 0.8 / 2.0	W 1852 1.0	28	0656 2.2 / 0.6	TH 1920 2.2 / 0.7
14	0706 1.9 / 0.9	TH 1929 1.0	29	0749 2.1 / 0.7	F 2016 2.1 / 0.8
15	0744 1.9 / 1.0	F 2012 1.2 / 1.9	30	0845 2.0 / 0.8	SA 2116 2.1 / 0.9
31	0946 1.9 / 0.8	SU 2221 2.0 / 1.0			

JUNE

Day	Time m	Time m	Day	Time m	Time m
1	1052 1.9 / 0.9	M 2330 2.0 / 1.0	16	0941 1.8 / 1.0	TU 2218 1.2 ◑
2	1158 1.8 / 0.9	TU 2324 1.2 ◑	17	1043 1.8 / 1.1	W 2324 1.9 / 1.2
3	0036 1.0	W 1300 1.8 / 0.9 / 2.0	18	1149 1.8 / 1.0	TH 1.9
4	0136 0.9 / 1.9	TH 1355 0.9 / 2.0	19	0031 1.0 / 1.8	F 1255 1.0 / 2.0
5	0228 0.9 / 1.9	F 1444 0.9 / 2.0	20	0134 0.9 / 1.9	SA 1355 0.9 / 2.0
6	0313 0.8 / 2.0	SA 1528 0.9 / 2.0	21	0231 0.8 / 2.0	SU 1452 0.8 / 2.1
7	0355 0.8 / 2.0	SU 1609 0.8 / 2.1	22	0326 0.7 / 2.1	M 1547 0.7 / 2.2
8	0434 0.8 / 2.0	M 1649 0.8 / 2.0	23	0418 0.6 / 2.2	TU 1639 0.7 / 2.3
9	0511 0.8 / 2.0	TU 1726 0.8	24	0510 0.5 / 2.3	W 1731 0.6
10	0545 2.0 / 0.8	W 1801 2.0 / 0.9	25	0600 2.3 / 0.4	TH 1821 2.3 / 0.6 ●
11	0618 2.0 / 0.8	TH 1836 2.0 / 0.9	26	0649 2.2 / 0.5	F 1911 2.3 / 0.6
12	0651 0.8 / 2.0	F 1910 2.0 / 1.0	27	0738 2.1 / 0.6	SA 2001 2.3 / 0.7
13	0725 1.9 / 0.9	SA 1947 1.9 / 1.0	28	0827 2.0 / 0.6	SU 2052 2.1 / 0.8
14	0803 1.9 / 0.9	SU 2029 1.1	29	0916 2.0 / 0.8	M 2146 2.1 / 0.9
15	0848 1.8 / 1.0	M 2119 1.9 / 1.2	30	1010 1.9 / 0.9	TU 2246 2.0 / 1.0

JULY

Day	Time m	Time m	Day	Time m	Time m
1	1109 1.8 / 1.0	W 2352 1.9 / 1.1	16	0954 1.8 / 1.0	TH 2234 1.1
2	1215 1.8 / 1.1	TH 1.9	17	1103 1.8 / 1.1	F 2352 1.9 / 1.1
3	0059 1.1 / 1.8	F 1320 1.1 / 1.9	18	1222 1.8 / 1.1	SA 1.9 ○
4	0200 1.0 / 1.8	SA 1418 1.1 / 1.9 ◑	19	0112 1.0 / 1.8	SU 1338 1.0 / 2.0
5	0251 1.0 / 1.9	SU 1507 1.0 / 2.0	20	0220 0.9 / 1.9	M 1443 0.9 / 2.1
6	0336 0.9 / 2.0	M 1551 0.9 / 2.0	21	0319 0.7 / 2.1	TU 1540 0.8 / 2.2
7	0416 0.8 / 2.0	TU 1631 0.9 / 2.0	22	0412 0.6 / 2.3	W 1632 0.6 / 2.3
8	0454 0.8 / 2.0	W 1709 0.8	23	0501 0.4 / 2.3	TH 1721 0.6 / 2.3
9	0529 2.0 / 0.7	TH 1744 2.0 / 0.8	24	0548 0.4 / 2.3	F 1808 2.4 / 0.5
10	0602 2.0 / 0.7	F 1817 2.0 / 0.8	25	0634 2.3 / 0.4	SA 1854 2.3 / 0.6
11	0633 2.0 / 0.8	SA 1848 2.0 / 0.9 ○	26	0717 2.2 / 0.4	SU 1938 2.3 / 0.6 ●
12	0703 2.0 / 0.8	SU 1920 2.0 / 0.9	27	0759 2.1 / 0.7	M 2021 2.2 / 0.7
13	0735 1.9 / 0.8	M 1956 2.0 / 0.9	28	0841 2.0 / 0.8	TU 2107 2.1 / 0.9
14	0813 1.9 / 0.9	TU 2039 2.0 / 1.0	29	0926 1.9 / 0.9	W 2159 1.9 / 1.0
15	0858 1.9 / 0.9	W 2130 1.9 / 1.0	30	1022 1.8 / 1.2	TH 2306 1.8 / 1.2
31	1134 1.6 / 1.3	F 1.7			

AUGUST

Day	Time m	Time m	Day	Time m	Time m
1	0025 1.3 / 1.6	SA 1253 1.3 / 1.8	16	1211 1.7 / 1.2	SU 1.8
2	0137 1.2 / 1.8	SU 1400 1.2 / 1.8 ◑	17	0105 1.1 / 1.8	M 1335 1.1 / 1.9
3	0233 1.0 / 1.9	M 1452 1.1 / 1.9	18	0216 0.9 / 2.0	TU 1439 0.9 / 2.1
4	0317 0.9 / 2.0	TU 1534 1.0 / 2.0	19	0311 0.7 / 2.1	W 1532 0.7 / 2.2
5	0356 0.8 / 2.0	W 1612 0.9 / 2.0	20	0400 0.5 / 2.3	TH 1620 0.6 / 2.3
6	0433 0.7 / 2.1	TH 1649 0.8 / 2.0	21	0446 0.4 / 2.3	F 1705 0.5
7	0508 0.7 / 2.1	F 1722 0.8	22	0529 2.3 / 0.3	SA 1748 2.4 / 0.4
8	0540 2.0 / 0.7	SA 1753 2.1 / 0.8	23	0611 2.3 / 0.4	SU 1829 2.4 / 0.4
9	0609 2.0 / 0.7	SU 1822 2.1 / 0.8 ○	24	0650 2.3 / 0.4	M 1908 2.3 / 0.6
10	0637 2.0 / 0.7	M 1852 2.1 / 0.8	25	0726 2.1 / 0.6	TU 1946 2.2 / 0.7 ●
11	0707 2.0 / 0.7	TU 1926 2.1 / 0.8	26	0803 2.0 / 0.8	W 2025 2.0 / 0.9
12	0741 2.0 / 0.8	W 2005 2.0 / 0.9	27	0843 1.9 / 0.9	TH 2111 1.9 / 1.1
13	0823 1.9 / 0.9	TH 2054 2.0 / 1.0	28	0936 1.8 / 1.0	F 2218 1.8 / 1.3
14	0918 1.8 / 1.1	F 2200 1.9 / 1.2	29	1058 1.6 / 1.4	SA 2352 1.6 / 1.3
15	1034 1.8 / 1.2	SA 2331 1.8 / 1.2	30	1232 1.6 / 1.4	SU 1.6
31	0114 1.3 / 1.8	M 1343 1.3 / 1.8			

Chart Datum: 1·40 metres below Ordnance Datum (Newlyn)
HAT is 2·6 metres above Chart Datum

TIME ZONE (UT)	ENGLAND – POOLE HARBOUR	Dates in amber are SPRINGS
For Summer Time add ONE hour in **non-shaded areas**	LAT 50°42'N LONG 1°59'W	Dates in yellow are NEAPS
	TIMES AND HEIGHTS OF HIGH AND LOW WATERS	**2009**

SEPTEMBER

Time	m		Time	m
1 TU 0211 / 1432	1.1 1.9 1.2 1.9	**16** W 0205 / 1428	0.9 2.1 0.9 2.1
2 W 0253 / 1512	0.9 2.0 1.0 2.0	**17** TH 0256 / 1517	0.7 2.2 0.7 2.2
3 TH 0331 / 1548	0.8 2.1 0.8 2.0	**18** F 0342 / 1601 ●	0.5 2.3 0.6 2.3
4 F 0406 / 1622 ○	0.7 2.1 0.8 2.1	**19** SA 0424 / 1643	0.4 2.4 0.5 2.3
5 SA 0440 / 1655	0.7 2.1 0.7 2.1	**20** SU 0505 / 1723	0.4 2.4 0.4
6 SU 0512 / 1725	0.6 2.1 0.7	**21** M 0543 / 1801	2.3 0.4 2.3 0.5
7 M 0541 / 1754	2.1 0.6 2.1 0.7	**22** TU 0619 / 1836	2.3 0.4 2.3 0.6
8 TU 0609 / 1825	2.1 0.7 2.1 0.7	**23** W 0653 / 1910	2.1 0.7 2.1 0.8
9 W 0640 / 1859	2.1 0.7 2.1 0.8	**24** TH 0727 / 1946	2.0 0.9 2.0 0.9
10 TH 0715 / 1939	2.0 0.8 2.0 0.9	**25** F 0806 / 2027	1.1 1.9 1.1
11 F 0759 / 2029	2.0 1.0 1.9 1.0	**26** SA 0857 / 2130 ☽	1.3 1.7 1.3
12 SA 0857 / 2141 ☽	1.8 1.2 1.8 1.2	**27** SU 1023 / 2310	1.6 1.4 1.4
13 SU 1025 / 2325	1.8 1.3 1.8 1.2	**28** M 1202	1.6 1.4
14 M 1211	1.8 1.3 1.8	**29** TU 0038 / 1314	1.3 1.9 1.3 1.7
15 TU 0059 / 1330	1.1 1.9 1.1 1.9	**30** W 0137 / 1402	1.2 1.9 1.2 1.9

OCTOBER

Time	m		Time	m
1 TH 0220 / 1441	1.0 2.0 1.0 2.0	**16** F 0232 / 1455	0.7 2.3 0.7 2.2
2 F 0258 / 1516	0.8 2.1 0.8 2.0	**17** SA 0317 / 1538	0.6 2.3 0.6 2.3
3 SA 0333 / 1550	0.7 2.1 0.8 2.1	**18** SU 0358 / 1618 ●	0.6 2.3 0.6 2.3
4 SU 0407 / 1622 ○	0.7 2.1 0.7 2.1	**19** M 0437 / 1657	0.6 2.3 0.6 2.3
5 M 0439 / 1654	0.7 2.2 0.7 2.2	**20** TU 0515 / 1734	0.6 2.3 0.6
6 TU 0511 / 1726	0.7 2.2 0.7	**21** W 0550 / 1807	2.2 0.7 2.2 0.7
7 W 0543 / 1801	2.2 0.7 2.2 0.7	**22** TH 0624 / 1841	2.1 0.8 2.1 0.8
8 TH 0619 / 1839	2.1 0.7 2.1 0.8	**23** F 0659 / 1916	2.1 0.9 2.0 0.9
9 F 0659 / 1924	2.1 0.7 2.1 0.8	**24** SA 0738 / 1956	2.0 1.1 1.9 1.1
10 SA 0748 / 2019	2.0 0.8 2.0 1.0	**25** SU 0826 / 2049	1.8 1.3 1.8 1.3
11 SU 0854 / 2136 ☽	1.8 1.2 1.8 1.3	**26** M 0939 / 2211 ☽	1.7 1.4 1.6 1.4
12 M 1024 / 2313	1.8 1.3 1.2	**27** TU 1111 / 2340	1.7 1.4 1.6 1.3
13 TU 1158	1.8 1.2	**28** W 1225	1.8 1.4 1.6
14 W 0038 / 1312	1.0 2.0 1.0 2.0	**29** TH 0045 / 1318	1.2 1.9 1.2 1.8
15 TH 0142 / 1407	0.9 2.1 0.9 2.1	**30** F 0135 / 1400	1.1 2.0 1.0 1.9
		31 SA 0216 / 1438	0.9 2.0 0.9 2.0

NOVEMBER

Time	m		Time	m
1 SU 0254 / 1513	0.8 2.1 0.8 2.1	**16** M 0332 / 1556 ●	0.7 2.3 0.7 2.2
2 M 0330 / 1549 ○	0.8 2.2 0.7 2.1	**17** TU 0412 / 1635	0.7 2.3 0.7 2.2
3 TU 0406 / 1626	0.7 2.2 0.7 2.2	**18** W 0451 / 1712	0.8 2.2 0.7
4 W 0444 / 1705	0.7 2.3 0.7	**19** TH 0527 / 1747	2.1 0.8 2.1 0.8
5 TH 0523 / 1745	2.3 0.7 2.3 0.7	**20** F 0603 / 1821	2.1 0.9 2.1
6 F 0606 / 1830	2.2 0.8 2.2 0.7	**21** SA 0639 / 1856	2.1 1.0 1.9
7 SA 0653 / 1920	2.1 0.9 2.0 0.8	**22** SU 0716 / 1933	2.0 1.1 1.9 1.0
8 SU 0748 / 2019	2.1 1.0 2.0 0.9	**23** M 0758 / 2016	1.9 1.2 1.8 1.2
9 M 0853 / 2128 ☽	2.0 1.1 1.9 1.1	**24** TU 0850 / 2111 ☽	1.8 1.3 1.7 1.2
10 TU 1010 / 2246	1.9 1.2 1.9 1.3	**25** W 0956 / 2220	1.8 1.4 1.6 1.3
11 W 1130 / 2331	1.9 1.2 1.9	**26** TH 1110 / 2331	1.9 1.4 1.6 1.5
12 TH 0002 / 1240	1.0 2.0 1.0 1.9	**27** F 1215	1.8 1.3 1.7
13 F 0107 / 1339	0.9 2.1 0.9 2.0	**28** SA 0032 / 1308	1.2 1.9 1.2 1.8
14 SA 0201 / 1429	0.8 2.2 0.8 2.1	**29** SU 0125 / 1355	1.0 2.0 1.0 1.9
15 SU 0248 / 1514	0.8 2.3 0.8 2.1	**30** M 0211 / 1438	0.9 2.1 0.9 2.0

DECEMBER

Time	m		Time	m
1 TU 0255 / 1522	0.9 2.2 0.8 2.1	**16** W 0353 / 1619 ●	0.9 2.1 0.8 2.1
2 W 0340 / 1606 ○	0.8 2.3 0.7 2.2	**17** TH 0433 / 1657	0.9 2.1 0.8
3 TH 0425 / 1652	0.7 2.3 0.6	**18** F 0511 / 1733	2.1 0.9 2.1 0.8
4 F 0511 / 1739	2.3 0.7 2.3 0.6	**19** SA 0547 / 1807	2.1 0.9 2.1 0.8
5 SA 0559 / 1827	2.3 0.7 2.2 0.6	**20** SU 0622 / 1840	2.1 0.9 2.0 0.8
6 SU 0650 / 1918	2.3 0.8 2.1 0.7	**21** M 0655 / 1912	2.0 1.0 2.0 0.9
7 M 0743 / 2012	2.2 0.8 2.1 0.8	**22** TU 0730 / 1946	2.0 1.0 1.9 0.9
8 TU 0841 / 2109	2.1 0.9 2.0 0.8	**23** W 0807 / 2025	1.9 1.1 1.8 1.0
9 W 0944 / 2212 ☽	2.1 1.0 1.9 0.9	**24** TH 0851 / 2111 ☽	1.9 1.2 1.8 1.1
10 TH 1052 / 2318	2.0 1.0 1.9 1.0	**25** F 0946 / 2210	1.8 1.3 1.7 1.2
11 F 1201	2.0 1.1 1.9	**26** SA 1054 / 2318	1.8 1.3 1.7 1.2
12 SA 0025 / 1306	1.0 2.0 1.0 1.9	**27** SU 1206	1.9 1.2 1.8
13 SU 0127 / 1403	1.0 2.0 1.0 1.9	**28** M 0029 / 1313	1.2 1.9 1.1 1.9
14 M 0221 / 1453	1.0 2.1 0.9 2.0	**29** TU 0134 / 1412	1.0 2.0 0.9 2.0
15 TU 0310 / 1538	0.9 2.1 0.8 2.0	**30** W 0232 / 1505	0.9 2.1 0.8 2.1
		31 TH 0324 / 1556 ○	0.8 2.2 0.7 2.2

Chart Datum: 1·40 metres below Ordnance Datum (Newlyn)
HAT is 2·6 metres above Chart Datum

TIDES

SOUTHAMPTON

MEAN SPRING AND NEAP CURVES

Springs occur 2 days after New and Full Moon

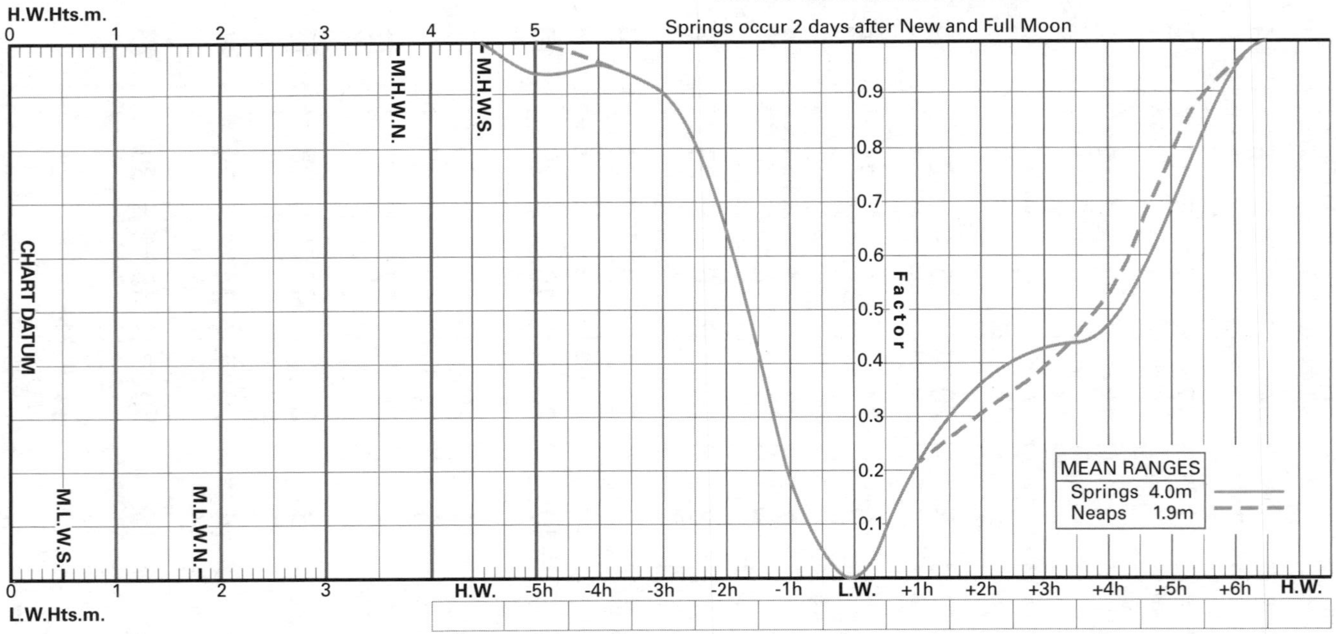

MEAN RANGES	
Springs	4.0m
Neaps	1.9m

Factor

0.9 0.8 0.7 0.6 0.5 0.4 0.3 0.2 0.1

H.W. +6h +5h +4h +3h +2h +1h L.W. -1h -2h -3h -4h -5h H.W.

M.H.W.S.
M.H.W.N.

M.L.W.N.
M.L.W.S.

CHART DATUM

H.W.Hts.m.

L.W.Hts.m.

Note - Double HWs occur at Southampton. The predictions are for the first HW.

TIME ZONE (UT)	ENGLAND – SOUTHAMPTON	Dates in amber are SPRINGS
For Summer Time add ONE hour in **non-shaded areas**	**LAT 50°54′N LONG 1°24′W** TIMES AND HEIGHTS OF HIGH AND LOW WATERS	Dates in yellow are NEAPS **2009**

JANUARY

Day	Time	m	Time	m
1 TH	0115 / 0701 / 1326 / 1917	4.3 / 1.3 / 4.2 / 1.1	**16** F — 0207 / 0801 / 1421 / 2020	4.5 / 0.9 / 4.4 / 0.8
2 F	0153 / 0737 / 1404 / 1954	4.2 / 1.4 / 4.1 / 1.2	**17** SA — 0251 / 0843 / 1505 / 2100	4.3 / 1.2 / 4.1 / 1.2
3 SA	0234 / 0817 / 1445 / 2036	4.1 / 1.5 / 4.1 / 1.4	**18** SU — 0337 / 0928 / 1552 / 2147	4.1 / 1.5 / 3.9 / 1.5
4 SU	0319 / 0905 / 1534 / 2127	4.1 / 1.6 / 4.0 / 1.5	**19** M — 0429 / 1023 / 1651 / 2247	3.9 / 1.8 / 3.7 / 1.9
5 M	0414 / 1004 / 1635 / 2231	4.0 / 1.7 / 3.9 / 1.7	**20** TU — 0533 / 1135 / 1808	3.8 / 2.0 / 3.6
6 TU	0520 / 1117 / 1749 / 2347	4.0 / 1.8 / 3.8 / 1.7	**21** W — 0005 / 0651 / 1255 / 1934	2.0 / 3.7 / 2.0 / 3.6
7 W	0632 / 1235 / 1906	4.0 / 1.7 / 3.9	**22** TH — 0122 / 0804 / 1402 / 2042	2.0 / 3.8 / 1.8 / 3.8
8 TH	0104 / 0742 / 1348 / 2016	1.6 / 4.2 / 1.4 / 4.1	**23** F — 0223 / 0900 / 1454 / 2131	1.8 / 4.0 / 1.6 / 4.0
9 F	0213 / 0845 / 1451 / 2117	1.4 / 4.4 / 1.1 / 4.3	**24** SA — 0311 / 0944 / 1537 / 2210	1.6 / 4.1 / 1.3 / 4.1
10 SA	0313 / 0941 / 1549 / 2212	1.1 / 4.5 / 0.8 / 4.5	**25** SU — 0353 / 1021 / 1616 / 2244	1.4 / 4.3 / 1.1 / 4.3
11 SU	0409 / 1033 / 1641 / 2303	0.9 / 4.7 / 0.6 / 4.6	**26** M — 0431 / 1054 / 1652 / 2315	1.1 / 4.3 / 0.9 / 4.3
12 M	0501 / 1122 / 1730 / 2351	0.7 / 4.7 / 0.4 / 4.7	**27** TU — 0507 / 1125 / 1726 / 2346	1.0 / 4.4 / 0.8 / 4.4
13 TU	0550 / 1209 / 1816	0.6 / 4.7 / 0.3	**28** W — 0540 / 1156 / 1758	0.9 / 4.4 / 0.7
14 W	0038 / 0636 / 1254 / 1859	4.7 / 0.6 / 4.7 / 0.4	**29** TH — 0017 / 0611 / 1229 / 1827	4.4 / 0.9 / 4.4 / 0.7
15 TH	0123 / 0719 / 1338 / 1940	4.6 / 0.7 / 4.6 / 0.6	**30** F — 0050 / 0641 / 1302 / 1857	4.4 / 0.9 / 4.4 / 0.8
			31 SA — 0124 / 0712 / 1336 / 1928	4.3 / 1.0 / 4.3 / 0.9

FEBRUARY

Day	Time	m	Time	m
1 SU	0200 / 0747 / 1413 / 2005	4.3 / 1.1 / 4.2 / 1.1	**16** M — 0249 / 0839 / 1507 / 2055	4.1 / 1.3 / 3.9 / 1.5
2 M	0240 / 0829 / 1456 / 2050	4.2 / 1.3 / 4.1 / 1.3	**17** TU — 0332 / 0922 / 1557 / 2146	3.8 / 1.7 / 3.6 / 1.9
3 TU	0329 / 0921 / 1552 / 2148	4.0 / 1.5 / 3.9 / 1.6	**18** W — 0428 / 1030 / 1711 / 2314	3.6 / 2.0 / 3.4 / 2.2
4 W	0434 / 1033 / 1709 / 2310	3.9 / 1.8 / 3.7 / 1.8	**19** TH — 0554 / 1211 / 1900	3.5 / 2.1 / 3.4
5 TH	0557 / 1207 / 1842	3.8 / 1.8 / 3.8	**20** F — 0057 / 0734 / 1337 / 2022	2.2 / 3.5 / 2.0 / 3.7
6 F	0046 / 0723 / 1337 / 2006	1.8 / 3.9 / 1.5 / 3.9	**21** SA — 0207 / 0840 / 1433 / 2112	2.0 / 3.8 / 1.7 / 3.9
7 SA	0206 / 0837 / 1446 / 2112	1.5 / 4.2 / 1.2 / 4.2	**22** SU — 0254 / 0925 / 1515 / 2149	1.6 / 4.0 / 1.3 / 4.1
8 SU	0310 / 0935 / 1543 / 2206	1.1 / 4.4 / 0.8 / 4.5	**23** M — 0333 / 1000 / 1553 / 2221	1.3 / 4.2 / 1.0 / 4.2
9 M	0404 / 1025 / 1632 / 2253	0.8 / 4.6 / 0.4 / 4.6	**24** TU — 0410 / 1031 / 1629 / 2250	1.0 / 4.3 / 0.8 / 4.3
10 TU	0453 / 1110 / 1718 / 2336	0.5 / 4.7 / 0.2 / 4.7	**25** W — 0444 / 1101 / 1703 / 2319	0.8 / 4.4 / 0.6 / 4.4
11 W	0537 / 1152 / 1759	0.3 / 4.7 / 0.1	**26** TH — 0517 / 1131 / 1735 / 2349	0.7 / 4.4 / 0.5 / 4.4
12 TH	0017 / 0618 / 1232 / 1837	4.8 / 0.2 / 4.7 / 0.2	**27** F — 0548 / 1202 / 1805	0.6 / 4.5 / 0.5
13 F	0056 / 0655 / 1310 / 1913	4.7 / 0.4 / 4.6 / 0.4	**28** SA — 0021 / 0618 / 1236 / 1834	4.5 / 0.6 / 4.5 / 0.6
14 SA	0134 / 0730 / 1348 / 1946	4.5 / 0.6 / 4.4 / 0.7		
15 SU	0211 / 0804 / 1426 / 2018	4.3 / 0.9 / 4.2 / 1.1		

MARCH

Day	Time	m	Time	m
1 SU	0056 / 0649 / 1311 / 1906	4.5 / 0.7 / 4.4 / 0.7	**16** M — 0134 / 0728 / 1353 / 1941	4.3 / 0.9 / 4.1 / 1.2
2 M	0132 / 0724 / 1348 / 1942	4.4 / 0.9 / 4.3 / 1.0	**17** TU — 0209 / 0758 / 1431 / 2014	4.0 / 1.2 / 3.9 / 1.6
3 TU	0212 / 0804 / 1432 / 2025	4.2 / 1.1 / 4.1 / 1.3	**18** W — 0247 / 0835 / 1518 / 2058	3.8 / 1.6 / 3.6 / 2.0
4 W	0300 / 0855 / 1530 / 2125	4.0 / 1.4 / 3.9 / 1.6	**19** TH — 0337 / 0931 / 1626 / 2221	3.5 / 2.0 / 3.4 / 2.3
5 TH	0406 / 1010 / 1652 / 2256	3.8 / 1.7 / 3.7 / 1.9	**20** F — 0454 / 1115 / 1810	3.4 / 2.2 / 3.4
6 F	0539 / 1156 / 1835	3.7 / 1.8 / 3.7	**21** SA — 0019 / 0642 / 1254 / 1943	2.3 / 3.4 / 2.0 / 3.6
7 SA	0043 / 0716 / 1330 / 2002	1.8 / 3.8 / 1.5 / 3.9	**22** SU — 0134 / 0802 / 1355 / 2036	2.0 / 3.6 / 1.7 / 3.8
8 SU	0203 / 0830 / 1436 / 2104	1.5 / 4.1 / 1.1 / 4.2	**23** M — 0222 / 0850 / 1440 / 2114	1.7 / 3.9 / 1.4 / 4.1
9 M	0302 / 0925 / 1529 / 2152	1.1 / 4.3 / 0.7 / 4.5	**24** TU — 0302 / 0926 / 1519 / 2146	1.3 / 4.1 / 1.0 / 4.2
10 TU	0351 / 1010 / 1615 / 2235	0.7 / 4.5 / 0.4 / 4.7	**25** W — 0338 / 0958 / 1556 / 2216	1.0 / 4.2 / 0.8 / 4.4
11 W	0435 / 1051 / 1656 / 2314	0.4 / 4.6 / 0.2 / 4.7	**26** TH — 0413 / 1030 / 1631 / 2247	0.7 / 4.4 / 0.6 / 4.5
12 TH	0516 / 1129 / 1735 / 2350	0.2 / 4.7 / 0.1 / 4.7	**27** F — 0448 / 1102 / 1705 / 2320	0.5 / 4.5 / 0.5 / 4.6
13 F	0553 / 1206 / 1811	0.2 / 4.6 / 0.2	**28** SA — 0522 / 1136 / 1739 / 2354	0.4 / 4.5 / 0.5 / 4.6
14 SA	0026 / 0627 / 1242 / 1843	4.6 / 0.3 / 4.5 / 0.4	**29** SU — 0555 / 1212 / 1812	0.5 / 4.6 / 0.5
15 SU	0100 / 0658 / 1317 / 1912	4.5 / 0.6 / 4.3 / 0.8	**30** M — 0031 / 0630 / 1251 / 1848	4.6 / 0.6 / 4.5 / 0.7
			31 TU — 0111 / 0708 / 1333 / 1928	4.5 / 0.8 / 4.3 / 1.0

APRIL

Day	Time	m	Time	m
1 W	0155 / 0752 / 1423 / 2017	4.3 / 1.1 / 4.1 / 1.4	**16** TH — 0217 / 0804 / 1452 / 2030	3.8 / 1.5 / 3.7 / 2.0
2 TH	0248 / 0849 / 1527 / 2123	4.0 / 1.4 / 3.9 / 1.7	**17** F — 0304 / 0855 / 1552 / 2139	3.6 / 1.8 / 3.6 / 2.2
3 F	0400 / 1008 / 1655 / 2258	3.8 / 1.7 / 3.7 / 1.9	**18** SA — 0409 / 1014 / 1712 / 2319	3.5 / 2.0 / 3.5 / 2.2
4 SA	0534 / 1148 / 1833	3.7 / 1.7 / 3.8	**19** SU — 0534 / 1149 / 1838	3.4 / 2.0 / 3.6
5 SU	0035 / 0705 / 1313 / 1949	1.7 / 3.8 / 1.4 / 4.1	**20** M — 0039 / 0658 / 1300 / 1940	2.0 / 3.5 / 1.8 / 3.8
6 M	0148 / 0813 / 1415 / 2045	1.4 / 4.1 / 1.1 / 4.3	**21** TU — 0134 / 0757 / 1352 / 2025	1.7 / 3.8 / 1.4 / 4.0
7 TU	0243 / 0905 / 1505 / 2131	1.0 / 4.3 / 0.7 / 4.5	**22** W — 0218 / 0841 / 1436 / 2103	1.4 / 4.0 / 1.1 / 4.2
8 W	0329 / 0949 / 1548 / 2211	0.7 / 4.6 / 0.5 / 4.6	**23** TH — 0259 / 0920 / 1517 / 2139	1.0 / 4.2 / 0.9 / 4.4
9 TH	0411 / 1028 / 1629 / 2248	0.5 / 4.5 / 0.4 / 4.6	**24** F — 0338 / 0957 / 1556 / 2216	0.8 / 4.4 / 0.7 / 4.6
10 F	0449 / 1104 / 1706 / 2323	0.4 / 4.5 / 0.4 / 4.6	**25** SA — 0417 / 1035 / 1635 / 2253	0.6 / 4.5 / 0.6 / 4.6
11 SA	0525 / 1139 / 1741 / 2356	0.4 / 4.5 / 0.5 / 4.5	**26** SU — 0456 / 1114 / 1715 / 2333	0.5 / 4.6 / 0.5 / 4.7
12 SU	0559 / 1214 / 1813	0.5 / 4.4 / 0.7	**27** M — 0536 / 1155 / 1755	0.5 / 4.6 / 0.6
13 M	0029 / 0629 / 1250 / 1842	4.4 / 0.7 / 4.3 / 1.0	**28** TU — 0014 / 0616 / 1240 / 1837	4.6 / 0.6 / 4.5 / 0.8
14 TU	0103 / 0657 / 1326 / 1912	4.2 / 0.9 / 4.1 / 1.3	**29** W — 0100 / 0701 / 1329 / 1924	4.5 / 0.7 / 4.4 / 1.1
15 W	0138 / 0728 / 1406 / 1946	4.0 / 1.2 / 3.9 / 1.6	**30** TH — 0150 / 0751 / 1425 / 2019	4.2 / 1.0 / 4.2 / 1.4

Chart Datum: 2·74 metres below Ordnance Datum (Newlyn)
HAT is 5·0 metres above Chart Datum

TIME ZONE (UT)
For Summer Time add ONE hour in **non-shaded areas**

ENGLAND – SOUTHAMPTON
LAT 50°54'N   LONG 1°24'W
TIMES AND HEIGHTS OF HIGH AND LOW WATERS

Dates in amber are **SPRINGS**
Dates in yellow are **NEAPS**

2009

MAY

Day	Time	m	Time	m		Day	Time	m	Time	m
1 F	0248	4.1	1533	4.0		**16** SA	0241	3.8	1523	3.8
	0851	1.3	2128	1.6			0829	1.6	2105	2.0
2 SA	0400	3.9	1653	3.9		**17** SU	0335	3.6	1623	3.7
	1005	1.5	2250	1.7			0927	1.8	2215	2.0
3 SU	0522	3.8	1814	4.0		**18** M	0439	3.6	1730	3.7
	1127	1.5					1039	1.8	◑ 2329	2.0
4 M	0010	1.6	1241	1.4		**19** TU	0550	3.6	1835	3.9
	0640	3.9	◑ 1922	4.1			1152	1.7		
5 TU	0118	1.4	1341	1.2		**20** W	0033	1.7	1254	1.5
	0745	4.0	2017	4.3			0656	3.7	1931	4.0
6 W	0212	1.2	1432	1.0		**21** TH	0128	1.5	1348	1.3
	0838	4.2	2104	4.4			0753	3.9	2019	4.2
7 TH	0259	1.0	1517	0.8		**22** F	0217	1.2	1437	1.1
	0923	4.3	2145	4.5			0842	4.1	2104	4.4
8 F	0342	0.8	1558	0.8		**23** SA	0303	0.9	1524	0.9
	1004	4.3	2222	4.5			0927	4.3	2148	4.5
9 SA	0421	0.7	1637	0.8		**24** SU	0349	0.7	1610	0.7
	1041	4.3	2257	4.4			1012	4.5	2232	4.6
10 SU	0458	0.7	1714	0.8		**25** M	0435	0.6	1657	0.7
	1117	4.3	2331	4.4			1058	4.5	2317	4.7
11 M	0532	0.7	1748	1.0		**26** TU	0522	0.5	1744	0.7
	1153	4.2	○				1145	4.6	●	
12 TU	0005	4.3	1230	4.2		**27** W	0005	4.6	1236	4.5
	0604	0.9	1820	1.2			0609	0.5	1832	0.8
13 W	0041	4.2	1307	4.1		**28** TH	0055	4.5	1329	4.4
	0635	1.0	1853	1.4			0658	0.7	1924	1.0
14 TH	0117	4.0	1348	4.0		**29** F	0148	4.4	1425	4.3
	0708	1.2	1928	1.6			0750	0.8	2019	1.2
15 F	0157	3.9	1432	3.9		**30** SA	0245	4.2	1527	4.2
	0744	1.4	2011	1.8			0846	1.0	2119	1.4
						31 SU	0347	4.0	1632	4.1
							0947	1.2	2225	1.5

JUNE

Day	Time	m	Time	m		Day	Time	m	Time	m
1 M	0454	3.9	1740	4.1		**16** TU	0352	3.7	1632	3.9
	1052	1.4	2333	1.6			0942	1.6	◑ 2224	1.8
2 TU	0604	3.9	1845	4.1		**17** W	0452	3.7	1734	3.9
	1158	1.4	◑				1046	1.7	2330	1.7
3 W	0038	1.5	1301	1.4		**18** TH	0600	3.7	1838	4.0
	0709	3.9	1943	4.2			1155	1.6		
4 TH	0137	1.4	1356	1.3		**19** F	0037	1.6	1302	1.5
	0808	4.0	2034	4.2			0706	3.9	1938	4.1
5 F	0228	1.3	1446	1.3		**20** SA	0139	1.4	1402	1.3
	0859	4.0	2119	4.3			0808	4.0	2034	4.3
6 SA	0314	1.1	1531	1.2		**21** SU	0236	1.1	1459	1.1
	0944	4.1	2200	4.3			0904	4.2	2127	4.5
7 SU	0356	1.0	1613	1.1		**22** M	0330	0.8	1554	0.9
	1025	4.1	2237	4.3			0957	4.4	2218	4.6
8 M	0435	1.0	1653	1.1		**23** TU	0423	0.6	1647	0.6
	1102	4.2	2313	4.2			1049	4.5	2308	4.6
9 TU	0513	0.9	1731	1.0		**24** W	0514	0.5	1738	0.7
	1139	4.2	○ 2348	4.2			1140	4.6	2358	4.6
10 W	0548	0.9	1807	1.2		**25** TH	0605	0.4	1829	0.7
	1215	4.2					1230	4.6	●	
11 TH	0024	4.2	1252	4.2		**26** F	0048	4.6	1322	4.6
	0620	1.0	1840	1.3			0653	0.4	1918	0.8
12 F	0101	4.1	1329	4.1		**27** SA	0138	4.5	1412	4.5
	0653	1.1	1915	1.4			0741	0.6	2007	0.9
13 SA	0138	4.0	1409	4.0		**28** SU	0229	4.4	1504	4.4
	0727	1.2	1951	1.6			0829	0.8	2057	1.1
14 SU	0218	3.9	1451	4.0		**29** M	0321	4.2	1558	4.2
	0804	1.4	2033	1.7			0917	1.0	2150	1.3
15 M	0302	3.8	1538	3.9		**30** TU	0416	4.0	1656	4.1
	0849	1.5	2124	1.8			1011	1.3	2249	1.5

JULY

Day	Time	m	Time	m		Day	Time	m	Time	m
1 W	0519	3.8	1759	4.0		**16** TH	0402	3.8	1640	3.9
	1111	1.6	2354	1.7			0953	1.6	2236	1.7
2 TH	0628	3.7	1905	3.9		**17** F	0510	3.8	1751	3.9
	1217	1.7					1103	1.8	2354	1.7
3 F	0100	1.7	1324	1.7		**18** SA	0628	3.8	1905	4.0
	0738	3.8	2006	4.0			1224	1.7		
4 SA	0202	1.6	1423	1.7		**19** SU	0111	1.5	1341	1.6
	0840	3.9	◑ 2100	4.0			0744	3.9	2013	4.2
5 SU	0253	1.4	1513	1.5		**20** M	0221	1.2	1447	1.3
	0932	4.0	2145	4.1			0851	4.1	2114	4.4
6 M	0338	1.3	1558	1.4		**21** TU	0321	0.9	1546	1.0
	1015	4.1	2224	4.2			0949	4.4	2208	4.5
7 TU	0419	1.1	1639	1.3		**22** W	0416	0.6	1641	0.7
	1052	4.2	2300	4.2			1041	4.6	2258	4.7
8 W	0457	1.0	1717	1.2		**23** TH	0507	0.4	1731	0.6
	1126	4.2	2333	4.2			1130	4.7	2346	4.7
9 TH	0533	0.9	1753	1.1		**24** F	0555	0.2	1819	0.5
	1159	4.2					1217	4.7		
10 F	0006	4.2	1232	4.2		**25** SA	0032	4.7	1303	4.7
	0606	0.9	1825	1.1			0640	0.2	1903	0.5
11 SA	0041	4.2	1306	4.2		**26** SU	0118	4.6	1348	4.6
	0637	0.9	○ 1856	1.2			0722	0.3	● 1945	0.7
12 SU	0115	4.1	1340	4.2		**27** M	0202	4.5	1432	4.5
	0706	1.0	1927	1.3			0803	0.6	2027	0.9
13 M	0150	4.1	1416	4.1		**28** TU	0247	4.2	1517	4.3
	0738	1.1	2001	1.4			0843	1.0	2111	1.3
14 TU	0227	4.0	1456	4.1		**29** W	0335	4.0	1607	4.0
	0814	1.3	2042	1.5			0927	1.4	2202	1.6
15 W	0310	3.9	1542	4.0		**30** TH	0431	3.8	1708	3.8
	0858	1.5	2132	1.6			1021	1.7	2307	1.9
						31 F	0544	3.6	1824	3.7
							1135	2.0		

AUGUST

Day	Time	m	Time	m		Day	Time	m	Time	m
1 SA	0028	2.0	1300	2.1		**16** SU	0605	3.7	1846	3.9
	0713	3.6	1943	3.8			1206	1.9		
2 SU	0143	1.9	1409	2.0		**17** M	0100	1.7	1334	1.7
	0828	3.7	◑ 2045	3.9			0734	3.9	◑ 2003	4.1
3 M	0239	1.6	1501	1.7		**18** TU	0215	1.3	1443	1.3
	0921	3.9	2132	4.1			0844	4.2	2105	4.4
4 TU	0324	1.4	1544	1.5		**19** W	0314	0.9	1539	1.0
	1002	4.1	2210	4.2			0940	4.4	2157	4.6
5 W	0403	1.1	1622	1.2		**20** TH	0406	0.5	1630	0.6
	1037	4.2	2242	4.3			1028	4.7	2244	4.7
6 TH	0439	0.9	1658	1.1		**21** F	0453	0.2	1716	0.4
	1107	4.3	2313	4.3			1113	4.8	2328	4.8
7 F	0514	0.8	1732	1.0		**22** SA	0537	0.1	1800	0.3
	1136	4.3	2343	4.3			1156	4.8		
8 SA	0546	0.8	1803	0.9		**23** SU	0010	4.8	1237	4.8
	1205	4.3					0618	0.1	1839	0.4
9 SU	0014	4.3	1236	4.3		**24** M	0051	4.7	1317	4.7
	0615	0.8	○ 1831	1.0			0656	0.3	1917	0.6
10 M	0046	4.3	1308	4.3		**25** TU	0131	4.5	1356	4.5
	0642	0.9	1859	1.0			0732	0.6	● 1953	0.9
11 TU	0119	4.3	1342	4.3		**26** W	0211	4.3	1436	4.2
	0711	1.0	1930	1.2			0807	1.0	2030	1.3
12 W	0154	4.2	1418	4.2		**27** TH	0254	4.0	1521	4.0
	0744	1.1	2007	1.3			0844	1.5	2114	1.7
13 TH	0233	4.1	1502	4.1		**28** F	0346	3.7	1617	3.7
	0823	1.4	2054	1.6			0934	1.9	2217	2.0
14 F	0324	3.9	1559	4.0		**29** SA	0501	3.5	1740	3.6
	0915	1.6	2157	1.8			1055	2.3	2354	2.2
15 SA	0435	3.8	1717	3.9		**30** SU	0647	3.5	1917	3.6
	1029	1.9	2326	1.9			1238	2.3		
						31 M	0121	2.1	1353	2.1
							0809	3.7	2025	3.8

Chart Datum: 2·74 metres below Ordnance Datum (Newlyn)
HAT is 5·0 metres above Chart Datum

TIME ZONE (UT)	ENGLAND – SOUTHAMPTON	Dates in amber are **SPRINGS**
For Summer Time add ONE hour in **non-shaded areas**	**LAT 50°54′N LONG 1°24′W**	Dates in yellow are **NEAPS**
	TIMES AND HEIGHTS OF HIGH AND LOW WATERS	**2009**

SEPTEMBER

Time	m		Time	m
1 0218	1.8	**16** 0205	1.3
0901	4.0	0834	4.3
TU 1442	1.8	W 1433	1.3
2110	4.0	2054	4.4
2 0301	1.5	**17** 0300	0.9
0938	4.2	0925	4.6
W 1521	1.5	TH 1524	0.9
2146	4.2	2141	4.6
3 0338	1.1	**18** 0348	0.5
1010	4.3	1009	4.8
TH 1557	1.2	F 1611	0.6
2216	4.3	● 2224	4.8
4 0413	0.9	**19** 0432	0.3
1038	4.4	1050	4.8
F 1631	1.0	SA 1654	0.4
○ 2245	4.4	2304	4.8
5 0446	0.8	**20** 0513	0.2
1105	4.4	1129	4.8
SA 1704	0.9	SU 1734	0.4
2314	4.4	2343	4.8
6 0518	0.7	**21** 0551	0.3
1134	4.5	1207	4.8
SU 1734	0.8	M 1811	0.5
2344	4.5		
7 0548	0.7	**22** 0021	4.6
1204	4.5	0626	0.5
M 1804	0.8	TU 1244	4.6
		1846	0.7
8 0016	4.5	**23** 0100	4.5
0616	0.8	0700	0.8
TU 1237	4.5	W 1321	4.4
1832	0.9	1918	1.0
9 0050	4.4	**24** 0138	4.3
0646	0.9	0732	1.2
W 1311	4.4	TH 1358	4.2
1904	1.1	1951	1.4
10 0126	4.3	**25** 0219	4.0
0719	1.1	0807	1.7
TH 1350	4.3	F 1439	3.9
1942	1.3	2030	1.8
11 0208	4.2	**26** 0309	3.8
0800	1.4	0853	2.1
F 1435	4.1	SA 1531	3.7
2030	1.6	◑ 2127	2.1
12 0302	4.0	**27** 0419	3.6
0855	1.7	1012	2.4
SA 1537	4.0	SU 1649	3.5
◑ 2138	1.8	2305	2.3
13 0420	3.8	**28** 0601	3.5
1017	2.0	1202	2.4
SU 1703	3.8	M 1831	3.6
2318	1.9		
14 0559	3.8	**29** 0039	2.2
1204	2.0	0729	3.7
M 1839	3.9	TU 1318	2.2
		1946	3.8
15 0055	1.7	**30** 0140	1.9
0728	4.0	0822	4.0
TU 1330	1.7	W 1407	1.9
1956	4.2	2034	4.0

OCTOBER

Time	m		Time	m
1 0224	1.6	**16** 0235	1.0
0900	4.2	0903	4.6
TH 1446	1.5	F 1501	1.0
2111	4.2	2120	4.6
2 0302	1.2	**17** 0321	0.7
0932	4.3	0945	4.8
F 1522	1.2	SA 1545	0.7
2142	4.4	2201	4.7
3 0338	1.0	**18** 0404	0.6
1002	4.5	1025	4.8
SA 1557	1.0	SU 1627	0.6
2212	4.5	● 2240	4.7
4 0413	0.8	**19** 0444	0.5
1031	4.5	1102	4.8
SU 1631	0.8	M 1706	0.6
○ 2243	4.6	2318	4.7
5 0447	0.7	**20** 0522	0.6
1102	4.6	1138	4.7
M 1704	0.8	TU 1742	0.7
2316	4.6	2355	4.6
6 0519	0.7	**21** 0557	0.8
1135	4.6	1214	4.5
TU 1737	0.8	W 1816	0.9
2351	4.6		
7 0552	0.8	**22** 0033	4.4
1210	4.6	0630	1.1
W 1810	0.9	TH 1250	4.4
		1848	1.1
8 0028	4.6	**23** 0112	4.3
0626	1.0	0703	1.4
TH 1249	4.5	F 1327	4.2
1846	1.0	1920	1.4
9 0109	4.4	**24** 0153	4.1
0704	1.2	0738	1.7
F 1332	4.4	SA 1408	4.0
1929	1.3	1957	1.7
10 0157	4.3	**25** 0241	3.9
0751	1.5	0823	2.0
SA 1423	4.2	SU 1456	3.8
2022	1.6	2047	2.0
11 0258	4.0	**26** 0341	3.7
0853	1.8	0930	2.3
SU 1530	4.0	M 1600	3.6
◑ 2135	1.8	◑ 2202	2.2
12 0420	3.9	**27** 0458	3.7
1020	2.0	1103	2.4
M 1658	3.9	TU 1722	3.6
2311	1.9	2334	2.2
13 0555	3.9	**28** 0622	3.8
1156	1.9	1222	2.2
TU 1828	4.0	W 1843	3.7
14 0038	1.6	**29** 0043	2.0
0714	4.1	0725	4.0
W 1313	1.6	TH 1318	1.9
1939	4.2	1942	3.9
15 0143	1.3	**30** 0135	1.7
0814	4.4	0811	4.2
TH 1412	1.3	F 1403	1.6
2034	4.4	2027	4.1
		31 0219	1.4
		0849	4.3
		SA 1443	1.3
		2105	4.3

NOVEMBER

Time	m		Time	m
1 0259	1.2	**16** 0335	0.9
0924	4.5	1001	4.6
SU 1521	1.1	M 1601	0.9
2140	4.5	● 2220	4.5
2 0337	1.0	**17** 0416	0.9
0959	4.6	1039	4.6
M 1559	0.9	TU 1640	0.8
○ 2216	4.6	2258	4.5
3 0415	0.8	**18** 0455	1.0
1034	4.7	1115	4.5
TU 1637	0.8	W 1718	0.9
2253	4.7	2336	4.4
4 0453	0.8	**19** 0532	1.1
1112	4.7	1151	4.5
W 1715	0.8	TH 1753	1.0
2333	4.7		
5 0532	0.9	**20** 0014	4.4
1152	4.7	0607	1.2
TH 1755	0.8	F 1228	4.3
		1826	1.1
6 0015	4.6	**21** 0053	4.3
0613	1.0	0642	1.4
F 1236	4.6	SA 1305	4.2
1837	1.0	1859	1.3
7 0103	4.5	**22** 0133	4.2
0658	1.2	0718	1.6
SA 1324	4.4	SU 1345	4.1
1925	1.2	1934	1.5
8 0156	4.3	**23** 0217	4.1
0750	1.5	0759	1.9
SU 1419	4.3	M 1428	3.9
2021	1.4	2016	1.7
9 0259	4.2	**24** 0306	3.9
0854	1.7	0850	2.0
M 1525	4.1	TU 1519	3.8
◑ 2130	1.6	◑ 2109	1.9
10 0414	4.1	**25** 0403	3.9
1011	1.8	0954	2.2
TU 1643	4.0	W 1619	3.7
2248	1.7	2217	2.0
11 0534	4.1	**26** 0508	3.8
1131	1.8	1108	2.1
W 1802	4.0	TH 1729	3.7
		2331	2.0
12 0004	1.6	**27** 0615	3.9
0646	4.2	1216	2.0
TH 1243	1.6	F 1838	3.8
1911	4.2		
13 0109	1.4	**28** 0036	1.8
0746	4.4	0714	4.1
F 1342	1.4	SA 1312	1.8
2008	4.3	1937	4.0
14 0203	1.3	**29** 0131	1.6
0836	4.5	0804	4.3
SA 1433	1.2	SU 1402	1.5
2056	4.4	2027	4.2
15 0251	1.0	**30** 0219	1.4
0920	4.6	0848	4.5
SU 1519	1.0	M 1447	1.2
2140	4.5	2111	4.4

DECEMBER

Time	m		Time	m
1 0304	1.2	**16** 0355	1.2
0931	4.6	1023	4.4
TU 1532	1.0	W 1622	1.0
2154	4.5	● 2247	4.3
2 0349	1.0	**17** 0437	1.2
1013	4.7	1100	4.4
W 1616	0.8	TH 1701	1.0
○ 2238	4.6	2324	4.4
3 0434	0.9	**18** 0516	1.1
1056	4.7	1136	4.4
TH 1701	0.7	F 1737	0.9
2322	4.7		
4 0519	0.9	**19** 0000	4.4
1141	4.7	0552	1.2
F 1746	0.7	SA 1212	4.4
		1811	1.0
5 0009	4.6	**20** 0037	4.3
0606	0.9	0627	1.3
SA 1229	4.7	SU 1247	4.3
1833	0.8	1843	1.1
6 0059	4.6	**21** 0114	4.3
0655	1.0	0701	1.4
SU 1319	4.6	M 1324	4.2
1922	0.9	1915	1.2
7 0152	4.5	**22** 0151	4.2
0747	1.2	0735	1.5
M 1412	4.4	TU 1401	4.1
2015	1.1	1948	1.4
8 0250	4.4	**23** 0231	4.1
0843	1.4	0812	1.7
TU 1509	4.2	W 1442	4.0
2111	1.2	2027	1.5
9 0352	4.3	**24** 0315	4.0
0945	1.5	0857	1.8
W 1613	4.1	TH 1528	3.8
◑ 2214	1.4	◑ 2114	1.7
10 0458	4.2	**25** 0406	3.9
1052	1.7	0952	1.9
TH 1721	4.0	F 1623	3.8
2321	1.5	2214	1.9
11 0607	4.2	**26** 0506	3.9
1202	1.7	1100	2.0
F 1832	4.0	SA 1731	3.7
		2326	1.9
12 0027	1.5	**27** 0613	3.9
0711	4.2	1214	1.9
SA 1307	1.6	SU 1843	3.8
1936	4.0		
13 0129	1.5	**28** 0039	1.8
0808	4.3	0718	4.1
SU 1405	1.5	M 1321	1.7
2033	4.1	1949	4.0
14 0223	1.4	**29** 0142	1.6
0858	4.4	0816	4.3
M 1455	1.3	TU 1419	1.4
2123	4.2	2046	4.2
15 0311	1.3	**30** 0239	1.3
0943	4.4	0909	4.4
TU 1541	1.2	W 1512	1.1
2207	4.3	2138	4.4
		31 0331	1.1
		0958	4.6
		TH 1603	0.8
		○ 2227	4.5

Chart Datum: 2·74 metres below Ordnance Datum (Newlyn)
HAT is 5·0 metres above Chart Datum

TIDES

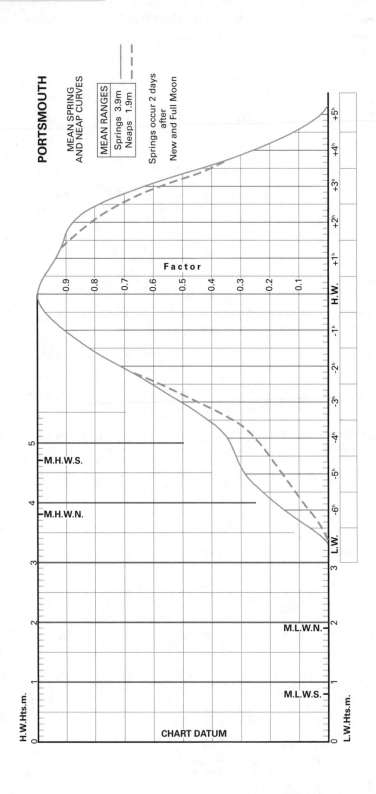

PORTSMOUTH

MEAN SPRING
AND NEAP CURVES

MEAN RANGES
Springs 3.9m Neaps 1.9m

Springs occur 2 days
after
New and Full Moon

Factor

0.9 0.8 0.7 0.6 0.5 0.4 0.3 0.2 0.1

H.W. -1ʰ -2ʰ -3ʰ -4ʰ -5ʰ -6ʰ L.W.

+5ʰ +4ʰ +3ʰ +2ʰ +1ʰ

H.W.Hts.m.

M.H.W.S.

M.H.W.N.

5 4 3 2 1 0

M.L.W.N.

M.L.W.S.

CHART DATUM

L.W.Hts.m.

3 2 1 0

ENGLAND – PORTSMOUTH

LAT 50°48′N   LONG 1°07′W

TIMES AND HEIGHTS OF HIGH AND LOW WATERS

Dates in amber are **SPRINGS**
Dates in yellow are **NEAPS**

2009

JANUARY

Time	m		Time	m
1 TH 0149	4.4	**16** F 0250	4.7
0709	1.4	0813	1.0
1353	4.3	1502	4.4
1928	1.2	2034	1.0
2 F 0226	4.4	**17** SA 0332	4.5
0746	1.5	0857	1.3
1430	4.2	1545	4.2
2005	1.3	2115	1.3
3 SA 0306	4.3	**18** SU 0414	4.3
0827	1.5	0944	1.6
1511	4.1	1630	4.0
2048	1.4	2203	1.6
4 SU 0351	4.2	**19** M 0500	4.1
0917	1.6	1041	1.8
1600	4.1	1723	3.8
2140	1.5	2302	1.9
5 M 0444	4.2	**20** TU 0557	3.9
1017	1.7	1153	2.0
1700	4.0	1834	3.6
2244	1.6		
6 TU 0550	4.1	**21** W 0017	2.1
1129	1.8	0710	3.8
1814	3.9	1309	2.0
2357	1.7	2002	3.7
7 W 0704	4.2	**22** TH 0133	2.0
1247	1.7	0825	3.9
1935	4.0	1413	1.9
		2111	3.9
8 TH 0114	1.6	**23** F 0234	1.9
0814	4.3	0922	4.1
1400	1.5	1504	1.6
2048	4.2	2200	4.1
9 F 0224	1.4	**24** SA 0322	1.6
0916	4.5	1007	4.2
1503	1.2	1546	1.4
2152	4.5	2240	4.3
10 SA 0324	1.2	**25** SU 0403	1.4
1013	4.7	1044	4.3
1559	0.9	1625	1.2
2249	4.7	2315	4.4
11 SU 0419	1.0	**26** M 0441	1.3
1106	4.8	1120	4.4
1651	0.7	1702	1.0
2342	4.8	2349	4.4
12 M 0510	0.8	**27** TU 0516	1.1
1157	4.8	1154	4.4
1740	0.5	1736	0.9
13 TU 0033	4.9	**28** W 0022	4.5
0558	0.8	0548	1.1
1246	4.8	1228	4.4
1826	0.5	1808	0.9
14 W 0121	4.9	**29** TH 0055	4.5
0645	0.8	0619	1.1
1334	4.8	1302	4.4
1910	0.6	1837	0.9
15 TH 0207	4.8	**30** F 0128	4.5
0730	0.9	0649	1.0
1419	4.6	1335	4.4
1953	0.7	1907	0.9
		31 SA 0201	4.5
		0722	1.1
		1410	4.4
		1941	1.0

FEBRUARY

Time	m		Time	m
1 SU 0236	4.4	**16** M 0324	4.3
0800	1.2	0853	1.4
1447	4.3	1546	4.0
2019	1.1	2111	1.6
2 M 0315	4.3	**17** TU 0402	4.0
0843	1.3	0938	1.8
1530	4.2	1633	3.8
2106	1.4	2205	2.0
3 TU 0402	4.2	**18** W 0452	3.8
0938	1.6	1050	2.1
1627	4.0	1739	3.6
2206	1.6	2333	2.2
4 W 0506	4.0	**19** TH 0606	3.6
1052	1.8	1229	2.1
1744	3.8	1924	3.5
2329	1.8		
5 TH 0630	4.0	**20** F 0108	2.2
1228	1.8	0749	3.6
1917	3.9	1347	2.0
		2049	3.8
6 F 0104	1.8	**21** SA 0217	2.0
0755	4.1	0901	3.9
1355	1.5	1441	1.7
2042	4.1	2140	4.0
7 SA 0223	1.6	**22** SU 0305	1.7
0907	4.3	0947	4.1
1500	1.2	1524	1.4
2148	4.4	2219	4.2
8 SU 0324	1.2	**23** M 0344	1.4
1006	4.5	1025	4.2
1554	0.8	1602	1.1
2243	4.6	2253	4.4
9 M 0415	0.9	**24** TU 0420	1.1
1057	4.7	1100	4.3
1643	0.6	1638	0.9
2332	4.8	2325	4.5
10 TU 0502	0.7	**25** W 0454	1.0
1145	4.8	1134	4.4
1727	0.4	1712	0.8
		2358	4.5
11 W 0017	4.9	**26** TH 0526	0.8
0545	0.6	1207	4.5
1231	4.8	1744	0.7
1809	0.4		
12 TH 0101	4.9	**27** F 0030	4.6
0626	0.6	0556	0.8
1314	4.8	1242	4.5
1848	0.4	1814	0.7
13 F 0140	4.8	**28** SA 0102	4.6
0705	0.6	0627	0.8
1353	4.7	1316	4.5
1924	0.6	1845	0.7
14 SA 0216	4.7		
0741	0.8		
1431	4.5		
1958	0.9		
15 SU 0250	4.5		
0816	1.1		
1507	4.3		
2032	1.2		

MARCH

Time	m		Time	m
1 SU 0135	4.6	**16** M 0211	4.5
0700	0.8	0738	1.0
1351	4.5	1435	4.3
1918	0.9	1955	1.2
2 M 0209	4.5	**17** TU 0243	4.3
0737	0.9	0810	1.3
1429	4.4	1512	4.1
1957	1.1	2031	1.6
3 TU 0248	4.4	**18** W 0319	4.0
0819	1.2	0849	1.7
1513	4.2	1557	3.8
2043	1.4	2119	2.0
4 W 0335	4.1	**19** TH 0406	3.7
0913	1.5	0948	2.0
1611	4.0	1700	3.6
2146	1.7	2250	2.3
5 TH 0440	3.9	**20** F 0515	3.5
1033	1.8	1142	2.1
1733	3.8	1835	3.5
2322	2.0		
6 F 0610	3.8	**21** SA 0037	2.3
1222	1.8	0657	3.5
1913	3.8	1310	2.0
		2011	3.7
7 SA 0106	1.9	**22** SU 0148	2.0
0746	3.9	0825	3.7
1349	1.5	1407	1.7
2037	4.1	2104	4.0
8 SU 0221	1.5	**23** M 0236	1.7
0859	4.2	0914	3.9
1451	1.1	1451	1.4
2138	4.4	2144	4.2
9 M 0317	1.1	**24** TU 0315	1.3
0954	4.5	0953	4.1
1541	0.8	1530	1.1
2228	4.7	2219	4.4
10 TU 0403	0.8	**25** W 0350	1.1
1043	4.6	1029	4.3
1625	0.5	1606	0.9
2313	4.8	2253	4.5
11 W 0446	0.6	**26** TH 0424	0.9
1127	4.7	1105	4.4
1707	0.4	1641	0.8
2354	4.9	2327	4.6
12 TH 0526	0.5	**27** F 0457	0.7
1209	4.8	1141	4.5
1745	0.4	1715	0.7
13 F 0033	4.9	**28** SA 0001	4.6
0602	0.5	0530	0.6
1249	4.7	1218	4.6
1820	0.5	1748	0.7
14 SA 0108	4.8	**29** SU 0036	4.7
0637	0.6	0604	0.6
1325	4.6	1256	4.6
1853	0.7	1823	0.7
15 SU 0141	4.7	**30** M 0112	4.7
0708	0.8	0640	0.7
1400	4.5	1336	4.6
1924	0.9	1900	0.9
		31 TU 0149	4.6
		0722	0.8
		1418	4.5
		1943	1.1

APRIL

Time	m		Time	m
1 W 0231	4.4	**16** TH 0248	4.0
0807	1.1	0819	1.6
1507	4.3	1531	3.9
2035	1.4	2050	2.0
2 TH 0322	4.1	**17** F 0333	3.8
0906	1.4	0911	1.9
1610	4.0	1628	3.7
2145	1.8	2203	2.2
3 F 0431	3.9	**18** SA 0435	3.6
1030	1.7	1040	2.0
1733	3.9	1745	3.7
2321	1.9	2345	2.2
4 SA 0601	3.8	**19** SU 0557	3.5
1211	1.7	1215	2.0
1907	4.0	1908	3.8
5 SU 0055	1.8	**20** M 0059	2.0
0733	3.9	0721	3.6
1331	1.4	1319	1.7
2021	4.2	2009	4.0
6 M 0205	1.4	**21** TU 0151	1.7
0841	4.2	0822	3.8
1429	1.1	1406	1.5
2117	4.5	2056	4.2
7 TU 0257	1.1	**22** W 0233	1.4
0934	4.4	0908	4.1
1517	0.8	1448	1.2
2205	4.7	2136	4.4
8 W 0341	0.8	**23** TH 0311	1.1
1021	4.6	0950	4.3
1600	0.7	1527	1.0
2248	4.8	2215	4.5
9 TH 0422	0.6	**24** F 0348	0.9
1104	4.6	1032	4.4
1640	0.6	1605	0.8
2327	4.8	2254	4.6
10 F 0501	0.6	**25** SA 0425	0.7
1144	4.7	1113	4.6
1717	0.6	1643	0.7
		2333	4.7
11 SA 0003	4.8	**26** SU 0504	0.6
0536	0.6	1156	4.7
1222	4.6	1723	0.7
1751	0.7		
12 SU 0037	4.7	**27** M 0013	4.7
0608	0.7	0544	0.6
1258	4.6	1240	4.7
1823	0.8	1805	0.8
13 M 0108	4.6	**28** TU 0055	4.7
0639	0.8	0627	0.7
1333	4.5	1325	4.7
1855	1.1	1849	0.9
14 TU 0139	4.4	**29** W 0138	4.6
0709	1.1	0713	0.8
1408	4.3	1414	4.5
1927	1.3	1938	1.1
15 W 0212	4.2	**30** TH 0225	4.4
0741	1.3	0806	1.0
1446	4.1	1508	4.4
2003	1.6	2035	1.2

Chart Datum: 2·73 metres below Ordnance Datum (Newlyn)
HAT is 5·1 metres above Chart Datum

TIDES

TIME ZONE (UT)
For Summer Time add ONE hour in **non-shaded areas**

ENGLAND – PORTSMOUTH

LAT 50°48′N   LONG 1°07′W

TIMES AND HEIGHTS OF HIGH AND LOW WATERS

Dates in amber are **SPRINGS**
Dates in yellow are **NEAPS**

2009

MAY

Time	m		Time	m
1 0321	4.2	**16** 0308	3.9
0907	1.3	0845	1.7
F 1612	4.2	SA 1558	3.9
2144	1.6	2121	2.0
2 0428	4.0	**17** 0400	3.7
1022	1.5	0944	1.8
SA 1728	4.1	SU 1657	3.9
2305	1.7	2231	2.1
3 0549	3.9	**18** 0504	3.7
1144	1.5	1058	1.8
SU 1845	4.2	M 1803	3.9
		◑ 2346	2.0
4 0026	1.6	**19** 0614	3.7
0707	4.0	1208	1.7
M 1257	1.4	TU 1907	4.0
◐ 1951	4.3		
5 0133	1.4	**20** 0048	1.8
0812	4.2	0720	3.8
TU 1356	1.2	W 1307	1.6
2047	4.5	2002	4.2
6 0227	1.2	**21** 0140	1.5
0907	4.3	0818	4.0
W 1446	1.0	TH 1357	1.4
2136	4.6	2052	4.3
7 0313	1.0	**22** 0227	1.3
0955	4.4	0911	4.2
TH 1529	0.9	F 1444	1.2
2220	4.6	2139	4.5
8 0355	0.9	**23** 0312	1.0
1039	4.5	1001	4.4
F 1610	0.8	SA 1531	1.0
2259	4.6	2225	4.6
9 0434	0.8	**24** 0358	0.8
1120	4.5	1049	4.6
SA 1648	0.9	SU 1617	0.9
2335	4.6	2310	4.7
10 0511	0.9	**25** 0444	0.7
1158	4.6	1138	4.7
SU 1725	1.0	M 1705	0.8
		2356	4.8
11 0008	4.6	**26** 0532	0.6
0544	0.9	1228	4.7
M 1234	4.5	TU 1754	0.8
○ 1759	1.1	●	
12 0041	4.5	**27** 0043	4.8
0616	1.0	0620	0.7
TU 1309	4.4	W 1319	4.7
1833	1.2	1843	0.9
13 0114	4.4	**28** 0132	4.7
0648	1.1	0711	0.7
W 1346	4.3	TH 1411	4.7
1907	1.4	1935	1.0
14 0148	4.2	**29** 0223	4.5
0721	1.3	0804	0.9
TH 1425	4.1	F 1506	4.6
1944	1.6	2031	1.2
15 0225	4.1	**30** 0318	4.4
0759	1.5	0900	1.1
F 1508	4.1	SA 1605	4.5
2027	1.8	2131	1.4
		31 0419	4.2
		1001	1.3
		SU 1707	4.4
		2236	1.5

JUNE

Time	m		Time	m
1 0524	4.1	**16** 0417	3.9
1107	1.4	0956	1.6
M 1811	4.3	TU 1705	4.0
2345	1.5	◑ 2233	1.8
2 0632	4.0	**17** 0516	3.9
1213	1.4	1058	1.7
TU 1914	4.3	W 1805	4.0
◐		2339	1.8
3 0051	1.5	**18** 0623	3.9
0736	4.0	1204	1.6
W 1315	1.4	TH 1910	4.1
2012	4.3		
4 0151	1.4	**19** 0046	1.6
0836	4.1	0732	4.0
TH 1410	1.4	F 1310	1.5
2105	4.4	2011	4.3
5 0243	1.3	**20** 0149	1.4
0930	4.2	0838	4.2
F 1459	1.3	SA 1410	1.4
2152	4.4	2108	4.4
6 0328	1.2	**21** 0246	1.2
1017	4.3	0938	4.4
SA 1543	1.3	SU 1507	1.2
2234	4.4	2202	4.6
7 0410	1.1	**22** 0341	0.9
1100	4.4	1034	4.6
SU 1624	1.2	M 1602	1.0
2311	4.5	2253	4.7
8 0449	1.1	**23** 0433	0.7
1139	4.4	1127	4.7
M 1704	1.2	TU 1654	0.9
2346	4.4	2344	4.8
9 0526	1.1	**24** 0525	0.6
1215	4.4	1220	4.8
TU 1741	1.2	W 1746	0.8
○			
10 0019	4.4	**25** 0034	4.8
0600	1.1	0615	0.5
W 1251	4.4	TH 1312	4.9
1816	1.3	● 1836	0.8
11 0054	4.4	**26** 0125	4.7
0633	1.1	0704	0.6
TH 1327	4.4	F 1404	4.8
1851	1.4	1926	0.8
12 0129	4.3	**27** 0216	4.6
0706	1.2	0753	0.7
F 1405	4.3	SA 1454	4.8
1925	1.5	2016	1.0
13 0206	4.2	**28** 0306	4.5
0740	1.3	0842	0.8
SA 1444	4.2	SU 1544	4.6
2002	1.6	2107	1.1
14 0244	4.1	**29** 0356	4.3
0818	1.4	0931	1.1
SU 1525	4.1	M 1634	4.5
2044	1.7	2201	1.3
15 0327	4.0	**30** 0449	4.1
0903	1.5	1025	1.3
M 1612	4.1	TU 1728	4.3
2134	1.8	2301	1.5

JULY

Time	m		Time	m
1 0548	4.0	**16** 0430	4.0
1124	1.6	1009	1.6
W 1827	4.2	TH 1711	4.1
		2249	1.7
2 0007	1.7	**17** 0537	3.9
0655	3.9	1118	1.7
TH 1230	1.7	F 1822	4.1
1931	4.1		
3 0114	1.7	**18** 0007	1.7
0806	3.9	0658	3.9
F 1335	1.7	SA 1237	1.7
2033	4.1	◑ 1938	4.1
4 0215	1.6	**19** 0127	1.5
0910	4.0	0818	4.1
SA 1433	1.7	SU 1353	1.6
◐ 2127	4.2	2047	4.3
5 0306	1.5	**20** 0235	1.3
1002	4.1	0926	4.3
SU 1522	1.6	M 1458	1.3
2213	4.3	2146	4.5
6 0351	1.3	**21** 0334	0.9
1046	4.3	1024	4.6
M 1606	1.4	TU 1555	1.1
2252	4.3	2241	4.7
7 0431	1.2	**22** 0427	0.7
1124	4.3	1118	4.8
TU 1646	1.3	W 1647	0.8
2327	4.4	2332	4.8
8 0509	1.1	**23** 0516	0.5
1159	4.4	1210	4.9
W 1724	1.2	TH 1736	0.7
2344	4.8		
9 0002	4.4	**24** 0022	4.8
0544	1.0	0603	0.4
TH 1234	4.4	F 1259	5.0
1759	1.2	1823	0.6
10 0036	4.4	**25** 0111	4.8
0617	1.0	0649	0.4
F 1308	4.4	SA 1346	4.9
1832	1.2	1909	0.7
11 0111	4.3	**26** 0157	4.7
0648	1.1	0732	0.5
SA 1342	4.4	SU 1430	4.9
○ 1903	1.3	● 1953	0.8
12 0145	4.3	**27** 0242	4.6
0718	1.1	0814	0.8
SU 1417	4.4	M 1512	4.7
1935	1.3	2036	1.0
13 0219	4.2	**28** 0325	4.4
0750	1.2	0856	1.1
M 1452	4.3	TU 1553	4.5
2011	1.4	2122	1.3
14 0256	4.2	**29** 0410	4.1
0828	1.3	0941	1.4
TU 1530	4.3	W 1638	4.2
2054	1.5	2214	1.6
15 0338	4.1	**30** 0501	3.9
0913	1.4	1037	1.8
W 1614	4.2	TH 1731	4.0
2145	1.6	2321	1.9
		31 0609	3.7
		1149	2.0
		F 1843	3.8

AUGUST

Time	m		Time	m
1 0040	2.0	**16** 0641	3.8
0740	3.7	1226	1.9
SA 1308	2.1	SU 1918	4.0
2005	3.9		
2 0152	1.9	**17** 0120	1.7
0856	3.9	0810	4.0
SU 1415	1.9	M 1350	1.5
◐ 2109	4.0	◑ 2035	4.2
3 0248	1.6	**18** 0231	1.3
0949	4.1	0919	4.4
M 1507	1.7	TU 1454	1.4
2156	4.2	2136	4.5
4 0332	1.4	**19** 0326	0.9
1031	4.3	1015	4.6
TU 1549	1.5	W 1547	1.0
2235	4.3	2228	4.7
5 0411	1.2	**20** 0415	0.6
1107	4.4	1105	4.6
W 1627	1.3	TH 1635	0.7
2310	4.4	2317	4.8
6 0448	1.0	**21** 0501	0.4
1140	4.5	1152	5.0
TH 1704	1.2	F 1720	0.6
2342	4.4		
7 0523	0.9	**22** 0004	4.9
1212	4.5	0544	0.3
F 1737	1.1	SA 1237	5.0
		1803	0.5
8 0015	4.4	**23** 0049	4.9
0555	0.9	0626	0.4
SA 1244	4.5	SU 1319	5.0
1808	1.1	1844	0.6
9 0048	4.4	**24** 0131	4.8
0624	0.9	0705	0.5
SU 1315	4.5	M 1358	4.9
○ 1837	1.1	1923	0.7
10 0121	4.4	**25** 0211	4.6
0652	0.9	0741	0.8
M 1347	4.5	TU 1434	4.7
1907	1.1	● 2001	1.0
11 0153	4.4	**26** 0250	4.4
0722	1.0	0818	1.1
TU 1419	4.5	W 1510	4.4
1941	1.2	2040	1.3
12 0228	4.3	**27** 0331	4.1
0756	1.2	0858	1.5
W 1454	4.4	TH 1548	4.1
2020	1.3	2126	1.7
13 0307	4.0	**28** 0418	3.9
0838	1.4	0951	1.9
TH 1535	4.2	F 1636	3.9
2109	1.5	2233	2.0
14 0358	4.0	**29** 0524	3.6
0933	1.7	1113	2.2
F 1631	4.1	SA 1748	3.7
2215	1.8		
15 0509	3.9	**30** 0007	2.1
1049	1.9	0715	3.6
SA 1748	4.0	SU 1247	2.3
2346	1.8	1939	3.7
		31 0129	2.0
		0838	3.9
		M 1358	2.0
		2050	3.9

Chart Datum: 2·73 metres below Ordnance Datum (Newlyn)
HAT is 5·1 metres above Chart Datum

ENGLAND – PORTSMOUTH

LAT 50°48′N   LONG 1°07′W

TIMES AND HEIGHTS OF HIGH AND LOW WATERS

Dates in amber are **SPRINGS**
Dates in yellow are **NEAPS**

2009

	SEPTEMBER			OCTOBER			NOVEMBER			DECEMBER	
	Time m	Time m		Time m	Time m		Time m	Time m		Time m	Time m

SEPTEMBER

1 TU 0226 1.7 / 0928 4.1 / 1447 1.8 / 2136 4.1   **16** W 0220 1.3 / 0907 4.5 / 1443 1.3 / 2122 4.5

2 W 0308 1.4 / 1007 4.3 / 1527 1.5 / 2213 4.3   **17** TH 0311 0.9 / 0958 4.7 / 1532 1.0 / 2212 4.7

3 TH 0346 1.2 / 1041 4.5 / 1603 1.2 / 2245 4.4   **18** F 0357 0.6 / 1044 4.9 / 1616 0.7 / ● 2257 4.9

4 F 0421 1.0 / 1112 4.5 / 1637 1.1 / ○ 2317 4.5   **19** SA 0439 0.4 / 1128 5.0 / 1658 0.6 / 2341 4.9

5 SA 0455 0.9 / 1143 4.6 / 1710 1.0 / 2349 4.5   **20** SU 0520 0.4 / 1209 5.0 / 1738 0.5

6 SU 0527 0.8 / 1214 4.6 / 1740 0.9   **21** M 0023 4.9 / 0558 0.5 / 1248 4.9 / 1816 0.6

7 M 0022 4.5 / 0556 0.8 / 1245 4.6 / 1809 0.9   **22** TU 0103 4.8 / 0634 0.7 / 1323 4.8 / 1851 0.8

8 TU 0055 4.5 / 0624 0.9 / 1317 4.6 / 1840 1.0   **23** W 0141 4.6 / 0708 1.0 / 1357 4.6 / 1925 1.1

9 W 0129 4.5 / 0655 1.0 / 1349 4.5 / 1914 1.1   **24** TH 0218 4.4 / 0742 1.3 / 1431 4.4 / 2001 1.4

10 TH 0205 4.4 / 0730 1.2 / 1425 4.4 / 1954 1.3   **25** F 0256 4.2 / 0821 1.7 / 1507 4.1 / 2042 1.7

11 F 0246 4.2 / 0814 1.5 / 1508 4.2 / 2044 1.6   **26** SA 0342 3.9 / 0912 2.1 / 1554 3.8 / ◑ 2145 2.1

12 SA 0340 4.0 / 0912 1.8 / 1607 4.0 / ◑ 2156 1.8   **27** SU 0446 3.7 / 1038 2.3 / 1701 3.6 / 2325 2.2

13 SU 0456 3.9 / 1040 2.0 / 1730 3.9 / 2340 1.9   **28** M 0629 3.6 / 1217 2.3 / 1852 3.6

14 M 0634 3.9 / 1226 2.0 / 1907 4.0   **29** TU 0053 2.1 / 0802 3.9 / 1329 2.1 / 2016 3.8

15 TU 0114 1.7 / 0803 4.1 / 1345 1.7 / 2025 4.2   **30** W 0152 1.8 / 0853 4.1 / 1417 1.8 / 2103 4.1

OCTOBER

1 TH 0235 1.5 / 0931 4.3 / 1456 1.5 / 2139 4.3   **16** F 0247 1.0 / 0934 4.8 / 1510 1.0 / 2150 4.7

2 F 0313 1.2 / 1004 4.5 / 1531 1.2 / 2213 4.4   **17** SA 0332 0.8 / 1019 4.9 / 1553 0.8 / 2235 4.8

3 SA 0348 1.0 / 1036 4.6 / 1605 1.1 / 2246 4.5   **18** SU 0413 0.7 / 1101 4.9 / 1633 0.7 / ● 2317 4.8

4 SU 0422 0.9 / 1109 4.6 / 1637 0.9 / ○ 2320 4.6   **19** M 0452 0.7 / 1140 4.9 / 1712 0.7 / 2358 4.8

5 M 0454 0.9 / 1141 4.7 / 1709 0.9 / 2355 4.7   **20** TU 0530 0.8 / 1217 4.8 / 1749 0.8

6 TU 0526 0.9 / 1215 4.7 / 1741 0.9   **21** W 0036 4.7 / 0605 0.9 / 1252 4.7 / 1822 1.0

7 W 0031 4.7 / 0558 0.9 / 1250 4.7 / 1816 0.9   **22** TH 0113 4.6 / 0639 1.2 / 1325 4.6 / 1856 1.2

8 TH 0109 4.6 / 0634 1.0 / 1326 4.6 / 1854 1.1   **23** F 0150 4.5 / 0714 1.4 / 1359 4.4 / 1931 1.4

9 F 0149 4.5 / 0714 1.2 / 1406 4.5 / 1939 1.3   **24** SA 0229 4.3 / 0753 1.7 / 1436 4.1 / 2011 1.7

10 SA 0236 4.4 / 0803 1.5 / 1454 4.1 / 2034 1.6   **25** SU 0314 4.0 / 0841 2.0 / 1521 3.9 / 2104 2.0

11 SU 0335 4.1 / 0909 1.8 / 1556 4.0 / ◑ 2151 1.8   **26** M 0411 3.8 / 0954 2.3 / 1621 3.7 / ● 2226 2.2

12 M 0453 4.0 / 1039 2.0 / 1720 3.9 / 2328 1.8   **27** TU 0527 3.8 / 1126 2.3 / 1741 3.6 / 2355 2.1

13 TU 0626 4.0 / 1213 1.9 / 1853 4.0   **28** W 0653 3.9 / 1240 2.2 / 1908 3.7

14 W 0053 1.6 / 0745 4.3 / 1327 1.6 / 2006 4.3   **29** TH 0100 1.9 / 0755 4.1 / 1333 1.9 / 2009 3.9

15 TH 0157 1.3 / 0845 4.6 / 1422 1.3 / 2102 4.5   **30** F 0150 1.7 / 0841 4.3 / 1415 1.6 / 2054 4.2

31 SA 0231 1.4 / 0920 4.4 / 1453 1.4 / 2134 4.4

NOVEMBER

1 SU 0309 1.2 / 0957 4.6 / 1528 1.2 / 2212 4.5   **16** M 0347 1.0 / 1036 4.8 / 1611 1.0 / ● 2257 4.7

2 M 0345 1.1 / 1034 4.7 / 1604 1.0 / ○ 2251 4.6   **17** TU 0427 1.0 / 1115 4.8 / 1650 1.0 / 2338 4.7

3 TU 0421 1.0 / 1111 4.7 / 1641 0.9 / 2331 4.7   **18** W 0506 1.1 / 1151 4.7 / 1727 1.0

4 W 0459 1.0 / 1149 4.8 / 1720 0.9   **19** TH 0016 4.6 / 0542 1.2 / 1226 4.6 / 1802 1.1

5 TH 0012 4.6 / 0538 1.0 / 1229 4.8 / 1800 0.9   **20** F 0053 4.6 / 0618 1.3 / 1259 4.5 / 1836 1.2

6 F 0056 4.7 / 0621 1.1 / 1311 4.7 / 1845 1.0   **21** SA 0129 4.5 / 0654 1.5 / 1334 4.3 / 1911 1.4

7 SA 0142 4.6 / 0708 1.3 / 1357 4.5 / 1935 1.2   **22** SU 0207 4.3 / 0731 1.7 / 1412 4.2 / 1948 1.6

8 SU 0234 4.5 / 0803 1.5 / 1449 4.3 / 2034 1.4   **23** M 0249 4.2 / 0813 1.9 / 1453 4.0 / 2031 1.8

9 M 0334 4.3 / 0908 1.7 / 1552 4.2 / ◐ 2143 1.6   **24** TU 0337 4.0 / 0905 2.1 / 1542 3.8 / ◐ 2126 1.9

10 TU 0446 4.2 / 1025 1.8 / 1707 4.1 / 2301 1.6   **25** W 0434 3.9 / 1011 2.2 / 1642 3.7 / 2235 2.0

11 W 0605 4.2 / 1145 1.8 / 1827 4.1   **26** TH 0539 3.9 / 1125 2.2 / 1751 3.7 / 2346 2.0

12 TH 0017 1.5 / 0715 4.4 / 1255 1.6 / 1937 4.2   **27** F 0645 4.0 / 1230 2.0 / 1900 3.8

13 F 0122 1.4 / 0815 4.6 / 1354 1.4 / 2036 4.4   **28** SA 0047 1.8 / 0743 4.2 / 1323 1.8 / 2000 4.0

14 SA 0216 1.2 / 0907 4.7 / 1444 1.2 / 2127 4.5   **29** SU 0140 1.6 / 0833 4.3 / 1410 1.6 / 2053 4.2

15 SU 0303 1.1 / 0953 4.6 / 1529 1.1 / 2214 4.6   **30** M 0226 1.4 / 0920 4.5 / 1453 1.3 / 2141 4.4

DECEMBER

1 TU 0310 1.3 / 1004 4.7 / 1537 1.1 / 2228 4.6   **16** W 0408 1.3 / 1056 4.6 / 1634 1.1 / ● 2325 4.5

2 W 0355 1.1 / 1047 4.8 / 1621 0.9 / ○ 2314 4.7   **17** TH 0448 1.3 / 1132 4.6 / 1712 1.0

3 TH 0440 1.0 / 1131 4.8 / 1707 0.8   **18** F 0002 4.5 / 0526 1.3 / 1207 4.5 / 1748 1.1

4 F 0000 4.8 / 0526 1.0 / 1216 4.8 / 1754 0.8   **19** SA 0037 4.5 / 0602 1.3 / 1241 4.5 / 1822 1.1

5 SA 0049 4.8 / 0614 1.0 / 1303 4.7 / 1842 0.8   **20** SU 0112 4.5 / 0637 1.4 / 1316 4.4 / 1855 1.2

6 SU 0139 4.8 / 0705 1.1 / 1352 4.6 / 1933 0.9   **21** M 0147 4.4 / 0710 1.5 / 1351 4.3 / 1927 1.3

7 M 0231 4.7 / 0758 1.2 / 1445 4.5 / 2027 1.1   **22** TU 0225 4.3 / 0745 1.6 / 1428 4.1 / 2001 1.4

8 TU 0327 4.6 / 0856 1.4 / 1542 4.3 / 2124 1.2   **23** W 0304 4.2 / 0822 1.7 / 1507 4.0 / 2040 1.6

9 W 0427 4.5 / 0959 1.6 / 1643 4.2 / ◐ 2227 1.4   **24** TH 0346 4.1 / 0906 1.9 / 1551 3.9 / ◐ 2126 1.7

10 TH 0531 4.4 / 1107 1.6 / 1751 4.1 / 2333 1.5   **25** F 0436 4.0 / 1001 2.0 / 1645 3.8 / 2225 1.8

11 F 0637 4.3 / 1216 1.7 / 1900 4.1   **26** SA 0536 4.0 / 1109 2.0 / 1752 3.8 / 2333 1.9

12 SA 0040 1.6 / 0740 4.4 / 1321 1.6 / 2006 4.1   **27** SU 0643 4.1 / 1221 1.9 / 1907 3.9

13 SU 0142 1.5 / 0838 4.4 / 1418 1.5 / 2106 4.2   **28** M 0044 1.8 / 0748 4.2 / 1328 1.7 / 2016 4.1

14 M 0236 1.5 / 0930 4.5 / 1508 1.4 / 2158 4.4   **29** TU 0149 1.6 / 0847 4.4 / 1427 1.4 / 2117 4.3

15 TU 0325 1.4 / 1015 4.6 / 1553 1.2 / 2244 4.4   **30** W 0247 1.4 / 0940 4.6 / 1520 1.1 / 2211 4.5

31 TH 0339 1.2 / 1030 4.7 / 1611 0.9 / ○ 2302 4.7

Chart Datum: 2·73 metres below Ordnance Datum (Newlyn)
HAT is 5·1 metres above Chart Datum

TIDES

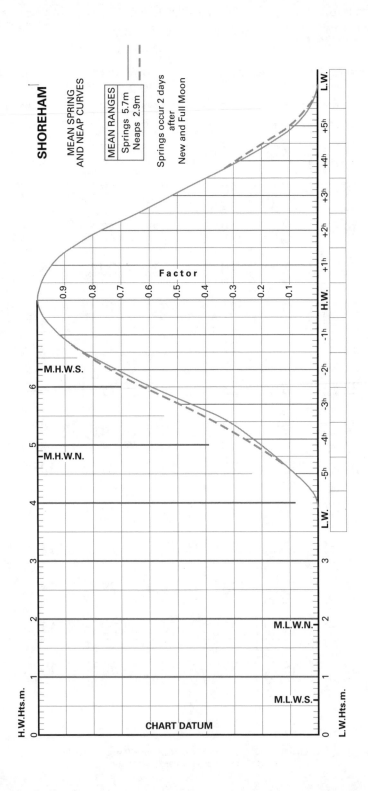

SHOREHAM

MEAN SPRING
AND NEAP CURVES

MEAN RANGES
Springs 5.7m
Neaps 2.9m

Springs occur 2 days
after
New and Full Moon

Factor

0.9 0.8 0.7 0.6 0.5 0.4 0.3 0.2 0.1

H.W.Hts.m.

CHART DATUM

L.W.Hts.m.

M.H.W.S.

M.H.W.N.

M.L.W.N.

M.L.W.S.

L.W.   -5ʰ   -4ʰ   -3ʰ   -2ʰ   -1ʰ   H.W.   +1ʰ   +2ʰ   +3ʰ   +4ʰ   +5ʰ   L.W.

TIME ZONE (UT)
For Summer Time add ONE hour in **non-shaded areas**

ENGLAND – SHOREHAM
LAT 50°50'N   LONG 0°15'W
TIMES AND HEIGHTS OF HIGH AND LOW WATERS

Dates in amber are **SPRINGS**
Dates in yellow are **NEAPS**
2009

JANUARY

Time	m	Time	m
1 0133	5.8	**16** 0242	6.3
0748	1.3	0850	0.9
TH 1344	5.7	F 1456	5.9
2006	1.2	2111	0.9
2 0208	5.7	**17** 0324	6.0
0823	1.4	0934	1.2
F 1421	5.6	SA 1539	5.6
2040	1.3	2154	1.2
3 0247	5.7	**18** 0407	5.6
0903	1.5	1019	1.5
SA 1503	5.5	SU 1626	5.2
2122	1.4	◑ 2239	1.6
4 0332	5.5	**19** 0455	5.3
0952	1.6	1112	1.8
SU 1543	5.3	M 1720	4.9
◐ 2213	1.6	2337	2.0
5 0426	5.4	**20** 0553	4.9
1052	1.7	1226	2.0
M 1654	5.1	TU 1826	4.6
2316	1.7		
6 0534	5.2	**21** 0100	2.2
1205	1.8	0701	4.8
TU 1813	5.0	W 1348	2.0
		1948	4.6
7 0035	1.8	**22** 0218	2.1
0655	5.3	0820	4.9
W 1323	1.7	TH 1451	1.9
1937	5.2	2106	4.9
8 0154	1.7	**23** 0316	1.9
0809	5.5	0923	5.1
TH 1433	1.4	F 1541	1.6
2046	5.5	2157	5.2
9 0301	1.4	**24** 0402	1.6
0912	5.8	1009	5.4
F 1534	1.1	SA 1624	1.3
2148	5.8	2237	5.5
10 0400	1.1	**25** 0442	1.4
1009	6.1	1046	5.6
SA 1629	0.8	SU 1701	1.1
2244	6.1	2312	5.8
11 0453	0.8	**26** 0518	1.2
1102	6.3	1119	5.8
SU 1720	0.6	M 1737	1.0
○ 2337	6.4	◐ 2344	5.9
12 0543	0.7	**27** 0552	1.1
1153	6.4	1150	5.9
M 1810	0.4	TU 1811	0.9
13 0027	6.5	**28** 0014	6.0
0631	0.6	0625	1.0
TU 1243	6.5	W 1221	5.9
1857	0.4	1844	0.9
14 0115	6.6	**29** 0043	6.0
0718	0.6	0656	1.0
W 1329	6.4	TH 1252	6.0
1944	0.5	1914	0.9
15 0200	6.5	**30** 0112	6.0
0805	0.7	0726	1.0
TH 1414	6.2	F 1324	6.0
2028	0.6	1942	0.9
		31 0145	6.0
		0756	1.0
		SA 1358	5.9
		2013	1.0

FEBRUARY

Time	m	Time	m
1 0220	6.0	**16** 0320	5.6
0832	1.1	0927	1.4
SU 1436	5.8	M 1538	5.3
2051	1.1	◑ 2146	1.6
2 0301	5.8	**17** 0400	5.2
0915	1.3	1010	1.8
M 1520	5.5	TU 1629	4.8
◐ 2137	1.4	2235	2.0
3 0349	5.5	**18** 0457	4.7
1010	1.6	1110	2.1
TU 1616	5.2	W 1738	4.5
2237	1.7	2347	2.3
4 0451	5.2	**19** 0613	4.5
1124	1.8	1301	2.3
W 1733	4.9	TH 1859	4.4
5 0003	1.9	**20** 0149	2.3
0622	5.0	0737	4.5
TH 1259	1.8	F 1426	2.1
1919	4.9	2041	4.7
6 0140	1.8	**21** 0254	2.0
0756	5.0	0901	4.9
F 1423	1.6	SA 1518	1.7
2041	5.2	2136	5.1
7 0256	1.5	**22** 0341	1.7
0908	5.5	0948	5.2
SA 1528	1.1	SU 1600	1.3
2146	5.7	2215	5.5
8 0354	1.1	**23** 0420	1.3
1006	6.0	1024	5.6
SU 1622	0.7	M 1637	1.1
2241	6.1	2248	5.8
9 0444	0.8	**24** 0454	1.1
1058	6.3	1056	5.8
M 1710	0.5	TU 1712	0.9
○ 2329	6.5	2319	5.9
10 0531	0.5	**25** 0528	1.0
1145	6.5	1127	6.0
TU 1755	0.3	W 1746	0.8
		● 2348	6.1
11 0014	6.6	**26** 0601	0.9
0615	0.4	1159	6.1
W 1230	6.5	TH 1819	0.7
1838	0.3		
12 0057	6.7	**27** 0018	6.2
0658	0.4	0632	0.8
TH 1311	6.5	F 1231	6.1
1919	0.4	1848	0.7
13 0136	6.6	**28** 0049	6.2
0738	0.5	0702	0.7
F 1350	6.3	SA 1303	6.2
1957	0.5	1918	0.7
14 0212	6.4		
0815	0.7		
SA 1425	6.0		
2033	0.8		
15 0246	6.0		
0850	1.0		
SU 1500	5.7		
2108	1.1		

MARCH

Time	m	Time	m
1 0121	6.2	**16** 0207	5.9
0733	0.8	0813	1.0
SU 1337	6.1	M 1424	5.7
1950	0.8	2030	1.2
2 0156	6.1	**17** 0235	5.6
0810	0.9	0847	1.3
M 1415	5.9	TU 1458	5.3
2029	1.0	2107	1.6
3 0236	5.9	**18** 0309	5.1
0852	1.1	0928	1.7
TU 1458	5.6	W 1543	4.9
2116	1.3	◑ 2154	2.0
4 0323	5.5	**19** 0400	4.7
0947	1.5	1024	2.1
W 1554	5.1	TH 1657	4.5
◐ 2218	1.7	2302	2.4
5 0426	5.0	**20** 0530	4.3
1104	1.8	1146	2.3
TH 1721	4.7	F 1819	4.4
2352	2.0		
6 0611	4.7	**21** 0059	2.4
1249	1.9	0653	4.3
F 1916	4.8	SA 1348	2.2
		1946	4.6
7 0135	1.9	**22** 0223	2.1
0752	5.0	0815	4.7
SA 1417	1.6	SU 1445	1.8
2039	5.2	2056	5.0
8 0249	1.5	**23** 0310	1.7
0904	5.4	0910	5.1
SU 1519	1.1	M 1527	1.4
2139	5.8	2137	5.4
9 0343	1.0	**24** 0348	1.3
0958	5.9	0948	5.5
M 1608	0.7	TU 1604	1.1
2228	6.2	2211	5.8
10 0430	0.7	**25** 0423	1.1
1045	6.2	1023	5.8
TU 1652	0.4	W 1640	0.9
2312	6.5	2244	6.0
11 0513	0.5	**26** 0457	0.9
1129	6.4	1058	6.0
W 1733	0.3	TH 1715	0.7
○ 2353	6.6	● 2317	6.2
12 0554	0.4	**27** 0531	0.7
1210	6.5	1133	6.1
TH 1813	0.3	F 1749	0.7
		2350	6.3
13 0031	6.6	**28** 0605	0.6
0632	0.4	1207	6.2
F 1248	6.3	SA 1822	0.6
1850	0.4		
14 0107	6.5	**29** 0024	6.3
0708	0.5	0639	0.6
SA 1322	6.3	SU 1243	6.3
1925	0.6	1857	0.6
15 0139	6.3	**30** 0100	6.3
0741	0.7	0716	0.6
SU 1353	6.0	M 1320	6.2
1957	0.8	1935	0.7
		31 0137	6.1
		0756	0.6
		TU 1401	5.9
		2018	1.0

APRIL

Time	m	Time	m
1 0219	5.8	**16** 0237	5.1
0843	1.1	0900	1.0
W 1449	5.6	TH 1514	5.0
2109	1.4	2127	1.9
2 0311	5.4	**17** 0324	4.7
0941	1.4	0953	1.9
TH 1552	5.1	F 1621	4.7
◐ 2218	1.8	◐ 2229	2.2
3 0422	4.9	**18** 0447	4.4
1101	1.9	1103	2.1
F 1726	4.8	SA 1739	4.5
2352	2.0	2351	2.3
4 0607	4.7	**19** 0609	4.4
1241	1.8	1231	2.1
SA 1907	4.9	SU 1851	4.7
5 0125	1.8	**20** 0124	2.1
0741	5.0	0718	4.6
SU 1401	1.5	M 1351	1.8
2023	5.4	1954	5.0
6 0232	1.4	**21** 0223	1.8
0847	5.4	0816	5.0
M 1458	1.1	TU 1441	1.5
2118	5.8	2044	5.4
7 0323	1.0	**22** 0306	1.4
0939	5.8	0903	5.4
TU 1545	0.7	W 1523	1.2
2205	6.2	2127	5.7
8 0408	0.7	**23** 0344	1.1
1024	6.1	0945	5.7
W 1628	0.6	TH 1601	1.0
2247	6.4	2206	6.0
9 0449	0.5	**24** 0422	0.9
1106	6.2	1025	6.0
TH 1708	0.5	F 1639	0.8
○ 2327	6.4	2244	6.2
10 0528	0.5	**25** 0500	0.7
1145	6.2	1105	6.1
F 1746	0.5	SA 1718	0.7
		● 2323	6.3
11 0003	6.4	**26** 0539	0.6
0605	0.5	1146	6.2
SA 1222	6.2	SU 1759	0.6
1822	0.6		
12 0037	6.3	**27** 0002	6.3
0640	0.6	0620	0.5
SU 1255	6.1	M 1228	6.3
1855	0.8	1841	0.7
13 0107	6.1	**28** 0043	6.3
0712	0.8	0703	0.6
M 1326	5.9	TU 1311	6.2
1928	1.0	1926	0.8
14 0134	5.8	**29** 0126	6.1
0744	1.0	0750	0.7
TU 1357	5.7	W 1358	6.0
2002	1.2	2015	1.0
15 0203	5.5	**30** 0214	5.8
0819	1.3	0842	1.0
W 1431	5.4	TH 1453	5.7
2040	1.6	2111	1.3

Chart Datum: 3·27 metres below Ordnance Datum (Newlyn)
HAT is 6·9 metres above Chart Datum

TIDES

TIME ZONE (UT)
For Summer Time add ONE hour in **non-shaded areas**

ENGLAND – SHOREHAM
LAT 50°50'N   LONG 0°15'W
TIMES AND HEIGHTS OF HIGH AND LOW WATERS

Dates in amber are **SPRINGS**
Dates in yellow are NEAPS
2009

MAY

	Time m		Time m
1	0312 5.4 / 0943 1.3 / F 1600 5.3 / 2219 1.6	**16**	0300 4.9 / 0927 1.7 / SA 1542 5.0 / 2158 1.9
2	0425 1.5 / 1058 1.5 / SA 1720 5.2 / 2341 1.7	**17**	0353 4.7 / 1024 1.9 / SU 1648 4.8 / 2302 2.0
3	0552 5.0 / 1220 1.5 / SU 1842 5.2	**18**	0516 4.6 / 1130 1.9 / M 1757 4.9 ●
4	0100 1.6 / 0714 5.1 / M 1331 1.4 / ○ 1951 5.5	**19**	0012 2.0 / 0625 4.7 / TU 1239 1.8 / 1858 5.0
5	0203 1.3 / 0818 5.4 / TU 1428 1.1 / 2047 5.7	**20**	0118 1.8 / 0725 5.0 / W 1341 1.6 / 1954 5.3
6	0255 1.0 / 0911 5.6 / W 1516 1.0 / 2135 6.0	**21**	0213 1.5 / 0819 5.3 / TH 1434 1.4 / 2043 5.6
7	0341 0.9 / 0958 5.8 / TH 1600 0.8 / 2219 6.1	**22**	0301 1.2 / 0908 5.6 / F 1521 1.1 / 2129 5.9
8	0423 0.8 / 1041 5.9 / F 1641 0.8 / 2259 6.1	**23**	0347 0.9 / 0955 5.8 / SA 1607 0.9 / 2215 6.1
9	0503 0.7 / 1121 6.0 / SA 1721 0.8 / 2336 6.1	**24**	0432 0.7 / 1042 6.1 / SU 1654 0.8 / 2300 6.3
10	0541 0.8 / 1158 6.0 / SU 1758 0.9	**25**	0519 0.6 / 1130 6.2 / M 1741 0.7 / 2346 6.3
11	0009 6.0 / 0616 0.8 / M 1232 5.9 / ○ 1833 0.9	**26**	0606 0.5 / 1218 6.3 / TU 1830 0.7 ●
12	0041 5.9 / 0650 0.9 / TU 1305 5.8 / 1907 1.1	**27**	0033 6.3 / 0655 0.6 / W 1308 6.2 / 1919 0.8
13	0111 5.7 / 0724 1.1 / W 1338 5.6 / 1942 1.3	**28**	0123 6.1 / 0746 0.6 / TH 1400 6.1 / 2012 0.9
14	0142 5.5 / 0800 1.2 / TH 1412 5.4 / 2021 1.5	**29**	0215 5.9 / 0840 0.8 / F 1455 5.9 / 2108 1.1
15	0217 5.2 / 0840 1.5 / F 1452 5.2 / 2105 1.7	**30**	0312 5.7 / 0938 1.2 / SA 1554 5.7 / 2210 1.3
		31	0415 5.4 / 1041 1.2 / SU 1657 5.6 / 2317 1.4

JUNE

	Time m		Time m
1	0522 5.2 / 1148 1.3 / M 1803 5.4	**16**	0410 5.0 / 1034 1.7 / TU 1646 5.1 / ◐ 2313 1.8
2	0025 1.4 / 0632 5.1 / TU 1253 1.4 / ◐ 1909 5.4	**17**	0514 4.9 / 1135 1.7 / W 1753 5.1
3	0127 1.4 / 0740 5.2 / W 1352 1.4 / 2010 5.5	**18**	0018 1.7 / 0628 5.0 / TH 1243 1.7 / 1902 5.2
4	0223 1.3 / 0839 5.3 / TH 1446 1.3 / 2103 5.6	**19**	0123 1.6 / 0736 5.1 / F 1349 1.5 / 2004 5.5
5	0313 1.2 / 0931 5.5 / F 1534 1.2 / 2151 5.7	**20**	0224 1.3 / 0836 5.4 / SA 1450 1.3 / 2100 5.7
6	0359 1.1 / 1017 5.6 / SA 1619 1.2 / 2234 5.8	**21**	0320 1.1 / 0932 5.7 / SU 1545 1.1 / 2154 6.0
7	0442 1.0 / 1100 5.7 / SU 1701 1.1 / 2312 5.8	**22**	0413 0.8 / 1027 6.0 / M 1638 0.9 / 2246 6.2
8	0522 1.0 / 1138 5.8 / M 1740 1.1 / 2348 5.8	**23**	0505 0.6 / 1120 6.2 / TU 1730 0.7 / 2337 6.3
9	0559 1.0 / 1214 5.8 / TU 1816 1.1 / ○	**24**	0556 0.5 / 1213 6.3 / W 1821 0.6
10	0021 5.7 / 0634 1.0 / W 1248 5.8 / 1851 1.1	**25**	0028 6.3 / 0647 0.5 / TH 1305 6.4 / ● 1911 0.6
11	0053 5.6 / 0709 1.1 / TH 1321 5.7 / 1926 1.3	**26**	0120 6.3 / 0738 0.5 / F 1355 6.4 / 2002 0.7
12	0125 5.5 / 0744 1.2 / F 1353 5.6 / 2003 1.4	**27**	0210 6.2 / 0829 0.6 / SA 1445 6.3 / 2054 0.8
13	0158 5.4 / 0821 1.3 / SA 1426 5.5 / 2041 1.5	**28**	0300 5.9 / 0920 0.8 / SU 1534 6.1 / 2148 1.0
14	0235 5.2 / 0859 1.4 / SU 1505 5.3 / 2124 1.6	**29**	0351 5.7 / 1013 1.0 / M 1623 5.8 / 2243 1.2
15	0318 5.1 / 0942 1.5 / M 1551 5.2 / 2214 1.7	**30**	0444 5.4 / 1108 1.3 / TU 1716 5.5 / 2343 1.5

JULY

	Time m		Time m
1	0542 5.1 / 1210 1.5 / W 1815 5.3	**16**	0421 5.1 / 1041 1.6 / TH 1656 5.2 / 2324 1.7
2	0048 1.6 / 0649 4.9 / TH 1315 1.7 / 1922 5.1	**17**	0530 5.0 / 1153 1.8 / F 1812 5.1
3	0152 1.6 / 0803 4.9 / F 1418 1.7 / 2030 5.2	**18**	0043 1.7 / 0659 5.0 / SA 1317 1.7 / ◐ 1934 5.3
4	0249 1.6 / 0908 5.1 / SA 1513 1.6 / ◐ 2127 5.3	**19**	0159 1.5 / 0816 5.2 / SU 1432 1.5 / 2043 5.6
5	0340 1.4 / 1000 5.3 / SU 1602 1.5 / 2214 5.5	**20**	0306 1.2 / 0921 5.6 / M 1534 1.2 / 2143 5.9
6	0425 1.2 / 1044 5.5 / M 1645 1.3 / 2255 5.6	**21**	0403 0.9 / 1019 6.0 / TU 1629 0.9 / 2238 6.2
7	0505 1.1 / 1122 5.7 / TU 1723 1.2 / 2331 5.7	**22**	0455 0.6 / 1114 6.3 / W 1720 0.7 / 2330 6.4
8	0542 1.0 / 1158 5.8 / W 1800 1.2	**23**	0545 0.4 / 1205 6.5 / TH 1809 0.5
9	0004 5.7 / 0617 1.0 / TH 1231 5.8 / 1834 1.1	**24**	0020 6.5 / 0633 0.3 / F 1254 6.6 / 1857 0.5
10	0035 5.7 / 0652 1.0 / F 1301 5.8 / 1908 1.2	**25**	0109 6.5 / 0721 0.3 / SA 1340 6.6 / 1944 0.5
11	0105 5.7 / 0725 1.0 / SA 1329 5.8 / ○ 1941 1.2	**26**	0154 6.4 / 0807 0.4 / SU 1423 6.5 / ● 2030 0.7
12	0135 5.6 / 0757 1.1 / SU 1358 5.8 / 2013 1.3	**27**	0237 6.1 / 0852 0.7 / M 1504 6.2 / 2115 0.9
13	0208 5.6 / 0827 1.2 / M 1432 5.7 / 2047 1.3	**28**	0320 5.8 / 0935 1.0 / TU 1546 5.9 / 2200 1.2
14	0245 5.5 / 0902 1.3 / TU 1511 5.6 / 2128 1.5	**29**	0405 5.4 / 1020 1.4 / W 1632 5.5 / 2251 1.6
15	0328 5.3 / 0946 1.4 / W 1558 5.4 / 2219 1.6	**30**	0456 5.0 / 1114 1.8 / TH 1726 5.1 / 2358 1.9
		31	0600 4.7 / 1232 2.1 / F 1832 4.8

AUGUST

	Time m		Time m
1	0121 2.0 / 0723 4.6 / SA 1354 2.1 / 1957 4.8	**16**	0017 1.9 / 0643 4.8 / SU 1302 2.0 / 1921 5.0
2	0229 1.9 / 0851 4.8 / SU 1456 1.9 / ● 2110 5.0	**17**	0149 1.7 / 0809 5.1 / M 1425 1.6 / ◐ 2037 5.4
3	0323 1.6 / 0946 5.2 / M 1546 1.6 / 2200 5.3	**18**	0300 1.3 / 0917 5.6 / TU 1527 1.2 / 2138 5.9
4	0407 1.3 / 1028 5.5 / TU 1627 1.4 / 2239 5.6	**19**	0354 0.8 / 1013 6.1 / W 1619 0.8 / 2231 6.2
5	0446 1.1 / 1105 5.7 / W 1704 1.2 / 2313 5.7	**20**	0443 0.5 / 1103 6.5 / TH 1706 0.6 / 2319 6.5
6	0521 1.0 / 1137 5.9 / TH 1739 1.1 / 2344 5.8	**21**	0529 0.3 / 1149 6.7 / F 1751 0.4
7	0556 0.9 / 1207 5.9 / F 1812 1.0	**22**	0005 6.6 / 0613 0.3 / SA 1234 6.8 / 1835 0.4
8	0012 5.9 / 0629 0.9 / SA 1234 6.0 / 1845 1.0	**23**	0049 6.6 / 0656 0.3 / SU 1315 6.7 / 1918 0.5
9	0041 5.9 / 0700 0.9 / SU 1301 6.0 / ○ 1915 1.0	**24**	0130 6.4 / 0737 0.5 / M 1354 6.5 / 1958 0.7
10	0110 5.9 / 0728 1.0 / M 1330 6.0 / 1943 1.1	**25**	0208 6.2 / 0816 0.7 / TU 1430 6.2 / ● 2036 0.9
11	0141 5.9 / 0755 1.0 / TU 1402 5.9 / 2014 1.1	**26**	0245 5.8 / 0853 1.1 / W 1507 5.8 / 2114 1.3
12	0216 5.8 / 0829 1.1 / W 1439 5.8 / 2053 1.3	**27**	0325 5.4 / 0932 1.5 / TH 1548 5.3 / 2157 1.7
13	0256 5.6 / 0912 1.4 / TH 1522 5.5 / 2142 1.5	**28**	0415 5.0 / 1021 2.0 / F 1642 4.9 / 2255 2.1
14	0346 5.2 / 1007 1.7 / F 1618 5.2 / 2247 1.8	**29**	0520 4.6 / 1132 2.3 / SA 1752 4.5
15	0455 4.9 / 1123 1.9 / SA 1740 4.9	**30**	0045 2.3 / 0641 4.5 / SU 1330 2.4 / 1920 4.5
		31	0206 2.1 / 0831 4.7 / M 1436 2.1 / 2052 4.9

Chart Datum: 3·27 metres below Ordnance Datum (Newlyn)
HAT is 6·9 metres above Chart Datum

ENGLAND – SHOREHAM

LAT 50°50′N LONG 0°15′W

TIMES AND HEIGHTS OF HIGH AND LOW WATERS

Dates in amber are **SPRINGS**
Dates in yellow are **NEAPS**

2009

SEPTEMBER

#	Day	Time m	Time m	Time m	Time m		#	Day	Time m	Time m	Time m	Time m
1	TU	0301 1.8	0925 5.2	1524 1.7	2139 5.3		16	W	0249 1.3	0908 5.8	1515 1.1	2128 5.9
2	W	0343 1.4	1004 5.5	1603 1.4	2215 5.6		17	TH	0340 0.8	0958 6.3	1602 0.7	2217 6.3
3	TH	0420 1.1	1038 5.8	1639 1.2	2246 5.8		18	F	0424 0.5	1044 6.6	1646 0.5 ●	2301 6.5
4	F	0455 1.0	1108 6.0	1712 1.0	2315 6.0 ○		19	SA	0507 0.4	1126 6.7	1728 0.4	2344 6.6
5	SA	0528 0.9	1136 6.1	1745 1.0	2344 6.0		20	SU	0548 0.4	1207 6.8	1809 0.4	
6	SU	0601 0.9	1203 6.1	1817 0.9			21	M	0024 6.6	0627 0.5	1246 6.6	1848 0.6
7	M	0014 6.1	0631 0.9	1236 6.2	1846 0.9		22	TU	0103 6.4	0705 0.7	1322 6.4	1925 0.8
8	TU	0045 6.1	0659 0.9	1302 6.2	1915 0.9		23	W	0138 6.1	0741 0.9	1355 6.1	2000 1.0
9	W	0116 6.1	0729 1.0	1335 6.1	1948 1.0		24	TH	0212 5.8	0816 1.2	1427 5.7	2035 1.4
10	TH	0151 5.9	0805 1.1	1412 5.9	2028 1.2		25	F	0249 5.4	0854 1.6	1505 5.3	2117 1.8
11	F	0232 5.6	0850 1.4	1456 5.5	2119 1.6		26	SA	0337 5.0	0942 2.1	1600 4.8	2212 2.2 ◑
12	SA	0323 5.2	0949 1.8	1554 5.1	2229 1.9 ◐		27	SU	0445 4.6	1049 2.4	1716 4.5	2333 2.4
13	SU	0441 4.8	1113 2.1	1731 4.8			28	M	0603 4.5	1250 2.5	1837 4.5	
14	M	0007 2.0	0639 4.8	1258 2.0	1916 5.0		29	TU	0131 2.3	0741 4.7	1405 2.2	2012 4.8
15	TU	0143 1.7	0805 5.2	1418 1.6	2031 5.4		30	W	0228 1.9	0847 5.1	1454 1.8	2103 5.2

OCTOBER

#	Day	Time m	Time m	Time m	Time m		#	Day	Time m	Time m	Time m	Time m
1	TH	0312 1.5	0926 5.5	1532 1.4	2138 5.6		16	F	0317 0.9	0935 6.3	1540 0.8	2155 6.2
2	F	0348 1.2	1004 5.8	1607 1.2	2209 5.8		17	SA	0401 0.7	1019 6.5	1622 0.6	2239 6.4
3	SA	0423 1.0	1029 6.0	1641 1.0	2241 6.0		18	SU	0442 0.6	1100 6.6	1704 0.5 ●	2320 6.5
4	SU	0457 0.9	1059 6.2	1714 0.9	2314 6.1 ○		19	M	0522 0.6	1139 6.6	1743 0.6	2359 6.4
5	M	0530 0.9	1130 6.3	1747 0.9	2347 6.2		20	TU	0601 0.7	1216 6.4	1821 0.7	
6	TU	0602 0.9	1203 6.3	1820 0.8			21	W	0036 6.3	0637 0.9	1250 6.2	1857 0.9
7	W	0021 6.2	0634 0.9	1237 6.3	1854 0.9		22	TH	0110 6.1	0712 1.1	1322 6.0	1931 1.1
8	TH	0056 6.2	0710 1.0	1313 6.1	1932 1.0		23	F	0144 5.8	0747 1.4	1354 5.6	2007 1.4
9	F	0135 6.0	0751 1.2	1353 5.9	2016 1.3		24	SA	0221 5.5	0827 1.7	1431 5.3	2048 1.7
10	SA	0220 5.7	0841 1.6	1442 5.5	2111 1.6		25	SU	0306 5.1	0914 2.0	1522 4.9	2141 2.0
11	SU	0318 5.3	0945 1.8	1547 5.1	2224 1.9		26	M	0410 4.8	1015 2.3	1637 4.6	2248 2.3 ◑
12	M	0447 5.0	1111 2.1	1729 4.9	2358 1.9		27	TU	0522 4.7	1133 2.4	1752 4.5	
13	TU	0629 5.0	1246 1.9	1904 5.1			28	W	0014 2.3	0632 4.8	1309 2.2	1902 4.7
14	W	0125 1.7	0747 5.4	1359 1.5	2013 5.5		29	TH	0136 2.1	0747 5.1	1408 1.9	2002 5.1
15	TH	0228 1.3	0846 5.9	1454 1.1	2108 5.9		30	F	0227 1.7	0829 5.4	1452 1.6	2048 5.4
							31	SA	0309 1.5	0926 5.7	1530 1.3	2128 5.7

NOVEMBER

#	Day	Time m	Time m	Time m	Time m		#	Day	Time m	Time m	Time m	Time m
1	SU	0346 1.2	0948 6.0	1606 1.1	2207 6.0		16	M	0419 0.9	1034 6.3	1641 0.8	2258 6.2 ●
2	M	0423 1.1	1024 6.2	1642 0.9	2245 6.2 ○		17	TU	0500 0.9	1114 6.3	1722 0.8	2338 6.2
3	TU	0459 1.0	1101 6.3	1720 0.8	2323 6.3		18	W	0540 1.0	1151 6.2	1801 0.9	
4	W	0537 0.9	1139 6.3	1758 0.8			19	TH	0014 6.1	0616 1.1	1226 6.0	1836 1.0
5	TH	0003 6.3	0616 0.9	1218 6.3	1839 0.8		20	F	0050 6.0	0652 1.2	1259 5.9	1911 1.1
6	F	0044 6.2	0659 1.0	1300 6.2	1924 0.9		21	SA	0124 5.8	0727 1.4	1332 5.7	1948 1.3
7	SA	0129 6.1	0746 1.2	1346 5.9	2013 1.1		22	SU	0200 5.6	0806 1.6	1407 5.4	2027 1.5
8	SU	0220 5.8	0840 1.4	1439 5.6	2110 1.4		23	M	0239 5.4	0850 1.8	1449 5.1	2113 1.8
9	M	0322 5.5	0944 1.7	1547 5.3	2219 1.6 ◐		24	TU	0326 5.1	0941 2.0	1543 4.8	2206 2.0 ◑
10	TU	0440 5.3	1100 1.8	1712 5.1	2338 1.7		25	W	0427 4.9	1042 2.2	1656 4.7	2309 2.1
11	W	0603 5.3	1220 1.7	1835 5.2			26	TH	0535 4.9	1149 2.2	1805 4.7	
12	TH	0054 1.6	0715 5.5	1329 1.5	1944 5.4		27	F	0016 2.1	0638 5.0	1257 2.0	1906 4.9
13	F	0157 1.4	0815 5.8	1425 1.2	2041 5.7		28	SA	0122 1.9	0735 5.3	1356 1.7	2000 5.2
14	SA	0249 1.1	0906 6.1	1514 1.0	2130 5.9		29	SU	0218 1.7	0825 5.5	1446 1.5	2050 5.5
15	SU	0336 1.0	0952 6.2	1559 0.9	2216 6.1		30	M	0306 1.5	0911 5.8	1531 1.2	2136 5.8

DECEMBER

#	Day	Time m	Time m	Time m	Time m		#	Day	Time m	Time m	Time m	Time m
1	TU	0350 1.2	0954 6.1	1614 1.0	2221 6.1		16	W	0444 1.2	1056 6.0	1707 1.0	2323 5.9 ●
2	W	0434 1.1	1038 6.3	1658 0.9	2306 6.2 ○		17	TH	0525 1.2	1134 6.0	1746 1.0	
3	TH	0518 0.9	1122 6.4	1743 0.7	2352 6.3		18	F	0000 6.0	0601 1.2	1209 5.9	1822 1.0
4	F	0604 0.9	1207 6.4	1830 0.7			19	SA	0035 6.0	0637 1.2	1242 5.8	1857 1.1
5	SA	0039 6.3	0651 0.9	1254 6.3	1918 0.8		20	SU	0108 5.9	0711 1.3	1314 5.7	1932 1.2
6	SU	0128 6.3	0741 1.0	1344 6.1	2009 0.9		21	M	0139 5.8	0747 1.4	1345 5.6	2007 1.3
7	M	0220 6.1	0835 1.1	1437 5.9	2104 1.0		22	TU	0210 5.6	0824 1.5	1418 5.4	2044 1.5
8	TU	0316 5.9	0933 1.3	1536 5.6	2203 1.2		23	W	0243 5.5	0905 1.7	1456 5.2	2123 1.6
9	W	0418 5.7	1037 1.5	1642 5.4	2308 1.4 ◐		24	TH	0323 5.3	0950 1.8	1541 5.0	2209 1.8 ◑
10	TH	0523 5.6	1145 1.6	1752 5.3			25	F	0413 5.1	1045 2.0	1639 4.9	2305 1.9
11	F	0015 1.5	0631 5.5	1252 1.6	1903 5.2		26	SA	0518 5.0	1149 2.0	1758 4.8	
12	SA	0120 1.5	0737 5.5	1354 1.5	2008 5.3		27	SU	0013 2.0	0635 5.1	1258 1.9	1912 5.0
13	SU	0219 1.5	0836 5.6	1449 1.3	2106 5.5		28	M	0125 1.7	0742 5.3	1403 1.7	2015 5.3
14	M	0312 1.4	0928 5.8	1539 1.2	2156 5.7		29	TU	0229 1.7	0840 5.6	1502 1.4	2111 5.6
15	TU	0400 1.3	1014 5.9	1624 1.1	2242 5.8		30	W	0326 1.4	0932 5.9	1554 1.1	2204 5.9
							31	TH	0417 1.1	1022 6.2	1644 0.8	2255 6.2 ○

Chart Datum: 3·27 metres below Ordnance Datum (Newlyn)
HAT is 6·9 metres above Chart Datum

TIDES

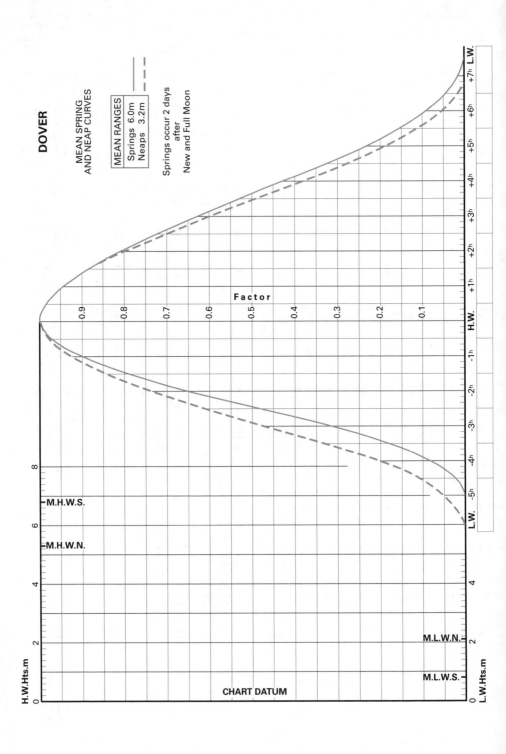

DOVER

MEAN SPRING
AND NEAP CURVES

MEAN RANGES	
Springs	6.0m
Neaps	3.2m

Springs occur 2 days
after
New and Full Moon

Factor

0.9
0.8
0.7
0.6
0.5
0.4
0.3
0.2
0.1

H.W.Hts.m

M.H.W.S.
M.H.W.N.

CHART DATUM

L.W.Hts.m

M.L.W.N.
M.L.W.S.

L.W.

H.W.

L.W.

+7ʰ +6ʰ +5ʰ +4ʰ +3ʰ +2ʰ +1ʰ

-1ʰ -2ʰ -3ʰ -4ʰ -5ʰ

TIME ZONE (UT)	ENGLAND – DOVER	Dates in amber are SPRINGS
For Summer Time add ONE hour in **non-shaded areas**	LAT 51°07′N LONG 1°19′E	Dates in yellow are NEAPS
	TIMES AND HEIGHTS OF HIGH AND LOW WATERS	**2009**

JANUARY

Time	m	Time	m
1 0122 0845 TH 1336 2056	6.3 1.4 6.1 1.5	**16** 0220 0957 F 1447 2208	6.7 0.8 6.2 1.2
2 0155 0921 F 1411 2132	6.3 1.5 6.0 1.6	**17** 0305 1035 SA 1533 2244	6.5 1.1 6.0 1.5
3 0234 0959 SA 1453 2211	6.2 1.6 5.9 1.7	**18** 0352 1115 SU 1625 ◐ 2325	6.2 1.5 5.6 1.9
4 0320 1041 SU 1544 ◐ 2257	6.1 1.7 5.8 1.9	**19** 0445 1201 M 1725	5.8 1.9 5.3
5 0416 1135 M 1648 2358	5.9 1.8 5.6 2.1	**20** 0020 0548 TU 1301 1835	2.2 5.4 2.1 5.2
6 0526 1244 TU 1813	5.8 1.9 5.5	**21** 0131 0704 W 1407 1950	2.4 5.3 2.2 5.2
7 0117 0646 W 1402 1934	2.1 5.8 1.9 5.6	**22** 0244 0823 TH 1512 2057	2.3 5.3 2.1 5.3
8 0237 0759 TH 1516 2040	1.9 5.9 1.7 5.9	**23** 0349 0927 F 1611 2148	2.0 5.6 1.9 5.7
9 0348 0904 F 1626 2139	1.6 6.2 1.4 6.2	**24** 0443 1013 SA 1700 2229	1.7 5.8 1.7 6.0
10 0454 1003 SA 1733 2233	1.3 6.4 1.2 6.5	**25** 0527 1048 SU 1742 2303	1.5 6.0 1.5 6.2
11 0557 1058 SU 1833 ○ 2322	1.0 6.6 1.0 6.7	**26** 0606 1118 M 1820 ● 2334	1.3 6.1 1.3 6.4
12 0655 1147 M 1927	0.8 6.7 0.8	**27** 0643 1148 TU 1857	1.2 6.2 1.3
13 0007 0748 TU 1234 2014	6.9 0.6 6.7 0.8	**28** 0003 0719 W 1217 1932	6.4 1.2 6.3 1.4
14 0052 0836 W 1318 2056	6.9 0.5 6.6 0.8	**29** 0031 0755 TH 1245 2006	6.5 1.1 6.3 1.2
15 0139 0918 TH 1402 2133	6.9 0.6 6.5 1.0	**30** 0100 0829 F 1313 2038	6.5 1.1 6.3 1.2
		31 0131 0901 SA 1345 2110	6.6 1.1 6.4 1.2

FEBRUARY

Time	m	Time	m
1 0207 0933 SU 1423 2145	6.6 1.2 6.3 1.4	**16** 0312 1024 M 1538 ◐ 2229	6.2 1.5 5.7 1.8
2 0248 1010 M 1509 ◐ 2227	6.4 1.4 6.0 1.6	**17** 0359 1058 TU 1635 2311	5.7 1.9 5.3 2.2
3 0338 1058 TU 1606 2321	6.1 1.7 5.7 2.0	**18** 0501 1156 W 1747	5.3 2.3 5.0
4 0442 1203 W 1730	5.7 2.0 5.3	**19** 0031 0618 TH 1323 1908	2.5 5.0 2.5 5.0
5 0039 0621 TH 1332 1922	2.2 5.5 2.1 5.3	**20** 0204 0750 F 1439 2029	2.5 5.0 2.4 5.2
6 0212 0757 F 1459 2038	2.1 5.6 1.9 5.6	**21** 0317 0909 SA 1543 2126	2.2 5.3 2.0 5.6
7 0334 0909 SA 1621 2140	1.8 5.9 1.6 6.0	**22** 0416 0953 SU 1636 2205	1.8 5.7 1.7 5.9
8 0450 1009 SU 1733 2232	1.3 6.3 1.2 6.5	**23** 0504 1024 M 1721 2236	1.5 6.0 1.4 6.2
9 0556 1059 M 1830 ○ 2316	0.9 6.6 0.8 6.8	**24** 0545 1052 TU 1801 2306	1.3 6.2 1.3 6.4
10 0651 1143 TU 1918 2357	0.6 6.7 0.6 7.0	**25** 0623 1121 W 1837 ● 2335	1.1 6.3 1.1 6.5
11 0739 1222 W 2000	0.4 6.8 0.6	**26** 0700 1150 TH 1912	1.0 6.4 1.0
12 0036 0819 TH 1300 2034	7.0 0.3 6.7 0.6	**27** 0004 0734 F 1219 1945	6.6 0.9 6.5 1.0
13 0115 0855 F 1336 2105	7.0 0.4 6.6 0.8	**28** 0035 0807 SA 1248 2017	6.7 0.9 6.6 1.0
14 0154 0927 SA 1414 2133	6.8 0.7 6.4 1.0		
15 0232 0956 SU 1454 2159	6.6 1.1 6.1 1.4		

MARCH

Time	m	Time	m
1 0106 0838 SU 1322 2049	6.8 0.9 6.6 1.0	**16** 0200 0915 M 1419 2119	6.5 1.1 6.2 1.4
2 0142 0910 M 1400 2124	6.7 1.1 6.4 1.2	**17** 0235 0936 TU 1458 2146	6.1 1.5 5.8 1.7
3 0223 0947 TU 1445 2206	6.5 1.4 6.1 1.5	**18** 0317 1006 W 1551 ◐ 2224	5.7 1.9 5.4 2.1
4 0312 1034 W 1543 ◐ 2301	6.1 1.7 5.6 1.9	**19** 0422 1053 TH 1705 2328	5.2 2.3 5.0 2.5
5 0421 1140 TH 1721	5.5 2.1 5.2	**20** 0542 1231 F 1825	4.9 2.6 4.9
6 0023 0624 F 1319 1915	2.2 5.3 2.3 5.2	**21** 0123 0705 SA 1404 1944	2.6 4.9 2.5 5.1
7 0201 0758 SA 1454 2032	2.1 5.5 2.0 5.6	**22** 0241 0825 SU 1510 2045	2.3 5.2 2.1 5.5
8 0329 0908 SU 1621 2131	1.7 5.9 1.5 6.1	**23** 0340 0912 M 1604 2126	1.9 5.6 1.8 5.9
9 0447 1003 M 1724 2219	1.2 6.3 1.1 6.5	**24** 0429 0946 TU 1650 2159	1.5 5.9 1.5 6.2
10 0547 1048 TU 1815 2301	0.6 6.6 0.8 6.8	**25** 0513 1017 W 1731 2231	1.2 6.2 1.2 6.4
11 0636 1126 W 1858 ○ 2339	0.5 6.7 0.6 7.0	**26** 0554 1049 TH 1810 ● 2303	1.0 6.4 1.1 6.6
12 0718 1201 TH 1934	0.3 6.8 0.6	**27** 0633 1120 F 1847 2335	0.9 6.5 1.0 6.7
13 0015 0754 F 1235 2006	7.0 0.4 6.7 0.9	**28** 0710 1152 SA 1922	0.8 6.6 0.9
14 0051 0825 SA 1309 2033	6.9 0.5 6.6 0.8	**29** 0008 0744 SU 1225 1956	6.8 0.8 6.7 0.9
15 0126 0852 SU 1344 2057	6.8 0.8 6.4 1.1	**30** 0044 0817 M 1302 2031	6.8 0.9 6.6 0.9
		31 0123 0852 TU 1345 2110	6.7 1.1 6.4 1.2

APRIL

Time	m	Time	m
1 0207 0933 W 1435 2156	6.4 1.4 6.1 1.5	**16** 0247 0935 TH 1516 2158	5.6 1.9 5.5 2.0
2 0303 1023 TH 1543 ◐ 2256	5.9 1.8 5.6 1.9	**17** 0350 1021 F 1625 ◐ 2255	5.2 2.2 5.2 2.3
3 0429 1135 F 1723	5.4 2.2 5.3	**18** 0506 1131 SA 1739	5.0 2.5 5.1
4 0022 0622 SA 1315 1859	2.1 5.3 2.2 5.4	**19** 0032 0620 SU 1317 1849	2.5 5.0 2.5 5.2
5 0155 0748 SU 1446 2014	1.9 5.5 1.9 5.7	**20** 0154 0727 M 1426 1949	2.2 5.2 2.2 5.5
6 0319 0854 M 1602 2111	1.5 5.9 1.5 6.1	**21** 0254 0820 TU 1521 2036	1.9 5.5 1.8 5.8
7 0429 0945 TU 1700 2157	1.1 6.2 1.1 6.5	**22** 0346 0901 W 1610 2115	1.5 5.9 1.5 6.1
8 0524 1026 W 1748 2238	0.8 6.5 0.9 6.7	**23** 0434 0939 TH 1655 2152	1.3 6.2 1.3 6.4
9 0611 1102 TH 1828 ○ 2315	0.6 6.6 0.7 6.8	**24** 0520 1014 F 1739 2229	1.1 6.4 1.1 6.6
10 0651 1136 F 1904 2352	0.6 6.6 0.7 6.8	**25** 0604 1050 SA 1820 ● 2307	0.9 6.6 1.0 6.8
11 0725 1209 SA 1935	0.6 6.6 0.8	**26** 0646 1127 SU 1900 2345	0.8 6.7 0.9 6.8
12 0027 0753 SU 1244 2001	6.7 0.8 6.5 1.0	**27** 0725 1207 M 1940	0.8 6.7 0.8
13 0101 0817 TU 1318 2024	6.6 1.0 6.4 1.2	**28** 0027 0803 TU 1251 2021	6.8 0.9 6.6 0.9
14 0134 0838 TU 1352 2048	6.3 1.3 6.2 1.4	**29** 0112 0844 W 1340 2106	6.6 1.1 6.4 1.1
15 0207 0902 W 1428 2118	6.0 1.6 5.9 1.7	**30** 0205 0930 TH 1438 2158	6.3 1.4 6.1 1.4

Chart Datum: 3·67 metres below Ordnance Datum (Newlyn)
HAT is 7·3 metres above Chart Datum

TIDES

ENGLAND – DOVER
LAT 51°07′N   LONG 1°19′E
TIMES AND HEIGHTS OF HIGH AND LOW WATERS

Dates in amber are **SPRINGS**
Dates in yellow are NEAPS

2009

MAY

Day	Time	m	Time	m	Day	Time	m	Time	m
1 F	0312	5.9	1026	1.7	**16** SA	0317	5.4	1001	2.0
	1547	5.8	2302	1.7		1539	5.5	2234	2.1
2 SA	0435	5.6	1140	2.0	**17** SU	0422	5.2	1056	2.2
	1705	5.6				1643	5.4	2341	2.2
3 SU	0020	1.8	0605	5.5	**18** M	0530	5.2	1212	2.3
	1302	2.0	1828	5.6		1749	5.4		
4 M	0138	1.7	0723	5.6	**19** TU	0058	2.1	0633	5.3
	1417	1.8	1942	5.8		1329	2.2	1850	5.5
5 TU	0250	1.4	0826	5.8	**20** W	0203	1.9	0728	5.5
	1524	1.5	2040	6.1		1431	1.9	1943	5.8
6 W	0356	1.2	0916	6.0	**21** TH	0259	1.6	0816	5.8
	1623	1.3	2128	6.3		1526	1.7	2030	6.1
7 TH	0452	1.0	0957	6.2	**22** F	0353	1.4	0900	6.1
	1713	1.1	2211	6.5		1618	1.4	2115	6.3
8 F	0539	0.9	1035	6.3	**23** SA	0446	1.2	0942	6.3
	1755	1.0	2251	6.5		1708	1.2	2159	6.5
9 SA	0619	0.9	1111	6.4	**24** SU	0537	1.0	1026	6.5
	1832	1.0	2329	6.5		1757	1.0	2244	6.7
10 SU	0653	1.0	1147	6.4	**25** M	0626	0.9	1110	6.6
	1905	1.1				1844	0.9	2331	6.7
11 M	0005	6.4	0721	1.1	**26** TU	0713	0.9	1157	6.7
	1223	6.4	1933	1.2		1932	0.8		
12 TU	0041	6.3	0747	1.3	**27** W	0019	6.7	0759	0.9
	1259	6.3	2000	1.3		1247	6.7	2020	0.9
13 W	0115	6.1	0812	1.4	**28** TH	0111	6.5	0847	1.1
	1334	6.2	2028	1.4		1340	6.6	2111	1.0
14 TH	0149	5.9	0841	1.6	**29** F	0209	6.3	0937	1.2
	1408	6.0	2102	1.6		1436	6.4	2205	1.1
15 F	0227	5.7	0917	1.8	**30** SA	0312	6.1	1031	1.4
	1447	5.8	2143	1.9		1535	6.2	2302	1.3
					31 SU	0419	5.9	1130	1.6
						1637	6.0		

JUNE

Day	Time	m	Time	m	Day	Time	m	Time	m
1 M	0003	1.4	0530	5.7	**16** TU	0414	5.5	1117	2.0
	1233	1.7	1744	5.9		1640	5.7	2358	1.9
2 TU	0106	1.5	0641	5.6	**17** W	0523	5.4	1221	2.1
	1336	1.7	1856	5.8		1746	5.6		
3 W	0208	1.5	0745	5.7	**18** TH	0105	1.9	0631	5.5
	1438	1.4	2001	5.9		1335	2.0	1851	5.7
4 TH	0310	1.4	0839	5.8	**19** F	0213	1.8	0733	5.6
	1539	1.6	2057	6.0		1442	1.8	1951	5.9
5 F	0410	1.4	0927	5.9	**20** SA	0316	1.6	0828	5.9
	1635	1.5	2146	6.1		1544	1.6	2048	6.2
6 SA	0502	1.3	1009	6.1	**21** SU	0417	1.3	0921	6.1
	1723	1.4	2230	6.2		1643	1.3	2142	6.4
7 SU	0545	1.3	1050	6.2	**22** M	0516	1.2	1013	6.4
	1803	1.3	2311	6.2		1740	1.1	2235	6.6
8 M	0622	1.3	1128	6.3	**23** TU	0613	1.1	1104	6.6
	1839	1.3	2349	6.2		1835	0.9	2327	6.7
9 TU	0654	1.4	1205	6.3	**24** W	0709	0.9	1153	6.7
	1912	1.3				1930	0.7		
10 W	0024	6.1	0724	1.4	**25** TH	0018	6.7	0802	0.8
	1242	6.3	1943	1.3		1243	6.8	2023	0.7
11 TH	0059	6.1	0755	1.4	**26** F	0110	6.6	0851	0.9
	1315	6.2	2016	1.4		1332	6.8	2113	0.6
12 F	0131	5.9	0828	1.5	**27** SA	0202	6.5	0936	0.9
	1347	6.1	2051	1.5		1422	6.7	2200	0.7
13 SA	0203	5.8	0904	1.6	**28** SU	0255	6.3	1019	1.1
	1418	6.0	2130	1.6		1512	6.5	2246	0.9
14 SU	0237	5.7	0943	1.7	**29** M	0348	6.1	1104	1.3
	1456	5.9	2212	1.7		1604	6.3	2334	1.2
15 M	0319	5.6	1026	1.9	**30** TU	0444	5.8	1153	1.6
	1543	5.8	2259	1.8		1700	6.0		

JULY

Day	Time	m	Time	m	Day	Time	m	Time	m
1 W	0026	1.5	0545	5.6	**16** TH	0414	5.6	1127	2.0
	1249	1.8	1803	5.7		1648	5.8		
2 TH	0123	1.7	0654	5.5	**17** F	0007	1.9	0528	5.4
	1351	2.0	1915	5.6		1238	2.1	1806	5.6
3 F	0224	1.8	0800	5.5	**18** SA	0128	2.0	0700	5.5
	1455	1.9	2026	5.6		1404	2.0	1927	5.7
4 SA	0326	1.8	0859	5.6	**19** SU	0246	1.8	0813	5.7
	1559	1.8	2127	5.8		1519	1.8	2037	6.0
5 SU	0425	1.7	0950	5.8	**20** M	0357	1.6	0915	6.0
	1654	1.6	2217	5.9		1626	1.4	2139	6.3
6 M	0515	1.6	1033	6.1	**21** TU	0504	1.3	1010	6.4
	1739	1.5	2258	6.0		1729	1.1	2236	6.5
7 TU	0556	1.5	1112	6.2	**22** W	0608	1.0	1100	6.7
	1818	1.4	2334	6.1		1830	0.8	2327	6.7
8 W	0633	1.4	1148	6.3	**23** TH	0706	0.8	1147	6.9
	1853	1.3				1927	0.6		
9 TH	0007	6.1	0706	1.4	**24** F	0014	6.8	0755	0.7
	1222	6.3	1927	1.3		1232	7.0	2016	0.4
10 F	0038	6.1	0739	1.4	**25** SA	0059	6.8	0839	0.7
	1252	6.3	2001	1.3		1316	7.0	2100	0.4
11 SA	0107	6.1	0813	1.4	**26** SU	0143	6.7	0917	0.7
	1320	6.3	2036	1.3		1400	6.9	2139	0.5
12 SU	0133	6.0	0847	1.4	**27** M	0227	6.5	0953	0.9
	1347	6.3	2110	1.3		1445	6.7	2217	0.8
13 M	0201	6.0	0921	1.5	**28** TU	0312	6.2	1028	1.2
	1420	6.2	2145	1.4		1531	6.4	2256	1.2
14 TU	0235	5.9	0956	1.6	**29** W	0401	5.9	1108	1.6
	1500	6.1	2222	1.6		1621	6.0	2340	1.7
15 W	0319	5.8	1036	1.8	**30** TH	0457	5.5	1158	2.0
	1548	6.0	2307	1.8		1719	5.6		
					31 F	0036	2.0	0604	5.3
						1306	2.3	1831	5.3

AUGUST

Day	Time	m	Time	m	Day	Time	m	Time	m
1 SA	0144	2.2	0722	5.2	**16** SU	0052	2.2	0649	5.3
	1420	2.3	2000	5.3		1338	2.2	1924	5.5
2 SU	0252	2.2	0837	5.4	**17** M	0229	2.1	0808	5.6
	1530	2.1	2117	5.5		1503	1.9	2038	5.9
3 M	0356	2.0	0934	5.7	**18** TU	0348	1.7	0911	6.0
	1631	1.8	2207	5.8		1616	1.4	2139	6.3
4 TU	0451	1.7	1017	6.0	**19** W	0459	1.4	1004	6.5
	1720	1.5	2244	6.0		1723	1.0	2232	6.6
5 W	0535	1.5	1053	6.3	**20** TH	0600	1.0	1050	6.8
	1759	1.4	2314	6.1		1822	0.7	2318	6.8
6 TH	0613	1.4	1126	6.4	**21** F	0652	0.7	1133	7.0
	1834	1.3	2342	6.2		1913	0.4	2359	6.9
7 F	0647	1.3	1155	6.4	**22** SA	0737	0.6	1213	7.2
	1908	1.2				1957	0.3		
8 SA	0010	6.2	0719	1.3	**23** SU	0037	6.9	0815	0.6
	1224	6.5	1941	1.2		1254	7.1	2036	0.4
9 SU	0037	6.2	0752	1.2	**24** M	0116	6.8	0848	0.7
	1249	6.5	2014	1.1		1334	7.0	2110	0.6
10 M	0101	6.3	0823	1.2	**25** TU	0155	6.6	0919	1.0
	1316	6.5	2045	1.2		1414	6.8	2141	1.0
11 TU	0128	6.3	0855	1.3	**26** W	0236	6.3	0949	1.3
	1348	6.5	2116	1.3		1457	6.4	2213	1.4
12 W	0202	6.3	0927	1.4	**27** TH	0323	5.9	1020	1.7
	1425	6.4	2149	1.5		1545	5.9	2248	1.9
13 TH	0243	6.1	1004	1.6	**28** F	0418	5.5	1102	2.2
	1510	6.3	2230	1.7		1643	5.5	2342	2.3
14 F	0334	5.8	1052	1.9	**29** SA	0525	5.2	1217	2.5
	1608	5.8	2326	2.0		1756	5.1		
15 SA	0447	5.4	1200	2.2	**30** SU	0106	2.6	0645	5.1
	1739	5.5				1348	2.6	1931	5.1
					31 M	0225	2.5	0811	5.0
						1506	2.3	2101	5.4

Chart Datum: 3·67 metres below Ordnance Datum (Newlyn)
HAT is 7·3 metres above Chart Datum

TIME ZONE (UT)	ENGLAND – DOVER	Dates in amber are SPRINGS
For Summer Time add ONE hour in non-shaded areas	LAT 51°07'N LONG 1°19'E	Dates in yellow are NEAPS
	TIMES AND HEIGHTS OF HIGH AND LOW WATERS	2009

SEPTEMBER

Time	m	Time	m
1 0332 / 0911 / TU 1608 / 2147	2.1 / 5.7 / 1.9 / 5.8	**16** 0342 / 0858 / W 1608 / 2130	1.7 / 6.1 / 1.4 / 6.3
2 0428 / 0953 / W 1655 / 2219	1.8 / 6.0 / 1.6 / 6.0	**17** 0448 / 0948 / TH 1711 / 2218	1.3 / 6.6 / 0.9 / 6.6
3 0511 / 1026 / TH 1733 / 2244	1.5 / 6.3 / 1.3 / 6.2	**18** 0542 / 1032 / F 1804 / ● 2259	0.9 / 6.9 / 0.6 / 6.8
4 0548 / 1055 / F 1808 / ○ 2310	1.4 / 6.5 / 1.2 / 6.3	**19** 0628 / 1112 / SA 1850 / 2336	0.7 / 7.1 / 0.5 / 6.9
5 0621 / 1123 / SA 1841 / 2337	1.3 / 6.5 / 1.1 / 6.4	**20** 0709 / 1150 / SU 1930	0.7 / 7.2 / 0.5
6 0653 / 1150 / SU 1915	1.2 / 6.6 / 1.1	**21** 0011 / 0744 / M 1228 / 2005	6.9 / 0.7 / 7.1 / 0.6
7 0004 / 0725 / M 1218 / 1947	6.4 / 1.2 / 6.6 / 1.1	**22** 0047 / 0815 / TU 1306 / 2035	6.8 / 0.9 / 6.9 / 0.9
8 0030 / 0757 / TU 1246 / 2018	6.5 / 1.2 / 6.7 / 1.1	**23** 0124 / 0844 / W 1344 / 2103	6.6 / 1.1 / 6.6 / 1.2
9 0100 / 0828 / W 1319 / 2048	6.5 / 1.4 / 6.7 / 1.3	**24** 0204 / 0910 / TH 1424 / 2127	6.3 / 1.4 / 6.3 / 1.6
10 0135 / 0902 / TH 1356 / 2122	6.4 / 1.4 / 6.5 / 1.5	**25** 0248 / 0937 / F 1511 / 2155	6.0 / 1.8 / 5.8 / 2.0
11 0217 / 0941 / F 1442 / 2204	6.2 / 1.6 / 6.1 / 1.8	**26** 0343 / 1014 / SA 1612 / ◑ 2239	5.6 / 2.2 / 5.4 / 2.5
12 0310 / 1030 / SA 1544 / ◑ 2302	5.8 / 2.0 / 5.7 / 2.2	**27** 0450 / 1117 / SU 1724	5.2 / 2.6 / 5.1
13 0436 / 1141 / SU 1747	5.3 / 2.3 / 5.3	**28** 0016 / 0605 / M 1310 / 1847	2.8 / 5.1 / 2.7 / 5.0
14 0035 / 0641 / M 1326 / 1921	2.4 / 5.5 / 2.3 / 5.5	**29** 0151 / 0727 / TU 1430 / 2020	2.4 / 5.3 / 2.4 / 5.3
15 0221 / 0757 / TU 1454 / 2033	2.2 / 5.7 / 1.9 / 5.9	**30** 0300 / 0832 / W 1530 / 2107	2.3 / 5.6 / 2.0 / 5.7

OCTOBER

Time	m	Time	m
1 0354 / 0914 / TH 1617 / 2137	1.9 / 6.0 / 1.6 / 6.0	**16** 0424 / 0925 / F 1649 / 2155	1.3 / 6.6 / 0.9 / 6.6
2 0437 / 0946 / F 1657 / 2204	1.6 / 6.3 / 1.4 / 6.2	**17** 0515 / 1008 / SA 1739 / 2234	1.0 / 6.8 / 0.7 / 6.7
3 0515 / 1016 / SA 1734 / 2233	1.4 / 6.5 / 1.2 / 6.4	**18** 0559 / 1048 / SU 1822 / ● 2310	0.9 / 7.0 / 0.7 / 6.8
4 0550 / 1046 / SU 1811 / ○ 2302	1.3 / 6.6 / 1.1 / 6.5	**19** 0638 / 1126 / M 1900 / 2345	0.9 / 7.0 / 0.8 / 6.8
5 0625 / 1116 / M 1847 / 2332	1.2 / 6.7 / 1.1 / 6.6	**20** 0713 / 1203 / TU 1933	0.9 / 6.9 / 0.9
6 0659 / 1147 / TU 1921	1.1 / 6.8 / 1.1	**21** 0022 / 0744 / W 1241 / 2001	6.7 / 1.1 / 6.7 / 1.1
7 0002 / 0733 / W 1220 / 1953	6.7 / 1.1 / 6.8 / 1.1	**22** 0059 / 0812 / TH 1318 / 2026	6.6 / 1.3 / 6.5 / 1.4
8 0037 / 0807 / TH 1256 / 2026	6.7 / 1.2 / 6.7 / 1.3	**23** 0138 / 0838 / F 1357 / 2050	6.4 / 1.5 / 6.1 / 1.7
9 0117 / 0844 / F 1338 / 2104	6.5 / 1.4 / 6.5 / 1.5	**24** 0219 / 0907 / SA 1443 / 2121	6.1 / 1.8 / 5.8 / 2.0
10 0204 / 0928 / SA 1429 / 2150	6.2 / 1.6 / 6.1 / 1.9	**25** 0309 / 0945 / SU 1542 / 2204	5.7 / 2.2 / 5.4 / 2.4
11 0305 / 1022 / SU 1547 / ◑ 2252	5.8 / 2.0 / 5.6 / 2.3	**26** 0411 / 1039 / M 1650 / 2307	5.4 / 2.5 / 5.1 / 2.7
12 0445 / 1138 / M 1745	5.5 / 2.2 / 5.4	**27** 0520 / 1211 / TU 1802	5.2 / 2.6 / 5.1
13 0030 / 0621 / TU 1317 / 1908	2.4 / 5.3 / 2.1 / 5.6	**28** 0055 / 0630 / W 1337 / 1911	2.7 / 5.3 / 2.4 / 5.3
14 0208 / 0736 / W 1440 / 2016	2.1 / 5.8 / 1.7 / 5.9	**29** 0210 / 0733 / TH 1438 / 2006	2.4 / 5.5 / 2.1 / 5.6
15 0323 / 0836 / TH 1550 / 2110	1.7 / 6.2 / 1.3 / 6.3	**30** 0306 / 0821 / F 1529 / 2047	2.1 / 5.9 / 1.7 / 5.9
		31 0354 / 0859 / SA 1615 / 2122	1.8 / 6.1 / 1.5 / 6.2

NOVEMBER

Time	m	Time	m
1 0437 / 0934 / SU 1658 / 2156	1.5 / 6.4 / 1.3 / 6.4	**16** 0529 / 1025 / M 1753 / ● 2247	1.2 / 6.6 / 1.0 / 6.6
2 0518 / 1009 / M 1740 / ○ 2230	1.3 / 6.6 / 1.1 / 6.6	**17** 0610 / 1105 / TU 1831 / 2325	1.1 / 6.7 / 1.1 / 6.6
3 0558 / 1045 / TU 1820 / 2305	1.2 / 6.7 / 1.1 / 6.7	**18** 0647 / 1143 / W 1904	1.2 / 6.6 / 1.2
4 0637 / 1122 / W 1858 / 2342	1.1 / 6.8 / 1.1 / 6.8	**19** 0002 / 0719 / TH 1221 / 1933	6.6 / 1.2 / 6.5 / 1.4
5 0715 / 1201 / TH 1936	1.1 / 6.8 / 1.1	**20** 0041 / 0749 / F 1258 / 2000	6.5 / 1.4 / 6.3 / 1.5
6 0023 / 0755 / F 1244 / 2015	6.7 / 1.1 / 6.7 / 1.3	**21** 0118 / 0818 / SA 1336 / 2027	6.4 / 1.5 / 6.1 / 1.7
7 0110 / 0837 / SA 1333 / 2058	6.6 / 1.3 / 6.4 / 1.5	**22** 0155 / 0850 / SU 1416 / 2101	6.2 / 1.7 / 5.8 / 1.9
8 0203 / 0926 / SU 1433 / 2149	6.3 / 1.6 / 6.1 / 1.8	**23** 0235 / 0928 / M 1504 / 2142	5.9 / 1.9 / 5.5 / 2.1
9 0309 / 1025 / M 1554 / ◐ 2253	6.0 / 1.7 / 5.8 / 2.1	**24** 0322 / 1014 / TU 1603 / 2231	5.7 / 2.1 / 5.3 / 2.3
10 0427 / 1138 / TU 1725	5.8 / 1.9 / 5.6	**25** 0421 / 1114 / W 1708 / 2336	5.5 / 2.3 / 5.2 / 2.5
11 0016 / 0548 / W 1258 / 1842	2.2 / 5.8 / 1.8 / 5.7	**26** 0526 / 1228 / TH 1813	5.4 / 2.3 / 5.2
12 0137 / 0702 / TH 1410 / 1947	2.0 / 5.9 / 1.7 / 5.9	**27** 0057 / 0629 / F 1338 / 1910	2.5 / 5.5 / 2.1 / 5.4
13 0247 / 0804 / F 1517 / 2042	1.8 / 6.1 / 1.4 / 6.1	**28** 0207 / 0724 / SA 1438 / 1959	2.3 / 5.7 / 1.9 / 5.7
14 0349 / 0856 / SA 1617 / 2128	1.5 / 6.4 / 1.2 / 6.3	**29** 0306 / 0812 / SU 1532 / 2042	2.0 / 6.0 / 1.6 / 6.0
15 0443 / 0943 / SU 1709 / 2209	1.3 / 6.6 / 1.1 / 6.5	**30** 0358 / 0856 / M 1624 / 2124	1.7 / 6.2 / 1.4 / 6.2

DECEMBER

Time	m	Time	m
1 0448 / 0939 / TU 1713 / 2205	1.4 / 6.5 / 1.2 / 6.5	**16** 0547 / 1051 / W 1806 / ● 2310	1.4 / 6.3 / 1.4 / 6.4
2 0534 / 1022 / W 1759 / ○ 2247	1.2 / 6.7 / 1.1 / 6.7	**17** 0627 / 1130 / TH 1842 / 2348	1.3 / 6.3 / 1.4 / 6.5
3 0619 / 1106 / TH 1844 / 2332	1.1 / 6.8 / 1.1 / 6.8	**18** 0701 / 1207 / F 1913	1.3 / 6.3 / 1.4
4 0705 / 1152 / F 1929	1.0 / 6.8 / 1.1	**19** 0025 / 0733 / SA 1243 / 1943	6.5 / 1.4 / 6.2 / 1.5
5 0018 / 0751 / SA 1240 / 2014	6.8 / 1.0 / 6.7 / 1.2	**20** 0100 / 0804 / SU 1316 / 2013	6.4 / 1.4 / 6.1 / 1.5
6 0108 / 0840 / SU 1332 / 2102	6.7 / 1.0 / 6.5 / 1.3	**21** 0132 / 0837 / M 1348 / 2046	6.3 / 1.5 / 5.9 / 1.6
7 0201 / 0932 / M 1431 / 2153	6.6 / 1.2 / 6.3 / 1.5	**22** 0201 / 0912 / TU 1419 / 2122	6.2 / 1.6 / 5.8 / 1.7
8 0258 / 1026 / TU 1536 / 2247	6.4 / 1.3 / 6.0 / 1.7	**23** 0232 / 0950 / W 1453 / 2202	6.0 / 1.7 / 5.6 / 1.9
9 0400 / 1124 / W 1646 / ◐ 2348	6.2 / 1.5 / 5.8 / 1.9	**24** 0312 / 1033 / TH 1539 / ◐ 2247	5.9 / 1.9 / 5.5 / 2.1
10 0505 / 1226 / TH 1759	6.0 / 1.6 / 5.7	**25** 0403 / 1123 / F 1642 / 2342	5.7 / 2.0 / 5.3 / 2.2
11 0053 / 0616 / F 1329 / 1906	1.9 / 5.9 / 1.6 / 5.7	**26** 0509 / 1229 / SA 1803	5.5 / 2.1 / 5.3
12 0159 / 0725 / SA 1433 / 2007	1.9 / 5.9 / 1.6 / 5.8	**27** 0056 / 0623 / SU 1343 / 1911	2.3 / 5.6 / 2.0 / 5.4
13 0305 / 0827 / SU 1538 / 2101	1.8 / 6.0 / 1.6 / 5.9	**28** 0215 / 0729 / M 1451 / 2009	2.2 / 5.7 / 1.8 / 5.7
14 0408 / 0921 / M 1638 / 2148	1.6 / 6.1 / 1.5 / 6.1	**29** 0321 / 0827 / TU 1553 / 2102	1.9 / 6.0 / 1.6 / 6.0
15 0502 / 1009 / TU 1726 / 2231	1.5 / 6.2 / 1.4 / 6.3	**30** 0420 / 0920 / W 1651 / 2152	1.6 / 6.1 / 1.3 / 6.3
		31 0515 / 1011 / TH 1745 / ○ 2240	1.2 / 6.5 / 1.1 / 6.6

Chart Datum: 3·67 metres below Ordnance Datum (Newlyn)
HAT is 7·3 metres above Chart Datum

TIDES

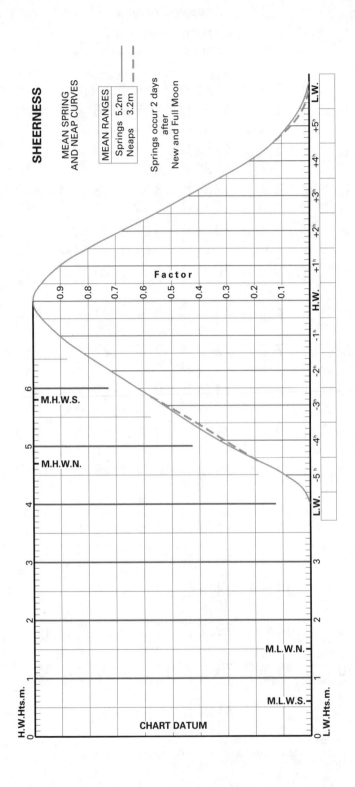

SHEERNESS

MEAN SPRING
AND NEAP CURVES

MEAN RANGES	
Springs	5.2m
Neaps	3.2m

Springs occur 2 days
after
New and Full Moon

TIME ZONE (UT)
For Summer Time add ONE hour in **non-shaded areas**

ENGLAND – SHEERNESS
LAT 51°27′N   LONG 0°45′E
TIMES AND HEIGHTS OF HIGH AND LOW WATERS

Dates in amber are **SPRINGS**
Dates in yellow are **NEAPS**
2009

JANUARY

Day	Time m	Time m	Day	Time m	Time m
1 TH	0256 5.4 / 1529 5.4	2118 1.1	16 F	0350 5.7 / 1023 0.5	1624 5.6 / 2214 1.1
2 F	0331 5.4 / 0951 0.9	1606 5.3 / 2153 1.2	17 SA	0433 5.5 / 1058 0.7	1708 5.3 / 2250 1.2
3 SA	0408 5.3 / 1024 1.0	1647 5.2 / 2230 1.3	18 SU	0517 5.3 / 1135 0.9	1754 5.0 / ◐2332 1.4
4 SU	0449 5.2 / 1100 1.1	1733 5.0 / ◖2314 1.4	19 M	0609 5.0 / 1219 1.2	1847 4.8
5 M	0538 5.1 / 1145 1.1	1830 4.9	20 TU	0029 1.6 / 0711 4.8	1323 1.5 / 1950 4.6
6 TU	0011 1.5 / 0639 5.0	1247 1.2 / 1939 4.9	21 W	0148 1.7 / 0827 4.6	1437 1.6 / 2103 4.6
7 W	0125 1.5 / 0757 5.0	1414 1.3 / 2053 5.0	22 TH	0311 1.6 / 0944 4.7	1544 1.5 / 2212 4.7
8 TH	0254 1.4 / 0915 5.1	1540 1.2 / 2202 5.1	23 F	0421 1.4 / 1048 4.9	1641 1.4 / 2307 5.0
9 F	0411 1.3 / 1026 5.3	1649 1.1 / 2304 5.3	24 SA	0519 1.2 / 1138 5.1	1728 1.3 / 2351 5.2
10 SA	0521 0.9 / 1130 5.6	1751 1.0	25 SU	0605 1.0 / 1219 5.3	1807 1.2
11 SU	0001 5.5 / 0625 0.7	1228 5.8 / ○1845 0.9	26 M	0028 5.3 / 0643 0.9	●1255 5.4 / 1842 1.0
12 M	0052 5.7 / 0723 0.4	1320 6.0 / 1934 0.8	27 TU	0103 5.4 / 0718 0.8	1328 5.5 / 1916 0.9
13 TU	0140 5.8 / 0814 0.3	1409 6.0 / 2019 0.8	28 W	0135 5.5 / 0753 0.7	1401 5.6 / 1952 0.9
14 W	0225 5.8 / 0901 0.2	1455 6.0 / 2100 0.8	29 TH	0207 5.6 / 0828 0.6	1434 5.6 / 2028 0.8
15 TH	0308 5.8 / 0944 0.3	1540 5.8 / 2138 0.9	30 F	0238 5.6 / 0903 0.6	1507 5.6 / 2101 0.9
			31 SA	0310 5.6 / 0933 0.7	1542 5.5 / 2131 1.0

FEBRUARY

Day	Time m	Time m	Day	Time m	Time m
1 SU	0343 5.5 / 0959 0.8	1618 5.3 / 2200 1.1	16 M	0436 5.4 / 1043 1.0	1703 5.1 / ○2245 1.3
2 M	0421 5.4 / 1023 0.9	1659 5.1 / ◐2237 1.2	17 TU	0519 5.0 / 1119 1.3	1747 4.7 / 2331 1.5
3 TU	0505 5.3 / 1101 1.1	1750 4.9 / 2329 1.3	18 W	0616 4.6 / 1214 1.6	1845 4.4
4 W	0604 5.1 / 1201 1.3	1858 4.7	19 TH	0043 1.7 / 0735 4.4	1344 1.8 / 2007 4.4
5 TH	0044 1.5 / 0724 4.9	1339 1.5 / 2021 4.7	20 F	0235 1.7 / 0911 4.4	1511 1.8 / 2136 4.5
6 F	0232 1.5 / 0856 4.9	1523 1.4 / 2143 4.9	21 SA	0357 1.5 / 1024 4.7	1616 1.5 / 2239 4.8
7 SA	0402 1.2 / 1019 5.2	1639 1.2 / 2253 5.2	22 SU	0459 1.2 / 1115 5.1	1707 1.3 / 2326 5.1
8 SU	0520 0.8 / 1126 5.5	1744 1.0 / 2351 5.5	23 M	0545 1.0 / 1155 5.3	1749 1.1
9 M	0624 0.5 / 1221 5.8	1837 0.8	24 TU	0004 5.3 / 0623 0.8	1231 5.5 / 1824 1.0
10 TU	0040 5.7 / 0715 0.3	1310 6.0 / 1922 0.7	25 W	0039 5.5 / 0658 0.7	●1304 5.6 / 1858 0.9
11 W	0124 5.9 / 0801 0.1	1354 6.0 / 2003 0.7	26 TH	0111 5.6 / 0733 0.6	1336 5.7 / 1933 0.8
12 TH	0205 5.9 / 0842 0.1	1435 6.0 / 2040 0.7	27 F	0143 5.7 / 0808 0.5	1409 5.7 / 2009 0.7
13 F	0244 5.9 / 0918 0.2	1513 5.8 / 2113 0.8	28 SA	0214 5.7 / 0841 0.5	1442 5.7 / 2042 0.8
14 SA	0321 5.8 / 0950 0.4	1550 5.6 / 2143 0.9			
15 SU	0358 5.6 / 1017 0.7	1626 5.4 / 2212 1.1			

MARCH

Day	Time m	Time m	Day	Time m	Time m
1 SU	0247 5.7 / 0910 0.6	1516 5.6 / 2111 0.8	16 M	0327 5.6 / 0938 0.8	1546 5.4 / 2140 1.0
2 M	0321 5.7 / 0933 0.8	1551 5.4 / 2139 0.9	17 TU	0402 5.3 / 1002 1.1	1619 5.1 / 2208 1.2
3 TU	0400 5.6 / 0958 0.9	1632 5.2 / 2216 1.1	18 W	0442 5.0 / 1035 1.3	1657 4.8 / ◐2249 1.4
4 W	0446 5.3 / 1039 1.1	1721 4.9 / ◐2311 1.2	19 TH	0532 4.6 / 1125 1.7	1749 4.5 / 2350 1.7
5 TH	0547 5.0 / 1145 1.4	1831 4.6	20 F	0646 4.3 / 1244 2.0	1910 4.2
6 F	0034 1.4 / 0712 4.8	1333 1.6 / 2003 4.6	21 SA	0148 1.8 / 0823 4.3	1432 1.9 / 2047 4.3
7 SA	0230 1.4 / 0850 4.9	1514 1.5 / 2132 4.8	22 SU	0321 1.5 / 0944 4.6	1542 1.6 / 2158 4.7
8 SU	0401 1.0 / 1015 5.2	1632 1.2 / 2241 5.2	23 M	0423 1.2 / 1038 5.0	1635 1.3 / 2249 5.0
9 M	0516 0.7 / 1117 5.6	1733 1.0 / 2336 5.5	24 TU	0511 1.0 / 1120 5.3	1718 1.1 / 2330 5.3
10 TU	0612 0.4 / 1208 5.8	1821 0.8	25 W	0552 0.8 / 1158 5.5	1756 1.0
11 W	0021 5.7 / 0657 0.2	1258 5.9 / 1901 0.7	26 TH	0006 5.5 / 0628 0.7	●1233 5.6 / 1833 0.8
12 TH	0102 5.9 / 0737 0.2	1331 6.0 / 1939 0.6	27 F	0041 5.6 / 0705 0.6	1307 5.7 / 1910 0.7
13 F	0140 6.0 / 0813 0.2	1408 5.9 / 2014 0.6	28 SA	0115 5.7 / 0741 0.5	1342 5.8 / 1947 0.7
14 SA	0217 5.9 / 0845 0.3	1442 5.8 / 2046 0.7	29 SU	0149 5.8 / 0816 0.5	1416 5.8 / 2023 0.7
15 SU	0252 5.8 / 0914 0.6	1515 5.6 / 2115 0.8	30 M	0225 5.8 / 0847 0.6	1452 5.6 / 2057 0.7
			31 TU	0304 5.8 / 0916 0.8	1530 5.5 / 2131 0.8

APRIL

Day	Time m	Time m	Day	Time m	Time m
1 W	0348 5.6 / 0949 1.0	1613 5.2 / 2215 1.0	16 TH	0415 5.0 / 1004 1.4	1621 4.9 / 2221 1.3
2 TH	0439 5.3 / 1038 1.3	1708 4.9 / ◐2315 1.2	17 F	0503 4.7 / 1050 1.6	1710 4.6 / ◑2316 1.5
3 F	0546 5.0 / 1149 1.6	1822 4.7	18 SA	0605 4.4 / 1156 1.9	1819 4.4
4 SA	0047 1.3 / 0713 4.9	1331 1.7 / 1953 4.6	19 SU	0040 1.6 / 0726 4.4	1331 1.9 / 1948 4.4
5 SU	0230 1.1 / 0844 5.0	1500 1.5 / 2116 4.9	20 M	0225 1.5 / 0845 4.6	1450 1.7 / 2104 4.6
6 M	0353 0.8 / 1000 5.3	1613 1.2 / 2221 5.3	21 TU	0331 1.2 / 0947 4.9	1548 1.4 / 2201 5.0
7 TU	0459 0.6 / 1058 5.6	1710 1.0 / 2313 5.5	22 W	0424 1.0 / 1036 5.2	1636 1.2 / 2248 5.3
8 W	0550 0.4 / 1146 5.8	1756 0.9 / 2357 5.7	23 TH	0510 0.8 / 1119 5.5	1720 1.0 / 2329 5.5
9 TH	0631 0.4 / 1226 5.8	1835 0.7	24 F	0553 0.7 / 1159 5.6	1803 0.9
10 F	0036 5.8 / 0707 0.4	1304 5.8 / 1911 0.7	25 SA	0009 5.6 / 0633 0.7	●1238 5.7 / 1845 0.8
11 SA	0114 5.9 / 0740 0.4	1338 5.8 / 1947 0.6	26 SU	0049 5.8 / 0713 0.6	1316 5.8 / 1927 0.7
12 SU	0150 5.8 / 0810 0.5	1411 5.7 / 2020 0.6	27 M	0128 5.9 / 0752 0.6	1355 5.8 / 2010 0.6
13 M	0226 5.7 / 0839 0.7	1442 5.6 / 2050 0.8	28 TU	0210 5.8 / 0830 0.7	1435 5.7 / 2051 0.6
14 TU	0301 5.5 / 0904 0.9	1512 5.4 / 2115 1.0	29 W	0255 5.8 / 0908 0.8	1518 5.5 / 2135 0.7
15 W	0336 5.3 / 0931 1.1	1544 5.2 / 2142 1.1	30 TH	0345 5.6 / 0951 1.1	1606 5.3 / 2226 0.8

Chart Datum: 2·90 metres below Ordnance Datum (Newlyn)
HAT is 6·3 metres above Chart Datum

TIDES

TIDES

TIME ZONE (UT)
For Summer Time add ONE hour in **non-shaded areas**

ENGLAND – SHEERNESS

LAT 51°27'N   LONG 0°45'E

TIMES AND HEIGHTS OF HIGH AND LOW WATERS

Dates in amber are **SPRINGS**
Dates in yellow are NEAPS

2009

MAY

Time m	Time m
1 0442 5.4 / 1043 1.3 / F 1705 5.0 / 2331 0.9	**16** 0440 4.9 / 1026 1.5 / SA 1643 4.8 / 2255 1.3
2 0550 5.2 / 1152 1.3 / SA 1817 4.9	**17** 0532 4.7 / 1120 1.7 / SU 1739 4.7 / 2356 1.4
3 0053 1.0 / 0707 5.1 / SU 1315 1.5 / 1935 4.9	**18** 0634 4.6 / 1227 1.7 / M 1848 4.6 / ☽
4 0215 0.9 / 0825 5.2 / M 1432 1.4 / ◐ 2049 5.1	**19** 0111 1.4 / 0743 4.7 / TU 1343 1.7 / 2002 4.7
5 0326 0.7 / 0933 5.4 / TU 1539 1.3 / 2152 5.3	**20** 0226 1.2 / 0849 4.9 / W 1450 1.5 / 2106 4.9
6 0428 0.6 / 1030 5.5 / W 1636 1.1 / 2245 5.4	**21** 0328 1.1 / 0947 5.2 / TH 1548 1.3 / 2202 5.2
7 0518 0.6 / 1118 5.6 / TH 1724 1.0 / 2331 5.5	**22** 0423 0.9 / 1039 5.4 / F 1642 1.1 / 2253 5.4
8 0558 0.7 / 1159 5.6 / F 1806 0.9	**23** 0515 0.8 / 1126 5.6 / SA 1734 0.9 / 2341 5.6
9 0012 5.6 / 0632 0.7 / SA 1237 5.6 / 1844 0.8	**24** 0604 0.8 / 1212 5.7 / SU 1824 0.8
10 0052 5.7 / 0705 0.7 / SU 1312 5.6 / 1922 0.7	**25** 0027 5.8 / 0650 0.7 / M 1256 5.7 / 1913 0.6
11 0129 5.6 / 0738 0.8 / M 1344 5.6 / ○ 1958 0.8	**26** 0114 5.9 / 0735 0.7 / TU 1340 5.7 / ● 2003 0.5
12 0206 5.6 / 0809 0.9 / TU 1416 5.5 / 2030 0.8	**27** 0202 5.9 / 0820 0.8 / W 1425 5.7 / 2052 0.5
13 0242 5.4 / 0838 1.0 / W 1447 5.3 / 2058 1.0	**28** 0252 5.9 / 0905 0.9 / TH 1512 5.6 / 2143 0.5
14 0318 5.2 / 0908 1.2 / TH 1520 5.2 / 2128 1.1	**29** 0345 5.8 / 0951 1.0 / F 1603 5.4 / 2235 0.6
15 0357 5.1 / 0942 1.3 / F 1558 5.0 / 2206 1.2	**30** 0441 5.6 / 1042 1.2 / SA 1659 5.3 / 2333 0.6
	31 0541 5.4 / 1139 1.3 / SU 1801 5.2

JUNE

Time m	Time m
1 0037 0.7 / 0646 5.3 / M 1244 1.4 / 1907 5.1	**16** 0550 4.9 / 1139 1.5 / TU 1757 4.9 / ◑
2 0143 0.8 / 0753 5.2 / TU 1352 1.4 / ◑ 2014 5.2	**17** 0014 1.2 / 0648 4.8 / W 1239 1.6 / 1859 4.8
3 0246 0.8 / 0857 5.2 / W 1456 1.3 / 2118 5.2	**18** 0117 1.2 / 0754 4.9 / TH 1349 1.5 / 2011 4.9
4 0346 0.9 / 0957 5.3 / TH 1557 1.2 / 2216 5.3	**19** 0231 1.2 / 0901 5.0 / F 1502 1.4 / 2119 5.1
5 0438 0.9 / 1049 5.3 / F 1652 1.1 / 2307 5.3	**20** 0341 1.1 / 1002 5.3 / SA 1608 1.2 / 2221 5.3
6 0522 1.0 / 1134 5.4 / SA 1740 1.0 / 2353 5.4	**21** 0444 1.0 / 1059 5.4 / SU 1710 1.0 / 2319 5.5
7 0600 1.0 / 1215 5.4 / SU 1824 0.9	**22** 0541 0.9 / 1152 5.6 / M 1810 0.8
8 0036 5.4 / 0636 1.0 / M 1252 5.4 / 1905 0.8	**23** 0014 5.7 / 0634 0.8 / TU 1242 5.7 / 1906 0.6
9 0116 5.5 / 0711 1.0 / TU 1326 5.4 / ○ 1942 0.8	**24** 0107 5.9 / 0724 0.8 / W 1330 5.8 / 2000 0.4
10 0153 5.4 / 0745 1.0 / W 1359 5.4 / 2016 0.9	**25** 0158 6.0 / 0813 0.8 / TH 1418 5.8 / ● 2052 0.3
11 0228 5.4 / 0817 1.1 / TH 1431 5.4 / 2048 0.9	**26** 0248 6.0 / 0859 0.8 / F 1505 5.8 / 2141 0.2
12 0304 5.3 / 0851 1.1 / F 1505 5.3 / 2121 0.9	**27** 0338 5.9 / 0944 0.9 / SA 1552 5.7 / 2229 0.3
13 0340 5.2 / 0927 1.2 / SA 1541 5.2 / 2157 1.0	**28** 0428 5.8 / 1027 1.0 / SU 1641 5.6 / 2316 0.5
14 0419 5.1 / 1006 1.3 / SU 1620 5.1 / 2237 1.1	**29** 0519 5.6 / 1113 1.2 / M 1732 5.5
15 0502 5.0 / 1049 1.4 / M 1705 5.0 / 2322 1.1	**30** 0004 0.7 / 0613 5.3 / TU 1203 1.3 / 1829 5.3

JULY

Time m	Time m
1 0057 0.9 / 0712 5.1 / W 1303 1.4 / 1932 5.1	**16** 0601 5.0 / 1145 1.5 / TH 1810 4.9
2 0157 1.1 / 0815 5.0 / TH 1411 1.5 / 2040 5.0	**17** 0017 1.3 / 0704 4.9 / F 1252 1.6 / 1921 4.9
3 0258 1.2 / 0920 5.0 / F 1521 1.4 / 2148 5.0	**18** 0136 1.4 / 0819 4.9 / SA 1422 1.5 / ◑ 2043 5.0
4 0357 1.3 / 1020 5.1 / SA 1626 1.3 / 2249 5.1	**19** 0309 1.3 / 0932 5.1 / SU 1545 1.3 / 2159 5.2
5 0450 1.2 / 1113 5.2 / SU 1724 1.1 / 2340 5.2	**20** 0422 1.2 / 1039 5.3 / M 1656 1.0 / 2306 5.5
6 0536 1.2 / 1158 5.3 / M 1812 1.0	**21** 0526 1.0 / 1138 5.5 / TU 1803 0.7
7 0025 5.3 / 0615 1.2 / TU 1237 5.4 / 1853 0.9	**22** 0006 5.8 / 0623 0.9 / W 1231 5.7 / 1902 0.5
8 0104 5.4 / 0652 1.1 / W 1312 5.4 / 1930 0.8	**23** 0059 6.0 / 0715 0.8 / TH 1319 5.9 / 1954 0.2
9 0139 5.4 / 0726 1.0 / TH 1345 5.4 / 2004 0.8	**24** 0148 6.1 / 0802 0.7 / F 1404 6.0 / 2042 0.1
10 0213 5.5 / 0800 1.0 / F 1417 5.5 / ● 2037 0.8	**25** 0235 6.1 / 0846 0.7 / SA 1448 6.0 / 2127 0.1
11 0246 5.5 / 0835 1.0 / SA 1449 5.5 / ○ 2111 0.8	**26** 0320 6.0 / 0926 0.8 / SU 1531 5.9 / 2207 0.2
12 0319 5.4 / 0910 1.1 / SU 1522 5.4 / 2144 0.8	**27** 0404 5.8 / 1003 0.9 / M 1613 5.8 / 2245 0.5
13 0354 5.3 / 0945 1.2 / M 1555 5.3 / 2216 0.9	**28** 0447 5.6 / 1039 1.1 / TU 1657 5.6 / 2321 0.8
14 0431 5.2 / 1019 1.3 / TU 1632 5.2 / 2248 1.0	**29** 0533 5.3 / 1119 1.3 / W 1747 5.3
15 0512 5.1 / 1056 1.4 / W 1715 5.1 / 2325 1.1	**30** 0002 1.1 / 0624 5.0 / TH 1210 1.5 / 1846 5.0
	31 0059 1.4 / 0725 4.8 / F 1324 1.6 / 2001 4.8

AUGUST

Time m	Time m
1 0212 1.6 / 0838 4.7 / SA 1450 1.6 / 2122 4.8	**16** 0059 1.6 / 0744 4.7 / SU 1359 1.6 / 2020 4.9
2 0324 1.6 / 0952 4.8 / SU 1608 1.4 / ◑ 2232 5.0	**17** 0250 1.5 / 0910 4.9 / M 1532 1.3 / ◑ 2147 5.2
3 0426 1.5 / 1053 5.0 / M 1712 1.2 / 2326 5.2	**18** 0409 1.3 / 1024 5.3 / TU 1650 0.9 / 2258 5.5
4 0517 1.3 / 1140 5.2 / TU 1800 1.0	**19** 0516 1.1 / 1124 5.6 / W 1757 0.6 / 2356 5.9
5 0009 5.4 / 0558 1.2 / W 1219 5.4 / 1838 0.9	**20** 0612 0.9 / 1215 5.8 / TH 1852 0.3
6 0046 5.5 / 0634 1.1 / TH 1253 5.5 / 1913 0.8	**21** 0046 6.1 / 0700 0.8 / F 1301 6.0 / 1939 0.2
7 0119 5.5 / 0708 1.0 / F 1325 5.6 / 1945 0.8	**22** 0131 6.1 / 0744 0.7 / SA 1343 6.1 / 2022 0.1
8 0150 5.6 / 0742 0.9 / SA 1356 5.6 / 2018 0.7	**23** 0213 6.1 / 0823 0.7 / SU 1423 6.1 / 2101 0.2
9 0222 5.6 / 0816 0.9 / SU 1426 5.6 / ○ 2051 0.7	**24** 0254 6.0 / 0900 0.8 / M 1503 6.0 / 2136 0.4
10 0253 5.6 / 0850 1.0 / M 1457 5.6 / 2122 0.8	**25** 0332 5.8 / 0934 0.9 / TU 1541 5.8 / ● 2206 0.7
11 0326 5.5 / 0921 1.1 / TU 1528 5.5 / 2149 0.9	**26** 0410 5.5 / 1005 1.1 / W 1621 5.6 / 2235 1.0
12 0400 5.4 / 0949 1.2 / W 1603 5.5 / 2212 1.0	**27** 0448 5.2 / 1037 1.3 / TH 1705 5.2 / 2309 1.3
13 0437 5.2 / 1020 1.3 / TH 1644 5.3 / 2243 1.2	**28** 0532 4.9 / 1121 1.6 / F 1801 4.8 / 2359 1.6
14 0523 5.0 / 1105 1.4 / F 1736 5.1 / 2334 1.4	**29** 0630 4.6 / 1230 1.8 / SA 1919 4.5
15 0623 4.8 / 1213 1.6 / SA 1849 4.9	**30** 0123 1.9 / 0750 4.5 / SU 1421 1.8 / 2052 4.6
	31 0253 1.8 / 0918 4.6 / M 1546 1.5 / 2208 4.9

Chart Datum: 2·90 metres below Ordnance Datum (Newlyn)
HAT is 6·3 metres above Chart Datum

TIME ZONE (UT)
For Summer Time add ONE hour in **non-shaded areas**

ENGLAND – SHEERNESS

LAT 51°27′N   LONG 0°45′E

TIMES AND HEIGHTS OF HIGH AND LOW WATERS

Dates in amber are **SPRINGS**
Dates in yellow are **NEAPS**

2009

SEPTEMBER

Time	m		Time	m
1 0401	1.6	**16** 0356	1.4
1024	4.9	1008	5.3
TU 1649	1.2	W 1642	0.8
2301	5.2	2246	5.6
2 0454	1.4	**17** 0501	1.1
1112	5.2	1106	5.6
W 1735	1.0	TH 1743	0.5
2343	5.4	2339	5.9
3 0536	1.2	**18** 0554	0.9
1151	5.4	1154	5.9
TH 1813	0.9	F 1832	0.3
		●	
4 0018	5.5	**19** 0025	6.1
0611	1.1	0638	0.8
F 1226	5.4	SA 1237	6.0
○ 1845	0.8	1914	0.3
5 0051	5.6	**20** 0107	6.1
0644	1.0	0718	0.7
SA 1257	5.7	SU 1317	6.1
1918	0.7	1953	0.3
6 0122	5.7	**21** 0146	6.1
0718	0.9	0756	0.7
SU 1328	5.7	M 1356	6.1
1951	0.7	2028	0.4
7 0153	5.7	**22** 0223	5.9
0753	0.9	0832	0.8
M 1359	5.8	TU 1434	6.0
2024	0.7	2059	0.6
8 0224	5.7	**23** 0258	5.7
0827	0.9	0904	0.9
TU 1430	5.7	W 1512	5.8
2055	0.8	2127	0.9
9 0257	5.6	**24** 0332	5.5
0857	1.0	0933	1.1
W 1503	5.7	TH 1550	5.5
2120	0.9	2153	1.2
10 0331	5.5	**25** 0407	5.2
0925	1.1	1001	1.3
TH 1540	5.6	F 1631	5.1
2142	1.1	2224	1.5
11 0409	5.3	**26** 0445	4.9
0957	1.2	1039	1.5
F 1623	5.4	SA 1723	4.8
2217	1.3	◑ 2311	1.8
12 0454	5.1	**27** 0537	4.6
0723	4.7	1139	1.8
SA 1719	5.1	SU 1835	4.5
◑ 2315	1.5		
13 0556	4.8	**28** 0025	2.1
1201	1.5	0655	4.4
SU 1835	4.9	M 1339	1.8
		2007	4.4
14 0050	1.8	**29** 0212	2.0
0723	4.7	0829	4.5
M 1354	1.5	TU 1509	1.6
2010	4.9	2127	4.7
15 0238	1.7	**30** 0324	1.8
0854	4.9	0941	4.8
TU 1526	1.2	W 1609	1.3
2138	5.2	2223	5.1

OCTOBER

Time	m		Time	m
1 0419	1.5	**16** 0435	1.2
1033	5.1	1041	5.6
TH 1657	1.1	F 1719	0.6
2306	5.4	2316	5.8
2 0502	1.3	**17** 0526	1.0
1114	5.4	1128	5.8
F 1736	0.9	SA 1805	0.5
2342	5.6		
3 0540	1.1	**18** 0000	5.9
1150	5.6	0609	0.9
SA 1811	0.8	SU 1211	5.9
		● 1844	0.2
4 0016	5.7	**19** 0040	5.9
0615	1.0	0649	0.8
SU 1224	5.7	M 1251	6.0
○ 1845	0.8	1919	0.6
5 0050	5.8	**20** 0118	5.9
0651	0.9	0728	0.7
M 1258	5.8	TU 1331	6.0
1919	0.7	1952	0.7
6 0123	5.8	**21** 0153	5.8
0727	0.9	0805	0.8
TU 1331	5.8	W 1409	5.9
1954	0.8	2023	0.8
7 0156	5.8	**22** 0227	5.7
0804	0.9	0838	0.9
W 1406	5.8	TH 1447	5.7
2026	0.8	2051	1.1
8 0231	5.7	**23** 0300	5.5
0838	0.9	0906	1.1
TH 1444	5.8	F 1525	5.4
2056	1.0	2118	1.3
9 0308	5.5	**24** 0332	5.2
0913	1.0	0933	1.3
F 1525	5.6	SA 1606	5.1
2127	1.2	2149	1.5
10 0349	5.3	**25** 0409	5.0
0953	1.1	1008	1.4
SA 1614	5.4	SU 1653	4.8
2211	1.4	2232	1.8
11 0438	5.1	**26** 0456	4.7
1047	1.3	1100	1.6
SU 1714	5.2	M 1753	4.6
◑ 2314	1.6	2334	2.0
12 0544	4.8	**27** 0602	4.5
1208	1.4	1220	1.7
M 1833	5.0	TU 1908	4.5
13 0046	1.8	**28** 0102	2.1
0710	4.8	0726	4.5
TU 1350	1.3	W 1408	1.6
2002	5.0	2024	4.6
14 0220	1.7	**29** 0229	1.9
0835	5.0	0842	4.7
W 1513	1.0	TH 1514	1.4
2122	5.3	2127	4.9
15 0333	1.4	**30** 0329	1.6
0945	5.3	0941	5.0
TH 1623	0.7	F 1606	1.2
2225	5.6	2217	5.2
		31 0418	1.4
		1029	5.3
		SA 1651	1.0
		2300	5.5

NOVEMBER

Time	m		Time	m
1 0501	1.2	**16** 0541	1.0
1111	5.5	1148	5.7
SU 1731	0.9	M 1811	0.8
2340	5.6	●	
2 0543	1.0	**17** 0015	5.7
1150	5.6	0623	0.9
M 1810	0.8	TU 1231	5.7
○		1846	0.8
3 0018	5.7	**18** 0053	5.7
0623	0.9	0704	0.8
TU 1229	5.8	W 1312	5.7
1848	0.8	1919	0.9
4 0056	5.8	**19** 0129	5.6
0704	0.9	0743	0.8
W 1309	5.9	TH 1352	5.7
1927	0.8	1952	1.0
5 0133	5.8	**20** 0203	5.5
0746	0.8	0818	0.9
TH 1349	5.9	F 1430	5.5
2004	0.9	2022	1.1
6 0212	5.7	**21** 0235	5.4
0828	0.8	0848	1.0
F 1432	5.8	SA 1507	5.4
2042	1.0	2052	1.3
7 0253	5.6	**22** 0308	5.3
0912	0.8	0916	1.2
SA 1519	5.7	SU 1546	5.2
2123	1.1	2124	1.4
8 0339	5.4	**23** 0344	5.1
1000	0.9	0950	1.2
SU 1612	5.5	M 1627	5.0
2212	1.3	2204	1.6
9 0432	5.2	**24** 0427	4.9
1058	1.1	1034	1.4
M 1714	5.3	TU 1715	4.8
◑ 2313	1.5	◑ 2254	1.7
10 0537	5.0	**25** 0518	4.8
1212	1.1	1129	1.5
TU 1826	5.2	W 1811	4.7
		2355	1.8
11 0029	1.6	**26** 0621	4.6
0652	5.0	1238	1.5
W 1333	1.1	TH 1916	4.6
1942	5.2		
12 0149	1.6	**27** 0107	1.9
0807	5.1	0733	4.7
TH 1446	0.9	F 1357	1.5
2054	5.3	2022	4.8
13 0258	1.4	**28** 0222	1.7
0914	5.3	0840	4.8
F 1551	0.8	SA 1504	1.3
2156	5.5	2123	5.0
14 0400	1.3	**29** 0325	1.5
1012	5.5	0939	5.1
SA 1647	0.8	SU 1601	1.2
2249	5.6	2216	5.3
15 0454	1.1	**30** 0420	1.3
1103	5.6	1032	5.3
SU 1733	0.8	M 1651	1.1
2334	5.6	2305	5.5

DECEMBER

Time	m		Time	m
1 0511	1.1	**16** 0607	1.0
1120	5.5	1219	5.5
TU 1739	0.9	W 1820	1.1
2350	5.6	●	
2 0600	0.9	**17** 0036	5.4
1207	5.7	0650	0.9
W 1824	0.9	TH 1301	5.5
○		1855	1.0
3 0034	5.7	**18** 0113	5.5
0648	0.8	0729	0.8
TH 1253	5.8	F 1340	5.5
1908	0.8	1929	1.1
4 0117	5.7	**19** 0147	5.4
0736	0.7	0805	0.9
F 1339	5.9	SA 1416	5.5
1952	0.8	2001	1.1
5 0201	5.7	**20** 0220	5.4
0826	0.6	0836	0.9
SA 1427	5.9	SU 1451	5.4
2036	0.9	2033	1.1
6 0246	5.7	**21** 0252	5.4
0915	0.6	0905	1.0
SU 1517	5.8	M 1526	5.3
2121	1.0	2106	1.2
7 0334	5.6	**22** 0326	5.3
1006	0.6	0937	1.0
M 1609	5.7	TU 1602	5.2
2209	1.1	2142	1.3
8 0425	5.4	**23** 0402	5.2
1059	0.7	1013	1.1
TU 1706	5.5	W 1640	5.0
2301	1.3	2222	1.4
9 0521	5.3	**24** 0441	5.0
1156	0.9	1053	1.2
W 1807	5.3	TH 1724	4.9
◑		◑ 2306	1.5
10 0000	1.4	**25** 0527	4.8
0624	5.2	1139	1.3
TH 1300	0.9	F 1815	4.8
1912	5.2	2359	1.7
11 0106	1.5	**26** 0624	4.8
0732	5.2	1236	1.4
F 1405	1.0	SA 1919	4.7
2018	5.2		
12 0215	1.5	**27** 0107	1.7
0839	5.2	0735	4.8
SA 1509	1.0	SU 1352	1.4
2122	5.2	2028	4.8
13 0321	1.4	**28** 0228	1.6
0943	5.2	0849	4.9
SU 1608	1.1	M 1512	1.3
2220	5.2	2134	5.0
14 0423	1.3	**29** 0341	1.4
1041	5.3	0956	5.1
M 1659	1.1	TU 1617	1.2
2311	5.3	2234	5.3
15 0519	1.1	**30** 0444	1.1
1133	5.4	1056	5.4
TU 1742	1.1	W 1714	1.0
2356	5.4	2329	5.5
		31 0542	0.9
		1151	5.6
		TH 1807	0.9
		○	

Chart Datum: 2·90 metres below Ordnance Datum (Newlyn)
HAT is 6·3 metres above Chart Datum

TIDES

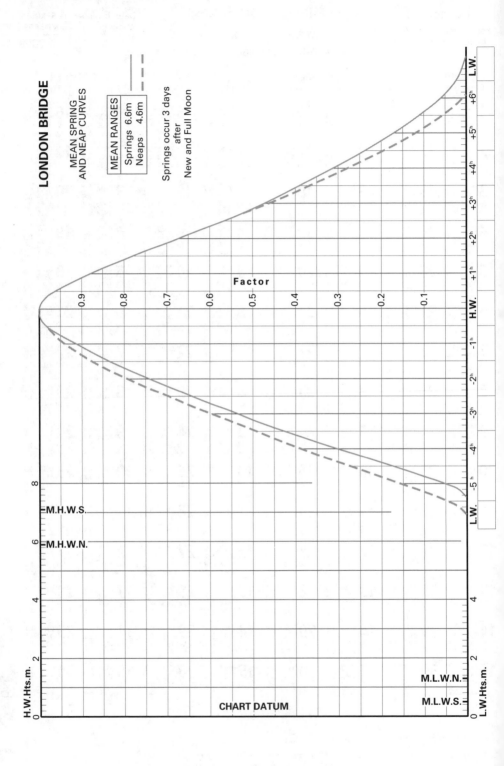

LONDON BRIDGE

MEAN SPRING
AND NEAP CURVES

MEAN RANGES	
Springs	6.6m
Neaps	4.6m

Springs occur 3 days
after
New and Full Moon

TIME ZONE (UT)	ENGLAND – LONDON BRIDGE	Dates in amber are SPRINGS
For Summer Time add ONE hour in **non-shaded areas**	**LAT 51°30′N LONG 0°05′W**	Dates in yellow are NEAPS
	TIMES AND HEIGHTS OF HIGH AND LOW WATERS	**2009**

JANUARY

Time m · Time m

Day	DoW	T1	h1	T2	h2	T3	h3	T4	h4
1	TH	0411	6.5	1040	1.1	1649	6.5	2246	1.1
16	F	0509	6.9	1156	0.3	1744	7.0	2352	0.9
2	F	0447	6.5	1112	1.0	1728	6.5	2323	1.1
17	SA	0548	6.7	1228	0.6	1826	6.6		
3	SA	0527	6.5	1148	0.9	1811	6.5		
18	SU	0023	1.1	0628	6.5	1301	0.9	1908	6.3
4	SU	0003	1.1	0611	6.4	1230	1.0	1858	6.3
19	M	0059	1.3	0715	6.1	1342	1.2	1956	5.9
5	M	0049	1.3	0704	6.3	1318	1.1	1953	6.1
20	TU	0146	1.6	0817	5.8	1434	1.5	2058	5.6
6	TU	0144	1.5	0805	6.1	1419	1.3	2057	5.9
21	W	0247	1.8	0938	5.6	1537	1.7	2210	5.6
7	W	0259	1.6	0917	6.0	1542	1.5	2210	5.9
22	TH	0357	1.8	1052	5.7	1647	1.6	2315	5.8
8	TH	0429	1.6	1032	6.1	1713	1.4	2321	6.1
23	F	0514	1.6	1153	6.0	1754	1.5		
9	F	0551	1.3	1144	6.4	1828	1.2		
24	SA	0012	6.1	0639	1.3	1246	6.3	1852	1.3
10	SA	0023	6.4	0704	1.0	1248	6.7	1930	1.0
25	SU	0101	6.3	0734	1.1	1331	6.5	1942	1.0
11	SU	0119	6.7	0807	0.6	1345	7.0	2026	0.9
26	M	0143	6.5	0821	0.9	1411	6.6	2026	1.1
12	M	0211	6.8			1439	7.2	2116	0.8
27	TU	0221	6.5	0903	0.9	1448	6.6	2105	1.2
13	TU	0259	6.9	0954	0.2	1529	7.3	2202	0.7
28	W	0255	6.5	0940	1.0	1521	6.6	2137	1.2
14	W	0345	7.0	1040	0.1	1617	7.3	2243	0.8
29	TH	0326	6.5	1011	1.0	1555	6.6	2206	1.2
15	TH	0428	7.0	1121	0.2	1702	7.2	2319	0.8
30	F	0356	6.6	1034	1.0	1629	6.7	2235	1.1
31	SA	0428	6.7	1057	0.9	1705	6.7	2306	0.9

FEBRUARY

Time m · Time m

Day	DoW	T1	h1	T2	h2	T3	h3	T4	h4
1	SU	0505	6.7	1125	0.8	1744	6.6	2339	0.9
16	M	0547	6.7	1214	0.9	1814	6.4	◑	
2	M	0547	6.5	1159	0.9	1828	6.4	◑	
17	TU	0012	1.1	0627	6.3	1246	1.2	1852	6.0
3	TU	0017	1.1	0635	6.5	1240	1.1	1917	6.1
18	W	0050	1.4	0716	5.8	1336	1.6	1940	5.6
4	W	0105	1.3	0732	6.1	1334	1.4	2017	5.7
19	TH	0152	1.7	0828	5.3	1446	1.9	2054	5.3
5	TH	0210	1.7	0844	5.8	1453	1.8	2134	5.6
20	F	0312	1.9	1021	5.3	1602	1.9	2240	5.4
6	F	0358	1.8	1009	5.8	1655	1.8	2300	5.7
21	SA	0429	1.7	1129	5.7	1717	1.6	2345	5.8
7	SA	0548	1.5	1134	6.1	1820	1.4		
22	SU	0610	1.4	1222	6.2	1826	1.3		
8	SU	0011	6.1	0703	1.0	1242	6.5	1922	1.1
23	M	0036	6.2	0712	1.0	1308	6.5	1920	1.1
9	M	0109	6.5	0801	0.5	1338	7.0	2016	0.8
24	TU	0121	6.5	0759	0.4	1348	6.6	2006	1.1
10	TU	0159	6.8	0853	0.1	1427	7.2	2104	0.6
25	W	0159	6.6	0843	0.8	1424	6.7	2048	1.1
11	W	0244	7.0	0940	-0.1	1513	7.3	2148	0.5
26	TH	0234	6.5	0922	0.8	1458	6.7	2124	1.1
12	TH	0325	7.1	1021	-0.1	1555	7.3	2226	0.6
27	F	0305	6.6	0954	0.9	1532	6.7	2154	1.0
13	F	0403	7.1	1057	0.1	1634	7.2	2259	0.6
28	SA	0335	6.7	1019	0.9	1605	6.7	2222	1.0
14	SA	0438	7.1	1126	0.3	1709	7.0	2324	0.8
15	SU	0512	6.9	1150	0.6	1741	6.7	2346	0.9

MARCH

Time m · Time m

Day	DoW	T1	h1	T2	h2	T3	h3	T4	h4
1	SU	0408	6.8	1038	0.8	1640	6.7	2249	0.8
16	M	0442	7.0	1113	0.7	1701	6.7	2312	0.8
2	M	0445	6.9	1102	0.8	1718	6.6	2319	0.8
17	TU	0516	6.7	1132	0.9	1734	6.5	2334	0.9
3	TU	0527	6.8	1134	0.8	1800	6.4	2354	1.0
18	W	0556	6.3	1159	1.2	1812	6.1		
4	W	0615	6.5	1214	1.1	1848	6.0	◑	
19	TH	0008	1.2	0643	5.8	1244	1.6	1859	5.7
5	TH	0039	1.3	0712	6.0	1308	1.6	1947	5.6
20	F	0104	1.6	0744	5.3	1359	2.0	2000	5.3
6	F	0145	1.7	0826	5.6	1429	2.0	2110	5.4
21	SA	0235	1.9	0934	5.2	1542	2.0	2154	5.3
7	SA	0356	1.9	1005	5.6	1653	1.9	2247	5.6
22	SU	0354	1.7	1056	5.6	1637	1.8	2310	5.7
8	SU	0549	1.3	1130	6.1	1810	1.4	2357	6.1
23	M	0514	1.4	1150	6.1	1747	1.4		
9	M	0652	0.7	1231	6.6	1907	1.0		
24	TU	0003	6.1	0633	1.1	1236	6.4	1845	1.2
10	TU	0052	6.6	0744	0.2	1323	7.1	1956	0.6
25	W	0049	6.4	0725	0.9	1316	6.6	1935	1.0
11	W	0139	6.9	0832	0.0	1409	7.3	2043	0.5
26	TH	0128	6.5	0810	0.8	1354	6.7	2019	1.0
12	TH	0221	7.1	0915	-0.1	1450	7.3	2125	0.4
27	F	0204	6.6	0851	0.8	1430	6.8	2059	0.9
13	F	0300	7.2	0953	0.0	1528	7.2	2202	0.5
28	SA	0238	6.7	0927	0.8	1505	6.8	2136	0.9
14	SA	0336	7.2	1026	0.2	1602	7.1	2233	0.6
29	SU	0313	6.8	0956	0.8	1541	6.8	2208	0.8
15	SU	0409	7.1	1053	0.4	1632	6.9	2256	0.7
30	M	0350	7.0	1020	0.8	1618	6.8	2237	0.7
31	TU	0431	7.0	1046	0.8	1658	6.6	2307	0.8

APRIL

Time m · Time m

Day	DoW	T1	h1	T2	h2	T3	h3	T4	h4
1	W	0515	6.8	1120	0.9	1740	6.3	2344	1.0
16	TH	0533	6.2	1129	1.2	1743	6.2	2343	1.1
2	TH	0606	6.4	1203	1.3	1829	5.9	◑	
17	F	0619	5.9	1211	1.5	1829	5.8	◑	
3	F	0033	1.3	0707	5.9	1300	1.7	1933	5.5
18	SA	0034	1.4	0715	5.5	1315	1.8	1926	5.5
4	SA	0153	1.7	0829	5.6	1431	2.0	2106	5.4
19	SU	0157	1.6	0828	5.3	1438	1.9	2046	5.4
5	SU	0407	1.6	1003	5.8	1636	1.8	2230	5.8
20	M	0316	1.6	1001	5.5	1552	1.8	2217	5.6
6	M	0529	1.0	1114	6.3	1745	1.3	2333	6.3
21	TU	0426	1.4	1104	5.9	1658	1.5	2318	5.9
7	TU	0627	0.5	1210	6.8	1840	0.9		
22	W	0536	1.1	1154	6.3	1759	1.2		
8	W	0026	6.7	0716	0.1	1259	7.1	1929	0.6
23	TH	0006	6.3	0637	0.9	1238	6.6	1854	1.0
9	TH	0113	7.0	0801	0.0	1343	7.2	2015	0.4
24	F	0050	6.5	0729	0.8	1320	6.8	1945	0.9
10	F	0155	7.1	0843	0.0	1423	7.2	2058	0.4
25	SA	0131	6.7	0815	0.7	1400	6.8	2031	0.8
11	SA	0235	7.1	0921	0.2	1459	7.0	2136	0.5
26	SU	0212	6.9	0856	0.7	1440	6.9	2114	0.7
12	SU	0311	7.0	0954	0.4	1530	6.9	2208	0.6
27	M	0253	7.0	0932	0.7	1520	6.8	2154	0.6
13	M	0345	6.9	1021	0.7	1559	6.8	2230	0.8
28	TU	0337	7.0	1006	0.7	1602	6.8	2232	0.6
14	TU	0418	6.8	1041	0.8	1629	6.7	2246	0.8
29	W	0423	7.0	1039	0.8	1645	6.6	2310	0.7
15	W	0454	6.5	1100	1.0	1703	6.5	2308	0.9
30	TH	0512	6.8	1117	1.0	1731	6.3	2354	0.9

Chart Datum: 3·20 metres below Ordnance Datum (Newlyn)
HAT is 7·6 metres above Chart Datum

TIDES

TIME ZONE (UT)	ENGLAND – LONDON BRIDGE	Dates in amber are SPRINGS
For Summer Time add ONE hour in **non-shaded areas**	LAT 51°30'N LONG 0°05'W	Dates in yellow are NEAPS
	TIMES AND HEIGHTS OF HIGH AND LOW WATERS	2009

MAY

Time	m	Time	m
1 0607	6.4	**16** 0600	6.0
1204	1.3	1151	1.3
F 1825	6.0	SA 1805	6.0
2 0051	1.1	**17** 0017	1.2
0712	6.1	0649	5.8
SA 1305	1.6	SU 1244	1.5
1934	5.8	1856	5.8
3 0211	1.2	**18** 0119	1.3
0829	6.0	0747	5.7
SU 1429	1.8	M 1350	1.7
2054	5.8	◑ 1958	5.6
4 0342	1.1	**19** 0230	1.4
0943	6.2	0854	5.7
M 1600	1.6	TU 1502	1.7
◑ 2203	6.1	2111	5.7
5 0454	0.8	**20** 0338	1.3
1046	6.5	1004	5.9
TU 1710	1.2	W 1610	1.5
2303	6.4	2220	5.9
6 0551	0.5	**21** 0445	1.1
1141	6.8	1105	6.2
W 1807	0.9	TH 1714	1.3
2356	6.7	2319	6.2
7 0641	0.3	**22** 0550	1.0
1230	7.0	1158	6.5
TH 1859	0.7	F 1815	1.0
8 0045	6.9	**23** 0012	6.5
0726	0.3	0649	0.8
F 1315	7.0	SA 1247	6.7
1946	0.5	1912	0.8
9 0130	6.9	**24** 0102	6.8
0809	0.4	0741	0.7
SA 1356	6.9	SU 1333	6.9
2030	0.5	2006	0.7
10 0212	6.9	**25** 0150	7.0
0848	0.5	0829	0.7
SU 1432	6.8	M 1419	6.9
2110	0.6	2057	0.5
11 0251	6.7	**26** 0239	7.1
0923	0.7	0914	0.7
M 1504	6.6	TU 1504	6.9
○ 2144	0.7	● 2145	0.4
12 0326	6.6	**27** 0328	7.1
0953	0.9	0957	0.7
TU 1533	6.6	W 1550	6.8
2211	0.9	2232	0.4
13 0401	6.5	**28** 0418	7.1
1015	1.0	1039	0.8
W 1605	6.5	TH 1638	6.7
2231	0.9	2319	0.4
14 0437	6.4	**29** 0511	6.9
1038	1.1	1122	1.0
TH 1640	6.4	F 1727	6.5
2255	0.9		
15 0516	6.2	**30** 0006	0.5
1110	1.2	0605	6.7
F 1720	6.2	SA 1209	1.1
2330	1.0	1821	6.3
		31 0058	0.7
		0705	6.5
		SU 1302	1.3
		1922	6.2

JUNE

Time	m	Time	m
1 0156	0.8	**16** 0044	1.0
0809	6.4	0712	6.0
M 1403	1.4	TU 1309	1.4
2027	6.2	◐ 1919	6.0
2 0300	0.9	**17** 0139	1.1
0912	6.4	0808	5.9
TU 1511	1.4	W 1410	1.5
◐ 2130	6.2	2020	5.9
3 0406	0.8	**18** 0244	1.2
1012	6.4	0913	5.9
W 1622	1.3	TH 1521	1.5
2229	6.3	2128	5.9
4 0507	0.8	**19** 0357	1.2
1108	6.5	1020	6.1
TH 1728	1.2	F 1633	1.4
2326	6.5	2236	6.1
5 0601	0.7	**20** 0510	1.1
1200	6.6	1123	6.3
F 1826	1.0	SA 1741	1.2
		2340	6.4
6 0019	6.6	**21** 0617	0.9
0650	0.7	1220	6.6
SA 1248	6.7	SU 1847	0.9
1917	0.8		
7 0108	6.6	**22** 0038	6.7
0735	0.7	0716	0.8
SU 1331	6.7	M 1313	6.8
2004	0.8	1949	0.6
8 0154	6.6	**23** 0134	6.9
0818	0.8	0811	0.7
M 1410	6.6	TU 1403	6.9
2048	0.8	2047	0.4
9 0236	6.6	**24** 0228	7.1
0857	0.9	0903	0.7
TU 1445	6.5	W 1452	6.9
2127	0.8	○ 2141	0.2
10 0314	6.5	**25** 0320	7.2
0931	1.0	0952	0.7
W 1517	6.4	TH 1541	7.0
2159	0.9	● 2231	0.1
11 0348	6.4	**26** 0411	7.2
0958	1.1	1037	0.7
TH 1549	6.4	F 1628	6.9
2225	1.0	2317	0.1
12 0423	6.3	**27** 0501	7.2
1024	1.1	1119	0.7
F 1623	6.4	SA 1715	6.9
2250	1.0		
13 0459	6.3	**28** 0000	0.1
1055	1.1	0551	7.0
SA 1701	6.4	SU 1201	0.8
2321	0.9	1802	6.7
14 0539	6.3	**29** 0042	0.3
1133	1.2	0642	6.8
SU 1741	6.4	M 1242	1.0
2359	0.9	1853	6.6
15 0623	6.3	**30** 0124	0.5
1217	1.2	0736	6.5
M 1827	6.1	TU 1328	1.2
		1948	6.3

JULY

Time	m	Time	m
1 0210	0.8	**16** 0053	1.0
0834	6.3	0728	6.1
W 1419	1.4	TH 1323	1.4
2050	6.1	1938	6.1
2 0305	1.0	**17** 0148	1.2
0934	6.1	0828	5.9
TH 1520	1.5	F 1432	1.6
2154	6.1	2045	5.9
3 0408	1.2	**18** 0305	1.4
1033	6.1	0939	5.8
F 1631	1.5	SA 1556	1.6
2257	6.1	◑ 2159	6.0
4 0515	1.2	**19** 0436	1.4
1129	6.2	1053	6.0
SA 1749	1.3	SU 1716	1.4
◑ 2356	6.3	2315	6.2
5 0614	1.1	**20** 0555	1.2
1222	6.3	1159	6.3
SU 1852	1.1	M 1834	1.0
6 0050	6.4	**21** 0024	6.5
0705	1.0	0702	0.9
M 1310	6.5	TU 1257	6.6
1944	0.9	1942	0.6
7 0139	6.5	**22** 0124	6.9
0753	0.9	0801	0.7
TU 1353	6.5	W 1350	6.9
2031	0.8	2041	0.3
8 0222	6.6	**23** 0218	7.2
0837	1.0	0855	0.6
W 1431	6.5	TH 1439	7.1
2114	0.8	2133	0.0
9 0300	6.5	**24** 0308	7.3
0916	1.1	0943	0.5
TH 1505	6.5	F 1526	7.1
2151	0.9	2221	-0.1
10 0333	6.4	**25** 0356	7.4
0948	1.2	1027	0.5
F 1536	6.4	SA 1610	7.2
2221	1.0	2303	-0.2
11 0406	6.4	**26** 0442	7.3
1014	1.2	1106	0.5
SA 1608	6.4	SU 1652	7.1
○ 2244	1.0	● 2340	0.0
12 0439	6.5	**27** 0525	7.2
1042	1.1	1141	0.7
SU 1640	6.5	M 1733	7.0
2307	0.9		
13 0515	6.5	**28** 0013	0.2
1114	1.1	0608	6.9
M 1716	6.5	TU 1214	0.8
2336	0.8	1813	6.8
14 0554	6.4	**29** 0045	0.6
1151	1.1	0651	6.5
TU 1756	6.4	W 1249	1.1
		1858	6.4
15 0011	0.9	**30** 0122	0.9
0637	6.3	0740	6.1
W 1233	1.2	TH 1332	1.4
1842	6.3	1955	6.0
		31 0211	1.3
		0842	5.7
		F 1428	1.6
		2113	5.7

AUGUST

Time	m	Time	m
1 0313	1.6	**16** 0216	1.7
0954	5.6	0900	5.6
SA 1537	1.8	SU 1528	1.8
2231	5.7	2132	5.7
2 0425	1.6	**17** 0330	1.8
1059	5.8	1028	5.7
SU 1700	1.6	M 1707	1.5
◐ 2336	6.0	◐ 2302	6.0
3 0540	1.4	**18** 0546	1.4
1157	6.1	1144	6.1
M 1833	1.3	TU 1831	1.0
4 0031	6.3	**19** 0015	6.5
0641	1.2	0653	1.2
TU 1249	6.4	W 1244	6.6
1927	0.9	1934	0.5
5 0120	6.6	**20** 0113	7.0
0733	1.0	0749	0.7
W 1333	6.6	TH 1334	7.0
2013	0.8	2028	0.1
6 0202	6.7	**21** 0204	7.3
0819	1.0	0840	0.5
TH 1413	6.6	F 1421	7.3
2056	0.7	2116	-0.2
7 0239	6.7	**22** 0250	7.4
0900	1.0	0926	0.4
F 1448	6.6	SA 1504	7.3
2135	0.8	2200	-0.2
8 0312	6.6	**23** 0334	7.5
0935	1.1	1008	0.4
SA 1519	6.5	SU 1544	7.3
2208	0.9	2239	-0.1
9 0343	6.5	**24** 0414	7.3
1002	1.2	1047	0.6
SU 1547	6.5	M 1622	7.3
○ 2231	1.0	2311	0.1
10 0414	6.6	**25** 0452	7.1
1026	1.1	1115	0.6
M 1616	6.6	TU 1658	7.1
2247	1.0	● 2338	0.4
11 0447	6.6	**26** 0526	6.8
1054	1.0	1142	0.8
TU 1649	6.7	W 1734	6.9
2308	0.9		
12 0523	6.5	**27** 0003	0.7
1124	1.0	0600	6.5
W 1727	6.7	TH 1209	1.1
2338	0.8	1813	6.4
13 0603	6.4	**28** 0034	1.0
1159	1.1	0636	6.0
TH 1812	6.5	F 1246	1.4
		1901	5.9
14 0015	1.0	**29** 0119	1.5
0650	6.1	0724	5.6
F 1244	1.3	SA 1344	1.7
1905	6.2	2017	5.4
15 0104	1.3	**30** 0227	1.9
0747	5.7	0900	5.3
SA 1346	1.7	SU 1459	1.9
2011	5.9	2205	5.4
		31 0345	1.9
		1029	5.5
		M 1618	1.8
		2313	5.8

Chart Datum: 3·20 metres below Ordnance Datum (Newlyn)
HAT is 7·6 metres above Chart Datum

TIME ZONE (UT)	ENGLAND – LONDON BRIDGE	Dates in amber are SPRINGS
For Summer Time add ONE hour in **non-shaded areas**	LAT 51°30'N LONG 0°05'W	Dates in yellow are NEAPS
	TIMES AND HEIGHTS OF HIGH AND LOW WATERS	**2009**

SEPTEMBER

Time	m		Time	m
1 TU 0507 1131 1809	1.7 6.0 1.3		**16** W 0535 1148 1819	1.5 6.1 0.8
2 W 0007 0616 1222 1901	6.3 1.3 6.4 0.9		**17** TH 0003 0636 1224 1915	6.6 1.0 6.7 0.3
3 TH 0054 0709 1307 1946	6.6 1.0 6.6 0.7		**18** F 0056 0728 1312 ● 2005	7.1 0.6 7.1 0.0
4 F 0135 0754 1346 ○ 2029	6.8 0.9 6.7 0.7		**19** SA 0143 0817 1356 2050	7.4 0.4 7.3 -0.2
5 SA 0211 0836 1421 2108	6.8 1.0 6.6 0.8		**20** SU 0227 0902 1437 2132	7.5 0.3 7.3 -0.1
6 SU 0244 0912 1452 2142	6.7 1.1 6.6 0.9		**21** M 0307 0943 1516 2208	7.4 0.4 7.3 0.1
7 M 0315 0942 1520 2206	6.6 1.1 6.6 1.0		**22** TU 0343 1018 1553 2238	7.2 0.5 7.2 0.4
8 TU 0346 1008 1550 2222	6.6 1.1 6.7 1.0		**23** W 0416 1048 1627 2303	7.0 0.7 7.1 0.7
9 W 0418 1033 1624 2242	6.7 1.0 6.8 0.9		**24** TH 0446 1110 1703 2324	6.8 0.9 6.8 0.9
10 TH 0454 1101 1704 2310	6.6 1.0 6.8 0.9		**25** F 0517 1132 1741 2349	6.5 1.1 6.4 1.2
11 F 0533 1134 1750 2348	6.4 1.1 6.6 1.1		**26** SA 0553 1205 1827	6.1 1.4 5.9
12 SA 0619 1217 1844 ○	6.1 1.3 6.2		**27** SU 0029 0637 1303 1929	1.6 5.7 1.7 5.4
13 SU 0037 0715 1321 1951	1.5 5.7 1.7 5.7		**28** M 0139 0741 1425 2127	2.0 5.3 1.9 5.3
14 M 0149 0831 1520 2121	1.9 5.4 1.8 5.6		**29** TU 0304 0950 1542 2239	2.1 5.3 1.8 5.6
15 TU 0407 1012 1707 2256	2.0 5.6 1.4 6.0		**30** W 0423 1056 1709 2334	1.9 5.8 1.4 6.1

OCTOBER

Time	m		Time	m
1 TH 0535 1148 1819	1.5 6.2 1.1		**16** F 0609 1156 1846	1.0 6.7 0.3
2 F 0020 0631 1233 1907	6.5 1.2 6.5 0.9		**17** SA 0031 0701 1245 1934	7.1 0.7 7.1 0.1
3 SA 0101 0718 1312 1951	6.7 1.0 6.6 0.8		**18** SU 0118 0749 1329 ● 2018	7.3 0.5 7.2 0.1
4 SU 0137 0800 1348 ○ 2031	6.8 1.0 6.7 0.8		**19** M 0200 0834 1411 2059	7.3 0.4 7.2 0.2
5 M 0211 0840 1421 2107	6.8 1.0 6.7 0.9		**20** TU 0238 0916 1451 2135	7.2 0.5 7.1 0.4
6 TU 0245 0916 1453 2135	6.7 1.0 6.7 1.0		**21** W 0313 0953 1528 2206	7.0 0.6 7.0 0.7
7 W 0318 0948 1528 2158	6.7 1.0 6.9 1.0		**22** TH 0344 1023 1604 2231	6.8 0.8 6.8 0.9
8 TH 0353 1018 1607 2222	6.7 0.9 6.9 0.9		**23** F 0413 1045 1640 2251	6.7 1.0 6.6 1.1
9 F 0431 1048 1650 2254	6.6 1.0 6.8 1.0		**24** SA 0445 1105 1719 2316	6.5 1.1 6.3 1.3
10 SA 0512 1124 1739 2334	6.4 1.1 6.5 1.2		**25** SU 0522 1137 1803 2353	6.2 1.3 5.9 1.6
11 SU 0558 1211 1836 ○	6.1 1.3 6.1		**26** M 0606 1228 1857 ●	5.9 1.6 5.6
12 M 0027 0656 1328 1947	1.6 5.7 1.6 5.8		**27** TU 0051 0701 1328 2008	1.9 5.5 1.6 5.4
13 TU 0143 0822 1522 2119	2.0 5.5 1.6 5.8		**28** W 0212 0826 1459 2142	2.1 5.3 1.7 5.5
14 W 0351 0954 1649 2239	1.9 5.8 1.1 6.2		**29** TH 0329 1003 1607 2245	2.0 5.6 1.5 5.9
15 TH 0510 1102 1753 2340	1.5 6.3 0.6 6.7		**30** F 0436 1101 1712 2335	1.7 5.9 1.2 6.2
			31 SA 0536 1149 1812	1.4 6.3 1.0

NOVEMBER

Time	m		Time	m
1 SU 0019 0630 1232 1903	6.5 1.1 6.5 0.9		**16** M 0050 0721 1305 ● 1945	7.0 0.7 7.0 0.5
2 M 0100 0719 1312 ○ 1949	6.7 1.0 6.7 0.9		**17** TU 0134 0808 1350 2027	7.0 0.6 7.0 0.6
3 TU 0139 0805 1351 2030	6.8 0.9 6.8 0.9		**18** W 0213 0851 1432 2106	6.9 0.7 6.9 0.8
4 W 0217 0849 1431 2107	6.9 0.8 6.9 0.9		**19** TH 0248 0931 1511 2140	6.7 0.8 6.7 1.0
5 TH 0256 0931 1513 2141	6.9 0.8 7.0 0.9		**20** F 0319 1003 1548 2206	6.6 1.0 6.6 1.1
6 F 0335 1010 1558 2214	6.8 0.8 7.0 1.0		**21** SA 0349 1028 1623 2228	6.5 1.1 6.4 1.2
7 SA 0417 1050 1645 2251	6.7 1.0 6.8 1.1		**22** SU 0422 1050 1701 2254	6.5 1.2 6.3 1.3
8 SU 0501 1133 1737 2334	6.5 1.0 6.6 1.3		**23** M 0459 1120 1742 2330	6.3 1.2 6.1 1.4
9 M 0550 1228 1836 ◐	6.2 1.1 6.3		**24** TU 0541 1202 1828 ◐	6.1 1.3 5.9
10 TU 0028 0651 1341 1945	1.6 5.9 1.3 6.1		**25** W 0016 0629 1258 1920	1.6 5.9 1.5 5.7
11 W 0141 0811 1502 2102	1.8 5.8 1.2 6.1		**26** TH 0115 0728 1404 2021	1.8 5.7 1.5 5.7
12 TH 0315 0927 1616 2211	1.8 6.0 1.0 6.3		**27** F 0226 0840 1511 2131	1.8 5.6 1.5 5.8
13 F 0433 1031 1718 2310	1.5 6.3 0.7 6.7		**28** SA 0338 0954 1616 2237	1.7 5.8 1.4 6.0
14 SA 0536 1127 1812	1.1 6.6 0.5		**29** SU 0444 1056 1719 2333	1.5 6.1 1.2 6.3
15 SU 0002 0631 1218 1900	6.9 0.9 6.9 0.4		**30** M 0545 1818	1.2 1.0

DECEMBER

Time	m		Time	m
1 TU 0023 0642 1239 1912	6.6 1.0 6.7 0.9		**16** W 0111 0746 1334 ● 2000	6.6 0.9 6.7 0.9
2 W 0110 0736 1327 ○ 2001	6.8 0.8 6.9 0.8		**17** TH 0153 0832 1419 2042	6.6 0.8 6.6 1.0
3 TH 0155 0829 1414 2048	6.9 0.7 7.0 0.8		**18** F 0231 0915 1459 2120	6.5 0.9 6.6 1.1
4 F 0239 0919 1503 2132	6.9 0.6 7.1 0.9		**19** SA 0303 0952 1535 2151	6.5 1.0 6.5 1.2
5 SA 0323 1009 1552 2214	6.9 0.6 7.1 0.9		**20** SU 0334 1022 1608 2214	6.5 1.1 6.4 1.3
6 SU 0409 1056 1642 2256	6.8 0.6 7.0 1.0		**21** M 0406 1042 1642 2238	6.4 1.1 6.4 1.2
7 M 0456 1143 1734 2339	6.6 0.6 6.9 1.1		**22** TU 0440 1105 1719 2310	6.4 1.1 6.4 1.2
8 TU 0545 1232 1829	6.5 0.7 6.6		**23** W 0518 1137 1759 2348	6.4 1.1 6.3 1.1
9 W 0027 0640 1326 ◐ 1928	1.3 6.3 0.8 6.4		**24** TH 0600 1217 1843 ◐	6.2 1.1 6.2
10 TH 0122 0745 1424 2032	1.5 6.2 1.0 6.3		**25** F 0033 0647 1305 1933	1.4 6.1 1.2 6.0
11 F 0226 0852 1529 2136	1.6 6.1 1.0 6.3		**26** SA 0127 0744 1405 2032	1.5 5.9 1.4 5.9
12 SA 0340 0957 1636 2236	1.6 6.2 0.9 6.3		**27** SU 0236 0851 1518 2139	1.7 5.8 1.5 5.9
13 SU 0454 1057 1733 2332	1.4 6.4 1.0 6.4		**28** M 0355 1003 1633 2249	1.6 5.9 1.4 6.0
14 M 0600 1153 1826	1.2 6.5 0.9		**29** TU 0507 1111 1742 2351	1.4 6.2 1.2 6.3
15 TU 0023 0655 1246 1914	6.6 1.0 6.6 0.9		**30** W 0613 1212 1845	1.2 6.6 1.0
			31 TH 0046 0717 1309 ○ 1943	6.6 0.8 6.9 0.9

Chart Datum: 3·20 metres below Ordnance Datum (Newlyn)
HAT is 7·6 metres above Chart Datum

TIDES

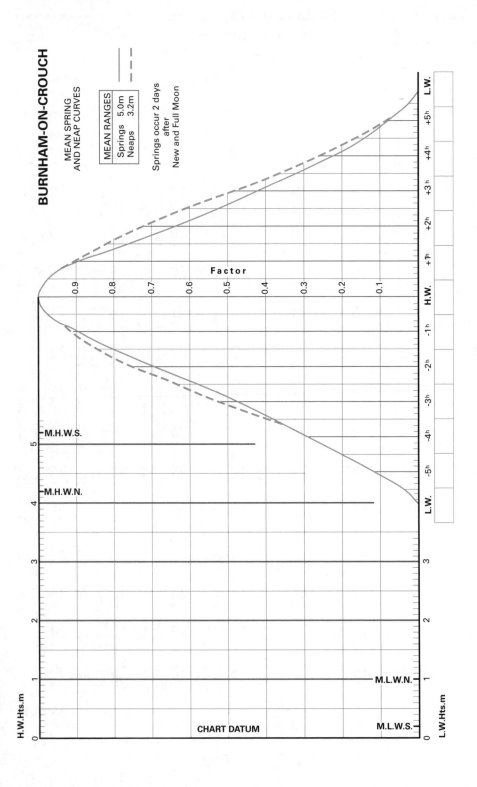

BURNHAM-ON-CROUCH

MEAN SPRING
AND NEAP CURVES

MEAN RANGES	
Springs	5.0m
Neaps	3.2m

Springs occur 2 days
after
New and Full Moon

ENGLAND – BURNHAM-ON-CROUCH
LAT 51°37′N   LONG 0°48′E
TIMES AND HEIGHTS OF HIGH AND LOW WATERS

Dates in amber are **SPRINGS**
Dates in yellow are **NEAPS**

2009

JANUARY

Time m

Day	Readings	Day	Readings
1	0238 4.9 / 0904 0.6 / TH 1518 4.8 / 2110 0.8	**16**	0345 5.1 / 1025 -0.2 / F 1622 5.0 / 2227 0.6
2	0319 4.9 / 0945 0.6 / F 1601 4.8 / 2154 0.9	**17**	0428 4.9 / 1109 0.1 / SA 1708 4.8 / 2311 0.8
3	0404 4.8 / 1030 0.7 / SA 1649 4.7 / 2242 1.0	**18**	0515 4.7 / 1154 0.3 / SU 1757 4.5 / ◑ 2358 1.0
4	0452 4.7 / 1119 0.8 / SU 1740 4.6 / ◑ 2334 1.1	**19**	0608 4.4 / 1243 0.6 / M 1851 4.2
5	0545 4.5 / 1214 0.9 / M 1837 4.5	**20**	0050 1.1 / 0711 4.2 / TU 1336 0.9 / 1952 4.1
6	0033 1.3 / 0644 4.4 / TU 1321 1.0 / 1942 4.3	**21**	0152 1.2 / 0825 4.0 / W 1437 1.0 / 2057 4.1
7	0148 1.3 / 0756 4.3 / W 1439 1.1 / 2053 4.4	**22**	0308 1.2 / 0936 4.1 / TH 1543 1.1 / 2158 4.2
8	0313 1.2 / 0916 4.4 / TH 1558 1.0 / 2202 4.5	**23**	0423 1.0 / 1035 4.2 / F 1641 1.0 / 2252 4.4
9	0432 1.0 / 1027 4.6 / F 1704 0.8 / 2303 4.7	**24**	0520 0.8 / 1127 4.4 / SA 1730 1.0 / 2339 4.6
10	0537 0.6 / 1129 4.9 / SA 1800 0.6 / 2357 5.0	**25**	0607 0.7 / 1211 4.5 / SU 1811 0.9
11	0632 0.2 / 1224 5.2 / SU 1850 0.5 / ○	**26**	0019 4.7 / 0646 0.5 / M 1251 4.6 / ● 1846 0.8
12	0047 5.2 / 0722 -0.1 / M 1315 5.4 / 1936 0.4	**27**	0054 4.8 / 0721 0.4 / TU 1324 4.7 / 1917 0.7
13	0135 5.3 / 0810 -0.3 / TU 1404 5.5 / 2020 0.3	**28**	0124 4.8 / 0752 0.4 / W 1355 4.8 / 1948 0.6
14	0219 5.3 / 0856 -0.4 / W 1451 5.5 / 2103 0.4	**29**	0153 4.9 / 0822 0.3 / TH 1426 4.9 / 2021 0.6
15	0302 5.3 / 0941 -0.4 / TH 1536 5.3 / 2145 0.5	**30**	0226 5.0 / 0854 0.4 / F 1501 4.9 / 2056 0.6
		31	0302 5.0 / 0928 0.4 / SA 1541 4.9 / 2133 0.6

FEBRUARY

Time m

Day	Readings	Day	Readings
1	0343 5.0 / 1003 0.5 / SU 1624 4.8 / 2212 0.7	**16**	0434 4.8 / 1104 0.4 / M 1707 4.4 / ◑ 2306 0.8
2	0427 4.9 / 1041 0.6 / M 1711 4.6 / ● 2255 0.9	**17**	0518 4.4 / 1144 0.8 / TU 1751 4.1 / 2349 1.0
3	0515 4.7 / 1122 0.8 / TU 1802 4.4 / 2345 1.1	**18**	0611 4.0 / 1231 1.0 / W 1844 3.9
4	0611 4.4 / 1216 1.1 / W 1903 4.1	**19**	0042 1.2 / 0726 3.7 / TH 1329 1.3 / 1959 3.7
5	0049 1.3 / 0718 4.2 / TH 1341 1.2 / 2020 4.0	**20**	0154 1.3 / 0901 3.7 / F 1447 1.3 / 2123 3.8
6	0242 1.3 / 0852 4.1 / F 1546 1.2 / 2143 4.1	**21**	0340 1.2 / 1010 3.9 / SA 1607 1.2 / 2225 4.1
7	0426 0.9 / 1016 4.4 / SA 1658 0.9 / 2250 4.5	**22**	0450 0.9 / 1104 4.2 / SU 1704 1.0 / 2316 4.4
8	0530 0.4 / 1119 4.8 / SU 1752 0.5 / 2345 4.9	**23**	0539 0.6 / 1149 4.5 / M 1748 0.8 / 2358 4.6
9	0622 0.0 / 1213 5.2 / M 1839 0.3 / ○	**24**	0620 0.4 / 1228 4.7 / TU 1827 0.6
10	0034 5.2 / 0709 -0.4 / TU 1302 5.4 / 1921 0.1	**25**	0035 4.8 / 0656 0.3 / W 1303 4.9 / ● 1901 0.5
11	0118 5.4 / 0753 -0.6 / W 1347 5.5 / 2002 0.1	**26**	0108 4.9 / 0730 0.2 / TH 1336 5.0 / 1934 0.4
12	0200 5.5 / 0835 -0.6 / TH 1429 5.4 / 2040 0.1	**27**	0139 5.0 / 0802 0.2 / F 1408 5.0 / 2006 0.4
13	0239 5.4 / 0914 -0.4 / F 1510 5.3 / 2116 0.2	**28**	0211 5.1 / 0834 0.2 / SA 1442 5.1 / 2039 0.4
14	0317 5.3 / 0951 -0.2 / SA 1549 5.0 / 2152 0.4		
15	0355 5.1 / 1028 0.1 / SU 1627 4.7 / 2228 0.6		

MARCH

Time m

Day	Readings	Day	Readings
1	0246 5.1 / 0905 0.3 / SU 1520 5.0 / 2113 0.4	**16**	0323 5.0 / 0943 0.3 / M 1545 4.6 / 2148 0.5
2	0325 5.1 / 0937 0.4 / M 1600 4.8 / 2150 0.5	**17**	0359 4.7 / 1015 0.6 / TU 1619 4.4 / 2223 0.7
3	0407 4.9 / 1012 0.6 / TU 1644 4.6 / 2232 0.7	**18**	0438 4.4 / 1052 0.8 / W 1657 4.2 / ◑ 2303 0.8
4	0455 4.7 / 1054 0.8 / W 1732 4.3 / ◑ 2321 0.9	**19**	0523 4.0 / 1137 1.1 / TH 1741 3.9 / 2353 1.0
5	0550 4.4 / 1148 1.1 / TH 1830 4.0	**20**	0621 3.7 / 1233 1.3 / F 1839 3.7
6	0024 1.1 / 0659 4.1 / F 1303 1.3 / 1952 3.8	**21**	0058 1.2 / 0806 3.5 / SA 1349 1.4 / 2024 3.6
7	0230 1.2 / 0843 4.0 / SA 1538 1.2 / 2130 4.0	**22**	0235 1.2 / 0934 3.8 / SU 1519 1.3 / 2147 3.9
8	0415 0.7 / 1007 4.4 / SU 1644 0.8 / 2236 4.4	**23**	0403 0.9 / 1030 4.1 / M 1625 1.0 / 2241 4.2
9	0514 0.2 / 1107 4.8 / M 1734 0.4 / 2329 4.8	**24**	0458 0.6 / 1115 4.5 / TU 1715 0.8 / 2326 4.5
10	0603 -0.2 / 1157 5.2 / TU 1818 0.2	**25**	0543 0.4 / 1156 4.6 / W 1757 0.5
11	0015 5.2 / 0647 -0.5 / W 1243 5.4 / ○ 1859 0.0	**26**	0006 4.8 / 0622 0.2 / TH 1234 5.0 / ● 1835 0.4
12	0058 5.4 / 0728 -0.5 / TH 1325 5.4 / 1937 0.0	**27**	0043 5.0 / 0700 0.1 / F 1310 5.1 / 1911 0.3
13	0137 5.5 / 0806 -0.5 / F 1403 5.3 / 2012 0.0	**28**	0118 5.1 / 0735 0.2 / SA 1345 5.1 / 1946 0.3
14	0213 5.4 / 0841 -0.2 / SA 1439 5.1 / 2045 0.1	**29**	0154 5.2 / 0809 0.2 / SU 1422 5.1 / 2021 0.3
15	0248 5.2 / 0913 0.0 / SU 1512 4.9 / 2116 0.3	**30**	0231 5.2 / 0842 0.4 / M 1500 5.0 / 2058 0.3
		31	0312 5.1 / 0916 0.5 / TU 1540 4.8 / 2138 0.4

APRIL

Time m

Day	Readings	Day	Readings
1	0356 4.9 / 0955 0.7 / W 1623 4.5 / 2223 0.6	**16**	0406 4.3 / 1011 0.9 / TH 1616 4.3 / 2230 0.8
2	0446 4.6 / 1042 0.9 / TH 1712 4.2 / ◑ 2317 0.7	**17**	0450 4.1 / 1057 1.1 / F 1700 4.1 / ◑ 2321 0.9
3	0543 4.3 / 1141 1.2 / F 1811 3.9	**18**	0543 3.9 / 1153 1.2 / SA 1753 3.9
4	0030 0.9 / 0659 4.1 / SA 1309 1.3 / 1937 3.8	**19**	0025 1.0 / 0652 3.7 / SU 1303 1.3 / 1901 3.8
5	0227 0.8 / 0836 4.2 / SU 1512 1.1 / 2110 4.0	**20**	0147 1.0 / 0830 3.8 / M 1425 1.3 / 2040 3.9
6	0350 0.4 / 0950 4.5 / M 1617 0.8 / 2213 4.5	**21**	0307 0.8 / 0939 4.1 / TU 1536 1.1 / 2151 4.1
7	0447 0.1 / 1045 4.9 / TU 1707 0.4 / 2305 4.8	**22**	0410 0.6 / 1031 4.5 / W 1633 0.9 / 2243 4.5
8	0535 -0.2 / 1134 5.1 / W 1751 0.2 / 2350 5.1	**23**	0501 0.4 / 1117 4.8 / TH 1721 0.6 / 2329 4.7
9	0618 -0.3 / 1217 5.3 / TH 1833 0.1 / ○	**24**	0547 0.3 / 1159 5.0 / F 1806 0.5
10	0032 5.3 / 0657 -0.3 / F 1258 5.2 / 1910 0.0	**25**	0012 5.0 / 0628 0.2 / SA 1241 5.1 / ● 1847 0.4
11	0112 5.3 / 0733 -0.1 / SA 1335 5.1 / 1945 0.1	**26**	0054 5.1 / 0708 0.3 / SU 1322 5.2 / 1928 0.3
12	0148 5.2 / 0805 0.1 / SU 1407 4.9 / 2016 0.3	**27**	0136 5.2 / 0747 0.4 / M 1402 5.1 / 2009 0.3
13	0222 5.0 / 0833 0.4 / M 1437 4.7 / 2045 0.4	**28**	0218 5.2 / 0825 0.5 / TU 1443 4.9 / 2052 0.3
14	0254 4.8 / 0901 0.6 / TU 1505 4.6 / 2114 0.5	**29**	0303 5.1 / 0904 0.6 / W 1525 4.8 / 2137 0.4
15	0328 4.5 / 0933 0.7 / W 1537 4.5 / 2149 0.6	**30**	0351 4.9 / 0949 0.8 / TH 1611 4.5 / 2229 0.4

Chart Datum: 2·35 metres below Ordnance Datum (Newlyn)

TIDES

ENGLAND – BURNHAM-ON-CROUCH

TIME ZONE (UT)
For Summer Time add ONE hour in **non-shaded areas**

LAT 51°37'N   LONG 0°48'E
TIMES AND HEIGHTS OF HIGH AND LOW WATERS

Dates in amber are **SPRINGS**
Dates in yellow are **NEAPS**

2009

MAY

Day	Time	m	Time	m	Time	m	Time	m	Day	Time	m	Time	m	Time	m	Time	m
1 F	0444	4.7	1042	1.0	1702	4.3	2331	0.5	16 SA	0425	4.2	1025	1.0	1631	4.4	2258	0.8
2 SA	0545	4.5	1146	1.1	1803	4.1			17 SU	0515	4.1	1120	1.1	1723	4.2	2359	0.8
3 SU	0045	0.5	0657	4.3	1308	1.2	1921	4.1	18 M	0614	4.0	1223	1.2	1821	4.1		
4 M	0207	0.4	0815	4.4	1433	1.0	2039	4.3	19 TU	0108	0.9	0723	4.1	1334	1.2	1932	4.1
5 TU	0317	0.2	0921	4.6	1539	0.7	2142	4.6	20 W	0219	0.8	0837	4.2	1445	1.2	2050	4.2
6 W	0414	0.0	1016	4.9	1634	0.5	2235	4.8	21 TH	0324	0.7	0941	4.4	1549	1.0	2156	4.4
7 TH	0503	0.0	1105	5.0	1722	0.3	2323	5.0	22 F	0422	0.5	1036	4.7	1647	0.8	2252	4.7
8 F	0547	0.0	1150	5.1	1806	0.2			23 SA	0514	0.4	1126	4.9	1739	0.6	2343	4.9
9 SA	0007	5.1	0627	0.1	1231	5.0	1847	0.3	24 SU	0603	0.4	1214	5.0	1829	0.5		
10 SU	0049	5.0	0703	0.3	1307	4.9	1923	0.4	25 M	0032	5.1	0648	0.4	1300	5.1	1917	0.3
11 M	0126	4.9	0733	0.5	1339	4.7	1954	0.6	26 TU	0120	5.2	0733	0.5	1345	5.1	2004	0.2
12 TU	0200	4.7	0758	0.7	1405	4.6	2020	0.6	27 W	0207	5.2	0817	0.5	1429	5.0	2053	0.2
13 W	0231	4.5	0824	0.8	1432	4.6	2048	0.6	28 TH	0255	5.2	0903	0.6	1514	4.9	2143	0.1
14 TH	0303	4.4	0857	0.8	1505	4.5	2123	0.7	29 F	0345	5.0	0951	0.8	1601	4.7	2237	0.1
15 F	0341	4.3	0938	0.9	1545	4.5	2207	0.7	30 SA	0438	4.9	1044	0.9	1652	4.6	2333	0.2
									31 SU	0536	4.7	1141	0.9	1749	4.4		

JUNE

Day	Time	m	Time	m	Time	m	Time	m	Day	Time	m	Time	m	Time	m	Time	m
1 M	0034	0.2	0638	4.6	1245	0.9	1854	4.4	16 TU	0542	4.4	1143	1.0	1749	4.4		
2 TU	0138	0.2	0743	4.5	1352	0.9	2003	4.4	17 W	0027	0.8	0640	4.4	1245	1.1	1848	4.3
3 W	0240	0.2	0846	4.6	1459	0.8	2108	4.5	18 TH	0133	0.8	0746	4.3	1355	1.2	1959	4.2
4 TH	0339	0.2	0943	4.7	1600	0.7	2205	4.7	19 F	0241	0.8	0855	4.3	1507	1.1	2114	4.3
5 F	0431	0.3	1035	4.8	1655	0.5	2258	4.8	20 SA	0348	0.8	1000	4.5	1617	1.0	2221	4.5
6 SA	0519	0.3	1123	4.8	1745	0.5	2346	4.8	21 SU	0451	0.7	1059	4.7	1721	0.7	2320	4.8
7 SU	0603	0.5	1206	4.8	1830	0.5			22 M	0547	0.6	1152	4.9	1818	0.5		
8 M	0030	4.8	0640	0.6	1245	4.7	1910	0.5	23 TU	0014	5.1	0638	0.5	1242	5.0	1910	0.2
9 TU	0110	4.7	0711	0.7	1317	4.6	1944	0.6	24 W	0106	5.2	0726	0.4	1330	5.1	2000	0.0
10 W	0145	4.5	0734	0.8	1342	4.5	2009	0.7	25 TH	0156	5.3	0812	0.4	1415	5.1	2049	-0.2
11 TH	0214	4.4	0759	0.8	1408	4.6	2033	0.7	26 F	0245	5.4	0858	0.4	1500	5.1	2137	-0.2
12 F	0244	4.4	0833	0.8	1442	4.6	2107	0.7	27 SA	0333	5.3	0943	0.5	1546	5.0	2225	-0.2
13 SA	0320	4.4	0914	0.8	1522	4.7	2148	0.7	28 SU	0422	5.1	1030	0.6	1633	4.9	2315	-0.1
14 SU	0402	4.4	0959	0.9	1607	4.6	2236	0.7	29 M	0513	4.9	1119	0.7	1724	4.7		
15 M	0450	4.4	1048	0.9	1656	4.6	2328	0.7	30 TU	0006	0.1	0607	4.7	1212	0.8	1820	4.6

JULY

Day	Time	m	Time	m	Time	m	Time	m	Day	Time	m	Time	m	Time	m	Time	m
1 W	0101	0.3	0705	4.5	1309	0.9	1925	4.4	16 TH	0604	4.4	1155	1.0	1812	4.4		
2 TH	0159	0.4	0807	4.4	1414	0.9	2033	4.4	17 F	0035	0.9	0703	4.3	1258	1.2	1916	4.2
3 F	0301	0.6	0909	4.3	1525	0.9	2138	4.4	18 SA	0150	1.0	0814	4.1	1423	1.2	2037	4.2
4 SA	0401	0.7	1006	4.3	1631	0.8	2237	4.5	19 SU	0319	1.1	0930	4.2	1557	1.1	2158	4.3
5 SU	0455	0.7	1059	4.5	1727	0.7	2329	4.6	20 M	0437	0.9	1037	4.4	1711	0.7	2304	4.7
6 M	0543	0.7	1146	4.5	1817	0.6			21 TU	0538	0.7	1135	4.7	1809	0.3		
7 TU	0016	4.6	0624	0.7	1228	4.6	1859	0.5	22 W	0001	5.0	0629	0.4	1227	5.0	1900	-0.1
8 W	0058	4.6	0659	0.6	1303	4.6	1934	0.5	23 TH	0054	5.3	0716	0.3	1314	5.2	1948	-0.4
9 TH	0133	4.5	0725	0.8	1329	4.6	2001	0.6	24 F	0142	5.5	0800	0.2	1358	5.3	2034	-0.5
10 F	0200	4.5	0749	0.7	1354	4.6	2025	0.5	25 SA	0228	5.5	0842	0.1	1441	5.3	2117	-0.5
11 SA	0228	4.6	0820	0.7	1424	4.7	2054	0.5	26 SU	0313	5.4	0923	0.2	1523	5.3	2200	-0.4
12 SU	0301	4.6	0856	0.6	1502	4.8	2129	0.5	27 M	0357	5.2	1004	0.3	1606	5.1	2243	-0.2
13 M	0340	4.7	0936	0.6	1544	4.8	2209	0.5	28 TU	0442	4.9	1046	0.5	1652	4.9	2328	0.1
14 TU	0424	4.7	1018	0.7	1629	4.8	2252	0.6	29 W	0530	4.6	1131	0.6	1742	4.6		
15 W	0512	4.6	1104	0.9	1718	4.6	2339	0.8	30 TH	0015	0.5	0621	4.3	1222	0.8	1842	4.3
									31 F	0108	0.8	0721	4.1	1321	1.0	1957	4.0

AUGUST

Day	Time	m	Time	m	Time	m	Time	m	Day	Time	m	Time	m	Time	m	Time	m
1 SA	0212	1.0	0830	4.0	1440	1.1	2114	4.0	16 SU	0045	1.2	0734	3.9	1337	1.2	2008	4.0
2 SU	0326	1.1	0938	4.0	1606	1.0	2218	4.2	17 M	0256	1.3	0904	3.9	1548	1.0	2143	4.2
3 M	0431	1.0	1036	4.2	1708	0.7	2313	4.4	18 TU	0429	1.0	1020	4.5	1701	0.5	2252	4.6
4 TU	0522	0.9	1126	4.4	1757	0.6			19 W	0526	0.6	1119	4.7	1756	0.0	2348	5.1
5 W	0000	4.5	0604	0.8	1210	4.5	1837	0.4	20 TH	0614	0.3	1209	5.0	1844	-0.4		
6 TH	0041	4.6	0640	0.7	1246	4.6	1912	0.4	21 F	0037	5.4	0657	0.1	1254	5.3	1927	-0.6
7 F	0115	4.7	0710	0.6	1315	4.7	1940	0.3	22 SA	0123	5.6	0739	0.0	1337	5.5	2009	-0.7
8 SA	0143	4.7	0737	0.6	1340	4.8	2006	0.3	23 SU	0206	5.6	0818	0.0	1417	5.5	2049	-0.6
9 SU	0210	4.8	0806	0.5	1409	4.9	2034	0.3	24 M	0247	5.4	0856	0.0	1457	5.4	2128	-0.3
10 M	0241	4.9	0838	0.6	1443	5.0	2105	0.4	25 TU	0327	5.2	0933	0.2	1536	5.2	2205	0.0
11 TU	0318	4.9	0913	0.5	1521	5.0	2139	0.4	26 W	0407	4.9	1010	0.4	1618	4.9	2243	0.3
12 W	0358	4.9	0950	0.5	1604	4.9	2214	0.6	27 TH	0448	4.6	1050	0.6	1703	4.5	2324	0.7
13 TH	0443	4.7	1031	0.7	1650	4.7	2253	0.7	28 F	0532	4.2	1134	0.8	1757	4.1		
14 F	0531	4.5	1117	0.9	1742	4.4	2341	1.0	29 SA	0011	1.0	0624	3.9	1228	1.0	1912	3.8
15 SA	0626	4.2	1213	1.1	1844	4.2			30 SU	0111	1.3	0740	3.7	1341	1.2	2047	3.7
									31 M	0234	1.4	0906	3.6	1530	1.1	2157	3.9

Chart Datum: 2·35 metres below Ordnance Datum (Newlyn)

ENGLAND – BURNHAM-ON-CROUCH
LAT 51°37'N   LONG 0°48'E
TIMES AND HEIGHTS OF HIGH AND LOW WATERS

2009

SEPTEMBER

Day	Time m		Day	Time m	
1 TU	0356 1.2 / 1010 4.1 / 1637 0.8 / 2250 4.2		**16** W	0411 1.0 / 1003 4.3 / 1643 0.3 / 2237 4.7	
2 W	0451 1.0 / 1101 4.3 / 1725 0.6 / 2335 4.5		**17** TH	0505 0.6 / 1108 4.6 / 1734 -0.1 / 2329 5.1	
3 TH	0534 0.8 / 1144 4.6 / 1804 0.4		**18** F	0550 0.3 / 1146 5.1 / 1819 -0.4	
4 F	0015 4.7 / 0611 0.6 / 1221 4.7 / 1838 0.3 ○		**19** SA	0015 5.4 / 0632 0.0 / 1231 5.4 / 1900 -0.6	
5 SA	0049 4.8 / 0644 0.5 / 1253 4.8 / 1910 0.2		**20** SU	0059 5.5 / 0712 -0.1 / 1312 5.6 / 1940 -0.5	
6 SU	0119 4.9 / 0715 0.4 / 1321 4.9 / 1939 0.2		**21** M	0140 5.5 / 0750 0.0 / 1351 5.5 / 2017 -0.3	
7 M	0149 5.0 / 0746 0.4 / 1351 5.0 / 2009 0.2		**22** TU	0218 5.3 / 0826 0.1 / 1429 5.4 / 2052 -0.1	
8 TU	0220 5.0 / 0817 0.4 / 1424 5.1 / 2039 0.3		**23** W	0255 5.1 / 0901 0.2 / 1507 5.1 / 2125 0.2	
9 W	0256 5.0 / 0851 0.4 / 1502 5.0 / 2110 0.4		**24** TH	0330 4.8 / 0936 0.5 / 1546 4.8 / 2200 0.6	
10 TH	0334 4.9 / 0927 0.5 / 1544 4.9 / 2145 0.6		**25** F	0406 4.5 / 1013 0.7 / 1628 4.4 / 2238 0.9	
11 F	0417 4.7 / 1009 0.6 / 1630 4.7 / 2226 0.8		**26** SA	0444 4.2 / 1055 0.9 / 1715 4.0 / 2323 1.1 ◑	
12 SA	0504 4.4 / 1057 0.8 / 1723 4.4 / 2318 1.1 ◑		**27** SU	0529 3.9 / 1147 1.1 / 1819 3.7	
13 SU	0557 4.1 / 1156 1.0 / 1825 4.1		**28** M	0021 1.4 / 0629 3.7 / 1256 1.2 / 2004 3.6	
14 M	0024 1.3 / 0705 3.9 / 1327 1.1 / 1955 4.0		**29** TU	0137 1.5 / 0815 3.7 / 1433 1.1 / 2122 3.8	
15 TU	0240 1.4 / 0845 3.9 / 1538 0.8 / 2132 4.2		**30** W	0303 1.3 / 0932 4.0 / 1550 0.9 / 2215 4.1	

OCTOBER

Day	Time m		Day	Time m	
1 TH	0407 1.1 / 1024 4.3 / 1640 0.6 / 2259 4.5		**16** F	0435 0.6 / 1032 4.9 / 1705 -0.1 / 2303 5.2	
2 F	0454 0.8 / 1108 4.6 / 1723 0.4 / 2339 4.8		**17** SA	0522 0.3 / 1120 5.2 / 1750 -0.3 / 2349 5.3	
3 SA	0535 0.6 / 1147 4.8 / 1801 0.3		**18** SU	0605 0.1 / 1205 5.4 / 1832 -0.3 ●	
4 SU	0015 4.9 / 0613 0.5 / 1223 5.0 / 1836 0.2 ○		**19** M	0032 5.4 / 0646 0.1 / 1247 5.5 / 1910 -0.2	
5 M	0050 5.1 / 0648 0.4 / 1257 5.1 / 1910 0.2		**20** TU	0112 5.3 / 0724 0.1 / 1327 5.4 / 1945 0.1	
6 TU	0124 5.1 / 0723 0.4 / 1332 5.1 / 1943 0.3		**21** W	0149 5.1 / 0800 0.3 / 1405 5.2 / 2018 0.3	
7 W	0159 5.1 / 0758 0.4 / 1408 5.1 / 2015 0.4		**22** TH	0223 4.9 / 0833 0.4 / 1442 5.0 / 2048 0.6	
8 TH	0235 5.0 / 0834 0.4 / 1448 5.1 / 2048 0.6		**23** F	0254 4.7 / 0905 0.6 / 1518 4.6 / 2120 0.8	
9 F	0315 4.8 / 0913 0.5 / 1531 4.9 / 2127 0.7		**24** SA	0326 4.5 / 0940 0.8 / 1557 4.3 / 2158 1.0	
10 SA	0357 4.6 / 0958 0.7 / 1620 4.7 / 2213 1.0		**25** SU	0403 4.3 / 1022 0.9 / 1641 4.0 / 2244 1.2	
11 SU	0445 4.3 / 1051 0.8 / 1715 4.4 / 2310 1.2 ◑		**26** M	0446 4.1 / 1114 1.1 / 1734 3.8 / 2341 1.4 ◑	
12 M	0540 4.1 / 1159 1.0 / 1821 4.2		**27** TU	0539 3.9 / 1220 1.2 / 1846 3.7	
13 TU	0024 1.3 / 0651 3.9 / 1340 0.9 / 1949 4.2		**28** W	0050 1.4 / 0608 3.8 / 1338 1.1 / 2016 3.8	
14 W	0219 1.3 / 0825 4.1 / 1515 0.6 / 2112 4.5		**29** TH	0206 1.4 / 0823 3.9 / 1451 0.9 / 2121 4.1	
15 TH	0340 0.9 / 0937 4.4 / 1616 0.2 / 2213 4.8		**30** F	0314 1.2 / 0931 4.2 / 1549 0.7 / 2211 4.5	
			31 SA	0409 0.9 / 1023 4.5 / 1639 0.5 / 2256 4.8	

NOVEMBER

Day	Time m		Day	Time m	
1 SU	0458 0.7 / 1108 4.8 / 1723 0.4 / 2338 5.0		**16** M	0541 0.2 / 1142 5.3 / 1805 0.1 ●	
2 M	0542 0.5 / 1151 5.0 / 1805 0.3 ○		**17** TU	0006 5.2 / 0625 0.2 / 1227 5.3 / 1845 0.3	
3 TU	0019 5.1 / 0623 0.4 / 1233 5.2 / 1844 0.4		**18** W	0047 5.1 / 0707 0.3 / 1309 5.2 / 1920 0.5	
4 W	0059 5.2 / 0704 0.4 / 1314 5.2 / 1922 0.5		**19** TH	0124 4.9 / 0744 0.4 / 1347 5.0 / 1950 0.7	
5 TH	0139 5.1 / 0745 0.4 / 1356 5.2 / 1959 0.6		**20** F	0155 4.7 / 0816 0.6 / 1422 4.7 / 2017 0.9	
6 F	0219 5.0 / 0826 0.4 / 1439 5.1 / 2037 0.7		**21** SA	0222 4.6 / 0843 0.7 / 1455 4.5 / 2047 1.0	
7 SA	0300 4.8 / 0911 0.5 / 1525 5.0 / 2121 0.9		**22** SU	0252 4.5 / 0915 0.8 / 1531 4.4 / 2124 1.1	
8 SU	0344 4.6 / 1002 0.6 / 1616 4.8 / 2212 1.1		**23** M	0329 4.4 / 0955 0.9 / 1612 4.2 / 2210 1.2	
9 M	0433 4.4 / 1101 0.7 / 1713 4.6 / 2313 1.2 ◑		**24** TU	0413 4.3 / 1045 1.0 / 1659 4.1 / 2304 1.3 ◑	
10 TU	0530 4.3 / 1211 0.7 / 1818 4.5		**25** W	0503 4.2 / 1144 1.0 / 1755 4.1	
11 W	0027 1.2 / 0638 4.2 / 1329 0.6 / 1932 4.5		**26** TH	0006 1.4 / 0600 4.1 / 1250 1.0 / 1900 4.1	
12 TH	0150 1.1 / 0757 4.3 / 1443 0.4 / 2043 4.6		**27** F	0114 1.3 / 0709 4.1 / 1356 1.0 / 2011 4.2	
13 F	0303 0.9 / 0906 4.6 / 1543 0.2 / 2143 4.9		**28** SA	0221 1.2 / 0826 4.2 / 1459 0.9 / 2116 4.5	
14 SA	0402 0.6 / 1004 4.9 / 1635 0.1 / 2235 5.1		**29** SU	0324 1.1 / 0933 4.4 / 1557 0.7 / 2212 4.7	
15 SU	0454 0.4 / 1055 5.2 / 1722 0.0 / 2322 5.2		**30** M	0422 0.9 / 1031 4.7 / 1650 0.6 / 2303 5.0	

DECEMBER

Day	Time m		Day	Time m	
1 TU	0516 0.7 / 1122 5.0 / 1739 0.5 / 2351 5.1		**16** W	0614 0.4 / 1212 5.0 / 1828 0.6 ●	
2 W	0606 0.5 / 1211 5.2 / 1826 0.5 ○		**17** TH	0028 4.9 / 0658 0.4 / 1257 4.9 / 1905 0.7	
3 TH	0037 5.2 / 0654 0.4 / 1258 5.3 / 1910 0.6		**18** F	0106 4.8 / 0738 0.5 / 1336 4.8 / 1935 0.9	
4 F	0122 5.2 / 0741 0.3 / 1345 5.3 / 1953 0.7		**19** SA	0136 4.7 / 0811 0.6 / 1409 4.6 / 1957 0.9	
5 SA	0205 5.1 / 0829 0.3 / 1432 5.3 / 2038 0.8		**20** SU	0159 4.6 / 0834 0.7 / 1437 4.5 / 2023 1.0	
6 SU	0249 5.0 / 0917 0.2 / 1520 5.2 / 2124 0.8		**21** M	0227 4.6 / 0909 0.7 / 1508 4.5 / 2059 1.0	
7 M	0334 4.8 / 1008 0.3 / 1610 5.0 / 2214 0.9		**22** TU	0303 4.7 / 0933 0.8 / 1546 4.5 / 2141 1.0	
8 TU	0422 4.7 / 1102 0.3 / 1704 4.9 / 2309 1.0		**23** W	0345 4.7 / 1016 0.8 / 1630 4.5 / 2228 1.1	
9 W	0516 4.6 / 1200 0.3 / 1802 4.7 ◑		**24** TH	0433 4.6 / 1105 0.8 / 1719 4.4 / 2321 1.2 ◑	
10 TH	0010 1.0 / 0616 4.5 / 1303 0.4 / 1905 4.7		**25** F	0524 4.5 / 1201 0.9 / 1814 4.4	
11 F	0116 1.0 / 0724 4.5 / 1406 0.4 / 2010 4.7		**26** SA	0020 1.2 / 0621 4.3 / 1303 1.0 / 1916 4.3	
12 SA	0225 0.9 / 0833 4.6 / 1509 0.4 / 2111 4.7		**27** SU	0127 1.3 / 0729 4.2 / 1410 1.0 / 2025 4.4	
13 SU	0331 0.7 / 0936 4.7 / 1606 0.4 / 2207 4.9		**28** M	0239 1.2 / 0845 4.3 / 1519 1.0 / 2133 4.5	
14 M	0431 0.6 / 1033 4.9 / 1658 0.4 / 2258 4.9		**29** TU	0351 1.1 / 0957 4.5 / 1624 0.9 / 2234 4.7	
15 TU	0525 0.4 / 1124 5.0 / 1745 0.5 / 2345 4.9		**30** W	0457 0.8 / 1058 4.8 / 1723 0.7 / 2329 4.9	
			31 TH	0555 0.5 / 1154 5.1 / 1816 0.6 ○	

Chart Datum: 2·35 metres below Ordnance Datum (Newlyn)

TIDES

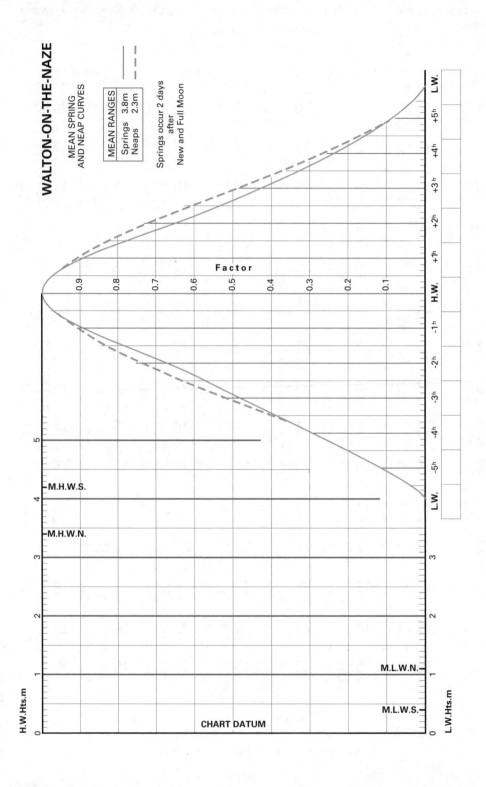

WALTON-ON-THE-NAZE

MEAN SPRING
AND NEAP CURVES

MEAN RANGES	
Springs	3.8m
Neaps	2.3m

Springs occur 2 days
after
New and Full Moon

Factor

0.9 0.8 0.7 0.6 0.5 0.4 0.3 0.2 0.1

H.W.Hts.m

-M.H.W.S.

-M.H.W.N.

CHART DATUM

L.W.Hts.m

M.L.W.N.-

M.L.W.S.-

+5ʰ +4ʰ +3ʰ +2ʰ +1ʰ H.W. -1ʰ -2ʰ -3ʰ -4ʰ -5ʰ L.W.

L.W.

TIME ZONE (UT)	ENGLAND – WALTON-ON-THE-NAZE	Dates in amber are SPRINGS
For Summer Time add ONE hour in non-shaded areas	LAT 51°51′N LONG 1°17′E	Dates in yellow are NEAPS
	TIMES AND HEIGHTS OF HIGH AND LOW WATERS	2009

JANUARY

Time	m	Time	m
1 0159	3.9	**16** 0259	4.2
0818	0.6	0922	0.2
TH 1431	3.9	F 1530	4.1
2020	0.9	2117	0.9
2 0237	3.9	**17** 0340	4.1
0856	0.6	1006	0.4
F 1512	3.8	SA 1614	3.9
2059	0.9	2201	1.0
3 0318	3.8	**18** 0424	3.9
0936	0.7	1052	0.6
SA 1557	3.8	SU 1700	3.6
2143	1.0	◐ 2250	1.1
4 0404	3.8	**19** 0515	3.7
1024	0.7	1143	0.9
SU 1648	3.7	M 1752	3.4
◐ 2235	1.1	2351	1.2
5 0457	3.7	**20** 0618	3.5
1121	0.8	1242	1.1
M 1747	3.5	TU 1857	3.3
2338	1.1		
6 0602	3.6	**21** 0107	1.3
1229	0.9	0733	3.3
TU 1852	3.5	W 1348	1.2
		2009	3.3
7 0049	1.1	**22** 0230	1.2
0713	3.6	0847	3.4
W 1343	1.0	TH 1453	1.2
2002	3.5	2115	3.4
8 0205	1.1	**23** 0339	1.0
0825	3.7	0948	3.6
TH 1453	0.9	F 1548	1.1
2110	3.7	2209	3.6
9 0318	0.9	**24** 0432	0.8
0933	3.9	1038	3.8
F 1557	0.8	SA 1634	1.0
2211	3.8	2254	3.8
10 0425	0.7	**25** 0515	0.7
1035	4.1	1121	3.9
SA 1652	0.7	SU 1713	0.9
2306	4.0	2334	3.9
11 0523	0.4	**26** 0551	0.6
1131	4.2	1158	3.9
SU 1741	0.7	M 1747	0.9
○ 2357	4.2		
12 0616	0.3	**27** 0009	3.9
1224	4.4	0622	0.6
M 1827	0.7	TU 1233	4.0
		1819	0.8
13 0046	4.2	**28** 0041	3.9
0706	0.1	0652	0.5
TU 1314	4.4	W 1304	4.0
1911	0.7	1851	0.8
14 0133	4.3	**29** 0111	4.0
0753	0.1	0723	0.6
W 1401	4.4	TH 1336	4.0
1954	0.7	1924	0.8
15 0216	4.3	**30** 0142	4.0
0838	0.1	0755	0.6
TH 1447	4.3	F 1410	4.0
2036	0.8	1957	0.7
		31 0216	4.0
		0828	0.5
		SA 1447	4.0
		2033	0.7

FEBRUARY

Time	m	Time	m
1 0251	4.0	**16** 0343	4.0
0904	0.5	1000	0.4
SU 1527	3.9	M 1608	3.7
2113	0.7	◑ 2201	0.9
2 0332	4.0	**17** 0426	3.7
0944	0.6	1046	0.6
M 1613	3.7	TU 1650	3.4
◑ 2159	0.9	2253	1.1
3 0420	3.8	**18** 0522	3.4
1034	0.8	1147	1.2
TU 1706	3.5	W 1745	3.2
2256	1.0		
4 0520	3.6	**19** 0008	1.3
1144	1.0	0645	3.2
W 1812	3.3	TH 1300	1.4
		1913	3.1
5 0012	1.1	**20** 0149	1.3
0639	3.4	0819	3.2
TH 1314	1.1	F 1417	1.3
1932	3.3	2042	3.2
6 0145	1.1	**21** 0314	1.1
0810	3.5	0927	3.5
F 1441	1.1	SA 1523	1.2
2055	3.4	2143	3.5
7 0317	0.9	**22** 0410	0.9
0939	3.7	1018	3.7
SA 1549	0.9	SU 1612	1.0
2203	3.7	2231	3.7
8 0425	0.6	**23** 0451	0.7
1033	4.0	1100	3.9
SU 1643	0.6	M 1651	0.9
2258	4.0	2311	3.9
9 0519	0.3	**24** 0526	0.6
1126	4.2	1137	4.0
M 1729	0.7	TU 1725	0.8
		○ 2347	4.2
10 0607	0.1	**25** 0557	0.5
1214	4.4	1210	4.0
TU 1811	0.6	W 1757	0.8
		●	
11 0032	4.5	**26** 0018	4.0
0651	0.0	0627	0.4
W 1259	4.4	TH 1242	4.0
1852	0.6	1828	0.7
12 0114	4.4	**27** 0050	4.0
0732	0.0	0658	0.4
TH 1341	4.3	F 1313	4.1
1932	0.6	1901	0.6
13 0153	4.4	**28** 0121	4.1
0811	0.1	0730	0.4
F 1420	4.2	SA 1346	4.1
2009	0.6	1935	0.6
14 0230	4.3		
0847	0.3		
SA 1457	4.1		
2045	0.7		
15 0306	4.2		
0922	0.4		
SU 1532	3.9		
2121	0.8		

MARCH

Time	m	Time	m
1 0153	4.2	**16** 0235	4.1
0802	0.4	0843	0.5
SU 1422	4.0	M 1453	3.9
2012	0.5	2049	0.7
2 0229	4.2	**17** 0311	4.0
0836	0.4	0917	0.8
M 1501	3.9	TU 1526	3.7
2051	0.6	2126	0.8
3 0309	4.1	**18** 0351	3.7
0915	0.6	1000	1.0
TU 1543	3.7	W 1605	3.5
2135	0.7	◑ 2215	1.0
4 0357	3.9	**19** 0442	3.4
1004	0.9	1100	1.3
W 1634	3.5	TH 1656	3.3
◑ 2233	0.9	2326	1.2
5 0458	3.6	**20** 0556	3.1
1117	1.2	1219	1.4
TH 1742	3.2	F 1812	3.1
2355	1.1		
6 0625	3.3	**21** 0101	1.2
1302	1.3	0742	3.1
F 1914	3.1	SA 1340	1.4
		1957	3.1
7 0147	1.1	**22** 0233	1.1
0811	3.4	0856	3.4
SA 1435	1.2	SU 1450	1.3
2045	3.4	2106	3.4
8 0317	0.8	**23** 0332	0.9
0930	3.7	0948	3.7
SU 1539	1.0	M 1541	1.1
2151	3.7	2156	3.6
9 0417	0.4	**24** 0415	0.7
1026	4.1	1030	3.9
M 1628	0.8	TU 1620	0.9
2243	4.0	2237	3.8
10 0505	0.2	**25** 0451	0.5
1114	4.3	1106	4.0
TU 1710	0.6	W 1655	0.8
2328	4.2	2313	3.9
11 0548	0.1	**26** 0524	0.5
1157	4.4	1140	4.1
W 1751	0.5	TH 1729	0.7
○		● 2348	4.0
12 0010	4.3	**27** 0558	0.4
0627	0.1	1213	4.1
TH 1238	4.3	F 1803	0.6
1829	0.5		
13 0050	4.3	**28** 0022	4.1
0704	0.1	0631	0.4
F 1315	4.2	SA 1248	4.1
1907	0.5	1839	0.5
14 0126	4.3	**29** 0057	4.2
0739	0.2	0705	0.4
SA 1350	4.1	SU 1323	4.1
1943	0.5	1916	0.5
15 0200	4.2	**30** 0134	4.2
0811	0.4	0740	0.4
SU 1422	4.0	M 1400	4.0
2016	0.6	1956	0.4
		31 0213	4.2
		0817	0.5
		TU 1440	3.9
		2038	0.5

APRIL

Time	m	Time	m
1 0258	4.1	**16** 0326	3.7
0859	0.7	0924	1.0
W 1525	3.7	TH 1534	3.6
2126	0.6	2150	0.9
2 0350	3.8	**17** 0415	3.4
0951	1.0	1020	1.3
TH 1618	3.4	F 1626	3.4
◑ 2229	0.9	◑ 2256	1.1
3 0457	3.5	**18** 0518	3.2
1110	1.3	1137	1.4
F 1731	3.2	SA 1733	3.2
4 0003	1.0	**19** 0016	1.1
0629	3.4	0644	3.2
SA 1256	1.3	SU 1256	1.4
1903	3.2	1857	3.2
5 0148	0.9	**20** 0134	1.0
0804	3.5	0806	3.3
SU 1419	1.2	M 1403	1.3
2025	3.4	2011	3.3
6 0303	0.6	**21** 0238	0.9
0914	3.8	0903	3.6
M 1519	1.0	TU 1457	1.1
2127	3.7	2107	3.5
7 0358	0.3	**22** 0328	0.7
1007	4.1	0948	3.8
TU 1606	0.8	W 1541	0.9
2218	4.0	2152	3.7
8 0443	0.2	**23** 0410	0.6
1052	4.2	1027	4.0
W 1647	0.6	TH 1620	0.8
2303	4.1	2234	3.9
9 0523	0.2	**24** 0449	0.5
1133	4.2	1105	4.1
TH 1728	0.6	F 1659	0.7
○ 2345	4.2	2314	4.0
10 0600	0.2	**25** 0528	0.4
1212	4.2	1143	4.1
F 1806	0.5	SA 1739	0.6
		● 2354	4.1
11 0023	4.2	**26** 0606	0.4
0634	0.3	1223	4.1
SA 1247	4.1	SU 1820	0.5
1844	0.5		
12 0100	4.2	**27** 0036	4.2
0707	0.4	0645	0.4
SU 1320	4.0	M 1303	4.1
1919	0.5	1903	0.4
13 0134	4.1	**28** 0120	4.2
0738	0.5	0725	0.5
M 1350	3.9	TU 1345	4.0
1952	0.6	1948	0.4
14 0209	4.0	**29** 0206	4.2
0810	0.7	0807	0.6
TU 1420	3.9	W 1429	3.9
2025	0.6	2036	0.4
15 0246	3.9	**30** 0256	4.1
0844	0.8	0854	0.8
W 1454	3.8	TH 1518	3.7
2103	0.7	2131	0.5

Chart Datum: 2·16 metres below Ordnance Datum (Newlyn)
HAT is 4·6 metres above Chart Datum

TIDES

267

TIDES

TIME ZONE (UT)
For Summer Time add ONE hour in **non-shaded areas**

LAT 51°51′N   LONG 1°17′E

TIMES AND HEIGHTS OF HIGH AND LOW WATERS

Dates in amber are **SPRINGS**
Dates in yellow are **NEAPS**

2009

MAY

Day	Time	m	Time	m	Time	m	Time	m
1	0354	3.8	0951	1.1	F 1617	3.5	2240	0.7
2	0503	3.6	1107	1.3	SA 1728	3.4		
3	0006	0.7	0621	3.6	SU 1234	1.3	1843	3.4
4	0128	0.6	0737	3.6	M 1349	1.2	◐1952	3.6
5	0236	0.5	0843	3.8	TU 1448	1.0	2054	3.8
6	0330	0.4	0937	4.0	W 1538	0.8	2147	3.9
7	0415	0.3	1024	4.1	TH 1623	0.7	2235	4.0
8	0454	0.4	1106	4.1	F 1705	0.6	2318	4.0
9	0531	0.5	1145	4.0	SA 1746	0.6	2359	4.0
10	0605	0.6	1221	4.0	SU 1825	0.6		
11	0037	4.0	0638	0.6	M 1254	3.9	○1901	0.6
12	0114	3.9	0711	0.7	TU 1325	3.9	1936	0.6
13	0150	3.9	0744	0.8	W 1356	3.8	2010	0.6
14	0226	3.8	0819	0.9	TH 1430	3.8	2047	0.7
15	0306	3.7	0858	1.0	F 1512	3.6	2132	0.8
16	0351	3.5	0946	1.2	SA 1601	3.5	2228	0.9
17	0445	3.4	1049	1.3	SU 1700	3.4	2332	0.9
18	0548	3.3	1200	1.3	M 1806	3.3	◐	
19	0038	0.9	0656	3.4	TU 1306	1.3	1911	3.4
20	0140	0.8	0801	3.5	W 1404	1.2	2011	3.5
21	0237	0.7	0857	3.7	TH 1456	1.0	2105	3.7
22	0328	0.6	0946	3.9	F 1545	0.8	2155	3.9
23	0416	0.5	1032	4.0	SA 1632	0.7	2244	4.1
24	0501	0.5	1117	4.1	SU 1719	0.6	2332	4.2
25	0546	0.5	1202	4.1	M 1807	0.4		
26	0020	4.2	0630	0.5	TU 1249	4.1	●1856	0.4
27	0111	4.3	0715	0.6	W 1336	4.1	1946	0.3
28	0202	4.2	0801	0.7	TH 1425	4.0	2039	0.3
29	0256	4.2	0850	0.8	F 1516	3.9	2136	0.4
30	0352	4.0	0945	1.0	SA 1612	3.8	2239	0.4
31	0453	3.9	1048	1.1	SU 1712	3.7	2346	0.5

JUNE

Day	Time	m	Time	m	Time	m	Time	m
1	0556	3.8	1158	1.2	M 1814	3.7		
2	0053	0.5	0701	3.7	TU 1308	1.2	◐1916	3.7
3	0157	0.6	0804	3.7	W 1412	1.1	2018	3.7
4	0253	0.6	0903	3.8	TH 1509	0.9	2115	3.8
5	0342	0.6	0954	3.9	F 1600	0.6	2208	3.9
6	0425	0.7	1040	3.9	SA 1647	0.7	2256	3.9
7	0504	0.7	1122	3.9	SU 1731	0.6	2340	3.9
8	0541	0.8	1200	3.9	M 1812	0.6		
9	0021	3.9	0615	0.8	TU 1236	3.9	○1849	0.6
10	0059	3.8	0650	0.8	W 1308	3.8	1924	0.6
11	0134	3.8	0724	0.9	TH 1339	3.8	1957	0.6
12	0209	3.8	0758	0.9	F 1413	3.8	2032	0.7
13	0246	3.7	0834	1.0	SA 1452	3.7	2111	0.7
14	0327	3.7	0915	1.0	SU 1536	3.7	2155	0.7
15	0413	3.6	1004	1.1	M 1626	3.6	2247	0.8
16	0505	3.5	1101	1.2	TU 1721	3.5	◐2345	0.8
17	0604	3.5	1206	1.2	W 1822	3.5		
18	0047	0.8	0706	3.5	TH 1311	1.2	1923	3.6
19	0150	0.8	0810	3.6	F 1414	1.1	2025	3.7
20	0251	0.7	0910	3.8	SA 1514	0.9	2125	3.9
21	0348	0.7	1005	3.9	SU 1611	0.7	2222	4.0
22	0441	0.6	1057	4.0	M 1706	0.6	2317	4.2
23	0531	0.6	1148	4.1	TU 1800	0.6		
24	0011	4.3	0618	0.6	W 1238	4.2	1852	0.3
25	0104	4.3	0705	0.6	TH 1328	4.2	●1944	0.2
26	0156	4.3	0751	0.7	F 1416	4.2	2035	0.2
27	0247	4.3	0838	0.8	SA 1504	4.2	2125	0.2
28	0338	4.2	0926	0.9	SU 1553	4.1	2217	0.3
29	0429	4.0	1017	1.0	M 1644	4.0	2311	0.4
30	0523	3.8	1116	1.1	TU 1738	3.8		

JULY

Day	Time	m	Time	m	Time	m	Time	m
1	0009	0.6	0620	3.7	W 1222	1.2	1838	3.7
2	0109	0.8	0722	3.6	TH 1332	1.2	1942	3.6
3	0210	0.9	0826	3.6	F 1440	1.1	2047	3.6
4	0307	0.9	0925	3.6	SA 1541	0.9	◐2147	3.7
5	0357	0.9	1017	3.8	SU 1634	0.8	2240	3.8
6	0442	0.9	1103	3.9	M 1720	0.7	2326	3.9
7	0521	0.9	1144	3.9	TU 1801	0.6		
8	0008	3.9	0557	0.9	W 1221	3.9	1837	0.6
9	0045	3.9	0631	0.9	TH 1254	3.9	1908	0.6
10	0119	3.8	0704	0.9	F 1324	3.9	1939	0.6
11	0150	3.8	0736	0.9	SA 1355	3.9	○2010	0.6
12	0223	3.8	0810	0.9	SU 1429	3.9	2044	0.6
13	0259	3.8	0846	0.9	M 1507	3.9	2120	0.6
14	0340	3.8	0927	1.0	TU 1549	3.8	2202	0.7
15	0427	3.7	1014	1.1	W 1637	3.7	2252	0.8
16	0521	3.6	1113	1.2	TH 1735	3.6	2355	0.9
17	0623	3.5	1223	1.2	F 1842	3.6		
18	0108	1.0	0731	3.5	SA 1338	1.2	◐1954	3.6
19	0222	0.9	0842	3.6	SU 1454	1.0	2105	3.8
20	0330	0.8	0947	3.8	M 1602	0.8	2210	4.0
21	0428	0.8	1045	4.0	TU 1702	0.5	2309	4.2
22	0519	0.7	1137	4.2	W 1755	0.3		
23	0003	4.3	0605	0.6	TH 1227	4.3	1844	0.2
24	0054	4.4	0650	0.6	F 1314	4.4	1932	0.1
25	0140	4.4	0734	0.6	SA 1359	4.4	2017	0.1
26	0228	4.4	0817	0.7	SU 1442	4.4	●2101	0.1
27	0313	4.3	0859	0.8	M 1524	4.3	2144	0.2
28	0357	4.1	0943	0.9	TU 1608	4.1	2228	0.5
29	0442	3.8	1029	1.0	W 1657	3.9	2318	0.8
30	0533	3.6	1132	1.2	TH 1756	3.6		
31	0016	1.0	0634	3.4	F 1248	1.3	1907	3.4

AUGUST

Day	Time	m	Time	m	Time	m	Time	m
1	0122	1.2	0746	3.3	SA 1411	1.2	2023	3.4
2	0231	1.2	0857	3.5	SU 1523	1.1	◐2130	3.6
3	0332	1.2	0955	3.7	M 1620	0.9	2224	3.8
4	0421	1.1	1043	3.9	TU 1705	0.7	2310	3.9
5	0502	1.0	1125	4.0	W 1743	0.6	2350	4.0
6	0537	0.9	1202	4.0	TH 1816	0.6		
7	0026	4.0	0609	0.9	F 1235	4.0	1845	0.6
8	0057	3.9	0641	0.9	SA 1303	4.0	1913	0.6
9	0126	3.9	0712	0.8	SU 1332	4.0	○1943	0.6
10	0156	4.0	0745	0.8	M 1402	4.0	2014	0.6
11	0230	4.0	0819	0.8	TU 1436	4.0	2046	0.6
12	0308	3.9	0857	0.8	W 1513	4.0	2122	0.7
13	0351	3.8	0939	0.9	TH 1558	3.9	2207	0.8
14	0441	3.6	1033	1.1	F 1654	3.7	2308	1.0
15	0543	3.4	1147	1.2	SA 1807	3.5		
16	0035	1.2	0659	3.3	SU 1317	1.2	1934	3.5
17	0205	1.2	0824	3.5	M 1448	1.0	◐2058	3.7
18	0320	1.0	0936	3.7	TU 1559	0.7	2206	4.0
19	0416	0.9	1033	4.0	W 1654	0.4	2301	4.2
20	0504	0.7	1122	4.3	TH 1742	0.2	2351	4.4
21	0548	0.6	1208	4.4	F 1828	0.1		
22	0037	4.5	0630	0.6	SA 1252	4.5	1910	0.1
23	0121	4.5	0711	0.6	SU 1334	4.5	1950	0.1
24	0202	4.4	0752	0.6	M 1413	4.4	2028	0.2
25	0241	4.2	0831	0.7	TU 1451	4.3	●2105	0.4
26	0319	4.1	0910	0.8	W 1531	4.1	2143	0.7
27	0357	3.8	0952	1.0	TH 1615	3.8	2228	1.0
28	0440	3.6	1046	1.2	F 1711	3.5	2325	1.2
29	0537	3.3	1205	1.3	SA 1832	3.3		
30	0038	1.4	0702	3.2	SU 1341	1.3	1959	3.3
31	0156	1.5	0825	3.4	M 1459	1.1	2108	3.5

Chart Datum: 2·16 metres below Ordnance Datum (Newlyn)
HAT is 4·6 metres above Chart Datum

TIME ZONE (UT)
For Summer Time add ONE hour in **non-shaded areas**

ENGLAND–WALTON-ON-THE-NAZE
LAT 51°51′N   LONG 1°17′E
TIMES AND HEIGHTS OF HIGH AND LOW WATERS

Dates in amber are SPRINGS
Dates in yellow are NEAPS

2009

SEPTEMBER

#	Time	m	#	Time	m
1 TU	0305 / 1555 / 2202	1.3 / 3.6 / 0.9 / 3.8	**16** W	0306 / 0920 / 1548 / 2156	1.1 / 3.8 / 0.6 / 4.1
2 W	0357 / 1016 / 1639 / 2246	1.2 / 3.9 / 0.7 / 4.0	**17** TH	0359 / 1014 / 1638 / 2246	0.9 / 4.1 / 0.3 / 4.3
3 TH	0438 / 1058 / 1715 / 2324	1.0 / 4.0 / 0.6 / 4.1	**18** F ●	0444 / 1101 / 1722 / 2331	0.7 / 4.3 / 0.2 / 4.4
4 F ○	0512 / 1134 / 1746 / 2359	0.9 / 4.1 / 0.6 / 4.1	**19** SA	0526 / 1144 / 1803	0.6 / 4.4 / 0.1
5 SA	0544 / 1206 / 1815	0.9 / 4.1 / 0.6	**20** SU	0014 / 0607 / 1226 / 1842	4.4 / 0.6 / 4.5 / 0.2
6 SU	0029 / 0615 / 1235 / 1843	4.1 / 0.8 / 4.1 / 0.6	**21** M	0054 / 0647 / 1305 / 1919	4.4 / 0.6 / 4.4 / 0.3
7 M	0058 / 0647 / 1304 / 1913	4.0 / 0.8 / 4.1 / 0.6	**22** TU	0132 / 0726 / 1343 / 1954	4.3 / 0.6 / 4.4 / 0.4
8 TU	0128 / 0720 / 1335 / 1944	4.1 / 0.7 / 4.1 / 0.6	**23** W	0207 / 0804 / 1420 / 2028	4.2 / 0.7 / 4.2 / 0.6
9 W	0202 / 0756 / 1408 / 2016	4.1 / 0.7 / 4.1 / 0.6	**24** TH	0241 / 0842 / 1458 / 2103	4.0 / 0.8 / 4.0 / 0.8
10 TH	0238 / 0833 / 1447 / 2052	4.0 / 0.8 / 4.1 / 0.8	**25** F	0315 / 0921 / 1540 / 2144	3.8 / 0.8 / 3.8 / 1.1
11 F ○	0319 / 0916 / 1532 / 2136	3.8 / 0.9 / 3.9 / 0.9	**26** SA ○	0353 / 1012 / 1632 / 2241	3.6 / 1.1 / 3.5 / 1.4
12 SA ○	0407 / 1010 / 1629 / 2238	3.6 / 1.1 / 3.6 / 1.2	**27** SU	0443 / 1127 / 1750 / 2356	3.4 / 1.3 / 3.2 / 1.5
13 SU	0510 / 1129 / 1749	3.4 / 1.2 / 3.4	**28** M	0606 / 1301 / 1925	3.2 / 1.3 / 3.2
14 M	0016 / 0637 / 1314 / 1929	1.4 / 3.3 / 1.2 / 3.4	**29** TU	0117 / 0743 / 1420 / 2036	1.6 / 3.3 / 1.2 / 3.5
15 TU	0155 / 0810 / 1444 / 2055	1.3 / 3.4 / 0.9 / 3.7	**30** W	0229 / 0849 / 1517 / 2129	1.4 / 3.5 / 1.0 / 3.7

OCTOBER

#	Time	m	#	Time	m
1 TH	0323 / 0940 / 1601 / 2213	1.2 / 3.8 / 0.8 / 3.9	**16** F	0335 / 0947 / 1614 / 2223	0.9 / 4.1 / 0.3 / 4.3
2 F	0405 / 1021 / 1637 / 2251	1.1 / 3.9 / 0.7 / 4.1	**17** SA	0420 / 1034 / 1657 / 2306	0.8 / 4.3 / 0.3 / 4.3
3 SA	0440 / 1058 / 1709 / 2324	0.9 / 4.0 / 0.6 / 4.1	**18** SU ●	0503 / 1118 / 1736 / 2347	0.7 / 4.3 / 0.3 / 4.3
4 SU ○	0514 / 1131 / 1741 / 2355	0.9 / 4.1 / 0.6 / 4.1	**19** M	0544 / 1159 / 1813	0.6 / 4.3 / 0.4
5 M	0547 / 1203 / 1813	0.8 / 4.1 / 0.6	**20** TU	0025 / 0625 / 1239 / 1848	4.2 / 0.6 / 4.3 / 0.5
6 TU	0027 / 0622 / 1237 / 1845	4.1 / 0.7 / 4.2 / 0.6	**21** W	0102 / 0705 / 1317 / 1922	4.1 / 0.6 / 4.2 / 0.6
7 W	0101 / 0659 / 1312 / 1919	4.1 / 0.7 / 4.2 / 0.6	**22** TH	0135 / 0743 / 1354 / 1956	4.1 / 0.7 / 4.1 / 0.8
8 TH	0137 / 0737 / 1350 / 1954	4.1 / 0.6 / 4.2 / 0.7	**23** F	0207 / 0819 / 1432 / 2030	4.0 / 0.7 / 3.9 / 1.0
9 F	0215 / 0819 / 1432 / 2034	4.0 / 0.6 / 4.1 / 0.8	**24** SA	0240 / 0858 / 1513 / 2109	3.9 / 0.9 / 3.7 / 1.1
10 SA	0257 / 0905 / 1521 / 2121	3.8 / 0.8 / 3.9 / 1.1	**25** SU	0318 / 0946 / 1601 / 2200	3.7 / 1.0 / 3.5 / 1.4
11 SU ○	0347 / 1005 / 1623 / 2227	3.6 / 0.9 / 3.6 / 1.3	**26** M ○	0406 / 1051 / 1703 / 2310	3.5 / 1.1 / 3.3 / 1.5
12 M	0454 / 1130 / 1747	3.4 / 1.1 / 3.4	**27** TU	0512 / 1209 / 1828	3.3 / 1.2 / 3.2
13 TU	0005 / 0623 / 1309 / 1921	1.5 / 3.3 / 1.0 / 3.5	**28** W	0028 / 0640 / 1322 / 1945	1.6 / 3.3 / 1.1 / 3.4
14 W	0135 / 0748 / 1427 / 2037	1.4 / 3.5 / 0.7 / 3.8	**29** TH	0138 / 0754 / 1423 / 2043	1.5 / 3.4 / 1.0 / 3.6
15 TH	0242 / 0853 / 1526 / 2134	1.2 / 3.6 / 0.5 / 4.1	**30** F	0236 / 0850 / 1511 / 2129	1.3 / 3.6 / 0.8 / 3.8
			31 SA	0322 / 0936 / 1553 / 2209	1.1 / 3.8 / 0.7 / 4.0

NOVEMBER

#	Time	m	#	Time	m
1 SU	0403 / 1016 / 1631 / 2246	1.0 / 3.9 / 0.6 / 4.1	**16** M ●	0441 / 1054 / 1708 / 2322	0.7 / 4.2 / 0.5 / 4.1
2 M ○	0441 / 1055 / 1708 / 2322	0.8 / 4.1 / 0.6 / 4.1	**17** TU	0525 / 1137 / 1746	0.6 / 4.2 / 0.6
3 TU	0520 / 1133 / 1745	0.7 / 4.2 / 0.6	**18** W	0000 / 0607 / 1218 / 1821	4.1 / 0.6 / 4.1 / 0.7
4 W	0000 / 0600 / 1214 / 1822	4.2 / 0.6 / 4.2 / 0.6	**19** TH	0037 / 0648 / 1257 / 1856	4.0 / 0.6 / 4.0 / 0.8
5 TH	0039 / 0642 / 1255 / 1901	4.2 / 0.6 / 4.2 / 0.7	**20** F	0110 / 0727 / 1335 / 1930	4.0 / 0.6 / 3.9 / 0.9
6 F	0119 / 0726 / 1339 / 1942	4.1 / 0.5 / 4.2 / 0.7	**21** SA	0142 / 0803 / 1412 / 2004	3.9 / 0.7 / 3.9 / 1.0
7 SA	0201 / 0813 / 1427 / 2026	4.0 / 0.6 / 4.1 / 0.9	**22** SU	0215 / 0839 / 1451 / 2041	3.9 / 0.8 / 3.7 / 1.1
8 SU	0247 / 0905 / 1521 / 2117	3.9 / 0.6 / 3.9 / 1.1	**23** M	0253 / 0921 / 1533 / 2124	3.8 / 0.9 / 3.6 / 1.2
9 M ◗	0341 / 1008 / 1624 / 2221	3.7 / 0.7 / 3.7 / 1.3	**24** TU ◖	0337 / 1012 / 1622 / 2219	3.6 / 1.0 / 3.5 / 1.4
10 TU	0447 / 1126 / 1739 / 2343	3.6 / 0.8 / 3.6 / 1.4	**25** W	0432 / 1113 / 1720 / 2326	3.5 / 1.0 / 3.4 / 1.4
11 W	0604 / 1247 / 1856	3.5 / 0.8 / 3.6	**26** TH	0536 / 1216 / 1826	3.4 / 1.1 / 3.4
12 TU	0102 / 0716 / 1358 / 2005	1.3 / 3.6 / 0.6 / 3.8	**27** F	0033 / 0645 / 1318 / 1933	1.4 / 3.4 / 1.0 / 3.5
13 F	0209 / 0821 / 1457 / 2104	1.2 / 3.6 / 0.5 / 3.9	**28** SA	0136 / 0749 / 1415 / 2032	1.3 / 3.5 / 0.9 / 3.6
14 SA	0306 / 0917 / 1546 / 2154	1.0 / 3.8 / 0.5 / 4.1	**29** SU	0231 / 0846 / 1507 / 2123	1.2 / 3.6 / 0.8 / 3.8
15 SU	0356 / 1007 / 1629 / 2240	0.8 / 4.1 / 0.5 / 4.1	**30** M	0323 / 0936 / 1554 / 2209	1.0 / 3.9 / 0.7 / 4.0

DECEMBER

#	Time	m	#	Time	m
1 TU	0411 / 1023 / 1639 / 2254	0.8 / 4.0 / 0.7 / 4.1	**16** W ●	0513 / 1122 / 1724 / 2342	0.7 / 4.0 / 0.8 / 3.9
2 W ○	0458 / 1110 / 1723 / 2338	0.7 / 4.2 / 0.6 / 4.1	**17** TH	0557 / 1205 / 1801	0.6 / 4.0 / 0.9
3 TH	0545 / 1156 / 1806	0.6 / 4.3 / 0.7	**18** F	0020 / 0637 / 1244 / 1836	3.9 / 0.6 / 4.0 / 0.9
4 F	0022 / 0633 / 1245 / 1849	4.2 / 0.5 / 4.3 / 0.7	**19** SA	0054 / 0714 / 1320 / 1909	3.9 / 0.6 / 3.9 / 0.9
5 SA	0108 / 0722 / 1334 / 1934	4.1 / 0.4 / 4.3 / 0.8	**20** SU	0125 / 0747 / 1354 / 1942	3.9 / 0.6 / 3.8 / 0.9
6 SU	0155 / 0812 / 1424 / 2020	3.9 / 0.4 / 4.2 / 0.8	**21** M	0156 / 0819 / 1428 / 2016	3.9 / 0.7 / 3.8 / 1.0
7 M	0243 / 0904 / 1518 / 2109	4.0 / 0.4 / 4.1 / 1.0	**22** TU	0231 / 0853 / 1504 / 2053	3.8 / 0.7 / 3.7 / 1.0
8 TU	0335 / 1002 / 1614 / 2205	3.9 / 0.5 / 3.9 / 1.1	**23** W	0310 / 0933 / 1546 / 2135	3.8 / 0.8 / 3.7 / 1.1
9 W ◗	0432 / 1105 / 1716 / 2309	3.8 / 0.6 / 3.8 / 1.2	**24** TH ◖	0355 / 1020 / 1633 / 2226	3.7 / 0.9 / 3.6 / 1.2
10 TH	0534 / 1212 / 1820	3.7 / 0.6 / 3.7	**25** F	0447 / 1115 / 1728 / 2327	3.6 / 0.9 / 3.5 / 1.3
11 F	0020 / 0640 / 1319 / 1926	1.2 / 3.7 / 0.7 / 3.7	**26** SA	0547 / 1217 / 1830	3.5 / 1.0 / 3.4
12 SA	0130 / 0745 / 1420 / 2029	1.2 / 3.7 / 0.7 / 3.7	**27** SU	0034 / 0652 / 1321 / 1936	1.3 / 3.5 / 1.0 / 3.5
13 SU	0235 / 0848 / 1515 / 2126	1.1 / 3.8 / 0.7 / 3.8	**28** M	0141 / 0759 / 1424 / 2041	1.3 / 3.6 / 0.9 / 3.6
14 M	0333 / 0945 / 1603 / 2216	0.9 / 3.9 / 0.8 / 3.9	**29** TU	0245 / 0902 / 1524 / 2139	1.0 / 3.7 / 0.8 / 3.7
15 TU	0425 / 1036 / 1645 / 2301	0.8 / 4.0 / 0.8 / 3.9	**30** W	0346 / 1000 / 1618 / 2232	0.9 / 3.9 / 0.8 / 4.0
			31 TH ○	0443 / 1054 / 1707 / 2323	0.7 / 4.1 / 0.7 / 4.1

Chart Datum: 2·16 metres below Ordnance Datum (Newlyn)
HAT is 4·6 metres above Chart Datum

TIDES

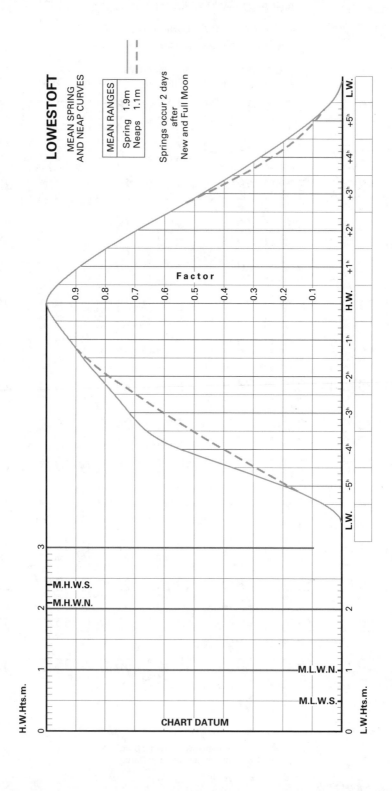

LOWESTOFT

MEAN SPRING
AND NEAP CURVES

MEAN RANGES

Spring 1.9m
Neaps 1.1m

Springs occur 2 days
after
New and Full Moon

ENGLAND – LOWESTOFT

LAT 52°28′N   LONG 1°45′E

TIMES AND HEIGHTS OF HIGH AND LOW WATERS

Dates in amber are **SPRINGS**
Dates in yellow are **NEAPS**

2009

JANUARY

Time m   Time m

Day	Time	m	Time	m	Time	m	Time	m
1 TH	0618	0.7	1227	2.2	1805	1.0		
2 F	0025	2.5	0656	0.8	1306	2.2	1845	1.1
3 SA	0105	2.5	0736	0.8	1348	2.2	1929	1.1
4 SU ☽	0148	2.4	0821	0.8	1438	2.1	2019	1.2
5 M	0235	2.4	0915	0.9	1549	2.1	2117	1.2
6 TU	0333	2.4	1027	0.9	1712	2.2	2235	1.2
7 W	0455	2.3	1140	0.9	1810	2.2	2359	1.1
8 TH	0610	2.4	1241	0.9	1902	2.3		
9 F	0106	1.0	0714	2.4	1338	0.9	1951	2.4
10 SA	0208	0.8	0817	2.5	1433	0.8	2039	2.4
11 SU ○	0308	0.6	0917	2.5	1526	0.8	2126	2.6
12 M	0403	0.4	1011	2.6	1615	0.8	2212	2.7
13 TU	0454	0.3	1100	2.5	1700	0.9	2258	2.7
14 W	0541	0.2	1148	2.5	1741	0.9	2343	2.7
15 TH	0625	0.3	1234	2.4	1820	0.9		
16 F	0027	2.7	0709	0.4	1323	2.2	1858	1.0
17 SA	0112	2.6	0754	0.6	1415	2.1	1938	1.1
18 SU ☽	0200	2.5	0843	0.8	1522	2.1	2026	1.2
19 M	0257	2.4	0943	0.9	1630	2.1	2134	1.3
20 TU	0415	2.2	1053	1.1	1730	2.1	2321	1.3
21 W	0536	2.2	1157	1.2	1829	2.1		
22 TH	0035	1.2	0659	2.2	1254	1.2	1921	2.2
23 F	0136	1.1	0804	2.2	1343	1.2	2003	2.3
24 SA	0224	0.9	0849	2.2	1424	1.1	2037	2.4
25 SU	0304	0.8	0925	2.3	1459	1.1	2108	2.4
26 M	0340	0.7	0956	2.3	1530	1.0	2140	2.5
27 TU	0414	0.7	1025	2.3	1602	0.9	2214	2.5
28 W	0448	0.6	1055	2.3	1636	0.9	2249	2.6
29 TH	0522	0.6	1126	2.3	1711	0.8	2325	2.6
30 F	0556	0.6	1159	2.3	1746	0.9		
31 SA	0000	2.6	0629	0.6	1235	2.2	1821	0.9

FEBRUARY

Time m   Time m

Day	Time	m	Time	m	Time	m	Time	m
1 SU	0037	2.5	0703	0.7	1313	2.2	1901	1.0
2 M ☽	0117	2.5	0742	0.8	1357	2.2	1947	1.0
3 TU	0204	2.4	0830	0.9	1452	2.1	2043	1.1
4 W	0304	2.3	0936	1.0	1614	2.1	2200	1.1
5 TH	0435	2.3	1113	1.1	1734	2.1	2343	1.0
6 F	0603	2.3	1226	1.1	1835	2.2		
7 SA	0056	0.9	0717	2.4	1329	1.0	1930	2.3
8 SU	0202	0.7	0822	2.4	1427	0.9	2022	2.5
9 M ○	0302	0.5	0914	2.5	1518	0.9	2109	2.6
10 TU	0352	0.3	1000	2.5	1602	0.8	2155	2.7
11 W	0437	0.2	1042	2.5	1642	0.7	2238	2.8
12 TH	0519	0.2	1123	2.4	1719	0.7	2321	2.8
13 F	0559	0.3	1203	2.3	1755	0.8		
14 SA	0003	2.7	0636	0.4	1243	2.2	1829	0.9
15 SU	0045	2.6	0713	0.6	1321	2.2	1907	1.0
16 M ☽	0129	2.4	0752	0.9	1403	2.1	1950	1.1
17 TU	0222	2.3	0837	1.1	1456	2.1	2047	1.2
18 W	0345	2.1	0950	1.3	1618	2.0	2246	1.2
19 TH	0519	2.1	1131	1.3	1730	2.1		
20 F	0013	1.1	0648	2.1	1238	1.3	1835	2.1
21 SA	0114	1.0	0750	2.2	1330	1.2	1929	2.2
22 SU	0200	0.9	0831	2.2	1409	1.2	2007	2.3
23 M	0239	0.8	0903	2.3	1441	1.0	2041	2.4
24 TU	0314	0.7	0930	2.3	1511	0.9	2114	2.5
25 W ●	0347	0.6	0957	2.3	1543	0.8	2149	2.5
26 TH	0421	0.5	1027	2.4	1617	0.7	2224	2.6
27 F	0455	0.5	1058	2.4	1652	0.7	2300	2.6
28 SA	0529	0.5	1131	2.3	1726	0.7	2336	2.6

MARCH

Time m   Time m

Day	Time	m	Time	m	Time	m	Time	m
1 SU	0601	0.5	1206	2.3	1801	0.8		
2 M	0013	2.5	0634	0.6	1245	2.3	1839	0.8
3 TU	0055	2.5	0712	0.8	1328	2.2	1926	0.9
4 W ☽	0146	2.4	0800	0.9	1421	2.1	2025	1.0
5 TH	0254	2.3	0906	1.1	1533	2.1	2154	1.0
6 F	0443	2.2	1059	1.2	1701	2.1	2337	0.9
7 SA	0612	2.2	1219	1.2	1810	2.2		
8 SU	0048	0.7	0725	2.3	1324	1.1	1910	2.3
9 M	0153	0.5	0819	2.4	1418	1.0	2002	2.5
10 TU	0247	0.4	0902	2.4	1502	0.9	2049	2.6
11 W ○	0333	0.3	0940	2.4	1542	0.7	2133	2.7
12 TH	0414	0.2	1018	2.4	1619	0.7	2216	2.7
13 F	0452	0.3	1055	2.4	1655	0.7	2258	2.7
14 SA	0528	0.4	1131	2.3	1730	0.7	2339	2.6
15 SU	0602	0.5	1206	2.3	1804	0.8		
16 M	0020	2.5	0634	0.7	1240	2.2	1840	0.8
17 TU	0103	2.3	0707	0.9	1316	2.2	1922	1.0
18 W ☽	0155	2.2	0744	1.1	1400	2.1	2014	1.1
19 TH	0321	2.0	0833	1.3	1458	2.1	2157	1.1
20 F	0457	2.0	1055	1.4	1623	2.0	2340	1.1
21 SA	0616	2.1	1212	1.4	1738	2.1		
22 SU	0035	0.9	0718	2.1	1301	1.3	1837	2.1
23 M	0122	0.8	0759	2.2	1338	1.2	1924	2.2
24 TU	0201	0.7	0830	2.3	1410	1.0	2004	2.3
25 W	0237	0.6	0858	2.3	1442	0.9	2042	2.4
26 TH	0313	0.5	0926	2.3	1517	0.8	2119	2.5
27 F	0349	0.4	0957	2.4	1554	0.7	2157	2.6
28 SA	0425	0.4	1030	2.4	1631	0.6	2235	2.6
29 SU	0501	0.5	1105	2.4	1708	0.6	2314	2.6
30 M	0536	0.5	1142	2.4	1746	0.7	2356	2.5
31 TU	0612	0.7	1221	2.3	1829	0.7		

APRIL

Time m   Time m

Day	Time	m	Time	m	Time	m	Time	m
1 W	0043	2.4	0653	0.9	1307	2.3	1920	0.8
2 TH ☽	0142	2.3	0744	1.1	1402	2.2	2027	0.8
3 F	0308	2.2	0852	1.2	1511	2.1	2203	0.8
4 SA	0456	2.2	1047	1.3	1633	2.1	2327	0.7
5 SU	0614	2.3	1205	1.2	1744	2.2		
6 M	0033	0.6	0717	2.3	1306	1.1	1845	2.3
7 TU	0133	0.5	0804	2.3	1357	1.0	1938	2.4
8 W	0223	0.4	0842	2.4	1440	0.9	2026	2.5
9 TH ○	0307	0.3	0917	2.4	1519	0.7	2111	2.6
10 F	0346	0.4	0952	2.4	1556	0.6	2155	2.6
11 SA	0422	0.4	1027	2.4	1633	0.6	2237	2.5
12 SU	0456	0.5	1101	2.4	1709	0.6	2319	2.4
13 M	0528	0.7	1134	2.3	1744	0.7		
14 TU	0000	2.3	0557	0.9	1206	2.3	1819	0.8
15 W	0044	2.2	0627	1.0	1242	2.3	1900	0.9
16 TH	0135	2.1	0704	1.2	1325	2.2	1950	0.9
17 F	0255	2.0	0750	1.3	1418	2.1	2102	1.0
18 SA	0424	2.0	0850	1.4	1522	2.1	2251	1.0
19 SU	0530	2.0	1111	1.4	1642	2.1	2348	0.9
20 M	0629	2.1	1208	1.3	1746	2.1		
21 TU	0034	0.8	0714	2.2	1250	1.2	1838	2.2
22 W	0116	0.7	0749	2.2	1328	1.1	1924	2.3
23 TH	0156	0.6	0821	2.3	1407	0.9	2007	2.4
24 F	0236	0.5	0854	2.4	1448	0.8	2049	2.5
25 SA ●	0316	0.5	0928	2.4	1530	0.7	2131	2.5
26 SU	0356	0.5	1004	2.4	1612	0.6	2214	2.5
27 M	0436	0.5	1042	2.4	1655	0.6	2259	2.5
28 TU	0516	0.6	1122	2.4	1740	0.5	2348	2.5
29 W	0558	0.8	1205	2.4	1829	0.6		
30 TH	0043	2.4	0643	0.9	1254	2.3	1925	0.6

Chart Datum: 1·50 metres below Ordnance Datum (Newlyn)
HAT is 2·9 metres above Chart Datum

TIDES

TIME ZONE (UT)
For Summer Time add ONE hour in **non-shaded areas**

ENGLAND – LOWESTOFT
LAT 52°28'N LONG 1°45'E
TIMES AND HEIGHTS OF HIGH AND LOW WATERS

Dates in amber are **SPRINGS**
Dates in yellow are NEAPS

2009

MAY

Day				
1 F	0150 2.3	0736 1.1	1349 2.3	2034 0.6
2 SA	0325 2.2	0842 1.3	1453 2.2	2155 0.6
3 SU	0449 2.2	1017 1.3	1605 2.2	2306 0.6
4 M	0557 2.3	1133 1.3	1716 2.3	☽
5 TU	0007 0.5	0654 2.3	1235 1.2	1818 2.3
6 W	0104 0.5	0740 2.3	1328 1.0	1914 2.4
7 TH	0154 0.5	0817 2.3	1414 0.9	2004 2.4
8 F	0237 0.5	0852 2.4	1456 0.8	2052 2.4
9 SA	0316 0.6	0927 2.4	1536 0.7	2138 2.4
10 SU	0352 0.6	1001 2.4	1615 0.6	2223 2.4
11 M	0426 0.7	1035 2.4	1652 0.6	2305 2.3 ○
12 TU	0457 0.8	1107 2.4	1728 0.7	2347 2.2
13 W	0526 0.9	1139 2.4	1805 0.7	
14 TH	0029 2.2	0557 1.0	1216 2.3	1844 0.8
15 F	0115 2.1	0635 1.1	1258 2.3	1929 0.8
16 SA	0212 2.0	0720 1.2	1347 2.2	2024 0.9
17 SU	0334 2.0	0812 1.3	1441 2.2	2135 0.9
18 M	0441 2.0	0914 1.4	1542 2.2	2247 0.9 ☾
19 TU	0535 2.1	1038 1.3	1652 2.2	2342 0.8
20 W	0623 2.1	1151 1.2	1753 2.2	
21 TH	0030 0.7	0705 2.2	1245 1.1	1845 2.3
22 F	0116 0.6	0745 2.3	1333 1.0	1934 2.3
23 SA	0201 0.6	0823 2.3	1421 0.8	2022 2.4
24 SU	0246 0.6	0901 2.4	1509 0.7	2110 2.5
25 M	0332 0.6	0941 2.5	1558 0.6	2200 2.5
26 TU	0417 0.6	1023 2.5	1647 0.5	2252 2.5 ●
27 W	0503 0.7	1107 2.5	1738 0.4	2347 2.5
28 TH	0549 0.8	1153 2.5	1831 0.4	
29 F	0044 2.4	0635 1.0	1243 2.5	1925 0.4
30 SA	0149 2.3	0725 1.1	1335 2.4	2025 0.4
31 SU	0311 2.2	0821 1.2	1432 2.4	2131 0.5

JUNE

Day				
1 M	0425 2.2	0930 1.3	1536 2.4	2236 0.5
2 TU	0527 2.2	1049 1.3	1646 2.4	2336 0.6 ☽
3 W	0623 2.2	1157 1.2	1752 2.3	
4 TH	0032 0.7	0711 2.2	1258 1.1	1853 2.3
5 F	0123 0.7	0753 2.3	1351 0.9	1951 2.3
6 SA	0208 0.8	0830 2.3	1439 0.8	2044 2.3
7 SU	0249 0.8	0906 2.4	1522 0.7	2132 2.3
8 M	0327 0.9	0940 2.4	1603 0.7	2216 2.3
9 TU	0401 0.9	1013 2.4	1641 0.7	2257 2.3 ○
10 W	0432 0.9	1045 2.5	1717 0.7	2335 2.2
11 TH	0502 1.0	1119 2.4	1753 0.7	
12 F	0011 2.2	0535 1.0	1156 2.4	1829 0.7
13 SA	0049 2.1	0613 1.1	1236 2.4	1908 0.7
14 SU	0130 2.1	0654 1.1	1319 2.4	1950 0.8
15 M	0216 2.1	0740 1.2	1404 2.3	2039 0.8
16 TU	0318 2.0	0832 1.2	1454 2.3	2137 0.8 ☾
17 W	0436 2.1	0932 1.3	1552 2.2	2245 0.8
18 TH	0534 2.1	1050 1.3	1705 2.2	2346 0.8
19 F	0624 2.2	1204 1.1	1810 2.3	
20 SA	0041 0.8	0710 2.3	1304 1.0	1907 2.3
21 SU	0133 0.7	0754 2.3	1359 0.8	2003 2.4
22 M	0223 0.7	0838 2.4	1454 0.7	2100 2.5
23 TU	0314 0.7	0922 2.5	1549 0.5	2155 2.5
24 W	0404 0.7	1007 2.6	1642 0.4	2249 2.5
25 TH	0452 0.8	1053 2.6	1733 0.3	2341 2.5 ●
26 F	0538 0.8	1140 2.7	1822 0.2	
27 SA	0033 2.4	0622 0.9	1227 2.7	1911 0.3
28 SU	0128 2.3	0706 1.0	1315 2.6	2002 0.4
29 M	0232 2.2	0751 1.1	1406 2.5	2057 0.5
30 TU	0345 2.2	0844 1.2	1504 2.4	2158 0.7

JULY

Day				
1 W	0448 2.1	0956 1.2	1616 2.3	2301 0.8
2 TH	0545 2.2	1121 1.2	1730 2.3	
3 F	0001 0.9	0639 2.2	1233 1.1	1842 2.2
4 SA	0056 1.0	0729 2.3	1336 1.0	1951 2.2 ☽
5 SU	0146 1.0	0811 2.3	1428 0.9	2045 2.2
6 M	0231 1.0	0848 2.4	1512 0.8	2129 2.3
7 TU	0309 1.0	0921 2.4	1552 0.7	2207 2.3
8 W	0343 1.0	0953 2.5	1628 0.7	2242 2.3
9 TH	0414 1.0	1026 2.5	1702 0.6	2314 2.3
10 F	0444 0.9	1100 2.5	1735 0.6	2345 2.2
11 SA	0517 0.9	1135 2.5	1808 0.6 ○	
12 SU	0017 2.2	0552 1.0	1212 2.5	1841 0.7
13 M	0053 2.2	0630 1.0	1250 2.5	1917 0.7
14 TU	0131 2.2	0711 1.1	1330 2.4	1957 0.8
15 W	0215 2.1	0756 1.1	1414 2.4	2043 0.8
16 TH	0311 2.1	0850 1.2	1506 2.3	2144 0.9
17 F	0435 2.1	0959 1.2	1620 2.3	2305 0.9
18 SA	0542 2.2	1131 1.2	1744 2.3 ☾	
19 SU	0013 0.9	0637 2.3	1242 1.0	1852 2.3
20 M	0112 0.9	0728 2.4	1344 0.8	1956 2.4
21 TU	0208 0.9	0817 2.5	1444 0.6	2057 2.5
22 W	0302 0.8	0904 2.6	1541 0.4	2150 2.5
23 TH	0353 0.8	0951 2.7	1632 0.2	2238 2.5
24 F	0439 0.8	1036 2.8	1719 0.2	2324 2.5
25 SA	0522 0.8	1121 2.8	1804 0.2 ●	2345 2.2
26 SU	0010 2.4	0601 0.8	1206 2.8	1847 0.3
27 M	0056 2.3	0640 0.9	1251 2.7	1930 0.4
28 TU	0145 2.2	0721 1.0	1338 2.6	2016 0.6
29 W	0242 2.2	0807 1.1	1433 2.4	2110 0.9
30 TH	0354 2.1	0908 1.2	1550 2.3	2221 1.1
31 F	0459 2.1	1049 1.2	1715 2.2	2333 1.2

AUGUST

Day				
1 SA	0600 2.2	1214 1.2	1840 2.2	
2 SU	0036 1.2	0659 2.2	1323 1.0	1950 2.2 ☽
3 M	0133 1.2	0748 2.3	1415 0.9	2037 2.3
4 TU	0218 1.2	0826 2.4	1456 0.8	2115 2.3
5 W	0255 1.1	0858 2.5	1532 0.7	2148 2.3
6 TH	0325 1.0	0929 2.5	1606 0.6	2217 2.3
7 F	0354 1.0	1002 2.6	1638 0.6	2245 2.3
8 SA	0425 0.9	1036 2.6	1709 0.6	2314 2.3
9 SU	0457 0.9	1110 2.6	1741 0.6	2345 2.3 ○
10 M	0531 0.9	1145 2.6	1812 0.6	
11 TU	0019 2.3	0605 0.9	1221 2.6	1844 0.7
12 W	0055 2.3	0643 1.0	1259 2.5	1919 0.8
13 TH	0137 2.2	0726 1.1	1343 2.4	2002 0.9
14 F	0226 2.2	0819 1.1	1437 2.4	2059 1.0
15 SA	0334 2.2	0928 1.2	1556 2.3	2227 1.1
16 SU	0501 2.2	1111 1.1	1734 2.3	2354 1.1
17 M	0607 2.3	1227 0.9	1850 2.4 ☾	
18 TU	0058 1.1	0703 2.4	1333 0.7	1956 2.4
19 W	0157 1.0	0755 2.5	1433 0.5	2050 2.5
20 TH	0251 0.9	0843 2.7	1527 0.3	2136 2.6
21 F	0337 0.8	0929 2.8	1614 0.2	2218 2.6
22 SA	0420 0.8	1014 2.9	1657 0.2	2300 2.5
23 SU	0459 0.7	1058 2.9	1738 0.2	2341 2.5
24 M	0537 0.8	1142 2.7	1817 0.4 ○	
25 TU	0021 2.4	0614 0.8	1226 2.7	1854 0.6 ●
26 W	0102 2.3	0653 0.9	1312 2.6	1934 0.8
27 TH	0145 2.2	0738 1.0	1406 2.4	2018 1.1
28 F	0238 2.2	0835 1.2	1530 2.2	2121 1.3
29 SA	0355 2.2	1021 1.2	1702 2.2	2306 1.4
30 SU	0508 2.2	1153 1.1	1827 2.2	
31 M	0019 1.4	0612 2.2	1257 1.0	1933 2.2

Chart Datum: 1·50 metres below Ordnance Datum (Newlyn)
HAT is 2·9 metres above Chart Datum

ENGLAND – LOWESTOFT

LAT 52°28′N   LONG 1°45′E

TIMES AND HEIGHTS OF HIGH AND LOW WATERS

Dates in amber are **SPRINGS**
Dates in yellow are **NEAPS**

2009

SEPTEMBER

Day	Time m	Day	Time m
1 TU	0115 1.3 / 0709 2.3 / 1346 0.9 / 2017 2.3	**16** W	0045 1.2 / 0636 2.4 / 1319 0.6 / 1949 2.5
2 W	0157 1.2 / 0751 2.4 / 1426 0.8 / 2051 2.3	**17** TH	0143 1.1 / 0730 2.6 / 1416 0.5 / 2035 2.5
3 TH	0230 1.1 / 0825 2.5 / 1501 0.7 / 2119 2.4	**18** F	0232 1.0 / 0819 2.7 / 1505 0.3 / ● 2115 2.6
4 F	0259 1.0 / 0858 2.6 / 1533 0.6 / ○ 2145 2.4	**19** SA	0316 0.9 / 0905 2.8 / 1549 0.3 / 2153 2.6
5 SA	0328 0.9 / 0932 2.6 / 1605 0.6 / 2212 2.4	**20** SU	0356 0.8 / 0951 2.9 / 1629 0.3 / 2232 2.5
6 SU	0400 0.9 / 1007 2.7 / 1637 0.6 / 2242 2.4	**21** M	0435 0.7 / 1035 2.8 / 1708 0.4 / 2310 2.5
7 M	0434 0.8 / 1042 2.7 / 1709 0.6 / 2314 2.4	**22** TU	0513 0.7 / 1119 2.8 / 1744 0.6 / 2348 2.4
8 TU	0508 0.8 / 1118 2.6 / 1741 0.6 / 2348 2.4	**23** W	0551 0.8 / 1203 2.6 / 1819 0.8
9 W	0543 0.9 / 1154 2.6 / 1813 0.7	**24** TH	0024 2.4 / 0630 0.9 / 1249 2.5 / 1853 1.0
10 TH	0025 2.4 / 0620 0.9 / 1235 2.5 / 1848 0.8	**25** F	0103 2.3 / 0713 1.0 / 1344 2.3 / 1931 1.2
11 F	0107 2.3 / 0705 1.0 / 1322 2.4 / 1933 1.0	**26** SA	0147 2.3 / 0808 1.1 / 1512 2.2 / ◑ 2019 1.4
12 SA	0156 2.3 / 0801 1.1 / 1424 2.3 / ◑ 2030 1.2	**27** SU	0244 2.2 / 0945 1.2 / 2211 1.5
13 SU	0300 2.1 / 0918 1.1 / 1559 2.3 / 2201 1.3	**28** M	0404 2.2 / 1120 1.1 / 1755 2.2 / 2349 1.5
14 M	0423 2.3 / 1103 1.0 / 1738 2.3 / 2340 1.3	**29** TU	0516 2.2 / 1217 1.0 / 1900 2.3
15 TU	0537 2.3 / 1215 0.8 / 1851 2.4	**30** W	0041 1.4 / 0614 2.3 / 1305 0.9 / 1944 2.3

OCTOBER

Day	Time m	Day	Time m
1 TH	0122 1.3 / 0702 2.4 / 1345 0.8 / 2017 2.4	**16** F	0119 1.2 / 0703 2.6 / 1350 0.5 / 2013 2.5
2 F	0154 1.2 / 0743 2.5 / 1421 0.7 / 2044 2.4	**17** SA	0207 1.0 / 0754 2.7 / 1438 0.4 / 2050 2.5
3 SA	0225 1.1 / 0822 2.5 / 1454 0.7 / 2110 2.4	**18** SU	0251 0.9 / 0842 2.8 / 1520 0.5 / ● 2127 2.5
4 SU	0258 0.9 / 0859 2.6 / 1528 0.6 / ○ 2139 2.5	**19** M	0333 0.8 / 0929 2.8 / 1600 0.5 / 2204 2.6
5 M	0333 0.8 / 0937 2.7 / 1603 0.6 / 2211 2.5	**20** TU	0413 0.7 / 1015 2.7 / 1637 0.6 / 2241 2.5
6 TU	0410 0.8 / 1015 2.7 / 1638 0.6 / 2245 2.5	**21** W	0453 0.7 / 1100 2.6 / 1711 0.8 / 2317 2.5
7 W	0448 0.8 / 1053 2.6 / 1712 0.7 / 2321 2.5	**22** TH	0532 0.8 / 1145 2.5 / 1744 0.9 / 2352 2.5
8 TH	0526 0.8 / 1134 2.6 / 1748 0.8	**23** F	0611 0.9 / 1231 2.3 / 1816 1.1
9 F	0000 2.5 / 0608 0.8 / 1220 2.5 / 1827 0.9	**24** SA	0028 2.4 / 0653 0.9 / 1326 2.2 / 1851 1.3
10 SA	0044 2.4 / 0657 0.9 / 1314 2.4 / 1915 1.1	**25** SU	0111 2.4 / 0744 1.0 / 1443 2.1 / 1935 1.4
11 SU	0135 2.4 / 0758 0.9 / 1424 2.3 / ◑ 2014 1.3	**26** M	0202 2.3 / 0854 1.1 / 1605 2.1 / ◑ 2030 1.5
12 M	0238 2.3 / 0921 0.9 / 1615 2.3 / 2142 1.4	**27** TU	0304 2.3 / 1032 1.1 / 1711 2.2 / 2225 1.6
13 TU	0352 2.3 / 1051 0.8 / 1736 2.3 / 2319 1.4	**28** W	0417 2.3 / 1131 1.0 / 1810 2.2 / 2347 1.5
14 W	0507 2.4 / 1157 0.7 / 1840 2.4	**29** TH	0522 2.3 / 1217 0.9 / 1858 2.3
15 TH	0023 1.3 / 0608 2.5 / 1257 0.6 / 1931 2.5	**30** F	0031 1.4 / 0615 2.4 / 1259 0.8 / 1933 2.3
		31 SA	0109 1.2 / 0702 2.4 / 1337 0.8 / 2004 2.4

NOVEMBER

Day	Time m	Day	Time m
1 SU	0147 1.1 / 0746 2.5 / 1414 0.7 / 2035 2.5	**16** M	0229 0.9 / 0824 2.6 / 1452 0.7 / ● 2103 2.5
2 M	0226 1.0 / 0827 2.6 / 1452 0.6 / ○ 2108 2.5	**17** TU	0314 0.8 / 0914 2.6 / 1532 0.7 / 2140 2.6
3 TU	0307 0.9 / 0909 2.6 / 1531 0.6 / 2143 2.5	**18** W	0357 0.7 / 1002 2.5 / 1609 0.8 / 2217 2.6
4 W	0349 0.8 / 0951 2.6 / 1611 0.7 / 2220 2.6	**19** TH	0438 0.7 / 1048 2.5 / 1643 0.9 / 2252 2.6
5 TH	0432 0.7 / 1035 2.6 / 1650 0.7 / 2259 2.6	**20** F	0518 0.8 / 1133 2.4 / 1714 1.0 / 2325 2.5
6 F	0517 0.7 / 1122 2.6 / 1732 0.9 / 2341 2.5	**21** SA	0557 0.8 / 1217 2.3 / 1745 1.1
7 SA	0605 0.7 / 1214 2.5 / 1816 1.0	**22** SU	0001 2.5 / 0636 0.9 / 1302 2.2 / 1819 1.2
8 SU	0027 2.5 / 0659 0.7 / 1314 2.4 / 1905 1.2	**23** M	0042 2.4 / 0719 0.9 / 1355 2.1 / 1901 1.3
9 M	0120 2.5 / 0801 0.7 / 1429 2.3 / ◐ 2002 1.3	**24** TU	0129 2.4 / 0809 1.0 / 1506 2.1 / ◐ 1949 1.4
10 TU	0218 2.4 / 0915 0.7 / 1608 2.3 / 2115 1.4	**25** W	0220 2.3 / 0911 1.0 / 1617 2.1 / 2045 1.5
11 W	0324 2.4 / 1029 0.7 / 1718 2.3 / 2243 1.4	**26** TH	0317 2.3 / 1024 1.0 / 1713 2.1 / 2155 1.5
12 TH	0436 2.4 / 1132 0.7 / 1817 2.4 / 2351 1.3	**27** F	0424 2.3 / 1122 1.0 / 1802 2.2 / 2322 1.4
13 F	0541 2.5 / 1229 0.6 / 1907 2.4	**28** SA	0529 2.3 / 1210 0.9 / 1846 2.3
14 SA	0049 1.2 / 0639 2.5 / 1322 0.6 / 1949 2.4	**29** SU	0021 1.3 / 0623 2.4 / 1255 0.8 / 1925 2.4
15 SU	0141 1.0 / 0733 2.6 / 1409 0.6 / 2026 2.5	**30** M	0111 1.1 / 0713 2.4 / 1338 0.8 / 2002 2.4

DECEMBER

Day	Time m	Day	Time m
1 TU	0158 1.0 / 0800 2.5 / 1422 0.7 / 2040 2.5	**16** W	0304 0.8 / 0912 2.4 / 1511 0.9 / ● 2121 2.5
2 W	0245 0.8 / 0848 2.5 / 1506 0.7 / ○ 2119 2.5	**17** TH	0348 0.7 / 0958 2.4 / 1548 1.0 / 2157 2.5
3 TH	0333 0.7 / 0936 2.6 / 1551 0.7 / 2159 2.6	**18** F	0428 0.7 / 1041 2.4 / 1622 1.0 / 2231 2.5
4 F	0423 0.6 / 1026 2.6 / 1636 0.8 / 2242 2.6	**19** SA	0506 0.7 / 1120 2.3 / 1652 1.0 / 2305 2.5
5 SA	0513 0.5 / 1118 2.5 / 1722 0.9 / 2327 2.6	**20** SU	0542 0.7 / 1156 2.3 / 1722 1.1 / 2340 2.5
6 SU	0605 0.5 / 1212 2.5 / 1808 1.0	**21** M	0617 0.8 / 1232 2.2 / 1756 1.1
7 M	0014 2.6 / 0657 0.5 / 1309 2.4 / 1854 1.1	**22** TU	0018 2.5 / 0652 0.8 / 1309 2.2 / 1834 1.1
8 TU	0105 2.6 / 0752 0.5 / 1414 2.3 / 1944 1.2	**23** W	0059 2.5 / 0730 0.9 / 1350 2.1 / 1917 1.2
9 W	0157 2.6 / 0852 0.6 / 1538 2.2 / ◐ 2041 1.3	**24** TH	0143 2.4 / 0813 0.9 / 1439 2.1 / ◐ 2004 1.3
10 TH	0256 2.5 / 0958 0.6 / 1648 2.2 / 2153 1.3	**25** F	0230 2.3 / 0904 1.0 / 1554 2.1 / 2059 1.3
11 F	0405 2.5 / 1101 0.7 / 1746 2.3 / 2313 1.3	**26** SA	0325 2.3 / 1010 1.0 / 1705 2.1 / 2209 1.3
12 SA	0517 2.4 / 1200 0.8 / 1839 2.3	**27** SU	0436 2.3 / 1120 1.0 / 1759 2.2 / 2335 1.3
13 SU	0020 1.2 / 0621 2.4 / 1255 0.8 / 1925 2.3	**28** M	0547 2.3 / 1217 0.9 / 1847 2.3
14 M	0121 1.1 / 0722 2.4 / 1345 0.9 / 2006 2.4	**29** TU	0039 1.1 / 0646 2.3 / 1309 0.9 / 1932 2.4
15 TU	0215 0.9 / 0820 2.4 / 1430 0.9 / 2044 2.5	**30** W	0135 1.0 / 0741 2.4 / 1359 0.8 / 2015 2.4
		31 TH	0228 0.8 / 0836 2.5 / 1448 0.8 / ○ 2059 2.5

Chart Datum: 1·50 metres below Ordnance Datum (Newlyn)
HAT is 2·9 metres above Chart Datum

TIDES

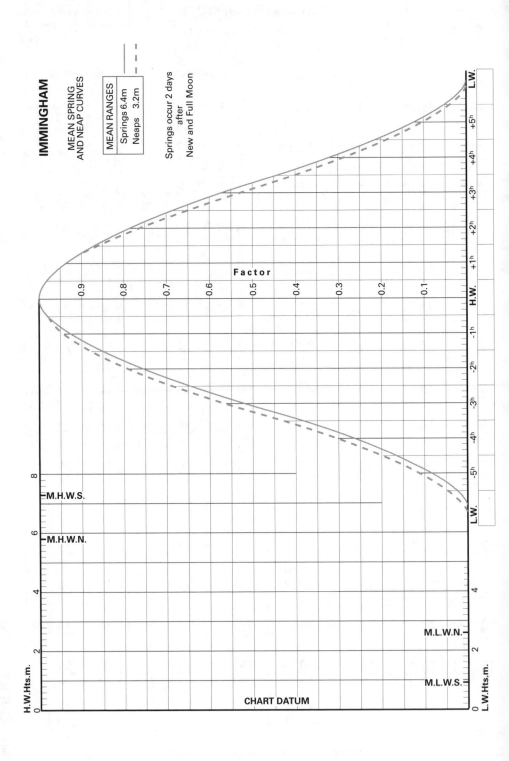

ENGLAND – IMMINGHAM

LAT 53°38′N   LONG 0°11′W

TIMES AND HEIGHTS OF HIGH AND LOW WATERS

Dates in amber are **SPRINGS**
Dates in yellow are **NEAPS**

2009

JANUARY

Day				
1 TH	0236 1.6	0839 6.4	1438 1.9	2038 6.8
16 F	0339 0.9	0939 6.7	1535 1.7	2138 7.1
2 F	0309 1.7	0915 6.3	1514 2.1	2114 6.7
17 SA	0419 1.3	1023 6.4	1613 2.0	2225 6.7
3 SA	0346 1.8	0955 6.2	1555 2.2	2157 6.5
18 SU	0500 1.8	1110 6.0	1655 2.4	☽ 2319 6.2
4 SU	0430 1.9	1043 6.0	1645 2.4	☽ 2249 6.4
19 M	0545 2.3	1205 5.7	1747 2.7	
5 M	0525 2.0	1141 5.9	1747 2.5	2352 6.3
20 TU	0024 5.9	0641 2.6	1308 5.6	1854 2.9
6 TU	0630 2.2	1253 5.8	1901 2.6	
21 W	0139 5.6	0751 2.7	1414 5.6	2034 2.9
7 W	0106 6.2	0744 2.2	1412 5.9	2019 2.4
22 TH	0254 5.7	0904 2.7	1517 5.9	2150 2.6
8 TH	0228 6.3	0858 2.1	1521 6.2	2134 2.1
23 F	0358 5.8	1002 2.5	1610 6.2	2243 2.2
9 F	0343 6.5	1006 1.9	1621 6.6	2242 1.6
24 SA	0450 6.1	1051 2.2	1655 6.5	2328 1.9
10 SA	0450 6.8	1106 1.6	1714 6.9	2342 1.2
25 SU	0532 6.3	1134 2.0	1734 6.7	
11 SU	0549 7.1	1200 1.4	1803 7.3	O
26 M	0009 1.6	0607 6.5	1214 1.8	1809 6.9
12 M	0037 0.8	0642 7.3	1250 1.2	1848 7.5
27 TU	0047 1.5	0641 6.6	1250 1.7	1843 7.0
13 TU	0127 0.5	0730 7.3	1335 1.1	1931 7.6
28 W	0122 1.4	0713 6.7	1322 1.6	1916 7.1
14 W	0213 0.5	0815 7.3	1417 1.2	2013 7.6
29 TH	0153 1.3	0745 6.7	1351 1.6	1947 7.1
15 TH	0257 0.6	0857 7.0	1457 1.4	2054 7.4
30 F	0222 1.3	0816 6.7	1421 1.6	2017 7.1
31 SA	0249 1.4	0847 6.6	1452 1.7	2050 7.0

FEBRUARY

Day				
1 SU	0318 1.5	0921 6.5	1527 1.8	2129 6.8
16 M	0408 1.8	1006 6.1	1608 2.2	☽ 2226 6.1
2 M	0353 1.7	1001 6.2	1609 2.0	☽ 2216 6.6
17 TU	0446 2.4	1050 5.7	1653 2.6	2327 5.6
3 TU	0440 2.0	1052 6.0	1706 2.3	2316 6.2
18 W	0537 2.8	1201 5.4	1756 2.9	
4 W	0545 2.3	1201 5.7	1825 2.6	
19 TH	0058 5.3	0649 3.1	1330 5.4	1924 3.0
5 TH	0035 5.9	0710 2.5	1337 5.7	1957 2.5
20 F	0228 5.3	0830 3.0	1445 5.6	2131 2.7
6 F	0219 5.9	0841 2.4	1503 6.0	2126 2.1
21 SA	0339 5.6	0943 2.7	1544 6.0	2223 2.2
7 SA	0346 6.2	0957 2.1	1610 6.4	2239 1.6
22 SU	0432 6.0	1033 2.3	1631 6.3	2307 1.8
8 SU	0453 6.7	1058 1.7	1704 6.9	2337 1.0
23 M	0512 6.3	1116 1.9	1710 6.6	2347 1.5
9 M	0548 7.0	1150 1.3	1752 7.3	O
24 TU	0546 6.5	1154 1.7	1745 6.9	
10 TU	0027 0.6	0635 7.3	1237 1.1	1834 7.6
25 W	0025 1.3	0618 6.7	1230 1.5	● 1819 7.0
11 W	0113 0.3	0716 7.4	1319 0.9	1915 7.7
26 TH	0100 1.1	0649 6.8	1302 1.4	1851 7.2
12 TH	0155 0.3	0753 7.3	1358 1.0	1953 7.7
27 F	0132 1.1	0719 6.9	1333 1.3	1923 7.3
13 F	0233 0.5	0828 7.1	1433 1.1	2030 7.5
28 SA	0200 1.1	0749 6.9	1403 1.3	1955 7.3
14 SA	0307 0.9	0900 6.8	1504 1.4	2106 7.1
15 SU	0338 1.3	0932 6.5	1534 1.8	2143 6.7

MARCH

Day				
1 SU	0227 1.1	0819 6.8	1433 1.3	2029 7.2
16 M	0259 1.4	0849 6.6	1502 1.6	2109 6.5
2 M	0254 1.3	0852 6.7	1507 1.5	2108 6.9
17 TU	0327 1.9	0917 6.3	1533 2.0	2146 6.0
3 TU	0327 1.6	0931 6.4	1548 1.8	2155 6.5
18 W	0401 2.4	0954 5.9	1616 2.4	☽ 2239 5.5
4 W	0412 2.0	1021 6.0	1645 2.2	☽ 2258 6.0
19 TH	0450 2.8	1053 5.5	1718 2.8	
5 TH	0518 2.5	1132 5.6	1811 2.5	
20 F	0019 5.1	0602 3.2	1243 5.3	1841 3.0
6 F	0033 5.7	0655 2.8	1320 5.6	1953 2.4
21 SA	0158 5.2	0741 3.2	1409 5.5	2053 2.7
7 SA	0228 5.9	0835 2.6	1451 5.9	2124 1.9
22 SU	0308 5.5	0913 2.8	1510 5.8	2149 2.2
8 SU	0348 6.2	0949 2.2	1555 6.4	2229 1.3
23 M	0400 5.9	1004 2.3	1557 6.2	2233 1.8
9 M	0447 6.7	1045 1.7	1647 6.9	2321 0.8
24 TU	0440 6.3	1046 2.0	1636 6.6	2313 1.5
10 TU	0535 7.0	1133 1.3	1733 7.3	2352 1.2
25 W	0515 6.5	1124 1.7	1713 6.8	
11 W	0008 0.5	0615 7.2	1217 1.0	O 1814 7.5
26 TH	0548 6.8	1201 1.4	● 1748 7.1	
12 TH	0051 0.4	0652 7.3	1257 0.9	1853 7.6
27 F	0029 1.0	0619 6.9	1237 1.2	1823 7.2
13 F	0129 0.4	0724 7.2	1334 0.9	1930 7.6
28 SA	0103 0.9	0651 7.0	1311 1.1	1859 7.4
14 SA	0202 0.6	0755 7.0	1406 1.0	2004 7.3
29 SU	0135 1.0	0723 7.1	1345 1.1	1935 7.4
15 SU	0232 1.0	0822 6.9	1435 1.3	2037 7.0
30 M	0205 1.1	0755 7.0	1419 1.1	2014 7.2
31 TU	0237 1.3	0831 6.8	1457 1.4	2057 6.9

APRIL

Day				
1 W	0314 1.7	0913 6.5	1543 1.7	2150 6.4
16 TH	0330 2.3	0922 6.0	1552 2.3	2211 5.5
2 TH	0402 2.2	1006 6.1	1648 2.1	☽ 2303 5.9
17 F	0417 2.8	1014 5.6	1651 2.6	☽ 2334 5.2
3 F	0514 2.7	1124 5.7	1816 2.3	
18 SA	0523 3.1	1145 5.4	1808 2.7	
4 SA	0053 5.7	0651 2.8	1309 5.7	1950 2.1
19 SU	0111 5.2	0646 3.1	1316 5.5	1933 2.6
5 SU	0224 5.9	0821 2.6	1430 6.1	2107 1.6
20 M	0222 5.5	0811 2.9	1420 5.7	2049 2.2
6 M	0334 6.3	0928 2.1	1532 6.5	2205 1.2
21 TU	0315 5.8	0913 2.5	1511 6.1	2143 1.8
7 TU	0427 6.7	1021 1.7	1623 6.9	2255 0.9
22 W	0358 6.2	1002 2.1	1554 6.4	2229 1.5
8 W	0511 6.9	1108 1.3	1708 7.2	2340 0.7
23 TH	0437 6.5	1045 1.7	1636 6.8	2312 1.3
9 TH	0548 7.1	1152 1.1	1750 7.3	O
24 F	0513 6.7	1127 1.4	1716 7.0	2354 1.1
10 F	0021 0.7	0622 7.1	1232 1.0	1829 7.3
25 SA	0549 6.9	1208 1.2	1758 7.2	●
11 SA	0058 0.8	0654 7.1	1309 1.0	1906 7.2
26 SU	0033 1.0	0625 7.1	1249 1.0	1839 7.3
12 SU	0131 1.0	0723 7.0	1341 1.1	1941 7.0
27 M	0111 1.0	0701 7.1	1330 0.9	1922 7.3
13 M	0200 1.2	0750 6.9	1410 1.3	2013 6.7
28 TU	0149 1.1	0739 7.1	1412 1.0	2007 7.1
14 TU	0227 1.6	0817 6.7	1438 1.6	2045 6.4
29 W	0227 1.4	0819 6.9	1457 1.2	2057 6.8
15 W	0256 1.9	0846 6.4	1510 1.9	2121 5.9
30 TH	0311 1.7	0906 6.6	1550 1.5	2157 6.3

Chart Datum: 3·90 metres below Ordnance Datum (Newlyn)
HAT is 8·0 metres above Chart Datum

TIDES

ENGLAND – IMMINGHAM
LAT 53°38′N   LONG 0°11′W
TIMES AND HEIGHTS OF HIGH AND LOW WATERS

TIME ZONE (UT)
For Summer Time add ONE hour in **non-shaded areas**

Dates in amber are **SPRINGS**
Dates in yellow are **NEAPS**

2009

MAY

Day	Time	m	Time	m
1 F	0404	2.2	1004	6.3
			1657	1.7
	2318	6.0		
2 SA	0514	2.5	1121	6.0
			1814	1.8
3 SU	0046	5.9	0635	2.6
	1248	6.0	1930	1.7
4 M ☾	0201	6.1	0752	2.4
	1400	6.2	2036	1.5
5 TU	0304	6.3	0856	2.1
	1501	6.5	2132	1.3
6 W	0356	6.5	0950	1.8
	1554	6.7	2222	1.2
7 TH	0439	6.7	1040	1.5
	1642	6.9	2307	1.1
8 F	0517	6.8	1125	1.4
	1727	6.9	2349	1.1
9 SA	0552	6.9	1207	1.3
	1808	6.9		
10 SU	0027	1.2	0625	6.9
	1246	1.2	1846	6.8
11 M ○	0102	1.3	0656	6.9
	1321	1.3	1922	6.7
12 TU	0134	1.5	0726	6.8
	1352	1.4	1956	6.5
13 W	0203	1.7	0756	6.7
	1422	1.6	2030	6.2
14 TH	0234	2.0	0827	6.5
	1456	1.8	2107	6.0
15 F	0309	2.2	0904	6.2
	1537	2.1	2153	5.7
16 SA	0352	2.5	0951	5.9
	1630	2.3	2253	5.5
17 SU	0447	2.8	1055	5.7
	1733	2.4		
18 M ☽	0008	5.4	0554	2.9
	1211	5.7	1839	2.3
19 TU	0118	5.5	0704	2.8
	1318	5.8	1944	2.1
20 W	0218	5.8	0810	2.5
	1417	6.1	2045	1.9
21 TH	0309	6.1	0909	2.2
	1510	6.4	2141	1.6
22 F	0356	6.4	1003	1.9
	1600	6.7	2232	1.4
23 SA	0440	6.6	1054	1.5
	1649	6.9	2321	1.2
24 SU	0523	6.9	1144	1.2
	1738	7.1		
25 M	0008	1.1	0604	7.1
	1233	1.0	1827	7.2
26 TU ●	0053	1.4	0647	7.2
	1321	0.8	1916	7.2
27 W	0137	1.1	0729	7.2
	1409	0.8	2007	7.1
28 TH	0222	1.3	0814	7.1
	1459	0.9	2101	6.8
29 F	0309	1.6	0903	6.9
	1554	1.1	2202	6.5
30 SA	0401	1.9	1000	6.6
	1653	1.3	2311	6.3
31 SU	0501	2.2	1107	6.4
	1756	1.4		

JUNE

Day	Time	m	Time	m
1 M	0019	6.1	0606	2.4
	1218	6.3	1858	1.6
2 TU ◑	0123	6.1	0714	2.4
	1324	6.3	1959	1.6
3 W	0222	6.1	0819	2.3
	1426	6.3	2056	1.6
4 TH	0316	6.2	0918	2.1
	1525	6.4	2148	1.6
5 F	0403	6.4	1012	1.9
	1618	6.4	2235	1.6
6 SA	0445	6.5	1102	1.7
	1707	6.5	2320	1.6
7 SU	0524	6.6	1147	1.6
	1752	6.5		
8 M	0001	1.6	0601	6.7
	1230	1.5	1832	6.5
9 TU ○	0039	1.7	0636	6.8
	1307	1.5	1908	6.5
10 W	0114	1.7	0709	6.8
	1342	1.5	1943	6.4
11 TH	0147	1.8	0742	6.7
	1414	1.6	2017	6.3
12 F	0219	1.9	0815	6.6
	1448	1.7	2052	6.1
13 SA	0252	2.1	0850	6.4
	1524	1.8	2132	6.0
14 SU	0330	2.2	0930	6.3
	1606	1.9	2217	5.9
15 M	0414	2.4	1016	6.1
	1655	2.0	2310	5.7
16 TU	0507	2.5	1112	6.0
	1750	2.1		
17 W	0011	5.7	0608	2.6
	1215	6.0	1849	2.1
18 TH	0117	5.8	0715	2.5
	1322	6.1	1953	2.0
19 F	0221	5.9	0822	2.3
	1428	6.2	2058	1.9
20 SA	0319	6.2	0927	2.0
	1531	6.5	2159	1.7
21 SU	0413	6.5	1029	1.7
	1632	6.7	2257	1.5
22 M	0503	6.8	1128	1.3
	1729	7.0	2350	1.3
23 TU	0551	7.1	1223	0.9
	1824	7.2		
24 W	0041	1.2	0637	7.3
	1316	0.6	1916	7.3
25 TH ●	0129	1.1	0723	7.4
	1406	0.5	2007	7.2
26 F	0215	1.2	0808	7.4
	1455	0.5	2057	7.1
27 SA	0301	1.3	0855	7.3
	1544	0.7	2149	6.8
28 SU	0347	1.6	0946	7.0
	1634	1.0	2244	6.5
29 M	0436	1.9	1041	6.8
	1726	1.3	2339	6.2
30 TU	0529	2.2	1141	6.5
	1820	1.7		

JULY

Day	Time	m	Time	m
1 W	0035	6.0	0628	2.4
	1245	6.2	1917	2.0
2 TH	0133	5.9	0736	2.5
	1351	6.0	2017	2.2
3 F	0232	5.9	0847	2.4
	1457	6.0	2116	2.2
4 SA ◑	0327	6.0	0950	2.2
	1600	6.1	2209	2.1
5 SU	0417	6.2	1045	2.0
	1654	6.2	2257	2.0
6 M	0501	6.5	1133	1.8
	1740	6.3	2342	1.9
7 TU	0541	6.7	1216	1.6
	1820	6.4		
8 W	0022	1.8	0617	6.8
	1257	1.5	1854	6.5
9 TH	0100	1.7	0653	6.9
	1333	1.4	1927	6.5
10 F	0133	1.7	0726	6.9
	1406	1.4	1959	6.5
11 SA ○	0204	1.8	0759	6.8
	1436	1.5	2032	6.4
12 SU	0235	1.8	0832	6.7
	1506	1.6	2105	6.3
13 M	0307	1.9	0905	6.6
	1538	1.7	2141	6.2
14 TU	0343	2.1	0942	6.5
	1614	1.8	2222	6.1
15 W	0426	2.2	1028	6.3
	1700	2.0	2312	5.9
16 TH	0520	2.4	1124	6.2
	1759	2.1		
17 F	0017	5.8	0628	2.5
	1234	6.0	1910	2.2
18 SA ◑	0137	5.8	0746	2.5
	1358	6.1	2026	2.2
19 SU	0251	6.0	0903	2.2
	1518	6.3	2138	2.0
20 M	0355	6.4	1016	1.7
	1627	6.6	2242	1.7
21 TU	0451	6.8	1120	1.2
	1729	6.9	2339	1.4
22 W	0541	7.2	1217	0.8
	1823	7.2		
23 TH	0030	1.2	0627	7.5
	1308	0.4	1912	7.4
24 F	0118	1.0	0653	7.6
	1355	0.2	1957	7.4
25 SA	0201	1.0	0755	7.7
	1440	0.3	2040	7.3
26 SU ●	0243	1.1	0838	7.6
	1523	0.5	2122	7.0
27 M	0323	1.4	0921	7.3
	1604	1.0	2204	6.6
28 TU	0403	1.7	1008	6.9
	1645	1.5	2250	6.3
29 W	0444	2.1	1101	6.4
	1730	2.0	2343	5.9
30 TH	0533	2.5	1204	6.0
	1824	2.4		
31 F	0043	5.7	0639	2.8
	1318	5.7	1934	2.7

AUGUST

Day	Time	m	Time	m
1 SA	0150	5.6	0819	2.8
	1435	5.6	2049	2.7
2 SU ◑	0255	5.8	0936	2.5
	1545	5.8	2150	2.5
3 M	0352	6.1	1031	2.1
	1642	6.0	2240	2.2
4 TU	0439	6.4	1117	1.8
	1726	6.3	2324	2.0
5 W	0520	6.7	1159	1.5
	1802	6.5		
6 TH	0005	1.8	0556	6.9
	1239	1.4	1834	6.6
7 F	0043	1.7	0631	7.0
	1315	1.3	1905	6.7
8 SA	0116	1.6	0705	7.0
	1347	1.3	1935	6.7
9 SU ○	0146	1.6	0737	7.0
	1416	1.3	2005	6.7
10 M	0214	1.6	0807	7.0
	1441	1.4	2035	6.6
11 TU	0242	1.7	0838	6.9
	1506	1.5	2106	6.5
12 W	0314	1.8	0912	6.8
	1536	1.7	2142	6.3
13 TH	0351	2.0	0954	6.5
	1616	2.0	2227	6.0
14 F	0442	2.3	1049	6.2
	1714	2.3	2330	5.8
15 SA	0556	2.6	1205	5.9
	1837	2.6		
16 SU	0103	5.7	0724	2.6
	1349	5.7	2008	2.6
17 M ◑	0234	5.9	0855	2.2
	1519	6.2	2129	2.2
18 TU	0342	6.4	1012	1.9
	1627	6.6	2233	1.8
19 W	0437	6.9	1112	1.1
	1723	7.0	2327	1.4
20 TH	0526	7.3	1204	0.6
	1812	7.3		
21 F	0015	1.1	0611	7.6
	1252	0.3	1855	7.5
22 SA	0100	0.9	0653	7.8
	1335	0.2	1935	7.5
23 SU	0141	0.9	0734	7.8
	1415	0.3	2011	7.3
24 M ○	0219	1.0	0813	7.7
	1452	0.7	2046	7.1
25 TU ●	0254	1.3	0852	7.3
	1526	1.1	2120	6.7
26 W	0326	1.7	0933	6.8
	1559	1.7	2157	6.3
27 TH	0400	2.1	1019	6.3
	1635	2.3	2243	5.9
28 F	0443	2.5	1122	5.7
	1723	2.8	2351	5.6
29 SA	0544	2.9	1208	5.4
	1838	3.1		
30 SU	0112	5.5	0749	3.0
	1413	5.4	2024	3.1
31 M	0226	5.7	0919	2.6
	1525	5.7	2130	2.7

Chart Datum: 3·90 metres below Ordnance Datum (Newlyn)
HAT is 8·0 metres above Chart Datum

ENGLAND – IMMINGHAM

LAT 53°38′N   LONG 0°11′W

TIMES AND HEIGHTS OF HIGH AND LOW WATERS

Dates in amber are **SPRINGS**
Dates in yellow are **NEAPS**

2009

SEPTEMBER

Day	Time m	Time m	Time m	Time m
1 TU	0326 6.1	1009 2.2	1620 6.1	2219 2.3
16 W	0324 6.5	1000 1.5	1617 6.7	2217 1.8
2 W	0414 6.4	1053 1.8	1701 6.4	2302 2.0
17 TH	0418 7.0	1054 0.9	1707 7.1	2307 1.4
3 TH	0454 6.7	1133 1.5	1736 6.6	2342 1.7
18 F	0505 7.4	1142 0.6	1751 7.4	●2353 1.1
4 F	0530 6.9	1211 1.3	1807 6.7	○
19 SA	0548 7.7	1227 0.4	1830 7.5	○
5 SA	0018 1.6	0604 7.1	1247 1.2	1836 6.9
20 SU	0036 0.9	0629 7.8	1308 0.6	1905 7.4
6 SU	0051 1.5	0637 7.2	1319 1.2	1906 6.9
21 M	0116 0.9	0709 7.7	1345 0.6	1938 7.3
7 M	0121 1.5	0709 7.2	1348 1.2	1935 6.9
22 TU	0152 1.0	0747 7.5	1418 0.9	2009 7.1
8 TU	0150 1.5	0740 7.2	1413 1.3	2004 6.8
23 W	0224 1.3	0824 7.2	1448 1.4	2039 6.8
9 W	0219 1.5	0812 7.1	1438 1.5	2034 6.7
24 TH	0253 1.6	0901 6.7	1516 1.9	2110 6.4
10 TH	0250 1.7	0848 6.9	1507 1.7	2110 6.5
25 F	0324 2.1	0943 6.2	1548 2.4	2148 6.0
11 F	0328 1.9	0932 6.5	1547 2.1	2156 6.1
26 SA	0405 2.5	1042 5.6	1634 2.9	◐2251 5.6
12 SA	0421 2.3	1031 6.1	1647 2.6	◐2301 5.8
27 SU	0506 2.9	1216 5.3	1746 3.3	
13 SU	0541 2.6	1201 5.7	1819 2.9	
28 M	0031 5.5	0638 3.0	1342 5.3	1939 3.3
14 M	0044 5.7	0718 2.5	1355 5.8	2000 2.8
29 TU	0151 5.7	0844 2.7	1452 5.7	2059 2.9
15 TU	0219 6.0	0852 2.1	1515 6.2	2119 2.3
30 W	0252 6.0	0935 2.2	1546 6.0	2149 2.4

OCTOBER

Day	Time m	Time m	Time m	Time m
1 TH	0340 6.4	1017 1.8	1627 6.4	2231 2.1
16 F	0352 7.0	1026 1.0	1642 7.0	2241 1.5
2 F	0420 6.7	1057 1.5	1701 6.6	2309 1.8
17 SA	0439 7.3	1113 0.8	1723 7.2	2327 1.2
3 SA	0456 6.9	1135 1.3	1733 6.8	2346 1.6
18 SU	0524 7.5	1157 0.7	1800 7.3	●
4 SU	0532 7.1	1211 1.2	1804 7.0	○
19 M	0010 1.1	0606 7.5	1237 0.8	1834 7.3
5 M	0020 1.5	0607 7.2	1246 1.2	1835 7.1
20 TU	0050 1.1	0646 7.4	1313 1.0	1907 7.2
6 TU	0054 1.4	0642 7.3	1317 1.2	1906 7.1
21 W	0126 1.2	0725 7.3	1345 1.3	1938 7.1
7 W	0127 1.3	0717 7.3	1346 1.3	1937 7.0
22 TH	0158 1.4	0801 6.9	1414 1.6	2007 6.9
8 TH	0200 1.4	0754 7.2	1416 1.5	2011 6.9
23 F	0227 1.7	0834 6.5	1442 2.0	2037 6.6
9 F	0236 1.6	0834 6.9	1450 1.8	2049 6.6
24 SA	0259 2.0	0916 6.1	1515 2.4	2113 6.2
10 SA	0319 1.8	0924 6.5	1534 2.2	2138 6.3
25 SU	0339 2.4	1007 5.7	1559 2.8	2205 5.9
11 SU	0418 2.2	1031 6.0	1637 2.7	◐2248 5.9
26 M	0436 2.7	1128 5.4	1701 3.2	◐2332 5.6
12 M	0541 2.4	1213 5.8	1809 2.9	
27 TU	0553 2.8	1254 5.4	1825 3.3	
13 TU	0029 5.9	0712 2.3	1347 6.0	1943 2.8
28 W	0058 5.7	0722 2.7	1403 5.6	1956 3.0
14 W	0155 6.2	0833 1.8	1458 6.3	2055 2.3
29 TH	0203 5.9	0836 2.4	1459 5.9	2059 2.7
15 TH	0258 6.6	0935 1.4	1555 6.7	2152 1.9
30 F	0254 6.2	0927 2.0	1543 6.3	2146 2.3
31 SA	0338 6.5	1011 1.7	1621 6.6	2228 2.0

NOVEMBER

Day	Time m	Time m	Time m	Time m
1 SU	0418 6.8	1053 1.5	1657 6.8	2309 1.7
16 M	0502 7.1	1126 1.3	1731 7.0	●2347 1.4
2 M	0458 7.0	1133 1.3	1732 7.0	○2349 1.5
17 TU	0547 7.1	1207 1.3	1807 7.0	
3 TU	0539 7.2	1211 1.2	1807 7.1	
18 W	0028 1.3	0628 7.0	1245 1.4	1841 7.1
4 W	0028 1.3	0619 7.3	1249 1.2	1842 7.2
19 TH	0107 1.4	0707 6.9	1318 1.6	1914 7.1
5 TH	0108 1.2	0700 7.3	1325 1.3	1918 7.2
20 F	0140 1.5	0744 6.7	1349 1.8	1945 6.9
6 F	0148 1.2	0744 7.2	1402 1.5	1956 7.1
21 SA	0211 1.7	0820 6.5	1419 2.0	2017 6.7
7 SA	0231 1.4	0831 6.9	1443 1.8	2039 6.8
22 SU	0243 1.9	0856 6.2	1452 2.3	2052 6.5
8 SU	0321 1.6	0926 6.5	1531 2.2	2132 6.5
23 M	0321 2.1	0939 5.9	1532 2.6	2135 6.2
9 M	0422 1.8	1036 6.2	1633 2.5	◑2240 6.3
24 TU	0409 2.4	1034 5.6	1622 2.8	◑2233 5.9
10 TU	0536 2.0	1203 6.0	1751 2.7	
25 W	0509 2.5	1143 5.5	1725 3.0	2346 5.8
11 W	0005 6.2	0651 1.9	1320 6.1	1911 2.7
26 TH	0614 2.5	1253 5.6	1836 3.0	
12 TH	0122 6.3	0801 1.7	1425 6.3	2021 2.4
27 F	0055 5.8	0720 2.4	1355 5.8	1945 2.8
13 F	0226 6.6	0901 1.5	1522 6.6	2121 2.1
28 SA	0156 6.0	0822 2.2	1450 6.0	2047 2.5
14 SA	0322 6.8	0954 1.3	1610 6.8	2213 1.8
29 SU	0250 6.3	0918 2.0	1537 6.3	2141 2.2
15 SU	0414 7.0	1042 1.3	1652 6.9	2301 1.5
30 M	0340 6.6	1009 1.7	1621 6.6	2232 1.9

DECEMBER

Day	Time m	Time m	Time m	Time m
1 TU	0429 6.8	1057 1.5	1704 6.9	2321 1.5
16 W	0534 6.7	1143 1.7	1745 6.9	●
2 W	0517 7.1	1143 1.4	1745 7.1	○
17 TH	0014 1.5	0617 6.7	1223 1.7	1822 7.0
3 TH	0009 1.3	0604 7.2	1228 1.3	1825 7.2
18 F	0054 1.5	0655 6.7	1259 1.7	1856 7.0
4 F	0056 1.1	0652 7.3	1311 1.3	1906 7.3
19 SA	0130 1.5	0730 6.6	1332 1.8	1929 7.0
5 SA	0143 1.0	0740 7.2	1354 1.4	1949 7.3
20 SU	0202 1.6	0803 6.5	1403 1.9	2002 6.9
6 SU	0231 1.0	0830 7.0	1438 1.6	2034 7.2
21 M	0233 1.7	0836 6.5	1434 2.0	2034 6.7
7 M	0321 1.2	0925 6.8	1526 1.9	2125 6.9
22 TU	0305 1.8	0911 6.2	1508 2.2	2110 6.5
8 TU	0417 1.4	1027 6.5	1620 2.2	2225 6.7
23 W	0342 2.0	0950 6.0	1546 2.4	2151 6.3
9 W	0517 1.6	1134 6.3	1722 2.4	○2333 6.5
24 TH	0424 2.2	1036 5.8	1633 2.6	◑2240 6.1
10 TH	0620 1.7	1240 6.1	1831 2.5	
25 F	0516 2.3	1133 5.7	1731 2.7	2339 6.0
11 F	0042 6.4	0723 1.8	1342 6.1	1941 2.5
26 SA	0615 2.4	1240 5.7	1839 2.8	
12 SA	0150 6.4	0824 1.9	1441 6.2	2048 2.3
27 SU	0047 6.0	0720 2.4	1351 5.8	1949 2.7
13 SU	0253 6.6	0921 1.9	1535 6.4	2147 2.1
28 M	0200 6.1	0827 2.2	1455 6.0	2058 2.4
14 M	0352 6.5	1012 1.8	1623 6.5	2241 1.9
29 TU	0307 6.3	0931 2.0	1551 6.3	2202 2.0
15 TU	0446 6.6	1100 1.8	1706 6.7	2329 1.7
30 W	0408 6.6	1029 1.8	1642 6.7	2301 1.6
31 TH	0505 6.9	1123 1.5	1729 7.0	○2357 1.2

TIDES

Chart Datum: 3·90 metres below Ordnance Datum (Newlyn)
HAT is 8·0 metres above Chart Datum

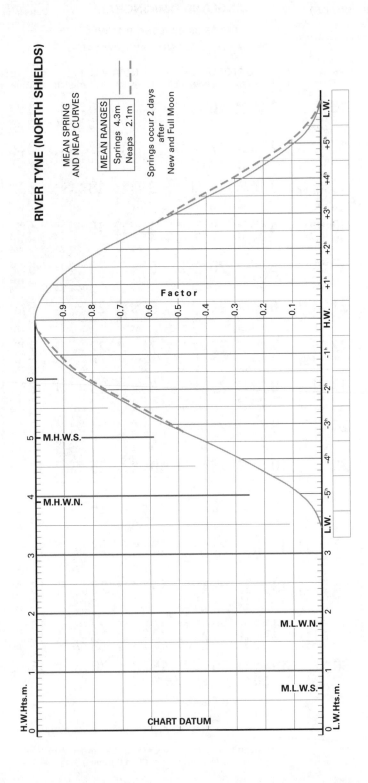

RIVER TYNE (NORTH SHIELDS)

MEAN SPRING
AND NEAP CURVES

MEAN RANGES
Springs 4.3m
Neaps   2.1m

Springs occur 2 days
after
New and Full Moon

ENGLAND – NORTH SHIELDS

LAT 55°01′N   LONG 1°26′W

TIMES AND HEIGHTS OF HIGH AND LOW WATERS

Dates in amber are **SPRINGS**
Dates in yellow are **NEAPS**

2009

JANUARY

Time	m	Time	m
1 TH	0007 1.1 / 0612 4.5 / 1208 1.5 / 1810 4.8	**16** F	0104 0.7 / 0705 4.7 / 1303 1.4 / 1910 5.0
2 F	0044 1.2 / 0650 4.4 / 1245 1.6 / 1849 4.7	**17** SA	0148 1.0 / 0752 4.4 / 1346 1.6 / 2001 4.7
3 SA	0124 1.3 / 0733 4.3 / 1326 1.7 / 1933 4.6	**18** SU	0234 1.4 / 0842 4.2 / 1437 1.9 / 2058 4.4
4 SU	0209 1.4 / 0822 4.2 / 1416 1.9 / 2025 4.5	**19** M	0327 1.7 / 0940 4.0 / 1543 2.1 / 2205 4.1
5 M	0303 1.5 / 0920 4.2 / 1519 2.0 / 2128 4.4	**20** TU	0431 2.0 / 1046 3.9 / 1707 2.2 / 2323 4.0
6 TU	0408 1.6 / 1027 4.2 / 1635 2.0 / 2239 4.4	**21** W	0545 2.1 / 1158 4.0 / 1834 2.1
7 W	0521 1.6 / 1137 4.3 / 1754 1.8 / 2356 4.5	**22** TH	0040 4.0 / 0655 2.0 / 1303 4.1 / 1937 1.9
8 TH	0633 1.5 / 1244 4.5 / 1906 1.5	**23** F	0141 4.2 / 0748 1.9 / 1353 4.3 / 2023 1.6
9 F	0108 4.7 / 0739 1.4 / 1343 4.7 / 2010 1.2	**24** SA	0228 4.3 / 0830 1.7 / 1434 4.5 / 2102 1.4
10 SA	0211 4.9 / 0836 1.2 / 1435 5.0 / 2106 0.8	**25** SU	0306 4.5 / 0907 1.5 / 1509 4.7 / 2136 1.2
11 SU	0307 5.1 / 0928 1.1 / 1522 5.2 / 2159 0.5	**26** M	0340 4.6 / 0941 1.4 / 1541 4.8 / 2209 1.0
12 M	0358 5.2 / 1015 1.0 / 1608 5.3 / 2248 0.3	**27** TU	0412 4.7 / 1012 1.3 / 1611 4.9 / 2241 0.9
13 TU	0447 5.2 / 1100 1.0 / 1653 5.4 / 2335 0.3	**28** W	0443 4.8 / 1044 1.2 / 1642 5.0 / 2313 0.8
14 W	0534 5.1 / 1142 1.0 / 1738 5.4	**29** TH	0514 4.8 / 1115 1.2 / 1713 5.0 / 2345 0.8
15 TH	0020 0.4 / 0619 4.9 / 1223 1.2 / 1823 5.2	**30** F	0546 4.7 / 1146 1.2 / 1746 5.0
		31 SA	0018 0.9 / 0619 4.6 / 1219 1.3 / 1821 4.9

FEBRUARY

Time	m	Time	m
1 SU	0052 1.0 / 0656 4.5 / 1255 1.4 / 1902 4.8	**16** M	0143 1.4 / 0749 4.5 / 1347 1.7 / 2012 4.3
2 M	0131 1.2 / 0740 4.4 / 1338 1.6 / 1950 4.6	**17** TU	0227 1.8 / 0840 4.0 / 1444 2.0 / 2116 3.9
3 TU	0219 1.5 / 0834 4.2 / 1436 1.8 / 2052 4.4	**18** W	0328 2.1 / 0946 3.8 / 1610 2.2 / 2239 3.7
4 W	0324 1.7 / 0943 4.1 / 1557 1.9 / 2212 4.2	**19** TH	0455 2.3 / 1109 3.8 / 1801 2.2
5 TH	0451 1.9 / 1107 4.1 / 1734 1.8 / 2346 4.2	**20** F	0013 3.8 / 0628 2.2 / 1232 3.9 / 1916 1.9
6 F	0621 1.8 / 1229 4.3 / 1900 1.5	**21** SA	0122 4.0 / 0729 2.0 / 1330 4.2 / 2003 1.6
7 SA	0107 4.5 / 0734 1.6 / 1334 4.6 / 2006 1.1	**22** SU	0209 4.2 / 0812 1.7 / 1412 4.4 / 2041 1.3
8 SU	0210 4.8 / 0831 1.3 / 1426 4.9 / 2101 0.7	**23** M	0245 4.4 / 0848 1.5 / 1447 4.6 / 2114 1.1
9 M	0302 5.0 / 0918 1.1 / 1511 5.2 / 2149 0.4	**24** TU	0317 4.6 / 0920 1.3 / 1517 4.8 / 2145 0.9
10 TU	0347 5.2 / 1002 0.9 / 1554 5.4 / 2233 0.2	**25** W	0347 4.8 / 0951 1.1 / 1547 5.0 / 2217 0.7
11 W	0429 5.2 / 1041 0.8 / 1635 5.5 / 2315 0.2	**26** TH	0416 4.8 / 1021 1.0 / 1616 5.1 / 2248 0.6
12 TH	0510 5.1 / 1119 0.8 / 1715 5.4 / 2353 0.4	**27** F	0446 4.9 / 1052 0.9 / 1647 5.1 / 2319 0.6
13 F	0549 4.9 / 1154 0.9 / 1756 5.3	**28** SA	0517 4.9 / 1123 0.9 / 1721 5.1 / 2351 0.7
14 SA	0030 0.7 / 0627 4.7 / 1230 1.1 / 1837 5.0		
15 SU	0106 1.0 / 0706 4.5 / 1306 1.4 / 1921 4.7		

MARCH

Time	m	Time	m
1 SU	0550 4.8 / 1156 1.0 / 1757 5.0	**16** M	0026 1.1 / 0626 4.5 / 1234 1.3 / 1849 4.5
2 M	0024 0.9 / 0626 4.7 / 1233 1.2 / 1839 4.9	**17** TU	0059 1.5 / 0704 4.3 / 1313 1.6 / 1937 4.2
3 TU	0102 1.2 / 0710 4.5 / 1317 1.4 / 1930 4.6	**18** W	0139 1.8 / 0750 4.1 / 1404 1.9 / 2037 3.9
4 W	0149 1.5 / 0803 4.2 / 1417 1.6 / 2037 4.3	**19** TH	0234 2.2 / 0852 3.8 / 1519 2.1 / 2157 3.6
5 TH	0259 1.9 / 0917 4.0 / 1546 1.8 / 2208 4.1	**20** F	0402 2.4 / 1014 3.7 / 1708 2.1 / 2332 3.7
6 F	0441 2.0 / 1051 4.0 / 1731 1.7 / 2348 4.1	**21** SA	0549 2.3 / 1145 3.8 / 1837 1.9
7 SA	0618 1.9 / 1217 4.2 / 1856 1.3	**22** SU	0047 3.9 / 0656 2.1 / 1252 4.0 / 1927 1.6
8 SU	0105 4.4 / 0727 1.6 / 1322 4.6 / 1957 0.9	**23** M	0135 4.1 / 0741 1.8 / 1337 4.3 / 2006 1.3
9 M	0202 4.7 / 0818 1.3 / 1412 4.9 / 2047 0.6	**24** TU	0212 4.4 / 0818 1.5 / 1413 4.6 / 2041 1.0
10 TU	0248 4.9 / 0902 1.0 / 1455 5.2 / 2131 0.3	**25** W	0244 4.6 / 0851 1.2 / 1444 4.8 / 2113 0.8
11 W	0328 5.1 / 0941 0.8 / 1534 5.3 / 2211 0.2	**26** TH	0314 4.8 / 0922 1.0 / 1515 5.0 / 2145 0.6
12 TH	0405 5.1 / 1018 0.7 / 1612 5.4 / 2248 0.2	**27** F	0345 4.9 / 0955 0.8 / 1547 5.1 / 2218 0.5
13 F	0441 5.0 / 1053 0.7 / 1650 5.3 / 2322 0.5	**28** SA	0416 5.0 / 1028 0.8 / 1622 5.2 / 2252 0.6
14 SA	0516 4.9 / 1126 0.8 / 1728 5.1 / 2354 0.8	**29** SU	0449 5.0 / 1100 0.8 / 1659 5.1 / 2326 0.7
15 SU	0550 4.8 / 1159 1.0 / 1808 4.9	**30** M	0525 4.9 / 1139 0.8 / 1741 5.0
		31 TU	0002 0.9 / 0604 4.7 / 1221 1.0 / 1828 4.8

APRIL

Time	m	Time	m
1 W	0045 1.3 / 0651 4.5 / 1312 1.2 / 1926 4.5	**16** TH	0105 1.8 / 0715 4.2 / 1338 1.7 / 2007 3.9
2 TH	0138 1.6 / 0749 4.3 / 1420 1.5 / 2041 4.2	**17** F	0156 2.1 / 0811 3.9 / 1442 1.9 / 2117 3.7
3 F	0256 2.0 / 0907 4.1 / 1550 1.6 / 2212 4.0	**18** SA	0311 2.3 / 0923 3.8 / 1608 1.9 / 2236 3.7
4 SA	0437 2.1 / 1039 4.1 / 1725 1.4 / 2341 4.2	**19** SU	0447 2.3 / 1043 3.8 / 1733 1.8 / 2350 3.8
5 SU	0605 1.9 / 1200 4.3 / 1841 1.1	**20** M	0603 2.1 / 1154 4.0 / 1834 1.6
6 M	0050 4.4 / 0707 1.6 / 1302 4.6 / 1938 0.8	**21** TU	0045 4.1 / 0655 1.8 / 1247 4.2 / 1919 1.3
7 TU	0143 4.6 / 0756 1.3 / 1351 4.8 / 2025 0.6	**22** W	0127 4.3 / 0736 1.5 / 1328 4.5 / 1958 1.0
8 W	0225 4.8 / 0838 1.0 / 1433 5.0 / 2106 0.5	**23** TH	0204 4.5 / 0814 1.2 / 1406 4.7 / 2035 0.8
9 TH	0303 4.9 / 0917 0.9 / 1511 5.1 / 2143 0.5	**24** F	0238 4.7 / 0850 1.0 / 1442 4.9 / 2112 0.7
10 F	0338 5.0 / 0953 0.8 / 1549 5.1 / 2218 0.6	**25** SA	0313 4.9 / 0927 0.8 / 1520 5.1 / 2149 0.6
11 SA	0411 4.9 / 1028 0.8 / 1627 5.1 / 2250 0.7	**26** SU	0348 5.0 / 1006 0.7 / 1601 5.1 / 2228 0.6
12 SU	0445 4.9 / 1102 0.8 / 1705 4.9 / 2321 1.0	**27** M	0426 5.0 / 1047 0.6 / 1645 5.1 / 2308 0.8
13 M	0519 4.7 / 1136 1.0 / 1744 4.7 / 2352 1.2	**28** TU	0506 4.9 / 1131 0.7 / 1734 5.0 / 2351 0.9
14 TU	0554 4.6 / 1211 1.2 / 1826 4.4	**29** W	0551 4.8 / 1220 0.8 / 1828 4.7
15 W	0025 1.5 / 0631 4.4 / 1250 1.4 / 1912 4.1	**30** TH	0040 1.3 / 0643 4.6 / 1317 1.0 / 1931 4.5

Chart Datum: 2·60 metres below Ordnance Datum (Newlyn)
HAT is 5·7 metres above Chart Datum

TIDES

TIME ZONE (UT)
For Summer Time add ONE hour in **non-shaded areas**

ENGLAND – NORTH SHIELDS
LAT 55°01'N   LONG 1°26'W
TIMES AND HEIGHTS OF HIGH AND LOW WATERS

Dates in amber are **SPRINGS**
Dates in yellow are **NEAPS**

2009

MAY

Day	Time	m	Time	m	Time	m	Time	m
1 F	0139	1.6	0744	4.4	1426	1.2	2044	4.3
2 SA	0253	1.9	0859	4.3	1545	1.2	2203	4.2
3 SU	0418	1.9	1018	4.3	1704	1.2	2318	4.2
4 M ☽	0535	1.8	1132	4.4	1813	1.0		
5 TU	0022	4.3	0637	1.6	1234	4.6	1909	0.9
6 W	0114	4.5	0728	1.4	1325	4.7	1956	0.8
7 TH	0158	4.6	0812	1.2	1410	4.8	2037	0.8
8 F	0236	4.7	0853	1.0	1451	4.9	2114	0.8
9 SA	0312	4.8	0931	0.9	1530	4.9	2149	0.9
10 SU	0346	4.8	1008	0.9	1609	4.8	2222	1.0
11 M ○	0420	4.8	1043	0.9	1648	4.7	2254	1.2
12 TU	0454	4.7	1118	1.0	1727	4.5	2327	1.3
13 W	0530	4.6	1154	1.2	1807	4.4		
14 TH	0001	1.5	0607	4.5	1233	1.3	1851	4.2
15 F	0041	1.7	0649	4.3	1318	1.5	1940	4.0
16 SA	0127	1.9	0739	4.1	1411	1.6	2037	3.9
17 SU	0226	2.1	0837	4.0	1515	1.7	2140	3.8
18 M ☽	0339	2.1	0943	4.0	1624	1.7	2245	3.9
19 TU	0453	2.1	1048	4.0	1728	1.5	2345	4.0
20 W	0555	1.9	1147	4.2	1823	1.3		
21 TH	0036	4.2	0647	1.6	1239	4.4	1912	1.1
22 F	0121	4.5	0734	1.4	1327	4.6	1957	1.0
23 SA	0203	4.7	0819	1.1	1413	4.8	2042	0.8
24 SU	0244	4.9	0904	0.9	1459	5.0	2126	0.8
25 M	0326	5.0	0950	0.7	1548	5.1	2212	0.8
26 TU ●	0409	5.0	1038	0.5	1638	5.1	2258	0.9
27 W	0455	5.0	1129	0.5	1732	5.0	2346	1.1
28 TH	0544	4.9	1221	0.6	1828	4.8		
29 F	0037	1.3	0636	4.8	1318	0.7	1928	4.6
30 SA	0133	1.5	0735	4.7	1419	0.8	2031	4.4
31 SU	0235	1.7	0840	4.5	1524	1.0	2137	4.3

JUNE

Day	Time	m	Time	m	Time	m	Time	m
1 M	0344	1.8	0948	4.5	1631	1.1	2242	4.2
2 TU	0454	1.8	1057	4.4	1736	1.2	2345	4.2
3 W	0600	1.7	1201	4.4	1835	1.2		
4 TH	0041	4.3	0658	1.5	1259	4.5	1926	1.2
5 F	0129	4.4	0749	1.4	1350	4.5	2010	1.2
6 SA	0212	4.5	0834	1.2	1435	4.6	2049	1.2
7 SU	0251	4.6	0915	1.1	1517	4.6	2126	1.2
8 M	0327	4.7	0953	1.0	1557	4.6	2201	1.2
9 TU	0402	4.7	1029	1.0	1635	4.6	2235	1.3
10 W	0436	4.7	1104	1.0	1712	4.5	2308	1.4
11 TH	0511	4.7	1139	1.1	1749	4.4	2343	1.4
12 F	0547	4.6	1216	1.1	1828	4.3		
13 SA	0019	1.5	0625	4.5	1256	1.2	1909	4.2
14 SU	0100	1.7	0708	4.4	1340	1.3	1955	4.1
15 M	0146	1.8	0755	4.3	1429	1.5	2047	4.0
16 TU	0239	1.9	0848	4.2	1525	1.5	2144	4.0
17 W	0343	1.9	0947	4.2	1626	1.5	2244	4.0
18 TH	0452	1.9	1050	4.2	1729	1.5	2345	4.2
19 F	0558	1.7	1154	4.3	1829	1.3		
20 SA	0042	4.4	0658	1.5	1256	4.5	1926	1.2
21 SU	0135	4.6	0755	1.2	1354	4.7	2020	1.0
22 M	0223	4.8	0849	0.9	1448	4.9	2112	0.9
23 TU	0311	5.0	0942	0.6	1541	5.1	2202	0.9
24 W ○	0357	5.1	1033	0.4	1633	5.1	2250	0.9
25 TH	0444	5.2	1124	0.3	1726	5.1	2338	0.9
26 F	0533	5.2	1214	0.3	1818	5.0		
27 SA	0025	1.1	0623	5.1	1305	0.4	1910	4.8
28 SU	0113	1.3	0716	5.0	1357	0.7	2004	4.5
29 M	0204	1.5	0812	4.8	1451	0.9	2100	4.3
30 TU	0301	1.6	0913	4.6	1549	1.2	2200	4.2

JULY

Day	Time	m	Time	m	Time	m	Time	m
1 W	0407	1.8	1018	4.4	1652	1.5	2303	4.1
2 TH	0519	1.8	1128	4.2	1757	1.6		
3 F	0006	4.1	0630	1.8	1236	4.2	1857	1.6
4 SA	0104	4.3	0731	1.6	1335	4.3	1948	1.6
5 SU	0153	4.4	0821	1.4	1424	4.4	2031	1.5
6 M	0235	4.5	0903	1.3	1507	4.5	2109	1.4
7 TU	0312	4.7	0941	1.1	1545	4.5	2145	1.4
8 W	0346	4.7	1016	1.0	1620	4.6	2218	1.3
9 TH	0419	4.8	1049	0.9	1654	4.6	2251	1.3
10 F	0452	4.8	1122	0.9	1727	4.6	2323	1.3
11 SA	0525	4.8	1155	0.9	1801	4.5	2357	1.3
12 SU	0559	4.8	1230	1.0	1837	4.4		
13 M	0031	1.4	0635	4.7	1307	1.1	1915	4.3
14 TU	0109	1.5	0716	4.6	1347	1.3	1958	4.2
15 W	0153	1.7	0802	4.5	1434	1.4	2050	4.1
16 TH	0248	1.8	0858	4.3	1532	1.5	2151	4.1
17 F	0358	1.9	1005	4.2	1643	1.6	2300	4.1
18 SA	0519	1.8	1122	4.3	1758	1.6		
19 SU	0012	4.3	0635	1.6	1239	4.4	1908	1.4
20 M	0116	4.5	0742	1.2	1346	4.7	2009	1.2
21 TU	0210	4.8	0841	0.8	1443	4.9	2103	1.0
22 W	0259	5.1	0934	0.5	1534	5.1	2152	0.9
23 TH	0345	5.3	1024	0.2	1623	5.2	2237	0.8
24 F	0430	5.4	1111	0.1	1710	5.2	2321	0.8
25 SA	0515	5.4	1157	0.1	1756	5.1		
26 SU	0003	0.9	0600	5.3	1242	0.3	1841	4.9
27 M	0045	1.1	0648	5.1	1325	0.7	1928	4.6
28 TU	0128	1.3	0738	4.9	1411	1.1	2018	4.4
29 W	0216	1.6	0834	4.5	1502	1.5	2113	4.1
30 TH	0318	1.8	0939	4.2	1603	1.8	2217	4.0
31 F	0438	2.0	1055	4.0	1717	2.0	2329	4.0

AUGUST

Day	Time	m	Time	m	Time	m	Time	m
1 SA	0608	2.0	1216	4.0	1833	2.0		
2 SU ○	0039	4.1	0719	1.8	1323	4.1	1931	1.9
3 M	0135	4.3	0809	1.5	1413	4.3	2016	1.7
4 TU	0218	4.5	0849	1.3	1453	4.5	2054	1.5
5 W	0255	4.7	0924	1.1	1527	4.6	2128	1.3
6 TH	0327	4.6	0956	0.9	1559	4.7	2159	1.2
7 F	0358	4.9	1027	0.8	1629	4.7	2230	1.1
8 SA	0428	5.0	1058	0.8	1700	4.7	2300	1.1
9 SU ○	0459	5.0	1129	0.8	1730	4.7	2331	1.1
10 M	0530	5.0	1201	0.9	1803	4.6		
11 TU	0003	1.2	0604	4.9	1234	1.0	1837	4.5
12 W	0038	1.3	0642	4.8	1309	1.2	1917	4.4
13 TH	0118	1.5	0727	4.6	1352	1.4	2006	4.3
14 F	0210	1.7	0824	4.4	1450	1.7	2110	4.1
15 SA	0324	1.9	0938	4.2	1612	1.9	2229	4.1
16 SU	0458	1.9	1109	4.2	1744	1.8	2353	4.2
17 M ○	0626	1.6	1235	4.4	1901	1.6		
18 TU	0102	4.5	0735	1.1	1341	4.7	2001	1.3
19 W	0157	4.9	0832	0.7	1434	5.0	2051	1.1
20 TH	0244	5.2	0921	0.3	1520	5.2	2135	0.8
21 F	0327	5.4	1007	0.1	1604	5.3	2217	0.7
22 SA	0409	5.4	1050	0.1	1645	5.2	2257	0.7
23 SU	0451	5.4	1131	0.2	1726	5.1	2335	0.8
24 M ○	0534	5.4	1210	0.5	1806	4.9		
25 TU ●	0013	1.0	0617	5.1	1248	0.8	1847	4.7
26 W	0053	1.3	0704	4.8	1327	1.3	1932	4.4
27 TH	0137	1.6	0757	4.4	1412	1.7	2024	4.2
28 F	0233	2.0	0902	4.1	1511	2.1	2129	4.0
29 SA	0356	2.1	1022	3.8	1635	2.3	2249	3.9
30 SU	0543	2.1	1153	3.8	1808	2.2		
31 M	0010	4.0	0700	1.8	1304	4.0	1911	2.0

Chart Datum: 2·60 metres below Ordnance Datum (Newlyn)
HAT is 5·7 metres above Chart Datum

ENGLAND – NORTH SHIELDS

LAT 55°01'N   LONG 1°26'W

TIMES AND HEIGHTS OF HIGH AND LOW WATERS

Dates in amber are **SPRINGS**
Dates in yellow are **NEAPS**

2009

SEPTEMBER

Day	Time	m	Time	m	Time	m	Time	m
1 TU	0111	4.2	0748	1.6	1352	4.3	1955	1.8
2 W	0155	4.5	0825	1.3	1429	4.5	2031	1.5
3 TH	0230	4.7	0858	1.1	1501	4.7	2104	1.3
4 F ○	0301	4.9	0929	0.9	1531	4.8	2134	1.1
5 SA	0330	5.0	0959	0.8	1600	4.9	2204	1.0
6 SU	0400	5.1	1029	0.7	1629	4.9	2234	1.0
7 M	0430	5.1	1059	0.7	1659	4.9	2305	1.0
8 TU	0502	5.1	1130	0.8	1730	4.8	2337	1.1
9 W	0537	5.0	1202	1.0	1805	4.7		
10 TH	0013	1.2	0617	4.9	1238	1.2	1845	4.6
11 F	0055	1.4	0705	4.6	1322	1.5	1936	4.4
12 SA ◐	0152	1.7	0807	4.3	1425	1.9	2043	4.2
13 SU	0312	1.8			1559	2.1	2212	4.1
14 M	0452	1.8	1109	4.2	1738	2.0	2340	4.3
15 TU	0619	1.4	1230	4.4	1852	1.7		
16 W	0048	4.6	0724	1.0	1330	4.8	1946	1.4
17 TH	0141	5.0	0816	0.6	1418	5.0	2032	1.1
18 F ●	0225	5.3	0902	0.3	1500	5.2	2114	0.9
19 SA	0306	5.5	0944	0.2	1539	5.3	2153	0.7
20 SU	0346	5.6	1024	0.2	1617	5.2	2231	0.7
21 M	0426	5.5	1101	0.4	1654	5.1	2308	0.8
22 TU	0507	5.3	1138	0.7	1731	5.0	2345	1.0
23 W	0549	5.0	1210	1.1	1809	4.7		
24 TH	0022	1.3	0634	4.7	1246	1.5	1850	4.5
25 F	0105	1.6	0725	4.3	1326	1.9	1938	4.2
26 SA ◐	0157	1.9	0827	4.0	1421	2.2	2040	4.0
27 SU	0313	2.1	0945	3.8	1547	2.5	2200	3.9
28 M	0458	2.1	1101	3.8	1729	2.4	2326	4.0
29 TU	0621	1.9	1209	4.0	1838	2.2		
30 W	0033	4.2	0711	1.6	1318	4.2	1923	1.9

OCTOBER

Day	Time	m	Time	m	Time	m	Time	m
1 TH	0119	4.5	0750	1.4	1356	4.5	2000	1.6
2 F	0156	4.7	0823	1.1	1428	4.7	2033	1.4
3 SA	0228	4.9	0855	0.9	1458	4.8	2104	1.2
4 SU	0258	5.0	0926	0.8	1527	5.0	2136	1.0
5 M	0329	5.2	0957	0.7	1557	5.0	2208	0.9
6 TU	0402	5.2	1029	0.8	1629	5.0	2242	0.9
7 W	0438	5.2	1103	0.9	1703	5.0	2318	1.0
8 TH	0518	5.1	1138	1.1	1741	4.9	2358	1.1
9 F	0603	4.9	1217	1.4	1825	4.7		
10 SA	0047	1.3	0657	4.6	1308	1.7	1919	4.5
11 SU ◐	0150	1.5	0806	4.3	1417	2.0	2030	4.3
12 M	0313	1.7	0933	4.2	1552	2.2	2158	4.2
13 TU	0445	1.6	1101	4.3	1723	2.0	2320	4.4
14 W	0603	1.3	1214	4.5	1831	1.7		
15 TH	0026	4.7	0704	1.0	1311	4.7	1924	1.4
16 F	0119	5.0	0754	0.7	1356	5.0	2009	1.2
17 SA	0204	5.2	0838	0.6	1436	5.1	2051	1.0
18 SU ●	0245	5.4	0918	0.5	1513	5.2	2130	0.9
19 M	0325	5.4	0955	0.6	1549	5.2	2208	0.8
20 TU	0405	5.3	1031	0.8	1625	5.1	2245	0.9
21 W	0446	5.1	1104	1.0	1701	5.0	2322	1.1
22 TH	0528	4.9	1137	1.3	1738	4.8	2359	1.3
23 F	0611	4.6	1211	1.6	1817	4.6		
24 SA	0040	1.5	0659	4.3	1251	1.9	1901	4.3
25 SU	0128	1.8	0755	4.0	1340	2.2	1957	4.2
26 M ◐	0231	2.0	0903	3.9	1452	2.4	2107	4.0
27 TU	0354	2.1	1019	3.8	1625	2.4	2225	4.0
28 W	0516	1.9	1132	3.9	1742	2.3	2335	4.1
29 TH	0617	1.7	1229	4.2	1837	2.0		
30 F	0030	4.4	0703	1.5	1312	4.4	1919	1.7
31 SA	0113	4.6	0741	1.4	1349	4.6	1957	1.5

NOVEMBER

Day	Time	m	Time	m	Time	m	Time	m
1 SU	0150	4.8	0817	1.1	1422	4.8	2032	1.3
2 M ○	0226	5.0	0852	0.9	1455	5.0	2108	1.1
3 TU	0302	5.1	0928	0.9	1529	5.1	2146	1.0
4 W	0341	5.2	1005	0.9	1604	5.1	2225	0.9
5 TH	0422	5.2	1043	1.0	1643	5.1	2308	0.9
6 F	0508	5.1	1124	1.2	1726	5.0	2355	1.0
7 SA	0559	4.9	1210	1.4	1814	4.8		
8 SU	0048	1.1	0657	4.7	1305	1.7	1910	4.6
9 M ◑	0152	1.3	0806	4.4	1411	2.0	2019	4.5
10 TU	0306	1.4	0922	4.3	1532	2.1	2136	4.4
11 W	0424	1.3	1038	4.3	1652	2.0	2252	4.5
12 TH	0535	1.2	1146	4.5	1800	1.8	2358	4.7
13 F	0637	1.1	1243	4.6	1857	1.6		
14 SA	0054	4.9	0728	1.0	1331	4.8	1946	1.4
15 SU	0143	5.0	0813	0.9	1413	4.9	2030	1.2
16 M ●	0228	5.1	0853	1.0	1451	5.0	2112	1.1
17 TU	0310	5.1	0930	1.0	1527	5.0	2151	1.0
18 W	0351	5.0	1005	1.1	1603	5.0	2229	1.0
19 TH	0431	4.9	1040	1.3	1638	5.0	2306	1.1
20 F	0512	4.7	1113	1.5	1714	4.8	2342	1.3
21 SA	0552	4.6	1147	1.6	1752	4.7		
22 SU	0021	1.4	0635	4.4	1224	1.8	1832	4.5
23 M	0104	1.6	0722	4.2	1308	2.0	1920	4.4
24 TU ◑	0153	1.7	0817	4.1	1401	2.2	2016	4.3
25 W	0253	1.9	0918	3.9	1510	2.3	2120	4.1
26 TH	0401	1.9	1023	3.9	1626	2.3	2226	4.1
27 F	0507	1.8	1125	4.1	1734	2.1	2327	4.2
28 SA	0605	1.7	1219	4.3	1830	1.9		
29 SU	0022	4.4	0654	1.5	1306	4.5	1917	1.7
30 M	0111	4.6	0739	1.3	1348	4.7	2002	1.4

DECEMBER

Day	Time	m	Time	m	Time	m	Time	m
1 TU	0157	4.8	0822	1.1	1427	4.9	2046	1.2
2 W ○	0242	5.0	0905	1.0	1507	5.1	2130	1.0
3 TH	0327	5.1	0949	1.0	1548	5.2	2216	0.8
4 F	0415	5.2	1033	1.0	1630	5.2	2304	0.7
5 SA	0505	5.1	1119	1.2	1716	5.2	2354	0.7
6 SU	0557	5.1	1207	1.3	1805	5.1		
7 M	0047	0.8	0653	4.9	1258	1.5	1859	4.9
8 TU	0144	0.9	0753	4.6	1354	1.7	2000	4.8
9 W ◑	0245	1.1	0857	4.4	1459	1.9	2107	4.7
10 TH	0351	1.3	1003	4.3	1610	1.9	2216	4.6
11 F	0458	1.4	1109	4.3	1722	1.9	2326	4.6
12 SA	0603	1.4	1211	4.4	1828	1.8		
13 SU	0031	4.6	0701	1.4	1306	4.5	1926	1.6
14 M	0128	4.7	0750	1.4	1353	4.7	2017	1.4
15 TU	0218	4.7	0834	1.4	1434	4.8	2101	1.3
16 W ●	0302	4.8	0912	1.4	1512	4.9	2141	1.2
17 TH	0343	4.8	0948	1.4	1548	4.9	2218	1.1
18 F	0421	4.8	1022	1.4	1622	4.9	2253	1.1
19 SA	0458	4.7	1055	1.4	1656	4.9	2327	1.1
20 SU	0534	4.6	1128	1.5	1731	4.8		
21 M	0002	1.2	0610	4.5	1203	1.6	1807	4.7
22 TU	0039	1.3	0649	4.4	1239	1.7	1847	4.6
23 W	0118	1.5	0732	4.3	1320	1.9	1930	4.5
24 TH ◑	0203	1.6	0820	4.3	1408	2.0	2020	4.3
25 F	0255	1.7	0914	4.0	1508	2.2	2118	4.2
26 SA	0356	1.8	1016	4.0	1620	2.2	2222	4.2
27 SU	0502	1.8	1120	4.1	1733	2.1	2330	4.3
28 M	0607	1.7	1221	4.3	1839	1.8		
29 TU	0036	4.4	0707	1.5	1317	4.5	1937	1.5
30 W	0136	4.6	0801	1.2	1406	4.8	2030	1.2
31 TH ○	0230	4.9	0851	1.2	1451	5.0	2120	0.9

Chart Datum: 2·60 metres below Ordnance Datum (Newlyn)
HAT is 5·7 metres above Chart Datum

TIDES

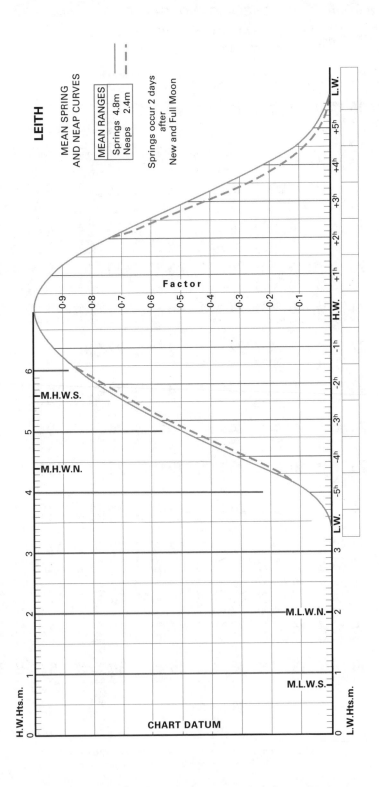

LEITH

MEAN SPRING
AND NEAP CURVES

MEAN RANGES
Springs 4.8m
Neaps 2.4m

Springs occur 2 days
after
New and Full Moon

Factor

0·9 0·8 0·7 0·6 0·5 0·4 0·3 0·2 0·1

H.W.Hts.m.

M.H.W.S.

M.H.W.N.

M.L.W.N.

M.L.W.S.

CHART DATUM

L.W.Hts.m.

L.W.   H.W.   L.W.

-5ʰ -4ʰ -3ʰ -2ʰ -1ʰ   +1ʰ +2ʰ +3ʰ +4ʰ +5ʰ

TIME ZONE (UT)
For Summer Time add ONE hour in **non-shaded areas**

SCOTLAND – LEITH

LAT 55°59′N   LONG 3°11′W

TIMES AND HEIGHTS OF HIGH AND LOW WATERS

Dates in amber are **SPRINGS**
Dates in yellow are **NEAPS**

2009

JANUARY

Time	m	Time	m	Time	m	Time	m
1 TH	0523 5.0 / 1049 1.6 / 1725 5.1 / 2319 1.3	**16** F	0612 5.2 / 1147 1.4 / 1831 5.4				
2 F	0603 4.9 / 1120 1.7 / 1803 5.0 / 2353 1.4	**17** SA	0031 1.1 / 0700 4.9 / 1217 1.7 / 1923 5.1				
3 SA	0646 4.8 / 1154 1.8 / 1845 4.9	**18**	0104 1.5 / 0752 4.6 / 1300 2.0 / ☽ 2021 4.8				
4 SU	0032 1.5 / 0733 4.7 / 1241 2.0 / ☽ 1934 4.8	**19**	0148 1.9 / 0847 4.4 / 1405 2.2 / 2122 4.5				
5 M	0123 1.7 / 0829 4.6 / 1349 2.1 / 2034 4.7	**20** TU	0303 2.2 / 0947 4.3 / 1545 2.4 / 2228 4.4				
6 TU	0230 1.8 / 0935 4.6 / 1516 2.1 / 2150 4.7	**21** W	0431 2.3 / 1054 4.3 / 1714 2.2 / 2341 4.4				
7 W	0356 1.8 / 1044 4.7 / 1643 2.0 / 2307 4.8	**22** TH	0538 2.2 / 1206 4.5 / 1821 2.0				
8 TH	0521 1.7 / 1150 4.9 / 1755 1.6	**23** F	0047 4.5 / 0627 2.0 / 1304 4.7 / 1909 1.8				
9 F	0016 5.1 / 0628 1.5 / 1250 5.1 / 1900 1.3	**24** SA	0137 4.7 / 0707 1.8 / 1347 4.9 / 1947 1.5				
10 SA	0117 5.4 / 0728 1.3 / 1343 5.4 / 2000 0.9	**25** SU	0216 4.9 / 0744 1.6 / 1423 5.1 / 2020 1.3				
11 SU	0212 5.6 / 0821 1.1 / 1432 5.7 / ○ 2055 0.5	**26** M	0249 5.1 / 0819 1.4 / 1455 5.2 / ● 2052 1.1				
12 M	0302 5.8 / 0910 1.0 / 1519 5.8 / 2146 0.3	**27** TU	0320 5.2 / 0855 1.2 / 1526 5.3 / 2126 0.9				
13 TU	0350 5.8 / 0956 0.9 / 1606 5.9 / 2232 0.3	**28** W	0352 5.2 / 0930 1.1 / 1557 5.4 / 2159 0.8				
14 W	0437 5.7 / 1038 1.0 / 1653 5.8 / 2316 0.4	**29** TH	0424 5.2 / 1003 1.1 / 1628 5.4 / 2231 0.9				
15 TH	0524 5.5 / 1115 1.1 / 1741 5.6 / 2356 0.7	**30** F	0459 5.0 / 1031 1.2 / 1701 5.4 / 2258 1.0				
		31 SA	0534 5.1 / 1054 1.3 / 1736 5.3 / 2321 1.1				

FEBRUARY

Time	m	Time	m
1 SU	0613 5.0 / 1119 1.4 / 1816 5.2 / 2349 1.3	**16** M	0005 1.5 / 0702 4.6 / 1207 1.8 / ☽ 1934 4.7
2 M	0656 4.8 / 1157 1.6 / 1902 5.0 / ●	**17** TU	0043 1.9 / 0753 4.4 / 1259 2.1 / 2034 4.3
3 TU	0031 1.5 / 0747 4.6 / 1253 1.9 / 1959 4.8	**18** W	0144 2.3 / 0853 4.2 / 1439 2.4 / 2142 4.1
4 W	0135 1.9 / 0852 4.5 / 1421 2.1 / 2118 4.6	**19** TH	0344 2.5 / 1002 4.1 / 1655 2.3 / 2303 4.1
5 TH	0320 2.1 / 1013 4.5 / 1628 2.0 / 2248 4.6	**20** F	0514 2.4 / 1126 4.2 / 1811 2.1
6 F	0516 2.0 / 1132 4.7 / 1756 1.6	**21** SA	0026 4.3 / 0610 2.1 / 1239 4.5 / 1858 1.7
7 SA	0008 4.4 / 0627 1.7 / 1240 5.0 / 1902 1.2	**22** SU	0117 4.6 / 0653 1.8 / 1325 4.8 / 1933 1.5
8 SU	0113 5.2 / 0723 1.4 / 1334 5.4 / 1958 0.7	**23** M	0154 4.9 / 0729 1.6 / 1401 5.0 / 2004 1.2
9 M	0204 5.5 / 0811 1.1 / 1420 5.7 / ○ 2047 0.3	**24** TU	0226 5.1 / 0803 1.3 / 1432 5.2 / 2035 0.9
10 TU	0249 5.8 / 0856 0.8 / 1504 5.9 / 2132 0.1	**25** W	0256 5.2 / 0837 1.1 / 1503 5.4 / ● 2106 0.7
11 W	0332 5.8 / 0936 0.7 / 1547 6.0 / 2213 0.1	**26** TH	0326 5.3 / 0911 0.9 / 1533 5.5 / 2138 0.6
12 TH	0415 5.7 / 1014 0.7 / 1630 5.9 / 2250 0.3	**27** F	0358 5.4 / 0943 0.9 / 1604 5.5 / 2208 0.6
13 F	0456 5.5 / 1046 0.9 / 1713 5.7 / 2321 0.6	**28** SA	0431 5.3 / 1010 0.9 / 1637 5.5 / 2233 0.8
14 SA	0538 5.2 / 1109 1.1 / 1757 5.4 / 2344 1.1		
15 SU	0619 4.8 / 1132 1.4 / 1843 5.0		

MARCH

Time	m	Time	m
1 SU	0507 5.3 / 1031 1.0 / 1714 5.4 / 2251 1.0	**16** M	0542 4.9 / 1058 1.3 / 1810 4.9 / 2321 1.5
2 M	0545 5.1 / 1055 1.2 / 1756 5.3 / 2318 1.2	**17** TU	0621 4.7 / 1129 1.6 / 1857 4.6 / 2355 1.9
3 TU	0627 4.9 / 1133 1.4 / 1844 5.0	**18** W	0708 4.4 / 1215 2.0 / 1953 4.3
4 W	0000 1.6 / 0717 4.6 / 1231 1.7 / ☽ 1944 4.7	**19** TH	0053 2.4 / 0805 4.2 / 1337 2.3 / 2057 4.1
5 TH	0109 2.0 / 0824 4.4 / 1415 2.0 / 2107 4.5	**20** F	0249 2.6 / 0915 4.1 / 1626 2.3 / 2213 4.0
6	0331 2.3 / 0955 4.4 / 1635 1.9 / 2242 4.5	**21** SA	0443 2.5 / 1034 4.1 / 1739 2.0 / 2342 4.2
7 SA	0514 2.1 / 1120 4.6 / 1756 1.5	**22** SU	0541 2.2 / 1154 4.4 / 1825 1.7
8 SU	0003 4.8 / 0618 1.7 / 1228 5.0 / 1856 1.0	**23** M	0040 4.5 / 0624 1.8 / 1247 4.7 / 1901 1.4
9 M	0103 5.2 / 0708 1.3 / 1319 5.4 / 1946 0.6	**24** TU	0119 4.8 / 0701 1.5 / 1326 5.0 / 1933 1.1
10 TU	0150 5.4 / 0752 1.0 / 1403 5.6 / 2030 0.3	**25** W	0152 5.1 / 0736 1.2 / 1359 5.2 / 2004 0.9
11 W	0230 5.6 / 0833 0.7 / 1444 5.8 / ○ 2109 0.2	**26** TH	0224 5.3 / 0810 1.0 / 1432 5.4 / ● 2037 0.7
12 TH	0309 5.6 / 0912 0.6 / 1524 5.9 / 2146 0.2	**27** F	0256 5.4 / 0844 0.8 / 1504 5.5 / 2109 0.6
13 F	0348 5.6 / 0947 0.6 / 1605 5.8 / 2219 0.4	**28** SA	0329 5.5 / 0918 0.7 / 1538 5.6 / 2141 0.6
14 SA	0426 5.4 / 1017 0.8 / 1646 5.6 / 2245 0.8	**29** SU	0404 5.4 / 0949 0.7 / 1616 5.6 / 2209 0.7
15 SU	0504 5.2 / 1038 1.0 / 1727 5.3 / 2301 1.2	**30** M	0441 5.4 / 1017 0.9 / 1657 5.5 / 2232 1.0
		31 TU	0522 5.2 / 1048 1.1 / 1743 5.3 / 2304 1.4

APRIL

Time	m	Time	m
1 W	0607 4.9 / 1134 1.3 / 1836 5.0 / 2354 1.8	**16** TH	0632 4.5 / 1152 1.8 / 1919 4.3
2 TH	0701 4.7 / 1248 1.6 / 1942 4.7 / ☽	**17** F	0020 2.3 / 0726 4.3 / 1300 2.1 / ☽ 2017 4.1
3 F	0128 2.2 / 0815 4.4 / 1446 1.8 / 2107 4.5	**18** SA	0150 2.5 / 0831 4.2 / 1459 2.2 / 2123 4.1
4 SA	0335 2.3 / 0945 4.5 / 1630 1.6 / 2234 4.6	**19** SU	0349 2.6 / 0944 4.2 / 1642 2.0 / 2234 4.2
5 SU	0456 2.0 / 1103 4.7 / 1741 1.2 / 2348 4.8	**20** M	0454 2.2 / 1054 4.3 / 1732 1.7 / 2339 4.4
6 M	0554 1.7 / 1207 5.0 / 1837 0.9	**21** TU	0541 1.9 / 1153 4.6 / 1813 1.4
7 TU	0044 5.1 / 0643 1.4 / 1258 5.3 / 1923 0.7	**22** W	0029 4.7 / 0620 1.6 / 1240 4.9 / 1848 1.2
8 W	0128 5.3 / 0726 1.0 / 1341 5.5 / 2004 0.5	**23** TH	0110 5.0 / 0658 1.3 / 1320 5.1 / 1924 0.9
9 TH	0207 5.4 / 0806 0.8 / 1422 5.6 / ○ 2041 0.4	**24** F	0148 5.2 / 0736 1.0 / 1358 5.4 / 2000 0.7
10 F	0244 5.4 / 0845 0.7 / 1502 5.6 / 2115 0.5	**25** SA	0225 5.4 / 0815 0.8 / 1436 5.5 / ● 2038 0.6
11 SA	0321 5.4 / 0921 0.7 / 1543 5.5 / 2145 0.7	**26** SU	0301 5.5 / 0855 0.7 / 1516 5.6 / 2117 0.7
12 SU	0358 5.3 / 0951 0.8 / 1623 5.3 / 2209 1.0	**27** M	0340 5.5 / 0937 0.7 / 1559 5.6 / 2156 0.9
13 M	0434 5.1 / 1015 1.1 / 1703 5.1 / 2227 1.3	**28** TU	0421 5.4 / 1020 0.7 / 1646 5.5 / 2237 1.1
14 TU	0510 4.9 / 1037 1.3 / 1744 4.8 / 2250 1.6	**29** W	0506 5.3 / 1109 0.9 / 1737 5.3 / 2324 1.5
15 W	0548 4.7 / 1107 1.6 / 1828 4.6 / 2326 1.9	**30** TH	0556 5.0 / 1205 1.2 / 1834 5.0

Chart Datum: 2·90 metres below Ordnance Datum (Newlyn)
HAT is 6·3 metres above Chart Datum

SCOTLAND – LEITH

TIME ZONE (UT)
For Summer Time add ONE hour in **non-shaded areas**

LAT 55°59'N   LONG 3°11'W

TIMES AND HEIGHTS OF HIGH AND LOW WATERS

Dates in amber are **SPRINGS**
Dates in yellow are **NEAPS**

2009

MAY

Day	Time	m	Time	m
1 F	0025 / 0655 / 1317 / 1942	1.8 / 4.8 / 1.4 / 4.8	16 SA 0652 / 1234 / 1939	4.5 / 4.8 / 4.3
2 SA	0144 / 0810 / 1445 / 2059	2.1 / 4.7 / 1.4 / 4.6	17 SU 0104 / 0748 / 1342 / 2036	2.3 / 4.4 / 1.9 / 4.3
3 SU	0311 / 0929 / 1606 / 2213	2.1 / 4.7 / 1.3 / 4.7	18 M 0227 / 0851 / 1505 / 2138	2.3 / 4.3 / 1.9 / 4.3
4 M	0422 / 1039 / 1711 / 2321	1.9 / 4.8 / 1.2 / 4.8	19 TU 0346 / 0957 / 1618 / 2240	2.2 / 4.4 / 1.7 / 4.5
5 TU	0519 / 1140 / 1807	1.7 / 5.0 / 1.0	20 W 0445 / 1057 / 1711 / 2336	2.0 / 4.6 / 1.5 / 4.7
6 W	0016 / 0610 / 1233 / 1854	5.0 / 1.5 / 5.2 / 0.9	21 TH 0534 / 1152 / 1758	1.7 / 4.8 / 1.3
7 TH	0103 / 0656 / 1319 / 1933	5.1 / 1.2 / 5.3 / 0.9	22 F 0027 / 0619 / 1242 / 1842	4.9 / 1.4 / 5.1 / 1.1
8 F	0143 / 0739 / 1402 / 2009	5.2 / 1.0 / 5.3 / 0.9	23 SA 0113 / 0704 / 1328 / 1927	5.2 / 1.1 / 5.3 / 0.9
9 SA	0221 / 0820 / 1444 / 2042	5.2 / 0.9 / 5.3 / 0.9	24 SU 0156 / 0750 / 1414 / 2014	5.3 / 0.9 / 5.5 / 0.8
10 SU	0258 / 0857 / 1524 / 2112	5.2 / 0.9 / 5.3 / 1.1	25 M 0238 / 0840 / 1500 / 2103	5.5 / 0.7 / 5.6 / 0.8
11 M	0334 / 0930 / 1603 / 2139	5.2 / 1.0 / 5.2 / 1.2	26 TU 0322 / 0932 / 1548 / 2152	5.5 / 0.6 / 5.7 / 0.9
12 TU	0409 / 0958 / 1642 / 2205	5.1 / 1.1 / 5.0 / 1.4	27 W 0408 / 1024 / 1639 / 2242	5.5 / 0.6 / 5.6 / 1.1
13 W	0444 / 1026 / 1721 / 2234	5.0 / 1.3 / 4.8 / 1.6	28 TH 0456 / 1117 / 1732 / 2332	5.4 / 0.6 / 5.4 / 1.4
14 TH	0522 / 1059 / 1803 / 2311	4.8 / 1.4 / 4.7 / 1.8	29 F 0549 / 1212 / 1829	5.3 / 0.8 / 5.2
15 F	0604 / 1141 / 1848 / 2359	4.7 / 1.6 / 4.5 / 2.1	30 SA 0025 / 0648 / 1312 / 1931	1.6 / 5.1 / 1.0 / 5.0
			31 SU 0125 / 0756 / 1419 / 2037	1.8 / 5.0 / 1.2 / 4.8

JUNE

Day	Time	m	Time	m
1 M	0232 / 0904 / 1528 / 2143	1.9 / 4.9 / 1.3 / 4.7	16 TU 0121 / 0758 / 1354 / 2048	2.1 / 4.6 / 1.7 / 4.5
2 TU	0338 / 1009 / 1632 / 2245	1.9 / 4.9 / 1.3 / 4.7	17 W 0230 / 0858 / 1459 / 2148	2.1 / 4.5 / 1.7 / 4.5
3 W	0440 / 1110 / 1730 / 2343	1.8 / 4.9 / 1.4 / 4.8	18 TH 0342 / 1004 / 1608 / 2250	2.0 / 4.6 / 1.6 / 4.6
4 TH	0537 / 1207 / 1819	1.7 / 4.9 / 1.4	19 F 0447 / 1108 / 1713 / 2349	1.8 / 4.7 / 1.5 / 4.8
5 F	0035 / 0629 / 1259 / 1900	4.9 / 1.5 / 5.0 / 1.3	20 SA 0546 / 1209 / 1812	1.6 / 4.9 / 1.3
6 SA	0121 / 0717 / 1347 / 1937	5.0 / 1.3 / 5.0 / 1.3	21 SU 0043 / 0641 / 1306 / 1907	5.0 / 1.4 / 5.2 / 1.2
7 SU	0202 / 0800 / 1430 / 2011	5.0 / 1.2 / 5.1 / 1.3	22 M 0134 / 0737 / 1359 / 2002	5.3 / 0.9 / 5.5 / 1.0
8 M	0240 / 0838 / 1509 / 2044	5.1 / 1.1 / 5.1 / 1.3	23 TU 0222 / 0834 / 1449 / 2055	5.5 / 0.6 / 5.7 / 0.9
9 TU	0316 / 0912 / 1547 / 2116	5.1 / 1.1 / 5.0 / 1.3	24 W 0309 / 0929 / 1539 / 2146	5.6 / 0.4 / 5.7 / 0.9
10 W	0350 / 0944 / 1623 / 2149	5.1 / 1.1 / 5.0 / 1.4	25 TH 0357 / 1021 / 1629 / 2235	5.7 / 0.3 / 5.7 / 0.9
11 TH	0425 / 1016 / 1659 / 2223	5.1 / 1.2 / 4.9 / 1.5	26 F 0446 / 1111 / 1720 / 2321	5.6 / 0.3 / 5.6 / 1.1
12 F	0501 / 1050 / 1738 / 2258	5.0 / 1.2 / 4.8 / 1.6	27 SA 0537 / 1200 / 1813	5.6 / 0.5 / 5.4
13 SA	0540 / 1127 / 1819 / 2338	4.9 / 1.4 / 4.7 / 1.8	28 SU 0005 / 0631 / 1249 / 1907	1.3 / 5.4 / 0.7 / 5.1
14 SU	0621 / 1209 / 1903	4.8 / 1.5 / 4.6	29 M 0051 / 0730 / 1339 / 2005	1.5 / 5.2 / 1.1 / 4.8
15 M	0023 / 0706 / 1257 / 1952	1.9 / 4.6 / 1.6 / 4.5	30 TU 0141 / 0832 / 1435 / 2105	1.7 / 5.0 / 1.4 / 4.7

JULY

Day	Time	m	Time	m
1 W	0245 / 0934 / 1540 / 2205	1.9 / 4.8 / 1.7 / 4.5	16 TH 0116 / 0807 / 1353 / 2101	1.9 / 4.7 / 1.7 / 4.5
2 TH	0359 / 1037 / 1646 / 2307	2.0 / 4.7 / 1.8 / 4.5	17 F 0235 / 0915 / 1511 / 2209	2.0 / 4.6 / 1.8 / 4.5
3 F	0510 / 1142 / 1744	1.9 / 4.6 / 1.8	18 SA 0407 / 1033 / 1645 / 2318	2.0 / 4.6 / 1.8 / 4.7
4 SA	0008 / 0613 / 1243 / 1831	4.6 / 1.7 / 4.7 / 1.7	19 SU 0527 / 1146 / 1759	1.7 / 4.8 / 1.6
5 SU	0103 / 0705 / 1335 / 1911	4.8 / 1.5 / 4.8 / 1.6	20 M 0022 / 0633 / 1252 / 1900	4.9 / 1.3 / 5.1 / 1.3
6 M	0148 / 0748 / 1418 / 1947	4.9 / 1.4 / 4.9 / 1.5	21 TU 0119 / 0734 / 1348 / 1955	5.2 / 0.9 / 5.5 / 1.1
7 TU	0227 / 0825 / 1456 / 2023	5.0 / 1.2 / 5.0 / 1.4	22 W 0209 / 0830 / 1439 / 2046	5.5 / 0.5 / 5.7 / 0.9
8 W	0301 / 0858 / 1530 / 2058	5.1 / 1.1 / 5.1 / 1.3	23 TH 0255 / 0921 / 1526 / 2133	5.8 / 0.2 / 5.8 / 0.7
9 TH	0333 / 0930 / 1602 / 2133	5.2 / 1.0 / 5.1 / 1.3	24 F 0341 / 1009 / 1613 / 2217	5.9 / 0.0 / 5.8 / 0.7
10 F	0406 / 1003 / 1636 / 2208	5.2 / 1.0 / 5.1 / 1.3	25 SA 0428 / 1054 / 1659 / 2259	5.9 / 0.1 / 5.7 / 0.8
11 SA	0440 / 1036 / 1712 / 2241	5.2 / 1.0 / 5.0 / 1.3	26 SU 0515 / 1136 / 1747 / 2336	5.8 / 0.3 / 5.4 / 1.0
12 SU	0515 / 1108 / 1749 / 2312	5.1 / 1.1 / 4.9 / 1.5	27 M 0605 / 1215 / 1835	5.6 / 0.7 / 5.1
13 M	0551 / 1140 / 1828 / 2342	5.0 / 1.2 / 4.8 / 1.6	28 TU 0009 / 0657 / 1251 / 1926	1.3 / 5.3 / 1.2 / 4.8
14 TU	0630 / 1213 / 1912	4.9 / 1.4 / 4.7	29 W 0047 / 0754 / 1330 / 2021	1.7 / 4.9 / 1.6 / 4.6
15 W	0020 / 0714 / 1255 / 2001	1.8 / 4.8 / 1.5 / 4.6	30 TH 0144 / 0857 / 1433 / 2121	2.0 / 4.6 / 2.0 / 4.4
			31 F 0317 / 1003 / 1603 / 2227	2.2 / 4.4 / 2.2 / 4.4

AUGUST

Day	Time	m	Time	m
1 SA	0453 / 1116 / 1718 / 2340	2.1 / 4.4 / 2.2 / 4.4	16 SU 0351 / 1012 / 1640 / 2256	2.0 / 4.6 / 2.0 / 4.6
2 SU	0610 / 1227 / 1812	1.9 / 4.5 / 2.0	17 M 0525 / 1134 / 1755	1.7 / 4.8 / 1.8
3 M	0044 / 0702 / 1322 / 1854	4.6 / 1.7 / 4.7 / 1.8	18 TU 0007 / 0631 / 1243 / 1852	4.9 / 1.2 / 5.2 / 1.4
4 TU	0132 / 0741 / 1403 / 1931	4.9 / 1.4 / 4.9 / 1.6	19 W 0105 / 0729 / 1337 / 1942	5.3 / 0.7 / 5.5 / 1.1
5 W	0210 / 0812 / 1438 / 2006	5.1 / 1.2 / 5.0 / 1.4	20 TH 0153 / 0819 / 1423 / 2028	5.7 / 0.3 / 5.8 / 0.8
6 TH	0242 / 0842 / 1508 / 2040	5.2 / 1.0 / 5.1 / 1.3	21 F 0237 / 0906 / 1507 / 2112	5.9 / 0.0 / 5.9 / 0.6
7 F	0313 / 0913 / 1539 / 2115	5.3 / 0.9 / 5.2 / 1.1	22 SA 0320 / 0949 / 1550 / 2153	6.1 / 0.0 / 5.8 / 0.6
8 SA	0344 / 0944 / 1610 / 2148	5.4 / 0.8 / 5.2 / 1.1	23 SU 0404 / 1029 / 1633 / 2231	6.0 / 0.1 / 5.7 / 0.7
9 SU	0415 / 1015 / 1643 / 2218	5.4 / 0.8 / 5.2 / 1.1	24 M 0449 / 1105 / 1716 / 2302	5.9 / 0.4 / 5.4 / 0.9
10 M	0447 / 1043 / 1718 / 2242	5.3 / 0.9 / 5.1 / 1.2	25 TU 0535 / 1136 / 1800 / 2328	5.6 / 0.9 / 5.1 / 1.3
11 TU	0521 / 1105 / 1755 / 2304	5.2 / 1.0 / 5.0 / 1.4	26 W 0624 / 1159 / 1846 / 2359	5.2 / 1.4 / 4.8 / 1.6
12 W	0559 / 1128 / 1835 / 2336	5.1 / 1.2 / 4.9 / 1.6	27 TH 0718 / 1231 / 1938	4.8 / 1.8 / 4.5
13 TH	0643 / 1204 / 1922	5.0 / 1.5 / 4.7	28 F 0050 / 0818 / 1330 / 2038	2.0 / 4.5 / 2.3 / 4.3
14 F	0024 / 0735 / 1300 / 2020	1.8 / 4.8 / 1.8 / 4.5	29 SA 0230 / 0926 / 1523 / 2146	2.3 / 4.2 / 2.5 / 4.3
15 SA	0146 / 0845 / 1434 / 2137	2.0 / 4.6 / 2.1 / 4.5	30 SU 0446 / 1044 / 1656 / 2305	2.3 / 4.2 / 2.4 / 4.3
			31 M 0600 / 1206 / 1754	2.0 / 4.5 / 2.2

Chart Datum: 2·90 metres below Ordnance Datum (Newlyn)
HAT is 6·3 metres above Chart Datum

SCOTLAND – LEITH

LAT 55°59′N   LONG 3°11′W

TIMES AND HEIGHTS OF HIGH AND LOW WATERS

Dates in amber are **SPRINGS**
Dates in yellow are **NEAPS**

2009

SEPTEMBER				OCTOBER				NOVEMBER				DECEMBER			
Time	m	Time	m	Time	m	Time	m	Time	m	Time	m	Time	m	Time	m

SEPTEMBER

1 0018 4.6 / 0646 1.7 / TU 1301 4.7 / 1835 1.9
16 0623 1.1 / 1230 5.2 / W 1836 1.4

2 0107 4.9 / 0720 1.4 / W 1340 4.9 / 1911 1.6
17 0047 5.4 / 0714 0.7 / TH 1320 5.5 / 1921 1.1

3 0144 5.1 / 0750 1.2 / TH 1411 5.1 / 1944 1.3
18 0133 5.8 / 0800 0.3 / F 1402 5.7 / ● 2005 0.8

4 0216 5.3 / 0818 0.9 / F 1440 5.2 / ○ 2018 1.1
19 0215 6.0 / 0843 0.2 / SA 1443 5.8 / 2046 0.6

5 0246 5.4 / 0847 0.8 / SA 1510 5.3 / 2051 1.0
20 0257 6.1 / 0922 0.2 / SU 1523 5.8 / 2126 0.6

6 0316 5.5 / 0918 0.7 / SU 1541 5.4 / 2123 0.9
21 0340 6.0 / 0959 0.4 / M 1604 5.6 / 2202 0.7

7 0347 5.5 / 0947 0.7 / M 1613 5.4 / 2152 1.0
22 0424 5.8 / 1031 0.7 / TU 1644 5.4 / 2231 1.0

8 0419 5.5 / 1012 0.8 / TU 1648 5.3 / 2214 1.1
23 0508 5.5 / 1054 1.1 / W 1725 5.1 / 2253 1.3

9 0455 5.4 / 1030 1.0 / W 1724 5.2 / 2236 1.3
24 0554 5.1 / 1111 1.6 / TH 1808 4.9 / 2321 1.7

10 0536 5.2 / 1053 1.3 / TH 1805 5.0 / 2310 1.5
25 0645 4.7 / 1143 2.0 / F 1856 4.6

11 0622 5.0 / 1130 1.6 / F 1853 4.8
26 0008 2.0 / 0742 4.4 / SA 1239 2.4 / ◐ 1955 4.4

12 0002 1.8 / 0718 4.8 / SA 1231 2.0 / ◐ 1954 4.6
27 0132 2.4 / 0847 4.2 / SU 1428 2.7 / 2105 4.3

13 0140 2.0 / 0832 4.6 / SU 1442 2.3 / 2117 4.5
28 0418 2.3 / 1000 4.2 / M 1624 2.6 / 2220 4.3

14 0358 2.0 / 1003 4.6 / M 1637 2.2 / 2242 4.7
29 0526 2.0 / 1123 4.3 / TU 1722 2.3 / 2334 4.5

15 0522 1.5 / 1125 4.9 / TU 1744 1.8 / 2352 5.0
30 0610 1.8 / 1223 4.6 / W 1805 2.0

OCTOBER

1 0027 4.8 / 0645 1.5 / TH 1303 4.9 / 1841 1.7
16 0025 5.5 / 0652 0.8 / F 1258 5.4 / 1855 1.2

2 0107 5.1 / 0715 1.2 / F 1335 5.1 / 1915 1.4
17 0111 5.7 / 0735 0.6 / SA 1339 5.6 / 1939 0.9

3 0141 5.3 / 0744 1.0 / SA 1406 5.3 / 1949 1.1
18 0154 5.8 / 0815 0.5 / SU 1419 5.7 / ● 2021 0.8

4 0213 5.4 / 0814 0.8 / SU 1438 5.4 / ○ 2023 1.0
19 0236 5.9 / 0853 0.6 / M 1458 5.6 / 2101 0.8

5 0246 5.6 / 0845 0.7 / M 1510 5.5 / 2056 0.9
20 0319 5.8 / 0927 0.8 / TU 1537 5.5 / 2137 0.9

6 0319 5.6 / 0915 0.8 / TU 1544 5.5 / 2128 0.9
21 0402 5.6 / 0955 1.1 / W 1616 5.4 / 2207 1.1

7 0355 5.6 / 0942 0.9 / W 1620 5.4 / 2157 1.0
22 0445 5.3 / 1016 1.4 / TH 1654 5.2 / 2230 1.4

8 0435 5.5 / 1006 1.1 / TH 1659 5.3 / 2227 1.2
23 0529 5.0 / 1037 1.7 / F 1734 4.9 / 2259 1.7

9 0520 5.3 / 1036 1.4 / F 1743 5.1 / 2308 1.4
24 0615 4.7 / 1111 2.0 / SA 1820 4.7 / 2342 1.9

10 0611 5.1 / 1120 1.8 / SA 1834 4.9
25 0707 4.5 / 1202 2.4 / SU 1915 4.5

11 0018 1.7 / 0711 4.8 / SU 1244 2.2 / ◐ 1939 4.7
26 0046 2.2 / 0805 4.3 / M 1333 2.6 / 2019 4.4

12 0204 1.9 / 0828 4.6 / M 1448 2.4 / 2105 4.6
27 0252 2.3 / 0909 4.2 / TU 1523 2.6 / 2129 4.4

13 0351 1.7 / 0953 4.7 / TU 1618 2.2 / 2226 4.8
28 0428 2.1 / 1017 4.3 / W 1633 2.4 / 2235 4.5

14 0505 1.4 / 1109 4.9 / W 1719 1.8 / 2331 5.1
29 0518 1.9 / 1121 4.5 / TH 1722 2.1 / 2333 4.7

15 0603 1.0 / 1210 5.2 / TH 1810 1.5
30 0557 1.6 / 1211 4.8 / F 1803 1.8

31 0021 5.0 / 0631 1.4 / SA 1252 5.1 / 1840 1.5

NOVEMBER

1 0102 5.2 / 0704 1.2 / SU 1330 5.3 / 1917 1.3
16 0137 5.5 / 0747 1.0 / M 1358 5.4 / ● 2000 1.1

2 0140 5.4 / 0738 1.0 / M 1406 5.5 / ○ 1954 1.1
17 0221 5.5 / 0823 1.0 / TU 1437 5.5 / 2041 1.0

3 0218 5.5 / 0813 0.9 / TU 1442 5.6 / 2032 0.9
18 0304 5.5 / 0856 1.2 / W 1516 5.4 / 2118 1.1

4 0256 5.6 / 0849 0.9 / W 1519 5.6 / 2112 0.9
19 0346 5.4 / 0925 1.3 / TH 1553 5.3 / 2149 1.2

5 0338 5.7 / 0927 1.0 / TH 1559 5.5 / 2155 0.9
20 0426 5.2 / 0951 1.5 / F 1630 5.2 / 2216 1.4

6 0422 5.6 / 1006 1.3 / F 1642 5.4 / 2243 1.1
21 0506 5.0 / 1019 1.7 / SA 1707 5.0 / 2246 1.5

7 0511 5.4 / 1051 1.5 / SA 1729 5.3 / 2337 1.3
22 0548 4.8 / 1053 1.9 / SU 1749 4.9 / 2325 1.7

8 0604 5.2 / 1148 1.9 / SU 1823 5.1
23 0633 4.6 / 1137 2.1 / M 1836 4.7

9 0042 1.5 / 0706 5.0 / M 1302 2.1 / ◐ 1930 4.9
24 0013 1.9 / 0722 4.5 / TU 1234 2.4 / ◐ 1930 4.5

10 0201 1.6 / 0818 4.8 / TU 1426 2.2 / 2049 4.9
25 0115 2.1 / 0817 4.4 / W 1350 2.5 / 2032 4.5

11 0325 1.5 / 0934 4.8 / W 1543 2.1 / 2202 5.0
26 0233 2.1 / 0917 4.4 / TH 1516 2.5 / 2135 4.5

12 0435 1.4 / 1043 4.9 / TH 1646 1.9 / 2305 5.1
27 0356 2.0 / 1018 4.5 / F 1624 2.3 / 2236 4.6

13 0534 1.2 / 1143 5.1 / F 1740 1.7
28 0455 1.8 / 1115 4.7 / SA 1717 2.0 / 2332 4.8

14 0001 5.3 / 0624 1.1 / SA 1234 5.2 / 1829 1.4
29 0542 1.6 / 1208 4.9 / SU 1803 1.7

15 0051 5.5 / 0708 1.0 / SU 1317 5.4 / 1916 1.2
30 0023 5.0 / 0624 1.4 / M 1255 5.2 / 1847 1.5

DECEMBER

1 0111 5.2 / 0707 1.2 / TU 1339 5.4 / 1931 1.2
16 0212 5.2 / 0759 1.4 / W 1425 5.3 / ● 2029 1.2

2 0155 5.5 / 0750 1.1 / W 1420 5.5 / ○ 2017 1.0
17 0254 5.2 / 0832 1.4 / TH 1502 5.3 / 2105 1.2

3 0240 5.6 / 0835 1.1 / TH 1501 5.6 / 2106 0.8
18 0332 5.2 / 0904 1.4 / F 1537 5.3 / 2136 1.2

4 0326 5.7 / 0923 1.1 / F 1544 5.7 / 2157 0.7
19 0409 5.2 / 0934 1.5 / SA 1611 5.2 / 2205 1.2

5 0413 5.7 / 1012 1.2 / SA 1630 5.6 / 2249 0.7
20 0445 5.1 / 1006 1.5 / SU 1646 5.2 / 2235 1.3

6 0503 5.6 / 1101 1.4 / SU 1719 5.5 / 2342 0.9
21 0521 5.0 / 1039 1.6 / M 1723 5.1 / 2308 1.4

7 0556 5.4 / 1151 1.6 / M 1813 5.4
22 0600 4.8 / 1114 1.8 / TU 1802 4.9 / 2345 1.6

8 0037 1.0 / 0653 5.2 / TU 1245 1.8 / 1913 5.2
23 0643 4.7 / 1152 2.0 / W 1845 4.8

9 0137 1.2 / 0757 4.9 / W 1347 2.0 / ◖ 2023 5.1
24 0027 1.7 / 0729 4.5 / TH 1241 2.2 / ◖ 1933 4.6

10 0244 1.4 / 0904 4.8 / TH 1456 2.1 / 2132 5.0
25 0118 1.9 / 0822 4.5 / F 1345 2.3 / 2030 4.5

11 0353 1.5 / 1010 4.8 / F 1605 2.0 / 2236 5.0
26 0221 2.0 / 0921 4.4 / SA 1504 2.3 / 2137 4.5

12 0458 1.6 / 1112 4.8 / SA 1709 1.9 / 2338 5.0
27 0336 2.0 / 1024 4.5 / SU 1623 2.2 / 2244 4.6

13 0555 1.5 / 1209 4.9 / SU 1809 1.7
28 0452 1.9 / 1126 4.7 / M 1728 1.9 / 2347 4.8

14 0034 5.1 / 0643 1.5 / M 1300 5.1 / 1902 1.5
29 0554 1.7 / 1224 4.9 / TU 1824 1.6

15 0126 5.2 / 0723 1.5 / TU 1344 5.2 / 1948 1.3
30 0046 5.1 / 0648 1.5 / W 1317 5.2 / 1918 1.3

31 0140 5.4 / 0739 1.4 / TH 1404 5.5 / ○ 2011 0.9

Chart Datum: 2·90 metres below Ordnance Datum (Newlyn)
HAT is 6·3 metres above Chart Datum

TIDES

285

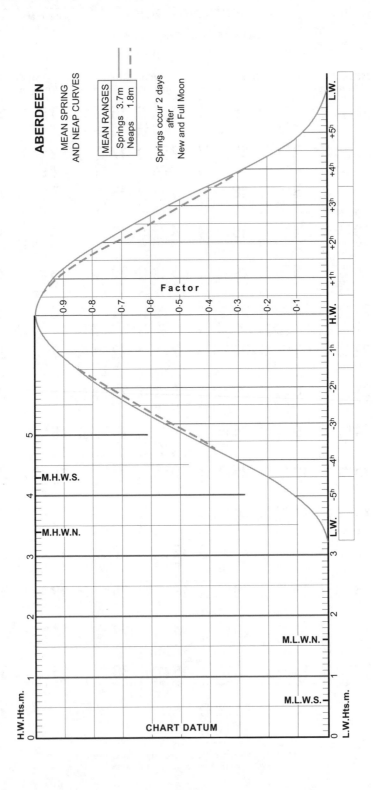

ABERDEEN

MEAN SPRING
AND NEAP CURVES

MEAN RANGES	
Springs	3.7m
Neaps	1.8m

Springs occur 2 days
after
New and Full Moon

Factor

JANUARY

Time m — Time m

Day	Time m	Time m	Time m	Time m
1 TH	0408 3.8	0947 1.4	1604 4.1	2221 1.1
16 F	0500 4.0	1041 1.3	1706 4.3	2324 0.9
2 F	0448 3.7	1024 1.5	1643 4.0	2300 1.2
17 SA	0548 3.8	1126 1.5	1757 4.0	
3 SA	0531 3.7	1107 1.6	1728 3.9	2346 1.3
18 SU	0011 1.2	0639 3.6	1219 1.7	1854 3.7 ◑
4 SU	0621 3.6	1158 1.7	1821 3.8 ◐	
19 M	0105 1.5	0736 3.4	1324 1.9	2001 3.5
5 M	0041 1.4	0719 3.6	1303 1.8	1924 3.7
20 TU	0209 1.8	0843 3.4	1449 2.0	2120 3.4
6 TU	0146 1.5	0824 3.6	1417 1.8	2036 3.7
21 W	0330 1.9	0955 3.4	1619 1.9	2236 3.4
7 W	0257 1.5	0933 3.7	1534 1.7	2151 3.8
22 TH	0440 1.8	1057 3.6	1718 1.7	2335 3.6
8 TH	0410 1.4	1038 3.8	1646 1.4	2302 4.0
23 F	0529 1.7	1146 3.7	1802 1.5	
9 F	0516 1.3	1135 4.0	1748 1.1	
24 SA	0021 3.7	0609 1.6	1227 3.9	1839 1.3
10 SA	0005 4.2	0612 1.2	1227 4.2	1842 0.8
25 SU	0100 3.8	0645 1.4	1301 4.0	1913 1.1
11 SU	0101 4.3	0702 1.0	1313 4.4 ○	1933 0.5
26 M	0134 3.9	0718 1.3	1334 4.1 ●	1945 1.0
12 M	0152 4.4	0751 0.8	1401 4.6	2022 0.4
27 TU	0206 4.0	0750 1.2	1404 4.2	2017 0.9
13 TU	0241 4.4	0834 0.7	1446 4.6	2109 0.3
28 W	0237 4.0	0821 1.1	1435 4.3	2049 0.8
14 W	0328 4.4	0917 1.0	1532 4.6	2154 0.4
29 TH	0309 4.0	0852 1.1	1506 4.3	2120 0.8
15 TH	0414 4.2	0958 1.1	1618 4.5	2239 0.6
30 F	0341 4.0	0923 1.1	1539 4.2	2153 0.9
31 SA	0415 3.9	0957 1.2	1615 4.2	2227 1.0

FEBRUARY

Time m — Time m

Day	Time m	Time m	Time m	Time m
1 SU	0453 3.8	1034 1.3	1657 4.1	2307 1.1
16 M	0546 3.6	1129 1.5	1809 3.6 ◐	
2 M	0538 3.7	1119 1.4	1746 3.9	2357 1.3 ◐
17 TU	0007 1.6	0637 3.4	1228 1.8	1914 3.3
3 TU	0633 3.6	1219 1.6	1850 3.7	
18 W	0109 1.9	0743 3.3	1355 2.0	2038 3.2
4 W	0103 1.5	0742 3.5	1340 1.7	2010 3.6
19 TH	0239 2.1	0905 3.2	1555 1.9	2210 3.2
5 TH	0228 1.7	0902 3.5	1515 1.7	2139 3.6
20 F	0417 2.0	1025 3.4	1659 1.7	2317 3.4
6 F	0400 1.6	1020 3.6	1641 1.4	2300 3.8
21 SA	0511 1.8	1122 3.6	1743 1.4	
7 SA	0512 1.5	1125 3.9	1744 1.0	
22 SU	0002 3.6	0551 1.6	1204 3.8	1818 1.2
8 SU	0003 4.1	0606 1.2	1218 4.2	1836 0.7
23 M	0039 3.8	0625 1.4	1239 3.9	1850 1.0
9 M	0055 4.3	0653 0.8	1304 4.4 ○	1923 0.4
24 TU	0111 3.9	0656 1.2	1310 4.1	1921 0.8
10 TU	0141 4.4	0735 0.8	1346 4.6	2007 0.2
25 W	0141 4.0	0726 1.0	1340 4.2	1951 0.7
11 W	0223 4.4	0815 0.8	1428 4.7	2048 0.2
26 TH	0210 4.1	0757 0.9	1410 4.3	2022 0.6
12 TH	0303 4.3	0853 0.8	1509 4.6	2127 0.4
27 F	0240 4.1	0827 0.8	1442 4.4	2052 0.6
13 F	0343 4.2	0930 0.9	1550 4.5	2205 0.6
28 SA	0311 4.1	0859 0.9	1515 4.3	2124 0.7
14 SA	0422 4.0	1006 1.0	1632 4.2	2242 0.9
15 SU	0502 3.8	1045 1.3	1717 3.9	2321 1.3

MARCH

Time m — Time m

Day	Time m	Time m	Time m	Time m
1 SU	0345 4.0	0932 0.9	1553 4.3	2158 0.8
16 M	0420 3.8	1012 1.1	1644 3.8	2237 1.3
2 M	0422 3.9	1009 1.1	1635 4.1	2238 1.1
17 TU	0458 3.6	1053 1.4	1734 3.5	2319 1.7
3 TU	0506 3.8	1055 1.2	1727 3.9	2328 1.4
18 W	0545 3.4	1145 1.7	1836 3.2	
4 W	0601 3.6	1158 1.5	1836 3.6 ◐	
19 TH	0016 1.9	0648 3.2	1305 1.9	1954 3.1
5 TH	0039 1.7	0715 3.4	1327 1.6	2003 3.5
20 F	0147 2.1	0808 3.1	1506 1.8	2128 3.1
6 F	0218 1.8	0843 3.4	1513 1.5	2139 3.5
21 SA	0339 2.0	0937 3.2	1625 1.6	2242 3.3
7 SA	0359 1.7	1008 3.6	1636 1.2	2259 3.7
22 SU	0440 1.8	1043 3.4	1710 1.4	2329 3.5
8 SU	0505 1.5	1113 3.9	1734 0.8	2356 4.0
23 M	0521 1.6	1129 3.6	1745 1.1	
9 M	0554 1.2	1203 4.1	1822 0.5	
24 TU	0006 3.7	0555 1.3	1206 3.8	1817 0.9
10 TU	0041 4.2	0636 0.9	1247 4.4	1905 0.3
25 W	0038 3.9	0626 1.1	1238 4.0	1848 0.7
11 W	0121 4.3	0715 0.8	1327 4.5 ○	1944 0.3
26 TH	0108 4.0	0657 0.9	1310 4.2 ●	1919 0.6
12 TH	0158 4.3	0752 0.7	1405 4.6	2021 0.3
27 F	0139 4.1	0729 0.8	1342 4.3	1951 0.5
13 F	0234 4.2	0827 0.7	1444 4.5	2056 0.5
28 SA	0210 4.2	0802 0.7	1417 4.4	2024 0.5
14 SA	0309 4.1	0901 0.9	1523 4.3	2129 0.7
29 SU	0244 4.2	0837 0.7	1455 4.3	2059 0.6
15 SU	0344 4.0	0936 0.9	1602 4.1	2202 1.0
30 M	0319 4.1	0914 0.8	1536 4.2	2137 0.9
31 TU	0359 4.0	0956 0.9	1624 4.0	2221 1.1

APRIL

Time m — Time m

Day	Time m	Time m	Time m	Time m
1 W	0445 3.8	1049 1.1	1723 3.8	2317 1.5
16 TH	0508 3.5	1118 1.5	1807 3.2	2338 1.9
2 TH	0544 3.6	1159 1.3	1838 3.5 ◐	
17 F	0606 3.3	1225 1.7	1914 3.1 ◐	
3 F	0035 1.7	0702 3.4	1331 1.4	2005 3.4
18 SA	0055 2.0	0717 3.2	1354 1.7	2031 3.1
4 SA	0217 1.8	0829 3.4	1508 1.3	2136 3.5
19 SU	0232 2.0	0834 3.2	1521 1.6	2146 3.2
5 SU	0345 1.7	0951 3.6	1621 1.0	2246 3.7
20 M	0347 1.8	0947 3.3	1618 1.4	2241 3.4
6 M	0446 1.4	1054 3.8	1715 0.8	2337 3.9
21 TU	0436 1.6	1041 3.5	1659 1.1	2323 3.6
7 TU	0533 1.2	1143 4.1	1801 0.6	
22 W	0515 1.4	1123 3.7	1735 0.9	2359 3.8
8 W	0019 4.0	0614 0.9	1225 4.2	1841 0.5
23 TH	0550 1.1	1200 3.9	1810 0.7	
9 TH	0056 4.1	0652 0.6	1304 4.3 ○	1917 0.5
24 F	0033 4.0	0625 0.9	1238 4.1	1846 0.6
10 F	0131 4.2	0728 0.7	1343 4.3	1952 0.5
25 SA	0107 4.1	0702 0.7	1316 4.3 ●	1923 0.5
11 SA	0204 4.1	0803 0.7	1421 4.3	2025 0.7
26 SU	0143 4.2	0741 0.6	1357 4.3	2001 0.6
12 SU	0238 4.1	0838 0.8	1459 4.1	2057 0.9
27 M	0220 4.2	0821 0.6	1441 4.3	2042 0.7
13 M	0311 4.0	0912 0.9	1539 3.9	2130 1.1
28 TU	0300 4.1	0906 0.6	1528 4.2	2126 0.9
14 TU	0346 3.8	0948 1.1	1621 3.7	2205 1.4
29 W	0344 4.0	0956 0.7	1623 4.0	2216 1.2
15 W	0423 3.7	1029 1.3	1709 3.4	2245 1.6
30 TH	0436 3.9	1055 0.9	1727 3.8	2317 1.5

Chart Datum: 2·25 metres below Ordnance Datum (Newlyn)
HAT is 4·8 metres above Chart Datum

TIDES

TIDES

SCOTLAND – ABERDEEN
LAT 57°09'N   LONG 2°05'W
TIMES AND HEIGHTS OF HIGH AND LOW WATERS

Dates in amber are **SPRINGS**
Dates in yellow are **NEAPS**

2009

MAY

Time	m		Time	m
1 0539	3.7		**16** 0533	3.5
1205	1.0		1151	1.4
F 1839	3.6		SA 1835	3.2
2 0033	1.7		**17** 0009	1.8
0652	3.6		0632	3.3
SA 1325	1.1		SU 1256	1.5
1956	3.5		1935	3.2
3 0157	1.7		**18** 0122	1.9
0809	3.6		0736	3.3
SU 1445	1.0		M 1405	1.5
2114	3.5		◐ 2039	3.2
4 0314	1.6		**19** 0234	1.8
0924	3.7		0840	3.4
M 1553	0.9		TU 1508	1.4
◐ 2219	3.6		2141	3.4
5 0416	1.4		**20** 0336	1.6
1027	3.8		0941	3.5
TU 1648	0.8		W 1602	1.2
2310	3.8		2233	3.6
6 0506	1.2		**21** 0427	1.4
1118	3.9		1035	3.7
W 1734	0.8		TH 1649	1.0
2352	3.9		2317	3.8
7 0550	1.0		**22** 0512	1.2
1203	4.0		1123	3.9
TH 1814	0.7		F 1733	0.9
			2358	3.9
8 0029	4.0		**23** 0556	1.0
0629	0.9		1209	4.0
F 1244	4.1		SA 1817	0.7
1850	0.8			
9 0105	4.0		**24** 0039	4.1
0707	0.8		0640	0.8
SA 1324	4.1		SU 1256	4.2
1925	0.8		1901	0.7
10 0139	4.0		**25** 0120	4.2
0744	0.8		0726	0.6
SU 1403	4.0		M 1344	4.3
1959	0.9		1946	0.7
11 0213	4.0		**26** 0203	4.2
0820	0.8		0814	0.5
M 1442	3.9		TU 1433	4.3
○ 2033	1.1		● 2033	0.8
12 0247	3.9		**27** 0248	4.2
0856	0.9		0904	0.5
TU 1522	3.8		W 1526	4.2
2107	1.2		2122	1.0
13 0321	3.8		**28** 0336	4.1
0933	1.0		0957	0.5
W 1603	3.6		TH 1623	4.0
2142	1.4		2214	1.2
14 0359	3.7		**29** 0430	4.0
1012	1.2		1055	0.6
TH 1648	3.5		F 1724	3.9
2222	1.6		2311	1.3
15 0441	3.6		**30** 0530	3.9
1057	1.3		1157	0.8
F 1739	3.3		SA 1826	3.7
2309	1.7			
			31 0014	1.5
			0633	3.8
			SU 1303	0.9
			1931	3.6

JUNE

Time	m		Time	m
1 0123	1.6		**16** 0022	1.7
0741	3.7		0643	3.5
M 1409	1.0		TU 1303	1.3
2038	3.5		◐ 1940	3.3
2 0232	1.6		**17** 0127	1.7
0850	3.7		0742	3.5
TU 1516	1.1		W 1404	1.3
◑ 2142	3.6		2040	3.4
3 0339	1.5		**18** 0234	1.7
0956	3.7		0845	3.5
W 1615	1.1		TH 1506	1.3
2238	3.6		2141	3.5
4 0438	1.4		**19** 0338	1.5
1054	3.7		0950	3.6
TH 1706	1.1		F 1607	1.2
2325	3.7		2238	3.7
5 0528	1.2		**20** 0439	1.3
1144	3.8		1052	3.8
F 1749	1.1		SA 1704	1.1
			2329	3.9
6 0006	3.8		**21** 0534	1.1
0612	1.1		1150	4.0
SA 1230	3.8		SU 1758	1.0
1828	1.1			
7 0044	3.9		**22** 0017	4.0
0653	1.0		0626	0.8
SU 1312	3.8		M 1244	4.1
1905	1.1		1848	0.9
8 0120	4.0		**23** 0104	4.2
0731	0.9		0717	0.6
M 1352	3.8		TU 1336	4.3
1940	1.1		1937	0.8
9 0155	4.0		**24** 0151	4.3
0808	0.9		0808	0.4
TU 1430	3.8		W 1429	4.3
○ 2015	1.2		2026	0.8
10 0229	4.0		**25** 0238	4.4
0843	0.9		0859	0.3
W 1508	3.8		TH 1521	4.3
2049	1.2		● 2113	0.9
11 0303	3.9		**26** 0326	4.4
0918	1.0		0950	0.3
TH 1546	3.7		F 1613	4.2
2124	1.3		2201	1.0
12 0339	3.9		**27** 0417	4.3
0955	1.0		1042	0.4
F 1625	3.6		SA 1705	4.0
2201	1.4		2251	1.1
13 0418	3.8		**28** 0510	4.2
1034	1.1		1134	0.6
SA 1708	3.5		SU 1759	3.8
2241	1.5		2343	1.3
14 0501	3.7		**29** 0607	4.0
1118	1.2		1228	0.8
SU 1754	3.4		M 1855	3.6
2327	1.6			
15 0549	3.6		**30** 0041	1.5
1207	1.3		0707	3.8
M 1845	3.4		TU 1327	1.1
			1955	3.5

JULY

Time	m		Time	m
1 0146	1.6		**16** 0031	1.6
0813	3.7		0655	3.6
W 1430	1.3		TH 1311	1.4
2100	3.5		1950	3.4
2 0300	1.6		**17** 0142	1.7
0925	3.7		0803	3.6
TH 1539	1.4		F 1420	1.4
2203	3.5		2058	3.5
3 0414	1.6		**18** 0300	1.6
1033	3.5		0919	3.6
F 1640	1.5		SA 1536	1.4
2259	3.6		◐ 2207	3.6
4 0513	1.4		**19** 0417	1.4
1131	3.6		1034	3.7
SA 1729	1.4		SU 1648	1.3
◑ 2347	3.7		2309	3.8
5 0601	1.3		**20** 0523	1.1
1220	3.7		1140	3.9
SU 1812	1.4		M 1748	1.1
6 0028	3.8		**21** 0002	4.0
0642	1.1		0618	0.8
M 1303	3.7		TU 1238	4.2
1849	1.3		1839	1.0
7 0106	3.9		**22** 0052	4.3
0719	1.0		0709	0.4
TU 1341	3.8		W 1329	4.3
1925	1.2		1927	0.8
8 0140	4.0		**23** 0138	4.5
0754	0.9		0758	0.2
W 1416	3.8		TH 1418	4.4
1958	1.2		2012	0.8
9 0213	4.0		**24** 0224	4.6
0827	0.9		0846	0.1
TH 1450	3.8		F 1505	4.4
2031	1.2		2056	0.8
10 0245	4.0		**25** 0309	4.6
0900	0.8		0932	0.2
F 1523	3.8		SA 1551	4.3
2103	1.2		2139	0.8
11 0318	4.0		**26** 0355	4.5
0933	0.9		1017	0.3
SA 1557	3.8		SU 1636	4.1
○ 2136	1.2		● 2221	1.0
12 0353	4.0		**27** 0443	4.3
1007	0.9		1102	0.6
SU 1633	3.7		M 1721	3.8
2211	1.3		2307	1.2
13 0429	3.9		**28** 0534	4.1
1043	1.0		1148	1.0
M 1713	3.6		TU 1814	3.7
2249	1.4		2358	1.4
14 0510	3.8		**29** 0631	3.8
1124	1.1		1240	1.3
TU 1757	3.5		W 1910	3.5
2334	1.5			
15 0558	3.7		**30** 0059	1.6
1212	1.3		0736	3.5
W 1849	3.5		TH 1341	1.6
			2014	3.4
			31 0220	1.8
			0854	3.4
			F 1500	1.8
			2126	3.4

AUGUST

Time	m		Time	m
1 0356	1.7		**16** 0239	1.6
1014	3.4		0904	3.5
SA 1619	1.8		SU 1523	1.9
2234	3.5		2145	3.6
2 0501	1.6		**17** 0409	1.6
1119	3.5		1028	3.7
SU 1714	1.7		M 1642	1.5
◑ 2329	3.6		◐ 2254	3.8
3 0549	1.4		**18** 0516	1.0
1209	3.6		1135	4.0
M 1756	1.5		TU 1739	1.2
			2350	4.1
4 0011	3.8		**19** 0609	0.7
0627	1.2		1228	4.2
TU 1248	3.7		W 1828	1.0
1832	1.4			
5 0048	3.9		**20** 0037	4.4
0702	1.0		0657	0.3
W 1323	3.8		TH 1315	4.4
1906	1.2		1911	0.8
6 0121	4.1		**21** 0121	4.6
0734	0.9		0742	0.2
TH 1354	3.9		F 1358	4.5
1938	1.1		1952	0.7
7 0152	4.1		**22** 0203	4.7
0805	0.8		0824	0.1
F 1425	4.0		SA 1440	4.4
2008	1.0		2032	0.7
8 0222	4.2		**23** 0246	4.7
0835	0.7		0905	0.2
SA 1455	4.0		SU 1521	4.3
2038	1.0		2111	0.7
9 0253	4.2		**24** 0328	4.6
0905	0.7		0945	0.5
SU 1526	3.9		M 1601	4.1
○ 2109	1.0		2150	0.9
10 0325	4.2		**25** 0413	4.3
0936	0.8		1024	0.8
M 1558	3.9		TU 1644	3.9
2141	1.1		● 2231	1.1
11 0359	4.1		**26** 0501	4.0
1008	0.9		1105	1.2
TU 1634	3.8		W 1729	3.7
2216	1.2		2317	1.4
12 0438	4.0		**27** 0555	3.7
1045	1.1		1152	1.5
W 1715	3.7		TH 1822	3.5
2257	1.4			
13 0524	3.9		**28** 0017	1.7
1130	1.3		0700	3.4
TH 1806	3.6		F 1252	1.9
2352	1.5		1926	3.4
14 0622	3.7		**29** 0141	1.9
1229	1.5		0821	3.3
F 1910	3.5		SA 1418	2.0
			2044	3.3
15 0107	1.7		**30** 0336	1.8
0738	3.5		0951	3.3
SA 1350	1.7		SU 1557	2.0
2026	3.5		2204	3.4
			31 0443	1.6
			1101	3.4
			M 1654	1.8
			2303	3.5

Chart Datum: 2·25 metres below Ordnance Datum (Newlyn)
HAT is 4·8 metres above Chart Datum

SCOTLAND – ABERDEEN

LAT 57°09′N LONG 2°05′W

TIMES AND HEIGHTS OF HIGH AND LOW WATERS

Dates in amber are **SPRINGS**
Dates in yellow are **NEAPS**

2009

SEPTEMBER

Time	m	Time	m
1 0528	1.4	**16** 0504	0.9
1147	3.6	1125	4.0
TU 1735	1.6	W 1725	1.3
2347	3.8	2333	4.2
2 0604	1.2	**17** 0554	0.6
1224	3.8	1212	4.1
W 1810	1.4	TH 1809	1.0
3 0022	4.0	**18** 0018	4.5
0636	1.0	0638	0.4
TH 1256	3.9	F 1255	4.4
1841	1.2	● 1849	0.8
4 0054	4.1	**19** 0100	4.6
0706	0.8	0719	0.3
F 1326	4.0	SA 1333	4.4
○ 1911	1.1	1928	0.7
5 0124	4.2	**20** 0140	4.7
0735	0.7	0758	0.3
SA 1354	4.1	SU 1411	4.4
1941	1.0	2006	0.7
6 0154	4.3	**21** 0221	4.7
0804	0.7	0835	0.4
SU 1423	4.1	M 1448	4.3
2011	0.9	2043	0.8
7 0225	4.3	**22** 0302	4.5
0834	0.7	0911	0.7
M 1454	4.1	TU 1526	4.2
2041	0.9	2121	0.8
8 0257	4.2	**23** 0345	4.2
0904	0.8	0947	1.0
TU 1526	4.1	W 1604	4.0
2114	1.0	2200	1.2
9 0333	4.2	**24** 0431	3.9
0937	0.9	1024	1.4
W 1601	4.0	TH 1646	3.8
2149	1.1	2244	1.4
10 0414	4.1	**25** 0524	3.6
1013	1.1	1107	1.7
TH 1643	4.0	F 1735	3.6
2233	1.3	2340	1.7
11 0503	3.9	**26** 0628	3.4
1100	1.4	1205	2.0
F 1734	3.7	SA 1839	3.4
2331	1.5	◐	
12 0607	3.7	**27** 0058	1.9
1204	1.7	0744	3.2
SA 1843	3.5	SU 1330	2.2
◐		1955	3.3
13 0053	1.6	**28** 0252	1.9
0729	3.5	0912	3.2
SU 1337	1.9	M 1517	2.1
2006	3.5	2118	3.4
14 0235	1.6	**29** 0409	1.7
0901	3.5	1025	3.4
M 1519	1.8	TU 1621	1.9
2130	3.6	2224	3.6
15 0402	1.3	**30** 0454	1.4
1024	3.8	1113	3.6
TU 1632	1.6	W 1704	1.7
2240	3.9	2311	3.8

OCTOBER

Time	m	Time	m
1 0530	1.2	**16** 0532	0.7
1150	3.8	1151	4.2
TH 1739	1.5	F 1747	1.1
2348	4.0	2357	4.4
2 0602	1.0	**17** 0615	0.6
1222	4.0	1230	4.3
F 1810	1.3	SA 1827	0.9
3 0021	4.1	**18** 0038	4.5
0631	0.9	0653	0.5
SA 1252	4.1	SU 1307	4.4
1841	1.1	● 1905	0.8
4 0053	4.3	**19** 0119	4.6
0701	0.8	0730	0.6
SU 1322	4.2	M 1343	4.4
○ 1912	0.9	1943	0.8
5 0125	4.4	**20** 0200	4.5
0732	0.7	0806	0.8
M 1352	4.3	TU 1419	4.3
1944	0.9	2021	0.9
6 0158	4.4	**21** 0241	4.3
0804	0.7	0841	1.0
TU 1424	4.3	W 1455	4.2
2018	0.9	2059	1.0
7 0235	4.4	**22** 0323	4.1
0837	0.8	0915	1.2
W 1458	4.2	TH 1531	4.0
2054	0.9	2138	1.2
8 0315	4.3	**23** 0408	3.9
0913	1.0	0952	1.5
TH 1536	4.1	F 1610	3.9
2134	1.0	2220	1.4
9 0400	4.1	**24** 0458	3.6
0954	1.2	1032	1.8
F 1620	4.0	SA 1656	3.7
2224	1.2	2310	1.6
10 0455	3.9	**25** 0556	3.4
1046	1.5	1124	2.0
SA 1715	3.8	SU 1754	3.5
2329	1.4		
11 0605	3.7	**26** 0015	1.8
1157	1.8	0701	3.3
SU 1828	3.6	M 1237	2.2
◐		◑ 1903	3.4
12 0053	1.5	**27** 0139	1.8
0727	3.6	0814	3.3
M 1331	1.9	TU 1407	2.2
1950	3.6	2016	3.4
13 0227	1.4	**28** 0304	1.7
0928	3.4	0928	3.4
TU 1503	1.8	W 1525	2.0
2111	3.7	2127	3.5
14 0345	1.2	**29** 0403	1.5
1010	3.8	1024	3.5
W 1611	1.6	TH 1618	1.8
2219	4.0	2223	3.7
15 0444	0.9	**30** 0445	1.4
1106	4.0	1107	3.7
TH 1703	1.3	F 1659	1.6
2311	4.2	2306	3.9
		31 0520	1.2
		1143	3.9
		SA 1734	1.4
		2344	4.1

NOVEMBER

Time	m	Time	m
1 0554	1.0	**16** 0021	4.3
1216	4.1	0630	0.9
SU 1809	1.2	M 1244	4.2
		● 1848	1.0
2 0021	4.2	**17** 0104	4.3
0627	0.9	0707	1.0
M 1250	4.2	TU 1320	4.3
○ 1844	1.0	1927	1.0
3 0058	4.3	**18** 0145	4.2
0703	0.8	0743	1.1
TU 1324	4.3	W 1356	4.3
1922	0.9	2006	1.0
4 0137	4.4	**19** 0226	4.1
0740	0.8	0818	1.2
W 1359	4.3	TH 1431	4.2
2001	0.8	2043	1.1
5 0219	4.4	**20** 0307	4.0
0818	0.9	0853	1.4
TH 1438	4.3	F 1507	4.1
2044	0.9	2121	1.2
6 0304	4.3	**21** 0349	3.9
0900	1.1	0928	1.5
F 1520	4.2	SA 1545	4.0
2131	0.9	2200	1.3
7 0355	4.1	**22** 0434	3.7
0947	1.3	1007	1.7
SA 1608	4.1	SU 1626	3.9
2226	1.1	2244	1.4
8 0454	4.0	**23** 0522	3.5
1043	1.6	1051	1.8
SU 1705	3.9	M 1715	3.7
2330	1.2	2334	1.6
9 0603	3.8	**24** 0616	3.4
1151	1.8	1145	2.0
M 1815	3.8	TU 1812	3.6
◑		◐	
10 0045	1.3	**25** 0034	1.7
0716	3.7	0714	3.4
TU 1312	1.9	W 1253	2.1
1929	3.8	1914	3.5
11 0204	1.2	**26** 0142	1.7
0832	3.7	0817	3.4
W 1431	1.8	TH 1407	2.1
2043	3.9	2018	3.5
12 0315	1.1	**27** 0247	1.6
0942	3.8	0920	3.5
TH 1539	1.7	F 1514	1.9
2151	4.0	2121	3.6
13 0416	1.0	**28** 0344	1.5
1039	3.9	1015	3.6
F 1636	1.5	SA 1609	1.8
2248	4.1	2217	3.8
14 0507	1.0	**29** 0432	1.4
1125	4.1	1101	3.8
SA 1724	1.3	SU 1656	1.5
2337	4.2	2307	3.9
15 0550	0.9	**30** 0516	1.2
1206	4.2	1142	4.0
SU 1808	1.1	M 1740	1.3
		2352	4.1

DECEMBER

Time	m	Time	m
1 0558	1.1	**16** 0056	4.0
1221	4.2	0650	1.3
TU 1823	1.1	W 1305	4.2
		● 1918	1.1
2 0037	4.2	**17** 0137	4.1
0641	1.0	0727	1.3
W 1301	4.3	TH 1341	4.2
○ 1906	0.9	1955	1.0
3 0123	4.4	**18** 0216	4.0
0724	1.0	0802	1.3
TH 1342	4.4	F 1416	4.2
1952	0.8	2031	1.0
4 0210	4.4	**19** 0254	4.0
0809	1.0	0836	1.3
F 1424	4.4	SA 1450	4.2
2039	0.7	2106	1.1
5 0259	4.4	**20** 0330	3.9
0855	1.1	0909	1.4
SA 1509	4.4	SU 1524	4.1
2130	0.7	2141	1.1
6 0352	4.2	**21** 0408	3.8
0943	1.2	0943	1.5
SU 1559	4.3	M 1601	4.0
2223	0.8	2217	1.2
7 0449	4.1	**22** 0447	3.7
1035	1.4	1020	1.6
M 1654	4.1	TU 1641	3.9
2321	0.9	2257	1.3
8 0548	3.9	**23** 0530	3.6
1133	1.6	1101	1.7
TU 1755	4.1	W 1725	3.8
		2341	1.5
9 0023	1.0	**24** 0619	3.5
0651	3.8	1150	1.8
W 1239	1.7	TH 1816	3.7
◑ 1900	4.0	◐	
10 0129	1.2	**25** 0033	1.6
0757	3.7	0712	3.4
TH 1348	1.8	F 1251	1.9
2009	3.9	1914	3.6
11 0236	1.3	**26** 0134	1.6
0904	3.7	0813	3.4
F 1500	1.7	SA 1402	2.0
2120	3.9	2018	3.6
12 0342	1.3	**27** 0239	1.6
1007	3.8	0916	3.5
SA 1608	1.6	SU 1513	1.9
2225	3.9	2126	3.6
13 0441	1.3	**28** 0344	1.6
1100	3.9	1017	3.7
SU 1706	1.5	M 1618	1.7
2321	4.0	2232	3.8
14 0530	1.3	**29** 0444	1.4
1147	4.0	1111	3.9
M 1755	1.3	TU 1716	1.4
		2330	4.0
15 0011	4.0	**30** 0538	1.3
0612	1.3	1159	4.1
TU 1228	4.1	W 1807	1.1
1838	1.2		
		31 0023	4.2
		0627	1.1
		TH 1244	4.3
		○ 1856	0.8

TIDES

Chart Datum: 2·25 metres below Ordnance Datum (Newlyn)
HAT is 4·8 metres above Chart Datum

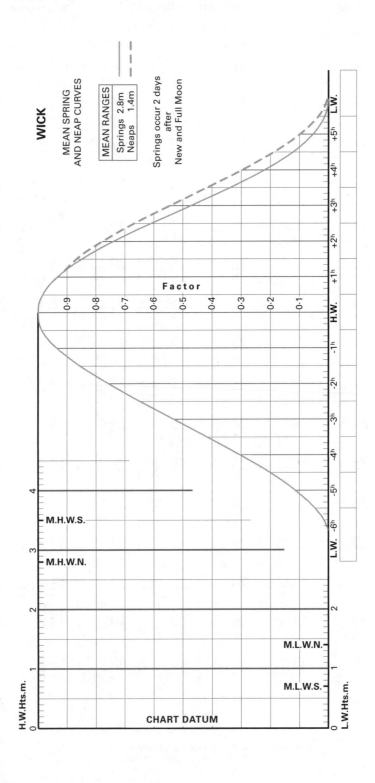

WICK

MEAN SPRING AND NEAP CURVES

MEAN RANGES	
Springs	2.8m
Neaps	1.4m

Springs occur 2 days after New and Full Moon

Factor

0·9 0·8 0·7 0·6 0·5 0·4 0·3 0·2 0·1

H.W. Hts. m.

L.W. Hts. m.

M.H.W.S.
M.H.W.N.

M.L.W.N.
M.L.W.S.

CHART DATUM

L.W.

H.W.

L.W.

SCOTLAND – WICK

LAT 58°26′N   LONG 3°05′W

TIMES AND HEIGHTS OF HIGH AND LOW WATERS

Dates in amber are **SPRINGS**
Dates in yellow are **NEAPS**

2009

JANUARY

Time	m	Time	m
1 0157	3.1	**16** 0251	3.2
0729	1.2	0818	1.1
TH 1357	3.4	F 1459	3.5
2006	1.0	2110	0.9
2 0235	3.0	**17** 0335	3.0
0806	1.3	0900	1.0
F 1435	3.3	SA 1548	3.3
2045	1.1	2158	1.1
3 0317	2.9	**18** 0423	2.9
0846	1.4	0950	1.5
SA 1518	3.2	SU 1642	3.1
2129	1.1	☽ 2254	1.3
4 0406	2.9	**19** 0518	2.8
0935	1.5	1103	1.6
SU 1609	3.1	M 1745	2.9
☾ 2226	1.2		
5 0504	2.9	**20** 0002	1.5
1042	1.6	0621	2.8
M 1711	3.1	TU 1241	1.7
2339	1.3	1900	2.8
6 0610	2.9	**21** 0122	1.6
1208	1.6	0734	2.8
TU 1822	3.1	W 1414	1.6
		2019	2.8
7 0053	1.3	**22** 0229	1.5
0718	3.0	0841	2.9
W 1327	1.5	TH 1511	1.4
1937	3.1	2121	2.9
8 0203	3.1	**23** 0317	1.5
0825	3.1	0932	3.1
TH 1437	1.3	F 1554	1.3
2050	3.2	2208	3.0
9 0305	1.2	**24** 0357	1.4
0925	3.3	1014	3.2
F 1538	1.0	SA 1630	1.1
2155	3.4	2248	3.1
10 0400	1.1	**25** 0431	1.3
1019	3.5	1050	3.3
SA 1632	0.7	SU 1703	1.0
2253	3.5	2323	3.2
11 0449	1.0	**26** 0503	1.2
1109	3.7	1124	3.4
SU 1722	0.5	M 1734	0.9
○ 2345	3.6	● 2356	3.2
12 0534	0.9	**27** 0534	1.1
1157	3.8	1157	3.5
M 1810	0.4	TU 1805	0.8
13 0034	3.6	**28** 0029	3.2
0617	0.9	0604	1.0
TU 1244	3.8	W 1230	3.5
1856	0.4	1835	0.7
14 0122	3.5	**29** 0101	3.2
0658	0.9	0635	1.0
W 1329	3.8	TH 1302	3.5
1941	0.4	1906	0.7
15 0207	3.4	**30** 0134	3.2
0739	1.0	0707	1.0
TH 1414	3.7	F 1335	3.5
2025	0.6	1939	0.8
		31 0207	3.1
		0741	1.0
		SA 1410	3.4
		2013	0.9

FEBRUARY

Time	m	Time	m
1 0244	3.1	**16** 0332	2.9
0816	1.1	0901	1.3
SU 1449	3.3	M 1557	3.0
2051	1.0	☽ 2145	1.4
2 0326	3.0	**17** 0420	2.8
0858	1.3	0958	1.5
M 1537	3.2	TU 1657	2.7
☾ 2138	1.2	2251	1.6
3 0419	2.9	**18** 0523	2.7
0954	1.4	1148	1.7
TU 1637	3.0	W 1818	2.6
2247	1.3		
4 0526	2.8	**19** 0029	1.7
1129	1.5	0642	2.6
W 1755	2.9	TH 1350	1.6
		1955	2.6
5 0024	1.4	**20** 0205	1.7
0644	2.8	0806	2.7
TH 1312	1.4	F 1452	1.4
1923	2.9	2103	2.7
6 0153	1.4	**21** 0300	1.5
0804	3.0	0906	2.9
F 1435	1.2	SA 1534	1.2
2048	3.1	2150	2.9
7 0303	1.3	**22** 0338	1.4
0913	3.2	0950	3.1
SA 1536	0.9	SU 1608	1.0
2154	3.3	2227	3.0
8 0355	1.1	**23** 0411	1.2
1009	3.4	1027	3.2
SU 1626	0.6	M 1639	0.9
2247	3.4	2300	3.1
9 0439	0.9	**24** 0441	1.0
1058	3.7	1101	3.3
M 1711	0.4	TU 1709	0.7
○ 2334	3.5	2332	3.2
10 0520	0.8	**25** 0511	0.9
1143	3.8	1134	3.5
TU 1754	0.3	W 1738	0.6
		●	
11 0018	3.6	**26** 0004	3.3
0558	0.7	0540	0.8
W 1227	3.9	TH 1206	3.5
1834	0.3	1808	0.5
12 0059	3.5	**27** 0035	3.3
0635	0.7	0612	0.7
TH 1308	3.8	F 1239	3.6
1912	0.4	1839	0.5
13 0137	3.4	**28** 0107	3.3
0710	0.8	0644	0.8
F 1348	3.7	SA 1313	3.5
1949	0.6	1911	0.6
14 0214	3.2		
0745	0.9		
SA 1428	3.5		
2024	0.9		
15 0252	3.1		
0821	1.1		
SU 1509	3.2		
2101	1.1		

MARCH

Time	m	Time	m
1 0140	3.2	**16** 0211	3.1
0717	0.8	0751	1.0
SU 1348	3.4	M 1436	3.1
1944	0.7	2016	1.1
2 0215	3.2	**17** 0247	2.9
0754	0.9	0829	1.2
M 1429	3.3	TU 1519	2.8
2022	0.9	2053	1.4
3 0257	3.0	**18** 0330	2.8
0836	1.1	0920	1.4
TU 1518	3.1	W 1616	2.6
2108	1.2	☽ 2149	1.6
4 0348	2.9	**19** 0428	2.6
0935	1.3	1059	1.5
W 1622	2.9	TH 1737	2.4
☾ 2219	1.4	2333	1.7
5 0458	2.8	**20** 0547	2.6
1122	1.4	1301	1.5
TH 1747	2.8	F 1918	2.5
6 0014	1.5	**21** 0123	1.7
0623	2.8	0715	2.6
F 1312	1.2	SA 1416	1.3
1925	2.8	2032	2.6
7 0151	1.5	**22** 0227	1.5
0751	2.9	0825	2.7
SA 1431	1.0	SU 1500	1.1
2048	3.0	2118	2.8
8 0256	1.3	**23** 0308	1.3
0901	3.1	0914	2.9
SU 1527	0.7	M 1535	0.9
2147	3.2	2155	2.9
9 0342	1.1	**24** 0341	1.1
0954	3.4	0953	3.1
M 1612	0.5	TU 1606	0.8
2234	3.3	2229	3.1
10 0422	0.9	**25** 0412	1.0
1041	3.6	1029	3.3
TU 1652	0.3	W 1636	0.6
2315	3.4	2301	3.2
11 0458	0.7	**26** 0442	0.8
1124	3.7	1103	3.4
W 1730	0.3	TH 1706	0.5
○ 2354	3.5	● 2333	3.3
12 0534	0.6	**27** 0514	0.7
1204	3.7	1139	3.5
TH 1806	0.3	F 1738	0.4
13 0030	3.4	**28** 0006	3.4
0609	0.6	0547	0.6
F 1243	3.7	SA 1215	3.5
1840	0.4	1811	0.5
14 0105	3.4	**29** 0040	3.4
0643	0.7	0622	0.6
SA 1320	3.5	SU 1252	3.5
1913	0.6	1845	0.6
15 0138	3.2	**30** 0116	3.3
0717	0.8	0700	0.6
SU 1357	3.3	M 1333	3.4
1944	0.9	1923	0.7
		31 0154	3.2
		0741	0.8
		TU 1418	3.2
		2004	1.0

APRIL

Time	m	Time	m
1 0238	3.1	**16** 0255	2.8
0831	0.9	0859	1.2
W 1512	3.0	TH 1545	2.5
2056	1.2	2112	1.5
2 0332	2.9	**17** 0347	2.7
0943	1.1	1018	1.3
TH 1622	2.8	F 1655	2.4
☾ 2220	1.5	☽ 2238	1.7
3 0444	2.8	**18** 0456	2.6
1131	1.1	1153	1.3
F 1750	2.7	SA 1819	2.4
4 0009	1.5	**19** 0015	1.6
0610	2.8	0614	2.6
SA 1305	1.0	SU 1313	1.2
1923	2.8	1936	2.5
5 0136	1.4	**20** 0131	1.5
0733	2.9	0726	2.7
SU 1415	0.8	M 1408	1.1
2035	2.9	2031	2.7
6 0236	1.2	**21** 0222	1.3
0840	3.1	0822	2.8
M 1507	0.6	TU 1449	0.9
2127	3.1	2112	2.8
7 0321	1.0	**22** 0301	1.1
0933	3.2	0909	3.0
TU 1550	0.5	W 1525	0.8
2211	3.2	2150	3.0
8 0359	0.8	**23** 0336	0.9
1019	3.4	0950	3.2
W 1627	0.4	TH 1559	0.6
2250	3.3	2226	3.2
9 0435	0.7	**24** 0411	0.8
1101	3.5	1031	3.3
TH 1702	0.4	F 1633	0.5
○ 2326	3.3	2302	3.3
10 0510	0.6	**25** 0448	0.6
1141	3.5	1112	3.4
F 1736	0.5	SA 1709	0.5
		● 2339	3.4
11 0001	3.3	**26** 0526	0.5
0546	0.6	1153	3.5
SA 1219	3.4	SU 1747	0.5
1809	0.6		
12 0034	3.3	**27** 0017	3.4
0621	0.7	0606	0.5
SU 1255	3.4	M 1237	3.4
1841	0.8	1827	0.6
13 0106	3.2	**28** 0057	3.3
0655	0.8	0651	0.5
M 1332	3.1	TU 1324	3.3
1912	1.0	1910	0.8
14 0138	3.1	**29** 0140	3.2
0730	0.9	0740	0.6
TU 1409	2.9	W 1415	3.2
1944	1.2	1958	1.0
15 0214	3.0	**30** 0228	3.1
0809	1.1	0840	0.7
W 1452	2.7	TH 1514	3.0
2021	1.4	2057	1.3

Chart Datum: 1·71 metres below Ordnance Datum (Newlyn)
HAT is 4·0 metres above Chart Datum

TIDES

TIME ZONE (UT)
For Summer Time add ONE hour in **non-shaded areas**

SCOTLAND – WICK
LAT 58°26′N   LONG 3°05′W
TIMES AND HEIGHTS OF HIGH AND LOW WATERS

Dates in amber are **SPRINGS**
Dates in yellow are **NEAPS**
2009

MAY

	Time	m		Time	m
1	0326	3.0	**16**	0316	2.8
	0958	0.9		0940	1.1
F	1625	2.8	SA	1615	2.5
	2219	1.4		2147	1.5
2	0436	2.9	**17**	0412	2.7
	1123	0.9		1051	1.2
SA	1743	2.7	SU	1720	2.5
	2346	1.4		2307	1.5
3	0552	2.9	**18**	0517	2.6
	1241	0.8		1201	1.2
SU	1900	2.8	M	1827	2.5
4	0103	1.4	**19**	0021	1.5
	0706	2.9		0622	2.7
M	1348	0.7	TU	1303	1.1
	2006	2.9		1927	2.6
5	0205	1.2	**20**	0123	1.4
	0812	3.1		0724	2.8
TU	1440	0.7	W	1355	1.0
	2058	3.0		2020	2.8
6	0253	1.0	**21**	0214	1.2
	0907	3.2		0820	2.9
W	1522	0.6	TH	1440	0.8
	2143	3.1		2107	3.0
7	0335	0.9	**22**	0300	1.0
	0955	3.2		0912	3.1
TH	1600	0.6	F	1522	0.7
	2222	3.2		2150	3.1
8	0413	0.8	**23**	0343	0.8
	1039	3.3		1001	3.2
F	1635	0.6	SA	1604	0.6
	2259	3.2		2233	3.3
9	0451	0.7	**24**	0426	0.7
	1120	3.3		1050	3.4
SA	1709	0.7	SU	1647	0.6
	2334	3.3		2315	3.4
10	0528	0.7	**25**	0512	0.5
	1158	3.2		1138	3.4
SU	1743	0.8	M	1731	0.6
				2359	3.4
11	0007	3.2	**26**	0559	0.4
	0605	0.7		1228	3.4
M	1236	3.1	TU	1817	0.7
○	1816	0.9	●		
12	0041	3.2	**27**	0044	3.4
	0641	0.8		0649	0.4
TU	1312	3.0	W	1320	3.3
	1849	1.0		1905	0.9
13	0114	3.1	**28**	0132	3.4
	0718	0.9		0744	0.4
W	1350	2.9	TH	1414	3.2
	1923	1.2		1955	1.0
14	0150	3.0	**29**	0223	3.3
	0757	1.0		0844	0.5
TH	1431	2.7	F	1512	3.0
	2000	1.3		2051	1.2
15	0230	2.9	**30**	0319	3.2
	0843	1.1		0950	0.6
F	1519	2.6	SA	1613	2.9
	2046	1.4		2156	1.3
			31	0421	3.1
				1058	0.7
			SU	1717	2.8
				2308	1.3

JUNE

	Time	m		Time	m
1	0526	3.0	**16**	0427	2.8
	1206	0.8		1054	1.1
M	1822	2.8	TU	1725	2.6
			☽	2312	1.4
2	0019	1.3	**17**	0526	2.8
	0632	3.0		1159	1.1
TU	1310	0.9	W	1826	2.7
☽	1925	2.8			
3	0128	1.3	**18**	0024	1.4
	0739	3.0		0630	2.8
W	1407	0.9	TH	1301	1.1
	2023	2.9		1927	2.8
4	0226	1.2	**19**	0129	1.3
	0840	3.0		0735	2.9
TH	1454	0.9	F	1359	1.0
	2113	3.0		2025	2.9
5	0316	1.0	**20**	0228	1.1
	0934	3.0		0839	3.0
F	1535	0.9	SA	1453	0.9
	2156	3.1		2119	3.1
6	0359	0.9	**21**	0322	0.9
	1021	3.0		0939	3.2
SA	1612	0.9	SU	1544	0.8
	2236	3.1		2209	3.3
7	0439	0.9	**22**	0414	0.7
	1104	3.1		1036	3.3
SU	1648	0.9	M	1634	0.8
	2313	3.2		2258	3.4
8	0518	0.8	**23**	0505	0.5
	1143	3.0		1130	3.4
M	1724	1.0	TU	1722	0.7
	2348	3.2		2346	3.5
9	0555	0.8	**24**	0556	0.3
	1220	3.0		1222	3.4
TU	1758	1.0	W	1810	0.7
○					
10	0022	3.2	**25**	0034	3.6
	0630	0.8		0646	0.3
W	1257	3.0	TH	1314	3.4
	1832	1.0	●	1856	0.8
11	0056	3.2	**26**	0123	3.6
	0706	0.8		0738	0.3
TH	1333	2.9	F	1405	3.3
	1906	1.1		1943	0.9
12	0132	3.1	**27**	0212	3.5
	0742	0.8		0830	0.4
F	1411	2.8	SA	1456	3.2
	1942	1.2		2030	1.0
13	0209	3.1	**28**	0303	3.4
	0821	0.9		0924	0.5
SA	1451	2.7	SU	1548	3.0
	2021	1.2		2121	1.1
14	0249	3.0	**29**	0356	3.3
	0904	1.0		1021	0.7
SU	1536	2.7	M	1641	2.9
	2105	1.3		2220	1.3
15	0334	2.9	**30**	0454	3.1
	0954	1.0		1121	0.9
M	1627	2.6	TU	1738	2.8
	2201	1.4		2331	1.4

JULY

	Time	m		Time	m
1	0557	2.9	**16**	0441	2.9
	1225	1.1		1057	1.2
W	1839	2.7	TH	1734	2.7
				2330	1.4
2	0049	1.4	**17**	0548	2.8
	0705	2.8		1215	1.2
TH	1331	1.2	F	1842	2.8
	1944	2.8			
3	0205	1.3	**18**	0054	1.4
	0816	2.8		0703	2.9
F	1429	1.2	SA	1329	1.2
	2044	2.9	☽	1951	2.9
4	0304	1.2	**19**	0209	1.2
	0917	2.8		0819	3.0
SA	1516	1.2	SU	1437	1.1
☽	2134	3.0		2056	3.1
5	0351	1.1	**20**	0314	0.9
	1008	2.9		0929	3.1
SU	1557	1.2	M	1535	1.0
	2217	3.1		2153	3.3
6	0431	1.0	**21**	0409	0.7
	1051	3.0		1028	3.3
M	1634	1.1	TU	1626	0.9
	2256	3.2		2245	3.5
7	0508	0.9	**22**	0459	0.4
	1130	3.0		1122	3.5
TU	1709	1.1	W	1712	0.8
	2332	3.2		2334	3.6
8	0542	0.8	**23**	0547	0.2
	1206	3.0		1212	3.5
W	1742	1.0	TH	1756	0.7
9	0006	3.3	**24**	0021	3.8
	0615	0.7		0633	0.1
TH	1240	3.0	F	1259	3.5
	1814	1.0		1838	0.7
10	0039	3.3	**25**	0107	3.8
	0647	0.7		0718	0.2
F	1314	3.0	SA	1345	3.4
	1846	1.0		1920	0.8
11	0112	3.3	**26**	0153	3.7
	0720	0.7		0803	0.3
SA	1347	3.0	SU	1429	3.3
○	1919	1.0	●	2000	0.9
12	0146	3.2	**27**	0238	3.5
	0753	0.8		0848	0.6
SU	1422	2.9	M	1513	3.1
	1953	1.1		2043	1.0
13	0222	3.2	**28**	0326	3.3
	0828	0.8		0935	0.8
M	1459	2.8	TU	1559	2.9
	2030	1.2		2132	1.2
14	0300	3.1	**29**	0418	3.1
	0907	0.9		1028	1.1
TU	1542	2.8	W	1651	2.8
	2112	1.3		2240	1.4
15	0346	3.0	**30**	0519	2.8
	0954	1.1		1133	1.3
W	1633	2.7	TH	1752	2.7
	2208	1.4			
			31	0013	1.5
				0633	2.7
			F	1252	1.5
				1903	2.7

AUGUST

	Time	m		Time	m
1	0152	1.4	**16**	0038	1.4
	0757	2.7		0647	2.8
SA	1408	1.5	SU	1316	1.4
	2016	2.8		1928	2.9
2	0255	1.3	**17**	0205	1.2
	0905	2.8		0814	2.9
SU	1502	1.4	M	1432	1.3
☽	2114	3.0	☽	2040	3.1
3	0340	1.1	**18**	0309	0.9
	0955	2.9		0925	3.1
M	1543	1.3	TU	1528	1.1
	2159	3.1		2139	3.3
4	0417	1.0	**19**	0400	0.6
	1036	3.0		1020	3.3
TU	1618	1.2	W	1614	0.9
	2237	3.2		2230	3.6
5	0450	0.9	**20**	0446	0.3
	1112	3.0		1109	3.5
W	1650	1.1	TH	1655	0.8
	2312	3.3		2317	3.8
6	0522	0.7	**21**	0529	0.2
	1145	3.1		1154	3.6
TH	1721	1.0	F	1735	0.6
	2345	3.4			
7	0552	0.7	**22**	0002	3.9
	1217	3.1		0610	0.1
F	1752	0.9	SA	1236	3.6
				1814	0.6
8	0017	3.4	**23**	0045	3.9
	0621	0.6		0651	0.2
SA	1248	3.2	SU	1317	3.5
	1822	0.9		1852	0.7
9	0049	3.4	**24**	0128	3.8
	0651	0.6		0729	0.4
SU	1319	3.1	M	1355	3.3
○	1853	0.9		1930	0.8
10	0121	3.4	**25**	0209	3.5
	0722	0.7		0807	0.7
M	1351	3.1	TU	1434	3.2
	1925	0.9	●	2008	1.0
11	0154	3.3	**26**	0253	3.3
	0754	0.8		0845	1.0
TU	1425	3.0	W	1516	3.0
	1959	1.0		2050	1.2
12	0231	3.2	**27**	0342	3.0
	0828	0.9		0930	1.3
W	1504	3.0	TH	1604	2.8
	2038	1.2		2151	1.4
13	0314	3.1	**28**	0443	2.7
	0910	1.1		1034	1.6
TH	1552	2.9	F	1705	2.7
	2128	1.3		2338	1.6
14	0409	3.0	**29**	0601	2.6
	1008	1.3		1208	1.7
F	1653	2.8	SA	1821	2.7
	2251	1.4			
15	0521	2.8	**30**	0133	1.5
	1208	2.8		0736	2.6
SA	1808	2.8	SU	1345	1.6
				1944	2.8
			31	0237	1.3
				0847	2.7
			M	1442	1.5
				2047	2.9

Chart Datum: 1·71 metres below Ordnance Datum (Newlyn)
HAT is 4·0 metres above Chart Datum

SCOTLAND – WICK
LAT 58°26′N   LONG 3°05′W
TIMES AND HEIGHTS OF HIGH AND LOW WATERS

Dates in amber are **SPRINGS**
Dates in yellow are **NEAPS**

2009

SEPTEMBER

Day	Time m	Time m	Day	Time m	Time m
1 TU	0319 1.1 / 0934 2.9	1522 1.4 / 2133 3.1	**16** W	0257 0.8 / 0915 3.2	1513 1.1 / 2123 3.4
2 W	0353 1.0 / 1012 3.0	1555 1.2 / 2211 3.2	**17** TH	0344 0.5 / 1005 3.4	1555 0.9 / 2212 3.6
3 TH	0424 0.8 / 1046 3.1	1625 1.1 / 2245 3.3	**18** F	0426 0.3 / 1049 3.5	1634 0.8 / ●2257 3.8
4 F	0453 0.7 / 1118 3.2	1655 0.9 / ○2318 3.4	**19** SA	0505 0.3 / 1129 3.6	1711 0.7 / 2339 3.9
5 SA	0522 0.6 / 1148 3.3	1725 0.9 / 2349 3.5	**20** SU	0543 0.3 / 1208 3.6	1749 0.6
6 SU	0551 0.6 / 1218 3.3	1755 0.8	**21** M	0021 3.8 / 0619 0.4	1245 3.5 / 1825 0.7
7 M	0021 3.5 / 0620 0.6	1249 3.3 / 1826 0.8	**22** TU	0101 3.7 / 0655 0.6	1321 3.4 / 1902 0.8
8 TU	0054 3.5 / 0651 0.7	1321 3.3 / 1859 0.9	**23** W	0141 3.4 / 0729 0.9	1357 3.2 / 1939 1.0
9 W	0129 3.4 / 0723 0.8	1355 3.2 / 1934 1.0	**24** TH	0222 3.2 / 0803 1.2	1435 3.1 / 2020 1.2
10 TH	0208 3.3 / 0758 1.0	1434 3.1 / 2015 1.1	**25** F	0309 2.9 / 0841 1.4	1519 2.9 / 2116 1.4
11 F	0254 3.1 / 0841 1.2	1523 3.0 / 2109 1.3	**26** SA	0407 2.7 / 0937 1.7	1618 2.8 / ◑2257 1.6
12 SA	0353 2.9 / 0942 1.4	1626 2.9 / ◑2246 1.4	**27** SU	0526 2.6 / 1115 1.8	1734 2.7
13 SU	0512 2.8 / 1133 1.6	1747 2.8	**28** M	0049 1.5 / 0700 2.6	1301 1.8 / 1857 2.8
14 M	0036 1.3 / 0645 2.8	1311 1.5 / 1912 2.9	**29** TU	0201 1.4 / 0814 2.7	1408 1.6 / 2007 2.9
15 TU	0158 1.1 / 0812 3.0	1422 1.3 / 2025 3.2	**30** W	0245 1.2 / 0902 2.9	1450 1.4 / 2056 3.1

OCTOBER

Day	Time m	Time m	Day	Time m	Time m
1 TH	0319 1.0 / 0939 3.0	1524 1.3 / 2136 3.2	**16** F	0322 0.6 / 0942 3.4	1532 1.0 / 2150 3.6
2 F	0350 0.9 / 1013 3.2	1555 1.1 / 2211 3.4	**17** SA	0402 0.5 / 1024 3.5	1611 0.9 / 2235 3.7
3 SA	0420 0.8 / 1044 3.3	1626 1.0 / 2246 3.5	**18** SU	0439 0.5 / 1103 3.5	1649 0.8 / ●2317 3.7
4 SU	0449 0.7 / 1116 3.4	1657 0.8 / ○2320 3.6	**19** M	0515 0.6 / 1140 3.5	1727 0.7 / 2358 3.7
5 SU	0519 0.6 / 1147 3.4	1729 0.8 / 2355 3.6	**20** TU	0550 0.7 / 1215 3.5	1805 0.8
6 TU	0550 0.6 / 1220 3.4	1803 0.8	**21** W	0037 3.5 / 0624 0.9	1250 3.4 / 1842 0.9
7 W	0031 3.6 / 0623 0.7	1255 3.4 / 1839 0.8	**22** TH	0117 3.3 / 0658 1.1	1325 3.3 / 1920 1.0
8 TH	0111 3.5 / 0659 0.9	1332 3.3 / 1919 0.9	**23** F	0157 3.1 / 0731 1.3	1402 3.2 / 2001 1.2
9 F	0154 3.3 / 0739 1.1	1414 3.2 / 2007 1.1	**24** SA	0241 2.9 / 0808 1.5	1444 3.1 / 2052 1.4
10 SA	0245 3.1 / 0826 1.3	1505 3.1 / 2111 1.2	**25** SU	0335 2.7 / 0857 1.7	1536 2.9 / 2208 1.5
11 SU	0349 2.9 / 0936 1.5	1611 3.0 / ◑2254 1.3	**26** M	0443 2.6 / 1015 1.8	1643 2.8 / 2338 1.5
12 M	0512 2.8 / 1125 1.6	1733 2.9	**27** TU	0603 2.6 / 1150 1.8	1825 2.8
13 TU	0027 1.2 / 0718 2.7	1254 1.6 / 1853 3.0	**28** W	0057 1.4 / 0718 2.7	1309 1.7 / 1908 2.9
14 W	0141 1.0 / 0758 3.0	1401 1.4 / 2004 3.2	**29** TH	0154 1.3 / 0814 2.8	1404 1.5 / 2005 3.0
15 TH	0237 0.8 / 0855 3.2	1451 1.2 / 2101 3.4	**30** F	0235 1.1 / 0856 3.0	1445 1.4 / 2052 3.1
			31 SA	0310 1.0 / 0933 3.2	1521 1.2 / 2133 3.3

NOVEMBER

Day	Time m	Time m	Day	Time m	Time m
1 SU	0343 0.9 / 1008 3.3	1555 1.0 / 2212 3.4	**16** M	0415 0.8 / 1038 3.5	1633 0.9 / ●2259 3.5
2 M	0415 0.8 / 1043 3.4	1630 0.9 / ○2252 3.5	**17** TU	0451 0.9 / 1115 3.5	1712 0.9 / 2340 3.5
3 TU	0449 0.7 / 1119 3.5	1707 0.8 / 2332 3.6	**18** W	0527 1.0 / 1151 3.5	1751 0.9
4 W	0525 0.8 / 1155 3.6	1746 0.8	**19** TH	0020 3.4 / 0601 1.1	1227 3.5 / 1829 1.0
5 TH	0014 3.6 / 0603 0.8	1235 3.5 / 1828 0.8	**20** F	0059 3.2 / 0635 1.2	1301 3.4 / 1907 1.0
6 F	0100 3.5 / 0645 1.0	1316 3.5 / 1915 0.8	**21** SA	0138 3.1 / 0709 1.3	1337 3.3 / 1946 1.1
7 SA	0148 3.4 / 0730 1.2	1402 3.4 / 2010 0.9	**22** SU	0218 3.0 / 0746 1.5	1417 3.2 / 2029 1.2
8 SU	0244 3.2 / 0823 1.4	1456 3.3 / 2119 1.0	**23** M	0304 2.8 / 0828 1.6	1502 3.1 / 2122 1.3
9 M	0349 3.0 / 0932 1.6	1601 3.2 / ◑2244 1.1	**24** TU	0358 2.7 / 0921 1.7	1554 3.0 / ◑2228 1.4
10 TU	0503 2.9 / 1101 1.6	1714 3.1	**25** W	0500 2.7 / 1034 1.8	1657 2.9 / 2338 1.4
11 W	0002 1.0 / 0618 2.9	1221 1.6 / 1827 3.2	**26** TH	0606 2.7 / 1154 1.7	1802 2.9
12 TH	0112 1.0 / 0728 3.0	1329 1.4 / 1935 3.3	**27** F	0043 1.4 / 0707 2.8	1302 1.7 / 1904 2.9
13 F	0210 0.9 / 0826 3.1	1424 1.3 / 2036 3.4	**28** SA	0138 1.3 / 0802 2.9	1358 1.5 / 2001 3.1
14 SA	0257 0.8 / 0915 3.3	1510 1.1 / 2128 3.5	**29** SU	0224 1.2 / 0849 3.1	1445 1.3 / 2053 3.2
15 SU	0338 0.8 / 0958 3.4	1552 1.0 / 2215 3.5	**30** M	0306 1.1 / 0932 3.3	1527 1.2 / 2142 3.3

DECEMBER

Day	Time m	Time m	Day	Time m	Time m
1 TU	0346 1.0 / 1013 3.4	1609 1.0 / 2229 3.5	**16** W	0435 1.1 / 1058 3.4	1705 1.0 / ●2329 3.3
2 W	0426 0.9 / 1055 3.5	1652 0.8 / ○2316 3.6	**17** TH	0510 1.2 / 1135 3.5	1742 1.0
3 TH	0509 0.9 / 1137 3.6	1738 0.7	**18** F	0007 3.3 / 0545 1.2	1210 3.5 / 1818 0.9
4 F	0004 3.6 / 0552 0.9	1221 3.7 / 1825 0.7	**19** SA	0044 3.2 / 0618 1.2	1244 3.5 / 1853 1.0
5 SA	0054 3.6 / 0638 1.0	1306 3.6 / 1915 0.6	**20** SU	0120 3.1 / 0652 1.2	1319 3.4 / 1928 1.0
6 SU	0145 3.4 / 0725 1.1	1355 3.6 / 2010 0.7	**21** M	0156 3.1 / 0725 1.3	1354 3.3 / 2004 1.1
7 M	0239 3.3 / 0816 1.3	1447 3.5 / 2111 0.8	**22** TU	0233 3.0 / 0801 1.4	1431 3.2 / 2042 1.2
8 TU	0337 3.2 / 0913 1.4	1545 3.4 / 2218 0.9	**23** W	0315 2.9 / 0840 1.5	1513 3.1 / 2126 1.3
9 W	0439 3.0 / 1021 1.5	1648 3.3 / ◑2326 1.0	**24** TH	0401 2.8 / 0927 1.6	1601 3.0 / ◑2221 1.4
10 TH	0542 3.0 / 1135 1.6	1755 3.2	**25** F	0456 2.8 / 1030 1.7	1658 3.0 / 2327 1.4
11 F	0033 1.1 / 0647 3.0	1250 1.5 / 1903 3.2	**26** SA	0558 2.9 / 1152 1.7	1803 2.9
12 SA	0137 1.1 / 0751 3.0	1358 1.4 / 2010 3.2	**27** SU	0035 1.4 / 0701 2.9	1306 1.6 / 1910 3.0
13 SU	0232 1.1 / 0847 3.1	1455 1.3 / 2110 3.2	**28** M	0138 1.3 / 0803 3.0	1410 1.5 / 2016 3.1
14 M	0317 1.2 / 0936 3.3	1543 1.2 / 2202 3.3	**29** TU	0234 1.2 / 0858 3.2	1506 1.2 / 2118 3.2
15 TU	0358 1.2 / 1019 3.4	1625 1.1 / 2247 3.3	**30** W	0325 1.1 / 0949 3.4	1556 1.0 / 2214 3.4
			31 TH	0413 1.0 / 1037 3.5	1644 0.8 / ○2306 3.5

Chart Datum: 1·71 metres below Ordnance Datum (Newlyn)
HAT is 4·0 metres above Chart Datum

TIDES

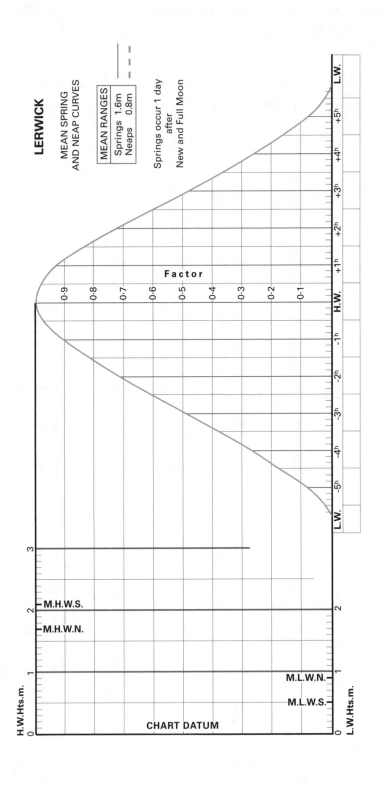

LERWICK

MEAN SPRING
AND NEAP CURVES

MEAN RANGES
Springs 1.6m
Neaps 0.8m

Springs occur 1 day
after
New and Full Moon

Factor

SCOTLAND – LERWICK

LAT 60°09′N   LONG 1°08′W

TIMES AND HEIGHTS OF HIGH AND LOW WATERS

Dates in amber are **SPRINGS**
Dates in yellow are **NEAPS**

2009

JANUARY

Day	Time m	Time m	Time m	Time m
1 TH	0138 1.9	0718 0.9	1332 2.1	1955 0.7
16 F	0230 2.0	0808 0.8	1437 2.2	2050 0.6
2 F	0216 1.9	0756 0.9	1412 2.0	2035 0.7
17 SA	0312 1.8	0853 0.9	1524 2.0	2139 0.8
3 SA	0259 1.8	0839 1.0	1457 2.0	2121 0.8
18 SU	0357 1.8	0945 1.0	1616 1.9	◑ 2236 0.9
4 SU	0348 1.8	0930 1.0	1550 1.9	◐ 2215 0.8
19 M	0450 1.7	1104 1.1	1721 1.7	2351 1.0
5 M	0445 1.8	1034 1.1	1652 1.9	2323 0.9
20 TU	0559 1.7	1248 1.1	1846 1.7	
6 TU	0549 1.8	1159 1.1	1804 1.9	
21 W	0110 1.1	0716 1.7	1405 1.0	2003 1.7
7 W	0040 0.9	0659 1.8	1318 1.0	1923 1.9
22 TH	0213 1.1	0820 1.8	1500 0.9	2102 1.8
8 TH	0148 0.9	0804 2.0	1422 0.8	2033 2.0
23 F	0303 1.0	0910 1.9	1543 0.8	2148 1.8
9 F	0248 0.8	0901 2.1	1520 0.7	2136 2.1
24 SA	0343 1.0	0951 2.0	1618 0.8	2227 1.9
10 SA	0342 0.8	0954 2.2	1613 0.5	2234 2.2
25 SU	0417 0.9	1028 2.1	1649 0.7	2303 2.0
11 SU	0432 0.7	1045 2.3	1702 0.3	○ 2328 2.2
26 M	0450 0.8	1103 2.1	1720 0.6	● 2337 2.0
12 M	0518 0.7	1134 2.4	1750 0.3	
27 TU	0521 0.7	1135 2.2	1750 0.5	
13 TU	0017 2.2	0602 0.6	1222 2.4	1835 0.2
28 W	0009 2.0	0551 0.7	1207 2.2	1821 0.5
14 W	0104 2.2	0644 0.7	1308 2.4	1920 0.3
29 TH	0041 2.0	0623 0.7	1238 2.2	1853 0.5
15 TH	0147 2.1	0726 0.7	1353 2.3	2005 0.4
30 F	0112 2.0	0656 0.7	1310 2.2	1926 0.5
31 SA	0145 1.9	0731 0.7	1346 2.1	2003 0.6

FEBRUARY

Day	Time m	Time m	Time m	Time m
1 SU	0222 1.9	0810 0.8	1426 2.0	2044 0.7
16 M	0306 1.8	0859 0.9	1531 1.8	◑ 2133 0.9
2 M	0306 1.8	0856 0.9	1515 1.9	◑ 2133 0.8
17 TU	0350 1.7	1003 1.0	1627 1.6	2239 1.1
3 TU	0359 1.8	0954 1.0	1617 1.8	2236 0.9
18 W	0448 1.6	1206 1.1	1803 1.5	
4 W	0504 1.7	1118 1.0	1735 1.6	
19 TH	0025 1.1	0629 1.6	1342 1.0	1945 1.6
5 TH	0009 1.0	0625 1.7	1301 0.9	1911 1.8
20 F	0150 1.1	0754 1.7	1441 0.9	2046 1.6
6 F	0138 1.0	0747 1.8	1416 0.8	2033 1.9
21 SA	0244 1.0	0847 1.8	1522 0.8	2129 1.7
7 SA	0244 0.9	0852 2.0	1516 0.6	2136 2.0
22 SU	0323 0.9	0929 1.9	1554 0.7	2204 1.8
8 SU	0336 0.6	0947 2.1	1606 0.4	2229 2.1
23 M	0356 0.8	1005 2.0	1624 0.6	2238 1.9
9 M	0421 0.6	1036 2.3	1651 0.2	○ 2316 2.2
24 TU	0426 0.7	1039 2.1	1653 0.5	2310 2.0
10 TU	0503 0.6	1122 2.4	1733 0.1	2359 2.4
25 W	0457 0.6	1111 2.1	1722 0.4	● 2341 2.0
11 W	0542 0.5	1205 2.4	1814 0.1	
26 TH	0528 0.5	1142 2.2	1753 0.3	
12 TH	0038 2.1	0621 0.5	1246 2.4	1853 0.2
27 F	0011 2.0	0559 0.5	1214 2.2	1824 0.4
13 F	0116 2.1	0659 0.5	1326 2.3	1932 0.4
28 SA	0042 2.0	0633 0.5	1247 2.2	1858 0.4
14 SA	0152 2.0	0737 0.6	1405 2.1	2010 0.6
15 SU	0227 1.9	0815 0.7	1446 2.0	2049 0.8

MARCH

Day	Time m	Time m	Time m	Time m
1 SU	0114 2.0	0709 0.5	1323 2.1	1935 0.5
16 M	0145 1.9	0745 0.6	1412 1.8	2006 0.8
2 M	0150 1.9	0749 0.6	1403 2.0	2016 0.6
17 TU	0220 1.8	0826 0.8	1456 1.7	2043 0.9
3 TU	0231 1.9	0835 0.7	1454 1.9	2104 0.8
18 W	0301 1.7	0923 0.9	1549 1.5	◑ 2137 1.1
4 W	0323 1.8	0935 0.8	1600 1.7	◐ 2209 0.9
19 TH	0353 1.6	1111 1.0	1706 1.4	2333 1.1
5 TH	0432 1.7	1106 0.9	1728 1.6	
20 F	0505 1.5	1255 0.9	1914 1.5	
6 F	0001 1.0	0603 1.7	1257 0.8	1916 1.7
21 SA	0108 1.1	0712 1.6	1402 0.8	2015 1.5
7 SA	0134 1.0	0737 1.8	1410 0.6	2033 1.8
22 SU	0209 1.0	0812 1.6	1444 0.7	2056 1.6
8 SU	0236 0.8	0841 1.9	1505 0.4	2127 1.9
23 M	0250 0.9	0855 1.8	1517 0.6	2131 1.8
9 M	0323 0.7	0933 2.1	1550 0.3	2213 2.0
24 TU	0323 0.7	0932 1.9	1547 0.5	2204 1.9
10 TU	0403 0.6	1020 2.2	1631 0.2	2255 2.1
25 W	0355 0.6	1006 2.0	1618 0.4	2236 1.9
11 W	0442 0.4	1102 2.3	1710 0.1	○ 2332 2.1
26 TH	0428 0.5	1040 2.1	1650 0.3	● 2308 2.0
12 TH	0519 0.4	1142 2.3	1747 0.2	
27 F	0501 0.4	1114 2.1	1723 0.3	2340 2.0
13 F	0008 2.1	0555 0.3	1220 2.3	1823 0.3
28 SA	0535 0.4	1149 2.2	1757 0.3	
14 SA	0041 2.0	0632 0.4	1257 2.1	1858 0.4
29 SU	0013 2.1	0611 0.4	1226 2.1	1833 0.4
15 SU	0120 2.0	0708 0.5	1334 2.0	1932 0.6
30 M	0048 2.0	0651 0.4	1306 2.1	1913 0.5
31 TU	0125 2.0	0735 0.5	1353 1.9	1956 0.7

APRIL

Day	Time m	Time m	Time m	Time m
1 W	0208 1.9	0827 0.6	1451 1.8	2049 0.8
16 TH	0226 1.7	0858 0.6	1522 1.5	2059 1.0
2 TH	0304 1.8	0933 0.7	1603 1.6	◑ 2201 1.0
17 F	0316 1.6	1019 0.8	1625 1.4	◐ 2236 1.1
3 F	0417 1.7	1112 0.7	1734 1.6	2358 1.0
18 SA	0418 1.5	1146 0.8	1810 1.4	
4 SA	0550 1.6	1245 0.6	1912 1.6	
19 SU	0008 1.0	0541 1.5	1255 0.8	1924 1.5
5 SU	0118 0.9	0718 1.7	1353 0.5	2016 1.7
20 M	0114 1.0	0717 1.6	1347 0.7	2009 1.6
6 M	0216 0.8	0821 1.9	1445 0.4	2106 1.8
21 TU	0203 0.8	0808 1.7	1428 0.6	2047 1.7
7 TU	0301 0.6	0912 2.0	1528 0.3	2148 1.9
22 W	0243 0.7	0849 1.8	1505 0.5	2123 1.8
8 W	0341 0.5	0957 2.1	1607 0.2	2227 2.0
23 TH	0320 0.6	0928 1.9	1540 0.4	2158 1.9
9 TH	0419 0.4	1039 2.1	1643 0.2	○ 2302 2.0
24 F	0357 0.5	1007 2.0	1617 0.3	2234 2.0
10 F	0456 0.4	1118 2.1	1718 0.3	2335 2.0
25 SA	0434 0.4	1047 2.1	1654 0.3	● 2311 2.1
11 SA	0533 0.4	1155 2.1	1753 0.4	
26 SU	0513 0.3	1128 2.1	1733 0.3	2348 2.1
12 SU	0006 2.0	0608 0.4	1231 2.0	1826 0.5
27 M	0555 0.3	1212 2.1	1814 0.4	
13 M	0038 2.0	0645 0.5	1308 1.9	1859 0.7
28 TU	0027 2.1	0639 0.3	1301 2.0	1858 0.6
14 TU	0111 1.9	0723 0.6	1347 1.7	1932 0.8
29 W	0111 2.0	0729 0.4	1355 1.9	1947 0.7
15 W	0146 1.8	0805 0.7	1431 1.6	2008 0.9
30 TH	0200 1.9	0826 0.4	1457 1.7	2044 0.8

Chart Datum: 1·22 metres below Ordnance Datum (Local)
HAT is 2·5 metres above Chart Datum

TIDES

TIDES

For Summer Time add ONE hour in **non-shaded areas**

SCOTLAND – LERWICK
LAT 60°09'N   LONG 1°08'W
TIMES AND HEIGHTS OF HIGH AND LOW WATERS

Dates in amber are **SPRINGS**
Dates in yellow are **NEAPS**
2009

	MAY			JUNE			JULY			AUGUST		
	Time m	Time m		Time m	Time m		Time m	Time m		Time m	Time m	

MAY

1 0301 1.8 / 0935 0.5 / F 1606 1.6 / 2157 0.9
16 0249 1.7 / 0933 0.7 / SA 1551 1.5 / 2137 1.0

2 0411 1.7 / 1102 0.5 / SA 1724 1.6 / 2332 0.9
17 0344 1.6 / 1041 0.7 / SU 1651 1.4 / 2300 1.0

3 0532 1.7 / 1220 0.5 / SU 1843 1.6
18 0445 1.6 / 1147 0.7 / M 1804 1.5

4 0047 0.9 / 0650 1.7 / M 1325 0.5 / ☽ 1944 1.7
19 0013 0.9 / 0555 1.6 / TU 1245 0.7 / 1908 1.5

5 0147 0.8 / 0752 1.8 / TU 1417 0.4 / 2034 1.7
20 0111 0.8 / 0706 1.6 / W 1335 0.6 / 1957 1.7

6 0235 0.6 / 0846 1.9 / W 1501 0.4 / 2117 1.8
21 0200 0.7 / 0802 1.7 / TH 1421 0.5 / 2041 1.8

7 0318 0.5 / 0933 1.9 / TH 1540 0.4 / 2157 1.9
22 0245 0.6 / 0851 1.8 / F 1504 0.5 / 2123 1.9

8 0358 0.5 / 1017 2.0 / F 1617 0.4 / 2232 1.9
23 0328 0.5 / 0938 2.0 / SA 1548 0.4 / 2204 2.0

9 0437 0.4 / 1057 1.9 / SA 1652 0.5 / 2306 2.0
24 0412 0.4 / 1026 2.0 / SU 1631 0.4 / 2247 2.1

10 0514 0.4 / 1135 1.9 / SU 1726 0.5 / 2339 2.0
25 0457 0.3 / 1115 2.1 / M 1714 0.4 / 2330 2.1

11 0551 0.5 / 1212 1.9 / M 1801 0.6 / ○
26 0544 0.3 / 1206 2.1 / TU 1802 0.5 / ●

12 0013 2.0 / 0628 0.5 / TU 1251 1.8 / 1834 0.7
27 0016 2.1 / 0633 0.2 / W 1301 2.0 / 1850 0.6

13 0047 1.9 / 0707 0.6 / W 1330 1.7 / 1909 0.8
28 0106 2.1 / 0726 0.3 / TH 1357 1.9 / 1941 0.7

14 0123 1.8 / 0749 0.6 / TH 1412 1.6 / 1948 0.9
29 0159 2.0 / 0822 0.3 / F 1454 1.8 / 2035 0.8

15 0202 1.7 / 0836 0.7 / F 1459 1.5 / 2035 0.9
30 0257 1.9 / 0924 0.4 / SA 1552 1.7 / 2136 0.8

31 0357 1.8 / 1033 0.5 / SU 1655 1.6 / 2249 0.9

JUNE

1 0503 1.8 / 1144 0.5 / M 1800 1.6
16 0404 1.7 / 1038 0.7 / TU 1659 1.5 / ☽ 2259 0.9

2 0006 0.8 / 0614 1.7 / TU 1250 0.5 / ☾ 1902 1.6
17 0502 1.6 / 1142 0.7 / W 1801 1.6

3 0114 0.8 / 0720 1.7 / W 1346 0.6 / 1957 1.7
18 0014 0.9 / 0608 1.7 / TH 1245 0.7 / 1904 1.7

4 0211 0.7 / 0819 1.8 / TH 1434 0.6 / 2045 1.8
19 0118 0.8 / 0718 1.7 / F 1342 0.7 / 2001 1.8

5 0300 0.6 / 0912 1.8 / F 1516 0.6 / 2129 1.8
20 0213 0.7 / 0820 1.8 / SA 1435 0.6 / 2052 1.9

6 0344 0.6 / 0959 1.8 / SA 1555 0.6 / 2209 1.9
21 0305 0.6 / 0918 1.9 / SU 1527 0.6 / 2141 2.0

7 0424 0.5 / 1042 1.8 / SU 1632 0.7 / 2246 2.0
22 0356 0.4 / 1013 2.0 / M 1617 0.5 / 2230 2.1

8 0503 0.5 / 1121 1.8 / M 1708 0.7 / 2321 2.0
23 0447 0.3 / 1108 2.1 / TU 1706 0.5 / 2319 2.2

9 0540 0.5 / 1200 1.8 / TU 1743 0.7 / ○ 2356 2.0
24 0537 0.2 / 1203 2.1 / W 1753 0.5

10 0617 0.5 / 1237 1.8 / W 1818 0.7
25 0009 2.2 / 0626 0.1 / TH 1256 2.0 / ● 1840 0.5

11 0031 1.9 / 0653 0.5 / TH 1314 1.7 / 1853 0.8
26 0100 2.2 / 0715 0.1 / F 1347 2.0 / 1927 0.6

12 0106 1.9 / 0730 0.5 / F 1352 1.7 / 1930 0.8
27 0150 2.1 / 0806 0.2 / SA 1436 1.9 / 2015 0.7

13 0143 1.8 / 0810 0.6 / SA 1432 1.6 / 2009 0.8
28 0241 2.1 / 0858 0.3 / SU 1525 1.8 / 2105 0.7

14 0224 1.8 / 0853 0.6 / SU 1515 1.6 / 2055 0.9
29 0333 2.0 / 0954 0.5 / M 1616 1.7 / 2203 0.8

15 0311 1.7 / 0941 0.7 / M 1604 1.5 / 2150 0.9
30 0430 1.8 / 1058 0.6 / TU 1712 1.6 / 2318 0.9

JULY

1 0535 1.7 / 1207 0.7 / W 1816 1.6
16 0421 1.7 / 1042 0.8 / TH 1710 1.6 / 2316 0.9

2 0042 0.9 / 0648 1.7 / TH 1313 0.8 / 1919 1.7
17 0527 1.7 / 1157 0.8 / F 1818 1.7

3 0152 0.8 / 0756 1.7 / F 1410 0.8 / 2017 1.7
18 0042 0.9 / 0644 1.7 / SA 1313 0.8 / 1929 1.8

4 0248 0.8 / 0856 1.7 / SA 1458 0.8 / ☾ 2108 1.8
19 0152 0.8 / 0802 1.8 / SU 1418 0.8 / 2031 1.9

5 0336 0.7 / 0947 1.7 / SU 1541 0.8 / 2152 1.9
20 0253 0.6 / 0908 1.9 / M 1516 0.7 / 2127 2.0

6 0417 0.6 / 1030 1.8 / M 1619 0.8 / 2231 2.0
21 0347 0.4 / 1007 2.0 / TU 1607 0.6 / 2219 2.2

7 0453 0.6 / 1109 1.8 / TU 1655 0.7 / 2308 2.0
22 0438 0.3 / 1102 2.1 / W 1655 0.5 / 2309 2.3

8 0527 0.5 / 1145 1.8 / W 1729 0.7 / 2342 2.0
23 0525 0.1 / 1152 2.1 / TH 1739 0.5 / 2358 2.3

9 0600 0.5 / 1220 1.8 / TH 1801 0.7
24 0611 0.1 / 1239 2.1 / F 1822 0.5

10 0015 2.0 / 0633 0.5 / F 1254 1.8 / 1833 0.7
25 0044 2.3 / 0656 0.1 / SA 1324 2.0 / 1904 0.5

11 0048 2.0 / 0705 0.5 / SA 1326 1.8 / ○ 1906 0.7
26 0130 2.3 / 0740 0.2 / SU 1407 1.9 / ● 1947 0.6

12 0121 2.0 / 0739 0.5 / SU 1400 1.7 / 1941 0.7
27 0216 2.2 / 0825 0.4 / M 1449 1.8 / 2031 0.7

13 0157 1.9 / 0816 0.6 / M 1438 1.7 / 2020 0.8
28 0303 2.0 / 0912 0.6 / TU 1533 1.7 / 2122 0.8

14 0238 1.9 / 0856 0.6 / TU 1521 1.7 / 2106 0.8
29 0354 1.8 / 1006 0.8 / W 1622 1.7 / 2231 0.8

15 0325 1.7 / 0943 0.7 / W 1612 1.7 / 2201 0.9
30 0454 1.7 / 1117 0.9 / TH 1724 1.6

31 0014 0.9 / 0616 1.6 / F 1240 1.0 / 1843 1.6

AUGUST

1 0138 0.9 / 0740 1.6 / SA 1350 1.0 / 1954 1.7
16 0023 0.9 / 0629 1.7 / SU 1301 1.0 / 1908 1.8

2 0239 0.8 / 0845 1.7 / SU 1444 1.0 / ☾ 2050 1.8
17 0144 0.8 / 0758 1.8 / M 1412 0.9 / ☾ 2019 1.9

3 0326 0.7 / 0934 1.7 / M 1527 0.9 / 2135 1.9
18 0246 0.6 / 0904 1.9 / TU 1508 0.8 / 2116 2.1

4 0403 0.7 / 1014 1.8 / TU 1604 0.8 / 2214 2.0
19 0338 0.4 / 0959 2.1 / W 1555 0.6 / 2207 2.2

5 0435 0.6 / 1049 1.9 / W 1637 0.7 / 2249 2.0
20 0424 0.2 / 1048 2.1 / TH 1638 0.5 / 2254 2.4

6 0506 0.5 / 1123 1.9 / TH 1708 0.7 / 2322 2.1
21 0507 0.1 / 1132 2.2 / F 1719 0.4 / 2339 2.4

7 0536 0.5 / 1155 1.9 / F 1738 0.6 / 2354 2.1
22 0549 0.1 / 1214 2.2 / SA 1759 0.4

8 0606 0.4 / 1225 1.9 / SA 1809 0.6
23 0022 2.4 / 0629 0.2 / SU 1254 2.1 / 1838 0.5

9 0023 2.1 / 0636 0.4 / SU 1256 1.9 / ○ 1840 0.6
24 0104 2.3 / 0710 0.3 / M 1332 2.0 / 1918 0.5

10 0055 2.1 / 0708 0.5 / M 1326 1.9 / 1914 0.6
25 0146 2.2 / 0750 0.5 / TU 1409 1.9 / ● 2000 0.7

11 0128 2.0 / 0742 0.5 / TU 1400 1.9 / 1951 0.7
26 0230 2.0 / 0831 0.7 / W 1449 1.8 / 2046 0.8

12 0206 2.0 / 0820 0.6 / W 1440 1.8 / 2034 0.8
27 0318 1.8 / 0917 0.9 / TH 1534 1.7 / 2151 1.0

13 0251 1.9 / 0905 0.8 / TH 1529 1.8 / 2128 0.9
28 0415 1.7 / 1022 1.1 / F 1631 1.7 / 2348 1.0

14 0349 1.8 / 1001 0.9 / F 1629 1.7 / 2241 0.9
29 0543 1.6 / 1205 1.1 / SA 1801 1.7

15 0500 1.7 / 1123 1.0 / SA 1743 1.7
30 0119 1.0 / 0724 1.6 / SU 1327 1.1 / 1930 1.7

31 0220 0.9 / 0828 1.6 / M 1424 1.0 / 2027 1.8

Chart Datum: 1·22 metres below Ordnance Datum (Local)
HAT is 2·5 metres above Chart Datum

TIME ZONE (UT)	SCOTLAND – LERWICK	Dates in amber are SPRINGS
For Summer Time add ONE hour in **non-shaded areas**	LAT 60°09′N LONG 1°08′W	Dates in yellow are NEAPS
	TIMES AND HEIGHTS OF HIGH AND LOW WATERS	**2009**

SEPTEMBER

Time	m	Time	m	Time	m	Time	m
1 0304	0.8	**16** 0234	0.5				
0912	1.8	0854	2.0				
TU 1505	0.9	W 1453	0.8				
2111	1.9	2101	2.1				
2 0338	0.7	**17** 0321	0.4				
0948	1.8	0942	2.1				
W 1539	0.8	TH 1536	0.6				
2148	2.0	2149	2.3				
3 0408	0.6	**18** 0404	0.2				
1021	1.9	1026	2.2				
TH 1610	0.7	F 1616	0.5				
2223	2.1	● 2234	2.4				
4 0436	0.5	**19** 0444	0.2				
1053	2.0	1106	2.2				
F 1640	0.6	SA 1655	0.5				
○ 2255	2.1	2316	2.4				
5 0505	0.4	**20** 0523	0.2				
1124	2.0	1144	2.2				
SA 1710	0.6	SU 1734	0.4				
2325	2.2	2357	2.4				
6 0534	0.4	**21** 0601	0.3				
1153	2.0	1219	2.2				
SU 1742	0.6	M 1813	0.5				
2356	2.2						
7 0605	0.4	**22** 0037	2.3				
1222	2.1	0638	0.5				
M 1814	0.6	TU 1254	2.1				
		1852	0.6				
8 0027	2.2	**23** 0117	2.1				
0637	0.5	0715	0.7				
TU 1253	2.0	W 1329	2.0				
1849	0.6	1932	0.7				
9 0102	2.1	**24** 0159	2.0				
0712	0.6	0753	0.9				
W 1327	2.0	TH 1407	1.9				
1928	0.7	2018	0.9				
10 0141	2.0	**25** 0246	1.8				
0751	0.7	0833	1.0				
TH 1406	1.9	F 1451	1.8				
2013	0.8	2119	1.0				
11 0229	1.9	**26** 0341	1.7				
0836	0.9	0931	1.2				
F 1455	1.9	SA 1545	1.7				
2109	0.9	◐ 2306	1.0				
12 0331	1.8	**27** 0500	1.6				
0936	1.0	1119	1.2				
SA 1600	1.8	SU 1700	1.7				
◐ 2229	0.9						
13 0451	1.7	**28** 0040	1.0				
1111	1.1	0653	1.6				
SU 1721	1.7	M 1249	1.2				
		1852	1.7				
14 0020	0.9	**29** 0144	0.9				
0632	1.7	0755	1.7				
M 1257	1.0	TU 1350	1.1				
1856	1.8	1953	1.8				
15 0136	0.7	**30** 0228	0.8				
0756	1.8	0837	1.8				
TU 1403	0.9	W 1432	1.0				
2007	2.0	2037	1.9				

OCTOBER

Time	m	Time	m
1 0302	0.7	**16** 0300	0.4
0913	1.9	0918	2.1
TH 1506	0.9	F 1514	0.7
2115	2.0	2128	2.3
2 0331	0.6	**17** 0341	0.4
0946	2.0	1000	2.1
F 1538	0.8	SA 1554	0.6
2149	2.1	2212	2.3
3 0401	0.5	**18** 0420	0.4
1018	2.1	1038	2.2
SA 1610	0.7	SU 1633	0.5
2222	2.2	● 2254	2.3
4 0431	0.5	**19** 0457	0.4
1049	2.1	1113	2.2
SU 1642	0.6	M 1712	0.5
○ 2255	2.2	2334	2.3
5 0503	0.5	**20** 0534	0.5
1120	2.2	1148	2.2
M 1716	0.6	TU 1751	0.6
2329	2.3		
6 0536	0.5	**21** 0014	2.2
1152	2.2	0610	0.7
TU 1751	0.6	W 1222	2.2
		1831	0.6
7 0005	2.2	**22** 0054	2.1
0610	0.6	0645	0.8
W 1225	2.2	TH 1257	2.1
1829	0.6	1912	0.7
8 0044	2.2	**23** 0136	1.9
0648	0.7	0721	1.0
TH 1302	2.1	F 1335	2.0
1912	0.7	1957	0.9
9 0128	2.1	**24** 0221	1.8
0730	0.8	0800	1.1
F 1343	2.0	SA 1418	1.9
2002	0.7	2052	1.0
10 0222	1.9	**25** 0313	1.7
0820	1.0	0852	1.2
SA 1436	1.9	SU 1508	1.8
2103	0.8	2210	1.0
11 0331	1.8	**26** 0415	1.6
0925	1.1	1020	1.3
SU 1545	1.8	M 1610	1.7
◐ 2229	0.9	◐ 2333	1.0
12 0453	1.7	**27** 0550	1.6
1108	1.1	1149	1.2
M 1709	1.8	TU 1734	1.7
13 0009	0.8	**28** 0042	1.0
0628	1.8	0704	1.7
TU 1241	1.1	W 1256	1.1
1839	1.9	1901	1.8
14 0119	0.7	**29** 0134	0.9
0740	1.9	0752	1.8
W 1343	1.0	TH 1346	1.0
1946	2.0	1952	1.9
15 0214	0.5	**30** 0214	0.8
0833	2.0	0831	1.9
TH 1431	0.8	F 1427	0.9
2040	2.1	2034	2.0
		31 0249	0.7
		0906	2.0
		SA 1503	0.8
		2112	2.1

NOVEMBER

Time	m	Time	m
1 0323	0.6	**16** 0357	0.6
0941	2.1	1012	2.2
SU 1539	0.7	M 1618	0.6
2150	2.2	● 2237	2.2
2 0358	0.6	**17** 0435	0.7
1015	2.2	1049	2.2
M 1616	0.6	TU 1658	0.6
○ 2228	2.2	2319	2.2
3 0434	0.6	**18** 0512	0.7
1050	2.2	1124	2.2
TU 1654	0.6	W 1737	0.6
2307	2.3	2359	2.1
4 0511	0.6	**19** 0548	0.8
1127	2.3	1200	2.2
W 1734	0.6	TH 1817	0.7
2349	2.3		
5 0551	0.7	**20** 0038	2.0
1205	2.3	0623	0.9
TH 1817	0.6	F 1236	2.2
		1857	0.7
6 0035	2.2	**21** 0119	1.9
0633	0.8	0659	1.0
F 1247	2.2	SA 1313	2.1
1904	0.6	1939	0.8
7 0127	2.1	**22** 0201	1.9
0720	0.9	0737	1.1
SA 1334	2.1	SU 1353	2.0
1958	0.7	2025	0.9
8 0227	2.0	**23** 0245	1.8
0813	1.0	0821	1.1
SU 1431	2.0	M 1437	1.8
2100	0.7	2117	1.0
9 0332	1.9	**24** 0335	1.7
0917	1.1	0917	1.2
M 1538	2.0	TU 1529	1.8
◑ 2218	0.7	◑ 2221	1.0
10 0443	1.8	**25** 0432	1.7
1042	1.1	1033	1.2
TU 1653	1.9	W 1627	1.8
2342	0.7	2328	1.0
11 0601	1.8	**26** 0542	1.7
1208	1.1	1150	1.2
W 1811	2.0	TH 1734	1.8
12 0051	0.7	**27** 0028	0.9
0709	1.9	0650	1.7
TH 1314	1.0	F 1253	1.1
1919	2.0	1848	1.8
13 0148	0.6	**28** 0120	0.9
0803	1.9	0741	1.8
F 1407	0.9	SA 1344	1.0
2016	2.1	1946	1.9
14 0236	0.6	**29** 0205	0.8
0850	2.0	0824	1.9
SA 1454	0.8	SU 1429	0.9
2107	2.2	2035	2.0
15 0318	0.6	**30** 0247	0.8
0933	2.1	0905	2.0
SU 1537	0.7	M 1511	0.8
2154	2.2	2121	2.1

DECEMBER

Time	m	Time	m
1 0329	0.7	**16** 0420	0.8
0946	2.2	1034	2.2
TU 1554	0.7	W 1651	0.7
2206	2.2	● 2310	2.1
2 0411	0.7	**17** 0457	0.9
1027	2.3	1111	2.2
W 1638	0.6	TH 1729	0.7
○ 2253	2.2	2348	2.0
3 0454	0.7	**18** 0533	0.9
1109	2.3	1147	2.2
TH 1723	0.5	F 1806	0.7
2342	2.3		
4 0539	0.7	**19** 0025	2.0
1153	2.3	0608	0.9
F 1810	0.5	SA 1222	2.2
		1842	0.7
5 0034	2.2	**20** 0102	2.0
0625	0.8	0642	0.9
SA 1241	2.3	SU 1256	2.1
1900	0.5	1918	0.7
6 0128	2.1	**21** 0138	1.9
0713	0.8	0716	0.9
SU 1331	2.3	M 1331	2.1
1952	0.5	1954	0.8
7 0223	2.0	**22** 0215	1.8
0804	0.9	0751	1.0
M 1426	2.2	TU 1408	2.0
2048	0.6	2033	0.8
8 0319	1.9	**23** 0255	1.8
0858	1.0	0831	1.0
TU 1524	2.1	W 1450	1.9
2151	0.6	2117	0.9
9 0417	1.9	**24** 0340	1.7
1002	1.0	0920	1.1
W 1627	2.0	TH 1539	1.9
◑ 2303	0.7	◑ 2209	0.9
10 0521	1.8	**25** 0431	1.7
1121	1.1	1023	1.1
TH 1736	2.0	F 1635	1.8
		2314	1.0
11 0015	0.8	**26** 0531	1.7
0628	1.8	1147	1.1
F 1241	1.0	SA 1740	1.8
1847	2.0		
12 0119	0.8	**27** 0023	1.0
0729	1.9	0639	1.8
SA 1345	0.9	SU 1259	1.1
1952	2.0	1853	1.8
13 0212	0.8	**28** 0123	0.9
0823	2.0	0741	1.9
SU 1440	0.9	M 1357	1.0
2051	2.0	2001	1.9
14 0259	0.8	**29** 0217	0.9
0911	2.0	0834	2.0
M 1527	0.8	TU 1449	0.8
2142	2.0	2059	2.0
15 0341	0.8	**30** 0308	0.8
0954	2.1	0923	2.1
TU 1611	0.7	W 1539	0.7
2228	2.1	2153	2.1
		31 0357	0.8
		1011	2.2
		TH 1627	0.5
		○ 2245	2.2

Chart Datum: 1·22 metres below Ordnance Datum (Local)
HAT is 2·5 metres above Chart Datum

TIDES

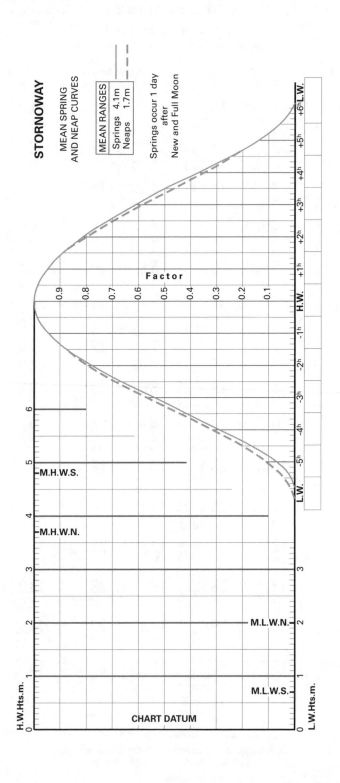

STORNOWAY

MEAN SPRING
AND NEAP CURVES

MEAN RANGES	
Springs	4.1m
Neaps	1.7m

Springs occur 1 day
after
New and Full Moon

SCOTLAND – STORNOWAY

LAT 58°12′N   LONG 6°23′W

TIMES AND HEIGHTS OF HIGH AND LOW WATERS

Dates in amber are **SPRINGS**
Dates in yellow are **NEAPS**

2009

JANUARY

Day	Time m	Time m	Time m	Time m
1 TH	0333 1.3	0930 4.3	1604 1.2	2154 3.9
2 F	0411 1.5	1010 4.2	1644 1.3	2239 3.7
3 SA	0453 1.6	1058 4.0	1730 1.4	2337 3.7
4 SU	0543 1.8	1157 4.0	1822 1.5	
5 M	0043 3.6	0641 1.9	1302 3.9	1921 1.6
6 TU	0152 3.7	0750 1.9	1411 3.9	2029 1.6
7 W	0300 3.8	0907 1.8	1522 4.0	2141 1.5
8 TH	0404 4.1	1022 1.6	1629 4.2	2247 1.4
9 F	0501 4.4	1127 1.3	1729 4.4	2345 1.2
10 SA	0553 4.7	1224 1.0	1823 4.6	
11 SU	0036 1.0	0641 4.9	1316 0.7	1911 4.8
12 M	0124 0.8	0726 5.1	1403 0.4	1956 4.8
13 TU	0207 0.7	0810 5.2	1447 0.4	2039 4.7
14 W	0249 0.7	0853 5.1	1529 0.4	2121 4.5
15 TH	0330 0.9	0936 4.9	1612 0.7	2205 4.3
16 F	0412 1.1	1022 4.6	1655 1.0	2254 4.0
17 SA	0456 1.4	1115 4.3	1742 1.4	2353 3.7
18 SU	0545 1.7	1221 3.9	1834 1.7	
19 M	0108 3.5	0644 2.0	1344 3.7	1939 2.0
20 TU	0228 3.5	0805 2.2	1504 3.5	2102 2.1
21 W	0337 3.6	0941 2.1	1613 3.5	2215 2.0
22 TH	0432 3.8	1050 2.0	1706 3.6	2309 1.8
23 F	0516 4.0	1141 1.7	1748 3.7	2352 1.6
24 SA	0555 4.2	1222 1.5	1823 3.9	
25 SU	0031 1.3	0628 4.4	1258 1.2	1853 4.0
26 M	0106 1.1	0659 4.5	1330 1.0	1921 4.2
27 TU	0138 1.0	0729 4.6	1400 0.8	1949 4.2
28 W	0209 0.9	0757 4.7	1431 0.7	2017 4.3
29 TH	0239 0.8	0826 4.6	1503 0.7	2045 4.2
30 F	0310 0.9	0856 4.5	1536 0.8	2115 4.1
31 SA	0343 1.0	0930 4.4	1612 0.9	2150 4.0

FEBRUARY

Day	Time m	Time m	Time m	Time m
1 SU	0420 1.2	1011 4.2	1652 1.1	2235 3.8
2 M	0503 1.4	1106 4.0	1738 1.4	2340 3.6
3 TU	0556 1.7	1221 3.8	1836 1.6	
4 W	0108 3.6	0707 1.8	1347 3.7	1950 1.8
5 TH	0235 3.6	0846 1.9	1512 3.8	2123 1.7
6 F	0352 3.9	1021 1.6	1627 4.0	2243 1.5
7 SA	0455 4.2	1126 1.2	1731 3.7	2334 1.6
8 SU	0546 4.6	1221 0.8	1815 4.5	
9 M	0028 0.9	0630 4.9	1305 0.4	1857 4.7
10 TU	0112 0.6	0711 5.2	1347 0.2	1936 4.8
11 W	0152 0.5	0749 5.2	1426 0.2	2012 4.8
12 TH	0229 0.5	0825 5.2	1503 0.3	2048 4.6
13 F	0306 0.6	0901 4.9	1540 0.5	2124 4.4
14 SA	0343 0.9	0938 4.6	1617 0.9	2202 4.1
15 SU	0422 1.2	1019 4.2	1657 1.3	2247 3.8
16 M	0503 1.6	1111 3.8	1740 1.7	2352 3.5
17 TU	0552 1.9	1245 3.4	1835 2.1	
18 W	0138 3.4	0702 2.2	1435 3.3	2009 2.3
19 TH	0302 3.4	0914 2.3	1553 3.3	2151 2.2
20 F	0406 3.6	1039 2.0	1650 3.5	2251 1.9
21 SA	0455 3.9	1126 1.7	1731 3.7	2334 1.6
22 SU	0534 4.1	1203 1.4	1803 3.9	
23 M	0011 1.3	0606 4.3	1236 1.1	1830 4.1
24 TU	0045 1.1	0636 4.6	1305 0.9	1856 4.3
25 W	0115 0.8	0703 4.7	1334 0.6	1922 4.5
26 TH	0144 0.7	0730 4.8	1403 0.5	1948 4.5
27 F	0214 0.6	0758 4.8	1434 0.5	2015 4.5
28 SA	0245 0.6	0828 4.7	1507 0.5	2045 4.4

MARCH

Day	Time m	Time m	Time m	Time m
1 SU	0318 0.7	0902 4.6	1542 0.7	2118 4.2
2 M	0354 0.9	0943 4.3	1620 1.0	2200 4.0
3 TU	0436 1.2	1040 4.0	1705 1.3	2302 3.7
4 W	0529 1.6	1206 3.7	1801 1.7	
5 TH	0049 3.5	0647 1.8	1344 3.5	1926 1.9
6 F	0225 3.6	0852 1.8	1513 3.6	2122 1.9
7 SA	0345 3.9	1021 1.5	1624 3.9	2237 1.6
8 SU	0446 4.2	1119 1.0	1717 4.2	2329 1.2
9 M	0534 4.6	1205 0.7	1800 4.5	
10 TU	0013 0.9	0614 4.9	1247 0.4	1837 4.7
11 W	0053 0.6	0650 5.1	1324 0.2	1911 4.8
12 TH	0130 0.5	0724 5.1	1359 0.2	1944 4.8
13 F	0206 0.5	0757 5.0	1434 0.4	2015 4.7
14 SA	0241 0.6	0807 4.6	1507 0.6	2048 4.5
15 SU	0316 0.8	0903 4.6	1542 1.0	2122 4.2
16 M	0352 1.2	0939 4.1	1617 1.4	2202 3.9
17 TU	0431 1.5	1025 3.7	1656 1.8	2257 3.7
18 W	0517 1.9	1140 3.4	1745 2.2	
19 TH	0033 3.5	0618 2.2	1356 3.2	1904 2.4
20 F	0216 3.4	0827 2.3	1521 3.3	2116 2.3
21 SA	0328 3.6	1007 2.1	1621 3.4	2221 2.1
22 SU	0421 3.8	1055 1.8	1702 3.7	2305 1.8
23 M	0502 4.1	1131 1.4	1733 4.0	2341 1.4
24 TU	0535 4.3	1202 1.1	1800 4.2	
25 W	0013 1.1	0604 4.6	1232 0.8	1825 4.5
26 TH	0045 0.9	0633 4.8	1302 0.6	1852 4.6
27 F	0115 0.7	0702 4.9	1333 0.4	1920 4.7
28 SA	0148 0.6	0733 4.9	1406 0.4	1950 4.7
29 SU	0221 0.6	0807 4.7	1440 0.5	2023 4.6
30 M	0257 0.7	0846 4.6	1517 0.7	2100 4.4
31 TU	0337 0.9	0933 4.3	1557 1.1	2147 4.1

APRIL

Day	Time m	Time m	Time m	Time m
1 W	0423 1.2	1039 3.9	1643 1.5	2303 3.8
2 TH	0523 1.5	1212 3.6	1744 1.8	
3 F	0046 3.7	0659 1.8	1344 3.5	1923 2.0
4 SA	0214 3.7	0850 1.6	1506 3.6	2111 1.9
5 SU	0330 4.0	1006 1.3	1612 3.9	2218 1.6
6 M	0429 4.3	1059 1.0	1700 4.2	2308 1.3
7 TU	0515 4.5	1143 0.7	1740 4.4	2350 1.0
8 W	0553 4.7	1221 0.5	1814 4.6	
9 TH	0029 0.8	0628 4.8	1258 0.5	1845 4.7
10 F	0106 0.7	0700 4.8	1332 0.5	1916 4.7
11 SA	0142 0.7	0732 4.7	1405 0.7	1947 4.6
12 SU	0217 0.8	0803 4.5	1438 0.9	2020 4.5
13 M	0252 1.0	0837 4.3	1511 1.1	2055 4.3
14 TU	0329 1.3	0916 4.0	1546 1.5	2137 4.1
15 W	0408 1.6	1003 3.6	1624 1.8	2232 3.8
16 TH	0454 1.8	1113 3.4	1711 2.1	2347 3.6
17 F	0552 2.1	1254 3.2	1819 2.3	
18 SA	0112 3.6	0715 2.0	1428 3.3	2009 2.4
19 SU	0230 3.6	0903 2.1	1535 3.4	2131 2.2
20 M	0330 3.8	1002 1.8	1620 3.7	2220 1.9
21 TU	0416 4.0	1043 1.5	1653 4.0	2259 1.6
22 W	0454 4.3	1118 1.2	1723 4.2	2334 1.3
23 TH	0528 4.5	1152 0.9	1753 4.5	
24 F	0009 1.0	0602 4.7	1228 0.7	1823 4.7
25 SA	0046 0.8	0636 4.9	1304 0.6	1856 4.8
26 SU	0123 0.7	0714 4.9	1341 0.5	1931 4.8
27 M	0203 0.6	0755 4.8	1419 0.6	2011 4.7
28 TU	0245 0.7	0841 4.6	1459 0.9	2056 4.5
29 W	0331 0.9	0937 4.3	1543 1.2	2154 4.3
30 TH	0425 1.2	1049 3.9	1634 1.5	2312 4.1

Chart Datum: 2·71 metres below Ordnance Datum (Local)
HAT is 5·5 metres above Chart Datum

TIDES

TIDES

TIME ZONE (UT)
For Summer Time add ONE hour in **non-shaded areas**

SCOTLAND – STORNOWAY

LAT 58°12′N   LONG 6°23′W

TIMES AND HEIGHTS OF HIGH AND LOW WATERS

Dates in amber are **SPRINGS**
Dates in yellow are **NEAPS**

2009

MAY

Day	Time	m	Time	m	Time	m	Time	m
1 F	0534	1.4	1209	3.7	1741	1.8		
2 SA	0035	3.9	0658	1.5	1328	3.6	1911	2.0
3 SU	0152	3.9	0823	1.5	1444	3.7	2039	1.9
4 M	0304	4.1	0934	1.3	1548	3.8	◑ 2147	1.7
5 TU	0403	4.2	1029	1.1	1637	4.0	2239	1.4
6 W	0451	4.3	1114	1.0	1716	4.2	2324	1.2
7 TH	0531	4.4	1154	0.9	1750	4.4		
8 F	0005	1.1	0606	4.5	1231	0.9	1822	4.5
9 SA	0044	1.0	0640	4.4	1306	0.9	1854	4.5
10 SU	0122	1.0	0713	4.4	1341	1.0	1927	4.5
11 M	0159	1.0	0748	4.2	1414	1.1	○ 2002	4.5
12 TU	0235	1.1	0824	4.1	1449	1.3	2039	4.3
13 W	0313	1.3	0905	3.9	1524	1.5	2122	4.2
14 TH	0353	1.5	0952	3.7	1603	1.7	2213	4.0
15 F	0437	1.7	1049	3.5	1648	1.9	2312	3.8
16 SA	0528	1.8	1156	3.4	1744	2.1		
17 SU	0016	3.7	0628	1.9	1308	3.3	1854	2.2
18 M	0119	3.7	0735	1.9	1419	3.4	◐ 2010	2.2
19 TU	0221	3.8	0843	1.8	1517	3.6	2114	2.0
20 W	0317	3.9	0940	1.6	1602	3.9	2205	1.8
21 TH	0405	4.1	1028	1.3	1641	4.1	2250	1.5
22 F	0450	4.4	1113	1.1	1719	4.4	2335	1.2
23 SA	0533	4.6	1156	0.9	1758	4.6		
24 SU	0020	1.0	0617	4.7	1239	0.8	1837	4.8
25 M	0106	0.8	0703	4.7	1323	0.7	1920	4.9
26 TU	0153	0.7	0751	4.7	1406	0.8	● 2006	4.8
27 W	0242	0.7	0843	4.6	1451	0.9	2057	4.7
28 TH	0333	0.8	0939	4.3	1538	1.1	2154	4.6
29 F	0428	0.9	1041	4.1	1630	1.4	2300	4.4
30 SA	0528	1.1	1147	3.9	1730	1.6		
31 SU	0010	4.2	0633	1.3	1257	3.7	1840	1.8

JUNE

Day	Time	m	Time	m	Time	m	Time	m
1 M	0120	4.1	0742	1.4	1407	3.7	1955	1.8
2 TU	0229	4.0	0850	1.4	1514	3.7	◐ 2106	1.8
3 W	0333	4.0	0952	1.3	1608	3.8	2207	1.6
4 TH	0427	4.0	1044	1.3	1652	4.0	2259	1.5
5 F	0512	4.0	1128	1.3	1730	4.1	2346	1.4
6 SA	0552	4.1	1209	1.2	1805	4.3		
7 SU	0029	1.3	0629	4.1	1248	1.2	1840	4.4
8 M	0109	1.2	0705	4.0	1324	1.1	1914	4.4
9 TU	0147	1.2	0740	4.0	1359	1.2	○ 1950	4.4
10 W	0224	1.2	0816	4.0	1434	1.2	2026	4.4
11 TH	0300	1.2	0852	3.9	1509	1.3	2105	4.3
12 F	0337	1.3	0934	3.8	1545	1.5	2147	4.1
13 SA	0417	1.4	1019	3.6	1625	1.7	2234	4.0
14 SU	0500	1.5	1109	3.5	1710	1.8	2326	3.8
15 M	0547	1.6	1206	3.5	1803	2.0		
16 TU	0021	3.8	0639	1.6	1306	3.5	◐ 1902	2.0
17 W	0119	3.8	0737	1.6	1407	3.6	2005	2.0
18 TH	0218	3.9	0838	1.6	1506	3.8	2109	1.8
19 F	0319	4.0	0940	1.5	1600	4.0	2211	1.6
20 SA	0417	4.1	1038	1.3	1651	4.2	2309	1.4
21 SU	0513	4.3	1132	1.1	1739	4.5		
22 M	0004	1.1	0606	4.5	1224	1.0	1825	4.7
23 TU	0058	0.8	0658	4.6	1312	0.8	1912	4.9
24 W	0149	0.6	0748	4.7	1358	0.6	2000	5.0
25 TH	0238	0.5	0837	4.6	1444	0.8	● 2048	5.0
26 F	0326	0.5	0926	4.5	1529	0.9	2138	4.8
27 SA	0415	0.6	1017	4.3	1616	1.1	2233	4.6
28 SU	0505	0.8	1113	4.0	1706	1.4	2334	4.3
29 M	0558	1.1	1215	3.8	1802	1.6		
30 TU	0041	4.1	0655	1.4	1324	3.6	1906	1.8

JULY

Day	Time	m	Time	m	Time	m	Time	m
1 W	0152	3.9	0801	1.6	1435	3.6	2022	1.9
2 TH	0303	3.8	0912	1.7	1539	3.7	2139	1.9
3 F	0407	3.7	1016	1.7	1631	3.8	2243	1.7
4 SA	0500	3.7	1109	1.6	1715	4.0	2336	1.6
5 SU	0545	3.8	1154	1.5	1753	4.1		
6 M	0020	1.4	0623	3.8	1235	1.3	1828	4.3
7 TU	0101	1.3	0658	3.9	1312	1.2	1902	4.4
8 W	0137	1.1	0730	4.0	1346	1.1	1935	4.5
9 TH	0210	1.0	0801	4.0	1419	1.1	2007	4.5
10 F	0242	1.0	0833	4.0	1451	1.1	2040	4.4
11 SA	0315	1.0	0906	4.0	1523	1.2	○ 2114	4.3
12 SU	0349	1.0	0941	3.9	1557	1.3	2150	4.1
13 M	0426	1.1	1020	3.7	1634	1.5	2232	4.0
14 TU	0507	1.3	1108	3.6	1717	1.7	2324	3.9
15 W	0553	1.4	1206	3.6	1809	1.8		
16 TH	0027	3.8	0645	1.6	1313	3.6	1911	1.9
17 F	0136	3.8	0748	1.6	1422	3.7	2026	1.9
18 SA	0248	3.8	0901	1.6	1530	3.9	◐ 2147	1.7
19 SU	0400	4.0	1016	1.5	1632	4.1	2259	1.4
20 M	0505	4.2	1120	1.3	1727	4.5	2358	1.0
21 TU	0600	4.4	1214	1.0	1816	4.8		
22 W	0051	0.7	0649	4.7	1303	0.8	1902	5.1
23 TH	0139	0.4	0735	4.8	1347	0.6	1945	5.2
24 F	0224	0.2	0819	4.8	1430	0.6	2028	5.2
25 SA	0307	0.2	0901	4.7	1511	0.7	2111	5.0
26 SU	0349	0.4	0945	4.5	1552	0.9	● 2157	4.8
27 M	0432	0.7	1033	4.2	1635	1.2	2250	4.4
28 TU	0517	1.1	1129	3.9	1723	1.5	2357	4.0
29 W	0608	1.5	1239	3.6	1819	1.9		
30 TH	0118	3.7	0708	1.8	1357	3.5	1936	2.1
31 F	0239	3.5	0831	2.0	1511	3.6	2120	2.1

AUGUST

Day	Time	m	Time	m	Time	m	Time	m
1 SA	0353	3.5	0954	2.0	1612	3.7	2237	1.9
2 SU	0452	3.6	1053	1.8	1659	3.9	◐ 2329	1.7
3 M	0536	3.7	1139	1.6	1738	4.1		
4 TU	0010	1.5	0611	3.8	1219	1.4	1812	4.3
5 W	0046	1.2	0642	4.0	1255	1.2	1844	4.5
6 TH	0117	1.0	0710	4.1	1327	1.0	1913	4.6
7 F	0147	0.9	0737	4.2	1357	0.9	1941	4.6
8 SA	0215	0.8	0804	4.2	1426	0.9	2009	4.6
9 SU	0245	0.7	0832	4.2	1456	1.0	○ 2038	4.5
10 M	0317	0.8	0902	4.1	1526	1.1	2108	4.4
11 TU	0351	0.9	0933	4.0	1600	1.3	2144	4.2
12 W	0428	1.1	1013	3.8	1639	1.5	2233	4.0
13 TH	0511	1.4	1110	3.7	1727	1.7	2347	3.8
14 F	0603	1.6	1233	3.6	1831	1.9		
15 SA	0113	3.7	0709	1.8	1357	3.6	2003	1.9
16 SU	0239	3.7	0839	1.9	1516	3.8	2146	1.7
17 M	0357	3.9	1009	1.7	1623	4.2	◐ 2257	1.3
18 TU	0459	4.2	1112	1.4	1717	4.6	2351	0.9
19 W	0550	4.5	1203	1.0	1804	5.0		
20 TH	0038	0.5	0634	4.8	1248	0.8	1845	5.2
21 F	0121	0.3	0715	4.9	1329	0.6	1925	5.4
22 SA	0201	0.2	0754	4.9	1408	0.5	2003	5.3
23 SU	0240	0.2	0831	4.8	1446	0.6	2041	5.1
24 M	0318	0.5	0910	4.6	1525	0.8	○ 2120	4.8
25 TU	0357	0.8	0951	4.3	1604	1.2	● 2204	4.3
26 W	0437	1.3	1041	4.0	1647	1.6	2304	3.9
27 TH	0522	1.7	1152	3.7	1737	2.0		
28 F	0046	3.6	0616	2.1	1321	3.6	1850	2.3
29 SA	0216	3.4	0747	2.3	1440	3.6	2106	2.3
30 SU	0335	3.4	0932	2.3	1546	3.8	2227	2.1
31 M	0436	3.6	1033	2.0	1637	4.0	2312	1.8

Chart Datum: 2·71 metres below Ordnance Datum (Local)
HAT is 5·5 metres above Chart Datum

SCOTLAND – STORNOWAY
LAT 58°12′N   LONG 6°23′W
TIMES AND HEIGHTS OF HIGH AND LOW WATERS

2009

SEPTEMBER
Time m   Time m

1 0518 3.7 / 1118 1.8 / TU 1716 4.2 / 2348 1.5   **16** 0449 4.3 / 1059 1.4 / W 1704 4.7 / 2335 0.8

2 0549 3.9 / 1156 1.5 / W 1749 4.4   **17** 0534 4.6 / 1145 1.1 / TH 1747 5.0

3 0019 1.3 / 0617 4.2 / TH 1230 1.2 / 1819 4.6   **18** 0017 0.5 / 0614 4.8 / F 1227 0.8 / ● 1826 5.3

4 0049 1.0 / 0643 4.3 / F 1300 1.0 / ○ 1846 4.7   **19** 0057 0.4 / 0651 5.0 / SA 1306 0.7 / 1902 5.3

5 0116 0.8 / 0708 4.5 / SA 1329 0.9 / 1912 4.8   **20** 0134 0.3 / 0726 5.0 / SU 1344 0.6 / 1937 5.2

6 0144 0.7 / 0733 4.5 / SU 1357 0.8 / 1939 4.8   **21** 0211 0.4 / 0801 4.9 / M 1421 0.7 / 2012 5.0

7 0213 0.6 / 0800 4.5 / M 1427 0.9 / 2007 4.7   **22** 0246 0.7 / 0836 4.7 / TU 1458 1.0 / 2048 4.7

8 0245 0.7 / 0828 4.5 / TU 1458 1.0 / 2038 4.6   **23** 0322 1.1 / 0914 4.4 / W 1536 1.3 / 2128 4.3

9 0318 0.9 / 0859 4.3 / W 1532 1.2 / 2115 4.3   **24** 0400 1.5 / 0959 4.1 / TH 1617 1.7 / 2220 3.9

10 0355 1.1 / 0937 4.1 / TH 1612 1.4 / 2207 4.0   **25** 0441 1.9 / 1105 3.9 / F 1705 2.1

11 0438 1.4 / 1036 3.8 / F 1701 1.7 / 2334 3.7   **26** 0005 3.5 / 0531 2.3 / SA 1237 3.7 / ◐ 1811 2.4

12 0531 1.8 / 1217 3.7 / SA 1812 1.9 / ◐   **27** 0142 3.4 / 0654 2.5 / SU 1358 3.7 / 2026 2.4

13 0112 3.6 / 0646 2.0 / SU 1347 3.7 / 2009 2.0   **28** 0302 3.4 / 0827 2.5 / M 1507 3.8 / 2154 2.2

14 0239 3.7 / 0807 2.0 / M 1508 4.0 / 2147 1.6   **29** 0404 3.6 / 1002 2.2 / TU 1602 4.0 / 2239 1.9

15 0352 4.0 / 1003 1.8 / TU 1613 4.3 / 2248 1.2   **30** 0446 3.8 / 1047 1.9 / W 1644 4.2 / 2313 1.6

OCTOBER
Time m   Time m

1 0518 4.1 / 1124 1.6 / TH 1718 4.5 / 2344 1.3   **16** 0514 4.6 / 1122 1.2 / F 1727 4.9 / 2353 0.7

2 0546 4.3 / 1157 1.4 / F 1748 4.7   **17** 0552 4.8 / 1203 1.0 / SA 1805 5.1

3 0012 1.1 / 0611 4.5 / SA 1228 1.2 / 1816 4.8   **18** 0031 0.7 / 0626 4.9 / SU 1243 0.9 / ● 1840 5.1

4 0041 0.9 / 0636 4.7 / SU 1258 1.0 / 1844 4.9   **19** 0107 0.7 / 0700 4.9 / M 1321 0.9 / 1914 5.0

5 0111 0.7 / 0703 4.8 / M 1329 0.9 / 1913 5.0   **20** 0143 0.8 / 0734 4.9 / TU 1358 1.0 / 1949 4.8

6 0143 0.7 / 0732 4.8 / TU 1401 0.9 / 1945 4.9   **21** 0218 1.0 / 0809 4.7 / W 1436 1.2 / 2025 4.5

7 0217 0.8 / 0803 4.7 / W 1436 1.0 / 2021 4.7   **22** 0253 1.3 / 0847 4.5 / TH 1514 1.4 / 2105 4.2

8 0253 0.9 / 0839 4.5 / TH 1514 1.1 / 2105 4.4   **23** 0330 1.6 / 0931 4.3 / F 1555 1.7 / 2155 3.9

9 0332 1.2 / 0924 4.3 / F 1558 1.4 / 2207 4.1   **24** 0410 1.9 / 1030 4.1 / SA 1642 2.0 / 2312 3.6

10 0416 1.6 / 1035 4.0 / SA 1654 1.7 / 2340 3.8   **25** 0458 2.3 / 1145 3.9 / SU 1740 2.3

11 0513 1.9 / 1213 3.9 / SU 1819 1.9 / ◐   **26** 0046 3.5 / 0605 2.5 / M 1301 3.8 / ○ 1905 2.4

12 0109 3.7 / 0639 2.2 / M 1336 3.9 / 2008 1.8   **27** 0208 3.5 / 0750 2.5 / TU 1411 3.8 / 2047 2.3

13 0229 3.8 / 0827 2.1 / TU 1452 4.1 / 2131 1.5   **28** 0315 3.6 / 0912 2.4 / W 1512 4.0 / 2146 2.0

14 0337 4.1 / 0944 1.8 / W 1555 4.4 / 2227 1.2   **29** 0404 3.8 / 1003 2.1 / TH 1600 4.2 / 2226 1.8

15 0431 4.3 / 1037 1.5 / TH 1645 4.7 / 2312 0.9   **30** 0439 4.1 / 1043 1.8 / F 1639 4.4 / 2300 1.5

31 0509 4.3 / 1118 1.6 / SA 1713 4.6 / 2333 1.3

NOVEMBER
Time m   Time m

1 0537 4.6 / 1152 1.4 / SU 1745 4.8   **16** 0007 1.0 / 0605 4.7 / M 1224 1.2 / ● 1823 4.6

2 0006 1.0 / 0606 4.8 / M 1228 1.2 / ○ 1818 4.9   **17** 0044 1.0 / 0640 4.7 / TU 1304 1.1 / 1859 4.6

3 0041 0.9 / 0638 4.9 / TU 1304 1.0 / 1854 4.9   **18** 0121 1.1 / 0715 4.8 / W 1343 1.2 / 1935 4.5

4 0118 0.8 / 0712 4.9 / W 1343 0.9 / 1932 4.9   **19** 0157 1.2 / 0751 4.7 / TH 1421 1.3 / 2012 4.3

5 0156 0.9 / 0750 4.9 / TH 1424 1.0 / 2016 4.7   **20** 0233 1.4 / 0830 4.6 / F 1500 1.4 / 2052 4.1

6 0235 1.0 / 0831 4.8 / F 1508 1.1 / 2108 4.4   **21** 0310 1.6 / 0912 4.4 / SA 1540 1.6 / 2137 3.9

7 0318 1.3 / 0927 4.5 / SA 1558 1.3 / 2215 4.2   **22** 0349 1.8 / 1001 4.2 / SU 1622 1.8 / 2231 3.7

8 0406 1.6 / 1038 4.3 / SU 1700 1.5 / 2333 3.9   **23** 0433 2.0 / 1057 4.1 / M 1711 1.9 / 2336 3.6

9 0507 1.9 / 1158 4.2 / M 1817 1.7   **24** 0526 2.2 / 1158 3.9 / TU 1808 2.1 / ◑

10 0050 3.8 / 0627 2.1 / TU 1314 4.1 / 1940 1.6   **25** 0047 3.5 / 0632 2.4 / W 1300 3.9 / 1912 2.1

11 0204 3.9 / 0755 2.0 / W 1425 4.2 / 2056 1.5   **26** 0159 3.6 / 0746 2.4 / TH 1401 3.9 / 2020 2.0

12 0311 4.0 / 0910 1.9 / TH 1529 4.4 / 2156 1.3   **27** 0301 3.7 / 0855 2.2 / F 1458 4.0 / 2120 1.9

13 0406 4.2 / 1009 1.6 / F 1622 4.5 / 2245 1.2   **28** 0348 3.9 / 0949 2.0 / SA 1549 4.2 / 2209 1.6

14 0451 4.4 / 1058 1.4 / SA 1707 4.6 / 2327 1.1   **29** 0427 4.2 / 1035 1.8 / SU 1634 4.3 / 2253 1.4

15 0530 4.6 / 1142 1.3 / SU 1747 4.6   **30** 0503 4.4 / 1119 1.6 / M 1717 4.5 / 2335 1.3

DECEMBER
Time m   Time m

1 0541 4.6 / 1203 1.3 / TU 1759 4.7   **16** 0029 1.3 / 0628 4.5 / W 1256 1.3 / ● 1852 4.2

2 0017 1.1 / 0619 4.8 / W 1248 1.1 / ○ 1843 4.8   **17** 0107 1.2 / 0704 4.6 / TH 1335 1.2 / 1928 4.2

3 0100 0.9 / 0700 4.9 / TH 1333 0.9 / 1928 4.8   **18** 0144 1.2 / 0739 4.7 / F 1412 1.2 / 2002 4.2

4 0143 0.9 / 0744 5.0 / F 1420 0.8 / 2017 4.7   **19** 0219 1.2 / 0815 4.6 / SA 1447 1.2 / 2037 4.1

5 0227 1.0 / 0831 4.9 / SA 1507 0.8 / 2108 4.6   **20** 0254 1.3 / 0851 4.5 / SU 1523 1.3 / 2113 4.0

6 0312 1.1 / 0924 4.8 / SU 1558 0.9 / 2205 4.3   **21** 0330 1.4 / 0930 4.4 / M 1600 1.4 / 2153 3.9

7 0400 1.3 / 1023 4.6 / M 1653 1.1 / 2309 4.1   **22** 0408 1.6 / 1013 4.2 / TU 1640 1.5 / 2239 3.7

8 0455 1.6 / 1130 4.4 / TU 1754 1.3   **23** 0450 1.8 / 1101 4.0 / W 1724 1.7 / 2334 3.6

9 0016 3.9 / 0558 1.8 / W 1240 4.3 / ◑ 1859 1.5   **24** 0538 2.0 / 1155 3.9 / TH 1813 1.8

10 0127 3.8 / 0711 1.9 / TH 1349 4.2 / 2009 1.5   **25** 0035 3.5 / 0634 2.1 / F 1253 3.8 / 1909 1.9

11 0236 3.8 / 0827 1.9 / F 1458 4.1 / 2118 1.5   **26** 0140 3.6 / 0737 2.2 / SA 1353 3.8 / 2011 1.8

12 0338 4.0 / 0937 1.8 / SA 1559 4.1 / 2216 1.5   **27** 0243 3.7 / 0846 2.1 / SU 1457 3.9 / 2116 1.8

13 0429 4.1 / 1037 1.7 / SU 1652 4.2 / 2306 1.4   **28** 0341 3.8 / 0953 1.9 / M 1559 4.1 / 2217 1.6

14 0513 4.3 / 1128 1.5 / M 1736 4.3 / 2349 1.3   **29** 0433 4.2 / 1053 1.6 / TU 1656 4.3 / 2312 1.4

15 0552 4.4 / 1213 1.4 / TU 1816 4.2   **30** 0521 4.5 / 1147 1.3 / W 1748 4.5

31 0002 1.2 / 0607 4.6 / TH 1239 1.0 / ○ 1837 4.7

Chart Datum: 2·71 metres below Ordnance Datum (Local)
HAT is 5·5 metres above Chart Datum

TIDES

301

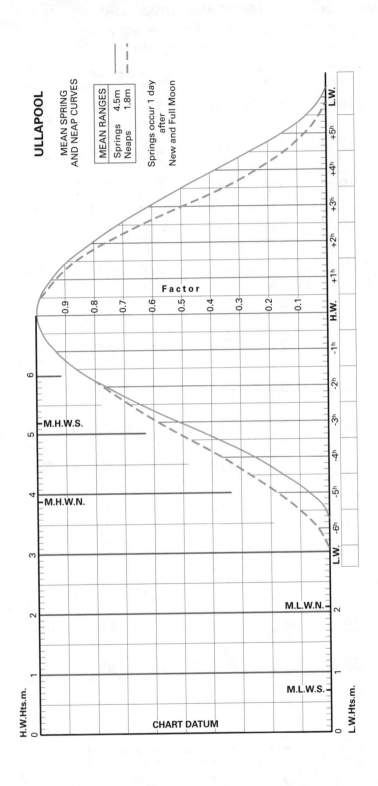

ULLAPOOL

MEAN SPRING
AND NEAP CURVES

MEAN RANGES	
Springs	4.5m
Neaps	1.8m

Springs occur 1 day
after
New and Full Moon

TIME ZONE (UT)	SCOTLAND – ULLAPOOL	Dates in amber are SPRINGS
For Summer Time add ONE hour in non-shaded areas	LAT 57°54'N LONG 5°10'W	Dates in yellow are NEAPS
	TIMES AND HEIGHTS OF HIGH AND LOW WATERS	2009

JANUARY

Day	Time m				Day	Time m			
1 TH	0339 1.6	0932 4.9	1607 1.5	2158 4.5	16 F	0424 1.2	1028 5.0	1702 1.2	2305 4.5
2 F	0416 1.7	1012 4.7	1646 1.6	2241 4.3	17 SA	0508 1.6	1120 4.6	1747 1.6	
3 SA	0457 1.9	1059 4.6	1730 1.7	2335 4.2	18 SU	0002 4.2	0556 1.9	1225 4.3	1838 2.0 ☽
4 SU	0546 2.0	1156 4.4	1822 1.8 ☽		19 M	0112 4.0	0655 2.3	1345 4.0	1944 2.3
5 M	0043 4.1	0646 2.2	1307 4.3	1924 1.9	20 TU	0230 3.9	0815 2.5	1510 3.9	2109 2.4
6 TU	0158 4.1	0802 2.3	1420 4.3	2038 2.0	21 W	0344 4.0	0949 2.5	1621 4.0	2226 2.3
7 W	0308 4.3	0921 2.1	1531 4.4	2152 1.8	22 TH	0442 4.2	1059 2.3	1715 4.1	2321 2.1
8 TH	0413 4.5	1033 1.9	1639 4.6	2258 1.6	23 F	0527 4.4	1148 2.0	1757 4.3	
9 F	0510 4.8	1134 1.5	1738 4.9	2354 1.4	24 SA	0004 1.9	0604 4.7	1229 1.7	1831 4.5
10 SA	0600 5.1	1229 1.1	1831 5.1		25 SU	0041 1.6	0636 4.8	1304 1.5	1901 4.6
11 SU	0045 1.1	0646 5.4	1320 0.8	1918 5.3 ○	26 M	0115 1.5	0706 5.0	1336 1.3	1929 4.7 ●
12 M	0132 0.9	0731 5.6	1407 0.6	2003 5.4	27 TU	0146 1.3	0734 5.1	1407 1.1	1956 4.8
13 TU	0217 0.8	0814 5.6	1453 0.6	2048 5.3	28 W	0217 1.2	0803 5.2	1438 1.0	2023 4.8
14 W	0300 0.8	0855 5.5	1536 0.6	2131 5.1	29 TH	0247 1.2	0833 5.2	1509 1.0	2053 4.8
15 TH	0342 1.0	0942 5.3	1619 0.9	2216 4.8	30 F	0318 1.2	0905 5.1	1541 1.0	2126 4.7
					31 SA	0351 1.3	0941 5.0	1615 1.2	2203 4.6

FEBRUARY

Day	Time m				Day	Time m			
1 SU	0427 1.5	1021 4.8	1654 1.4	2247 4.4	16 M	0513 1.8	1117 4.1	1744 2.0 ☽	
2 M	0510 1.7	1112 4.5	1739 1.6	2347 4.2 ☽	17 TU	0004 4.0	0601 2.2	1243 3.8	1837 2.3
3 TU	0603 2.0	1223 4.3	1837 1.9		18 W	0133 3.8	0713 2.5	1428 3.6	2013 2.6
4 W	0112 4.0	0717 2.2	1353 4.1	1958 2.1	19 TH	0304 3.8	0916 2.6	1559 3.7	2204 2.5
5 TH	0241 4.1	0857 2.2	1521 4.2	2135 2.1	20 F	0415 4.0	1044 2.3	1658 3.9	2304 2.2
6 F	0402 4.3	1028 1.9	1638 4.4	2253 1.8	21 SA	0504 4.2	1132 2.0	1739 4.2	2345 1.9
7 SA	0505 4.7	1133 1.5	1737 4.8	2349 1.4	22 SU	0542 4.5	1208 1.6	1811 4.4	
8 SU	0554 5.0	1225 1.0	1824 5.1		23 M	0020 1.6	0613 4.8	1241 1.3	1837 4.6
9 M	0037 1.1	0636 5.4	1311 0.6	1905 5.3 ○	24 TU	0053 1.3	0641 5.0	1312 1.1	1903 4.8
10 TU	0120 0.8	0716 5.6	1353 0.4	1944 5.4	25 W	0123 1.1	0708 5.2	1342 0.9	1928 4.9 ●
11 W	0200 0.6	0754 5.7	1433 0.3	2021 5.4	26 TH	0153 0.9	0736 5.3	1411 0.7	1955 5.0
12 TH	0239 0.6	0832 5.6	1510 0.4	2058 5.1	27 F	0223 0.8	0806 5.3	1441 0.7	2024 5.0
13 F	0317 0.7	0909 5.3	1547 0.7	2135 4.9	28 SA	0253 0.9	0838 5.2	1513 0.7	2056 4.9
14 SA	0354 1.0	0947 5.0	1624 1.1	2214 4.6					
15 SU	0432 1.4	1027 4.5	1702 1.5	2259 4.2					

MARCH

Day	Time m				Day	Time m			
1 SU	0327 1.0	0914 5.1	1547 0.9	2132 4.8	16 M	0401 1.3	0949 4.4	1623 1.5	2212 4.3
2 M	0403 1.2	0955 4.8	1625 1.2	2215 4.5	17 TU	0439 1.7	1032 4.0	1700 1.9	2304 4.0
3 TU	0445 1.5	1049 4.5	1709 1.6	2313 4.2	18 W	0523 2.1	1148 3.7	1747 2.3 ☽	
4 W	0538 1.9	1208 4.1	1806 2.0		19 TH	0033 3.7	0624 2.4	1339 3.5	1908 2.6
5 TH	0048 4.0	0657 2.1	1347 4.0	1936 2.3	20 F	0210 3.7	0825 2.5	1520 3.5	2127 2.5
6 F	0229 4.0	0855 2.1	1520 4.0	2132 2.2	21 SA	0333 3.8	1009 2.3	1626 3.8	2233 2.2
7 SA	0354 4.2	1026 1.7	1635 4.3	2246 1.8	22 SU	0428 4.1	1058 1.9	1708 4.0	2314 1.9
8 SU	0455 4.6	1125 1.3	1727 4.7	2338 1.4	23 M	0508 4.3	1134 1.6	1739 4.3	2349 1.6
9 M	0540 5.0	1211 0.8	1808 5.0		24 TU	0540 4.6	1207 1.2	1805 4.6	
10 TU	0021 1.0	0619 5.3	1253 0.5	1844 5.2	25 W	0021 1.3	0608 4.9	1238 0.9	1830 4.8
11 W	0101 0.7	0655 5.5	1331 0.3	1919 5.3 ○	26 TH	0053 1.0	0637 5.1	1309 0.7	1857 5.0
12 TH	0139 0.5	0730 5.5	1407 0.3	1952 5.3	27 F	0124 0.8	0707 5.3	1341 0.5	1926 5.1
13 F	0215 0.5	0804 5.4	1441 0.5	2025 5.1	28 SA	0156 0.7	0739 5.3	1413 0.5	1957 5.1
14 SA	0250 0.7	0838 5.1	1515 0.7	2058 4.9	29 SU	0230 0.7	0815 5.2	1447 0.6	2032 5.0
15 SU	0325 0.9	0913 4.8	1548 1.1	2133 4.6	30 M	0306 0.8	0856 5.0	1524 0.8	2111 4.8
					31 TU	0346 1.0	0945 4.7	1604 1.2	2159 4.5

APRIL

Day	Time m				Day	Time m			
1 W	0433 1.4	1050 4.3	1651 1.6	2307 4.2	16 TH	0458 1.9	1119 3.7	1715 2.2	2344 3.8
2 TH	0532 1.7	1217 4.0	1754 2.0 ☽		17 F	0554 2.2	1247 3.5	1821 2.4	
3 F	0044 4.0	0700 2.0	1346 3.9	1932 2.2	18 SA	0111 3.7	0721 2.3	1416 3.5	2017 2.5
4 SA	0217 4.0	0852 1.9	1512 4.0	2119 2.1	19 SU	0230 3.8	0902 2.2	1530 3.7	2139 2.3
5 SU	0337 4.2	1010 1.5	1619 4.3	2227 1.7	20 M	0334 3.9	1004 1.9	1620 3.9	2228 2.0
6 M	0435 4.5	1104 1.1	1707 4.6	2316 1.3	21 TU	0420 4.2	1047 1.6	1655 4.2	2308 1.6
7 TU	0519 4.8	1148 0.8	1746 4.8	2358 1.0	22 W	0457 4.5	1124 1.2	1726 4.5	2343 1.3
8 W	0557 5.1	1227 0.6	1820 5.0		23 TH	0531 4.7	1159 1.0	1756 4.8	
9 TH	0038 0.8	0632 5.2	1305 0.5	1853 5.1 ○	24 F	0019 1.0	0604 5.0	1235 0.7	1827 5.0
10 F	0115 0.7	0706 5.2	1339 0.6	1925 5.1	25 SA	0055 0.8	0640 5.1	1311 0.6	1900 5.1 ●
11 SA	0151 0.7	0740 5.1	1412 0.7	1957 5.0	26 SU	0132 0.7	0719 5.2	1348 0.5	1936 5.1
12 SU	0225 0.7	0814 4.8	1445 0.9	2030 4.8	27 M	0211 0.6	0802 5.1	1427 0.7	2017 5.0
13 M	0300 1.0	0848 4.5	1518 1.2	2104 4.6	28 TU	0253 0.7	0851 4.9	1508 0.9	2104 4.8
14 TU	0336 1.3	0927 4.2	1552 1.5	2143 4.3	29 W	0339 0.9	0950 4.6	1554 1.2	2200 4.6
15 W	0414 1.6	1013 3.9	1630 1.9	2232 4.1	30 TH	0432 1.2	1100 4.3	1646 1.6	2313 4.3

Chart Datum: 2·75 metres below Ordnance Datum (Newlyn)
HAT is 5·9 metres above Chart Datum

TIDES

TIME ZONE (UT)
For Summer Time add ONE hour in **non-shaded areas**

SCOTLAND – ULLAPOOL
LAT 57°54′N   LONG 5°10′W
TIMES AND HEIGHTS OF HIGH AND LOW WATERS

Dates in amber are **SPRINGS**
Dates in yellow are **NEAPS**

2009

MAY

Day	Time m	Time m	Time m	Time m		Day	Time m	Time m	Time m	Time m
1 F	0538 1.5	1216 4.1	1753 1.9			16 SA	0529 1.9	1157 3.7	1747 2.2	
2 SA	0035 4.2	0700 1.6	1333 4.0	1920 2.0		17 SU	0014 3.9	0630 2.0	1308 3.6	1901 2.3
3 SU	0156 4.2	0826 1.6	1448 4.0	2047 1.9		18 M	0125 3.9	0744 2.0	1417 3.7	2023 2.2
4 M	0309 4.3	0937 1.4	1551 4.2	2154 1.7		19 TU	0229 3.9	0853 1.9	1516 3.9	2128 2.0
5 TU	0408 4.4	1033 1.2	1640 4.4	2247 1.4		20 W	0324 4.1	0949 1.6	1604 4.1	2218 1.8
6 W	0455 4.6	1119 1.1	1721 4.6	2333 1.2		21 TH	0411 4.3	1037 1.4	1645 4.4	2303 1.5
7 TH	0536 4.7	1200 0.9	1757 4.8			22 F	0454 4.6	1121 1.1	1723 4.7	2346 1.2
8 F	0014 1.1	0612 4.8	1239 0.9	1831 4.9		23 SA	0537 4.8	1203 0.9	1801 4.9	
9 SA	0054 1.0	0648 4.8	1314 0.9	1904 4.9		24 SU	0029 0.9	0620 5.0	1246 0.7	1841 5.1
10 SU	0131 1.0	0723 4.7	1348 1.0	1937 4.9		25 M	0114 0.7	0707 5.0	1330 0.7	1924 5.1
11 M	0206 1.0	0759 4.6	1422 1.1	2011 4.8		26 TU	0200 0.6	0757 5.0	1414 0.8	2011 5.1
12 TU	0242 1.2	0836 4.4	1456 1.2	2046 4.6		27 W	0248 0.7	0852 4.9	1500 0.9	2103 5.0
13 W	0319 1.3	0915 4.2	1531 1.5	2125 4.4		28 TH	0338 0.8	0951 4.7	1549 1.1	2200 4.8
14 TH	0357 1.5	1000 4.0	1609 1.8	2211 4.2		29 F	0433 1.0	1053 4.4	1643 1.4	2305 4.6
15 F	0440 1.7	1053 3.8	1653 2.0	2307 4.0		30 SA	0533 1.2	1157 4.2	1743 1.6	
						31 SU	0014 4.4	0638 1.4	1304 4.1	1851 1.8

JUNE

Day	Time m	Time m	Time m	Time m		Day	Time m	Time m	Time m	Time m
1 M	0125 4.3	0746 1.5	1412 4.1	2004 1.9		16 TU	0022 4.1	0641 1.8	1311 3.8	1910 2.1
2 TU	0235 4.2	0854 1.5	1517 4.1	2114 1.8		17 W	0127 4.0	0744 1.8	1415 3.9	2020 2.1
3 W	0338 4.3	0956 1.5	1612 4.2	2216 1.7		18 TH	0230 4.1	0849 1.7	1514 4.0	2127 1.9
4 TH	0432 4.3	1049 1.4	1658 4.4	2309 1.6		19 F	0328 4.2	0951 1.6	1607 4.3	2227 1.7
5 F	0519 4.4	1135 1.4	1738 4.6	2356 1.4		20 SA	0425 4.4	1048 1.4	1657 4.5	2321 1.4
6 SA	0601 4.4	1217 1.3	1816 4.7			21 SU	0519 4.6	1140 1.2	1744 4.8	
7 SU	0038 1.3	0639 4.5	1256 1.3	1850 4.7		22 M	0013 1.1	0611 4.8	1231 1.0	1830 5.0
8 M	0117 1.2	0716 4.5	1332 1.3	1924 4.8		23 TU	0104 0.8	0703 5.0	1319 0.8	1917 5.2
9 TU	0154 1.2	0751 4.4	1407 1.3	2005 4.8		24 W	0154 0.6	0753 5.1	1406 0.7	2005 5.3
10 W	0230 1.2	0826 4.4	1441 1.4	2032 4.7		25 TH	0243 0.5	0844 5.0	1453 0.8	2054 5.2
11 TH	0305 1.3	0901 4.3	1516 1.5	2108 4.6		26 F	0332 0.5	0936 4.9	1540 0.9	2145 5.1
12 F	0342 1.3	0939 4.2	1552 1.6	2147 4.4		27 SA	0421 0.6	1029 4.7	1628 1.1	2240 4.9
13 SA	0420 1.4	1020 4.0	1631 1.7	2231 4.3		28 SU	0511 0.9	1125 4.4	1719 1.4	2341 4.6
14 SU	0501 1.6	1108 3.9	1714 1.9	2323 4.2		29 M	0604 1.2	1225 4.2	1815 1.6	
15 M	0548 1.7	1205 3.8	1807 2.0			30 TU	0047 4.3	0700 1.5	1331 4.0	1917 1.9

JULY

Day	Time m	Time m	Time m	Time m		Day	Time m	Time m	Time m	Time m
1 W	0158 4.1	0805 1.8	1439 4.0	2030 2.0		16 TH	0031 4.1	0647 1.8	1320 3.9	1923 2.1
2 TH	0310 4.0	0916 1.9	1543 4.1	2146 2.0		17 F	0145 4.1	0756 1.9	1432 4.0	2043 2.1
3 F	0415 4.0	1022 1.8	1638 4.2	2251 1.9		18 SA	0259 4.1	0914 1.8	1540 4.2	2202 1.9
4 SA	0509 4.1	1116 1.8	1724 4.4	2344 1.7		19 SU	0410 4.3	1027 1.7	1642 4.5	2308 1.5
5 SU	0554 4.2	1202 1.6	1803 4.5			20 M	0513 4.5	1128 1.4	1735 4.8	
6 M	0028 1.5	0632 4.3	1243 1.5	1838 4.7		21 TU	0005 1.1	0607 4.8	1221 1.1	1822 5.1
7 TU	0107 1.4	0707 4.4	1319 1.4	1911 4.8		22 W	0057 0.7	0655 5.1	1310 0.8	1907 5.4
8 W	0142 1.2	0738 4.5	1353 1.3	1942 4.8		23 TH	0145 0.4	0740 5.2	1355 0.7	1951 5.5
9 TH	0216 1.2	0808 4.5	1426 1.3	2013 4.8		24 F	0230 0.3	0825 5.2	1439 0.6	2034 5.5
10 F	0249 1.1	0838 4.5	1458 1.3	2045 4.8		25 SA	0314 0.3	0909 5.1	1521 0.7	2119 5.3
11 SA	0321 1.1	0909 4.4	1531 1.4	2119 4.7		26 SU	0357 0.5	0954 4.8	1604 0.9	2206 5.0
12 SU	0354 1.2	0943 4.3	1604 1.5	2155 4.6		27 M	0439 0.8	1043 4.6	1648 1.2	2259 4.6
13 M	0430 1.3	1022 4.2	1641 1.6	2237 4.4		28 TU	0524 1.2	1139 4.3	1736 1.6	
14 TU	0508 1.4	1108 4.1	1724 1.8	2327 4.3		29 W	0003 4.3	0613 1.6	1246 4.0	1831 2.0
15 W	0553 1.6	1208 4.0	1816 2.0			30 TH	0120 3.9	0713 2.0	1401 3.9	1945 2.2
						31 F	0244 3.8	0834 2.2	1517 3.9	2121 2.3

AUGUST

Day	Time m	Time m	Time m	Time m		Day	Time m	Time m	Time m	Time m
1 SA	0401 3.8	1001 2.2	1620 4.1	2241 2.1		16 SU	0248 4.0	0853 2.1	1527 4.1	2154 1.9
2 SU	0459 3.9	1103 2.0	1709 4.3	2334 1.9		17 M	0407 4.2	1020 1.9	1634 4.5	2304 1.5
3 M	0543 4.1	1149 1.8	1748 4.5			18 TU	0509 4.5	1121 1.5	1726 4.9	2357 1.0
4 TU	0015 1.6	0618 4.3	1228 1.6	1821 4.7		19 W	0558 4.9	1210 1.1	1810 5.3	
5 W	0051 1.4	0649 4.5	1302 1.4	1851 4.9		20 TH	0044 0.6	0640 5.2	1255 0.8	1850 5.5
6 TH	0124 1.2	0716 4.6	1334 1.2	1920 5.0		21 F	0128 0.3	0719 5.3	1337 0.6	1929 5.7
7 F	0155 1.0	0742 4.7	1405 1.1	1948 5.0		22 SA	0209 0.2	0758 5.4	1417 0.5	2008 5.6
8 SA	0224 0.9	0809 4.7	1434 1.1	2017 5.0		23 SU	0248 0.2	0836 5.4	1456 0.6	2048 5.4
9 SU	0254 0.9	0837 4.7	1504 1.1	2047 5.0		24 M	0326 0.5	0916 5.0	1536 0.8	2129 5.0
10 M	0324 1.0	0907 4.6	1535 1.2	2120 4.8		25 TU	0405 0.9	0958 4.7	1616 1.2	2214 4.6
11 TU	0357 1.1	0941 4.5	1610 1.4	2159 4.6		26 W	0444 1.3	1047 4.3	1659 1.6	2313 4.1
12 W	0432 1.3	1022 4.3	1649 1.6	2245 4.4		27 TH	0527 1.8	1154 4.0	1750 2.1	
13 TH	0514 1.5	1115 4.1	1737 1.9	2350 4.2		28 F	0040 3.8	0621 2.2	1320 3.9	1901 2.4
14 F	0605 1.8	1235 4.0	1843 2.1			29 SA	0217 3.6	0749 2.5	1446 3.9	2058 2.5
15 SA	0120 4.0	0716 2.1	1406 4.0	2017 2.2		30 SU	0342 3.7	0941 2.4	1555 4.0	2227 2.2
						31 M	0442 3.9	1045 2.2	1646 4.2	2315 1.9

Chart Datum: 2·75 metres below Ordnance Datum (Newlyn)
HAT is 5·9 metres above Chart Datum

TIME ZONE (UT)	SCOTLAND – ULLAPOOL	Dates in amber are SPRINGS
For Summer Time add ONE hour in **non-shaded areas**	LAT 57°54′N LONG 5°10′W	Dates in yellow are NEAPS
	TIMES AND HEIGHTS OF HIGH AND LOW WATERS	**2009**

SEPTEMBER

Time m

Day		Time m	Day		Time m
1	TU	0523 4.1 / 1724 4.5 / 2352 1.6	**16**	W	0457 4.6 / 1107 1.5 / 1711 5.0 / 2342 0.9
2	W	0555 4.4 / 1204 1.6 / 1756 4.7	**17**	TH	0541 5.0 / 1153 1.1 / 1751 5.3
3	TH	0025 1.3 / 0622 4.6 / 1237 1.4 / 1824 4.9	**18**	F	0024 0.6 / 0619 5.3 / 1235 0.8 / ● 1829 5.6
4	F	0056 1.1 / 0647 4.8 / 1307 1.2 / ○ 1851 5.1	**19**	SA	0105 0.4 / 0655 5.4 / 1314 0.6 / 1905 5.6
5	SA	0125 0.9 / 0712 4.9 / 1337 1.0 / 1918 5.2	**20**	SU	0143 0.3 / 0730 5.4 / 1352 0.6 / 1942 5.5
6	SU	0154 0.8 / 0737 5.0 / 1406 1.0 / 1947 5.2	**21**	M	0219 0.4 / 0805 5.3 / 1430 0.7 / 2019 5.3
7	M	0223 0.8 / 0804 5.0 / 1436 1.0 / 2017 5.1	**22**	TU	0255 0.7 / 0841 5.1 / 1508 0.9 / 2057 4.9
8	TU	0253 0.8 / 0834 4.9 / 1508 1.1 / 2051 5.0	**23**	W	0331 1.1 / 0918 4.8 / 1546 1.3 / 2137 4.5
9	W	0326 1.0 / 0908 4.8 / 1543 1.3 / 2130 4.7	**24**	TH	0408 1.5 / 1000 4.4 / 1627 1.7 / 2229 4.1
10	TH	0402 1.2 / 0949 4.6 / 1623 1.5 / 2220 4.4	**25**	F	0448 1.9 / 1059 4.1 / 1715 2.1 / 2356 3.8
11	F	0443 1.6 / 1043 4.3 / 1713 1.9 / 2336 4.1	**26**	SA	0537 2.4 / 1229 3.9 / 1821 2.4
12	SA	0536 1.9 / 1212 4.0 / 1824 2.1 ◑	**27**	SU	0136 3.6 / 0659 2.6 / 1400 3.9 / 2014 2.5
13	SU	0115 4.0 / 0654 2.3 / 1354 4.0 / 2013 2.2	**28**	M	0307 3.7 / 0904 2.6 / 1517 4.0 / 2151 2.3
14	M	0245 4.0 / 0849 2.2 / 1518 4.2 / 2151 1.8	**29**	TU	0410 3.9 / 1012 2.3 / 1611 4.2 / 2240 2.0
15	TU	0402 4.3 / 1012 1.9 / 1622 4.6 / 2253 1.4	**30**	W	0452 4.1 / 1056 2.0 / 1651 4.4 / 2317 1.7

OCTOBER

Time m

Day		Time m	Day		Time m
1	TH	0523 4.4 / 1131 1.7 / 1723 4.7 / 2350 1.4	**16**	F	0519 5.0 / 1130 1.2 / 1731 5.2
2	F	0550 4.6 / 1204 1.4 / 1753 4.9	**17**	SA	0000 0.8 / 0556 5.2 / 1212 1.0 / 1808 5.4
3	SA	0020 1.1 / 0615 4.9 / 1235 1.2 / 1820 5.1	**18**	SU	0040 0.7 / 0631 5.3 / 1252 0.8 / ● 1844 5.4
4	SU	0051 0.9 / 0640 5.0 / 1306 1.0 / ○ 1849 5.3	**19**	M	0117 0.7 / 0705 5.4 / 1330 0.8 / 1920 5.3
5	M	0122 0.8 / 0707 5.1 / 1338 0.9 / 1919 5.3	**20**	TU	0153 0.8 / 0739 5.3 / 1407 0.9 / 1957 5.1
6	TU	0153 0.8 / 0736 5.2 / 1410 0.9 / 1953 5.2	**21**	W	0228 1.0 / 0814 5.1 / 1445 1.1 / 2034 4.8
7	W	0226 0.8 / 0809 5.1 / 1445 1.0 / 2031 5.0	**22**	TH	0303 1.3 / 0850 4.8 / 1523 1.4 / 2115 4.5
8	TH	0301 1.0 / 0846 4.9 / 1524 1.2 / 2117 4.8	**23**	F	0339 1.7 / 0931 4.6 / 1603 1.7 / 2203 4.1
9	F	0340 1.3 / 0931 4.7 / 1608 1.5 / 2217 4.4	**24**	SA	0418 2.0 / 1021 4.3 / 1649 2.0 / 2310 3.9
10	SA	0425 1.7 / 1033 4.4 / 1704 1.8 / 2342 4.2	**25**	SU	0505 2.3 / 1132 4.1 / 1746 2.3
11	SU	0523 2.1 / 1206 4.2 / ○ 1823 2.1	**26**	M	0036 3.7 / 0610 2.6 / 1258 3.9 / ● 1909 2.4
12	M	0111 4.1 / 0648 2.3 / 1340 4.2 / 2009 2.0	**27**	TU	0204 3.7 / 0754 2.6 / 1417 4.0 / 2043 2.3
13	TU	0235 4.1 / 0836 2.2 / 1500 4.4 / 2133 1.7	**28**	W	0317 3.8 / 0917 2.5 / 1519 4.1 / 2146 2.1
14	W	0345 4.4 / 0951 2.0 / 1602 4.7 / 2231 1.3	**29**	TH	0406 4.1 / 1010 2.2 / 1606 4.4 / 2230 1.8
15	TH	0437 4.7 / 1045 1.6 / 1650 5.0 / 2318 1.0	**30**	F	0443 4.3 / 1051 1.9 / 1644 4.6 / 2308 1.5
			31	SA	0513 4.6 / 1127 1.6 / 1717 4.8 / 2342 1.3

NOVEMBER

Time m

Day		Time m	Day		Time m
1	SU	0542 4.9 / 1201 1.4 / 1749 5.1	**16**	M	0017 1.1 / 0613 5.2 / 1233 1.2 / ● 1831 5.1
2	M	0016 1.1 / 0611 5.1 / 1237 1.2 / ○ 1822 5.2	**17**	TU	0055 1.1 / 0648 5.2 / 1313 1.2 / 1908 5.0
3	TU	0051 0.9 / 0642 5.2 / 1313 1.0 / 1859 5.3	**18**	W	0132 1.2 / 0723 5.2 / 1351 1.2 / 1945 4.9
4	W	0127 0.9 / 0716 5.3 / 1351 1.0 / 1939 5.2	**19**	TH	0207 1.3 / 0758 5.1 / 1429 1.3 / 2023 4.7
5	TH	0205 0.9 / 0754 5.2 / 1431 1.0 / 2024 5.1	**20**	F	0243 1.5 / 0833 4.9 / 1506 1.5 / 2101 4.5
6	F	0245 1.1 / 0837 5.1 / 1515 1.2 / 2118 4.8	**21**	SA	0319 1.7 / 0911 4.7 / 1545 1.7 / 2143 4.3
7	SA	0328 1.4 / 0929 4.9 / 1605 1.4 / 2222 4.6	**22**	SU	0357 1.9 / 0954 4.5 / 1627 1.9 / 2231 4.1
8	SU	0418 1.7 / 1034 4.6 / 1705 1.6 / 2337 4.3	**23**	M	0439 2.1 / 1045 4.3 / 1715 2.1 / 2330 3.9
9	M	0518 2.0 / 1155 4.5 / ◐ 1820 1.8	**24**	TU	0530 2.4 / 1149 4.2 / ● 1811 2.2
10	TU	0053 4.2 / 0636 2.2 / 1316 4.4 / 1943 1.8	**25**	W	0042 3.8 / 0635 2.5 / 1302 4.1 / 1919 2.3
11	W	0209 4.3 / 0803 2.2 / 1431 4.5 / 2059 1.7	**26**	TH	0157 3.9 / 0756 2.5 / 1410 4.1 / 2030 2.2
12	TH	0317 4.4 / 0917 2.0 / 1536 4.7 / 2200 1.5	**27**	F	0301 4.0 / 0906 2.4 / 1509 4.3 / 2131 2.0
13	F	0412 4.6 / 1016 1.7 / 1628 4.8 / 2251 1.3	**28**	SA	0352 4.2 / 1001 2.2 / 1558 4.4 / 2220 1.8
14	SA	0457 4.8 / 1106 1.5 / 1713 5.0 / 2336 1.1	**29**	SU	0433 4.5 / 1047 1.9 / 1641 4.7 / 2304 1.5
15	SU	0537 5.0 / 1151 1.3 / 1753 5.1	**30**	M	0510 4.8 / 1130 1.6 / 1722 4.9 / 2346 1.3

DECEMBER

Time m

Day		Time m	Day		Time m
1	TU	0547 5.0 / 1212 1.3 / 1804 5.1	**16**	W	0041 1.5 / 0638 5.0 / 1304 1.4 / ● 1904 4.8
2	W	0027 1.1 / 0624 5.2 / 1255 1.1 / ○ 1847 5.2	**17**	TH	0119 1.4 / 0713 5.1 / 1342 1.4 / 1939 4.8
3	TH	0109 1.0 / 0704 5.3 / 1339 1.0 / 1934 5.2	**18**	F	0155 1.4 / 0746 5.1 / 1418 1.4 / 2012 4.7
4	F	0152 1.0 / 0748 5.4 / 1424 0.9 / 2023 5.2	**19**	SA	0229 1.5 / 0819 5.0 / 1453 1.4 / 2045 4.6
5	SA	0236 1.1 / 0835 5.3 / 1512 1.0 / 2117 5.0	**20**	SU	0303 1.6 / 0853 4.9 / 1528 1.5 / 2119 4.5
6	SU	0323 1.2 / 0926 5.2 / 1603 1.1 / 2214 4.8	**21**	M	0338 1.7 / 0928 4.8 / 1604 1.6 / 2155 4.4
7	M	0413 1.5 / 1024 5.0 / 1658 1.3 / 2316 4.6	**22**	TU	0414 1.8 / 1007 4.6 / 1643 1.7 / 2236 4.2
8	TU	0507 1.7 / 1130 4.8 / 1759 1.5	**23**	W	0453 2.0 / 1052 4.5 / 1725 1.9 / 2327 4.1
9	W	0022 4.4 / 0609 1.9 / 1242 4.6 / ◐ 1813 2.0	**24**	TH	0539 2.2 / 1148 4.3 / ◐ 1813 2.0
10	TH	0132 4.3 / 0720 2.1 / 1355 4.5 / 2015 1.8	**25**	F	0033 4.0 / 0635 2.4 / 1256 4.2 / 1912 2.1
11	F	0241 4.3 / 0834 2.1 / 1505 4.5 / 2123 1.8	**26**	SA	0147 4.0 / 0747 2.4 / 1405 4.2 / 2020 2.1
12	SA	0344 4.4 / 0944 2.0 / 1608 4.5 / 2224 1.7	**27**	SU	0253 4.1 / 0902 2.4 / 1509 4.3 / 2129 2.0
13	SU	0437 4.6 / 1045 1.8 / 1700 4.6 / 2315 1.6	**28**	M	0352 4.3 / 1007 2.1 / 1609 4.4 / 2229 1.8
14	M	0522 4.8 / 1137 1.7 / 1746 4.7	**29**	TU	0443 4.6 / 1104 1.8 / 1703 4.5 / 2322 1.6
15	TU	0000 1.5 / 0602 4.9 / 1223 1.5 / 1826 4.8	**30**	W	0529 4.9 / 1155 1.5 / 1754 4.9
			31	TH	0011 1.3 / 0613 5.2 / 1244 1.1 / ○ 1842 5.2

Chart Datum: 2·75 metres below Ordnance Datum (Newlyn)
HAT is 5·9 metres above Chart Datum

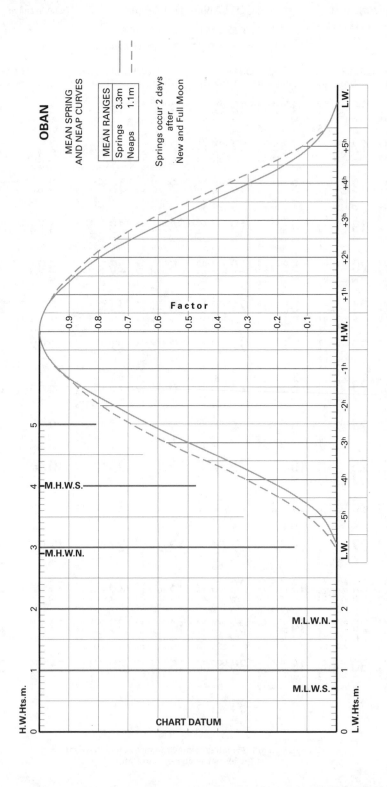

OBAN

MEAN SPRING
AND NEAP CURVES

MEAN RANGES	
Springs	3.3m
Neaps	1.1m

Springs occur 2 days
after
New and Full Moon

Factor

SCOTLAND – OBAN
LAT 56°25′N   LONG 5°29′W
TIMES AND HEIGHTS OF HIGH AND LOW WATERS

Dates in amber are **SPRINGS**
Dates in yellow are **NEAPS**

2009

JANUARY

Time	m		Time	m
1 0219	1.4		**16** 0306	0.7
0825	3.7		0901	3.8
TH 1448	1.6		F 1549	1.3
2028	3.5		2123	3.4
2 0249	1.4		**17** 0350	1.0
0900	3.6		0940	3.5
F 1522	1.7		SA 1632	1.5
2102	3.4		2204	3.2
3 0324	1.5		**18** 0436	1.3
0938	3.5		1023	3.2
SA 1604	1.7		SU 1721	1.8
2144	3.3		○ 2254	3.0
4 0410	1.6		**19** 0527	1.6
1027	3.4		1118	3.0
SU 1659	1.6		M 1820	1.9
○ 2235	3.2			
5 0508	1.7		**20** 0019	2.9
1130	3.3		0626	1.8
M 1807	1.8		TU 1254	2.8
2342	3.1		1935	2.0
6 0622	1.7		**21** 0158	2.9
1301	3.3		0742	1.9
TU 1919	1.8		W 1513	2.9
			2106	1.9
7 0114	3.1		**22** 0309	3.1
0744	1.7		0927	1.9
W 1435	3.4		TH 1604	3.0
2029	1.6		2206	1.7
8 0248	3.3		**23** 0400	3.3
0907	1.5		1031	1.8
TH 1543	3.6		F 1630	3.2
2132	1.3		2248	1.5
9 0353	3.6		**24** 0442	3.5
1019	1.3		1113	1.6
F 1637	3.7		SA 1703	3.4
2229	1.1		2325	1.3
10 0446	3.8		**25** 0521	3.7
1118	1.0		1148	1.4
SA 1724	3.9		SU 1737	3.6
2320	0.8		2358	1.2
11 0533	4.1		**26** 0558	3.8
1209	0.8		1220	1.3
SU 1807	4.0		M 1812	3.7
○				
12 0008	0.6		**27** 0030	1.1
0617	4.2		0632	3.9
M 1257	0.7		TU 1253	1.2
1848	4.0		1843	3.8
13 0055	0.5		**28** 0101	1.0
0700	4.2		0704	4.0
TU 1342	0.7		W 1324	1.1
1928	3.9		1911	3.8
14 0140	0.5		**29** 0128	1.0
0741	4.2		0733	4.0
W 1425	0.8		TH 1353	1.1
2007	3.8		1935	3.7
15 0223	0.6		**30** 0153	1.0
0821	4.0		0800	3.9
TH 1507	1.0		F 1418	1.2
2045	3.6		2002	3.7
			31 0220	1.1
			0829	3.8
			SA 1447	1.3
			2033	3.6

FEBRUARY

Time	m		Time	m
1 0254	1.2		**16** 0356	1.3
0904	3.6		0931	3.2
SU 1525	1.4		M 1630	1.7
2110	3.4		○ 2154	3.1
2 0335	1.3		**17** 0443	1.6
0946	3.4		1009	2.9
M 1614	1.6		TU 1726	1.9
○ 2154	3.3		2250	2.9
3 0429	1.5		**18** 0542	1.9
1043	3.2		1112	2.7
TU 1720	1.7		W 1839	2.0
2255	3.1			
4 0549	1.7		**19** 0115	2.8
1218	3.0		0658	2.1
W 1844	1.8		TH 1536	2.7
			2030	2.4
5 0038	3.0		**20** 0258	2.9
0729	1.8		0932	2.0
TH 1439	3.1		F 1615	2.9
2006	1.6		2151	1.8
6 0250	3.1		**21** 0351	3.1
0911	1.6		1026	1.8
F 1552	3.3		SA 1626	3.1
2120	1.4		2234	1.5
7 0400	3.5		**22** 0429	3.4
1026	1.3		1100	1.5
SA 1643	3.6		SU 1649	3.3
2221	1.0		2308	1.2
8 0448	3.8		**23** 0503	3.6
1119	0.9		1130	1.3
SU 1724	3.8		M 1720	3.6
2312	0.7		2338	1.0
9 0530	4.1		**24** 0537	3.8
1203	0.7		1158	1.1
M 1801	3.9		TU 1751	3.7
○ 2358	0.5			
10 0608	4.2		**25** 0007	0.9
1244	0.6		0609	4.0
TU 1835	4.0		W 1228	0.9
			● 1820	3.8
11 0041	0.3		**26** 0034	0.8
0645	4.3		0639	4.0
W 1323	0.6		TH 1256	0.8
1909	4.0		1844	3.8
12 0122	0.3		**27** 0101	0.7
0721	4.2		0706	4.0
TH 1400	0.7		F 1323	0.8
1942	3.9		1907	3.8
13 0201	0.4		**28** 0127	0.7
0754	4.0		0733	4.0
F 1435	0.9		SA 1349	0.9
2013	3.8		1935	3.8
14 0239	0.6			
0826	3.8			
SA 1509	1.1			
2044	3.6			
15 0316	0.9			
0858	3.5			
SU 1546	1.4			
2116	3.3			

MARCH

Time	m		Time	m
1 0157	0.8		**16** 0246	1.0
0802	3.8		0822	3.5
SU 1420	1.0		M 1509	1.3
2007	3.7		2043	3.4
2 0232	1.0		**17** 0324	1.4
0837	3.6		0852	3.2
M 1459	1.1		TU 1552	1.6
2044	3.5		2121	3.2
3 0314	1.2		**18** 0410	1.7
0919	3.3		0925	2.9
TU 1548	1.4		W 1648	1.8
2128	3.3		○ 2211	2.9
4 0412	1.5		**19** 0510	2.0
1016	3.0		1010	2.6
W 1655	1.6		TH 1800	2.0
○ 2230	3.0			
5 0545	1.7		**20** 0012	2.7
1213	2.8		0629	2.1
TH 1824	1.7		F 1439	2.6
			1935	2.0
6 0037	2.9		**21** 0233	2.8
0734	1.7		0905	2.0
F 1441	2.9		SA 1529	2.8
1952	1.6		2114	1.8
7 0253	3.1		**22** 0324	3.1
0922	1.5		0956	1.7
SA 1545	3.2		SU 1553	3.0
2109	1.3		2200	1.5
8 0352	3.5		**23** 0401	3.3
1022	1.1		1026	1.4
SU 1632	3.6		M 1620	3.2
2209	0.9		2234	1.2
9 0435	3.8		**24** 0434	3.6
1107	0.8		1055	1.2
M 1709	3.7		TU 1650	3.5
2257	0.6		2304	1.0
10 0513	4.0		**25** 0507	3.8
1145	0.6		1124	0.9
TU 1741	3.9		W 1720	3.7
2341	0.4		2333	0.8
11 0548	4.2		**26** 0539	4.0
1222	0.5		1153	0.7
W 1812	4.0		TH 1748	3.8
○			●	
12 0021	0.3		**27** 0001	0.6
0621	4.2		0609	4.0
TH 1257	0.6		F 1223	0.6
1842	4.0		1812	3.9
13 0100	0.3		**28** 0032	0.6
0653	4.1		0637	4.0
F 1330	0.7		SA 1252	0.6
1913	4.0		1839	3.9
14 0136	0.5		**29** 0104	0.6
0724	4.0		0707	4.0
SA 1401	0.8		SU 1325	0.6
1942	3.9		1912	3.8
15 0211	0.7		**30** 0141	0.7
0753	3.7		0742	3.8
SU 1434	1.1		M 1402	0.8
2011	3.7		1948	3.7
			31 0222	0.9
			0821	3.5
			TU 1445	1.0
			2030	3.5

APRIL

Time	m		Time	m
1 0312	1.1		**16** 0346	1.8
0908	3.2		0904	2.9
W 1538	1.2		TH 1616	1.8
2120	3.3		2152	3.0
2 0422	1.4		**17** 0446	2.0
1014	2.9		0954	2.7
TH 1648	1.4		F 1721	1.9
○ 2233	3.0		○ 2313	2.8
3 0552	1.6		**18** 0602	2.0
1243	2.7		1240	2.5
F 1810	1.5		SA 1837	1.9
4 0051	2.9		**19** 0138	2.9
0740	1.6		0734	2.0
SA 1424	2.8		SU 1427	2.7
1934	1.4		1959	1.8
5 0232	3.2		**20** 0239	3.0
0908	1.3		0850	1.7
SU 1524	3.1		M 1506	2.9
2049	1.2		2101	1.6
6 0328	3.4		**21** 0319	3.3
1002	1.1		0934	1.5
M 1608	3.4		TU 1540	3.1
2147	0.9		2143	1.3
7 0411	3.7		**22** 0356	3.5
1043	0.9		1009	1.2
TU 1642	3.6		W 1612	3.4
2234	0.7		2218	1.1
8 0447	3.9		**23** 0431	3.7
1120	0.7		1043	0.9
W 1713	3.8		TH 1643	3.6
2317	0.5		2252	0.8
9 0521	4.0		**24** 0505	3.9
1154	0.7		1116	0.7
TH 1744	3.9		F 1712	3.7
○ 2357	0.5		2328	0.7
10 0554	4.0		**25** 0539	4.0
1226	0.7		1150	0.6
F 1814	4.0		SA 1743	3.8
			●	
11 0035	0.5		**26** 0006	0.6
0624	3.9		0613	4.0
SA 1259	0.8		SU 1227	0.5
1844	3.9		1817	3.9
12 0111	0.7		**27** 0048	0.6
0655	3.8		0649	3.9
SU 1331	0.9		M 1306	0.6
1915	3.9		1856	3.9
13 0145	0.9		**28** 0133	0.7
0725	3.6		0730	3.7
M 1404	1.1		TU 1350	0.7
1946	3.7		1939	3.7
14 0220	1.2		**29** 0223	0.8
0756	3.4		0816	3.4
TU 1441	1.3		W 1439	0.8
2021	3.5		2027	3.5
15 0259	1.5		**30** 0320	1.1
0828	3.2		0910	3.1
W 1524	1.6		TH 1534	1.0
2101	3.2		2124	3.3

Chart Datum: 2·10 metres below Ordnance Datum (Newlyn)
HAT is 4·5 metres above Chart Datum

TIDES

307

TIME ZONE (UT)	SCOTLAND – OBAN	Dates in amber are SPRINGS
For Summer Time add ONE hour in **non-shaded areas**	**LAT 56°25'N LONG 5°29'W**	Dates in yellow are NEAPS
	TIMES AND HEIGHTS OF HIGH AND LOW WATERS	**2009**

MAY

#	Time	m	#	Time	m
1	0428	1.3	16	0421	1.9
	1021	2.9		0946	2.8
F	1638	1.2	SA	1637	1.8
	2237	3.1		2233	3.0
2	0549	1.4	17	0523	1.9
	1223	2.8		1053	2.7
SA	1751	1.3	SU	1734	1.8
				2351	3.0
3	0028	3.1	18	0631	1.9
	0721	1.4		1239	2.7
SU	1350	2.9	M	1836	1.8
	1907	1.3	◐		
4	0157	3.2	19	0119	3.1
	0838	1.3		0737	1.7
M	1451	3.0	TU	1357	2.9
◑	2018	1.2		1938	1.7
5	0256	3.3	20	0222	3.2
	0932	1.2		0832	1.5
TU	1535	3.2	W	1445	3.0
	2118	1.0		2035	1.5
6	0341	3.5	21	0310	3.4
	1014	1.1		0918	1.3
W	1610	3.4	TH	1526	3.2
	2208	0.9		2126	1.2
7	0419	3.6	22	0353	3.6
	1051	1.0		1000	1.1
TH	1643	3.6	F	1604	3.5
	2252	0.8		2215	1.0
8	0453	3.7	23	0435	3.8
	1125	0.9		1041	0.9
F	1716	3.8	SA	1643	3.7
	2333	0.8		2302	0.8
9	0527	3.7	24	0516	3.9
	1157	0.9		1124	0.7
SA	1749	3.8	SU	1724	3.8
				2350	0.7
10	0011	0.9	25	0558	3.9
	0559	3.7		1207	0.6
SU	1231	1.0	M	1806	3.9
	1821	3.9			
11	0048	1.0	26	0039	0.6
	0632	3.6		0641	3.8
M	1306	1.1	TU	1253	0.5
○	1855	3.8	●	1851	3.9
12	0124	1.2	27	0130	0.7
	0707	3.5		0727	3.7
TU	1342	1.2	W	1341	0.6
	1931	3.7		1938	3.8
13	0202	1.4	28	0223	0.8
	0741	3.4		0816	3.5
W	1420	1.3	TH	1431	0.7
	2008	3.5		2028	3.7
14	0242	1.6	29	0320	1.0
	0818	3.2		0910	3.2
TH	1501	1.5	F	1524	0.8
	2049	3.4		2123	3.5
15	0328	1.7	30	0421	1.2
	0857	3.0		1014	3.0
F	1546	1.7	SA	1622	1.0
	2136	3.2		2226	3.3
			31	0529	1.3
				1137	2.9
			SU	1724	1.1
				2343	3.2

JUNE

#	Time	m	#	Time	m
1	0643	1.4	16	0529	1.8
	1259	2.9		1100	2.9
M	1830	1.2	TU	1729	1.7
			◐	2347	3.2
2	0108	3.1	17	0629	1.7
	0755	1.4		1207	2.9
TU	1404	3.0	W	1831	1.7
◑	1938	1.3			
3	0216	3.1	18	0105	3.2
	0855	1.4		0730	1.6
W	1456	3.1	TH	1329	3.0
	2042	1.3		1937	1.6
4	0309	3.2	19	0221	3.3
	0943	1.3		0830	1.5
TH	1538	3.3	F	1440	3.2
	2139	1.2		2045	1.4
5	0352	3.3	20	0323	3.4
	1024	1.3		0925	1.2
F	1616	3.4	SA	1537	3.4
	2228	1.2		2150	1.2
6	0431	3.4	21	0417	3.6
	1100	1.2		1017	1.0
SA	1653	3.6	SU	1628	3.6
	2312	1.2		2250	1.0
7	0508	3.5	22	0506	3.7
	1135	1.2		1107	0.8
SU	1730	3.7	M	1717	3.8
	2353	1.2		2345	0.8
8	0544	3.5	23	0553	3.8
	1211	1.1		1155	0.6
M	1807	3.8	TU	1804	4.0
9	0031	1.2	24	0037	0.7
	0620	3.5		0639	3.8
TU	1249	1.1	W	1244	0.5
	1844	3.8	○	1849	4.0
10	0110	1.3	25	0129	0.6
	0657	3.5		0724	3.7
W	1326	1.2	TH	1332	0.4
	1921	3.7	●	1936	4.0
11	0149	1.4	26	0219	0.7
	0734	3.4		0810	3.6
TH	1403	1.3	F	1420	0.5
	1958	3.6		2022	3.9
12	0228	1.5	27	0309	0.8
	0810	3.3		0857	3.4
F	1438	1.4	SA	1508	0.6
	2036	3.5		2109	3.7
13	0308	1.6	28	0400	1.0
	0845	3.2		0947	3.2
SA	1513	1.5	SU	1558	0.8
	2114	3.4		2159	3.5
14	0349	1.7	29	0453	1.2
	0923	3.1		1044	3.1
SU	1551	1.6	M	1651	1.0
	2156	3.3		2254	3.2
15	0435	1.7	30	0552	1.4
	1007	3.0		1153	2.9
M	1635	1.7	TU	1747	1.3
	2245	3.2			

JULY

#	Time	m	#	Time	m
1	0001	3.0	16	0531	1.7
	0657	1.6		1107	3.0
W	1308	2.9	TH	1742	1.7
	1850	1.5			
2	0124	2.9	17	0001	3.1
	0808	1.7		0642	1.7
TH	1414	2.9	F	1228	3.0
	1959	1.6		1901	1.7
3	0241	2.9	18	0149	3.1
	0913	1.6		0756	1.6
F	1511	3.1	SA	1416	3.1
	2112	1.6	◑	2025	1.6
4	0340	3.0	19	0316	3.3
	1004	1.5		0904	1.4
SA	1558	3.2	SU	1532	3.3
◑	2214	1.6		2146	1.3
5	0422	3.1	20	0417	3.5
	1046	1.4		1005	1.1
SU	1640	3.4	M	1628	3.6
	2303	1.5		2252	1.0
6	0500	3.3	21	0507	3.7
	1124	1.3		1058	0.8
M	1720	3.6	TU	1716	3.9
	2344	1.4		2346	0.8
7	0537	3.4	22	0552	3.8
	1200	1.2		1147	0.5
TU	1758	3.7	W	1800	4.1
8	0021	1.3	23	0034	0.6
	0614	3.5		0633	3.9
W	1236	1.1	TH	1234	0.3
	1834	3.8		1843	4.2
9	0058	1.3	24	0120	0.5
	0649	3.6		0713	3.9
TH	1311	1.1	F	1319	0.3
	1909	3.8		1924	4.2
10	0134	1.3	25	0203	0.6
	0723	3.6		0753	3.8
F	1344	1.1	SA	1403	0.3
	1943	3.8		2004	4.0
11	0209	1.3	26	0246	0.7
	0753	3.5		0832	3.6
SA	1413	1.2	SU	1446	0.5
○	2015	3.7	●	2043	3.8
12	0241	1.3	27	0328	0.9
	0821	3.4		0911	3.4
SU	1439	1.3	M	1530	0.7
	2046	3.6		2122	3.5
13	0311	1.4	28	0412	1.2
	0851	3.3		0953	3.2
M	1509	1.4	TU	1616	1.1
	2119	3.5		2203	3.2
14	0345	1.5	29	0500	1.5
	0927	3.2		1043	3.0
W	1547	1.5	W	1705	1.4
	2159	3.4		2252	2.9
15	0430	1.6	30	0557	1.7
	1011	3.1		1203	2.8
TH	1637	1.6	TH	1803	1.7
	2250	3.2			
			31	0012	2.7
				0710	1.8
			F	1340	2.8
				1915	1.8

AUGUST

#	Time	m	#	Time	m
1	0258	2.7	16	0158	3.0
	0846	1.8		0736	1.6
SA	1457	3.0	SU	1428	3.1
	2100	1.9		2030	1.7
2	0422	2.9	17	0324	3.2
	0952	1.6		0853	1.4
SU	1550	3.2	M	1539	3.4
◑	2215	1.7	◑	2155	1.4
3	0432	3.0	18	0419	3.4
	1037	1.4		0956	1.0
M	1631	3.4	TU	1627	3.7
	2300	1.6		2251	1.0
4	0454	3.3	19	0503	3.7
	1114	1.2		1049	0.7
TU	1707	3.6	W	1709	4.0
	2335	1.4		2337	0.7
5	0526	3.5	20	0541	3.9
	1148	1.1		1135	0.4
W	1743	3.8	TH	1748	4.2
6	0007	1.2	21	0019	0.5
	0559	3.6		0616	4.0
TH	1220	1.0	F	1219	0.2
	1818	3.9		1825	4.3
7	0039	1.1	22	0100	0.5
	0632	3.7		0651	4.0
F	1250	0.9	SA	1301	0.2
	1850	4.0		1901	4.3
8	0111	1.0	23	0138	0.5
	0701	3.7		0725	4.0
SA	1319	0.9	SU	1341	0.3
	1920	4.0		1936	4.1
9	0141	1.0	24	0215	0.7
	0726	3.7		0759	3.8
SU	1343	1.0	M	1421	0.5
○	1947	3.9		2010	3.9
10	0208	1.0	25	0252	0.9
	0750	3.6		0832	3.6
M	1407	1.1	TU	1500	0.8
	2014	3.8	●	2042	3.6
11	0233	1.2	26	0330	1.2
	0818	3.5		0906	3.4
TU	1435	1.2	W	1541	1.2
	2044	3.6		2116	3.2
12	0305	1.3	27	0415	1.5
	0851	3.4		0947	3.1
W	1512	1.3	TH	1629	1.6
	2121	3.4		2154	2.9
13	0348	1.5	28	0511	1.8
	0932	3.2		1050	2.9
TH	1600	1.5	F	1727	1.9
	2208	3.2		2253	2.6
14	0449	1.6	29	0624	1.9
	1027	3.1		1318	2.8
F	1711	1.7	SA	1842	2.1
	2323	3.0			
15	0612	1.7	30	0319	2.6
	1156	2.9		0816	1.9
SA	1849	1.8	SU	1450	2.9
				2109	2.0
			31	0408	2.8
				0932	1.7
			M	1540	3.2
				2208	1.8

Chart Datum: 2·10 metres below Ordnance Datum (Newlyn)
HAT is 4·5 metres above Chart Datum

SCOTLAND – OBAN
LAT 56°25′N   LONG 5°29′W
TIMES AND HEIGHTS OF HIGH AND LOW WATERS

Dates in amber are **SPRINGS**
Dates in yellow are **NEAPS**

2009

SEPTEMBER

Day				
1 TU	0418 3.0	1017 1.4	1614 3.4	2243 1.5
2 W	0434 3.3	1053 1.2	1646 3.7	2312 1.3
3 TH	0503 3.5	1125 1.0	1719 3.9	2341 1.1
4 F	0534 3.7	1154 0.9	1752 4.0	○
5 SA	0010 1.0	0604 3.8	1222 0.8	1823 4.1
6 SU	0040 0.9	0630 3.9	1248 0.8	1850 4.1
7 M	0108 0.9	0653 3.8	1313 0.9	1916 4.0
8 TU	0135 0.9	0718 3.8	1339 1.0	1943 3.9
9 W	0202 1.0	0748 3.8	1410 1.1	2015 3.7
10 TH	0237 1.2	0823 3.5	1449 1.3	2053 3.4
11 F	0322 1.4	0906 3.3	1542 1.6	2143 3.1
12 SA	0425 1.6	1004 3.1	1707 1.6	◑ 2311 2.8
13 SU	0554 1.7	1158 2.9	1856 1.8	
14 M	0207 2.9	1430 3.2	2042 1.6	
15 TU	0316 3.1	0840 1.4	1528 3.5	2150 1.3
16 W	0405 3.4	0941 1.0	1611 3.8	2237 1.0
17 TH	0444 3.7	1031 0.7	1649 4.1	2318 0.7
18 F	0519 3.9	1116 0.4	1725 4.3	● 2356 0.6
19 SA	0550 4.0	1158 0.3	1759 4.3	
20 SU	0032 0.5	0622 4.1	1238 0.3	1832 4.3
21 M	0107 0.6	0654 4.1	1317 0.5	1905 4.1
22 TU	0142 0.8	0726 3.9	1354 0.7	1935 3.9
23 W	0217 1.0	0758 3.7	1431 1.0	2006 3.6
24 TH	0255 1.3	0831 3.5	1511 1.4	2038 3.3
25 F	0339 1.6	0912 3.3	1559 1.7	2112 3.0
26 SA	0435 1.8	1008 3.0	1659 2.0	◐ 2201 2.7
27 SU	0547 2.0	1255 2.9	1818 2.2	
28 M	0220 2.6	0725 2.0	1404 3.0	2044 2.1
29 TU	0315 2.8	0856 1.8	1512 3.2	2137 1.8
30 W	0339 3.0	0944 1.5	1545 3.5	2208 1.6

OCTOBER

Day				
1 TH	0403 3.3	1020 1.3	1617 3.7	2237 1.3
2 F	0432 3.5	1051 1.1	1649 3.9	2306 1.1
3 SA	0503 3.7	1120 0.9	1721 4.0	2335 0.9
4 SU	0532 3.8	1148 0.9	1751 4.1	○
5 M	0005 0.8	0556 3.9	1216 0.8	1819 4.1
6 TU	0035 0.8	0622 3.9	1246 0.8	1847 4.0
7 W	0106 0.8	0652 3.9	1319 0.9	1919 3.9
8 TH	0141 0.9	0727 3.8	1357 1.1	1956 3.7
9 F	0221 1.1	0807 3.6	1444 1.3	2039 3.4
10 SA	0311 1.3	0855 3.4	1548 1.6	2137 3.0
11 SU	0416 1.5	1003 3.2	1717 1.8	2319 2.8
12 M	0537 1.6	1216 3.1	1858 1.8	
13 TU	0149 2.9	0701 1.5	1407 3.0	2031 1.6
14 W	0253 3.1	0817 1.3	1503 3.6	2130 1.3
15 TH	0341 3.4	0918 1.0	1547 3.8	2214 1.0
16 F	0419 3.7	1008 0.8	1624 4.0	2252 0.9
17 SA	0451 3.9	1053 0.6	1658 4.2	2328 0.8
18 SU	0522 4.0	1135 0.6	1732 4.2	●
19 M	0003 0.8	0554 4.1	1215 0.6	1804 4.1
20 TU	0037 0.8	0627 4.1	1253 0.8	1835 4.0
21 W	0112 1.0	0659 4.0	1330 1.0	1907 3.8
22 TH	0148 1.1	0733 3.9	1407 1.3	1940 3.6
23 F	0227 1.4	0809 3.6	1448 1.6	2013 3.3
24 SA	0311 1.6	0851 3.4	1536 1.9	2051 3.1
25 SU	0404 1.8	0945 3.2	1634 2.1	2142 2.8
26 M	0507 2.0	1114 3.0	1747 2.2	◑ 2341 2.7
27 TU	0622 2.0	1337 3.1	1918 2.1	
28 W	0212 2.8	0748 1.9	1430 3.3	2034 1.9
29 TH	0251 3.0	0852 1.7	1508 3.5	2118 1.7
30 F	0323 3.2	0934 1.5	1541 3.7	2153 1.4
31 SA	0355 3.5	1615 3.8	2226 1.2	

NOVEMBER

Day				
1 SU	0427 3.6	1041 1.1	1648 4.0	2258 1.0
2 M	0457 3.8	1053 1.0	1721 4.1	○ 2331 0.9
3 TU	0527 3.9	1148 0.9	1753 4.1	●
4 W	0006 0.8	0559 4.0	1227 0.9	1827 4.0
5 TH	0045 0.8	0635 4.0	1309 1.0	1905 3.9
6 F	0126 0.8	0716 3.9	1356 1.1	1948 3.7
7 SA	0212 1.0	0802 3.7	1441 1.3	2037 3.4
8 SU	0305 1.1	0856 3.5	1554 1.5	2137 3.1
9 M	0405 1.3	1003 3.4	1710 1.6	◑ 2306 2.9
10 TU	0515 1.4	1143 3.3	1837 1.7	
11 W	0110 3.0	0630 1.4	1329 3.4	1958 1.6
12 TH	0219 3.1	0744 1.3	1431 3.5	2059 1.4
13 F	0310 3.3	0848 1.2	1519 3.7	2146 1.3
14 SA	0349 3.5	0942 1.1	1558 3.8	2226 1.2
15 SU	0423 3.7	1030 1.0	1634 3.9	2302 1.1
16 M	0457 3.9	1113 1.0	1708 3.9	● 2337 1.1
17 TU	0531 4.0	1154 1.0	1742 3.9	
18 W	0012 1.1	0606 4.0	1234 1.1	1815 3.9
19 TH	0049 1.1	0641 4.0	1312 1.3	1849 3.8
20 F	0127 1.2	0718 3.9	1350 1.5	1925 3.6
21 SA	0206 1.4	0756 3.8	1430 1.7	2001 3.4
22 SU	0248 1.5	0837 3.6	1515 1.9	2040 3.3
23 M	0333 1.7	0924 3.4	1606 2.0	2125 3.1
24 TU	0422 1.9	1704 2.1	◐ 2223 2.9	
25 W	0518 2.0	1135 3.2	1809 2.1	2351 2.9
26 TH	0620 2.0	1311 3.2	1915 2.0	
27 F	0132 3.0	0723 1.9	1414 3.4	2013 1.9
28 SA	0229 3.1	0823 1.8	1459 3.5	2101 1.6
29 SU	0312 3.3	0915 1.6	1540 3.7	2143 1.4
30 M	0351 3.5	1001 1.4	1620 3.9	2223 1.2

DECEMBER

Day				
1 TU	0429 3.7	1046 1.2	1659 4.0	2304 1.0
2 W	0507 3.9	1131 1.0	1738 4.0	○ 2346 0.8
3 TH	0547 4.0	1217 0.9	1818 4.0	
4 F	0029 0.7	0629 4.0	1305 0.9	1900 3.9
5 SA	0116 0.7	0714 4.0	1355 1.0	1945 3.7
6 SU	0203 0.8	0801 3.9	1448 1.1	2033 3.5
7 M	0254 0.9	0852 3.8	1545 1.3	2126 3.3
8 TU	0349 1.0	0949 3.6	1647 1.5	2231 3.1
9 W	0448 1.2	1058 3.6	1756 1.6	◑ 2358 3.0
10 TH	0554 1.3	1229 3.3	1910 1.7	
11 F	0124 3.0	0703 1.4	1350 3.3	2019 1.6
12 SA	0229 3.2	0812 1.4	1451 3.4	2116 1.6
13 SU	0319 3.3	0916 1.4	1539 3.5	2202 1.5
14 M	0400 3.5	1011 1.4	1619 3.5	2242 1.4
15 TU	0439 3.7	1059 1.3	1655 3.6	2319 1.3
16 W	0517 3.8	1142 1.3	1730 3.7	● 2356 1.2
17 TH	0554 4.0	1221 1.3	1806 3.7	
18 F	0034 1.2	0631 4.0	1300 1.4	1841 3.7
19 SA	0112 1.2	0707 4.0	1337 1.5	1916 3.7
20 SU	0149 1.3	0744 3.9	1415 1.6	1951 3.6
21 M	0226 1.4	0821 3.8	1452 1.7	2026 3.5
22 TU	0301 1.5	0858 3.6	1531 1.8	2100 3.4
23 W	0336 1.7	0937 3.5	1614 1.9	2138 3.2
24 TH	0415 1.8	1021 3.4	1703 2.0	◐ 2224 3.1
25 F	0503 1.9	1117 3.3	1801 2.0	2322 3.0
26 SA	0603 2.0	1239 3.2	1904 1.9	
27 SU	0044 3.0	0712 1.9	1309 3.3	2005 1.8
28 M	0219 3.1	0823 1.8	1513 3.5	2103 1.6
29 TU	0322 3.3	0932 1.6	1604 3.6	2156 1.3
30 W	0413 3.6	1033 1.3	1649 3.8	2245 1.0
31 TH	0459 3.8	1126 1.1	1732 3.9	○ 2332 0.8

Chart Datum: 2·10 metres below Ordnance Datum (Newlyn)
HAT is 4·5 metres above Chart Datum

TIDES

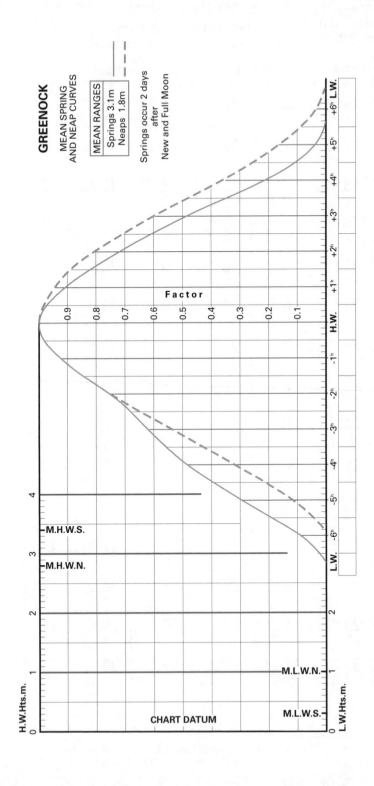

SCOTLAND – GREENOCK

LAT 55°57′N   LONG 4°46′W

TIMES AND HEIGHTS OF HIGH AND LOW WATERS

Dates in amber are **SPRINGS**
Dates in yellow are **NEAPS**

2009

JANUARY

Day	Time	m	Time	m	Time	m	Time	m
1 TH	0300	3.2	0822	0.8	1510	3.6	2051	0.6
2 F	0339	3.2	0903	0.8	1548	3.5	2134	0.6
3 SA	0419	3.2	0948	0.9	1629	3.4	2223	0.7
4 SU	0501	3.1	1037	1.0	1714	3.3	◑2318	0.7
5 M	0546	3.1	1133	1.1	1808	3.2		
6 TU	0019	0.8	0639	3.0	1238	1.1	1916	3.1
7 W	0125	0.8	0752	3.0	1350	1.1	2043	3.0
8 TH	0235	0.8	0918	3.1	1502	0.9	2203	3.1
9 F	0338	0.7	1025	3.2	1605	0.6	2308	3.3
10 SA	0434	0.5	1121	3.4	1659	0.4		
11 SU	0006	3.4	0524	0.4	1212	3.6	○1748	0.2
12 M	0102	3.4	0613	0.4	1301	3.7	1835	0.1
13 TU	0154	3.4	0701	0.4	1347	3.8	1922	0.1
14 W	0242	3.4	0820	0.4	1432	3.9	2008	0.1
15 TH	0327	3.4	0834	0.4	1515	3.8	2054	0.2
16 F	0409	3.3	0920	0.5	1557	3.7	2141	0.4
17 SA	0449	3.2	1008	0.6	1639	3.6	2231	0.6
18 SU	0529	3.1	1100	0.8	1722	3.4	◑2327	0.8
19 M	0612	3.0	1201	1.0	1809	3.1		
20 TU	0034	1.0	0703	2.9	1318	1.1	1901	2.9
21 W	0152	1.1	0816	2.8	1435	1.0	2015	2.8
22 TH	0258	1.1	0945	2.9	1536	0.9	2205	2.8
23 F	0352	1.0	1045	3.2	1624	0.7	2304	2.9
24 SA	0437	0.9	1130	3.3	1706	0.6	2348	3.0
25 SU	0515	0.8	1209	3.5	1742	0.5		
26 M	0026	3.1	0548	0.8	1244	3.5	●1815	0.5
27 TU	0101	3.1	0619	0.7	1315	3.5	1845	0.5
28 W	0134	3.2	0648	0.7	1345	3.5	1914	0.5
29 TH	0206	3.2	0720	0.6	1416	3.4	1945	0.4
30 F	0239	3.3	0756	0.6	1450	3.4	2021	0.4
31 SA	0313	3.3	0835	0.5	1526	3.6	2101	0.4

FEBRUARY

Day	Time	m	Time	m	Time	m	Time	m
1 SU	0348	3.3	0917	0.6	1603	3.5	2147	0.5
2 M	0425	3.3	1004	0.7	1644	3.3	◑2240	0.6
3 TU	0505	3.1	1057	0.8	1732	3.1	2340	0.8
4 W	0553	3.0	1201	1.0	1833	2.9		
5 TH	0051	0.9	0655	2.9	1320	1.0	2017	2.8
6 F	0216	0.9	0846	2.9	1450	0.9	2203	2.9
7 SA	0330	0.8	1015	3.1	1559	0.6	2310	3.1
8 SU	0427	0.6	1114	3.3	1652	0.3		
9 M	0005	3.3	0515	0.4	1204	3.5	○1737	0.1
10 TU	0055	3.4	0600	0.3	1250	3.7	1820	0.0
11 W	0141	3.4	0643	0.2	1335	3.7	1901	0.0
12 TH	0223	3.4	0725	0.2	1416	3.8	1941	0.1
13 F	0301	3.4	0806	0.2	1455	3.8	2021	0.2
14 SA	0334	3.3	0846	0.3	1532	3.7	2101	0.3
15 SU	0407	3.2	0927	0.4	1609	3.5	2143	0.5
16 M	0441	3.1	1012	0.6	1647	3.3	◐2230	0.8
17 TU	0520	3.0	1105	0.8	1729	3.0	2326	1.1
18 W	0606	2.8	1223	1.0	1818	2.8		
19 TH	0058	1.3	0706	2.7	1406	1.1	1919	2.6
20 F	0233	1.3	0904	2.7	1512	0.9	2150	2.6
21 SA	0332	1.1	1022	3.0	1601	0.7	2249	2.8
22 SU	0417	0.9	1108	3.2	1642	0.5	2330	2.9
23 M	0454	0.7	1146	3.3	1717	0.4		
24 TU	0006	3.0	0526	0.6	1221	3.4	1748	0.3
25 W	0041	3.1	0554	0.6	1253	3.4	●1816	0.3
26 TH	0113	3.1	0621	0.5	1323	3.4	1843	0.3
27 F	0142	3.2	0652	0.4	1354	3.5	1915	0.2
28 SA	0212	3.3	0728	0.3	1429	3.5	1952	0.2

MARCH

Day	Time	m	Time	m	Time	m	Time	m
1 SU	0245	3.4	0808	0.3	1505	3.5	2034	0.2
2 M	0319	3.4	0851	0.3	1543	3.5	2120	0.4
3 TU	0356	3.3	0938	0.5	1623	3.3	2213	0.6
4 W	0436	3.2	1033	0.6	1710	3.0	◑2315	0.8
5 TH	0523	3.0	1140	0.8	1812	2.8		
6 F	0034	1.0	0624	2.8	1310	0.9	2026	2.6
7 SA	0210	1.0	0831	2.8	1446	0.7	2208	2.9
8 SU	0323	0.8	1006	3.0	1550	0.4	2304	3.1
9 M	0417	0.5	1101	3.3	1639	0.1	2352	3.3
10 TU	0502	0.3	1148	3.5	1720	0.0		
11 W	0036	3.3	0543	0.2	1233	3.6	○1759	0.0
12 TH	0118	3.4	0622	0.1	1315	3.6	1836	0.0
13 F	0155	3.3	0700	0.1	1354	3.6	1912	0.1
14 SA	0227	3.3	0736	0.1	1430	3.6	1948	0.2
15 SU	0257	3.3	0812	0.2	1504	3.5	2025	0.2
16 M	0329	3.3	0850	0.3	1539	3.4	2103	0.6
17 TU	0403	3.2	0932	0.5	1617	3.2	2145	0.8
18 W	0440	3.1	1022	0.7	1658	2.9	◑2235	1.1
19 TH	0525	2.9	1134	1.0	1748	2.7	2348	1.3
20 F	0622	2.7	1325	1.0	1849	2.5		
21 SA	0152	1.4	0751	2.6	1437	0.8	2100	2.5
22 SU	0258	1.2	0944	2.8	1527	0.6	2215	2.7
23 M	0345	0.9	1033	3.0	1608	0.4	2257	2.9
24 TU	0423	0.7	1112	3.2	1643	0.3	2334	3.0
25 W	0454	0.6	1147	3.2	1715	0.1		
26 TH	0009	3.1	0522	0.5	1221	3.3	●1742	0.2
27 F	0041	3.2	0551	0.4	1255	3.3	1812	0.1
28 SA	0112	3.2	0625	0.3	1331	3.4	1848	0.1
29 SU	0144	3.4	0704	0.2	1409	3.5	1929	0.2
30 M	0219	3.5	0746	0.2	1448	3.5	2014	0.2
31 TU	0256	3.5	0831	0.2	1529	3.4	2104	0.4

APRIL

Day	Time	m	Time	m	Time	m	Time	m
1 W	0334	3.4	0922	0.3	1613	3.2	2159	0.6
2 TH	0415	3.3	1022	0.5	1704	2.9	◑2306	0.9
3 F	0505	3.0	1138	0.7	1821	2.7		
4 SA	0030	1.0	0614	2.8	1311	0.7	2039	2.7
5 SU	0156	0.9	0823	2.8	1431	0.5	2152	2.9
6 M	0304	0.7	0946	3.1	1530	0.3	2243	3.1
7 TU	0357	0.5	1039	3.3	1617	0.1	2328	3.2
8 W	0442	0.3	1125	3.4	1657	0.0		
9 TH	0010	3.3	0522	0.1	1209	3.5	○1734	0.1
10 F	0048	3.3	0559	0.1	1250	3.5	1809	0.2
11 SA	0123	3.3	0634	0.1	1328	3.4	1843	0.3
12 SU	0153	3.4	0708	0.2	1403	3.4	1918	0.4
13 M	0224	3.4	0743	0.2	1437	3.4	1955	0.5
14 TU	0256	3.4	0821	0.3	1512	3.2	2034	0.6
15 W	0331	3.3	0903	0.5	1551	3.1	2116	0.8
16 TH	0408	3.1	0953	0.6	1634	2.9	2204	1.0
17 F	0451	2.9	1059	0.8	1724	2.7	◑2305	1.2
18 SA	0545	2.7	1226	0.9	1825	2.5		
19 SU	0031	1.3	0657	2.6	1344	0.8	1950	2.5
20 M	0158	1.2	0837	2.7	1440	0.6	2119	2.7
21 TU	0256	1.0	0942	2.9	1524	0.4	2211	2.9
22 W	0339	0.8	1027	3.0	1602	0.3	2253	3.0
23 TH	0415	0.6	1106	3.2	1635	0.2	2330	3.1
24 F	0449	0.4	1145	3.2	1709	0.1		
25 SA	0006	3.2	0524	0.3	1226	3.3	●1745	0.1
26 SU	0042	3.3	0603	0.2	1308	3.4	1826	0.1
27 M	0120	3.4	0645	0.1	1352	3.4	1912	0.2
28 TU	0159	3.5	0731	0.2	1436	3.4	2002	0.3
29 W	0239	3.6	0821	0.2	1522	3.3	2056	0.4
30 TH	0320	3.5	0916	0.3	1613	3.1	2155	0.6

TIDES

Chart Datum: 1·62 metres below Ordnance Datum (Newlyn)
HAT is 3·9 metres above Chart Datum

TIDES

TIME ZONE (UT)
For Summer Time add ONE hour in **non-shaded areas**

SCOTLAND – GREENOCK
LAT 55°57'N   LONG 4°46'W
TIMES AND HEIGHTS OF HIGH AND LOW WATERS

Dates in amber are **SPRINGS**
Dates in yellow are **NEAPS**

2009

MAY

Date	Time	m	Time	m	Time	m	Time	m
1 F	0406	3.3	1021	0.4	1715	2.9	2302	0.8
2 SA	0501	3.1	1137	0.5	1841	2.8		
3 SU	0015	0.9	0617	3.0	1254	0.5	2013	2.8
4 M	0128	0.8	0757	2.9	1403	0.4	☽2119	2.9
5 TU	0234	0.7	0914	3.1	1501	0.3	2211	3.1
6 W	0330	0.5	1009	3.2	1549	0.2	2257	3.2
7 TH	0418	0.3	1057	3.3	1631	0.2	2339	3.2
8 F	0500	0.2	1141	3.3	1709	0.3		
9 SA	0017	3.3	0538	0.2	1223	3.3	1744	0.4
10 SU	0052	3.3	0613	0.2	1301	3.3	1819	0.5
11 M	0124	3.4	0647	0.3	○1336	3.2	1854	0.5
12 TU	0156	3.4	0722	0.6	1412	3.2	1933	0.6
13 W	0230	3.4	0800	0.4	1449	3.1	2013	0.7
14 TH	0304	3.4	0842	0.5	1529	3.0	2056	0.8
15 F	0341	3.2	0930	0.6	1612	2.9	2143	0.9
16 SA	0422	3.1	1026	0.7	1701	2.8	2234	1.0
17 SU	0511	2.9	1131	0.7	1756	2.7	2334	1.1
18 M	0610	2.8	1238	0.7	1858	2.7 ☽		
19	0040	1.1	0720	2.8	1338	0.6	2008	2.7
20 W	0147	1.0	0834	2.8	1430	0.5	2112	2.8
21 TH	0245	0.9	0934	3.0	1516	0.3	2204	3.0
22 F	0334	0.7	1025	3.1	1558	0.2	2250	3.1
23 SA	0419	0.5	1113	3.2	1640	0.2	2333	3.2
24 SU	0502	0.3	1201	3.3	1724	0.2		
25 M	0016	3.4	0546	0.2	1250	3.3	1811	0.2
26 TU	0100	3.5	0633	0.1	●1340	3.3	1901	0.3
27 W	0144	3.6	0722	0.1	1431	3.3	1954	0.3
28 TH	0228	3.6	0815	0.1	1523	3.2	2049	0.4
29 F	0314	3.6	0912	0.1	1619	3.1	2146	0.6
30 SA	0402	3.5	1013	0.2	1721	3.0	2246	0.6
31 SU	0458	3.3	1118	0.3	1826	2.9	2348	0.7

JUNE

Date	Time	m	Time	m	Time	m	Time	m
1 M	0603	3.1	1224	0.4	1932	2.9		
2 TU	0052	0.7	0717	3.1	1329	0.4	☽2034	2.9
3 W	0158	0.7	0832	3.0	1427	0.4	2131	3.0
4 TH	0259	0.6	0936	3.1	1519	0.4	2222	3.0
5 F	0353	0.5	1029	3.1	1605	0.5	2308	3.1
6 SA	0439	0.4	1116	3.1	1647	0.5	2350	3.2
7 SU	0521	0.4	1159	3.1	1726	0.6		
8 M	0028	3.3	0558	0.5	1239	3.1	1802	0.6
9 TU	0103	3.4	0634	0.4	○1315	3.1	1838	0.6
10 W	0136	3.4	0709	0.4	1351	3.0	1916	0.7
11 TH	0209	3.4	0745	0.6	1429	3.0	1955	0.7
12 F	0243	3.4	0824	0.6	1509	3.0	2036	0.7
13 SA	0318	3.3	0905	0.5	1550	3.0	2118	0.7
14 SU	0356	3.2	0951	0.5	1634	2.9	2203	0.8
15 M	0438	3.1	1042	0.6	1720	2.9	2252	0.9
16 TU	0527	3.0	1139	0.6	1809	2.9	☽2347	0.9
17 W	0625	2.9	1237	0.6	1904	2.8		
18 TH	0048	1.0	0732	2.9	1336	0.5	2006	2.9
19 F	0154	0.9	0845	2.9	1433	0.5	2114	2.9
20 SA	0257	0.7	0951	3.0	1527	0.4	2214	3.1
21 SU	0354	0.5	1049	3.1	1618	0.3	2308	3.2
22 M	0446	0.3	1144	3.2	1709	0.3	2357	3.4
23 TU	0535	0.1	1239	3.2	1759	0.2		
24 W	0046	3.5	0623	0.0	1334	3.3	1851	0.3
25 TH	0134	3.6	0713	0.0	1428	3.2	●1942	0.3
26 F	0220	3.7	0804	0.0	1521	3.2	2034	0.3
27 SA	0306	3.7	0856	0.0	1613	3.2	2126	0.3
28 SU	0353	3.6	0949	0.1	1703	3.1	2219	0.4
29 M	0442	3.5	1046	0.2	1752	3.0	2315	0.5
30 TU	0533	3.3	1147	0.4	1842	2.9		

JULY

Date	Time	m	Time	m	Time	m	Time	m
1 W	0014	0.7	0628	3.1	1250	0.5	1937	2.9
2 TH	0121	0.8	0734	2.9	1353	0.6	2042	2.8
3 F	0229	0.8	0854	2.8	1452	0.7	2147	2.9
4 SA	0330	0.7	1004	2.9	1545	0.7	☽2243	3.1
5 SU	0422	0.5	1059	2.9	1631	0.7	2331	3.2
6 M	0507	0.4	1146	2.9	1713	0.7		
7 TU	0012	3.3	0546	0.4	1226	2.9	1750	0.7
8 W	0048	3.4	0621	0.4	1302	3.0	1824	0.7
9 TH	0121	3.4	0654	0.4	1336	3.0	1858	0.7
10 F	0152	3.4	0726	0.4	1411	3.0	1932	0.6
11 SA	0223	3.4	0759	0.4	1446	3.1	○2009	0.6
12 SU	0256	3.4	0834	0.4	1523	3.1	2048	0.6
13 M	0331	3.4	0913	0.4	1601	3.1	2129	0.6
14 TU	0408	3.3	0958	0.4	1641	3.1	2215	0.7
15 W	0449	3.1	1050	0.5	1724	3.0	2306	0.8
16 TH	0538	3.0	1148	0.6	1812	2.9		
17 F	0004	0.9	0641	2.9	1251	0.6	1910	2.9
18 SA	0113	0.9	0803	2.8	1359	0.6	☽2028	2.9
19 SU	0227	0.8	0929	2.8	1505	0.6	2147	3.0
20 M	0337	0.6	1039	3.0	1605	0.4	2250	3.2
21 TU	0435	0.3	1139	3.1	1658	0.3	2345	3.4
22 W	0525	0.1	1234	3.2	1748	0.2		
23 TH	0035	3.5	0612	-0.1	1328	3.2	1836	0.2
24 F	0123	3.7	0658	-0.1	1419	3.3	1924	0.2
25 SA	0209	3.7	0744	-0.1	1506	3.3	2011	0.2
26 SU	0253	3.7	0830	0.0	1549	3.2	●2058	0.2
27 M	0335	3.7	0917	0.1	1629	3.2	2146	0.3
28 TU	0417	3.6	1006	0.3	1707	3.1	2236	0.5
29 W	0459	3.3	1100	0.5	1747	3.0	2333	0.7
30 TH	0543	3.1	1204	0.8	1833	2.9		
31 F	0042	0.8	0634	2.8	1320	0.9	1934	2.8

AUGUST

Date	Time	m	Time	m	Time	m	Time	m
1 SA	0203	0.9	0743	2.6	1430	1.0	2111	2.8
2 SU	0311	0.8	0950	2.6	1528	0.9	☽2224	3.0
3 M	0405	0.6	1051	2.8	1617	0.8	2314	3.2
4 TU	0450	0.5	1136	2.9	1658	0.7	2355	3.3
5 W	0528	0.4	1213	2.9	1734	0.7		
6 TH	0031	3.4	0602	0.3	1247	3.0	1805	0.6
7 F	0103	3.4	0633	0.3	1318	3.0	1833	0.6
8 SA	0131	3.4	0700	0.3	1348	3.1	1903	0.6
9 SU	0200	3.4	0728	0.3	1419	3.1	○1937	0.5
10 M	0232	3.5	0800	0.3	1452	3.2	2015	0.5
11 TU	0306	3.5	0837	0.3	1527	3.2	2056	0.5
12 W	0342	3.4	0921	0.4	1604	3.2	2141	0.6
13 TH	0420	3.3	1011	0.5	1644	3.1	2231	0.7
14 F	0503	3.1	1110	0.7	1731	3.0	2331	0.9
15 SA	0601	2.9	1218	0.8	1828	2.9		
16 SU	0043	1.0	0732	2.7	1339	0.9	1952	2.9
17 M	0211	0.9	0926	2.8	1456	0.7	☽2131	3.0
18 TU	0329	0.6	1040	3.0	1556	0.5	2240	3.2
19 W	0425	0.3	1135	3.2	1647	0.3	2334	3.5
20 TH	0512	0.0	1225	3.3	1733	0.2		
21 F	0022	3.6	0555	-0.1	1313	3.3	1817	0.1
22 SA	0108	3.7	0637	-0.1	1357	3.3	1900	0.1
23 SU	0152	3.8	0718	-0.1	1438	3.3	1943	0.2
24 M	0232	3.8	0758	0.0	1514	3.3	2025	0.2
25 TU	0311	3.7	0840	0.2	1547	3.3	●2108	0.3
26 W	0348	3.6	0922	0.4	1621	3.2	2154	0.5
27 TH	0426	3.3	1010	0.7	1659	3.1	2248	0.7
28 F	0507	3.0	1108	1.0	1744	2.9		
29 SA	0004	0.9	0555	2.7	1245	1.2	1840	2.8
30 SU	0139	1.0	0657	2.5	1409	1.2	2021	2.8
31 M	0248	0.9	0939	2.5	1508	1.1	2200	3.0

Chart Datum: 1·62 metres below Ordnance Datum (Newlyn)
HAT is 3·9 metres above Chart Datum

TIME ZONE (UT)	SCOTLAND – GREENOCK	Dates in amber are SPRINGS
For Summer Time add ONE hour in **non-shaded areas**	LAT 55°57′N LONG 4°46′W	Dates in yellow are NEAPS
	TIMES AND HEIGHTS OF HIGH AND LOW WATERS	**2009**

SEPTEMBER

Time	m	Time	m
1 TU 0341 1556 2249	0.7 0.9 3.2	**16** W 0319 1545 2227	0.6 0.6 3.3
1 TU 1035	2.7	**16** W 1033	3.1
2 W 0425 1636 2329	0.5 0.7 3.3	**17** TH 0411 1632 2317	0.2 0.4 3.6
2 W 1114	2.9	**17** TH 1121	3.3
3 TH 0502 1709	0.3 0.6	**18** F 0454 1206 1715	0.0 3.4 0.2
3 TH 1148	3.0	**18** F	
4 ○ 0004 0534 1221 1738	3.4 0.3 3.1 0.6	**19** SA 0003 0534 1249 1755	3.7 0.0 3.4 0.2
5 SA 0036 0603 1251 1804	3.4 0.3 3.1 0.6	**20** SU 0047 0612 1328 1835	3.7 0.2 3.4 0.2
6 SU 0105 0603 1319 1832	3.4 0.3 3.2 0.5	**21** M 0129 0650 1403 1913	3.8 0.1 3.4 0.2
7 M 0135 0656 1348 1906	3.5 0.3 3.3 0.5	**22** TU 0207 0727 1435 1952	3.7 0.3 3.4 0.3
8 TU 0208 0729 1421 1945	3.5 0.3 3.4 0.4	**23** W 0244 0805 1508 2033	3.6 0.4 3.4 0.4
9 W 0244 0808 1456 2027	3.5 0.3 3.4 0.5	**24** TH 0320 0845 1543 2116	3.5 0.5 3.3 0.6
10 TH 0320 0852 1533 2113	3.5 0.4 3.4 0.6	**25** F 0357 0928 1622 2209	3.3 0.9 3.2 0.8
11 F 0359 0943 1614 2206	3.3 0.6 3.3 0.7	**26** SA ◑ 0439 1019 1707 2324	3.0 1.2 3.0 1.0
12 SA ◑ 0442 1044 1701 2309	3.1 0.9 3.0 0.9	**27** SU 0528 1143 1803	2.7 1.4 2.9
13 SU 0541 1159 1800	2.8 1.0 3.0	**28** M 0106 0631 1335 1925	1.1 2.5 1.4 2.8
14 M 0031 0728 1332 1933	1.0 2.7 1.1 2.9	**29** TU 0216 0849 1437 2119	0.9 2.6 1.2 3.0
15 TU 0207 0933 1448 2122	1.0 2.8 0.9 3.1	**30** W 0308 0958 1526 2213	0.7 2.8 1.0 3.2

OCTOBER

Time	m	Time	m
1 TH 0351 1605 2253	0.5 0.8 3.3	**16** F 0349 1613 2254	0.3 0.4 3.6
1 TH 1039	3.0	**16** F 1058	3.4
2 F 0429 1638 2328	0.4 0.7 3.4	**17** SA 0432 1655 2339	0.2 0.3 3.7
2 F 1114	3.1	**17** SA 1140	3.5
3 SA 0502 1707	0.3 0.6	**18** SU 0512 1735	0.2 0.3
3 SA 1147	3.2	**18** SU 1219	3.5
4 ○ 0001 0530 1218 1733	3.4 0.3 3.3 0.6	**19** M 0023 0548 1257 1812	3.7 0.3 3.5 0.3
5 SU 0035 0557 1247 1805	3.5 0.4 3.3 0.5	**20** TU 0104 0624 1330 1848	3.7 0.4 3.5 0.3
6 M 0109 0628 1319 1841	3.5 0.4 3.5 0.5	**21** W 0142 0700 1403 1926	3.6 0.5 3.5 0.4
7 TU 0147 0705 1355 1922	3.5 0.4 3.6 0.4	**22** TH 0218 0737 1437 2005	3.5 0.6 3.5 0.5
8 W 0225 0748 1432 2006	3.5 0.5 3.6 0.5	**23** F 0255 0817 1513 2049	3.4 0.8 3.5 0.7
9 TH 0305 0835 1511 2055	3.5 0.6 3.6 0.6	**24** SA 0334 0859 1552 2140	3.2 1.0 3.4 0.8
10 F 0347 0928 1553 2152	3.3 0.8 3.5 0.7	**25** SU 0416 0947 1636 2246	3.0 1.2 3.2 1.0
11 SA ◑ 0436 1032 1642 2302	3.1 1.0 3.4 0.9	**26** M ● 0506 1050 1730	2.8 1.4 3.0
12 SU 0544 1152 1747	2.9 1.2 3.3	**27** TU 0013 0608 1224 1838	1.1 2.7 1.5 2.9
13 M 0029 0745 1319 1924	0.9 2.8 1.1 3.0	**28** W 0128 0736 1346 2008	1.0 2.7 1.4 3.0
14 TU 0154 0918 1430 2102	0.8 3.0 0.9 3.2	**29** TH 0224 0859 1441 2119	0.9 2.9 1.2 3.1
15 W 0259 1012 1526 2204	0.6 3.2 0.7 3.4	**30** F 0311 0952 1525 2207	0.7 3.2 1.0 3.3
		31 SA 0350 1034 1601 2248	0.5 3.2 0.9 3.4

NOVEMBER

Time	m	Time	m
1 SU 0425 1634 2326	0.5 0.7 3.4	**16** M 0450 1717	0.5 0.4
1 SU 1111	3.3	**16** M ●	
2 M ○ 0458 1707	0.4 0.6	**17** TU 0000 0528 1230 1754	3.6 0.5 3.6 0.4
2 M 1145	3.4	**17** TU	
3 TU 0005 0530 1219 1743	3.5 0.4 3.5 0.5	**18** W 0042 0605 1305 1831	3.5 0.4 3.6 0.5
4 W 0047 0607 1256 1823	3.5 0.4 3.6 0.5	**19** TH 0120 0641 1339 1908	3.3 0.7 3.7 0.6
5 TH 0129 0649 1335 1907	3.5 0.5 3.7 0.4	**20** F 0157 0718 1414 1947	3.4 0.8 3.7 0.6
6 F 0213 0735 1415 1955	3.5 0.6 3.8 0.5	**21** SA 0235 0758 1450 2029	3.3 0.9 3.6 0.7
7 SA 0257 0826 1457 2047	3.5 0.7 3.7 0.6	**22** SU 0315 0839 1528 2116	3.2 1.0 3.5 0.8
8 SU 0345 0922 1543 2147	3.3 0.8 3.6 0.7	**23** M 0358 0923 1610 2209	3.1 1.1 3.4 0.9
9 M ◑ 0440 1025 1635 2257	3.1 1.0 3.5 0.8	**24** TU ◐ 0445 1013 1657 2311	3.0 1.3 3.2 1.0
10 TU 0553 1137 1740	0.5 1.1 3.3	**25** W 0538 1114 1753	0.5 1.4 3.1
11 W ● 0013 0727 1252 1903	0.8 2.9 1.1 3.2	**26** TH 0019 0640 1220 1856	1.0 2.9 1.4 3.0
12 TH 0127 0844 1401 2029	0.7 3.1 1.0 3.3	**27** F 0124 0750 1330 2006	1.0 2.9 1.4 3.0
13 F 0231 0941 1500 2135	0.6 3.2 0.8 3.4	**28** SA 0219 0855 1430 2111	0.9 3.0 1.2 3.1
14 SA 0323 1029 1551 2228	0.5 3.4 0.8 3.5	**29** SU 0306 0949 1519 2206	0.7 3.1 1.0 3.3
15 SU 0409 1112 1636 2315	0.4 3.5 0.5 3.6	**30** M 0348 1034 1603 2254	0.6 3.3 0.8 3.4

DECEMBER

Time	m	Time	m
1 TU 0428 1644 2341	0.5 0.7 3.4	**16** W 0515 1744	0.7 0.5
1 TU 1116	3.4	**16** W 1212 ●	3.6
2 W 0509 1727	0.5 0.5	**17** TH 0028 0553 1250 1821	3.3 0.8 3.6 0.5
2 W ○ 1156	3.6	**17** TH	
3 TH 0029 0551 1238 1810	3.5 0.5 3.7 0.4	**18** F 0107 0629 1325 1857	3.3 0.8 3.7 0.5
4 F 0117 0638 1321 1857	3.5 0.5 3.8 0.4	**19** SA 0144 0704 1358 1933	3.3 0.8 3.7 0.6
5 SA 0206 0727 1405 1947	3.5 0.5 3.9 0.4	**20** SU 0221 0740 1433 2010	3.2 0.8 3.7 0.6
6 SU 0255 0818 1450 2040	3.4 0.6 3.9 0.4	**21** M 0258 0818 1508 2049	3.2 0.8 3.6 0.7
7 M 0346 0912 1537 2137	3.3 0.7 3.8 0.5	**22** TU 0338 0857 1545 2132	3.2 0.9 3.5 0.7
8 TU 0441 1009 1629 2238	3.2 0.8 3.7 0.6	**23** W 0418 0938 1625 2218	3.1 1.0 3.4 0.8
9 W ◐ 0542 1111 1726 2344	3.1 0.9 3.5 0.7	**24** TH 0501 1024 1710 2310	3.1 1.1 3.2 0.9
10 TH 0649 1217 1831	0.9 1.0 3.4	**25** F 0547 1116 1802	3.0 1.2 3.1
11 F 0052 0756 1326 1944	0.7 3.1 1.0 3.3	**26** SA 0009 0639 1218 1902	1.0 3.0 1.3 3.0
12 SA 0158 0900 1431 2059	0.7 3.1 0.9 3.3	**27** SU 0113 0743 1327 2014	1.0 2.9 1.3 3.0
13 SU 0256 0957 1529 2202	0.7 3.2 0.8 3.3	**28** M 0216 0855 1435 2127	0.9 3.0 1.1 3.1
14 M 0348 1047 1619 2256	0.7 3.4 0.6 3.3	**29** TU 0313 0958 1535 2230	0.8 3.2 0.9 3.2
15 TU 0433 1132 1703 2344	0.7 3.5 0.6 3.3	**30** W 0405 1051 1626 2326	0.7 3.4 0.7 3.3
		31 TH ○ 0453 1138 1714	0.5 3.4 0.4

Chart Datum: 1·62 metres below Ordnance Datum (Newlyn)
HAT is 3·9 metres above Chart Datum

TIDES

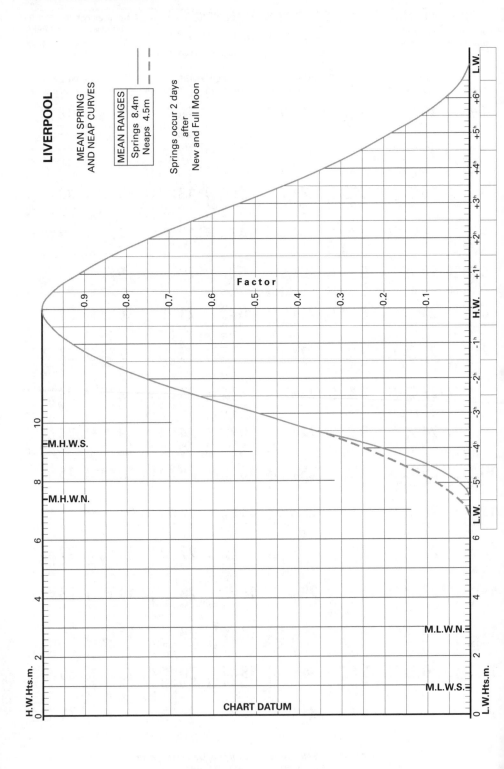

LIVERPOOL

MEAN SPRING
AND NEAP CURVES

MEAN RANGES
Springs 8.4m
Neaps 4.5m

Springs occur 2 days
after
New and Full Moon

Factor

0.9
0.8
0.7
0.6
0.5
0.4
0.3
0.2
0.1

L.W. +6ʰ +5ʰ +4ʰ +3ʰ +2ʰ +1ʰ H.W. -1ʰ -2ʰ -3ʰ -4ʰ -5ʰ L.W.

M.H.W.S.
M.H.W.N.

M.L.W.N.
M.L.W.S.

H.W.Hts.m.
L.W.Hts.m.

10
8
6
4
2
0

CHART DATUM

ENGLAND – LIVERPOOL (ALFRED DK)

LAT 53°24'N   LONG 3°01'W

TIMES AND HEIGHTS OF HIGH AND LOW WATERS

Dates in amber are **SPRINGS**
Dates in yellow are **NEAPS**

2009

JANUARY

Day	Time m	Time m	Time m	Time m
1 TH	0143 8.5	0809 2.1	1401 8.8	2038 2.0
16 F	0238 9.0	0909 1.5	1456 9.2	2147 1.3
2 F	0221 8.4	0846 2.3	1440 8.7	2116 2.1
17 SA	0320 8.6	0950 2.0	1539 8.7	2228 1.9
3 SA	0302 8.2	0927 2.5	1524 8.5	2157 2.3
18 SU	0405 8.1	1034 2.5	1627 8.1	◐ 2314 2.6
4 SU	0348 8.0	1015 2.7	1614 8.3	◐ 2248 2.6
19 M	0457 7.6	1127 3.0	1724 7.5	
5 M	0444 7.8	1113 2.9	1713 8.1	2352 2.7
20 TU	0009 3.0	0605 7.2	1231 3.3	1840 7.2
6 TU	0549 7.6	1226 3.0	1820 8.0	
21 W	0116 3.3	0725 7.2	1346 3.3	2001 7.2
7 W	0109 2.7	0701 7.8	1347 2.8	1931 8.1
22 TH	0229 3.2	0833 7.6	1507 3.1	2105 7.6
8 TH	0225 2.5	0813 8.1	1502 2.4	2043 8.5
23 F	0333 2.9	0927 8.0	1607 2.7	2154 7.9
9 F	0333 2.4	0916 8.7	1609 1.8	2147 8.9
24 SA	0423 2.5	1011 8.5	1652 2.3	2236 8.3
10 SA	0432 1.6	1013 9.2	1708 1.4	2243 9.3
25 SU	0503 2.1	1050 8.8	1731 1.9	2312 8.5
11 SU	0526 1.2	1104 9.6	1802 0.7	○ 2335 9.5
26 M	0540 1.9	1126 9.0	1806 1.7	● 2346 8.7
12 M	0616 1.0	1154 9.9	1853 0.4	
27 TU	0614 1.7	1159 9.1	1840 1.5	
13 TU	0023 9.7	0703 0.9	1242 10.0	1940 0.3
28 W	0017 8.8	0647 1.6	1232 9.1	1913 1.4
14 W	0110 9.6	0747 0.9	1328 9.9	2024 0.5
29 TH	0050 8.8	0719 1.6	1305 9.2	1945 1.4
15 TH	0155 9.4	0829 1.1	1412 9.7	2106 0.8
30 F	0123 8.9	0751 1.6	1339 9.2	2016 1.5
31 SA	0157 8.8	0824 1.7	1416 9.1	2047 1.6

FEBRUARY

Day	Time m	Time m	Time m	Time m
1 SU	0233 8.7	0859 1.9	1455 8.9	2122 1.9
16 M	0318 8.2	0951 2.3	1539 8.1	◐ 2221 2.7
2 M	0314 8.4	0938 2.3	1540 8.6	◐ 2204 2.3
17 TU	0401 7.7	1037 2.9	1628 7.4	2313 3.3
3 TU	0404 8.0	1030 2.7	1637 8.1	2302 2.8
18 W	0459 7.1	1142 3.4	1741 6.8	
4 W	0510 7.6	1144 3.1	1748 7.7	
19 TH	0024 3.6	0635 6.9	1301 3.6	1929 6.8
5 TH	0027 3.1	0630 7.4	1322 3.0	1912 7.7
20 F	0145 3.6	0805 7.2	1431 3.3	2043 7.2
6 F	0203 2.9	0756 7.8	1452 2.5	2036 8.0
21 SA	0307 3.2	0904 7.7	1547 2.8	2134 7.7
7 SA	0323 2.4	0909 8.4	1604 1.8	2143 8.6
22 SU	0404 2.6	0949 8.3	1633 2.2	2214 8.2
8 SU	0426 1.7	1006 9.1	1702 1.1	2236 9.2
23 M	0446 2.1	1028 8.7	1710 1.8	2250 8.6
9 M	0519 1.2	1055 9.6	1753 0.5	○ 2323 9.6
24 TU	0522 1.7	1103 9.0	1744 1.4	● 2323 8.8
10 TU	0606 0.8	1140 10.0	1839 0.0	
25 W	0555 1.5	1136 9.2	1817 1.2	2354 9.0
11 W	0007 9.7	0649 0.6	1224 10.1	1921 0.1
26 TH	0627 1.3	1208 9.3	1849 1.1	
12 TH	0049 9.7	0729 0.6	1305 10.0	2000 0.3
27 F	0025 9.1	0658 1.2	1241 9.4	1920 1.0
13 F	0128 9.5	0806 0.8	1344 9.7	2037 0.7
28 SA	0058 9.1	0730 1.2	1315 9.4	1950 1.1
14 SA	0205 9.2	0841 1.2	1422 9.3	2110 1.3
15 SU	0241 8.8	0915 1.7	1459 8.7	2144 2.0

MARCH

Day	Time m	Time m	Time m	Time m
1 SU	0131 9.1	0802 1.3	1352 9.3	2020 1.4
16 M	0205 8.8	0840 1.7	1424 8.6	2059 2.1
2 M	0207 8.9	0836 1.6	1431 9.0	2054 1.7
17 TU	0240 8.3	0912 2.2	1502 8.0	2130 2.7
3 TU	0248 8.6	0915 2.0	1517 8.5	2136 2.3
18 W	0319 7.8	0954 2.8	1547 7.3	◐ 2218 3.3
4 W	0337 8.1	1007 2.5	1615 7.9	◐ 2235 2.9
19 TH	0410 7.2	1059 3.3	1651 6.7	2336 3.7
5 TH	0445 7.5	1126 3.0	1733 7.4	
20 F	0537 6.8	1221 3.5	1846 6.5	
6 F	0004 3.3	0615 7.3	1315 3.0	1909 7.4
21 SA	0101 3.7	0724 7.0	1344 3.3	2008 7.0
7 SA	0153 3.1	0750 7.7	1448 2.4	2033 7.9
22 SU	0225 3.3	0828 7.5	1503 2.8	2101 7.6
8 SU	0317 2.4	0900 8.4	1556 1.6	2134 8.6
23 M	0328 2.7	0916 8.1	1554 2.2	2142 8.1
9 M	0416 1.7	0953 9.1	1649 0.8	2222 9.2
24 TU	0413 2.2	0955 8.6	1634 1.7	2218 8.5
10 TU	0504 1.1	1039 9.6	1735 0.3	○ 2305 9.6
25 W	0450 1.7	1031 8.9	1710 1.3	● 2251 8.9
11 W	0548 0.7	1121 9.9	1817 0.1	2345 9.7
26 TH	0525 1.3	1105 9.2	1745 1.0	2324 9.1
12 TH	0628 0.5	1201 10.0	1855 0.2	
27 F	0600 1.1	1139 9.4	1819 0.9	2357 9.2
13 F	0022 9.6	0704 0.5	1239 9.8	1930 0.4
28 SA	0635 0.9	1215 9.5	1852 0.9	
14 SA	0058 9.5	0739 0.8	1315 9.5	2003 0.9
29 SU	0032 9.3	0709 0.9	1253 9.5	1925 1.0
15 SU	0131 9.2	0811 1.2	1349 9.1	2032 1.5
30 M	0109 9.3	0744 1.1	1332 9.3	1959 1.3
31 TU	0148 9.1	0822 1.4	1416 8.9	2037 1.7

APRIL

Day	Time m	Time m	Time m	Time m
1 W	0232 8.7	0906 1.8	1505 8.4	2123 2.3
16 TH	0250 7.9	0923 2.7	1517 7.4	2138 3.2
2 TH	0326 8.1	1004 2.4	1608 7.8	◐ 2226 2.9
17 F	0338 7.4	1023 3.1	1614 6.9	◐ 2249 3.6
3 F	0437 7.6	1129 2.8	1731 7.3	2358 3.2
18 SA	0445 7.0	1139 3.3	1743 6.6	
4 SA	0609 7.5	1309 2.7	1904 7.5	
19 SU	0012 3.6	0623 7.0	1252 3.1	1914 6.9
5 SU	0141 3.0	0734 7.8	1434 2.1	2017 8.0
20 M	0126 3.3	0736 7.4	1400 2.7	2013 7.4
6 M	0259 2.3	0839 8.5	1536 1.4	2113 8.6
21 TU	0231 2.8	0829 7.9	1458 2.2	2058 7.9
7 TU	0355 1.7	0931 9.0	1626 0.9	2159 9.1
22 W	0323 2.3	0912 8.4	1547 1.7	2137 8.4
8 W	0441 1.2	1017 9.4	1710 0.6	2240 9.3
23 TH	0408 1.8	0952 8.8	1630 1.3	2214 8.8
9 TH	0523 0.9	1058 9.6	1749 0.5	○ 2318 9.4
24 F	0450 1.4	1031 9.1	1710 1.0	○ 2251 9.1
10 F	0602 0.8	1136 9.5	1825 0.6	2353 9.4
25 SA	0530 1.0	1110 9.4	1749 0.9	● 2329 9.3
11 SA	0638 0.8	1212 9.4	1858 0.9	
26 SU	0611 0.9	1151 9.5	1827 0.8	
12 SU	0027 9.2	0711 1.0	1246 9.1	1928 1.3
27 M	0009 9.4	0652 0.6	1235 9.4	1905 1.0
13 M	0101 9.0	0742 1.3	1320 8.8	1955 1.7
28 TU	0052 9.3	0733 0.9	1320 9.2	1945 1.3
14 TU	0134 8.8	0811 1.7	1355 8.4	2020 2.2
29 W	0137 9.1	0818 1.2	1409 8.9	2028 1.7
15 W	0210 8.3	0842 2.2	1433 7.9	2052 2.7
30 TH	0227 8.8	0910 1.6	1503 8.4	2120 2.2

Chart Datum: 4·93 metres below Ordnance Datum (Newlyn)
HAT is 10·5m above Chart Datum

TIDES

TIME ZONE (UT)
For Summer Time add ONE hour in **non-shaded areas**

ENGLAND – LIVERPOOL (ALFRED DK)

LAT 53°24′N   LONG 3°01′W

TIMES AND HEIGHTS OF HIGH AND LOW WATERS

Dates in amber are **SPRINGS**
Dates in yellow are NEAPS

2009

MAY

1	0325 8.3 / 1013 2.0 / F 1608 7.9 / 2226 2.7	16	0314 7.8 / 0954 2.7 / SA 1544 7.3 / 2210 3.2
2	0435 8.0 / 1129 2.3 / SA 1724 7.6 / 2347 2.9	17	0408 7.5 / 1055 2.9 / SU 1645 7.0 / 2319 3.3
3	0553 7.9 / 1250 2.2 / SU 1841 7.7	18	0513 7.3 / 1200 2.9 / M 1759 7.1
4	0113 2.7 / 0706 8.0 / M 1404 1.9 / 1947 8.0	19	0028 3.2 / 0624 7.5 / TU 1303 2.6 / 1908 7.3
5	0227 2.3 / 0809 8.4 / TU 1506 1.6 / 2043 8.4	20	0132 2.9 / 0727 7.8 / W 1404 2.3 / 2004 7.8
6	0325 1.9 / 0903 8.7 / W 1557 1.3 / 2131 8.8	21	0231 2.4 / 0821 8.2 / TH 1500 1.9 / 2052 8.3
7	0413 1.5 / 0951 9.0 / TH 1640 1.1 / 2213 9.0	22	0325 2.0 / 0910 8.6 / F 1551 1.5 / 2137 8.7
8	0455 1.3 / 1033 9.0 / F 1718 1.1 / 2251 9.1	23	0416 1.5 / 0958 9.0 / SA 1639 1.2 / 2221 9.1
9	0534 1.2 / 1112 9.0 / SA 1753 1.2 / 2327 9.1	24	0505 1.2 / 1045 9.2 / SU 1724 1.0 / 2306 9.3
10	0611 1.3 / 1148 8.9 / SU 1826 1.4	25	0553 0.9 / 1133 9.4 / M 1809 1.0 / 2352 9.4
11	0001 9.0 / 0645 1.4 / M 1223 8.7 / 1856 1.6	26	0642 0.8 / 1222 9.4 / TU 1853 1.0 ●
12	0035 8.9 / 0717 1.6 / TU 1257 8.5 / 1924 1.9	27	0040 9.4 / 0730 0.8 / W 1313 9.2 / 1939 1.2
13	0111 8.7 / 0749 1.8 / W 1334 8.3 / 1953 2.2	28	0131 9.3 / 0821 0.9 / TH 1405 9.0 / 2027 1.5
14	0148 8.4 / 0823 2.1 / TH 1412 8.0 / 2028 2.5	29	0224 9.1 / 0914 1.2 / F 1459 8.7 / 2119 1.9
15	0228 8.1 / 0903 2.4 / F 1455 7.6 / 2112 2.9	30	0320 8.8 / 1011 1.5 / SA 1557 8.3 / 2217 2.2
		31	0420 8.5 / 1111 1.7 / SU 1700 8.0 / 2322 2.5

JUNE

1	0525 8.2 / 1215 2.0 / M 1806 7.9	16	0427 7.9 / 1109 2.6 / TU 1658 7.5 / ☽ 2333 3.0
2	0031 2.6 / 0630 8.1 / TU 1322 2.1 / ☽ 1910 7.9	17	0525 7.8 / 1210 2.6 / W 1801 7.5
3	0142 2.5 / 0734 8.1 / W 1426 2.0 / 2009 8.1	18	0039 2.9 / 0627 7.9 / TH 1315 2.5 / 1906 7.7
4	0248 2.3 / 0833 8.2 / TH 1522 1.9 / 2101 8.3	19	0146 2.6 / 0731 8.1 / F 1419 2.2 / 2009 8.1
5	0342 2.1 / 0925 8.4 / F 1608 1.8 / 2147 8.5	20	0251 2.2 / 0834 8.4 / SA 1520 1.9 / 2106 8.5
6	0429 1.9 / 1011 8.5 / SA 1648 1.8 / 2228 8.7	21	0351 1.8 / 0932 8.7 / SU 1615 1.5 / 2158 9.0
7	0510 1.8 / 1053 8.5 / SU 1725 1.8 / 2306 8.8	22	0448 1.3 / 1028 9.1 / M 1707 1.2 / 2249 9.3
8	0549 1.7 / 1130 8.5 / M 1800 1.8 / 2342 8.8	23	0543 0.9 / 1121 9.3 / TU 1758 1.0 / 2340 9.5
9	0625 1.7 / 1206 8.5 / TU 1832 1.9 ○	24	0636 0.7 / 1213 9.4 / W 1847 1.0
10	0017 8.8 / 0700 1.8 / W 1241 8.4 / 1903 2.0	25	0031 9.6 / 0727 0.5 / TH 1304 9.4 / ● 1935 1.0
11	0054 8.7 / 0734 1.9 / TH 1317 8.3 / 1935 2.1	26	0122 9.6 / 0817 0.5 / F 1354 9.3 / 2022 1.2
12	0131 8.6 / 0808 2.0 / F 1354 8.2 / 2011 2.3	27	0212 9.5 / 0906 0.7 / SA 1444 9.1 / 2109 1.4
13	0209 8.4 / 0845 2.1 / SA 1433 8.0 / 2051 2.5	28	0302 9.2 / 0953 1.0 / SU 1533 8.7 / 2157 1.8
14	0250 8.2 / 0927 2.3 / SU 1515 7.8 / 2137 2.7	29	0354 8.8 / 1042 1.5 / M 1625 8.3 / 2248 2.2
15	0335 8.0 / 1014 2.4 / M 1603 7.6 / 2231 2.9	30	0448 8.4 / 1134 2.0 / TU 1723 7.9 / 2346 2.6

JULY

1	0549 8.0 / 1231 2.4 / W 1827 7.6	16	0441 8.0 / 1115 2.6 / TH 1712 7.6 / 2350 3.0
2	0051 2.8 / 0655 7.7 / TH 1336 2.6 / 1932 7.6	17	0544 7.9 / 1227 2.8 / F 1822 7.6
3	0203 2.8 / 0803 7.7 / F 1442 2.6 / 2033 7.8	18	0110 2.9 / 0655 7.8 / SA 1346 2.6 / ☽ 1935 7.8
4	0313 2.6 / 0903 7.8 / SA 1538 2.5 / ☽ 2126 8.1	19	0227 2.5 / 0809 8.1 / SU 1457 2.3 / 2044 8.3
5	0408 2.4 / 0954 8.0 / SU 1625 2.3 / 2211 8.4	20	0337 2.0 / 0918 8.5 / M 1601 1.8 / 2144 8.9
6	0453 2.1 / 1038 8.2 / M 1705 2.1 / 2251 8.7	21	0439 1.3 / 1017 9.0 / TU 1658 1.3 / 2238 9.4
7	0534 1.9 / 1117 8.3 / TU 1742 2.0 / 2328 8.8	22	0535 0.8 / 1111 9.3 / W 1750 1.0 / 2329 9.8
8	0611 1.8 / 1153 8.4 / W 1816 1.9	23	0628 0.4 / 1201 9.6 / TH 1838 0.8
9	0003 8.8 / 0646 1.7 / TH 1227 8.4 / 1848 1.9	24	0017 9.9 / 0716 0.1 / F 1249 9.6 / 1924 0.7
10	0038 8.8 / 0719 1.7 / F 1300 8.5 / 1920 1.9	25	0105 10.0 / 0802 0.2 / SA 1335 9.6 / 2007 0.8
11	0112 8.8 / 0751 1.7 / SA 1333 8.4 / ○ 1953 1.9	26	0151 9.8 / 0845 0.4 / SU 1419 9.3 / ● 2047 1.1
12	0147 8.7 / 0824 1.8 / SU 1408 8.4 / 2028 2.1	27	0235 9.5 / 0926 0.9 / M 1501 8.9 / 2128 1.6
13	0224 8.6 / 0858 1.9 / M 1444 8.3 / 2106 2.3	28	0320 8.9 / 1006 1.5 / TU 1545 8.4 / 2212 2.1
14	0303 8.5 / 0936 2.1 / TU 1525 8.1 / 2149 2.5	29	0406 8.3 / 1050 2.2 / W 1634 7.8 / 2303 2.7
15	0348 8.3 / 1019 2.3 / W 1613 7.8 / 2241 2.8	30	0501 7.7 / 1143 2.8 / TH 1736 7.4
		31	0006 3.1 / 0613 7.2 / F 1247 3.2 / 1855 7.2

AUGUST

1	0122 3.3 / 0736 7.1 / SA 1401 3.2 / 2009 7.5	16	0047 3.1 / 0634 7.5 / SU 1323 3.0 / 1916 7.6
2	0250 3.1 / 0845 7.4 / SU 1514 3.0 / ☽ 2107 7.9	17	0216 2.7 / 0800 7.8 / M 1446 2.6 / ☽ 2034 8.2
3	0356 2.6 / 0938 7.8 / M 1608 2.6 / 2154 8.4	18	0330 2.0 / 0911 8.2 / TU 1553 1.9 / 2135 9.0
4	0441 2.2 / 1022 8.1 / TU 1650 2.2 / 2234 8.7	19	0431 1.2 / 1008 9.0 / W 1648 1.3 / 2226 9.6
5	0520 1.9 / 1100 8.4 / W 1727 1.9 / 2311 8.9	20	0524 0.5 / 1058 9.5 / TH 1738 0.8 / 2313 10.0
6	0555 1.7 / 1134 8.5 / TH 1801 1.8 / 2344 9.0	21	0612 0.1 / 1143 9.7 / F 1823 0.6 / 2358 10.1
7	0627 1.5 / 1206 8.6 / F 1832 1.7	22	0656 0.0 / 1226 9.8 / SA 1905 0.5
8	0016 9.0 / 0658 1.5 / SA 1237 8.7 / 1901 1.6	23	0041 10.1 / 0737 0.1 / SU 1308 9.6 / 1944 0.7
9	0048 9.0 / 0728 1.4 / SU 1308 8.7 / ○ 1932 1.6	24	0123 9.8 / 0816 0.5 / M 1347 9.3 / 2020 1.0
10	0121 9.0 / 0758 1.5 / M 1340 8.7 / 2004 1.7	25	0203 9.4 / 0852 1.1 / TU 1425 8.9 / ● 2056 1.5
11	0155 8.9 / 0828 1.6 / TU 1413 8.6 / 2037 1.9	26	0242 8.8 / 0927 1.7 / W 1503 8.4 / 2135 2.2
12	0231 8.8 / 0901 1.9 / W 1451 8.4 / 2114 2.3	27	0323 8.0 / 1006 2.5 / TH 1545 7.8 / 2222 2.8
13	0314 8.5 / 0939 2.3 / TH 1536 8.1 / 2200 2.7	28	0412 7.4 / 1057 3.1 / F 1642 7.3 / 2326 3.4
14	0407 8.1 / 1030 2.7 / F 1635 7.7 / 2309 3.1	29	0527 6.9 / 1205 3.6 / SA 1815 7.0
15	0514 7.7 / 1147 3.1 / SA 1751 7.5	30	0047 3.5 / 0710 6.8 / SU 1326 3.6 / 1942 7.3
		31	0227 3.3 / 0823 7.2 / M 1450 3.2 / 2043 7.8

Chart Datum: 4·93 metres below Ordnance Datum (Newlyn)
HAT is 10·5m above Chart Datum

TIME ZONE (UT)
For Summer Time add ONE hour in **non-shaded areas**

ENGLAND – LIVERPOOL (ALFRED DK)
LAT 53°24'N   LONG 3°01'W
TIMES AND HEIGHTS OF HIGH AND LOW WATERS

Dates in amber are **SPRINGS**
Dates in yellow are **NEAPS**

2009

SEPTEMBER

Day	Time m	Time m	Time m	Time m	Day	Time m	Time m	Time m	Time m
1 TU	0336 2.7	0915 7.7	1547 2.7	2130 8.3	**16** W	0321 1.8	0901 8.5	1541 1.9	2121 9.1
2 W	0419 2.2	0958 8.2	1629 2.2	2210 8.8	**17** TH	0417 1.0	0953 9.1	1633 1.2	2209 9.7
3 TH	0455 1.8	1034 8.5	1705 1.9	2246 8.9	**18** F	0505 0.4	1038 9.6	1719 0.8	● 2253 10.0
4 F	0528 1.5	1108 8.7	1737 1.6	○ 2318 9.2	**19** SA	0549 0.2	1120 9.8	1801 0.6	2335 10.1
5 SA	0559 1.3	1138 8.8	1808 1.5	2349 9.2	**20** SU	0630 0.2	1200 9.7	1841 0.6	
6 SU	0629 1.2	1208 8.9	1838 1.4		**21** M	0015 9.9	0708 0.4	1238 9.6	1917 0.8
7 M	0020 9.2	0659 1.2	1239 9.0	1908 1.4	**22** TU	0053 9.6	0743 0.8	1314 9.3	1952 1.2
8 TU	0052 9.2	0729 1.5	1310 8.9	1940 1.5	**23** W	0130 9.2	0816 1.4	1349 8.9	2025 1.7
9 W	0127 9.1	0800 1.5	1345 8.8	2013 1.8	**24** TH	0207 8.6	0848 2.1	1425 8.4	2100 2.3
10 TH	0205 8.9	0832 1.9	1423 8.6	2050 2.1	**25** F	0246 8.0	0922 2.7	1505 7.9	2144 2.9
11 F	0249 8.5	0911 2.3	1510 8.2	2138 2.6	**26** SA	0332 7.3	1010 3.3	1557 7.4	◐ 2249 3.4
12 SA	0344 7.9	1004 2.9	1612 7.4	◑ 2251 3.1	**27** SU	0439 6.8	1123 3.8	1724 7.0	
13 SU	0457 7.5	1126 3.3	1734 7.4		**28** M	0011 3.6	0623 6.6	1247 3.8	1905 7.1
14 M	0038 3.1	0628 7.4	1311 3.2	1908 7.7	**29** TU	0138 3.3	0750 7.0	1411 3.4	2009 7.6
15 TU	0211 2.6	0757 7.6	1437 2.6	2024 8.3	**30** W	0253 2.8	0842 7.6	1512 2.9	2057 8.2

OCTOBER

Day	Time m	Time m	Time m	Time m	Day	Time m	Time m	Time m	Time m
1 TH	0340 2.3	0924 8.1	1556 2.3	2137 8.7	**16** F	0355 1.0	0930 9.1	1611 1.4	2148 9.5
2 F	0417 1.8	1001 8.6	1632 1.9	2213 9.0	**17** SA	0441 0.7	1014 9.5	1655 1.0	2231 9.7
3 SA	0451 1.5	1034 8.8	1706 1.6	2246 9.2	**18** SU	0523 0.5	1054 9.6	1737 0.8	● 2311 9.8
4 SU	0524 1.2	1106 9.0	1739 1.4	○ 2318 9.3	**19** M	0601 0.6	1132 9.6	1815 0.9	2349 9.6
5 M	0557 1.1	1137 9.1	1812 1.3	2351 9.4	**20** TU	0637 0.9	1208 9.4	1852 1.1	
6 TU	0630 1.1	1210 9.2	1846 1.2		**21** W	0026 9.3	0711 1.3	1244 9.2	1926 1.4
7 W	0027 9.4	0703 1.3	1245 9.2	1921 1.4	**22** TH	0102 8.9	0742 1.8	1319 8.9	1959 1.8
8 TH	0105 9.2	0737 1.5	1324 9.0	1958 1.6	**23** F	0138 8.5	0813 2.3	1356 8.5	2033 2.3
9 F	0148 8.9	0813 1.9	1407 8.7	2040 2.0	**24** SA	0217 8.0	0845 2.8	1436 8.1	2114 2.8
10 SA	0236 8.4	0857 2.4	1458 8.3	2134 2.5	**25** SU	0302 7.5	0929 3.3	1524 7.6	2212 3.2
11 SU	0335 7.9	0955 2.9	1602 7.8	◑ 2253 2.9	**26** M	0359 7.0	1035 3.7	1629 7.2	2325 3.4
12 M	0452 7.5	1119 3.3	1726 7.6		**27** TU	0529 6.7	1155 3.8	1804 7.2	
13 TU	0031 2.8	0623 7.5	1257 3.1	1854 7.9	**28** W	0038 3.3	0656 7.0	1310 3.5	1917 7.5
14 W	0156 2.3	0741 8.0	1419 2.6	2004 8.5	**29** TH	0146 2.9	0756 7.4	1415 3.1	2011 7.9
15 TH	0302 1.6	0841 8.6	1520 1.9	2100 9.1	**30** F	0243 2.5	0842 8.0	1507 2.6	2055 8.4
					31 SA	0329 2.0	0922 8.4	1550 2.1	2134 8.8

NOVEMBER

Day	Time m	Time m	Time m	Time m	Day	Time m	Time m	Time m	Time m
1 SU	0410 1.6	0958 8.8	1630 1.7	2211 9.1	**16** M	0456 1.2	1031 9.3	1714 1.3	● 2251 9.2
2 M	0449 1.3	1032 9.1	1710 1.4	○ 2248 9.3	**17** TU	0534 1.2	1109 9.3	1753 1.3	2329 9.1
3 TU	0527 1.2	1108 9.3	1749 1.2	2327 9.4	**18** W	0610 1.4	1145 9.2	1831 1.5	
4 W	0605 1.2	1146 9.4	1830 1.2		**19** TH	0005 9.0	0644 1.7	1221 9.1	1906 1.7
5 TH	0008 9.4	0643 1.3	1227 9.3	1910 1.3	**20** F	0041 8.7	0716 2.0	1257 8.9	1941 1.9
6 F	0052 9.2	0723 1.5	1311 9.2	1954 1.5	**21** SA	0118 8.5	0748 2.3	1335 8.7	2015 2.2
7 SA	0140 9.0	0805 1.8	1400 8.9	2043 1.8	**22** SU	0156 8.1	0820 2.6	1415 8.4	2053 2.5
8 SU	0232 8.6	0854 2.3	1454 8.6	2141 2.1	**23** M	0238 7.8	0900 3.0	1459 8.0	2139 2.8
9 M	0332 8.1	0953 2.7	1557 8.2	◑ 2252 2.4	**24** TU	0326 7.4	0952 3.3	1549 7.7	◐ 2236 3.0
10 TU	0444 7.8	1107 2.9	1711 8.1		**25** W	0424 7.2	1056 3.5	1650 7.5	2339 3.1
11 W	0010 2.4	0601 7.8	1228 2.9	1826 8.1	**26** TH	0535 7.1	1204 3.5	1759 7.5	
12 TH	0126 2.2	0712 8.0	1346 2.6	1934 8.4	**27** F	0042 3.0	0647 7.3	1310 3.2	1905 7.7
13 F	0232 1.8	0813 8.4	1451 2.2	2033 8.8	**28** SA	0144 2.7	0747 7.7	1411 2.9	2002 8.1
14 SA	0327 1.5	0904 8.8	1545 1.8	2124 9.1	**29** SU	0240 2.3	0836 8.1	1506 2.4	2052 8.5
15 SU	0414 1.2	0950 9.1	1631 1.5	2209 9.2	**30** M	0332 1.9	0920 8.6	1557 1.9	2138 8.9

DECEMBER

Day	Time m	Time m	Time m	Time m	Day	Time m	Time m	Time m	Time m
1 TU	0419 1.6	1003 9.0	1645 1.6	2223 9.2	**16** W	0513 1.8	1053 9.0	1738 1.7	● 2316 8.8
2 W	0504 1.3	1046 9.3	1732 1.3	○ 2309 9.4	**17** TH	0550 1.8	1129 9.1	1817 1.7	2352 8.7
3 TH	0548 1.2	1130 9.5	1820 1.1	2356 9.4	**18** F	0626 1.8	1206 9.1	1854 1.7	
4 F	0632 1.2	1216 9.5	1908 1.0		**19** SA	0027 8.7	0700 1.9	1242 9.0	1928 1.8
5 SA	0045 9.4	0717 1.3	1305 9.5	1956 1.1	**20** SU	0102 8.6	0731 2.1	1319 8.9	2001 2.0
6 SU	0135 9.2	0803 1.5	1355 9.4	2046 1.2	**21** M	0138 8.4	0803 2.3	1356 8.7	2033 2.1
7 M	0227 8.9	0852 1.8	1448 9.1	2139 1.5	**22** TU	0216 8.2	0837 2.5	1434 8.5	2109 2.3
8 TU	0322 8.6	0945 2.1	1544 8.8	2235 1.8	**23** W	0255 8.0	0918 2.7	1515 8.2	2151 2.6
9 W	0421 8.3	1044 2.4	1644 8.5	◑ 2337 2.1	**24** TH	0339 7.7	1005 3.0	1602 8.0	◐ 2241 2.8
10 TH	0526 8.0	1149 2.7	1750 8.3		**25** F	0430 7.5	1103 3.2	1656 7.8	2341 2.9
11 F	0043 2.3	0634 7.9	1301 2.7	1858 8.2	**26** SA	0531 7.4	1210 3.3	1758 7.7	
12 SA	0153 2.3	0739 8.1	1414 2.6	2004 8.3	**27** SU	0048 2.9	0639 7.4	1320 3.1	1905 7.8
13 SU	0256 2.2	0838 8.3	1518 2.3	2102 8.4	**28** M	0156 2.7	0747 7.8	1428 2.7	2011 8.1
14 M	0348 2.0	0928 8.6	1611 2.1	2152 8.6	**29** TU	0259 2.3	0846 8.3	1530 2.2	2111 8.5
15 TU	0433 1.9	1013 8.8	1657 1.9	2237 8.7	**30** W	0355 1.9	0940 8.8	1628 1.7	2206 9.0
					31 TH	0448 1.5	1030 9.4	1722 1.2	○ 2257 9.3

Chart Datum: 4·93 metres below Ordnance Datum (Newlyn)
HAT is 10·5m above Chart Datum

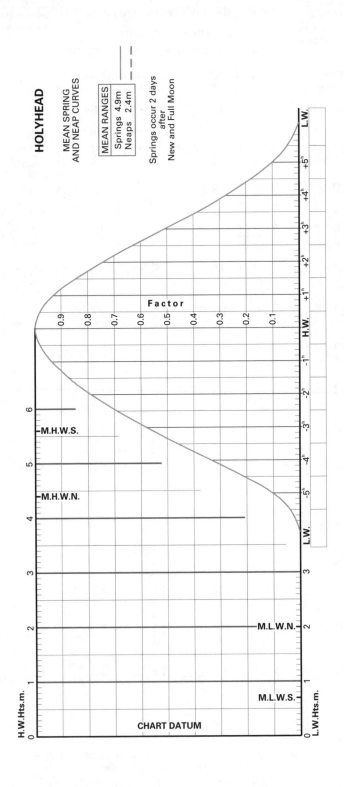

HOLYHEAD

MEAN SPRING
AND NEAP CURVES

MEAN RANGES
Springs 4.9m
Neaps 2.4m

Springs occur 2 days
after
New and Full Moon

WALES – HOLYHEAD

LAT 53°19'N   LONG 4°37'W

TIMES AND HEIGHTS OF HIGH AND LOW WATERS

2009

JANUARY

Time	m	Time	m
1 0050 0650 1304 1918 TH	5.0 1.5 5.4 1.4	**16** 0144 0740 1359 2020 F	5.2 1.2 5.6 1.1
2 0128 0728 1343 1958 F	4.9 1.6 5.2 1.4	**17** 0230 0828 1447 2110 SA	5.0 1.5 5.2 1.3
3 0209 0811 1426 2044 SA	4.8 1.7 5.1 1.6	**18** 0320 0921 1541 2207 SU ◑	4.7 1.8 4.9 1.8
4 0256 0901 1517 2137 SU ◑	4.7 1.9 4.9 1.7	**19** 0420 1026 1647 2314 M	4.5 2.1 4.6 2.1
5 0354 1002 1617 2241 M	4.6 2.0 4.9 1.7	**20** 0532 1143 1808 TU	4.4 2.3 4.4
6 0506 1114 1730 2352 TU	4.6 2.0 4.8 1.7	**21** 0026 0649 1302 1927 W	2.2 4.4 2.3 4.4
7 0621 1228 1846 W	4.7 1.9 4.9	**22** 0134 0754 1409 2028 TH	2.1 4.6 2.1 4.6
8 0101 0728 1337 1954 TH	1.6 4.8 1.6 5.1	**23** 0229 0843 1459 2113 F	2.0 4.9 1.8 4.9
9 0204 0827 1438 2054 F	1.4 5.2 1.2 5.4	**24** 0312 0923 1538 2150 SA	1.7 5.1 1.5 4.9
10 0301 0919 1533 2148 SA	1.2 5.5 0.9 5.6	**25** 0348 0957 1611 2222 SU	1.5 5.3 1.3 5.0
11 0352 1008 1624 2238 SU ○	0.9 5.8 0.6 5.7	**26** 0420 1028 1642 2251 M ●	1.3 5.4 1.1 5.2
12 0440 1055 1713 2326 M	0.8 6.0 0.4 5.7	**27** 0450 1100 1711 2321 TU	1.2 5.5 1.0 5.2
13 0526 1141 1800 TU	0.7 6.1 0.4	**28** 0521 1132 1744 2352 W	1.1 5.6 0.9 5.2
14 0013 0610 1228 1846 W	5.6 0.8 6.0 0.5	**29** 0553 1205 1816 TH	1.0 5.6 0.9
15 0058 0655 1313 1932 TH	5.5 0.9 5.8 0.7	**30** 0025 0625 1239 1849 F	5.2 1.1 5.6 1.0
		31 0059 0700 1315 1925 SA	5.2 1.2 5.5 1.1

FEBRUARY

Time	m	Time	m
1 0136 0738 1353 2005 SU	5.0 1.3 5.3 1.3	**16** 0228 0834 1451 2109 M ◐	4.8 1.7 4.7 1.9
2 0217 0824 1438 2055 M ◑	4.9 1.6 5.1 1.5	**17** 0318 0931 1549 2212 TU	4.5 2.1 4.3 2.3
3 0308 0921 1537 2158 TU	4.7 1.8 4.9 1.8	**18** 0426 1051 1717 2339 W	4.3 2.4 4.1 2.5
4 0418 1038 1657 2320 W	4.5 2.0 4.6 1.9	**19** 0559 1227 1904 TH	4.2 2.4 4.1
5 0550 1208 1832 TH	4.5 1.9 4.7	**20** 0105 0724 1346 2012 F	2.4 4.4 2.1 4.4
6 0046 0713 1329 1951 F	1.8 4.6 1.6 4.9	**21** 0209 0820 1438 2057 SA	2.1 4.5 1.8 4.6
7 0157 0819 1434 2052 SA	1.6 5.1 1.2 5.2	**22** 0252 0901 1516 2131 SU	1.8 4.8 1.5 4.9
8 0255 0911 1527 2142 SU	1.2 5.5 0.8 5.5	**23** 0326 0934 1547 2200 M	1.5 5.2 1.2 5.0
9 0343 0957 1614 2227 M ○	0.9 5.8 0.4 5.6	**24** 0357 1005 1617 2227 TU	1.2 5.4 1.0 5.2
10 0426 1041 1658 2309 TU	0.6 6.0 0.3 5.7	**25** 0426 1035 1646 2255 W ●	1.0 5.6 0.8 5.3
11 0508 1123 1739 2349 W	0.5 6.1 0.2 5.7	**26** 0456 1106 1716 2325 TH	0.8 5.7 0.7 5.4
12 0548 1204 1820 TH	0.5 6.0 0.4	**27** 0527 1139 1747 2357 F	0.8 5.7 0.7 5.4
13 0029 0627 1245 1859 F	5.5 0.7 5.8 0.7	**28** 0559 1213 1820 SA	0.8 5.7 0.8
14 0108 0707 1325 1939 SA	5.3 0.9 5.5 1.0		
15 0147 0748 1406 2021 SU	5.1 1.3 5.1 1.5		

MARCH

Time	m	Time	m
1 0031 0634 1249 1855 SU	5.4 0.9 5.6 0.9	**16** 0110 0715 1330 1939 M	5.1 1.2 5.0 1.5
2 0108 0713 1328 1936 M	5.2 1.1 5.4 1.1	**17** 0147 0758 1411 2022 TU	4.9 1.6 4.6 1.9
3 0149 0759 1415 2026 TU	5.0 1.3 5.1 1.5	**18** 0231 0849 1503 2117 W ◑	4.6 2.0 4.3 2.3
4 0240 0859 1517 2133 W ◑	4.8 1.7 4.7 1.9	**19** 0331 1001 1627 2242 TH	4.3 2.3 4.0 2.6
5 0353 1023 1648 2305 TH	4.5 1.9 4.5 2.1	**20** 0459 1141 1823 F	4.2 2.4 4.0
6 0534 1201 1832 F	4.5 1.8 4.5	**21** 0022 0634 1304 1939 SA	2.5 4.3 2.1 4.2
7 0038 0703 1323 1949 SA	2.0 4.7 1.5 4.8	**22** 0131 0740 1400 2024 SU	2.2 4.5 1.8 4.5
8 0150 0808 1425 2044 SU	1.6 5.1 1.0 5.1	**23** 0218 0824 1439 2058 M	1.9 4.8 1.4 4.8
9 0244 0858 1514 2129 M	1.2 5.4 0.7 5.4	**24** 0253 0900 1512 2127 TU	1.5 5.1 1.1 5.0
10 0328 0941 1557 2208 TU	0.9 5.7 0.4 5.6	**25** 0324 0932 1542 2155 W	1.2 5.3 0.9 5.2
11 0407 1021 1636 2245 W ○	0.6 5.9 0.3 5.6	**26** 0355 1004 1613 2225 TH ●	0.9 5.5 0.7 5.4
12 0445 1100 1713 2322 TH	0.5 6.0 0.3 5.6	**27** 0426 1037 1645 2257 F	0.7 5.7 0.6 5.5
13 0523 1139 1750 2358 F	0.5 5.9 0.5 5.5	**28** 0500 1112 1718 2331 SA	0.6 5.7 0.6 5.5
14 0600 1216 1826 SA	0.6 5.7 0.8	**29** 0535 1149 1754 SU	0.6 5.7 0.7
15 0034 0634 1254 1901 SU	5.4 0.9 5.4 1.1	**30** 0007 0614 1229 1834 M	5.5 0.7 5.6 0.9
		31 0048 0658 1314 1919 TU	5.3 0.9 5.3 1.2

APRIL

Time	m	Time	m
1 0133 0750 1407 2013 W	5.1 1.2 5.0 1.6	**16** 0159 0820 1432 2040 TH	4.7 1.8 4.3 2.2
2 0230 0856 1517 2126 TH ◑	4.8 1.5 4.6 1.9	**17** 0252 0922 1543 2150 F ◑	4.5 2.1 4.1 2.5
3 0347 1024 1653 2259 F	4.6 1.7 4.4 2.1	**18** 0406 1043 1719 2320 SA	4.3 2.2 4.0 2.5
4 0524 1154 1827 SA	4.3 1.6 4.5	**19** 0531 1204 1841 SU	4.3 2.0 4.2
5 0025 0646 1308 1935 SU	1.9 4.8 1.3 4.8	**20** 0034 0641 1305 1934 M	2.3 4.5 1.8 4.4
6 0132 0748 1406 2026 M	1.6 5.1 1.0 5.1	**21** 0127 0734 1350 2013 TU	1.9 4.7 1.5 4.7
7 0223 0837 1453 2107 TU	1.2 5.4 0.7 5.3	**22** 0209 0816 1428 2047 W	1.6 5.0 1.2 5.0
8 0306 0919 1533 2144 W	0.9 5.6 0.6 5.4	**23** 0245 0854 1504 2120 TH	1.3 5.3 0.9 5.2
9 0345 0958 1610 2220 TH ○	0.7 5.7 0.5 5.5	**24** 0321 0931 1539 2154 F	1.0 5.5 0.7 5.4
10 0422 1036 1646 2255 F	0.6 5.7 0.6 5.5	**25** 0357 1008 1615 2230 SA ●	0.7 5.6 0.6 5.6
11 0459 1114 1721 2331 SA	0.6 5.6 0.7 5.5	**26** 0436 1048 1654 2309 SU	0.6 5.7 0.6 5.6
12 0535 1151 1756 SU	0.8 5.4 1.0	**27** 0517 1131 1736 2351 M	0.6 5.6 0.7 5.6
13 0005 0612 1227 1830 M	5.4 1.0 5.1 1.2	**28** 0603 1218 1821 TU	0.8 5.5 0.9
14 0041 0650 1303 1907 TU	5.2 1.3 4.9 1.6	**29** 0036 0652 1309 1911 W	5.4 1.0 5.2 1.2
15 0117 0731 1343 1948 W	5.0 1.6 4.6 1.9	**30** 0128 0751 1409 2011 TH	5.2 1.1 4.9 1.5

Chart Datum: 3·05 metres below Ordnance Datum (Newlyn)
HAT is 6·3m above Chart Datum

TIDES

WALES – HOLYHEAD

TIME ZONE (UT)
For Summer Time add ONE hour in **non-shaded areas**

LAT 53°19'N   LONG 4°37'W

TIMES AND HEIGHTS OF HIGH AND LOW WATERS

Dates in amber are **SPRINGS**
Dates in yellow are **NEAPS**

2009

MAY

Time	m	Time	m
1 F 0229 / 0859 / 1521 / 2122	5.0 / 1.3 / 4.7 / 1.8	**16** SA 0224 / 0850 / 1505 / 2108	4.7 / 1.8 / 4.3 / 2.2
2 SA 0343 / 1017 / 1645 / 2243	4.8 / 1.4 / 4.5 / 1.9	**17** SU 0322 / 0951 / 1615 / 2216	4.5 / 1.9 / 4.2 / 2.3
3 SU 0505 / 1134 / 1804 / 2359	4.8 / 1.4 / 4.6 / 1.8	**18** M 0430 / 1058 / 1728 / 2326 ☽	4.3 / 1.9 / 4.2 / 2.2
4 M 0619 / 1242 / 1908 ●	4.9 / 1.2 / 4.8	**19** TU 0538 / 1201 / 1831	4.5 / 1.7 / 4.4
5 TU 0103 / 0720 / 1339 / 1959	1.6 / 5.1 / 1.1 / 4.9	**20** W 0027 / 0637 / 1255 / 1921	2.0 / 4.7 / 1.5 / 4.6
6 W 0156 / 0811 / 1426 / 2041	1.4 / 5.2 / 1.0 / 5.1	**21** TH 0119 / 0729 / 1342 / 2005	1.7 / 4.9 / 1.3 / 4.9
7 TH 0242 / 0855 / 1508 / 2119	1.1 / 5.3 / 0.9 / 5.2	**22** F 0205 / 0816 / 1426 / 2046	1.4 / 5.1 / 1.1 / 5.1
8 F 0323 / 0936 / 1546 / 2156	1.0 / 5.4 / 0.9 / 5.3	**23** SA 0249 / 0900 / 1509 / 2126	1.1 / 5.3 / 0.9 / 5.4
9 SA 0401 / 1015 / 1622 / 2232	0.9 / 5.3 / 0.9 / 5.4	**24** SU 0333 / 0945 / 1552 / 2209	0.9 / 5.5 / 0.7 / 5.5
10 SU 0439 / 1053 / 1657 / 2307	0.9 / 5.3 / 1.0 / 5.4	**25** M 0419 / 1032 / 1637 / 2253	0.7 / 5.6 / 0.7 / 5.6
11 M 0516 / 1130 / 1732 / 2343 ○	1.0 / 5.1 / 1.2 / 5.3	**26** TU 0506 / 1121 / 1724 / 2340 ●	0.6 / 5.6 / 0.8 / 5.7
12 TU 0553 / 1206 / 1807	1.1 / 5.0 / 1.4	**27** W 0557 / 1212 / 1814	0.6 / 5.5 / 0.9
13 W 0018 / 0631 / 1244 / 1844	5.2 / 1.3 / 4.8 / 1.6	**28** TH 0030 / 0651 / 1307 / 1907	5.6 / 0.7 / 5.3 / 1.1
14 TH 0055 / 0712 / 1323 / 1925	5.1 / 1.5 / 4.6 / 1.8	**29** F 0124 / 0748 / 1405 / 2004	5.5 / 0.8 / 5.1 / 1.3
15 F 0137 / 0757 / 1409 / 2012	4.9 / 1.6 / 4.4 / 2.0	**30** SA 0222 / 0850 / 1509 / 2106	5.3 / 1.0 / 4.8 / 1.6
		31 SU 0326 / 0956 / 1618 / 2214	5.1 / 1.2 / 4.7 / 1.7

JUNE

Time	m	Time	m
1 M 0435 / 1103 / 1727 / 2323	5.0 / 1.3 / 4.6 / 1.7	**16** TU 0336 / 0958 / 1619 / 2223 ◗	4.7 / 1.7 / 4.4 / 2.0
2 TU 0544 / 1207 / 1831 ●	4.9 / 1.3 / 4.7	**17** W 0437 / 1058 / 1725 / 2328	4.6 / 1.7 / 4.4 / 2.0
3 W 0028 / 0648 / 1306 / 1927	1.7 / 4.9 / 1.3 / 4.8	**18** TH 0542 / 1200 / 1829	4.7 / 1.6 / 4.6
4 TH 0127 / 0745 / 1358 / 2015	1.6 / 4.9 / 1.3 / 4.9	**19** F 0031 / 0644 / 1300 / 1926	1.8 / 4.8 / 1.5 / 4.8
5 F 0219 / 0834 / 1444 / 2057	1.5 / 5.0 / 1.3 / 5.0	**20** SA 0130 / 0743 / 1355 / 2017	1.6 / 5.0 / 1.3 / 5.0
6 SA 0305 / 0919 / 1525 / 2136	1.3 / 5.0 / 1.3 / 5.2	**21** SU 0225 / 0839 / 1447 / 2106	1.3 / 5.2 / 1.1 / 5.3
7 SU 0347 / 1000 / 1603 / 2214	1.2 / 5.0 / 1.2 / 5.3	**22** M 0317 / 0931 / 1537 / 2154	1.0 / 5.4 / 0.9 / 5.5
8 M 0426 / 1038 / 1639 / 2250	1.2 / 5.0 / 1.3 / 5.3	**23** TU 0408 / 1023 / 1626 / 2242	0.7 / 5.5 / 0.8 / 5.7
9 TU 0503 / 1115 / 1714 / 2325 ○	1.2 / 5.0 / 1.3 / 5.3	**24** W 0459 / 1114 / 1715 / 2331	0.5 / 5.6 / 0.7 / 5.8
10 W 0539 / 1150 / 1749	1.2 / 4.9 / 1.4	**25** TH 0550 / 1205 / 1804 ●	0.4 / 5.5 / 0.8
11 TH 0000 / 0615 / 1226 / 1825	5.3 / 1.2 / 4.9 / 1.5	**26** F 0020 / 0641 / 1256 / 1854	5.8 / 0.4 / 5.4 / 0.9
12 F 0037 / 0653 / 1303 / 1903	5.2 / 1.3 / 4.8 / 1.6	**27** SA 0111 / 0733 / 1348 / 1945	5.7 / 0.5 / 5.2 / 1.1
13 SA 0116 / 0733 / 1344 / 1944	5.1 / 1.4 / 4.6 / 1.7	**28** SU 0203 / 0827 / 1442 / 2039	5.5 / 0.8 / 5.0 / 1.3
14 SU 0157 / 0816 / 1428 / 2030	4.9 / 1.5 / 4.5 / 1.9	**29** M 0258 / 0923 / 1539 / 2137	5.3 / 1.1 / 4.8 / 1.5
15 M 0243 / 0904 / 1519 / 2122	4.8 / 1.6 / 4.4 / 2.0	**30** TU 0358 / 1024 / 1642 / 2242	5.0 / 1.3 / 4.6 / 1.8

JULY

Time	m	Time	m
1 W 0504 / 1127 / 1748 / 2351	4.8 / 1.6 / 4.5 / 1.9	**16** TH 0344 / 1005 / 1626 / 2238	4.8 / 1.7 / 4.5 / 2.0
2 TH 0614 / 1231 / 1854	4.7 / 1.7 / 4.6	**17** F 0452 / 1114 / 1742 / 2353	4.7 / 1.7 / 4.5 / 1.9
3 F 0059 / 0722 / 1332 / 1952	1.9 / 4.6 / 1.7 / 4.7	**18** SA 0610 / 1227 / 1856 ○	4.7 / 1.7 / 4.7
4 SA 0202 / 0820 / 1426 / 2041 ☽	1.8 / 4.7 / 1.7 / 4.9	**19** SU 0106 / 0724 / 1335 / 1959	1.7 / 4.8 / 1.5 / 5.0
5 SU 0255 / 0909 / 1511 / 2122	1.6 / 4.7 / 1.6 / 5.0	**20** M 0211 / 0828 / 1434 / 2053	1.3 / 5.1 / 1.3 / 5.3
6 M 0338 / 0950 / 1550 / 2200	1.4 / 4.8 / 1.4 / 5.2	**21** TU 0308 / 0924 / 1527 / 2143	0.9 / 5.3 / 1.0 / 5.6
7 TU 0416 / 1027 / 1625 / 2234	1.3 / 4.9 / 1.3 / 5.3	**22** W 0400 / 1014 / 1615 / 2230	0.6 / 5.5 / 0.7 / 5.8
8 W 0450 / 1100 / 1658 / 2308	1.2 / 5.0 / 1.3 / 5.3	**23** TH 0448 / 1102 / 1702 / 2317	0.3 / 5.6 / 0.6 / 6.0
9 TH 0523 / 1132 / 1731 / 2341	1.1 / 5.0 / 1.2 / 5.4	**24** F 0536 / 1148 / 1747	0.2 / 5.7 / 0.6
10 F 0555 / 1205 / 1804 ●	1.1 / 5.0 / 1.3	**25** SA 0003 / 0622 / 1235 / 1832	6.0 / 0.2 / 5.6 / 0.7
11 SA 0015 / 0629 / 1239 / 1838 ○	5.3 / 1.1 / 4.9 / 1.3	**26** SU 0050 / 0708 / 1320 / 1917	5.9 / 0.4 / 5.4 / 0.9
12 SU 0051 / 0704 / 1314 / 1914	5.3 / 1.2 / 4.9 / 1.4	**27** M 0136 / 0755 / 1406 / 2005	5.7 / 0.7 / 5.1 / 1.2
13 M 0127 / 0740 / 1351 / 1953	5.2 / 1.3 / 4.8 / 1.6	**28** TU 0224 / 0844 / 1456 / 2057	5.3 / 1.1 / 4.8 / 1.5
14 TU 0206 / 0821 / 1433 / 2037	5.1 / 1.4 / 4.7 / 1.7	**29** W 0317 / 0939 / 1552 / 2159	5.0 / 1.3 / 4.6 / 1.9
15 W 0251 / 0908 / 1523 / 2131	4.9 / 1.5 / 4.6 / 1.9	**30** TH 0421 / 1044 / 1701 / 2315	4.6 / 1.9 / 4.4 / 2.1
		31 F 0539 / 1156 / 1819	4.4 / 2.1 / 4.4

AUGUST

Time	m	Time	m
1 SA 0035 / 0704 / 1309 / 1931	2.1 / 4.3 / 2.1 / 4.6	**16** SU 0554 / 1208 / 1838	4.5 / 1.9 / 4.7
2 SU 0149 / 0811 / 1411 / 2025 ◗	2.0 / 4.5 / 1.9 / 4.8	**17** M 0055 / 0718 / 1324 / 1947 ☽	1.7 / 4.7 / 1.7 / 5.0
3 M 0244 / 0900 / 1457 / 2108	1.7 / 4.6 / 1.7 / 5.0	**18** TU 0204 / 0823 / 1425 / 2042	1.3 / 5.1 / 1.3 / 5.4
4 TU 0325 / 0938 / 1535 / 2143	1.5 / 4.8 / 1.5 / 5.2	**19** W 0259 / 0915 / 1515 / 2129	0.8 / 5.7 / 1.0 / 5.7
5 W 0359 / 1010 / 1607 / 2215	1.3 / 5.0 / 1.3 / 5.3	**20** TH 0347 / 1000 / 1600 / 2214	0.5 / 5.6 / 0.7 / 6.0
6 TH 0430 / 1040 / 1637 / 2246	1.1 / 5.1 / 1.2 / 5.5	**21** F 0431 / 1043 / 1642 / 2257	0.2 / 5.7 / 0.5 / 6.1
7 F 0459 / 1108 / 1707 / 2317	1.0 / 5.1 / 1.1 / 5.5	**22** SA 0514 / 1125 / 1723 / 2340	0.2 / 5.7 / 0.5 / 6.1
8 SA 0529 / 1138 / 1738 / 2349	0.9 / 5.2 / 1.1 / 5.5	**23** SU 0556 / 1206 / 1805	0.3 / 5.6 / 0.6
9 SU 0600 / 1209 / 1809 ○	0.9 / 5.2 / 1.1	**24** M 0022 / 0637 / 1248 / 1847	5.9 / 0.5 / 5.5 / 0.8
10 M 0022 / 0631 / 1242 / 1842	5.5 / 1.0 / 5.1 / 1.2	**25** TU 0106 / 0719 / 1329 / 1931 ●	5.7 / 0.9 / 5.2 / 1.2
11 TU 0056 / 0705 / 1317 / 1918	5.4 / 1.1 / 5.0 / 1.3	**26** W 0149 / 0803 / 1413 / 2019	5.3 / 1.3 / 4.9 / 1.6
12 W 0133 / 0742 / 1355 / 2000	5.2 / 1.3 / 4.9 / 1.5	**27** TH 0237 / 0852 / 1504 / 2118	4.8 / 1.8 / 4.6 / 2.0
13 TH 0214 / 0827 / 1441 / 2053	5.0 / 1.5 / 4.7 / 1.8	**28** F 0337 / 0955 / 1611 / 2237	4.4 / 2.2 / 4.4 / 2.3
14 F 0307 / 0924 / 1544 / 2203	4.8 / 1.7 / 4.6 / 2.0	**29** SA 0503 / 1118 / 1739	4.2 / 2.4 / 4.3
15 SA 0420 / 1041 / 1710 / 2332	4.6 / 1.9 / 4.5 / 2.0	**30** SU 0009 / 0646 / 1244 / 1904	2.3 / 4.2 / 2.4 / 4.5
		31 M 0128 / 0756 / 1349 / 2002	2.1 / 4.6 / 2.1 / 4.7

Chart Datum: 3·05 metres below Ordnance Datum (Newlyn)
HAT is 6·3m above Chart Datum

TIME ZONE (UT)
For Summer Time add ONE hour in **non-shaded areas**

WALES – HOLYHEAD
LAT 53°19'N   LONG 4°37'W
TIMES AND HEIGHTS OF HIGH AND LOW WATERS

Dates in amber are **SPRINGS**
Dates in yellow are **NEAPS**

2009

SEPTEMBER

Time	m	Time	m
1 0222 1.8	TU 1435 1.9 / 0841 4.6 / 2044 5.0	**16** 0153 1.2	W 1411 1.4 / 0813 5.1 / 2027 5.5
2 0301 1.5	W 1510 1.6 / 0916 4.9 / 2118 5.2	**17** 0244 0.8	TH 1458 1.0 / 0900 5.4 / 2111 5.8
3 0332 1.2	TH 1541 1.3 / 0945 5.0 / 2148 5.4	**18** 0328 0.5	F 1539 0.7 / 0941 5.5 / ● 2153 6.0
4 0401 1.0	F 1609 1.1 / 1012 5.2 / ○ 2217 5.6	**19** 0409 0.3	SA 1619 0.5 / 1020 5.8 / 2234 6.1
5 0429 0.9	SA 1638 1.0 / 1039 5.3 / 2248 5.6	**20** 0448 0.3	SU 1658 0.5 / 1058 5.8 / 2315 6.0
6 0458 0.8	SU 1708 0.9 / 1107 5.3 / 2319 5.7	**21** 0527 0.5	M 1738 0.7 / 1137 5.7 / 2355 5.8
7 0528 0.8	M 1740 1.0 / 1139 5.4 / 2353 5.6	**22** 0606 0.8	TU 1819 0.9 / 1215 5.5
8 0559 0.9	TU 1814 1.1 / 1211 5.3	**23** 0036 5.5	W 1255 5.3 / 0644 1.1 / 1900 1.3
9 0027 5.5	W 1247 5.2 / 0633 1.0 / 1851 1.2	**24** 0117 5.1	TH 1335 5.0 / 0724 1.5 / 1946 1.7
10 0105 5.3	TH 1326 5.1 / 0712 1.3 / 1935 1.5	**25** 0201 4.7	F 1421 4.7 / 0809 2.0 / 2041 2.0
11 0150 5.1	F 1414 4.9 / 0758 1.6 / 2031 1.8	**26** 0257 4.4	SA 1523 4.5 / 0907 2.4 / ◑ 2155 2.3
12 0247 4.8	SA 1521 4.6 / 0859 1.9 / ◑ 2149 2.0	**27** 0421 4.1	SU 1648 4.4 / 1030 2.6 / 2329 2.4
13 0410 4.5	SU 1655 4.5 / 1025 2.1 / 2325 2.0	**28** 0609 4.1	M 1818 4.5 / 1203 2.6
14 0553 4.5	M 1827 4.8 / 1159 2.1	**29** 0048 2.2	TU 1312 2.3 / 0722 4.4 / 1922 4.7
15 0048 1.6	TU 1314 1.8 / 0714 4.8 / 1934 5.1	**30** 0143 1.9	W 1400 2.0 / 0808 4.6 / 2007 5.0

OCTOBER

Time	m	Time	m
1 0224 1.6	TH 1436 1.7 / 0842 4.9 / 2042 5.2	**16** 0223 0.9	F 1436 1.1 / 0839 5.4 / 2050 5.8
2 0256 1.3	F 1507 1.4 / 0911 5.1 / 2114 5.4	**17** 0305 0.7	SA 1517 0.9 / 0918 5.6 / 2131 5.9
3 0326 1.1	SA 1537 1.2 / 0939 5.3 / 2145 5.6	**18** 0345 0.6	SU 1557 0.8 / 0956 5.7 / ● 2212 5.9
4 0355 0.9	SU 1608 1.0 / 1007 5.4 / ○ 2217 5.7	**19** 0423 0.7	M 1636 0.8 / 1033 5.7 / 2252 5.8
5 0425 0.8	M 1640 0.9 / 1037 5.5 / 2251 5.7	**20** 0500 0.8	TU 1716 0.9 / 1111 5.7 / 2332 5.6
6 0457 0.8	TU 1714 0.9 / 1110 5.6 / 2327 5.7	**21** 0538 1.0	W 1756 1.1 / 1148 5.6
7 0532 0.9	W 1752 1.0 / 1146 5.5	**22** 0011 5.3	TH 1226 5.4 / 0614 1.3 / 1836 1.4
8 0005 5.6	TH 1225 5.4 / 0609 1.1 / 1834 1.2	**23** 0051 5.0	F 1305 5.2 / 0653 1.7 / 1920 1.7
9 0049 5.4	F 1309 5.2 / 0652 1.3 / 1923 1.4	**24** 0132 4.7	SA 1348 4.9 / 0736 2.0 / 2010 2.0
10 0139 5.1	SA 1402 5.0 / 0744 1.7 / 2026 1.7	**25** 0223 4.4	SU 1442 4.7 / 0828 2.3 / 2113 2.2
11 0243 4.8	SU 1513 4.8 / 0850 2.0 / ◑ 2147 1.9	**26** 0333 4.2	M 1553 4.5 / 0936 2.6 / 2232 2.3
12 0412 4.6	M 1645 4.7 / 1017 2.2 / 2316 1.8	**27** 0504 4.2	TU 1714 4.6 / 1102 2.6 / 2349 2.2
13 0547 4.6	TU 1809 4.9 / 1145 2.1	**28** 0623 4.3	W 1824 4.7 / 1215 2.5
14 0032 1.5	W 1255 1.8 / 0659 4.9 / 1914 5.2	**29** 0049 2.0	TH 1310 2.2 / 0718 4.6 / 1917 4.9
15 0133 1.2	TH 1350 1.4 / 0754 5.2 / 2005 5.5	**30** 0135 1.7	F 1353 1.9 / 0758 4.8 / 2000 5.1
		31 0213 1.4	SA 1429 1.6 / 0832 5.1 / 2037 5.3

NOVEMBER

Time	m	Time	m
1 0248 1.2	SU 1504 1.3 / 0904 5.3 / 2113 5.5	**16** 0324 1.0	M 1541 1.1 / 0935 5.6 / ● 2155 5.6
2 0321 1.0	M 1539 1.1 / 0937 5.5 / ○ 2149 5.7	**17** 0402 1.0	TU 1621 1.1 / 1013 5.6 / 2235 5.5
3 0356 0.9	TU 1616 1.0 / 1011 5.6 / 2227 5.7	**18** 0440 1.1	W 1701 1.1 / 1051 5.6 / 2314 5.4
4 0433 0.9	W 1656 0.9 / 1048 5.7 / 2308 5.7	**19** 0517 1.3	TH 1740 1.3 / 1128 5.6 / 2353 5.2
5 0512 0.9	TH 1739 1.0 / 1128 5.7 / 2353 5.6	**20** 0553 1.5	F 1819 1.4 / 1205 5.4
6 0556 1.1	F 1827 1.1 / 1212 5.6	**21** 0030 5.0	SA 1242 5.3 / 0630 1.7 / 1859 1.6
7 0041 5.4	SA 1301 5.4 / 0643 1.3 / 1921 1.3	**22** 0110 4.8	SU 1322 5.1 / 0710 1.9 / 1943 1.8
8 0137 5.1	SU 1358 5.2 / 0739 1.6 / 2025 1.5	**23** 0154 4.6	M 1408 4.9 / 0755 2.1 / 2033 2.0
9 0243 4.9	M 1506 5.1 / 0844 1.9 / ◐ 2139 1.6	**24** 0246 4.4	TU 1503 4.7 / 0848 2.3 / ◑ 2131 2.1
10 0403 4.7	TU 1625 5.0 / 1001 2.0 / 2255 1.6	**25** 0352 4.3	W 1608 4.6 / 0952 2.5 / 2236 2.1
11 0523 4.7	W 1741 5.1 / 1118 2.0	**26** 0505 4.3	TH 1716 4.7 / 1102 2.4 / 2341 2.0
12 0005 1.4	TH 1227 1.8 / 0632 4.9 / 1846 5.2	**27** 0611 4.5	F 1818 4.8 / 1207 2.3
13 0106 1.3	F 1324 1.6 / 0728 5.1 / 1941 5.4	**28** 0037 1.9	SA 1302 2.0 / 0705 4.7 / 1912 5.0
14 0158 1.1	SA 1414 1.3 / 0815 5.3 / 2029 5.5	**29** 0126 1.7	SU 1350 1.8 / 0750 4.9 / 2000 5.2
15 0243 1.0	SU 1459 1.2 / 0856 5.4 / 2113 5.6	**30** 0210 1.4	M 1433 1.5 / 0831 5.2 / 2044 5.3

DECEMBER

Time	m	Time	m
1 0252 1.2	TU 1516 1.2 / 0910 5.4 / 2127 5.5	**16** 0349 1.3	W 1613 1.3 / 1000 5.5 / ● 2225 5.2
2 0333 1.1	W 1600 1.0 / 0950 5.6 / ○ 2211 5.6	**17** 0427 1.3	TH 1651 1.2 / 1037 5.5 / 2302 5.2
3 0416 1.0	TH 1645 0.8 / 1032 5.8 / 2258 5.7	**18** 0502 1.3	F 1727 1.3 / 1113 5.5 / 2338 5.1
4 0501 0.9	F 1733 0.8 / 1117 5.8 / 2346 5.6	**19** 0536 1.4	SA 1802 1.3 / 1147 5.5
5 0548 1.0	SA 1823 0.8 / 1204 5.8	**20** 0012 5.1	SU 1838 1.4 / 0611 1.5 / 1223 5.4
6 0037 5.5	SU 1255 5.7 / 0637 1.2 / 1917 0.9	**21** 0047 5.0	M 1259 5.3 / 0647 1.6 / 1916 1.5
7 0132 5.3	M 1349 5.6 / 0730 1.4 / 2014 1.1	**22** 0125 4.8	TU 1338 5.2 / 0725 1.8 / 1956 1.6
8 0230 5.1	TU 1448 5.4 / 0828 1.6 / 2117 1.3	**23** 0205 4.7	W 1420 5.0 / 0807 1.9 / 2040 1.8
9 0336 4.9	W 1554 5.2 / 0933 1.8 / ◐ 2224 1.4	**24** 0251 4.6	TH 1509 4.8 / 0855 2.1 / ◑ 2131 1.9
10 0446 4.8	TH 1705 5.1 / 1042 1.9 / 2331 1.5	**25** 0347 4.4	F 1606 4.7 / 0952 2.2 / 2230 2.0
11 0555 4.8	F 1814 5.1 / 1151 1.9	**26** 0455 4.4	SA 1714 4.7 / 1059 2.3 / 2335 2.0
12 0034 1.5	SA 1257 1.8 / 0657 4.9 / 1917 5.1	**27** 0605 4.5	SU 1823 4.7 / 1208 2.2
13 0133 1.5	SU 1355 1.6 / 0752 5.0 / 2013 5.1	**28** 0039 1.9	M 1312 1.9 / 0708 4.7 / 1926 4.9
14 0224 1.5	M 1447 1.5 / 0839 5.2 / 2102 5.2	**29** 0137 1.7	TU 1408 1.6 / 0802 5.0 / 2022 5.1
15 0309 1.4	TU 1532 1.4 / 0921 5.4 / 2145 5.2	**30** 0229 1.4	W 1500 1.3 / 0850 5.3 / 2113 5.4
		31 0318 1.2	TH 1549 0.9 / 0936 5.6 / ○ 2202 5.6

Chart Datum: 3·05 metres below Ordnance Datum (Newlyn)
HAT is 6·3m above Chart Datum

TIDES

321

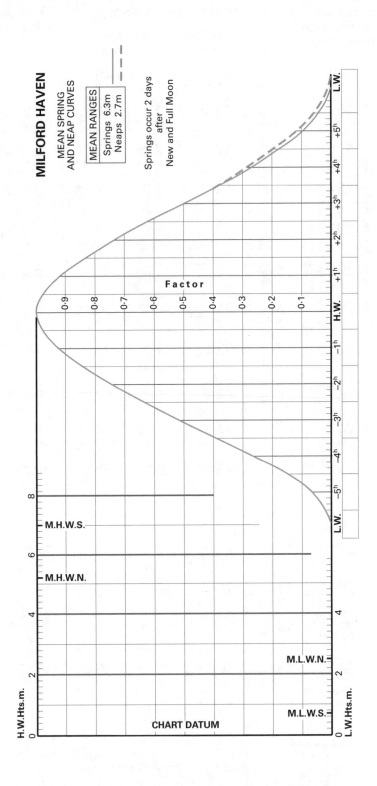

MILFORD HAVEN
MEAN SPRING
AND NEAP CURVES

MEAN RANGES
Springs 6.3m
Neaps 2.7m

Springs occur 2 days
after
New and Full Moon

Factor

0·9 0·8 0·7 0·6 0·5 0·4 0·3 0·2 0·1

+5ʰ +4ʰ +3ʰ +2ʰ +1ʰ H.W. −1ʰ −2ʰ −3ʰ −4ʰ −5ʰ L.W.

L.W.

H.W.Hts.m.
8 6 4 2 0

M.H.W.S.
M.H.W.N.

CHART DATUM

L.W.Hts.m.
4 2 0

M.L.W.N.
M.L.W.S.

WALES – MILFORD HAVEN

LAT 51°42′N   LONG 5°03′W

TIMES AND HEIGHTS OF HIGH AND LOW WATERS

Dates in amber are **SPRINGS**
Dates in yellow are **NEAPS**

2009

JANUARY

Day	Time	m	Day	Time	m
1 TH	0244 / 0853 / 1510 / 2110	1.6 / 6.4 / 1.5 / 6.1	**16** F	0342 / 0949 / 1611 / 2210	1.1 / 6.8 / 1.3 / 6.3
2 F	0320 / 0930 / 1547 / 2148	1.7 / 6.3 / 1.7 / 5.9	**17** SA	0423 / 1031 / 1652 / 2253	1.5 / 6.3 / 1.7 / 5.9
3 SA	0359 / 1011 / 1628 / 2231	1.9 / 6.1 / 1.9 / 5.8	**18** SU	0506 / 1116 / 1737 / 2342	1.9 / 5.9 / 2.2 / 5.5
4 SU	0443 / 1058 / 1717 / 2323	2.1 / 5.9 / 2.1 / 5.6	**19** M	0558 / 1209 / 1836	2.4 / 5.4 / 2.5
5 M	0537 / 1156 / 1818	2.3 / 5.7 / 2.2	**20** TU	0046 / 0707 / 1321 / 1954	5.2 / 2.6 / 5.1 / 2.7
6 TU	0028 / 0648 / 1306 / 1934	5.5 / 2.4 / 5.6 / 2.2	**21** W	0207 / 0834 / 1444 / 2115	5.1 / 2.7 / 5.1 / 2.6
7 W	0145 / 0812 / 1423 / 2052	5.5 / 2.3 / 5.7 / 2.1	**22** TH	0325 / 0948 / 1556 / 2216	5.3 / 2.5 / 5.3 / 2.3
8 TH	0300 / 0930 / 1536 / 2202	5.8 / 2.0 / 6.0 / 1.7	**23** F	0425 / 1043 / 1650 / 2304	5.7 / 2.1 / 5.6 / 2.0
9 F	0407 / 1036 / 1640 / 2302	6.2 / 1.5 / 6.4 / 1.4	**24** SA	0510 / 1127 / 1731 / 2343	6.0 / 1.8 / 5.9 / 1.7
10 SA	0507 / 1135 / 1738 / 2356	6.7 / 1.1 / 6.7 / 1.0	**25** SU	0549 / 1205 / 1808	6.3 / 1.5 / 6.2
11 SU	0602 / 1228 / 1831 / O	7.1 / 0.7 / 7.0	**26** M	0018 / 0623 / 1240 / ● 1841	1.5 / 6.5 / 1.3 / 6.4
12 M	0047 / 0651 / 1319 / 1919	0.7 / 7.3 / 0.5 / 7.2	**27** TU	0051 / 0656 / 1312 / 1912	1.3 / 6.7 / 1.1 / 6.5
13 TU	0134 / 0739 / 1405 / 2004	0.6 / 7.4 / 0.5 / 7.1	**28** W	0123 / 0728 / 1344 / 1943	1.1 / 6.8 / 1.0 / 6.6
14 W	0219 / 0824 / 1449 / 2048	0.6 / 7.4 / 0.6 / 7.0	**29** TH	0155 / 0800 / 1416 / 2015	1.1 / 6.8 / 1.0 / 6.6
15 TH	0301 / 0907 / 1531 / 2129	0.8 / 7.2 / 0.9 / 6.7	**30** F	0227 / 0832 / 1448 / 2047	1.1 / 6.8 / 1.1 / 6.5
			31 SA	0259 / 0906 / 1521 / 2121	1.2 / 6.6 / 1.2 / 6.3

FEBRUARY

Day	Time	m	Day	Time	m
1 SU	0333 / 0942 / 1557 / 2158	1.4 / 6.4 / 1.5 / 6.1	**16** M	0418 / 1026 / 1639 / ◐ 2247	1.8 / 5.8 / 2.1 / 5.5
2 M	0410 / 1023 / 1638 / ◐ 2243	1.7 / 6.1 / 1.8 / 5.8	**17** TU	0459 / 1110 / 1725 / 2340	2.3 / 5.3 / 2.6 / 5.1
3 TU	0457 / 1115 / 1732 / 2343	2.0 / 5.8 / 2.1 / 5.5	**18** W	0601 / 1214 / 1844	2.7 / 4.9 / 2.9
4 W	0604 / 1226 / 1851	2.3 / 5.4 / 2.4	**19** TH	0110 / 0743 / 1403 / 2038	4.8 / 2.9 / 4.7 / 2.9
5 TH	0108 / 0742 / 1359 / 2031	5.3 / 2.4 / 5.4 / 2.3	**20** F	0255 / 0923 / 1534 / 2154	5.0 / 2.7 / 5.0 / 2.5
6 F	0242 / 0919 / 1527 / 2152	5.5 / 2.1 / 5.7 / 1.9	**21** SA	0402 / 1023 / 1630 / 2243	5.4 / 2.2 / 5.4 / 2.1
7 SA	0400 / 1032 / 1637 / 2256	6.0 / 1.6 / 6.2 / 1.4	**22** SU	0448 / 1107 / 1710 / 2322	5.9 / 1.8 / 5.9 / 1.7
8 SU	0502 / 1130 / 1732 / 2348	6.6 / 1.0 / 6.7 / 0.9	**23** M	0526 / 1143 / 1745 / 2357	6.3 / 1.4 / 6.2 / 1.3
9 M	0554 / 1220 / 1820 / O	7.1 / 0.6 / 7.0	**24** TU	0600 / 1216 / 1817	6.6 / 1.1 / 6.5
10 TU	0035 / 0639 / 1305 / 1903	0.6 / 7.4 / 0.3 / 7.2	**25** W	0029 / 0632 / 1248 / ● 1848	1.1 / 6.8 / 0.9 / 6.7
11 W	0119 / 0722 / 1346 / 1944	0.4 / 7.5 / 0.2 / 7.3	**26** TH	0101 / 0703 / 1320 / 1918	0.9 / 6.9 / 0.7 / 6.8
12 TH	0159 / 0802 / 1424 / 2022	0.4 / 7.5 / 0.4 / 7.1	**27** F	0132 / 0735 / 1352 / 1950	0.8 / 7.0 / 0.7 / 6.9
13 F	0236 / 0840 / 1500 / 2058	0.5 / 7.2 / 0.7 / 6.8	**28** SA	0204 / 0808 / 1424 / 2022	0.8 / 7.0 / 0.8 / 6.8
14 SA	0311 / 0915 / 1533 / 2133	0.9 / 6.8 / 1.1 / 6.4			
15 SU	0344 / 0950 / 1605 / 2208	1.3 / 6.4 / 1.6 / 6.0			

MARCH

Day	Time	m	Day	Time	m
1 SU	0237 / 0841 / 1456 / 2055	0.9 / 6.8 / 1.0 / 6.6	**16** M	0310 / 0913 / 1525 / 2129	1.3 / 6.3 / 1.6 / 6.1
2 M	0310 / 0917 / 1531 / 2132	1.1 / 6.6 / 1.3 / 6.3	**17** TU	0341 / 0947 / 1555 / 2205	1.7 / 5.8 / 2.1 / 5.6
3 TU	0348 / 0958 / 1611 / 2217	1.5 / 6.2 / 1.7 / 5.9	**18** W	0418 / 1026 / 1633 / 2252	2.2 / 5.3 / 2.5 / 5.1
4 W	0435 / 1050 / 1705 / 2318	1.9 / 5.7 / 2.2 / 5.5	**19** TH	0511 / 1122 / 1740	2.7 / 4.8 / 2.9
5 TH	0545 / 1207 / 1830	2.3 / 5.3 / 2.5	**20** F	0009 / 0650 / 1309 / 1944	4.8 / 2.9 / 4.5 / 3.0
6 F	0051 / 0736 / 1351 / 2022	5.2 / 2.4 / 5.2 / 2.4	**21** SA	0210 / 0840 / 1456 / 2115	4.8 / 2.7 / 4.8 / 2.7
7 SA	0235 / 0915 / 1523 / 2145	5.4 / 2.0 / 5.6 / 1.9	**22** SU	0324 / 0947 / 1554 / 2208	5.3 / 2.3 / 5.3 / 2.2
8 SU	0353 / 1024 / 1628 / 2245	6.0 / 1.5 / 6.1 / 1.3	**23** M	0412 / 1032 / 1636 / 2249	5.7 / 1.8 / 5.8 / 1.7
9 M	0450 / 1118 / 1718 / 2334	6.6 / 0.9 / 6.7 / 0.8	**24** TU	0451 / 1109 / 1711 / 2325	6.2 / 1.4 / 6.2 / 1.3
10 TU	0538 / 1203 / 1802	7.1 / 0.5 / 7.0	**25** W	0527 / 1144 / 1744 / 2359	6.5 / 1.1 / 6.5 / 1.0
11 W	0017 / 0619 / 1243 / O 1841	0.5 / 7.3 / 0.3 / 7.2	**26** TH	0600 / 1217 / 1817	6.8 / 0.8 / 6.8
12 TH	0056 / 0659 / 1320 / 1918	0.3 / 7.4 / 0.3 / 7.2	**27** F	0032 / 0634 / 1252 / 1850	0.8 / 7.0 / 0.6 / 7.0
13 F	0132 / 0735 / 1354 / 1952	0.4 / 7.3 / 0.5 / 7.1	**28** SA	0107 / 0708 / 1326 / 1924	0.6 / 7.1 / 0.6 / 7.0
14 SA	0207 / 0809 / 1426 / 2025	0.5 / 7.1 / 0.7 / 6.8	**29** SU	0142 / 0743 / 1400 / 1959	0.6 / 7.1 / 0.7 / 6.9
15 SU	0239 / 0842 / 1456 / 2057	0.9 / 6.7 / 1.1 / 6.5	**30** M	0217 / 0820 / 1436 / 2036	0.8 / 6.9 / 0.9 / 6.7
			31 TU	0255 / 0900 / 1514 / 2117	1.1 / 6.5 / 1.3 / 6.4

APRIL

Day	Time	m	Day	Time	m
1 W	0337 / 0946 / 1559 / 2207	1.4 / 6.1 / 1.7 / 5.9	**16** TH	0352 / 0957 / 1604 / 2222	2.1 / 5.3 / 2.4 / 5.3
2 TH	0431 / 1045 / 1658 / ◐ 2315	1.9 / 5.6 / 2.2 / 5.5	**17** F	0442 / 1049 / 1701 / ◑ 2327	2.5 / 4.9 / 2.8 / 5.0
3 F	0549 / 1206 / 1829	2.2 / 5.2 / 2.4	**18** SA	0602 / 1208 / 1840	2.7 / 4.7 / 2.9
4 SA	0048 / 0735 / 1345 / 2011	5.4 / 2.2 / 5.2 / 2.3	**19** SU	0101 / 0737 / 1352 / 2012	4.9 / 2.7 / 4.8 / 2.7
5 SU	0223 / 0901 / 1508 / 2127	5.6 / 1.9 / 5.6 / 1.8	**20** M	0226 / 0849 / 1500 / 2116	5.2 / 2.3 / 5.2 / 2.3
6 M	0334 / 1005 / 1607 / 2224	6.1 / 1.4 / 6.1 / 1.3	**21** TU	0321 / 0942 / 1548 / 2203	5.6 / 1.9 / 5.6 / 1.9
7 TU	0428 / 1054 / 1655 / 2310	6.6 / 1.0 / 6.6 / 0.9	**22** W	0406 / 1025 / 1628 / 2244	6.0 / 1.5 / 6.1 / 1.4
8 W	0514 / 1137 / 1736 / 2351	6.9 / 0.7 / 6.9 / 0.7	**23** TH	0446 / 1105 / 1706 / 2323	6.4 / 1.1 / 6.5 / 1.1
9 TH	0554 / 1215 / 1814 / O	7.1 / 0.6 / 7.0	**24** F	0524 / 1144 / 1744 / O	6.7 / 0.9 / 6.8
10 F	0029 / 0631 / 1250 / 1849	0.6 / 7.1 / 0.6 / 7.0	**25** SA	0002 / 0603 / 1223 / ● 1821	0.8 / 7.0 / 0.7 / 7.0
11 SA	0105 / 0706 / 1323 / 1923	0.6 / 7.0 / 0.7 / 6.9	**26** SU	0042 / 0643 / 1302 / 1900	0.7 / 7.1 / 0.6 / 7.1
12 SU	0138 / 0740 / 1355 / 1955	0.8 / 6.8 / 1.0 / 6.7	**27** M	0122 / 0724 / 1342 / 1941	0.7 / 7.0 / 0.7 / 7.0
13 M	0211 / 0812 / 1425 / 2027	1.0 / 6.5 / 1.3 / 6.4	**28** TU	0204 / 0807 / 1423 / 2025	0.8 / 6.8 / 0.9 / 6.8
14 TU	0242 / 0844 / 1455 / 2100	1.4 / 6.1 / 1.6 / 6.1	**29** W	0248 / 0853 / 1507 / 2113	1.0 / 6.5 / 1.3 / 6.5
15 W	0315 / 0918 / 1526 / 2136	1.8 / 5.7 / 2.0 / 5.7	**30** TH	0338 / 0946 / 1558 / 2209	1.4 / 6.1 / 1.7 / 6.1

Chart Datum: 3·71 metres below Ordnance Datum (Newlyn)
HAT is 7·8m above Chart Datum

TIDES

TIDES

WALES – MILFORD HAVEN
LAT 51°42′N   LONG 5°03′W
TIMES AND HEIGHTS OF HIGH AND LOW WATERS

Dates in amber are **SPRINGS**
Dates in yellow are **NEAPS**

2009

MAY

Time	m	Time	m
1 0437	1.7	**16** 0421	2.2
1047	5.7	1025	5.2
F 1701	2.0	SA 1635	2.5
2317	5.8	2254	5.4
2 0553	1.9	**17** 0520	2.4
1201	5.4	1124	5.0
SA 1823	2.2	SU 1741	2.6
		2359	5.2
3 0036	5.7	**18** 0632	2.4
0717	2.0	1235	5.0
SU 1323	5.5	M 1901	2.6
1946	2.1	◑	
4 0155	5.8	**19** 0112	5.3
0832	1.8	0742	2.3
M 1436	5.7	TU 1349	5.2
◐ 2056	1.8	2010	2.4
5 0302	6.1	**20** 0218	5.5
0933	1.5	0842	2.0
TU 1535	6.0	W 1450	5.5
2153	1.5	2108	2.0
6 0357	6.3	**21** 0314	5.9
1023	1.2	0936	1.7
W 1624	6.3	TH 1541	5.9
2241	1.2	2200	1.6
7 0444	6.5	**22** 0403	6.2
1107	1.1	1025	1.3
TH 1708	6.5	F 1627	6.3
2323	1.1	2248	1.3
8 0527	6.6	**23** 0450	6.6
1145	1.0	1111	1.1
F 1747	6.7	SA 1712	6.7
		2335	1.0
9 0002	1.0	**24** 0537	6.8
0605	6.6	1157	0.9
SA 1222	1.0	SU 1758	6.9
1823	6.7		
10 0039	1.0	**25** 0021	0.8
0641	6.6	0623	6.9
SU 1256	1.1	M 1243	0.8
1858	6.6	1844	7.0
11 0114	1.1	**26** 0109	0.7
0715	6.4	0711	6.9
M 1329	1.2	TU 1329	0.8
○ 1932	6.5	● 1931	7.0
12 0148	1.3	**27** 0157	0.7
0749	6.3	0800	6.8
TU 1401	1.4	W 1416	0.9
2006	6.4	2020	6.9
13 0222	1.5	**28** 0247	0.9
0823	6.0	0851	6.6
W 1433	1.7	TH 1504	1.1
2040	6.1	2112	6.7
14 0257	1.7	**29** 0339	1.1
0858	5.8	0944	6.3
TH 1507	1.9	F 1556	1.4
2118	5.9	2207	6.4
15 0335	2.0	**30** 0436	1.4
0938	5.5	1040	6.0
F 1546	2.2	SA 1654	1.7
2201	5.6	2306	6.2
		31 0538	1.6
		1141	5.7
		SU 1800	1.9

JUNE

Time	m	Time	m
1 0010	6.0	**16** 0534	2.1
0644	1.8	1139	5.3
M 1248	5.6	TU 1755	2.3
1908	1.9	◐	
2 0117	5.9	**17** 0010	5.5
0751	1.8	0636	2.2
TU 1354	5.6	W 1242	5.3
◑ 2015	1.9	1903	2.3
3 0222	5.9	**18** 0116	5.5
0853	1.8	0742	2.1
W 1456	5.8	TH 1350	5.5
2116	1.8	2013	2.2
4 0321	6.0	**19** 0223	5.7
0948	1.7	0848	1.9
TH 1551	6.0	F 1455	5.7
2210	1.7	2119	1.9
5 0414	6.0	**20** 0325	6.0
1036	1.6	0949	1.6
F 1640	6.1	SA 1554	6.1
2257	1.5	2219	1.5
6 0502	6.1	**21** 0423	6.3
1119	1.5	1046	1.3
SA 1724	6.3	SU 1649	6.5
2340	1.4	2315	1.2
7 0544	6.2	**22** 0518	6.6
1158	1.4	1139	1.0
SU 1803	6.4	M 1742	6.8
8 0019	1.4	**23** 0008	0.9
0622	6.2	0611	6.8
M 1236	1.4	TU 1230	0.8
1840	6.4	1833	7.0
9 0056	1.4	**24** 0101	0.6
0659	6.2	0703	6.9
TU 1310	1.4	W 1320	0.7
○ 1916	6.4	1924	7.2
10 0132	1.4	**25** 0151	0.5
0734	6.1	0753	6.9
W 1344	1.5	TH 1408	0.7
1950	6.3	● 2014	7.2
11 0206	1.5	**26** 0241	0.6
0808	6.0	0842	6.8
TH 1417	1.6	F 1456	0.8
2025	6.2	2103	7.0
12 0241	1.6	**27** 0330	0.8
0843	5.9	0931	6.6
F 1451	1.7	SA 1544	1.0
2101	6.1	2152	6.8
13 0318	1.7	**28** 0418	1.1
0919	5.8	1019	6.3
SA 1528	1.9	SU 1633	1.3
2140	5.9	2241	6.5
14 0357	1.9	**29** 0508	1.4
0959	5.6	1109	6.0
SU 1609	2.0	M 1725	1.6
2223	5.7	2334	6.1
15 0442	2.0	**30** 0602	1.7
1045	5.4	1204	5.7
M 1657	2.2	TU 1823	1.9
2313	5.6		

JULY

Time	m	Time	m
1 0032	5.8	**16** 0540	2.1
0702	2.0	1149	5.4
W 1308	5.5	TH 1806	2.3
1928	2.2		
2 0138	5.5	**17** 0024	5.5
0808	2.2	0647	2.2
TH 1415	5.4	F 1300	5.4
2038	2.2	1925	2.3
3 0245	5.5	**18** 0141	5.5
0914	2.1	0808	2.2
F 1521	5.6	SA 1420	5.5
2143	2.1	◑ 2049	2.1
4 0349	5.6	**19** 0259	5.7
1012	2.0	0925	1.9
SA 1619	5.8	SU 1533	5.9
◐ 2238	1.9	2202	1.7
5 0444	5.7	**20** 0408	6.1
1100	1.8	1030	1.5
SU 1707	6.0	M 1636	6.4
2324	1.7	2304	1.2
6 0530	5.9	**21** 0509	6.5
1142	1.6	1127	1.1
M 1749	6.2	TU 1733	6.8
7 0005	1.6	**22** 0000	0.8
0609	6.1	0603	6.8
TU 1220	1.5	W 1220	0.7
1826	6.4	1824	7.2
8 0042	1.4	**23** 0052	0.5
0645	6.2	0653	7.1
W 1255	1.4	TH 1309	0.5
1901	6.5	1913	7.4
9 0117	1.3	**24** 0140	0.3
0719	6.2	0740	7.2
TH 1328	1.4	F 1355	0.4
1935	6.5	1959	7.5
10 0150	1.3	**25** 0225	0.3
0751	6.2	0824	7.1
F 1400	1.4	SA 1438	0.5
2007	6.5	2044	7.3
11 0222	1.3	**26** 0308	0.5
0823	6.2	0907	6.9
SA 1432	1.4	SU 1521	0.8
○ 2040	6.4	● 2126	7.0
12 0256	1.4	**27** 0349	0.9
0856	6.1	0948	6.5
SU 1506	1.5	M 1602	1.1
2114	6.3	2209	6.6
13 0330	1.5	**28** 0430	1.4
0930	6.0	1031	6.1
M 1541	1.7	TU 1645	1.6
2151	6.1	2253	6.1
14 0407	1.7	**29** 0513	1.9
1008	5.8	1118	5.7
TU 1619	1.9	W 1733	2.1
2232	5.9	2343	5.6
15 0448	1.9	**30** 0606	2.3
1053	5.6	1216	5.3
W 1706	2.1	TH 1837	2.4
2321	5.7		
		31 0049	5.2
		0718	2.6
		F 1334	5.1
		2002	2.6

AUGUST

Time	m	Time	m
1 0212	5.1	**16** 0114	5.3
0845	2.6	0745	2.4
SA 1456	5.2	SU 1400	5.4
2123	2.5	2038	2.2
2 0332	5.2	**17** 0248	5.5
0953	2.3	0914	2.1
SU 1603	5.6	M 1523	5.8
◑ 2224	2.2	◑ 2156	1.7
3 0431	5.5	**18** 0402	6.0
1045	2.0	1022	1.6
M 1653	5.9	TU 1629	6.4
2310	1.8	2257	1.2
4 0515	5.8	**19** 0501	6.5
1126	1.7	1117	1.0
TU 1733	6.2	W 1723	7.0
2349	1.5	2349	0.7
5 0553	6.1	**20** 0551	7.0
1203	1.5	1206	0.6
W 1809	6.5	TH 1811	7.4
6 0024	1.3	**21** 0036	0.3
0626	6.3	0636	7.3
TH 1236	1.3	F 1251	0.4
1841	6.6	1855	7.6
7 0056	1.2	**22** 0120	0.2
0657	6.4	0719	7.3
F 1307	1.2	SA 1334	0.3
1913	6.7	1937	7.6
8 0127	1.1	**23** 0200	0.3
0727	6.5	0759	7.3
SA 1338	1.1	SU 1413	0.4
1943	6.7	2017	7.4
9 0158	1.0	**24** 0238	0.5
0757	6.5	0837	7.0
SU 1409	1.1	M 1451	0.7
○ 2014	6.7	2055	7.0
10 0229	1.1	**25** 0314	1.0
0828	6.4	0914	6.6
M 1440	1.2	TU 1527	1.2
2046	6.4	● 2132	6.5
11 0301	1.2	**26** 0349	1.5
0859	6.3	0951	6.2
TU 1512	1.4	W 1604	1.7
2119	6.4	2211	6.0
12 0334	1.5	**27** 0425	2.0
0934	6.1	1032	5.7
W 1547	1.7	TH 1646	2.2
2156	6.1	2255	5.4
13 0411	1.8	**28** 0511	2.5
1015	5.8	1125	5.2
TH 1629	2.0	F 1746	2.7
2243	5.8	2357	4.9
14 0459	2.1	**29** 0625	2.9
1108	5.5	1249	4.9
F 1727	2.3	SA 1926	2.9
2346	5.4		
15 0607	2.4	**30** 0140	4.8
1224	5.3	0816	2.9
SA 1856	2.5	SU 1432	5.1
		2104	2.7
		31 0314	5.0
		0934	2.6
		M 1542	5.5
		2205	2.3

Chart Datum: 3·71 metres below Ordnance Datum (Newlyn)
HAT is 7·8m above Chart Datum

WALES – MILFORD HAVEN
LAT 51°42′N   LONG 5°03′W
TIMES AND HEIGHTS OF HIGH AND LOW WATERS

Dates in amber are **SPRINGS**
Dates in yellow are **NEAPS**

2009

SEPTEMBER

Day	Time m	Day	Time m
1 TU	0411 5.4 / 1024 2.1 / 1630 5.9 / 2249 1.9	16 W	0354 6.1 / 1011 1.5 / 1617 6.6 / 2245 1.1
2 W	0453 5.9 / 1104 1.7 / 1708 6.3 / 2325 1.5	17 TH	0447 6.6 / 1102 1.0 / 1707 7.1 / 2332 0.6
3 TH	0528 6.2 / 1138 1.4 / 1742 6.6 / 2358 1.2	18 F	0532 7.1 / 1147 0.6 / 1751 7.4
4 F ○	0600 6.5 / 1210 1.2 / 1814 6.8	19 SA	0015 0.4 / 0614 7.3 / 1229 0.4 / 1832 7.6
5 SA	0029 1.0 / 0629 6.6 / 1241 1.0 / 1845 6.9	20 SU	0055 0.3 / 0653 7.4 / 1308 0.4 / 1911 7.5
6 SU	0100 0.9 / 0659 6.8 / 1312 0.9 / 1915 7.0	21 M	0132 0.5 / 0730 7.3 / 1345 0.6 / 1948 7.3
7 M	0131 0.9 / 0729 6.8 / 1343 0.9 / 1946 6.9	22 TU	0207 0.8 / 0806 7.0 / 1421 0.9 / 2023 6.9
8 TU	0202 1.0 / 0800 6.7 / 1415 1.1 / 2018 6.8	23 W	0240 1.2 / 0840 6.6 / 1455 1.3 / 2058 6.4
9 W	0234 1.1 / 0832 6.6 / 1447 1.3 / 2052 6.5	24 TH	0312 1.6 / 0915 6.2 / 1529 1.8 / 2134 5.9
10 TH	0307 1.4 / 0907 6.3 / 1523 1.6 / 2131 6.2	25 F	0345 2.1 / 0954 5.7 / 1608 2.3 / 2215 5.4
11 F	0345 1.8 / 0949 6.0 / 1607 2.0 / 2219 5.8	26 SA ◑	0425 2.6 / 1043 5.3 / 1704 2.8 / 2312 4.9
12 SA ◑	0434 2.2 / 1045 5.6 / 1710 2.4 / 2328 5.3	27 SU	0533 3.0 / 1201 4.9 / 1842 3.0
13 SU	0549 2.5 / 1209 5.3 / 1852 2.5	28 M	0055 4.7 / 0731 3.1 / 1353 5.0 / 2027 2.8
14 M	0107 5.2 / 0740 2.5 / 1354 5.4 / 2036 2.2	29 TU	0238 4.9 / 0859 2.7 / 1506 5.4 / 2131 2.4
15 TU	0244 5.5 / 0907 2.1 / 1516 6.0 / 2149 1.7	30 W	0337 5.4 / 0951 2.3 / 1555 5.9 / 2215 2.0

OCTOBER

Day	Time m	Day	Time m
1 TH	0419 5.8 / 1032 1.9 / 1634 6.3 / 2252 1.6	16 F	0424 6.6 / 1040 1.1 / 1644 7.0 / 2309 0.9
2 F	0454 6.2 / 1107 1.5 / 1709 6.6 / 2326 1.3	17 SA	0509 7.0 / 1124 0.8 / 1728 7.2 / 2350 0.7
3 SA	0527 6.5 / 1139 1.2 / 1742 6.8 / 2358 1.0	18 SU ●	0549 7.2 / 1204 0.7 / 1808 7.3
4 SU ○	0558 6.8 / 1212 1.0 / 1814 7.0	19 M	0027 0.7 / 0627 7.2 / 1243 0.7 / 1845 7.2
5 M	0030 0.9 / 0629 6.9 / 1245 0.9 / 1846 7.1	20 TU	0104 0.8 / 0703 7.1 / 1319 0.9 / 1921 7.0
6 TU	0104 0.9 / 0701 7.0 / 1319 0.9 / 1920 7.0	21 W	0138 1.1 / 0738 6.9 / 1355 1.2 / 1956 6.7
7 W	0137 0.9 / 0735 6.9 / 1354 1.1 / 1956 6.9	22 TH	0211 1.4 / 0813 6.6 / 1429 1.5 / 2031 6.3
8 TH	0212 1.1 / 0811 6.8 / 1430 1.3 / 2034 6.6	23 F	0243 1.8 / 0848 6.2 / 1504 1.9 / 2106 5.9
9 F	0249 1.5 / 0851 6.5 / 1512 1.6 / 2118 6.2	24 SA	0316 2.2 / 0926 5.9 / 1542 2.3 / 2147 5.4
10 SA	0332 1.8 / 0938 6.1 / 1602 2.0 / 2213 5.8	25 SU	0354 2.6 / 1013 5.5 / 1633 2.7 / 2239 5.1
11 SU ◑	0428 2.3 / 1041 5.7 / 1713 2.4 / 2328 5.4	26 M	0451 2.9 / 1117 5.2 / 1751 2.9 / 2355 4.8
12 M	0549 2.5 / 1208 5.5 / 1855 2.4	27 TU	0626 3.1 / 1247 5.1 / 1923 2.8
13 TU	0103 5.3 / 0732 2.5 / 1343 5.7 / 2024 2.1	28 W	0135 4.9 / 0757 2.9 / 1410 5.3 / 2036 2.5
14 W	0230 5.7 / 0851 2.0 / 1458 6.1 / 2131 1.6	29 TH	0245 5.3 / 0901 2.5 / 1507 5.7 / 2128 2.2
15 TH	0334 6.2 / 0951 1.6 / 1556 6.6 / 2224 1.2	30 F	0333 5.7 / 0951 2.1 / 1551 6.1 / 2210 1.8
		31 SA	0413 6.1 / 1028 1.7 / 1630 6.4 / 2248 1.4

NOVEMBER

Day	Time m	Day	Time m
1 SU	0449 6.5 / 1106 1.4 / 1707 6.7 / 2325 1.2	16 M ●	0526 6.8 / 1143 1.1 / 1746 6.8
2 M ○	0525 6.8 / 1143 1.2 / 1744 6.9	17 TU	0004 1.2 / 0605 6.9 / 1222 1.1 / 1825 6.8
3 TU	0002 1.0 / 0601 7.0 / 1221 1.0 / 1821 7.1	18 W	0041 1.2 / 0643 6.9 / 1300 1.2 / 1902 6.7
4 W	0040 0.9 / 0639 7.1 / 1300 1.0 / 1901 7.1	19 TH	0116 1.3 / 0719 6.7 / 1336 1.4 / 1937 6.5
5 TH	0119 1.0 / 0718 7.0 / 1341 1.0 / 1943 6.9	20 F	0150 1.5 / 0755 6.6 / 1411 1.6 / 2013 6.2
6 F	0159 1.1 / 0800 6.9 / 1424 1.2 / 2027 6.6	21 SA	0223 1.8 / 0830 6.3 / 1446 1.8 / 2048 6.0
7 SA	0242 1.4 / 0846 6.6 / 1511 1.5 / 2117 6.3	22 SU	0257 2.0 / 0908 6.1 / 1524 2.1 / 2127 5.7
8 SU	0331 1.7 / 0929 6.3 / 1607 1.8 / 2216 5.9	23 M	0334 2.3 / 0949 5.8 / 1607 2.3 / 2211 5.4
9 M ◑	0429 2.1 / 1044 6.0 / 1717 2.1 / 2325 5.6	24 TU ◑	0419 2.6 / 1039 5.5 / 1701 2.6 / 2305 5.2
10 TU	0544 2.3 / 1158 5.9 / 1839 2.1	25 W	0520 2.8 / 1139 5.4 / 1810 2.7
11 W	0043 5.6 / 0708 2.3 / 1317 5.9 / 1956 2.0	26 TH	0012 5.1 / 0638 2.8 / 1251 5.3 / 1922 2.6
12 TH	0159 5.8 / 0821 2.0 / 1420 6.2 / 2101 1.7	27 F	0128 5.2 / 0751 2.7 / 1400 5.5 / 2026 2.4
13 F	0303 6.1 / 0923 1.7 / 1527 6.4 / 2156 1.5	28 SA	0233 5.5 / 0853 2.4 / 1458 5.8 / 2121 2.1
14 SA	0357 6.4 / 1015 1.4 / 1619 6.7 / 2243 1.3	29 SU	0325 5.8 / 0945 2.0 / 1547 6.1 / 2209 1.7
15 SU	0444 6.7 / 1101 1.2 / 1704 6.8 / 2325 1.2	30 M	0411 6.2 / 1032 1.7 / 1633 6.5 / 2254 1.4

DECEMBER

Day	Time m	Day	Time m
1 TU	0455 6.6 / 1117 1.4 / 1718 6.7 / 2338 1.2	16 W ●	0552 6.6 / 1208 1.5 / 1813 6.6
2 W ○	0539 6.9 / 1202 1.1 / 1804 6.9	17 TH	0025 1.4 / 0630 6.6 / 1247 1.4 / 1850 6.4
3 TH	0022 1.0 / 0623 7.1 / 1248 0.9 / 1849 7.0	18 F	0101 1.4 / 0707 6.7 / 1323 1.4 / 1925 6.4
4 F	0107 0.9 / 0709 7.1 / 1334 0.9 / 1937 7.0	19 SA	0135 1.5 / 0742 6.6 / 1357 1.5 / 1959 6.3
5 SA	0152 1.0 / 0756 7.1 / 1422 1.0 / 2025 6.8	20 SU	0208 1.6 / 0816 6.5 / 1431 1.6 / 2032 6.2
6 SU	0239 1.1 / 0846 7.0 / 1511 1.1 / 2116 6.6	21 M	0240 1.7 / 0850 6.3 / 1505 1.7 / 2106 6.0
7 M	0328 1.4 / 0938 6.7 / 1605 1.4 / 2209 6.3	22 TU	0314 1.9 / 0925 6.1 / 1541 1.9 / 2142 5.8
8 TU	0422 1.6 / 1033 6.5 / 1703 1.6 / 2306 6.0	23 W	0350 2.1 / 1004 5.9 / 1621 2.1 / 2223 5.6
9 W ◑	0523 1.9 / 1134 6.2 / 1807 1.9	24 TH ◑	0433 2.2 / 1048 5.7 / 1707 2.3 / 2311 5.4
10 TH	0010 5.8 / 0630 2.1 / 1240 6.0 / 1915 2.0	25 F	0525 2.5 / 1141 5.5 / 1805 2.5
11 F	0118 5.7 / 0741 2.1 / 1348 6.0 / 2023 2.0	26 SA	0010 5.3 / 0632 2.6 / 1246 5.4 / 1915 2.5
12 SA	0226 5.8 / 0849 2.0 / 1454 6.0 / 2125 1.9	27 SU	0122 5.3 / 0749 2.6 / 1358 5.5 / 2027 2.3
13 SU	0327 6.0 / 0949 1.9 / 1553 6.1 / 2218 1.8	28 M	0234 5.5 / 0901 2.3 / 1506 5.8 / 2132 2.0
14 M	0422 6.2 / 1041 1.7 / 1646 6.2 / 2305 1.6	29 TU	0336 5.9 / 1003 1.9 / 1605 6.1 / 2229 1.7
15 TU	0509 6.4 / 1127 1.6 / 1731 6.3 / 2347 1.5	30 W	0432 6.3 / 1058 1.5 / 1700 6.5 / 2321 1.3
		31 TH ○	0524 6.8 / 1150 1.1 / 1752 6.8

Chart Datum: 3·71 metres below Ordnance Datum (Newlyn)
HAT is 7·8m above Chart Datum

TIDES

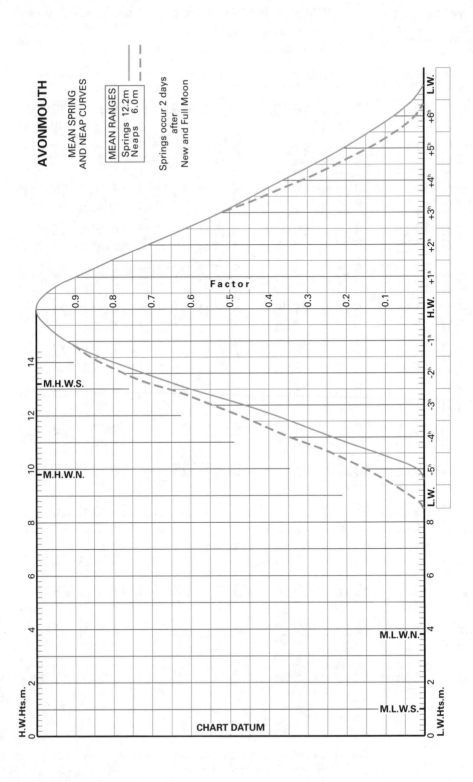

AVONMOUTH

MEAN SPRING
AND NEAP CURVES

MEAN RANGES
Springs 12.2m
Neaps 6.0m

Springs occur 2 days
after
New and Full Moon

Factor

0.9 0.8 0.7 0.6 0.5 0.4 0.3 0.2 0.1

H.W.Hts.m.

M.H.W.S.

M.H.W.N.

CHART DATUM

H.W.

L.W.

L.W.Hts.m.

M.L.W.N.

M.L.W.S.

TIME ZONE (UT)
For Summer Time add ONE hour in **non-shaded areas**

ENGLAND – AVONMOUTH
LAT 51°30′N   LONG 2°44′W
TIMES AND HEIGHTS OF HIGH AND LOW WATERS

Dates in amber are **SPRINGS**
Dates in yellow are **NEAPS**

2009

JANUARY

Time m	Time m
1 0356 2.5 / 0947 11.8 / TH 1622 2.5 / 2206 11.6	**16** 0500 1.4 / 1043 13.0 / F 1720 1.7 / 2304 12.3
2 0426 2.5 / 1021 11.7 / F 1653 2.5 / 2241 11.5	**17** 0527 1.9 / 1120 12.2 / SA 1745 2.2 / 2339 11.6
3 0501 2.6 / 1100 11.5 / SA 1730 2.6 / 2322 11.3	**18** 0556 2.4 / 1159 11.4 / SU 1817 2.8 ☽
4 0542 2.8 / 1146 11.2 / SU 1814 2.8 ☽	**19** 0019 10.7 / 0633 3.1 / M 1247 10.5 / 1858 3.4
5 0011 10.9 / 0630 3.1 / M 1243 10.8 / 1907 3.2	**20** 0114 10.0 / 0724 3.7 / TU 1355 9.9 / 1955 4.0
6 0112 10.5 / 0731 3.5 / TU 1352 10.5 / 2018 3.5	**21** 0236 9.6 / 0835 4.1 / W 1517 9.7 / 2116 4.1
7 0229 10.4 / 0858 3.7 / W 1516 10.6 / 2156 3.4	**22** 0355 9.9 / 1005 3.9 / TH 1627 10.1 / 2248 3.7
8 0356 10.8 / 1038 3.3 / TH 1636 11.2 / 2317 2.8	**23** 0457 10.5 / 1121 3.2 / F 1725 10.7 / 2351 2.9
9 0507 11.6 / 1151 2.6 / F 1741 11.9	**24** 0549 11.3 / 1217 2.6 / SA 1814 11.3
10 0022 2.1 / 0606 12.5 / SA 1255 1.9 / 1838 12.7	**25** 0044 2.4 / 0634 11.9 / SU 1308 2.2 / 1856 11.8
11 0121 1.5 / 0659 13.2 / SU 1354 1.4 / ○ 1931 13.2	**26** 0133 2.1 / 0715 12.3 / M 1356 2.0 / 1936 12.1
12 0217 1.1 / 0750 13.7 / M 1448 1.0 / 2020 13.6	**27** 0219 2.0 / 0753 12.4 / TU 1441 1.9 / 2014 12.2
13 0307 0.8 / 0838 13.9 / TU 1536 0.7 / 2107 13.6	**28** 0300 2.0 / 0829 12.4 / W 1520 2.0 / 2048 12.2
14 0352 0.8 / 0921 13.9 / W 1618 0.8 / 2149 13.4	**29** 0332 2.1 / 0901 12.4 / TH 1551 2.1 / 2119 12.2
15 0429 1.0 / 1005 13.6 / TH 1653 1.2 / 2228 13.0	**30** 0355 2.2 / 0932 12.4 / F 1614 2.1 / 2148 12.2
	31 0415 2.1 / 1003 12.3 / SA 1636 2.0 / 2220 12.2

FEBRUARY

Time m	Time m
1 0443 2.1 / 1038 12.1 / SU 1705 2.1 / 2257 11.9	**16** 0515 2.1 / 1112 11.5 / M 1730 2.5 / ○ 2327 10.9
2 0516 2.2 / 1119 11.7 / M 1741 2.4 / ☽ 2339 11.4	**17** 0546 2.8 / 1147 10.4 / TU 1804 3.2
3 0556 2.7 / 1208 11.0 / TU 1826 3.0	**18** 0007 10.0 / 0629 3.6 / W 1240 9.5 / 1854 4.0
4 0033 10.6 / 0647 3.4 / W 1314 10.3 / 1927 3.7	**19** 0118 9.2 / 0739 4.3 / TH 1420 8.9 / 2018 4.6
5 0148 10.0 / 0806 4.0 / TH 1447 10.0 / 2124 4.0	**20** 0316 9.2 / 0915 4.4 / F 1558 9.4 / 2209 4.2
6 0333 10.2 / 1024 3.8 / F 1625 10.5 / 2304 3.2	**21** 0430 10.0 / 1054 3.6 / SA 1701 10.2 / 2329 3.2
7 0457 11.1 / 1145 2.8 / SA 1735 11.6	**22** 0526 10.9 / 1156 2.7 / SU 1751 11.2
8 0013 2.3 / 0559 12.2 / SU 1249 1.8 / 1831 12.6	**23** 0023 2.5 / 0611 11.8 / M 1248 2.1 / 1834 11.8
9 0113 1.4 / 0651 13.2 / M 1345 1.0 / ○ 1921 13.4	**24** 0113 2.0 / 0652 12.3 / TU 1337 1.7 / 1913 12.3
10 0206 0.7 / 0738 13.9 / TU 1437 0.5 / 2006 13.9	**25** 0200 1.8 / 0730 12.6 / W 1423 1.6 / ● 1950 12.5
11 0254 0.4 / 0823 14.2 / W 1522 0.3 / 2048 14.0	**26** 0243 1.7 / 0806 12.8 / TH 1503 1.6 / 2024 12.6
12 0336 0.3 / 0904 14.2 / TH 1600 0.4 / 2126 13.8	**27** 0318 1.8 / 0839 12.8 / F 1535 1.7 / 2056 12.7
13 0410 0.6 / 0940 13.8 / F 1629 0.9 / 2200 13.3	**28** 0343 1.8 / 0910 12.8 / SA 1557 1.8 / 2126 12.7
14 0435 1.1 / 1013 13.2 / SA 1648 1.5 / 2229 12.6	
15 0453 1.6 / 1042 12.4 / SU 1705 2.0 / 2256 11.8	

MARCH

Time m	Time m
1 0400 1.8 / 0942 12.7 / SU 1615 1.8 / 2158 12.6	**16** 0420 1.6 / 1007 12.2 / M 1627 2.0 / 2219 11.8
2 0423 1.8 / 1017 12.5 / M 1641 1.9 / 2234 12.2	**17** 0440 2.1 / 1033 11.3 / TU 1649 2.4 / 2245 11.0
3 0453 2.0 / 1057 11.8 / TU 1714 2.3 / 2315 11.5	**18** 0508 2.6 / 1103 10.4 / W 1718 3.1 / ☽ 2319 10.1
4 0530 2.6 / 1144 10.9 / W 1756 3.0	**19** 0545 3.4 / 1144 9.4 / TH 1801 3.9
5 0007 10.6 / 0619 3.4 / TH 1251 10.0 / 1856 3.9	**20** 0014 9.1 / 0650 4.3 / F 1315 8.7 / 1925 4.7
6 0126 9.8 / 0742 4.2 / F 1441 9.6 / 2122 4.2	**21** 0231 8.9 / 0833 4.5 / SA 1520 9.0 / 2123 4.5
7 0327 9.9 / 1024 3.7 / SA 1620 10.4 / 2256 3.2	**22** 0355 9.6 / 1014 3.8 / SU 1628 10.0 / 2258 3.5
8 0448 11.0 / 1136 2.5 / SU 1726 11.6 / 2359 2.0	**23** 0452 10.7 / 1125 2.8 / M 1719 11.0 / 2354 2.6
9 0547 12.3 / 1233 1.4 / M 1817 12.7	**24** 0539 11.6 / 1218 2.1 / TU 1803 11.8
10 0054 1.1 / 0635 13.3 / TU 1325 0.7 / 1902 13.5	**25** 0043 2.0 / 0621 12.2 / W 1307 1.7 / 1842 12.4
11 0145 0.5 / 0719 13.9 / W 1413 0.3 / ○ 1944 13.9	**26** 0131 1.7 / 0700 12.7 / TH 1353 1.5 / 1920 12.7
12 0231 0.2 / 0801 14.2 / TH 1456 0.2 / 2023 13.9	**27** 0214 1.6 / 0737 12.9 / F 1434 1.4 / 1956 12.9
13 0311 0.2 / 0838 14.0 / F 1532 0.5 / 2058 13.7	**28** 0251 1.5 / 0813 13.1 / SA 1508 1.5 / 2030 13.0
14 0344 0.6 / 0912 13.6 / SA 1559 1.1 / 2128 13.2	**29** 0321 1.5 / 0848 13.1 / SU 1534 1.5 / 2104 13.0
15 0406 1.2 / 0941 12.9 / SU 1614 1.6 / 2154 12.5	**30** 0344 1.6 / 0924 12.9 / M 1557 1.6 / 2139 12.8
	31 0408 1.6 / 1002 12.5 / TU 1624 1.8 / 2217 12.3

APRIL

Time m	Time m
1 0439 2.0 / 1043 11.7 / W 1658 2.3 / 2300 11.5	**16** 0441 2.6 / 1034 10.4 / TH 1649 2.9 / 2249 10.2
2 0518 2.6 / 1134 10.8 / TH 1742 3.2 / ● 2356 10.5	**17** 0518 3.2 / 1115 9.7 / F 1729 3.7 / ☽ 2339 9.5
3 0613 3.5 / 1246 9.8 / F 1851 4.0	**18** 0616 3.9 / 1224 9.0 / SA 1839 4.4
4 0127 9.8 / 0811 4.1 / SA 1441 9.8 / 2115 3.9	**19** 0119 9.0 / 0748 4.2 / SU 1418 9.0 / 2026 4.4
5 0317 10.2 / 1005 3.3 / SU 1602 10.6 / 2233 2.9	**20** 0304 9.5 / 0915 3.8 / M 1538 9.8 / 2157 3.8
6 0427 11.3 / 1110 2.2 / M 1703 11.7 / 2332 1.9	**21** 0406 10.4 / 1032 3.0 / TU 1635 10.7 / 2307 2.9
7 0523 12.3 / 1204 1.4 / TU 1752 12.7	**22** 0457 11.3 / 1134 2.4 / W 1723 11.6
8 0025 1.1 / 0610 13.1 / W 1255 0.8 / 1836 13.3	**23** 0001 2.3 / 0543 12.0 / TH 1227 1.9 / 1806 12.3
9 0114 0.6 / 0653 13.5 / TH 1341 0.5 / ○ 1916 13.6	**24** 0051 1.9 / 0625 12.6 / F 1315 1.5 / 1847 12.8
10 0159 0.5 / 0733 13.6 / F 1423 0.6 / 1953 13.5	**25** 0137 1.6 / 0707 12.9 / SA 1359 1.4 / ● 1927 13.1
11 0240 0.6 / 0810 13.4 / SA 1459 0.9 / 2027 13.2	**26** 0219 1.4 / 0748 13.1 / SU 1439 1.3 / 2006 13.2
12 0313 1.0 / 0843 13.0 / SU 1526 1.4 / 2057 12.7	**27** 0257 1.3 / 0829 13.1 / M 1514 1.3 / 2046 13.2
13 0336 1.5 / 0912 12.4 / M 1542 1.9 / 2124 12.2	**28** 0331 1.4 / 0911 12.9 / TU 1546 1.5 / 2127 12.9
14 0353 1.9 / 0938 11.8 / TU 1557 2.2 / 2149 11.6	**29** 0405 1.6 / 0954 12.4 / W 1619 1.8 / 2210 12.3
15 0413 2.2 / 1005 11.1 / W 1619 2.4 / 2216 11.0	**30** 0441 2.0 / 1041 11.8 / TH 1658 2.4 / 2258 11.6

TIDES

Chart Datum: 6·50 metres below Ordnance Datum (Newlyn)
HAT is 14·7m above Chart Datum

TIDES

ENGLAND – AVONMOUTH

LAT 51°30'N   LONG 2°44'W

TIMES AND HEIGHTS OF HIGH AND LOW WATERS

Dates in amber are **SPRINGS**
Dates in yellow are **NEAPS**

2009

MAY

#	Time m	#	Time m
1 F	0526 2.6 / 1135 10.9 / F 1748 3.1 / 2359 10.8	**16** SA	0506 2.9 / 1102 10.2 / SA 1716 3.2 / 2321 10.1
2 SA	0630 3.2 / 1248 10.5 / SA 1906 3.6	**17** SU	0557 3.3 / 1155 9.8 / SU 1812 3.7
3 SU	0126 10.4 / 0804 3.4 / SU 1418 10.3 / 2045 3.4	**18** M	0026 9.7 / 0704 3.6 / M 1307 9.6 / ◑ 1928 3.9
4 M	0250 10.7 / 0927 2.9 / M 1529 10.8 / ◑ 2156 2.7	**19** TU	0149 9.8 / 0818 3.5 / TU 1427 9.9 / 2050 3.7
5 TU	0354 11.3 / 1031 2.3 / TU 1628 11.5 / 2256 2.0	**20** W	0304 10.3 / 0930 3.1 / W 1538 10.5 / 2205 3.2
6 W	0450 12.0 / 1127 1.8 / W 1719 12.2 / 2349 1.5	**21** TH	0406 11.0 / 1040 2.7 / TH 1637 11.3 / 2312 2.6
7 TH	0539 12.5 / 1218 1.4 / TH 1805 12.6	**22** F	0502 11.7 / 1142 2.1 / F 1729 12.0
8 F	0038 1.2 / 0623 12.8 / F 1305 1.2 / 1845 12.9	**23** SA	0010 2.0 / 0552 12.3 / SA 1237 1.7 / 1817 12.6
9 SA	0125 1.1 / 0704 12.8 / SA 1348 1.3 / 1923 12.8	**24** SU	0102 1.6 / 0640 12.8 / SU 1328 1.4 / 1902 13.1
10 SU	0207 1.2 / 0742 12.6 / SU 1426 1.5 / 1959 12.6	**25** M	0152 1.4 / 0728 13.0 / M 1415 1.2 / 1948 13.3
11 M	0243 1.5 / 0817 12.3 / M 1457 1.9 / ○ 2032 12.3	**26** TU	0240 1.2 / 0816 13.1 / TU 1500 1.2 / ● 2034 13.3
12 TU	0312 1.8 / 0849 11.9 / TU 1520 2.1 / 2102 11.9	**27** W	0325 1.2 / 0904 13.0 / W 1542 1.3 / 2121 13.1
13 W	0334 2.1 / 0919 11.5 / W 1539 2.3 / 2131 11.5	**28** TH	0408 1.4 / 0952 12.7 / TH 1623 1.6 / 2208 12.7
14 TH	0358 2.3 / 0949 11.1 / TH 1603 2.5 / 2200 11.0	**29** F	0451 1.7 / 1040 12.2 / F 1706 2.0 / 2258 12.1
15 F	0428 2.6 / 1021 10.6 / F 1635 2.8 / 2235 10.5	**30** SA	0538 2.0 / 1132 11.6 / SA 1755 2.4 / 2355 11.6
		31 SU	0630 2.4 / 1223 11.1 / SU 1852 2.8

JUNE

#	Time m	#	Time m
1 M	0102 11.1 / 0730 2.7 / M 1340 10.8 / 1959 3.0 ◐	**16** TU	0627 2.9 / 1222 10.4 / TU 1843 3.3 ◑
2 TU	0212 11.0 / 0835 2.8 / TU 1446 10.8 / ◑ 2108 2.9	**17** W	0051 10.4 / 0725 3.1 / W 1324 10.3 / 1949 3.5
3 W	0314 11.1 / 0942 2.8 / W 1547 11.0 / 2212 2.6	**18** TH	0201 10.4 / 0833 3.2 / TH 1436 10.4 / 2109 3.4
4 TH	0412 11.3 / 1044 2.5 / TH 1642 11.4 / 2310 2.3	**19** F	0314 10.7 / 0951 3.0 / F 1551 10.9 / 2228 2.9
5 F	0505 11.6 / 1139 2.3 / F 1731 11.8	**20** SA	0424 11.3 / 1104 2.5 / SA 1656 11.6 / 2337 2.4
6 SA	0003 2.0 / 0553 11.8 / SA 1230 2.0 / 1816 12.0	**21** SU	0526 11.9 / 1207 2.0 / SU 1753 12.3
7 SU	0052 1.8 / 0637 11.9 / SU 1316 1.9 / 1858 12.2	**22** M	0037 1.8 / 0621 12.5 / M 1305 1.6 / 1845 12.9
8 M	0137 1.8 / 0719 11.9 / M 1358 1.9 / 1937 12.2	**23** TU	0135 1.4 / 0715 12.9 / TU 1401 1.3 / 1936 13.3
9 TU	0218 1.9 / 0757 11.8 / TU 1436 2.1 / ○ 2013 12.0	**24** W	0231 1.2 / 0807 13.1 / W 1453 1.1 / 2026 13.5
10 W	0255 2.1 / 0834 11.6 / W 1507 2.3 / 2048 11.8	**25** TH	0323 1.0 / 0857 13.2 / TH 1541 1.0 / ● 2114 13.5
11 TH	0326 2.3 / 0908 11.4 / TH 1533 2.4 / 2121 11.5	**26** F	0410 0.9 / 0945 13.2 / F 1625 1.1 / 2202 13.3
12 F	0353 2.4 / 0940 11.2 / F 1557 2.5 / 2152 11.3	**27** SA	0452 1.1 / 1031 12.9 / SA 1704 1.3 / 2247 12.9
13 SA	0422 2.5 / 1012 11.1 / SA 1627 2.6 / 2225 11.1	**28** SU	0531 1.4 / 1115 12.4 / SU 1743 1.7 / 2334 12.3
14 SU	0457 2.5 / 1048 10.9 / SU 1704 2.7 / 2304 10.8	**29** M	0609 1.8 / 1202 11.7 / M 1822 2.2
15 M	0538 2.7 / 1130 10.7 / M 1749 3.0 / 2352 10.6	**30** TU	0025 11.6 / 0648 2.4 / TU 1254 11.1 / 1906 2.7

JULY

#	Time m	#	Time m
1 W	0124 11.0 / 0734 2.9 / W 1355 10.6 / 2002 3.2	**16** TH	0011 10.8 / 0639 2.9 / TH 1240 10.6 / 1859 3.3
2 TH	0228 10.6 / 0833 3.3 / TH 1501 10.4 / 2114 3.4	**17** F	0114 10.5 / 0740 3.3 / F 1348 10.3 / 2015 3.6
3 F	0332 10.5 / 0950 3.4 / F 1604 10.5 / 2229 3.2	**18** SA	0232 10.3 / 0906 3.4 / SA 1513 10.4 / ◑ 2156 3.5
4 SA	0433 10.6 / 1101 3.1 / SA 1701 10.9 / ◑ 2331 2.8	**19** SU	0357 10.7 / 1038 3.1 / SU 1633 11.1 / 2318 2.8
5 SU	0527 11.0 / 1158 2.7 / SU 1752 11.4	**20** M	0510 11.4 / 1150 2.4 / M 1738 12.0
6 M	0024 2.3 / 0616 11.3 / M 1249 2.3 / 1837 11.8	**21** TU	0026 2.0 / 0611 12.3 / TU 1254 1.7 / 1834 12.9
7 TU	0113 2.1 / 0700 11.6 / TU 1337 2.1 / 1919 12.0	**22** W	0128 1.4 / 0705 13.0 / W 1353 1.2 / 1926 13.5
8 W	0200 2.0 / 0741 11.7 / W 1422 2.1 / 1959 12.1	**23** TH	0225 0.9 / 0757 13.4 / TH 1447 0.8 / 2015 13.9
9 TH	0243 2.0 / 0820 11.7 / TH 1501 2.2 / 2035 12.0	**24** F	0317 0.5 / 0845 13.7 / F 1534 0.5 / 2102 14.0
10 F	0321 2.2 / 0855 11.7 / F 1533 2.3 / 2108 11.9	**25** SA	0401 0.4 / 0929 13.7 / SA 1615 0.6 / 2145 13.9
11 SA	0352 2.3 / 0927 11.6 / SA 1557 2.4 / ○ 2139 11.7	**26** SU	0440 0.6 / 1010 13.4 / SU 1650 0.9 / ● 2225 13.4
12 SU	0417 2.3 / 0957 11.6 / SU 1624 2.4 / 2208 11.6	**27** M	0511 1.1 / 1048 12.8 / M 1718 1.4 / 2303 12.6
13 M	0443 2.3 / 1027 11.5 / M 1648 2.4 / 2242 11.5	**28** TU	0536 1.7 / 1125 12.0 / TU 1745 2.1 / 2342 11.7
14 TU	0514 2.3 / 1103 11.3 / TU 1724 2.5 / 2322 11.2	**29** W	0603 2.4 / 1203 11.1 / W 1818 2.8
15 W	0553 2.5 / 1146 11.0 / W 1806 2.8	**30** TH	0026 10.7 / 0639 3.1 / TH 1253 10.3 / 1903 3.5
		31 F	0130 9.9 / 0730 3.8 / F 1410 9.7 / 2009 4.0

AUGUST

#	Time m	#	Time m
1 SA	0254 9.6 / 0845 4.1 / SA 1530 9.8 / 2145 4.0	**16** SU	0205 9.8 / 0831 4.0 / SU 1451 10.0 / 2144 4.0
2 SU	0406 9.8 / 1027 3.8 / SU 1637 10.3 / ◑ 2306 3.3	**17** M	0348 10.2 / 1028 3.5 / M 1623 10.8 / ◑ 2316 3.0
3 M	0507 10.5 / 1135 3.1 / M 1732 11.1	**18** TU	0504 11.3 / 1143 2.5 / TU 1730 12.0
4 TU	0003 2.6 / 0557 11.1 / TU 1229 2.4 / 1819 11.8	**19** W	0021 1.9 / 0602 12.4 / W 1245 1.5 / 1824 13.1
5 W	0055 2.1 / 0642 11.7 / W 1319 2.0 / 1901 12.2	**20** TH	0119 1.0 / 0654 13.2 / TH 1341 0.8 / 1913 13.9
6 TH	0143 1.8 / 0722 12.0 / TH 1406 1.9 / 1940 12.4	**21** F	0212 0.5 / 0741 13.8 / F 1432 0.4 / 1959 14.3
7 F	0229 1.8 / 0800 12.1 / F 1449 1.9 / 2016 12.4	**22** SA	0300 0.1 / 0825 14.0 / SA 1517 0.2 / 2042 14.3
8 SA	0309 1.9 / 0834 12.1 / SA 1525 2.1 / 2048 12.3	**23** SU	0342 0.2 / 0906 13.9 / SU 1555 0.4 / 2121 14.0
9 SU	0342 2.0 / 0905 12.0 / SU 1550 2.3 / ○ 2118 12.2	**24** M	0416 0.6 / 0943 13.5 / M 1626 0.9 / 2157 13.4
10 M	0406 2.2 / 0933 12.0 / M 1605 2.3 / 2146 12.1	**25** TU	0441 1.3 / 1016 12.8 / TU 1647 1.6 / ● 2229 12.6
11 TU	0423 2.2 / 1002 11.9 / TU 1627 2.2 / 2217 11.9	**26** W	0458 2.0 / 1045 12.0 / W 1706 2.2 / 2259 11.6
12 W	0447 2.2 / 1035 11.7 / W 1656 2.3 / 2254 11.6	**27** TH	0519 2.6 / 1116 11.0 / TH 1734 2.9 / 2333 10.5
13 TH	0519 2.4 / 1115 11.3 / TH 1732 2.7 / 2339 11.0	**28** F	0549 3.3 / 1156 10.0 / F 1813 3.7
14 F	0600 2.9 / 1205 10.7 / F 1819 3.3	**29** SA	0024 9.4 / 0635 4.1 / SA 1310 9.2 / 1919 4.5
15 SA	0039 10.3 / 0655 3.6 / SA 1313 10.1 / 1928 4.0	**30** SU	0216 8.9 / 0756 4.7 / SU 1504 9.2 / 2103 4.6
		31 M	0343 9.3 / 1002 4.3 / M 1614 10.0 / 2248 3.7

Chart Datum: 6·50 metres below Ordnance Datum (Newlyn)
HAT is 14·7m above Chart Datum

TIME ZONE (UT)	ENGLAND – AVONMOUTH	Dates in amber are SPRINGS
For Summer Time add ONE hour in **non-shaded areas**	LAT 51°30'N LONG 2°44'W	Dates in yellow are NEAPS
	TIMES AND HEIGHTS OF HIGH AND LOW WATERS	**2009**

SEPTEMBER

Time m	Time m
1 0444 10.2 / 1116 3.3 / TU 1709 11.0 / 2343 2.7	**16** 0454 11.4 / 1130 2.3 / W 1717 12.2
2 0534 11.1 / 1208 2.4 / W 1755 11.8	**17** 0005 1.6 / 0547 12.6 / TH 1227 1.3 / 1807 13.3
3 0032 2.0 / 0616 11.8 / TH 1256 1.9 / 1836 12.4	**18** 0058 0.8 / 0635 13.5 / F 1318 0.6 / ● 1853 14.0
4 0120 1.6 / 0655 12.3 / F 1343 1.7 / ○ 1914 12.7	**19** 0148 0.3 / 0718 14.0 / SA 1407 0.3 / 1936 14.3
5 0205 1.5 / 0732 12.4 / SA 1426 1.7 / 1949 12.7	**20** 0233 0.2 / 0759 14.0 / SU 1450 0.3 / 2016 14.2
6 0246 1.6 / 0806 12.5 / SU 1503 1.9 / 2022 12.6	**21** 0313 0.4 / 0837 13.8 / M 1527 0.6 / 2053 13.8
7 0320 1.8 / 0838 12.4 / M 1531 2.1 / 2052 12.5	**22** 0346 1.0 / 0911 13.3 / TU 1556 1.2 / 2126 13.1
8 0344 2.1 / 0907 12.4 / TU 1547 2.2 / 2121 12.4	**23** 0407 1.7 / 0942 12.6 / W 1614 1.9 / 2155 12.3
9 0400 2.1 / 0937 12.3 / W 1605 2.2 / 2154 12.2	**24** 0420 2.3 / 1009 11.8 / TH 1631 2.4 / 2222 11.3
10 0421 2.2 / 1011 12.0 / TH 1632 2.3 / 2231 11.7	**25** 0439 2.7 / 1036 10.9 / F 1657 3.0 / 2257 10.4
11 0452 2.4 / 1051 11.4 / F 1707 2.7 / 2316 10.9	**26** 0507 3.4 / 1111 10.0 / SA 1733 3.8 / ◐ 2332 9.3
12 0531 3.0 / 1140 10.6 / SA 1752 3.5 / ◐	**27** 0547 4.2 / 1211 9.1 / SU 1835 4.6
13 0017 10.0 / 0625 3.9 / SU 1252 9.9 / 1903 4.3	**28** 0117 8.6 / 0707 4.9 / M 1432 9.0 / 2019 4.8
14 0157 9.5 / 0827 4.4 / M 1449 9.9 / 2150 4.0	**29** 0311 9.1 / 0915 4.7 / TU 1542 9.8 / 2215 4.0
15 0346 10.2 / 1024 3.5 / TU 1615 10.9 / 2308 2.8	**30** 0412 10.0 / 1046 3.6 / W 1637 10.8 / 2313 2.9

OCTOBER

Time m	Time m
1 0501 11.0 / 1138 2.7 / TH 1723 11.7	**16** 0523 12.6 / 1158 1.3 / F 1743 13.2
2 0001 2.1 / 0544 11.8 / F 1225 2.0 / 1803 12.3	**17** 0028 0.9 / 0609 13.3 / SA 1248 0.8 / 1827 13.7
3 0048 1.7 / 0623 12.4 / SA 1311 1.8 / 1842 12.7	**18** 0117 0.6 / 0651 13.7 / SU 1335 0.6 / ● 1909 13.9
4 0132 1.5 / 0700 12.7 / SU 1354 1.7 / ○ 1918 12.9	**19** 0201 0.6 / 0730 13.7 / M 1419 0.7 / 1949 13.7
5 0214 1.5 / 0735 12.8 / M 1432 1.8 / 1953 12.9	**20** 0241 0.9 / 0808 13.4 / TU 1457 1.1 / 2026 13.3
6 0249 1.7 / 0809 12.8 / TU 1503 1.9 / 2027 12.8	**21** 0313 1.4 / 0842 13.0 / W 1526 1.6 / 2059 12.7
7 0317 1.9 / 0842 12.7 / W 1527 2.0 / 2101 12.7	**22** 0336 2.0 / 0913 12.4 / TH 1547 2.1 / 2128 12.0
8 0339 2.0 / 0916 12.5 / TH 1550 2.1 / 2137 12.3	**23** 0351 2.5 / 0941 11.7 / F 1606 2.6 / 2156 11.2
9 0404 2.2 / 0954 12.1 / F 1619 2.4 / 2218 11.7	**24** 0411 2.8 / 1009 11.0 / SA 1633 3.0 / 2225 10.4
10 0436 2.6 / 1036 11.5 / SA 1655 2.9 / 2305 10.9	**25** 0439 3.3 / 1043 10.2 / SU 1708 3.6 / 2304 9.7
11 0518 3.2 / 1129 10.7 / SU 1745 3.6 / ◐	**26** 0517 3.9 / 1133 9.5 / M 1802 4.2 / ●
12 0010 10.0 / 0617 4.0 / M 1248 10.0 / 1915 4.3	**27** 0011 9.0 / 0620 4.6 / TU 1325 9.1 / 1928 4.6
13 0158 9.7 / 0832 4.2 / TU 1442 10.2 / 2133 3.7	**28** 0211 9.0 / 0804 4.7 / W 1454 9.6 / 2058 4.2
14 0329 10.5 / 1002 3.3 / W 1555 11.2 / 2242 2.6	**29** 0324 9.7 / 0938 4.1 / TH 1552 10.4 / 2217 3.4
15 0431 11.6 / 1104 2.2 / TH 1653 12.3 / 2338 1.6	**30** 0418 10.6 / 1049 3.2 / F 1642 11.3 / 2317 2.6
	31 0505 11.5 / 1142 2.5 / SA 1726 12.0

NOVEMBER

Time m	Time m
1 0007 2.0 / 0547 12.2 / SU 1230 2.1 / 1807 12.5	**16** 0042 1.3 / 0623 13.0 / M 1303 1.3 / ● 1843 13.1
2 0054 1.7 / 0627 12.7 / M 1315 1.8 / ○ 1847 12.9	**17** 0128 1.3 / 0704 13.1 / TU 1348 1.3 / 1924 13.0
3 0137 1.6 / 0706 13.0 / TU 1357 1.7 / 1927 13.0	**18** 0210 1.4 / 0742 12.9 / W 1428 1.5 / 2003 12.7
4 0218 1.5 / 0744 13.1 / W 1436 1.7 / 2007 13.0	**19** 0246 1.8 / 0819 12.6 / TH 1502 1.9 / 2039 12.2
5 0254 1.6 / 0823 13.0 / TH 1512 1.8 / 2048 12.8	**20** 0314 2.2 / 0852 12.2 / F 1529 2.3 / 2111 11.8
6 0327 1.8 / 0900 12.8 / F 1545 2.0 / 2130 12.5	**21** 0334 2.5 / 0924 11.7 / SA 1552 2.6 / 2141 11.3
7 0400 2.1 / 0946 12.4 / SA 1621 2.3 / 2215 11.9	**22** 0357 2.8 / 0955 11.2 / SU 1620 2.9 / 2213 10.8
8 0437 2.5 / 1033 11.8 / SU 1703 2.7 / 2305 11.2	**23** 0425 3.0 / 1029 10.7 / M 1655 3.2 / 2249 10.3
9 0523 3.0 / 1129 11.1 / M 1758 3.3 / ◑	**24** 0502 3.4 / 1111 10.2 / TU 1740 3.5 / ◑ 2336 9.9
10 0009 10.6 / 0626 3.6 / TU 1244 10.7 / 1920 3.6	**25** 0551 3.8 / 1208 9.8 / W 1839 3.9
11 0136 10.3 / 0802 3.7 / W 1414 10.8 / 2052 3.4	**26** 0041 9.6 / 0658 4.1 / TH 1328 9.7 / 1951 3.9
12 0256 10.7 / 0923 3.2 / TH 1523 11.3 / 2202 2.8	**27** 0202 9.7 / 0819 4.1 / F 1445 10.1 / 2105 3.7
13 0358 11.4 / 1027 2.5 / F 1621 12.0 / 2301 2.1	**28** 0317 10.2 / 0938 3.7 / SA 1548 10.7 / 2217 3.2
14 0452 12.1 / 1123 1.9 / SA 1713 12.5 / 2354 1.6	**29** 0417 10.9 / 1048 3.1 / SU 1643 11.4 / 2320 2.6
15 0540 12.6 / 1215 1.5 / SU 1800 12.9	**30** 0509 11.7 / 1146 2.5 / M 1734 12.1

DECEMBER

Time m	Time m
1 0015 2.0 / 0556 12.4 / TU 1239 2.0 / 1820 12.6	**16** 0100 2.0 / 0642 12.4 / W 1322 1.9 / ● 1906 12.3
2 0105 1.7 / 0641 12.9 / W 1329 1.7 / ○ 1907 13.0	**17** 0145 1.9 / 0724 12.5 / TH 1406 1.9 / 1947 12.2
3 0152 1.5 / 0726 13.2 / TH 1417 1.6 / 1953 13.1	**18** 0226 1.9 / 0803 12.4 / F 1446 2.0 / 2025 12.1
4 0238 1.4 / 0811 13.3 / F 1503 1.5 / 2040 13.1	**19** 0302 2.2 / 0839 12.2 / SA 1520 2.3 / 2059 11.9
5 0321 1.5 / 0857 13.2 / SA 1547 1.6 / 2127 12.9	**20** 0329 2.4 / 0913 12.0 / SU 1548 2.5 / 2131 11.6
6 0403 1.7 / 0944 13.0 / SU 1630 1.8 / 2213 12.6	**21** 0352 2.6 / 0944 11.7 / M 1614 2.6 / 2201 11.4
7 0444 2.0 / 1032 12.6 / M 1713 2.1 / 2302 12.1	**22** 0416 2.7 / 1015 11.3 / TU 1643 2.7 / 2232 11.1
8 0528 2.3 / 1123 12.1 / TU 1800 2.4 / 2354 11.5	**23** 0448 2.8 / 1048 11.0 / W 1718 2.8 / 2308 10.8
9 0618 2.7 / 1222 11.5 / W 1853 2.8 / ◐	**24** 0526 3.0 / 1129 10.7 / TH 1800 3.1 / ◐ 2352 10.5
10 0057 11.0 / 0718 3.1 / TH 1332 11.2 / 1956 3.1	**25** 0612 3.4 / 1220 10.4 / F 1851 3.4
11 0210 10.8 / 0829 3.2 / F 1441 11.1 / 2109 3.2	**26** 0048 10.2 / 0710 3.7 / SA 1326 10.2 / 1956 3.6
12 0316 10.9 / 0941 3.1 / SA 1544 11.3 / 2218 3.0	**27** 0159 10.1 / 0827 3.9 / SU 1442 10.3 / 2117 3.6
13 0416 11.2 / 1046 2.8 / SU 1642 11.5 / 2318 2.6	**28** 0320 10.4 / 0954 3.6 / M 1559 10.8 / 2237 3.1
14 0510 11.7 / 1142 2.4 / M 1734 11.9	**29** 0432 11.1 / 1109 2.9 / TU 1704 11.5 / 2343 2.5
15 0011 2.2 / 0558 12.1 / TU 1234 2.0 / 1821 12.1	**30** 0531 12.0 / 1212 2.3 / W 1801 12.2
	31 0041 1.9 / 0623 12.7 / TH 1310 1.8 / ○ 1853 12.9

Chart Datum: 6·50 metres below Ordnance Datum (Newlyn)
HAT is 14·7m above Chart Datum

TIDES

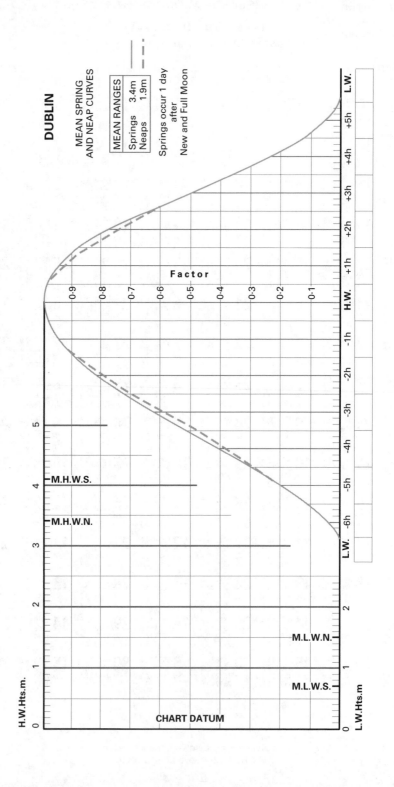

DUBLIN

MEAN SPRING
AND NEAP CURVES

MEAN RANGES	
Springs	3.4m
Neaps	1.9m

Springs occur 1 day
after
New and Full Moon

Factor

TIME ZONE (UT)	IRELAND – DUBLIN (NORTH WALL)	Dates in amber are SPRINGS
For Summer Time add ONE hour in **non-shaded areas**	LAT 53°21′N LONG 6°13′W	Dates in yellow are NEAPS
	TIMES AND HEIGHTS OF HIGH AND LOW WATERS	**2009**

JANUARY

Time	m		Time	m
1 0213	3.6	**16**	0304	3.7
0742	1.2		0830	1.0
TH 1425	3.9	F 1520	4.1
2013	0.9		2113	0.7
2 0256	3.6	**17**	0355	3.6
0825	1.2		0924	1.1
F 1508	3.9	SA 1614	3.9
2056	1.0		2205	1.0
3 0342	3.5	**18**	0451	3.5
0912	1.3		1022	1.4
SA 1554	3.8	SU 1714	3.6
2143	1.0	◓ 2301	1.3
4 0433	3.5	**19**	0553	3.4
1004	1.4		1127	1.5
SU 1645	3.7	M 1821	3.5
◓ 2237	1.1		
5 0530	3.4	**20**	0004	1.5
1104	1.4		0658	3.3
M 1742	3.6	TU 1242	1.6
2338	1.2		1929	3.4
6 0634	3.4	**21**	0120	1.6
1212	1.4		0801	3.4
TU 1847	3.6	W 1407	1.6
			2036	3.3
7 0049	1.2	**22**	0235	1.6
0741	3.5		0900	3.5
W 1324	1.4	TH 1513	1.5
1959	3.6		2137	3.4
8 0159	1.2	**23**	0329	1.5
0844	3.7		0950	3.7
TH 1430	1.2	F 1600	1.3
2107	3.8		2225	3.5
9 0301	1.1	**24**	0409	1.3
0941	3.9		1033	3.8
F 1530	0.9	SA 1638	1.1
2208	3.9		2303	3.6
10 0355	0.9	**25**	0443	1.2
1033	4.1		1109	3.9
SA 1624	0.6	SU 1709	1.0
2302	4.0		2336	3.6
11 0443	0.8	**26**	0513	1.1
1121	4.3		1140	3.9
SU 1713	0.4	M 1738	0.9
○ 2352	4.1	●	
12 0527	0.7	**27**	0005	3.7
1207	4.4		0540	1.0
M 1800	0.3	TU 1210	4.0
			1804	0.8
13 0039	4.1	**28**	0034	3.7
0610	0.7		0607	0.9
TU 1254	4.4	W 1241	4.0
1846	0.3		1830	0.7
14 0127	4.0	**29**	0105	3.8
0654	0.7		0637	0.8
W 1341	4.3	TH 1316	4.0
1934	0.4		1902	0.7
15 0215	3.9	**30**	0140	3.8
0740	0.8		0712	0.8
TH 1430	4.2	F 1355	4.0
2023	0.5		1939	0.7
		31	0220	3.8
			0751	0.9
		SA 1436	4.0
			2020	0.7

FEBRUARY

Time	m		Time	m
1 0303	3.7	**16**	0352	3.5
0835	1.0		0941	1.2
SU 1521	3.9	M 1626	3.5
2105	0.9	◑ 2212	1.3
2 0350	3.6	**17**	0451	3.3
0925	1.1		1043	1.4
M 1610	3.8	TU 1734	3.3
◑ 2156	1.0		2312	1.6
3 0445	3.5	**18**	0605	3.2
1023	1.3		1155	1.6
TU 1707	3.6	W 1852	3.1
2256	1.3		
4 0552	3.4	**19**	0025	1.7
1137	1.4		0719	3.2
W 1819	3.5	TH 1334	1.6
			2006	3.1
5 0015	1.4	**20**	0205	1.7
0712	3.4		0826	3.3
TH 1303	1.4	F 1451	1.4
1944	3.5		2113	3.2
6 0143	1.4	**21**	0308	1.5
0827	3.6		0923	3.5
F 1422	1.2	SA 1538	1.2
2102	3.6		2203	3.4
7 0256	1.2	**22**	0348	1.3
0931	3.8		1008	3.7
SA 1527	0.9	SU 1613	1.0
2205	3.8		2241	3.5
8 0352	1.0	**23**	0420	1.1
1025	4.0		1045	3.8
SU 1620	0.5	M 1642	0.9
2257	3.9		2312	3.6
9 0436	0.7	**24**	0447	0.9
1112	4.2		1115	3.9
M 1705	0.3	TU 1708	0.7
○ 2342	4.0		2339	3.7
10 0517	0.6	**25**	0513	0.8
1155	4.3		1143	4.0
TU 1747	0.2	W 1732	0.6
		●	
11 0023	4.0	**26**	0003	3.8
0554	0.5		0538	0.7
W 1236	4.3	TH 1213	4.0
1827	0.2		1758	0.5
12 0102	3.9	**27**	0033	3.8
0633	0.5		0608	0.6
TH 1317	4.3	F 1247	4.1
1908	0.3		1831	0.5
13 0141	3.9	**28**	0107	3.9
0714	0.6		0643	0.6
F 1359	4.1	SA 1326	4.1
1951	0.5		1908	0.5
14 0221	3.7		
0758	0.8		
SA 1444	4.0		
2034	0.7		
15 0304	3.6		
0846	1.0		
SU 1531	3.7		
2121	1.0		

MARCH

Time	m		Time	m
1 0147	3.9	**16**	0224	3.7
0723	0.6		0816	0.8
SU 1408	4.0	M 1458	3.6
1949	0.6		2043	1.0
2 0230	3.8	**17**	0307	3.5
0808	0.7		0908	1.2
M 1454	3.9	TU 1549	3.4
2036	0.8		2132	1.3
3 0318	3.7	**18**	0357	3.3
0900	0.9		1008	1.3
TU 1546	3.7	W 1653	3.1
2128	1.1	◑ 2231	1.6
4 0414	3.5	**19**	0508	3.2
1003	1.1		1118	1.5
W 1647	3.5	TH 1815	3.0
◑ 2233	1.3		2342	1.7
5 0524	3.4	**20**	0637	3.1
1124	1.3		1242	1.5
TH 1808	3.3	F 1933	3.0
2359	1.5		
6 0654	3.3	**21**	0110	1.7
1255	1.3		0750	3.2
F 1942	3.3	SA 1410	1.4
			2040	3.1
7 0135	1.5	**22**	0229	1.5
0815	3.5		0849	3.4
SA 1417	1.0	SU 1501	1.2
2100	3.5		2131	3.3
8 0249	1.2	**23**	0313	1.3
0921	3.7		0936	3.6
SU 1519	0.7	M 1536	1.0
2200	3.7		2209	3.5
9 0341	0.9	**24**	0346	1.1
1015	4.0		1013	3.7
M 1607	0.4	TU 1605	0.8
2249	3.8		2240	3.6
10 0423	0.7	**25**	0414	0.8
1101	4.1		1044	3.8
TU 1649	0.3	W 1631	0.6
2329	3.9		2306	3.7
11 0501	0.5	**26**	0441	0.7
1141	4.2		1112	3.9
W 1728	0.2	TH 1658	0.5
○		● 2331	3.8
12 0004	3.9	**27**	0509	0.5
0537	0.5		1144	4.0
TH 1218	4.2	F 1728	0.4
1805	0.2		
13 0035	3.9	**28**	0001	3.9
0612	0.5		0542	0.4
F 1254	4.1	SA 1221	4.1
1842	0.4		1802	0.4
14 0108	3.8	**29**	0038	4.0
0650	0.5		0619	0.4
SA 1332	4.0	SU 1302	4.1
1919	0.5		1842	0.5
15 0144	3.8	**30**	0120	3.9
0731	0.7		0702	0.5
SU 1414	3.8	M 1348	4.0
1959	0.8		1926	0.6
		31	0206	3.9
			0752	0.6
		TU 1439	3.8
			2016	0.9

APRIL

Time	m		Time	m
1 0258	3.7	**16**	0324	3.4
0851	0.8		0942	1.2
W 1536	3.6	TH 1621	3.1
2115	1.1		2158	1.5
2 0357	3.6	**17**	0424	3.3
1001	0.9		1046	1.3
TH 1644	3.4	F 1736	3.0
◑ 2226	1.4	◑ 2306	1.7
3 0512	3.4	**18**	0545	3.2
1122	1.1		1156	1.4
F 1811	3.3	SA 1851	3.0
2351	1.5		
4 0642	3.4	**19**	0018	1.7
1246	1.1		0703	3.2
SA 1936	3.4	SU 1307	1.3
			1955	3.1
5 0119	1.4	**20**	0128	1.5
0800	3.6		0804	3.3
SU 1401	0.9	M 1404	1.1
2048	3.5		2047	3.3
6 0228	1.2	**21**	0221	1.3
0905	3.8		0852	3.5
M 1459	0.6	TU 1446	0.9
2145	3.7		2128	3.5
7 0320	1.0	**22**	0300	1.1
1000	3.9		0932	3.6
TU 1547	0.5	W 1521	0.7
2232	3.8		2201	3.6
8 0403	0.8	**23**	0334	0.9
1046	4.0		1007	3.8
W 1628	0.4	TH 1553	0.6
2311	3.8		2230	3.8
9 0442	0.6	**24**	0407	0.7
1126	4.1		1041	3.9
TH 1707	0.4	F 1626	0.5
○ 2342	3.8		2300	3.9
10 0519	0.5	**25**	0441	0.5
1201	4.0		1119	4.0
F 1742	0.4	SA 1701	0.4
		● 2336	4.0
11 0010	3.8	**26**	0520	0.4
0554	0.5		1200	4.1
SA 1235	3.9	SU 1740	0.4
1817	0.5		
12 0041	3.8	**27**	0016	4.0
0631	0.6		0602	0.4
SU 1311	3.8	M 1247	4.0
1852	0.6		1823	0.5
13 0116	3.8	**28**	0102	4.0
0711	0.7		0651	0.4
M 1351	3.7	TU 1338	3.9
1930	0.9		1911	0.7
14 0155	3.7	**29**	0152	3.9
0755	0.8		0747	0.6
TU 1434	3.5	W 1433	3.8
2012	1.1		2006	0.9
15 0237	3.6	**30**	0248	3.8
0845	1.0		0850	0.7
W 1523	3.3	TH 1535	3.6
2100	1.3		2109	1.2

Chart Datum: 0·20 metres above Ordnance Datum (Dublin)
HAT is 4·5m above Chart Datum

TIDES

331

TIDES

TIME ZONE (UT)
For Summer Time add ONE hour in **non-shaded areas**

IRELAND – DUBLIN (NORTH WALL)
LAT 53°21′N   LONG 6°13′W
TIMES AND HEIGHTS OF HIGH AND LOW WATERS

Dates in amber are **SPRINGS**
Dates in yellow are **NEAPS**

2009

MAY

Time	m		Time	m
1 0352	3.7	**16**	0352	3.4
1000	0.8		1011	1.2
F 1646	3.5	SA	1649	3.2
2219	1.3		2225	1.5
2 0506	3.6	**17**	0451	3.3
1113	0.9		1109	1.3
SA 1803	3.4	SU	1754	3.1
2334	1.4		2327	1.6
3 0625	3.6	**18**	0557	3.3
1226	0.9		1208	1.2
SU 1917	3.4	M	1858	3.2
			◐	
4 0049	1.4	**19**	0028	1.5
0737	3.7		0701	3.3
M 1333	0.8	TU	1303	1.1
◐ 2023	3.5		1951	3.3
5 0156	1.2	**20**	0123	1.4
0841	3.8		0756	3.5
TU 1431	0.7	W	1352	1.0
2119	3.6		2037	3.4
6 0252	1.1	**21**	0210	1.2
0937	3.9		0844	3.6
W 1521	0.6	TH	1436	0.8
2207	3.7		2117	3.6
7 0339	0.9	**22**	0253	1.0
1026	3.9		0930	3.8
TH 1605	0.6	F	1517	0.7
2248	3.7		2155	3.8
8 0422	0.8	**23**	0335	0.8
1108	3.9		1014	3.9
F 1645	0.7	SA	1558	0.6
2320	3.8		2235	3.9
9 0502	0.8	**24**	0418	0.6
1144	3.8		1100	4.0
SA 1721	0.7	SU	1640	0.6
2348	3.8		2317	4.0
10 0540	0.7	**25**	0504	0.5
1218	3.8		1148	4.0
SU 1756	0.8	M	1724	0.6
11 0019	3.8	**26**	0002	4.1
0618	0.8		0552	0.4
M 1254	3.7	TU	1238	4.0
○ 1831	0.9	●	1810	0.6
12 0055	3.8	**27**	0051	4.1
0657	0.8		0644	0.4
TU 1332	3.6	W	1332	4.0
1908	1.0		1901	0.8
13 0133	3.8	**28**	0143	4.1
0739	0.9		0742	0.5
W 1414	3.5	TH	1429	3.8
1948	1.1		1956	0.9
14 0215	3.7	**29**	0241	4.0
0825	1.0		0844	0.6
TH 1459	3.4	F	1529	3.7
2033	1.3		2056	1.1
15 0300	3.6	**30**	0343	3.9
0916	1.1		0948	0.7
F 1550	3.3	SA	1634	3.6
2125	1.4		2200	1.2
		31	0451	3.9
			1052	0.8
		SU	1740	3.5
			2306	1.3

JUNE

Time	m		Time	m
1 0600	3.8	**16**	0502	3.5
1156	0.8		1107	1.1
M 1847	3.5	TU	1749	3.3
		◐	2325	1.4
2 0014	1.3	**17**	0600	3.5
0707	3.8		1204	1.2
TU 1301	0.9	W	1848	3.3
◐ 1949	3.5			
3 0120	1.3	**18**	0025	1.4
0811	3.8		0700	3.5
W 1400	0.9	TH	1301	1.1
2047	3.6		1945	3.4
4 0222	1.2	**19**	0123	1.3
0910	3.8		0802	3.6
TH 1455	1.0	F	1356	1.0
2138	3.6		2039	3.6
5 0317	1.2	**20**	0219	1.1
1003	3.7		0901	3.7
F 1542	1.0	SA	1449	0.9
2221	3.7		2129	3.8
6 0405	1.1	**21**	0312	0.9
1049	3.7		0956	3.9
SA 1624	1.0	SU	1539	0.8
2258	3.7		2217	4.0
7 0448	1.0	**22**	0403	0.7
1128	3.7		1048	4.0
SU 1702	1.0	M	1626	0.7
2330	3.8		2304	4.1
8 0528	1.0	**23**	0454	0.5
1202	3.7		1139	4.0
M 1738	1.0	TU	1713	0.6
			2351	4.2
9 0001	3.8	**24**	0544	0.4
0605	0.9		1229	4.1
TU 1236	3.6	W	1800	0.7
○ 1811	1.0			
10 0036	3.8	**25**	0039	4.3
0642	0.9		0635	0.3
W 1312	3.6	TH	1321	4.0
1846	1.1	●	1847	0.7
11 0113	3.8	**26**	0131	4.3
0720	1.0		0729	0.4
TH 1351	3.5	F	1414	3.9
1923	1.1		1939	0.8
12 0152	3.8	**27**	0225	4.2
0759	1.0		0826	0.4
F 1431	3.5	SA	1509	3.8
2002	1.2		2033	1.0
13 0234	3.7	**28**	0322	4.1
0841	1.0		0923	0.6
SA 1515	3.4	SU	1606	3.7
2046	1.3		2131	1.1
14 0320	3.7	**29**	0423	4.0
0925	1.1		1021	0.8
SU 1602	3.3	M	1706	3.6
2135	1.3		2231	1.2
15 0409	3.6	**30**	0527	3.8
1014	1.1		1120	0.9
M 1653	3.3	TU	1808	3.5
2228	1.4		2334	1.4

JULY

Time	m		Time	m
1 0634	3.7	**16**	0514	3.6
1222	1.1		1110	1.2
W 1910	3.5	TH	1757	3.4
			2334	1.4
2 0043	1.4	**17**	0619	3.5
0739	3.6		1216	1.3
TH 1327	1.2	F	1905	3.4
2010	3.5			
3 0154	1.4	**18**	0046	1.4
0843	3.6		0732	3.5
F 1429	1.3	SA	1326	1.2
2106	3.6	◐	2012	3.5
4 0259	1.4	**19**	0156	1.2
0941	3.6		0843	3.6
SA 1522	1.3	SU	1430	1.1
◐ 2155	3.7		2112	3.7
5 0353	1.2	**20**	0259	1.0
1031	3.6		0945	3.8
SU 1607	1.2	M	1527	1.0
2236	3.7		2205	4.0
6 0437	1.1	**21**	0356	0.7
1111	3.6		1039	3.9
M 1645	1.2	TU	1617	0.8
2311	3.8		2253	4.2
7 0515	1.0	**22**	0446	0.4
1145	3.6		1128	4.0
TU 1719	1.1	W	1702	0.6
2343	3.9		2339	4.3
8 0550	1.0	**23**	0534	0.3
1217	3.6		1215	4.1
W 1751	1.0	TH	1746	0.6
9 0015	3.9	**24**	0024	4.4
0621	0.9		0621	0.2
TH 1249	3.6	F	1302	4.0
1822	1.0		1829	0.6
10 0049	3.9	**25**	0111	4.4
0652	0.9		0709	0.3
F 1322	3.6	SA	1349	4.0
1853	1.0		1914	0.7
11 0125	3.9	**26**	0159	4.3
0723	0.9		0758	0.4
SA 1358	3.6	SU	1437	3.8
○ 1928	1.0		2003	0.8
12 0204	3.9	**27**	0250	4.1
0758	0.9		0850	0.6
SU 1438	3.6	M	1527	3.7
2007	1.1		2056	1.0
13 0246	3.8	**28**	0345	3.9
0838	0.9		0943	0.8
M 1520	3.5	TU	1621	3.6
2050	1.1		2153	1.2
14 0331	3.8	**29**	0446	3.7
0923	1.0		1038	1.1
TU 1606	3.5	W	1721	3.4
2137	1.2		2254	1.4
15 0419	3.7	**30**	0555	3.5
1013	1.1		1138	1.3
W 1658	3.4	TH	1827	3.4
2231	1.3			
		31	0004	1.5
			0707	3.4
		F	1248	1.5
			1933	3.4

AUGUST

Time	m		Time	m
1 0129	1.6	**16**	0025	1.4
0818	3.4		0716	3.4
SA 1403	1.5	SU	1308	1.6
2035	3.5		1953	3.5
2 0247	1.4	**17**	0147	1.2
0923	3.4		0835	3.5
SU 1504	1.5	M	1422	1.3
◐ 2130	3.6	◐	2059	3.7
3 0341	1.3	**18**	0255	0.9
1014	3.5		0938	3.7
M 1549	1.3	TU	1520	1.0
2215	3.8		2153	4.0
4 0422	1.1	**19**	0350	0.6
1053	3.6		1030	3.9
TU 1626	1.2	W	1607	0.8
2251	3.9		2240	4.2
5 0456	1.0	**20**	0437	0.3
1125	3.6		1116	4.0
W 1658	1.1	TH	1649	0.6
2323	3.9		2324	4.4
6 0526	0.9	**21**	0520	0.2
1154	3.7		1158	4.1
TH 1727	1.0	F	1728	0.5
2352	4.0			
7 0553	0.8	**22**	0005	4.4
1222	3.7		0601	0.1
F 1754	0.9	SA	1239	4.0
			1807	0.5
8 0021	4.0	**23**	0047	4.4
0617	0.8		0643	0.2
SA 1251	3.7	SU	1319	4.0
1822	0.8		1849	0.6
9 0055	4.0	**24**	0130	4.3
0645	0.8		0727	0.4
SU 1324	3.7	M	1400	3.9
○ 1854	0.8		1933	0.7
10 0132	4.0	**25**	0216	4.1
0719	0.8		0813	0.7
M 1402	3.7	TU	1445	3.7
1931	0.9	●	2022	0.9
11 0213	4.0	**26**	0306	3.8
0759	0.8		0903	1.0
TU 1443	3.7	W	1533	3.6
2013	1.0		2117	1.2
12 0256	3.9	**27**	0403	3.6
0843	0.9		0956	1.3
W 1528	3.6	TH	1630	3.4
2100	1.1		2219	1.4
13 0344	3.7	**28**	0515	3.3
0932	1.1		1055	1.5
TH 1618	3.5	F	1741	3.3
2154	1.2		2329	1.6
14 0440	3.6	**29**	0634	3.2
1031	1.3		1205	1.7
F 1719	3.4	SA	1856	3.3
2302	1.4			
15 0549	3.4	**30**	0102	1.6
1144	1.4		0752	3.2
SA 1835	3.4	SU	1333	1.7
			2004	3.4
		31	0228	1.5
			0902	3.3
		M	1441	1.6
			2103	3.6

Chart Datum: 0·20 metres above Ordnance Datum (Dublin)
HAT is 4·5m above Chart Datum

TIME ZONE (UT)	IRELAND – DUBLIN (NORTH WALL)	Dates in amber are SPRINGS
For Summer Time add ONE hour in **non-shaded areas**	**LAT 53°21'N LONG 6°13'W**	Dates in yellow are NEAPS
	TIMES AND HEIGHTS OF HIGH AND LOW WATERS	**2009**

SEPTEMBER

#	Day	Readings (Time m)	#	Readings (Time m)
1	TU	0320 1.2 / 0953 3.5 / 1526 1.4 / 2150 3.8	16	0247 0.8 / 0930 3.7 / 1508 1.0 / 2140 4.0
2	W	0358 1.1 / 1029 3.6 / 1602 1.2 / 2227 3.9	17	0338 0.5 / 1020 3.9 / 1553 0.8 / 2227 4.2
3	TH	0429 0.9 / 1100 3.7 / 1632 1.0 / 2258 4.0	18	0422 0.3 / 1102 4.0 / 1633 0.6 / ● 2308 4.3
4	F	0455 0.8 / 1128 3.7 / 1659 0.9 / ○ 2325 4.0	19	0502 0.2 / 1139 4.1 / 1710 0.5 / 2346 4.4
5	SA	0519 0.7 / 1153 3.8 / 1724 0.8 / 2352 4.1	20	0540 0.2 / 1214 4.0 / 1748 0.5
6	SU	0543 0.6 / 1219 3.8 / 1752 0.7	21	0024 4.3 / 0618 0.3 / 1250 4.0 / 1826 0.6
7	M	0024 4.1 / 0611 0.6 / 1252 3.9 / 1824 0.7	22	0105 4.2 / 0657 0.5 / 1328 3.9 / 1909 0.7
8	TU	0102 4.1 / 0645 0.7 / 1329 3.9 / 1901 0.7	23	0148 4.0 / 0740 0.8 / 1410 3.8 / 1956 0.9
9	W	0143 4.0 / 0725 0.8 / 1411 3.8 / 1944 0.9	24	0236 3.8 / 0826 1.1 / 1455 3.7 / 2049 1.1
10	TH	0228 3.9 / 0810 0.9 / 1457 3.7 / 2034 1.0	25	0330 3.5 / 0919 1.4 / 1548 3.5 / 2150 1.3
11	F	0319 3.7 / 0903 1.2 / 1550 3.6 / 2133 1.2	26	0439 3.3 / 1019 1.6 / 1656 3.4 / ◐ 2258 1.5
12	SA	0419 3.5 / 1007 1.4 / 1653 3.4 / ◐ 2249 1.4	27	0600 3.1 / 1128 1.8 / 1816 3.3
13	SU	0537 3.4 / 1129 1.5 / 1816 3.4	28	0022 1.6 / 0718 3.1 / 1250 1.8 / 1928 3.4
14	M	0018 1.4 / 0710 3.4 / 1258 1.5 / 1938 3.6	29	0152 1.4 / 0828 3.3 / 1405 1.6 / 2029 3.5
15	TU	0142 1.1 / 0829 3.5 / 1412 1.3 / 2045 3.8	30	0245 1.2 / 0919 3.5 / 1453 1.4 / 2118 3.7

OCTOBER

#	Day	Readings (Time m)	#	Readings (Time m)
1	TH	0324 1.0 / 0957 3.6 / 1530 1.2 / 2156 3.8	16	0318 0.6 / 1002 3.9 / 1533 0.9 / 2211 4.2
2	F	0354 0.9 / 1029 3.7 / 1600 1.0 / 2228 3.9	17	0402 0.4 / 1044 4.0 / 1615 0.7 / 2254 4.2
3	SA	0420 0.7 / 1057 3.8 / 1628 0.8 / 2256 4.0	18	0442 0.4 / 1121 4.0 / 1654 0.6 / ● 2332 4.2
4	SU	0444 0.6 / 1122 3.9 / 1655 0.7 / ○ 2324 4.1	19	0520 0.4 / 1153 4.0 / 1732 0.6
5	M	0511 0.6 / 1149 4.0 / 1725 0.7 / 2358 4.1	20	0008 4.1 / 0556 0.6 / 1227 4.0 / 1811 0.7
6	TU	0542 0.6 / 1222 4.0 / 1800 0.6	21	0047 4.0 / 0633 0.7 / 1304 4.0 / 1852 0.8
7	W	0036 4.1 / 0618 0.7 / 1302 4.0 / 1839 0.7	22	0129 3.9 / 0712 0.9 / 1344 3.9 / 1937 0.9
8	TH	0121 4.0 / 0659 0.8 / 1347 3.9 / 1926 0.8	23	0214 3.7 / 0757 1.2 / 1428 3.8 / 2028 1.1
9	F	0210 3.9 / 0748 1.0 / 1437 3.8 / 2021 1.0	24	0305 3.5 / 0847 1.4 / 1517 3.6 / 2124 1.3
10	SA	0306 3.7 / 0846 1.3 / 1533 3.7 / 2127 1.4	25	0407 3.3 / 0946 1.6 / 1616 3.5 / 2227 1.4
11	SU	0412 3.5 / 0956 1.5 / 1640 3.6 / ◐ 2245 1.2	26	0521 3.2 / 1052 1.7 / 1730 3.4 / ◐ 2336 1.5
12	M	0535 3.4 / 1119 1.6 / 1801 3.6	27	0635 3.2 / 1202 1.8 / 1843 3.4
13	TU	0009 1.2 / 0701 3.4 / 1242 1.5 / 1920 3.7	28	0049 1.5 / 0740 3.3 / 1311 1.7 / 1944 3.5
14	W	0126 1.0 / 0814 3.6 / 1351 1.3 / 2027 3.9	29	0152 1.3 / 0834 3.4 / 1407 1.4 / 2035 3.6
15	TH	0227 0.8 / 0913 3.8 / 1447 1.1 / 2123 4.1	30	0237 1.1 / 0917 3.6 / 1448 1.3 / 2117 3.7
			31	0311 1.0 / 0952 3.7 / 1523 1.1 / 2153 3.9

NOVEMBER

#	Day	Readings (Time m)	#	Readings (Time m)
1	SU	0342 0.8 / 1023 3.9 / 1555 0.9 / 2225 4.0	16	0424 0.7 / 1103 4.0 / 1641 0.9 / ● 2321 4.0
2	M	0411 0.7 / 1051 3.9 / 1627 0.8 / ○ 2300 4.1	17	0502 0.8 / 1137 4.0 / 1722 0.8 / 2357 4.0
3	TU	0443 0.6 / 1123 4.0 / 1703 0.7 / 2338 4.1	18	0539 0.8 / 1209 4.0 / 1801 0.8
4	W	0519 0.6 / 1200 4.1 / 1743 0.6	19	0034 3.9 / 0614 0.9 / 1245 4.0 / 1841 0.9
5	TH	0021 4.1 / 0558 0.7 / 1243 4.1 / 1827 0.7	20	0113 3.8 / 0652 1.1 / 1323 4.0 / 1923 1.0
6	F	0109 4.0 / 0643 0.9 / 1331 4.1 / 1918 0.7	21	0155 3.7 / 0732 1.2 / 1405 3.9 / 2007 1.1
7	SA	0202 3.9 / 0735 1.1 / 1424 4.0 / 2017 0.9	22	0242 3.5 / 0818 1.3 / 1450 3.8 / 2056 1.2
8	SU	0302 3.7 / 0836 1.3 / 1523 3.9 / 2123 1.0	23	0333 3.4 / 0910 1.5 / 1539 3.6 / 2149 1.3
9	M	0409 3.6 / 0945 1.4 / 1630 3.8 / ◑ 2234 1.0	24	0432 3.3 / 1009 1.6 / 1634 3.5 / ◑ 2246 1.4
10	TU	0525 3.5 / 1100 1.5 / 1743 3.8 / 2348 1.0	25	0539 3.2 / 1112 1.7 / 1737 3.4 / 2346 1.4
11	W	0640 3.6 / 1214 1.5 / 1855 3.9	26	0643 3.3 / 1213 1.7 / 1841 3.4
12	TH	0058 1.0 / 0748 3.7 / 1322 1.4 / 2001 3.9	27	0045 1.4 / 0740 3.4 / 1310 1.6 / 1939 3.5
13	F	0200 0.9 / 0847 3.8 / 1421 1.2 / 2101 3.9	28	0138 1.3 / 0828 3.5 / 1400 1.5 / 2029 3.6
14	SA	0254 0.8 / 0939 3.9 / 1512 1.1 / 2154 4.0	29	0223 1.1 / 0910 3.7 / 1443 1.3 / 2114 3.7
15	SU	0341 0.7 / 1024 4.0 / 1559 1.0 / 2240 4.1	30	0304 1.0 / 0948 3.8 / 1524 1.1 / 2158 3.9

DECEMBER

#	Day	Readings (Time m)	#	Readings (Time m)
1	TU	0343 0.9 / 1025 4.0 / 1605 0.9 / 2241 4.0	16	0448 1.0 / 1123 4.0 / 1714 1.0 / ● 2349 3.8
2	W	0422 0.8 / 1104 4.1 / 1647 0.7 / ○ 2325 4.1	17	0525 1.0 / 1155 4.0 / 1752 0.9
3	TH	0503 0.7 / 1145 4.2 / 1732 0.6	18	0022 3.8 / 0559 1.0 / 1229 4.0 / 1829 0.9
4	F	0012 4.1 / 0546 0.8 / 1231 4.2 / 1819 0.5	19	0057 3.7 / 0633 1.1 / 1304 4.0 / 1905 0.9
5	SA	0102 4.1 / 0633 0.8 / 1320 4.2 / 1911 0.6	20	0133 3.7 / 0708 1.1 / 1341 4.0 / 1942 1.0
6	SU	0155 4.0 / 0724 1.0 / 1413 4.2 / 2008 0.6	21	0212 3.6 / 0746 1.2 / 1421 3.9 / 2020 1.1
7	M	0253 3.9 / 0821 1.1 / 1510 4.1 / 2108 0.7	22	0254 3.5 / 0827 1.3 / 1503 3.8 / 2101 1.1
8	TU	0355 3.8 / 0924 1.3 / 1612 4.0 / 2211 0.8	23	0339 3.4 / 0913 1.4 / 1548 3.7 / 2145 1.2
9	W	0501 3.7 / 1030 1.4 / 1717 3.9 / ◑ 2316 1.0	24	0429 3.4 / 1005 1.5 / 1637 3.6 / ◑ 2235 1.3
10	TH	0608 3.6 / 1139 1.4 / 1825 3.9	25	0526 3.3 / 1103 1.6 / 1732 3.5 / 2332 1.4
11	F	0023 1.0 / 0714 3.6 / 1249 1.4 / 1932 3.8	26	0629 3.3 / 1206 1.6 / 1833 3.4
12	SA	0129 1.1 / 0816 3.7 / 1354 1.4 / 2036 3.8	27	0035 1.4 / 0731 3.4 / 1308 1.6 / 1938 3.5
13	SU	0230 1.1 / 0913 3.8 / 1454 1.3 / 2136 3.8	28	0136 1.3 / 0827 3.5 / 1406 1.4 / 2040 3.6
14	M	0323 1.1 / 1003 3.9 / 1547 1.2 / 2228 3.8	29	0231 1.2 / 0917 3.7 / 1459 1.2 / 2136 3.8
15	TU	0408 1.0 / 1046 3.9 / 1633 1.1 / 2312 3.8	30	0321 1.0 / 1004 3.9 / 1548 1.0 / 2227 3.9
			31	0408 1.0 / 1049 4.1 / 1636 0.6 / ○ 2316 4.0

Chart Datum: 0·20 metres above Ordnance Datum (Dublin)
HAT is 4·5m above Chart Datum

TIDES

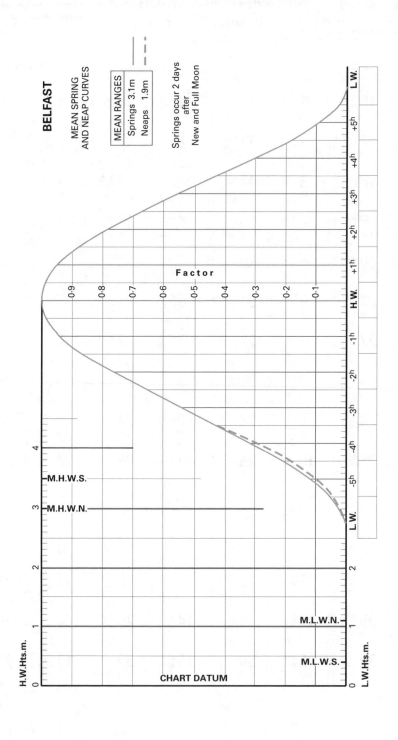

BELFAST

MEAN SPRING
AND NEAP CURVES

MEAN RANGES	
Springs	3.1m
Neaps	1.9m

Springs occur 2 days
after
New and Full Moon

Factor

TIME ZONE (UT)	NORTHERN IRELAND – BELFAST	Dates in amber are SPRINGS
For Summer Time add ONE hour in non-shaded areas	LAT 54°36′N LONG 5°55′W	Dates in yellow are NEAPS
	TIMES AND HEIGHTS OF HIGH AND LOW WATERS	2009

JANUARY

Day	Time m	Time m	Day	Time m	Time m
1 TH	0138 3.2 / 0736 0.9	1347 3.5 / 2007 0.7	**16** F	0245 3.2 / 0835 0.7	1453 3.7 / 2102 0.5
2 F	0218 3.1 / 0817 0.9	1427 3.5 / 2048 0.7	**17** SA	0333 3.1 / 0925 0.8	1542 3.6 / 2153 0.7
3 SA	0304 3.1 / 0900 1.0	1511 3.4 / 2135 0.8	**18** SU	0421 3.0 / 1020 1.0	1632 3.4 / 2251 0.9
4 SU	0355 3.1 / 0949 1.0	1601 3.3 / ◑2228 0.9	**19** M	0511 2.9 / 1124 1.1	1727 3.2 / 2355 1.1
5 M	0451 3.0 / 1044 1.1	1701 3.3 / 2330 0.9	**20** TU	0612 2.9 / 1232 1.2	1836 3.0
6 TU	0552 3.0 / 1148 1.2	1809 3.2	**21** W	0100 1.2 / 0730 2.9	1341 1.1 / 1959 2.9
7 W	0042 1.0 / 0656 3.1	1306 1.1 / 1921 3.2	**22** TH	0201 1.2 / 0838 3.0	1445 1.1 / 2103 3.0
8 TH	0154 0.9 / 0801 3.2	1421 1.0 / 2031 3.2	**23** F	0255 1.1 / 0931 3.2	1539 0.9 / 2153 3.1
9 F	0255 0.8 / 0903 3.3	1523 0.8 / 2135 3.3	**24** SA	0340 1.0 / 1015 3.3	1621 0.8 / 2234 3.1
10 SA	0349 0.8 / 0959 3.5	1617 0.6 / 2232 3.4	**25** SU	0418 0.9 / 1053 3.4	1654 0.7 / 2310 3.2
11 SU	0439 0.7 / 1051 3.7	1707 0.4 / ○2324 3.4	**26** M	0453 0.8 / 1127 3.5	1725 0.6 / ●2342 3.2
12 M	0527 0.6 / 1140 3.8	1754 0.3	**27** TU	0527 0.8 / 1156 3.5	1757 0.6
13 TU	0015 3.4 / 0613 0.6	1229 3.9 / 1840 0.2	**28** W	0010 3.1 / 0600 0.7	1219 3.5 / 1829 0.6
14 W	0105 3.3 / 0700 0.6	1317 3.9 / 1927 0.3	**29** TH	0034 3.1 / 0634 0.7	1243 3.5 / 1903 0.5
15 TH	0156 3.3 / 0747 0.7	1405 3.8 / 2014 0.4	**30** F	0104 3.2 / 0709 0.7	1317 3.5 / 1937 0.5
			31 SA	0142 3.2 / 0746 0.7	1357 3.5 / 2015 0.6

FEBRUARY

Day	Time m	Time m	Day	Time m	Time m
1 SU	0225 3.2 / 0826 0.7	1440 3.5 / 2058 0.6	**16** M	0333 3.1 / 0932 0.8	1554 3.2 / ◑2152 0.9
2 M	0312 3.1 / 0912 0.8	1529 3.3 / ◑2147 0.8	**17** TU	0419 3.0 / 1034 1.0	1645 3.0 / 2256 1.1
3 TU	0406 3.0 / 1005 0.9	1627 3.2 / 2247 0.9	**18** W	0512 2.8 / 1155 1.1	1746 2.8
4 W	0511 3.0 / 1111 1.1	1741 3.0	**19** TH	0018 1.3 / 0621 2.8	1308 1.1 / 1927 2.7
5 TH	0009 1.1 / 0625 2.9	1247 1.1 / 1903 2.9	**20** F	0128 1.3 / 0812 2.8	1415 1.0 / 2045 2.8
6 F	0142 1.0 / 0730 3.0	1415 0.9 / 2025 3.0	**21** SA	0227 1.1 / 0909 3.0	1511 0.8 / 2134 2.9
7 SA	0248 0.9 / 0852 3.2	1518 0.6 / 2132 3.1	**22** SU	0316 1.0 / 0953 3.2	1552 0.7 / 2213 3.0
8 SU	0342 0.7 / 0950 3.4	1611 0.4 / 2226 3.2	**23** M	0355 0.8 / 1029 3.3	1626 0.5 / 2247 3.1
9 M	0431 0.6 / 1039 3.6	1658 0.2 / ○2314 3.3	**24** TU	0430 0.7 / 1101 3.4	1658 0.5 / 2317 3.1
10 TU	0516 0.5 / 1126 3.7	1741 0.1 / 2359 3.3	**25** W	0503 0.6 / 1126 3.4	1730 0.4 / ●2339 3.1
11 W	0558 0.5 / 1211 3.8	1823 0.1	**26** TH	0535 0.5 / 1143 3.4	1802 0.4
12 TH	0044 3.2 / 0639 0.5	1257 3.8 / 1902 0.2	**27** F	0000 3.2 / 0607 0.5	1212 3.5 / 1833 0.4
13 F	0128 3.2 / 0720 0.5	1341 3.7 / 1942 0.3	**28** SA	0033 3.2 / 0641 0.5	1249 3.5 / 1907 0.4
14 SA	0211 3.2 / 0801 0.6	1425 3.6 / 2022 0.5			
15 SU	0251 3.1 / 0844 0.7	1509 3.5 / 2104 0.7			

MARCH

Day	Time m	Time m	Day	Time m	Time m
1 SU	0112 3.2 / 0717 0.5	1331 3.5 / 1945 0.5	**16** M	0214 3.2 / 0809 0.6	1437 3.3 / 2023 0.7
2 M	0154 3.2 / 0758 0.5	1416 3.4 / 2029 0.6	**17** TU	0253 3.1 / 0853 0.7	1522 3.1 / 2106 0.9
3 TU	0241 3.2 / 0845 0.6	1506 3.3 / 2119 0.8	**18** W	0338 3.0 / 0949 0.9	1612 2.9 / ◑2200 1.2
4 W	0335 3.1 / 0941 0.8	1609 3.0 / ◑2221 1.0	**19** TH	0430 2.9 / 1116 1.1	1710 2.7 / 2329 1.3
5 TH	0444 2.9 / 1052 1.0	1730 2.8 / 2356 1.2	**20** F	0532 2.7 / 1233 1.1	1824 2.6
6 F	0606 2.9 / 1248 1.0	1901 2.8	**21** SA	0050 1.3 / 0658 2.7	1338 1.0 / 2013 2.6
7 SA	0133 1.1 / 0730 3.0	1408 0.7 / 2026 2.9	**22** SU	0152 1.2 / 0832 2.9	1432 0.8 / 2102 2.8
8 SU	0238 0.9 / 0842 3.2	1508 0.5 / 2126 3.0	**23** M	0243 1.0 / 0917 3.0	1516 0.6 / 2140 2.9
9 M	0331 0.7 / 0937 3.4	1558 0.3 / 2214 3.1	**24** TU	0324 0.8 / 0952 3.1	1553 0.5 / 2211 3.0
10 TU	0418 0.5 / 1024 3.6	1642 0.2 / 2257 3.2	**25** W	0401 0.7 / 1020 3.2	1627 0.4 / 2239 3.1
11 W	0500 0.4 / 1108 3.7	1721 0.1 / ○2339 3.2	**26** TH	0435 0.6 / 1044 3.3	1659 0.3 / ●2303 3.2
12 TH	0539 0.4 / 1151 3.7	1758 0.0	**27** F	0507 0.5 / 1111 3.4	1731 0.3 / 2332 3.3
13 F	0019 3.2 / 0616 0.4	1234 3.6 / 1833 0.3	**28** SA	0541 0.4 / 1146 3.5	1805 0.4
14 SA	0059 3.2 / 0653 0.4	1315 3.6 / 1908 0.4	**29** SU	0008 3.3 / 0616 0.4	1227 3.5 / 1842 0.4
15 SU	0136 3.2 / 0730 0.5	1356 3.5 / 1945 0.6	**30** M	0049 3.4 / 0656 0.4	1312 3.4 / 1923 0.5
			31 TU	0134 3.3 / 0740 0.5	1402 3.3 / 2010 0.7

APRIL

Day	Time m	Time m	Day	Time m	Time m
1 W	0224 3.3 / 0830 0.6	1459 3.1 / 2104 0.9	**16** TH	0305 3.1 / 0916 0.9	1543 2.9 / 2125 1.1
2 TH	0321 3.1 / 0931 0.7	1609 2.9 / ◑2212 1.1	**17** F	0355 3.0 / 1030 1.0	1640 2.7 / 2231 1.3
3 F	0431 3.0 / 1054 0.9	1733 2.8 / 2352 1.2	**18** SA	0453 2.9 / 1152 1.0	1743 2.6 / 2359 1.3
4 SA	0554 2.9 / 1241 0.8	1903 2.8	**19** SU	0559 2.8 / 1255 0.9	1855 2.7
5 SU	0116 1.1 / 0718 3.0	1353 0.6 / 2014 2.9	**20** M	0106 1.2 / 0708 2.8	1349 0.8 / 1959 2.8
6 M	0221 0.9 / 0824 3.2	1451 0.4 / 2108 3.0	**21** TU	0200 1.1 / 0811 2.9	1435 0.6 / 2045 3.0
7 TU	0314 0.7 / 0917 3.4	1539 0.3 / 2153 3.1	**22** W	0246 0.9 / 0855 3.1	1515 0.5 / 2123 3.1
8 W	0359 0.5 / 1004 3.5	1620 0.2 / 2235 3.2	**23** TH	0326 0.8 / 0933 3.2	1551 0.4 / 2158 3.2
9 TH	0441 0.5 / 1047 3.6	1657 0.3 / ○2315 3.2	**24** F	0403 0.6 / 1008 3.3	1627 0.4 / 2232 3.3
10 F	0519 0.5 / 1129 3.5	1731 0.4 / 2353 3.3	**25** SA	0440 0.5 / 1046 3.4	1703 0.4 / ●2310 3.4
11 SA	0555 0.5 / 1209 3.5	1805 0.5	**26** SU	0518 0.4 / 1128 3.5	1741 0.4 / 2351 3.5
12 SU	0030 3.3 / 0630 0.5	1249 3.4 / 1838 0.6	**27** M	0559 0.4 / 1214 3.5	1824 0.5
13 M	0105 3.3 / 0705 0.6	1328 3.3 / 1913 0.7	**28** TU	0036 3.5 / 0643 0.4	1305 3.4 / 1910 0.6
14 TU	0142 3.3 / 0743 0.6	1409 3.2 / 1951 0.8	**29** W	0125 3.5 / 0731 0.4	1400 3.3 / 2001 0.8
15 W	0217 3.3 / 0825 0.7	1453 3.0 / 2034 1.0	**30** TH	0217 3.4 / 0827 0.6	1503 3.1 / 2101 0.9

Chart Datum: 2·01 metres below Ordnance Datum (Belfast)
HAT is 3·9m above Chart Datum

TIDES

NORTHERN IRELAND – BELFAST
LAT 54°36′N   LONG 5°55′W
TIMES AND HEIGHTS OF HIGH AND LOW WATERS

TIME ZONE (UT)
For Summer Time add ONE hour in **non-shaded areas**

Dates in amber are **SPRINGS**
Dates in yellow are **NEAPS**

2009

MAY

Day	Time m	Time m	Time m	Time m
1 F	0316 3.3	0932 0.6	1614 2.9	2212 1.1
16 SA	0322 3.2	0943 0.9	1610 2.8	2153 1.1
2 SA	0423 3.2	1055 0.7	1733 2.8	2333 1.1
17 SU	0414 3.0	1049 0.9	1707 2.8	2254 1.2
3 SU	0541 3.1	1220 0.6	1847 2.9	
18 M ◐	0512 2.9	1159 0.9	1805 2.8	
4 M ◑	0048 1.0	0656 3.2	1328 0.5	1949 3.0
19	0000 1.2	0612 2.9	1258 0.8	1900 2.9
5 TU	0153 0.9	0759 3.3	1425 0.4	2041 3.1
20 W	0104 1.1	0710 3.0	1348 0.7	1951 3.0
6 W	0248 0.8	0853 3.4	1512 0.4	2128 3.1
21 TH	0159 1.0	0804 3.1	1434 0.6	2038 3.1
7 TH	0337 0.7	0941 3.4	1554 0.4	2211 3.2
22 F	0248 0.9	0854 3.2	1516 0.5	2122 3.3
8 F	0420 0.6	1025 3.4	1631 0.5	2251 3.3
23 SA	0334 0.7	0941 3.4	1558 0.5	2207 3.4
9 SA	0500 0.6	1107 3.4	1706 0.6	2329 3.3
24 SU	0418 0.6	1028 3.4	1641 0.5	2252 3.5
10 SU	0538 0.6	1146 3.3	1740 0.7	
25 M	0503 0.4	1117 3.5	1725 0.5	2339 3.6
11 M ○	0004 3.4	0613 0.6	1224 3.3	1814 0.8
26 TU ●	0549 0.4	1207 3.4	1812 0.6	
12 TU	0039 3.4	0648 0.6	1302 3.2	1849 0.8
27 W	0028 3.6	0636 0.3	1301 3.4	1902 0.7
13 W	0116 3.4	0724 0.7	1343 3.1	1927 0.9
28 TH	0119 3.6	0728 0.3	1359 3.2	1957 0.8
14 TH	0156 3.4	0804 0.7	1427 3.0	2010 1.0
29 F	0212 3.6	0824 0.4	1501 3.1	2055 0.9
15 F	0237 3.3	0849 0.8	1516 2.9	2059 1.1
30 SA	0308 3.5	0927 0.6	1607 3.0	2159 0.9
31 SU	0409 3.4	1037 0.5	1714 3.0	2305 1.0

JUNE

Day	Time m	Time m	Time m	Time m
1 M	0516 3.3	1148 0.6	1818 2.9	
16 TU ◑	0419 3.1	1050 0.8	1719 2.9	2302 1.1
2 ◑	0012 1.0	0625 3.3	1253 0.6	1916 3.0
17 W	0516 3.1	1152 0.8	1813 3.0	
3 W	0116 0.9	0729 3.3	1350 0.6	2010 3.0
18 TH	0002 1.1	0618 3.1	1256 0.8	1906 3.0
4 TH	0217 0.9	0826 3.3	1441 0.7	2100 3.1
19 F	0109 1.0	0721 3.1	1355 0.7	1959 3.1
5 F	0312 0.8	0918 3.3	1527 0.7	2147 3.2
20 SA	0214 0.9	0822 3.2	1448 0.7	2053 3.3
6 SA	0401 0.7	1006 3.3	1607 0.8	2230 3.3
21 SU	0312 0.8	0920 3.3	1538 0.6	2145 3.4
7 SU	0445 0.7	1048 3.3	1645 0.8	2309 3.3
22 M	0404 0.6	1014 3.4	1627 0.6	2236 3.5
8 M	0524 0.7	1127 3.2	1720 0.8	2344 3.4
23 TU	0454 0.4	1106 3.4	1715 0.6	2326 3.6
9 TU ○	0559 0.7	1203 3.2	1754 0.9	
24 W	0542 0.3	1159 3.4	1803 0.6	
10 W	0019 3.4	0631 0.7	1240 3.1	1829 0.9
25 TH	0016 3.7	0630 0.2	1252 3.3	1853 0.6
11 TH	0055 3.4	0705 0.7	1319 3.1	1907 0.9
26 F	0107 3.7	0720 0.2	1348 3.2	1945 0.7
12 F	0131 3.4	0741 0.7	1401 3.0	1947 0.9
27 SA	0159 3.7	0812 0.2	1445 3.2	2038 0.7
13 SA	0208 3.4	0821 0.7	1446 3.0	2031 0.9
28 SU	0251 3.6	0907 0.3	1543 3.1	2134 0.8
14 SU	0247 3.3	0905 0.7	1535 2.9	2118 1.0
29 M	0345 3.5	1006 0.5	1641 3.0	2233 0.9
15 M	0329 3.2	0954 0.8	1627 2.9	2208 1.0
30 TU	0442 3.4	1109 0.6	1738 3.0	2335 0.9

JULY

Day	Time m	Time m	Time m	Time m
1 W	0544 3.3	1212 0.7	1837 3.0	
16 TH	0428 3.2	1055 0.8	1724 3.0	2314 1.0
2 TH	0039 1.0	0652 3.1	1314 0.8	1937 3.0
17 F	0534 3.1	1204 0.9	1825 3.0	
3 F	0145 1.0	0800 3.1	1410 0.9	2034 3.1
18 SA ◑	0026 1.1	0648 3.0	1325 0.9	1928 3.1
4 SA ◑	0248 0.9	0859 3.1	1502 0.9	2126 3.2
19 SU	0152 1.0	0800 3.1	1431 0.8	2029 3.2
5 SU	0344 0.8	0950 3.1	1547 0.9	2212 3.3
20 M	0300 0.8	0906 3.2	1526 0.7	2127 3.4
6 M	0430 0.7	1034 3.1	1626 0.9	2252 3.3
21 TU	0356 0.5	1004 3.3	1617 0.6	2220 3.5
7 TU	0508 0.7	1112 3.1	1701 0.9	2328 3.4
22 W	0446 0.3	1056 3.3	1704 0.5	2311 3.7
8 W	0540 0.7	1146 3.1	1734 0.9	
23 TH	0532 0.2	1146 3.3	1750 0.5	
9 TH	0001 3.4	0610 0.6	1220 3.1	1807 0.8
24 F ○	0000 3.7	0617 0.1	1236 3.3	1836 0.5
10 F	0033 3.4	0641 0.6	1253 3.1	1843 0.8
25 SA	0049 3.8	0702 0.1	1327 3.2	1923 0.6
11 SA ○	0102 3.4	0714 0.6	1348 3.2	1920 0.8
26 SU ●	0138 3.8	0748 0.2	1418 3.2	2011 0.6
12 SU	0133 3.4	0749 0.6	1405 3.2	1959 0.8
27 M	0227 3.7	0835 0.3	1508 3.1	2100 0.7
13 M	0208 3.4	0827 0.6	1447 3.0	2041 0.8
28 TU	0316 3.6	0925 0.5	1557 3.1	2154 0.8
14 TU	0248 3.3	0910 0.7	1534 3.0	2126 0.9
29 W	0406 3.4	1021 0.7	1647 3.0	2256 0.9
15 W	0334 3.3	0958 0.7	1626 3.0	2216 1.0
30 TH	0500 3.3	1128 0.9	1744 2.9	
31 F	0005 1.0	0605 2.9	1236 1.1	1856 2.9

AUGUST

Day	Time m	Time m	Time m	Time m
1 SA	0116 1.1	0734 2.8	1340 1.1	2009 3.0
16	0627 2.9	1308 1.1	1905 3.0	
2 SU ◑	0225 1.0	0844 2.9	1437 1.1	2107 3.1
17 M ◑	0143 1.0	0748 2.9	1420 0.9	2013 3.2
3 M	0326 0.9	0936 3.0	1525 1.0	2154 3.2
18 TU	0251 0.7	0900 3.1	1515 0.8	2114 3.4
4 TU	0411 0.7	1018 3.0	1604 0.9	2233 3.3
19 W	0345 0.4	0956 3.2	1604 0.6	2206 3.6
5 W	0446 0.6	1054 3.1	1638 0.8	2308 3.4
20 TH	0432 0.2	1044 3.3	1649 0.5	2254 3.7
6 TH	0514 0.6	1127 3.1	1710 0.8	2338 3.4
21 F	0516 0.1	1129 3.3	1732 0.5	2340 3.8
7 F	0543 0.6	1156 3.1	1742 0.7	
22 SA	0557 0.1	1215 3.3	1813 0.5	
8 SA	0002 3.4	0612 0.5	1220 3.1	1815 0.7
23 SU	0027 3.8	0636 0.2	1300 3.3	1855 0.5
9 SU ○	0024 3.4	0643 0.5	1247 3.1	1849 0.7
24 M	0114 3.7	0716 0.3	1345 3.3	1938 0.6
10 M	0055 3.4	0716 0.5	1322 3.1	1925 0.7
25 TU ●	0200 3.6	0757 0.5	1429 3.2	2023 0.7
11 TU	0132 3.4	0751 0.5	1403 3.2	2004 0.7
26 W	0245 3.5	0840 0.7	1513 3.2	2112 0.8
12 W	0214 3.4	0831 0.6	1448 3.1	2048 0.8
27 TH	0332 3.3	0928 0.9	1559 3.1	2214 1.0
13 TH	0259 3.3	0917 0.7	1540 3.1	2139 0.9
28 F	0422 3.0	1029 1.1	1652 3.0	2331 1.1
14 F	0353 3.2	1013 0.9	1643 3.0	2238 1.0
29 SA	0522 2.8	1154 1.3	1758 2.9	
15 SA	0504 3.0	1123 1.1	1753 3.0	2357 1.1
30 SU	0045 1.1	0704 2.7	1306 1.3	1941 2.9
31 M	0156 1.0	0825 2.8	1408 1.2	2043 3.1

Chart Datum: 2·01 metres below Ordnance Datum (Belfast)
HAT is 3·9m above Chart Datum

NORTHERN IRELAND – BELFAST

LAT 54°36′N   LONG 5°55′W

TIMES AND HEIGHTS OF HIGH AND LOW WATERS

Dates in amber are **SPRINGS**
Dates in yellow are **NEAPS**

2009

SEPTEMBER

Day	Time m	Time m	Time m	Time m
1 TU	0257 0.9	0916 2.9	1458 1.1	2130 3.2
2 W	0341 0.7	0956 3.0	1537 0.9	2208 3.3
3 TH	0414 0.6	1030 3.1	1611 0.8	2240 3.4
4 F	0443 0.6	1059 3.1	1643 0.7	○2306 3.4
5 SA	0512 0.5	1124 3.2	1714 0.7	2323 3.4
6 SU	0542 0.5	1144 3.2	1746 0.7	2347 3.5
7 M	0612 0.5	1212 3.3	1819 0.6	
8 TU	0022 3.5	0643 0.5	1249 3.3	1854 0.6
9 W	0103 3.5	0719 0.6	1330 3.3	1934 0.7
10 TH	0146 3.4	0800 0.7	1416 3.3	2020 0.8
11 F	0234 3.3	0848 0.9	1508 3.2	2113 0.9
12 SA	0333 3.1	0945 1.1	1614 3.1	◑2217 1.0
13 SU	0451 2.9	1101 1.2	1731 3.0	2351 1.1
14 M	0619 2.8	1257 1.2	1849 3.1	
15 TU	0134 0.9	0746 2.8	1406 1.0	2001 3.3
16 W	0237 0.6	0853 3.1	1501 0.8	2100 3.5
17 TH	0329 0.4	0942 3.2	1548 0.7	2150 3.6
18 F	0413 0.3	1027 3.3	1630 0.6	2236 3.7
19 SA	0454 0.2	1109 3.4	1710 0.5	2320 3.8
20 SU	0531 0.3	1151 3.4	1749 0.5	
21 M	0005 3.7	0607 0.4	1233 3.4	1827 0.6
22 TU	0049 3.7	0644 0.5	1313 3.4	1908 0.6
23 W	0132 3.6	0722 0.7	1354 3.4	1950 0.6
24 TH	0215 3.4	0802 0.9	1435 3.3	2037 0.8
25 F	0300 3.2	0846 1.1	1520 3.2	2134 1.0
26 SA	0350 3.0	0939 1.3	1612 3.1	◑2255 1.2
27 SU	0448 2.8	1101 1.4	1712 3.0	
28 M	0010 1.2	0601 2.7	1226 1.5	1830 2.9
29 TU	0117 1.1	0752 2.7	1330 1.3	2005 3.0
30 W	0214 0.9	0843 2.9	1422 1.2	2053 3.2

OCTOBER

Day	Time m	Time m	Time m	Time m
1 TH	0259 0.8	0922 3.0	1504 1.0	2131 3.3
2 F	0335 0.7	0955 3.2	1540 0.9	2202 3.4
3 SA	0408 0.6	1024 3.3	1613 0.8	2226 3.4
4 SU	0439 0.6	1049 3.3	1645 0.7	○2250 3.5
5 M	0510 0.6	1114 3.4	1718 0.7	2321 3.5
6 TU	0542 0.6	1146 3.5	1753 0.6	2359 3.6
7 W	0617 0.6	1225 3.5	1831 0.6	
8 TH	0042 3.5	0655 0.7	1309 3.5	1914 0.7
9 F	0130 3.4	0740 0.8	1357 3.4	2002 0.8
10 SA	0224 3.3	0831 1.0	1452 3.3	2059 0.9
11 SU	0329 3.1	0933 1.2	1559 3.2	◑2210 1.0
12 M	0450 2.9	1057 1.3	1716 3.1	2350 1.0
13 TU	0617 2.9	1236 1.3	1836 3.2	
14 W	0114 0.8	0736 3.0	1345 1.1	1946 3.4
15 TH	0216 0.6	0834 3.2	1440 0.9	2042 3.5
16 F	0306 0.5	0922 3.3	1527 0.8	2131 3.7
17 SA	0350 0.4	1006 3.4	1610 0.7	2217 3.7
18 SU	0428 0.5	1048 3.5	1649 0.6	●2301 3.7
19 M	0505 0.5	1128 3.5	1728 0.6	2343 3.7
20 TU	0540 0.7	1207 3.5	1807 0.7	
21 W	0025 3.6	0616 0.8	1245 3.5	1845 0.7
22 TH	0106 3.5	0653 0.9	1323 3.5	1926 0.8
23 F	0148 3.4	0732 1.0	1404 3.5	2010 0.9
24 SA	0233 3.2	0815 1.2	1448 3.4	2102 1.0
25 SU	0322 3.0	0905 1.3	1538 3.2	2209 1.1
26 M	0418 2.9	1008 1.4	1635 3.1	2326 1.2
27 TU	0520 2.8	1130 1.5	1738 3.0	
28 W	0030 1.1	0630 2.8	1241 1.4	1846 3.0
29 TH	0126 1.0	0740 2.9	1337 1.3	1950 3.1
30 F	0214 0.9	0834 3.1	1424 1.2	2038 3.2
31 SA	0255 0.6	0909 3.3	1505 1.0	2117 3.4

NOVEMBER

Day	Time m	Time m	Time m	Time m
1 SU	0331 0.7	0945 3.4	1542 0.9	2152 3.5
2 M	0407 0.7	1019 3.5	1619 0.8	○2227 3.5
3 TU	0442 0.7	1053 3.6	1656 0.7	2305 3.6
4 W	0519 0.7	1130 3.6	1736 0.7	2347 3.6
5 TH	0559 0.7	1212 3.7	1818 0.6	
6 F	0034 3.5	0642 0.8	1258 3.7	1904 0.6
7 SA	0126 3.4	0731 1.0	1348 3.6	1956 0.7
8 SU	0224 3.3	0826 1.1	1444 3.5	2056 0.8
9 M	0331 3.1	0930 1.2	1548 3.4	◐2207 0.9
10 TU	0448 3.0	1045 1.3	1701 3.4	2329 0.9
11 W	0605 3.0	1204 1.2	1816 3.4	
12 TH	0044 0.8	0711 3.1	1313 1.1	1922 3.5
13 F	0146 0.7	0808 3.2	1412 1.0	2020 3.5
14 SA	0238 0.7	0858 3.4	1504 0.9	2112 3.6
15 SU	0323 0.7	0944 3.4	1550 0.8	2159 3.6
16 M	0404 0.7	1028 3.5	1633 0.8	●2244 3.6
17 TU	0443 0.8	1108 3.6	1714 0.8	2326 3.5
18 W	0520 0.9	1146 3.6	1753 0.8	
19 TH	0006 3.5	0556 1.0	1223 3.6	1831 0.8
20 F	0045 3.4	0632 1.0	1300 3.6	1909 0.8
21 SA	0125 3.3	0710 1.1	1340 3.6	1949 0.9
22 SU	0209 3.2	0752 1.1	1422 3.5	2033 1.0
23 M	0256 3.1	0838 1.2	1508 3.4	2123 1.0
24 TU	0348 3.0	0930 1.3	1558 3.3	◐2221 1.1
25 W	0444 3.0	1028 1.4	1654 3.2	2327 1.1
26 TH	0542 3.0	1133 1.4	1752 3.1	
27 F	0029 1.1	0639 3.0	1238 1.3	1850 3.1
28 SA	0124 1.0	0733 3.1	1337 1.3	1946 3.2
29 SU	0212 0.9	0824 3.3	1428 1.1	2037 3.3
30 M	0257 0.8	0909 3.4	1515 1.0	2124 3.4

DECEMBER

Day	Time m	Time m	Time m	Time m
1 TU	0339 0.8	0953 3.5	1559 0.8	2209 3.5
2 W	0421 0.8	1035 3.6	1642 0.7	○2255 3.6
3 TH	0504 0.8	1118 3.7	1726 0.6	2342 3.6
4 F	0548 0.8	1203 3.8	1812 0.5	
5 SA	0031 3.5	0635 0.8	1251 3.8	1900 0.5
6 SU	0124 3.4	0725 0.9	1342 3.8	1952 0.5
7 M	0222 3.3	0819 1.0	1435 3.7	2048 0.6
8 TU	0325 3.2	0918 1.0	1534 3.6	2151 0.7
9 W	0431 3.1	1021 1.1	1638 3.5	◐2259 0.8
10 TH	0537 3.1	1129 1.1	1745 3.5	
11 F	0007 0.8	0639 3.1	1237 1.1	1852 3.4
12 SA	0111 0.9	0739 3.2	1341 1.1	1955 3.4
13 SU	0208 0.9	0834 3.2	1441 1.0	2052 3.4
14 M	0300 0.9	0925 3.4	1535 0.9	2144 3.4
15 TU	0346 0.9	1012 3.5	1622 0.8	2231 3.4
16 W	0427 1.0	1054 3.5	1705 0.8	●2313 3.4
17 TH	0505 1.0	1133 3.6	1743 0.8	2351 3.3
18 F	0541 1.0	1208 3.6	1818 0.8	
19 SA	0027 3.3	0615 1.0	1244 3.6	1851 0.8
20 SU	0105 3.2	0650 1.0	1320 3.6	1926 0.8
21 M	0145 3.2	0729 1.0	1357 3.5	2003 0.9
22 TU	0228 3.1	0810 1.0	1435 3.5	2044 0.9
23 W	0313 3.1	0855 1.1	1515 3.4	2130 0.9
24 TH	0402 3.1	0943 1.1	1600 3.3	◑2221 1.0
25 F	0454 3.0	1036 1.2	1654 3.2	2319 1.0
26 SA	0548 3.0	1136 1.3	1755 3.1	
27 SU	0026 1.1	0644 3.1	1246 1.3	1858 3.1
28 M	0132 1.2	0741 3.1	1355 1.2	2001 3.2
29 TU	0229 0.9	0837 3.3	1454 1.0	2100 3.3
30 W	0321 0.8	0930 3.4	1546 0.8	2154 3.4
31 TH	0408 0.8	1018 3.6	1634 0.6	○2245 3.4

Chart Datum: 2·01 metres below Ordnance Datum (Belfast)
HAT is 3·9m above Chart Datum

TIDES

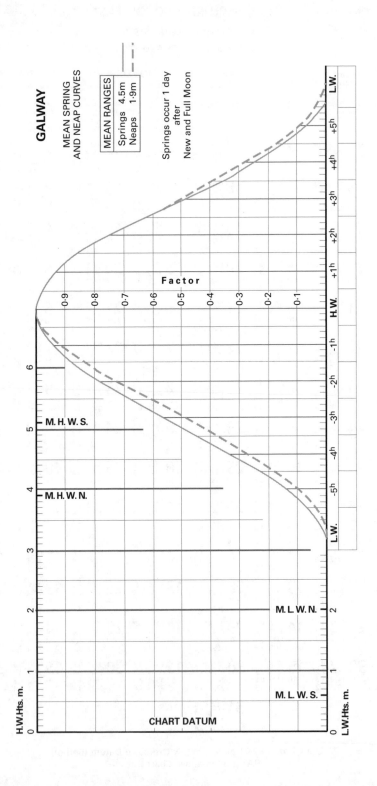

GALWAY

MEAN SPRING
AND NEAP CURVES

MEAN RANGES
Springs 4.5m
Neaps 1·9m

Springs occur 1 day
after
New and Full Moon

Factor

0·9 0·8 0·7 0·6 0·5 0·4 0·3 0·2 0·1

H.W.

L.W.

M. H. W. S.

M. H. W. N.

M. L. W. N.

M. L. W. S.

CHART DATUM

H.W.Hts. m.

L.W.Hts. m.

TIME ZONE (UT)
For Summer Time add ONE hour in **non-shaded areas**

IRELAND – GALWAY
LAT 53°16′N   LONG 9°03′W
TIMES AND HEIGHTS OF HIGH AND LOW WATERS

Dates in amber are **SPRINGS**
Dates in yellow are **NEAPS**
2009

JANUARY

Day	Time	m	Time	m	Day	Time	m	Time	m
1 TH	0128	1.4			**16** F	0206	1.0		
	0800	4.7				0842	4.8		
	1350	1.1				1432	0.9		
	2026	4.3				2113	4.5		
2 F	0206	1.6			**17** SA	0253	1.3		
	0836	4.6				0930	4.5		
	1428	1.2				1518	1.3		
	2106	4.2				2205	4.2		
3 SA	0249	1.7			**18** SU	0346	1.7		
	0916	4.5				1024	4.1		
	1512	1.4				1612	1.7		
	2153	4.2				◑ 2303	4.0		
4 SU	0339	1.8			**19** M	0452	2.0		
	1005	4.3				1123	3.8		
	1602	1.6				1723	2.0		
	◐ 2248	4.1							
5 M	0438	2.0			**20** TU	0006	3.8		
	1102	4.2				0608	2.1		
	1700	1.7				1236	3.6		
	2347	4.1				1852	2.1		
6 TU	0548	2.0			**21** W	0120	3.8		
	1205	4.2				0724	2.1		
	1810	1.8				1402	3.6		
						2007	2.0		
7 W	0053	4.2			**22** TH	0232	3.9		
	0709	1.8				0831	1.9		
	1320	4.2				1508	3.8		
	1932	1.7				2059	1.8		
8 TH	0203	4.4			**23** F	0324	4.1		
	0820	1.5				0921	1.6		
	1434	4.4				1555	4.0		
	2039	1.4				2140	1.6		
9 F	0305	4.6			**24** SA	0406	4.3		
	0917	1.2				1002	1.4		
	1535	4.7				1634	4.2		
	2133	1.1				2217	1.4		
10 SA	0359	4.9			**25** SU	0444	4.5		
	1008	0.8				1039	1.1		
	1629	4.9				1711	4.4		
	2222	0.9				2253	1.2		
11 SU	0450	5.2			**26** M	0521	4.7		
	1056	0.5				1114	0.9		
	1720	5.1				1746	4.5		
	○ 2309	0.7				● 2328	1.0		
12 M	0539	5.3			**27** TU	0557	4.8		
	1142	0.3				1149	0.7		
	1808	5.2				1820	4.6		
	2355	0.6							
13 TU	0627	5.4			**28** W	0002	0.9		
	1225	0.2				0631	4.8		
	1854	5.1				1221	0.6		
						1853	4.6		
14 W	0039	0.6			**29** TH	0034	0.9		
	0712	5.3				0705	4.9		
	1308	0.4				1253	0.6		
	1939	5.0				1925	4.6		
15 TH	0123	0.7			**30** F	0107	0.9		
	0756	5.1				0736	4.8		
	1349	0.5				1325	0.7		
	2024	4.8				1955	4.5		
					31 SA	0141	1.1		
						0807	4.7		
						1400	0.9		
						2025	4.4		

FEBRUARY

Day	Time	m	Day	Time	m
1 SU	0219	1.3	**16** M	0303	1.5
	0840	4.6		0936	4.0
	1439	1.1		1521	1.7
	2103	4.3		○ 2206	3.9
2 M	0304	1.5	**17** TU	0401	1.9
	0925	4.0		1028	3.7
	1525	1.4		1621	2.1
	◑ 2157	4.1		2306	3.6
3 TU	0358	1.7	**18** W	0525	2.1
	1026	4.1		1139	3.4
	1621	1.7		1806	2.3
	2305	3.9			
4 W	0506	1.9	**19** TH	0036	3.5
	1138	4.0		0650	2.1
	1731	1.9		1344	3.4
				1938	2.2
5 TH	0022	3.9	**20** F	0216	3.7
	0642	1.9		0808	1.9
	1302	3.9		1459	3.6
	1915	1.9		2041	1.9
6 F	0150	4.1	**21** SA	0311	3.9
	0815	1.6		0902	1.6
	1428	4.1		1542	3.9
	2036	1.5		2121	1.6
7 SA	0300	4.4	**22** SU	0351	4.2
	0915	1.1		0940	1.3
	1531	4.5		1617	4.2
	2129	1.2		2156	1.3
8 SU	0354	4.8	**23** M	0427	4.4
	1003	0.7		1015	0.9
	1622	4.8		1651	4.4
	2214	0.8		2231	1.0
9 M	0442	5.1	**24** TU	0502	4.6
	1047	0.4		1049	0.7
	1708	5.0		1724	4.6
	○ 2258	0.5		2305	0.7
10 TU	0528	5.3	**25** W	0536	4.8
	1128	0.1		1122	0.5
	1752	5.2		1756	4.7
	2339	0.3		● 2338	0.6
11 W	0612	5.4	**26** TH	0609	4.9
	1207	0.1		1154	0.4
	1834	5.2		1827	4.8
12 TH	0020	0.3	**27** F	0009	0.6
	0653	5.3		0640	4.9
	1245	0.2		1225	0.4
	1915	5.1		1855	4.8
13 F	0100	0.4	**28** SA	0042	0.6
	0734	5.1		0711	4.9
	1322	0.4		1257	0.5
	1954	4.8		1922	4.7
14 SA	0138	0.7			
	0813	4.8			
	1359	0.8			
	2034	4.5			
15 SU	0219	1.1			
	0853	4.4			
	1437	1.2			
	2117	4.3			

MARCH

Day	Time	m	Day	Time	m
1 SU	0116	0.7	**16** M	0149	1.0
	0741	4.8		0822	4.4
	1332	0.7		1402	1.3
	1950	4.6		2038	4.3
2 M	0154	0.9	**17** TU	0230	1.4
	0815	4.6		0902	4.0
	1411	1.0		1439	1.7
	2026	4.4		2123	3.9
3 TU	0237	1.3	**18** W	0321	1.8
	0900	4.3		0950	3.6
	1456	1.4		1529	2.1
	2118	4.1		○ 2218	3.6
4 W	0331	1.6	**19** TH	0451	2.1
	1006	4.0		1054	3.4
	1553	1.8		1734	2.3
	◑ 2236	3.9		2332	3.5
5 TH	0443	1.8	**20** F	0617	2.1
	1126	3.8		1314	3.3
	1711	2.0		1859	2.2
6 F	0006	3.8	**21** SA	0144	3.5
	0642	1.8		0727	1.9
	1259	3.8		1433	3.6
	1919	1.9		2003	2.0
7 SA	0146	4.0	**22** SU	0242	3.8
	0809	1.5		0824	1.6
	1425	4.1		1515	3.9
	2028	1.5		2048	1.6
8 SU	0253	4.4	**23** M	0322	4.1
	0904	1.0		0905	1.3
	1521	4.5		1549	4.2
	2117	1.1		2125	1.3
9 M	0342	4.7	**24** TU	0358	4.3
	0948	0.6		0942	0.9
	1607	4.8		1621	4.5
	2159	0.7		2201	0.9
10 TU	0427	5.0	**25** W	0432	4.6
	1028	0.3		1018	0.7
	1650	5.0		1653	4.7
	2239	0.4		2236	0.7
11 W	0510	5.2	**26** TH	0506	4.8
	1106	0.2		1051	0.5
	1730	5.2		1724	4.8
	○ 2319	0.3		● 2309	0.5
12 TH	0551	5.3	**27** F	0539	4.9
	1143	0.1		1123	0.4
	1810	5.2		1754	4.9
	2357	0.3		2342	0.4
13 F	0631	5.2	**28** SA	0612	5.0
	1219	0.3		1156	0.4
	1848	5.1		1824	4.9
14 SA	0034	0.4	**29** SU	0016	0.4
	0708	5.0		0646	5.0
	1254	0.5		1230	0.5
	1924	4.9		1855	4.9
15 SU	0112	0.7	**30** M	0054	0.6
	0745	4.7		0722	4.8
	1327	0.9		1308	0.7
	2000	4.6		1929	4.7
			31 TU	0134	0.8
				0803	4.6
				1349	1.0
				2010	4.5

APRIL

Day	Time	m	Day	Time	m
1 W	0221	1.1	**16** TH	0256	1.7
	0853	4.3		0926	3.7
	1437	1.4		1458	2.1
	2106	4.2		2147	3.8
2 TH	0318	1.5	**17** F	0415	2.0
	1001	4.0		1025	3.5
	1538	1.8		1653	2.3
	◑ 2227	3.9		○ 2249	3.6
3 F	0437	1.7	**18** SA	0537	2.0
	1122	3.8		1147	3.4
	1711	2.0		1815	2.3
4 SA	0001	3.9	**19** SU	0017	3.6
	0634	1.6		0640	1.9
	1252	3.9		1339	3.6
	1905	1.9		1915	2.0
5 SU	0130	4.1	**20** M	0149	3.7
	0748	1.4		0736	1.7
	1408	4.2		1430	3.9
	2008	1.5		2006	1.7
6 M	0233	4.4	**21** TU	0238	4.0
	0841	1.0		0823	1.4
	1501	4.6		1508	4.1
	2055	1.1		2049	1.4
7 TU	0321	4.8	**22** W	0317	4.3
	0924	0.7		0905	1.1
	1545	4.8		1542	4.4
	2137	0.8		2127	1.1
8 W	0405	5.0	**23** TH	0353	4.5
	1004	0.5		0942	0.8
	1626	5.0		1613	4.7
	2217	0.6		2204	0.8
9 TH	0447	5.1	**24** F	0429	4.7
	1042	0.4		1018	0.6
	1705	5.1		1645	4.9
	○ 2256	0.5		2240	0.6
10 F	0528	5.1	**25** SA	0506	4.9
	1118	0.5		1053	0.5
	1743	5.1		1720	5.0
	2334	0.5		● 2316	0.5
11 SA	0607	5.0	**26** SU	0546	5.0
	1152	0.6		1129	0.5
	1819	5.0		1756	5.1
				2355	0.4
12 SU	0011	0.6	**27** M	0627	5.0
	0644	4.8		1208	0.6
	1226	0.8		1836	5.0
	1855	4.9			
13 M	0048	0.8	**28** TU	0037	0.5
	0720	4.6		0709	4.9
	1259	1.1		1251	0.8
	1932	4.6		1918	4.9
14 TU	0126	1.1	**29** W	0123	0.7
	0758	4.3		0756	4.7
	1333	1.4		1336	1.1
	2011	4.3		2006	4.6
15 W	0206	1.4	**30** TH	0213	1.0
	0838	4.0		0850	4.4
	1411	1.8		1427	1.4
	2054	4.1		2106	4.3

TIDES

Chart Datum: 0·20 metres above Ordnance Datum (Dublin)
HAT is 5·6m above Chart Datum

IRELAND – GALWAY

TIME ZONE (UT)
For Summer Time add ONE hour in **non-shaded areas**

LAT 53°16′N   LONG 9°03′W
TIMES AND HEIGHTS OF HIGH AND LOW WATERS

Dates in amber are **SPRINGS**
Dates in yellow are **NEAPS**

2009

MAY

Day	Time	m
1 F	0313	1.3
	0956	4.1
	1532	1.8
	2223	4.1
2 SA	0433	1.5
	1111	4.0
	1705	1.9
	2346	4.1
3 SU	0607	1.5
	1228	4.1
	1836	1.8
4 M	0101	4.2
	0717	1.3
	1339	4.3
	1939	1.5
5 TU	0204	4.4
	0812	1.1
	1434	4.5
	2030	1.2
6 W	0256	4.6
	0858	1.0
	1519	4.7
	2113	1.0
7 TH	0341	4.8
	0939	0.9
	1600	4.9
	2154	0.9
8 F	0423	4.8
	1017	0.9
	1638	4.9
	2234	0.8
9 SA	0504	4.8
	1054	0.9
	1716	4.9
	2313	0.8
10 SU	0544	4.7
	1128	1.0
	1753	4.9
	2351	0.9
11 M	0622	4.6
	1202	1.2
	1831	4.8
12 TU	0029	1.0
	0700	4.5
	1237	1.3
	1909	4.6
13 W	0109	1.2
	0739	4.3
	1314	1.5
	1949	4.4
14 TH	0149	1.4
	0820	4.1
	1353	1.8
	2033	4.2
15 F	0235	1.6
	0905	3.9
	1438	2.0
	2121	4.0
16 SA	0331	1.7
	0956	3.7
	1543	2.2
	2215	3.9
17 SU	0439	1.8
	1053	3.7
	1717	2.2
	2312	3.8
18 M	0544	1.8
	1155	3.7
	1823	2.1
19 TU	0012	3.8
	0642	1.7
	1307	3.8
	1919	1.9
20 W	0120	4.0
	0735	1.5
	1406	4.1
	2008	1.6
21 TH	0220	4.2
	0823	1.3
	1451	4.4
	2052	1.3
22 F	0308	4.4
	0906	1.1
	1530	4.6
	2133	1.0
23 SA	0353	4.7
	0946	0.9
	1610	4.9
	2214	0.7
24 SU	0438	4.8
	1027	0.7
	1652	5.0
	2256	0.5
25 M	0525	5.0
	1109	0.6
	1737	5.1
	2341	0.4
26 TU	0612	5.0
	1154	0.7
	1823	5.1
27 W	0028	0.4
	0659	5.0
	1240	0.8
	1910	5.0
28 TH	0116	0.5
	0748	4.8
	1328	1.0
	2002	4.8
29 F	0207	0.7
	0842	4.6
	1420	1.3
	2100	4.6
30 SA	0303	1.0
	0942	4.3
	1520	1.5
	2208	4.4
31 SU	0410	1.2
	1047	4.2
	1635	1.7
	2318	4.2

JUNE

Day	Time	m
1 M	0527	1.4
	1154	4.2
	1756	1.7
2 TU	0026	4.2
	0638	1.4
	1301	4.2
	1905	1.6
3 W	0130	4.3
	0739	1.4
	1401	4.3
	2002	1.5
4 TH	0228	4.3
	0831	1.4
	1452	4.5
	2050	1.3
5 F	0317	4.4
	0915	1.3
	1535	4.6
	2134	1.2
6 SA	0402	4.4
	0955	1.3
	1615	4.7
	2215	1.1
7 SU	0445	4.5
	1033	1.3
	1654	4.7
	2256	1.1
8 M	0526	4.4
	1110	1.3
	1733	4.7
	2336	1.0
9 TU	0606	4.4
	1146	1.3
	1812	4.7
10 W	0015	1.1
	0644	4.4
	1222	1.4
	1851	4.6
11 TH	0053	1.1
	0723	4.3
	1258	1.4
	1931	4.5
12 F	0131	1.2
	0802	4.2
	1336	1.5
	2011	4.4
13 SA	0210	1.3
	0842	4.1
	1416	1.7
	2054	4.3
14 SU	0251	1.4
	0925	4.0
	1501	1.8
	2140	4.1
15 M	0337	1.5
	1011	3.9
	1555	1.9
	2230	4.0
16 TU	0428	1.6
	1100	3.9
	1701	2.0
	2322	4.0
17 W	0526	1.7
	1154	3.9
	1815	1.9
18 TH	0019	4.0
	0629	1.7
	1255	4.1
	1922	1.7
19 F	0124	4.1
	0735	1.5
	1359	4.2
	2018	1.5
20 SA	0229	4.3
	0832	1.3
	1455	4.5
	2109	1.1
21 SU	0326	4.5
	0922	1.1
	1545	4.6
	2156	0.8
22 M	0419	4.7
	1010	0.9
	1634	5.0
	2244	0.5
23 TU	0510	4.9
	1057	0.7
	1724	5.1
	2332	0.3
24 W	0600	5.0
	1144	0.6
	1813	5.2
25 TH	0019	0.2
	0648	5.0
	1231	0.6
	1902	5.1
26 F	0106	0.3
	0736	4.9
	1317	0.7
	1951	5.0
27 SA	0152	0.4
	0825	4.8
	1404	0.9
	2043	4.8
28 SU	0241	0.7
	0917	4.5
	1456	1.2
	2141	4.5
29 M	0335	1.0
	1014	4.3
	1555	1.5
	2244	4.2
30 TU	0438	1.4
	1114	4.1
	1707	1.7
	2347	4.1

JULY

Day	Time	m
1 W	0549	1.6
	1217	4.0
	1824	1.8
2 TH	0053	4.0
	0659	1.7
	1325	4.0
	1933	1.7
3 F	0200	3.9
	0802	1.7
	1427	4.1
	2031	1.6
4 SA	0259	4.0
	0853	1.7
	1518	4.3
	2118	1.4
5 SU	0348	4.1
	0937	1.6
	1601	4.4
	2201	1.3
6 M	0432	4.2
	1016	1.4
	1640	4.5
	2241	1.1
7 TU	0513	4.3
	1054	1.3
	1719	4.6
	2320	1.0
8 W	0552	4.4
	1131	1.2
	1758	4.6
	2357	0.9
9 TH	0629	4.4
	1206	1.1
	1835	4.7
10 F	0032	0.8
	0705	4.4
	1240	1.1
	1912	4.6
11 SA	0107	0.9
	0740	4.4
	1314	1.2
	1947	4.6
12 SU	0141	0.9
	0815	4.3
	1349	1.3
	2023	4.4
13 M	0216	1.1
	0849	4.2
	1426	1.5
	2101	4.3
14 TU	0255	1.2
	0926	4.1
	1510	1.6
	2147	4.2
15 W	0339	1.4
	1011	4.0
	1602	1.8
	2240	4.0
16 TH	0431	1.6
	1105	4.0
	1707	1.9
	2340	4.0
17 F	0532	1.7
	1207	4.0
	1831	1.8
18 SA	0048	3.9
	0649	1.7
	1320	4.1
	1956	1.6
19 SU	0205	4.1
	0809	1.6
	1433	4.3
	2056	1.2
20 M	0311	4.3
	0909	1.2
	1532	4.7
	2147	0.8
21 TU	0407	4.6
	0959	0.9
	1624	5.0
	2235	0.4
22 W	0458	4.9
	1046	0.6
	1713	5.2
	2320	0.2
23 TH	0547	5.1
	1132	0.4
	1801	5.3
24 F	0004	0.0
	0633	5.1
	1216	0.4
	1847	5.3
25 SA	0047	0.0
	0717	5.1
	1259	0.4
	1932	5.1
26 SU	0129	0.2
	0801	4.9
	1341	0.7
	2018	4.9
27 M	0212	0.6
	0846	4.6
	1426	1.0
	2107	4.5
28 TU	0258	1.0
	0935	4.3
	1515	1.4
	2203	4.2
29 W	0351	1.4
	1029	4.0
	1618	1.7
	2305	3.9
30 TH	0458	1.8
	1131	3.8
	1740	1.9
31 F	0016	3.7
	0618	2.0
	1247	3.7
	1904	1.9

AUGUST

Day	Time	m
1 SA	0138	3.6
	0733	2.0
	1408	3.8
	2017	1.8
2 SU	0249	3.7
	0832	1.9
	1506	4.0
	2107	1.5
3 M	0338	3.9
	0918	1.6
	1550	4.3
	2146	1.3
4 TU	0419	4.1
	0957	1.4
	1628	4.4
	2222	1.0
5 W	0457	4.3
	1034	1.2
	1705	4.6
	2257	0.8
6 TH	0533	4.4
	1110	1.0
	1740	4.7
	2332	0.7
7 F	0608	4.5
	1143	0.9
	1815	4.8
8 SA	0005	0.6
	0642	4.6
	1216	0.8
	1848	4.8
9 SU	0037	0.6
	0713	4.6
	1247	0.9
	1919	4.7
10 M	0109	0.7
	0743	4.5
	1319	1.0
	1949	4.6
11 TU	0142	0.9
	0810	4.4
	1354	1.2
	2021	4.4
12 W	0219	1.1
	0840	4.3
	1435	1.4
	2103	4.2
13 TH	0302	1.4
	0922	4.1
	1524	1.7
	2203	4.0
14 F	0353	1.7
	1023	4.0
	1627	1.9
	2313	3.8
15 SA	0457	1.9
	1134	3.9
	1758	1.9
16 SU	0029	3.8
	0626	1.9
	1257	4.0
	1950	1.6
17 M	0155	4.0
	0801	1.7
	1425	4.3
	2050	1.2
18 TU	0303	4.3
	0859	1.3
	1525	4.7
	2137	0.7
19 W	0356	4.7
	0947	0.9
	1613	5.0
	2220	0.3
20 TH	0443	5.0
	1031	0.5
	1659	5.3
	2302	0.1
21 F	0528	5.2
	1113	0.3
	1744	5.4
	2343	0.0
22 SA	0611	5.2
	1154	0.2
	1827	5.4
23 SU	0023	0.0
	0652	5.2
	1235	0.3
	1908	5.2
24 M	0102	0.3
	0733	5.0
	1315	0.6
	1949	4.9
25 TU	0141	0.6
	0813	4.7
	1355	0.9
	2032	4.5
26 W	0222	1.1
	0854	4.4
	1438	1.3
	2120	4.1
27 TH	0308	1.6
	0941	4.1
	1534	1.8
	2219	3.7
28 F	0414	2.0
	1038	3.8
	1701	2.1
	2340	3.5
29 SA	0546	2.2
	1204	3.6
	1835	2.1
30 SU	0122	3.5
	0704	2.2
	1350	3.7
	1959	1.9
31 M	0236	3.7
	0807	2.0
	1449	4.0
	2048	1.6

Chart Datum: 0·20 metres above Ordnance Datum (Dublin)
HAT is 5·6m above Chart Datum

TIME ZONE (UT)
For Summer Time add ONE hour in **non-shaded areas**

IRELAND – GALWAY
LAT 53°16′N LONG 9°03′W
TIMES AND HEIGHTS OF HIGH AND LOW WATERS

Dates in amber are **SPRINGS**
Dates in yellow are **NEAPS**

2009

SEPTEMBER

	Time m		Time m
1 TU	0321 3.9 / 0854 1.7 / 1531 4.2 / 2121 1.3	**16** W	0251 4.5 / 0844 1.3 / 1511 4.8 / 2119 0.7
2 W	0358 4.2 / 0932 1.4 / 1608 4.5 / 2154 1.0	**17** TH	0339 4.8 / 0928 0.9 / 1557 5.1 / 2200 0.4
3 TH	0433 4.4 / 1008 1.1 / 1642 4.7 / 2228 0.7	**18** F	0422 5.1 / 1010 0.5 / 1640 5.4 / 2239 0.2
4 F	0507 4.6 / 1043 0.9 / 1716 4.8 / 2302 0.6	**19** SA	0504 5.3 / 1051 0.4 / 1722 5.4 / 2318 0.2
5 SA	0540 4.7 / 1116 0.7 / 1748 4.9 / 2334 0.5	**20** SU	0545 5.3 / 1131 0.3 / 1803 5.4 / 2356 0.3
6 SU	0612 4.8 / 1148 0.7 / 1819 4.9	**21** M	0625 5.2 / 1210 0.4 / 1843 5.2
7 M	0005 0.6 / 0641 4.9 / 1218 0.7 / 1848 4.8	**22** TU	0033 0.5 / 0703 5.1 / 1248 0.7 / 1922 4.9
8 TU	0036 0.7 / 0708 4.7 / 1250 0.8 / 1918 4.7	**23** W	0110 0.9 / 0741 4.8 / 1327 1.0 / 2001 4.5
9 W	0110 0.9 / 0734 4.6 / 1326 1.0 / 1950 4.5	**24** TH	0148 1.3 / 0820 4.5 / 1408 1.4 / 2045 4.1
10 TH	0148 1.1 / 0805 4.4 / 1407 1.3 / 2033 4.3	**25** F	0231 1.8 / 0904 4.1 / 1458 1.8 / 2140 3.7
11 F	0232 1.5 / 0848 4.2 / 1457 1.6 / 2139 4.0	**26** SA	0335 2.2 / 0957 3.8 / 1625 2.1 / ☽ 2300 3.5
12 SA	0325 1.8 / 0953 4.0 / 1602 1.9 / ☽ 2258 3.8	**27** SU	0519 2.4 / 1108 3.6 / 1759 2.2
13 SU	0437 2.1 / 1115 3.9 / 1754 2.0	**28** M	0055 3.5 / 0632 2.3 / 1315 3.7 / 1912 2.0
14 M	0021 3.8 / 0632 2.0 / 1250 4.0 / 1941 1.6	**29** TU	0209 3.7 / 0732 2.1 / 1419 3.9 / 2007 1.7
15 TU	0148 4.1 / 0751 1.8 / 1417 4.4 / 2035 1.1	**30** W	0252 4.0 / 0821 1.8 / 1502 4.2 / 2046 1.4

OCTOBER

	Time m		Time m
1 TH	0328 4.3 / 0901 1.4 / 1538 4.5 / 2121 1.1	**16** F	0316 5.0 / 0907 1.0 / 1536 5.1 / 2137 0.6
2 F	0401 4.5 / 0938 1.2 / 1612 4.7 / 2156 0.8	**17** SA	0358 5.2 / 0948 0.7 / 1618 5.3 / 2215 0.5
3 SA	0434 4.7 / 1013 0.9 / 1644 4.8 / 2229 0.7	**18** SU	0438 5.3 / 1029 0.6 / 1659 5.3 / ● 2253 0.6
4 SU	0505 4.8 / 1047 0.8 / 1716 5.0 / 2301 0.6	**19** M	0518 5.3 / 1108 0.6 / 1739 5.2 / 2330 0.7
5 M	0536 4.9 / 1118 0.7 / 1747 5.0 / 2332 0.6	**20** TU	0557 5.2 / 1147 0.7 / 1819 5.1
6 TU	0606 4.9 / 1151 0.7 / 1820 5.0	**21** W	0006 0.9 / 0636 5.1 / 1226 0.9 / 1858 4.8
7 W	0006 0.7 / 0637 4.9 / 1226 0.8 / 1855 4.9	**22** TH	0043 1.2 / 0714 4.8 / 1304 1.2 / 1938 4.5
8 TH	0043 0.9 / 0710 4.8 / 1306 1.0 / 1935 4.7	**23** F	0121 1.6 / 0754 4.6 / 1345 1.5 / 2021 4.2
9 F	0125 1.2 / 0747 4.6 / 1350 1.2 / 2024 4.4	**24** SA	0204 1.9 / 0837 4.3 / 1433 1.8 / 2113 3.9
10 SA	0212 1.6 / 0835 4.4 / 1442 1.6 / 2131 4.1	**25** SU	0301 2.3 / 0927 4.0 / 1541 2.1 / 2219 3.7
11 SU	0309 1.9 / 0944 4.1 / 1549 1.8 / ☽ 2249 4.0	**26** M	0439 2.4 / 1026 3.8 / 1710 2.2 / ☽ 2349 3.6
12 M	0430 2.1 / 1107 4.1 / 1755 1.9	**27** TU	0552 2.4 / 1143 3.8 / 1819 2.1
13 TU	0011 4.0 / 0623 2.0 / 1238 4.2 / 1918 1.6	**28** W	0113 3.8 / 0650 2.2 / 1319 3.9 / 1915 1.9
14 W	0130 4.3 / 0730 1.7 / 1356 4.5 / 2012 1.2	**29** TH	0207 4.0 / 0741 2.0 / 1415 4.1 / 2003 1.6
15 TH	0229 4.7 / 0822 1.3 / 1450 4.9 / 2056 0.9	**30** F	0247 4.3 / 0826 1.7 / 1457 4.3 / 2044 1.3
		31 SA	0322 4.5 / 0906 1.4 / 1533 4.6 / 2121 1.1

NOVEMBER

	Time m		Time m
1 SU	0355 4.7 / 0942 1.1 / 1607 4.8 / 2156 0.9	**16** M	0414 5.1 / 1009 1.0 / 1639 5.0 / ● 2232 1.0
2 M	0426 4.9 / 1018 0.9 / 1642 5.0 / ○ 2230 0.8	**17** TU	0454 5.1 / 1050 1.0 / 1719 5.0 / 2309 1.1
3 TU	0500 5.0 / 1053 0.8 / 1719 5.1 / 2305 0.8	**18** W	0534 5.1 / 1130 1.0 / 1800 4.8 / 2346 1.3
4 W	0536 5.1 / 1130 0.7 / 1759 5.1 / 2344 0.9	**19** TH	0614 5.0 / 1209 1.1 / 1840 4.7
5 TH	0615 5.1 / 1210 0.7 / 1842 5.0	**20** F	0023 1.4 / 0654 4.8 / 1249 1.2 / 1920 4.5
6 F	0026 1.0 / 0656 5.0 / 1254 0.9 / 1928 4.8	**21** SA	0103 1.6 / 0734 4.7 / 1329 1.4 / 2003 4.3
7 SA	0111 1.2 / 0741 4.8 / 1341 1.1 / 2020 4.6	**22** SU	0144 1.9 / 0816 4.5 / 1412 1.6 / 2049 4.1
8 SU	0202 1.6 / 0833 4.6 / 1434 1.4 / 2123 4.3	**23** M	0232 2.1 / 0901 4.3 / 1500 1.8 / 2142 3.9
9 M	0301 1.9 / 0939 4.4 / 1540 1.6 / 2236 4.2	**24** TU	0334 2.3 / 0951 4.1 / 1601 2.0 / ☾ 2241 3.8
10 TU	0420 2.0 / 1055 4.3 / 1717 1.7 / 2350 4.3	**25** W	0452 2.3 / 1044 4.0 / 1711 2.0 / 2344 3.9
11 W	0554 2.0 / 1213 4.4 / 1845 1.6	**26** TH	0557 2.3 / 1140 4.0 / 1815 2.0
12 TH	0100 4.4 / 0702 1.8 / 1325 4.5 / 1944 1.4	**27** F	0048 4.0 / 0654 2.1 / 1244 4.0 / 1912 1.8
13 F	0201 4.7 / 0757 1.5 / 1424 4.8 / 2032 1.2	**28** SA	0146 4.1 / 0745 1.9 / 1352 4.2 / 2002 1.6
14 SA	0250 4.9 / 0845 1.3 / 1513 4.9 / 2114 1.0	**29** SU	0233 4.4 / 0831 1.6 / 1445 4.4 / 2046 1.4
15 SU	0334 5.1 / 0928 1.1 / 1557 5.0 / 2154 1.0	**30** M	0313 4.6 / 0914 1.4 / 1530 4.6 / 2126 1.2

DECEMBER

	Time m		Time m
1 TU	0352 4.9 / 0954 1.1 / 1614 4.9 / 2206 1.0	**16** W	0438 4.9 / 1037 1.2 / 1707 4.6 / ● 2255 1.3
2 W	0433 5.0 / 1035 0.8 / 1659 5.0 / ○ 2247 0.9	**17** TH	0519 4.9 / 1118 1.1 / 1747 4.6 / 2332 1.3
3 TH	0516 5.2 / 1118 0.7 / 1745 5.1 / 2331 0.9	**18** F	0559 4.9 / 1157 1.1 / 1827 4.6
4 F	0602 5.2 / 1202 0.6 / 1833 5.1	**19** SA	0010 1.4 / 0639 4.8 / 1234 1.1 / 1905 4.5
5 SA	0017 0.9 / 0648 5.2 / 1248 0.6 / 1920 5.0	**20** SU	0047 1.4 / 0718 4.8 / 1311 1.2 / 1944 4.4
6 SU	0104 1.0 / 0736 5.1 / 1335 0.8 / 2011 4.8	**21** M	0125 1.6 / 0756 4.7 / 1348 1.3 / 2024 4.3
7 M	0154 1.3 / 0827 4.9 / 1425 1.0 / 2108 4.6	**22** TU	0204 1.7 / 0835 4.6 / 1426 1.4 / 2106 4.2
8 TU	0249 1.5 / 0926 4.6 / 1522 1.3 / 2212 4.4	**23** W	0246 2.0 / 0915 4.3 / 1507 1.6 / 2152 4.1
9 W	0354 1.8 / 1032 4.5 / 1632 1.5 / ☽ 2319 4.3	**24** TH	0334 2.0 / 0959 4.2 / 1554 1.8 / ☾ 2242 4.0
10 TH	0511 1.9 / 1140 4.4 / 1757 1.6	**25** F	0432 2.2 / 1048 4.1 / 1648 1.9 / 2334 4.0
11 F	0025 4.4 / 0625 1.8 / 1250 4.4 / 1911 1.6	**26** SA	0542 2.2 / 1142 4.0 / 1753 1.9
12 SA	0129 4.5 / 0729 1.7 / 1356 4.4 / 2008 1.5	**27** SU	0032 4.0 / 0655 2.1 / 1246 4.0 / 1908 1.8
13 SU	0226 4.6 / 0824 1.6 / 1452 4.5 / 2055 1.5	**28** M	0137 4.2 / 0758 1.8 / 1359 4.2 / 2012 1.6
14 M	0314 4.7 / 0912 1.4 / 1541 4.6 / 2137 1.4	**29** TU	0237 4.4 / 0851 1.5 / 1503 4.4 / 2104 1.4
15 TU	0357 4.8 / 0955 1.3 / 1625 4.6 / 2216 1.4	**30** W	0328 4.7 / 0939 1.2 / 1556 4.7 / 2151 1.1
		31 TH	0416 4.9 / 1025 0.8 / 1646 4.9 / ○ 2237 0.9

Chart Datum: 0·20 metres above Ordnance Datum (Dublin)
HAT is 5·6m above Chart Datum

TIDES

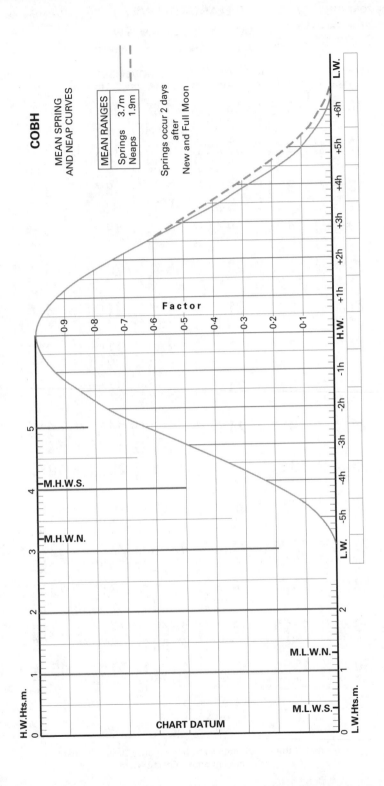

TIME ZONE (UT)	IRELAND – COBH	Dates in amber are SPRINGS
For Summer Time add ONE hour in **non-shaded areas**	LAT 51°51′N LONG 8°18′W	Dates in yellow are NEAPS
	TIMES AND HEIGHTS OF HIGH AND LOW WATERS	**2009**

JANUARY

Day	Time m	Time m	Time m	Time m	Day	Time m	Time m	Time m	Time m
1 TH	0205 0.9	0808 3.9	1429 1.0	2018 3.8	16 F	0308 0.5	0903 4.0	1535 0.7	2119 3.8
2 F	0246 1.0	0848 3.9	1510 1.1	2059 3.7	17 SA	0353 0.7	0947 3.8	1620 0.9	2202 3.6
3 SA	0330 1.1	0931 3.8	1554 1.2	2145 3.7	18 SU	0440 0.9	1032 3.6	1708 1.1	◑ 2250 3.5
4 SU	0419 1.2	1019 3.7	1644 1.3	◐ 2238 3.6	19 M	0531 1.2	1123 3.4	1803 1.3	2348 3.3
5 M	0516 1.3	1114 3.6	1744 1.3	2339 3.6	20 TU	0632 1.3	1227 3.2	1908 1.4	
6 TU	0623 1.3	1218 3.6	1856 1.4		21 W	0101 3.2	0740 1.4	1341 3.2	2017 1.4
7 W	0048 3.5	0736 1.3	1329 3.6	2009 1.2	22 TH	0217 3.3	0851 1.4	1450 3.3	2124 1.3
8 TH	0201 3.6	0849 1.1	1439 3.7	2120 1.0	23 F	0321 3.5	0955 1.2	1548 3.5	2220 1.1
9 F	0313 3.8	0958 0.9	1546 3.8	2223 0.8	24 SA	0414 3.7	1045 1.0	1635 3.7	2304 0.9
10 SA	0418 4.0	1058 0.7	1646 4.0	2318 0.5	25 SU	0458 3.9	1123 0.9	1716 3.8	2339 0.8
11 SU	0515 4.2	1150 0.4	1738 4.1	○	26 M	0536 4.0	1155 0.8	1751 3.9 ●	
12 M	0008 0.4	0604 4.3	1238 0.3	1825 4.2	27 TU	0009 0.7	0610 4.0	1226 0.7	1822 3.9
13 TU	0054 0.3	0651 4.3	1323 0.3	1910 4.2	28 W	0038 0.7	0641 4.1	1257 0.7	1851 3.9
14 W	0140 0.3	0736 4.3	1408 0.4	1954 4.1	29 TH	0109 0.7	0712 4.0	1330 0.8	1922 3.9
15 TH	0224 0.4	0820 4.1	1452 0.5	2037 4.0	30 F	0143 0.7	0744 4.0	1404 0.8	1954 3.9
					31 SA	0220 0.8	0819 4.0	1440 0.9	2030 3.9

FEBRUARY

Day	Time m	Time m	Time m	Time m	Day	Time m	Time m	Time m	Time m
1 SU	0300 0.9	0857 3.9	1519 1.0	2110 3.8	16 M	0354 0.9	0944 3.6	1617 1.1	◑ 2200 3.5
2 M	0343 1.0	0941 3.8	1603 1.1	◐ 2158 3.7	17 TU	0440 1.1	1027 3.3	1707 1.3	2251 3.2
3 TU	0435 1.2	1033 3.6	1658 1.3	2258 3.5	18 W	0537 1.4	1125 3.1	1814 1.5	
4 W	0542 1.3	1140 3.4	1813 1.4		19 TH	0004 3.1	0649 1.5	1254 3.0	1934 1.5
5 TH	0012 3.4	0703 1.4	1300 3.3	1941 1.4	20 F	0145 3.1	0811 1.4	1425 3.1	2054 1.3
6 F	0139 3.4	0831 1.2	1424 3.4	2104 1.1	21 SA	0259 3.3	0929 1.2	1528 3.3	2158 1.1
7 SA	0305 3.6	0948 0.9	1539 3.6	2213 0.8	22 SU	0353 3.6	1023 1.0	1616 3.6	2243 0.9
8 SU	0412 3.9	1049 0.6	1638 3.9	2308 0.5	23 M	0436 3.8	1102 0.8	1655 3.8	2318 0.7
9 M	0506 4.1	1139 0.3	1727 4.1	○ 2355 0.2	24 TU	0513 3.9	1133 0.6	1730 3.9	2346 0.6
10 TU	0551 4.3	1223 0.2	1810 4.2		25 W	0546 4.0	1202 0.6	1800 3.9 ●	
11 W	0038 0.1	0633 4.3	1304 0.2	1850 4.2	26 TH	0014 0.5	0616 4.1	1233 0.5	1828 4.0
12 TH	0119 0.1	0713 4.3	1343 0.2	1929 4.2	27 F	0045 0.5	0645 4.1	1304 0.6	1857 4.0
13 F	0158 0.2	0751 4.2	1422 0.4	2006 4.0	28 SA	0118 0.5	0717 4.0	1338 0.6	1929 4.0
14 SA	0236 0.4	0828 4.0	1459 0.6	2042 3.9					
15 SU	0314 0.6	0905 3.8	1537 0.8	2119 3.7					

MARCH

Day	Time m	Time m	Time m	Time m	Day	Time m	Time m	Time m	Time m
1 SU	0155 0.6	0751 4.0	1413 0.7	2004 3.9	16 M	0239 0.6	0828 3.7	1500 0.8	2043 3.7
2 M	0234 0.7	0829 3.9	1452 0.8	2044 3.8	17 TU	0316 0.9	0903 3.5	1536 1.0	2122 3.5
3 TU	0318 0.9	0913 3.7	1536 1.0	2131 3.7	18 W	0359 1.1	0944 3.3	1622 1.3	◑ 2210 3.2
4 W	0411 1.1	1006 3.5	1633 1.2	◐ 2232 3.4	19 TH	0455 1.4	1036 3.0	1728 1.4	2315 3.0
5 TH	0519 1.3	1116 3.2	1750 1.3	2352 3.3	20 F	0608 1.5	1156 2.9	1852 1.5	
6 F	0645 1.3	1245 3.1	1924 1.3		21 SA	0102 3.0	0729 1.4	1349 2.9	2013 1.4
7 SA	0131 3.3	0819 1.2	1418 3.3	2053 1.0	22 SU	0226 3.2	0845 1.2	1456 3.2	2118 1.1
8 SU	0259 3.5	0938 0.8	1530 3.6	2202 0.7	23 M	0320 3.4	0942 1.0	1544 3.5	2206 0.7
9 M	0401 3.9	1035 0.5	1625 3.9	2254 0.4	24 TU	0403 3.7	1024 0.7	1624 3.7	2243 0.7
10 TU	0449 4.1	1121 0.2	1710 4.1	2338 0.2	25 W	0440 3.8	1100 0.5	1658 3.8	2315 0.5
11 W	0532 4.2	1202 0.1	1750 4.2	○	26 TH	0513 4.0	1132 0.5	1730 3.9 ●	2346 0.4
12 TH	0017 0.1	0610 4.3	1240 0.1	1827 4.2	27 F	0545 4.0	1205 0.4	1801 4.0	
13 F	0054 0.1	0646 4.2	1316 0.2	1902 4.1	28 SA	0019 0.4	0617 4.0	1240 0.4	1833 4.0
14 SA	0130 0.2	0721 4.1	1351 0.4	1935 4.0	29 SU	0056 0.4	0652 4.0	1316 0.5	1908 4.0
15 SU	0204 0.4	0754 3.9	1425 0.6	2008 3.9	30 M	0135 0.5	0730 4.0	1354 0.5	1946 4.0
					31 TU	0218 0.6	0812 3.8	1437 0.7	2030 3.8

APRIL

Day	Time m	Time m	Time m	Time m	Day	Time m	Time m	Time m	Time m
1 W	0306 0.7	0900 3.6	1527 0.9	2121 3.6	16 TH	0328 1.1	0913 3.3	1550 1.2	2141 3.3
2 TH	0403 1.0	0957 3.4	1627 1.1	◐ 2224 3.4	17 F	0422 1.3	1003 3.1	1651 1.4	◑ 2240 3.1
3 F	0512 1.1	1109 3.2	1744 1.2	2348 3.2	18 SA	0530 1.4	1110 3.0	1808 1.4	
4 SA	0637 1.2	1238 3.1	1914 1.1		19 SU	0001 3.0	0644 1.4	1243 3.0	1922 1.3
5 SU	0125 3.3	0807 1.0	1405 3.3	2038 0.9	20 M	0130 3.1	0752 1.2	1401 3.1	2024 1.1
6 M	0242 3.6	0917 0.7	1511 3.6	2142 0.6	21 TU	0229 3.4	0849 1.0	1455 3.4	2115 0.9
7 TU	0339 3.8	1012 0.4	1602 3.8	2232 0.4	22 W	0316 3.6	0937 0.8	1538 3.6	2158 0.7
8 W	0426 4.0	1057 0.3	1647 4.0	2315 0.2	23 TH	0357 3.8	1020 0.6	1618 3.8	2239 0.5
9 TH	0508 4.1	1138 0.2	1727 4.1	○ 2354 0.2	24 F	0436 3.9	1100 0.5	1656 3.9	2318 0.4
10 F	0546 4.1	1215 0.2	1803 4.1		25 SA	0514 4.0	1140 0.4	1734 4.0 ●	2358 0.4
11 SA	0029 0.3	0620 4.0	1250 0.3	1836 4.0	26 SU	0554 4.0	1220 0.4	1813 4.0	
12 SU	0103 0.4	0652 3.9	1323 0.5	1908 3.9	27 M	0040 0.3	0635 4.0	1302 0.4	1854 4.0
13 M	0135 0.5	0724 3.8	1356 0.6	1940 3.8	28 TU	0124 0.4	0718 3.9	1346 0.5	1938 4.0
14 TU	0209 0.7	0756 3.7	1429 0.8	2015 3.7	29 W	0212 0.5	0806 3.8	1434 0.6	2027 3.8
15 W	0245 0.9	0832 3.5	1505 1.0	2055 3.5	30 TH	0304 0.6	0858 3.6	1528 0.7	2122 3.7

Chart Datum: 0·13 metres above Ordnance Datum (Dublin)
HAT is 4·5m above Chart Datum

TIDES

TIME ZONE (UT)
For Summer Time add ONE hour in **non-shaded areas**

IRELAND – COBH
LAT 51°51′N   LONG 8°18′W
TIMES AND HEIGHTS OF HIGH AND LOW WATERS

Dates in amber are **SPRINGS**
Dates in yellow are **NEAPS**

2009

MAY

Day	Time	m	Day	Time	m
1 F	0403 / 0957 / 1629 / 2226	0.8 / 3.4 / 0.9 / 3.5	16 SA	0353 / 0939 / 1619 / 2211	1.2 / 3.3 / 1.2 / 3.3
2 SA	0510 / 1105 / 1740 / 2343	0.9 / 3.3 / 1.0 / 3.4	17 SU	0451 / 1035 / 1721 / 2312	1.3 / 3.2 / 1.3 / 3.3
3 SU	0627 / 1222 / 1900	1.0 / 3.3 / 0.9	18 M	0556 / 1141 / 1828	1.3 / 3.2 / 1.2
4 M	0104 / 0743 / 1337 / 2013	3.4 / 0.9 / 3.4 / 0.8	19 TU	0019 / 0659 / 1251 / 1929	3.3 / 1.2 / 3.2 / 1.1
5 TU	0213 / 0847 / 1440 / 2113	3.6 / 0.7 / 3.6 / 0.6	20 W	0124 / 0757 / 1352 / 2024	3.4 / 1.1 / 3.4 / 1.0
6 W	0309 / 0941 / 1532 / 2205	3.7 / 0.6 / 3.7 / 0.5	21 TH	0220 / 0851 / 1446 / 2116	3.6 / 0.9 / 3.6 / 0.8
7 TH	0357 / 1029 / 1619 / 2250	3.8 / 0.5 / 3.9 / 0.4	22 F	0311 / 0942 / 1536 / 2206	3.7 / 0.7 / 3.7 / 0.6
8 F	0441 / 1111 / 1701 / 2329	3.9 / 0.4 / 3.9 / 0.4	23 SA	0400 / 1031 / 1625 / 2255	3.8 / 0.6 / 3.9 / 0.5
9 SA	0520 / 1150 / 1739	3.9 / 0.5 / 4.0	24 SU	0448 / 1119 / 1713 / 2343	3.9 / 0.5 / 4.0 / 0.4
10 SU	0005 / 0555 / 1226 / 1813	0.5 / 3.9 / 0.5 / 3.9	25 M	0536 / 1207 / 1800	4.0 / 0.4 / 4.1
11 M	0038 / 0628 / 1259 / 1846	0.6 / 3.8 / 0.6 / 3.9	26 TU	0030 / 0623 / 1254 / 1846	0.3 / 4.0 / 0.4 / 4.1
12 TU	0110 / 0700 / 1332 / 1919	0.7 / 3.7 / 0.7 / 3.8	27 W	0119 / 0712 / 1342 / 1935	0.3 / 3.9 / 0.4 / 4.0
13 W	0144 / 0733 / 1405 / 1955	0.8 / 3.6 / 0.9 / 3.7	28 TH	0209 / 0803 / 1433 / 2027	0.4 / 3.8 / 0.4 / 3.9
14 TH	0221 / 0810 / 1442 / 2035	0.9 / 3.5 / 1.0 / 3.6	29 F	0302 / 0855 / 1526 / 2121	0.5 / 3.8 / 0.5 / 3.8
15 F	0303 / 0851 / 1526 / 2119	1.1 / 3.4 / 1.1 / 3.4	30 SA	0358 / 0951 / 1623 / 2219	0.6 / 3.6 / 0.7 / 3.6
			31 SU	0458 / 1050 / 1725 / 2322	0.7 / 3.5 / 0.8 / 3.5

JUNE

Day	Time	m	Day	Time	m
1 M	0603 / 1153 / 1832	0.8 / 3.4 / 0.8	16 TU	0505 / 1055 / 1733 / 2326	1.2 / 3.4 / 1.2 / 3.5
2 TU	0029 / 0709 / 1259 / 1938	3.5 / 0.8 / 3.4 / 0.8	17 W	0605 / 1154 / 1835	1.2 / 3.4 / 1.1
3 W	0134 / 0810 / 1401 / 2038	3.5 / 0.8 / 3.5 / 0.8	18 TH	0027 / 0707 / 1258 / 1938	3.5 / 1.1 / 3.5 / 1.1
4 TH	0232 / 0906 / 1457 / 2133	3.6 / 0.8 / 3.6 / 0.7	19 F	0130 / 0809 / 1400 / 2040	3.5 / 1.0 / 3.6 / 0.9
5 F	0324 / 0958 / 1548 / 2222	3.6 / 0.7 / 3.7 / 0.7	20 SA	0231 / 0909 / 1501 / 2140	3.6 / 0.9 / 3.7 / 0.8
6 SA	0412 / 1045 / 1635 / 2306	3.7 / 0.7 / 3.8 / 0.7	21 SU	0331 / 1009 / 1601 / 2238	3.7 / 0.7 / 3.8 / 0.6
7 SU	0455 / 1127 / 1717 / 2343	3.7 / 0.7 / 3.8 / 0.7	22 M	0429 / 1104 / 1657 / 2332	3.9 / 0.5 / 4.1 / 0.4
8 M	0534 / 1204 / 1755	3.7 / 0.7 / 3.8	23 TU	0523 / 1156 / 1749	4.0 / 0.4 / 4.1
9 TU	0017 / 0609 / 1239 / 1829	0.8 / 3.7 / 0.7 / 3.8	24 W	0022 / 0614 / 1245 / 1839	0.3 / 4.0 / 0.3 / 4.1
10 W	0049 / 0643 / 1312 / 1904	0.8 / 3.7 / 0.8 / 3.8	25 TH	0111 / 0704 / 1334 / 1928	0.3 / 4.0 / 0.2 / 4.1
11 TH	0122 / 0717 / 1345 / 1939	0.8 / 3.7 / 0.8 / 3.7	26 F	0201 / 0753 / 1423 / 2017	0.3 / 4.0 / 0.3 / 4.0
12 F	0159 / 0753 / 1421 / 2016	0.9 / 3.6 / 0.9 / 3.7	27 SA	0250 / 0842 / 1512 / 2106	0.4 / 3.9 / 0.4 / 3.9
13 SA	0239 / 0832 / 1501 / 2057	1.0 / 3.6 / 1.0 / 3.6	28 SU	0341 / 0931 / 1603 / 2156	0.5 / 3.8 / 0.5 / 3.8
14 SU	0323 / 0915 / 1546 / 2142	1.1 / 3.5 / 1.1 / 3.6	29 M	0432 / 1021 / 1655 / 2249	0.6 / 3.6 / 0.7 / 3.6
15 M	0412 / 1002 / 1636 / 2231	1.1 / 3.5 / 1.1 / 3.5	30 TU	0527 / 1115 / 1752 / 2346	0.8 / 3.5 / 0.8 / 3.5

JULY

Day	Time	m	Day	Time	m
1 W	0626 / 1214 / 1853	0.9 / 3.4 / 1.0	16 TH	0510 / 1108 / 1744 / 2341	1.2 / 3.5 / 1.2 / 3.5
2 TH	0048 / 0727 / 1318 / 1956	3.4 / 1.0 / 3.4 / 1.0	17 F	0616 / 1213 / 1855	1.2 / 3.6 / 1.2
3 F	0152 / 0829 / 1421 / 2059	3.3 / 1.0 / 3.4 / 1.0	18 SA	0049 / 0731 / 1325 / 2009	3.4 / 1.2 / 3.5 / 1.1
4 SA	0252 / 0928 / 1520 / 2156	3.4 / 1.0 / 3.5 / 1.0	19 SU	0202 / 0844 / 1438 / 2121	3.5 / 1.1 / 3.6 / 0.9
5 SU	0346 / 1023 / 1613 / 2245	3.5 / 0.9 / 3.6 / 0.9	20 M	0312 / 0951 / 1546 / 2225	3.6 / 0.8 / 3.8 / 0.6
6 M	0435 / 1109 / 1659 / 2325	3.6 / 0.8 / 3.7 / 0.8	21 TU	0416 / 1051 / 1646 / 2320	3.8 / 0.5 / 4.0 / 0.4
7 TU	0517 / 1147 / 1739 / 2359	3.7 / 0.8 / 3.8 / 0.8	22 W	0511 / 1143 / 1738	4.0 / 0.3 / 4.2
8 W	0554 / 1220 / 1815	3.7 / 0.7 / 3.9	23 TH	0010 / 0601 / 1232 / 1825	0.2 / 4.1 / 0.2 / 4.2
9 TH	0029 / 0628 / 1251 / 1848	0.8 / 3.7 / 0.7 / 3.9	24 F	0057 / 0648 / 1318 / 1911	0.1 / 4.1 / 0.1 / 4.2
10 F	0101 / 0700 / 1322 / 1920	0.8 / 3.7 / 0.7 / 3.8	25 SA	0142 / 0733 / 1403 / 1955	0.2 / 4.1 / 0.1 / 4.2
11 SA	0136 / 0733 / 1356 / 1954	0.8 / 3.7 / 0.8 / 3.8	26 SU	0227 / 0817 / 1447 / 2039	0.3 / 4.0 / 0.3 / 4.0
12 SU	0212 / 0808 / 1432 / 2030	0.9 / 3.7 / 0.9 / 3.8	27 M	0312 / 0901 / 1532 / 2123	0.4 / 3.9 / 0.4 / 3.8
13 M	0251 / 0846 / 1512 / 2109	0.9 / 3.7 / 0.9 / 3.7	28 TU	0357 / 0945 / 1617 / 2208	0.6 / 3.7 / 0.7 / 3.6
14 TU	0332 / 0927 / 1555 / 2152	1.0 / 3.6 / 1.0 / 3.7	29 W	0444 / 1032 / 1706 / 2257	0.8 / 3.5 / 0.9 / 3.4
15 W	0417 / 1013 / 1644 / 2242	1.1 / 3.6 / 1.1 / 3.6	30 TH	0537 / 1126 / 1803 / 2357	1.1 / 3.3 / 1.1 / 3.2
			31 F	0640 / 1234 / 1910	1.2 / 3.2 / 1.3

AUGUST

Day	Time	m	Day	Time	m
1 SA	0112 / 0751 / 1351 / 2024	3.1 / 1.3 / 3.2 / 1.3	16 SU	0020 / 0702 / 1302 / 1948	3.3 / 1.3 / 3.3 / 1.2
2 SU	0225 / 0902 / 1459 / 2134	3.2 / 1.2 / 3.3 / 1.2	17 M	0144 / 0825 / 1427 / 2107	3.3 / 1.1 / 3.5 / 1.0
3 M	0326 / 1004 / 1554 / 2228	3.4 / 1.0 / 3.5 / 1.0	18 TU	0301 / 0937 / 1537 / 2212	3.6 / 0.8 / 3.8 / 0.6
4 TU	0417 / 1052 / 1640 / 2309	3.5 / 0.8 / 3.7 / 0.8	19 W	0404 / 1037 / 1634 / 2306	3.8 / 0.5 / 4.0 / 0.3
5 W	0459 / 1129 / 1720 / 2340	3.7 / 0.7 / 3.9 / 0.7	20 TH	0457 / 1127 / 1722 / 2352	4.0 / 0.2 / 4.2 / 0.2
6 TH	0536 / 1200 / 1755	3.8 / 0.6 / 3.9	21 F	0543 / 1212 / 1806	4.2 / 0.1 / 4.3
7 F	0008 / 0608 / 1227 / 1826	0.7 / 3.8 / 0.6 / 3.9	22 SA	0035 / 0626 / 1255 / 1848	0.1 / 4.2 / 0.0 / 4.3
8 SA	0037 / 0638 / 1255 / 1855	0.7 / 3.8 / 0.6 / 3.9	23 SU	0117 / 0707 / 1336 / 1928	0.1 / 4.2 / 0.1 / 4.2
9 SU	0108 / 0707 / 1326 / 1925	0.7 / 3.8 / 0.7 / 3.9	24 M	0158 / 0748 / 1416 / 2007	0.3 / 4.1 / 0.3 / 4.0
10 M	0142 / 0738 / 1401 / 1957	0.8 / 3.8 / 0.7 / 3.9	25 TU	0238 / 0827 / 1457 / 2045	0.4 / 3.9 / 0.5 / 3.8
11 TU	0218 / 0812 / 1438 / 2034	0.8 / 3.8 / 0.8 / 3.8	26 W	0319 / 0906 / 1537 / 2125	0.7 / 3.7 / 0.8 / 3.6
12 W	0256 / 0851 / 1519 / 2114	0.9 / 3.7 / 0.9 / 3.8	27 TH	0402 / 0949 / 1622 / 2209	0.9 / 3.5 / 1.0 / 3.3
13 TH	0338 / 0935 / 1606 / 2203	1.0 / 3.6 / 1.1 / 3.6	28 F	0452 / 1039 / 1717 / 2304	1.2 / 3.3 / 1.3 / 3.1
14 F	0429 / 1030 / 1705 / 2304	1.2 / 3.5 / 1.2 / 3.4	29 SA	0557 / 1151 / 1827	1.4 / 3.1 / 1.4
15 SA	0537 / 1139 / 1822	1.3 / 3.4 / 1.3	30 SU	0030 / 0715 / 1326 / 1950	3.0 / 1.4 / 3.1 / 1.4
			31 M	0202 / 0837 / 1439 / 2109	3.1 / 1.3 / 3.2 / 1.3

Chart Datum: 0·13 metres above Ordnance Datum (Dublin)
HAT is 4·5m above Chart Datum

IRELAND – COBH

LAT 51°51′N   LONG 8°18′W

TIMES AND HEIGHTS OF HIGH AND LOW WATERS

Dates in amber are **SPRINGS**
Dates in yellow are **NEAPS**

2009

SEPTEMBER

Day	Time m	Time m	Time m	Time m	Day	Time m	Time m	Time m	Time m
1 TU	0306 3.3	0941 1.1	1533 3.5	2204 1.0	16 W	0251 3.6	0924 0.7	1526 3.8	2157 0.6
2 W	0355 3.5	1028 0.8	1617 3.7	2243 0.8	17 TH	0350 3.9	1020 0.4	1618 4.1	2247 0.3
3 TH	0435 3.7	1103 0.7	1655 3.9	2314 0.9	18 F ●	0438 4.1	1108 0.2	1703 4.3	2331 0.2
4 F ○	0511 3.8	1132 0.6	1728 4.0	2340 0.6	19 SA	0522 4.2	1151 0.1	1744 4.3	
5 SA	0542 3.9	1157 0.6	1758 4.0		20 SU	0012 0.1	0602 4.3	1231 0.1	1822 4.3
6 SU	0008 0.6	0610 3.9	1225 0.6	1825 4.0	21 M	0051 0.2	0641 4.2	1309 0.2	1859 4.2
7 M	0040 0.6	0638 3.9	1257 0.6	1854 4.0	22 TU	0129 0.4	0717 4.1	1346 0.4	1934 4.0
8 TU	0113 0.7	0709 3.9	1332 0.7	1927 4.0	23 W	0206 0.6	0754 3.9	1423 0.6	2009 3.8
9 W	0149 0.7	0742 3.9	1410 0.8	2003 3.9	24 TH	0244 0.8	0831 3.7	1502 0.9	2046 3.6
10 TH	0227 0.9	0821 3.8	1452 0.9	2046 3.8	25 F	0325 1.0	0912 3.5	1545 1.2	2128 3.3
11 F	0311 1.0	0908 3.7	1542 1.1	2136 3.6	26 SA ◐	0414 1.3	1001 3.2	1639 1.4	2219 3.1
12 SA ◑	0406 1.2	1006 3.5	1645 1.3	2241 3.3	27 SU	0518 1.4	1108 3.0	1749 1.5	2337 2.9
13 SU	0518 1.3	1120 3.3	1805 1.3		28 M	0639 1.5	1252 3.0	1911 1.5	
14 M	0003 3.2	0646 1.3	1253 3.3	1935 1.2	29 TU	0127 3.0	0759 1.4	1409 3.2	2027 1.3
15 TU	0135 3.3	0813 1.1	1421 3.5	2055 0.9	30 W	0235 3.2	0902 1.1	1502 3.5	2123 1.1

OCTOBER

Day	Time m	Time m	Time m	Time m	Day	Time m	Time m	Time m	Time m
1 TH	0323 3.5	0949 0.9	1545 3.7	2204 0.9	16 F	0329 3.9	1000 0.5	1556 4.1	2225 0.4
2 F	0402 3.7	1026 0.7	1622 3.9	2237 0.7	17 SA	0417 4.1	1047 0.3	1641 4.2	2308 0.3
3 SA	0438 3.9	1057 0.6	1655 4.0	2309 0.6	18 SU ●	0500 4.2	1129 0.3	1721 4.2	2348 0.3
4 SU	0510 3.9	1126 0.6	1725 4.0	2340 0.6	19 M	0540 4.2	1208 0.3	1758 4.2	
5 M	0540 4.0	1158 0.6	1756 4.1		20 TU	0026 0.4	0616 4.2	1245 0.5	1832 4.1
6 TU	0013 0.6	0611 4.0	1233 0.6	1828 4.1	21 W	0102 0.5	0652 4.0	1320 0.6	1906 3.9
7 W	0050 0.6	0645 4.0	1311 0.6	1904 4.0	22 TH	0138 0.7	0727 3.9	1355 0.8	1939 3.8
8 TH	0128 0.7	0723 4.0	1352 0.7	1945 3.9	23 F	0214 0.9	0804 3.7	1432 1.0	2015 3.6
9 F	0211 0.8	0806 3.8	1439 0.9	2031 3.7	24 SA	0253 1.1	0844 3.5	1513 1.2	2056 3.4
10 SA	0300 1.0	0857 3.7	1533 1.1	2125 3.5	25 SU	0339 1.3	0931 3.3	1605 1.4	2145 3.2
11 SU ◑	0359 1.1	0959 3.5	1638 1.2	2233 3.3	26 M	0440 1.4	1030 3.2	1709 1.6	2249 3.1
12 M	0512 1.2	1115 3.4	1757 1.3	2355 3.3	27 TU	0554 1.5	1151 3.1	1824 1.5	
13 TU	0637 1.2	1246 3.4	1925 1.2		28 W	0018 3.1	0707 1.4	1315 3.2	1933 1.4
14 W	0122 3.4	0759 1.0	1407 3.6	2039 0.9	29 TH	0140 3.2	0809 1.2	1414 3.5	2030 1.2
15 TH	0233 3.7	0906 0.7	1507 3.9	2136 0.6	30 F	0235 3.5	0859 1.0	1500 3.7	2117 1.0
					31 SA	0319 3.7	0942 0.9	1540 3.8	2159 0.8

NOVEMBER

Day	Time m	Time m	Time m	Time m	Day	Time m	Time m	Time m	Time m
1 SU	0358 3.9	1021 0.7	1618 4.0	2238 0.7	16 M ●	0438 4.1	1109 0.6	1659 4.1	2327 0.6
2 M ○	0436 4.0	1059 0.6	1654 4.1	2316 0.6	17 TU	0519 4.1	1148 0.5	1737 4.0	
3 TU	0514 4.1	1138 0.6	1732 4.1	2355 0.6	18 W	0005 0.6	0557 4.1	1225 0.7	1811 4.0
4 W	0552 4.1	1217 0.6	1811 4.1		19 TH	0041 0.7	0633 4.0	1258 0.8	1844 3.9
5 TH	0035 0.6	0631 4.1	1300 0.6	1852 4.0	20 F	0115 0.8	0708 3.9	1332 1.0	1917 3.8
6 F	0118 0.7	0715 4.0	1346 0.7	1937 3.9	21 SA	0150 0.9	0744 3.8	1407 1.1	1953 3.7
7 SA	0205 0.7	0803 3.9	1436 0.8	2027 3.8	22 SU	0226 1.1	0823 3.6	1447 1.2	2032 3.6
8 SU	0258 0.9	0857 3.8	1531 1.0	2123 3.6	23 M	0308 1.2	0907 3.6	1533 1.4	2118 3.4
9 M	0357 1.0	0958 3.6	1634 1.1	2227 3.5	24 TU ◐	0400 1.3	0957 3.4	1628 1.5	2211 3.3
10 TU	0505 1.1	1109 3.5	1747 1.2	2340 3.4	25 W	0500 1.4	1054 3.4	1730 1.5	2314 3.3
11 W	0621 1.1	1226 3.5	1905 1.1		26 TH	0607 1.4	1159 3.4	1836 1.5	
12 TH	0056 3.5	0737 1.0	1338 3.7	2013 0.9	27 F	0023 3.3	0710 1.4	1305 3.5	1936 1.3
13 F	0205 3.7	0841 0.8	1438 3.8	2110 0.8	28 SA	0130 3.5	0807 1.2	1402 3.6	2031 1.2
14 SA	0302 3.8	0936 0.7	1530 4.0	2201 0.7	29 SU	0226 3.6	0900 1.0	1453 3.8	2122 1.0
15 SU	0352 4.0	1025 0.6	1617 4.0	2246 0.6	30 M	0318 3.8	0950 0.9	1542 3.9	2211 0.8

DECEMBER

Day	Time m	Time m	Time m	Time m	Day	Time m	Time m	Time m	Time m
1 TU	0406 4.0	1038 0.8	1628 4.0	2258 0.7	16 W ●	0503 4.0	1133 0.8	1721 3.9	2349 0.8
2 W ○	0453 4.1	1124 0.8	1714 4.1	2343 0.6	17 TH	0543 4.0	1209 0.9	1757 3.9	
3 TH	0539 4.2	1210 0.8	1800 4.1		18 F	0024 0.8	0619 4.0	1242 0.9	1830 3.9
4 F	0028 0.5	0625 4.2	1256 0.6	1845 4.1	19 SA	0057 0.8	0654 3.9	1313 0.9	1902 3.9
5 SA	0114 0.5	0712 4.2	1343 0.6	1933 4.0	20 SU	0129 0.9	0728 3.9	1346 1.0	1936 3.8
6 SU	0202 0.6	0802 4.1	1433 0.7	2023 3.9	21 M	0203 1.0	0804 3.9	1423 1.1	2012 3.7
7 M	0253 0.7	0854 4.0	1525 0.8	2116 3.8	22 TU	0240 1.1	0842 3.8	1503 1.2	2051 3.7
8 TU	0348 0.8	0949 3.8	1621 0.9	2212 3.7	23 W	0322 1.2	0923 3.7	1547 1.3	2136 3.6
9 W ◐	0447 0.9	1048 3.7	1723 1.0	2313 3.6	24 TH	0410 1.3	1009 3.6	1637 1.4	2226 3.5
10 TH	0552 1.0	1152 3.6	1831 1.1		25 F	0505 1.4	1100 3.6	1735 1.4	2323 3.5
11 F	0019 3.5	0701 1.0	1259 3.6	1937 1.1	26 SA	0608 1.4	1200 3.5	1840 1.4	
12 SA	0126 3.6	0808 1.0	1403 3.6	2039 1.0	27 SU	0028 3.5	0715 1.4	1304 3.5	1946 1.3
13 SU	0229 3.7	0909 1.0	1501 3.7	2135 0.9	28 M	0136 3.5	0820 1.3	1409 3.6	2049 1.2
14 M	0326 3.8	1004 0.9	1553 3.8	2226 0.9	29 TU	0241 3.7	0923 1.1	1511 3.9	2148 1.0
15 TU	0417 3.9	1052 0.9	1640 3.9	2310 0.8	30 W	0342 3.9	1021 0.9	1609 3.9	2243 0.8
					31 TH ○	0438 4.0	1114 0.6	1702 4.0	2332 0.6

Chart Datum: 0·13 metres above Ordnance Datum (Dublin)
HAT is 4·5m above Chart Datum

TIDES

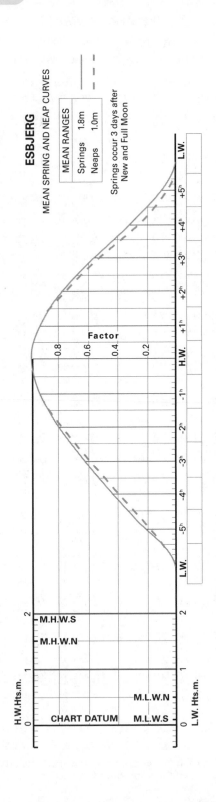

ESBJERG

MEAN SPRING AND NEAP CURVES

MEAN RANGES	
Springs	1.8m
Neaps	1.0m

Springs occur 3 days after
New and Full Moon

TIME ZONE -0100
(Danish Standard Time)
Subtract 1 hour for UT
For Danish Summer Time add
ONE hour in **non-shaded areas**

DENMARK – ESBJERG

LAT 55°28'N   LONG 8°26'E

TIMES AND HEIGHTS OF HIGH AND LOW WATERS

Dates in amber are **SPRINGS**
Dates in yellow are **NEAPS**

2009

JANUARY

Day	Time	m	Day	Time	m
1 TH	0516	1.8	**16** F	0618	1.8
	1133	0.1		1223	0.0
	1742	1.5		1850	1.5
	2338	0.1			
2 F	0549	1.8	**17** SA	0030	0.0
	1211	0.1		0704	1.8
	1819	1.5		1309	0.0
				1935	1.5
3 SA	0019	0.1	**18** SU	0117	0.1
	0628	1.8		0754	1.7
	1254	0.1		1357	0.1
	1901	1.5		◑ 2024	1.4
4 SU	0104	0.1	**19** M	0209	0.1
	0714	1.8		0848	1.7
	1340	0.1		1451	0.2
	◑ 1951	1.5		2120	1.4
5 M	0154	0.1	**20** TU	0308	0.2
	0807	1.8		0951	1.6
	1433	0.1		1554	0.3
	2046	1.5		2223	1.5
6 TU	0250	0.2	**21** W	0420	0.2
	0909	1.7		1057	1.5
	1531	0.2		1704	0.3
	2151	1.5		2328	1.5
7 W	0354	0.2	**22** TH	0538	0.2
	1021	1.6		1202	1.5
	1637	0.2		1811	0.3
	2306	1.5			
8 TH	0506	0.2	**23** F	0029	1.5
	1142	1.6		0645	0.2
	1747	0.3		1301	1.5
				1906	0.3
9 F	0020	1.5	**24** SA	0124	1.6
	0620	0.2		0739	0.1
	1258	1.6		1354	1.5
	1854	0.2		1952	0.2
10 SA	0127	1.6	**25** SU	0213	1.6
	0727	0.1		0825	0.1
	1405	1.6		1440	1.5
	1951	0.2		2032	0.2
11 SU	0224	1.7	**26** M	0256	1.7
	0825	0.0		0903	0.1
	1503	1.6		● 1521	1.5
	○ 2043	0.1		2106	0.1
12 M	0317	1.7	**27** TU	0332	1.7
	0918	-0.1		0936	0.1
	1555	1.6		1555	1.5
	2131	0.1		2138	0.1
13 TU	0405	1.8	**28** W	0403	1.7
	1006	-0.1		1006	0.0
	1642	1.6		1626	1.5
	2216	0.0		2209	0.0
14 W	0451	1.8	**29** TH	0432	1.7
	1052	-0.1		1037	0.0
	1725	1.5		1655	1.5
	2300	0.0		2242	0.0
15 TH	0534	1.9	**30** F	0500	1.7
	1138	-0.1		1111	-0.1
	1808	1.5		1724	1.5
	2345	0.0		2318	-0.1
			31 SA	0533	1.7
				1148	-0.1
				1757	1.5
				2357	-0.1

FEBRUARY

Day	Time	m	Day	Time	m
1 SU	0609	1.7	**16** M	0044	-0.1
	1227	-0.1		0714	1.6
	1834	1.5		1313	0.1
				◑ 1932	1.4
2 M	0040	-0.1	**17** TU	0130	0.0
	0651	1.7		0801	1.5
	1312	0.0		1358	0.2
	1918	1.5		2021	1.4
3 TU	0127	0.0	**18** W	0222	0.1
	0742	1.6		0859	1.4
	1400	0.0		1452	0.3
	◑ 2009	1.4		2124	1.4
4 W	0221	0.0	**19** TH	0330	0.2
	0841	1.6		1009	1.3
	1457	0.2		1605	0.3
	2111	1.4		2237	1.4
5 TH	0325	0.1	**20** F	0503	0.2
	0957	1.4		1122	1.3
	1604	0.2		1732	0.3
	2232	1.4		2348	1.4
6 F	0444	0.2	**21** SA	0619	0.2
	1129	1.4		1227	1.3
	1724	0.3		1835	0.2
	2359	1.4			
7 SA	0608	0.1	**22** SU	0049	1.5
	1249	1.4		0714	0.1
	1838	0.2		1323	1.4
				1924	0.1
8 SU	0111	1.5	**23** M	0142	1.5
	0718	0.0		0758	0.0
	1356	1.4		1412	1.4
	1937	0.1		2004	0.1
9 M	0211	1.6	**24** TU	0227	1.6
	0815	-0.1		0836	0.0
	1451	1.5		1454	1.4
	○ 2028	0.0		2039	0.0
10 TU	0303	1.7	**25** W	0306	1.6
	0904	-0.2		0909	-0.1
	1539	1.5		● 1530	1.5
	2115	-0.1		2112	-0.1
11 W	0350	1.8	**26** TH	0339	1.6
	0949	-0.2		0939	-0.1
	1603	1.5		1603	1.5
	2157	-0.1		2145	-0.1
12 TH	0433	1.8	**27** F	0411	1.6
	1032	-0.2		1012	-0.2
	1700	1.5		1633	1.5
	2239	-0.2		2220	-0.2
13 F	0513	1.8	**28** SA	0442	1.7
	1112	-0.2		1046	-0.2
	1737	1.5		1703	1.5
	2320	-0.2		2257	-0.2
14 SA	0552	1.7			
	1152	-0.1			
	1813	1.5			
15 SU	0001	-0.2			
	0632	1.7			
	1232	0.0			
	1851	1.4			

MARCH

Day	Time	m	Day	Time	m
1 SU	0515	1.7	**16** M	0559	1.5
	1123	-0.2		1156	-0.1
	1735	1.5		1809	1.4
	2336	-0.2			
2 M	0551	1.6	**17** TU	0012	-0.2
	1202	-0.2		0635	1.4
	1810	1.4		1232	0.0
				1845	1.4
3 TU	0018	-0.2	**18** W	0054	-0.1
	0634	1.6		0716	1.3
	1245	-0.1		1311	0.1
	1851	1.4		◑ 1927	1.4
4 W	0106	-0.2	**19** TH	0141	0.0
	0724	1.5		0806	1.2
	1334	0.0		1357	0.2
	◑ 1942	1.4		2022	1.3
5 TH	0200	0.0	**20** F	0239	0.2
	0827	1.4		0913	1.2
	1430	0.1		1457	0.3
	2045	1.3		2135	1.3
6 F	0308	0.1	**21** SA	0409	0.2
	0952	1.3		1034	1.1
	1542	0.2		1628	0.3
	2215	1.3		2257	1.3
7 SA	0435	0.1	**22** SU	0538	0.1
	1125	1.2		1145	1.2
	1708	0.3		1749	0.2
	2345	1.4			
8 SU	0600	0.0	**23** M	0005	1.4
	1241	1.3		0635	0.0
	1822	0.1		1245	1.3
				1844	0.1
9 M	0056	1.5	**24** TU	0101	1.4
	0706	-0.1		0720	-0.1
	1342	1.4		1336	1.3
	1920	0.0		1927	0.0
10 TU	0154	1.6	**25** W	0150	1.5
	0758	-0.2		0758	-0.1
	1433	1.4		1421	1.4
	2009	-0.1		2006	-0.1
11 W	0245	1.7	**26** TH	0232	1.5
	0845	-0.3		0834	-0.2
	1518	1.5		● 1500	1.4
	○ 2054	-0.2		2043	-0.2
12 TH	0330	1.7	**27** F	0311	1.6
	0927	-0.3		0909	-0.3
	1557	1.5		1536	1.4
	2136	-0.3		2119	-0.2
13 F	0411	1.7	**28** SA	0347	1.6
	1006	-0.3		0944	-0.3
	1633	1.5		1609	1.4
	2216	-0.3		2157	-0.3
14 SA	0449	1.7	**29** SU	0422	1.6
	1044	-0.2		1021	-0.3
	1706	1.4		1642	1.4
	2255	-0.3		2236	-0.3
15 SU	0524	1.6	**30** M	0459	1.5
	1120	-0.2		1059	-0.2
	1737	1.4		1715	1.4
	2333	-0.2		2317	-0.3
			31 TU	0539	1.5
				1140	-0.2
				1751	1.4

APRIL

Day	Time	m	Day	Time	m
1 W	0001	-0.3	**16** TH	0024	-0.1
	0624	1.4		0637	1.2
	1224	-0.1		1233	0.0
	1835	1.4		1845	1.4
2 TH	0051	-0.2	**17** F	0107	0.0
	0718	1.3		0723	1.1
	1314	0.0		1316	0.1
	● 1927	1.3		◑ 1935	1.3
3 F	0149	-0.1	**18** SA	0200	0.1
	0827	1.2		0821	1.0
	1413	0.1		1409	0.2
	2038	1.3		2036	1.3
4 SA	0301	0.0	**19** SU	0307	0.1
	0954	1.1		0936	1.0
	1528	0.2		1520	0.2
	2207	1.3		2152	1.3
5 SU	0429	0.0	**20** M	0430	0.1
	1116	1.2		1054	1.1
	1651	0.2		1642	0.2
	2329	1.4		2309	1.3
6 M	0545	-0.1	**21** TU	0539	0.0
	1224	1.2		1159	1.2
	1801	0.0		1749	0.1
7 TU	0036	1.5	**22** W	0012	1.4
	0645	-0.2		0631	-0.1
	1320	1.3		1254	1.3
	1857	-0.1		1842	0.0
8 W	0133	1.6	**23** TH	0107	1.4
	0736	-0.3		0716	-0.2
	1409	1.4		1343	1.3
	1947	-0.2		1929	-0.1
9 TH	0223	1.6	**24** F	0156	1.5
	0821	-0.3		0758	-0.2
	1452	1.4		1427	1.4
	○ 2032	-0.3		2012	-0.2
10 F	0308	1.6	**25** SA	0241	1.5
	0902	-0.3		0838	-0.3
	1530	1.4		● 1507	1.4
	2114	-0.3		2053	-0.3
11 SA	0348	1.6	**26** SU	0324	1.5
	0940	-0.3		0917	-0.3
	1605	1.4		1545	1.4
	2154	-0.3		2135	-0.3
12 SU	0424	1.5	**27** M	0405	1.5
	1016	-0.2		0957	-0.3
	1636	1.4		1623	1.4
	2231	-0.3		2218	-0.3
13 M	0458	1.4	**28** TU	0448	1.4
	1049	-0.1		1039	-0.2
	1706	1.4		1700	1.4
	2309	-0.2		2303	-0.3
14 TU	0529	1.3	**29** W	0532	1.4
	1122	-0.1		1122	-0.2
	1734	1.4		1742	1.4
	2345	-0.2		2351	-0.3
15 W	0600	1.3	**30** TH	0621	1.3
	1156	0.0		1209	-0.1
	1806	1.4		1828	1.4

Chart Datum: 0·69 metres below Dansk Normal Null
HAT is 2·2 metres above Chart Datum

TIDES

TIDES

TIME ZONE -0100
(Danish Standard Time)
Subtract 1 hour for UT
For Danish Summer Time add
ONE hour in **non-shaded areas**

DENMARK – ESBJERG

LAT 55°28′N   LONG 8°26′E

TIMES AND HEIGHTS OF HIGH AND LOW WATERS

Dates in amber are **SPRINGS**
Dates in yellow are **NEAPS**

2009

MAY

Day	Time m	Day	Time m
1	0043 -0.2, 0720 1.2, F 1300 0.0, 1925 1.4	16	0041 0.0, 0650 1.1, SA 1246 0.0, 1900 1.4
2	0143 -0.2, 0828 1.1, SA 1400 0.1, 2036 1.4	17	0127 0.0, 0741 1.1, SU 1336 0.1, 1954 1.4
3	0254 -0.1, 0944 1.1, SU 1511 0.1, 2154 1.4	18	0223 0.0, 0843 1.1, M 1434 0.1, 2056 1.4
4	0412 -0.1, 1054 1.2, M 1626 0.1, 2306 1.4	19	0326 0.0, 0954 1.1, TU 1541 0.1, 2206 1.4
5	0521 -0.2, 1157 1.2, TU 1733 0.0	20	0433 0.0, 1103 1.2, W 1650 0.1, 2317 1.4
6	0011 1.5, 0618 -0.2, W 1251 1.3, 1831 -0.2	21	0536 -0.1, 1206 1.3, TH 1754 0.0
7	0108 1.5, 0709 -0.3, TH 1341 1.4, 1923 -0.2	22	0021 1.4, 0632 -0.1, F 1303 1.4, 1850 -0.1
8	0159 1.6, 0755 -0.3, F 1425 1.4, 2010 -0.3	23	0120 1.4, 0721 -0.2, SA 1354 1.4, 1942 -0.2
9	0245 1.5, 0837 -0.3, SA 1505 1.4, 2054 -0.3	24	0213 1.5, 0809 -0.2, SU 1441 1.5, 2030 -0.2
10	0327 1.5, 0915 -0.2, SU 1541 1.4, 2135 -0.3	25	0303 1.4, 0854 -0.2, M 1525 1.4, 2118 -0.3
11	0403 1.4, 0951 -0.2, M 1614 1.4, 2213 -0.1	26	0352 1.4, 0938 -0.2, TU 1608 1.5, 2205 -0.3
12	0436 1.3, 1024 -0.1, TU 1642 1.4, 2249 -0.2	27	0440 1.4, 1023 -0.2, W 1651 1.5, 2253 -0.3
13	0506 1.2, 1055 0.0, W 1710 1.4, 2324 -0.1	28	0529 1.3, 1109 -0.1, TH 1736 1.5, 2343 -0.3
14	0535 1.2, 1128 0.0, TH 1739 1.4	29	0620 1.3, 1157 -0.1, F 1825 1.5
15	0000 -0.1, 0608 1.2, F 1204 0.0, 1815 1.4	30	0036 -0.2, 0715 1.2, SA 1248 0.0, 1921 1.5
		31	0133 -0.2, 0814 1.2, SU 1344 0.0, 2022 1.5

JUNE

Day	Time m	Day	Time m
1	0235 -0.2, 0918 1.2, M 1446 0.0, 2130 1.5	16	0147 -0.1, 0800 1.3, TU 1359 0.0, 2013 1.5
2	0342 -0.1, 1021 1.2, TU 1554 0.0, 2237 1.5	17	0239 0.0, 0858 1.2, W 1456 0.0, 2115 1.5
3	0448 -0.1, 1121 1.3, W 1701 0.0, 2341 1.5	18	0339 0.0, 1005 1.3, TH 1559 0.0, 2224 1.4
4	0548 -0.1, 1218 1.3, TH 1804 -0.1	19	0443 0.0, 1115 1.3, F 1707 0.0, 2339 1.4
5	0040 1.5, 0642 -0.2, F 1310 1.4, 1900 0.0	20	0548 0.0, 1221 1.3, SA 1815 0.0
6	0134 1.5, 0731 -0.2, SA 1358 1.4, 1952 -0.2	21	0048 1.4, 0649 0.0, SU 1322 1.4, 1917 -0.1
7	0224 1.5, 0815 -0.1, SU 1442 1.5, 2039 -0.2	22	0151 1.4, 0745 -0.1, M 1418 1.4, 2013 -0.2
8	0308 1.4, 0856 -0.1, M 1522 1.5, 2121 -0.2	23	0249 1.4, 0835 -0.1, TU 1509 1.5, 2106 -0.2
9	0346 1.3, 0932 -0.1, TU 1557 1.5, 2200 -0.1	24	0342 1.4, 0923 -0.1, W 1556 1.6, 2155 -0.3
10	0420 1.3, 1004 0.0, W 1627 1.5, 2234 -0.1	25	0433 1.4, 1009 -0.1, TH 1642 1.6, 2244 -0.3
11	0449 1.2, 1036 0.0, TH 1654 1.5, 2307 -0.1	26	0521 1.4, 1055 -0.1, F 1728 1.6, 2332 -0.3
12	0517 1.2, 1107 0.0, F 1721 1.5, 2340 -0.1	27	0607 1.3, 1142 -0.1, SA 1815 1.6
13	0547 1.2, 1143 0.0, SA 1754 1.5	28	0021 -0.2, 0655 1.3, SU 1230 -0.1, 1905 1.6
14	0018 -0.1, 0624 1.2, SU 1223 0.0, 1833 1.5	29	0112 -0.2, 0745 1.3, M 1321 -0.1, 1959 1.6
15	0100 -0.1, 0708 1.2, M 1308 0.0, 1920 1.5	30	0205 -0.1, 0840 1.3, TU 1415 0.0, 2058 1.6

JULY

Day	Time m	Day	Time m
1	0303 0.0, 0939 1.3, W 1517 0.0, 2202 1.5	16	0203 0.0, 0813 1.4, TH 1420 0.0, 2036 1.6
2	0407 0.0, 1040 1.3, TH 1626 0.0, 2308 1.5	17	0257 0.0, 0913 1.4, F 1519 0.1, 2143 1.5
3	0513 0.0, 1141 1.4, F 1736 0.0	18	0400 0.1, 1025 1.3, SA 1630 0.1, 2304 1.4
4	0011 1.5, 0614 0.0, SA 1239 1.4, 1841 0.0	19	0511 0.2, 1145 1.4, SU 1748 0.1
5	0109 1.5, 0709 0.0, SU 1333 1.5, 1937 -0.1	20	0027 1.4, 0623 0.1, M 1257 1.4, 1900 0.0
6	0202 1.4, 0757 0.0, M 1421 1.5, 2027 -0.1	21	0137 1.4, 0726 0.1, TU 1359 1.5, 2001 -0.1
7	0248 1.4, 0839 0.0, TU 1504 1.6, 2109 -0.1	22	0238 1.5, 0820 0.0, W 1454 1.6, 2054 -0.2
8	0329 1.4, 0915 0.0, W 1541 1.6, 2146 0.0	23	0331 1.5, 0909 0.0, TH 1543 1.7, 2143 -0.2
9	0404 1.3, 0948 0.0, TH 1612 1.6, 2218 0.0	24	0419 1.5, 0954 -0.1, F 1629 1.8, 2229 -0.3
10	0433 1.3, 1018 0.0, F 1639 1.6, 2248 0.0	25	0503 1.5, 1038 -0.1, SA 1712 1.8, 2313 -0.2
11	0500 1.3, 1049 0.0, SA 1706 1.6, 2319 0.0	26	0545 1.5, 1122 -0.2, SU 1756 1.8, 2357 -0.2
12	0528 1.3, 1123 0.0, SU 1734 1.6, 2353 -0.1	27	0626 1.5, 1206 -0.1, M 1841 1.8
13	0600 1.4, 1200 -0.1, M 1809 1.6	28	0042 -0.1, 0709 1.4, TU 1253 -0.1, 1929 1.7
14	0031 -0.1, 0638 1.4, TU 1242 -0.1, 1851 1.6	29	0130 0.0, 0756 1.4, W 1342 0.0, 2021 1.6
15	0115 -0.1, 0722 1.4, W 1328 0.0, 1939 1.6	30	0221 0.1, 0850 1.4, TH 1439 0.1, 2123 1.5
		31	0320 0.3, 0953 1.4, F 1548 0.2, 2231 1.5

AUGUST

Day	Time m	Day	Time m
1	0432 0.3, 1100 1.5, SA 1709 0.2, 2339 1.4	16	0325 0.6, 0946 1.4, SU 1603 0.2, 2246 1.4
2	0545 0.3, 1205 1.5, SU 1823 0.1	17	0442 0.3, 1118 1.5, M 1731 0.2
3	0042 1.4, 0645 0.2, M 1304 1.5, 1921 0.1	18	0015 1.4, 0603 0.3, TU 1237 1.5, 1848 0.1
4	0137 1.4, 0736 0.2, TU 1357 1.6, 2009 0.1	19	0125 1.5, 0709 0.2, W 1342 1.7, 1948 0.0
5	0226 1.5, 0818 0.1, W 1442 1.6, 2051 0.0	20	0224 1.6, 0803 0.1, TH 1436 1.8, 2039 -0.1
6	0307 1.5, 0854 0.1, TH 1520 1.7, 2125 0.0	21	0314 1.6, 0850 0.0, F 1525 1.9, 2124 -0.1
7	0343 1.5, 0927 0.1, F 1553 1.7, 2155 0.0	22	0358 1.6, 0934 -0.1, SA 1610 1.9, 2208 -0.2
8	0414 1.5, 0957 0.0, SA 1621 1.7, 2224 0.0	23	0438 1.6, 1017 -0.1, SU 1651 1.9, 2249 -0.2
9	0441 1.5, 1027 0.0, SU 1647 1.7, 2254 0.0	24	0515 1.6, 1059 -0.2, M 1732 1.9, 2330 -0.1
10	0508 1.5, 1100 0.0, M 1715 1.7, 2327 0.0	25	0553 1.6, 1141 -0.1, TU 1812 1.8
11	0536 1.5, 1137 -0.1, TU 1748 1.7	26	0010 0.0, 0630 1.6, W 1224 0.0, 1855 1.7
12	0004 0.0, 0610 1.5, W 1217 -0.1, 1827 1.7	27	0052 0.1, 0712 1.6, TH 1309 0.1, 1942 1.6
13	0045 0.0, 0650 1.5, TH 1301 0.0, 1913 1.7	28	0137 0.3, 0759 1.5, F 1401 0.2, 2039 1.5
14	0131 0.1, 0737 1.5, F 1351 0.2, 2008 1.6	29	0229 0.4, 0900 1.5, SA 1507 0.3, 2148 1.4
15	0223 0.2, 0833 1.5, SA 1451 0.1, 2116 1.5	30	0339 0.6, 1013 1.5, SU 1639 0.3, 2303 1.4
		31	0507 0.5, 1127 1.5, M 1758 0.3

Chart Datum: 0·69 metres below Dansk Normal Null
HAT is 2·2 metres above Chart Datum

TIME ZONE -0100
(Danish Standard Time)
Subtract 1 hour for UT
For Danish Summer Time add
ONE hour in **non-shaded areas**

DENMARK – ESBJERG

LAT 55°28′N   LONG 8°26′E

TIMES AND HEIGHTS OF HIGH AND LOW WATERS

Dates in amber are **SPRINGS**
Dates in yellow are **NEAPS**

2009

SEPTEMBER

Day	Time m	Time m	Day	Time m	Time m
1 TU	0009 1.4 · 0615 0.4	1230 1.6 · 1856 0.2	**16** W	0003 1.5 · 0545 0.4	1219 1.7 · 1833 0.1
2 W	0106 1.5 · 0707 0.3	1324 1.7 · 1942 0.2	**17** TH	0109 1.6 · 0649 0.3	1322 1.8 · 1929 0.0
3 TH	0156 1.5 · 0750 0.2	1412 1.7 · 2022 0.1	**18** F	0203 1.6 · 0742 0.1	1416 1.9 · 2018 -0.1 ●
4 F	0239 1.6 · 0827 0.2	1451 1.8 · 2055 0.1	**19** SA	0251 1.7 · 0829 0.0	1504 2.0 · 2101 -0.1
5 SA	0316 1.6 · 0900 0.1	1526 1.8 · 2126 0.1	**20** SU	0333 1.7 · 0912 -0.1	1548 2.0 · 2143 -0.1
6 SU	0348 1.6 · 0931 0.1	1557 1.8 · 2155 0.0	**21** M	0411 1.7 · 0954 -0.1	1629 1.9 · 2222 0.0
7 M	0418 1.6 · 1003 0.0	1627 1.8 · 2227 0.0	**22** TU	0446 1.7 · 1035 -0.1	1707 1.8 · 2300 0.1
8 TU	0445 1.6 · 1038 0.0	1657 1.8 · 2301 0.0	**23** W	0520 1.7 · 1115 0.0	1744 1.8 · 2338 0.2
9 W	0515 1.7 · 1115 0.0	1730 1.8 · 2339 0.0	**24** TH	0554 1.7 · 1157 0.1	1822 1.7
10 TH	0547 1.7 · 1155 0.0	1809 1.8	**25** F	0015 0.3 · 0630 1.7	1239 0.2 · 1904 1.6
11 F	0020 0.1 · 0625 1.6	1240 0.0 · 1856 1.7	**26** SA	0056 0.4 · 0712 1.7	1327 0.3 · 1954 1.5 ◑
12 SA	0106 0.2 · 0711 1.6	1331 0.1 · 1952 1.6 ◐	**27** SU	0142 0.5 · 0806 1.6	1427 0.4 · 2059 1.4
13 SU	0158 0.3 · 0808 0.2	1433 0.2 · 2106 1.5	**28**	0241 0.5 · 0916 1.6	1552 0.5 · 2216 1.4
14 M	0303 0.4 · 0925 1.5	1551 0.3 · 2241 1.5	**29** TU	0407 0.6 · 1036 1.6	1718 0.4 · 2327 1.5
15 TU	0424 0.5 · 1100 1.6	1721 0.3	**30** W	0530 0.5 · 1145 1.6	1818 0.3

OCTOBER

Day	Time m	Time m	Day	Time m	Time m
1 TH	0027 1.5 · 0627 0.4	1243 1.7 · 1904 0.3	**16** F	0046 1.6 · 0624 0.3	1300 1.9 · 1905 0.1
2 F	0118 1.6 · 0712 0.3	1333 1.8 · 1944 0.2	**17** SA	0139 1.7 · 0718 0.1	1354 2.0 · 1953 0.0
3 SA	0203 1.7 · 0751 0.2	1416 1.8 · 2019 0.1	**18** SU	0225 1.8 · 0806 0.1	1442 2.0 · 2037 0.0 ●
4 SU	0244 1.7 · 0828 0.2	1455 1.8 · 2053 0.1	**19** M	0306 1.8 · 0851 0.0	1526 1.9 · 2118 0.1
5 M	0320 1.7 · 0903 0.1	1531 1.8 · 2126 0.1	**20** TU	0345 1.8 · 0933 0.0	1606 1.9 · 2157 0.1
6 TU	0352 1.7 · 0939 0.1	1606 1.8 · 2200 0.1	**21** W	0420 1.8 · 1014 0.0	1644 1.8 · 2233 0.2
7 W	0424 1.7 · 1016 0.0	1640 1.8 · 2237 0.1	**22** TH	0453 1.8 · 1054 0.1	1718 1.7 · 2309 0.3
8 TH	0456 1.7 · 1056 0.0	1718 1.8 · 2317 0.1	**23** F	0524 1.8 · 1133 0.2	1753 1.6 · 2344 0.3
9 F	0530 1.7 · 1139 0.1	1800 1.7	**24** SA	0557 1.8 · 1214 0.3	1830 1.6
10 SA	0000 0.2 · 0610 1.7	1226 0.1 · 1849 1.6	**25** SU	0021 0.4 · 0635 1.7	1258 0.3 · 1913 1.5
11 SU	0047 0.3 · 0658 1.7	1320 0.2 · 1951 1.6 ◐	**26** M	0104 0.5 · 0722 1.7	1349 0.4 · 2009 1.5
12 M	0142 0.4 · 0759 1.7	1424 0.3 · 2108 1.5	**27** TU	0155 0.5 · 0821 1.7	1454 0.5 · 2118 1.4
13 TU	0248 0.5 · 0919 1.7	1544 0.3 · 2233 1.5	**28** W	0301 0.6 · 0932 1.7	1611 0.5 · 2232 1.5
14 W	0406 0.5 · 1046 1.7	1705 0.2 · 2345 1.6	**29** TH	0419 0.5 · 1046 1.7	1719 0.4 · 2336 1.5
15 TH	0522 0.4 · 1158 1.8	1810 0.2	**30** F	0528 0.5 · 1151 1.7	1813 0.3
			31 SA	0033 1.6 · 0624 0.4	1247 1.8 · 1858 0.2

NOVEMBER

Day	Time m	Time m	Day	Time m	Time m
1 SU	0124 1.7 · 0711 0.3	1337 1.8 · 1940 0.2	**16** M	0158 1.8 · 0745 0.1	1421 1.9 · 2013 0.1 ●
2 M	0209 1.7 · 0754 0.2	1423 1.8 · 2019 0.2 ○	**17** TU	0242 1.8 · 0832 0.1	1506 1.8 · 2055 0.2
3 TU	0250 1.8 · 0836 0.2	1506 1.8 · 2058 0.1	**18** W	0323 1.8 · 0917 0.1	1548 1.8 · 2134 0.2
4 W	0328 1.8 · 0916 0.1	1547 1.8 · 2137 0.1	**19** TH	0400 1.8 · 0958 0.1	1625 1.7 · 2211 0.3
5 TH	0405 1.8 · 0958 0.1	1628 1.8 · 2218 0.2	**20** F	0433 1.8 · 1038 0.2	1658 1.6 · 2245 0.3
6 F	0442 1.8 · 1042 0.1	1712 1.7 · 2300 0.2	**21** SA	0503 1.8 · 1115 0.2	1730 1.5 · 2319 0.3
7 SA	0521 1.8 · 1128 0.1	1758 1.7 · 2345 0.3	**22** SU	0533 1.8 · 1153 0.3	1802 1.5 · 2354 0.4
8 SU	0605 1.8 · 1218 0.1	1851 1.6	**23** M	0607 1.8 · 1232 0.3	1839 1.5
9 M	0034 0.3 · 0656 1.8	1314 0.2 · 1951 1.5 ◑	**24** TU	0035 0.4 · 0648 1.8	1315 0.3 · 1926 1.5 ◑
10 TU	0130 0.4 · 0757 1.8	1417 0.2 · 2100 1.5	**25** W	0121 0.4 · 0737 1.7	1405 0.4 · 2022 1.5
11 W	0233 0.4 · 0909 1.8	1527 0.2 · 2212 1.5	**26** TH	0214 0.4 · 0835 1.7	1503 0.4 · 2127 1.5
12 TH	0343 0.4 · 1024 1.8	1639 0.2 · 2318 1.6	**27** F	0315 0.4 · 0940 1.7	1606 0.4 · 2236 1.5
13 F	0454 0.4 · 1133 1.8	1742 0.3	**28** SA	0422 0.4 · 1050 1.7	1709 0.3 · 2340 1.5
14 SA	0017 1.7 · 0557 0.3	1234 1.9 · 1838 0.1	**29** SU	0527 0.4 · 1157 1.7	1807 0.3
15 SU	0110 1.7 · 0654 0.2	1330 1.9 · 1928 0.1	**30** M	0039 1.6 · 0627 0.3	1257 1.7 · 1900 0.2

DECEMBER

Day	Time m	Time m	Day	Time m	Time m
1 TU	0132 1.7 · 0721 0.2	1353 1.8 · 1948 0.2	**16** W	0221 1.8 · 0819 0.1	1449 1.7 · 2037 0.2 ●
2 W	0221 1.7 · 0811 0.2	1444 1.8 · 2033 0.2 ○	**17** TH	0305 1.8 · 0906 0.1	1533 1.6 · 2118 0.2
3 TH	0306 1.8 · 0859 0.1	1533 1.7 · 2118 0.2	**18** F	0344 1.8 · 0947 0.2	1610 1.6 · 2154 0.2
4 F	0350 1.8 · 0945 0.1	1620 1.7 · 2202 0.2	**19** SA	0418 1.8 · 1025 0.2	1642 1.5 · 2227 0.3
5 SA	0432 1.8 · 1032 0.0	1707 1.7 · 2247 0.2	**20** SU	0448 1.8 · 1059 0.2	1711 1.5 · 2259 0.3
6 SU	0515 1.8 · 1120 0.0	1755 1.6 · 2333 0.2	**21** M	0515 1.8 · 1132 0.2	1739 1.5 · 2332 0.2
7 M	0601 1.9 · 1210 0.0	1845 1.6	**22** TU	0545 1.8 · 1206 0.2	1811 1.5
8 TU	0022 0.2 · 0651 1.9	1303 0.1 · 1939 1.5	**23** W	0009 0.2 · 0620 1.8	1244 0.2 · 1850 1.5
9 W	0114 0.2 · 0748 1.8	1400 0.1 · 2038 1.5 ◑	**24** TH	0051 0.2 · 0702 1.8	1326 0.2 · 1936 1.5 ◑
10 TH	0211 0.3 · 0851 1.8	1501 0.2 · 2141 1.5	**25** F	0136 0.2 · 0751 1.7	1414 0.2 · 2030 1.5
11 F	0314 0.3 · 0957 1.8	1606 0.2 · 2244 1.6	**26** SA	0229 0.3 · 0848 1.7	1509 0.2 · 2132 1.5
12 SA	0421 0.3 · 1105 1.8	1713 0.2 · 2344 1.6	**27** SU	0329 0.3 · 0953 1.7	1610 0.3 · 2242 1.5
13 SU	0529 0.2 · 1208 1.8	1811 0.2	**28** M	0436 0.3 · 1107 1.6	1717 0.3 · 2352 1.5
14 M	0041 1.7 · 0631 0.2	1307 1.8 · 1904 0.2	**29** TU	0546 0.3 · 1221 1.6	1822 0.3
15 TU	0133 1.7 · 0727 0.1	1401 1.7 · 1953 0.2	**30** W	0057 1.6 · 0653 0.2	1327 1.6 · 1921 0.2
			31 TH	0155 1.7 · 0751 0.1	1427 1.6 · 2013 0.2 ○

Chart Datum: 0·69 metres below Dansk Normal Null
HAT is 2·2 metres above Chart Datum

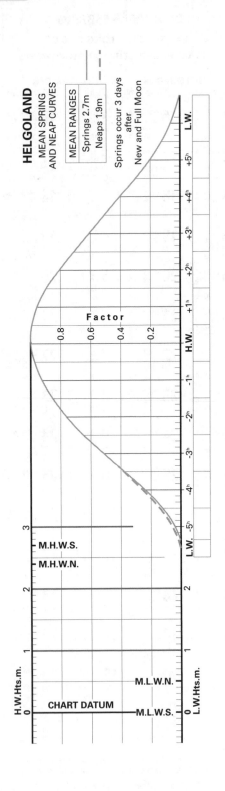

HELGOLAND

MEAN SPRING
AND NEAP CURVES

MEAN RANGES
Springs 2.7m
Neaps 1.9m

Springs occur 3 days
after
New and Full Moon

TIME ZONE -0100
(German Standard Time)
Subtract 1 hour for UT
For German Summer Time add
ONE hour in **non-shaded areas**

GERMANY – HELGOLAND
LAT 54°11'N   LONG 7°53'E
TIMES AND HEIGHTS OF HIGH AND LOW WATERS

Dates in amber are **SPRINGS**
Dates in yellow are **NEAPS**

2009

JANUARY

Day	Time	m	Time	m	Time	m	Time	m	Moon
1 TH	0221	3.2	0912	0.5	1446	2.9	2115	0.6	
2 F	0254	3.2	0945	0.6	1520	2.9	2150	0.7	
3 SA	0331	3.1	1020	0.6	1558	2.8	2227	0.7	
4 SU	0410	3.1	1057	0.6	1639	2.8	2308	0.8	◑
5 M	0455	3.0	1141	0.7	1729	2.8			
6 TU	0003	0.9	0553	3.0	1242	0.9	1834	2.8	
7 W	0114	0.9	0706	3.0	1356	1.0	1949	2.9	
8 TH	0235	0.9	0824	3.0	1513	1.0	2104	3.0	
9 F	0354	0.8	0941	3.1	1626	0.8	2213	3.1	
10 SA	0507	0.7	1050	3.1	1732	0.7	2314	3.2	
11 SU	0610	0.6	1150	3.1	1829	0.6			○
12 M	0008	3.3	0707	0.5	1242	3.1	1921	0.6	
13 TU	0059	3.4	0800	0.4	1333	3.1	2011	0.5	
14 W	0149	3.4	0851	0.4	1422	3.0	2058	0.4	
15 TH	0235	3.4	0935	0.3	1506	2.9	2138	0.4	
16 F	0315	3.3	1012	0.3	1545	2.9	2216	0.5	
17 SA	0354	3.3	1047	0.5	1624	2.9	2254	0.6	
18 SU	0435	3.2	1123	0.7	1706	2.8	2335	0.7	◑
19 M	0522	3.0	1205	0.8	1754	2.8			
20 TU	0027	0.9	0619	2.9	1302	1.0	1855	2.8	
21 W	0136	1.0	0730	2.9	1415	1.1	2008	2.9	
22 TH	0255	1.0	0847	2.9	1531	1.1	2119	3.0	
23 F	0409	1.0	0957	2.9	1636	1.0	2219	3.1	
24 SA	0509	0.9	1053	3.0	1727	0.9	2308	3.2	
25 SU	0558	0.8	1137	3.0	1811	0.8	2351	3.2	
26 M	0641	0.7	1217	3.0	1850	0.7			●
27 TU	0028	3.2	0719	0.6	1253	3.0	1927	0.6	
28 W	0102	3.3	0753	0.5	1326	3.0	2000	0.5	
29 TH	0133	3.3	0825	0.5	1357	3.0	2029	0.5	
30 F	0203	3.3	0854	0.4	1426	2.9	2058	0.4	
31 SA	0235	3.2	0925	0.4	1459	2.9	2132	0.5	

FEBRUARY

Day	Time	m	Time	m	Time	m	Time	m	Moon
1 SU	0311	3.2	0959	0.5	1533	2.9	2206	0.6	
2 M	0346	3.2	1030	0.6	1607	2.9	2238	0.7	
3 TU	0423	3.1	1103	0.7	1647	2.9	2323	0.8	
4 W	0514	3.0	1156	0.9	1747	2.8			
5 TH	0034	0.9	0629	2.9	1316	1.0	1910	2.9	
6 F	0206	0.9	0801	2.9	1449	0.9	2040	2.9	
7 SA	0340	0.8	0930	2.9	1614	0.8	2201	3.1	
8 SU	0500	0.6	1046	3.0	1725	0.7	2306	3.2	
9 M	0606	0.5	1145	3.1	1823	0.6			
10 TU	0000	3.3	0700	0.4	1234	3.1	1913	0.5	
11 W	0048	3.4	0748	0.3	1318	3.0	1958	0.4	
12 TH	0133	3.4	0832	0.3	1400	3.0	2040	0.4	
13 F	0215	3.4	0910	0.3	1439	3.0	2116	0.3	
14 SA	0252	3.3	0942	0.4	1513	3.0	2148	0.4	
15 SU	0326	3.3	1011	0.5	1546	3.0	2219	0.5	
16 M	0359	3.2	1039	0.7	1619	2.9	2251	0.7	◑
17 TU	0435	3.0	1111	0.8	1658	2.9	2333	0.8	
18 W	0522	2.8	1200	1.0	1753	2.8			
19 TH	0037	0.9	0632	2.7	1314	1.1	1910	2.8	
20 F	0204	1.0	0759	2.7	1443	1.1	2035	2.9	
21 SA	0334	0.9	0924	2.7	1604	1.0	2149	3.0	
22 SU	0445	0.8	1030	2.8	1705	0.8	2245	3.1	
23 M	0538	0.7	1117	2.9	1751	0.7	2328	3.2	
24 TU	0621	0.6	1155	3.0	1831	0.6			○
25 W	0006	3.2	0658	0.5	1229	3.0	1906	0.5	●
26 TH	0039	3.2	0731	0.4	1302	3.0	1938	0.4	
27 F	0110	3.3	0800	0.3	1332	3.0	2008	0.4	
28 SA	0141	3.3	0830	0.3	1402	3.0	2039	0.3	

MARCH

Day	Time	m	Time	m	Time	m	Time	m	Moon
1 SU	0214	3.2	0902	0.3	1434	3.0	2113	0.4	
2 M	0250	3.2	0935	0.4	1508	3.0	2148	0.4	
3 TU	0327	3.1	1007	0.5	1542	3.0	2221	0.5	
4 W	0406	3.0	1040	0.7	1622	2.9	2306	0.6	◑
5 TH	0457	2.9	1133	0.8	1723	2.9			
6 F	0018	0.8	0614	2.8	1258	1.0	1851	2.9	
7 SA	0157	0.8	0752	2.8	1438	0.9	2028	3.0	
8 SU	0336	0.7	0925	2.8	1608	0.8	2152	3.1	
9 M	0455	0.5	1038	2.9	1716	0.6	2256	3.2	
10 TU	0555	0.4	1132	3.0	1811	0.5	2346	3.3	
11 W	0643	0.3	1216	3.0	1857	0.4			○
12 TH	0030	3.3	0726	0.2	1255	3.0	1938	0.3	
13 F	0111	3.3	0804	0.3	1332	3.1	2015	0.3	
14 SA	0149	3.3	0838	0.3	1406	3.1	2048	0.3	
15 SU	0224	3.2	0908	0.4	1438	3.0	2119	0.3	
16 M	0256	3.1	0935	0.5	1508	3.0	2148	0.4	
17 TU	0327	3.0	1001	0.6	1539	3.0	2218	0.5	
18 W	0359	2.9	1030	0.8	1614	2.9	2254	0.7	◑
19 TH	0440	2.7	1111	0.9	1704	2.8	2350	0.8	
20 F	0543	2.6	1219	1.0	1816	2.7			
21 SA	0114	0.9	0709	2.5	1351	1.0	1946	2.7	
22 SU	0250	0.8	0840	2.6	1522	0.9	2109	2.8	
23 M	0410	0.6	0954	2.7	1631	0.7	2210	3.0	
24 TU	0506	0.5	1044	2.8	1720	0.6	2255	3.1	
25 W	0548	0.4	1122	2.9	1759	0.5	2333	3.2	
26 TH	0625	0.4	1157	3.0	1835	0.4			●
27 F	0008	3.2	0659	0.3	1231	3.0	1909	0.3	
28 SA	0041	3.2	0730	0.3	1303	3.0	1943	0.3	
29 SU	0115	3.2	0803	0.3	1336	3.1	2019	0.3	
30 M	0152	3.2	0838	0.3	1411	3.1	2057	0.3	
31 TU	0233	3.1	0914	0.4	1448	3.1	2136	0.4	

APRIL

Day	Time	m	Time	m	Time	m	Time	m	Moon
1 W	0315	3.0	0951	0.5	1528	3.1	2217	0.4	
2 TH	0401	2.9	1033	0.6	1615	3.0	2308	0.5	◑
3 F	0457	2.8	1130	0.8	1719	2.9			
4 SA	0021	0.6	0614	2.7	1254	0.9	1845	2.9	
5 SU	0156	0.7	0747	2.7	1431	0.9	2018	3.0	
6 M	0329	0.6	0914	2.8	1556	0.7	2137	3.1	
7 TU	0441	0.4	1020	2.9	1659	0.5	2235	3.2	
8 W	0532	0.3	1107	2.9	1748	0.4	2322	3.2	
9 TH	0615	0.3	1149	3.0	1833	0.4			○
10 F	0006	3.2	0655	0.3	1228	3.0	1914	0.3	
11 SA	0046	3.2	0732	0.3	1303	3.1	1949	0.3	
12 SU	0122	3.2	0805	0.4	1334	3.1	2021	0.3	
13 M	0155	3.1	0835	0.4	1405	3.1	2052	0.3	
14 TU	0227	3.0	0903	0.4	1437	3.0	2123	0.3	
15 W	0300	2.9	0931	0.5	1510	3.0	2155	0.4	
16 TH	0334	2.8	1001	0.6	1546	2.9	2231	0.6	
17 F	0413	2.6	1039	0.8	1630	2.8	2318	0.7	◑
18 SA	0506	2.5	1137	0.9	1732	2.7			
19 SU	0029	0.7	0620	2.4	1259	0.9	1852	2.7	
20 M	0157	0.6	0745	2.5	1427	0.8	2014	2.8	
21 TU	0317	0.5	0901	2.6	1541	0.6	2120	2.9	
22 W	0417	0.4	0957	2.7	1634	0.5	2209	3.0	
23 TH	0502	0.4	1041	2.9	1718	0.5	2251	3.1	
24 F	0543	0.4	1119	3.0	1759	0.4	2332	3.2	
25 SA	0622	0.3	1156	3.1	1838	0.4			●
26 SU	0010	3.2	0659	0.3	1232	3.1	1919	0.3	
27 M	0051	3.2	0737	0.3	1311	3.1	2003	0.3	
28 TU	0135	3.1	0818	0.4	1353	3.1	2048	0.3	
29 W	0222	3.0	0901	0.4	1437	3.1	2133	0.3	
30 TH	0310	2.9	0945	0.5	1523	3.1	2221	0.4	

Chart Datum: 1·68 metres below Normal Null (German reference level)
HAT is 3·0 metres above Chart Datum

GERMANY – HELGOLAND

TIME ZONE -0100
(German Standard Time)
Subtract 1 hour for UT
For German Summer Time add
ONE hour in **non-shaded areas**

LAT 54°11′N   LONG 7°53′E

TIMES AND HEIGHTS OF HIGH AND LOW WATERS

Dates in amber are **SPRINGS**
Dates in yellow are **NEAPS**

2009

MAY

Day	Time m	Time m	Time m	Time m
1	0402 2.8	1034 0.6	F 1615 3.1	2316 0.4
2	0501 2.7	1134 0.7	SA 1719 3.0	
3	0025 0.5	0612 2.6	SU 1250 0.7	1837 3.0
4	0148 0.5	0734 2.7	M 1416 0.7	◑2000 3.0
5	0309 0.5	0851 2.8	TU 1533 0.6	2112 3.1
6	0412 0.4	0951 2.9	W 1630 0.5	2207 3.1
7	0458 0.3	1036 2.9	TH 1717 0.5	2253 3.1
8	0540 0.4	1117 3.0	F 1804 0.5	2338 3.1
9	0623 0.4	1159 3.1	SA 1848 0.4	
10	0021 3.1	0702 0.4	SU 1236 3.1	1925 0.4
11	0057 3.1	0736 0.4	M 1308 3.1	○1957 0.3
12	0130 3.0	0808 0.4	TU 1340 3.1	2031 0.3
13	0204 2.9	0839 0.4	W 1415 3.0	2106 0.3
14	0240 2.8	0909 0.5	TH 1450 3.0	2140 0.4
15	0316 2.7	0942 0.6	F 1526 3.0	2215 0.5
16	0354 2.7	1019 0.7	SA 1606 2.9	2256 0.6
17	0438 2.6	1106 0.7	SU 1655 2.8	2350 0.6
18	0535 2.5	1210 0.7	M 1759 2.8	◐
19	0100 0.5	0646 2.5	TU 1326 0.7	1912 2.8
20	0213 0.5	0758 2.6	W 1438 0.6	2020 2.9
21	0317 0.4	0901 2.7	TH 1539 0.5	2116 3.0
22	0409 0.4	0953 2.9	F 1632 0.5	2207 3.1
23	0459 0.4	1040 3.0	SA 1723 0.5	2257 3.2
24	0547 0.4	1124 3.1	SU 1812 0.4	2345 3.2
25	0632 0.4	1207 3.2	M 1900 0.3	
26	0033 3.1	0718 0.4	TU 1253 3.2	●1952 0.3
27	0124 3.1	0807 0.4	W 1342 3.2	2043 0.3
28	0217 3.0	0859 0.4	TH 1431 3.2	2133 0.2
29	0308 2.9	0942 0.4	F 1520 3.2	2223 0.3
30	0359 2.8	1033 0.5	SA 1612 3.1	2317 0.3
31	0456 2.7	1130 0.5	SU 1712 3.1	

JUNE

Day	Time m	Time m	Time m	Time m
1	0017 0.4	0559 2.6	M 1234 0.6	1819 3.0
2	0122 0.4	0706 2.7	TU 1345 0.6	◑1930 3.0
3	0230 0.5	0814 2.8	W 1455 0.6	2037 3.0
4	0331 0.5	0913 2.9	TH 1555 0.6	2134 3.1
5	0422 0.5	1002 2.9	F 1646 0.6	2224 3.1
6	0508 0.5	1047 3.0	SA 1735 0.6	2313 3.1
7	0554 0.6	1133 3.1	SU 1823 0.5	2358 3.0
8	0637 0.5	1214 3.1	M 1904 0.4	
9	0037 3.1	0714 0.5	TU 1249 3.1	○1940 0.4
10	0113 2.9	0748 0.5	W 1323 3.1	2016 0.4
11	0148 2.9	0822 0.5	TH 1358 3.1	2052 0.4
12	0223 2.8	0854 0.5	F 1432 3.1	2125 0.4
13	0258 2.8	0926 0.5	SA 1506 3.1	2159 0.5
14	0334 2.7	1002 0.5	SU 1543 3.0	2236 0.5
15	0413 2.7	1041 0.6	M 1624 2.9	2316 0.5
16	0457 2.6	1104 0.6	TU 1712 2.9	◐
17	0006 0.5	0550 2.6	W 1226 0.7	1812 2.9
18	0107 0.5	0654 2.6	TH 1334 0.7	1918 2.9
19	0213 0.5	0801 2.7	F 1443 0.6	2025 2.9
20	0317 0.5	0905 2.9	SA 1549 0.6	2129 3.0
21	0419 0.5	1004 3.0	SU 1653 0.6	2231 3.1
22	0519 0.5	1059 3.1	M 1753 0.5	2329 3.1
23	0615 0.5	1151 3.2	TU 1850 0.4	
24	0024 3.1	0708 0.5	W 1242 3.3	○1945 0.3
25	0118 3.0	0800 0.5	TH 1335 3.3	●2039 0.2
26	0211 3.0	0851 0.3	F 1425 3.3	2129 0.2
27	0301 2.9	0937 0.3	SA 1512 3.2	2215 0.2
28	0348 2.8	1023 0.3	SU 1559 3.2	2302 0.3
29	0437 2.8	1002 0.4	M 1651 3.1	2350 0.4
30	0529 2.7	1204 0.5	TU 1747 3.1	

JULY

Day	Time m	Time m	Time m	Time m
1	0040 0.5	0625 2.7	W 1301 0.6	1848 3.0
2	0138 0.6	0725 2.8	TH 1406 0.7	1953 3.0
3	0242 0.7	0829 2.9	F 1515 0.7	2059 3.0
4	0346 0.7	0929 3.0	SA 1617 0.7	◑2159 3.0
5	0441 0.7	1022 3.1	SU 1713 0.7	2252 3.0
6	0531 0.7	1111 3.1	M 1803 0.6	2340 3.0
7	0616 0.7	1155 3.2	TU 1847 0.5	
8	0021 3.0	0657 0.6	W 1234 3.2	1926 0.5
9	0058 3.0	0734 0.5	TH 1309 3.2	2002 0.5
10	0133 3.0	0808 0.5	F 1341 3.2	2035 0.4
11	0205 2.9	0838 0.4	SA 1412 3.2	○2106 0.4
12	0236 2.8	0907 0.4	SU 1444 3.1	2137 0.4
13	0310 2.8	0941 0.5	M 1519 3.1	2212 0.5
14	0346 2.8	1017 0.5	TU 1557 3.1	2245 0.5
15	0423 2.8	1053 0.6	W 1635 3.0	2321 0.5
16	0503 2.7	1136 0.7	TH 1722 2.9	
17	0009 0.6	0557 2.7	F 1238 0.7	1826 2.9
18	0117 0.7	0707 2.8	SA 1355 0.7	◑1944 2.9
19	0235 0.7	0825 2.9	SU 1517 0.7	2103 2.9
20	0352 0.7	0939 3.0	M 1634 0.6	2217 3.0
21	0503 0.6	1045 3.1	TU 1743 0.5	2322 3.1
22	0605 0.5	1142 3.2	W 1843 0.4	
23	0018 3.1	0700 0.5	TH 1234 3.3	1938 0.3
24	0109 3.0	0751 0.4	F 1324 3.4	2029 0.2
25	0158 3.0	0840 0.3	SA 1411 3.3	●2115 0.2
26	0244 2.9	0923 0.2	SU 1455 3.3	2154 0.2
27	0326 2.9	1002 0.3	M 1537 3.2	2232 0.3
28	0407 2.9	1042 0.4	TU 1621 3.2	2310 0.5
29	0449 2.9	1123 0.6	W 1707 3.1	2351 0.7
30	0535 2.8	1211 0.7	TH 1800 2.9	
31	0042 0.8	0631 2.8	F 1313 0.8	1905 2.9

AUGUST

Day	Time m	Time m	Time m	Time m
1	0150 0.9	0740 2.8	SA 1431 0.9	2022 2.8
2	0307 1.0	0855 2.9	SU 1550 0.9	◑2136 2.9
3	0417 0.9	1000 3.0	M 1654 0.8	2236 2.9
4	0513 0.8	1053 3.1	TU 1745 0.7	2324 2.9
5	0558 0.7	1137 3.2	W 1829 0.6	
6	0004 3.0	0639 0.6	TH 1215 3.2	1908 0.5
7	0040 3.0	0716 0.5	F 1250 3.2	1942 0.5
8	0113 3.0	0749 0.5	SA 1320 3.2	2013 0.4
9	0142 3.0	0817 0.4	SU 1349 3.2	○2040 0.4
10	0210 2.9	0845 0.4	M 1419 3.2	2110 0.4
11	0241 2.9	0917 0.4	TU 1454 3.1	2143 0.5
12	0316 2.9	0952 0.5	W 1531 3.1	2215 0.5
13	0350 2.9	1024 0.6	TH 1606 3.0	2244 0.6
14	0425 2.9	1100 0.7	F 1648 2.9	2327 0.8
15	0516 2.8	1159 0.8	SA 1753 2.9	
16	0037 0.9	0631 2.8	SU 1325 0.8	1920 2.8
17	0208 0.9	0800 2.9	M 1500 0.9	◑2052 2.9
18	0338 0.8	0926 3.0	TU 1626 0.6	2211 2.9
19	0453 0.7	1036 3.2	W 1736 0.5	2315 3.1
20	0555 0.6	1132 3.3	TH 1833 0.4	
21	0007 3.1	0648 0.5	F 1222 3.4	1923 0.3
22	0053 3.0	0736 0.4	SA 1308 3.4	2008 0.2
23	0136 3.1	0820 0.3	SU 1351 3.4	2049 0.3
24	0218 3.0	0900 0.3	M 1431 3.3	2124 0.3
25	0255 3.0	0934 0.3	TU 1509 3.2	●2156 0.4
26	0330 3.0	1008 0.4	W 1547 3.1	2228 0.6
27	0406 2.9	1043 0.6	TH 1627 3.0	2303 0.8
28	0446 2.9	1122 0.7	F 1714 2.8	2348 1.0
29	0539 2.8	1223 0.9	SA 1818 2.7	
30	0056 1.1	0651 2.8	SU 1345 1.0	1941 2.7
31	0224 1.1	0816 2.9	M 1516 1.0	2107 2.7

Chart Datum: 1·68 metres below Normal Null (German reference level)
HAT is 3·0 metres above Chart Datum

SEPTEMBER

Time	m	Time	m
1 0348	1.0	**16** 0330	0.9
TU 0934	3.0	W 0917	3.1
1632	0.8	1620	0.6
2216	2.8	2204	2.9
2 0451	0.8	**17** 0443	0.7
W 1031	3.1	TH 1024	3.2
1724	0.6	1724	0.5
2303	2.9	2302	3.0
3 0536	0.7	**18** 0539	0.6
TH 1113	3.2	F 1117	3.3
1804	0.5	1814	0.4
2339	3.0	● 2348	3.1
4 0614	0.6	**19** 0629	0.5
F 1149	3.2	SA 1203	3.3
1840	0.5	1858	0.3
○			
5 0013	3.0	**20** 0030	3.1
SA 0649	0.5	SU 0713	0.4
1913	0.4	1247	3.3
		1939	0.3
6 0045	3.0	**21** 0109	3.1
SU 0721	0.5	M 0754	0.4
1254	3.2	1327	3.3
1942	0.4	2016	0.4
7 0115	3.0	**22** 0146	3.1
M 0750	0.4	TU 0831	0.4
1323	3.2	1405	3.3
2011	0.4	2050	0.5
8 0142	3.0	**23** 0222	3.1
TU 0820	0.4	W 0905	0.4
1355	3.2	1440	3.2
2041	0.5	2120	0.5
9 0212	3.0	**24** 0255	3.0
W 0853	0.4	TH 0936	0.5
1429	3.1	1515	3.1
2113	0.5	2150	0.7
10 0246	3.0	**25** 0328	3.0
TH 0928	0.5	F 1009	0.6
1507	3.1	1551	2.9
2146	0.6	2222	0.9
11 0322	3.0	**26** 0406	2.9
F 1002	0.6	SA 1047	0.8
1546	3.0	1635	2.7
2219	0.7	◑ 2303	1.0
12 0400	3.0	**27** 0455	2.9
SA 1042	0.7	SU 1140	0.9
1632	2.9	1734	2.6
◑ 2304	0.9		
13 0454	2.9	**28** 0006	1.2
SU 1143	0.8	M 0603	2.8
1740	2.7	1258	1.0
		1855	2.6
14 0018	1.0	**29** 0133	1.2
M 0614	2.9	TU 0730	2.8
1314	0.9	1431	1.0
1912	2.8	2025	2.6
15 0156	1.0	**30** 0305	1.1
TU 0749	3.0	W 0854	2.9
1455	0.8	1554	0.8
2047	2.9	2139	2.7

OCTOBER

Time	m	Time	m
1 0415	0.9	**16** 0425	0.8
TH 0956	3.0	F 1006	3.2
1650	0.6	1701	0.5
2229	2.9	2239	3.0
2 0503	0.7	**17** 0516	0.6
F 1038	3.1	SA 1054	3.3
1728	0.5	1745	0.5
2305	2.9	2321	3.1
3 0539	0.6	**18** 0603	0.6
SA 1114	3.2	SU 1140	3.3
1802	0.5	1828	0.5
2339	3.0		
4 0614	0.6	**19** 0003	3.1
SU 1149	3.2	M 0647	0.5
1836	0.5	1223	3.3
○		1908	0.6
5 0012	3.0	**20** 0041	3.2
M 0648	0.5	TU 0727	0.5
1223	3.2	1303	3.3
1908	0.4	1945	0.6
6 0044	3.1	**21** 0117	3.2
TU 0722	0.5	W 0803	0.5
1256	3.2	1338	3.2
1940	0.5	2018	0.6
7 0115	3.1	**22** 0151	3.2
W 0758	0.5	TH 0837	0.5
1332	3.2	1413	3.1
2013	0.6	2049	0.6
8 0147	3.2	**23** 0225	3.1
TH 0834	0.5	F 0911	0.5
1410	3.1	1448	3.0
2048	0.6	2119	0.7
9 0223	3.1	**24** 0300	3.0
F 0912	0.5	SA 0944	0.6
1451	3.1	1524	2.8
2125	0.7	2150	0.8
10 0303	3.1	**25** 0337	3.0
SA 0951	0.6	SU 1020	0.8
1536	3.0	1604	2.7
2205	0.8	2228	1.0
11 0348	3.1	**26** 0421	2.9
SU 1038	0.7	M 1106	0.9
1629	2.9	1656	2.6
◑ 2257	1.0	◑ 2323	1.1
12 0447	3.0	**27** 0519	2.8
M 1143	0.8	TU 1211	1.0
1738	2.7	1805	2.5
13 0012	1.1	**28** 0039	1.2
TU 0607	3.0	W 0634	2.8
1311	0.8	1333	1.0
1906	2.8	1927	2.6
14 0146	1.1	**29** 0205	1.1
W 0739	3.1	TH 0756	2.9
1447	0.6	1455	0.8
2037	2.8	2043	2.7
15 0317	0.9	**30** 0320	0.9
TH 0903	3.2	F 0904	2.9
1606	0.7	1557	0.7
2148	2.9	2140	2.8
		31 0415	0.8
		SA 0953	3.0
		1640	0.6
		2223	2.9

NOVEMBER

Time	m	Time	m
1 0456	0.7	**16** 0536	0.7
SU 1033	3.1	M 1115	3.2
1718	0.6	1758	0.7
2300	3.0	● 2337	3.2
2 0536	0.7	**17** 0623	0.7
M 1113	3.2	TU 1201	3.2
1757	0.6	1840	0.7
○ 2338	3.1		
3 0616	0.6	**18** 0018	3.2
TU 1152	3.2	W 0704	0.6
1834	0.6	1241	3.2
		1918	0.7
4 0014	3.2	**19** 0054	3.2
W 0657	0.6	TH 0740	0.6
1231	3.2	1317	3.1
1912	0.6	1952	0.7
5 0051	3.2	**20** 0128	3.2
TH 0739	0.6	F 0816	0.6
1314	3.2	1352	3.0
1953	0.7	2025	0.7
6 0130	3.3	**21** 0204	3.2
F 0823	0.6	SA 0852	0.6
1359	3.1	1428	2.9
2034	0.7	2057	0.7
7 0212	3.3	**22** 0239	3.1
SA 0906	0.7	SU 0926	0.6
1444	3.0	1503	2.8
2115	0.7	2128	0.8
8 0255	3.2	**23** 0314	3.1
SU 0950	0.6	M 1000	0.8
1532	2.9	1540	2.8
2201	0.8	2203	0.9
9 0343	3.2	**24** 0352	3.0
M 1041	0.7	TU 1039	0.9
1628	2.8	1622	2.7
◐ 2256	0.9	◐ 2247	1.0
10 0443	3.1	**25** 0438	0.9
TU 1145	0.7	W 1127	0.9
1734	2.7	1715	2.6
		2345	1.1
11 0006	1.0	**26** 0537	0.9
W 0557	3.1	TH 1229	0.9
1301	0.8	1820	2.6
1852	2.7		
12 0129	1.0	**27** 0056	1.1
TH 0720	3.1	F 0647	2.9
1424	0.8	1341	0.9
2012	2.8	1932	2.7
13 0251	0.9	**28** 0210	1.0
F 0840	3.1	SA 0757	2.9
1536	0.7	1449	0.8
2120	2.9	2038	2.8
14 0357	0.8	**29** 0315	0.9
SA 0939	3.2	SU 0857	3.0
1629	0.6	1544	0.7
2211	3.0	2133	2.9
15 0448	0.7	**30** 0409	0.8
SU 1029	3.2	M 0949	3.1
1714	0.6	1633	0.7
2254	3.1	2221	3.1

DECEMBER

Time	m	Time	m
1 0459	0.8	**16** 0603	0.8
TU 1038	3.2	W 1142	3.2
1721	0.7	1819	0.8
2305	3.2	●	
2 0548	0.7	**17** 0000	3.3
W 1126	3.2	TH 0647	0.7
1807	0.7	1224	3.1
○ 2348	3.2	1858	0.8
3 0637	0.6	**18** 0037	3.3
TH 1213	3.2	F 0724	0.7
1853	0.7	1301	3.1
		1934	0.7
4 0033	3.3	**19** 0112	3.3
F 0727	0.6	SA 0801	0.7
1303	3.2	1337	3.0
1941	0.7	2009	0.7
5 0121	3.3	**20** 0147	3.3
SA 0818	0.6	SU 0837	0.6
1353	3.1	1412	3.0
2028	0.7	2041	0.7
6 0207	3.3	**21** 0221	3.2
SU 0906	0.5	M 0910	0.6
1442	3.0	1444	2.9
2113	0.6	2110	0.7
7 0252	3.3	**22** 0253	3.2
M 0951	0.5	TU 0941	0.7
1529	2.9	1516	2.9
2159	0.7	2142	0.7
8 0338	3.3	**23** 0326	3.1
TU 1040	0.6	W 1013	0.7
1621	2.9	1551	2.8
2251	0.8	2218	0.8
9 0433	3.2	**24** 0402	3.1
W 1135	0.6	TH 1048	0.8
1719	2.8	1630	2.8
◐ 2351	0.8	◐ 2259	0.9
10 0536	3.0	**25** 0445	3.0
TH 1236	0.7	F 1131	0.8
1824	2.8	1718	2.7
		2351	1.0
11 0058	0.9	**26** 0540	2.9
F 0647	3.1	SA 1228	0.9
1344	0.8	1820	2.7
1934	2.8		
12 0211	0.9	**27** 0058	1.0
SA 0800	3.1	SU 0647	2.9
1452	0.9	1336	0.9
2041	2.9	1930	2.8
13 0320	0.9	**28** 0211	1.0
SU 0906	3.1	M 0758	3.0
1553	0.8	1445	0.9
2139	3.0	2039	2.9
14 0420	0.9	**29** 0321	0.9
M 1003	3.2	TU 0906	3.0
1646	0.8	1551	0.8
2229	3.1	2142	3.0
15 0513	0.8	**30** 0427	0.8
TU 1055	3.2	W 1010	3.1
1734	0.8	1653	0.8
2316	3.2	2239	3.2
		31 0528	0.7
		TH 1109	3.1
		1750	0.7
		○ 2331	3.3

Chart Datum: 1·68 metres below Normal Null (German reference level)
HAT is 3·0 metres above Chart Datum

TIDES

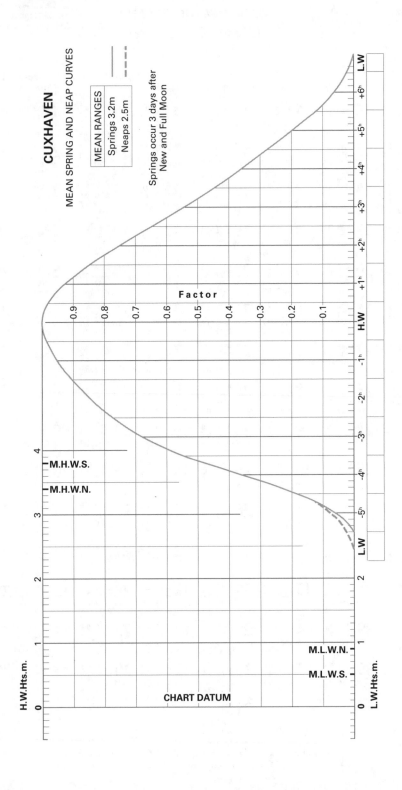

CUXHAVEN

MEAN SPRING AND NEAP CURVES

MEAN RANGES
Springs 3.2m
Neaps 2.5m

Springs occur 3 days after
New and Full Moon

Factor

0.9 0.8 0.7 0.6 0.5 0.4 0.3 0.2 0.1

H.W.Hts.m.

M.H.W.S.
M.H.W.N.

M.L.W.N.
M.L.W.S.

CHART DATUM

L.W.Hts.m.

TIME ZONE -0100
(German Standard Time)
Subtract 1 hour for UT
For German Summer Time add
ONE hour in **non-shaded areas**

GERMANY – CUXHAVEN

LAT 53°52′N   LONG 8°43′E

TIMES AND HEIGHTS OF HIGH AND LOW WATERS

Dates in amber are **SPRINGS**
Dates in yellow are **NEAPS**

2009

JANUARY		FEBRUARY		MARCH		APRIL	
Time m	Time m	Time m	Time m	Time m	Time m	Time m	Time m
1 0337 3.8 1034 0.5 TH 1602 3.5 2237 0.5	**16** 0427 3.9 1137 0.3 F 1659 3.4 2338 0.5	**1** 0423 3.8 1121 0.5 SU 1649 3.5 2328 0.4	**16** 0514 3.7 1200 0.6 M 1733 3.5 ☽	**1** 0325 3.9 1023 0.3 SU 1549 3.6 2235 0.4	**16** 0409 3.7 1057 0.4 M 1622 3.6 2306 0.4	**1** 0428 3.7 1111 0.5 W 1643 3.7 2334 0.4	**16** 0449 3.3 1115 0.6 TH 1659 3.5 2341 0.6
2 0410 3.8 1106 0.6 F 1637 3.4 2310 0.7	**17** 0508 3.9 1210 0.5 SA 1739 3.4	**2** 0458 3.8 1151 0.6 M 1721 3.5	**17** 0007 0.6 0549 3.6 TU 1227 0.8 1811 3.4	**2** 0402 3.8 1057 0.4 M 1624 3.6 2310 0.5	**17** 0441 3.6 1120 0.6 TU 1653 3.5 2333 0.5	**2** 0514 3.6 1150 0.6 TH 1729 3.6 ☽	**17** 0527 3.2 1148 0.8 F 1742 3.4 ☽
3 0445 3.7 1141 0.6 SA 1713 3.4 2347 0.8	**18** 0013 0.6 0549 3.7 SU 1243 0.6 ☽ 1820 3.3	**3** 0000 0.7 0535 3.7 TU 1221 0.7 ☽ 1800 3.4	**18** 0043 0.8 0636 3.4 W 1310 1.0 1905 3.3	**3** 0440 3.8 1128 0.5 TU 1657 3.6 2341 0.5	**18** 0514 3.5 1144 0.7 W 1728 3.4 ☽	**3** 0020 0.5 0610 3.3 F 1244 0.8 1832 3.5	**18** 0025 0.7 0619 3.1 SA 1242 0.9 1844 3.3
4 0522 3.7 1216 0.7 SU 1753 3.3 ☽	**19** 0051 0.7 0634 3.6 M 1322 0.8 1907 3.3	**4** 0041 0.8 0625 3.6 W 1311 0.9 1900 3.4	**19** 0143 1.0 0744 3.2 TH 1422 1.1 2021 3.3	**4** 0517 3.6 1158 0.6 W 1736 3.5 ☽	**19** 0004 0.7 0554 3.3 TH 1219 0.9 1816 3.3	**4** 0129 0.6 0726 3.2 SA 1405 0.9 1957 3.5	**19** 0134 0.7 0732 3.0 SU 1403 0.9 2004 3.3
5 0027 0.9 0607 3.6 M 1259 0.8 1843 3.3	**20** 0139 0.9 0730 3.5 TU 1416 1.0 2008 3.3	**5** 0148 0.9 0739 3.5 TH 1429 1.0 2021 3.4	**20** 0310 1.0 0909 3.2 F 1553 1.1 2146 3.4	**5** 0021 0.6 0608 3.4 TH 1247 0.8 1836 3.4	**20** 0055 0.8 0655 3.1 F 1323 1.0 1927 3.2	**5** 0303 0.6 0859 3.2 SU 1544 0.8 2129 3.6	**20** 0302 0.6 0856 3.0 M 1535 0.8 2125 3.4
6 0121 1.0 0705 3.6 TU 1358 0.9 1947 3.3	**21** 0246 1.0 0841 3.4 W 1530 1.1 2120 3.4	**6** 0319 0.9 0909 3.5 F 1604 0.9 2151 3.5	**21** 0444 0.9 1032 3.3 SA 1719 1.0 2300 3.5	**6** 0128 0.7 0724 3.3 F 1409 0.9 2003 3.4	**21** 0217 0.9 0819 3.1 SA 1456 1.0 2056 3.3	**6** 0441 0.6 1027 3.4 M 1714 0.7 2247 3.7	**21** 0427 0.5 1011 3.1 TU 1654 0.6 2231 3.5
7 0232 1.0 0817 3.6 W 1512 0.9 2101 3.4	**22** 0407 1.1 0957 3.5 TH 1648 1.1 2231 3.5	**7** 0455 0.8 1039 3.6 SA 1734 0.8 2311 3.7	**22** 0602 0.7 1138 3.4 SU 1824 0.8 2356 3.7	**7** 0305 0.8 0900 3.3 SA 1551 0.9 2138 3.6	**22** 0356 0.8 0949 3.1 SU 1632 0.9 2219 3.4	**7** 0557 0.4 1134 3.5 TU 1820 0.5 2345 3.8	**22** 0532 0.4 1108 3.3 W 1752 0.5 2320 3.6
8 0353 0.9 0935 3.6 TH 1632 0.9 2216 3.5	**23** 0526 1.0 1107 3.5 F 1756 1.0 2331 3.7	**8** 0620 0.6 1155 3.6 SU 1849 0.6	**23** 0658 0.6 1228 3.5 M 1913 0.7	**8** 0448 0.7 1034 3.4 SU 1726 0.8 2301 3.7	**23** 0522 0.6 1102 3.3 M 1747 0.7 2321 3.6	**8** 0652 0.3 1223 3.6 W 1910 0.4	**23** 0620 0.3 1153 3.5 TH 1839 0.5
9 0514 0.8 1051 3.7 F 1748 0.8 2326 3.7	**24** 0630 0.9 1203 3.6 SA 1849 0.9	**9** 0017 3.9 0728 0.5 M 1257 3.7 ○ 1949 0.6	**24** 0039 3.8 0742 0.5 TU 1309 3.6 1954 0.6	**9** 0613 0.4 1149 3.5 M 1839 0.6	**24** 0623 0.4 1154 3.4 TU 1840 0.6	**9** 0032 3.9 0736 0.3 TH 1304 3.6 ○ 1955 0.4	**24** 0002 3.8 0703 0.3 F 1234 3.6 1922 0.5
10 0629 0.7 1201 3.7 SA 1857 0.7	**25** 0020 3.8 0721 0.7 SU 1249 3.6 1934 0.8	**10** 0111 4.0 0823 0.4 TU 1348 3.7 2038 0.5	**25** 0116 3.8 0819 0.4 W 1345 3.6 ● 2031 0.5	**10** 0005 3.9 0716 0.4 TU 1246 3.6 1935 0.5	**25** 0005 3.7 0707 0.4 W 1236 3.5 1922 0.5	**10** 0116 3.9 0818 0.3 F 1342 3.7 2036 0.3	**25** 0043 3.9 0742 0.3 SA 1311 3.7 ● 2001 0.4
11 0027 3.9 0733 0.6 SU 1302 3.7 ○ 1955 0.6	**26** 0101 3.8 0804 0.6 M 1330 3.6 ● 2015 0.7	**11** 0158 4.0 0912 0.3 W 1433 3.6 2123 0.4	**26** 0150 3.9 0853 0.4 TH 1418 3.6 2104 0.4	**11** 0056 3.9 0806 0.3 W 1331 3.6 ○ 2021 0.4	**26** 0043 3.8 0745 0.3 TH 1312 3.6 ● 1959 0.4	**11** 0157 3.9 0855 0.3 SA 1416 3.7 2112 0.3	**26** 0122 3.9 0819 0.3 SU 1347 3.8 2040 0.3
12 0120 4.0 0830 0.5 M 1357 3.7 2047 0.6	**27** 0139 3.8 0841 0.6 TU 1408 3.6 2053 0.6	**12** 0243 4.1 0957 0.3 TH 1515 3.6 2204 0.4	**27** 0221 3.9 0923 0.3 F 1447 3.6 2134 0.4	**12** 0140 4.0 0849 0.2 TH 1410 3.6 2102 0.3	**27** 0118 3.8 0820 0.3 F 1346 3.7 2034 0.3	**12** 0234 3.8 0927 0.4 SU 1447 3.7 2143 0.3	**27** 0203 3.9 0857 0.4 M 1425 3.8 2122 0.3
13 0211 4.1 0924 0.4 TU 1448 3.7 2137 0.5	**28** 0214 3.9 0917 0.5 W 1442 3.5 2127 0.5	**13** 0325 4.0 1036 0.3 F 1552 3.6 2240 0.3	**28** 0252 3.9 0952 0.3 SA 1516 3.6 2203 0.4	**13** 0222 4.0 0928 0.3 F 1446 3.7 2139 0.3	**28** 0151 3.9 0852 0.3 SA 1417 3.7 2107 0.3	**13** 0307 3.7 0956 0.4 M 1518 3.7 2212 0.3	**28** 0248 3.8 0939 0.4 TU 1507 3.8 2206 0.3
14 0300 4.1 1016 0.4 W 1537 3.6 2223 0.5	**29** 0246 3.9 0948 0.4 TH 1512 3.6 2155 0.5	**14** 0403 3.9 1108 0.3 SA 1627 3.5 2310 0.4		**14** 0300 4.0 1002 0.3 SA 1519 3.7 2211 0.3	**29** 0226 3.9 0920 0.3 SU 1449 3.7 2141 0.3	**14** 0341 3.6 1023 0.4 TU 1550 3.6 2240 0.3	**29** 0335 3.7 1021 0.4 W 1551 3.8 2250 0.3
15 0345 4.0 1101 0.3 TH 1620 3.5 2302 0.4	**30** 0317 3.9 1017 0.4 F 1542 3.5 2222 0.5	**15** 0439 3.8 1135 0.4 SU 1700 3.5 2338 0.5		**15** 0335 3.9 1032 0.4 SU 1551 3.6 2240 0.3	**30** 0303 3.9 0958 0.3 M 1524 3.7 2218 0.3	**15** 0414 3.5 1049 0.5 W 1624 3.6 2310 0.5	**30** 0425 3.5 1105 0.5 TH 1638 3.8 2336 0.4
	31 0348 3.8 1047 0.4 SA 1615 3.5 2254 0.5				**31** 0345 3.8 1034 0.4 TU 1603 3.7 2255 0.4		

Chart Datum: 1·66 metres below Normal Null (German reference level)
HAT is 3·6 metres above Chart Datum

TIDES

355

TIDES

TIME ZONE -0100
(German Standard Time)
Subtract 1 hour for UT
For German Summer Time add
ONE hour in **non-shaded areas**

GERMANY – CUXHAVEN
LAT 53°52′N   LONG 8°43′E
TIMES AND HEIGHTS OF HIGH AND LOW WATERS

Dates in amber are **SPRINGS**
Dates in yellow are **NEAPS**
2009

MAY

Time	m		Time	m
1 0517	3.5		**16** 0508	3.2
1151	0.6		1132	0.7
F 1730	3.7		SA 1720	3.5
2 0028	0.4		**17** 0008	0.6
0616	3.3		0552	3.1
SA 1248	0.7		SU 1215	0.8
1833	3.6		1810	3.4
3 0135	0.5		**18** 0059	0.6
0728	3.2		0650	3.0
SU 1402	0.7		M 1317	0.8
1951	3.6		◗ 1913	3.3
4 0257	0.5		**19** 0208	0.5
0850	3.2		0801	3.0
M 1528	0.7		TU 1433	0.7
◗ 2113	3.7		2025	3.4
5 0421	0.5		**20** 0324	0.5
1007	3.3		0912	3.1
TU 1649	0.6		W 1550	0.6
2224	3.7		2132	3.5
6 0528	0.4		**21** 0431	0.4
1106	3.5		1014	3.3
W 1750	0.5		TH 1655	0.6
2318	3.8		2229	3.6
7 0618	0.4		**22** 0527	0.4
1151	0.6		1106	3.5
TH 1837	0.5		F 1752	0.6
			2321	3.7
8 0004	3.8		**23** 0618	0.4
0701	0.4		1154	3.6
F 1232	3.7		SA 1844	0.5
1924	0.5			
9 0050	3.8		**24** 0010	3.8
0745	0.4		0707	0.5
SA 1313	3.7		SU 1239	3.8
2009	0.4		1932	0.5
10 0133	3.8		**25** 0058	3.8
0825	0.4		0753	0.4
SU 1349	3.7		M 1323	3.9
2047	0.4		2019	0.4
11 0210	3.7		**26** 0148	3.8
0857	0.4		0839	0.5
M 1421	3.7		TU 1408	3.9
○ 2119	0.3		● 2109	0.3
12 0244	3.6		**27** 0239	3.8
0927	0.4		0928	0.5
TU 1453	3.7		W 1457	3.9
2150	0.3		2201	0.3
13 0319	3.5		**28** 0332	3.7
0957	0.5		1016	0.4
W 1527	3.7		TH 1545	3.9
2222	0.3		2251	0.3
14 0354	3.4		**29** 0425	3.5
1026	0.5		1103	0.5
TH 1603	3.6		F 1634	3.8
2255	0.4		2340	0.3
15 0430	3.3		**30** 0518	3.4
1057	0.6		1151	0.5
F 1640	3.6		SA 1727	3.8
2329	0.5			
			31 0032	0.4
			0614	3.3
			SU 1246	0.6
			1826	3.7

JUNE

Time	m		Time	m
1 0130	0.4		**16** 0031	0.5
0717	3.2		0614	3.2
M 1348	0.6		TU 1240	0.7
1932	3.6		◗ 1829	3.5
2 0235	0.4		**17** 0119	0.5
0824	3.2		0708	3.2
TU 1458	0.6		W 1337	0.7
◗ 2043	3.6		1928	3.5
3 0344	0.5		**18** 0220	0.6
0931	3.3		0811	3.2
W 1609	0.6		TH 1446	0.7
2150	3.7		2034	3.5
4 0448	0.5		**19** 0327	0.6
1029	3.5		0917	3.3
TH 1712	0.6		F 1557	0.7
2247	3.7		2140	3.6
5 0541	0.5		**20** 0433	0.6
1118	3.6		1019	3.5
F 1805	0.6		SA 1706	0.6
2337	3.7		2244	3.6
6 0629	0.6		**21** 0538	0.6
1203	3.7		1119	3.6
SA 1856	0.6		SU 1812	0.6
			2345	3.8
7 0026	3.7		**22** 0640	0.6
0716	0.6		1214	3.8
SU 1247	3.8		M 1912	0.5
1945	0.6			
8 0111	3.7		**23** 0043	3.8
0759	0.5		0737	0.5
M 1327	3.8		TU 1307	3.9
2026	0.5		2008	0.4
9 0152	3.6		**24** 0139	3.8
0835	0.5		0830	0.5
TU 1403	3.8		W 1358	4.0
○ 2101	0.4		2103	0.3
10 0228	3.6		**25** 0235	3.7
0908	0.5		0923	0.5
W 1437	3.8		TH 1449	4.0
2136	0.4		● 2159	0.3
11 0304	3.5		**26** 0329	3.6
0941	0.5		1013	0.4
TH 1511	3.8		F 1539	4.0
2209	0.4		2250	0.2
12 0339	3.4		**27** 0419	3.5
1012	0.5		1101	0.4
F 1547	3.7		SA 1626	3.9
2242	0.4		2335	0.2
13 0414	3.4		**28** 0507	3.4
1044	0.5		1143	0.4
SA 1623	3.7		SU 1715	3.8
2316	0.5			
14 0450	3.3		**29** 0021	0.3
1118	0.6		0557	3.3
SU 1701	3.6		M 1229	0.5
2352	0.5		1806	3.8
15 0529	3.3		**30** 0107	0.4
1156	0.7		0648	3.3
M 1741	3.6		TU 1319	0.5
			1901	3.7

JULY

Time	m		Time	m
1 0157	0.5		**16** 0038	0.6
0743	3.3		0621	3.3
W 1414	0.6		TH 1252	0.7
2001	3.6		1840	3.6
2 0253	0.6		**17** 0124	0.7
0842	3.4		0716	3.3
TH 1518	0.7		F 1351	0.8
2108	3.6		1944	3.5
3 0358	0.7		**18** 0230	0.8
0945	3.5		0825	3.3
F 1628	0.8		SA 1508	0.8
2214	3.6		◗ 2100	3.5
4 0503	0.8		**19** 0349	0.7
1045	3.6		0941	3.4
SA 1734	0.8		SU 1631	0.7
◗ 2315	3.6		2218	3.5
5 0601	0.7		**20** 0510	0.7
1138	3.7		1054	3.6
SU 1833	0.7		M 1751	0.6
			2331	3.6
6 0008	3.6		**21** 0624	0.7
0652	0.7		1200	3.8
M 1226	3.8		TU 1902	0.5
1925	0.6			
7 0055	3.6		**22** 0036	3.7
0737	0.7		0729	0.6
TU 1310	3.8		W 1257	3.9
2009	0.6		2003	0.4
8 0137	3.6		**23** 0134	3.7
0818	0.6		0824	0.5
W 1348	3.8		TH 1349	4.0
2047	0.5		2058	0.3
9 0215	3.6		**24** 0228	3.6
0855	0.5		0916	0.4
TH 1424	3.8		F 1439	4.1
2123	0.5		2151	0.3
10 0251	3.6		**25** 0318	3.6
0930	0.5		1004	0.4
F 1457	3.9		SA 1526	4.0
2156	0.5		2238	0.2
11 0323	3.5		**26** 0403	3.6
0959	0.5		1045	0.3
SA 1529	3.8		SU 1610	3.9
○ 2226	0.4		● 2318	0.2
12 0353	3.4		**27** 0444	3.5
1027	0.5		1123	0.3
SU 1602	3.8		M 1653	3.8
2257	0.5		2355	0.3
13 0427	3.4		**28** 0525	3.4
1059	0.5		1201	0.5
M 1637	3.7		TU 1737	3.8
2331	0.5			
14 0504	3.4		**29** 0031	0.5
1136	0.6		0608	3.4
TU 1714	3.7		W 1240	0.6
			1822	3.6
15 0004	0.5		**30** 0109	0.7
0540	3.5		0653	3.4
W 1211	0.7		TH 1324	0.7
1752	3.6		1915	3.5
			31 0156	0.8
			0748	3.4
			F 1423	0.9
			2021	3.4

AUGUST

Time	m		Time	m
1 0302	1.0		**16** 0151	0.9
0857	3.4		0748	3.3
SA 1542	1.0		SU 1437	0.9
2138	3.4		2035	3.4
2 0421	1.0		**17** 0322	0.9
1011	3.5		0917	3.4
SU 1704	0.9		M 1613	0.8
◗ 2252	3.5		◗ 2206	3.4
3 0535	0.9		**18** 0456	0.8
1117	3.6		1041	3.6
M 1813	0.8		TU 1743	0.6
2353	3.5		2326	3.5
4 0633	0.8		**19** 0616	0.7
1209	3.7		1150	3.8
TU 1908	0.7		W 1856	0.5
5 0040	3.5		**20** 0031	3.6
0719	0.7		0721	0.6
W 1252	3.8		TH 1246	3.9
1952	0.6		1956	0.4
6 0121	3.6		**21** 0125	3.7
0801	0.6		0814	0.5
TH 1331	3.8		F 1336	4.0
2030	0.5		2046	0.3
7 0158	3.6		**22** 0212	3.7
0840	0.5		0901	0.4
F 1406	3.8		SA 1422	4.0
2105	0.5		2132	0.3
8 0232	3.6		**23** 0256	3.7
0913	0.5		0944	0.3
SA 1437	3.9		SU 1506	4.0
2135	0.4		2214	0.3
9 0301	3.6		**24** 0336	3.7
0941	0.5		1023	0.3
SU 1506	3.9		M 1547	3.9
○ 2202	0.4		2249	0.3
10 0328	3.5		**25** 0413	3.6
1006	0.5		1057	0.4
M 1536	3.8		TU 1626	3.8
2231	0.4		● 2320	0.4
11 0359	3.5		**26** 0448	3.5
1037	0.5		1129	0.5
TU 1610	3.8		W 1704	3.7
2304	0.5		2350	0.6
12 0434	3.5		**27** 0525	3.5
1113	0.6		1201	0.6
W 1647	3.8		TH 1743	3.6
2336	0.6			
13 0508	3.5		**28** 0020	0.8
1145	0.7		0604	3.4
TH 1722	3.7		F 1238	0.8
			1829	3.4
14 0004	0.7		**29** 0100	1.0
0543	3.4		0656	3.3
F 1219	0.7		SA 1332	0.9
1805	3.5		1933	3.2
15 0043	0.8		**30** 0205	1.1
0634	3.3		0807	3.2
SA 1314	0.8		SU 1453	1.1
1910	3.4		2057	3.2
			31 0334	1.2
			0932	3.2
			M 1628	1.0
			2223	3.3

Chart Datum: 1·66 metres below Normal Null (German reference level)
HAT is 3·6 metres above Chart Datum

GERMANY – CUXHAVEN

LAT 53°52′N   LONG 8°43′E

TIMES AND HEIGHTS OF HIGH AND LOW WATERS

2009

TIME ZONE -0100
(German Standard Time)
Subtract 1 hour for UT
For German Summer Time add
ONE hour in **non-shaded areas**

Dates in amber are **SPRINGS**
Dates in yellow are **NEAPS**

SEPTEMBER

Day	Dow	Time m	Time m	Time m	Time m
1	TU	0502 1.1	1049 3.6	1749 0.8	2331 3.4
2	W	0610 0.9	1147 3.7	1846 0.6	
3	TH	0019 3.5	0658 0.7	1229 3.7	1927 0.5
4	F	0057 3.5	0737 0.6	1305 3.8	○ 2003 0.5
5	SA	0131 3.6	0814 0.6	1338 3.8	2036 0.4
6	SU	0204 3.6	0847 0.5	1409 3.9	2106 0.4
7	M	0233 3.6	0917 0.5	1438 3.9	2134 0.5
8	TU	0300 3.6	0944 0.5	1509 3.8	2202 0.5
9	W	0330 3.6	1014 0.5	1544 3.8	2235 0.6
10	TH	0404 3.6	1049 0.6	1622 3.7	2308 0.8
11	F	0439 3.6	1123 0.6	1701 3.6	2339 0.8
12	SA	0517 3.5	1200 0.7	1747 3.5	◑
13	SU	0021 0.9	0610 3.4	1257 0.8	1856 3.3
14	M	0132 1.0	0730 3.4	1426 0.9	2027 3.3
15	TU	0310 1.1	0905 3.5	1608 0.8	2202 3.4
16	W	0449 0.9	1031 3.7	1738 0.7	2320 3.5
17	TH	0608 0.7	1139 3.8	1845 0.5	
18	F	0019 3.6	0706 0.6	1231 3.9	● 1937 0.4
19	SA	0106 3.7	0755 0.5	1317 4.0	2023 0.3
20	SU	0148 3.7	0839 0.4	1400 4.0	2104 0.3
21	M	0227 3.7	0919 0.4	1442 4.0	2142 0.4
22	TU	0304 3.7	0955 0.4	1521 3.9	2215 0.5
23	W	0338 3.7	1027 0.4	1557 3.8	2244 0.5
24	TH	0412 3.6	1057 0.5	1633 3.6	2311 0.7
25	F	0446 3.5	1127 0.6	1709 3.4	2338 0.9
26	SA	0522 3.5	1201 0.8	1750 3.2	◐
27	SU	0014 1.1	0610 3.4	1250 1.0	1849 3.1
28	M	0113 1.2	0718 3.3	1405 1.1	2009 3.1
29	TU	0241 1.2	0843 3.4	1541 1.0	2138 3.1
30	W	0417 1.1	1007 3.5	1709 0.8	2253 3.3

OCTOBER

Day	Dow	Time m	Time m	Time m	Time m
1	TH	0534 0.9	1110 3.6	1810 0.6	2345 3.4
2	F	0624 0.7	1153 3.6	1851 0.5	
3	SA	0022 3.5	0703 0.6	1228 3.7	1925 0.5
4	SU	0056 3.5	0740 0.6	1303 3.8	○ 1959 0.5
5	M	0130 3.6	0815 0.5	1337 3.8	2032 0.5
6	TU	0201 3.7	0849 0.5	1410 3.9	2103 0.5
7	W	0231 3.7	0922 0.5	1445 3.8	2136 0.6
8	TH	0304 3.8	0956 0.6	1524 3.7	2211 0.6
9	F	0341 3.7	1032 0.5	1605 3.6	2247 0.7
10	SA	0420 3.7	1110 0.6	1650 3.6	2326 0.8
11	SU	0504 3.6	1155 0.7	1743 3.4	◑
12	M	0015 1.0	0602 3.5	1257 0.8	1853 3.3
13	TU	0127 1.1	0721 3.5	1424 0.8	2022 3.3
14	W	0302 1.0	0853 3.6	1602 0.8	2153 3.4
15	TH	0437 1.0	1017 3.7	1725 0.7	2306 3.5
16	F	0550 0.8	1119 3.8	1824 0.5	2357 3.6
17	SA	0642 0.6	1208 3.9	1910 0.5	
18	SU	0039 3.7	0728 0.6	1253 3.9	● 1953 0.5
19	M	0119 3.7	0813 0.5	1336 3.9	2035 0.5
20	TU	0157 3.8	0853 0.5	1417 3.9	2111 0.6
21	W	0233 3.8	0928 0.5	1454 3.8	2143 0.6
22	TH	0306 3.7	1001 0.5	1530 3.6	2212 0.6
23	F	0340 3.7	1031 0.5	1605 3.5	2239 0.7
24	SA	0414 3.6	1102 0.6	1641 3.3	2307 0.7
25	SU	0451 3.5	1136 0.8	1720 3.2	2341 1.0
26	M	0534 3.5	1219 0.9	1810 3.1	◐
27	TU	0032 1.2	0632 3.4	1321 1.0	1918 3.0
28	W	0147 1.2	0747 3.3	1444 1.0	2039 3.1
29	TH	0316 1.1	0908 3.4	1609 0.8	2156 3.2
30	F	0437 0.9	1015 3.5	1715 0.7	2254 3.3
31	SA	0535 0.8	1105 3.6	1802 0.6	2338 3.4

NOVEMBER

Day	Dow	Time m	Time m	Time m	Time m
1	SU	0620 0.7	1146 3.7	1842 0.6	
2	M	0017 3.6	0702 0.7	1226 3.8	○ 1921 0.6
3	TU	0054 3.7	0742 0.6	1305 3.8	1958 0.6
4	W	0130 3.8	0822 0.6	1346 3.8	2036 0.6
5	TH	0207 3.8	0903 0.6	1428 3.8	2117 0.7
6	F	0246 3.9	0945 0.6	1512 3.7	2158 0.7
7	SA	0328 3.9	1026 0.6	1559 3.6	2239 0.7
8	SU	0411 3.8	1109 0.6	1647 3.5	2323 0.8
9	M	0459 3.8	1158 0.7	1743 3.4	◑
10	TU	0015 0.9	0557 3.7	1300 0.7	1850 3.2
11	W	0122 1.0	0710 3.6	1417 0.8	2008 3.2
12	TH	0245 1.0	0832 3.7	1542 0.8	2129 3.4
13	F	0410 1.0	0949 3.7	1657 0.7	2236 3.5
14	SA	0520 0.8	1051 3.8	1753 0.7	2327 3.6
15	SU	0613 0.8	1141 3.8	1839 0.7	
16	M	0009 3.7	0701 0.7	1229 3.8	● 1924 0.7
17	TU	0051 3.7	0748 0.7	1314 3.8	2007 0.7
18	W	0131 3.8	0830 0.6	1355 3.8	2044 0.7
19	TH	0206 3.8	0905 0.6	1432 3.7	2117 0.7
20	F	0240 3.8	0939 0.6	1508 3.6	2148 0.7
21	SA	0316 3.8	1013 0.6	1544 3.4	2218 0.7
22	SU	0351 3.7	1045 0.6	1619 3.3	2247 0.7
23	M	0428 3.6	1119 0.8	1655 3.3	2320 0.9
24	TU	0506 3.6	1155 0.9	1736 3.2	◐
25	W	0000 1.0	0551 3.5	1241 0.9	1828 3.1
26	TH	0056 1.1	0649 3.4	1343 0.9	1933 3.1
27	F	0208 1.1	0758 3.4	1456 0.9	2045 3.2
28	SA	0325 1.0	0908 3.5	1605 0.8	2151 3.2
29	SU	0434 0.9	1009 3.6	1704 0.7	2246 3.5
30	M	0532 0.8	1101 3.7	1755 0.7	2335 3.6

DECEMBER

Day	Dow	Time m	Time m	Time m	Time m
1	TU	0624 0.8	1151 3.7	1845 0.7	
2	W	0020 3.7	0713 0.7	1239 3.8	○ 1931 0.7
3	TH	0104 3.8	0800 0.7	1327 3.8	2018 0.7
4	F	0148 3.9	0849 0.6	1417 3.8	2106 0.7
5	SA	0235 4.0	0941 0.6	1508 3.8	2154 0.7
6	SU	0321 4.0	1028 0.5	1556 3.6	2237 0.7
7	M	0406 4.0	1113 0.5	1645 3.5	2321 0.7
8	TU	0453 3.9	1200 0.6	1737 3.4	◑
9	W	0011 0.8	0547 3.8	1253 0.6	1834 3.3
10	TH	0108 0.8	0649 3.7	1355 0.7	1939 3.3
11	F	0214 0.9	0758 3.7	1503 0.8	2048 3.4
12	SA	0328 0.9	0910 3.7	1613 0.8	2154 3.5
13	SU	0439 0.9	1016 3.7	1716 0.9	2252 3.6
14	M	0541 0.9	1115 3.7	1811 0.8	2342 3.7
15	TU	0636 0.9	1208 3.7	1900 0.8	
16	W	0029 3.8	0728 0.8	1256 3.7	● 1945 0.8
17	TH	0110 3.8	0812 0.7	1338 3.7	2024 0.7
18	F	0147 3.8	0849 0.7	1415 3.7	2059 0.7
19	SA	0222 3.8	0924 0.6	1452 3.6	2133 0.7
20	SU	0258 3.9	0959 0.6	1526 3.5	2204 0.7
21	M	0333 3.8	1031 0.6	1559 3.4	2232 0.7
22	TU	0407 3.8	1101 0.7	1632 3.4	2302 0.7
23	W	0441 3.7	1133 0.8	1706 3.3	2335 0.9
24	TH	0516 3.6	1207 0.9	1744 3.3	◐
25	F	0014 0.9	0558 3.5	1248 0.9	1832 3.2
26	SA	0105 1.0	0651 3.5	1343 0.9	1932 3.2
27	SU	0211 1.0	0757 3.5	1450 0.9	2041 3.3
28	M	0326 1.0	0909 3.5	1601 0.9	2150 3.4
29	TU	0440 0.9	1018 3.6	1710 0.8	2254 3.6
30	W	0549 0.8	1122 3.7	1815 0.8	2352 3.7
31	TH	0651 0.9	1220 3.8	1914 0.8	○

Chart Datum: 1·66 metres below Normal Null (German reference level)
HAT is 3·6 metres above Chart Datum

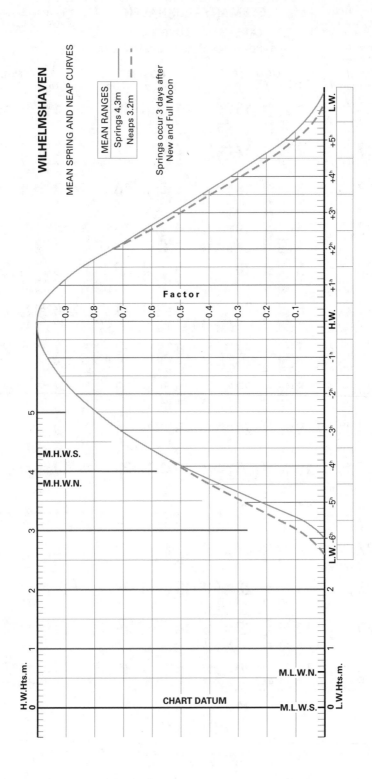

WILHELMSHAVEN

MEAN SPRING AND NEAP CURVES

MEAN RANGES
Springs 4.3m
Neaps 3.2m

Springs occur 3 days after
New and Full Moon

Factor

0.9 0.8 0.7 0.6 0.5 0.4 0.3 0.2 0.1

H.W. -1ʰ -2ʰ -3ʰ -4ʰ -5ʰ -6ʰ L.W.

+5ʰ +4ʰ +3ʰ +2ʰ +1ʰ H.W.

L.W.

M.H.W.S.
M.H.W.N.

H.W.Hts.m.

M.L.W.N.
CHART DATUM
M.L.W.S.
L.W.Hts.m.

TIME ZONE -0100
(German Standard Time)
Subtract 1 hour for UT
For German Summer Time add
ONE hour in **non-shaded areas**

GERMANY – WILHELMSHAVEN

LAT 53°31'N   LONG 8°09'E

TIMES AND HEIGHTS OF HIGH AND LOW WATERS

Dates in amber are **SPRINGS**
Dates in yellow are **NEAPS**

2009

JANUARY

Time	m		Time	m
1 0322	4.8	**16**	0419	5.0
0943	0.6		1041	0.4
TH 1547	4.4	F	1649	4.4
2144	0.7		2244	0.6
2 0355	4.8	**17**	0457	4.9
1015	0.7		1115	0.6
F 1621	4.4	SA	1725	4.4
2217	0.8		2318	0.7
3 0431	4.7	**18**	0535	4.8
1049	0.7		1149	0.8
SA 1656	4.3	SU	1803	4.3
2253	0.9		◑ 2356	0.9
4 0508	4.6	**19**	0618	4.6
1124	0.8		1227	1.0
SU 1735	4.3	M	1847	4.2
◑ 2332	1.0			
5 0551	4.6	**20**	0043	1.1
1206	0.9		0713	4.4
M 1824	4.2	TU	1321	1.2
			1946	4.3
6 0023	1.1	**21**	0148	1.3
0647	4.5		0822	4.4
TU 1303	1.1	W	1433	1.3
1927	4.2		2059	4.4
7 0131	1.2	**22**	0308	1.4
0759	4.5		0939	4.4
W 1415	1.1	TH	1552	1.3
2041	4.3		2211	4.6
8 0251	1.2	**23**	0426	1.3
0919	4.5		1050	4.5
TH 1534	1.1	F	1700	1.2
2159	4.5		2312	4.6
9 0413	1.0	**24**	0531	1.1
1037	4.6		1147	4.5
F 1651	1.0	SA	1756	1.1
2311	4.7			
10 0530	0.9	**25**	0002	4.8
1148	4.7		0624	1.0
SA 1801	0.9	SU	1235	4.6
			1843	1.0
11 0014	4.9	**26**	0046	4.8
0639	0.7		0709	0.8
SU 1251	4.7	M	1317	4.6
○ 1902	0.8		● 1924	0.8
12 0110	5.0	**27**	0126	4.9
0737	0.6		0749	0.7
M 1347	4.7	TU	1357	4.6
1955	0.7		2002	0.7
13 0202	5.1	**28**	0202	4.9
0832	0.5		0826	0.6
TU 1439	4.7	W	1432	4.6
2046	0.6		2035	0.7
14 0252	5.1	**29**	0235	4.9
0923	0.5		0858	0.5
W 1528	4.6	TH	1502	4.5
2132	0.5		2103	0.6
15 0338	5.1	**30**	0306	4.9
1006	0.4		0927	0.5
TH 1611	4.5	F	1531	4.5
2210	0.5		2130	0.5
		31	0338	4.8
			0957	0.5
		SA	1602	4.5
			2202	0.6

FEBRUARY

Time	m		Time	m
1 0414	4.8	**16**	0501	4.8
1030	0.6		1110	0.7
SU 1635	4.5	M	1716	4.4
2236	0.7		◑ 2315	0.8
2 0447	4.8	**17**	0534	4.5
1100	0.7		1136	1.0
M 1706	4.4	TU	1752	4.3
2306	0.8		2350	1.0
3 0521	4.6	**18**	0618	4.3
1131	0.8		1217	1.2
TU 1743	4.3	W	1844	4.2
◑ 2344	0.9			
4 0609	4.5	**19**	0047	1.2
1218	1.0		0725	4.2
W 1841	4.3	TH	1327	1.4
			2001	4.2
5 0047	1.1	**20**	0211	1.4
0723	4.4		0851	4.1
TH 1332	1.2	F	1457	1.4
2003	4.3		2127	4.4
6 0216	1.2	**21**	0344	1.3
0854	4.4		1016	4.2
F 1504	1.2	SA	1622	1.3
2134	4.5		2243	4.5
7 0352	1.0	**22**	0502	1.0
1025	4.5		1124	4.4
SA 1635	1.1	SU	1729	1.1
2257	4.7		2340	4.7
8 0520	0.8	**23**	0600	0.8
1143	4.6		1216	4.5
SU 1752	0.9	M	1819	0.9
9 0006	4.8	**24**	0025	4.8
0632	0.7		0646	0.7
M 1247	4.6	TU	1258	4.6
○ 1855	0.8		1902	0.8
10 0102	5.0	**25**	0105	4.8
0730	0.5		0726	0.6
TU 1340	4.7	W	1336	4.6
1947	0.6		● 1939	0.6
11 0152	5.1	**26**	0141	4.9
0820	0.4		0802	0.5
W 1427	4.7	TH	1410	4.6
2033	0.5		2012	0.5
12 0238	5.1	**27**	0213	4.9
0905	0.3		0834	0.4
TH 1509	4.7	F	1440	4.6
2114	0.4		2043	0.4
13 0320	5.1	**28**	0244	4.9
0944	0.3		0904	0.4
F 1546	4.6	SA	1509	4.6
2148	0.4		2112	0.4
14 0357	5.0			
1016	0.4			
SA 1618	4.6			
2218	0.4			
15 0430	4.9			
1043	0.5			
SU 1647	4.5			
2247	0.6			

MARCH

Time	m		Time	m
1 0318	4.9	**16**	0401	4.8
0935	0.4		1008	0.5
SU 1541	4.6	M	1611	4.6
2144	0.5		2216	0.5
2 0355	4.8	**17**	0431	4.6
1008	0.5		1031	0.7
M 1613	4.6	TU	1639	4.5
2218	0.5		2241	0.6
3 0430	4.8	**18**	0500	4.4
1039	0.6		1055	0.9
TU 1644	4.6	W	1710	4.4
2248	0.6		◑ 2312	0.9
4 0506	4.6	**19**	0538	4.2
1108	0.8		1128	1.1
W 1720	4.5	TH	1757	4.2
◑ 2324	0.7			
5 0554	4.4	**20**	0001	1.1
1154	1.0		0637	4.0
TH 1819	4.4	F	1229	1.3
			1909	4.2
6 0028	1.0	**21**	0120	1.2
0709	4.3		0802	3.9
F 1312	1.2	SA	1359	1.4
1946	4.4		2039	4.2
7 0203	1.1	**22**	0256	1.1
0846	4.3		0934	4.0
SA 1452	1.2	SU	1534	1.2
2124	4.5		2204	4.4
8 0346	1.0	**23**	0421	0.9
1021	4.4		1050	4.2
SU 1626	1.0	M	1649	1.0
2250	4.7		2307	4.6
9 0513	0.7	**24**	0523	0.7
1138	4.5		1145	4.4
M 1742	0.8	TU	1743	0.8
2356	4.9		2353	4.7
10 0620	0.5	**25**	0610	0.5
1236	4.6		1227	4.5
TU 1841	0.5	W	1828	0.7
11 0050	5.0	**26**	0034	4.8
0713	0.4		0651	0.4
W 1325	4.6	TH	1305	4.6
○ 1930	0.5		● 1907	0.5
12 0136	5.0	**27**	0112	4.9
0758	0.3		0729	0.4
TH 1406	4.7	F	1340	4.7
2012	0.4		1942	0.4
13 0218	5.0	**28**	0146	4.9
0838	0.3		0803	0.3
F 1442	4.7	SA	1413	4.7
2049	0.3		2017	0.4
14 0256	5.0	**29**	0221	4.9
0913	0.4		0836	0.4
SA 1514	4.7	SU	1445	4.7
2121	0.3		2051	0.4
15 0330	4.9	**30**	0258	4.8
0943	0.4		0911	0.4
SU 1543	4.7	M	1519	4.7
2149	0.3		2127	0.4
		31	0339	4.8
			0947	0.5
		TU	1555	4.7
			2204	0.4

APRIL

Time	m		Time	m
1 0421	4.7	**16**	0436	4.3
1022	0.6		1024	0.8
W 1632	4.6	TH	1644	4.5
2241	0.5		2249	0.7
2 0504	4.5	**17**	0511	4.1
1059	0.8		1057	1.0
TH 1715	4.6	F	1725	4.3
◑ 2324	0.6		◑ 2332	0.9
3 0557	4.3	**18**	0602	4.0
1150	1.0		1148	1.1
F 1817	4.5	SA	1827	4.2
4 0030	0.8	**19**	0038	1.0
0712	4.2		0716	3.9
SA 1308	1.1	SU	1306	1.2
1943	4.5		1949	4.2
5 0202	0.9	**20**	0203	0.9
0846	4.2		0842	3.9
SU 1445	1.1	M	1436	1.1
2117	4.6		2113	4.3
6 0340	0.8	**21**	0327	0.7
1015	4.3		1000	4.1
M 1615	0.9	TU	1554	0.9
2238	4.7		2220	4.5
7 0459	0.6	**22**	0432	0.5
1124	4.4		1059	4.3
TU 1723	0.7	W	1654	0.7
2339	4.8		2311	4.6
8 0556	0.4	**23**	0523	0.5
1215	4.6		1146	4.5
W 1816	0.6	TH	1744	0.6
			2355	4.8
9 0028	4.9	**24**	0609	0.4
0643	0.3		1227	4.6
TH 1259	4.7	F	1830	0.6
○ 1903	0.5			
10 0113	4.9	**25**	0038	4.8
0727	0.3		0651	0.4
F 1339	4.7	SA	1307	4.7
1946	0.4		● 1910	0.4
11 0155	4.9	**26**	0118	4.9
0806	0.4		0731	0.4
SA 1413	4.7	SU	1344	4.8
2022	0.4		1950	0.4
12 0231	4.9	**27**	0159	4.9
0839	0.4		0810	0.4
SU 1442	4.8	M	1423	4.8
2052	0.3		2032	0.4
13 0303	4.8	**28**	0244	4.8
0908	0.5		0851	0.4
M 1511	4.7	TU	1503	4.8
2120	0.3		2115	0.3
14 0334	4.6	**29**	0331	4.7
0933	0.5		0933	0.5
TU 1541	4.6	W	1545	4.8
2148	0.4		2158	0.4
15 0405	4.4	**30**	0419	4.6
0958	0.6		1014	0.6
W 1612	4.6	TH	1629	4.7
2217	0.6		2243	0.5

Chart Datum: 2·26 metres below Normal Null (German reference level)
HAT is 4·5 metres above Chart Datum

TIDES

TIDES

TIME ZONE -0100
(German Standard Time)
Subtract 1 hour for UT
For German Summer Time add
ONE hour in **non-shaded areas**

GERMANY – WILHELMSHAVEN

LAT 53°31′N   LONG 8°09′E

TIMES AND HEIGHTS OF HIGH AND LOW WATERS

Dates in amber are **SPRINGS**
Dates in yellow are NEAPS

2009

MAY

Time	m		Time	m
1 0509	4.4	**16** 0454	4.2
1058	0.8	1040	0.8
F 1719	4.7	SA 1705	4.5
2333	0.5	2315	0.7
2 0606	4.3	**17** 0537	4.0
1153	0.9	1122	0.9
SA 1821	4.6	SU 1755	4.3
3 0037	0.6	**18** 0005	0.7
0716	4.1	0635	3.9
SU 1305	1.0	M 1221	1.0
1939	4.6	☽ 1900	4.3
4 0157	0.7	**19** 0111	0.7
0838	4.2	0746	3.9
M 1430	0.9	TU 1336	1.0
☽ 2103	4.6	2014	4.3
5 0322	0.6	**20** 0225	0.7
0956	4.3	0859	4.1
TU 1551	0.8	W 1452	0.9
2216	4.7	2123	4.5
6 0431	0.5	**21** 0332	0.6
1058	4.4	1003	4.2
W 1653	0.6	TH 1558	0.8
2312	4.8	2222	4.6
7 0522	0.4	**22** 0430	0.5
1144	4.6	1058	4.4
TH 1743	0.6	F 1656	0.7
		2314	4.7
8 0000	4.8	**23** 0525	0.5
0608	0.4	1148	4.6
F 1226	4.7	SA 1751	0.6
1831	0.6		
9 0046	4.8	**24** 0005	4.8
0654	0.5	0616	0.5
SA 1308	4.7	SU 1235	4.8
1917	0.5	1841	0.5
10 0130	4.8	**25** 0055	4.8
0735	0.5	0703	0.5
SU 1344	4.8	M 1320	4.9
1955	0.4	1929	0.4
11 0207	4.7	**26** 0145	4.8
0809	0.5	0750	0.5
M 1416	4.8	TU 1404	4.9
○ 2026	0.4	● 2019	0.4
12 0240	4.6	**27** 0236	4.7
0838	0.5	0839	0.5
TU 1447	4.7	W 1454	4.9
2057	0.4	2111	0.3
13 0312	4.5	**28** 0329	4.6
0906	0.6	0927	0.5
W 1520	4.7	TH 1541	4.9
2129	0.4	2159	0.3
14 0346	4.4	**29** 0420	4.5
0934	0.6	1012	0.5
TH 1553	4.6	F 1629	4.8
2202	0.5	2246	0.3
15 0419	4.3	**30** 0510	4.4
1005	0.7	1058	0.6
F 1627	4.6	SA 1719	4.8
2236	0.7	2336	0.4
		31 0605	4.3
		1150	0.7
		SU 1816	4.7

JUNE

Time	m		Time	m
1 0033	0.5	**16** 0559	4.1
0706	4.2	1147	0.8
M 1251	0.7	TU 1816	4.4
1922	4.7	☽	
2 0137	0.5	**17** 0026	0.6
0812	4.2	0652	4.1
TU 1401	0.8	W 1243	0.9
☽ 2033	4.6	1916	4.4
3 0246	0.6	**18** 0125	0.7
0919	4.3	0756	4.1
W 1511	0.8	TH 1350	0.9
2141	4.7	2024	4.5
4 0352	0.6	**19** 0231	0.7
1019	4.5	0903	4.3
TH 1614	0.7	F 1501	0.9
2239	4.7	2131	4.5
5 0446	0.6	**20** 0339	0.7
1109	4.6	1009	4.4
F 1709	0.7	SA 1610	0.8
2331	4.7	2236	4.6
6 0535	0.6	**21** 0445	0.7
1154	4.7	1111	4.6
SA 1801	0.5	SU 1717	0.7
		2339	4.7
7 0020	4.7	**22** 0548	0.7
0625	0.7	1209	4.8
SU 1239	4.7	M 1820	0.6
1851	0.6		
8 0106	4.7	**23** 0040	4.8
0709	0.6	0646	0.6
M 1320	4.8	TU 1303	4.9
1933	0.5	1917	0.5
9 0147	4.6	**24** 0136	4.7
0745	0.6	0740	0.6
TU 1356	4.8	W 1355	5.0
○ 2008	0.5	2013	0.4
10 0223	4.6	**25** 0232	4.7
0819	0.6	0833	0.5
W 1431	4.8	TH 1447	5.0
2043	0.5	● 2109	0.3
11 0257	4.5	**26** 0325	4.6
0851	0.6	0923	0.5
TH 1505	4.8	F 1536	5.0
2118	0.5	2158	0.2
12 0331	4.4	**27** 0415	4.5
0921	0.6	1007	0.4
F 1539	4.8	SA 1623	4.9
2151	0.5	2241	0.2
13 0404	4.3	**28** 0501	4.4
0951	0.6	1050	0.5
SA 1613	4.7	SU 1709	4.9
2225	0.6	2326	0.3
14 0438	4.3	**29** 0548	4.3
1026	0.7	1135	0.6
SU 1648	4.6	M 1758	4.8
2300	0.6		
15 0515	4.2	**30** 0012	0.5
1104	0.8	0637	4.3
M 1728	4.5	TU 1223	0.6
2339	0.6	1850	4.7

JULY

Time	m		Time	m
1 0102	0.6	**16** 0605	4.2
0729	4.3	1200	0.8
W 1318	0.6	TH 1826	4.5
1949	4.6		
2 0158	0.7	**17** 0033	0.8
0828	4.3	0658	4.2
TH 1422	0.9	F 1257	1.0
2055	4.6	1931	4.5
3 0304	0.9	**18** 0137	0.9
0932	4.4	0808	4.3
F 1531	1.0	SA 1411	1.0
2203	4.6	☽ 2048	4.4
4 0410	0.9	**19** 0255	0.9
1033	4.6	0927	4.4
SA 1638	0.9	SU 1533	0.9
☽ 2304	4.6	2208	4.5
5 0508	0.9	**20** 0415	0.8
1127	4.7	1044	4.6
SU 1737	0.8	M 1655	0.8
2359	4.6	2324	4.6
6 0601	0.8	**21** 0531	0.8
1215	4.8	1152	4.8
M 1830	0.7	TU 1809	0.6
7 0047	4.6	**22** 0031	4.7
0649	0.8	0637	0.7
TU 1259	4.8	W 1252	5.0
1916	0.7	1913	0.5
8 0130	4.6	**23** 0130	4.7
0730	0.7	0734	0.6
W 1340	4.8	TH 1345	5.1
1955	0.6	2009	0.4
9 0208	4.6	**24** 0224	4.7
0807	0.6	0827	0.5
TH 1417	4.9	F 1436	5.1
2033	0.6	2101	0.3
10 0244	4.6	**25** 0314	4.7
0841	0.6	0914	0.4
F 1451	4.9	SA 1524	5.1
2107	0.5	2147	0.2
11 0315	4.5	**26** 0359	4.6
0909	0.5	0955	0.3
SA 1522	4.9	SU 1607	5.0
○ 2137	0.5	● 2226	0.2
12 0345	4.4	**27** 0439	4.5
0936	0.5	1032	0.3
SU 1554	4.8	M 1648	4.9
2207	0.5	2303	0.4
13 0417	4.4	**28** 0517	4.4
1008	0.6	1109	0.5
M 1628	4.7	TU 1728	4.8
2241	0.5	2340	0.6
14 0451	4.3	**29** 0555	4.4
1045	0.7	1147	0.7
TU 1703	4.7	W 1810	4.7
2314	0.6		
15 0526	4.3	**30** 0018	0.8
1120	0.7	0637	4.3
W 1740	4.6	TH 1230	0.8
2348	0.6	1900	4.5
		31 0104	1.0
		0730	4.3
		F 1328	1.0
		2004	4.4

AUGUST

Time	m		Time	m
1 0210	1.2	**16** 0058	1.1
0840	4.4	0729	4.3
SA 1445	1.2	SU 1338	1.1
2122	4.4	2021	4.3
2 0329	1.2	**17** 0227	1.1
0956	4.5	0859	4.4
SU 1607	1.1	M 1514	1.0
☽ 2237	4.4	☽ 2154	4.4
3 0443	1.1	**18** 0400	1.0
1102	4.6	1027	4.6
M 1717	1.0	TU 1645	0.8
2339	4.5	2315	4.5
4 0542	1.0	**19** 0522	0.9
1155	4.7	1140	4.8
TU 1813	0.8	W 1802	0.6
5 0029	4.5	**20** 0022	4.6
0631	0.9	0629	0.7
W 1239	4.8	TH 1240	5.0
1859	0.7	1905	0.5
6 0111	4.6	**21** 0119	4.7
0714	0.7	0725	0.6
TH 1320	4.8	F 1332	5.0
1939	0.6	1957	0.3
7 0150	4.6	**22** 0208	4.7
0751	0.6	0813	0.4
F 1358	4.9	SA 1419	5.1
2016	0.5	2043	0.3
8 0224	4.6	**23** 0252	4.7
0825	0.6	0856	0.3
SA 1430	4.9	SU 1503	5.1
2048	0.5	2126	0.3
9 0253	4.6	**24** 0332	4.7
0852	0.5	0934	0.3
SU 1459	4.9	M 1542	5.0
○ 2115	0.4	2201	0.3
10 0320	4.5	**25** 0406	4.6
0917	0.5	1007	0.4
M 1529	4.8	TU 1619	4.9
2143	0.5	● 2231	0.5
11 0350	4.5	**26** 0439	4.5
0947	0.5	1038	0.5
TU 1603	4.8	W 1654	4.7
2216	0.5	2302	0.7
12 0423	4.5	**27** 0510	4.5
1023	0.6	1110	0.7
W 1637	4.7	TH 1729	4.5
2248	0.6	2332	1.0
13 0454	4.4	**28** 0546	4.4
1055	0.7	1145	0.9
TH 1709	4.6	F 1812	4.3
2316	0.7		
14 0526	4.4	**29** 0010	1.2
1127	0.8	0635	4.3
F 1750	4.5	SA 1237	1.1
2353	0.9	1913	4.2
15 0615	4.3	**30** 0113	1.4
1218	1.0	0746	4.2
SA 1854	4.4	SU 1356	1.3
		2036	4.1
		31 0240	1.5
		0913	4.4
		M 1530	1.3
		2203	4.2

Chart Datum: 2·26 metres below Normal Null (German reference level)
HAT is 4·5 metres above Chart Datum

TIME ZONE -0100
(German Standard Time)
Subtract 1 hour for UT
For German Summer Time add
ONE hour in **non-shaded areas**

GERMANY – WILHELMSHAVEN

LAT 53°31'N   LONG 8°09'E

TIMES AND HEIGHTS OF HIGH AND LOW WATERS

Dates in amber are **SPRINGS**
Dates in yellow are **NEAPS**

2009

SEPTEMBER

Time	m		Time	m
1 0409	1.3	**16** 0352	1.2	
1032	4.5	1015	4.6	
TU 1652	1.1	W 1641	0.8	
2315	4.3	2307	4.4	
2 0518	1.1	**17** 0512	0.9	
1131	4.7	1126	4.8	
W 1750	0.8	TH 1751	0.6	
3 0005	4.4	**18** 0008	4.6	
0607	0.9	0614	0.7	
TH 1214	4.7	F 1222	4.9	
1834	0.7	● 1847	0.5	
4 0045	4.5	**19** 0058	4.6	
0648	0.7	0706	0.6	
F 1252	4.8	SA 1310	5.0	
○ 1912	0.6	1934	0.4	
5 0121	4.5	**20** 0143	4.7	
0725	0.6	0751	0.5	
SA 1329	4.8	SU 1355	5.0	
1947	0.5	2017	0.4	
6 0155	4.6	**21** 0222	4.7	
0759	0.6	0832	0.4	
SU 1401	4.9	M 1436	5.0	
2019	0.5	2056	0.4	
7 0224	4.6	**22** 0257	4.7	
0828	0.5	0907	0.4	
M 1431	4.9	TU 1513	4.9	
2047	0.5	2129	0.5	
8 0252	4.6	**23** 0330	4.7	
0856	0.5	0938	0.6	
TU 1502	4.8	W 1547	4.8	
2116	0.5	2157	0.6	
9 0321	4.6	**24** 0400	4.6	
0925	0.5	1007	0.6	
W 1537	4.7	TH 1620	4.6	
2148	0.6	2222	0.8	
10 0353	4.6	**25** 0430	4.5	
0959	0.6	1036	0.7	
TH 1612	4.6	F 1653	4.4	
2220	0.7	2249	1.0	
11 0425	4.5	**26** 0503	4.4	
1032	0.7	1108	0.9	
F 1647	4.6	SA 1731	4.2	
2250	0.8	◑ 2324	1.3	
12 0459	4.5	**27** 0548	4.3	
1107	0.8	1155	1.2	
SA 1730	4.4	SU 1826	4.0	
◑ 2330	1.0			
13 0550	4.3	**28** 0021	1.5	
1200	1.0	0655	4.2	
SU 1837	4.2	M 1309	1.4	
		1946	3.9	
14 0038	1.3	**29** 0146	1.6	
0709	4.3	0822	4.3	
M 1326	1.1	TU 1442	1.3	
2009	4.2	2116	4.0	
15 0214	1.3	**30** 0321	1.4	
0845	4.5	0948	4.4	
TU 1509	1.1	W 1610	1.1	
2146	4.3	2234	4.2	

OCTOBER

Time	m		Time	m
1 0437	1.1	**16** 0453	0.9	
1053	4.5	1104	4.8	
TH 1712	0.8	F 1729	0.6	
2328	4.3	2344	4.5	
2 0530	0.9	**17** 0549	0.7	
1137	4.6	1156	4.9	
F 1755	0.6	SA 1818	0.5	
3 0008	4.4	**18** 0029	4.6	
0611	0.8	0638	0.7	
SA 1215	4.7	SU 1243	4.9	
1833	0.6	● 1904	0.5	
4 0043	4.5	**19** 0111	4.7	
0650	0.7	0724	0.6	
SU 1252	4.8	M 1328	4.9	
○ 1910	0.5	1947	0.5	
5 0118	4.6	**20** 0149	4.7	
0726	0.6	0804	0.6	
M 1327	4.8	TU 1409	4.9	
1944	0.5	2024	0.6	
6 0151	4.7	**21** 0223	4.8	
0801	0.6	0838	0.5	
TU 1401	4.8	W 1444	4.8	
2017	0.6	2056	0.7	
7 0222	4.7	**22** 0255	4.7	
0834	0.6	0910	0.5	
W 1437	4.6	TH 1518	4.6	
2050	0.6	2123	0.7	
8 0254	4.7	**23** 0327	4.6	
0907	0.6	0939	0.6	
TH 1515	4.7	F 1551	4.5	
2124	0.7	2148	0.8	
9 0329	4.7	**24** 0359	4.6	
0941	0.6	1010	0.7	
F 1555	4.6	SA 1624	4.3	
2159	0.8	2216	1.0	
10 0405	4.7	**25** 0432	4.6	
1019	0.6	1043	0.9	
SA 1637	4.5	SU 1659	4.1	
2235	1.0	2250	1.2	
11 0447	4.6	**26** 0512	4.4	
1101	0.8	1125	1.1	
SU 1726	4.3	M 1747	4.0	
◑ 2322	1.2	◑ 2339	1.4	
12 0542	4.5	**27** 0609	4.3	
1200	1.0	1225	1.2	
M 1833	4.2	TU 1854	3.9	
13 0032	1.3	**28** 0050	1.5	
0700	4.5	0725	4.2	
TU 1324	1.1	W 1345	1.3	
2002	4.2	2016	3.9	
14 0205	1.4	**29** 0218	1.4	
0833	4.6	0848	4.3	
W 1502	1.0	TH 1509	1.1	
2134	4.3	2134	4.1	
15 0339	1.2	**30** 0338	1.2	
0959	4.7	0958	4.5	
TH 1628	0.8	F 1615	0.9	
2249	4.4	2235	4.3	
		31 0437	1.0	
		1049	4.6	
		SA 1705	0.7	
		2320	4.4	

NOVEMBER

Time	m		Time	m
1 0525	0.9	**16** 0607	0.8	
1131	4.7	1216	4.8	
SU 1748	0.7	M 1833	0.8	
		●		
2 0001	4.5	**17** 0039	4.7	
0610	0.8	0656	0.8	
M 1213	4.7	TU 1303	4.8	
○ 1830	0.7	1918	0.8	
3 0040	4.6	**18** 0119	4.8	
0652	0.7	0738	0.7	
TU 1254	4.8	W 1344	4.7	
1910	0.7	1955	0.7	
4 0118	4.7	**19** 0154	4.8	
0733	0.7	0813	0.7	
W 1334	4.8	TH 1420	4.7	
1949	0.7	2027	0.8	
5 0156	4.8	**20** 0227	4.8	
0814	0.7	0846	0.7	
TH 1417	4.8	F 1455	4.6	
2030	0.7	2058	0.8	
6 0235	4.9	**21** 0302	4.7	
0856	0.7	0920	0.7	
F 1502	4.7	SA 1529	4.4	
2110	0.8	2126	0.8	
7 0315	4.8	**22** 0336	4.7	
0936	0.7	0952	0.7	
SA 1548	4.6	SU 1602	4.3	
2149	0.8	2154	0.9	
8 0357	4.7	**23** 0410	4.6	
1017	0.7	1026	0.9	
SU 1634	4.4	M 1635	4.2	
2231	1.0	2227	1.1	
9 0443	4.7	**24** 0446	4.5	
1104	0.8	1102	1.0	
M 1726	4.3	TU 1714	4.1	
◐ 2320	1.1	◐ 2307	1.2	
10 0540	4.6	**25** 0530	4.4	
1202	0.9	1147	1.1	
TU 1830	4.2	W 1805	4.0	
11 0026	1.2	**26** 0000	1.3	
0651	4.6	0628	4.3	
W 1316	1.0	TH 1246	1.1	
1948	4.1	1910	4.0	
12 0147	1.3	**27** 0109	1.4	
0813	4.6	0738	4.3	
TH 1441	1.0	F 1356	1.1	
2108	4.3	2023	4.1	
13 0311	1.2	**28** 0226	1.3	
0931	4.7	0849	4.4	
F 1558	0.9	SA 1506	1.0	
2218	4.4	2130	4.2	
14 0421	1.0	**29** 0335	1.1	
1035	4.8	0951	4.5	
SA 1657	0.7	SU 1606	0.9	
2311	4.6	2227	4.4	
15 0517	0.9	**30** 0434	1.0	
1127	4.8	1045	4.6	
SU 1745	0.7	M 1701	0.9	
2356	4.7	2318	4.6	

DECEMBER

Time	m		Time	m
1 0529	0.9	**16** 0013	4.8	
1136	4.7	0632	1.0	
TU 1752	0.8	W 1242	4.7	
		● 1854	0.9	
2 0006	4.7	**17** 0056	4.8	
0621	0.8	0717	0.9	
W 1226	4.7	TH 1325	4.7	
○ 1841	0.8	1934	0.9	
3 0051	4.8	**18** 0133	4.8	
0709	0.8	0755	0.8	
TH 1315	4.7	F 1403	4.6	
1928	0.8	2008	0.8	
4 0137	4.9	**19** 0209	4.8	
0759	0.7	0831	0.7	
F 1406	4.7	SA 1439	4.6	
2017	0.8	2042	0.8	
5 0224	5.0	**20** 0245	4.9	
0851	0.7	0907	0.7	
SA 1457	4.7	SU 1512	4.5	
2104	0.8	2112	0.8	
6 0310	5.0	**21** 0319	4.8	
0938	0.6	0939	0.7	
SU 1545	4.6	M 1543	4.4	
2147	0.8	2139	0.8	
7 0354	4.9	**22** 0351	4.7	
1020	0.6	1010	0.8	
M 1633	4.4	TU 1613	4.3	
2229	0.8	2208	0.9	
8 0441	4.9	**23** 0423	4.7	
1105	0.7	1041	0.9	
TU 1722	4.3	W 1646	4.3	
2316	0.9	2242	1.0	
9 0533	4.8	**24** 0458	4.6	
1156	0.7	1114	0.9	
W 1818	4.2	TH 1723	4.2	
◐		◐ 2320	1.1	
10 0011	1.0	**25** 0539	4.5	
0633	4.7	1154	1.0	
TH 1255	0.8	F 1810	4.1	
1920	4.2			
11 0116	1.1	**26** 0009	1.2	
0741	4.7	0633	4.4	
F 1403	0.9	SA 1247	1.1	
2027	4.3	1910	4.1	
12 0228	1.1	**27** 0113	1.3	
0853	4.7	0739	4.4	
SA 1514	1.0	SU 1353	1.2	
2134	4.4	2020	4.2	
13 0339	1.1	**28** 0227	1.3	
1000	4.7	0851	4.4	
SU 1619	1.0	M 1504	1.1	
2234	4.5	2131	4.4	
14 0442	1.1	**29** 0340	1.1	
1059	4.7	1001	4.5	
M 1715	1.0	TU 1614	1.0	
2326	4.7	2237	4.5	
15 0539	1.0	**30** 0450	1.0	
1153	4.7	1106	4.6	
TU 1807	1.0	W 1720	1.0	
		2338	4.7	
		31 0555	0.9	
		1207	4.7	
		TH 1821	0.9	
		○		

Chart Datum: 2·26 metres below Normal Null (German reference level)
HAT is 4·5 metres above Chart Datum

TIDES

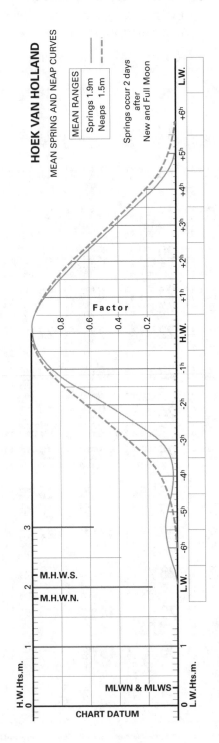

HOEK VAN HOLLAND

MEAN SPRING AND NEAP CURVES

MEAN RANGES

Springs 1.9m
Neaps 1.5m

Springs occur 2 days
after
New and Full Moon

Note - Double LWs often occur.
The predictions are for the lower
LW which is usually the first.

TIME ZONE -0100
(Dutch Standard Time)
Subtract 1 hour for UT
For Dutch Summer Time add
ONE hour in **non-shaded areas**

NETHERLANDS – HOEK VAN HOLLAND

LAT 51°59′N   LONG 4°07′E

TIMES AND HEIGHTS OF HIGH AND LOW WATERS

Dates in amber are **SPRINGS**
Dates in yellow are **NEAPS**

2009

JANUARY

Time	m		Time	m
1 0040	0.5	**16** 0157	0.5
0536	2.0	0615	2.1
TH 1045	0.2	F 1125	0.1
1749	2.2	1835	2.3
2 0125	0.5	**17** 0247	0.6
0610	2.0	0706	2.1
F 1126	0.2	SA 1224	0.1
1825	2.2	1925	2.2
3 0157	0.5	**18** 0136	0.5
0645	2.0	0749	2.0
SA 1205	0.1	SU 1330	0.1
1916	2.2	☽ 2026	2.0
4 0220	0.6	**19** 0226	0.5
0735	2.0	0845	1.9
SU 1254	0.1	M 1435	0.2
☽ 2005	2.1	2125	1.9
5 0227	0.6	**20** 0315	0.5
0840	1.9	1000	1.8
M 1354	0.2	TU 1604	0.3
2116	2.1	2244	1.8
6 0315	0.5	**21** 0445	0.5
0946	1.9	1125	1.8
TU 1505	0.2	W 1714	0.4
2226	2.0		
7 0416	0.5	**22** 0003	1.8
1055	1.9	0534	0.4
W 1625	0.3	TH 1230	1.8
2336	2.0	1805	0.5
8 0504	0.5	**23** 0110	1.9
1200	2.0	0635	0.4
TH 1735	0.3	F 1330	1.9
		1904	0.5
9 0035	2.0	**24** 0154	1.9
0610	0.4	0720	0.3
F 1300	2.1	SA 1404	2.0
1824	0.4	1950	0.5
10 0129	2.1	**25** 0239	2.0
0656	0.4	0745	0.3
SA 1349	2.2	SU 1445	2.1
1914	0.4	2020	0.5
11 0221	2.1	**26** 0316	2.0
0736	0.3	0819	0.3
SU 1438	2.3	M 1520	2.2
○ 2235	0.5	● 2050	0.5
12 0308	2.1	**27** 0334	2.1
0816	0.2	0839	0.2
M 1526	2.4	TU 1544	2.2
2336	0.5	2240	0.5
13 0355	2.1	**28** 0404	2.1
0855	0.1	0903	0.2
TU 1615	2.4	W 1618	2.3
		2334	0.5
14 0014	0.5	**29** 0445	2.1
0445	2.1	0939	0.2
W 0939	0.1	TH 1651	2.3
1657	2.4		
15 0116	0.5	**30** 0020	0.4
0528	2.1	0515	0.1
TH 1029	0.1	F 1016	0.1
1745	2.4	1725	2.2
		31 0100	0.4
		0545	0.1
		SA 1044	0.1
		1802	2.2

FEBRUARY

Time	m		Time	m
1 0145	0.5	**16** 0030	0.4
0620	2.1	0709	2.1
SU 1125	0.1	M 1300	0.2
1839	2.2	◑ 1935	1.9
2 0000	0.5	**17** 0130	0.4
0705	2.1	0754	2.0
M 1213	0.1	TU 1404	0.3
1930	2.1	2023	1.8
3 0039	0.4	**18** 0225	0.4
0755	2.0	0854	1.8
TU 1330	0.1	W 1540	0.4
◑ 2024	2.0	2134	1.6
4 0227	0.4	**19** 0426	0.4
0900	2.0	1025	1.6
W 1454	0.2	TH 1644	0.4
2145	1.9	2345	1.6
5 0334	0.4	**20** 0526	0.3
1026	1.9	1205	1.7
TH 1615	0.3	F 1754	0.4
2303	1.8		
6 0444	0.4	**21** 0050	1.7
1139	1.9	0609	0.3
F 1724	0.4	SA 1305	1.9
		1845	0.5
7 0030	1.8	**22** 0146	1.8
0550	0.4	0654	0.3
SA 1244	2.0	SU 1349	2.0
2055	0.4	2155	0.4
8 0125	1.9	**23** 0213	1.9
0633	0.3	0955	0.3
SU 1338	2.2	M 1425	2.1
2150	0.4	2230	0.5
9 0215	2.0	**24** 0250	2.0
0718	0.2	0755	0.3
M 1427	2.3	TU 1455	2.2
○ 2214	0.5	2250	0.5
10 0259	2.1	**25** 0316	2.0
0755	0.1	0809	0.2
TU 1511	2.4	W 1519	2.2
2316	0.5	● 2240	0.5
11 0338	2.1	**26** 0334	2.1
0835	0.1	0835	0.2
W 1555	2.4	TH 1551	2.3
		2305	0.4
12 0006	0.5	**27** 0416	2.1
0426	2.2	0905	0.1
TH 0915	0.1	F 1625	2.3
1637	2.4	2354	0.4
13 0056	0.5	**28** 0446	2.1
0500	2.2	0939	0.1
F 1006	0.1	SA 1657	2.3
1718	2.3		
14 0146	0.5		
0546	2.2		
SA 1055	0.1		
1806	2.2		
15 0220	0.5		
0625	2.1		
SU 1144	0.1		
1849	2.1		

MARCH

Time	m		Time	m
1 0034	0.4	**16** 0156	0.3
0516	2.1	0556	2.2
SU 1020	0.1	M 1350	0.2
1735	2.2	1815	2.0
2 0120	0.4	**17** 0000	0.3
0551	2.2	0636	2.1
M 1059	0.1	TU 1300	0.3
1816	2.2	1855	1.9
3 0145	0.3	**18** 0040	0.2
0636	2.2	0715	2.0
TU 1155	0.1	W 1344	0.3
1902	2.1	◐ 1935	1.7
4 0004	0.3	**19** 0135	0.2
0719	2.1	0815	1.8
W 1405	0.2	TH 1510	0.4
◑ 1955	1.9	2034	1.5
5 0215	0.3	**20** 0406	0.3
0825	2.0	0934	1.6
TH 1454	0.2	F 1636	0.4
2126	1.7	2220	1.4
6 0305	0.3	**21** 0455	0.2
1005	1.8	1136	1.6
F 1605	0.4	SA 1724	0.4
2254	1.6		
7 0430	0.3	**22** 0005	1.5
1136	1.9	0544	0.2
SA 1920	0.4	SU 1236	1.8
		1825	0.4
8 0014	1.7	**23** 0106	1.7
0524	0.3	0634	0.2
SU 1245	2.0	M 1326	2.0
2044	0.3	2055	0.4
9 0115	1.8	**24** 0134	1.8
0916	0.2	0926	0.2
M 1328	2.2	TU 1349	2.1
2125	0.4	2206	0.3
10 0158	1.9	**25** 0204	1.9
0955	0.2	1005	0.2
TU 1415	2.3	W 1415	2.2
2210	0.4	2225	0.4
11 0238	2.0	**26** 0235	2.0
0735	0.1	0735	0.2
W 1450	2.3	TH 1445	2.2
○ 2234	0.5	● 2240	0.4
12 0319	2.1	**27** 0305	2.1
0816	0.1	0806	0.2
TH 1532	2.3	F 1522	2.3
2330	0.4	2305	0.4
13 0357	2.2	**28** 0339	2.2
0856	0.1	0835	0.1
F 1612	2.3	SA 1555	2.3
		2334	0.4
14 0025	0.4	**29** 0415	2.2
0438	2.2	0916	0.1
SA 1305	0.1	SU 1632	2.2
1656	2.2	2135	0.3
15 0116	0.4	**30** 0452	2.2
0515	2.2	0955	0.1
SU 1325	0.2	M 1711	2.2
1736	2.1	2220	0.3
		31 0527	2.2
		1045	0.2
		TU 1756	2.1
		2303	0.2

APRIL

Time	m		Time	m
1 0611	2.2	**16** 0005	0.2
1330	0.2	0646	1.9
W 1842	1.9	TH 1337	0.4
		1855	1.7
2 0020	0.2	**17** 0105	0.2
0706	2.1	0734	1.8
TH 1354	0.2	F 1450	0.4
◐ 1935	1.7	◐ 1954	1.6
3 0155	0.2	**18** 0341	0.2
0815	1.9	0905	1.7
F 1444	0.3	SA 1605	0.4
2105	1.6	2120	1.5
4 0255	0.2	**19** 0436	0.2
1006	1.9	1019	1.7
SA 1740	0.4	SU 1705	0.4
2244	1.5	2245	1.5
5 0404	0.2	**20** 0536	0.2
1125	1.9	1134	1.8
SU 1905	0.3	M 1810	0.4
6 0005	1.6	**21** 0016	1.6
0745	0.2	0614	0.2
M 1225	2.1	TU 1224	2.0
2025	0.3	2020	0.3
7 0055	1.8	**22** 0055	1.8
0834	0.1	0817	0.2
TU 1315	2.2	W 1306	2.1
2114	0.3	2125	0.3
8 0139	1.9	**23** 0126	1.9
0935	0.1	0931	0.2
W 1351	2.2	TH 1339	2.2
2144	0.4	2155	0.3
9 0215	2.0	**24** 0155	2.0
0716	0.2	0703	0.2
TH 1427	2.2	F 1416	2.2
○ 2226	0.4	2240	0.4
10 0255	2.1	**25** 0232	2.1
0755	0.2	0740	0.2
F 1511	2.2	SA 1451	2.3
2254	0.4	● 2005	0.4
11 0336	2.2	**26** 0309	2.2
1130	0.2	0816	0.2
SA 1551	2.2	SU 1528	2.2
2344	0.3	2034	0.3
12 0408	2.2	**27** 0350	2.3
1205	0.2	0855	0.2
SU 1628	2.1	M 1611	2.2
		2120	0.3
13 0046	0.2	**28** 0429	2.3
0445	2.2	1215	0.2
M 1306	0.2	TU 1656	2.1
1709	2.0	2205	0.2
14 0126	0.2	**29** 0515	2.3
0526	2.1	1245	0.2
TU 1320	0.3	W 1739	1.9
1745	1.9	2254	0.2
15 0135	0.2	**30** 0559	2.2
0601	2.1	1315	0.2
W 1320	0.3	TH 1831	1.8
1826	1.8		

Chart Datum: 0·84 metres below NAP Datum
HAT is 2·4 metres above Chart Datum

TIDES

363

TIME ZONE -0100
(Dutch Standard Time)
Subtract 1 hour for UT
For Dutch Summer Time add
ONE hour in **non-shaded areas**

NETHERLANDS – HOEK VAN HOLLAND

LAT 51°59'N   LONG 4°07'E

TIMES AND HEIGHTS OF HIGH AND LOW WATERS

Dates in amber are **SPRINGS**
Dates in yellow are **NEAPS**

2009

MAY

Day	Time	m		Day	Time	m
1 F	0020 / 0658 / 1355 / 1944	0.1 / 2.1 / 0.4 / 1.7		**16** SA	0024 / 0715 / 1430 / 1924	0.1 / 1.9 / 0.4 / 1.7
2 SA	0135 / 0815 / 1500 / 2110	0.1 / 2.0 / 0.3 / 1.6		**17** SU	0130 / 0826 / 1527 / 2035	0.1 / 1.8 / 0.4 / 1.6
3 SU	0229 / 0955 / 1745 / 2236	0.1 / 2.0 / 0.3 / 1.6		**18** M	0354 / 0923 / 1630 / ◑ 2145	0.2 / 1.8 / 0.4 / 1.6
4 M	0334 / 1054 / 1906 / ◔ 2335	0.1 / 2.0 / 0.3 / 1.7		**19** TU	0505 / 1036 / 1715 / 2256	0.2 / 1.9 / 0.4 / 1.7
5 TU	0715 / 1159 / 2015	0.1 / 2.1 / 0.3		**20** W	0550 / 1129 / 1850 / 2349	0.2 / 2.0 / 0.4 / 1.8
6 W	0030 / 0826 / 1244 / 2105	1.8 / 0.1 / 2.1 / 0.3		**21** TH	0524 / 1214 / 2045	0.2 / 2.1 / 0.3
7 TH	0111 / 0915 / 1328 / 2115	1.9 / 0.2 / 2.1 / 0.4		**22** F	0039 / 0553 / 1306 / 2136	1.9 / 0.2 / 2.2 / 0.3
8 F	0155 / 0659 / 1416 / 2154	2.0 / 0.2 / 2.1 / 0.4		**23** SA	0125 / 0640 / 1346 / 1904	2.0 / 0.2 / 2.2 / 0.3
9 SA	0231 / 0744 / 1450 / 2004	2.1 / 0.3 / 2.1 / 0.3		**24** SU	0206 / 0714 / 1428 / 1945	2.1 / 0.2 / 2.2 / 0.3
10 SU	0311 / 1040 / 1535 / 2336	2.1 / 0.3 / 2.0 / 0.2		**25** M	0247 / 0759 / 1511 / 2021	2.2 / 0.2 / 2.1 / 0.2
11 M	0349 / 1127 / 1611 / ○	2.2 / 0.4 / 2.0		**26** TU	0332 / 0845 / 1555 / ● 2108	2.3 / 0.3 / 2.1 / 0.2
12 TU	0004 / 0429 / 1224 / 1649	0.2 / 2.2 / 0.3 / 1.9		**27** W	0415 / 1220 / 1640 / 2155	2.3 / 0.3 / 2.0 / 0.1
13 W	0044 / 0505 / 1247 / 1726	0.1 / 2.1 / 0.4 / 1.9		**28** TH	0501 / 1300 / 1735 / 2249	2.3 / 0.3 / 1.9 / 0.1
14 TH	0107 / 0546 / 1310 / 1800	0.1 / 2.0 / 0.4 / 1.8		**29** F	0555 / 1337 / 1835 / 2354	2.2 / 0.3 / 1.8 / 0.0
15 F	0000 / 0626 / 1337 / 1840	0.1 / 2.0 / 0.4 / 1.8		**30** SA	0655 / 1437 / 1935	2.2 / 0.3 / 1.8
				31 SU	0105 / 0804 / 1604 / 2046	0.0 / 2.1 / 0.4 / 1.8

JUNE

Day	Time	m		Day	Time	m
1 M	0204 / 0845 / 1705 / 2150	0.0 / 2.1 / 0.4 / 1.7		**16** TU	0134 / 0920 / 1520 / ◐ 2106	0.1 / 2.1 / 0.4 / 1.8
2 TU	0304 / 1025 / 1835 / ◐ 2255	0.1 / 2.0 / 0.3 / 1.8		**17** W	0225 / 0946 / 1600 / 2206	0.1 / 2.0 / 0.4 / 1.8
3 W	0634 / 1130 / 1930 / 2356	0.1 / 2.0 / 0.3 / 1.8		**18** TH	0330 / 1035 / 1635 / 2306	0.2 / 2.0 / 0.4 / 1.8
4 TH	0734 / 1226 / 2035	0.2 / 2.0 / 0.3		**19** F	0425 / 1136 / 1714	0.2 / 2.0 / 0.4
5 F	0048 / 0820 / 1315 / 2107	1.9 / 0.2 / 2.0 / 0.4		**20** SA	0002 / 0530 / 1229 / 1810	1.9 / 0.2 / 2.1 / 0.3
6 SA	0135 / 0704 / 1359 / 1915	2.0 / 0.3 / 2.0 / 0.3		**21** SU	0056 / 0626 / 1326 / 1850	2.0 / 0.2 / 2.1 / 0.3
7 SU	0215 / 0800 / 1446 / 1955	2.0 / 0.3 / 2.0 / 0.3		**22** M	0145 / 0705 / 1411 / 1929	2.1 / 0.3 / 2.1 / 0.3
8 M	0254 / 0850 / 1526 / 2035	2.1 / 0.4 / 2.0 / 0.2		**23** TU	0228 / 0755 / 1457 / 2009	2.2 / 0.3 / 2.1 / 0.2
9 TU	0335 / 1010 / 1606 / ○ 2115	2.1 / 0.4 / 2.0 / 0.2		**24** W	0317 / 1124 / 1547 / 2115	2.3 / 0.4 / 2.0 / 0.2
10 W	0416 / 1140 / 1633 / 2154	2.1 / 0.4 / 1.9 / 0.1		**25** TH	0405 / 1210 / 1638 / ● 2135	2.3 / 0.4 / 2.0 / 0.1
11 TH	0448 / 1217 / 1704 / 2229	2.1 / 0.4 / 1.9 / 0.1		**26** F	0450 / 1306 / 1725 / 2229	2.3 / 0.4 / 1.9 / 0.0
12 F	0524 / 1300 / 1756 / 2325	2.1 / 0.4 / 1.9 / 0.0		**27** SA	0546 / 1356 / 1819 / 2325	2.3 / 0.4 / 1.9 / 0.0
13 SA	0136 / 0605 / 1334 / 1814	0.1 / 2.0 / 0.4 / 1.8		**28** SU	0634 / 1437 / 1915	2.3 / 0.4 / 1.9
14 SU	0000 / 0645 / 1407 / 1915	0.1 / 2.0 / 0.4 / 1.8		**29** M	0024 / 0739 / 1537 / 2010	0.0 / 2.2 / 0.4 / 1.9
15 M	0044 / 0735 / 1450 / 1955	0.1 / 2.0 / 0.4 / 1.8		**30** TU	0134 / 0834 / 1650 / 2116	0.0 / 2.1 / 0.4 / 1.9

JULY

Day	Time	m		Day	Time	m
1 W	0239 / 0945 / 1740 / 2216	0.1 / 2.0 / 0.4 / 1.8		**16** TH	0134 / 0847 / 1445 / 2110	0.1 / 2.0 / 0.4 / 1.9
2 TH	0344 / 1156 / 1640 / 2326	0.2 / 1.9 / 0.4 / 1.8		**17** F	0255 / 0950 / 1534 / 2225	0.2 / 2.0 / 0.4 / 1.9
3 F	0504 / 1154 / 1740	0.3 / 1.9 / 0.4		**18** SA	0354 / 1100 / 1656 / ◔ 2324	0.2 / 2.0 / 0.4 / 1.9
4 SA	0026 / 0605 / 1254 / ◔ 1824	1.9 / 0.3 / 1.9 / 0.3		**19** SU	0504 / 1205 / 1756	0.3 / 1.9 / 0.4
5 SU	0125 / 0700 / 1356 / 1905	1.9 / 0.4 / 1.9 / 0.3		**20** M	0036 / 0615 / 1310 / 1835	2.0 / 0.3 / 2.0 / 0.3
6 M	0204 / 0734 / 1445 / 1943	2.0 / 0.4 / 2.0 / 0.2		**21** TU	0129 / 0700 / 1358 / 1915	2.2 / 0.4 / 2.0 / 0.2
7 TU	0249 / 0820 / 1513 / 2030	2.1 / 0.5 / 2.0 / 0.2		**22** W	0215 / 0745 / 1449 / 1955	2.3 / 0.4 / 2.0 / 0.2
8 W	0330 / 0855 / 1544 / 2055	2.1 / 0.5 / 2.0 / 0.2		**23** TH	0305 / 1116 / 1532 / 2036	2.4 / 0.5 / 2.1 / 0.1
9 TH	0359 / 0925 / 1615 / 2125	2.2 / 0.5 / 2.0 / 0.1		**24** F	0347 / 1144 / 1618 / 2115	2.4 / 0.5 / 2.1 / 0.1
10 F	0435 / 1150 / 1656 / 2153	2.2 / 0.5 / 2.0 / 0.1		**25** SA	0433 / 1245 / 1706 / 2201	2.4 / 0.5 / 2.1 / 0.0
11 SA	0504 / 1225 / 1725 / ○ 2229	2.2 / 0.5 / 2.0 / 0.1		**26** SU	0521 / 1325 / 1748 / ● 2256	2.4 / 0.5 / 2.1 / 0.1
12 SU	0539 / 1315 / 1754 / 2310	2.1 / 0.5 / 1.9 / 0.1		**27** M	0608 / 1430 / 1835 / 2310	2.3 / 0.5 / 2.1 / 0.1
13 M	0611 / 1356 / 1829 / 2344	2.1 / 0.5 / 1.9 / 0.1		**28** TU	0705 / 1510 / 1925	2.2 / 0.5 / 2.0
14 TU	0656 / 1417 / 1915	2.1 / 0.5 / 1.9		**29** W	0054 / 0755 / 1400 / 2014	0.1 / 2.1 / 0.5 / 2.0
15 W	0035 / 0740 / 1420 / 2016	0.1 / 2.1 / 0.5 / 1.9		**30** TH	0204 / 0900 / 1445 / 2125	0.2 / 1.9 / 0.4 / 1.9
				31 F	0336 / 1015 / 1610 / 2245	0.3 / 1.8 / 0.4 / 1.8

AUGUST

Day	Time	m		Day	Time	m
1 SA	0444 / 1135 / 1720	0.4 / 1.8 / 0.4		**16** SU	0356 / 1036 / 1615 / 2310	0.3 / 1.8 / 0.4 / 1.9
2 SU	0005 / 0555 / 1245 / ◐ 1804	1.8 / 0.4 / 1.8 / 0.3		**17** M	0454 / 1155 / 1725 / ◐	0.4 / 1.8 / 0.4
3 M	0109 / 0645 / 1346 / 1844	1.9 / 0.5 / 1.9 / 0.3		**18** TU	0026 / 0554 / 1255 / 1809	2.0 / 0.5 / 1.9 / 0.3
4 TU	0154 / 0736 / 1430 / 1935	2.0 / 0.5 / 2.0 / 0.3		**19** W	0118 / 0926 / 1349 / 1855	2.2 / 0.5 / 2.0 / 0.2
5 W	0233 / 0754 / 1506 / 2005	2.1 / 0.6 / 2.0 / 0.2		**20** TH	0202 / 0955 / 1436 / 1929	2.3 / 0.5 / 2.0 / 0.2
6 TH	0310 / 0830 / 1524 / 2023	2.2 / 0.6 / 2.0 / 0.2		**21** F	0245 / 1050 / 1516 / 2009	2.4 / 0.6 / 2.1 / 0.1
7 F	0335 / 0900 / 1554 / 2056	2.2 / 0.6 / 2.1 / 0.2		**22** SA	0329 / 1135 / 1557 / 2049	2.4 / 0.6 / 2.2 / 0.1
8 SA	0405 / 1120 / 1630 / 2119	2.2 / 0.6 / 2.1 / 0.2		**23** SU	0412 / 1214 / 1637 / 2135	2.4 / 0.6 / 2.2 / 0.1
9 SU	0439 / 1155 / 1655 / ○ 2151	2.3 / 0.5 / 2.1 / 0.2		**24** M	0455 / 1304 / 1718 / 2225	2.4 / 0.6 / 2.2 / 0.2
10 M	0509 / 1245 / 1728 / 2230	2.2 / 0.5 / 2.1 / 0.2		**25** TU	0541 / 1355 / 1801 / ● 2315	2.3 / 0.5 / 2.2 / 0.2
11 TU	0541 / 1325 / 1755 / 2305	2.2 / 0.5 / 2.1 / 0.1		**26** W	0626 / 1145 / 1846	2.1 / 0.5 / 2.1
12 W	0615 / 1126 / 1835 / 2345	2.2 / 0.5 / 2.1 / 0.1		**27** TH	0025 / 0715 / 1300 / 1935	0.3 / 2.0 / 0.4 / 2.0
13 TH	0659 / 1205 / 1920	2.2 / 0.5 / 2.1		**28** F	0150 / 0810 / 1355 / 2034	0.3 / 1.8 / 0.4 / 1.9
14 F	0035 / 0749 / 1340 / 2015	0.2 / 2.1 / 0.4 / 2.0		**29** SA	0255 / 0914 / 1550 / 2204	0.4 / 1.7 / 0.4 / 1.7
15 SA	0230 / 0906 / 1516 / 2146	0.2 / 1.9 / 0.4 / 1.9		**30** SU	0436 / 1126 / 1706 / 2345	0.5 / 1.6 / 0.4 / 1.8
				31 M	0524 / 1225 / 1745	0.5 / 1.7 / 0.4

Chart Datum: 0·84 metres below NAP Datum
HAT is 2·4 metres above Chart Datum

TIME ZONE -0100
(Dutch Standard Time)
Subtract 1 hour for UT
For Dutch Summer Time add
ONE hour in **non-shaded areas**

NETHERLANDS – HOEK VAN HOLLAND

LAT 51°59′N   LONG 4°07′E

TIMES AND HEIGHTS OF HIGH AND LOW WATERS

Dates in amber are **SPRINGS**
Dates in yellow are **NEAPS**

2009

SEPTEMBER

Time m	Time m
1 0044 1.9 / 0625 0.6 / TU 1314 1.9 / 1834 0.3	**16** 0009 2.1 / 0805 0.5 / W 1243 1.8 / 2025 0.3
2 0146 2.1 / 0946 0.5 / W 1359 2.0 / 1915 0.3	**17** 0106 2.2 / 0907 0.5 / TH 1336 2.0 / 1825 0.3
3 0209 2.2 / 1025 0.5 / TH 1446 2.0 / 1935 0.3	**18** 0146 2.3 / 0934 0.5 / F 1416 2.1 / ● 1905 0.2
4 0235 2.2 / 1100 0.6 / F 1454 2.1 / ○ 2000 0.3	**19** 0227 2.4 / 1020 0.6 / SA 1451 2.2 / 1946 0.2
5 0305 2.3 / 0824 0.6 / SA 1525 2.1 / 2025 0.3	**20** 0307 2.4 / 1105 0.6 / SU 1531 2.3 / 2028 0.2
6 0338 2.3 / 0845 0.6 / SU 1555 2.2 / 2049 0.2	**21** 0347 2.4 / 0850 0.6 / M 1607 2.3 / 2109 0.2
7 0405 2.3 / 1134 0.5 / M 1625 2.2 / 2119 0.2	**22** 0431 2.3 / 0929 0.5 / TU 1648 2.3 / 2155 0.3
8 0439 2.3 / 1220 0.5 / TU 1658 2.2 / 2158 0.2	**23** 0515 2.2 / 1015 0.5 / W 1728 2.3 / 2245 0.4
9 0515 2.3 / 1015 0.5 / W 1729 2.2 / 2236 0.2	**24** 0555 2.1 / 1105 0.4 / TH 1816 2.2
10 0550 2.3 / 1056 0.4 / TH 1806 2.3 / 2319 0.2	**25** 0010 0.5 / 0638 2.0 / F 1204 0.4 / 1900 2.1
11 0629 2.2 / 1140 0.4 / F 1849 2.2	**26** 0120 0.5 / 0720 1.8 / SA 1320 0.4 / ◐ 2005 1.9
12 0014 0.3 / 0719 2.0 / SA 1250 0.4 / ◐ 1945 2.1	**27** 0237 0.6 / 0820 1.7 / SU 1530 0.4 / 2114 1.7
13 0230 0.4 / 0836 1.8 / SU 1446 0.4 / 2105 1.9	**28** 0404 0.6 / 1000 1.5 / M 1635 0.4 / 2315 1.8
14 0325 0.5 / 1016 1.7 / M 1544 0.4 / 2255 1.9	**29** 0504 0.6 / 1156 1.7 / TU 1724 0.3
15 0640 0.5 / 1135 1.7 / TU 1654 0.4	**30** 0026 1.9 / 0620 0.6 / W 1250 1.8 / 1820 0.3

OCTOBER

Time m	Time m
1 0106 2.1 / 0906 0.5 / TH 1330 1.9 / 1900 0.4	**16** 0045 2.3 / 0854 0.5 / F 1305 2.0 / 2110 0.3
2 0135 2.2 / 0935 0.5 / F 1400 2.0 / 2135 0.4	**17** 0126 2.3 / 0924 0.6 / SA 1348 2.1 / 1845 0.3
3 0206 2.2 / 1015 0.5 / SA 1419 2.1 / 1924 0.4	**18** 0205 2.4 / 0945 0.6 / SU 1427 2.2 / ● 1930 0.3
4 0236 2.3 / 0755 0.6 / SU 1449 2.2 / ○ 1945 0.3	**19** 0247 2.4 / 0749 0.6 / M 1507 2.3 / 2004 0.3
5 0305 2.4 / 0814 0.6 / M 1518 2.3 / 2026 0.3	**20** 0327 2.3 / 0825 0.5 / TU 1547 2.3 / 2049 0.4
6 0337 2.4 / 0846 0.5 / TU 1556 2.3 / 2055 0.3	**21** 0408 2.2 / 0909 0.5 / W 1626 2.3
7 0413 2.4 / 0915 0.5 / W 1627 2.3 / 2135 0.3	**22** 0040 0.5 / 0455 2.1 / TH 0955 0.4 / 1708 2.3
8 0449 2.3 / 0955 0.4 / TH 1707 2.4 / 2216 0.3	**23** 0120 0.5 / 0525 2.0 / F 1034 0.4 / 1745 2.2
9 0527 2.2 / 1040 0.4 / F 1746 2.3 / 2305 0.4	**24** 0020 0.6 / 0605 2.0 / SA 1134 0.3 / 1824 2.1
10 0612 2.1 / 1125 0.4 / SA 1831 2.3	**25** 0100 0.6 / 0645 1.9 / SU 1235 0.3 / 1925 2.0
11 0146 0.4 / 0706 1.9 / SU 1300 0.4 / ◐ 1929 2.1	**26** 0210 0.6 / 0734 1.7 / M 1420 0.4 / ◐ 2035 1.8
12 0224 0.5 / 0815 1.7 / M 1420 0.4 / 2110 2.0	**27** 0325 0.7 / 0850 1.6 / TU 1616 0.4 / 2154 1.8
13 0324 0.6 / 1006 1.6 / TU 1525 0.4 / 2246 2.0	**28** 0435 0.6 / 1015 1.6 / W 1705 0.4 / 2325 1.9
14 0640 0.5 / 1114 1.7 / W 1855 0.4 / 2344 2.1	**29** 0540 0.6 / 1155 1.7 / TH 1755 0.4
15 0805 0.5 / 1221 1.9 / TH 2025 0.3	**30** 0016 2.0 / 0805 0.5 / F 1246 1.9 / 2000 0.4
	31 0056 2.2 / 0905 0.5 / SA 1309 2.0 / 2100 0.4

NOVEMBER

Time m	Time m
1 0126 2.2 / 0955 0.5 / SU 1339 2.1 / 1855 0.4	**16** 0147 2.2 / 0946 0.6 / M 1409 2.2 / ● 1919 0.4
2 0156 2.3 / 1036 0.5 / M 1415 2.2 / ○ 1926 0.4	**17** 0235 2.2 / 0745 0.5 / TU 1452 2.3 / 2004 0.5
3 0235 2.4 / 0756 0.5 / TU 1451 2.3 / 1955 0.4	**18** 0312 2.0 / 0825 0.4 / W 1528 2.3 / 2045 0.5
4 0312 2.4 / 0826 0.5 / W 1529 2.4 / 2035 0.4	**19** 0358 2.2 / 0905 0.4 / TH 1608 2.3 / 2350 0.6
5 0352 2.3 / 0900 0.4 / TH 1607 2.4 / 2114 0.4	**20** 0435 2.1 / 0945 0.3 / F 1648 2.3
6 0431 2.2 / 0939 0.4 / F 1647 2.4 / 2205 0.5	**21** 0040 0.6 / 0511 2.0 / SA 1029 0.3 / 1729 2.2
7 0512 2.1 / 1029 0.3 / SA 1736 2.4	**22** 0030 0.6 / 0544 2.0 / SU 1114 0.3 / 1809 2.1
8 0110 0.5 / 0601 2.0 / SU 1125 0.3 / 1825 2.3	**23** 0040 0.7 / 0623 1.9 / M 1204 0.3 / 1900 2.0
9 0137 0.5 / 0706 1.9 / M 1234 0.3 / ◑ 1936 2.2	**24** 0140 0.7 / 0705 1.8 / TU 1254 0.3 / ◑ 2000 1.9
10 0230 0.6 / 0825 1.8 / TU 1344 0.3 / 2100 2.1	**25** 0250 0.7 / 0816 1.8 / W 1400 0.3 / 2055 1.9
11 0500 0.6 / 0940 1.7 / W 1445 0.3 / 2214 2.1	**26** 0347 0.6 / 0920 1.7 / TH 1630 0.4 / 2205 1.9
12 0636 0.6 / 1056 1.8 / TH 1834 0.3 / 2326 2.2	**27** 0454 0.6 / 1025 1.8 / F 1724 0.4 / 2316 2.0
13 0737 0.5 / 1156 1.9 / F 1950 0.4	**28** 0550 0.6 / 1136 1.8 / SA 1840 0.4
14 0014 2.2 / 0834 0.5 / SA 1245 2.0 / 2040 0.3	**29** 0005 2.1 / 0815 0.5 / SU 1219 2.0 / 1744 0.4
15 0106 2.2 / 0910 0.6 / SU 1328 2.1 / 1835 0.4	**30** 0046 2.2 / 0916 0.5 / M 1305 2.1 / 1824 0.4

DECEMBER

Time m	Time m
1 0128 2.3 / 0653 0.5 / TU 1348 2.2 / 1905 0.4	**16** 0225 2.1 / 0756 0.4 / W 1438 2.2 / ● 2015 0.5
2 0207 2.3 / 0736 0.5 / W 1427 2.3 / ○ 1943 0.4	**17** 0309 2.1 / 0825 0.3 / TH 1525 2.2 / 2104 0.5
3 0256 2.3 / 0810 0.4 / TH 1511 2.4 / 2025 0.4	**18** 0355 2.1 / 0855 0.3 / F 1559 2.3 / 2210 0.6
4 0336 2.2 / 0850 0.3 / F 1556 2.4 / 2116 0.5	**19** 0425 2.1 / 0934 0.2 / SA 1635 2.3 / 2350 0.6
5 0421 2.2 / 0929 0.3 / SA 1639 2.4	**20** 0505 2.1 / 1005 0.2 / SU 1715 2.2
6 0030 0.5 / 0509 2.1 / SU 1014 0.2 / 1727 2.4	**21** 0030 0.6 / 0536 2.0 / M 1045 0.2 / 1755 2.2
7 0115 0.5 / 0558 2.0 / M 1116 0.2 / 1826 2.3	**22** 0100 0.6 / 0604 2.0 / TU 1124 0.2 / 1824 2.1
8 0200 0.5 / 0659 1.9 / TU 1214 0.2 / 1925 2.2	**23** 0127 0.6 / 0645 2.0 / W 1214 0.2 / 1904 2.0
9 0250 0.6 / 0805 1.9 / W 1336 0.2 / ◑ 2035 2.2	**24** 0200 0.6 / 0725 1.9 / TH 1255 0.2 / ◑ 2006 2.0
10 0440 0.6 / 0910 1.9 / TH 1430 0.2 / 2146 2.1	**25** 0230 0.6 / 0836 1.9 / F 1354 0.3 / 2106 2.0
11 0606 0.6 / 1016 1.9 / F 1525 0.3 / 2244 2.1	**26** 0310 0.6 / 0929 1.9 / SA 1506 0.3 / 2211 2.0
12 0700 0.6 / 1126 1.9 / SA 1916 0.3 / 2355 2.1	**27** 0410 0.6 / 1036 1.9 / SU 1555 0.3 / 2316 2.0
13 0811 0.6 / 1215 2.0 / SU 1957 0.4	**28** 0504 0.6 / 1135 1.9 / M 1705 0.4
14 0045 2.1 / 0845 0.5 / M 1309 2.1 / 1834 0.4	**29** 0004 2.1 / 0554 0.5 / TU 1235 2.0 / 1804 0.4
15 0139 2.1 / 0655 0.5 / TU 1355 2.1 / 1924 0.5	**30** 0101 2.1 / 0635 0.4 / W 1328 2.2 / 1900 0.4
	31 0151 2.1 / 0715 0.4 / TH 1411 2.3 / ○ 1934 0.4

Chart Datum: 0·84 metres below NAP Datum
HAT is 2·4 metres above Chart Datum

TIDES

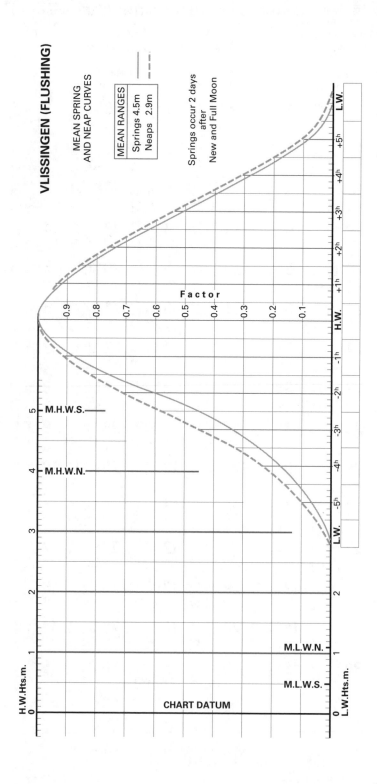

VLISSINGEN (FLUSHING)

MEAN SPRING
AND NEAP CURVES

MEAN RANGES
Springs 4.5m
Neaps 2.9m

Springs occur 2 days
after
New and Full Moon

TIME ZONE -0100
(Dutch Standard Time)
Subtract 1 hour for UT
For Dutch Summer Time add
ONE hour in **non-shaded areas**

NETHERLANDS – VLISSINGEN

LAT 51°27′N   LONG 3°36′E

TIMES AND HEIGHTS OF HIGH AND LOW WATERS

Dates in amber are **SPRINGS**
Dates in yellow are **NEAPS**

2009

JANUARY

Time m		Time m	
1 0445 4.7		**16** 0527 4.9	
1110 0.6		1151 0.4	
TH 1702 4.7		F 1752 4.9	
2316 1.0			
2 0517 4.6		**17** 0000 0.9	
1146 0.7		0616 4.8	
F 1737 4.7		SA 1235 0.5	
2351 1.1		1846 4.7	
3 0555 4.5		**18** 0046 1.0	
1221 0.7		0706 4.5	
SA 1822 4.6		SU 1326 0.7	
		◐ 1935 4.4	
4 0030 1.1		**19** 0135 1.2	
0641 4.4		0801 4.3	
SU 1310 0.8		M 1414 1.0	
◑ 1915 4.5		2035 4.1	
5 0126 1.1		**20** 0245 1.3	
0746 4.3		0905 4.2	
M 1406 0.8		TU 1525 1.2	
2026 4.4		2201 3.9	
6 0226 1.2		**21** 0415 1.4	
0852 4.3		1036 3.9	
TU 1516 0.9		W 1644 1.3	
2136 4.3		2316 3.9	
7 0335 1.2		**22** 0530 1.3	
1006 4.3		1145 4.0	
W 1620 0.9		TH 1806 1.3	
2239 4.4			
8 0449 1.1		**23** 0016 4.1	
1110 4.5		0637 1.1	
TH 1736 0.9		F 1245 4.2	
2346 4.5		1846 1.2	
9 0605 0.9		**24** 0105 4.3	
1212 4.7		0714 1.0	
F 1836 0.8		SA 1326 4.4	
		1925 1.1	
10 0045 4.7		**25** 0145 4.4	
0708 0.7		0800 0.8	
SA 1307 4.9		SU 1405 4.6	
1932 0.7		1959 1.0	
11 0135 4.8		**26** 0218 4.6	
0759 0.5		0836 0.7	
SU 1356 5.1		M 1431 4.7	
○ 2020 0.7		2037 1.0	
12 0226 4.9		**27** 0246 4.7	
0851 0.4		0905 0.6	
M 1442 5.2		TU 1501 4.8	
2107 0.7		2110 0.9	
13 0309 5.0		**28** 0316 4.8	
0939 0.3		0942 0.5	
TU 1530 5.3		W 1532 4.9	
2152 0.7		2146 0.8	
14 0355 5.0		**29** 0347 4.9	
1025 0.2		1018 0.4	
W 1616 5.2		TH 1605 4.9	
2236 0.8		2215 0.8	
15 0437 5.0		**30** 0422 4.8	
1109 0.3		1056 0.5	
TH 1706 5.1		F 1637 4.9	
2318 0.8		2256 0.8	
		31 0452 4.8	
		1126 0.5	
		SA 1711 4.8	
		2328 0.9	

FEBRUARY

Time m		Time m	
1 0527 4.8		**16** 0006 0.9	
1200 0.5		0617 4.6	
SU 1752 4.7		M 1235 0.8	
		◐ 1848 4.3	
2 0002 0.9		**17** 0050 1.0	
0610 4.7		0706 4.3	
M 1240 0.6		TU 1326 1.0	
1837 4.6		1938 4.0	
3 0050 0.9		**18** 0155 1.2	
0657 4.5		0806 3.9	
TU 1330 0.7		W 1446 1.3	
◑ 1935 4.4		2035 3.7	
4 0156 1.1		**19** 0326 1.4	
0810 4.3		0935 3.7	
W 1436 0.9		TH 1605 1.4	
2055 4.2		2245 3.6	
5 0306 1.2		**20** 0445 1.3	
0936 4.2		1115 3.8	
TH 1555 1.0		F 1726 1.4	
2216 4.1		2349 3.9	
6 0424 1.1		**21** 0606 1.1	
1036 4.3		1220 4.1	
F 1718 1.0		SA 1819 1.2	
2336 4.2			
7 0556 0.9		**22** 0042 4.2	
1205 4.5		0700 0.9	
SA 1826 0.9		SU 1305 4.4	
		1905 1.1	
8 0036 4.5		**23** 0126 4.4	
0659 0.7		0746 0.8	
SU 1259 4.8		M 1338 4.6	
1919 0.8		1934 1.0	
9 0125 4.7		**24** 0152 4.6	
0755 0.4		0809 0.6	
M 1346 5.0		TU 1408 4.8	
○ 2011 0.7		2016 0.9	
10 0209 4.9		**25** 0219 4.7	
0842 0.3		0842 0.5	
TU 1428 5.2		W 1436 4.9	
2052 0.7		2045 0.8	
11 0252 5.0		**26** 0247 4.9	
0925 0.2		0918 0.4	
W 1513 5.2		TH 1506 5.0	
2136 0.7		2119 0.7	
12 0333 5.1		**27** 0319 5.0	
1007 0.2		0952 0.3	
TH 1556 5.2		F 1537 5.0	
2216 0.7		2158 0.7	
13 0415 5.1		**28** 0352 5.0	
1048 0.2		1028 0.3	
F 1637 5.1		SA 1609 5.0	
2252 0.7		2232 0.7	
14 0455 5.0			
1125 0.4			
SA 1718 4.9			
2330 0.8			
15 0538 4.8			
1159 0.5			
SU 1801 4.6			

MARCH

Time m		Time m	
1 0426 5.0		**16** 0502 4.8	
1102 0.4		1128 0.6	
SU 1645 4.9		M 1726 4.5	
2306 0.7		2336 0.8	
2 0503 4.9		**17** 0541 4.6	
1135 0.5		1155 0.9	
M 1723 4.8		TU 1805 4.3	
2347 0.7			
3 0542 4.8		**18** 0004 0.9	
1215 0.6		0622 4.3	
TU 1809 4.6		W 1235 1.1	
		◑ 1846 4.0	
4 0030 0.8		**19** 0106 1.1	
0631 4.6		0715 3.9	
W 1305 0.8		TH 1335 1.4	
◑ 1905 4.3		1946 3.7	
5 0136 0.9		**20** 0255 1.3	
0746 4.3		0835 3.6	
TH 1416 1.0		F 1525 1.5	
2030 4.0		2114 3.4	
6 0249 1.1		**21** 0416 1.3	
0916 4.1		1046 3.7	
F 1535 1.2		SA 1645 1.4	
2206 3.8		2316 3.7	
7 0426 1.1		**22** 0520 1.1	
1045 4.2		1146 4.0	
SA 1704 1.1		SU 1756 1.2	
2325 4.1			
8 0556 0.9		**23** 0006 4.0	
1156 4.5		0626 0.9	
SU 1814 1.0		M 1230 4.3	
		1836 1.0	
9 0026 4.4		**24** 0045 4.3	
0655 0.6		0706 0.7	
M 1245 4.8		TU 1306 4.6	
1912 0.8		1916 0.9	
10 0109 4.7		**25** 0116 4.6	
0742 0.3		0734 0.6	
TU 1330 5.0		W 1332 4.8	
1956 0.7		1945 0.8	
11 0151 4.9		**26** 0146 4.8	
0822 0.2		0809 0.5	
W 1410 5.1		TH 1406 4.9	
○ 2033 0.6		2016 0.7	
12 0229 5.0		**27** 0217 4.9	
0906 0.2		0846 0.4	
TH 1450 5.1		F 1435 5.1	
2111 0.6		2056 0.6	
13 0308 5.1		**28** 0249 5.0	
0943 0.2		0922 0.3	
F 1530 5.1		SA 1506 5.1	
2149 0.6		2132 0.5	
14 0346 5.1		**29** 0325 5.1	
1019 0.3		0959 0.3	
SA 1611 5.0		SU 1546 5.0	
2228 0.6		2209 0.5	
15 0425 5.0		**30** 0403 5.1	
1056 0.5		1038 0.4	
SU 1647 4.8		M 1626 4.9	
2306 0.7		2252 0.5	
		31 0441 5.0	
		1121 0.5	
		TU 1705 4.8	
		2335 0.6	

APRIL

Time m		Time m	
1 0526 4.9		**16** 0556 4.3	
1206 0.6		1159 1.1	
W 1752 4.5		TH 1816 4.1	
2 0019 0.7		**17** 0024 1.0	
0618 4.6		0651 4.0	
TH 1255 0.8		F 1249 1.3	
◐ 1855 4.1		◐ 1916 3.8	
3 0125 0.8		**18** 0216 1.2	
0735 4.3		0754 3.8	
F 1405 1.1		SA 1456 1.4	
2019 3.9		2025 3.6	
4 0256 0.9		**19** 0336 1.1	
0910 4.1		0925 3.7	
SA 1525 1.2		SU 1600 1.3	
2149 3.8		2211 3.7	
5 0425 0.9		**20** 0435 1.0	
1036 4.3		1056 4.0	
SU 1705 1.1		M 1654 1.2	
2309 4.1		2315 4.0	
6 0546 0.7		**21** 0536 0.9	
1145 4.5		1146 4.3	
M 1804 0.9		TU 1745 1.0	
7 0006 4.4		**22** 0000 4.3	
0640 0.5		0625 0.7	
TU 1236 4.8		W 1218 4.6	
1858 0.8		1836 0.9	
8 0049 4.6		**23** 0036 4.5	
0725 0.3		0655 0.6	
W 1310 4.9		TH 1256 4.8	
1935 0.7		1910 0.7	
9 0127 4.8		**24** 0110 4.6	
0802 0.3		0736 0.5	
TH 1351 5.0		F 1328 5.0	
○ 2012 0.6		1948 0.6	
10 0206 4.9		**25** 0145 5.0	
0839 0.3		0816 0.4	
F 1429 5.0		SA 1405 5.1	
2049 0.6		● 2028 0.5	
11 0245 5.0		**26** 0221 5.1	
0918 0.4		0856 0.3	
SA 1507 4.9		SU 1443 5.1	
2128 0.5		2110 0.5	
12 0323 5.0		**27** 0300 5.1	
0951 0.5		0936 0.4	
SU 1546 4.8		M 1525 5.0	
2206 0.6		2153 0.4	
13 0401 4.9		**28** 0343 5.1	
1026 0.6		1018 0.4	
M 1621 4.7		TU 1606 4.9	
2246 0.6		2238 0.4	
14 0435 4.8		**29** 0426 5.0	
1055 0.8		1059 0.5	
TU 1656 4.5		W 1652 4.7	
2316 0.7		2326 0.5	
15 0516 4.5		**30** 0515 4.8	
1131 0.9		1150 0.7	
W 1731 4.3		TH 1747 4.4	
2346 0.9			

Chart Datum: 2·32 metres below NAP Datum
HAT is 5·2 metres above Chart Datum

TIDES

TIDES

TIME ZONE -0100
(Dutch Standard Time)
Subtract 1 hour for UT
For Dutch Summer Time add
ONE hour in **non-shaded areas**

NETHERLANDS – VLISSINGEN

LAT 51°27'N   LONG 3°36'E

TIMES AND HEIGHTS OF HIGH AND LOW WATERS

Dates in amber are **SPRINGS**
Dates in yellow are **NEAPS**

2009

MAY

Day	Time	m	Time	m	Time	m	Time	m
1 F	0015	0.5	0618	4.6	1245	0.9	1901	4.2
2 SA	0125	0.6	0741	4.4	1355	1.0	2016	4.0
3 SU	0245	0.7	0855	4.3	1515	1.1	2130	4.0
4 M ◑	0405	0.7	1015	4.4	1651	1.1	2246	4.2
5 TU	0526	0.6	1115	4.6	1745	0.9	2336	4.4
6 W	0616	0.5	1209	4.7	1835	0.8		
7 TH	0025	4.6	0700	0.4	1248	4.8	1916	0.8
8 F	0105	4.7	0736	0.5	1331	4.8	1949	0.7
9 SA	0145	4.8	0816	0.5	1408	4.8	2031	0.6
10 SU	0225	4.8	0849	0.6	1447	4.8	2106	0.5
11 M ○	0302	4.9	0925	0.6	1527	4.7	2146	0.5
12 TU	0341	4.8	0959	0.6	1601	4.6	2226	0.6
13 W	0419	4.7	1036	0.9	1636	4.5	2300	0.7
14 TH	0455	4.5	1106	1.0	1715	4.3	2336	0.8
15 F	0536	4.3	1139	1.1	1756	4.2		
16 SA	0015	0.9	0626	4.2	1224	1.2	1846	4.0
17 SU	0120	1.0	0726	4.0	1340	1.3	1950	3.9
18 M	0247	1.0	0835	4.0	1517	1.3	2055	3.9
19 TU	0340	0.9	0942	4.1	1616	1.2	2205	4.0
20 W	0436	0.8	1046	4.3	1706	1.1	2305	4.3
21 TH	0525	0.7	1136	4.6	1745	0.9	2351	4.5
22 F	0616	0.6	1217	4.8	1836	0.8		
23 SA	0036	4.8	0700	0.5	1259	4.9	1918	0.6
24 SU	0116	4.9	0746	0.4	1342	5.0	2007	0.5
25 M	0201	5.1	0830	0.4	1425	5.0	2052	0.4
26 TU ●	0245	5.1	0915	0.5	1511	4.9	2142	0.4
27	0331	5.1	1002	0.5	1557	4.8	2228	0.3
28 TH	0419	5.0	1045	0.6	1647	4.7	2322	0.3
29 F	0510	4.9	1138	0.7	1745	4.5		
30 SA	0016	0.3	0616	4.8	1236	0.9	1848	4.4
31 SU	0116	0.4	0721	4.7	1335	1.0	1949	4.3

JUNE

Day	Time	m	Time	m	Time	m	Time	m
1 M	0220	0.5	0825	4.5	1445	1.1	2058	4.2
2 TU ◐	0335	0.6	0940	4.5	1555	1.1	2205	4.3
3 W	0446	0.6	1045	4.5	1704	1.0	2308	4.3
4 TH	0546	0.6	1139	4.5	1808	0.9	2359	4.4
5 F	0632	0.6	1236	4.6	1850	0.8		
6 SA	0050	4.5	0716	0.7	1315	4.6	1929	0.7
7 SU	0131	4.6	0750	0.7	1358	4.6	2009	0.7
8 M	0215	4.7	0825	0.8	1435	4.6	2050	0.6
9 TU ○	0251	4.7	0902	0.8	1516	4.6	2124	0.6
10 W	0329	4.7	0941	0.9	1546	4.6	2210	0.6
11 TH	0405	4.7	1015	0.9	1621	4.6	2245	0.6
12 F	0441	4.6	1050	1.0	1655	4.5	2326	0.7
13 SA	0519	4.5	1125	1.1	1735	4.4		
14 SU	0006	0.7	0555	4.4	1205	1.1	1818	4.3
15 M	0040	0.8	0646	4.3	1245	1.2	1905	4.2
16 TU ◐	0125	0.8	0746	4.2	1344	1.2	2005	4.1
17 W	0225	0.8	0848	4.3	1505	1.2	2116	4.2
18 TH	0336	0.8	0945	4.3	1554	1.1	2216	4.3
19 F	0436	0.8	1050	4.5	1659	1.0	2316	4.5
20 SA	0535	0.7	1146	4.6	1800	0.8		
21 SU	0007	4.7	0630	0.6	1237	4.8	1859	0.7
22 M	0057	4.9	0722	0.6	1326	4.9	1948	0.5
23 TU	0146	5.0	0812	0.5	1412	4.9	2039	0.4
24 W	0235	5.1	0900	0.6	1501	4.9	2129	0.3
25 TH ●	0320	5.2	0945	0.6	1546	4.9	2222	0.2
26 F	0411	5.1	1036	0.7	1636	4.8	2309	0.2
27 SA	0506	5.1	1126	0.8	1729	4.8	2359	0.2
28 SU	0557	5.0	1215	0.8	1825	4.7		
29 M	0056	0.3	0655	4.8	1305	0.9	1920	4.6
30 TU	0145	0.4	0756	4.6	1406	1.0	2021	4.4

JULY

Day	Time	m	Time	m	Time	m	Time	m
1 W	0246	0.6	0901	4.4	1504	1.1	2126	4.3
2 TH	0344	0.8	1005	4.3	1636	1.1	2236	4.2
3 F	0516	0.9	1116	4.3	1736	1.1	2340	4.3
4 SA ◐	0605	0.9	1216	4.4	1830	0.9		
5 SU	0040	4.4	0650	0.9	1305	4.4	1920	0.8
6 M	0125	4.5	0735	1.0	1345	4.5	2000	0.7
7 TU	0205	4.6	0805	1.0	1426	4.6	2036	0.7
8 W	0241	4.7	0842	0.9	1456	4.6	2115	0.6
9 TH	0315	4.7	0920	0.9	1529	4.7	2156	0.5
10 F	0350	4.8	0955	0.9	1605	4.7	2230	0.5
11 SA ○	0421	4.8	1030	0.9	1646	4.6	2306	0.6
12 SU	0455	4.7	1106	1.0	1709	4.6	2340	0.6
13 M	0525	4.6	1136	1.0	1741	4.5		
14 TU	0015	0.7	0606	4.5	1216	1.0	1826	4.5
15 W	0050	0.7	0649	4.5	1301	1.0	1916	4.4
16 TH	0135	0.8	0756	4.4	1356	1.1	2020	4.3
17 F	0246	0.8	0900	4.3	1506	1.1	2136	4.3
18 SA	0356	0.9	1010	4.3	1626	1.1	2242	4.4
19 SU	0459	0.9	1120	4.4	1736	0.9	2348	4.6
20 M	0605	0.8	1222	4.6	1840	0.7		
21 TU	0042	4.8	0709	0.7	1312	4.8	1938	0.5
22 W	0135	5.0	0758	0.7	1400	4.9	2032	0.3
23 TH	0222	5.2	0845	0.6	1446	5.0	2120	0.2
24 F	0306	5.2	0932	0.7	1532	5.0	2205	0.2
25 SA	0355	5.3	1015	0.9	1616	5.0	2251	0.2
26 SU ●	0440	5.2	1100	0.9	1702	5.0	2338	0.2
27 M	0529	5.0	1146	0.8	1749	4.9		
28 TU	0019	0.4	0619	4.8	1225	0.9	1840	4.7
29 W	0106	0.6	0711	4.6	1315	1.0	1936	4.5
30 TH	0200	0.7	0816	4.3	1419	1.2	2046	4.2
31 F	0306	1.0	0925	4.0	1533	1.2	2159	4.0

AUGUST

Day	Time	m	Time	m	Time	m	Time	m
1 SA	0415	1.2	1050	4.0	1655	1.2	2326	4.1
2 SU ◐	0541	1.2	1156	4.1	1816	1.1		
3 M	0026	4.3	0635	1.1	1249	4.4	1906	0.9
4 TU	0115	4.5	0715	1.1	1331	4.5	1945	0.8
5 W	0156	4.6	0756	1.0	1406	4.6	2022	0.7
6 TH	0225	4.7	0826	1.0	1435	4.7	2055	0.6
7 F	0251	4.8	0858	0.9	1506	4.8	2130	0.5
8 SA	0325	4.9	0932	0.9	1537	4.9	2205	0.5
9 SU ○	0352	4.9	1006	0.9	1607	4.9	2235	0.5
10 M	0422	4.9	1035	0.9	1637	4.8	2309	0.6
11 TU	0452	4.8	1110	0.9	1710	4.8	2346	0.6
12 W	0527	4.8	1139	0.9	1745	4.7		
13 TH	0016	0.7	0608	4.6	1226	1.0	1829	4.6
14 F	0100	0.8	0701	4.5	1321	1.0	1930	4.4
15 SA	0206	0.9	0818	4.2	1430	1.2	2055	4.2
16 SU	0315	1.1	0934	4.1	1606	1.1	2220	4.2
17 M ◐	0434	1.1	1105	4.2	1714	1.0	2335	4.5
18 TU	0555	1.0	1209	4.4	1836	0.8		
19 W	0036	4.8	0658	0.8	1257	4.7	1930	0.5
20 TH	0126	5.1	0746	0.8	1345	4.9	2018	0.3
21 F	0206	5.2	0830	0.7	1428	5.1	2106	0.2
22 SA	0246	5.3	0912	0.7	1509	5.1	2145	0.2
23 SU	0330	5.3	0956	0.7	1550	5.2	2228	0.3
24 M	0415	5.2	1036	0.8	1632	5.1	2306	0.4
25 TU ●	0457	5.0	1111	0.8	1716	5.0	2345	0.6
26 W	0540	4.8	1156	0.9	1759	4.8		
27 TH	0026	0.8	0626	4.5	1241	1.0	1845	4.5
28 F	0116	1.0	0720	4.1	1346	1.2	1945	4.1
29 SA	0226	1.3	0825	3.8	1506	1.3	2126	3.8
30 SU	0346	1.4	1020	3.7	1636	1.3	2306	3.9
31 M	0454	1.4	1135	4.0	1751	1.1		

Chart Datum: 2·32 metres below NAP Datum
HAT is 5·2 metres above Chart Datum

TIME ZONE -0100
(Dutch Standard Time)
Subtract 1 hour for UT
For Dutch Summer Time add
ONE hour in **non-shaded areas**

NETHERLANDS – VLISSINGEN

LAT 51°27'N   LONG 3°36'E

TIMES AND HEIGHTS OF HIGH AND LOW WATERS

Dates in amber are **SPRINGS**
Dates in yellow are **NEAPS**

2009

SEPTEMBER

Time	m		Time	m
1 0005	4.2	**16** 0544	1.1
0603	1.3	1155	4.4
TU 1225	4.3	W 1826	0.7
1846	0.9		
2 0056	4.5	**17** 0018	4.8
0656	1.1	0646	1.0
W 1307	4.5	TH 1240	4.7
1925	0.8	1918	0.5
3 0130	4.7	**18** 0105	5.1
0725	1.1	0730	0.8
TH 1342	4.7	F 1325	4.9
2000	0.7	● 2000	0.4
4 0156	4.8	**19** 0146	5.2
0800	1.0	0812	0.8
F 1406	4.8	SA 1403	5.1
○ 2028	0.6	2042	0.3
5 0222	4.9	**20** 0226	5.2
0829	0.9	0852	0.7
SA 1436	4.9	SU 1445	5.2
2100	0.6	2122	0.3
6 0251	5.0	**21** 0306	5.2
0901	0.8	0930	0.7
SU 1505	5.0	M 1526	5.1
2136	0.5	2200	0.4
7 0321	5.0	**22** 0346	5.1
0935	0.8	1008	0.7
M 1535	5.0	TU 1606	5.1
2208	0.5	2235	0.6
8 0352	5.0	**23** 0429	4.9
1016	0.8	1046	0.8
TU 1606	5.0	W 1646	5.0
2246	0.6	2316	0.8
9 0425	5.0	**24** 0510	4.7
1045	0.8	1126	0.9
W 1639	5.0	TH 1727	4.7
2316	0.6	2345	1.0
10 0501	4.9	**25** 0545	4.4
1126	0.9	1154	0.8
TH 1716	4.9	F 1810	4.4
2356	0.7		
11 0541	4.7	**26** 0019	1.2
1200	0.9	0631	4.1
F 1801	4.8	SA 1255	1.2
		◐ 1906	4.1
12 0036	0.9	**27** 0130	1.5
0635	4.4	0725	3.8
SA 1255	1.0	SU 1436	1.4
◐ 1859	4.4	2036	3.8
13 0141	1.1	**28** 0316	1.6
0742	4.1	0920	3.6
SU 1416	1.2	M 1550	1.4
2035	4.2	2214	3.8
14 0300	1.3	**29** 0414	1.6
0920	3.9	1101	3.8
M 1556	1.4	TU 1705	1.2
2206	4.2	2324	4.1
15 0430	1.3	**30** 0537	1.6
1049	4.1	1149	4.1
TU 1715	1.0	W 1810	1.0
2326	4.5		

OCTOBER

Time	m		Time	m
1 0016	4.4	**16** 0001	4.8
0614	1.2	0625	1.0
TH 1236	4.4	F 1218	4.6
1855	0.8	1858	0.5
2 0051	4.7	**17** 0046	5.0
0655	1.1	0709	0.9
F 1301	4.6	SA 1300	4.9
1926	0.8	1938	0.5
3 0118	4.8	**18** 0125	5.1
0730	1.0	0750	0.8
SA 1331	4.8	SU 1340	5.0
1955	0.7	● 2017	0.5
4 0149	5.0	**19** 0206	5.1
0800	0.9	0831	0.7
SU 1402	5.0	M 1420	5.1
○ 2025	0.6	2055	0.5
5 0220	5.1	**20** 0245	5.1
0835	0.8	0908	0.7
M 1431	5.1	TU 1500	5.1
2102	0.5	2136	0.6
6 0249	5.1	**21** 0325	5.0
0912	0.7	0945	0.7
TU 1506	5.1	W 1540	5.1
2138	0.5	2208	0.8
7 0326	5.1	**22** 0406	4.8
0948	0.7	1026	0.8
W 1541	5.2	TH 1621	4.9
2216	0.6	2246	0.9
8 0400	5.0	**23** 0446	4.6
1026	0.7	1054	0.9
TH 1616	5.1	F 1658	4.7
2252	0.7	2315	1.1
9 0439	4.9	**24** 0519	4.4
1109	0.8	1135	1.0
F 1658	5.0	SA 1741	4.4
2336	0.8	2350	1.3
10 0526	4.6	**25** 0606	4.2
1152	0.8	1215	1.2
SA 1746	4.8	SU 1831	4.1
11 0020	1.0	**26** 0040	1.5
0615	4.3	0655	3.9
SU 1250	1.0	M 1344	1.3
◐ 1849	4.4	◐ 1939	3.9
12 0125	1.2	**27** 0214	1.7
0735	4.0	0754	3.7
M 1405	1.1	TU 1506	1.3
2026	4.2	2105	3.8
13 0245	1.4	**28** 0341	1.6
0906	3.9	0934	3.7
TU 1546	1.1	W 1604	1.2
2149	4.3	2236	4.0
14 0426	1.4	**29** 0440	1.4
1024	4.1	1106	4.0
W 1705	0.9	TH 1715	1.1
2310	4.5	2331	4.3
15 0546	1.2	**30** 0536	1.3
1131	4.4	1147	4.3
TH 1810	0.7	F 1806	0.9
		31 0008	4.6
		0615	1.1
		SA 1219	4.5
		1846	0.8

NOVEMBER

Time	m		Time	m
1 0042	4.8	**16** 0105	4.9
0649	1.0	0728	0.9
SU 1253	4.8	M 1322	4.9
1915	0.7	● 1956	0.7
2 0112	5.0	**17** 0149	4.9
0728	0.9	0810	0.8
M 1327	5.0	TU 1403	5.0
○ 1956	0.6	2029	0.7
3 0148	5.1	**18** 0227	4.9
0806	0.8	0851	0.7
TU 1406	5.1	W 1445	5.0
2030	0.6	2108	0.8
4 0223	5.1	**19** 0310	4.8
0849	0.7	0930	0.7
W 1440	5.2	TH 1527	5.0
2110	0.6	2145	0.9
5 0303	5.1	**20** 0347	4.8
0925	0.6	1008	0.7
TH 1519	5.2	F 1606	4.8
2152	0.6	2215	1.0
6 0345	5.0	**21** 0425	4.6
1012	0.6	1046	0.8
F 1602	5.1	SA 1646	4.7
2236	0.7	2256	1.2
7 0427	4.8	**22** 0502	4.5
1101	0.7	1126	0.9
SA 1648	5.1	SU 1725	4.5
2320	0.9	2326	1.3
8 0517	4.6	**23** 0539	4.3
1145	0.7	1206	1.0
SU 1741	4.8	M 1810	4.3
9 0010	1.0	**24** 0005	1.4
0618	4.4	0631	4.2
M 1245	0.8	TU 1255	1.1
◑ 1851	4.6	◑ 1906	4.1
10 0116	1.2	**25** 0055	1.5
0730	4.2	0726	4.0
TU 1405	0.9	W 1405	1.2
2016	4.4	2006	4.0
11 0225	1.4	**26** 0241	1.6
0846	4.1	0831	3.9
W 1515	0.9	TH 1516	1.2
2125	4.4	2116	4.0
12 0355	1.4	**27** 0347	1.5
0955	4.2	0935	4.0
TH 1647	0.9	F 1604	1.1
2235	4.5	2220	4.2
13 0505	1.3	**28** 0435	1.4
1101	4.4	1046	4.2
F 1746	0.8	SA 1706	1.0
2336	4.7	2315	4.4
14 0606	1.1	**29** 0525	1.2
1155	4.6	1136	4.4
SA 1832	0.7	SU 1755	0.9
15 0022	4.8	**30** 0000	4.7
0651	1.0	0609	1.0
SU 1239	4.7	M 1216	4.7
1913	0.7	1841	0.8

DECEMBER

Time	m		Time	m
1 0041	4.9	**16** 0139	4.7
0656	0.9	0756	0.8
TU 1257	4.9	W 1355	4.8
1922	0.7	● 2009	0.9
2 0126	5.0	**17** 0218	4.7
0742	0.8	0835	0.7
W 1341	5.0	TH 1437	4.8
○ 2007	0.6	2046	0.9
3 0205	5.0	**18** 0255	4.7
0825	0.6	0915	0.7
TH 1423	5.1	F 1515	4.8
2050	0.6	2125	1.0
4 0246	5.0	**19** 0336	4.7
0917	0.6	0956	0.6
F 1508	5.2	SA 1551	4.8
2135	0.7	2158	1.0
5 0333	4.9	**20** 0409	4.7
1006	0.5	1036	0.7
SA 1556	5.2	SU 1629	4.7
2219	0.8	2236	1.1
6 0421	4.8	**21** 0446	4.6
1055	0.5	1105	0.7
SU 1642	5.1	M 1705	4.6
2311	0.9	2306	1.1
7 0516	4.7	**22** 0520	4.5
1146	0.5	1139	0.8
M 1737	4.9	TU 1738	4.5
		2339	1.2
8 0000	1.0	**23** 0555	4.4
0609	4.6	1215	0.9
TU 1246	0.6	W 1826	4.4
1845	4.8		
9 0056	1.1	**24** 0015	1.3
0709	4.4	0645	4.3
W 1339	0.6	TH 1255	0.9
◑ 1945	4.6	◑ 1910	4.3
10 0200	1.2	**25** 0105	1.3
0816	4.3	0737	4.2
TH 1446	0.8	F 1343	1.0
2055	4.5	2016	4.2
11 0303	1.3	**26** 0204	1.4
0919	4.3	0836	4.1
F 1606	0.9	SA 1455	1.1
2206	4.4	2115	4.2
12 0425	1.3	**27** 0313	1.4
1030	4.3	0942	4.2
SA 1716	0.9	SU 1600	1.0
2305	4.3	2214	4.3
13 0536	1.2	**28** 0424	1.3
1125	4.4	1048	4.3
SU 1805	0.9	M 1706	1.0
		2322	4.5
14 0005	4.5	**29** 0535	1.1
0626	1.1	1145	4.5
M 1221	4.5	TU 1806	0.9
1849	0.9		
15 0052	4.6	**30** 0018	4.6
0709	0.9	0636	0.9
TU 1315	4.7	W 1237	4.5
1932	0.9	1858	0.8
		31 0107	4.8
		0725	0.7
		TH 1325	4.9
		○ 1946	0.7

Chart Datum: 2·32 metres below NAP Datum
HAT is 5·2 metres above Chart Datum

TIDES

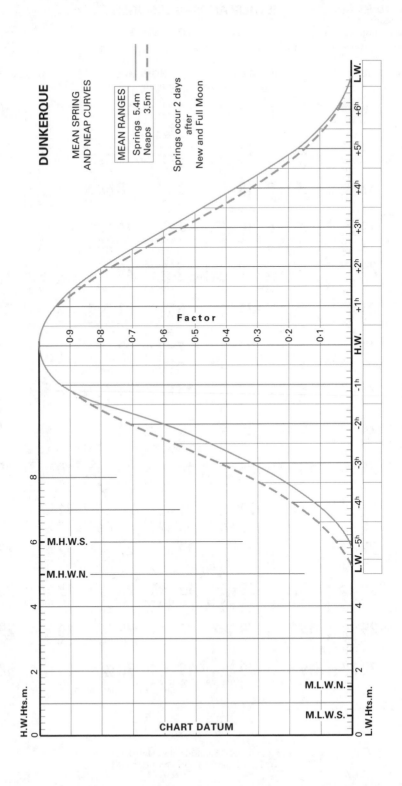

DUNKERQUE

MEAN SPRING
AND NEAP CURVES

MEAN RANGES
Springs 5.4m
Neaps 3.5m

Springs occur 2 days
after
New and Full Moon

Factor

0·9 0·8 0·7 0·6 0·5 0·4 0·3 0·2 0·1

L.W. +6ʰ +5ʰ +4ʰ +3ʰ +2ʰ +1ʰ H.W. -1ʰ -2ʰ -3ʰ -4ʰ -5ʰ L.W.

H.W.Hts.m.

M.H.W.S.
M.H.W.N.

M.L.W.N.
M.L.W.S.

L.W.Hts.m.

CHART DATUM

TIME ZONE -0100
(French Standard Time)
Subtract 1 hour for UT
For French Summer Time add
ONE hour in non-shaded areas

FRANCE – DUNKERQUE

LAT 51°03'N   LONG 2°22'E

TIMES AND HEIGHTS OF HIGH AND LOW WATERS

Dates in amber are SPRINGS
Dates in yellow are NEAPS

2009

JANUARY

Day	Time m	Day	Time m
1 TH	0318 5.6 / 1014 0.9 / 1543 5.6 / 2228 1.2	**16** F	0405 5.8 / 1110 0.6 / 1635 5.7 / 2326 1.1
2 F	0352 5.5 / 1050 1.0 / 1619 5.5 / 2305 1.2	**17** SA	0447 5.6 / 1153 0.8 / 1720 5.4
3 SA	0427 5.4 / 1129 1.1 / 1659 5.4 / 2346 1.3	**18** SU	0009 1.3 / 0535 5.4 / 1240 1.1 / 1812 5.1 ◐
4 SU	0511 5.3 / 1213 1.2 / 1751 5.3 ◐	**19** M	0059 1.6 / 0632 5.1 / 1334 1.4 / 1915 4.8
5 M	0034 1.5 / 0608 5.2 / 1307 1.5 / 1852 5.2	**20** TU	0159 1.8 / 0745 4.8 / 1438 1.7 / 2029 4.7
6 TU	0133 1.6 / 0713 5.2 / 1417 1.4 / 1958 5.1	**21** W	0310 1.9 / 0902 4.7 / 1551 1.8 / 2141 4.7
7 W	0250 1.6 / 0823 5.2 / 1536 1.3 / 2111 5.1	**22** TH	0433 1.8 / 1013 4.8 / 1710 1.7 / 2245 4.8
8 TH	0407 1.5 / 0938 5.3 / 1647 1.2 / 2225 5.3	**23** F	0543 1.6 / 1115 5.0 / 1807 1.5 / 2338 5.1
9 F	0517 1.2 / 1049 5.5 / 1754 1.0 / 2327 5.6	**24** SA	0632 1.3 / 1203 5.3 / 1849 1.3
10 SA	0621 1.0 / 1149 5.8 / 1853 0.8	**25** SU	0019 5.3 / 0709 1.1 / 1241 5.5 / 1923 1.1
11 SU	0020 5.8 / 0717 0.7 / 1242 6.1 / 1945 0.7 ○	**26** M	0053 5.5 / 0742 0.9 / 1314 5.6 / 1955 1.0
12 M	0109 5.9 / 0807 0.5 / 1332 6.2 / 2032 0.7	**27** TU	0122 5.7 / 0815 0.8 / 1343 5.7 / 2028 0.9
13 TU	0155 6.0 / 0855 0.3 / 1420 6.2 / 2118 0.7	**28** W	0152 5.8 / 0848 0.7 / 1413 5.8 / 2101 0.8
14 W	0240 6.0 / 0941 0.3 / 1506 6.1 / 2202 0.8	**29** TH	0222 5.8 / 0922 0.6 / 1444 5.8 / 2134 0.8
15 TH	0323 5.9 / 1026 0.4 / 1551 5.9 / 2244 0.9	**30** F	0253 5.8 / 0954 0.6 / 1515 5.8 / 2206 0.9
		31 SA	0322 5.6 / 1027 0.7 / 1545 5.7 / 2239 0.9

FEBRUARY

Day	Time m	Day	Time m
1 SU	0352 5.7 / 1101 0.8 / 1620 5.6 / 2315 1.0	**16** M	0451 5.5 / 1152 1.1 / 1719 5.2 ◐
2 M	0431 5.6 / 1140 0.9 / 1705 5.4 / 2357 1.2	**17** TU	0006 1.4 / 0539 5.1 / 1238 1.5 / 1812 4.8
3 TU	0523 5.5 / 1228 1.2 / 1807 5.2	**18** W	0100 1.7 / 0644 4.7 / 1340 1.8 / 1929 4.4
4 W	0052 1.4 / 0632 5.2 / 1336 1.4 / 1922 5.0	**19** TH	0215 2.0 / 0817 4.4 / 1501 2.0 / 2102 4.3
5 TH	0210 1.6 / 0754 5.0 / 1505 1.5 / 2051 4.9	**20** F	0349 2.0 / 0946 4.5 / 1635 1.9 / 2220 4.6
6 F	0342 1.6 / 0931 5.1 / 1632 1.4 / 2221 5.1	**21** SA	0516 1.7 / 1055 4.8 / 1742 1.6 / 2316 4.9
7 SA	0507 1.3 / 1050 5.4 / 1749 1.1 / 2325 5.4	**22** SU	0609 1.3 / 1143 5.2 / 1826 1.3 / 2358 5.2
8 SU	0616 0.9 / 1148 5.8 / 1847 0.8	**23** M	0647 1.0 / 1221 5.5 / 1900 1.1
9 M	0016 5.7 / 0710 0.5 / 1237 6.0 / 1934 0.7 ○	**24** TU	0031 5.5 / 0718 0.8 / 1253 5.7 / 1931 0.9
10 TU	0059 5.9 / 0756 0.3 / 1321 6.2 / 2017 0.6	**25** W	0101 5.7 / 0750 0.6 / 1321 5.8 / 2003 0.8 ●
11 W	0139 6.0 / 0840 0.1 / 1403 6.2 / 2058 0.6	**26** TH	0128 5.8 / 0823 0.6 / 1348 5.9 / 2036 0.7
12 TH	0218 6.1 / 0921 0.2 / 1444 6.1 / 2137 0.7	**27** F	0155 5.9 / 0857 0.5 / 1416 5.9 / 2109 0.6
13 F	0255 6.1 / 1001 0.3 / 1522 6.0 / 2214 0.8	**28** SA	0223 6.0 / 0930 0.5 / 1445 5.9 / 2142 0.7
14 SA	0333 6.0 / 1038 0.5 / 1559 5.8 / 2250 0.9		
15 SU	0410 5.8 / 1114 0.8 / 1637 5.5 / 2326 1.1		

MARCH

Day	Time m	Day	Time m
1 SU	0253 6.0 / 1003 0.5 / 1516 5.9 / 2214 0.7	**16** M	0338 5.8 / 1038 0.8 / 1559 5.5 / 2250 1.0
2 M	0326 5.9 / 1036 0.6 / 1552 5.7 / 2250 0.9	**17** TU	0415 5.5 / 1112 1.1 / 1637 5.2 / 2327 1.3
3 TU	0406 5.8 / 1114 0.9 / 1638 5.5 / 2333 1.1	**18** W	0459 5.1 / 1153 1.5 / 1725 4.9 ◐
4 W	0459 5.5 / 1203 1.2 / 1742 5.1 ◐	**19** TH	0014 1.7 / 0559 4.7 / 1250 1.9 / 1835 4.4
5 TH	0029 1.4 / 0613 5.1 / 1314 1.5 / 1906 4.8	**20** F	0123 1.9 / 0725 4.4 / 1410 2.1 / 2010 4.2
6 F	0152 1.6 / 0747 4.9 / 1453 1.6 / 2050 4.7	**21** SA	0257 2.0 / 0906 4.4 / 1549 2.0 / 2140 4.4
7 SA	0332 1.5 / 0933 5.0 / 1627 1.4 / 2215 5.0	**22** SU	0431 1.7 / 1020 4.7 / 1702 1.6 / 2240 4.8
8 SU	0500 1.2 / 1045 5.4 / 1740 1.1 / 2315 5.4	**23** M	0530 1.3 / 1110 5.1 / 1750 1.3 / 2324 5.2
9 M	0605 0.8 / 1138 5.7 / 1832 0.8	**24** TU	0611 1.0 / 1149 5.4 / 1827 1.0 / 2359 5.5
10 TU	0001 5.7 / 0654 0.4 / 1223 6.0 / 1916 0.7	**25** W	0645 0.8 / 1221 5.7 / 1859 0.8
11 W	0040 5.9 / 0738 0.3 / 1302 6.1 / 1956 0.6 ●	**26** TH	0029 5.7 / 0719 0.6 / 1250 5.8 / 1933 0.7
12 TH	0115 6.0 / 0818 0.2 / 1339 6.1 / 2033 0.6	**27** F	0056 5.8 / 0754 0.5 / 1317 5.9 / 2008 0.6
13 F	0150 6.1 / 0856 0.3 / 1415 6.0 / 2109 0.6	**28** SA	0123 5.9 / 0829 0.4 / 1346 6.0 / 2043 0.6
14 SA	0226 6.0 / 0931 0.4 / 1450 5.9 / 2143 0.7	**29** SU	0155 6.0 / 0905 0.4 / 1418 6.0 / 2119 0.6
15 SU	0302 6.0 / 1005 0.6 / 1525 5.8 / 2217 0.9	**30** M	0229 6.0 / 0941 0.5 / 1454 5.9 / 2155 0.6
		31 TU	0308 6.0 / 1018 0.7 / 1536 5.7 / 2235 0.8

APRIL

Day	Time m	Day	Time m
1 W	0355 5.8 / 1100 0.9 / 1629 5.4 / 2322 1.0	**16** TH	0434 5.1 / 1123 1.5 / 1656 4.9 / 2345 1.5
2 TH	0457 5.4 / 1155 1.3 / 1741 5.0 ◐	**17** F	0531 4.8 / 1214 1.8 / 1800 4.5 ◐
3 F	0024 1.3 / 0615 5.1 / 1314 1.6 / 1903 4.7	**18** SA	0042 1.8 / 0642 4.5 / 1322 2.0 / 1915 4.4
4 SA	0153 1.5 / 0750 4.9 / 1450 1.6 / 2043 4.7	**19** SU	0200 1.8 / 0804 4.5 / 1451 1.9 / 2039 4.5
5 SU	0325 1.3 / 0925 5.1 / 1615 1.4 / 2159 5.0	**20** M	0330 1.7 / 0926 4.7 / 1608 1.7 / 2149 4.8
6 M	0445 1.0 / 1029 5.4 / 1721 1.1 / 2254 5.4	**21** TU	0436 1.3 / 1022 5.1 / 1702 1.3 / 2238 5.1
7 TU	0545 0.7 / 1119 5.7 / 1810 0.9 / 2337 5.6	**22** W	0525 1.0 / 1105 5.4 / 1745 1.1 / 2317 5.4
8 W	0632 0.5 / 1201 5.8 / 1852 0.8	**23** TH	0606 0.8 / 1141 5.6 / 1823 0.9 / 2349 5.6
9 TH	0014 5.8 / 0714 0.4 / 1237 5.9 / 1930 0.7 ○	**24** F	0644 0.6 / 1212 5.7 / 1901 0.7
10 F	0048 5.9 / 0752 0.4 / 1311 5.9 / 2006 0.7	**25** SA	0020 5.8 / 0723 0.5 / 1243 5.9 / 1940 0.6 ●
11 SA	0124 6.0 / 0827 0.5 / 1346 5.9 / 2041 0.7	**26** SU	0054 5.9 / 0802 0.5 / 1319 5.9 / 2019 0.6
12 SU	0200 6.0 / 0902 0.6 / 1421 5.8 / 2116 0.7	**27** M	0133 6.0 / 0843 0.5 / 1359 5.9 / 2101 0.5
13 M	0236 5.9 / 0935 0.7 / 1455 5.7 / 2150 0.8	**28** TU	0215 6.1 / 0925 0.6 / 1444 5.8 / 2144 0.6
14 TU	0312 5.7 / 1009 1.0 / 1530 5.5 / 2225 1.0	**29** W	0304 6.0 / 1009 0.6 / 1536 5.6 / 2231 0.7
15 W	0350 5.4 / 1043 1.2 / 1608 5.2 / 2301 1.3	**30** TH	0401 5.7 / 1059 1.0 / 1636 5.4 / 2325 0.9

Chart Datum: 2·69 metres below IGN Datum
HAT is 6·4 metres above Chart Datum

TIDES

TIME ZONE -0100
(French Standard Time)
Subtract 1 hour for UT
For French Summer Time add
ONE hour in **non-shaded areas**

FRANCE – DUNKERQUE

LAT 51°03′N   LONG 2°22′E

TIMES AND HEIGHTS OF HIGH AND LOW WATERS

Dates in amber are **SPRINGS**
Dates in yellow are **NEAPS**

2009

MAY

Time	m		Time	m
1 F 0505	5.5	**16** SA 0509	5.0
1200	1.3	1146	1.6
1740	5.1	1731	4.8
2 SA 0031	1.1	**17** SU 0012	1.5
0614	5.2	0606	4.8
1317	1.5	1241	1.7
1854	4.9	1831	4.7
3 SU 0150	1.2	**18** M 0111	1.5
0741	5.1	0708	4.7
1436	1.5	1347	1.7
2022	4.9	◐ 1934	4.7
4 M 0308	1.2	**19** TU 0224	1.5
0902	5.0	0815	4.8
1550	1.3	1503	1.6
◑ 2130	5.1	2040	4.8
5 TU 0419	0.9	**20** W 0336	1.3
1002	5.4	0919	5.0
1652	1.1	1607	1.4
2224	5.3	2139	5.0
6 W 0518	0.8	**21** TH 0434	1.1
1052	5.5	1011	5.3
1743	1.0	1659	1.2
2308	5.5	2227	5.3
7 TH 0606	0.7	**22** F 0525	0.9
1134	5.6	1056	5.5
1826	0.9	1746	1.0
2347	5.6	2309	5.5
8 F 0648	0.7	**23** SA 0611	0.8
1211	5.7	1136	5.7
1905	0.9	1831	0.8
		2349	5.7
9 SA 0025	5.7	**24** SU 0655	0.7
0725	0.7	1217	5.8
1247	5.7	1916	0.7
1942	0.8		
10 SU 0103	5.8	**25** M 0033	5.9
0801	0.8	0741	0.6
1324	5.7	1302	5.8
2018	0.8	2002	0.6
11 M 0141	5.8	**26** TU 0120	6.0
0836	0.8	0827	0.6
1359	5.7	1350	5.9
O 2055	0.8	● 2050	0.5
12 TU 0218	5.7	**27** W 0211	6.1
0912	0.9	0916	0.6
1435	5.6	1443	5.8
2131	0.9	2139	0.5
13 W 0255	5.6	**28** TH 0307	6.0
0947	1.1	1006	0.8
1511	5.4	1537	5.7
2207	1.0	2231	0.6
14 TH 0335	5.4	**29** F 0403	5.9
1023	1.2	1100	0.9
1551	5.2	1632	5.5
2243	1.2	2326	0.7
15 F 0419	5.2	**30** SA 0500	5.6
1101	1.4	1157	1.1
1638	5.0	1728	5.4
2324	1.3		
		31 SU 0026	0.8
		0602	5.4
		1301	1.3
		1832	5.2

JUNE

Time	m		Time	m
1 M 0132	0.9	**16** TU 0030	1.2
0715	5.3	0621	5.0
1407	1.4	1255	1.5
1946	5.1	◐ 1840	5.0
2 TU 0239	1.0	**17** W 0127	1.3
0827	5.2	0716	5.0
1512	1.4	1356	1.5
◐ 2052	5.2	1938	5.0
3 W 0344	1.0	**18** TH 0235	1.3
0927	5.2	0815	5.0
1615	1.3	1508	1.5
2148	5.2	2038	5.1
4 TH 0445	1.0	**19** F 0344	1.2
1020	5.3	0916	5.2
1712	1.2	1614	1.3
2239	5.3	2139	5.2
5 F 0538	1.0	**20** SA 0445	1.1
1107	5.4	1016	5.3
1802	1.1	1713	1.2
2326	5.4	2237	5.4
6 SA 0624	1.0	**21** SU 0542	0.9
1151	5.4	1111	5.5
1845	1.0	1808	0.9
		2331	5.7
7 SU 0009	5.5	**22** M 0636	0.8
0705	1.0	1203	5.7
1232	5.5	1900	0.7
1925	0.9		
8 M 0051	5.6	**23** TU 0023	5.9
0742	1.0	0727	0.7
1311	5.5	1254	5.8
2003	0.9	1952	0.5
9 TU 0131	5.6	**24** W 0115	6.0
0818	1.0	0818	0.6
1347	5.6	1345	5.9
2040	0.8	2042	0.4
10 W 0208	5.6	**25** TH 0208	6.1
0855	1.0	0908	0.6
1421	5.5	1436	5.9
2116	0.9	● 2133	0.3
11 TH 0243	5.6	**26** F 0301	6.1
0931	1.1	0958	0.7
1457	5.5	1526	5.9
2152	0.9	2223	0.3
12 F 0321	5.5	**27** SA 0353	6.0
1006	1.2	1047	0.8
1535	5.4	1614	5.8
2227	1.0	2314	0.4
13 SA 0401	5.4	**28** SU 0444	5.8
1042	1.2	1137	1.0
1616	5.3	1703	5.6
2303	1.1		
14 SU 0444	5.3	**29** M 0006	0.6
1120	1.3	0537	5.6
1659	5.1	1230	1.2
2343	1.1	1757	5.4
15 M 0530	5.1	**30** TU 0100	0.8
1204	1.4	0636	5.3
1747	5.0	1326	1.3
		1859	5.3

JULY

Time	m		Time	m
1 W 0159	1.0	**16** TH 0040	1.2
0741	5.1	0623	5.2
1427	1.5	1303	1.5
2007	5.1	1844	5.1
2 TH 0301	1.2	**17** F 0141	1.3
0845	5.0	0725	5.1
1533	1.5	1413	1.6
2112	5.1	1951	5.1
3 F 0407	1.3	**18** SA 0258	1.4
0947	5.0	0835	5.0
1642	1.4	1534	1.5
2214	5.1	◐ 2106	5.1
4 SA 0513	1.3	**19** SU 0414	1.3
1046	5.1	0952	5.1
1743	1.3	1647	1.3
◐ 2312	5.2	2223	5.3
5 SU 0607	1.3	**20** M 0523	1.1
1139	5.2	1102	5.4
1832	1.1	1754	1.0
		2326	5.7
6 M 0002	5.3	**21** TU 0626	0.9
0651	1.2	1158	5.6
1223	5.3	1853	0.7
1914	1.0		
7 TU 0045	5.5	**22** W 0020	5.9
0729	1.1	0720	0.7
1301	5.5	1247	5.9
1950	0.9	1944	0.4
8 W 0122	5.6	**23** TH 0109	6.1
0803	1.1	0809	0.6
1335	5.5	1334	6.0
2025	0.8	2033	0.3
9 TH 0156	5.6	**24** F 0158	6.2
0838	1.0	0855	0.6
1406	5.6	1419	6.0
2100	0.8	2119	0.2
10 F 0228	5.6	**25** SA 0245	6.2
0912	1.0	0940	0.6
1438	5.6	1503	6.0
2133	0.8	2205	0.2
11 SA 0300	5.6	**26** SU 0331	6.1
0946	1.0	1024	0.7
1511	5.6	1546	5.9
O 2206	0.8	● 2250	0.4
12 SU 0335	5.6	**27** M 0416	5.9
1018	1.0	1107	0.9
1546	5.5	1630	5.8
2239	0.8	2334	0.6
13 M 0411	5.5	**28** TU 0501	5.6
1052	1.1	1151	1.1
1619	5.4	1716	5.6
2314	0.9		
14 TU 0447	5.4	**29** W 0020	0.9
1129	1.2	0550	5.4
1655	5.3	1239	1.3
2353	1.0	1811	5.3
15 W 0529	5.3	**30** TH 0112	1.2
1211	1.3	0649	5.0
1743	5.2	1338	1.6
		1920	5.0
		31 F 0214	1.5
		0801	4.8
		1448	1.7
		2037	4.8

AUGUST

Time	m		Time	m
1 SA 0328	1.7	**16** SU 0225	1.6
0917	4.7	0811	4.9
1612	1.7	1506	1.6
2153	4.8	2054	5.0
2 SU 0449	1.6	**17** M 0355	1.5
1028	4.8	0946	5.0
1726	1.5	1633	1.4
◐ 2300	5.0	◐ 2221	5.3
3 M 0551	1.4	**18** TU 0515	1.2
1126	5.1	1057	5.4
1818	1.2	1746	1.0
2352	5.3	2322	5.7
4 TU 0636	1.3	**19** W 0618	0.9
1210	5.3	1150	5.7
1859	1.0	1843	0.6
5 W 0032	5.5	**20** TH 0011	6.0
0712	1.1	0708	0.7
1245	5.5	1234	5.9
1933	0.9	1931	0.3
6 TH 0106	5.6	**21** F 0056	6.2
0744	1.0	0752	0.6
1316	5.6	1314	6.1
2004	0.7	2016	0.2
7 F 0136	5.7	**22** SA 0138	6.3
0816	0.9	0834	0.6
1344	5.7	1353	6.2
2037	0.7	2059	0.2
8 SA 0204	5.8	**23** SU 0220	6.2
0848	0.9	0915	0.7
1412	5.8	1433	6.2
2109	0.6	2140	0.3
9 SU 0233	5.8	**24** M 0301	6.1
0920	0.9	0955	0.8
1441	5.8	1513	6.1
O 2140	0.7	2220	0.5
10 M 0303	5.8	**25** TU 0341	5.9
0951	0.9	1033	0.9
1509	5.7	1554	5.9
2211	0.7	● 2258	0.7
11 TU 0331	5.7	**26** W 0421	5.7
1022	1.0	1112	1.1
1536	5.7	1637	5.6
2243	0.8	2338	1.1
12 W 0400	5.6	**27** TH 0505	5.3
1056	1.1	1154	1.4
1609	5.6	1727	5.3
2319	1.0		
13 TH 0438	5.5	**28** F 0024	1.4
1135	1.2	0559	4.9
1654	5.4	1248	1.7
		1834	4.9
14 F 0003	1.2	**29** SA 0125	1.8
0532	5.2	0713	4.6
1224	1.4	1402	1.9
1758	5.2	2001	4.6
15 SA 0101	1.4	**30** SU 0246	2.0
0647	5.0	0843	4.5
1334	1.6	1538	1.9
1920	5.0	2131	4.6
		31 M 0421	1.9
		1005	4.7
		1701	1.6
		2242	4.9

Chart Datum: 2·69 metres below IGN Datum
HAT is 6·4 metres above Chart Datum

FRANCE – DUNKERQUE

LAT 51°03'N   LONG 2°22'E

TIMES AND HEIGHTS OF HIGH AND LOW WATERS

Dates in amber are **SPRINGS**
Dates in yellow are **NEAPS**

2009

SEPTEMBER

Time m	Time m
1 0528 1.6 / 1103 5.0 / TU 1755 1.3 / 2331 5.3	**16** 0505 1.3 / 1044 5.4 / W 1734 0.9 / 2310 5.8
2 0613 1.3 / 1145 5.3 / W 1835 1.0	**17** 0603 0.9 / 1133 5.8 / TH 1827 0.5 / 2356 6.1
3 0009 5.5 / 0647 1.1 / TH 1220 5.6 / 1907 0.8	**18** 0649 0.8 / 1213 6.0 / F 1912 0.3 ●
4 0041 5.7 / 0717 1.0 / F 1249 5.7 / ○ 1936 0.7	**19** 0036 6.2 / 0731 0.7 / SA 1249 6.1 / 1954 0.3
5 0109 5.8 / 0747 0.9 / SA 1315 5.8 / 2008 0.6	**20** 0113 6.2 / 0810 0.7 / SU 1325 6.2 / 2033 0.3
6 0134 5.9 / 0819 0.8 / SU 1339 5.9 / 2040 0.6	**21** 0150 6.2 / 0848 0.7 / M 1403 6.2 / 2111 0.5
7 0200 5.9 / 0851 0.8 / M 1406 5.9 / 2112 0.6	**22** 0228 6.1 / 0925 0.8 / TU 1442 6.1 / 2148 0.7
8 0227 5.9 / 0923 0.8 / TU 1433 5.9 / 2143 0.7	**23** 0306 5.9 / 1001 0.9 / W 1521 5.9 / 2224 0.9
9 0255 5.9 / 0954 0.9 / W 1504 5.9 / 2215 0.8	**24** 0344 5.6 / 1038 1.1 / TH 1602 5.6 / 2301 1.3
10 0326 5.7 / 1029 1.0 / TH 1540 5.8 / 2251 1.0	**25** 0424 5.3 / 1117 1.4 / F 1649 5.2 / 2343 1.6
11 0406 5.5 / 1108 1.2 / F 1627 5.5 / 2336 1.3	**26** 0514 4.9 / 1206 1.7 / SA 1752 4.8 ◐
12 0503 5.2 / 1200 1.4 / SA 1736 5.2 ◐	**27** 0038 2.0 / 0624 4.6 / SU 1314 2.0 / 1917 4.5
13 0038 1.6 / 0629 4.9 / SU 1315 1.7 / 1910 4.9	**28** 0158 2.2 / 0756 4.4 / M 1452 2.1 / 2055 4.5
14 0210 1.7 / 0804 4.8 / M 1454 1.6 / 2054 5.0	**29** 0337 2.1 / 0926 4.6 / TU 1620 1.8 / 2207 4.9
15 0346 1.6 / 0940 5.0 / TU 1624 1.3 / 2214 5.4	**30** 0448 1.7 / 1025 4.9 / W 1717 1.4 / 2256 5.2

OCTOBER

Time m	Time m
1 0536 1.4 / 1109 5.3 / TH 1758 1.1 / 2335 5.5	**16** 0541 1.0 / 1109 5.8 / F 1805 0.6 / 2334 6.0
2 0613 1.2 / 1145 5.6 / F 1832 0.9	**17** 0626 0.9 / 1148 6.0 / SA 1849 0.5
3 0007 5.7 / 0644 1.0 / SA 1215 5.7 / 1903 0.7	**18** 0011 6.1 / 0707 0.8 / SU 1224 6.1 / ● 1929 0.5
4 0035 5.9 / 0715 0.9 / SU 1240 5.9 / ○ 1936 0.7	**19** 0047 6.1 / 0745 0.8 / M 1300 6.1 / 2007 0.6
5 0059 6.0 / 0748 0.8 / M 1306 6.0 / 2009 0.6	**20** 0123 6.1 / 0822 0.8 / TU 1338 6.1 / 2044 0.7
6 0126 6.0 / 0822 0.8 / TU 1335 6.1 / 2044 0.7	**21** 0200 6.0 / 0859 0.9 / W 1417 6.0 / 2119 0.9
7 0156 6.0 / 0857 0.8 / W 1407 6.1 / 2118 0.7	**22** 0237 5.8 / 0935 1.0 / TH 1456 5.8 / 2155 1.1
8 0230 6.0 / 0933 0.9 / TH 1444 6.0 / 2154 0.9	**23** 0315 5.6 / 1012 1.2 / F 1537 5.6 / 2231 1.4
9 0308 5.8 / 1011 1.0 / F 1526 5.8 / 2234 1.1	**24** 0354 5.3 / 1050 1.4 / SA 1622 5.3 / 2311 1.7
10 0355 5.5 / 1055 1.2 / SA 1621 5.5 / 2323 1.4	**25** 0441 5.0 / 1134 1.7 / SU 1718 4.9
11 0501 5.2 / 1152 1.4 / SU 1740 5.2	**26** 0000 1.9 / 0541 4.7 / M 1230 1.9 / ◐ 1827 4.6
12 0032 1.7 / 0623 4.9 / M 1312 1.6 / 1907 5.0	**27** 0105 2.1 / 0654 4.5 / TU 1348 2.0 / 1950 4.6
13 0206 1.8 / 0755 4.8 / TU 1446 1.6 / 2045 5.1	**28** 0233 2.1 / 0819 4.6 / W 1518 1.8 / 2112 4.8
14 0334 1.6 / 0923 5.1 / W 1608 1.2 / 2157 5.5	**29** 0351 1.9 / 0931 4.8 / TH 1622 1.5 / 2207 5.1
15 0446 1.3 / 1023 5.5 / TH 1714 0.8 / 2250 5.8	**30** 0446 1.6 / 1022 5.2 / F 1711 1.2 / 2250 5.4
	31 0529 1.3 / 1102 5.5 / SA 1751 1.0 / 2326 5.6

NOVEMBER

Time m	Time m
1 0606 1.1 / 1135 5.7 / SU 1828 0.9 / 2357 5.8	**16** 0645 1.0 / 1203 5.9 / M 1907 0.8 ●
2 0642 1.0 / 1205 5.8 / M 1904 0.9 ○	**17** 0026 5.9 / 0724 0.9 / TU 1242 5.9 / 1945 0.9
3 0026 5.9 / 0719 0.9 / TU 1236 6.0 / 1942 0.7	**18** 0104 5.9 / 0802 0.9 / W 1322 5.9 / 2022 0.9
4 0058 6.0 / 0758 0.8 / W 1312 6.1 / 2021 0.7	**19** 0142 5.8 / 0840 0.9 / TH 1402 5.9 / 2058 1.0
5 0136 6.0 / 0838 0.8 / TH 1351 6.1 / 2101 0.8	**20** 0219 5.7 / 0917 1.0 / F 1441 5.8 / 2134 1.2
6 0217 6.0 / 0920 0.8 / F 1437 6.0 / 2143 0.9	**21** 0255 5.6 / 0954 1.1 / SA 1520 5.6 / 2210 1.4
7 0304 5.9 / 1004 0.9 / SA 1528 5.9 / 2230 1.1	**22** 0333 5.4 / 1030 1.3 / SU 1602 5.4 / 2247 1.5
8 0358 5.6 / 1055 1.1 / SU 1630 5.6 / 2324 1.4	**23** 0416 5.2 / 1109 1.4 / M 1649 5.1 / 2329 1.7
9 0502 5.3 / 1154 1.2 / M 1737 5.4 ◑	**24** 0506 5.0 / 1154 1.6 / TU 1743 4.9 ◑
10 0032 1.6 / 0610 5.1 / TU 1309 1.4 / 1854 5.2	**25** 0018 1.9 / 0603 4.8 / W 1249 1.7 / 1844 4.8
11 0152 1.7 / 0732 5.0 / W 1428 1.3 / 2022 5.3	**26** 0119 2.0 / 0706 4.7 / TH 1359 1.7 / 1950 4.8
12 0308 1.6 / 0853 5.2 / TH 1542 1.1 / 2129 5.4	**27** 0235 1.9 / 0813 4.8 / F 1515 1.6 / 2057 5.0
13 0416 1.4 / 0952 5.4 / F 1647 0.9 / 2223 5.6	**28** 0344 1.7 / 0917 5.0 / SA 1615 1.4 / 2153 5.2
14 0514 1.2 / 1041 5.6 / SA 1741 0.8 / 2309 5.8	**29** 0439 1.5 / 1010 5.3 / SU 1706 1.2 / 2240 5.4
15 0602 1.1 / 1124 5.8 / SU 1827 0.8 / 2349 5.8	**30** 0527 1.3 / 1054 5.5 / M 1753 1.0 / 2321 5.6

DECEMBER

Time m	Time m
1 0612 1.1 / 1134 5.7 / TU 1836 0.9	**16** 0015 5.6 / 0712 1.0 / W 1236 5.7 / ● 1931 1.1
2 0000 5.8 / 0656 0.9 / W 1215 5.9 / ○ 1920 0.8	**17** 0055 5.7 / 0751 0.9 / TH 1316 5.8 / 2008 1.0
3 0041 5.9 / 0740 0.8 / TH 1258 6.1 / 2005 0.8	**18** 0132 5.7 / 0828 0.9 / F 1354 5.8 / 2043 1.1
4 0125 6.0 / 0826 0.7 / F 1346 6.2 / 2051 0.8	**19** 0207 5.7 / 0904 0.9 / SA 1430 5.7 / 2118 1.1
5 0212 6.0 / 0914 0.6 / SA 1436 6.1 / 2139 0.9	**20** 0240 5.7 / 0938 1.0 / SU 1504 5.6 / 2152 1.2
6 0302 5.9 / 1003 0.7 / SU 1529 6.0 / 2228 1.0	**21** 0314 5.6 / 1012 1.0 / M 1540 5.5 / 2225 1.3
7 0354 5.7 / 1054 0.8 / M 1624 5.8 / 2321 1.2	**22** 0351 5.5 / 1045 1.1 / TU 1619 5.4 / 2300 1.4
8 0447 5.6 / 1150 0.9 / TU 1721 5.6	**23** 0431 5.3 / 1122 1.2 / W 1702 5.3 / 2339 1.5
9 0018 1.4 / 0545 5.4 / W 1252 1.1 / ◑ 1828 5.4	**24** 0515 5.2 / 1203 1.4 / TH 1750 5.1 ◑
10 0123 1.5 / 0654 5.2 / TH 1359 1.1 / 1943 5.3	**25** 0024 1.6 / 0607 5.0 / F 1254 1.5 / 1846 5.0
11 0230 1.6 / 0810 5.2 / F 1507 1.2 / 2052 5.3	**26** 0119 1.7 / 0706 4.9 / SA 1358 1.6 / 1946 4.9
12 0338 1.5 / 0916 5.3 / SA 1614 1.2 / 2152 5.3	**27** 0229 1.8 / 0809 4.9 / SU 1514 1.5 / 2051 5.0
13 0444 1.4 / 1013 5.4 / SU 1715 1.1 / 2245 5.4	**28** 0344 1.7 / 0915 5.1 / M 1621 1.4 / 2156 5.2
14 0541 1.3 / 1105 5.5 / M 1808 1.1 / 2333 5.5	**29** 0448 1.5 / 1019 5.3 / TU 1721 1.2 / 2254 5.4
15 0629 1.2 / 1153 5.6 / TU 1852 1.1	**30** 0546 1.4 / 1114 5.6 / W 1815 1.0 / 2345 5.6
	31 0639 0.9 / 1204 5.9 / TH 1906 0.9 ○

TIDES

Chart Datum: 2·69 metres below IGN Datum
HAT is 6·4 metres above Chart Datum

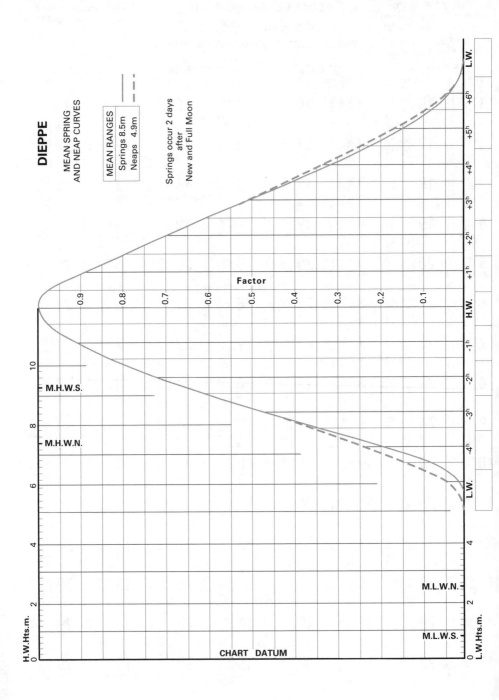

DIEPPE

MEAN SPRING
AND NEAP CURVES

MEAN RANGES
Springs 8.5m
Neaps 4.9m

Springs occur 2 days
after
New and Full Moon

Factor

TIME ZONE -0100
(French Standard Time)
Subtract 1 hour for UT
For French Summer Time add ONE hour in non-shaded areas

FRANCE – DIEPPE

LAT 49°56'N   LONG 1°05'E

TIMES AND HEIGHTS OF HIGH AND LOW WATERS

Dates in amber are **SPRINGS**
Dates in yellow are **NEAPS**

2009

JANUARY

Day				
1 TH	0214 8.5	0858 1.8	1428 8.5	2118 1.6
2 F	0249 8.3	0933 1.9	1504 8.3	2153 1.8
3 SA	0326 8.2	1011 2.1	1544 8.0	2232 2.0
4 SU	0408 7.9	1055 2.3	1629 7.8	◑ 2318 2.2
5 M	0458 7.8	1149 2.4	1726 7.6	
6 TU	0014 2.4	0601 7.6	1254 2.5	1839 7.5
7 W	0125 2.5	0720 7.6	1413 2.4	2000 7.6
8 TH	0248 2.3	0835 8.0	1533 2.0	2111 8.0
9 F	0403 1.9	0941 8.4	1640 1.5	2215 8.5
10 SA	0508 1.5	1040 8.8	1742 1.1	2313 8.9
11 SU	0607 1.2	1135 9.2	1841 0.8 ○	
12 M	0007 9.3	1227 9.5	1936 0.5	
13 TU	0056 9.4	0756 0.8	1315 9.6	2025 0.5
14 W	0143 9.4	0843 0.8	1400 9.5	2109 0.6
15 TH	0226 9.3	0925 1.0	1443 9.2	2148 0.9
16 F	0308 9.0	1003 1.3	1524 8.8	2222 1.4
17 SA	0348 8.6	1039 1.7	1606 8.3	2256 1.9
18 SU	0430 8.0	1117 2.2	1651 7.7	2336 2.4
19 M	0518 7.5	1205 2.6	1746 7.1	
20 TU	0029 2.9	0622 7.1	1309 3.0	1902 6.7
21 W	0143 3.1	0745 6.9	1431 3.0	2029 6.8
22 TH	0308 3.0	0901 7.1	1547 2.7	2136 7.2
23 F	0417 2.6	0958 7.6	1645 2.2	2225 7.6
24 SA	0509 2.2	1042 8.0	1733 1.8	2305 8.1
25 SU	0552 1.9	1120 8.3	1814 1.5	2341 8.4
26 M	0631 1.6	1155 8.6	1851 1.3 ●	
27 TU	0015 8.6	0706 1.4	1230 8.8	1927 1.2
28 W	0049 8.8	0740 1.3	1303 9.0	2000 1.1
29 TH	0122 8.9	0812 1.2	1336 9.0	2032 1.0
30 F	0154 8.9	0844 1.3	1409 8.9	2103 1.1
31 SA	0227 8.8	0916 1.4	1442 8.8	2133 1.3

FEBRUARY

Day				
1 SU	0300 8.7	0948 1.6	1517 8.5	2205 1.6
2 M	0336 8.4	1025 1.8	1557 8.2	2244 1.9
3 TU	0419 8.0	1112 2.2	1647 7.7	◑ 2335 2.3
4 W	0516 7.6	1214 2.5	1759 7.3	
5 TH	0046 2.6	0642 7.3	1340 2.6	1935 7.2
6 F	0221 2.6	0816 7.5	1514 2.2	2101 7.7
7 SA	0349 2.1	0933 8.1	1630 1.6	2211 8.3
8 SU	0459 1.6	1036 8.7	1736 1.1	2309 8.9
9 M	0602 1.1	1129 9.2	1835 0.6	2358 9.3
10 TU	0657 0.6	1216 9.6	1925 0.4 ○	
11 W	0042 9.6	0744 0.6	1259 9.7	2009 0.3
12 TH	0123 9.6	0825 0.6	1339 9.7	2046 0.5
13 F	0201 9.5	0901 0.8	1417 9.4	2118 0.8
14 SA	0237 9.2	0931 1.1	1452 9.0	2145 1.2
15 SU	0310 8.7	0959 1.5	1526 8.4	2211 1.8
16 M	0343 8.2	1029 2.0	1602 7.7	◑ 2243 2.3
17 TU	0421 7.5	1110 2.6	1646 7.0	2329 3.0
18 W	0514 6.9	1207 3.1	1759 6.4	
19 TH	0041 3.5	0647 6.4	1337 3.3	1952 6.3
20 F	0229 3.4	0831 6.6	1516 3.0	2113 6.8
21 SA	0352 2.9	0935 7.2	1622 2.4	2203 7.5
22 SU	0447 2.3	1020 7.8	1711 1.9	2243 8.0
23 M	0531 1.8	1058 8.3	1753 1.4	2318 8.5
24 TU	0610 1.4	1134 8.7	1831 1.1	2353 8.8
25 W	0646 1.2	1208 9.0	1906 0.9 ●	
26 TH	0026 9.0	0720 1.0	1241 9.2	1940 0.8
27 F	0058 9.2	0753 0.9	1313 9.3	2011 0.7
28 SA	0130 9.2	0825 0.9	1346 9.2	2042 0.8

MARCH

Day				
1 SU	0202 9.2	0857 1.0	1420 9.1	2112 1.0
2 M	0235 8.8	0928 1.2	1455 8.8	2143 1.4
3 TU	0311 8.6	1004 1.6	1535 8.3	2221 1.8
4 W	0353 8.1	1050 2.0	1625 7.7	◑ 2313 2.4
5 TH	0452 7.5	1154 2.5	1742 7.1	
6 F	0028 2.8	0627 7.1	1326 2.6	1931 7.1
7 SA	0213 2.7	0812 7.3	1507 2.2	2101 7.4
8 SU	0343 2.1	0930 8.0	1625 1.6	2206 8.4
9 M	0453 1.5	1028 8.7	1729 1.0	2256 9.0
10 TU	0552 1.0	1116 9.2	1821 0.6	2340 9.3
11 W	0640 0.7	1158 9.5	1906 0.4 ○	
12 TH	0020 9.5	0722 0.6	1238 9.6	1944 0.4
13 F	0057 9.5	0759 0.6	1313 9.5	2016 0.6
14 SA	0131 9.4	0830 0.8	1348 9.3	2044 0.9
15 SU	0204 9.1	0857 1.0	1420 8.9	2109 1.3
16 M	0235 8.7	0923 1.5	1451 8.4	2133 1.8
17 TU	0304 8.2	0951 1.9	1523 7.8	2203 2.4
18 W	0337 7.6	1027 2.5	1602 7.1	2245 3.0
19 TH	0421 6.9	1118 3.1	1705 6.4	2349 3.5
20 F	0546 6.3	1239 3.4	1901 6.2	
21 SA	0138 3.6	0746 6.4	1429 3.2	2032 6.7
22 SU	0311 3.0	0858 7.0	1543 2.6	2127 7.4
23 M	0409 2.4	0946 7.7	1634 1.9	2209 8.0
24 TU	0455 1.8	1026 8.3	1718 1.4	2246 8.6
25 W	0536 1.4	1103 8.7	1759 1.1	2322 8.9
26 TH	0616 1.1	1139 9.0	1837 0.9	● 2356 9.1
27 F	0653 0.9	1214 9.2	1913 0.7	
28 SA	0030 9.3	0729 0.8	1248 9.3	1947 0.6
29 SU	0104 9.4	0804 0.7	1323 9.3	2020 0.8
30 M	0139 9.3	0838 0.8	1400 9.2	2054 1.0
31 TU	0215 9.1	0914 1.1	1440 8.8	2129 1.4

APRIL

Day				
1 W	0255 8.6	0953 1.5	1523 8.3	2212 1.9
2 TH	0342 8.0	1043 2.0	1620 7.6	◑ 2308 2.4
3 F	0448 7.4	1150 2.4	1746 7.1	
4 SA	0028 2.8	0627 7.1	1325 2.5	1928 7.2
5 SU	0209 2.6	0803 7.5	1458 2.0	2048 7.8
6 M	0331 2.0	0914 8.1	1610 1.5	2146 8.4
7 TU	0436 1.4	1008 8.7	1708 1.0	2234 8.9
8 W	0530 1.1	1053 9.0	1756 0.8	2316 9.2
9 TH	0615 0.9	1134 9.2	1837 0.7	○ 2353 9.3
10 F	0653 0.8	1211 9.3	1912 0.8	
11 SA	0028 9.3	0727 0.8	1246 9.2	1943 0.9
12 SU	0101 9.2	0758 0.9	1319 9.0	2012 1.1
13 M	0133 9.0	0828 1.2	1352 8.7	2039 1.4
14 TU	0204 8.6	0856 1.5	1424 8.3	2106 1.9
15 W	0235 8.2	0924 1.9	1457 7.8	2136 2.4
16 TH	0308 7.6	0959 2.4	1536 7.2	2217 2.9
17 F	0351 7.0	1045 2.8	1632 6.7	◑ 2314 3.3
18 SA	0501 6.5	1153 3.2	1801 6.5	
19 SU	0039 3.4	0641 6.5	1325 3.1	1931 6.7
20 M	0209 3.1	0801 6.9	1444 2.6	2035 7.3
21 TU	0314 2.5	0857 7.5	1543 2.1	2124 7.9
22 W	0406 1.9	0944 8.1	1632 1.6	2206 8.4
23 TH	0454 1.5	1026 8.5	1718 1.2	2246 8.8
24 F	0539 1.2	1106 8.9	1802 1.0	2324 9.1
25 SA	0622 0.9	1145 9.1	1843 0.8 ●	
26 SU	0002 9.3	0703 0.8	1224 9.3	1923 0.8
27 M	0040 9.4	0744 0.7	1304 9.3	2001 0.8
28 TU	0120 9.3	0824 0.8	1347 9.1	2041 1.0
29 W	0202 9.1	0905 1.0	1432 8.8	2123 1.4
30 TH	0249 8.6	0951 1.3	1523 8.3	2211 1.8

Chart Datum: 4·45 metres below IGN Datum
HAT is 10·1 metres above Chart Datum

TIDES

TIME ZONE -0100
(French Standard Time)
Subtract 1 hour for UT
For French Summer Time add
ONE hour in **non-shaded areas**

FRANCE – DIEPPE
LAT 49°56'N   LONG 1°05'E
TIMES AND HEIGHTS OF HIGH AND LOW WATERS

Dates in amber are **SPRINGS**
Dates in yellow are **NEAPS**

2009

MAY

Time	m	Time	m
1 0343	8.1	**16** 0333	7.4
1045	1.8	1023	2.5
F 1626	7.8	SA 1607	7.2
2312	2.2	2248	2.8
2 0453	7.6	**17** 0428	7.0
1154	2.1	1118	2.7
SA 1744	7.5	SU 1710	7.0
		2350	2.9
3 0029	2.4	**18** 0537	6.9
0616	7.5	1225	2.7
SU 1316	2.1	M 1822	7.0
1905	7.6		
4 0152	2.2	**19** 0101	2.8
0736	7.6	0652	7.0
M 1432	1.9	TU 1336	2.6
2017	7.9	1931	7.3
5 0303	1.9	**20** 0210	2.5
0844	8.0	0758	7.4
TU 1539	1.6	W 1442	2.2
2116	8.3	2030	7.8
6 0405	1.6	**21** 0311	2.1
0940	8.4	0854	7.9
W 1636	1.4	TH 1541	1.8
2205	8.6	2121	8.2
7 0458	1.3	**22** 0408	1.7
1026	8.6	0945	8.3
TH 1724	1.2	F 1635	1.5
2247	8.8	2208	8.6
8 0543	1.2	**23** 0501	1.3
1108	8.8	1032	8.7
F 1803	1.2	SA 1726	1.2
2326	8.9	2253	8.9
9 0621	1.2	**24** 0552	1.1
1145	8.8	1118	8.9
SA 1839	1.2	SU 1815	1.0
		2337	9.1
10 0001	8.9	**25** 0640	0.9
0656	1.1	1204	9.1
SU 1221	8.8	M 1902	0.9
1912	1.3		
11 0034	8.9	**26** 0022	9.3
0731	1.2	0728	0.7
M 1255	8.7	TU 1251	9.2
1945	1.4	1948	0.9
12 0108	8.7	**27** 0109	9.3
0804	1.3	0815	0.7
TU 1330	8.5	W 1340	9.1
2017	1.6	2034	1.0
13 0142	8.5	**28** 0157	9.1
0835	1.5	0903	0.8
W 1405	8.3	TH 1430	8.9
2047	1.9	2123	1.2
14 0216	8.2	**29** 0248	8.8
0906	1.8	0953	1.1
TH 1440	7.9	F 1524	8.6
2119	2.2	2214	1.5
15 0251	7.8	**30** 0343	8.4
0940	2.1	1047	1.4
F 1519	7.5	SA 1621	8.3
2158	2.6	2311	1.8
		31 0443	8.1
		1145	1.7
		SU 1722	8.0

JUNE

Time	m	Time	m
1 0013	2.0	**16** 0446	7.4
0548	7.8	1137	2.3
M 1248	1.9	TU 1720	7.4
1828	7.8		
2 0118	2.1	**17** 0005	2.5
0656	7.7	0545	7.3
TU 1353	1.9	W 1235	2.4
1935	7.8	1823	7.4
3 0223	2.0	**18** 0108	2.5
0805	7.8	0653	7.4
W 1456	1.9	TH 1341	2.3
2038	8.0	1931	7.6
4 0325	1.9	**19** 0217	2.2
0907	7.9	0803	7.6
TH 1556	1.8	F 1450	2.1
2133	8.2	2036	7.9
5 0422	1.8	**20** 0325	1.9
0959	8.1	0906	8.0
F 1647	1.8	SA 1557	1.8
2220	8.3	2133	8.3
6 0510	1.6	**21** 0428	1.5
1044	8.2	1004	8.4
SA 1731	1.7	SU 1656	1.5
2301	8.4	2227	8.7
7 0553	1.5	**22** 0527	1.2
1125	8.4	1059	8.8
SU 1811	1.6	M 1753	1.2
2339	8.5	2319	9.0
8 0632	1.4	**23** 0623	0.9
1202	8.4	1151	9.1
M 1849	1.5	TU 1847	1.0
9 0014	8.6	**24** 0011	9.2
0709	1.4	0719	0.7
TU 1238	8.5	W 1243	9.2
1926	1.6	1941	0.9
10 0050	8.5	**25** 0102	9.3
0746	1.4	0812	0.6
W 1314	8.5	TH 1334	9.3
2001	1.6	2032	0.8
11 0125	8.5	**26** 0152	9.3
0820	1.5	0902	0.6
TH 1350	8.4	F 1424	9.2
2034	1.8	2121	0.9
12 0201	8.3	**27** 0241	9.2
0853	1.6	0949	0.7
F 1426	8.2	SA 1512	9.0
2106	1.9	2208	1.1
13 0237	8.1	**28** 0329	8.9
0926	1.8	1035	1.0
SA 1502	8.0	SU 1600	8.7
2141	2.1	2254	1.4
14 0315	7.9	**29** 0419	8.5
1004	2.0	1120	1.4
SU 1542	7.8	M 1650	8.3
2222	2.3	2341	1.8
15 0357	7.6	**30** 0511	8.0
1047	2.2	1209	1.8
M 1627	7.6	TU 1744	7.9
2310	2.4		

JULY

Time	m	Time	m
1 0034	2.1	**16** 0454	7.6
0610	7.6	1146	2.3
W 1304	2.2	TH 1726	7.6
1847	7.6		
2 0135	2.3	**17** 0018	2.4
0720	7.3	0557	7.4
TH 1408	2.4	F 1249	2.5
1957	7.5	1837	7.5
3 0242	2.4	**18** 0130	2.4
0833	7.3	0719	7.4
F 1516	2.4	SA 1408	2.4
2103	7.6	1958	7.6
4 0348	2.2	**19** 0252	2.2
0936	7.5	0838	7.7
SA 1617	2.2	SU 1529	2.1
2159	7.8	2109	8.0
5 0445	2.0	**20** 0405	1.7
1028	7.8	0947	8.2
SU 1709	2.0	M 1637	1.7
2244	8.1	2212	8.5
6 0532	1.8	**21** 0510	1.3
1111	8.1	1048	8.7
M 1753	1.8	TU 1739	1.2
2324	8.3	2309	9.0
7 0615	1.6	**22** 0613	0.9
1149	8.3	1143	9.1
TU 1833	1.7	W 1838	0.9
8 0000	8.4	**23** 0003	9.3
0654	1.4	0711	0.6
W 1224	8.5	TH 1234	9.4
1911	1.6	1933	0.7
9 0035	8.6	**24** 0052	9.6
0732	1.3	0804	0.4
TH 1259	8.6	F 1322	9.6
1946	1.5	2023	0.6
10 0110	8.6	**25** 0139	9.6
0806	1.3	0850	0.3
F 1333	8.6	SA 1407	9.5
2019	1.5	2107	0.7
11 0144	8.6	**26** 0223	9.5
0838	1.3	0932	0.5
SA 1406	8.6	SU 1449	9.3
2050	1.6	2147	0.9
12 0217	8.5	**27** 0305	9.1
0909	1.4	1009	0.9
SU 1439	8.4	M 1530	8.9
2122	1.7	2224	1.3
13 0251	8.4	**28** 0346	8.6
0941	1.6	1044	1.4
M 1513	8.3	TU 1611	8.4
2156	1.8	2302	1.8
14 0326	8.1	**29** 0430	8.0
1016	1.8	1122	2.0
TU 1549	8.1	W 1657	7.9
2235	2.0	2346	2.3
15 0406	7.9	**30** 0522	7.4
1056	2.0	1211	2.6
W 1632	7.8	TH 1755	7.3
2321	2.2		
		31 0045	2.7
		0633	6.9
		F 1320	2.9
		1914	7.0

AUGUST

Time	m	Time	m
1 0202	2.9	**16** 0057	2.6
0803	6.8	0651	7.1
SA 1443	2.9	SU 1341	2.7
2038	7.1	1936	7.4
2 0321	2.7	**17** 0232	2.4
0920	7.1	0825	7.5
SU 1556	2.6	M 1513	2.3
2142	7.5	2058	7.9
3 0426	2.3	**18** 0353	1.8
1014	7.6	0940	8.1
M 1653	2.2	TU 1625	1.7
2230	7.9	2204	8.5
4 0517	1.9	**19** 0501	1.2
1056	8.1	1040	8.8
TU 1738	1.8	W 1729	1.2
2308	8.3	2301	9.1
5 0600	1.6	**20** 0604	0.8
1132	8.4	1132	9.3
W 1818	1.6	TH 1828	0.8
2343	8.5	2350	9.5
6 0638	1.3	**21** 0659	0.6
1205	8.6	1219	9.6
TH 1854	1.4	F 1919	0.6
7 0017	8.7	**22** 0035	9.7
0714	1.2	0746	0.3
F 1238	8.8	SA 1301	9.7
1928	1.3	2004	0.5
8 0049	8.9	**23** 0117	9.7
0747	1.1	0828	0.4
SA 1310	8.9	SU 1342	9.6
1959	1.3	2044	0.6
9 0121	8.9	**24** 0157	9.5
0817	1.1	0904	0.6
SU 1341	8.9	M 1420	9.4
2029	1.3	2118	0.9
10 0152	8.9	**25** 0235	9.2
0847	1.2	0935	1.1
M 1411	8.8	TU 1456	9.0
2059	1.4	2148	1.4
11 0224	8.7	**26** 0311	8.6
0916	1.3	1003	1.6
TU 1443	8.7	W 1532	8.4
2130	1.5	2220	1.9
12 0257	8.5	**27** 0349	8.0
0946	1.6	1036	2.2
W 1516	8.4	TH 1611	7.8
2203	1.8	2259	2.5
13 0334	8.2	**28** 0435	7.2
1021	1.9	1122	2.9
TH 1555	8.1	F 1703	7.1
2245	2.1	2355	3.0
14 0418	7.8	**29** 0544	6.6
1108	2.3	1233	3.4
F 1645	7.7	SA 1828	6.6
2341	2.4		
15 0520	7.3	**30** 0120	3.3
1212	2.7	0733	6.5
SA 1759	7.3	SU 1413	3.4
		2012	6.7
		31 0255	3.0
		0900	6.9
		M 1535	2.9
		2120	7.2

Chart Datum: 4·45 metres below IGN Datum
HAT is 10·1 metres above Chart Datum

TIME ZONE -0100
(French Standard Time)
Subtract 1 hour for UT
For French Summer Time add
ONE hour in **non-shaded areas**

FRANCE – DIEPPE

LAT 49°56'N   LONG 1°05'E

TIMES AND HEIGHTS OF HIGH AND LOW WATERS

Dates in amber are **SPRINGS**
Dates in yellow are **NEAPS**

2009

SEPTEMBER

Time	m	Time	m
1 0404	2.4	**16** 0346	1.8
0951	7.5	0932	8.3
TU 1631	2.3	W 1617	1.6
2206	7.8	2154	8.6
2 0454	1.9	**17** 0452	1.2
1031	8.1	1026	9.0
W 1715	1.8	TH 1717	1.1
2244	8.3	2245	9.2
3 0536	1.5	**18** 0549	0.7
1105	8.5	1113	9.4
TH 1753	1.5	F 1810	0.7
2318	8.7	● 2331	9.5
4 0613	1.2	**19** 0638	0.5
1138	8.8	1156	9.6
F 1829	1.3	SA 1857	0.6
○ 2351	8.9		
5 0648	1.1	**20** 0013	9.7
1210	9.0	0721	0.5
SA 1902	1.2	SU 1236	9.7
		1938	0.6
6 0023	9.1	**21** 0052	9.6
0720	1.0	0758	0.6
SU 1242	9.1	M 1313	9.6
1934	1.1	2013	0.8
7 0054	9.1	**22** 0128	9.4
0751	1.0	0830	0.9
M 1312	9.1	TU 1348	9.3
2005	1.1	2045	1.1
8 0126	9.1	**23** 0204	9.0
0822	1.1	0859	1.3
TU 1343	9.1	W 1422	8.9
2036	1.2	2113	1.5
9 0158	9.0	**24** 0238	8.5
0851	1.2	0925	1.8
W 1415	8.9	TH 1455	8.4
2106	1.4	2143	2.0
10 0232	8.7	**25** 0314	7.9
0921	1.5	0957	2.4
TH 1449	8.6	F 1531	7.7
2139	1.7	2219	2.5
11 0310	8.3	**26** 0355	7.2
0956	2.0	1040	3.1
F 1529	8.2	SA 1619	7.0
2221	2.1	◑ 2310	3.1
12 0356	7.8	**27** 0459	6.6
1045	2.4	1147	3.6
SA 1622	7.6	SU 1740	6.5
◑ 2319	2.5		
13 0502	7.2	28 0031	3.5
1153	2.9	0646	6.4
SU 1743	7.2	M 1331	3.6
		1928	6.5
14 0042	2.8	**29** 0214	3.2
0645	7.1	0818	6.8
M 1332	2.9	TU 1457	3.1
1929	7.3	2041	7.1
15 0225	2.4	**30** 0325	2.6
0822	7.5	0912	7.4
TU 1506	2.3	W 1553	2.4
2051	7.9	2129	7.7

OCTOBER

Time	m	Time	m
1 0416	2.0	**16** 0432	1.2
0954	8.1	1004	9.0
TH 1638	1.9	F 1656	1.1
2209	8.3	2224	9.1
2 0459	1.6	**17** 0525	0.9
1030	8.5	1049	9.3
F 1718	1.5	SA 1746	0.9
2246	8.7	2307	9.3
3 0538	1.3	**18** 0610	0.8
1105	8.9	1130	9.5
SA 1756	1.3	SU 1829	0.9
2320	9.0	● 2348	9.4
4 0615	1.1	**19** 0650	0.9
1138	9.1	1208	9.5
SU 1832	1.1	M 1907	0.9
○ 2354	9.1		
5 0650	1.0	**20** 0025	9.3
1211	9.2	0725	1.0
M 1906	1.0	TU 1244	9.4
		1942	1.0
6 0026	9.2	**21** 0101	9.2
0723	1.0	0757	1.2
TU 1243	9.3	W 1318	9.1
1940	1.0	2014	1.2
7 0100	9.2	**22** 0136	8.9
0756	1.1	0828	1.6
W 1317	9.2	TH 1352	8.8
2014	1.1	2045	1.6
8 0136	9.1	**23** 0211	8.4
0829	1.3	0857	2.0
TH 1352	9.0	F 1426	8.3
2049	1.3	2115	2.0
9 0214	8.8	**24** 0247	7.9
0904	1.6	0929	2.5
F 1431	8.7	SA 1502	7.7
2126	1.7	2149	2.5
10 0256	8.3	**25** 0327	7.4
0945	2.0	1009	3.0
SA 1515	8.2	SU 1547	7.2
2212	2.1	2234	2.9
11 0348	7.8	**26** 0422	6.8
1037	2.5	1106	3.4
SU 1614	7.6	M 1653	6.7
◑ 2313	2.5	◑ 2339	3.3
12 0502	7.3	**27** 0544	6.6
1150	2.9	1229	3.5
M 1743	7.2	TU 1822	6.6
13 0040	2.7	**28** 0108	3.3
0643	7.3	0711	6.8
TU 1329	2.8	W 1355	3.2
1918	7.5	1941	6.9
14 0217	2.3	**29** 0226	2.9
0807	7.8	0816	7.3
W 1454	2.2	TH 1500	2.7
2035	8.0	2039	7.5
15 0331	1.7	**30** 0325	2.3
0912	8.4	0906	7.9
TH 1600	1.6	F 1551	2.1
2134	8.6	2125	8.0
		31 0413	1.9
		0949	8.4
		SA 1636	1.7
		2207	8.5

NOVEMBER

Time	m	Time	m
1 0457	1.5	**16** 0541	1.3
1028	8.8	1105	9.1
SU 1719	1.4	M 1801	1.2
2246	8.8	● 2325	8.9
2 0539	1.3	**17** 0620	1.3
1105	9.0	1143	9.1
M 1800	1.2	TU 1839	1.2
○ 2324	9.0		
3 0619	1.2	**18** 0003	8.9
1141	9.2	0656	1.3
TU 1840	1.1	W 1220	9.0
		1916	1.2
4 0001	9.2	**19** 0040	8.9
0657	1.1	0731	1.5
W 1218	9.3	TH 1255	8.9
1919	1.0	1951	1.3
5 0040	9.2	**20** 0116	8.7
0736	1.1	0805	1.7
TH 1257	9.3	F 1330	8.7
1958	1.0	2024	1.6
6 0121	9.1	**21** 0152	8.4
0815	1.3	0838	2.0
F 1338	9.1	SA 1406	8.4
2038	1.2	2056	1.9
7 0205	8.9	**22** 0228	8.1
0857	1.6	0910	2.3
SA 1423	8.8	SU 1443	8.0
2122	1.5	2128	2.2
8 0253	8.5	**23** 0306	7.7
0943	1.9	0946	2.6
SU 1514	8.3	M 1522	7.5
2213	1.9	2207	2.5
9 0350	8.0	**24** 0350	7.4
1039	2.3	1031	2.9
M 1617	7.8	TU 1611	7.2
◑ 2315	2.2	◐ 2256	2.8
10 0503	7.7	**25** 0446	7.1
1151	2.5	1129	3.1
TU 1734	7.6	W 1714	6.9
		2357	3.0
11 0033	2.3	**26** 0554	7.0
0622	7.6	1236	3.1
W 1313	2.5	TH 1825	7.0
1853	7.7		
12 0153	2.2	**27** 0107	2.9
0737	7.9	0706	7.2
TH 1428	2.1	F 1347	2.9
2005	8.0	1935	7.2
13 0303	1.8	**28** 0216	2.6
0842	8.3	0808	7.6
F 1533	1.7	SA 1452	2.5
2107	8.4	2034	7.6
14 0403	1.5	**29** 0319	2.2
0936	8.7	0902	8.0
SA 1629	1.4	SU 1550	2.0
2158	8.7	2125	8.1
15 0456	1.4	**30** 0414	1.9
1023	8.9	0949	8.4
SU 1718	1.3	M 1641	1.7
2244	8.9	2212	8.5

DECEMBER

Time	m	Time	m
1 0504	1.6	**16** 0557	1.7
1033	8.8	1126	8.7
TU 1730	1.3	W 1819	1.4
2257	8.8	● 2349	8.6
2 0551	1.3	**17** 0636	1.6
1116	9.1	1203	8.8
W 1817	1.1	TH 1858	1.4
○ 2341	9.1		
3 0637	1.2	**18** 0025	8.6
1200	9.3	0714	1.6
TH 1903	0.9	F 1239	8.8
		1935	1.3
4 0026	9.2	**19** 0101	8.6
0723	1.1	0750	1.6
F 1245	9.3	SA 1315	8.7
1950	0.9	2009	1.4
5 0113	9.2	**20** 0136	8.6
0809	1.2	0824	1.7
SA 1332	9.3	SU 1350	8.6
2036	0.9	2042	1.6
6 0202	9.1	**21** 0211	8.6
0856	1.3	0855	1.9
SU 1421	9.0	M 1424	8.3
2124	1.1	2112	1.8
7 0253	8.8	**22** 0245	8.2
0946	1.5	0926	2.1
M 1513	8.7	TU 1459	8.1
2215	1.4	2144	2.0
8 0347	8.5	**23** 0320	7.9
1039	1.8	1002	2.3
TU 1609	8.3	W 1536	7.8
2309	1.7	2222	2.2
9 0445	8.2	**24** 0359	7.7
1137	2.1	1044	2.5
W 1710	8.0	TH 1619	7.5
◐		◐ 2306	2.5
10 0009	2.0	**25** 0446	7.5
0548	7.9	1134	2.7
TH 1241	2.2	F 1712	7.3
1816	7.8	2359	2.7
11 0114	2.2	**26** 0546	7.3
0656	7.8	1234	2.8
F 1349	2.2	SA 1818	7.1
1927	7.7		
12 0223	2.2	**27** 0102	2.7
0805	7.9	0658	7.3
SA 1457	2.1	SU 1345	2.7
2035	7.9	1935	7.3
13 0328	2.1	**28** 0216	2.6
0907	8.1	0811	7.6
SU 1559	1.9	M 1500	2.4
2134	8.1	2044	7.6
14 0426	1.9	**29** 0330	2.3
1000	8.4	0912	8.0
M 1653	1.7	TU 1607	1.9
2225	8.3	2143	8.1
15 0515	1.8	**30** 0433	1.8
1046	8.6	1007	8.5
TU 1739	1.6	W 1705	1.5
2309	8.5	2237	8.6
		31 0529	1.5
		1059	8.9
		TH 1800	1.1
		○ 2328	9.0

Chart Datum: 4·45 metres below IGN Datum
HAT is 10·1 metres above Chart Datum

TIDES

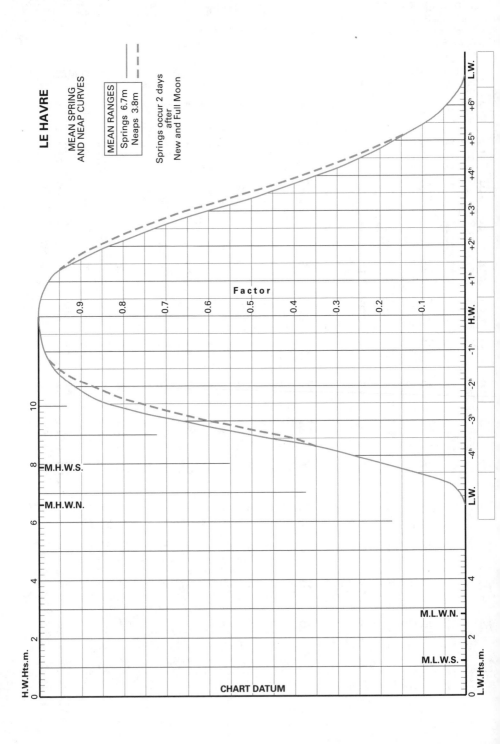

LE HAVRE

MEAN SPRING
AND NEAP CURVES

MEAN RANGES
Springs 6.7m
Neaps 3.8m

Springs occur 2 days
after
New and Full Moon

Factor

0.9 0.8 0.7 0.6 0.5 0.4 0.3 0.2 0.1

H.W.Hts.m.

M.H.W.S.
M.H.W.N.

CHART DATUM

M.L.W.N.
M.L.W.S.

L.W.Hts.m.

L.W.
+6ʰ +5ʰ +4ʰ +3ʰ +2ʰ +1ʰ H.W. -1ʰ -2ʰ -3ʰ -4ʰ L.W.

TIME ZONE -0100
(French Standard Time)
Subtract 1 hour for UT
For French Summer Time add
ONE hour in **non-shaded areas**

FRANCE – LE HAVRE

LAT 49°29'N   LONG 0°07'E

TIMES AND HEIGHTS OF HIGH AND LOW WATERS

Dates in amber are **SPRINGS**
Dates in yellow are **NEAPS**

2009

JANUARY		FEBRUARY		MARCH		APRIL	
Time m	Time m	Time m	Time m	Time m	Time m	Time m	Time m

1 0115 7.3 / 0810 2.2 / TH 1325 7.4 / 2028 1.9 — **16** 0212 7.6 / 0914 1.7 / F 1422 7.5 / 2133 1.7 — **1** 0203 7.4 / 0901 2.0 / SU 1417 7.4 / 2116 1.9 — **16** 0246 7.1 / 0936 2.4 / M 1502 6.9 / ◑ 2149 2.7 — **1** 0105 7.7 / 0809 1.4 / SU 1321 7.7 / 2024 1.4 — **16** 0137 7.5 / 0833 1.8 / M 1353 7.2 / 2042 2.2 — **1** 0159 7.4 / 0902 1.8 / W 1431 7.1 / 2119 2.2 — **16** 0212 6.7 / 0902 2.6 / TH 1443 6.4 / 2119 3.1

2 0151 7.2 / 0844 2.3 / F 1403 7.3 / 2102 2.1 — **17** 0253 7.3 / 0948 2.1 / SA 1504 7.2 / 2206 2.2 — **2** 0239 7.2 / 0936 2.2 / M 1456 7.1 / 2153 2.3 — **17** 0325 6.7 / 1011 2.9 / TU 1551 6.3 / 2231 3.2 — **2** 0139 7.6 / 0841 1.6 / M 1357 7.5 / 2055 1.8 — **17** 0207 7.1 / 0858 2.3 / TU 1426 6.8 / 2108 2.7 — **2** 0248 7.0 / 0948 2.3 / TH 1532 6.7 / ◑ 2213 2.7 — **17** 0257 6.3 / 0947 3.0 / F 1543 6.1 / ◑ 2218 3.5

3 0230 7.1 / 0921 2.5 / SA 1444 7.1 / 2140 2.3 — **18** 0335 7.0 / 1024 2.5 / SU 1550 6.8 / ◐ 2243 2.7 — **3** 0320 7.0 / 1020 2.6 / TU 1547 6.8 / ◐ 2242 2.6 — **18** 0424 6.3 / 1106 3.4 / W 1714 6.0 / 2342 3.7 — **3** 0214 7.4 / 0915 2.0 / TU 1438 7.2 / 2131 2.2 — **18** 0240 6.7 / 0930 2.8 / W 1508 6.3 / ◑ 2147 3.2 — **3** 0358 6.6 / 1055 2.7 / F 1705 6.5 / 2334 3.1 — **18** 0409 6.0 / 1058 3.3 / SA 1723 6.0 / 2355 3.6

4 0313 6.9 / 1004 2.7 / SU 1530 6.9 / ◑ 2225 2.5 — **19** 0425 6.7 / 1109 3.0 / M 1650 6.4 / 2333 3.1 — **4** 0420 6.8 / 1121 2.8 / W 1705 6.5 / 2353 3.0 — **19** 0601 6.0 / 1235 3.6 / TH 1907 5.9 — **4** 0256 7.1 / 0958 2.4 / W 1531 6.7 / ◑ 2220 2.7 — **19** 0329 6.2 / 1019 3.3 / TH 1611 5.9 / 2253 3.7 — **4** 0540 6.5 / 1232 2.7 / SA 1839 6.6 — **19** 0553 6.0 / 1235 3.2 / SU 1844 6.2

5 0403 6.8 / 1056 2.8 / M 1626 6.8 / 2321 2.7 — **20** 0531 6.5 / 1211 3.3 / TU 1811 6.2 — **5** 0554 6.6 / 1248 2.9 / TH 1848 6.5 — **20** 0135 3.7 / 0737 6.1 / F 1421 3.3 / 2024 6.2 — **5** 0359 6.6 / 1100 2.8 / TH 1659 6.4 / 2335 3.1 — **20** 0505 5.9 / 1142 3.6 / F 1819 5.8 — **5** 0121 2.9 / 0706 6.7 / SU 1406 2.4 / 1954 6.9 — **20** 0122 3.3 / 0706 6.3 / M 1351 2.8 / 1943 6.6

6 0507 6.8 / 1201 2.9 / TU 1741 6.7 — **21** 0048 3.4 / 0654 6.4 / W 1337 3.3 / 1943 6.2 — **6** 0132 2.9 / 0724 6.8 / F 1426 2.6 / 2011 6.9 — **21** 0300 3.2 / 0839 6.5 / SA 1529 2.7 / 2112 6.6 — **6** 0544 6.4 / 1234 2.9 / F 1845 6.5 — **21** 0047 3.8 / 0651 5.9 / SA 1334 3.4 / 1941 6.1 — **6** 0244 2.3 / 0813 7.1 / M 1521 1.8 / 2050 7.3 — **21** 0226 2.8 / 0800 6.7 / TU 1450 2.4 / 2029 7.0

7 0032 2.8 / 0626 6.8 / W 1322 2.8 / 1905 6.8 — **22** 0216 3.3 / 0809 6.5 / TH 1454 3.0 / 2048 6.5 — **7** 0301 2.5 / 0838 7.1 / SA 1542 2.0 / 2118 7.3 — **22** 0357 2.6 / 0922 6.9 / SU 1621 2.2 / 2148 7.0 — **7** 0124 3.0 / 0719 6.7 / SA 1417 2.5 / 2008 6.9 — **22** 0221 3.3 / 0759 6.3 / SU 1449 2.8 / 2034 6.6 — **7** 0351 1.7 / 0905 7.4 / TU 1621 1.4 / 2135 7.6 — **22** 0319 2.3 / 0845 7.1 / W 1541 2.0 / 2109 7.3

8 0158 2.7 / 0740 7.0 / TH 1445 2.4 / 2017 7.0 — **23** 0323 3.0 / 0903 6.8 / F 1553 2.6 / 2135 6.8 — **8** 0412 2.0 / 0937 7.5 / SU 1650 1.4 / 2212 7.7 — **23** 0444 2.2 / 0957 7.2 / M 1705 1.8 / 2220 7.3 — **8** 0256 2.5 / 0831 7.1 / SU 1536 1.9 / 2110 7.3 — **23** 0321 2.7 / 0847 6.8 / M 1543 2.3 / 2113 7.0 — **8** 0445 1.4 / 0949 7.7 / W 1710 1.2 / 2215 7.8 — **23** 0407 1.9 / 0925 7.4 / TH 1627 1.6 / 2147 7.5

9 0315 2.3 / 0844 7.3 / F 1553 1.9 / 2121 7.4 — **24** 0416 2.6 / 0944 7.1 / SA 1641 2.2 / 2211 7.1 — **9** 0518 1.5 / 1027 7.9 / M 1750 1.0 / ○ 2259 7.9 — **24** 0524 1.8 / 1031 7.5 / TU 1743 1.5 / 2253 7.5 — **9** 0409 1.9 / 0926 7.5 / M 1643 1.4 / 2158 7.7 — **24** 0409 2.1 / 0925 7.2 / TU 1630 1.8 / 2148 7.3 — **9** 0530 1.2 / 1030 7.8 / TH 1750 1.1 / ○ 2253 7.8 — **24** 0451 1.5 / 1004 7.6 / F 1710 1.4 / 2225 7.7

10 0420 1.9 / 0942 7.6 / SA 1655 1.5 / 2218 7.7 — **25** 0502 2.3 / 1020 7.3 / SU 1724 1.9 / 2245 7.3 — **10** 0613 1.1 / 1113 8.1 / TU 1840 0.7 / 2343 8.1 — **25** 0600 1.5 / 1104 7.7 / W 1817 1.3 / ● 2326 7.7 — **10** 0508 1.4 / 1012 7.8 / TU 1736 0.9 / 2240 7.9 — **25** 0452 1.8 / 1001 7.5 / W 1710 1.5 / 2222 7.6 — **10** 0607 1.1 / 1108 7.8 / F 1824 1.1 / 2328 7.8 — **25** 0534 1.2 / 1044 7.8 / SA 1752 1.2 / ● 2303 7.8

11 0520 1.5 / 1036 7.9 / SU 1755 1.1 / ○ 2310 7.9 — **26** 0542 2.0 / 1053 7.5 / M 1802 1.7 / ● 2317 7.4 — **11** 0658 0.9 / 1156 8.2 / W 1921 0.6 — **26** 0632 1.4 / 1137 7.8 / TH 1849 1.2 / 2358 7.8 — **11** 0556 1.0 / 1053 8.0 / W 1820 0.7 / ○ 2319 8.0 — **26** 0529 1.5 / 1036 7.7 / TH 1747 1.2 / ● 2257 7.7 — **11** 0640 1.1 / 1144 7.8 / SA 1854 1.2 — **26** 0614 1.1 / 1124 7.8 / SU 1832 1.1 / 2342 7.9

12 0618 1.3 / 1126 8.0 / M 1849 0.9 / 2359 8.0 — **27** 0618 1.8 / 1126 7.6 / TU 1837 1.5 / 2350 7.5 — **12** 0024 8.1 / 0737 0.9 / TH 1236 8.1 / 1957 0.8 — **27** 0704 1.3 / 1211 7.9 / F 1921 1.1 — **12** 0636 0.9 / 1133 8.1 / TH 1856 0.7 / 2357 8.0 — **27** 0604 1.2 / 1111 7.9 / F 1822 1.1 / 2331 7.8 — **12** 0002 7.8 / 0710 1.3 / SU 1220 7.7 / 1923 1.5 — **27** 0655 1.0 / 1207 7.8 / M 1912 1.2

13 0710 1.2 / 1213 8.1 / TU 1937 0.8 — **28** 0652 1.7 / 1159 7.7 / W 1910 1.4 — **13** 0103 8.0 / 0811 1.1 / F 1314 7.9 / 2029 1.1 — **28** 0031 7.8 / 0736 1.2 / SA 1245 7.9 / 1952 1.1 — **13** 0711 0.9 / 1210 8.0 / F 1928 0.9 — **28** 0640 1.1 / 1147 7.9 / SA 1856 1.0 — **13** 0035 7.6 / 0738 1.5 / M 1255 7.4 / 1949 1.8 — **28** 0023 7.8 / 0735 1.1 / TU 1251 7.7 / 1951 1.4

14 0046 8.0 / 0756 1.2 / W 1258 8.0 / 2020 0.9 — **29** 0022 7.6 / 0724 1.6 / TH 1232 7.7 / 1941 1.4 — **14** 0139 7.7 / 0841 1.5 / SA 1350 7.7 / 2056 1.6 — — **14** 0032 7.9 / 0741 1.1 / SA 1246 7.9 / 1956 1.2 — **29** 0006 7.9 / 0715 1.1 / SU 1224 7.9 / 1931 1.1 — **14** 0107 7.6 / 0805 1.8 / TU 1328 7.1 / 2014 2.2 — **29** 0106 7.7 / 0815 1.3 / W 1338 7.5 / 2032 1.8

15 0130 7.9 / 0837 1.4 / TH 1341 7.8 / 2058 1.2 — **30** 0055 7.6 / 0756 1.6 / F 1306 7.7 / 2013 1.5 — **15** 0213 7.4 / 0909 1.9 / SU 1425 7.3 / 2121 2.1 — — **15** 0106 7.7 / 0809 1.4 / SU 1320 7.6 / 2020 1.7 — **30** 0042 7.7 / 0750 1.2 / M 1304 7.7 / 2005 1.4 — **15** 0139 7.1 / 0831 2.2 / W 1403 6.8 / 2041 2.7 — **30** 0153 7.4 / 0858 1.7 / TH 1431 7.2 / 2118 2.2

31 0129 7.5 / 0828 1.7 / SA 1341 7.6 / 2044 1.7 — **31** 0119 7.6 / 0825 1.4 / TU 1345 7.5 / 2039 1.8

Chart Datum: 4·38 metres below IGN Datum
HAT is 8·4 metres above Chart Datum

TIDES

379

FRANCE – LE HAVRE

TIME ZONE -0100
(French Standard Time)
Subtract 1 hour for UT
For French Summer Time add
ONE hour in **non-shaded areas**

LAT 49°29'N   LONG 0°07'E

TIMES AND HEIGHTS OF HIGH AND LOW WATERS

Dates in amber are **SPRINGS**
Dates in yellow are **NEAPS**

2009

MAY

Day	Time m	Day	Time m
1 F	0247 7.1 / 0950 2.1 / 1536 6.8 / 2218 2.6	**16** SA	0236 6.6 / 0926 2.7 / 1513 6.4 / 2153 3.1
2 SA	0359 6.8 / 1059 2.4 / 1659 6.7 / 2338 2.8	**17** SU	0330 6.4 / 1021 2.9 / 1618 6.3 / 2302 3.2
3 SU	0524 6.7 / 1223 2.4 / 1817 6.8	**18** M	0441 6.3 / 1133 3.0 / 1737 6.3 ◐
4 M ◑	0102 2.6 / 0639 6.8 / 1339 2.2 / 1925 7.0	**19** TU	0016 3.1 / 0559 6.4 / 1244 2.8 / 1843 6.6
5 TU	0214 2.3 / 0745 7.0 / 1446 2.0 / 2021 7.3	**20** W	0122 2.8 / 0702 6.6 / 1347 2.5 / 1937 6.9
6 W	0317 2.0 / 0839 7.2 / 1546 1.7 / 2107 7.4	**21** TH	0222 2.5 / 0756 6.9 / 1446 2.2 / 2025 7.2
7 TH	0412 1.7 / 0925 7.4 / 1634 1.6 / 2148 7.6	**22** F	0319 2.1 / 0846 7.2 / 1542 1.9 / 2110 7.4
8 F	0456 1.6 / 1007 7.5 / 1715 1.6 / 2226 7.6	**23** SA	0412 1.7 / 0933 7.4 / 1634 1.6 / 2154 7.6
9 SA	0534 1.5 / 1046 7.6 / 1750 1.6 / 2302 7.6	**24** SU	0503 1.4 / 1019 7.6 / 1724 1.4 / 2238 7.7
10 SU	0609 1.5 / 1123 7.5 / 1823 1.6 / 2337 7.6	**25** M	0552 1.2 / 1106 7.7 / 1812 1.3 / 2323 7.8
11 M ○	0642 1.5 / 1159 7.4 / 1855 1.8	**26** TU ●	0639 1.0 / 1154 7.8 / 1859 1.3
12 TU	0011 7.5 / 0713 1.6 / 1235 7.3 / 1925 2.0	**27** W	0010 7.8 / 0727 1.0 / 1244 7.7 / 1945 1.4
13 W	0045 7.3 / 0743 1.8 / 1310 7.1 / 1955 2.3	**28** TH	0059 7.7 / 0814 1.2 / 1335 7.6 / 2033 1.7
14 TH	0119 7.1 / 0813 2.1 / 1346 6.9 / 2026 2.6	**29** F	0149 7.5 / 0903 1.4 / 1429 7.3 / 2125 1.9
15 F	0154 6.9 / 0845 2.4 / 1425 6.6 / 2103 2.9	**30** SA	0244 7.2 / 0956 1.7 / 1529 7.1 / 2221 2.2
		31 SU	0346 7.0 / 1053 2.0 / 1634 7.0 / 2323 2.4

JUNE

Day	Time m	Day	Time m
1 M	0453 6.9 / 1155 2.2 / 1740 6.9	**16** TU ◐	0348 6.7 / 1040 2.6 / 1625 6.6 / 2314 2.9
2 TU ◑	0027 2.5 / 0600 6.8 / 1259 2.3 / 1845 7.0	**17** W	0447 6.6 / 1139 2.7 / 1730 6.6
3 W	0132 2.4 / 0708 6.9 / 1402 2.3 / 1946 7.1	**18** TH	0017 2.8 / 0556 6.6 / 1245 2.6 / 1837 6.8
4 TH	0234 2.3 / 0810 7.0 / 1502 2.2 / 2038 7.2	**19** F	0126 2.6 / 0706 6.7 / 1355 2.5 / 1939 7.0
5 F	0331 2.1 / 0902 7.1 / 1554 2.1 / 2124 7.3	**20** SA	0236 2.3 / 0809 7.0 / 1504 2.2 / 2036 7.2
6 SA	0421 2.0 / 0948 7.2 / 1639 2.1 / 2205 7.4	**21** SU	0340 1.9 / 0907 7.2 / 1605 1.9 / 2129 7.5
7 SU	0503 1.9 / 1030 7.3 / 1720 2.0 / 2242 7.4	**22** M	0439 1.5 / 1002 7.5 / 1703 1.6 / 2221 7.7
8 M	0542 1.8 / 1107 7.3 / 1758 1.9 / 2317 7.5	**23** TU	0535 1.2 / 1055 7.7 / 1758 1.4 / 2311 7.8
9 TU	0619 1.7 / 1143 7.3 / 1834 2.0 / 2352 7.4	**24** W	0630 1.0 / 1146 7.8 / 1853 1.3
10 W	0654 1.7 / 1219 7.2 / 1908 2.0	**25** TH ●	0002 7.9 / 0723 0.9 / 1237 7.9 / 1945 1.2
11 TH	0027 7.3 / 0728 1.8 / 1254 7.2 / 1942 2.1	**26** F	0051 7.9 / 0813 0.9 / 1327 7.8 / 2033 1.3
12 F	0102 7.2 / 0800 1.9 / 1329 7.1 / 2015 2.3	**27** SA	0140 7.7 / 0900 1.1 / 1416 7.6 / 2120 1.5
13 SA	0137 7.1 / 0834 2.1 / 1405 6.9 / 2050 2.5	**28** SU	0229 7.5 / 0944 1.4 / 1506 7.4 / 2204 1.8
14 SU	0215 7.0 / 0909 2.3 / 1445 6.8 / 2130 2.7	**29** M	0319 7.3 / 1028 1.8 / 1557 7.1 / 2251 2.2
15 M	0258 6.8 / 0950 2.5 / 1531 6.7 / 2217 2.8	**30** TU	0413 7.0 / 1115 2.2 / 1652 6.9 / 2342 2.5

JULY

Day	Time m	Day	Time m
1 W	0514 6.7 / 1210 2.5 / 1756 6.8	**16** TH	0357 6.8 / 1048 2.6 / 1629 6.8 / 2325 2.8
2 TH	0044 2.7 / 0626 6.6 / 1315 2.7 / 1906 6.8	**17** F	0500 6.6 / 1151 2.8 / 1742 6.7
3 F	0152 2.7 / 0743 6.6 / 1421 2.8 / 2011 6.9	**18** SA ◐	0039 2.8 / 0625 6.6 / 1313 2.8 / 1904 6.8
4 SA	0256 2.6 / 0846 6.7 / 1521 2.6 / 2105 7.0	**19** SU	0205 2.5 / 0745 6.8 / 1438 2.5 / 2014 7.1
5 SU	0351 2.3 / 0936 6.9 / 1612 2.4 / 2149 7.2	**20** M	0318 2.1 / 0853 7.1 / 1547 2.0 / 2115 7.4
6 M	0439 2.1 / 1017 7.1 / 1659 2.2 / 2227 7.3	**21** TU	0422 1.6 / 0952 7.5 / 1650 1.7 / 2210 7.7
7 TU	0522 1.9 / 1054 7.2 / 1741 2.1 / 2302 7.4	**22** W	0526 1.2 / 1046 7.8 / 1752 1.3 / 2302 7.9
8 W	0603 1.8 / 1127 7.3 / 1820 2.0 / 2335 7.4	**23** TH	0625 0.9 / 1136 8.0 / 1847 1.1 / 2350 8.1
9 TH	0640 1.7 / 1201 7.3 / 1856 1.9	**24** F	0716 0.6 / 1223 8.0 / 1936 1.0
10 F ○	0009 7.5 / 0714 1.6 / 1234 7.3 / 1929 1.9	**25** SA ●	0037 8.1 / 0801 0.6 / 1308 8.0 / 2019 1.0
11 SA ○	0042 7.5 / 0746 1.7 / 1307 7.3 / 2001 2.0	**26** SU	0121 8.0 / 0842 0.9 / 1352 7.8 / 2058 1.3
12 SU	0116 7.4 / 0818 1.7 / 1340 7.3 / 2033 2.1	**27** M	0204 7.7 / 0918 1.3 / 1433 7.5 / 2134 1.7
13 M	0150 7.3 / 0849 1.9 / 1415 7.2 / 2106 2.2	**28** TU	0246 7.4 / 0953 1.8 / 1515 7.2 / 2211 2.2
14 TU	0228 7.1 / 0922 2.1 / 1453 7.0 / 2143 2.4	**29** W	0331 7.0 / 1029 2.3 / 1602 6.9 / 2253 2.6
15 W	0308 6.9 / 1000 2.3 / 1536 6.9 / 2228 2.6	**30** TH	0426 6.6 / 1115 2.9 / 1702 6.6 / 2351 3.0
		31 F	0542 6.3 / 1224 3.2 / 1824 6.4

AUGUST

Day	Time m	Day	Time m
1 SA	0111 3.1 / 0719 6.3 / 1347 3.2 / 1948 6.5	**16** SU	0006 2.9 / 0608 6.4 / 1247 3.0 / 1847 6.6
2 SU	0227 2.9 / 0832 6.5 / 1457 3.0 / 2048 6.7	**17** M	0147 2.7 / 0736 6.6 / 1424 2.7 / 2004 7.0
3 M ◑	0330 2.6 / 0922 6.8 / 1556 2.6 / 2133 7.0	**18** TU	0305 2.1 / 0847 7.2 / 1536 2.1 / 2107 7.5
4 TU	0422 2.2 / 1001 7.1 / 1645 2.3 / 2209 7.3	**19** W	0413 1.6 / 0944 7.6 / 1642 1.6 / 2200 7.8
5 W	0508 1.9 / 1034 7.3 / 1728 2.0 / 2242 7.5	**20** TH	0517 1.1 / 1034 7.9 / 1743 1.2 / 2247 8.1
6 TH	0548 1.7 / 1106 7.4 / 1806 1.8 / 2314 7.6	**21** F	0613 0.7 / 1118 8.1 / 1833 0.9 / 2332 8.2
7 F	0624 1.5 / 1137 7.5 / 1839 1.7 / 2347 7.7	**22** SA	0659 0.6 / 1201 8.1 / 1917 0.8
8 SA	0656 1.4 / 1209 7.5 / 1910 1.6	**23** SU	0014 8.2 / 0738 0.6 / 1242 8.1 / 1955 1.0
9 SU ○	0019 7.7 / 0726 1.4 / 1241 7.6 / 1940 1.6	**24** M	0055 8.1 / 0814 0.9 / 1321 7.9 / 2028 1.3
10 M	0051 7.6 / 0756 1.5 / 1313 7.5 / 2010 1.7	**25** TU ●	0134 7.8 / 0844 1.4 / 1358 7.6 / 2059 1.7
11 TU	0124 7.5 / 0826 1.6 / 1346 7.4 / 2042 1.9	**26** W	0212 7.5 / 0912 2.0 / 1434 7.2 / 2129 2.2
12 W	0159 7.3 / 0856 1.9 / 1420 7.2 / 2115 2.2	**27** TH	0251 6.9 / 0941 2.6 / 1515 6.9 / 2204 2.8
13 TH	0237 7.1 / 0929 2.2 / 1458 7.0 / 2154 2.5	**28** F	0341 6.5 / 1022 3.1 / 1611 6.4 / 2257 3.2
14 F	0322 6.8 / 1012 2.6 / 1548 6.8 / 2247 2.8	**29** SA	0501 6.0 / 1132 3.6 / 1742 6.1
15 SA	0428 6.5 / 1114 2.9 / 1708 6.6	**30** SU	0027 3.5 / 0652 6.0 / 1318 3.6 / 1920 6.2
		31 M	0202 3.2 / 0811 6.3 / 1437 3.2 / 2026 6.2

Chart Datum: 4·38 metres below IGN Datum
HAT is 8·4 metres above Chart Datum

TIME ZONE -0100
(French Standard Time)
Subtract 1 hour for UT
For French Summer Time add
ONE hour in non-shaded areas

FRANCE – LE HAVRE

LAT 49°29′N   LONG 0°07′E

TIMES AND HEIGHTS OF HIGH AND LOW WATERS

Dates in amber are **SPRINGS**
Dates in yellow are **NEAPS**

2009

SEPTEMBER

Time	m	Time	m
1 0308	2.7	**16** 0257	2.0
0900	6.7	0837	7.3
TU 1536	2.7	W 1528	2.0
2109	6.9	2054	7.5
2 0400	2.2	**17** 0403	1.5
0936	7.1	0928	7.7
W 1624	2.2	TH 1631	1.5
2144	7.3	2143	7.9
3 0445	1.8	**18** 0501	1.0
1007	7.4	1013	8.0
TH 1705	1.9	F 1725	1.1
2216	7.5	● 2227	8.1
4 0524	1.6	**19** 0551	0.8
1037	7.5	1054	8.1
F 1741	1.7	SA 1811	1.0
○ 2248	7.7	2309	8.2
5 0558	1.4	**20** 0632	0.8
1109	7.7	1134	8.1
SA 1814	1.5	SU 1850	1.0
2320	7.8	2349	8.1
6 0630	1.3	**21** 0708	0.9
1141	7.7	1213	8.0
SU 1844	1.4	M 1924	1.1
2352	7.8		
7 0700	1.3	**22** 0028	8.0
1212	7.7	0741	1.2
M 1915	1.4	TU 1249	7.9
		1956	1.4
8 0025	7.8	**23** 0105	7.7
0731	1.4	0809	1.7
TU 1244	7.7	W 1324	7.6
1947	1.5	2024	1.8
9 0100	7.7	**24** 0141	7.3
0802	1.6	0835	2.2
W 1318	7.5	TH 1358	7.2
2020	1.8	2051	2.3
10 0136	7.4	**25** 0219	6.9
0833	1.9	0902	2.7
TH 1353	7.4	F 1436	6.8
2053	2.1	2124	2.8
11 0215	7.1	**26** 0306	6.4
0907	2.3	0941	3.3
F 1432	7.1	SA 1527	6.4
2132	2.5	◑ 2213	3.3
12 0305	6.8	**27** 0421	6.0
0950	2.7	1047	3.7
SA 1528	6.7	SU 1658	6.0
◑ 2226	2.8	2338	3.6
13 0419	6.5	**28** 0608	6.0
1056	3.1	1239	3.8
SU 1659	6.5	M 1836	6.1
2352	3.0		
14 0606	6.4	**29** 0123	3.4
1240	3.2	0729	6.2
M 1840	6.6	TU 1404	3.3
		1946	6.4
15 0139	2.7	**30** 0232	2.8
0731	6.8	0821	6.7
TU 1418	2.6	W 1502	2.7
1955	7.1	2033	6.9

OCTOBER

Time	m	Time	m
1 0324	2.3	**16** 0342	1.5
0859	7.1	0906	7.7
TH 1549	2.2	F 1609	1.5
2110	7.2	2121	7.8
2 0409	1.9	**17** 0436	1.2
0932	7.4	0949	7.9
F 1631	1.9	SA 1659	1.3
2144	7.6	2205	8.0
3 0449	1.6	**18** 0522	1.1
1005	7.6	1029	8.0
SA 1709	1.7	SU 1742	1.2
2218	7.7	● 2246	8.0
4 0525	1.5	**19** 0601	1.2
1037	7.7	1107	8.0
SU 1743	1.5	M 1820	1.2
○ 2252	7.9	2325	8.0
5 0559	1.4	**20** 0636	1.3
1107	7.8	1144	7.9
M 1817	1.4	TU 1854	1.3
2326	7.9		
6 0632	1.3	**21** 0003	7.8
1144	7.8	0708	1.6
TU 1851	1.4	W 1220	7.8
		1925	1.6
7 0001	7.8	**22** 0040	7.6
0707	1.4	0738	1.9
W 1218	7.7	TH 1254	7.5
1926	1.4	1955	1.9
8 0039	7.7	**23** 0117	7.2
0741	1.6	0806	2.3
TH 1255	7.6	F 1329	7.2
2002	1.7	2024	2.3
9 0120	7.5	**24** 0155	6.9
0816	1.9	0836	2.8
F 1335	7.4	SA 1406	6.8
2038	2.0	2056	2.7
10 0206	7.2	**25** 0238	6.5
0854	2.4	0914	3.2
SA 1421	7.1	SU 1452	6.5
2120	2.4	2140	3.1
11 0301	6.8	**26** 0339	6.2
0942	2.8	1011	3.6
SU 1523	6.8	M 1603	6.1
◑ 2219	2.8	◑ 2249	3.4
12 0422	6.6	**27** 0510	6.1
1054	3.1	1141	3.7
M 1657	6.6	TU 1737	6.1
2350	2.9		
13 0600	6.6	**28** 0020	3.4
1239	3.0	0628	6.3
TU 1826	6.7	W 1306	3.4
		1849	6.3
14 0129	2.5	**29** 0135	3.0
0716	7.0	0727	6.6
W 1405	2.5	TH 1410	3.0
1937	7.1	1944	6.7
15 0241	2.0	**30** 0234	2.6
0817	7.4	0813	7.0
TH 1511	2.0	F 1502	2.5
2034	7.5	2028	7.1
		31 0323	2.2
		0852	7.3
		SA 1548	2.1
		2108	7.4

NOVEMBER

Time	m	Time	m
1 0407	1.9	**16** 0451	1.6
0928	7.6	1006	7.8
SU 1630	1.8	M 1713	1.6
2146	7.6	● 2227	7.7
2 0448	1.7	**17** 0531	1.6
1004	7.7	1044	7.8
M 1711	1.6	TU 1751	1.5
○ 2223	7.8	2307	7.7
3 0528	1.5	**18** 0607	1.7
1041	7.8	1121	7.8
TU 1750	1.4	W 1827	1.6
2302	7.8	2345	7.6
4 0607	1.5	**19** 0641	1.8
1118	7.9	1157	7.7
W 1830	1.3	TH 1901	1.7
2342	7.8		
5 0647	1.5	**20** 0022	7.5
1157	7.8	0714	2.0
TH 1910	1.4	F 1232	7.5
		1933	1.9
6 0025	7.7	**21** 0059	7.3
0726	1.7	0747	2.3
F 1240	7.7	SA 1308	7.3
1950	1.5	2005	2.2
7 0111	7.5	**22** 0135	7.0
0807	1.9	0819	2.6
SA 1326	7.5	SU 1344	7.0
2032	1.8	2038	2.5
8 0201	7.3	**23** 0213	6.8
0851	2.3	0855	3.0
SU 1417	7.3	M 1423	6.7
2120	2.2	2116	2.8
9 0301	7.0	**24** 0258	6.5
0945	2.6	0940	3.2
M 1521	7.0	TU 1511	6.5
◑ 2222	2.5	◑ 2204	3.0
10 0418	6.8	**25** 0356	6.4
1057	2.9	1040	3.4
TU 1642	6.8	W 1616	6.3
2342	2.6	2308	3.2
11 0537	6.9	**26** 0512	6.4
1222	2.8	1148	3.4
W 1800	6.9	TH 1734	6.4
12 0103	2.4	**27** 0016	3.1
0647	7.1	0621	6.5
TH 1338	2.5	F 1256	3.2
1908	7.1	1842	6.5
13 0212	2.1	**28** 0123	2.9
0748	7.3	0718	6.8
F 1443	2.1	SA 1400	2.8
2008	7.3	1938	6.8
14 0313	1.9	**29** 0226	2.6
0840	7.6	0806	7.1
SA 1540	1.9	SU 1459	2.5
2059	7.5	2028	7.1
15 0406	1.7	**30** 0322	2.2
0924	7.7	0851	7.4
SU 1630	1.7	M 1552	2.1
2145	7.7	2114	7.4

DECEMBER

Time	m	Time	m
1 0412	2.0	**16** 0506	2.1
0933	7.6	1029	7.6
TU 1641	1.7	W 1729	1.8
2159	7.6	● 2256	7.5
2 0500	1.7	**17** 0545	2.0
1016	7.7	1106	7.6
W 1728	1.5	TH 1807	1.7
○ 2244	7.7	2332	7.5
3 0547	1.6	**18** 0623	2.0
1059	7.9	1141	7.6
TH 1815	1.3	F 1843	1.7
2330	7.8		
4 0634	1.5	**19** 0006	7.4
1144	7.9	0659	2.0
F 1902	1.2	SA 1215	7.5
		1918	1.8
5 0017	7.8	**20** 0041	7.4
0720	1.5	0740	2.1
SA 1231	7.9	SU 1249	7.4
1948	1.3	1951	1.9
6 0106	7.7	**21** 0115	7.2
0808	1.7	0806	2.3
SU 1320	7.7	M 1323	7.3
2036	1.5	2023	2.1
7 0158	7.5	**22** 0148	7.1
0856	1.9	0838	2.5
M 1412	7.5	TU 1356	7.1
2125	1.7	2054	2.3
8 0253	7.3	**23** 0223	6.9
0948	2.2	0912	2.7
TU 1509	7.3	W 1434	6.9
2218	2.0	2129	2.5
9 0355	7.1	**24** 0303	6.8
1045	2.4	0952	2.9
W 1613	7.0	TH 1518	6.7
◑ 2316	2.3	◑ 2211	2.8
10 0501	7.0	**25** 0352	6.6
1147	2.6	1041	3.1
TH 1721	6.9	F 1612	6.6
		2304	2.9
11 0022	2.5	**26** 0453	6.6
0607	7.0	1140	3.1
F 1256	2.6	SA 1720	6.5
1831	6.9		
12 0131	2.5	**27** 0007	3.0
0713	7.1	0607	6.6
SA 1406	2.5	SU 1250	3.1
1941	7.0	1839	6.6
13 0237	2.4	**28** 0121	2.9
0813	7.2	0716	6.8
SU 1509	2.3	M 1407	2.8
2041	7.1	1948	6.8
14 0335	2.3	**29** 0238	2.6
0904	7.4	0815	7.1
M 1603	2.1	TU 1517	2.3
2131	7.3	2047	7.1
15 0424	2.2	**30** 0343	2.2
0949	7.5	0909	7.4
TU 1649	1.9	W 1617	1.9
2216	7.4	2141	7.4
		31 0440	1.9
		0959	7.7
		TH 1712	1.5
		○ 2232	7.7

Chart Datum: 4·38 metres below IGN Datum
HAT is 8·4 metres above Chart Datum

TIDES

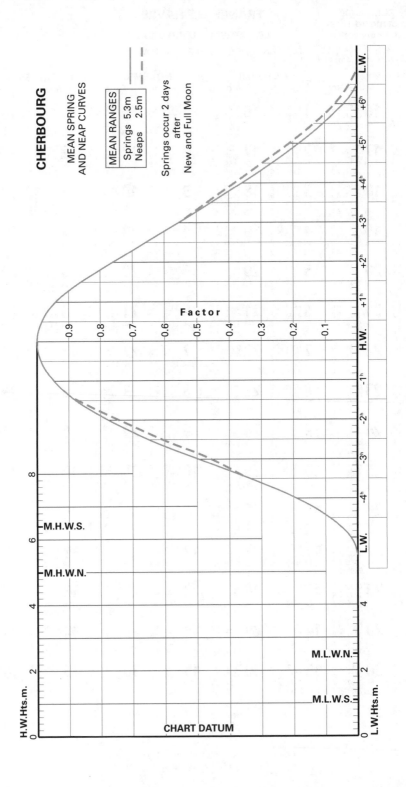

CHERBOURG

MEAN SPRING
AND NEAP CURVES

MEAN RANGES
Springs 5.3m
Neaps   2.5m

Springs occur 2 days
after
New and Full Moon

TIME ZONE -0100
(French Standard Time)
Subtract 1 hour for UT
For French Summer Time add
ONE hour in **non-shaded areas**

FRANCE – CHERBOURG

LAT 49°39′N   LONG 1°38′W

TIMES AND HEIGHTS OF HIGH AND LOW WATERS

Dates in amber are **SPRINGS**
Dates in yellow are **NEAPS**

2009

JANUARY

Day	Time m		Day	Time m	
1 TH	0556 1.9 / 1128 5.9 / 1817 1.7 / 2352 5.6		**16** F	0014 6.1 / 0654 1.6 / 1224 6.1 / 1917 1.5	
2 F	0632 2.0 / 1205 5.7 / 1853 1.8		**17** SA	0053 5.7 / 0735 1.9 / 1303 5.7 / 1956 1.9	
3 SA	0030 5.5 / 0711 2.2 / 1244 5.5 / 1935 2.0		**18** SU	0132 5.4 / 0818 2.3 / 1346 5.3 / 2041 2.4	
4 SU	0112 5.3 / 0758 2.3 / 1327 5.3 / 2023 2.2		**19** M	0220 5.1 / 0910 2.6 / 1440 4.9 / 2138 2.7	
5 M	0203 5.2 / 0855 2.5 / 1427 5.2 / 2124 2.3		**20** TU	0325 4.9 / 1020 2.8 / 1559 4.7 / 2257 2.9	
6 TU	0307 5.1 / 1005 2.6 / 1540 5.1 / 2237 2.4		**21** W	0448 4.8 / 1144 2.8 / 1732 4.7	
7 W	0423 5.2 / 1123 2.4 / 1702 5.2 / 2354 2.2		**22** TH	0019 2.8 / 0604 5.0 / 1257 2.6 / 1843 4.9	
8 TH	0540 5.5 / 1237 2.1 / 1817 5.5		**23** F	0123 2.6 / 0701 5.3 / 1352 2.3 / 1933 5.2	
9 F	0104 2.0 / 0646 5.8 / 1342 1.7 / 1922 5.8		**24** SA	0213 2.3 / 0746 5.6 / 1436 2.0 / 2013 5.5	
10 SA	0206 1.7 / 0744 6.1 / 1440 1.3 / 2021 6.2		**25** SU	0253 2.0 / 0825 5.8 / 1513 1.7 / 2049 5.7	
11 SU ○	0302 1.4 / 0838 6.4 / 1534 1.0 / 2114 6.4		**26** M ●	0329 1.8 / 0900 6.0 / 1548 1.5 / 2123 5.9	
12 M	0355 1.2 / 0930 6.6 / 1624 0.8 / 2204 6.5		**27** TU	0402 1.7 / 0933 6.1 / 1621 1.3 / 2154 6.0	
13 TU	0444 1.1 / 1018 6.7 / 1711 0.7 / 2251 6.5		**28** W	0435 1.5 / 1005 6.2 / 1653 1.2 / 2226 6.0	
14 W	0530 1.1 / 1103 6.6 / 1756 0.8 / 2334 6.3		**29** TH	0507 1.5 / 1038 6.2 / 1725 1.2 / 2258 6.0	
15 TH	0613 1.3 / 1145 6.4 / 1837 1.1		**30** F	0538 1.5 / 1110 6.2 / 1757 1.3 / 2330 6.0	
			31 SA	0611 1.6 / 1143 6.0 / 1829 1.4	

FEBRUARY

Day	Time m		Day	Time m	
1 SU	0002 5.8 / 0646 1.7 / 1215 5.8 / 1905 1.6		**16** M ◑	0043 5.5 / 0730 2.1 / 1257 5.3 / 1946 2.4	
2 M	0035 5.6 / 0726 2.0 / 1253 5.5 / 1948 1.9		**17** TU	0119 5.1 / 0812 2.5 / 1339 4.8 / 2032 2.8	
3 TU	0118 5.4 / 0816 2.3 / 1344 5.2 / 2042 2.3		**18** W	0213 4.8 / 0913 2.9 / 1456 4.5 / 2151 3.1	
4 W	0217 5.2 / 0923 2.5 / 1500 5.0 / 2157 2.5		**19** TH	0355 4.5 / 1053 3.0 / 1705 4.4 / 2345 3.1	
5 TH	0345 5.0 / 1052 2.5 / 1644 5.0 / 2331 2.5		**20** F	0537 4.7 / 1229 2.8 / 1826 4.7	
6 F	0525 5.2 / 1222 2.2 / 1813 5.3		**21** SA	0103 2.8 / 0640 5.0 / 1330 2.4 / 1913 5.1	
7 SA	0054 2.2 / 0639 5.6 / 1334 1.7 / 1920 5.7		**22** SU	0154 2.4 / 0725 5.4 / 1414 2.0 / 1952 5.5	
8 SU	0200 1.8 / 0739 6.0 / 1434 1.3 / 2017 6.1		**23** M	0233 2.0 / 0803 5.8 / 1451 1.6 / 2027 5.8	
9 M ○	0256 1.4 / 0832 6.4 / 1526 0.9 / 2106 6.4		**24** TU	0308 1.7 / 0839 6.0 / 1525 1.3 / 2100 6.0	
10 TU	0345 1.0 / 0920 6.7 / 1612 0.6 / 2151 6.5		**25** W	0340 1.4 / 0913 6.2 / 1557 1.1 / 2132 6.2	
11 W	0430 0.9 / 1004 6.8 / 1656 0.5 / 2232 6.6		**26** TH	0413 1.2 / 0945 6.4 / 1630 1.0 / 2204 6.2	
12 TH	0510 0.9 / 1043 6.7 / 1733 0.7 / 2308 6.4		**27** F	0445 1.1 / 1017 6.4 / 1701 0.9 / 2235 6.3	
13 F	0547 1.0 / 1119 6.5 / 1807 1.0 / 2342 6.2		**28** SA	0517 1.1 / 1050 6.4 / 1733 1.0 / 2306 6.2	
14 SA	0622 1.3 / 1152 6.2 / 1839 1.4				
15 SU	0012 5.9 / 0655 1.7 / 1224 5.8 / 1911 1.9				

MARCH

Day	Time m		Day	Time m	
1 SU	0549 1.2 / 1122 6.2 / 1805 1.2 / 2336 6.0		**16** M	0620 1.6 / 1149 5.7 / 1833 1.9	
2 M	0624 1.4 / 1154 6.0 / 1841 1.5		**17** TU	0002 5.6 / 0653 2.0 / 1219 5.3 / 1905 2.4	
3 TU	0009 5.8 / 0703 1.7 / 1232 5.6 / 1923 1.9		**18** W	0034 5.2 / 0731 2.4 / 1257 4.8 / 1947 2.8	
4 W	0050 5.5 / 0752 2.1 / 1323 5.2 / 2017 2.4		**19** TH	0119 4.8 / 0824 2.8 / 1402 4.4 / 2057 3.2	
5 TH	0151 5.1 / 0901 2.5 / 1448 4.8 / 2138 2.7		**20** F	0253 4.5 / 0955 3.0 / 1625 4.3 / 2258 3.2	
6 F	0330 4.9 / 1040 2.5 / 1648 4.8 / 2325 2.6		**21** SA	0456 4.5 / 1145 2.8 / 1751 4.6	
7 SA	0521 5.1 / 1217 2.2 / 1814 5.2		**22** SU	0026 2.8 / 0604 4.9 / 1251 2.4 / 1839 5.0	
8 SU	0050 2.2 / 0633 5.5 / 1327 1.7 / 1915 5.7		**23** M	0119 2.4 / 0651 5.3 / 1338 2.0 / 1918 5.4	
9 M	0153 1.7 / 0731 6.0 / 1423 1.2 / 2005 6.1		**24** TU	0159 2.0 / 0731 5.7 / 1416 1.6 / 1955 5.8	
10 TU	0244 1.3 / 0820 6.4 / 1510 0.8 / 2049 6.4		**25** W	0235 1.6 / 0809 6.0 / 1452 1.3 / 2030 6.0	
11 W ○	0329 1.0 / 0903 6.6 / 1552 0.7 / 2129 6.5		**26** TH ●	0310 1.3 / 0845 6.2 / 1527 1.0 / 2104 6.2	
12 TH	0408 0.8 / 0942 6.7 / 1629 0.7 / 2205 6.5		**27** F	0345 1.1 / 0920 6.4 / 1601 0.9 / 2137 6.4	
13 F	0445 0.8 / 1018 6.6 / 1703 0.8 / 2237 6.4		**28** SA	0420 1.0 / 0954 6.5 / 1635 0.8 / 2210 6.4	
14 SA	0518 1.0 / 1050 6.4 / 1735 1.1 / 2307 6.2		**29** SU	0454 0.9 / 1029 6.4 / 1710 0.9 / 2243 6.3	
15 SU	0550 1.2 / 1121 6.1 / 1804 1.5 / 2335 5.9		**30** M	0530 1.0 / 1105 6.3 / 1745 1.2 / 2317 6.2	
			31 TU	0608 1.3 / 1143 6.0 / 1824 1.6 / 2355 5.9	

APRIL

Day	Time m		Day	Time m	
1 W	0651 1.6 / 1226 5.6 / 1910 2.0		**16** TH	0008 5.3 / 0705 2.3 / 1235 4.9 / 1921 2.7	
2 TH ○	0042 5.5 / 0745 2.0 / 1325 5.1 / 2012 2.5		**17** F ◑	0052 4.9 / 0754 2.6 / 1334 4.6 / 2023 3.0	
3 F	0148 5.1 / 0859 2.3 / 1458 4.8 / 2140 2.7		**18** SA	0205 4.6 / 0907 2.9 / 1519 4.4 / 2158 3.1	
4 SA	0332 4.9 / 1037 2.4 / 1647 4.9 / 2321 2.5		**19** SU	0351 4.6 / 1040 2.7 / 1651 4.6 / 2325 2.9	
5 SU	0509 5.2 / 1205 2.0 / 1801 5.3		**20** M	0508 4.8 / 1153 2.4 / 1748 5.0	
6 M	0037 2.1 / 0617 5.6 / 1309 1.6 / 1856 5.7		**21** TU	0026 2.5 / 0603 5.1 / 1246 2.1 / 1833 5.3	
7 TU	0134 1.7 / 0711 6.0 / 1401 1.3 / 1942 6.1		**22** W	0113 2.1 / 0648 5.5 / 1331 1.7 / 1914 5.7	
8 W	0223 1.3 / 0757 6.2 / 1446 1.0 / 2024 6.3		**23** TH	0155 1.7 / 0731 5.9 / 1412 1.4 / 1953 6.0	
9 TH ○	0305 1.1 / 0839 6.4 / 1525 0.9 / 2101 6.4		**24** F	0235 1.4 / 0812 6.1 / 1452 1.1 / 2031 6.2	
10 F	0343 1.0 / 0916 6.4 / 1601 1.0 / 2135 6.4		**25** SA ●	0315 1.1 / 0852 6.3 / 1532 1.0 / 2108 6.4	
11 SA	0418 1.0 / 0951 6.3 / 1633 1.1 / 2206 6.3		**26** SU	0355 1.0 / 0931 6.4 / 1611 1.0 / 2146 6.4	
12 SU	0451 1.1 / 1023 6.2 / 1704 1.3 / 2236 6.1		**27** M	0435 0.9 / 1012 6.4 / 1651 1.1 / 2225 6.4	
13 M	0522 1.3 / 1054 5.9 / 1734 1.6 / 2305 5.9		**28** TU	0516 1.0 / 1054 6.2 / 1732 1.3 / 2306 6.2	
14 TU	0553 1.6 / 1124 5.6 / 1805 2.0 / 2334 5.6		**29** W	0600 1.2 / 1139 5.9 / 1818 1.6 / 2352 5.9	
15 W	0627 1.9 / 1156 5.3 / 1839 2.4		**30** TH	0649 1.5 / 1229 5.6 / 1911 2.0	

Chart Datum: 3·29 metres below IGN Datum
HAT is 7·0 metres above Chart Datum

TIDES

383

| TIME ZONE -0100 (French Standard Time) **Subtract 1 hour for UT** For French Summer Time add ONE hour in **non-shaded areas** | **FRANCE – CHERBOURG** **LAT 49°39'N   LONG 1°38'W** TIMES AND HEIGHTS OF HIGH AND LOW WATERS | Dates in amber are **SPRINGS** Dates in yellow are NEAPS **2009** |

MAY

Time	m		Time	m
1 0045 0748 F 1333 2017	5.6 1.8 5.2 2.4	**16**	0037 0732 SA 1313 1956	5.1 2.3 4.8 2.7
2 0152 0900 SA 1458 2139	5.3 2.1 5.0 2.5	**17**	0133 0829 SU 1418 2103	4.9 2.5 4.7 2.8
3 0320 1023 SU 1623 2301	5.1 2.1 5.1 2.4	**18**	0244 0936 M 1534 2217	4.8 2.5 4.7 2.7
4 0440 1137 M 1731 ☽	5.3 1.9 5.3	**19**	0357 1046 TU 1642 2323	4.8 2.4 4.9 2.5
5 0009 0546 TU 1239 1825	2.1 5.5 1.7 5.6	**20**	0501 1147 W 1737	5.1 2.1 5.2
6 0106 0641 W 1331 1912	1.8 5.7 1.5 5.9	**21**	0021 0557 TH 1242 1827	2.2 5.3 1.9 5.6
7 0155 0729 TH 1417 1954	1.6 5.9 1.4 6.0	**22**	0112 0648 F 1332 1913	1.8 5.6 1.6 5.9
8 0238 0812 F 1457 2032	1.4 6.0 1.4 6.1	**23**	0201 0738 SA 1419 1958	1.5 5.9 1.3 6.1
9 0317 0852 SA 1533 2107	1.3 6.0 1.4 6.1	**24**	0248 0825 SU 1506 2043	1.2 6.1 1.2 6.3
10 0353 0928 SU 1607 2140	1.3 6.0 1.5 6.1	**25**	0335 0913 M 1552 2128	1.0 6.3 1.1 6.4
11 0427 1002 M 1640 ○ 2212	1.4 5.9 1.6 6.0	**26**	0421 1000 TU 1638 ● 2214	0.9 6.3 1.1 6.4
12 0501 1035 TU 1713 2244	1.5 5.7 1.8 5.8	**27**	0508 1048 W 1726 2301	0.9 6.2 1.3 6.3
13 0534 1108 W 1746 2318	1.6 5.5 2.0 5.6	**28**	0557 1138 TH 1817 2351	1.0 6.0 1.5 6.1
14 0609 1143 TH 1822 2354	1.8 5.3 2.3 5.4	**29**	0649 1231 F 1912	1.3 5.8 1.8
15 0647 1223 F 1903	2.1 5.1 2.5	**30**	0045 0746 SA 1329 2012	5.8 1.5 5.5 2.1
		31	0144 0847 SU 1434 2118	5.6 1.8 5.3 2.2

JUNE

Time	m		Time	m
1 0250 0953 M 1542 2226	5.4 1.9 5.2 2.3	**16**	0152 0844 TU 1428 ◔ 2117	5.1 2.2 5.0 2.6
2 0400 1059 TU 1647 ◑ 2331	5.3 2.0 5.3 2.2	**17**	0251 0944 W 1530 2223	5.0 2.3 5.0 2.5
3 0505 1200 W 1746	5.3 2.0 5.4	**18**	0356 1050 TH 1636 2330	5.0 2.2 5.1 2.3
4 0031 0606 TH 1257 1838	2.1 5.4 1.9 5.6	**19**	0504 1155 F 1739	5.2 2.1 5.4
5 0125 0701 F 1346 1925	1.9 5.5 1.9 5.7	**20**	0034 0610 SA 1256 1839	2.0 5.4 1.9 5.7
6 0213 0750 SA 1431 2008	1.8 5.6 1.8 5.8	**21**	0132 0711 SU 1353 1933	1.7 5.7 1.6 6.0
7 0255 0833 SU 1511 2046	1.7 5.7 1.7 5.9	**22**	0227 0807 M 1447 2025	1.4 6.0 1.4 6.2
8 0334 0912 M 1548 2122	1.6 5.7 1.8 5.9	**23**	0320 0901 TU 1540 2116	1.1 6.2 1.2 6.4
9 0410 0947 TU 1623 ○ 2156	1.5 5.7 1.8 5.9	**24**	0412 0953 W 1631 ○ 2207	0.9 6.3 1.2 6.5
10 0446 1021 W 1658 2230	1.5 5.7 1.9 5.8	**25**	0502 1043 TH 1721 ● 2257	0.8 6.3 1.2 6.5
11 0521 1055 TH 1732 2305	1.6 5.6 2.0 5.7	**26**	0552 1133 F 1811 2345	0.8 6.2 1.3 6.4
12 0555 1130 F 1807 2341	1.7 5.5 2.1 5.6	**27**	0641 1221 SA 1901	1.0 6.0 1.5
13 0631 1206 SA 1844	1.8 5.3 2.2	**28**	0033 0729 SU 1308 1951	6.1 1.2 5.8 1.8
14 0019 0709 SU 1247 1927	5.4 2.0 5.2 2.4	**29**	0120 0819 M 1357 2044	5.8 1.6 5.5 2.0
15 0103 0752 M 1334 2017	5.2 2.1 5.1 2.5	**30**	0211 0912 TU 1452 2142	5.5 1.9 5.3 2.3

JULY

Time	m		Time	m
1 0309 1011 W 1554 2248	5.2 2.2 5.1 2.4	**16**	0157 0852 TH 1430 2130	5.1 2.2 5.1 2.5
2 0420 1117 TH 1703 2355	5.0 2.4 5.1 2.4	**17**	0301 0959 F 1540 2247	5.0 2.4 5.1 2.5
3 0533 1223 F 1807	5.0 2.4 5.2	**18**	0422 1117 SA 1702 ◑	5.0 2.3 5.2
4 0058 0641 SA 1321 1903	2.3 5.1 2.3 5.4	**19**	0004 0546 SU 1231 1818	2.2 5.2 2.1 5.5
5 0152 0736 SU 1412 1950	2.1 5.3 2.1 5.6	**20**	0113 0657 M 1337 1919	1.9 5.5 1.8 5.9
6 0239 0821 M 1455 2031	1.9 5.5 2.0 5.8	**21**	0214 0758 TU 1436 2015	1.4 5.9 1.5 6.2
7 0320 0859 TU 1534 2109	1.7 5.6 1.9 5.9	**22**	0310 0853 W 1530 2109	1.0 6.2 1.2 6.5
8 0357 0934 W 1610 2143	1.6 5.7 1.8 5.9	**23**	0402 0944 TH 1621 2159	0.8 6.4 1.0 6.7
9 0432 1007 TH 1644 2216	1.5 5.7 1.8 6.0	**24**	0451 1032 F 1709 2245	0.6 6.5 0.9 6.7
10 0505 1039 F 1716 ● 2248	1.5 5.7 1.8 5.9	**25**	0537 1117 SA 1754 2329	0.6 6.4 1.0 6.6
11 0537 1110 SA 1748 ○ 2321	1.5 5.7 1.8 5.9	**26**	0620 1158 SU 1837	0.8 6.3 1.2
12 0609 1143 SU 1820 2355	1.5 5.6 1.9 5.7	**27**	0009 0701 M 1237 1919	6.3 1.1 6.0 1.6
13 0641 1218 M 1856	1.6 5.5 2.0	**28**	0049 0741 TU 1315 2002	5.9 1.6 5.6 2.0
14 0031 0717 TU 1254 1937	5.5 1.8 5.4 2.2	**29**	0130 0824 W 1359 2053	5.5 2.0 5.3 2.4
15 0109 0759 TH 1336 2027	5.3 2.0 5.2 2.4	**30**	0220 0918 TH 1457 2159	5.0 2.4 5.0 2.7
		31	0332 1031 F 1619 2320	4.7 2.6 4.8 2.7

AUGUST

Time	m		Time	m
1 0510 1154 SA 1743	4.7 2.8 5.0	**16**	0402 1052 SU 1643 2348	4.8 2.6 5.0 2.4
2 0036 0630 SU 1303 ◑ 1847	2.5 4.9 2.6 5.2	**17**	0541 1220 M 1809 ◑	5.1 2.3 5.4
3 0136 0724 M 1357 1935	2.2 5.2 2.3 5.5	**18**	0103 0652 TU 1329 1911	1.9 5.5 1.9 5.9
4 0223 0806 TU 1441 2015	2.0 5.5 2.0 5.7	**19**	0204 0750 W 1426 2005	1.4 6.0 1.4 6.3
5 0303 0842 W 1518 2051	1.7 5.7 1.8 5.9	**20**	0258 0841 TH 1518 2056	0.9 6.3 1.1 6.7
6 0339 0915 TH 1552 2125	1.5 5.8 1.7 6.1	**21**	0347 0928 F 1605 2142	0.6 6.6 0.9 6.8
7 0411 0946 F 1623 2156	1.4 5.9 1.6 6.1	**22**	0432 1011 SA 1648 2224	0.5 6.6 0.8 6.8
8 0442 1016 SA 1653 2226	1.3 6.0 1.5 6.2	**23**	0513 1051 SU 1728 2303	0.6 6.6 0.9 6.7
9 0512 1045 SU 1723 ○ 2257	1.3 6.0 1.5 6.1	**24**	0550 1127 M 1805 2339	0.9 6.4 1.2 6.3
10 0542 1116 M 1754 2328	1.3 5.9 1.6 6.0	**25**	0626 1200 TU 1842 ●	1.3 6.0 1.6
11 0612 1146 TU 1826 2359	1.4 5.8 1.7 5.8	**26**	0013 0700 W 1232 1919	5.9 1.8 5.7 2.0
12 0645 1217 W 1903	1.6 5.6 2.0	**27**	0048 0736 TH 1308 2003	5.3 2.3 5.3 2.5
13 0033 0723 TH 1253 1948	5.5 1.9 5.4 2.2	**28**	0133 0824 F 1401 2106	4.9 2.8 4.9 2.8
14 0117 0812 F 1344 2050	5.2 2.3 5.2 2.5	**29**	0248 0943 SA 1537 2244	4.5 3.1 4.6 3.0
15 0223 0920 SA 1500 2216	4.9 2.6 5.0 2.6	**30**	0452 1129 SU 1721	4.5 3.1 4.8
		31	0013 0615 M 1244 1826	2.7 2.8 2.8 5.1

Chart Datum: 3·29 metres below IGN Datum
HAT is 7·0 metres above Chart Datum

TIME ZONE -0100
(French Standard Time)
Subtract 1 hour for UT
For French Summer Time add
ONE hour in **non-shaded areas**

FRANCE – CHERBOURG

LAT 49°39′N   LONG 1°38′W

TIMES AND HEIGHTS OF HIGH AND LOW WATERS

Dates in amber are **SPRINGS**
Dates in yellow are **NEAPS**

2009

SEPTEMBER

Date	Time	m	Time	m	Time	m	Time	m
1 TU	0114	2.4	0703	5.1	1336	2.4	1912	5.4
2 W	0159	2.0	0740	5.5	1417	2.0	1950	5.8
3 TH	0237	1.7	0814	5.8	1452	1.8	2025	6.0
4 F	0310	1.4	0847	6.0	1524	1.6	2058	6.2
5 SA	0342	1.3	0918	6.1	1555	1.4	2129	6.3
6 SU	0413	1.2	0948	6.2	1626	1.3	2200	6.3
7 M	0443	1.1	1016	6.2	1656	1.3	2230	6.3
8 TU	0513	1.2	1046	6.1	1727	1.4	2301	6.1
9 W	0544	1.4	1115	6.0	1800	1.6	2333	5.9
10 TH	0617	1.6	1146	5.8	1837	1.9		
11 F	0008	5.6	0656	2.0	1224	5.5	1923	2.2
12 SA ◖	0056	5.2	0746	2.4	1319	5.2	2027	2.5
13 SU	0210	4.9	0900	2.7	1445	4.9	2202	2.6
14 M	0406	4.8	1044	2.8	1641	5.1	2341	2.3
15 TU	0540	5.2	1214	2.4	1759	5.5		
16 W	0053	1.8	0643	5.6	1318	1.9	1859	6.0
17 TH	0150	1.3	0735	6.1	1412	1.4	1950	6.4
18 F ●	0240	0.9	0822	6.4	1459	1.1	2036	6.7
19 SA	0325	0.7	0904	6.6	1542	0.9	2119	6.8
20 SU	0406	0.7	0944	6.7	1622	0.9	2157	6.8
21 M	0443	0.8	1019	6.6	1659	1.0	2233	6.5
22 TU	0518	1.1	1052	6.4	1733	1.3	2307	6.2
23 W	0550	1.5	1122	6.1	1807	1.6	2339	5.8
24 TH	0622	2.0	1152	5.7	1841	2.1		
25 F	0012	5.4	0656	2.5	1227	5.3	1921	2.5
26 SA ◑	0053	4.9	0740	2.9	1314	4.9	2017	2.9
27 SU	0205	4.5	0854	3.2	1447	4.6	2155	3.1
28 M	0417	4.5	1051	3.2	1642	4.7	2336	2.9
29 TU	0539	4.7	1210	2.9	1750	5.0		
30 W	0037	2.5	0625	5.1	1302	2.5	1836	5.4

OCTOBER

Date	Time	m	Time	m	Time	m	Time	m
1 TH	0122	2.1	0703	5.5	1342	2.1	1915	5.7
2 F	0200	1.7	0738	5.8	1418	1.8	1951	6.0
3 SA	0234	1.5	0812	6.1	1451	1.5	2026	6.2
4 SU	0308	1.3	0844	6.2	1524	1.3	2059	6.4
5 M	0341	1.2	0916	6.3	1558	1.2	2132	6.4
6 TU	0414	1.1	0947	6.4	1631	1.2	2205	6.4
7 W	0447	1.2	1019	6.3	1705	1.3	2240	6.2
8 TH	0521	1.4	1052	6.2	1741	1.5	2317	6.0
9 F	0558	1.7	1129	5.9	1822	1.8	2359	5.6
10 SA	0641	2.1	1214	5.6	1912	2.1		
11 SU ◖	0054	5.2	0738	2.5	1314	5.3	2022	2.4
12 M	0216	4.9	0859	2.8	1444	5.0	2157	2.9
13 TU	0405	5.0	1040	2.7	1630	5.0	2328	2.2
14 W	0525	5.3	1200	2.3	1741	5.6		
15 TH	0035	1.8	0623	5.7	1300	1.8	1837	6.0
16 F	0129	1.4	0711	6.1	1351	1.5	1927	6.4
17 SA	0217	1.1	0756	6.4	1436	1.2	2012	6.5
18 SU	0259	1.1	0836	6.5	1517	1.1	2053	6.6
19 M	0338	1.0	0913	6.5	1556	1.1	2130	6.5
20 TU	0414	1.2	0948	6.4	1631	1.2	2205	6.3
21 W	0448	1.4	1020	6.3	1705	1.4	2239	6.1
22 TH	0520	1.7	1051	6.0	1739	1.7	2312	5.7
23 F	0553	2.1	1123	5.7	1813	2.1	2346	5.4
24 SA	0628	2.5	1158	5.4	1852	2.4		
25 SU	0028	5.0	0711	2.9	1244	5.0	1942	2.7
26 M ◖	0128	4.7	0812	3.1	1355	4.7	2056	2.9
27 TU	0307	4.6	0946	3.2	1534	4.7	2230	2.9
28 W	0434	4.7	1112	3.0	1650	4.9	2341	2.6
29 TH	0531	5.0	1211	2.6	1745	5.2		
30 F	0032	2.3	0615	5.4	1257	2.3	1830	5.6
31 SA	0115	1.9	0655	5.7	1337	1.9	1911	5.9

NOVEMBER

Date	Time	m	Time	m	Time	m	Time	m
1 SU	0154	1.6	0733	6.0	1415	1.6	1950	6.1
2 M ○	0232	1.4	0809	6.2	1453	1.4	2029	6.3
3 TU	0310	1.3	0845	6.4	1532	1.2	2107	6.4
4 W	0348	1.2	0921	6.4	1610	1.2	2145	6.4
5 TH	0427	1.3	0959	6.4	1650	1.2	2226	6.3
6 F	0507	1.5	1039	6.3	1732	1.4	2310	6.0
7 SA	0550	1.8	1123	6.1	1819	1.6	2359	5.7
8 SU	0640	2.1	1213	5.8	1913	1.9		
9 M ◑	0058	5.4	0740	2.4	1315	5.5	2021	2.2
10 TU	0214	5.2	0856	2.6	1434	5.3	2142	2.3
11 W	0341	5.2	1020	2.5	1601	5.3	2301	2.1
12 TH	0454	5.4	1133	2.3	1710	5.6		
13 F	0007	1.9	0552	5.7	1233	2.0	1809	5.8
14 SA	0102	1.7	0643	5.9	1326	1.7	1901	6.0
15 SU	0150	1.5	0728	6.2	1412	1.5	1947	6.2
16 M ●	0234	1.4	0809	6.3	1455	1.4	2030	6.2
17 TU	0313	1.5	0847	6.3	1533	1.4	2109	6.2
18 W	0350	1.6	0922	6.3	1610	1.4	2145	6.1
19 TH	0425	1.7	0956	6.2	1645	1.5	2219	5.9
20 F	0500	1.9	1030	6.0	1720	1.7	2254	5.7
21 SA	0534	2.1	1104	5.8	1755	1.9	2330	5.5
22 SU	0610	2.4	1140	5.5	1832	2.2		
23 M	0008	5.2	0649	2.6	1221	5.3	1915	2.4
24 TU ◐	0055	5.4	0737	2.8	1312	5.0	2006	2.6
25 W	0155	4.8	0837	3.0	1418	4.9	2111	2.7
26 TH	0307	4.8	0951	3.0	1533	4.9	2222	2.7
27 F	0418	4.9	1102	2.8	1637	5.0	2327	2.5
28 SA	0515	5.2	1202	2.5	1736	5.3		
29 SU	0023	2.2	0606	5.5	1253	2.2	1828	5.6
30 M	0113	1.9	0652	5.8	1341	1.8	1916	5.9

DECEMBER

Date	Time	m	Time	m	Time	m	Time	m
1 TU ●	0159	1.7	0737	6.1	1426	1.5	2002	6.1
2 W ○	0244	1.5	0819	6.3	1511	1.3	2047	6.3
3 TH	0329	1.4	0902	6.4	1556	1.1	2133	6.4
4 F	0414	1.3	0947	6.5	1642	1.1	2219	6.3
5 SA	0500	1.4	1032	6.5	1729	1.1	2308	6.2
6 SU	0549	1.6	1120	6.3	1818	1.3	2358	6.0
7 M	0640	1.8	1211	6.1	1911	1.5		
8 TU	0053	5.7	0735	2.0	1307	5.8	2008	1.8
9 W ◐	0154	5.5	0837	2.2	1409	5.6	2112	2.0
10 TH	0301	5.3	0945	2.4	1518	5.4	2221	2.2
11 F	0409	5.3	1055	2.4	1629	5.4	2330	2.2
12 SA	0514	5.4	1202	2.3	1736	5.4		
13 SU	0031	2.1	0612	5.6	1301	2.1	1836	5.6
14 M	0126	2.0	0703	5.8	1352	1.9	1929	5.7
15 TU	0213	1.9	0748	6.0	1437	1.7	2015	5.8
16 W ●	0256	1.8	0829	6.1	1518	1.6	2055	5.9
17 TH	0334	1.8	0907	6.1	1556	1.6	2132	5.9
18 F	0411	1.8	0942	6.1	1631	1.5	2206	5.9
19 SA	0446	1.8	1016	6.1	1706	1.6	2240	5.8
20 SU	0520	1.9	1050	6.0	1740	1.7	2313	5.7
21 M	0553	2.1	1124	5.8	1814	1.9	2347	5.5
22 TU	0627	2.2	1158	5.6	1848	2.0		
23 W	0023	5.3	0704	2.4	1236	5.4	1926	2.2
24 TH ◐	0105	5.2	0747	2.6	1321	5.2	2011	2.4
25 F	0154	5.0	0840	2.7	1416	5.0	2107	2.5
26 SA	0255	5.0	0946	2.8	1522	4.9	2215	2.6
27 SU	0404	5.0	1059	2.7	1636	5.0	2327	2.5
28 M	0514	5.2	1209	2.4	1747	5.3		
29 TU	0033	2.2	0617	5.5	1310	2.0	1848	5.6
30 W	0132	1.9	0712	5.9	1405	1.6	1943	5.9
31 TH ○	0226	1.6	0802	6.2	1457	1.3	2035	6.2

Chart Datum: 3·29 metres below IGN Datum
HAT is 7·0 metres above Chart Datum

TIDES

385

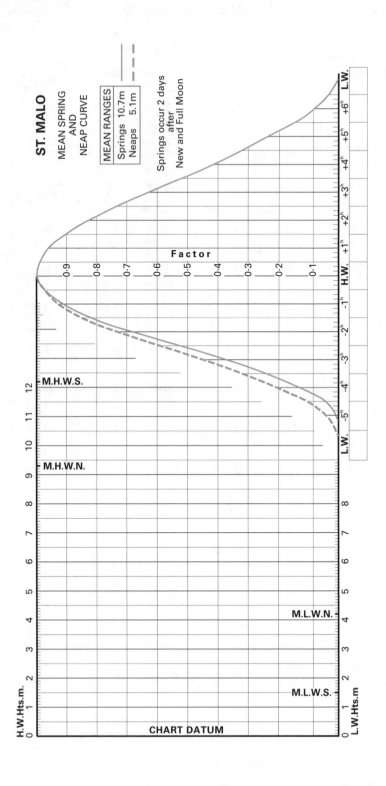

ST. MALO

MEAN SPRING
AND
NEAP CURVE

MEAN RANGES	
Springs	10.7m
Neaps	5.1m

Springs occur 2 days
after
New and Full Moon

Factor

TIME ZONE -0100
(French Standard Time)
Subtract 1 hour for UT
For French Summer Time add
ONE hour in **non-shaded areas**

FRANCE – ST MALO

LAT 48°38′N   LONG 2°02′W

TIMES AND HEIGHTS OF HIGH AND LOW WATERS

Dates in amber are **SPRINGS**
Dates in yellow are **NEAPS**

2009

JANUARY

Day				
1 TH	0412 2.9	0941 11.0	1637 2.7	2203 10.6
2 F	0446 3.1	1016 10.7	1712 3.0	2238 10.3
3 SA	0522 3.4	1053 10.3	1751 3.3	2317 9.9
4 SU	0604 3.7	1136 9.9	1835 3.7	
5 M	0005 9.6	0655 4.0	1232 9.6	1931 3.9
6 TU	0109 9.3	0802 4.2	1347 9.4	2043 4.0
7 W	0230 9.4	0924 4.0	1512 9.5	2205 3.7
8 TH	0351 9.8	1044 3.5	1630 10.0	2320 3.2
9 F	0502 10.5	1156 2.8	1739 10.7	
10 SA	0027 2.5	0604 11.3	1301 2.0	1840 11.4
11 SU ○	0128 1.9	0659 12.0	1401 1.5	1933 11.9
12 M	0224 1.5	0750 12.4	1455 1.1	2022 12.2
13 TU	0315 1.2	0837 12.6	1544 1.0	2107 12.2
14 W	0401 1.2	0921 12.5	1628 1.1	2149 12.0
15 TH	0443 1.5	1002 12.1	1708 1.6	2228 11.5
16 F	0521 2.1	1041 11.5	1744 2.3	2305 10.8
17 SA	0556 2.8	1119 10.8	1817 3.1	2342 10.1
18 SU ◐	0632 3.5	1159 9.9	1853 3.8	
19 M	0026 9.4	0715 4.2	1249 9.2	1941 4.5
20 TU	0127 8.9	0816 4.6	1403 8.6	2052 4.8
21 W	0255 8.7	0937 4.7	1536 8.6	2216 4.7
22 TH	0418 9.0	1053 4.4	1650 9.0	2326 4.3
23 F	0517 9.6	1154 3.8	1743 9.6	
24 SA	0020 3.7	0602 10.2	1243 3.2	1825 10.2
25 SU	0105 3.2	0640 10.7	1326 2.7	1902 10.6
26 M ●	0145 2.8	0716 11.1	1406 2.4	1937 11.0
27 TU	0222 2.4	0751 11.4	1443 2.1	2011 11.3
28 W	0257 2.2	0823 11.6	1518 1.9	2043 11.4
29 TH	0330 2.0	0855 11.7	1551 1.8	2115 11.4
30 F	0402 2.1	0927 11.6	1624 1.9	2145 11.3
31 SA	0434 2.3	0958 11.4	1655 2.2	2217 11.0

FEBRUARY

Day				
1 SU	0505 2.6	1031 11.0	1727 2.7	2250 10.6
2 M	0538 3.1	1106 10.4	1803 3.2	2329 10.1
3 TU ◐	0620 3.6	1152 9.8	1851 3.8	
4 W	0022 9.5	0720 4.1	1301 9.2	2000 4.2
5 TH	0146 9.1	0848 4.3	1446 9.0	2135 4.2
6 F	0332 9.3	1025 3.8	1625 9.5	2305 3.4
7 SA	0456 10.1	1147 3.0	1738 10.4	
8 SU	0020 2.7	0600 11.1	1256 2.0	1835 11.3
9 M	0122 1.9	0653 11.9	1355 1.3	1924 12.0
10 TU	0216 1.2	0740 12.5	1445 0.8	2009 12.4
11 W ○	0303 0.8	0823 12.8	1529 0.6	2049 12.5
12 TH	0344 0.8	0902 12.8	1608 0.8	2125 12.3
13 F	0421 1.1	0938 12.4	1641 1.3	2159 11.9
14 SA	0452 1.6	1011 11.8	1709 2.0	2230 11.2
15 SU	0520 2.4	1042 11.0	1733 2.9	2259 10.5
16 M	0546 3.2	1113 10.1	1758 3.7	◐ 2331 9.7
17 TU	0618 4.0	1149 9.2	1834 4.5	
18 W	0015 8.8	0708 4.8	1249 8.3	1937 5.2
19 TH	0147 8.2	0837 5.2	1451 8.0	2131 5.3
20 F	0347 8.4	1021 4.9	1628 8.5	2302 4.7
21 SA	0454 9.1	1131 4.1	1722 9.3	
22 SU	0000 3.9	0540 9.9	1222 3.3	1803 10.1
23 M	0045 3.2	0619 10.6	1306 2.6	1840 10.7
24 TU ○	0126 2.6	0655 11.2	1346 2.1	1916 11.2
25 W	0203 2.1	0730 11.7	1424 1.7	1950 11.6
26 TH ●	0239 1.7	0804 12.0	1459 1.4	2023 11.9
27 F	0313 1.5	0836 12.2	1532 1.3	2054 11.9
28 SA	0345 1.5	0907 12.1	1605 1.4	2124 11.9

MARCH

Day				
1 SU	0416 1.7	0938 11.9	1635 1.8	2155 11.5
2 M	0447 2.2	1010 11.4	1705 2.4	2227 11.0
3 TU	0519 2.8	1045 10.7	1739 3.1	2305 10.4
4 W ◐	0559 3.5	1130 9.8	1825 3.8	2357 9.6
5 TH	0658 4.1	1242 9.0	1937 4.5	
6 F	0130 8.9	0832 4.4	1447 8.8	2124 4.5
7 SA	0329 9.2	1021 3.9	1625 9.5	2301 3.7
8 SU	0450 10.1	1143 3.0	1730 10.5	
9 M	0012 2.7	0548 11.1	1246 2.0	1821 11.4
10 TU	0109 1.8	0637 12.0	1339 1.2	1906 12.1
11 W ○	0158 1.1	0721 12.5	1425 0.8	1946 12.4
12 TH	0242 0.8	0801 12.8	1505 0.7	2023 12.5
13 F	0319 0.8	0836 12.7	1538 0.9	2056 12.4
14 SA	0352 1.1	0910 12.3	1607 1.4	2127 12.0
15 SU	0420 1.6	0940 11.7	1632 2.1	2155 11.4
16 M	0444 2.3	1008 11.0	1652 2.9	2221 10.7
17 TU	0507 3.1	1035 10.1	1715 3.7	2249 9.8
18 W	0536 3.9	1106 9.2	1745 4.5	2325 9.0
19 TH	0618 4.7	1155 8.4	1837 5.3	
20 F	0038 8.2	0734 5.3	1354 7.9	2031 5.6
21 SA	0258 8.2	0935 5.1	1548 8.3	2224 5.1
22 SU	0416 8.8	1054 4.4	1647 9.1	2324 4.2
23 M	0505 9.7	1147 3.5	1729 10.0	
24 TU	0011 3.3	0546 10.5	1232 2.7	1808 10.7
25 W	0053 2.6	0625 11.2	1314 2.1	1846 11.4
26 TH ●	0133 2.0	0702 11.8	1354 1.6	1921 11.8
27 F	0212 1.6	0738 12.2	1432 1.3	1955 12.1
28 SA	0249 1.3	0812 12.4	1508 1.2	2028 12.3
29 SU	0324 1.3	0845 12.3	1542 1.3	2101 12.2
30 M	0358 1.5	0919 12.1	1615 1.7	2135 11.9
31 TU	0432 2.0	0955 11.5	1649 2.4	2212 11.3

APRIL

Day				
1 W	0508 2.7	1036 10.7	1726 3.2	2255 10.5
2 TH ●	0552 3.4	1128 9.8	1817 4.0	2355 9.6
3 F	0655 4.1	1253 9.0	1935 4.6	
4 SA	0135 9.1	0832 4.3	1445 9.0	2122 4.4
5 SU	0318 9.4	1013 3.8	1610 9.7	2248 3.6
6 M	0431 10.3	1126 2.9	1709 10.6	2352 2.7
7 TU	0526 11.1	1224 2.1	1757 11.4	
8 W	0045 1.9	0613 11.8	1313 1.6	1840 11.9
9 TH	0132 1.5	0655 12.2	1356 1.3	1918 12.2
10 F	0212 1.3	0733 12.3	1432 1.3	1953 12.2
11 SA	0248 1.3	0808 12.2	1504 1.5	2025 12.1
12 SU	0319 1.5	0840 11.9	1531 1.8	2055 11.9
13 M	0347 1.9	0910 11.5	1556 2.4	2124 11.4
14 TU	0413 2.4	0939 10.9	1620 3.0	2151 10.7
15 W	0439 3.1	1008 10.2	1646 3.7	2220 10.0
16 TH	0509 3.8	1041 9.4	1718 4.4	2258 9.2
17 F ○	0549 4.5	1128 8.7	1805 5.1	
18 SA	0000 8.5	0651 5.0	1255 8.2	1930 5.5
19 SU	0149 8.3	0828 5.0	1442 8.4	2119 5.1
20 M	0315 8.8	0956 4.5	1552 9.0	2230 4.4
21 TU	0414 9.5	1057 3.7	1643 9.8	2322 3.6
22 W	0502 10.3	1147 2.9	1727 10.6	
23 TH	0010 2.8	0546 11.0	1234 2.3	1808 11.3
24 F	0056 2.2	0627 11.6	1319 1.8	1848 11.8
25 SA	0140 1.7	0707 12.0	1402 1.5	1926 12.2
26 SU	0222 1.4	0746 12.3	1442 1.5	2003 12.4
27 M	0303 1.4	0825 12.3	1521 1.5	2042 12.3
28 TU	0342 1.5	0906 12.0	1600 1.8	2122 12.0
29 W	0422 1.9	0949 11.5	1640 2.4	2206 11.4
30 TH	0505 2.6	1038 10.7	1725 3.2	2257 10.7

Chart Datum: 6·29 metres below IGN Datum
HAT is 13·6 metres above Chart Datum

TIDES

TIDES

TIME ZONE -0100
(French Standard Time)
Subtract 1 hour for UT
For French Summer Time add
ONE hour in **non-shaded areas**

FRANCE – ST MALO

LAT 48°38'N   LONG 2°02'W

TIMES AND HEIGHTS OF HIGH AND LOW WATERS

Dates in amber are **SPRINGS**
Dates in yellow are **NEAPS**

2009

MAY

#	Time m	#	Time m
1	0556 3.2 / 1137 10.0 / F 1821 3.8	16	0533 4.0 / 1112 9.2 / SA 1748 4.6 / 2334 9.1
2	0003 10.0 / 0701 3.8 / SA 1255 9.4 / 1937 4.2	17	0624 4.4 / 1212 8.8 / SU 1850 4.9
3	0127 9.6 / 0825 4.0 / SU 1423 9.4 / 2104 4.1	18	0044 8.9 / 0731 4.6 / M 1328 8.7 / ◑ 2008 4.9
4	0251 9.8 / 0947 3.6 / M 1539 9.9 / ◐ 2218 3.6	19	0202 9.0 / 0847 4.4 / TU 1443 9.0 / 2123 4.4
5	0400 10.3 / 1055 3.1 / TU 1638 10.5 / 2320 3.0	20	0310 9.4 / 0956 3.9 / W 1545 9.6 / 2227 3.8
6	0456 10.8 / 1151 2.6 / W 1727 11.0	21	0409 10.0 / 1056 3.3 / TH 1638 10.3 / 2323 3.1
7	0012 2.5 / 0544 11.2 / TH 1239 2.3 / 1810 11.4	22	0501 10.6 / 1151 2.7 / F 1727 11.0
8	0059 2.2 / 0627 11.5 / F 1321 2.1 / 1848 11.7	23	0017 2.5 / 0551 11.2 / SA 1243 2.2 / 1814 11.6
9	0139 2.0 / 0706 11.5 / SA 1357 2.1 / 1924 11.7	24	0109 2.0 / 0639 11.7 / SU 1333 1.8 / 1859 12.0
10	0215 2.0 / 0741 11.5 / SU 1430 2.2 / 1957 11.7	25	0158 1.7 / 0726 12.0 / M 1420 1.6 / 1944 12.3
11	0248 2.1 / 0815 11.4 / M 1500 2.4 / ○ 2028 11.6	26	0246 1.5 / 0812 12.1 / TU 1506 1.6 / ● 2030 12.3
12	0319 2.3 / 0847 11.1 / TU 1529 2.7 / 2059 11.2	27	0333 1.5 / 0900 11.9 / W 1552 1.9 / 2117 12.1
13	0349 2.6 / 0918 10.7 / W 1558 3.1 / 2131 10.8	28	0420 1.8 / 0949 11.6 / TH 1639 2.3 / 2206 11.7
14	0420 3.0 / 0951 10.3 / TH 1629 3.6 / 2204 10.2	29	0508 2.2 / 1040 11.1 / F 1728 2.8 / 2259 11.2
15	0453 3.5 / 1028 9.7 / F 1703 4.1 / 2243 9.6	30	0600 2.7 / 1135 10.5 / SA 1822 3.3 / 2356 10.6
		31	0657 3.2 / 1236 10.0 / SU 1924 3.7

JUNE

#	Time m	#	Time m
1	0100 10.2 / 0800 3.6 / M 1345 9.8 / 2030 3.8	16	0649 3.9 / 1229 9.3 / TU 1913 4.4 / ◐
2	0210 10.0 / 0906 3.6 / TU 1455 9.8 / 2137 3.7	17	0055 9.4 / 0747 4.1 / W 1333 9.2 / 2019 4.3
3	0318 10.0 / 1011 3.5 / W 1558 10.1 / 2239 3.4	18	0204 9.4 / 0855 4.0 / TH 1443 9.5 / 2131 4.0
4	0419 10.2 / 1110 3.3 / TH 1653 10.5 / 2335 3.1	19	0314 9.7 / 1006 3.6 / F 1550 9.9 / 2240 3.5
5	0513 10.5 / 1202 3.1 / F 1740 10.8	20	0420 10.2 / 1112 3.2 / SA 1651 10.6 / 2344 2.9
6	0024 2.9 / 0601 10.7 / SA 1247 2.9 / 1822 11.0	21	0521 10.7 / 1213 2.6 / SU 1748 11.2
7	0108 2.7 / 0643 10.8 / SU 1327 2.8 / 1901 11.2	22	0044 2.3 / 0619 11.3 / M 1311 2.2 / 1842 11.8
8	0147 2.6 / 0721 10.9 / M 1404 2.7 / 1936 11.3	23	0142 1.8 / 0714 11.7 / TU 1406 1.8 / 1934 12.2
9	0224 2.5 / 0757 10.9 / TU 1438 2.7 / ○ 2010 11.3	24	0237 1.4 / 0807 12.0 / W 1459 1.6 / 2024 12.5
10	0259 2.5 / 0831 10.9 / W 1512 2.8 / 2044 11.2	25	0329 1.3 / 0857 12.1 / TH 1549 1.6 / ● 2113 12.4
11	0333 2.6 / 0905 10.8 / TH 1544 3.0 / 2117 10.9	26	0419 1.3 / 0945 12.0 / F 1637 1.7 / 2200 12.2
12	0407 2.8 / 0939 10.5 / F 1618 3.3 / 2151 10.6	27	0506 1.6 / 1031 11.6 / SA 1723 2.1 / 2247 11.7
13	0441 3.1 / 1014 10.2 / SA 1653 3.6 / 2228 10.2	28	0551 2.1 / 1117 11.1 / SU 1809 2.6 / 2334 11.1
14	0518 3.4 / 1052 9.9 / SU 1731 3.9 / 2308 9.9	29	0636 2.6 / 1204 10.5 / M 1856 3.2
15	0600 3.7 / 1136 9.5 / M 1817 4.2 / 2356 9.5	30	0024 10.5 / 0723 3.4 / TU 1257 9.9 / 1948 3.7

JULY

#	Time m	#	Time m
1	0121 9.9 / 0818 3.8 / W 1400 9.6 / 2049 4.0	16	0003 9.7 / 0659 3.8 / TH 1234 9.5 / 1926 4.2
2	0229 9.5 / 0921 4.1 / TH 1512 9.5 / 2156 4.1	17	0106 9.4 / 0801 4.1 / F 1346 9.3 / 2042 4.3
3	0341 9.5 / 1027 4.1 / F 1621 9.8 / 2300 3.8	18	0228 9.3 / 0920 4.1 / SA 1510 9.6 / 2206 3.9
4	0447 9.7 / 1129 3.8 / SA 1718 10.1 / ◐ 2357 3.5	19	0352 9.7 / 1042 3.6 / SU 1628 10.2 / 2321 3.2
5	0542 10.0 / 1221 3.5 / SU 1805 10.5	20	0507 10.3 / 1153 3.0 / M 1735 10.9
6	0045 3.1 / 0628 10.3 / M 1307 3.2 / 1845 10.9	21	0029 2.5 / 0611 11.0 / TU 1258 2.3 / 1834 11.7
7	0129 2.9 / 0708 10.6 / TU 1347 3.0 / 1922 11.1	22	0133 1.8 / 0708 11.7 / W 1358 1.7 / 1927 12.4
8	0208 2.6 / 0744 10.8 / W 1425 2.8 / 1957 11.3	23	0230 1.2 / 0759 12.2 / TH 1452 1.2 / 2016 12.8
9	0245 2.5 / 0818 11.0 / TH 1500 2.7 / 2030 11.3	24	0322 0.9 / 0846 12.4 / F 1541 1.1 / 2101 12.9
10	0320 2.4 / 0851 11.0 / F 1533 2.7 / 2103 11.3	25	0409 0.8 / 0930 12.4 / SA 1625 1.2 / 2144 12.7
11	0354 2.4 / 0923 11.0 / SA 1605 2.7 / ○ 2134 11.2	26	0451 1.2 / 1010 12.0 / SU 1705 1.6 / ● 2224 12.1
12	0427 2.5 / 0955 10.8 / SU 1637 2.9 / 2207 10.9	27	0529 1.8 / 1049 11.5 / M 1743 2.3 / 2303 11.4
13	0500 2.7 / 1027 10.5 / M 1710 3.2 / 2240 10.5	28	0604 2.6 / 1127 10.8 / TU 1819 3.1 / 2343 10.5
14	0534 3.1 / 1102 10.2 / TU 1746 3.6 / 2317 10.1	29	0639 3.4 / 1208 10.0 / W 1900 3.8
15	0612 3.5 / 1142 9.8 / W 1830 3.9	30	0030 9.7 / 0722 4.2 / TH 1302 9.3 / 1956 4.5
		31	0135 9.0 / 0826 4.7 / F 1424 9.0 / 2113 4.7

AUGUST

#	Time m	#	Time m
1	0306 8.7 / 0950 4.8 / SA 1555 9.1 / 2233 4.4	16	0200 9.0 / 0849 4.5 / SU 1450 9.3 / 2146 4.2
2	0430 9.0 / 1105 4.4 / SU 1701 9.7 / ◐ 2337 3.9	17	0345 9.3 / 1027 4.1 / M 1621 9.9 / ◑ 2312 3.4
3	0529 9.6 / 1204 3.9 / M 1750 10.2	18	0504 10.2 / 1145 3.1 / TU 1729 10.9
4	0029 3.3 / 0613 10.2 / TU 1252 3.3 / 1830 10.8	19	0022 2.4 / 0605 11.1 / W 1250 2.2 / 1825 11.9
5	0113 2.9 / 0651 10.6 / W 1333 2.9 / 1905 11.2	20	0124 1.5 / 0657 11.9 / TH 1348 1.4 / 1914 12.6
6	0153 2.5 / 0726 11.0 / TH 1411 2.6 / 1939 11.5	21	0218 0.9 / 0744 12.5 / F 1439 0.9 / 2001 13.0
7	0230 2.2 / 0759 11.3 / F 1445 2.4 / 2012 11.7	22	0306 0.6 / 0826 12.7 / SA 1524 0.8 / 2041 13.1
8	0304 2.0 / 0831 11.4 / SA 1517 2.2 / 2043 11.7	23	0348 0.7 / 0905 12.6 / SU 1603 1.0 / 2120 12.8
9	0336 2.0 / 0901 11.5 / SU 1547 2.2 / ○ 2112 11.7	24	0425 1.1 / 0941 12.3 / M 1638 1.5 / 2155 12.2
10	0407 2.0 / 0930 11.4 / M 1617 2.4 / 2142 11.5	25	0456 1.8 / 1015 11.7 / TU 1709 2.2 / ● 2229 11.4
11	0437 2.3 / 0959 11.1 / TU 1647 2.7 / 2212 11.1	26	0524 2.7 / 1047 10.9 / W 1738 3.1 / 2302 10.5
12	0507 2.7 / 1030 10.7 / W 1718 3.2 / 2244 10.6	27	0550 3.6 / 1121 10.0 / TH 1811 4.0 / 2340 9.5
13	0540 3.2 / 1104 10.3 / TH 1755 3.7 / 2324 10.0	28	0625 4.5 / 1206 9.2 / F 1859 4.8
14	0621 3.8 / 1151 9.7 / F 1847 4.2	29	0040 8.6 / 0726 5.2 / SA 1333 8.5 / 2025 5.2
15	0023 9.3 / 0720 4.3 / SA 1303 9.2 / 2006 4.5	30	0234 8.2 / 0914 5.0 / SU 1530 8.7 / 2208 4.9
		31	0411 8.6 / 1046 4.8 / M 1641 9.3 / 2317 4.2

Chart Datum: 6·29 metres below IGN Datum
HAT is 13·6 metres above Chart Datum

TIME ZONE -0100
(French Standard Time)
Subtract 1 hour for UT
For French Summer Time add
ONE hour in **non-shaded areas**

FRANCE – ST MALO

LAT 48°38′N   LONG 2°02′W

TIMES AND HEIGHTS OF HIGH AND LOW WATERS

Dates in amber are **SPRINGS**
Dates in yellow are **NEAPS**

2009

SEPTEMBER		OCTOBER		NOVEMBER		DECEMBER	
Time m	Time m	Time m	Time m	Time m	Time m	Time m	Time m
1 0508 9.4 1145 4.1 TU 1727 10.1	**16** 0455 10.4 1136 3.0 W 1717 11.1	**1** 0513 10.1 1154 3.5 TH 1730 10.6	**16** 0527 11.4 1214 2.2 F 1745 11.9	**1** 0014 2.7 0547 11.2 SU 1234 2.6 1807 11.5	**16** 0059 2.2 0627 11.8 M 1319 2.0 ● 1846 11.7	**1** 0020 2.6 0553 11.3 TU 1245 2.4 1818 11.4	**16** 0114 2.7 0647 11.3 W 1336 2.5 ● 1910 11.0
2 0007 3.4 0549 10.2 W 1230 3.3 1805 10.8	**17** 0012 2.3 0550 11.4 TH 1236 2.0 1808 12.1	**2** 0015 2.9 0550 10.8 F 1235 2.8 1807 11.3	**17** 0043 1.7 0612 12.0 SA 1304 1.6 1830 12.4	**2** 0056 2.2 0625 11.7 M 1317 2.2 ○ 1846 11.9	**17** 0139 2.1 0705 11.9 TU 1358 2.0 1925 11.7	**2** 0109 2.2 0637 11.8 W 1334 2.0 ○ 1903 11.8	**17** 0153 2.6 0725 11.4 TH 1414 2.4 1947 11.1
3 0050 2.8 0625 10.8 TH 1309 2.8 1840 11.3	**18** 0108 1.5 0637 12.1 F 1329 1.3 ● 1854 12.7	**3** 0055 2.4 0625 11.4 SA 1313 2.4 1842 11.8	**18** 0130 1.4 0653 12.3 SU 1348 1.4 ● 1910 12.5	**3** 0137 1.9 0702 12.0 TU 1358 1.9 1923 12.1	**18** 0214 2.2 0740 11.9 W 1434 2.1 2000 11.5	**3** 0156 1.9 0720 12.2 TH 1422 1.7 1948 12.0	**18** 0229 2.6 0800 11.4 F 1450 2.4 2021 11.1
4 0129 2.3 0659 11.3 F 1346 2.4 ○ 1914 11.7	**19** 0157 1.0 0720 12.6 SA 1416 1.0 1937 13.0	**4** 0133 2.0 0700 11.8 SU 1350 2.0 ○ 1917 12.1	**19** 0210 1.4 0731 12.4 M 1428 1.4 1948 12.4	**4** 0217 1.8 0739 12.2 W 1438 1.8 2000 12.1	**19** 0247 2.4 0814 11.7 TH 1507 2.3 2034 11.3	**4** 0241 1.8 0804 12.3 F 1508 1.7 2034 12.0	**19** 0303 2.6 0833 11.3 SA 1524 2.5 2054 11.0
5 0205 2.0 0732 11.6 SA 1421 2.1 1947 12.0	**20** 0241 0.8 0800 12.7 SU 1458 0.9 2015 13.0	**5** 0209 1.7 0733 12.0 M 1425 1.8 1950 12.2	**20** 0245 1.6 0805 12.3 TU 1502 1.6 2022 12.1	**5** 0255 1.8 0815 12.3 TH 1517 1.9 2039 12.0	**20** 0318 2.7 0846 11.4 F 1539 2.6 2107 10.9	**5** 0327 1.9 0850 12.2 SA 1555 1.8 2121 11.7	**20** 0336 2.8 0906 11.1 SU 1557 2.8 2126 10.7
6 0239 1.8 0804 11.8 SU 1453 1.9 2017 12.1	**21** 0318 1.0 0836 12.6 M 1534 1.2 2051 12.6	**6** 0243 1.7 0805 12.2 TU 1459 1.8 2021 12.2	**21** 0316 2.0 0837 12.0 W 1533 2.0 2055 11.7	**6** 0333 2.1 0854 12.1 F 1557 2.2 2121 11.6	**21** 0348 3.1 0919 11.0 SA 1610 3.1 2139 10.4	**6** 0413 2.2 0937 11.9 SU 1642 2.1 2210 11.3	**21** 0407 3.1 0938 10.8 M 1629 3.0 2158 10.4
7 0311 1.7 0834 11.9 M 1524 1.9 2047 12.0	**22** 0351 1.5 0909 12.3 TU 1606 1.7 2124 12.0	**7** 0317 1.8 0836 12.1 W 1533 2.0 2054 12.0	**22** 0344 2.5 0908 11.6 TH 1602 2.6 2126 11.0	**7** 0413 2.6 0937 11.6 SA 1638 2.7 2207 10.9	**22** 0418 3.6 0952 10.4 SU 1643 3.6 2214 9.9	**7** 0501 2.6 1027 11.5 M 1732 2.6 2301 10.8	**22** 0438 3.4 1010 10.4 TU 1702 3.3 2232 10.0
8 0342 1.8 0903 11.8 TU 1554 2.1 2116 11.8	**23** 0419 2.1 0940 11.7 W 1633 2.4 2155 11.2	**8** 0349 2.1 0908 11.9 TH 1606 2.3 2128 11.5	**23** 0409 3.1 0938 10.9 F 1629 3.2 2157 10.3	**8** 0456 3.2 1026 11.0 SU 1726 3.3 2302 10.2	**23** 0451 4.1 1028 9.8 M 1720 4.1 2254 9.3	**8** 0552 3.1 1121 10.9 TU 1825 3.1 2357 10.2	**23** 0512 3.8 1045 10.0 W 1738 3.7 2308 9.6
9 0412 2.1 0932 11.6 W 1624 2.4 2146 11.4	**24** 0442 3.0 1009 10.9 TH 1659 3.2 2225 10.3	**9** 0422 2.6 0944 11.4 F 1641 2.9 2207 10.8	**24** 0436 3.9 1009 10.2 SA 1700 4.0 2231 9.5	**9** 0549 3.8 1126 10.3 M 1826 3.8 ◐	**24** 0532 4.6 1113 9.3 TU 1806 4.5 ◑ 2346 8.9	**9** 0648 3.5 1221 10.3 W 1924 3.5 ◐	**24** 0550 4.1 1125 9.6 TH 1820 4.0 ◑ 2353 9.2
10 0441 2.6 1002 11.1 TH 1655 3.0 2219 10.8	**25** 0506 3.8 1039 10.1 F 1729 4.1 2258 9.4	**10** 0458 3.3 1025 10.7 SA 1723 3.6 2255 10.0	**25** 0508 4.6 1047 9.4 SU 1740 4.6 2317 8.8	**10** 0013 9.6 0657 4.3 TU 1244 9.8 1943 4.1	**25** 0626 5.0 1215 8.9 W 1907 4.8	**10** 0102 9.8 0751 3.8 TH 1329 10.0 2029 3.8	**25** 0638 4.4 1216 9.2 F 1912 4.3
11 0513 3.2 1037 10.5 F 1732 3.6 2300 10.0	**26** 0537 4.7 1118 9.2 SA 1811 4.9 ◑ 2350 8.5	**11** 0545 4.0 1120 9.9 SU 1820 4.2 ◑	**26** 0555 5.2 1147 8.7 M 1840 5.2 ◑	**11** 0139 9.4 0821 4.3 W 1409 9.8 2108 3.9	**26** 0058 8.7 0738 5.1 TH 1334 8.8 2020 4.7	**11** 0214 9.7 0900 3.9 F 1442 9.9 2138 3.7	**26** 0052 9.0 0739 4.6 SA 1325 9.0 2018 4.4
12 0555 3.9 1125 9.8 SA 1825 4.3 ◑	**27** 0630 5.4 1236 8.4 SU 1928 5.4	**12** 0009 9.2 0654 4.6 M 1251 9.3 1948 4.5	**27** 0040 8.3 0715 5.6 TU 1334 8.4 2013 5.3	**12** 0300 9.8 0941 3.8 TH 1524 10.2 2221 3.4	**27** 0217 8.8 0856 4.8 F 1449 9.1 2133 4.3	**12** 0325 9.8 1009 3.7 SA 1551 10.0 2244 3.5	**27** 0208 9.0 0849 4.5 SU 1446 9.1 2134 4.2
13 0003 9.2 0658 4.6 SU 1246 9.1 1948 4.7	**28** 0148 8.1 0822 5.8 M 1448 8.4 2127 5.3	**13** 0200 9.0 0836 4.7 TU 1437 9.5 2133 4.1	**28** 0227 8.4 0902 5.4 W 1502 8.8 2142 4.8	**13** 0405 10.4 1047 3.2 F 1625 10.8 2321 2.8	**28** 0324 9.3 1004 4.3 SA 1550 9.7 2235 3.8	**13** 0427 10.2 1111 3.3 SU 1651 10.5 2341 3.2	**28** 0324 9.4 1011 4.1 M 1558 9.6 2246 3.7
14 0200 8.8 0837 4.8 M 1447 9.2 2141 4.3	**29** 0334 8.5 1012 5.2 TU 1603 9.0 2243 4.5	**14** 0331 9.6 1009 4.0 W 1555 10.2 2250 3.3	**29** 0336 9.0 1014 4.7 TH 1559 9.5 2241 4.0	**14** 0458 11.0 1144 2.6 SA 1718 11.3	**29** 0419 10.0 1102 3.4 SU 1643 10.3 2330 3.1	**14** 0520 10.7 1206 3.0 M 1743 10.6	**29** 0429 10.0 1119 3.4 TU 1701 10.2 2349 3.1
15 0345 9.4 1022 4.1 TU 1614 10.0 2306 3.3	**30** 0432 9.3 1110 4.3 W 1651 9.8 2332 3.7	**15** 0435 10.5 1117 3.0 TH 1655 11.1 2351 2.4	**30** 0425 9.8 1105 3.9 F 1645 10.2 2329 3.3	**15** 0013 2.4 0545 11.5 SU 1235 2.2 1804 11.6	**30** 0507 10.7 1155 3.0 M 1731 10.9	**15** 0031 2.9 0606 11.0 TU 1254 2.7 1829 10.9	**30** 0527 10.8 1220 2.7 W 1759 10.9
			31 0508 10.5 1151 3.2 SA 1727 10.9				**31** 0047 2.6 0620 11.5 TH 1318 2.0 ○ 1852 11.5

Chart Datum: 6·29 metres below IGN Datum
HAT is 13·6 metres above Chart Datum

389

TIDES

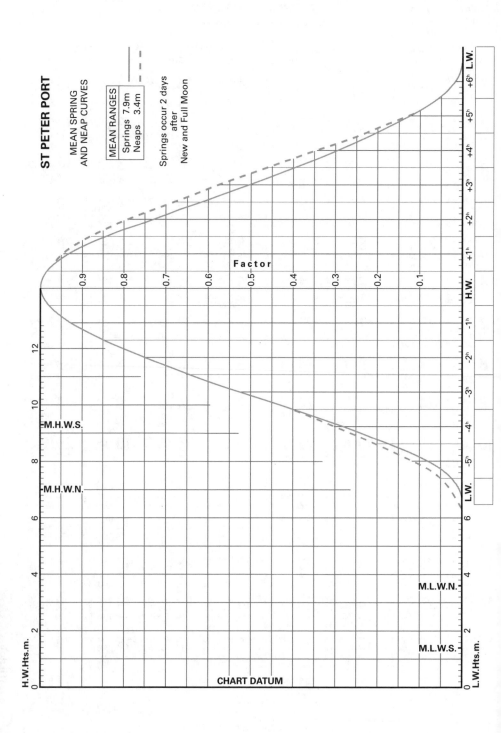

ST PETER PORT

MEAN SPRING
AND NEAP CURVES

MEAN RANGES	
Springs	7.9m
Neaps	3.4m

Springs occur 2 days
after
New and Full Moon

Factor

0.9 0.8 0.7 0.6 0.5 0.4 0.3 0.2 0.1

L.W. +6ʰ +5ʰ +4ʰ +3ʰ +2ʰ +1ʰ H.W. −1ʰ −2ʰ −3ʰ −4ʰ −5ʰ L.W.

M.H.W.S.
M.H.W.N.

M.L.W.N.
M.L.W.S.

H.W.Hts.m.
L.W.Hts.m.

CHART DATUM

CHANNEL ISLES – ST PETER PORT

LAT 49°27'N LONG 2°31'W

TIMES AND HEIGHTS OF HIGH AND LOW WATERS

Dates in amber are **SPRINGS**
Dates in yellow are NEAPS

2009

JANUARY
Time m Time m

Day	Time	m	Time	m	Time	m	Time	m
1 TH	0305	2.6	0907	8.3	1531	2.5	2127	8.0
16 F	0407	1.7	1003	9.0	1633	1.8	2227	8.4
2 F	0339	2.8	0942	8.1	1606	2.6	2203	7.8
17 SA	0445	2.3	1042	8.3	1711	2.4	2305	7.8
3 SA	0416	3.0	1022	7.9	1645	2.9	2245	7.6
18 SU	0525	2.9	1123	7.6	1751	3.1	2349	7.2
4 SU	0459	3.2	1109	7.7	1733	3.1	2336	7.4
19 M	0612	3.5	1213	7.0	1841	3.7		
5 M	0555	3.4	1207	7.5	1832	3.2		
20 TU	0048	6.8	0715	3.9	1324	6.6	1949	4.0
6 TU	0040	7.3	0707	3.5	1320	7.3	1947	3.3
21 W	0213	6.7	0839	4.0	1453	6.6	2116	4.0
7 W	0200	7.4	0833	3.3	1442	7.4	2109	3.1
22 TH	0334	6.9	1000	3.7	1606	6.9	2227	3.6
8 TH	0319	7.7	0953	2.9	1557	7.8	2223	2.7
23 F	0432	7.4	1058	3.3	1659	7.3	2318	3.2
9 F	0428	8.2	1101	2.3	1704	8.2	2326	2.2
24 SA	0519	7.8	1144	2.8	1743	7.7		
10 SA	0528	8.7	1201	1.7	1802	8.7		
25 SU	0001	2.8	0600	8.3	1225	2.4	1823	8.1
11 SU	0023	1.7	0622	9.3	1226	1.2	1855	9.1
26 M	0040	2.4	0638	8.6	1300	2.4	1900	8.4
12 M	0115	1.3	0712	9.6	1346	0.8	1944	9.4
27 TU	0116	2.1	0715	8.8	1339	1.8	1936	8.6
13 TU	0203	1.0	0759	9.8	1433	0.7	2029	9.5
28 W	0149	1.9	0748	8.9	1412	1.7	2008	8.7
14 W	0247	1.0	0843	9.8	1515	0.8	2110	9.3
29 TH	0221	1.8	0820	8.9	1443	1.7	2038	8.6
15 TH	0329	1.2	0924	9.5	1556	1.4	2149	8.9
30 F	0252	1.9	0850	8.8	1513	1.8	2107	8.5
31 SA	0322	2.1	0922	8.6	1543	2.1	2139	8.3

FEBRUARY
Time m Time m

Day	Time	m	Time	m	Time	m	Time	m
1 SU	0353	2.3	0956	8.4	1617	2.4	2215	8.0
16 M	0438	2.7	1034	7.7	1655	3.1	2251	7.4
2 M	0429	2.7	1037	8.0	1657	2.8	2258	7.7
17 TU	0513	3.4	1112	7.0	1732	3.7	2334	6.8
3 TU	0516	3.1	1129	7.5	1749	3.2	2356	7.3
18 W	0608	4.0	1211	6.4	1837	4.2		
4 W	0623	3.5	1241	7.1	1905	3.5		
19 TH	0055	6.3	0738	4.3	1403	6.1	2019	4.4
5 TH	0121	7.1	0803	3.6	1420	7.0	2048	3.5
20 F	0300	6.5	0928	4.0	1547	6.5	2203	4.0
6 F	0302	7.3	0944	3.1	1553	7.4	2215	3.0
21 SA	0412	7.0	1038	3.4	1641	7.1	2259	3.3
7 SA	0422	7.9	1057	2.4	1702	8.0	2321	2.3
22 SU	0500	7.6	1125	2.8	1724	7.7	2342	2.7
8 SU	0523	8.6	1156	1.7	1757	8.6		
23 M	0541	8.2	1205	2.3	1803	8.2		
9 M	0016	1.6	0614	9.3	1247	1.0	1845	9.3
24 TU	0020	2.2	0618	8.6	1242	1.8	1839	8.6
10 TU	0105	1.0	0700	9.8	1333	0.6	1929	9.6
25 W	0056	1.8	0654	9.0	1317	1.5	1914	8.9
11 W	0148	0.7	0743	10.0	1414	0.4	2009	9.7
26 TH	0130	1.5	0727	9.2	1350	1.3	1946	9.0
12 TH	0228	0.6	0823	10.0	1453	0.5	2046	9.6
27 F	0202	1.4	0759	9.3	1421	1.2	2015	9.0
13 F	0305	0.8	0859	9.6	1527	0.9	2119	9.2
28 SA	0232	1.4	0829	9.2	1450	1.4	2045	8.9
14 SA	0338	1.3	0932	9.1	1558	1.6	2149	8.6
15 SU	0408	1.9	1003	8.4	1626	2.3	2219	8.0

MARCH
Time m Time m

Day	Time	m	Time	m	Time	m	Time	m
1 SU	0301	1.6	0901	9.0	1520	1.7	2115	8.7
16 M	0334	1.9	0928	8.3	1547	2.4	2141	8.1
2 M	0332	1.9	0934	8.6	1552	2.1	2150	8.3
17 TU	0400	2.6	0957	7.7	1611	3.0	2210	7.5
3 TU	0407	2.4	1014	8.0	1631	2.7	2232	7.8
18 W	0429	3.3	1031	7.0	1641	3.7	2247	6.9
4 W	0453	3.0	1105	7.4	1723	3.3	2330	7.2
19 TH	0515	3.9	1122	6.4	1738	4.2	2352	6.4
5 TH	0601	3.5	1222	6.8	1844	3.7		
20 F	0651	4.3	1307	6.0	1930	4.5		
6 F	0102	6.9	0757	3.6	1419	6.8	2044	3.7
21 SA	0206	6.3	0840	4.1	1511	6.4	2119	4.1
7 SA	0258	7.1	0943	3.1	1553	7.4	2211	3.0
22 SU	0337	6.8	1001	3.5	1610	7.0	2224	3.4
8 SU	0415	7.9	1049	2.3	1653	8.1	2310	2.2
23 M	0427	7.4	1050	2.8	1653	7.6	2309	2.8
9 M	0510	8.6	1141	1.5	1742	8.8		
24 TU	0509	8.0	1131	2.2	1732	8.2	2348	2.2
10 TU	0000	1.4	0557	9.3	1228	0.9	1825	9.3
25 W	0548	8.6	1209	1.7	1809	8.6		
11 W	0045	0.9	0640	9.7	1310	0.7	1905	9.7
26 TH	0026	1.7	0624	9.0	1246	1.3	1844	9.0
12 TH	0126	0.6	0720	9.9	1349	0.4	1943	9.7
27 F	0102	1.3	0700	9.3	1321	1.1	1917	9.2
13 F	0203	0.6	0757	9.8	1424	0.6	2016	9.6
28 SA	0136	1.1	0734	9.4	1355	1.0	1950	9.3
14 SA	0237	0.9	0830	9.5	1455	1.1	2047	9.2
29 SU	0209	1.1	0807	9.2	1427	1.2	2022	9.2
15 SU	0307	1.3	0900	9.0	1522	1.7	2114	8.7
30 M	0242	1.3	0842	9.1	1500	1.5	2056	8.9
31 TU	0316	1.4	0919	8.6	1535	2.0	2134	8.5

APRIL
Time m Time m

Day	Time	m	Time	m	Time	m	Time	m
1 W	0355	2.3	1002	8.0	1618	2.7	2220	7.9
16 TH	0403	3.2	1007	7.1	1613	3.6	2220	7.0
2 TH	0446	2.9	1059	7.3	1715	3.3	2323	7.3
17 F	0447	3.7	1056	6.6	1705	4.1	2318	6.6
3 F	0603	3.4	1223	6.8	1846	3.7		
18 SA	0609	4.0	1218	6.3	1841	4.3		
4 SA	0058	7.0	0757	3.4	1416	6.9	2036	3.5
19 SU	0055	6.4	0745	4.0	1405	6.4	2016	4.1
5 SU	0244	7.3	0927	2.9	1535	7.5	2152	2.9
20 M	0234	6.7	0902	3.5	1517	6.9	2128	3.5
6 M	0354	7.9	1027	2.2	1630	8.2	2248	2.1
21 TU	0337	7.2	0959	2.9	1607	7.5	2221	2.9
7 TU	0446	8.6	1116	1.6	1716	8.7	2335	1.5
22 W	0425	7.8	1046	2.4	1650	8.0	2307	2.3
8 W	0532	9.1	1200	1.1	1758	9.2		
23 TH	0508	8.4	1129	1.9	1731	8.5	2349	1.8
9 TH	0018	1.1	0614	9.4	1242	0.9	1837	9.4
24 F	0549	8.8	1210	1.5	1810	8.9		
10 F	0058	0.9	0653	9.5	1319	0.9	1913	9.5
25 SA	0030	1.4	0629	9.1	1251	1.2	1848	9.2
11 SA	0135	0.9	0729	9.4	1353	1.1	1946	9.3
26 SU	0110	1.1	0709	9.3	1330	1.1	1926	9.4
12 SU	0208	1.1	0802	9.1	1424	1.4	2016	9.0
27 M	0150	1.1	0749	9.3	1408	1.2	2004	9.3
13 M	0238	1.5	0832	8.7	1450	1.9	2045	8.6
28 TU	0229	1.2	0829	9.0	1447	1.5	2045	9.0
14 TU	0305	2.0	0901	8.2	1515	2.5	2113	8.1
29 W	0310	1.6	0913	8.6	1529	2.0	2129	8.6
15 W	0332	2.6	0932	7.6	1541	3.1	2143	7.6
30 TH	0357	2.1	1003	8.1	1618	2.6	2220	8.1

Chart Datum: 5·06 metres below Ordnance Datum (Local)
HAT is 10·3 metres above Chart Datum

TIDES

TIDES

CHANNEL ISLES – ST PETER PORT
LAT 49°27'N   LONG 2°31'W
TIMES AND HEIGHTS OF HIGH AND LOW WATERS

Dates in **amber** are **SPRINGS**
Dates in yellow are **NEAPS**

2009

MAY

Day	Time	m	Time	m	Time	m	Time	m
1 F	0454	2.6	1103	7.5	1720	3.1	2325	7.6
2 SA	0610	3.0	1221	7.2	1842	3.4		
3 SU	0047	7.4	0737	3.0	1348	7.2	2009	3.3
4 M	0212	7.5	0855	2.7	1500	7.6	2121	2.8
5 TU	0320	7.9	0954	2.3	1556	8.0	2217	2.4
6 W	0415	8.3	1044	2.0	1644	8.4	2305	2.0
7 TH	0502	8.6	1129	1.7	1727	8.7	2349	1.7
8 F	0546	8.8	1211	1.6	1807	8.9		
9 SA	0029	1.5	0625	8.9	1249	1.6	1844	9.0
10 SU	0107	1.5	0703	8.8	1324	1.7	1918	8.9
11 M	0142	1.6	0737	8.6	1356	1.9	1951	8.7
12 TU	0214	1.9	0810	8.4	1426	2.2	2022	8.5
13 W	0244	2.2	0842	8.0	1454	2.6	2053	8.1
14 TH	0315	2.6	0916	7.6	1524	3.0	2126	7.7
15 F	0349	3.0	0953	7.3	1600	3.4	2205	7.3
16 SA	0432	3.3	1039	6.9	1646	3.7	2255	7.0
17 SU	0531	3.6	1138	6.7	1753	3.9		
18 M	0000	6.8	0646	3.6	1251	6.7	1912	3.9
19 TU	0117	6.9	0757	3.2	1405	6.9	2025	3.5
20 W	0230	7.2	0900	3.1	1508	7.3	2127	3.1
21 TH	0330	7.6	0956	2.6	1601	7.8	2222	2.5
22 F	0424	8.1	1047	2.2	1650	8.3	2312	2.0
23 SA	0514	8.5	1136	1.8	1736	8.8		
24 SU	0001	1.6	0601	8.9	1224	1.5	1822	9.1
25 M	0049	1.3	0649	9.1	1310	1.3	1907	9.3
26 TU	0136	1.1	0736	9.1	1356	1.3	1953	9.4
27 W	0223	1.2	0824	9.0	1442	1.5	2039	9.2
28 TH	0311	1.3	0912	8.8	1530	1.8	2127	8.9
29 F	0401	1.7	1003	8.4	1620	2.2	2219	8.5
30 SA	0456	2.1	1058	8.0	1716	2.6	2316	8.1
31 SU	0556	2.5	1200	7.7	1819	2.9		

JUNE

Day	Time	m	Time	m	Time	m	Time	m
1 M	0020	7.7	0702	2.7	1308	7.5	1929	3.1
2 TU	0130	7.6	0811	2.8	1416	7.5	2039	3.0
3 W	0239	7.6	0914	2.8	1517	7.7	2140	2.8
4 TH	0339	7.7	1009	2.6	1610	7.9	2233	2.6
5 F	0432	7.9	1058	2.5	1657	8.2	2320	2.4
6 SA	0519	8.1	1142	2.3	1739	8.4		
7 SU	0003	2.2	0601	8.2	1223	2.2	1819	8.5
8 M	0044	2.1	0641	8.3	1301	2.2	1857	8.6
9 TU	0121	2.0	0719	8.3	1336	2.2	1933	8.5
10 W	0156	2.1	0755	8.2	1409	2.4	2007	8.4
11 TH	0230	2.2	0830	8.1	1441	2.5	2040	8.2
12 F	0304	2.4	0904	7.8	1514	2.8	2114	8.0
13 SA	0338	2.7	0939	7.6	1548	3.0	2149	7.7
14 SU	0414	2.9	1017	7.4	1626	3.2	2230	7.5
15 M	0457	3.1	1101	7.2	1713	3.4	2318	7.3
16 TU	0549	3.3	1153	7.1	1811	3.5		
17 W	0017	7.2	0652	3.3	1256	7.1	1920	3.5
18 TH	0125	7.2	0800	3.2	1405	7.3	2032	3.2
19 F	0237	7.4	0908	2.9	1513	7.6	2140	2.8
20 SA	0344	7.8	1011	2.6	1614	8.1	2242	2.3
21 SU	0446	8.1	1109	2.1	1711	8.5	2340	1.8
22 M	0543	8.6	1205	1.8	1805	9.0		
23 TU	0035	1.4	0637	8.9	1259	1.4	1856	9.3
24 W	0129	1.1	0729	9.2	1350	1.2	1946	9.5
25 TH	0219	0.9	0819	9.3	1438	1.2	2034	9.5
26 F	0307	0.9	0906	9.2	1525	1.3	2120	9.4
27 SA	0354	1.1	0953	8.9	1610	1.6	2206	9.0
28 SU	0440	1.6	1039	8.5	1657	2.1	2254	8.5
29 M	0528	2.1	1128	8.0	1746	2.7	2344	7.9
30 TU	0619	2.6	1221	7.6	1841	3.0		

JULY

Day	Time	m	Time	m	Time	m	Time	m
1 W	0042	7.5	0718	3.1	1324	7.3	1946	3.3
2 TH	0151	7.1	0825	3.3	1433	7.2	2058	3.4
3 F	0303	7.1	0933	3.4	1537	7.3	2203	3.2
4 SA	0406	7.3	1031	3.2	1632	7.6	2257	3.0
5 SU	0459	7.5	1121	2.9	1719	7.9	2344	2.7
6 M	0545	7.8	1204	2.7	1802	8.2		
7 TU	0026	2.4	0626	8.0	1245	2.4	1841	8.4
8 W	0106	2.2	0705	8.2	1322	2.3	1919	8.6
9 TH	0143	2.1	0742	8.3	1356	2.2	1954	8.6
10 F	0217	2.0	0816	8.3	1428	2.2	2026	8.5
11 SA	0249	2.1	0848	8.2	1500	2.4	2057	8.4
12 SU	0320	2.2	0918	8.1	1530	2.5	2128	8.2
13 M	0351	2.4	0950	7.9	1602	2.7	2202	8.0
14 TU	0424	2.7	1026	7.7	1638	3.0	2242	7.7
15 W	0505	2.9	1109	7.5	1724	3.2	2332	7.5
16 TH	0556	3.2	1204	7.3	1824	3.4		
17 F	0035	7.3	0704	3.3	1315	7.2	1943	3.4
18 SA	0156	7.2	0827	3.3	1437	7.4	2110	3.1
19 SU	0319	7.5	0947	2.9	1552	7.8	2225	2.6
20 M	0432	7.9	1055	2.4	1657	8.4	2330	2.0
21 TU	0535	8.5	1156	1.9	1755	9.0		
22 W	0028	1.3	0630	9.0	1251	1.3	1847	9.5
23 TH	0121	0.8	0721	9.4	1341	0.8	1936	9.8
24 F	0209	0.5	0807	9.6	1427	0.8	2021	9.9
25 SA	0253	0.5	0850	9.6	1509	0.8	2103	9.8
26 SU	0334	0.8	0931	9.3	1549	1.2	2144	9.3
27 M	0414	1.3	1010	8.8	1628	1.8	2223	8.7
28 TU	0452	2.0	1049	8.2	1707	2.4	2303	8.0
29 W	0532	2.8	1131	7.6	1751	3.1	2349	7.3
30 TH	0620	3.4	1225	7.0	1848	3.7		
31 F	0054	6.7	0727	3.9	1344	6.7	2009	4.0

AUGUST

Day	Time	m	Time	m	Time	m	Time	m
1 SA	0228	6.5	0856	4.0	1510	6.8	2140	3.8
2 SU	0350	6.8	1013	3.7	1615	7.2	2243	3.4
3 M	0446	7.2	1106	3.3	1704	7.7	2330	2.9
4 TU	0531	7.7	1150	2.8	1746	8.2		
5 W	0011	2.4	0610	8.1	1229	2.4	1825	8.5
6 TH	0050	2.1	0648	8.4	1305	2.1	1901	8.8
7 F	0125	1.8	0723	8.6	1339	1.9	1935	8.9
8 SA	0157	1.7	0755	8.7	1410	1.7	2006	8.9
9 SU	0228	1.7	0825	8.6	1439	1.9	2035	8.8
10 M	0256	1.9	0853	8.5	1507	2.1	2104	8.6
11 TU	0324	2.1	0921	8.3	1535	2.4	2135	8.4
12 W	0354	2.4	0953	8.1	1607	2.7	2211	8.0
13 TH	0429	2.8	1032	7.7	1648	3.1	2256	7.6
14 F	0516	3.2	1124	7.4	1745	3.4		
15 SA	0000	7.2	0625	3.6	1240	7.1	1912	3.7
16 SU	0133	6.9	0806	3.6	1418	7.2	2100	3.4
17 M	0314	7.2	0939	3.2	1545	7.7	2222	2.7
18 TU	0430	7.9	1049	2.5	1651	8.4	2324	1.9
19 W	0528	8.6	1147	1.8	1745	9.2		
20 TH	0017	1.2	0618	9.2	1238	1.1	1834	9.7
21 F	0105	0.6	0704	9.7	1324	0.7	1919	10.1
22 SA	0149	0.3	0746	9.9	1407	0.5	2000	10.1
23 SU	0230	0.4	0826	9.8	1446	0.6	2039	9.9
24 M	0307	0.7	0902	9.5	1522	1.1	2115	9.4
25 TU	0341	1.4	0936	8.9	1555	1.7	2148	8.7
26 W	0413	2.1	1008	8.3	1627	2.5	2221	7.9
27 TH	0444	3.0	1042	7.6	1703	3.3	2258	7.1
28 F	0523	3.7	1127	6.9	1755	4.0	2355	6.5
29 SA	0628	4.3	1247	6.5	1922	4.3		
30 SU	0151	6.2	0818	4.4	1447	6.6	2118	4.1
31 M	0336	6.6	0956	4.0	1556	7.1	2226	3.6

Chart Datum: 5·06 metres below Ordnance Datum (Local)
HAT is 10·3 metres above Chart Datum

TIME ZONE (UT)	CHANNEL ISLES – ST PETER PORT	Dates in amber are SPRINGS
For Summer Time add ONE hour in **non-shaded areas**	LAT 49°27'N LONG 2°31'W	Dates in yellow are NEAPS
	TIMES AND HEIGHTS OF HIGH AND LOW WATERS	**2009**

SEPTEMBER

Day	Time m	Time m	Time m	Time m
1 TU	0428 7.1	1048 3.4	1643 7.6	2310 3.0
16 W	0421 8.1	1039 2.4	1638 8.6	2310 1.8
2 W	0509 7.7	1128 2.8	1724 8.2	2348 2.4
17 TH	0512 8.8	1130 1.7	1728 9.3	2358 1.1
3 TH	0546 8.2	1205 2.3	1801 8.6	
18 F	0558 9.4	1217 1.1	1813 9.8	
4 F	0024 2.0	0622 8.6	1240 1.9	1836 9.0 ○
19 SA	0042 0.7	0640 9.8	1301 0.7	1855 10.0
5 SA	0059 1.7	0656 8.9	1313 1.3	1910 9.1
20 SU	0124 0.5	0720 9.9	1342 0.6	1935 10.0
6 SU	0131 1.5	0728 9.0	1345 1.6	1941 9.2
21 M	0202 0.7	0757 9.8	1419 0.8	2011 9.7
7 M	0201 1.5	0757 9.0	1414 1.6	2010 9.1
22 TU	0237 1.1	0831 9.4	1452 1.3	2044 9.2
8 TU	0229 1.6	0825 8.9	1442 1.8	2039 8.9
23 W	0308 1.7	0901 8.9	1523 1.9	2115 8.6
9 W	0257 1.9	0854 8.7	1511 2.1	2110 8.6
24 TH	0335 2.4	0931 8.3	1552 2.6	2145 7.8
10 TH	0327 2.3	0926 8.3	1543 2.5	2146 8.1
25 F	0401 3.2	1002 7.6	1624 3.4	2219 7.1
11 F	0403 2.8	1006 7.9	1624 3.0	2233 7.8
26 SA	0433 3.9	1042 7.0	1710 4.0	2310 6.5 ◐
12 SA	0451 3.4	1100 7.4	1724 3.6	2341 7.0 ◐
27 SU	0533 4.4	1153 6.5	1840 4.4	
13 SU	0606 3.8	1203 7.0	1906 3.8	
28 M	0059 6.2	0729 4.6	1405 6.5	2033 4.3
14 M	0129 6.8	0803 3.8	1415 7.2	2101 3.4
29 TU	0302 6.5	0920 4.2	1522 6.9	2149 3.7
15 TU	0316 7.3	0936 3.2	1539 7.8	2215 2.6
30 W	0355 7.1	1014 3.6	1611 7.5	2235 3.1

OCTOBER

Day	Time m	Time m	Time m	Time m
1 TH	0436 7.7	1055 2.9	1651 8.1	2314 2.5
16 F	0448 8.8	1107 1.8	1704 9.2	2333 1.4
2 F	0513 8.2	1132 2.4	1729 8.6	2350 2.0
17 SA	0532 9.3	1152 1.3	1748 9.5	
3 SA	0549 8.7	1207 2.0	1805 9.0	
18 SU	0016 1.1	0612 9.6	1235 1.1	1829 9.7 ○
4 SU	0025 1.7	0623 9.0	1243 1.7	1839 9.2 ○
19 M	0056 1.0	0651 9.7	1315 1.1	1909 9.6
5 M	0059 1.5	0656 9.2	1316 1.5	1913 9.3
20 TU	0133 1.2	0728 9.5	1352 1.3	1944 9.3
6 TU	0132 1.4	0728 9.2	1349 1.5	1945 9.3
21 W	0207 1.6	0801 9.2	1425 1.6	2017 8.9
7 W	0204 1.6	0759 9.1	1421 1.7	2018 9.1
22 TH	0237 2.1	0832 8.8	1456 2.2	2048 8.4
8 TH	0236 1.9	0833 8.8	1454 2.0	2054 8.7
23 F	0305 2.6	0902 8.3	1526 2.7	2120 7.8
9 F	0310 2.3	0909 8.5	1531 2.5	2134 8.2
24 SA	0331 3.2	0934 7.7	1558 3.3	2156 7.2
10 SA	0349 2.8	0954 8.0	1617 3.0	2226 7.6
25 SU	0404 3.8	1014 7.2	1642 3.9	2243 6.7
11 SU	0443 3.4	1054 7.5	1725 3.5	2341 7.1 ◐
26 M	0455 4.3	1114 6.7	1756 4.2 ◐	
12 M	0606 3.9	1220 7.2	1910 3.6	
27 TU	0002 6.4	0631 4.5	1251 6.6	1927 4.2
13 TU	0128 7.0	0757 3.9	1403 7.4	2048 3.2
28 W	0150 6.5	0808 4.3	1422 6.8	2046 3.8
14 W	0259 7.5	0919 3.1	1519 8.0	2154 2.5
29 TH	0302 7.0	0918 3.8	1521 7.3	2143 3.3
15 TH	0359 8.2	1018 2.4	1615 8.6	2246 1.9
30 F	0350 7.5	1008 3.2	1607 7.8	2229 2.8
31 SA	0432 8.1	1050 2.7	1649 8.3	2310 2.3

NOVEMBER

Day	Time m	Time m	Time m	Time m
1 SU	0511 8.5	1131 2.2	1729 8.7	2349 1.9
16 M	0546 9.1	1210 1.7	1806 9.0 ●	
2 M	0549 8.9	1210 1.8	1808 9.0 ○	
17 TU	0030 1.7	0625 9.2	1251 1.7	1845 9.0
3 TU	0027 1.7	0625 9.2	1249 1.6	1846 9.2
18 W	0108 1.8	0703 9.2	1329 1.7	1923 8.8
4 W	0106 1.5	0702 9.3	1328 1.5	1925 9.2
19 TH	0143 2.0	0738 9.0	1404 2.0	1957 8.6
5 TH	0144 1.6	0740 9.3	1407 1.6	2005 9.1
20 F	0215 2.3	0811 8.7	1437 2.3	2031 8.3
6 F	0222 1.8	0820 9.1	1447 1.9	2047 8.8
21 SA	0244 2.7	0848 8.3	1510 2.7	2104 7.9
7 SA	0303 2.2	0903 8.8	1532 2.2	2134 8.3
22 SU	0315 3.1	0918 7.9	1544 3.1	2140 7.5
8 SU	0349 2.7	0953 8.3	1624 2.7	2229 7.8
23 M	0348 3.5	0956 7.5	1623 3.4	2222 7.1
9 M	0447 3.2	1054 7.9	1731 3.1	2339 7.4 ◑
24 TU	0431 3.9	1042 7.2	1714 3.7	2315 6.8 ◑
10 TU	0603 3.5	1210 7.6	1854 3.2	
25 W	0532 4.1	1146 6.9	1821 3.9	
11 W	0104 7.4	0731 3.5	1334 7.4	2015 3.0 ○
26 TH	0024 6.7	0651 4.2	1259 6.9	1932 3.8
12 TH	0225 7.6	0848 3.1	1446 7.9	2122 2.7
27 F	0142 6.9	0806 3.9	1412 7.1	2037 3.5
13 F	0327 8.1	0949 2.6	1545 8.3	2217 2.3
28 SA	0248 7.2	0909 3.5	1512 7.5	2135 3.1
14 SA	0418 8.5	1040 2.2	1636 8.7	2305 2.0
29 SU	0342 7.7	1004 3.0	1605 7.9	2226 2.7
15 SU	0504 8.9	1127 1.9	1723 8.9	2349 1.8
30 M	0430 8.2	1053 2.5	1653 8.3	2314 2.3

DECEMBER

Day	Time m	Time m	Time m	Time m
1 TU	0515 8.7	1141 2.1	1740 8.7	
16 W	0010 2.4	0606 8.7	1234 2.2	1829 8.4 ●
2 W	0001 1.9	0600 9.0	1228 1.7	1826 9.0 ○
17 TH	0050 2.3	0645 8.8	1313 2.1	1908 8.5
3 TH	0047 1.7	0644 9.3	1315 1.5	1912 9.1
18 F	0126 2.2	0722 8.8	1350 2.1	1944 8.4
4 F	0132 1.6	0729 9.4	1401 1.4	1959 9.1
19 SA	0200 2.3	0757 8.7	1424 2.2	2019 8.3
5 SA	0217 1.6	0815 9.4	1447 1.5	2045 9.0
20 SU	0232 2.5	0831 8.5	1457 2.4	2051 8.1
6 SU	0303 1.8	0902 9.2	1535 1.7	2134 8.7
21 M	0302 2.7	0903 8.3	1529 2.6	2124 7.9
7 M	0351 2.1	0951 8.8	1625 2.0	2225 8.3
22 TU	0334 2.9	0937 8.0	1602 2.9	2158 7.6
8 TU	0443 2.5	1045 8.4	1720 2.4	2321 7.9
23 W	0408 3.2	1013 7.7	1638 3.1	2235 7.4
9 W	0543 2.9	1145 8.0	1822 2.8 ◑	
24 TH	0448 3.5	1055 7.4	1721 3.4	2321 7.1 ◑
10 TH	0026 7.6	0650 3.2	1253 7.7	1930 3.0
25 F	0539 3.7	1148 7.2	1816 3.6	
11 F	0138 7.5	0805 3.2	1405 7.6	2041 3.0
26 SA	0019 7.0	0646 3.8	1254 7.1	1925 3.6
12 SA	0248 7.7	0914 3.1	1512 7.7	2144 2.9
27 SU	0132 7.1	0805 3.7	1410 7.2	2038 3.4
13 SU	0347 7.9	1013 2.8	1610 7.9	2238 2.7
28 M	0248 7.3	0918 3.3	1522 7.5	2146 3.1
14 M	0439 8.2	1104 2.6	1701 8.1	2326 2.5
29 TU	0353 7.8	1022 2.8	1624 7.9	2247 2.6
15 TU	0524 8.5	1151 2.3	1747 8.3	
30 W	0450 8.3	1120 2.3	1722 8.3	2343 2.1
31 TH	0543 8.8	1215 1.7	1815 8.8 ○	

TIDES

Chart Datum: 5·06 metres below Ordnance Datum (Local)
HAT is 10·3 metres above Chart Datum

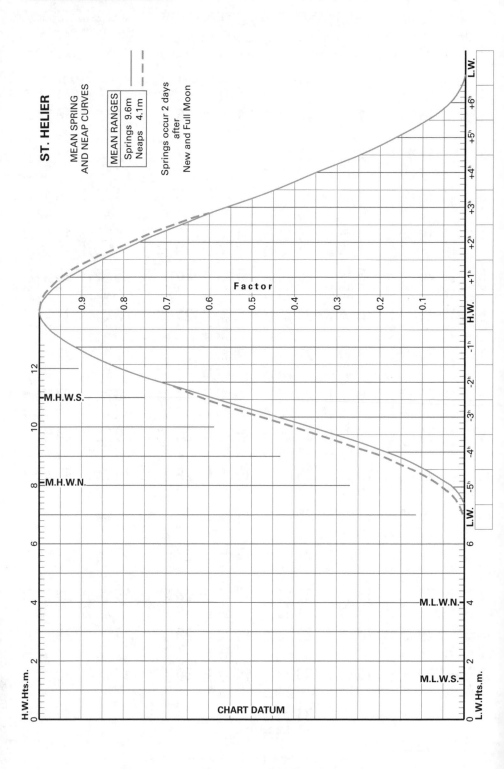

ST. HELIER

MEAN SPRING
AND NEAP CURVES

MEAN RANGES	
Springs	9.6m
Neaps	4.1m

Springs occur 2 days
after
New and Full Moon

Factor

TIME ZONE (UT)
For Summer Time add ONE hour in **non-shaded areas**

CHANNEL ISLES – ST HELIER
LAT 49°11'N   LONG 2°07'W
TIMES AND HEIGHTS OF HIGH AND LOW WATERS

Dates in amber are **SPRINGS**
Dates in yellow are **NEAPS**

2009

JANUARY

Time	m	Time	m
1 0312	2.6	**16** 0421	1.8
0857	9.9	0954	10.5
TH 1536	2.5	F 1644	2.0
2118	9.6	2218	9.9
2 0346	2.8	**17** 0456	2.5
0932	9.7	1031	9.8
F 1611	2.7	SA 1718	2.7
2154	9.3	2255	9.2
3 0423	3.1	**18** 0532	3.2
1010	9.3	1110	9.0
SA 1649	3.1	SU 1754	3.4
2234	9.0	◔ 2338	8.5
4 0505	3.4	**19** 0615	3.8
1054	8.9	1200	8.3
SU 1734	3.4	M 1842	4.1
◑ 2324	8.6		
5 0557	3.7	**20** 0039	8.0
1151	8.6	0717	4.3
M 1833	3.7	TU 1314	7.7
		1957	4.4
6 0028	8.4	**21** 0205	7.8
0706	3.9	0843	4.4
TU 1305	8.4	W 1445	7.7
1949	3.7	2124	4.3
7 0147	8.5	**22** 0327	8.1
0832	3.7	1003	4.0
W 1429	8.6	TH 1601	8.1
2112	3.5	2234	3.9
8 0307	8.9	**23** 0428	8.6
0953	3.2	1103	3.5
TH 1547	9.1	F 1657	8.6
2227	2.9	2326	3.3
9 0418	9.5	**24** 0516	9.2
1103	2.5	1150	2.9
F 1656	9.7	SA 1740	9.1
2333	2.3		
10 0520	10.3	**25** 0010	2.9
1207	1.8	0555	9.6
SA 1756	10.4	SU 1232	2.5
		1818	9.6
11 0032	1.7	**26** 0049	2.5
0615	10.9	0632	10.0
SU 1305	1.3	M 1311	2.1
○ 1849	10.9	● 1852	9.9
12 0127	1.3	**27** 0125	2.2
0706	11.3	0706	10.3
M 1358	0.9	TU 1346	1.9
1937	11.1	1925	10.1
13 0216	1.1	**28** 0159	2.0
0753	11.5	0738	10.5
TU 1446	0.8	W 1420	1.8
2022	11.2	1957	10.3
14 0302	1.1	**29** 0230	1.9
0836	11.4	0810	10.6
W 1530	0.9	TH 1451	1.7
2104	10.9	2028	10.3
15 0347	1.3	**30** 0301	1.9
0916	11.1	0842	10.5
TH 1609	1.3	F 1521	1.8
2142	10.5	2100	10.2
		31 0331	2.1
		0914	10.3
		SA 1552	2.0
		2131	9.9

FEBRUARY

Time	m	Time	m
1 0403	2.4	**16** 0444	3.0
0946	9.9	1023	9.0
SU 1624	2.5	M 1657	3.4
2205	9.5	◑ 2242	8.6
2 0437	2.9	**17** 0516	3.7
1023	9.4	1100	8.2
M 1700	3.0	TU 1732	4.1
◑ 2245	9.0	2328	7.9
3 0520	3.4	**18** 0607	4.4
1110	8.8	1203	7.4
TU 1749	3.6	W 1838	4.7
2341	8.5		
4 0622	3.8	**19** 0102	7.3
1221	8.2	0740	4.7
W 1904	4.0	TH 1406	7.1
		2037	4.4
5 0105	8.2	**20** 0258	7.5
0757	4.0	0931	4.4
TH 1403	8.1	F 1542	7.6
2047	3.9	2210	4.3
6 0248	8.4	**21** 0408	8.2
0938	3.5	1041	3.7
F 1542	8.6	SA 1638	8.4
2217	3.3	2306	3.5
7 0412	9.2	**22** 0456	8.9
1058	2.7	1129	3.0
SA 1654	9.4	SU 1720	9.0
2327	2.4	2350	2.8
8 0515	10.1	**23** 0535	9.6
1202	1.8	1211	2.4
SU 1751	10.3	M 1757	9.6
9 0025	1.6	**24** 0029	2.3
0608	10.9	0611	10.1
M 1258	1.0	TU 1251	1.9
○ 1839	11.0	1830	10.1
10 0117	1.0	**25** 0107	1.9
0654	11.5	0644	10.5
TU 1347	0.6	W 1327	1.6
1923	11.3	● 1903	10.4
11 0203	0.7	**26** 0141	1.6
0737	11.7	0717	10.8
W 1429	0.4	TH 1401	1.3
2002	11.4	1935	10.7
12 0243	0.7	**27** 0213	1.4
0816	11.7	0749	11.0
TH 1507	0.6	F 1432	1.3
2039	11.2	2006	10.8
13 0319	0.9	**28** 0243	1.4
0851	11.3	0822	10.9
F 1540	1.1	SA 1501	1.3
2111	10.8	2037	10.7
14 0350	1.5		
0923	10.7		
SA 1607	1.8		
2141	10.1		
15 0417	2.2		
0953	9.9		
SU 1632	2.6		
2210	9.4		

MARCH

Time	m	Time	m
1 0314	1.6	**16** 0341	2.1
0853	10.7	0919	9.8
SU 1531	1.7	M 1552	2.6
2108	10.4	2131	9.5
2 0344	2.0	**17** 0406	2.9
0925	10.2	0945	9.0
M 1602	2.2	TU 1615	3.4
2141	9.8	2158	8.7
3 0417	2.5	**18** 0435	3.6
1001	9.5	1017	8.1
TU 1637	2.9	W 1646	4.1
2219	9.2	◑ 2236	7.9
4 0459	3.2	**19** 0521	4.3
1047	8.7	1109	7.3
W 1725	3.6	TH 1743	4.8
◑ 2314	8.4	2355	7.3
5 0602	3.8	**20** 0644	4.8
1202	8.0	1317	7.0
TH 1845	4.2	F 1935	5.0
6 0047	8.0	**21** 0217	7.3
0746	4.1	0843	4.6
F 1403	7.8	SA 1506	7.4
2040	4.1	2129	4.5
7 0245	8.3	**22** 0333	8.0
0934	3.5	1002	3.9
SA 1542	8.5	SU 1604	8.2
2211	3.3	2231	3.7
8 0406	9.2	**23** 0422	8.7
1051	2.5	1054	3.1
SU 1646	9.5	M 1646	9.0
2317	2.3	2316	2.9
9 0504	10.1	**24** 0502	9.4
1150	1.5	1138	2.4
M 1736	10.4	TU 1724	9.6
		2358	2.3
10 0010	1.5	**25** 0540	10.1
0552	10.9	1219	1.8
TU 1241	1.0	W 1759	10.2
1820	11.0		
11 0058	0.9	**26** 0037	1.8
0635	11.4	0615	10.5
W 1325	0.6	TH 1258	1.4
● 1900	11.3	● 1833	10.6
12 0140	0.7	**27** 0115	1.4
0714	11.6	0650	10.9
TH 1403	0.6	F 1334	1.2
1936	11.4	1907	10.9
13 0217	0.7	**28** 0149	1.2
0750	11.5	0725	11.1
F 1437	0.8	SA 1407	1.1
2009	11.2	1941	11.0
14 0248	1.0	**29** 0222	1.2
0822	11.1	0800	11.0
SA 1505	1.2	SU 1440	1.2
2039	10.8	2015	10.9
15 0316	1.5	**30** 0255	1.4
0852	10.5	0835	10.7
SU 1530	1.9	M 1512	1.6
2106	10.2	2049	10.6
		31 0329	1.8
		0911	10.2
		TU 1547	2.2
		2125	10.0

APRIL

Time	m	Time	m
1 0407	2.4	**16** 0412	3.5
0952	9.4	0953	8.2
W 1627	2.9	TH 1622	4.0
2209	9.2	2207	8.1
2 0454	3.1	**17** 0456	4.1
1046	8.6	1043	7.6
TH 1721	3.6	F 1714	4.6
◑ 2311	8.5	◑ 2313	7.5
3 0604	3.7	**18** 0604	4.5
1210	8.0	1217	7.2
F 1846	4.1	SA 1839	4.8
4 0049	8.1	**19** 0109	7.4
0747	3.8	0737	4.5
SA 1403	8.0	SU 1404	7.5
2032	3.9	2022	4.6
5 0234	8.5	**20** 0236	7.8
0921	3.2	0902	4.0
SU 1525	8.8	M 1509	8.1
2153	3.1	2136	3.9
6 0346	9.3	**21** 0332	8.5
1030	2.4	1003	3.3
M 1624	9.6	TU 1558	8.8
2254	2.2	2229	3.2
7 0441	10.1	**22** 0418	9.2
1125	1.7	1053	2.6
TU 1711	10.3	W 1641	9.5
2345	1.6	2316	2.5
8 0528	10.7	**23** 0500	9.9
1213	1.3	1139	2.0
W 1754	10.8	TH 1721	10.1
9 0031	1.2	**24** 0000	1.9
0609	11.0	0540	10.4
TH 1255	1.1	F 1222	1.6
○ 1831	11.0	1800	10.6
10 0111	1.1	**25** 0043	1.5
0647	11.1	0620	10.8
F 1331	1.1	SA 1303	1.3
1906	11.1	● 1839	10.9
11 0146	1.2	**26** 0123	1.3
0721	11.0	0700	11.0
SA 1403	1.3	SU 1343	1.2
1938	10.9	1917	11.1
12 0216	1.4	**27** 0202	1.2
0753	10.7	0741	11.0
SU 1431	1.7	M 1421	1.3
2008	10.6	1957	11.0
13 0245	1.7	**28** 0242	1.4
0823	10.2	0823	10.7
M 1456	2.1	TU 1459	1.7
2035	10.1	2038	10.6
14 0312	2.3	**29** 0322	1.7
0851	9.6	0907	10.1
TU 1522	2.7	W 1541	2.2
2102	9.5	2121	10.1
15 0339	2.9	**30** 0408	2.3
0919	8.9	0956	9.5
W 1548	3.4	TH 1628	2.8
2130	8.8	2212	9.4

TIDES

Chart Datum: 5·88 metres below Ordnance Datum (Local)
HAT is 12·2 metres above Chart Datum

TIDES

CHANNEL ISLES – ST HELIER
LAT 49°11'N   LONG 2°07'W
TIMES AND HEIGHTS OF HIGH AND LOW WATERS

Dates in amber are **SPRINGS**
Dates in yellow are **NEAPS**

2009

MAY		JUNE		JULY		AUGUST	
Time m	Time m	Time m	Time m	Time m	Time m	Time m	Time m
1 0502 2.9 / 1055 8.8 / F 1728 3.4 / 2317 8.9	**16** 0439 3.7 / 1026 8.1 / SA 1654 4.1 / 2247 8.1	**1** 0011 9.1 / 0704 3.0 / M 1256 8.8 / 1932 3.2	**16** 0551 3.6 / 1143 8.3 / TU 1815 3.9	**1** 0029 8.8 / 0718 3.4 / W 1309 8.5 / 1948 3.6	**16** 0559 3.5 / 1150 8.5 / TH 1828 3.8	**1** 0215 7.7 / 0854 4.4 / SA 1500 8.0 / 2138 4.1	**16** 0118 8.0 / 0803 4.1 / SU 1406 8.3 / 2057 3.8
2 0612 3.3 / 1212 8.4 / SA 1845 3.7	**17** 0532 4.0 / 1128 7.8 / SU 1755 4.3 / 2359 7.9	**2** 0120 8.9 / 0809 3.1 / TU 1404 8.8 / 2038 3.2	**17** 0010 8.3 / 0650 3.7 / W 1248 8.3 / 1922 3.9	**2** 0137 8.4 / 0823 3.6 / TH 1419 8.4 / 2057 3.7	**17** 0023 8.4 / 0704 3.8 / F 1303 8.4 / 1945 3.9	**2** 0339 8.0 / 1013 4.0 / SU 1608 8.5 / 2245 3.6	**17** 0304 8.4 / 0938 3.5 / M 1536 9.0 / 2221 2.9
3 0039 8.6 / 0734 3.3 / SU 1338 8.5 / 2008 3.5	**18** 0639 4.1 / 1245 7.8 / M 1912 4.3	**3** 0228 8.9 / 0912 3.0 / W 1507 9.0 / 2140 3.0	**18** 0120 8.4 / 0759 3.6 / TH 1358 8.5 / 2035 3.6	**3** 0250 8.3 / 0931 3.7 / F 1527 8.6 / 2204 3.5	**18** 0145 8.3 / 0827 3.7 / SA 1426 8.6 / 2112 3.5	**3** 0440 8.5 / 1110 3.5 / M 1659 9.1 / 2336 3.0	**18** 0421 9.2 / 1052 2.7 / TU 1644 9.9 / 2329 2.0
4 0204 8.8 / 0851 3.0 / M 1451 8.9 / 2120 3.0	**19** 0119 8.0 / 0753 3.9 / TU 1400 8.1 / 2028 4.0	**4** 0330 9.1 / 1011 2.9 / TH 1602 9.3 / 2237 2.8	**19** 0230 8.7 / 0910 3.3 / F 1504 9.0 / 2145 3.2	**4** 0357 8.5 / 1034 3.5 / SA 1625 9.0 / 2303 3.2	**19** 0310 8.7 / 0949 3.2 / SU 1543 9.2 / 2228 2.8	**4** 0526 9.1 / 1156 3.0 / TU 1742 9.6	**19** 0521 10.2 / 1154 1.8 / W 1739 10.8
5 0313 9.3 / 0955 2.5 / TU 1549 9.4 / 2221 2.5	**20** 0228 8.4 / 0902 3.5 / W 1500 8.6 / 2133 3.4	**5** 0425 9.3 / 1104 2.7 / F 1651 9.6 / 2328 2.6	**20** 0336 9.2 / 1016 2.8 / SA 1605 9.5 / 2249 2.6	**5** 0453 8.9 / 1127 3.2 / SU 1715 9.3 / 2352 2.8	**20** 0424 9.3 / 1100 2.6 / M 1650 9.9 / 2336 2.1	**5** 0019 2.5 / 0604 9.5 / W 1236 2.6 / 1818 10.0	**20** 0027 1.2 / 0611 10.9 / TH 1248 1.2 / 1828 11.5
6 0409 9.7 / 1051 2.1 / W 1639 9.9 / 2313 2.1	**21** 0325 9.0 / 1001 2.9 / TH 1552 9.3 / 2220 2.8	**6** 0513 9.5 / 1150 2.6 / SA 1734 9.8	**21** 0438 9.7 / 1117 2.3 / SU 1703 10.1 / 2348 2.0	**6** 0540 9.2 / 1212 2.9 / M 1757 9.6	**21** 0528 10.0 / 1203 1.9 / TU 1749 10.6	**6** 0058 2.2 / 0639 9.8 / TH 1312 2.3 / 1853 10.3	**21** 0119 0.7 / 0657 11.4 / F 1337 0.7 / 1913 11.9
7 0457 10.1 / 1139 1.9 / TH 1722 10.3 / 2359 1.9	**22** 0416 9.6 / 1055 2.4 / F 1641 9.9 / 2322 2.2	**7** 0012 2.4 / 0555 9.6 / SU 1231 2.5 / 1813 10.0	**22** 0536 10.2 / 1215 1.9 / M 1757 10.6	**7** 0035 2.5 / 0620 9.5 / TU 1252 2.6 / 1835 9.9	**22** 0037 1.4 / 0623 10.7 / W 1301 1.4 / 1841 11.2	**7** 0133 2.0 / 0712 10.1 / F 1346 2.1 / 1925 10.4	**22** 0205 0.4 / 0739 11.6 / SA 1421 0.6 / 1954 11.9
8 0540 10.3 / 1221 1.8 / F 1801 10.4	**23** 0505 10.1 / 1146 1.9 / SA 1728 10.4	**8** 0051 2.3 / 0635 9.7 / M 1307 2.4 / 1850 10.0	**23** 0045 1.5 / 0630 10.6 / TU 1310 1.5 / 1849 11.0	**8** 0114 2.3 / 0657 9.7 / W 1328 2.5 / 1911 10.0	**23** 0134 0.9 / 0714 11.1 / TH 1354 1.0 / 1930 11.6	**8** 0206 1.8 / 0743 10.2 / SA 1417 2.0 / 1956 10.5	**23** 0246 0.5 / 0818 11.5 / SU 1500 0.8 / 2032 11.6
9 0039 1.8 / 0619 10.4 / SA 1259 1.9 / 1837 10.5	**24** 0012 1.8 / 0553 10.5 / SU 1235 1.6 / 1813 10.8	**9** 0128 2.2 / 0711 9.7 / TU 1342 2.5 / 1925 10.0	**24** 0141 1.2 / 0723 10.9 / W 1402 1.3 / 1940 11.2	**9** 0150 2.2 / 0732 9.8 / TH 1402 2.4 / 1944 10.1	**24** 0224 0.6 / 0800 11.3 / F 1441 0.8 / 2015 11.7	**9** 0237 1.8 / 0813 10.3 / SU 1447 2.0 / 2026 10.5	**24** 0323 0.9 / 0854 11.1 / M 1535 1.2 / 2107 11.0
10 0116 1.8 / 0655 10.3 / SU 1331 1.9 / 1910 10.5	**25** 0101 1.4 / 0641 10.8 / M 1322 1.4 / 1900 11.0	**10** 0202 2.3 / 0746 9.7 / W 1415 2.5 / 1958 9.9	**25** 0233 1.0 / 0813 10.9 / TH 1452 1.3 / ● 2029 11.2	**10** 0224 2.1 / 0804 9.8 / F 1435 2.4 / 2016 10.1	**25** 0310 0.6 / 0844 11.3 / SA 1525 0.9 / 2058 11.5	**10** 0307 1.8 / 0843 10.2 / M 1517 2.1 / 2056 10.3	**25** 0355 1.5 / 0926 10.5 / TU 1607 2.0 / ● 2140 10.2
11 0148 1.9 / 0728 10.1 / M 1401 2.1 / ○ 1942 10.3	**26** 0148 1.3 / 0729 10.8 / TU 1408 1.4 / ● 1946 11.0	**11** 0236 2.4 / 0819 9.5 / TH 1447 2.7 / 2031 9.7	**26** 0322 1.0 / 0901 10.8 / F 1539 1.4 / 2115 11.0	**11** 0256 2.2 / 0836 9.8 / SA 1506 2.4 / ○ 2048 10.0	**26** 0351 0.8 / 0924 10.9 / SU 1606 1.2 / ● 2137 11.0	**11** 0336 2.1 / 0913 10.0 / TU 1547 2.4 / 2127 9.9	**26** 0423 2.4 / 0957 9.7 / W 1636 2.8 / 2211 9.3
12 0219 2.1 / 0801 9.8 / TU 1431 2.4 / 2013 9.9	**27** 0235 1.3 / 0818 10.7 / W 1455 1.6 / 2033 10.8	**12** 0310 2.6 / 0853 9.3 / F 1520 2.9 / 2105 9.4	**27** 0409 1.3 / 0946 10.4 / SA 1624 1.7 / 2201 10.6	**12** 0328 2.3 / 0908 9.7 / SU 1538 2.6 / 2120 9.8	**27** 0428 1.4 / 1001 10.3 / M 1641 1.9 / 2214 10.2	**12** 0406 2.5 / 0943 9.6 / W 1619 2.9 / 2159 9.4	**27** 0450 3.3 / 1030 8.9 / TH 1709 3.6 / 2248 8.3
13 0250 2.4 / 0832 9.4 / W 1501 2.8 / 2043 9.5	**28** 0323 1.5 / 0907 10.3 / TH 1542 1.9 / 2122 10.4	**13** 0344 2.8 / 0927 9.0 / SA 1555 3.2 / 2141 9.1	**28** 0453 1.7 / 1031 10.0 / SU 1709 2.2 / 2246 10.0	**13** 0400 2.5 / 0940 9.4 / M 1611 2.8 / 2154 9.5	**28** 0503 2.2 / 1038 9.6 / TU 1717 2.7 / 2253 9.4	**13** 0439 3.0 / 1019 9.1 / TH 1657 3.4 / 2240 8.8	**28** 0524 4.1 / 1114 8.1 / F 1758 4.4 / 2348 7.5
14 0322 2.8 / 0904 9.0 / TH 1532 3.3 / 2116 9.0	**29** 0413 1.9 / 0958 9.9 / F 1632 2.4 / 2213 10.0	**14** 0421 3.1 / 1005 8.8 / SU 1633 3.5 / 2221 8.8	**29** 0538 2.3 / 1117 9.4 / M 1755 2.7 / 2334 9.4	**14** 0434 2.8 / 1015 9.1 / TU 1647 3.2 / 2231 9.1	**29** 0538 3.0 / 1118 8.9 / W 1757 3.4 / 2338 8.6	**14** 0522 3.5 / 1107 8.6 / F 1751 3.8 / 2342 8.2	**29** 0625 4.8 / 1241 7.5 / SA 1927 4.8
15 0357 3.2 / 0941 8.5 / F 1608 3.7 / 2155 8.5	**30** 0505 2.3 / 1052 9.4 / SA 1726 2.8 / 2309 9.5	**15** 0503 3.3 / 1050 8.5 / M 1719 3.7 / 2310 8.5	**30** 0624 2.9 / 1209 8.9 / TU 1847 3.2	**15** 0512 3.2 / 1056 8.8 / W 1730 3.5 / 2318 8.7	**30** 0621 3.8 / 1211 8.3 / TH 1853 4.0	**15** 0607 4.0 / 1223 8.2 / SA 1915 4.1	**30** 0146 7.2 / 0818 4.9 / SU 1439 7.6 / 2114 4.5
	31 0602 2.7 / 1151 9.0 / SU 1826 3.1				**31** 0042 7.9 / 0725 4.3 / F 1331 7.9 / 2013 4.3		**31** 0325 7.7 / 0953 4.4 / M 1551 8.3 / 2225 3.8

Chart Datum: 5·88 metres below Ordnance Datum (Local)
HAT is 12·2 metres above Chart Datum

CHANNEL ISLES – ST HELIER

LAT 49°11'N   LONG 2°07'W

TIMES AND HEIGHTS OF HIGH AND LOW WATERS

Dates in amber are **SPRINGS**
Dates in yellow are **NEAPS**

2009

SEPTEMBER

Day	Time	m		Day	Time	m
1 TU	0422	8.4		16 W	0413	9.4
	1050	3.6			1041	2.6
	1639	9.0			1632	10.1
	2313	3.1			2315	1.9
2 W	0504	9.1		17 TH	0506	10.4
	1133	3.0			1137	1.7
	1719	9.6			1723	11.0
	2354	2.5				
3 TH	0540	9.7		18 F	0008	1.2
	1211	2.4			0552	11.1
	1755	10.1			1228	1.1
					1808	11.5
4 F	0032	2.0		19 SA	0056	0.7
	0613	10.1			0634	11.5
	1248	2.1			1849	11.8
○	1827	10.5				
5 SA	0108	1.8		20 SU	0139	0.7
	0645	10.4			0713	11.6
	1322	1.8			1354	0.8
	1859	10.7			1928	11.7
6 SU	0141	1.6		21 M	0216	0.8
	0716	10.6			0749	11.4
	1354	1.7			1430	1.0
	1930	10.9			2004	11.4
7 M	0212	1.5		22 TU	0249	1.3
	0746	10.7			0821	11.0
	1424	1.7			1502	1.5
	2001	10.8			2036	10.8
8 TU	0242	1.6		23 W	0317	1.9
	0816	10.6			0851	10.4
	1454	1.8			1531	2.2
	2032	10.6			2106	10.0
9 W	0311	1.9		24 TH	0343	2.7
	0846	10.4			0919	9.7
	1524	2.2			1558	3.0
	2102	10.2			2135	9.1
10 TH	0341	2.4		25 F	0408	3.5
	0917	9.9			0949	8.9
	1556	2.7			1629	3.8
	2135	9.5			2208	8.3
11 F	0415	3.0		26 SA	0440	4.3
	0952	9.3			1027	8.1
	1635	3.3			1715	4.5
	2217	8.8		☾	2302	7.5
12 SA	0459	3.7		27 SU	0537	4.9
	1041	8.6			1147	7.4
	1732	3.9			1839	4.9
☾	2324	8.1				
13 SU	0610	4.2		28 M	0107	7.1
	1211	8.1			0729	5.2
	1906	4.2			1405	7.5
					2034	4.7
14 M	0119	7.8		29 TU	0253	7.6
	0757	4.3			0917	4.6
	1404	8.2			1519	8.1
	2054	3.8			2148	4.0
15 TU	0305	8.5		30 W	0349	8.3
	0932	3.5			1015	3.8
	1531	9.1			1607	8.9
	2214	2.8			2237	3.2

OCTOBER

Day	Time	m		Day	Time	m
1 TH	0430	9.1		16 F	0442	10.3
	1058	3.1			1113	1.8
	1646	9.6			1659	10.8
	2319	2.6			2342	1.5
2 F	0506	9.7		17 SA	0527	10.9
	1138	2.5			1201	1.4
	1722	10.1			1743	11.2
	2358	2.1				
3 SA	0541	10.2		18 SU	0027	1.2
	1215	2.1			0607	11.2
	1757	10.5			1245	1.2
				●	1823	11.3
4 SU	0035	1.8		19 M	0108	1.2
	0613	10.6			0644	11.3
	1252	1.8			1324	1.3
○	1830	10.8			1901	11.2
5 M	0111	1.6		20 TU	0143	1.4
	0646	10.8			0719	11.1
	1327	1.6			1359	1.5
	1903	11.0			1936	10.9
6 TU	0145	1.5		21 W	0215	1.8
	0718	11.0			0751	10.8
	1400	1.6			1430	1.9
	1936	10.9			2008	10.4
7 W	0217	1.6		22 TH	0243	2.3
	0751	10.9			0822	10.3
	1432	1.8			1500	2.4
	2010	10.7			2039	9.8
8 TH	0249	1.9		23 F	0311	2.9
	0824	10.6			0851	9.7
	1506	2.1			1529	3.0
	2046	10.2			2109	9.1
9 F	0323	2.4		24 SA	0339	3.6
	0859	10.1			0921	9.0
	1542	2.6			1602	3.7
	2125	9.5			2144	8.4
10 SA	0402	3.1		25 SU	0412	4.2
	0941	9.4			0959	8.3
	1628	3.3			1646	4.3
	2214	8.8			2233	7.7
11 SU	0453	3.7		26 M	0504	4.7
	1038	8.7			1102	7.7
	1724	3.9			1754	4.7
☾	2331	8.2		☾		
12 M	0610	4.2		27 TU	0001	7.3
	1207	8.3			0627	5.0
	1907	4.0			1254	7.5
					1926	4.7
13 TU	0120	8.1		28 W	0149	7.5
	0751	4.1			0809	4.8
	1354	8.5			1423	7.9
	2042	3.5			2049	4.2
14 W	0250	8.7		29 TH	0256	8.1
	0916	3.4			0921	4.2
	1512	9.3			1519	8.5
	2154	2.7			2147	3.6
15 TH	0352	9.6		30 F	0343	8.8
	1019	2.5			1012	3.5
	1610	10.1			1603	9.2
	2251	2.0			2234	2.9
				31 SA	0424	9.4
					1057	2.8
					1643	9.8
					2318	2.4

NOVEMBER

Day	Time	m		Day	Time	m
1 SU	0502	10.0		16 M	0540	10.6
	1139	2.3			1218	1.9
●	1721	10.3			1800	10.5
2 M	0000	2.0		17 TU	0039	2.0
	0539	10.5			0619	10.7
	1220	1.9			1258	1.9
○	1759	10.7			1838	10.5
3 TU	0040	1.7		18 W	0115	2.1
	0616	10.8			0655	10.9
	1300	1.7			1334	2.0
	1837	10.9			1914	10.4
4 W	0118	1.6		19 TH	0148	2.2
	0654	11.0			0729	10.5
	1338	1.6			1407	2.2
	1917	10.9			1949	10.1
5 TH	0156	1.7		20 F	0219	2.5
	0732	11.0			0801	10.2
	1416	1.7			1439	2.5
	1957	10.7			2022	9.7
6 F	0234	1.9		21 SA	0250	2.9
	0812	10.8			0833	9.8
	1457	2.0			1511	2.9
	2040	10.3			2054	9.2
7 SA	0315	2.3		22 SU	0321	3.3
	0855	10.3			0906	9.3
	1541	2.4			1545	3.3
	2127	9.7			2129	8.7
8 SU	0401	2.9		23 M	0355	3.8
	0943	9.7			0943	8.8
	1632	2.9			1625	3.8
	2223	9.1			2211	8.3
9 M	0456	3.4		24 TU	0438	4.2
	1043	9.2			1029	8.3
	1737	3.4			1714	4.1
◑	2332	8.6		☾	2306	7.9
10 TU	0608	3.7		25 W	0535	4.5
	1158	8.8			1133	7.9
	1855	3.5			1818	4.3
11 W	0055	8.5		26 TH	0018	7.8
	0729	3.7			0648	4.6
	1323	8.8			1255	7.9
	2014	3.3			1931	4.3
12 TH	0214	8.9		27 F	0137	7.9
	0845	3.3			0807	4.4
	1438	9.2			1409	8.2
	2122	2.9			2042	3.9
13 F	0318	9.4		28 SA	0242	8.4
	0948	2.8			0915	3.9
	1539	9.7			1508	8.7
	2220	2.4			2143	3.4
14 SA	0412	9.9		29 SU	0334	9.0
	1044	2.3			1011	3.3
	1631	10.1			1558	9.3
	2312	2.1			2236	2.9
15 SU	0458	10.3		30 M	0421	9.6
	1134	2.0			1102	2.7
	1718	10.4			1646	9.8
	2358	2.0			2325	2.4

DECEMBER

Day	Time	m		Day	Time	m
1 TU	0507	10.2		16 W	0018	2.5
	1150	2.2			0600	10.1
	1732	10.3			1240	2.3
				●	1823	9.9
2 W	0012	2.0		17 TH	0057	2.5
	0551	10.7			0639	10.2
	1237	1.8			1318	2.2
○	1818	10.7			1901	10.0
3 TH	0058	1.7		18 F	0132	2.4
	0636	11.0			0715	10.3
	1323	1.6			1353	2.2
	1905	10.8			1936	9.9
4 F	0143	1.7		19 SA	0205	2.5
	0722	11.1			0749	10.2
	1410	1.5			1426	2.3
	1952	10.8			2009	9.8
5 SA	0229	1.7		20 SU	0237	2.6
	0808	11.0			0821	10.0
	1456	1.6			1459	2.5
	2040	10.6			2041	9.6
6 SU	0315	1.9		21 M	0308	2.8
	0855	10.8			0853	9.7
	1544	1.8			1531	2.7
	2129	10.2			2113	9.3
7 M	0403	2.3		22 TU	0340	3.1
	0944	10.4			0926	9.4
	1635	2.2			1604	3.0
	2219	9.8			2147	9.0
8 TU	0454	2.7		23 W	0414	3.4
	1036	9.9			1001	9.0
	1728	2.6			1641	3.4
	2314	9.3			2225	8.6
9 W	0551	3.1		24 TH	0453	3.8
	1133	9.4			1042	8.6
	1827	3.0			1723	3.8
◑				☾	2310	8.3
10 TH	0015	8.9		25 F	0542	4.1
	0653	3.4			1134	8.2
	1239	9.0			1817	4.0
	1932	3.2				
11 F	0124	8.8		26 SA	0010	8.1
	0802	3.4			0646	4.3
	1351	8.9			1243	8.1
	2040	3.3			1926	4.1
12 SA	0234	8.9		27 SU	0124	8.1
	0910	3.3			0805	4.2
	1501	9.0			1401	8.2
	2144	3.1			2044	3.9
13 SU	0337	9.2		28 M	0238	8.5
	1013	3.0			0922	3.7
	1603	9.2			1513	8.7
	2243	2.9			2154	3.4
14 M	0432	9.5		29 TU	0343	9.1
	1109	2.7			1027	3.1
	1656	9.5			1616	9.3
	2334	2.7			2256	2.8
15 TU	0519	9.9		30 W	0441	9.8
	1158	2.5			1126	2.4
	1742	9.7			1714	9.9
					2352	2.2
				31 TH	0535	10.4
					1222	1.8
					1808	10.5
				○		

Chart Datum: 5·88 metres below Ordnance Datum (Local)
HAT is 12·2 metres above Chart Datum

TIDES

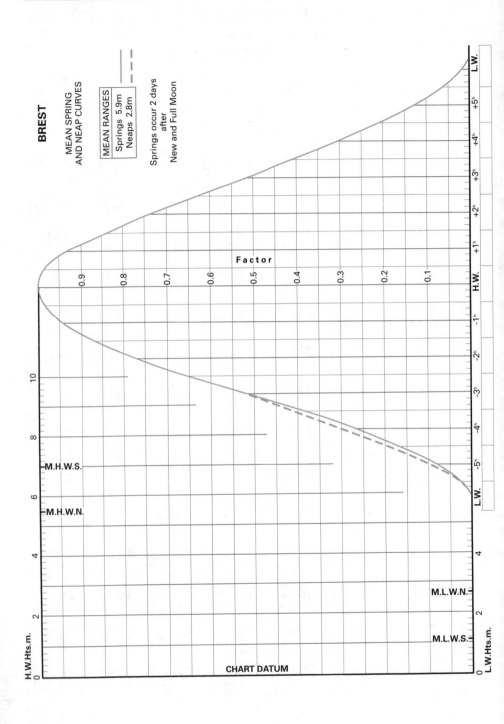

BREST

MEAN SPRING
AND NEAP CURVES

MEAN RANGES
Springs 5.9m
Neaps 2.8m

Springs occur 2 days
after
New and Full Moon

Factor

0.9 0.8 0.7 0.6 0.5 0.4 0.3 0.2 0.1

H.W.Hts.m.

M.H.W.S.

M.H.W.N.

CHART DATUM

M.L.W.N.

M.L.W.S.

L.W.Hts.m.

L.W.

H.W.

L.W.

TIME ZONE -0100
(French Standard Time)
Subtract 1 hour for UT
For French Summer Time add
ONE hour in **non-shaded areas**

FRANCE – BREST

LAT 48°23′N   LONG 4°30′W

TIMES AND HEIGHTS OF HIGH AND LOW WATERS

Dates in amber are **SPRINGS**
Dates in yellow are **NEAPS**

2009

JANUARY

Day	Time	m	Time	m	Time	m	Time	m
1 TH	0139	2.0	0738	6.5	1401	1.9	1955	6.1
2 F	0216	2.1	0815	6.3	1439	2.1	2034	6.0
3 SA	0256	2.3	0857	6.1	1522	2.2	2120	5.8
4 SU	0343	2.5	0946	5.9	1612	2.4	◑ 2215	5.7
5 M	0439	2.6	1046	5.7	1713	2.5	2321	5.6
6 TU	0546	2.7	1157	5.7	1823	2.5		
7 W	0033	5.7	0701	2.6	1313	5.8	1935	2.4
8 TH	0147	6.0	0815	2.2	1425	6.1	2044	2.1
9 F	0254	6.4	0921	1.8	1529	6.5	2145	1.7
10 SA	0354	6.8	1019	1.4	1625	6.8	2240	1.3
11 SU	0447	7.2	1112	1.0	1735	7.1	○ 2332	1.1
12 M	0538	7.4	1202	0.8	1805	7.2		
13 TU	0020	0.9	0625	7.5	1250	0.7	1851	7.2
14 W	0107	1.0	0710	7.4	1335	0.9	1934	7.0
15 TH	0151	1.2	0753	7.2	1419	1.2	2016	6.7
16 F	0235	1.5	0834	6.8	1503	1.7	2058	6.3
17 SA	0319	1.9	0916	6.3	1548	2.1	2143	5.9
18 SU	0406	2.3	1003	5.8	1638	2.6	◐ 2236	5.5
19 M	0500	2.7	1101	5.4	1737	2.9	2342	5.3
20 TU	0607	3.0	1217	5.2	1850	3.0		
21 W	0101	5.3	0727	3.0	1342	5.2	2006	2.9
22 TH	0215	5.5	0840	2.8	1449	5.4	2106	2.7
23 F	0311	5.8	0934	2.5	1538	5.7	2152	2.4
24 SA	0355	6.1	1017	2.2	1617	6.0	2232	2.1
25 SU	0433	6.4	1053	1.9	1652	6.3	2307	1.9
26 M	0508	6.6	1128	1.7	1725	6.4	● 2341	1.7
27 TU	0541	6.8	1200	1.5	1756	6.6		
28 W	0014	1.6	0613	6.9	1233	1.4	1828	6.6
29 TH	0046	1.5	0645	6.9	1305	1.4	1859	6.6
30 F	0119	1.5	0717	6.8	1338	1.5	1931	6.5
31 SA	0153	1.7	0751	6.7	1412	1.6	2006	6.4

FEBRUARY

Day	Time	m	Time	m	Time	m	Time	m
1 SU	0230	1.9	0827	6.4	1451	1.9	2045	6.1
2 M	0312	2.1	0910	6.1	1537	2.2	2134	5.9
3 TU	0403	2.4	1005	5.8	1633	2.5	◐ 2238	5.6
4 W	0508	2.7	1119	5.5	1746	2.7	2359	5.5
5 TH	0631	2.7	1250	5.5	1912	2.7		
6 F	0129	5.7	0801	2.4	1419	5.8	2033	2.3
7 SA	0247	6.2	0915	1.9	1525	6.3	2138	1.8
8 SU	0348	6.7	1013	1.3	1618	6.8	2232	1.3
9 M	0439	7.2	1103	0.9	1706	7.1	○ 2320	0.9
10 TU	0526	7.5	1149	0.6	1749	7.3		
11 W	0005	0.8	0609	7.6	1232	0.6	1830	7.3
12 TH	0047	0.8	0648	7.5	1312	0.8	1907	7.1
13 F	0127	1.0	0725	7.2	1350	1.1	1943	6.8
14 SA	0205	1.3	0800	6.8	1426	1.6	2017	6.4
15 SU	0242	1.6	0834	6.3	1503	2.1	2054	6.0
16 M	0322	2.3	0911	5.8	1545	2.6	◐ 2138	5.5
17 TU	0409	2.8	0959	5.3	1638	3.1	2241	5.2
18 W	0512	3.1	1115	4.9	1756	3.3		
19 TH	0013	5.0	0641	3.3	1307	4.9	1934	3.2
20 F	0148	5.2	0814	3.0	1433	5.2	2045	2.9
21 SA	0250	5.5	0913	2.6	1520	5.6	2131	2.5
22 SU	0334	5.9	0954	2.2	1557	6.0	2210	2.1
23 M	0411	6.3	1030	1.8	1630	6.3	2244	1.8
24 TU	0445	6.6	1104	1.5	1702	6.6	○ 2318	1.5
25 W	0518	6.9	1136	1.3	1733	6.8	● 2350	1.3
26 TH	0550	7.1	1208	1.1	1803	6.9		
27 F	0023	1.2	0621	7.1	1240	1.1	1834	6.9
28 SA	0056	1.2	0653	7.1	1313	1.2	1906	6.9

MARCH

Day	Time	m	Time	m	Time	m	Time	m
1 SU	0130	1.3	0727	6.9	1348	1.4	1940	6.6
2 M	0207	1.6	0803	6.6	1426	1.7	2019	6.3
3 TU	0250	1.9	0846	6.2	1512	2.2	2107	5.9
4 W	0342	2.3	0941	5.7	1609	2.6	◑ 2213	5.6
5 TH	0449	2.7	1101	5.3	1727	2.9	2344	5.4
6 F	0620	2.8	1248	5.3	1904	2.8		
7 SA	0126	5.6	0758	2.4	1417	5.7	2028	2.3
8 SU	0241	6.1	0907	1.8	1517	6.3	2128	1.8
9 M	0336	6.7	1001	1.3	1605	6.8	2218	1.3
10 TU	0424	7.1	1047	0.9	1648	7.1	2302	0.9
11 W	0506	7.4	1129	0.7	1727	7.3	○ 2344	0.8
12 TH	0546	7.5	1208	0.7	1803	7.3		
13 F	0022	0.8	0621	7.4	1244	0.9	1837	7.1
14 SA	0058	1.0	0654	7.1	1318	1.2	1908	6.9
15 SU	0133	1.3	0726	6.7	1350	1.7	1940	6.5
16 M	0208	1.8	0757	6.3	1424	2.1	2013	6.1
17 TU	0245	2.3	0831	5.8	1501	2.6	2052	5.6
18 W	0329	2.7	0913	5.3	1548	3.1	◐ 2149	5.2
19 TH	0426	3.1	1021	4.9	1701	3.4	2320	4.9
20 F	0549	3.3	1214	4.7	1845	3.4		
21 SA	0102	5.0	0728	3.1	1354	5.0	2007	3.0
22 SU	0212	5.4	0834	2.7	1446	5.5	2057	2.5
23 M	0258	5.8	0918	2.3	1523	5.9	2136	2.1
24 TU	0337	6.2	0956	1.8	1558	6.3	2212	1.7
25 W	0412	6.6	1031	1.5	1631	6.6	2247	1.4
26 TH	0447	6.9	1106	1.2	1703	6.9	● 2322	1.2
27 F	0521	7.1	1140	1.1	1736	7.1	2356	1.1
28 SA	0555	7.2	1214	1.0	1809	7.1		
29 SU	0032	1.1	0630	7.1	1249	1.1	1843	7.0
30 M	0110	1.2	0707	6.9	1327	1.4	1921	6.8
31 TU	0151	1.5	0747	6.6	1409	1.7	2004	6.4

APRIL

Day	Time	m	Time	m	Time	m	Time	m
1 W	0238	1.9	0835	6.1	1458	2.2	2057	6.0
2 TH	0334	2.3	0937	5.6	1600	2.6	● 2209	5.6
3 F	0446	2.6	1102	5.3	1722	2.8	2342	5.5
4 SA	0618	2.6	1244	5.4	1857	2.7		
5 SU	0115	5.7	0745	2.3	1401	5.8	2012	2.2
6 M	0223	6.2	0849	1.8	1456	6.3	2109	1.8
7 TU	0316	6.6	0939	1.4	1542	6.7	2156	1.4
8 W	0401	6.9	1024	1.1	1623	6.9	2239	1.1
9 TH	0441	7.1	1104	1.0	1700	7.1	2319	1.0
10 F	0519	7.1	1140	1.1	1734	7.1	2355	1.1
11 SA	0553	7.0	1214	1.2	1807	7.0		
12 SU	0030	1.3	0625	6.8	1247	1.5	1838	6.8
13 M	0105	1.5	0657	6.5	1320	1.8	1910	6.5
14 TU	0140	1.9	0729	6.1	1353	2.2	1944	6.1
15 W	0217	2.3	0804	5.7	1429	2.6	2023	5.7
16 TH	0259	2.6	0846	5.3	1514	3.0	2115	5.3
17 F	0351	2.9	0945	5.0	1615	3.2	○ 2231	5.1
18 SA	0500	3.1	1113	4.8	1741	3.3	2358	5.1
19 SU	0622	3.1	1243	5.0	1905	3.1		
20 M	0111	5.3	0733	2.8	1348	5.4	2005	2.7
21 TU	0206	5.7	0827	2.4	1435	5.8	2051	2.3
22 W	0252	6.1	0911	1.9	1516	6.2	2132	1.8
23 TH	0333	6.5	0952	1.6	1554	6.6	2212	1.5
24 F	0412	6.8	1031	1.3	1631	6.9	2251	1.2
25 SA	0451	7.0	1110	1.1	1708	7.1	● 2331	1.1
26 SU	0530	7.1	1149	1.1	1746	7.1		
27 M	0011	1.0	0611	7.1	1230	1.2	1827	7.1
28 TU	0055	1.2	0654	6.9	1313	1.4	1911	6.9
29 W	0141	1.4	0742	6.5	1401	1.7	2000	6.5
30 TH	0233	1.7	0836	6.1	1454	2.1	2059	6.1

TIDES

Chart Datum: 3·64 metres below IGN Datum
HAT is 7·8 metres above Chart Datum

TIME ZONE -0100
(French Standard Time)
Subtract 1 hour for UT
For French Summer Time add
ONE hour in **non-shaded areas**

FRANCE – BREST

LAT 48°23'N   LONG 4°30'W

TIMES AND HEIGHTS OF HIGH AND LOW WATERS

Dates in amber are **SPRINGS**
Dates in yellow are **NEAPS**

2009

MAY

Time m	Time m
1 0333 2.1 / 0941 5.7 / F 1558 2.4 / 2209 5.8	**16** 0321 2.6 / 0916 5.3 / SA 1540 2.9 / 2149 5.4
2 0444 2.3 / 1058 5.5 / SA 1714 2.6 / 2330 5.7	**17** 0416 2.8 / 1020 5.1 / SU 1644 3.0 / 2257 5.3
3 0603 2.4 / 1220 5.6 / SU 1834 2.5	**18** 0520 2.8 / 1132 5.2 / M 1756 3.0 ○
4 0048 5.9 / 0717 2.2 / M 1329 5.8 / ◑ 1943 2.2	**19** 0005 5.4 / 0627 2.7 / TU 1239 5.4 / 1902 2.7
5 0153 6.1 / 0819 1.9 / TU 1425 6.2 / 2041 1.9	**20** 0107 5.6 / 0728 2.4 / W 1338 5.7 / 1959 2.4
6 0246 6.4 / 0910 1.7 / W 1513 6.4 / 2130 1.7	**21** 0201 6.0 / 0822 2.1 / TH 1429 6.0 / 2049 2.0
7 0333 6.5 / 0955 1.5 / TH 1555 6.6 / 2214 1.5	**22** 0251 6.3 / 0911 1.8 / F 1516 6.4 / 2137 1.7
8 0414 6.6 / 1036 1.5 / F 1633 6.7 / 2254 1.5	**23** 0338 6.6 / 0958 1.5 / SA 1600 6.7 / 2223 1.4
9 0452 6.6 / 1113 1.5 / SA 1708 6.8 / 2331 1.5	**24** 0425 6.8 / 1044 1.3 / SU 1645 7.0 / 2310 1.1
10 0527 6.6 / 1148 1.6 / SU 1742 6.7	**25** 0511 6.9 / 1130 1.2 / M 1730 7.1 / 2357 1.0
11 0006 1.6 / 0601 6.5 / M 1222 1.8 / ○ 1816 6.6	**26** 0559 7.0 / 1216 1.2 / TU 1817 7.1 ●
12 0042 1.7 / 0635 6.3 / TU 1256 2.0 / 1850 6.4	**27** 0045 1.1 / 0648 6.8 / W 1305 1.3 / 1907 7.0
13 0118 1.9 / 0709 6.0 / W 1331 2.2 / 1925 6.1	**28** 0136 1.2 / 0739 6.6 / TH 1355 1.5 / 1959 6.7
14 0155 2.2 / 0746 5.8 / TH 1407 2.5 / 2004 5.9	**29** 0229 1.5 / 0834 6.3 / F 1449 1.8 / 2055 6.4
15 0235 2.4 / 0826 5.5 / F 1449 2.7 / 2051 5.6	**30** 0326 1.7 / 0932 6.0 / SA 1548 2.1 / 2157 6.2
	31 0428 2.0 / 1036 5.8 / SU 1653 2.3 / 2302 6.0

JUNE

Time m	Time m
1 0534 2.2 / 1142 5.7 / M 1800 2.4	**16** 0427 2.5 / 1031 5.4 / TU 1654 2.7 / ◑ 2303 5.6
2 0010 5.9 / 0639 2.2 / TU 1247 5.8 / ◑ 1906 2.3	**17** 0526 2.6 / 1135 5.5 / W 1759 2.7
3 0114 5.9 / 0741 2.2 / W 1348 5.9 / 2007 2.2	**18** 0007 5.6 / 0630 2.5 / TH 1240 5.6 / 1905 2.5
4 0213 6.0 / 0837 2.1 / TH 1441 6.1 / 2101 2.1	**19** 0111 5.8 / 0734 2.3 / F 1343 5.9 / 2008 2.2
5 0304 6.1 / 0927 2.0 / F 1528 6.2 / 2149 1.9	**20** 0213 6.0 / 0834 2.0 / SA 1441 6.2 / 2107 1.9
6 0350 6.1 / 1011 1.9 / SA 1610 6.4 / 2232 1.8	**21** 0311 6.3 / 0931 1.7 / SU 1537 6.6 / 2202 1.5
7 0431 6.2 / 1050 1.9 / SU 1648 6.5 / 2311 1.8	**22** 0407 6.6 / 1024 1.5 / M 1629 6.9 / 2255 1.2
8 0508 6.2 / 1127 1.9 / M 1724 6.5 / 2348 1.8	**23** 0459 6.8 / 1116 1.2 / TU 1720 7.1 / 2346 1.0
9 0544 6.2 / 1203 1.9 / TU 1800 6.5 / ○	**24** 0551 7.0 / 1206 1.1 / W 1811 7.2
10 0024 1.8 / 0619 6.2 / W 1238 2.0 / 1835 6.4	**25** 0037 0.9 / 0641 7.0 / TH 1256 1.1 / ● 1900 7.2
11 0100 1.8 / 0653 6.1 / TH 1312 2.1 / 1910 6.3	**26** 0127 0.9 / 0730 6.9 / F 1346 1.2 / 1949 7.1
12 0135 2.0 / 0728 6.0 / F 1348 2.2 / 1946 6.1	**27** 0217 1.1 / 0819 6.6 / SA 1435 1.4 / 2039 6.8
13 0212 2.1 / 0805 5.8 / SA 1426 2.4 / 2026 5.9	**28** 0308 1.4 / 0909 6.3 / SU 1527 1.7 / 2130 6.4
14 0251 2.3 / 0846 5.6 / SU 1508 2.5 / 2111 5.8	**29** 0400 1.8 / 1001 6.0 / M 1621 2.1 / 2224 6.0
15 0336 2.4 / 0934 5.5 / M 1556 2.6 / 2203 5.6	**30** 0455 2.1 / 1057 5.8 / TU 1719 2.4 / 2324 5.7

JULY

Time m	Time m
1 0555 2.4 / 1200 5.6 / W 1823 2.5	**16** 0436 2.4 / 1041 5.6 / TH 1708 2.6 / 2316 5.6
2 0030 5.5 / 0659 2.6 / TH 1307 5.6 / 1931 2.6	**17** 0540 2.6 / 1151 5.5 / F 1820 2.6
3 0139 5.5 / 0804 2.5 / F 1411 5.7 / 2036 2.5	**18** 0030 5.6 / 0653 2.5 / SA 1306 5.7 / ◑ 1936 2.4
4 0241 5.6 / 0902 2.4 / SA 1507 5.9 / ◑ 2130 2.3	**19** 0146 5.8 / 0807 2.3 / SU 1418 6.0 / 2047 2.0
5 0333 5.8 / 0951 2.3 / SU 1553 6.1 / 2216 2.1	**20** 0256 6.1 / 0913 1.9 / M 1523 6.5 / 2149 1.6
6 0416 5.9 / 1033 2.1 / M 1634 6.3 / 2256 1.9	**21** 0356 6.5 / 1011 1.5 / TU 1619 6.9 / 2245 1.1
7 0454 6.1 / 1111 2.0 / TU 1710 6.4 / 2332 1.8	**22** 0450 6.9 / 1105 1.1 / W 1711 7.2 / 2336 0.8
8 0529 6.2 / 1146 1.9 / W 1745 6.5	**23** 0540 7.1 / 1155 0.9 / TH 1800 7.5
9 0007 1.7 / 0602 6.3 / TH 1220 1.8 / 1818 6.5	**24** 0025 0.6 / 0626 7.2 / F 1242 0.8 / 1846 7.5
10 0040 1.7 / 0635 6.3 / F 1253 1.8 / 1851 6.5	**25** 0111 0.7 / 0711 7.1 / SA 1328 0.9 / 1930 7.3
11 0113 1.7 / 0707 6.2 / SA 1326 1.9 / ○ 1924 6.4	**26** 0156 0.9 / 0754 6.9 / SU 1412 1.2 / ● 2012 7.0
12 0146 1.8 / 0740 6.2 / SU 1400 2.0 / 1958 6.3	**27** 0240 1.3 / 0836 6.5 / M 1457 1.6 / 2055 6.5
13 0221 1.9 / 0815 6.0 / M 1436 2.1 / 2035 6.1	**28** 0324 1.8 / 0903 5.9 / TU 1544 2.0 / 2140 6.0
14 0259 2.1 / 0854 5.9 / TU 1518 2.3 / 2118 5.9	**29** 0412 2.3 / 1000 5.7 / W 1636 2.5 / 2234 5.5
15 0343 2.3 / 0942 5.7 / W 1607 2.5 / 2211 5.7	**30** 0508 2.7 / 1111 5.4 / TH 1740 2.8 / 2344 5.2
	31 0617 2.9 / 1228 5.3 / F 1856 2.9

AUGUST

Time m	Time m
1 0108 5.1 / 0735 2.9 / SA 1347 5.4 / 2014 2.8	**16** 0005 5.4 / 0627 2.7 / SU 1245 5.6 / 1919 2.6
2 0225 5.3 / 0843 2.7 / SU 1450 5.7 / ◑ 2114 2.5	**17** 0136 5.6 / 0753 2.4 / M 1409 6.0 / ◑ 2038 2.1
3 0320 5.6 / 0935 2.4 / M 1538 6.0 / 2200 2.2	**18** 0250 6.1 / 0903 2.0 / TU 1514 6.5 / 2140 1.5
4 0402 5.9 / 1016 2.2 / TU 1617 6.3 / 2238 1.9	**19** 0347 6.6 / 1000 1.4 / W 1608 7.0 / 2233 1.0
5 0437 6.1 / 1053 1.9 / W 1652 6.5 / 2313 1.7	**20** 0437 7.0 / 1051 1.0 / TH 1657 7.4 / 2321 0.6
6 0510 6.3 / 1126 1.7 / TH 1725 6.7 / 2345 1.5	**21** 0522 7.3 / 1138 0.7 / F 1742 7.6
7 0541 6.5 / 1158 1.6 / F 1756 6.8	**22** 0006 0.5 / 0605 7.4 / SA 1222 0.7 / 1824 7.6
8 0016 1.4 / 0611 6.5 / SA 1229 1.6 / 1827 6.8	**23** 0048 0.6 / 0645 7.3 / SU 1304 0.8 / 1903 7.4
9 0047 1.4 / 0641 6.6 / SU 1300 1.6 / ○ 1858 6.7	**24** 0128 0.9 / 0722 7.0 / M 1344 1.1 / 1940 7.0
10 0118 1.5 / 0711 6.5 / M 1332 1.7 / 1929 6.5	**25** 0207 1.4 / 0759 6.6 / TU 1424 1.6 / ● 2017 6.5
11 0151 1.6 / 0743 6.4 / TU 1407 1.8 / 2003 6.4	**26** 0246 1.9 / 0837 6.2 / W 1506 2.1 / 2056 5.9
12 0227 1.9 / 0819 6.2 / W 1446 2.1 / 2042 6.1	**27** 0328 2.4 / 0921 5.7 / TH 1554 2.6 / 2144 5.4
13 0308 2.1 / 0903 5.9 / TH 1533 2.4 / 2132 5.8	**28** 0420 2.9 / 1022 5.3 / F 1657 3.0 / 2258 5.0
14 0359 2.5 / 1000 5.6 / F 1632 2.6 / 2239 5.5	**29** 0533 3.2 / 1150 5.1 / SA 1821 3.2
15 0505 2.7 / 1117 5.5 / SA 1749 2.7	**30** 0040 4.9 / 0707 3.2 / SU 1324 5.2 / 1951 3.0
	31 0208 5.2 / 0822 2.9 / M 1430 5.6 / 2052 2.6

Chart Datum: 3·64 metres below IGN Datum
HAT is 7·8 metres above Chart Datum

TIME ZONE -0100
(French Standard Time)
Subtract 1 hour for UT
For French Summer Time add
ONE hour in **non-shaded areas**

FRANCE – BREST

LAT 48°23'N   LONG 4°30'W

TIMES AND HEIGHTS OF HIGH AND LOW WATERS

Dates in amber are **SPRINGS**
Dates in yellow are **NEAPS**

2009

SEPTEMBER

Day	Time m	Time m	Time m	Time m	Day	Time m	Time m	Time m	Time m
1 TU	0300 5.5	0912 2.5	1515 6.0	2136 2.2	**16** W	0240 6.2	0852 1.9	1502 6.6	2127 1.4
2 W	0339 5.9	0952 2.2	1552 6.3	2212 1.9	**17** TH	0332 6.7	0945 1.4	1552 7.1	2216 1.0
3 TH	0412 6.2	1026 1.9	1626 6.6	2245 1.6	**18** F	0418 7.1	1033 1.0	1637 7.5	2300 0.7
4 F	0443 6.5	1059 1.6	1658 6.8	○ 2317 1.4	**19** SA	0500 7.3	1116 0.8	1719 7.6	2342 0.7
5 SA	0513 6.7	1131 1.5	1729 7.0	2348 1.3	**20** SU	0539 7.4	1158 0.8	1758 7.5	
6 SU	0543 6.8	1202 1.4	1800 7.0		**21** M	0021 0.8	0615 7.3	1237 1.0	1834 7.2
7 M	0019 1.3	0613 6.8	1234 1.4	1830 7.0	**22** TU	0058 1.1	0650 7.0	1314 1.3	1908 6.8
8 TU	0050 1.3	0643 6.8	1306 1.5	1902 6.8	**23** W	0134 1.6	0724 6.6	1352 1.7	1942 6.4
9 W	0123 1.5	0715 6.6	1342 1.7	1936 6.5	**24** TH	0210 2.1	0759 6.2	1432 2.2	2019 5.9
10 TH	0200 1.8	0752 6.4	1422 2.0	2017 6.2	**25** F	0249 2.6	0841 5.7	1518 2.7	2103 5.4
11 F	0243 2.2	0836 6.0	1511 2.4	2108 5.8	**26** SA	0338 3.0	0938 5.3	1617 3.1	◑ 2213 5.0
12 SA	0336 2.5	0937 5.7	1613 2.7	◑ 2222 5.4	**27** SU	0448 3.3	1108 5.1	1739 3.3	2358 4.8
13 SU	0446 2.8	1102 5.5	1737 2.8	2359 5.3	**28** M	0625 3.4	1244 5.2	1911 3.1	
14 M	0617 2.9	1240 5.6	1914 2.5		**29** TU	0131 5.1	0746 3.1	1353 5.5	2015 2.7
15 TU	0134 5.7	0746 2.5	1402 6.1	2030 2.0	**30** W	0225 5.5	0837 2.6	1439 5.9	2059 2.3

OCTOBER

Day	Time m	Time m	Time m	Time m	Day	Time m	Time m	Time m	Time m
1 TH	0304 5.9	0917 2.2	1517 6.3	2136 1.9	**16** F	0310 6.7	0925 1.5	1530 7.0	2153 1.2
2 F	0338 6.3	0953 1.9	1552 6.6	2211 1.6	**17** SA	0354 7.0	1011 1.2	1614 7.2	2236 1.0
3 SA	0411 6.6	1027 1.6	1626 6.9	2245 1.4	**18** SU	0435 7.2	1053 1.0	1654 7.3	● 2316 1.0
4 SU	0443 6.8	1101 1.4	1659 7.0	○ 2318 1.3	**19** M	0513 7.2	1133 1.1	1731 7.2	2354 1.2
5 M	0514 7.0	1135 1.3	1732 7.1	2351 1.2	**20** TU	0548 7.1	1211 1.2	1807 7.0	
6 TU	0546 7.0	1209 1.3	1805 7.1		**21** W	0030 1.5	0623 6.9	1248 1.5	1841 6.6
7 W	0025 1.3	0619 7.0	1245 1.4	1840 6.9	**22** TH	0105 1.8	0657 6.6	1326 1.9	1915 6.3
8 TH	0102 1.5	0655 6.8	1324 1.6	1919 6.6	**23** F	0141 2.2	0732 6.2	1405 2.3	1952 5.8
9 F	0142 1.8	0735 6.5	1409 2.0	2005 6.2	**24** SA	0219 2.6	0813 5.8	1448 2.7	2035 5.4
10 SA	0229 2.2	0825 6.1	1502 2.3	2103 5.8	**25** SU	0304 3.0	0904 5.5	1540 3.0	2135 5.1
11 SU	0326 2.6	0931 5.8	1609 2.6	2222 5.4	**26** M	0404 3.3	1017 5.2	1648 3.2	◑ 2259 5.0
12 M	0440 2.8	1059 5.6	1734 2.7	2357 5.4	**27** TU	0524 3.3	1142 5.2	1807 3.1	
13 TU	0610 2.8	1232 5.8	1904 2.4		**28** W	0024 5.1	0645 3.2	1254 5.4	1916 2.9
14 W	0120 5.8	0732 2.4	1345 6.2	2012 1.9	**29** TH	0129 5.4	0746 2.8	1349 5.8	2009 2.5
15 TH	0221 6.3	0833 1.9	1442 6.7	2106 1.5	**30** F	0217 5.8	0833 2.4	1434 6.1	2053 2.1
					31 SA	0257 6.2	0914 2.1	1514 6.5	2133 1.8

NOVEMBER

Day	Time m	Time m	Time m	Time m	Day	Time m	Time m	Time m	Time m
1 SU	0335 6.5	0953 1.7	1553 6.8	2211 1.5	**16** M	0412 6.9	1033 1.5	1632 6.8	● 2253 1.5
2 M	0411 6.8	1031 1.5	1630 7.0	○ 2249 1.4	**17** TU	0451 6.9	1113 1.5	1710 6.8	2331 1.6
3 TU	0447 7.0	1109 1.3	1708 7.1	2327 1.3	**18** W	0528 6.9	1151 1.5	1747 6.7	
4 W	0524 7.1	1149 1.3	1747 7.0		**19** TH	0008 1.7	0603 6.8	1229 1.7	1822 6.5
5 TH	0006 1.3	0603 7.1	1230 1.3	1828 6.9	**20** F	0044 1.9	0639 6.6	1306 1.9	1857 6.2
6 F	0048 1.5	0645 6.9	1314 1.5	1913 6.6	**21** SA	0120 2.2	0715 6.4	1343 2.2	1934 6.0
7 SA	0133 1.8	0732 6.7	1404 1.7	2005 6.3	**22** SU	0157 2.4	0753 6.1	1423 2.4	2014 5.7
8 SU	0224 2.1	0826 6.3	1500 2.1	2106 5.9	**23** M	0238 2.7	0836 5.8	1507 2.7	2100 5.4
9 M	0323 2.4	0931 6.0	1606 2.3	◑ 2218 5.7	**24** TU	0325 2.9	0929 5.5	1558 2.9	◑ 2158 5.2
10 TU	0433 2.6	1048 5.9	1722 2.4	2337 5.7	**25** W	0422 3.1	1033 5.4	1659 3.0	2308 5.2
11 W	0551 2.6	1208 5.9	1838 2.3		**26** TH	0531 3.1	1143 5.4	1806 2.9	
12 TH	0051 5.9	0705 2.4	1317 6.2	1944 2.1	**27** F	0018 5.3	0639 3.0	1247 5.6	1909 2.7
13 F	0152 6.2	0807 2.1	1416 6.4	2040 1.8	**28** SA	0118 5.6	0739 2.7	1344 5.9	2004 2.4
14 SA	0244 6.5	0901 1.8	1506 6.7	2128 1.6	**29** SU	0211 6.0	0832 2.3	1434 6.2	2053 2.1
15 SU	0330 6.7	0949 1.6	1551 6.8	2213 1.5	**30** M	0258 6.3	0919 2.0	1521 6.5	2139 1.8

DECEMBER

Day	Time m	Time m	Time m	Time m	Day	Time m	Time m	Time m	Time m
1 TU	0342 6.6	1005 1.7	1605 6.8	2224 1.5	**16** W	0436 6.6	1059 1.7	1657 6.5	● 2315 1.8
2 W	0426 6.9	1049 1.4	1650 6.9	○ 2308 1.4	**17** TH	0514 6.7	1137 1.7	1733 6.5	2352 1.8
3 TH	0509 7.1	1135 1.2	1736 7.0	2353 1.3	**18** F	0550 6.7	1214 1.7	1808 6.4	
4 F	0555 7.2	1221 1.2	1822 7.0		**19** SA	0027 1.9	0625 6.7	1249 1.8	1842 6.3
5 SA	0040 1.3	0642 7.1	1309 1.2	1911 6.8	**20** SU	0102 2.0	0700 6.5	1323 1.9	1916 6.2
6 SU	0128 1.5	0731 7.0	1400 1.4	2003 6.6	**21** M	0137 2.1	0734 6.4	1358 2.1	1950 6.0
7 M	0220 1.7	0824 6.7	1454 1.7	2058 6.3	**22** TU	0212 2.3	0810 6.2	1435 2.3	2027 5.8
8 TU	0314 2.0	0920 6.4	1552 2.0	2158 6.0	**23** W	0250 2.5	0849 5.9	1514 2.5	2109 5.6
9 W	0415 2.2	1023 6.2	1656 2.2	◑ 2303 5.9	**24** TH	0333 2.7	0934 5.7	1601 2.7	◑ 2201 5.5
10 TH	0520 2.4	1131 6.0	1803 2.3		**25** F	0425 2.9	1031 5.5	1657 2.8	2304 5.4
11 F	0011 5.8	0629 2.4	1241 5.9	1909 2.3	**26** SA	0528 2.9	1138 5.5	1802 2.8	
12 SA	0117 5.9	0736 2.3	1346 6.0	2010 2.2	**27** SU	0013 5.5	0638 2.9	1248 5.6	1910 2.7
13 SU	0216 6.1	0837 2.2	1443 6.1	2105 2.1	**28** M	0121 5.7	0746 2.6	1354 5.8	2014 2.4
14 M	0308 6.3	0930 2.0	1533 6.3	2153 2.0	**29** TU	0222 6.0	0848 2.2	1454 6.2	2111 2.0
15 TU	0354 6.5	1017 1.8	1617 6.4	2236 1.9	**30** W	0318 6.4	0944 1.8	1548 6.5	2204 1.7
					31 TH	0410 6.8	1035 1.4	1639 6.9	○ 2255 1.4

Chart Datum: 3·64 metres below IGN Datum
HAT is 7·8 metres above Chart Datum

TIDES

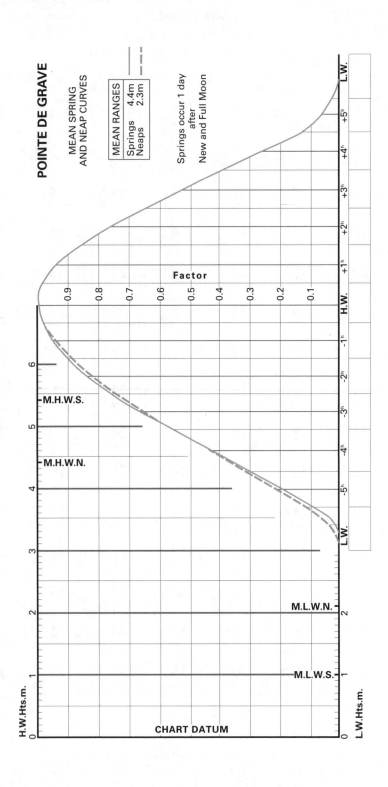

POINTE DE GRAVE

MEAN SPRING
AND NEAP CURVES

MEAN RANGES
Springs   4.4m
Neaps   2.3m

Springs occur 1 day
after
New and Full Moon

Factor

0.9 0.8 0.7 0.6 0.5 0.4 0.3 0.2 0.1

H.W.
-1ʰ
-2ʰ
-3ʰ
-4ʰ
-5ʰ
L.W.

+1ʰ +2ʰ +3ʰ +4ʰ +5ʰ L.W.

M.H.W.S.
M.H.W.N.

M.L.W.N.
M.L.W.S.

H.W.Hts.m.
L.W.Hts.m.

CHART DATUM

TIME ZONE -0100
(French Standard Time)
Subtract 1 hour for UT
For French Summer Time add
ONE hour in **non-shaded areas**

FRANCE – POINTE DE GRAVE

LAT 45°34'N   LONG 1°04'W

TIMES AND HEIGHTS OF HIGH AND LOW WATERS

Dates in amber are **SPRINGS**
Dates in yellow are **NEAPS**

2009

JANUARY

Day				
1 TH	0126 1.7	0740 5.1	1350 1.6	1957 4.7
2 F	0203 1.7	0819 4.9	1427 1.7	2038 4.6
3 SA	0244 1.8	0904 4.8	1510 1.8	2128 4.5
4 SU	0331 1.9	0958 4.7	1600 1.9	2231 4.4
5 M	0429 2.0	1104 4.6	1701 2.0	2345 4.4
6 TU	0536 2.0	1219 4.6	1811 2.0	
7 W	0101 4.6	0649 2.0	1334 4.7	1922 1.9
8 TH	0209 4.8	0759 1.8	1443 4.9	2029 1.7
9 F	0309 5.1	0906 1.5	1544 5.1	2131 1.5
10 SA	0005 5.4	1007 1.3	1639 5.4	2227 1.3
11 SU	0457 5.6	1102 1.0	1730 5.5	2319 1.1
12 M	0547 5.8	1153 0.9	1818 5.6	
13 TU	0008 1.0	0635 5.8	1241 0.9	1904 5.5
14 W	0054 1.1	0721 5.7	1325 1.0	1947 5.3
15 TH	0138 1.2	0804 5.5	1407 1.2	2029 5.1
16 F	0221 1.3	0845 5.2	1450 1.4	2109 4.8
17 SA	0306 1.6	0926 4.9	1535 1.7	2155 4.6
18 SU	0355 1.9	1016 4.6	1628 2.0	2256 4.4
19 M	0452 2.1	1126 4.3	1732 2.3	
20 TU	0014 4.3	0603 2.3	1255 4.2	1848 2.4
21 W	0130 4.3	0719 2.3	1413 4.2	1958 2.3
22 TH	0231 4.5	0826 2.2	1510 4.4	2054 2.1
23 F	0320 4.7	0919 2.0	1554 4.6	2139 1.9
24 SA	0400 4.9	1003 1.8	1630 4.8	2218 1.8
25 SU	0437 5.1	1041 1.6	1702 4.9	2254 1.6
26 M	0510 5.2	1116 1.5	1732 5.0	2328 1.5
27 TU	0542 5.2	1150 1.4	1801 5.1	
28 W	0002 1.4	0613 5.3	1223 1.3	1830 5.1
29 TH	0035 1.3	0644 5.3	1256 1.3	1900 5.1
30 F	0107 1.3	0717 5.3	1327 1.3	1931 5.0
31 SA	0140 1.4	0752 5.2	1401 1.4	2006 4.9

FEBRUARY

Day				
1 SU	0216 1.5	0832 5.0	1438 1.5	2048 4.7
2 M	0258 1.6	0920 4.8	1522 1.7	2142 4.5
3 TU	0351 1.8	1023 4.6	1619 1.9	2300 4.4
4 W	0459 2.0	1149 4.4	1733 2.1	
5 TH	0034 4.4	0622 2.0	1320 4.5	1859 2.1
6 F	0156 4.6	0747 1.9	1437 4.7	2019 1.9
7 SA	0303 5.0	0901 1.6	1539 5.0	2125 1.6
8 SU	0359 5.3	1001 1.2	1632 5.3	2220 1.3
9 M	0449 5.6	1053 0.9	1718 5.5	2309 1.0
10 TU	0534 5.8	1140 0.8	1801 5.6	2354 0.9
11 W	0616 5.8	1222 0.8	1840 5.6	
12 TH	0035 0.9	0655 5.7	1302 0.9	1916 5.4
13 F	0114 1.0	0731 5.5	1339 1.1	1948 5.2
14 SA	0152 1.2	0804 5.2	1415 1.4	2019 4.9
15 SU	0230 1.4	0836 4.9	1454 1.7	2054 4.7
16 M	0312 1.8	0915 4.5	1538 2.0	2143 4.4
17 TU	0402 2.1	1014 4.2	1636 2.4	2304 4.1
18 W	0511 2.4	1201 4.0	1758 2.6	
19 TH	0047 4.1	0640 2.5	1343 4.0	1926 2.5
20 F	0203 4.3	0800 2.3	1448 4.3	2030 2.3
21 SA	0258 4.5	0857 2.1	1533 4.5	2117 2.0
22 SU	0340 4.8	0940 1.8	1608 4.8	2156 1.7
23 M	0416 5.0	1017 1.6	1639 5.0	2232 1.5
24 TU	0448 5.2	1053 1.3	1708 5.1	2306 1.3
25 W	0519 5.4	1126 1.2	1737 5.2	2340 1.2
26 TH	0550 5.5	1159 1.1	1806 5.3	
27 F	0013 1.1	0621 5.5	1231 1.1	1835 5.3
28 SA	0045 1.1	0654 5.5	1303 1.1	1907 5.2

MARCH

Day				
1 SU	0118 1.2	0729 5.3	1335 1.2	1941 5.1
2 M	0154 1.3	0808 5.1	1412 1.4	2021 4.9
3 TU	0235 1.5	0856 4.8	1456 1.7	2114 4.6
4 W	0327 1.7	1002 4.5	1552 2.0	2235 4.4
5 TH	0438 2.0	1139 4.3	1712 2.2	
6 F	0022 4.4	0612 2.1	1317 4.4	1850 2.2
7 SA	0148 4.6	0745 1.9	1431 4.7	2014 1.9
8 SU	0254 5.0	0855 1.5	1530 5.0	2115 1.5
9 M	0348 5.3	0949 1.2	1617 5.3	2206 1.2
10 TU	0433 5.6	1036 0.9	1659 5.5	2251 1.0
11 W	0514 5.7	1118 0.8	1736 5.6	2333 0.8
12 TH	0552 5.7	1157 0.8	1810 5.5	
13 F	0011 0.8	0626 5.6	1234 0.9	1842 5.4
14 SA	0047 1.0	0658 5.4	1307 1.1	1911 5.3
15 SU	0121 1.1	0727 5.2	1340 1.4	1940 5.0
16 M	0156 1.4	0758 4.8	1415 1.7	2014 4.8
17 TU	0234 1.7	0834 4.5	1454 2.0	2058 4.5
18 W	0318 2.1	0926 4.2	1545 2.4	2206 4.2
19 TH	0421 2.4	1105 3.9	1704 2.6	2353 4.1
20 F	0552 2.5	1300 4.0	1840 2.6	
21 SA	0122 4.2	0719 2.4	1410 4.2	1951 2.4
22 SU	0222 4.5	0820 2.1	1457 4.5	2042 2.1
23 M	0307 4.7	0905 1.8	1534 4.7	2123 1.8
24 TU	0344 5.0	0944 1.5	1606 5.0	2200 1.5
25 W	0418 5.2	1020 1.3	1637 5.2	2237 1.3
26 TH	0450 5.4	1055 1.1	1708 5.3	2313 1.1
27 F	0523 5.5	1130 1.0	1739 5.4	2348 1.0
28 SA	0558 5.6	1204 1.0	1812 5.4	
29 SU	0023 1.0	0633 5.5	1239 1.0	1847 5.4
30 M	0059 1.0	0712 5.4	1314 1.2	1925 5.2
31 TU	0138 1.2	0755 5.1	1354 1.4	2010 5.0

APRIL

Day				
1 W	0222 1.4	0849 4.8	1441 1.7	2109 4.7
2 TH	0317 1.7	1003 4.5	1543 2.0	2234 4.5
3 F	0433 2.0	1141 4.4	1708 2.2	
4 SA	0014 4.5	0608 2.0	1309 4.5	1841 2.1
5 SU	0134 4.7	0733 1.8	1417 4.8	1957 1.8
6 M	0238 5.0	0836 1.5	1511 5.0	2055 1.5
7 TU	0329 5.3	0927 1.2	1555 5.2	2144 1.2
8 W	0412 5.4	1011 1.1	1633 5.4	2227 1.1
9 TH	0450 5.5	1052 1.0	1708 5.4	2308 1.0
10 F	0525 5.5	1129 1.0	1740 5.4	2345 1.0
11 SA	0558 5.4	1204 1.1	1811 5.4	
12 SU	0020 1.1	0629 5.2	1236 1.3	1842 5.2
13 M	0053 1.2	0700 5.0	1309 1.5	1914 5.0
14 TU	0127 1.5	0733 4.8	1343 1.7	1949 4.8
15 W	0204 1.7	0810 4.5	1421 2.0	2033 4.6
16 TH	0246 2.0	0900 4.2	1508 2.3	2130 4.3
17 F	0341 2.3	1016 4.0	1615 2.5	2252 4.2
18 SA	0458 2.4	1159 4.0	1740 2.5	
19 SU	0022 4.2	0621 2.3	1314 4.2	1854 2.4
20 M	0129 4.4	0726 2.1	1407 4.4	1951 2.1
21 TU	0220 4.7	0817 1.8	1449 4.7	2038 1.8
22 W	0302 4.9	0901 1.6	1526 4.9	2121 1.5
23 TH	0341 5.2	0941 1.3	1601 5.2	2202 1.3
24 F	0419 5.4	1021 1.2	1637 5.3	2242 1.1
25 SA	0457 5.5	1100 1.0	1715 5.4	2323 1.0
26 SU	0537 5.5	1139 1.0	1754 5.5	
27 M	0003 1.0	0619 5.5	1219 1.1	1835 5.4
28 TU	0045 1.0	0704 5.3	1300 1.2	1921 5.3
29 W	0129 1.2	0754 5.1	1345 1.4	2013 5.1
30 TH	0219 1.4	0853 4.8	1438 1.7	2116 4.9

Chart Datum: 2·83 metres below IGN Datum
HAT is 6·1 metres above Chart Datum

TIDES

TIME ZONE -0100
(French Standard Time)
Subtract 1 hour for UT
For French Summer Time add ONE hour in **non-shaded areas**

FRANCE – POINTE DE GRAVE

LAT 45°34'N   LONG 1°04'W

TIMES AND HEIGHTS OF HIGH AND LOW WATERS

Dates in amber are **SPRINGS**
Dates in yellow are **NEAPS**

2009

MAY

Time	m		Time	m
1 0318	1.6	**16**	0311	2.0
1007	4.6		0936	4.2
F 1543	1.9	SA	1535	2.2
2233	4.7		2203	4.4
2 0430	1.8	**17**	0410	2.1
1132	4.5		1047	4.1
SA 1659	2.0	SU	1641	2.3
2356	4.7		2312	4.3
3 0551	1.8	**18**	0517	2.1
1248	4.6		1201	4.2
SU 1818	2.0	M	1749	2.3
		◗		
4 0110	4.8	**19**	0021	4.4
0706	1.7		0622	2.0
M 1351	4.8	TU	1304	4.4
◗ 1928	1.8		1851	2.1
5 0213	4.9	**20**	0121	4.6
0807	1.5		0720	1.9
TU 1444	4.9	W	1356	4.6
2026	1.6		1947	1.9
6 0305	5.1	**21**	0214	4.8
0858	1.4		0812	1.6
W 1527	5.1	TH	1443	4.8
2117	1.4		2037	1.6
7 0348	5.1	**22**	0303	5.0
0943	1.3		0900	1.4
TH 1605	5.2	F	1527	5.1
2202	1.3		2126	1.4
8 0426	5.2	**23**	0349	5.2
1024	1.2		0947	1.3
F 1640	5.2	SA	1610	5.3
2243	1.2		2214	1.2
9 0501	5.2	**24**	0436	5.4
1102	1.3		1033	1.1
SA 1714	5.3	SU	1655	5.4
2320	1.2		2301	1.0
10 0536	5.1	**25**	0523	5.4
1137	1.3		1119	1.1
SU 1748	5.2	M	1741	5.5
2356	1.3		2348	0.9
11 0609	5.0	**26**	0611	5.4
1210	1.4		1205	1.1
M 1822	5.1	TU	1830	5.5
○		●		
12 0030	1.4	**27**	0036	1.0
0643	4.9		0702	5.3
TU 1243	1.6	W	1252	1.2
1856	5.0		1921	5.4
13 0104	1.5	**28**	0126	1.1
0717	4.7		0755	5.1
W 1318	1.7	TH	1342	1.3
1933	4.9		2015	5.3
14 0141	1.7	**29**	0217	1.2
0755	4.5		0853	4.9
TH 1356	1.9	F	1435	1.5
2015	4.7		2114	5.1
15 0223	1.8	**30**	0313	1.4
0839	4.3		0956	4.7
F 1441	2.1	SA	1534	1.7
2104	4.5		2217	4.9
		31	0413	1.6
			1105	4.6
		SU	1637	1.8
			2326	4.8

JUNE

Time	m		Time	m
1 0519	1.7	**16**	0420	1.9
1214	4.6		1051	4.3
M 1745	1.8	TU	1649	2.1
		◖ 2318	4.5
2 0036	4.7	**17**	0519	1.9
0628	1.8		1158	4.3
TU 1317	4.6	W	1753	2.0
◖ 1852	1.8			
3 0140	4.7	**18**	0023	4.5
0732	1.7		0623	1.9
W 1412	4.7	TH	1303	4.5
1954	1.7		1856	1.9
4 0237	4.7	**19**	0128	4.6
0827	1.6		0725	1.7
TH 1459	4.8	F	1403	4.7
2049	1.6		1957	1.7
5 0325	4.8	**20**	0229	4.8
0916	1.6		0823	1.6
F 1540	4.9	SA	1458	4.9
2137	1.5		2055	1.5
6 0406	4.8	**21**	0327	5.0
1000	1.5		0919	1.4
SA 1618	5.0	SU	1551	5.2
2221	1.5		2151	1.2
7 0444	4.9	**22**	0421	5.2
1039	1.5		1013	1.2
SU 1655	5.1	M	1642	5.4
2301	1.4		2246	1.0
8 0520	4.9	**23**	0514	5.3
1116	1.5		1105	1.1
M 1731	5.1	TU	1733	5.5
2337	1.4		2338	0.9
9 0555	4.9	**24**	0605	5.4
1150	1.5		1156	1.0
TU 1807	5.1	W	1824	5.6
○				
10 0012	1.4	**25**	0029	0.8
0629	4.8		0656	5.4
W 1224	1.6	TH	1245	1.0
1842	5.0	● 1915	5.6
11 0048	1.5	**26**	0118	0.9
0703	4.7		0746	5.3
TH 1300	1.6	F	1334	1.1
1917	4.9		2005	5.5
12 0124	1.5	**27**	0207	1.0
0737	4.6		0837	5.1
F 1336	1.7	SA	1422	1.2
1955	4.8		2056	5.3
13 0201	1.6	**28**	0255	1.2
0815	4.5		0928	4.9
SA 1416	1.8	SU	1513	1.4
2036	4.7		2148	5.0
14 0242	1.7	**29**	0346	1.4
0858	4.4		1024	4.6
SU 1500	1.9	M	1607	1.6
2123	4.6		2245	4.7
15 0327	1.8	**30**	0442	1.7
0950	4.3		1126	4.5
M 1550	2.0	TU	1707	1.8
2217	4.5		2351	4.5

JULY

Time	m		Time	m
1 0545	1.9	**16**	0426	1.8
1233	4.4		1102	4.3
W 1814	1.9	TH	1701	1.9
			2337	4.4
2 0102	4.4	**17**	0531	1.9
0653	1.9		1219	4.4
TH 1338	4.5	F	1814	1.9
1922	1.9			
3 0209	4.4	**18**	0053	4.4
0757	1.9		0644	1.9
F 1433	4.6	SA	1334	4.5
2024	1.9	◗ 1926	1.8
4 0306	4.5	**19**	0207	4.6
0853	1.8		0755	1.7
SA 1521	4.7	SU	1439	4.8
◗ 2118	1.8		2034	1.5
5 0352	4.6	**20**	0313	4.9
0940	1.7		0900	1.5
SU 1602	4.8	M	1538	5.1
2204	1.6		2138	1.3
6 0432	4.7	**21**	0411	5.1
1022	1.6		1000	1.3
M 1640	5.0	TU	1632	5.4
2245	1.5		2235	1.0
7 0508	4.8	**22**	0504	5.3
1059	1.5		1054	1.0
TU 1716	5.0	W	1722	5.6
2322	1.4		2328	0.8
8 0541	4.8	**23**	0554	5.5
1134	1.5		1145	0.9
W 1751	5.1	TH	1811	5.7
2357	1.4			
9 0612	4.8	**24**	0017	0.7
1208	1.5		0640	5.5
TH 1823	5.1	F	1232	0.8
			1858	5.7
10 0031	1.4	**25**	0103	0.7
0643	4.8		0725	5.5
F 1241	1.5	SA	1317	0.9
1856	5.0		1943	5.6
11 0104	1.4	**26**	0146	0.9
0713	4.8		0808	5.2
SA 1315	1.5	SU	1400	1.0
○ 1929	5.0	● 2026	5.3
12 0137	1.4	**27**	0228	1.1
0745	4.7		0850	4.9
SU 1349	1.5	M	1444	1.3
2005	4.9		2109	5.0
13 0211	1.5	**28**	0312	1.4
0821	4.6		0933	4.7
TU 1426	1.6	TU	1532	1.6
2045	4.7		2156	4.6
14 0249	1.6	**29**	0401	1.7
0903	4.5		1027	4.4
TU 1508	1.7	W	1622	1.9
2131	4.6		2257	4.3
15 0332	1.7	**30**	0500	2.0
0955	4.4		1141	4.2
W 1559	1.9	TH	1734	2.1
2228	4.5			
		31	0021	4.1
			0613	2.2
		F	1303	4.2
			1852	2.2

AUGUST

Time	m		Time	m
1 0145	4.1	**16**	0036	4.3
0729	2.2		0616	2.0
SA 1411	4.4	SU	1317	4.5
2004	2.1		1909	1.9
2 0250	4.2	**17**	0157	4.5
0833	2.0		0739	1.9
SU 1504	4.6	M	1428	4.8
◖ 2102	1.9	◗ 2025	1.6
3 0338	4.4	**18**	0304	4.8
0923	1.8		0850	1.6
M 1547	4.8	TU	1527	5.2
2148	1.7		2129	1.2
4 0416	4.6	**19**	0400	5.1
1004	1.7		0949	1.2
TU 1623	4.9	W	1619	5.5
2227	1.5		2223	0.9
5 0449	4.8	**20**	0449	5.4
1041	1.6		1041	1.0
W 1657	5.1	TH	1706	5.7
2302	1.4		2312	0.7
6 0519	4.9	**21**	0534	5.5
1115	1.4		1128	0.8
TH 1729	5.2	F	1751	5.8
2336	1.3		2357	0.7
7 0548	4.9	**22**	0616	5.5
1147	1.3		1212	0.7
F 1759	5.2	SA	1833	5.7
8 0008	1.2	**23**	0039	0.7
0615	5.0		0656	5.4
SA 1219	1.3	SU	1253	0.8
1829	5.2		1913	5.5
9 0039	1.2	**24**	0118	0.9
0643	4.9		0732	5.2
SU 1250	1.3	M	1332	1.0
○ 1900	5.1		1950	5.2
10 0109	1.2	**25**	0156	1.2
0713	4.9		0807	5.0
M 1321	1.3	TU	1412	1.3
1932	5.0	● 2025	4.9
11 0140	1.3	**26**	0235	1.5
0745	4.8		0843	4.7
TU 1355	1.4	W	1454	1.6
2009	4.9		2105	4.5
12 0214	1.4	**27**	0319	1.9
0822	4.7		0930	4.4
W 1433	1.6	TH	1545	2.0
2052	4.7		2203	4.2
13 0254	1.6	**28**	0414	2.2
0910	4.5		1045	4.2
TH 1520	1.7	F	1652	2.3
2149	4.5		2341	3.9
14 0344	1.8	**29**	0531	2.4
1018	4.3		1225	4.1
F 1622	1.9	SA	1820	2.4
2306	4.3			
15 0451	2.0	**30**	0120	4.0
1148	4.3		0700	2.4
SA 1743	2.0	SU	1345	4.2
			1942	2.3
		31	0227	4.2
			0809	2.2
		M	1441	4.5
			2040	2.0

Chart Datum: 2·83 metres below IGN Datum
HAT is 6·1 metres above Chart Datum

TIME ZONE -0100
(French Standard Time)
Subtract 1 hour for UT
For French Summer Time add
ONE hour in **non-shaded areas**

FRANCE – POINTE DE GRAVE
LAT 45°34'N   LONG 1°04'W
TIMES AND HEIGHTS OF HIGH AND LOW WATERS

Dates in amber are **SPRINGS**
Dates in yellow are **NEAPS**

2009

SEPTEMBER

Time	m		Time	m
1 0314	4.4	**16** 0252	4.9
TU 0859	1.9	0838	1.6
1523	5.3	W 1513	5.3
2123	1.8	2115	1.2
2 0350	4.6	**17** 0343	5.2
W 0939	1.7	0933	1.2
1559	5.0	TH 1602	5.5
2200	1.5	2205	1.0
3 0421	4.8	**18** 0428	5.4
TH 1014	1.5	1021	1.0
1630	5.1	F 1645	5.7
2234	1.4	● 2250	0.8
4 0449	5.0	**19** 0508	5.5
F 1048	1.3	1105	0.8
○ 1701	5.3	SA 1726	5.7
2307	1.2	2332	0.8
5 0517	5.1	**20** 0546	5.5
SA 1121	1.2	1147	0.8
1730	5.3	SU 1804	5.6
2339	1.2		
6 0544	5.1	**21** 0011	0.9
SU 1153	1.2	0622	5.4
1800	5.3	M 1226	0.9
		1840	5.4
7 0010	1.1	**22** 0047	1.1
0613	5.1	0655	5.3
M 1224	1.2	TU 1303	1.1
1830	5.3	1913	5.1
8 0040	1.2	**23** 0123	1.3
0642	5.1	0727	5.0
TU 1255	1.2	W 1340	1.4
1903	5.2	1946	4.8
9 0112	1.3	**24** 0159	1.7
0715	5.0	0802	4.8
W 1329	1.3	TH 1419	1.7
1940	5.0	2023	4.5
10 0146	1.4	**25** 0240	2.0
TH 0752	4.8	0847	4.5
1407	1.5	F 1505	2.1
2025	4.7	2119	4.1
11 0227	1.6	**26** 0331	2.3
F 0841	4.6	0957	4.2
1455	1.8	SA 1608	2.4
2127	4.4	◐ 2258	3.9
12 0318	1.9	**27** 0445	2.6
SA 0955	4.4	1139	4.1
1557	2.0	SU 1738	2.5
◐ 2255	4.3		
13 0429	2.1	**28** 0041	4.0
SU 1136	4.3	0617	2.6
1729	2.1	M 1305	4.2
		1904	2.4
14 0032	4.3	**29** 0149	4.2
M 0602	2.2	0730	2.4
1307	4.6	TU 1405	4.5
1903	1.9	2003	2.1
15 0150	4.6	**30** 0236	4.4
TU 0730	1.9	0822	2.1
1416	4.9	W 1449	4.7
2018	1.6	2047	1.9

OCTOBER

Time	m		Time	m
1 0313	4.7	**16** 0321	5.2
TH 0903	1.8	0910	1.3
1525	5.0	F 1542	5.5
2125	1.6	2141	1.1
2 0344	4.9	**17** 0403	5.4
F 0940	1.6	0958	1.0
1558	5.2	SA 1623	5.6
2200	1.4	2224	1.0
3 0414	5.1	**18** 0441	5.4
SA 1016	1.4	1041	1.0
1629	5.3	SU 1701	5.6
2234	1.3	● 2305	1.0
4 0443	5.3	**19** 0517	5.5
SU 1051	1.3	1122	1.0
1700	5.4	M 1738	5.5
○ 2307	1.2	2342	1.1
5 0514	5.5	**20** 0552	5.4
M 1125	1.2	1200	1.1
1732	5.4	TU 1812	5.3
2341	1.2		
6 0545	5.3	**21** 0018	1.3
TU 1159	1.2	0625	5.3
1806	5.4	W 1236	1.3
		1846	5.1
7 0014	1.2	**22** 0053	1.5
0619	5.3	0659	5.1
W 1234	1.3	TH 1312	1.5
1843	5.2	1919	4.8
8 0049	1.3	**23** 0128	1.8
0656	5.1	0736	4.9
TH 1311	1.3	F 1350	1.8
1924	5.0	1957	4.5
9 0127	1.5	**24** 0208	2.0
0735	4.9	0820	4.6
F 1353	1.5	SA 1434	2.1
2015	4.7	2048	4.2
10 0211	1.7	**25** 0255	2.3
SA 0835	4.7	0919	4.4
1444	1.8	SU 1529	2.3
2124	4.5	2207	4.0
11 0307	2.0	**26** 0358	2.5
SU 0953	4.5	1041	4.2
1553	2.0	M 1642	2.5
◐ 2257	4.3	◐ 2343	4.0
12 0423	2.2	**27** 0518	2.6
1129	4.5	1206	4.3
M 1724	2.0	TU 1804	2.5
13 0026	4.5	**28** 0055	4.2
0554	2.2	0632	2.5
TU 1324	4.4	W 1312	4.4
1852	1.9	1909	2.3
14 0136	4.7	**29** 0147	4.4
W 0714	1.9	0730	2.2
1400	5.0	TH 1403	4.7
2000	1.6	1959	2.0
15 0233	5.0	**30** 0228	4.6
TH 0817	1.6	0818	2.0
1455	5.3	F 1444	4.9
2054	1.3	2041	1.8
		31 0304	4.9
		0900	1.7
		SA 1521	5.1
		2121	1.5

NOVEMBER

Time	m		Time	m
1 0338	5.1	**16** 0417	5.3
SU 0940	1.5	1020	1.3
1557	5.3	M 1642	5.0
2159	1.4	● 2241	1.3
2 0412	5.2	**17** 0454	5.3
1020	1.3	1101	1.3
M 1633	5.4	TU 1719	5.2
○ 2236	1.3	2319	1.4
3 0448	5.4	**18** 0530	5.3
1059	1.2	1139	1.4
TU 1711	5.5	W 1754	5.1
2315	1.2	2354	1.5
4 0526	5.4	**19** 0606	5.3
1139	1.2	1216	1.5
W 1751	5.4	TH 1829	5.0
2353	1.3		
5 0606	5.4	**20** 0029	1.6
1220	1.2	0642	5.1
TH 1834	5.3	F 1252	1.6
		1903	4.8
6 0034	1.4	**21** 0105	1.8
0651	5.3	0719	5.0
F 1302	1.3	SA 1329	1.8
1923	5.1	1940	4.6
7 0118	1.5	**22** 0143	2.0
0741	5.1	0759	4.8
SA 1349	1.5	SU 1409	1.9
2019	4.8	2023	4.4
8 0207	1.8	**23** 0226	2.2
0840	5.0	0846	4.6
SU 1444	1.7	M 1455	2.1
2128	4.6	2117	4.3
9 0306	2.0	**24** 0317	2.3
0953	4.8	0944	4.5
M 1551	1.9	TU 1550	2.3
◑ 2250	4.5	◑ 2226	4.2
10 0418	2.1	**25** 0417	2.4
TU 1114	4.8	1052	4.4
1709	2.0	W 1654	2.3
		2340	4.2
11 0007	4.6	**26** 0524	2.4
0534	2.1	1202	4.4
W 1231	4.8	TH 1801	2.3
1826	1.9		
12 0113	4.8	**27** 0044	4.3
0647	1.9	0628	2.3
TU 1337	5.0	F 1304	4.5
1932	1.7	1901	2.1
13 0209	4.9	**28** 0137	4.5
0751	1.7	0725	2.1
F 1433	5.1	SA 1357	4.7
2028	1.5	1953	1.9
14 0257	5.1	**29** 0223	4.8
0846	1.5	0817	1.9
SA 1522	5.2	SU 1444	4.9
2116	1.4	2040	1.7
15 0339	5.2	**30** 0305	5.0
0935	1.4	0905	1.7
SU 1604	5.3	M 1529	5.1
2200	1.3	2125	1.5

DECEMBER

Time	m		Time	m
1 0348	5.2	**16** 0440	5.2
0952	1.5	1047	1.5
TU 1613	5.3	W 1709	5.0
2210	1.4	● 2302	1.6
2 0430	5.4	**17** 0517	5.2
1038	1.3	1126	1.5
W 1658	5.4	TH 1744	5.0
○ 2255	1.3	2338	1.6
3 0515	5.5	**18** 0553	5.2
1125	1.2	1202	1.5
TH 1744	5.4	F 1817	5.0
2340	1.3		
4 0602	5.5	**19** 0013	1.6
1212	1.1	0628	5.2
F 1833	5.4	SA 1236	1.5
		1849	4.9
5 0027	1.3	**20** 0047	1.7
0651	5.5	0702	5.1
SA 1300	1.2	SU 1311	1.6
1924	5.3	1921	4.8
6 0115	1.4	**21** 0123	1.8
0743	5.4	0737	5.0
SU 1349	1.3	M 1347	1.7
2018	5.1	1955	4.7
7 0206	1.5	**22** 0200	1.9
0838	5.3	0815	4.9
M 1441	1.5	TU 1425	1.8
2119	4.9	2033	4.5
8 0300	1.7	**23** 0240	2.0
0939	5.1	0857	4.7
TU 1538	1.7	W 1506	2.0
2225	4.7	2120	4.4
9 0400	1.8	**24** 0325	2.1
1047	4.9	0948	4.5
W 1641	1.8	TH 1553	2.1
◑ 2335	4.7	◑ 2218	4.3
10 0505	1.9	**25** 0418	2.2
1159	4.8	1048	4.4
TH 1750	1.9	F 1650	2.2
		2328	4.3
11 0042	4.7	**26** 0522	2.3
0613	2.0	1158	4.4
F 1308	4.8	SA 1755	2.2
1858	1.9		
12 0142	4.8	**27** 0039	4.4
0721	1.9	0630	2.2
SA 1412	4.8	SU 1307	4.5
2000	1.8	1901	2.1
13 0235	4.9	**28** 0143	4.6
0822	1.8	0734	2.0
SU 1506	4.9	M 1410	4.7
2054	1.7	2002	1.9
14 0321	5.0	**29** 0238	4.8
0916	1.7	0834	1.8
M 1552	4.9	TU 1507	4.9
2141	1.6	2058	1.7
15 0402	5.1	**30** 0330	5.1
1004	1.6	0930	1.5
TU 1632	5.0	W 1600	5.2
2223	1.6	2151	1.5
		31 0419	5.4
		1024	1.3
		TH 1650	5.4
		○ 2242	1.3

Chart Datum: 2·83 metres below IGN Datum
HAT is 6·1 metres above Chart Datum

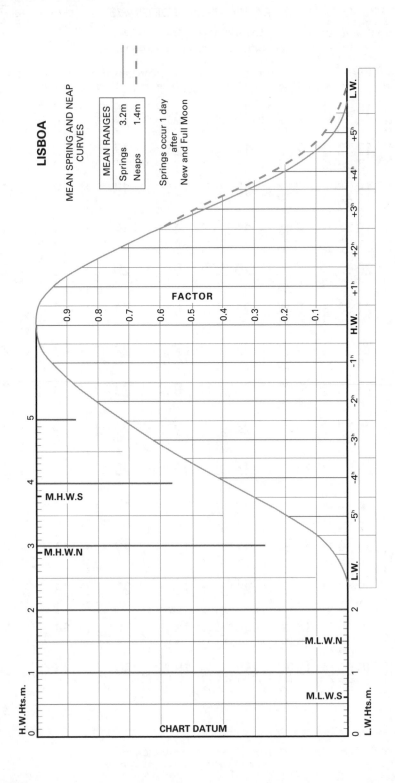

LISBOA

MEAN SPRING AND NEAP CURVES

MEAN RANGES	
Springs	3.2m
Neaps	1.4m

Springs occur 1 day after New and Full Moon

FACTOR

PORTUGAL – LISBOA
LAT 38°43'N LONG 9°07'W
TIMES AND HEIGHTS OF HIGH AND LOW WATERS

Dates in amber are **SPRINGS**
Dates in yellow are **NEAPS**

2009

JANUARY

Time	m		Time	m
1 0551	3.4		**16** 0014	0.7
TH 1146	0.9		F 0652	3.6
1813	3.2		1245	0.8
2355	1.0		1916	3.3
2 0630	3.3		**17** 0058	0.9
F 1225	1.0		SA 0736	3.6
1855	3.1		1330	1.0
			2003	3.0
3 0037	1.1		**18** 0149	1.1
SA 0713	3.2		SU 0827	3.0
1310	1.1		1422	1.2
1943	3.0		☽ 2100	2.9
4 0127	1.2		**19** 0251	1.4
SU 0805	3.1		M 0930	2.8
1404	1.1		1528	1.4
☽ 2041	2.9		2211	2.8
5 0229	1.3		**20** 0411	1.5
M 0907	3.0		TU 1048	2.7
1509	1.2		1646	1.5
2150	2.9		2327	2.8
6 0342	1.3		**21** 0535	1.4
TU 1020	3.0		W 1204	2.7
1621	1.2		1759	1.4
2303	3.0			
7 0500	1.2		**22** 0032	3.0
W 1135	3.1		TH 0641	1.3
1733	1.1		1304	2.8
			1854	1.3
8 0011	3.2		**23** 0123	3.1
TH 0611	1.0		F 0729	1.1
1244	3.2		1351	3.0
1837	0.9		1937	1.1
9 0113	3.5		**24** 0205	3.3
F 0714	0.7		SA 0807	1.0
1346	3.4		1430	3.1
1935	0.7		2014	1.0
10 0211	3.7		**25** 0242	3.4
SA 0811	0.5		SU 0841	0.8
1443	3.6		1505	3.2
2028	0.6		2047	0.9
11 0304	3.9		**26** 0316	3.5
SU 0903	0.3		M 0913	0.7
1535	3.7		● 1538	3.3
○ 2117	0.5		2120	0.8
12 0354	4.0		**27** 0350	3.6
M 0951	0.2		TU 0945	0.6
1623	3.8		1610	3.4
2204	0.4		2152	0.7
13 0441	4.1		**28** 0423	3.7
TU 1037	0.3		W 1016	0.6
1708	3.7		1643	3.4
2248	0.5		2224	0.7
14 0526	4.0		**29** 0457	3.7
W 1120	0.4		TH 1048	0.6
1751	3.6		1716	3.4
2331	0.6		2257	0.7
15 0609	3.8		**30** 0531	3.6
TH 1202	0.5		F 1121	0.6
1833	3.5		1750	3.4
			2331	0.7
			31 0607	3.5
			SA 1156	0.7
			1826	3.3

FEBRUARY

Time	m		Time	m
1 0008	0.8		**16** 0103	1.1
SU 0645	3.4		M 0733	3.0
1234	0.9		1325	1.3
1908	3.2		☽ 1959	2.9
2 0052	1.0		**17** 0157	1.4
M 0729	3.2		TU 0826	2.7
1321	1.0		1425	1.5
☽ 1959	3.0		2105	2.7
3 0148	1.1		**18** 0318	1.6
TU 0827	3.0		W 0951	2.5
1423	1.2		1555	1.6
2107	2.9		2239	2.7
4 0305	1.3		**19** 0504	1.6
W 0946	2.9		TH 1137	2.6
1544	1.3		1731	1.6
2232	3.0			
5 0438	1.2		**20** 0003	2.8
TH 1118	2.9		F 0620	1.4
1713	1.2		1246	2.7
2356	3.1		1834	1.4
6 0604	1.0		**21** 0100	3.0
F 1238	3.1		SA 0708	1.2
1829	1.0		1331	3.0
			1917	1.2
7 0106	3.4		**22** 0142	3.2
SA 0711	0.8		SU 0745	1.0
1342	3.4		1408	3.2
1929	0.8		1953	1.0
8 0204	3.7		**23** 0219	3.4
SU 0805	0.5		M 0818	0.8
1435	3.6		1442	3.3
2020	0.6		2026	0.8
9 0254	3.9		**24** 0253	3.6
M 0852	0.3		TU 0849	0.7
1522	3.8		1514	3.5
2105	0.4		2058	0.7
10 0340	4.1		**25** 0327	3.8
TU 0935	0.2		W 0920	0.6
1605	3.8		1547	3.6
2147	0.3		2130	0.6
11 0422	4.1		**26** 0401	3.8
W 1015	0.2		TH 0952	0.5
1645	3.8		1619	3.6
2227	0.3		2202	0.5
12 0502	4.0		**27** 0435	3.8
TH 1053	0.3		F 1023	0.5
1723	3.7		1652	3.6
2304	0.4		2235	0.5
13 0540	3.8		**28** 0509	3.8
F 1129	0.5		SA 1055	0.6
1759	3.6		1726	3.6
2342	0.6		2309	0.6
14 0617	3.6			
SA 1205	0.7			
1835	3.4			
15 0020	0.9			
SU 0653	3.3			
1242	1.0			
1913	3.1			

MARCH

Time	m		Time	m
1 0544	3.7		**16** 0616	3.3
SU 1129	0.7		M 1202	1.1
1802	3.5		1831	3.3
2346	0.8			
2 0622	3.5		**17** 0026	1.2
M 1207	0.8		TU 0651	3.0
1843	3.3		1240	1.4
			1910	3.0
3 0030	0.9		**18** 0115	1.5
TU 0707	3.2		W 0736	2.8
1253	1.1		1331	1.6
1933	3.2		☽ 2005	2.8
4 0127	1.2		**19** 0229	1.6
W 0808	3.0		TH 0851	2.6
1356	1.3		1500	1.8
☽ 2043	3.0		2135	2.7
5 0250	1.3		**20** 0418	1.7
TH 0935	2.8		F 1054	2.6
1528	1.4		1648	1.8
2219	3.0		2318	2.8
6 0435	1.3		**21** 0540	1.5
F 1117	2.9		SA 1211	2.8
1708	1.4		1758	1.6
2349	3.2			
7 0602	1.1		**22** 0022	3.0
SA 1235	3.2		SU 0632	1.3
1824	1.1		1258	3.0
			1844	1.3
8 0057	3.5		**23** 0107	3.3
SU 0703	0.8		M 0711	1.1
1332	3.5		1335	3.3
1919	0.9		1922	1.1
9 0151	3.8		**24** 0146	3.5
M 0751	0.6		TU 0745	0.9
1420	3.7		1410	3.5
2005	0.6		1956	0.9
10 0237	4.0		**25** 0223	3.7
TU 0834	0.4		W 0818	0.7
1502	3.8		1444	3.6
2046	0.5		2030	0.7
11 0319	4.1		**26** 0259	3.8
W 0912	0.3		TH 0851	0.6
1541	3.9		● 1518	3.8
○ 2125	0.4		2103	0.6
12 0359	4.1		**27** 0335	3.9
TH 0948	0.3		F 0923	0.5
1618	3.9		1553	3.8
2201	0.4		2137	0.5
13 0436	4.0		**28** 0411	3.9
F 1023	0.4		SA 0956	0.5
1653	3.8		1628	3.8
2237	0.5		2213	0.5
14 0510	3.8		**29** 0447	3.9
SA 1056	0.6		SU 1031	0.6
1726	3.7		1705	3.8
2312	0.7		2250	0.6
15 0543	3.6		**30** 0526	3.7
SU 1128	0.8		M 1108	0.7
1758	3.5		1744	3.7
2347	0.9		2332	0.8
			31 0609	3.5
			TU 1149	0.9
			1828	3.5

APRIL

Time	m		Time	m
1 0021	1.0		**16** 0045	1.5
W 0659	3.3		TH 0705	2.8
1240	1.2		1255	1.6
1924	3.3		1926	3.0
2 0125	1.2		**17** 0150	1.6
TH 0807	3.0		F 0810	2.7
1350	1.4		1411	1.8
☽ 2039	3.2		☽ 2039	2.9
3 0253	1.4		**18** 0319	1.6
F 0940	2.9		SA 0949	2.7
1526	1.5		1548	1.8
2214	3.2		2213	2.9
4 0432	1.3		**19** 0441	1.5
SA 1112	3.0		SU 1114	2.8
1700	1.4		1704	1.6
2337	3.3		2328	3.1
5 0548	1.1		**20** 0540	1.4
SU 1220	3.3		M 1210	3.0
1808	1.2		1758	1.4
6 0039	3.6		**21** 0022	3.3
M 0644	0.9		TU 0626	1.2
1312	3.5		1253	3.3
1859	0.9		1841	1.2
7 0130	3.8		**22** 0106	3.5
TU 0729	0.7		W 0705	1.0
1356	3.7		1332	3.5
1943	0.8		1920	1.0
8 0214	3.9		**23** 0147	3.7
W 0808	0.6		TH 0742	0.8
1436	3.8		1410	3.7
2023	0.6		1958	0.8
9 0255	4.0		**24** 0227	3.8
TH 0845	0.6		F 0818	0.7
1514	3.9		1447	3.8
○ 2100	0.6		2035	0.7
10 0333	3.9		**25** 0306	3.9
F 0920	0.6		SA 0854	0.6
1550	3.9		1526	3.9
2136	0.6		● 2114	0.6
11 0409	3.8		**26** 0347	3.9
SA 0953	0.7		SU 0932	0.6
1624	3.8		1606	3.9
2211	0.7		2155	0.6
12 0443	3.7		**27** 0429	3.8
SU 1025	0.8		M 1012	0.7
1657	3.7		1648	3.9
2246	0.9		2238	0.6
13 0515	3.5		**28** 0514	3.7
M 1057	1.0		TU 1054	0.8
1728	3.5		1733	3.8
2321	1.0		2326	0.8
14 0546	3.2		**29** 0604	3.5
TU 1130	1.2		W 1142	1.0
1800	3.3		1824	3.6
2359	1.3			
15 0621	3.0		**30** 0022	0.9
W 1207	1.4		TH 0701	3.3
1837	3.2		1239	1.2
			1923	3.5

HAT is 4·3 metres above Chart Datum

TIDES

TIME ZONE (UT)	PORTUGAL – LISBOA	Dates in amber are SPRINGS
For Summer Time add ONE hour in **non-shaded areas**	**LAT 38°43'N LONG 9°07'W**	Dates in yellow are NEAPS
	TIMES AND HEIGHTS OF HIGH AND LOW WATERS	**2009**

MAY

Time m   Time m

1 F	0129 1.1 / 0810 3.1 / 1350 1.4 / 2036 3.3	16 SA	0116 1.4 / 0739 2.8 / 1330 1.6 / 1959 3.0
2 SA	0250 1.2 / 0931 3.1 / 1515 1.5 / 2158 3.3	17 SU	0223 1.5 / 0849 2.8 / 1444 1.7 / 2112 3.0
3 SU	0411 1.2 / 1048 3.2 / 1635 1.4 / 2311 3.4	18 M	0334 1.5 / 1006 2.9 / 1558 1.6 / 2225 3.1
4 M	0519 1.1 / 1151 3.3 / 1739 1.2	19 TU	0438 1.4 / 1111 3.0 / 1701 1.5 / 2328 3.2
5 TU	0012 3.5 / 0614 1.0 / 1243 3.5 / 1832 1.0	20 W	0532 1.2 / 1203 3.2 / 1753 1.3
6 W	0103 3.6 / 0659 0.9 / 1328 3.6 / 1917 0.9	21 TH	0020 3.4 / 0619 1.0 / 1250 3.4 / 1840 1.1
7 TH	0148 3.7 / 0740 0.8 / 1409 3.7 / 1959 0.8	22 F	0108 3.5 / 0703 0.9 / 1334 3.6 / 1925 0.9
8 F	0229 3.7 / 0817 0.8 / 1448 3.8 / 2038 0.8	23 SA	0155 3.6 / 0746 0.8 / 1418 3.7 / 2010 0.7
9 SA	0308 3.7 / 0853 0.8 / 1525 3.8 / 2115 0.8	24 SU	0241 3.7 / 0829 0.7 / 1503 3.9 / 2056 0.6
10 SU	0345 3.6 / 0927 0.9 / 1600 3.7 / 2151 0.9	25 M	0329 3.8 / 0913 0.6 / 1550 3.9 / 2143 0.5
11 M	0420 3.5 / 1000 1.0 / 1633 3.6 / 2226 1.0	26 TU	0418 3.7 / 0959 0.7 / 1638 3.9 / 2233 0.6
12 TU	0453 3.3 / 1033 1.1 / 1705 3.5 / 2301 1.1	27 W	0509 3.7 / 1047 0.8 / 1728 3.9 / 2325 0.6
13 W	0526 3.2 / 1107 1.2 / 1738 3.4 / 2339 1.2	28 TH	0601 3.5 / 1139 0.8 / 1821 3.8
14 TH	0602 3.1 / 1145 1.4 / 1815 3.3	29 F	0021 0.8 / 0657 3.4 / 1235 1.1 / 1917 3.6
15 F	0023 1.3 / 0644 2.9 / 1231 1.5 / 1901 3.1	30 SA	0121 0.9 / 0758 3.3 / 1338 1.2 / 2020 3.5
		31 SU	0227 1.1 / 0904 3.2 / 1446 1.3 / 2127 3.3

JUNE

Time m   Time m

1 M	0334 1.1 / 1011 3.2 / 1556 1.3 / 2235 3.3	16 TU	0230 1.3 / 0902 2.9 / 1452 1.5 / 2124 3.1
2 TU	0439 1.2 / 1114 3.2 / 1703 1.3 / 2337 3.3	17 W	0333 1.3 / 1008 3.0 / 1559 1.4 / 2230 3.1
3 W	0537 1.1 / 1209 3.3 / 1801 1.2	18 TH	0435 1.2 / 1110 3.1 / 1703 1.3 / 2333 3.2
4 TH	0033 3.3 / 0628 1.1 / 1259 3.4 / 1853 1.1	19 F	0533 1.1 / 1208 3.3 / 1803 1.1
5 F	0122 3.4 / 0713 1.0 / 1344 3.5 / 1939 1.0	20 SA	0032 3.3 / 0628 1.0 / 1302 3.5 / 1859 0.9
6 SA	0207 3.4 / 0753 1.0 / 1426 3.5 / 2021 1.0	21 SU	0129 3.4 / 0720 0.8 / 1355 3.6 / 1953 0.7
7 SU	0249 3.3 / 0832 1.0 / 1505 3.6 / 2100 0.9	22 M	0224 3.6 / 0811 0.7 / 1448 3.8 / 2045 0.6
8 M	0327 3.3 / 0907 1.0 / 1541 3.6 / 2136 0.9	23 TU	0318 3.7 / 0901 0.6 / 1539 3.9 / 2136 0.4
9 TU	0403 3.3 / 0942 1.0 / 1615 3.5 / 2211 0.9	24 W	0410 3.7 / 0951 0.6 / 1630 4.0 / 2227 0.4
10 W	0437 3.2 / 1015 1.1 / 1648 3.5 / 2245 1.0	25 TH	0501 3.7 / 1040 0.6 / 1720 4.0 / 2317 0.4
11 TH	0510 3.2 / 1050 1.1 / 1721 3.4 / 2321 1.0	26 F	0551 3.6 / 1129 0.7 / 1809 3.9
12 F	0545 3.1 / 1127 1.2 / 1758 3.4	27 SA	0006 0.6 / 0640 3.5 / 1219 0.8 / 1859 3.7
13 SA	0000 1.1 / 0624 3.1 / 1207 1.3 / 1839 3.3	28 SU	0057 0.8 / 0731 3.4 / 1311 1.0 / 1951 3.5
14 SU	0044 1.2 / 0709 3.0 / 1254 1.4 / 1926 3.2	29 M	0150 0.9 / 0825 3.2 / 1408 1.1 / 2048 3.3
15 M	0133 1.3 / 0801 2.9 / 1349 1.4 / 2021 3.1	30 TU	0248 1.1 / 0925 3.1 / 1512 1.3 / 2152 3.1

JULY

Time m   Time m

1 W	0352 1.2 / 1030 3.1 / 1622 1.3 / 2259 3.0	16 TH	0233 1.2 / 0912 3.0 / 1504 1.4 / 2139 3.0
2 TH	0457 1.3 / 1135 3.1 / 1732 1.3	17 F	0341 1.3 / 1023 3.0 / 1621 1.3 / 2254 3.0
3 F	0004 3.0 / 0558 1.3 / 1233 3.2 / 1835 1.2	18 SA	0454 1.2 / 1134 3.2 / 1736 1.2
4 SA	0101 3.0 / 0651 1.2 / 1324 3.3 / 1926 1.1	19 SU	0008 3.1 / 0603 1.1 / 1241 3.4 / 1844 0.9
5 SU	0151 3.1 / 0736 1.1 / 1409 3.4 / 2009 1.0	20 M	0115 3.3 / 0705 0.9 / 1342 3.6 / 1944 0.7
6 M	0234 3.2 / 0816 1.0 / 1449 3.4 / 2047 1.0	21 TU	0215 3.5 / 0801 0.7 / 1437 3.8 / 2037 0.5
7 TU	0312 3.2 / 0852 1.0 / 1525 3.5 / 2121 0.9	22 W	0309 3.7 / 0852 0.6 / 1529 4.0 / 2127 0.3
8 W	0347 3.2 / 0926 1.0 / 1558 3.5 / 2154 0.8	23 TH	0359 3.8 / 0940 0.5 / 1617 4.1 / 2213 0.3
9 TH	0420 3.3 / 0959 0.9 / 1631 3.6 / 2227 0.8	24 F	0445 3.8 / 1025 0.4 / 1703 4.1 / 2258 0.3
10 F	0452 3.3 / 1032 0.9 / 1704 3.5 / 2300 0.8	25 SA	0529 3.8 / 1109 0.5 / 1748 4.0 / 2341 0.5
11 SA	0525 3.3 / 1106 0.9 / 1738 3.5 / 2334 0.9	26 SU	0612 3.6 / 1153 0.6 / 1831 3.8
12 SU	0600 3.2 / 1141 1.0 / 1815 3.4	27 M	0024 0.7 / 0656 3.5 / 1237 0.8 / 1916 3.5
13 M	0010 1.0 / 0637 3.2 / 1219 1.1 / 1854 3.3	28 TU	0109 0.9 / 0742 3.3 / 1327 1.1 / 2005 3.2
14 TU	0050 1.0 / 0720 3.1 / 1303 1.2 / 1939 3.2	29 W	0159 1.2 / 0836 3.1 / 1426 1.3 / 2105 3.0
15 W	0136 1.1 / 0810 3.0 / 1357 1.3 / 2033 3.1	30 TH	0301 1.4 / 0944 2.9 / 1542 1.5 / 2221 2.8
		31 F	0418 1.5 / 1101 2.9 / 1710 1.5 / 2341 2.8

AUGUST

Time m   Time m

1 SA	0535 1.5 / 1211 3.0 / 1823 1.4	16 SU	0433 1.4 / 1116 3.1 / 1726 1.2
2 SU	0047 2.9 / 0636 1.4 / 1307 3.2 / 1915 1.2	17 M	0001 3.1 / 0553 1.2 / 1231 3.4 / 1838 1.0
3 M	0138 3.0 / 0723 1.2 / 1352 3.3 / 1955 1.1	18 TU	0110 3.3 / 0658 1.0 / 1333 3.7 / 1936 0.7
4 TU	0218 3.1 / 0801 1.1 / 1430 3.4 / 2029 0.9	19 W	0206 3.6 / 0751 0.7 / 1430 4.0 / 2025 0.4
5 W	0253 3.3 / 0835 1.0 / 1504 3.6 / 2101 0.8	20 TH	0255 3.8 / 0839 0.5 / 1514 4.1 / 2110 0.3
6 TH	0326 3.4 / 0907 0.9 / 1537 3.7 / 2132 0.7	21 F	0340 4.0 / 0922 0.4 / 1558 4.2 / 2151 0.3
7 F	0357 3.4 / 0938 0.8 / 1609 3.7 / 2202 0.7	22 SA	0422 4.0 / 1004 0.3 / 1640 4.2 / 2231 0.3
8 SA	0428 3.5 / 1010 0.8 / 1642 3.7 / 2233 0.7	23 SU	0502 3.9 / 1043 0.4 / 1721 4.1 / 2310 0.5
9 SU	0500 3.5 / 1041 0.8 / 1715 3.7 / 2304 0.8	24 M	0541 3.8 / 1123 0.6 / 1800 3.8 / 2347 0.8
10 M	0533 3.4 / 1114 0.8 / 1748 3.6 / 2337 0.8	25 TU	0619 3.6 / 1204 0.9 / 1840 3.5
11 TU	0607 3.3 / 1148 0.9 / 1824 3.4	26 W	0027 1.0 / 0700 3.4 / 1248 1.1 / 1923 3.2
12 W	0012 0.9 / 0645 3.2 / 1228 1.1 / 1904 3.3	27 TH	0111 1.3 / 0748 3.1 / 1344 1.4 / 2017 2.9
13 TH	0054 1.1 / 0730 3.1 / 1317 1.2 / 1955 3.1	28 F	0210 1.6 / 0853 2.9 / 1504 1.6 / 2141 2.7
14 F	0148 1.3 / 0831 3.0 / 1426 1.4 / 2105 3.0	29 SA	0339 1.7 / 1027 2.8 / 1648 1.6 / 2321 2.7
15 SA	0303 1.4 / 0950 3.0 / 1556 1.4 / 2234 2.9	30 SU	0514 1.7 / 1147 3.0 / 1804 1.5
		31 M	0030 2.9 / 0617 1.6 / 1244 3.1 / 1853 1.3

HAT is 4·3 metres above Chart Datum

TIME ZONE (UT)	PORTUGAL – LISBOA	Dates in amber are SPRINGS
For Summer Time add ONE hour in non-shaded areas	LAT 38°43'N LONG 9°07'W	Dates in yellow are NEAPS
	TIMES AND HEIGHTS OF HIGH AND LOW WATERS	2009

SEPTEMBER

Time m	Time m
1 0116 3.1 / 0702 1.3 / TU 1327 3.3 / 1930 1.1	**16** 0100 3.5 / 0647 1.0 / W 1320 3.8 / 1921 0.7
2 0153 3.3 / 0738 1.1 / W 1403 3.5 / 2002 0.9	**17** 0150 3.8 / 0736 0.7 / TH 1408 4.1 / 2006 0.5
3 0226 3.4 / 0810 0.9 / TH 1437 3.7 / 2033 0.8	**18** 0234 3.9 / 0819 0.6 / F 1453 4.2 / ● 2047 0.4
4 0257 3.5 / 0841 0.8 / F 1510 3.8 / ○ 2104 0.7	**19** 0316 4.0 / 0900 0.4 / SA 1534 4.2 / 2125 0.4
5 0329 3.6 / 0913 0.7 / SA 1543 3.9 / 2134 0.7	**20** 0355 4.1 / 0939 0.4 / SU 1614 4.2 / 2202 0.5
6 0400 3.7 / 0944 0.7 / SU 1616 3.9 / 2204 0.7	**21** 0433 4.0 / 1017 0.5 / M 1652 4.0 / 2238 0.7
7 0432 3.7 / 1015 0.7 / M 1649 3.8 / 2235 0.7	**22** 0509 3.8 / 1055 0.7 / TU 1729 3.7 / 2313 0.9
8 0505 3.6 / 1047 0.8 / TU 1722 3.7 / 2306 0.8	**23** 0545 3.6 / 1135 1.0 / W 1806 3.4 / 2349 1.2
9 0540 3.5 / 1122 0.9 / W 1759 3.5 / 2342 1.0	**24** 0622 3.4 / 1215 1.3 / TH 1845 3.1
10 0618 3.4 / 1203 1.1 / TH 1840 3.3	**25** 0029 1.5 / 0704 3.2 / F 1306 1.5 / 1934 2.8
11 0024 1.2 / 0704 3.3 / F 1255 1.3 / 1935 3.1	**26** 0123 1.7 / 0802 3.0 / SA 1424 1.7 / ◑ 2054 2.7
12 0121 1.4 / 0808 3.1 / SA 1410 1.4 / ◑ 2054 3.0	**27** 0254 1.9 / 0934 2.8 / SU 1609 1.7 / 2245 2.7
13 0245 1.5 / 0936 3.0 / SU 1552 1.5 / 2234 3.0	**28** 0437 1.8 / 1107 3.0 / M 1727 1.6 / 2356 2.9
14 0427 1.5 / 1110 3.2 / M 1724 1.3 / 2358 3.2	**29** 0543 1.6 / 1207 3.2 / TU 1816 1.4
15 0548 1.3 / 1223 3.5 / TU 1830 1.0	**30** 0042 3.1 / 0628 1.4 / W 1252 3.4 / 1855 1.2

OCTOBER

Time m	Time m
1 0119 3.3 / 0705 1.2 / TH 1329 3.6 / 1929 1.0	**16** 0127 3.8 / 0715 0.8 / F 1346 4.0 / 1942 0.6
2 0153 3.5 / 0739 1.0 / F 1405 3.8 / 2001 0.8	**17** 0210 3.9 / 0757 0.7 / SA 1429 4.1 / 2021 0.6
3 0225 3.7 / 0812 0.9 / SA 1439 3.9 / 2032 0.8	**18** 0250 4.0 / 0837 0.6 / SU 1510 4.1 / ● 2058 0.6
4 0258 3.8 / 0844 0.8 / SU 1514 3.9 / ○ 2103 0.7	**19** 0329 4.0 / 0916 0.6 / M 1549 4.0 / 2134 0.7
5 0331 3.8 / 0917 0.7 / M 1548 3.9 / 2135 0.7	**20** 0406 3.9 / 0954 0.7 / TU 1627 3.8 / 2209 0.8
6 0405 3.8 / 0951 0.7 / TU 1624 3.9 / 2208 0.8	**21** 0442 3.8 / 1031 0.9 / W 1703 3.6 / 2243 1.0
7 0441 3.8 / 1027 0.8 / W 1701 3.7 / 2243 1.0	**22** 0517 3.6 / 1109 1.1 / TH 1738 3.3 / 2318 1.3
8 0519 3.7 / 1106 0.9 / TH 1742 3.6 / 2322 1.0	**23** 0551 3.4 / 1149 1.3 / F 1815 3.1 / 2357 1.5
9 0601 3.6 / 1152 1.1 / F 1830 3.3	**24** 0630 3.2 / 1236 1.5 / SA 1859 2.9
10 0009 1.2 / 0653 3.4 / SA 1250 1.3 / 1931 3.1	**25** 0046 1.7 / 0719 3.0 / SU 1340 1.6 / 2004 2.8
11 0112 1.5 / 0802 3.2 / SU 1411 1.4 / ◑ 2057 3.0	**26** 0200 1.8 / 0831 2.9 / M 1506 1.7 / 2139 2.7
12 0242 1.6 / 0932 3.2 / M 1549 1.4 / 2231 3.1	**27** 0334 1.8 / 1001 3.0 / TU 1626 1.6 / 2259 2.9
13 0419 1.5 / 1059 3.4 / TU 1711 1.2 / 2344 3.3	**28** 0449 1.7 / 1113 3.1 / W 1725 1.4 / 2354 3.1
14 0532 1.3 / 1205 3.6 / W 1811 1.0	**29** 0542 1.5 / 1205 3.3 / TH 1810 1.3
15 0040 3.6 / 0628 1.0 / TH 1259 3.8 / 1859 0.8	**30** 0036 3.3 / 0625 1.3 / F 1249 3.5 / 1849 1.1
	31 0114 3.5 / 0703 1.1 / SA 1328 3.7 / 1924 0.9

NOVEMBER

Time m	Time m
1 0150 3.6 / 0740 0.9 / SU 1406 3.8 / 1959 0.8	**16** 0227 3.8 / 0818 0.8 / M 1449 3.7 / ● 2035 0.8
2 0226 3.8 / 0816 0.8 / M 1445 3.8 / ○ 2033 0.7	**17** 0307 3.8 / 0858 0.6 / TU 1529 3.6 / 2112 0.9
3 0303 3.8 / 0853 0.7 / TU 1524 3.8 / 2109 0.7	**18** 0345 3.8 / 0937 0.8 / W 1607 3.5 / 2147 0.9
4 0342 3.9 / 0932 0.7 / W 1605 3.8 / 2147 0.7	**19** 0421 3.7 / 1014 0.9 / TH 1643 3.4 / 2222 1.1
5 0423 3.9 / 1013 0.7 / TH 1648 3.7 / 2228 0.8	**20** 0455 3.6 / 1050 1.0 / F 1717 3.2 / 2256 1.2
6 0507 3.8 / 1059 0.8 / F 1735 3.5 / 2313 1.0	**21** 0529 3.4 / 1128 1.2 / SA 1752 3.1 / 2334 1.3
7 0555 3.7 / 1150 1.0 / SA 1829 3.4	**22** 0605 3.3 / 1210 1.3 / SU 1832 3.0
8 0006 1.2 / 0651 3.5 / SU 1252 1.1 / 1933 3.2	**23** 0017 1.5 / 0647 3.2 / M 1259 1.4 / 1922 2.9
9 0111 1.4 / 0758 3.4 / M 1407 1.3 / ◐ 2049 3.1	**24** 0112 1.6 / 0741 3.0 / TU 1401 1.5 / ◐ 2027 2.9
10 0231 1.5 / 0917 3.3 / TU 1529 1.3 / 2208 3.2	**25** 0222 1.6 / 0849 3.0 / W 1511 1.5 / 2142 2.8
11 0354 1.4 / 1034 3.4 / W 1643 1.2 / 2316 3.3	**26** 0336 1.6 / 1003 3.0 / TH 1618 1.4 / 2250 2.9
12 0504 1.3 / 1139 3.5 / TH 1742 1.0	**27** 0441 1.5 / 1107 3.1 / F 1715 1.3 / 2344 3.1
13 0012 3.5 / 0602 1.1 / F 1234 3.7 / 1832 0.9	**28** 0536 1.3 / 1201 3.2 / SA 1802 1.2
14 0101 3.6 / 0651 0.9 / SA 1322 3.7 / 1916 0.8	**29** 0031 3.3 / 0623 1.2 / SU 1249 3.4 / 1845 1.0
15 0145 3.8 / 0736 0.8 / SU 1407 3.8 / 1957 0.8	**30** 0114 3.5 / 0707 1.0 / M 1334 3.5 / 1927 0.9

DECEMBER

Time m	Time m
1 0157 3.6 / 0751 0.8 / TU 1419 3.6 / 2008 0.8	**16** 0252 3.6 / 0848 0.9 / W 1516 3.3 / 2057 0.9
2 0241 3.8 / 0835 0.7 / W 1505 3.7 / ○ 2051 0.7	**17** 0331 3.6 / 0926 0.8 / TH 1554 3.3 / 2132 0.9
3 0326 3.8 / 0920 0.6 / TH 1553 3.7 / 2135 0.7	**18** 0406 3.6 / 1001 0.9 / F 1628 3.3 / 2206 1.0
4 0413 3.9 / 1007 0.6 / F 1642 3.7 / 2221 0.7	**19** 0439 3.5 / 1034 0.9 / SA 1700 3.2 / 2240 1.0
5 0501 3.9 / 1057 0.6 / SA 1732 3.6 / 2310 0.8	**20** 0511 3.5 / 1108 0.9 / SU 1733 3.2 / 2314 1.1
6 0551 3.8 / 1149 0.7 / SU 1825 3.5	**21** 0544 3.4 / 1144 1.0 / M 1807 3.1 / 2351 1.1
7 0003 0.9 / 0645 3.7 / M 1245 0.9 / 1922 3.3	**22** 0621 3.3 / 1223 1.1 / TU 1847 3.0
8 0100 1.1 / 0743 3.5 / TU 1346 1.0 / 2024 3.2	**23** 0033 1.3 / 0703 3.2 / W 1308 1.2 / 1933 2.9
9 0205 1.2 / 0848 3.4 / W 1452 1.1 / ◐ 2131 3.1	**24** 0122 1.3 / 0753 3.1 / TH 1400 1.3 / ◐ 2030 2.8
10 0315 1.3 / 0958 3.3 / TH 1601 1.2 / 2238 3.2	**25** 0221 1.4 / 0853 3.0 / F 1502 1.4 / 2136 2.8
11 0426 1.3 / 1105 3.3 / F 1706 1.1 / 2340 3.3	**26** 0329 1.5 / 1001 2.9 / SA 1608 1.3 / 2243 2.9
12 0533 1.2 / 1206 3.3 / SA 1803 1.1	**27** 0438 1.4 / 1108 3.0 / SU 1710 1.2 / 2345 3.1
13 0035 3.4 / 0631 1.1 / SU 1301 3.3 / 1854 1.0	**28** 0542 1.2 / 1210 3.1 / M 1807 1.1
14 0124 3.5 / 0722 1.0 / M 1350 3.4 / 1938 1.0	**29** 0041 3.3 / 0640 1.0 / TU 1308 3.3 / 1900 0.9
15 0210 3.5 / 0807 0.9 / TU 1435 3.4 / 2019 0.9	**30** 0134 3.5 / 0733 0.8 / W 1402 3.4 / 1951 0.8
	31 0225 3.7 / 0824 0.6 / TH 1455 3.6 / ○ 2040 0.6

HAT is 4·3 metres above Chart Datum

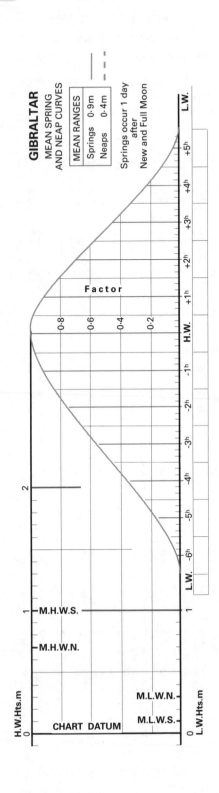

GIBRALTAR

MEAN SPRING
AND NEAP CURVES

MEAN RANGES	
Springs	0·9m
Neaps	0·4m

Springs occur 1 day
after
New and Full Moon

TIME ZONE -0100
(Gibraltar Standard Time)
Subtract 1 hour for UT
For Gibraltar Summer Time add
ONE hour in **non-shaded areas**

GIBRALTAR

LAT 36°08′N LONG 5°21′W

TIMES AND HEIGHTS OF HIGH AND LOW WATERS

Dates in amber are **SPRINGS**
Dates in yellow are **NEAPS**

2009

JANUARY

Day	Time	m	Time	m	Time	m	Time	m
1 TH	0545	0.9	1126	0.2	1806	0.8	2344	0.2
2 F	0625	0.8	1206	0.2	1848	0.8		
3 SA	0023	0.2	0711	0.8	1257	0.2	1937	0.7
4 SU	0114	0.3	0805	0.8	1358	0.3	☽2035	0.7
5 M	0220	0.3	0907	0.8	1511	0.3	2146	0.7
6 TU	0342	0.3	1018	0.8	1634	0.2	2307	0.7
7 W	0506	0.3	1132	0.8	1749	0.2		
8 TH	0020	0.8	0611	0.2	1237	0.8	1848	0.1
9 F	0120	0.8	0705	0.1	1334	0.9	1940	0.1
10 SA	0214	0.9	0755	0.1	1428	0.9	2029	0.0
11 SU	0304	0.9	0843	0.0	1520	1.0	○2115	0.0
12 M	0352	1.0	0931	0.0	1609	1.0	2159	0.0
13 TU	0438	1.0	1017	0.0	1656	1.0	2240	0.0
14 W	0523	1.0	1102	0.0	1742	0.9	2320	0.0
15 TH	0608	1.0	1146	0.1	1829	0.9		
16 F	0001	0.1	0654	0.9	1233	0.1	1916	0.8
17 SA	0044	0.2	0743	0.8	1323	0.2	2006	0.8
18 SU	0132	0.2	0836	0.8	1420	0.3	☽2101	0.7
19 M	0233	0.3	0935	0.7	1533	0.3	2207	0.6
20 TU	0401	0.3	1047	0.7	1706	0.3	2332	0.6
21 W	0533	0.3	1201	0.7	1815	0.3		
22 TH	0045	0.7	0631	0.3	1300	0.7	1901	0.2
23 F	0137	0.7	0713	0.2	1346	0.8	1941	0.2
24 SA	0216	0.8	0750	0.2	1426	0.8	2016	0.1
25 SU	0250	0.8	0824	0.2	1502	0.8	2050	0.1
26 M	0321	0.9	0857	0.1	1535	0.9	●2122	0.1
27 TU	0351	0.9	0929	0.1	1607	0.9	2152	0.1
28 W	0421	0.8	1001	0.1	1639	0.9	2221	0.1
29 TH	0452	0.9	1033	0.1	1712	0.9	2251	0.1
30 F	0525	0.9	1106	0.1	1746	0.9	2321	0.1
31 SA	0601	0.9	1142	0.1	1825	0.8	2356	0.1

FEBRUARY

Day	Time	m	Time	m	Time	m	Time	m
1 SU	0642	0.8	1223	0.2	1910	0.8		
2 M	0037	0.2	0731	0.8	1316	0.2	2005	0.7
3 TU	0133	0.2	0831	0.8	1428	0.2	☽2114	0.7
4 W	0259	0.3	0946	0.7	1615	0.2	2243	0.6
5 TH	0454	0.3	1115	0.7	1752	0.2		
6 F	0012	0.7	0611	0.2	1232	0.8	1852	0.1
7 SA	0117	0.8	0707	0.1	1332	0.8	1942	0.0
8 SU	0210	0.9	0755	0.0	1424	0.9	2026	0.0
9 M	0257	0.9	0840	0.0	1512	0.9	○2108	-0.1
10 TU	0340	1.0	0923	0.0	1557	1.0	2146	-0.1
11 W	0422	1.0	1004	-0.1	1640	1.0	2222	-0.1
12 TH	0502	1.0	1043	0.0	1722	0.9	2257	0.0
13 F	0542	0.9	1120	0.0	1803	0.9	2330	0.0
14 SA	0622	0.9	1157	0.1	1845	0.8		
15 SU	0005	0.1	0703	0.8	1237	0.2	1928	0.7
16 M	0043	0.2	0749	0.7	1324	0.2	☽2016	0.7
17 TU	0131	0.3	0843	0.7	1431	0.3	2115	0.6
18 W	0253	0.3	0955	0.6	1630	0.3	2243	0.6
19 TH	0512	0.4	1133	0.6	1757	0.3		
20 F	0023	0.6	0618	0.3	1244	0.7	1845	0.2
21 SA	0118	0.7	0659	0.2	1330	0.7	1922	0.2
22 SU	0155	0.7	0733	0.2	1407	0.8	1956	0.1
23 M	0226	0.8	0805	0.1	1441	0.8	2027	0.1
24 TU	0256	0.9	0837	0.1	1514	0.9	2058	0.1
25 W	0326	0.9	0908	0.1	1546	0.9	2128	0.0
26 TH	0357	0.9	0940	0.0	1619	0.9	2157	0.0
27 F	0429	0.9	1012	0.0	1652	0.9	2228	0.0
28 SA	0503	0.9	1045	0.0	1728	0.9	2259	0.1

MARCH

Day	Time	m	Time	m	Time	m	Time	m
1 SU	0540	0.9	1120	0.1	1807	0.8	2334	0.1
2 M	0620	0.9	1159	0.1	1853	0.8		
3 TU	0015	0.2	0709	0.8	1249	0.2	1948	0.7
4 W	0110	0.2	0810	0.7	1405	0.3	☽2058	0.7
5 TH	0246	0.3	0929	0.7	1617	0.3	2232	0.6
6 F	0457	0.3	1109	0.7	1751	0.3		
7 SA	0006	0.7	0611	0.2	1229	0.7	1846	0.1
8 SU	0108	0.8	0702	0.1	1326	0.8	1931	0.1
9 M	0157	0.9	0746	0.0	1413	0.9	2011	0.0
10 TU	0240	0.9	0827	0.0	1457	0.9	2048	0.0
11 W	0320	1.0	0906	-0.1	1539	1.0	○2123	0.0
12 TH	0359	1.0	0943	-0.1	1618	1.0	2156	0.0
13 F	0436	1.0	1018	0.0	1657	0.9	2228	0.0
14 SA	0512	0.9	1051	0.0	1735	0.9	2300	0.1
15 SU	0549	0.9	1124	0.1	1813	0.8	2331	0.1
16 M	0627	0.8	1159	0.1	1854	0.7		
17 TU	0006	0.2	0708	0.7	1239	0.2	1940	0.7
18 W	0049	0.3	0800	0.6	1339	0.3	☽2035	0.6
19 TH	0201	0.4	0908	0.6	1537	0.3	2150	0.6
20 F	0427	0.4	1046	0.6	1718	0.3	2330	0.6
21 SA	0548	0.3	1210	0.6	1810	0.3		
22 SU	0034	0.7	0629	0.2	1259	0.7	1848	0.1
23 M	0114	0.7	0702	0.1	1336	0.8	1921	0.1
24 TU	0147	0.8	0735	0.1	1410	0.8	1953	0.1
25 W	0220	0.9	0807	0.1	1444	0.9	2024	0.1
26 TH	0254	0.9	0840	0.0	1519	0.9	●2056	0.1
27 F	0329	1.0	0914	0.0	1555	0.9	2129	0.1
28 SA	0405	1.0	0949	0.0	1632	0.9	2203	0.1
29 SU	0442	1.0	1024	0.0	1711	0.9	2239	0.1
30 M	0521	0.9	1102	0.0	1753	0.9	2318	0.1
31 TU	0605	0.9	1144	0.1	1842	0.8		

APRIL

Day	Time	m	Time	m	Time	m	Time	m
1 W	0003	0.2	0656	0.8	1237	0.2	1941	0.8
2 TH	0107	0.3	0801	0.7	1404	0.3	☽2053	0.7
3 F	0252	0.3	0923	0.7	1607	0.3	2222	0.7
4 SA	0446	0.3	1100	0.7	1730	0.2	2347	0.6
5 SU	0556	0.2	1215	0.8	1823	0.2		
6 M	0046	0.8	0644	0.1	1308	0.8	1905	0.1
7 TU	0132	0.9	0726	0.1	1353	0.9	1943	0.1
8 W	0213	0.9	0804	0.0	1434	0.9	2018	0.0
9 TH	0253	0.9	0841	0.0	1514	0.9	2053	0.0
10 F	0331	0.9	0917	0.0	1553	0.9	2127	0.0
11 SA	0407	0.9	0951	0.0	1630	0.9	2159	0.1
12 SU	0443	0.9	1024	0.1	1707	0.9	2232	0.1
13 M	0519	0.8	1057	0.1	1745	0.8	2305	0.2
14 TU	0555	0.8	1131	0.2	1825	0.7	2341	0.2
15 W	0637	0.7	1210	0.2	1911	0.7		
16 TH	0024	0.3	0728	0.7	1307	0.3	2005	0.7
17 F	0130	0.4	0831	0.6	1444	0.3	☽2107	0.6
18 SA	0317	0.4	0948	0.6	1617	0.3	2221	0.6
19 SU	0449	0.3	1112	0.6	1718	0.3	2331	0.7
20 M	0543	0.3	1211	0.7	1801	0.2		
21 TU	0020	0.8	0622	0.2	1254	0.8	1837	0.2
22 W	0101	0.8	0658	0.2	1332	0.8	1912	0.1
23 TH	0140	0.9	0733	0.1	1410	0.9	1946	0.1
24 F	0219	0.9	0809	0.1	1449	0.9	2023	0.1
25 SA	0259	1.0	0847	0.1	1530	0.9	●2101	0.1
26 SU	0340	1.0	0927	0.0	1612	1.0	2141	0.1
27 M	0423	1.0	1007	0.1	1656	0.9	2223	0.1
28 TU	0507	0.9	1050	0.1	1743	0.9	2308	0.2
29 W	0555	0.9	1137	0.2	1835	0.9		
30 TH	0001	0.2	0650	0.8	1236	0.2	1935	0.8

Chart Datum: 0·25 metres below Alicante Datum (Mean Sea Level, Alicante)
HAT is 1·2 metres above Chart Datum

TIDES

TIDES

TIME ZONE -0100
(Gibraltar Standard Time)
Subtract 1 hour for UT
For Gibraltar Summer Time add ONE hour in **non-shaded areas**

GIBRALTAR

LAT 36°08'N   LONG 5°21'W

TIMES AND HEIGHTS OF HIGH AND LOW WATERS

Dates in amber are **SPRINGS**
Dates in yellow are **NEAPS**

2009

MAY

Day	Wk	Time m	Time m	Time m	Time m
1	F	0110 0.3	0756 0.8	1359 0.3	2044 0.8
2	SA	0241 0.3	0912 0.7	1532 0.3	2200 0.8
3	SU	0412 0.3	1035 0.7	1648 0.2	2314 0.8
4	M ◑	0523 0.2	1146 0.8	1745 0.2	
5	TU	0012 0.8	0616 0.2	1241 0.8	1830 0.2
6	W	0101 0.9	0659 0.1	1326 0.9	1910 0.1
7	TH	0143 0.9	0739 0.1	1408 0.9	1947 0.1
8	F	0223 0.9	0817 0.1	1449 0.9	2024 0.1
9	SA	0302 0.9	0853 0.1	1528 0.9	2100 0.1
10	SU	0340 0.9	0929 0.1	1606 0.9	2135 0.1
11	M ○	0418 0.9	1003 0.1	1644 0.8	2210 0.2
12	TU	0455 0.8	1038 0.1	1722 0.8	2246 0.2
13	W	0532 0.8	1113 0.2	1801 0.8	2323 0.2
14	TH	0613 0.7	1152 0.2	1844 0.7	
15	F	0005 0.3	0659 0.7	1241 0.3	1932 0.7
16	SA	0100 0.3	0753 0.7	1348 0.3	2024 0.7
17	SU	0211 0.3	0853 0.6	1502 0.3	2121 0.7
18	M ◐	0326 0.3	1001 0.7	1607 0.3	2223 0.7
19	TU	0434 0.3	1108 0.7	1729 0.2	2322 0.8
20	W	0530 0.2	1204 0.7	1749 0.2	
21	TH	0013 0.8	0616 0.2	1252 0.8	1830 0.2
22	F	0100 0.9	0659 0.1	1337 0.9	1912 0.2
23	SA	0145 0.9	0741 0.1	1422 0.9	1954 0.1
24	SU	0232 1.0	0825 0.1	1508 0.9	2039 0.1
25	M	0320 1.0	0910 0.1	1555 1.0	2125 0.1
26	TU ●	0408 1.0	0956 0.1	1643 1.0	2213 0.1
27	W	0457 1.0	1043 0.1	1733 0.9	2303 0.2
28	TH	0548 0.9	1132 0.1	1826 0.9	2357 0.2
29	F	0644 0.9	1228 0.2	1923 0.9	
30	SA	0100 0.2	0744 0.8	1334 0.2	2024 0.9
31	SU	0211 0.2	0849 0.8	1444 0.3	2127 0.8

JUNE

Day	Wk	Time m	Time m	Time m	Time m
1	M	0325 0.3	0958 0.8	1553 0.3	2233 0.8
2	TU ◑	0438 0.2	1108 0.8	1659 0.3	2334 0.8
3	W	0542 0.2	1208 0.8	1755 0.2	
4	TH	0027 0.8	0633 0.2	1300 0.8	1841 0.2
5	F	0115 0.9	0717 0.2	1346 0.8	1923 0.2
6	SA	0158 0.9	0757 0.1	1429 0.8	2002 0.2
7	SU	0240 0.9	0835 0.1	1510 0.8	2040 0.1
8	M	0320 0.9	0912 0.1	1549 0.8	2118 0.2
9	TU ○	0359 0.9	0948 0.1	1625 0.8	2154 0.2
10	W	0436 0.8	1022 0.1	1700 0.8	2230 0.2
11	TH	0512 0.8	1056 0.2	1735 0.8	2306 0.2
12	F	0548 0.8	1131 0.2	1812 0.8	2343 0.3
13	SA	0627 0.8	1208 0.2	1852 0.8	
14	SU	0025 0.3	0711 0.7	1253 0.3	1937 0.8
15	M	0116 0.3	0801 0.7	1346 0.3	2027 0.8
16	TU ◐	0214 0.3	0858 0.7	1447 0.3	2122 0.8
17	W	0319 0.3	1004 0.7	1553 0.3	2224 0.8
18	TH	0430 0.3	1113 0.7	1659 0.3	2327 0.8
19	F	0537 0.2	1215 0.8	1757 0.2	
20	SA	0025 0.9	0633 0.2	1310 0.8	1848 0.2
21	SU	0120 0.9	0723 0.1	1401 0.9	1937 0.1
22	M	0213 0.9	0812 0.1	1452 0.9	2027 0.1
23	TU	0305 1.0	0901 0.0	1542 1.0	2117 0.1
24	W	0357 1.0	0948 0.0	1631 1.0	2206 0.1
25	TH ●	0447 1.0	1034 0.0	1720 1.0	2255 0.1
26	F	0537 1.0	1120 0.1	1809 1.0	2345 0.1
27	SA	0628 0.9	1207 0.1	1901 1.0	
28	SU	0037 0.2	0722 0.9	1259 0.2	1954 0.9
29	M	0134 0.2	0819 0.8	1354 0.2	2050 0.9
30	TU	0236 0.2	0919 0.8	1456 0.3	2149 0.8

JULY

Day	Wk	Time m	Time m	Time m	Time m
1	W	0346 0.3	1026 0.7	1608 0.7	2254 0.8
2	TH	0507 0.3	1136 0.7	1723 0.3	2357 0.8
3	F	0613 0.3	1238 0.8	1821 0.3	
4	SA ◑	0053 0.8	0702 0.2	1331 0.8	1907 0.3
5	SU	0142 0.8	0743 0.2	1416 0.8	1948 0.2
6	M	0225 0.8	0821 0.2	1456 0.8	2026 0.2
7	TU	0305 0.8	0856 0.1	1532 0.9	2102 0.2
8	W	0342 0.9	0930 0.1	1605 0.9	2137 0.2
9	TH	0416 0.9	1002 0.1	1636 0.9	2210 0.2
10	F	0449 0.9	1033 0.1	1706 0.9	2243 0.2
11	SA ○	0521 0.8	1103 0.2	1738 0.9	2316 0.2
12	SU	0554 0.8	1133 0.2	1812 0.9	2351 0.2
13	M	0632 0.8	1208 0.2	1852 0.8	
14	TU	0032 0.2	0716 0.8	1249 0.3	1938 0.8
15	W	0121 0.2	0810 0.7	1342 0.3	2031 0.8
16	TH	0223 0.3	0914 0.7	1453 0.3	2134 0.8
17	F	0341 0.3	1031 0.7	1619 0.3	2248 0.8
18	SA ◐	0512 0.2	1149 0.7	1738 0.3	
19	SU	0001 0.8	0622 0.2	1254 0.8	1837 0.2
20	M	0104 0.9	0716 0.1	1349 0.9	1930 0.1
21	TU	0201 0.9	0805 0.1	1440 1.0	2020 0.1
22	W	0254 1.0	0851 0.0	1529 1.0	2108 0.0
23	TH	0345 1.0	0936 0.0	1616 1.1	2155 0.0
24	F	0432 1.0	1018 0.0	1701 1.1	2240 0.0
25	SA ●	0519 1.0	1058 0.0	1745 1.0	2323 0.1
26	SU	0605 1.0	1138 0.1	1831 1.0	
27	M	0007 0.1	0653 0.9	1220 0.2	1918 0.9
28	TU	0054 0.2	0744 0.8	1305 0.2	2008 0.9
29	W	0146 0.3	0839 0.8	1400 0.3	2103 0.8
30	TH	0251 0.3	0943 0.7	1514 0.4	2209 0.7
31	F	0428 0.3	1104 0.7	1655 0.4	2328 0.7

AUGUST

Day	Wk	Time m	Time m	Time m	Time m
1	SA	0556 0.3	1222 0.7	1807 0.4	
2	SU ◑	0037 0.8	0646 0.3	1318 0.8	1853 0.3
3	M	0129 0.8	0725 0.2	1401 0.8	1932 0.3
4	TU	0210 0.8	0800 0.2	1436 0.9	2007 0.2
5	W	0246 0.9	0833 0.2	1507 0.9	2041 0.2
6	TH	0319 0.9	0904 0.1	1537 0.9	2113 0.2
7	F	0350 0.9	0934 0.1	1606 1.0	2145 0.1
8	SA	0421 0.9	1003 0.1	1635 1.0	2216 0.1
9	SU ○	0452 0.9	1031 0.1	1705 1.0	2247 0.1
10	M	0524 0.9	1101 0.2	1738 1.0	2320 0.2
11	TU	0600 0.9	1133 0.2	1816 0.9	2357 0.2
12	W	0643 0.8	1210 0.2	1900 0.9	
13	TH	0041 0.2	0735 0.8	1259 0.3	1953 0.8
14	F	0142 0.3	0841 0.7	1413 0.4	2059 0.8
15	SA	0313 0.3	1004 0.7	1601 0.4	2222 0.8
16	SU	0508 0.3	1135 0.8	1733 0.4	2349 0.8
17	M ◐	0618 0.2	1244 0.8	1833 0.3	
18	TU	0056 0.9	0708 0.1	1338 0.9	1923 0.1
19	W	0151 1.0	0752 0.1	1426 1.0	2009 0.1
20	TH	0241 1.0	0834 0.0	1511 1.1	2053 0.0
21	F	0327 1.0	0914 0.0	1554 1.1	2136 0.0
22	SA	0412 1.1	0953 0.0	1635 1.1	2216 0.0
23	SU	0454 1.0	1029 0.0	1716 1.1	2255 0.1
24	M ○	0537 1.0	1105 0.1	1757 1.0	2333 0.1
25	TU ●	0620 0.9	1140 0.2	1839 0.9	
26	W	0012 0.2	0706 0.8	1220 0.3	1924 0.9
27	TH	0056 0.3	0758 0.8	1307 0.4	2016 0.8
28	F	0156 0.3	0859 0.7	1420 0.4	2121 0.7
29	SA	0341 0.3	1023 0.7	1623 0.4	2255 0.7
30	SU	0528 0.3	1158 0.7	1747 0.5	
31	M	0018 0.7	0620 0.3	1254 0.8	1831 0.3

Chart Datum: 0·25 metres below Alicante Datum (Mean Sea Level, Alicante)
HAT is 1·2 metres above Chart Datum

TIME ZONE -0100
(Gibraltar Standard Time)
Subtract 1 hour for UT
For Gibraltar Summer Time add
ONE hour in **non-shaded areas**

GIBRALTAR

LAT 36°08′N   LONG 5°21′W

TIMES AND HEIGHTS OF HIGH AND LOW WATERS

Dates in amber are **SPRINGS**
Dates in yellow are **NEAPS**

2009

SEPTEMBER

Time m	Time m
1 0109 0.8 / 0657 0.3 / TU 1332 0.9 / 1907 0.3	**16** 0047 0.9 / 0652 0.2 / W 1321 1.0 / 1908 0.1
2 0146 0.9 / 0730 0.2 / W 1404 0.9 / 1940 0.2	**17** 0138 1.0 / 0732 0.1 / TH 1405 1.1 / 1950 0.1
3 0218 0.9 / 0801 0.2 / TH 1434 1.0 / 2012 0.2	**18** 0222 1.0 / 0810 0.1 / F 1447 1.1 / ● 2031 0.0
4 0249 1.0 / 0831 0.2 / F 1503 1.0 / ○ 2044 0.2	**19** 0305 1.1 / 0847 0.1 / SA 1527 1.1 / 2110 0.0
5 0320 1.0 / 0901 0.1 / SA 1533 1.0 / 2115 0.1	**20** 0346 1.1 / 0923 0.1 / SU 1606 1.1 / 2148 0.0
6 0351 1.0 / 0930 0.1 / SU 1604 1.0 / 2147 0.1	**21** 0426 1.0 / 0957 0.1 / M 1644 1.1 / 2223 0.1
7 0424 1.0 / 1000 0.1 / M 1636 1.0 / 2219 0.1	**22** 0505 1.0 / 1031 0.2 / TU 1722 1.0 / 2258 0.2
8 0457 1.0 / 1032 0.2 / TU 1711 1.0 / 2253 0.2	**23** 0544 0.9 / 1105 0.2 / W 1800 0.9 / 2333 0.2
9 0535 1.0 / 1105 0.2 / W 1748 1.0 / 2329 0.2	**24** 0627 0.9 / 1142 0.3 / TH 1842 0.8
10 0618 0.9 / 1143 0.3 / TH 1833 0.9	**25** 0012 0.3 / 0715 0.8 / F 1226 0.4 / 1932 0.8
11 0012 0.3 / 0712 0.8 / F 1233 0.3 / 1928 0.9	**26** 0107 0.4 / 0816 0.7 / SA 1337 0.5 / ◖ 2037 0.7
12 0114 0.3 / 0821 0.8 / SA 1356 0.4 / ◖ 2038 0.8	**27** 0252 0.4 / 0933 0.7 / SU 1540 0.5 / 2207 0.7
13 0307 0.4 / 0948 0.8 / SU 1601 0.4 / 2209 0.8	**28** 0444 0.4 / 1108 0.7 / M 1709 0.4 / 2342 0.7
14 0504 0.3 / 1124 0.8 / M 1727 0.3 / 2343 0.8	**29** 0542 0.4 / 1211 0.8 / TU 1757 0.4
15 0606 0.2 / 1231 0.9 / TU 1823 0.2	**30** 0035 0.8 / 0621 0.3 / W 1251 0.9 / 1833 0.3

OCTOBER

Time m	Time m
1 0112 0.9 / 0654 0.3 / TH 1324 0.9 / 1906 0.2	**16** 0117 1.0 / 0706 0.2 / F 1339 1.0 / 1927 0.1
2 0144 0.9 / 0725 0.2 / F 1355 1.0 / 1939 0.2	**17** 0200 1.0 / 0743 0.1 / SA 1419 1.1 / 2006 0.1
3 0216 1.0 / 0756 0.2 / SA 1427 1.0 / 2011 0.2	**18** 0240 1.0 / 0818 0.1 / SU 1458 1.1 / ● 2043 0.1
4 0249 1.0 / 0827 0.2 / SU 1500 1.1 / ○ 2044 0.1	**19** 0319 1.0 / 0854 0.1 / M 1537 1.1 / 2120 0.1
5 0323 1.0 / 0859 0.2 / M 1535 1.1 / 2118 0.1	**20** 0358 1.0 / 0928 0.1 / TU 1615 1.0 / 2155 0.1
6 0358 1.0 / 0932 0.2 / TU 1611 1.1 / 2153 0.1	**21** 0435 1.0 / 1003 0.2 / W 1652 1.0 / 2229 0.2
7 0435 1.0 / 1007 0.2 / W 1649 1.1 / 2229 0.2	**22** 0513 0.9 / 1038 0.2 / TH 1729 0.9 / 2304 0.2
8 0516 1.0 / 1044 0.2 / TH 1730 1.0 / 2308 0.2	**23** 0553 0.9 / 1116 0.3 / F 1810 0.8 / 2343 0.3
9 0601 0.9 / 1127 0.3 / F 1817 0.9 / 2354 0.3	**24** 0639 0.8 / 1200 0.4 / SA 1859 0.8
10 0658 0.9 / 1223 0.4 / SA 1915 0.8	**25** 0033 0.4 / 0735 0.8 / SU 1306 0.4 / 2000 0.7
11 0101 0.4 / 0808 0.8 / SU 1357 0.4 / ◖ 2028 0.8	**26** 0203 0.4 / 0843 0.7 / M 1447 0.5 / ◖ 2114 0.7
12 0303 0.4 / 0934 0.8 / M 1550 0.4 / 2159 0.8	**27** 0344 0.4 / 0958 0.8 / TU 1613 0.4 / 2239 0.8
13 0442 0.3 / 1103 0.9 / TU 1708 0.3 / 2329 0.8	**28** 0452 0.4 / 1109 0.8 / W 1711 0.4 / 2346 0.8
14 0542 0.3 / 1208 0.9 / W 1802 0.2	**29** 0539 0.3 / 1159 0.9 / TH 1754 0.3
15 0030 0.9 / 0627 0.2 / TH 1257 1.0 / 1846 0.2	**30** 0030 0.8 / 0616 0.3 / F 1239 0.9 / 1830 0.3
	31 0108 0.9 / 0650 0.2 / SA 1316 1.0 / 1905 0.2

NOVEMBER

Time m	Time m
1 0143 1.0 / 0722 0.2 / SU 1352 1.0 / 1940 0.2	**16** 0219 1.0 / 0756 0.2 / M 1434 1.0 / ● 2023 0.1
2 0219 1.0 / 0756 0.2 / M 1431 1.1 / ○ 2017 0.1	**17** 0258 1.0 / 0832 0.2 / TU 1514 1.0 / 2100 0.1
3 0258 1.0 / 0832 0.2 / TU 1510 1.1 / 2054 0.1	**18** 0337 1.0 / 0909 0.2 / W 1553 1.0 / 2136 0.1
4 0337 1.0 / 0909 0.2 / W 1551 1.1 / 2133 0.1	**19** 0414 0.9 / 0945 0.2 / TH 1631 0.9 / 2212 0.2
5 0419 1.0 / 0950 0.2 / TH 1634 1.0 / 2214 0.2	**20** 0452 0.9 / 1022 0.2 / F 1710 0.9 / 2247 0.2
6 0503 1.0 / 1033 0.2 / F 1720 1.0 / 2257 0.2	**21** 0529 0.9 / 1100 0.3 / SA 1749 0.8 / 2325 0.3
7 0552 1.0 / 1122 0.3 / SA 1810 0.9 / 2348 0.3	**22** 0611 0.8 / 1143 0.3 / SU 1833 0.8
8 0648 0.9 / 1224 0.3 / SU 1909 0.9	**23** 0009 0.3 / 0658 0.8 / M 1236 0.4 / 1923 0.7
9 0056 0.9 / 0755 0.9 / M 1351 0.4 / ◑ 2019 0.8	**24** 0109 0.4 / 0753 0.8 / TU 1346 0.4 / ◑ 2021 0.7
10 0234 0.4 / 0911 0.9 / TU 1521 0.4 / 2139 0.8	**25** 0229 0.4 / 0853 0.8 / W 1502 0.4 / 2125 0.7
11 0401 0.3 / 1030 0.9 / W 1636 0.3 / ● 2301 0.8	**26** 0344 0.4 / 0956 0.8 / TH 1610 0.4 / 2236 0.7
12 0507 0.3 / 1136 0.9 / TH 1735 0.2	**27** 0445 0.4 / 1058 0.8 / F 1706 0.3 / 2339 0.8
13 0005 0.9 / 0558 0.2 / F 1229 1.0 / 1822 0.2	**28** 0534 0.3 / 1152 0.9 / SA 1754 0.2
14 0055 0.9 / 0640 0.2 / SA 1313 1.0 / 1905 0.1	**29** 0029 0.8 / 0615 0.3 / SU 1239 0.9 / 1835 0.2
15 0138 1.0 / 0719 0.2 / SU 1354 1.0 / 1944 0.1	**30** 0113 0.9 / 0653 0.2 / M 1322 1.0 / 1916 0.1

DECEMBER

Time m	Time m
1 0156 0.9 / 0732 0.2 / TU 1407 1.0 / 1957 0.1	**16** 0248 0.9 / 0822 0.2 / W 1502 0.9 / ● 2051 0.1
2 0239 1.0 / 0813 0.2 / W 1452 1.0 / 2040 0.1	**17** 0327 0.9 / 0859 0.2 / TH 1542 0.9 / 2127 0.1
3 0324 1.0 / 0856 0.2 / TH 1539 1.0 / 2123 0.1	**18** 0403 0.9 / 0936 0.2 / F 1620 0.9 / 2202 0.1
4 0409 1.0 / 0942 0.2 / F 1626 1.0 / 2201 0.1	**19** 0438 0.9 / 1012 0.2 / SA 1656 0.9 / 2236 0.2
5 0456 1.0 / 1030 0.2 / SA 1715 1.0 / 2255 0.1	**20** 0511 0.9 / 1047 0.2 / SU 1731 0.8 / 2310 0.2
6 0545 1.0 / 1121 0.2 / SU 1805 0.9 / 2345 0.2	**21** 0546 0.8 / 1124 0.2 / M 1807 0.8 / 2345 0.2
7 0638 1.0 / 1220 0.2 / M 1901 0.9	**22** 0624 0.8 / 1203 0.3 / TU 1847 0.8
8 0043 0.2 / 0737 0.9 / TU 1329 0.3 / 2002 0.8	**23** 0023 0.3 / 0706 0.8 / W 1251 0.3 / 1931 0.7
9 0154 0.3 / 0842 0.9 / W 1442 0.3 / ◑ 2109 0.8	**24** 0111 0.3 / 0756 0.8 / TH 1348 0.3 / ◑ 2024 0.7
10 0309 0.3 / 0951 0.9 / TH 1555 0.3 / 2222 0.8	**25** 0213 0.3 / 0852 0.7 / F 1454 0.3 / 2125 0.7
11 0424 0.3 / 1100 0.9 / F 1705 0.2 / 2334 0.8	**26** 0327 0.3 / 0955 0.7 / SA 1608 0.3 / 2239 0.7
12 0529 0.2 / 1200 0.9 / SA 1803 0.2	**27** 0443 0.2 / 1108 0.8 / SU 1714 0.2 / 2350 0.7
13 0033 0.8 / 0620 0.2 / SU 1252 0.9 / 1850 0.2	**28** 0544 0.2 / 1205 0.8 / M 1814 0.2
14 0123 0.9 / 0704 0.2 / M 1337 0.9 / 1933 0.2	**29** 0048 0.8 / 0633 0.2 / TU 1300 0.9 / 1902 0.1
15 0207 0.9 / 0744 0.2 / TU 1421 0.9 / 2013 0.1	**30** 0139 0.9 / 0719 0.2 / W 1352 0.9 / 1949 0.1
	31 0228 0.9 / 0805 0.2 / TH 1442 1.0 / ○ 2035 0.0

Chart Datum: 0·25 metres below Alicante Datum (Mean Sea Level, Alicante)
HAT is 1·2 metres above Chart Datum

TIDES

INDEX

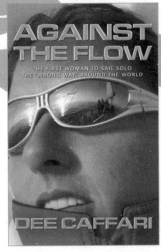